TEACHER'S EDITION

GRADE 7

Program Consultants:
Kylene Beers
Martha Hougen
Elena Izquierdo
Carol Jago
Erik Palmer
Robert E. Probst

Copyright © 2020 by Houghton Mifflin Harcourt Publishing Company

All rights reserved. No part of this work may be reproduced or transmitted in any form or by any means, electronic or mechanical, including photocopying or recording, or by any information storage or retrieval system, without the prior written permission of the copyright owner unless such copying is expressly permitted by federal copyright law. Requests for permission to make copies of any part of the work should be submitted through our Permissions website at https://customercare.hmhco.com/contactus/Permissions.html or mailed to Houghton Mifflin Harcourt Publishing Company, Attn: Intellectual Property Licensing, 9400 Southpark Center Loop, Orlando, Florida 32819-8647.

Front Cover Photo Credits: (outer ring): ©joyfull/Shutterstock, (inner ring): ©Vadim Georgiev/Shutterstock, (inset): ©Stockbyte/Getty Images, (c): ©Carrie Garcia/Houghton Mifflin Harcourt, (c overlay): ©Eyewire/Getty Images, (bc overlay): ©elenamiv/Shutterstock

Back Cover Photo Credits: (Units 1-6): ©Anthony Aneese Totah Jr./Dreamstime; ©Iryna Kuznetsova/Dreamstime; ©Dfikar/Dreamstime; ©StockTrek/Photodisc/Getty Images; ©Monkey Business Images/iStock/Getty Images; © Hemera Technologies/Ablestock/Getty Images

Printed in the U.S.A.

ISBN 978-1-328-47485-8

1 2 3 4 5 6 7 8 9 10 0690 27 26 25 24 23 22 21 20 19 18

4500718806 A B C D E F G

If you have received these materials as examination copies free of charge, Houghton Mifflin Harcourt Publishing Company retains title to the materials and they may not be resold. Resale of examination copies is strictly prohibited.

Possession of this publication in print format does not entitle users to convert this publication, or any portion of it, into electronic format.

Teacher's Edition Table of Contents

Program Consultants	T2
Into Literature Overview	T4
Maximize Growth through Data-Driven Differentiation and Assessment	T14
Build a Culture of Professional Growth	T16
Annotated Student Edition Table of Contents	T20
Into Literature Dashboard	T34
Into Literature Studios	T36
Featured Essays	
Positively Must Read: Notice & Note	T38
Reading and Writing Across Genres	T44

Unit 1	1
Unit 2	96
Unit 3	180
Unit 4	262
Unit 5	360
Unit 6	434

Student Resources	R1

PROGRAM CONSULTANTS

Kylene Beers

Nationally known lecturer and author on reading and literacy; coauthor with Robert Probst of *Disrupting Thinking, Notice & Note: Strategies for Close Reading,* and *Reading Nonfiction*; former president of the National Council of Teachers of English. Dr. Beers is the author of *When Kids Can't Read: What Teachers Can Do* and coeditor of *Adolescent Literacy: Turning Promise into Practice*, as well as articles in the Journal of Adolescent and Adult Literacy. Former editor of *Voices from the Middle*, she is the 2001 recipient of NCTE's Richard W. Halley Award, given for outstanding contributions to middle school literacy. She recently served as Senior Reading Researcher at the Comer School Development Program at Yale University as well as Senior Reading Advisor to Secondary Schools for the Reading and Writing Project at Teachers College.

Martha Hougen

National consultant, presenter, researcher, and author. Areas of expertise include differentiating instruction for students with learning difficulties, including those with learning disabilities and dyslexia; and teacher and leader preparation improvement. Dr. Hougen has taught at the middle school through graduate levels. In addition to peer-reviewed articles, curricular documents, and presentations, Dr. Hougen has published two college textbooks: *The Fundamentals of Literacy Instruction and Assessment Pre-K–6* (2012) and *The Fundamentals of Literacy Instruction and Assessment 6–12* (2014). Dr. Hougen has supported Educator Preparation Program reforms while working at the Meadows Center for Preventing Educational Risk at The University of Texas at Austin and at the CEEDAR Center, University of Florida.

Elena Izquierdo

Nationally recognized teacher educator and advocate for English language learners. Dr. Izquierdo is a linguist by training, with a Ph.D. in Applied Linguistics and Bilingual Education from Georgetown University. She has served on various state and national boards working to close the achievement gaps for bilingual students and English language learners. Dr. Izquierdo is a member of the Hispanic Leadership Council, which supports Hispanic students and educators at both the state and federal levels. She served as Vice President on the Executive Board of the National Association of Bilingual Education and as Publications and Professional Development Chair.

Carol Jago

Teacher of English with 32 years of experience at Santa Monica High School in California; author and nationally known lecturer; former president of the National Council of Teachers of English. Ms. Jago currently serves as Associate Director of the California Reading and Literature Project at UCLA. With expertise in standards assessment and secondary education, Ms. Jago is the author of numerous books on education, including *With Rigor for All* and *Papers, Papers, Papers*, and is active with the California Association of Teachers of English, editing its scholarly journal *California English* since 1996. Ms. Jago also served on the planning committee for the 2009 NAEP Readig Framework and the 2011 NAEP Writing Framework.

Erik Palmer

Veteran teacher and education consultant based in Denver, Colorado. Author of *Well Spoken: Teaching Speaking to All Students* and *Digitally Speaking: How to Improve Student Presentations with Technology*. His areas of focus include improving oral communication, promoting technology in classroom presentations, and updating instruction through the use of digital tools. He holds a bachelor's degree from Oberlin College and a master's degree in curriculum and instruction from the University of Colorado.

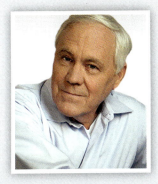

Robert E. Probst

Nationally respected authority on the teaching of literature; Professor Emeritus of English Education at Georgia State University. Dr. Probst's publications include numerous articles in *English Journal* and *Voices from the Middle*, as well as professional texts including (as coeditor) *Adolescent Literacy: Turning Promise into Practice* and (as coauthor with Kylene Beers) *Disrupting Thinking, Notice & Note: Strategies for Close Reading,* and *Reading Nonfiction*. He regularly speaks at national and international conventions including those of the International Literacy Association, the National Council of Teachers of English, the Association for Supervision and Curriculum Development, and the National Association of Secondary School Principals. He has served NCTE in various leadership roles, including the Conference on English Leadership Board of Directors, the Commission on Reading, and column editor of the NCTE journal *Voices from the Middle*. He is also the 2007 recipient of the CEL Outstanding Leadership Award.

Lead and Learn

Students who communicate...

- **Listen** actively
- **Present** effectively
- **Expand** vocabulary
- **Question** appropriately
- **Engage** constructively

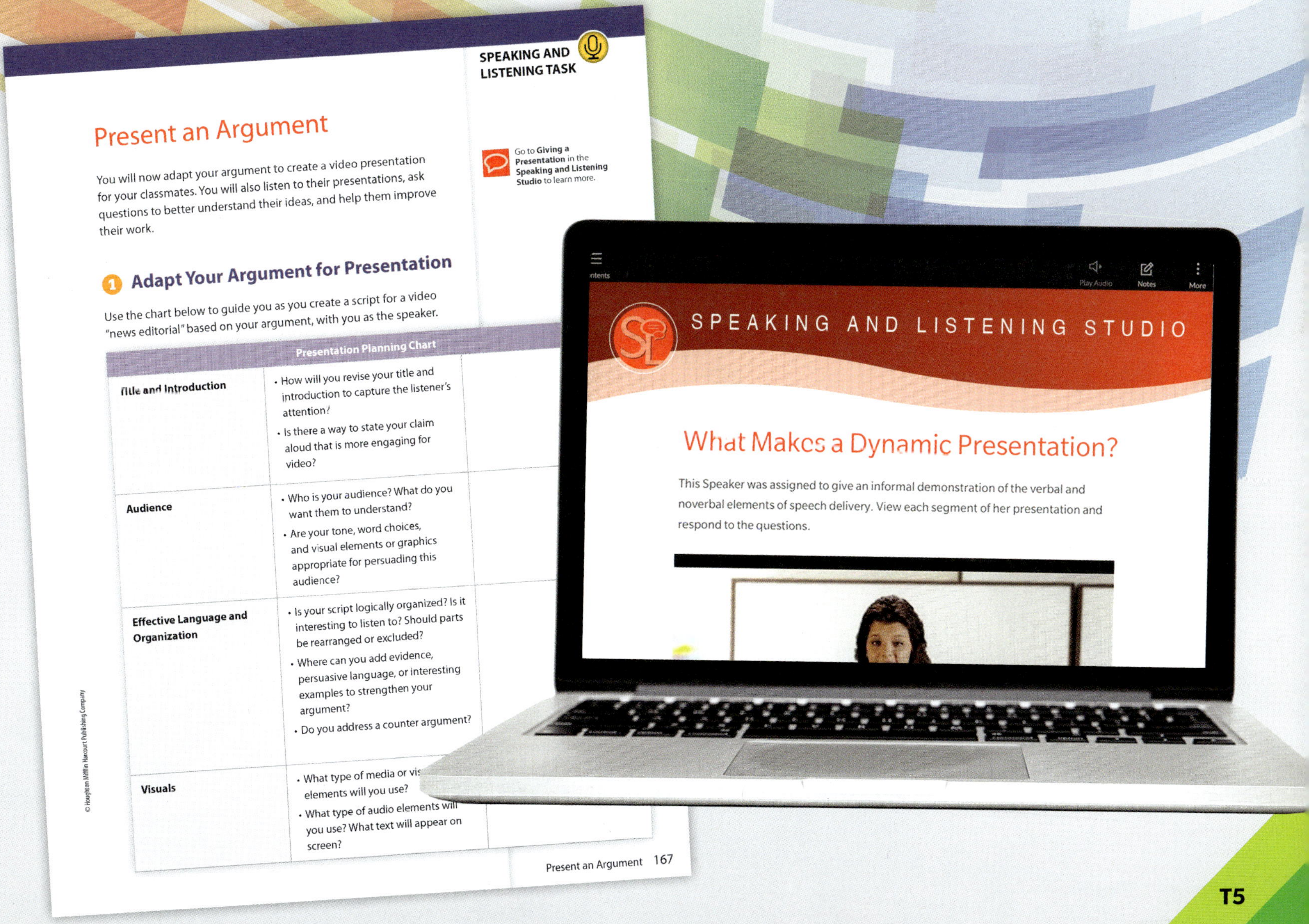
SPEAKING AND LISTENING TASK

Present an Argument

You will now adapt your argument to create a video presentation for your classmates. You will also listen to their presentations, ask questions to better understand their ideas, and help them improve their work.

Go to **Giving a Presentation** in the **Speaking and Listening Studio** to learn more.

1 Adapt Your Argument for Presentation

Use the chart below to guide you as you create a script for a video "news editorial" based on your argument, with you as the speaker.

Presentation Planning Chart		
Title and Introduction	• How will you revise your title and introduction to capture the listener's attention? • Is there a way to state your claim aloud that is more engaging for video?	
Audience	• Who is your audience? What do you want them to understand? • Are your tone, word choices, and visual elements or graphics appropriate for persuading this audience?	
Effective Language and Organization	• Is your script logically organized? Is it interesting to listen to? Should parts be rearranged or excluded? • Where can you add evidence, persuasive language, or interesting examples to strengthen your argument? • Do you address a counter argument?	
Visuals	• What type of media or vis[...] elements will you use? • What type of audio elements will you use? What text will appear on screen?	

© Houghton Mifflin Harcourt Publishing Company

Present an Argument 167

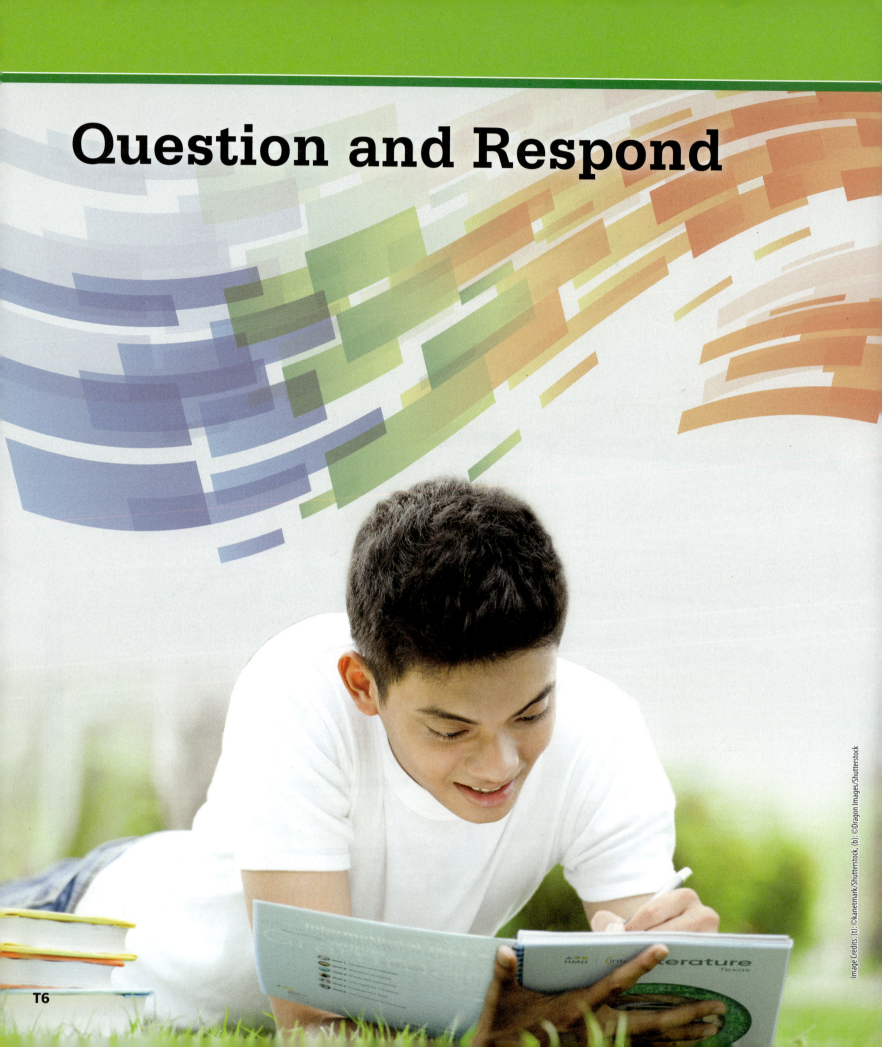
Question and Respond

Students who read...

- **Acquire** fluency
- **Choose** independently
- **Monitor** understanding
- **Annotate** and use evidence
- **Write** and discuss within and across texts

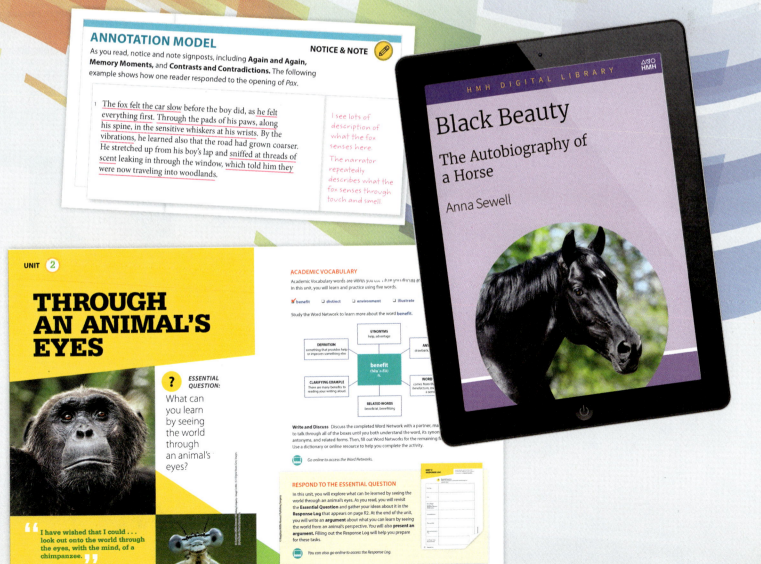

Connect Reading and Writing

Students who explore genre...

- **Analyze** features
- **Understand** effects of authors' choices
- **Emulate** craft
- **Use** mentor texts
- **Synthesize** ideas

GENRE ELEMENTS: INFORMATIONAL TEXT
- provides factual information
- includes evidence to support ideas
- often contains text features
- includes many forms, such as news articles and essays
- includes science writing, which explains complex scientific topics in language that is easy to understand

Craft and Communicate

Students who compose...

- **Inform,** argue, and connect
- **Create** in a literary genre
- **Imitate** mentor texts
- **Apply** conventions
- **Use** process and partners

Explore and Research

Students who inquire...

- **Generate** questions
- **Plan** and revise
- **Synthesize** information
- **Cite** sources
- **Deliver** results

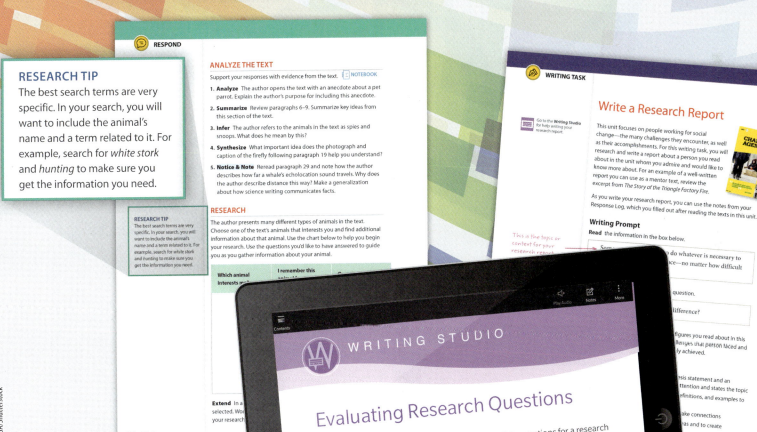

Maximize Growth through Data-Driven Differentiation and Assessment

Ongoing assessment and data reporting provide critical feedback loops to teachers and students, so that each experience encourages self-assessment and reflection, and drives positive learning outcomes for all students.

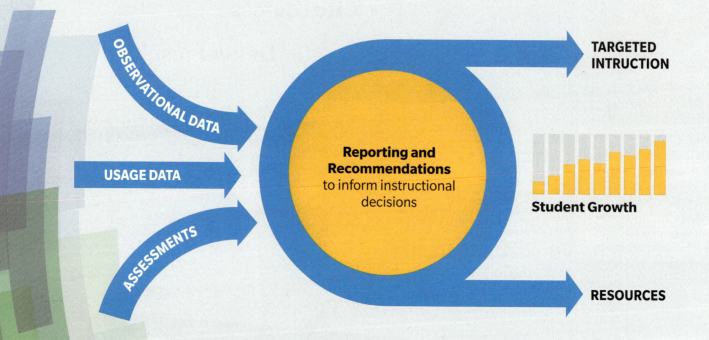

Actionable reports drive grouping and instructional recommendations appropriate for each learner.

Program Assessments

Adaptive Growth Measure

3 times per year

Adaptive Growth Measure allows teachers to gain an understanding of where students are on the learning continuum and identify students in need of intervention or enrichment.

Unit Assessments

6 times per year

Unit Assessments identify mastery of skills covered during the course of the unit across all literacy strands.

Ongoing Feedback from Daily Classroom Activities

Formative Assessment data is collected across a variety of student activities to help you make informed instructional decisions based on data.

- Check Your Understanding
- Selection Tests
- Writing Tasks
- Independent Reading
- Usage Data
- Online Essay Scoring
- Teacher Observations
- Research Projects

Assessments

HMH Into Literature has a comprehensive suite of assessments to help you determine what your students already know and how they are progressing through the program lessons.

Diagnostic Assessment for Reading is an informal, criterion-referenced assessment designed to diagnose the specific reading comprehension skills that need attention.

Skills-based Diagnostic Assessments will help you quickly gauge a student's mastery of common, grade-level appropriate skills.

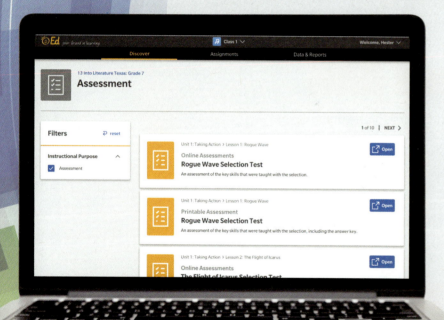

Every selection in the Into Literature program has a corresponding **Selection Test,** focusing on the skills taught in each lesson.
- Analyze & Apply
- Collaborate & Compare, and
- Independent Reading

A **Unit Test** assesses mastery of the skills taught in the entire Unit using new readings aligned with the Unit topic.

The **Diagnostic Screening Test** for Grammar, Usage, and Mechanics provides an assessment of strengths and weaknesses in the conventions of written English.

Each Module in the Grammar Studio has a **Diagnostic Assessment** and a **Summative Assessment,** for before and after instruction.

Foster a Learning Culture

As you encourage a culture of responsibility and collaboration, essential for students' success in the world of work, you will find learning activities that are social, active, and student owned.

Collaborate & Compare Designed to support individual accountability as well as team aptitude, this section requires students to read and annotate texts and compare their responses in small groups.

Peer Review is a critical part of students' creative process. Tools like Checklists for writing and listening and speaking tasks and the Revision Guide with questions, tips, and techniques offer practical support for peer interaction.

Learning Mindset notes and strategies in your Teacher's Edition are designed to help students acquire the attitude of perseverance through learning obstacles. Other resources like ongoing formative assessments, peer evaluation, and Reflect on the Unit questions encourage students to monitor their progress and develop metacognitive ability.

 **LEARNING MINDSET**

Seeking Challenges Explain that having a growth and learning mindset means taking risks. That involves trying new things and not being afraid to fail (or look silly) in front of friends. Emphasize that trying hard is important, but trying things that are hard is just as important. The brain needs to be stretched and challenged in much the same way as muscles do, and that's the way to think about difficult tasks, as challenges.

Build a Culture of Professional Growth

Embedded and on-going Professional Learning empowers you to develop high-impact learning experiences that provide all your students with opportunities for reading and writing success.

Build agency with purposeful, embedded teacher support and high-impact strategies

- Notice & Note Strategies for Close Reading
- Classroom Videos
- On-Demand Professional Learning Modules

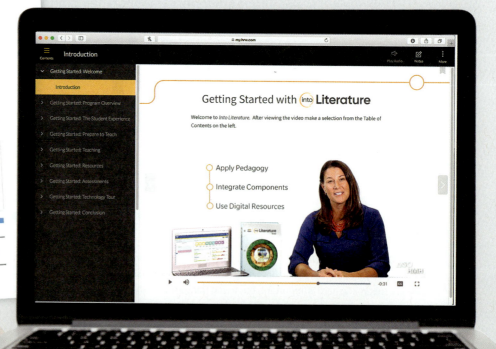

Grow Your Practice with Personalized Blended Professional Learning

- **Getting Started Course and Professional Learning Guide:** Learn the program components, pedagogy, and digital resources to successfully teach with *Into Literature*.

- **Follow-Up:** Choose from relevant instructional topics to create a personalized in-person or online Follow-Up experience to deepen program mastery and enhance teaching practices.

- **Coaching and Modeling:** Experience just-in-time support to ensure continuous professional learning that is student-centered and grounded in data.

- **askHMH:** Get on-demand access to program experts who will answer questions and provide personalized conferencing and digital demonstrations to support implementation.

- **Technical Services:** Plan, prepare, implement, and operate technology with ease.

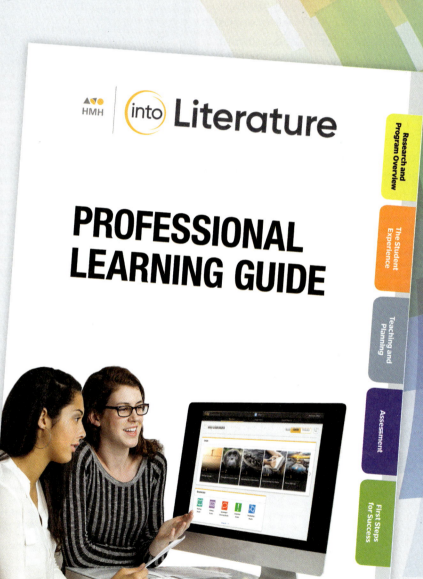

Annotated Student Edition Table of Contents

UNIT

Instructional Overview and Resources 1A

Topical Focus
Each unit reflects a topic linking selections, an Essential Question, a Quotation, and unit tasks for analysis, discussion, synthesis, and response.

Essential Question
Posing thought-provoking ideas for discussion and reflection as students read, the Essential Question stimulates analysis and synthesis, leading to a richer understanding of the unit's texts.

UNIT 1

TAKING ACTION
PAGE 1

? ESSENTIAL QUESTION

What helps people rise up to face difficulties?

ANALYZE & APPLY

NOTICE & NOTE
READING MODEL

 SHORT STORY
Rogue Wave 4
by Theodore Taylor

MYTH
The Flight of Icarus 24
retold by Sally Benson

 POEM
Icarus's Flight 36
by Stephen Dobyns

 HISTORY WRITING   MENTOR TEXT
Women in Aviation 44
by Patricia and Fredrick McKissack

COLLABORATE & COMPARE

 SHORT STORY
Thank You, M'am 58
by Langston Hughes

COMPARE CHARACTERS
AND PEOPLE

 ARTICLE
A Police Stop Changed This Teenager's Life 70
by Amy B Wang

FM6   Grade 7

T20

UNIT 1

Online Ed **INDEPENDENT READING**
These selections can be accessed through the digital edition.

LEGEND
from **Young Arthur**
by Robert D. San Souci

MYTH
Perseus and the Gorgon's Head
retold by Ann Turnbull

POEM
It Couldn't Be Done
by Edgar Albert Guest

POEM
Chemistry 101
by Marilyn Nelson

Suggested Novel Connection

NOVEL
Holes
by Louis Sachar

Additional Novel Connections
- **Flowers for Algernon**
  by Daniel Keyes
- **Buried Onions**
  by Gary Soto

Unit **1** **Tasks**
- Write an Informational Essay 86
- Present a Film Critique 93

Reflect on the Unit 95

Key Learning Objectives
In abbreviated form, each unit's main instructional goals are listed for planning and quick reference.

Key Learning Objectives
- Analyze plot
- Make Inferences
- Analyze myths
- Analyze form in poetry
- Analyze tone
- Determine author's purpose
- Analyze character
- Analyze setting and conflict
- Analyze structure

 Visit the Interactive Student Edition for:
- Unit and Selection Videos
- Media Selections
- Selection Audio Recordings
- Enhanced Digital Instruction

Contents FM7

UNIT 2

Instructional Overview and Resources 96A

UNIT 2
REALITY CHECK
PAGE 96

? ESSENTIAL QUESTION

What can blur the lines between what's real and what's not?

Analyze & Apply

This section of the Table of Contents groups a variety of selections for analysis, annotation, and application of the Notice & Note protocol, as well as standards instruction.

ANALYZE & APPLY

NOTICE & NOTE
READING MODEL

SHORT STORY
Heartbeat... 100
by David Yoo

ARTICLE   **MENTOR TEXT**
The Camera Does Lie...................................... 112
by Meg Moss

FOLK TALE
Two Legs or One?... 124
retold by Josepha Sherman

Collaborate & Compare

This section of the Table of Contents provides a comparative analysis of two selections linked by topic but different in genre, craft, or focus. Standards instruction and annotation are also applied.

COLLABORATE & COMPARE

COMPARE
MOODS

POEM
The Song of Wandering Aengus.......................... 134
by W. B. Yeats

POEM
Eldorado... 140
by Edgar Allan Poe

COMPARE
CHARACTERIZATION

DRAMA
The Governess *from* The Good Doctor.................. 146
by Neil Simon

PRODUCTION IMAGES
from The Governess...................................... 162
by Clackamas Community College

FM8   Grade 7

T22

UNIT 2

 INDEPENDENT READING
These selections can be accessed through the digital edition.

SHORT STORY
Way Too Cool
by Brenda Woods

INFORMATIONAL TEXT
Forever New
by Dan Risch

SHORT STORY
He—y, Come On Ou—t!
by Shinichi Hoshi

PERSONAL ESSAY
A Priceless Lesson in Humility
by Felipe Morales

Suggested Novel Connection

NOVEL
The Witch of Blackbird Pond
by Elizabeth George Speare

Unit 2 Task
- Create a Multimodal Presentation 172

Reflect on the Unit 179

Independent Reading
Interactive digital texts linked to the unit topic and in a wide range of genres and Lexile levels provide additional resources for students' independent reading, expanding student choice and experience.

Additional Novel Connections
- **The Westing Game**
  by Ellen Raskin
- **A Christmas Carol**
  by Charles Dickens

Key Learning Objectives
- Analyze character
- Analyze conflict
- Determine author's purpose
- Analyze folk tales
- Analyze humor
- Analyze rhyme
- Analyze sound devices and mood
- Analyze drama

 Visit the Interactive Student Edition for:
- Unit and Selection Videos
- Media Selections
- Selection Audio Recordings
- Enhanced Digital Instruction

Contents FM9

UNIT 3

Instructional Overview and Resources 180A

UNIT 3

INSPIRED BY NATURE
PAGE 180

? ESSENTIAL QUESTION

What does it mean to be in harmony with nature?

Notice & Note Reading Model
Using a gradual release model to teach the signposts referred to as Notice & Note, the Reading Model describes two to three signposts and illustrates them in a selection.

Mentor Text
This selection exemplifies genre characteristics and craft choices that will be used in end-of-unit writing tasks as models for students.

ANALYZE AND APPLY

NOTICE & NOTE READING MODEL

ARGUMENT
Never Retreat from Eyes Wide Open 184
by Paul Fleischman

MEMOIR   **MENTOR TEXT**
from Mississippi Solo 196
by Eddy Harris

POEM
The Drought 208
by Amy Helfrich

SHORT STORY
Allied with Green 216
by Naomi Shihab Nye

COLLABORATE & COMPARE

COMPARE FORMS AND ELEMENTS

POEM
Ode to enchanted light 228
by Pablo Neruda *translated by* Ken Krabbenhoft

POEM
Sleeping in the Forest 236
by Mary Oliver

COMPARE PERSUASIVE MEDIA

VIDEO
from Trash Talk 242
by the National Oceanic and Atmospheric Administration

POSTER
You're Part of the Solution 246

FM10 Grade 7

T24

UNIT 3

INDEPENDENT READING
These selections can be accessed through the digital edition.

MEMOIR
from **Unbowed**
by Wangari Muta Maathai

POEM
Problems with Hurricanes
by Victor Hernández Cruz

ARTICLE
Living Large Off the Grid
by Kristen Mascia

POETRY
Haiku
by Issa, Bashō, and Buson, *translated by* Richard Haas

Suggested Novel Connection

NOVEL
Peak
by Roland Smith

Unit Task
- Write a Personal Narrative 254

Reflect on the Unit 261

Additional Novel Connections

- **My Side of the Mountain**
  by Jean Craighead George

- **Kon-Tiki**
  by Thor Heyerdahl

Key Learning Objectives
- Analyze argument
- Analyze point of view
- Analyze memoir
- Analyze figurative language
- Analyze sonnets
- Analyze rhyme scheme
- Analyze theme
- Analyze odes
- Analyze lyric poetry
- Analyze media

Visit the Interactive Student Edition for:
- Unit and Selection Videos
- Media Selections
- Selection Audio Recordings
- Enhanced Digital Instruction

Contents FM11

UNIT 4

Instructional Overview
and Resources 262A

UNIT 4

THE TERROR AND WONDER OF SPACE

PAGE 262

ESSENTIAL QUESTION

Why is the idea of space exploration both inspiring and unnerving?

ANALYZE AND APPLY

NOTICE & NOTE
READING MODEL

SCIENCE WRITING
Martian Metropolis 266
by Meg Thacher

SCIENCE FICTION
Dark They Were, and Golden-Eyed 278
by Ray Bradbury

ARGUMENT   MENTOR TEXT
Challenges for Space Exploration 304
by Ann Leckie

POEM
What If We Were Alone? 314
by William Stafford

VIDEO
Seven Minutes of Terror 322
by the National Aeronautics and Space Administration

COLLABORATE & COMPARE

COMPARE
ARGUMENTS

ARGUMENT
Space Exploration Should Be More Science Than Fiction ... 326
by Claudia Alarcón

ARGUMENT
Humans Should Stay Home and Let Robots Take to the Stars 338
by Eiren Caffall

FM12   Grade 7

Variety of Genres

Each unit is comprised of different kinds of texts or genres. Essential characteristics of each genre are identified and illustrated. Students then apply those characteristics to their own writing.

UNIT 4

INDEPENDENT READING
These selections can be accessed through the digital edition.

ARGUMENT
Let's Aim for Mars
by Buzz Aldrin

PERSONAL ESSAY
An Optimistic View of the World
by Dan Tani

POEM
Your World
by Georgia Douglas Johnson

BIOGRAPHY
Sally Ride *from* Headstrong
by Rachel Swaby

Suggested Novel Connection

NOVEL
A Wrinkle in Time
by Madeleine L'Engle

Tasks
Each unit concludes with one or two culminating tasks that demonstrate essential understandings, synthesizing ideas and text references in oral and written responses.

Unit 4 Tasks
- Write an Argument 350
- Prepare a Podcast 357

Reflect on the Unit 359

Additional Novel Connections

- **Ender's Game**
  by Orson Scott Card
- **The Dark is Rising**
  by Susan Cooper

Key Learning Objectives
- Analyze structural elements
- Analyze organizational patterns
- Analyze author's purpose
- Analyze repetition
- Analyze science fiction
- Analyze mood
- Analyze graphical elements
- Analyze theme
- Analyze media
- Analyze rhetorical devices

 Visit the Interactive Student Edition for:
- Unit and Selection Videos
- Media Selections
- Selection Audio Recordings
- Enhanced Digital Instruction

Contents FM13

UNIT 5

Instructional Overview and Resources 360A

Cultural Diversity
Each unit includes a rich array of selections that represent multicultural authors and experiences.

UNIT 5

MORE THAN A GAME
PAGE 360

? ESSENTIAL QUESTION

How do sports bring together friends, families, and communities?

ANALYZE AND APPLY

NOTICE & NOTE READING MODEL

SHORT STORY   **MENTOR TEXT**
Ball Hawk 364
by Joseph Bruchac

INFORMATIONAL TEXT
Get in the Zone: The Psychology of Video Game Design 380
by Aaron Millar

INFORMATIONAL TEXT
It's Not Just a Game! 392
by Lori Calabrese

COLLABORATE & COMPARE

COMPARE THEME

NOVEL IN VERSE
from The Crossover 404
by Kwame Alexander

POEM
Double Doubles 414
by J. Patrick Lewis

FM14 Grade 7

UNIT 5

 INDEPENDENT READING

These selections can be accessed through the digital edition.

SHORT STORY
Batting After Sophie
by Sue Macy

SHORT STORY
Amigo Brothers
by Piri Thomas

BLOG
Bridging the Generational Divide Between a Football Father and Soccer Son
by John McCormick

SCIENCE WRITING
Arc of Triumph
by Nick D'Alto

Suggested Novel Connection

NOVEL
Slam!
by Walter Dean Myers

> **Suggested Novel Connection**
> One extended text is recommended for its topical and thematic connection to other texts in the unit.

Additional Novel Connections

- **Baseball in April and Other Stories**
  by Gary Soto

- **Bat 6**
  by Virginia Euwer Wolff

Unit 5 Task
- Write a Short Story 426

Reflect on the Unit 433

Key Learning Objectives
- Analyze point of view
- Make predictions
- Analyze organizational patterns
- Analyze novels in verse
- Analyze metaphor and personification
- Analyze voice in poetry
- Make inferences

 Visit the Interactive Student Edition for:
- Unit and Selection Videos
- Media Selections
- Selection Audio Recordings
- Enhanced Digital Instruction

Contents FM15

UNIT 6

Instructional Overview
and Resources 434A

UNIT 6

CHANGE AGENTS

PAGE 434

? ESSENTIAL QUESTION

What inspires you to make a difference?

ANALYZE AND APPLY

NOTICE & NOTE
READING MODEL

PERSONAL ESSAY
Craig Kielburger Reflects on Working Toward Peace 438
by Craig Kielburger

DOCUMENTARY
from It Takes a Child 450
by Judy Jackson

SHORT STORY
Sometimes a Dream Needs a Push 454
by Walter Dean Myers

POEM
A Poem for My Librarian, Mrs. Long 468
by Nikki Giovanni

COLLABORATE & COMPARE

COMPARE AUTHORS'
PURPOSES AND
MESSAGES

HISTORY WRITING
Frances Perkins and the Triangle Factory Fire 476
by David Brooks

HISTORY WRITING   **MENTOR TEXT**
from The Story of the Triangle Factory Fire 490
by Zachary Kent

FM16   Grade 7

UNIT 6

Online Ed **INDEPENDENT READING**
These selections can be accessed through the digital edition.

ARTICLE
Difference Maker: John Bergmann and Popcorn Park
by David Karas

AUTOBIOGRAPHY
from Walking with the Wind
by John Lewis

SHORT STORY
Doris Is Coming
by ZZ Packer

INFORMATIONAL TEXT
Seeing Is Believing
by Mary Morton Cowan

Suggested Novel Connection

NOVEL
Bud, Not Buddy
by Christopher Paul Curtis

Unit Tasks
- Write a Research Report.................................... 504
- Participate in a Panel Discussion 511

Reflect on the Unit 513

Additional Novel Connections
- **Lupita Manana**
  by Patricia Beatty
- **A Northern Light**
  by Jennifer Donnelly

> **Reflection**
> Students may pause and reflect on their process and understanding of the selections and the themes in each unit.

Key Learning Objectives
- Analyze author's point of view
- Analyze elements of documentary
- Analyze realistic fiction
- Analyze character qualities
- Analyze free verse in poetry
- Analyze theme
- Analyze history writing
- Determine key ideas
- Analyze text structure

 Visit the Interactive Student Edition for:
- Unit and Selection Videos
- Media Selections
- Selection Audio Recordings
- Enhanced Digital Instruction

Contents FM17

SELECTIONS BY GENRE

FICTION

SHORT STORY

Allied with Green Naomi Shihab Nye	216
Amigo Brothers Piri Thomas	Online
Ball Hawk Joseph Bruchac	364
Batting After Sophie Sue Macy	Online
Dark They Were, and Golden-Eyed Ray Bradbury SCIENCE FICTION	278
Doris Is Coming ZZ Packer	Online
Heartbeat David Yoo	100
He—y, Come On Ou—t! Shinichi Hoshi	Online
Rogue Wave Theodore Taylor	4
Sometimes a Dream Needs a Push Walter Dean Myers	454
Thank You, M'am Langston Hughes	58
Way Too Cool Brenda Woods	Online

ORAL TRADITION

The Flight of Icarus retold by Sally Benson MYTH	24
Perseus and the Gorgon's Head retold by Ann Turnbull MYTH	Online
Two Legs or One? retold by Josepha Sherman FOLK TALE	124
from Young Arthur Robert D. San Souci LEGEND	Online

NOVEL

from The Crossover Kwame Alexander NOVEL IN VERSE	404

NONFICTION

INFORMATIONAL TEXT

Arc of Triumph Nick D'Alto SCIENCE WRITING	Online
The Camera Does Lie Meg Moss	112
Difference Maker: John Bergmann and Popcorn Park David Karas	Online
Forever New Dan Risch	Online
Frances Perkins and the Triangle Factory Fire David Brooks HISTORY WRITING	476
Get in the Zone: The Psychology of Video Game Design Aaron Millar	380
It's Not Just a Game! Lori Calabrese	392
Living Large Off the Grid Kristen Mascia	Online
Martian Metropolis Meg Thatcher SCIENCE WRITING	266
A Police Stop Changed This Teenager's Life Amy B Wang	70
Seeing Is Believing Mary Morton Cowan	Online
from The Story of the Triangle Factory Fire Zachary Kent HISTORY WRITING	490
Women in Aviation Patricia and Fredrick McKissack HISTORY WRITING	44

ARGUMENT TEXT

Challenges for Space Exploration Ann Leckie	304
Human Should Stay Home and Let Robots Take to the Stars Eiren Caffall	338

Let's Aim for Mars Buzz Aldrin	Online
Never Retreat *from* **Eyes Wide Open** Paul Fleischman	184
Space Exploration Should Be More Science Than Fiction Claudia Alarcón	326

NARRATIVE NONFICTION

Bridging the Generational Divide Between a Football Father and Soccer Son John McCormick BLOG	Online
Craig Kielburger Reflects on Working Toward Peace Craig Kielburger PERSONAL ESSAY	438
An Optimistic View of the World Dan Tani PERSONAL ESSAY	Online
A Priceless Lesson in Humility Felipe Morales PERSONAL ESSAY	Online

AUTOBIOGRAPHY/MEMOIR

from **Mississippi Solo** Eddy Harris	196
from **Unbowed** Wangari Muta Maathai	Online
from **Walking with the Wind** John Lewis	Online

BIOGRAPHY

Sally Ride *from* **Headstrong** Rachel Swaby	Online

POETRY

Chemistry 101 Marilyn Nelson	Online
Double Doubles J. Patrick Lewis	414
The Drought Amy Helfrich	208
Eldorado Edgar Allan Poe	140
Haiku Issa, Bashō, and Buson *translated by* Richard Haas	Online
Icarus's Flight Stephen Dobyns	36
It Couldn't Be Done Edgar Albert Guest	Online
Ode to enchanted light Pablo Neruda	228
A Poem for My Librarian, Mrs. Long Nikki Giovanni	468
Problems with Hurricanes Victor Hernández Cruz	Online
Sleeping in the Forest Mary Oliver	236
The Song of Wandering Aengus W. B. Yeats	134
What If We Were Alone? William Stafford	314
Your World Georgia Douglas Johnson	Online

DRAMA

The Governess *from* **The Good Doctor** Neil Simon	146

MEDIA STUDY

from **The Governess** PRODUCTION IMAGES	162
from **It Takes a Child** Judy Jackson DOCUMENTARY	450
Seven Minutes of Terror National Aeronautics and Space Administration VIDEO	322
from **Trash Talk** National Oceanic and Atmospheric Administration VIDEO	242
You're Part of the Solution POSTER	246

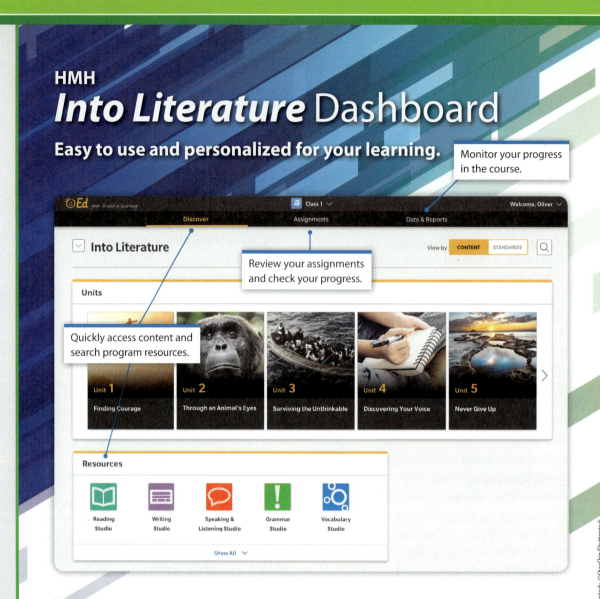

HMH
Into Literature Dashboard

Easy to use and personalized for your learning.

Monitor your progress in the course.

Review your assignments and check your progress.

Quickly access content and search program resources.

 Explore Online to Experience the Power of HMH Into Literature

All in One Place
Readings and assignments are supported by a variety of resources to bring literature to life and give you the tools you need to succeed.

Supporting 21st Century Skills
Whether you're working alone or collaborating with others, it takes effort to analyze the complex texts and competing ideas that bombard us in this fast-paced world. What will help you succeed? Staying engaged and organized. The digital tools in this program will help you take charge of your learning.

FM20

Ignite Your Investigation
You learn best when you're engaged. The **Stream to Start** videos at the beginning of every unit are designed to spark your interest before you read. Get curious and start reading!

Learn How to Close Read
Close reading effectively is all about examining the details. See how it's done by watching the **Close Read Screencasts** in your eBook. Hear modeled conversations on targeted passages.

Bring the Meaning into Focus
Text in Focus videos dig deeper into complex texts by offering visual explanations for potential stumbling blocks.

Personalized Annotations
My Notes encourages you to take notes as you read and allows you to mark the text in your own customized way. You can easily access annotations to review later as you prepare for exams.

Interactive Graphic Organizers
Graphic organizers help you process, summarize, and keep track of your learning and prepare for end-of-unit writing tasks. **Word Networks** help you learn academic vocabulary, and **Response Logs** help you explore and deepen your understanding of the **Essential Question** in each unit.

No Wi-Fi? No problem!
With HMH *Into Literature,* you always have access: download when you're online and access what you need when you're offline. Work offline and then upload when you're back online.

Communicate "Raise a Hand" to ask or answer questions without having to be in the same room as your teacher.

Collaborate Collaborate with your teacher via chat and work with a classmate to improve your writing.

FM21

HMH
Into Literature
STUDIOS

All the help you need to be successful in your literature class is one click away with the Studios. These digital-only lessons are here to tap into the skills that you already use and help you sharpen those skills for the future.

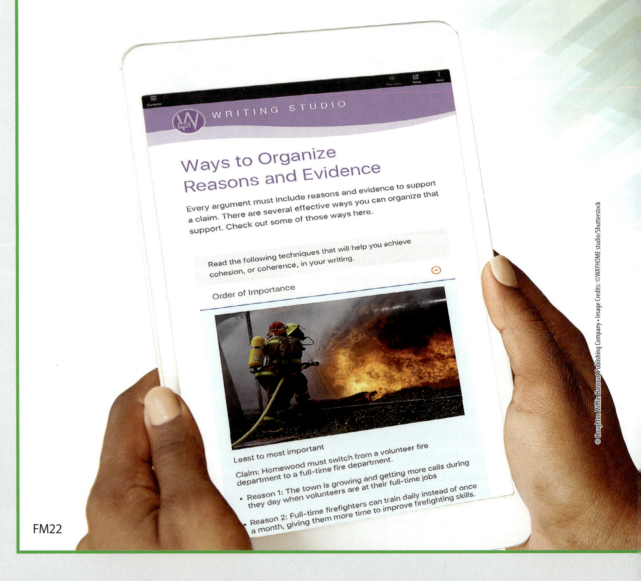

Online Ed Easy-to-find resources, organized in five separate STUDIOS. On demand and on ED!

Look for links in each lesson to take you to the appropriate Studio.

READING STUDIO

Go beyond the book with the Reading Studio. With over 100 full-length down-loadable titles to choose from, find the right story to continue your journey.

WRITING STUDIO

Being able to write clearly and effectively is a skill that will help you throughout life. The Writing Studio will help you become an expert communicator—in print or online.

SPEAKING & LISTENING STUDIO

Communication is more than just writing. The Speaking & Listening Studio will help you become an effective speaker and a focused listener.

GRAMMAR STUDIO

Go beyond traditional worksheets with the Grammar Studio. These engaging, interactive lessons will sharpen your grammar skills.

VOCABULARY STUDIO

Learn the skills you need to expand your vocabulary. The interactive lessons in the Vocabulary Studio will grow your vocabulary to improve your reading.

NOTICE & NOTE

This essay is an introduction to the Notice & Note signposts by program consultants Kylene Beers and Robert Probst. It is purposefully informal and designed to motivate students.

Ask students the following question:

What graphic elements let readers know that the essay's target is students? *Answer:* photos, drawings, questions and answers, color and underlining

---

An ABSOLUTELY, POSITIVELY, MUST READ ESSAY in the FRONT of your Literature Book

YOUR TEACHER AGREES!

BY TWO PEOPLE YOU HAVE NEVER HEARD OF
Dr. Kylene Beers and Dr. Robert E. Probst

If you are reading this essay when we think you are, it's early in the school year. You have this big book in front of you and, for some reason, your teacher has asked you to read these pages by two people you've never met.

Let's begin by telling you something about us.

From Dr. Beers:

"I've been a teacher all my adult life. I've worked with students at all grades and now I spend most of my time working with teachers, maybe even your teacher! I live in Texas and when I'm not on an airplane flying off to work in a school, I'm on my ranch, plowing a field. I like to read, cook, read, garden, read, spend time with my family and friends, and (did I mention?) read!"

Who are these people??

From Dr. Probst:

"I've also been a teacher all my adult life. When I first started teaching, I taught kids in middle school and high school, and then I spent most of my career teaching people how to be teachers. For many years now, Dr. Beers and I have written books together, books that are about teaching kids how to be better readers. I live in Florida and when I'm not in schools working with teachers and kids, I enjoy watching my grandkids play soccer and baseball and I love going out on my boat. And, like Dr. Beers, I love reading a great book, too."

So, we're teachers. And we're writers. Specifically, we write books for teachers, books teachers read so that they can help their students become better readers...

. . . and we're going to try to help you become a better reader this year.

We will because we both believe TWO things.

First, we've never met a kid who didn't want to get better at reading. <u>Reading is important for almost everything you do,</u> so doing it well is important.

Second, we believe that reading can change you. Reading something can open up your mind, your thinking, your ideas, your understanding of the world and all the people in it, so that you might choose to change yourself. <u>Reading can help you change yourself.</u>

We think too often it's easy to forget why reading is important. You can come to believe that you need to read better just so your grades will go up, or you need to read better so that you do well on a big state test. Those things are important—you bet—but they aren't as important as reading better so that you can become better. Yes, reading can help you change.

How would that happen—how can reading help you change yourself? Sometimes it is obvious. You read something about the importance of exercise and you <u>start walking a little more.</u>

Or, you read something about energy and the environment and you <u>decide to make sure you always turn off the lights</u> when you leave any room.

Other times, it might be less obvious. You might read *Wonder* and <u>begin to think about what it really means to be a good friend.</u> Maybe you walk over to that person sitting alone in the cafeteria and sit with him or her. Perhaps you'll read *Stella by Starlight* and that book helps you become someone who stands against racism. Or maybe it happens as you read *Mexican Whiteboy* and discover that <u>who you are is more about what you are on the inside than what anyone ever sees on the outside.</u> And when you realize that,

How can reading help me change myself?

FM25

Note that Beers and Probst list some of the standard reasons students want to be better readers: improve grades and enhance standardized test performance. But they add that reading "can help me change myself."

Ask students to use their consumable book's margins to complete a quick write answering this question:

How has reading led to personal change for you?

Encourage students to be specific.

Ask at least three to five students to share with the group.

Discuss with students the three "jobs" as readers Beers and Probst suggest.

"Hello! I wanted to discuss the Important Message with you!"

perhaps it will give you the courage you need to be truer to yourself, to be the person you really want to be.

Reading gives us moments to think, and as we think we just might discover something about ourselves that we want to change. And that's why we say reading can help us change ourselves.

Finding Important Messages

It sure would be easy to find important messages in the things we read if the authors would just label them and then maybe give us a call.

The reality is, though, that would make the reading less interesting. And it would mean that every reader is supposed to find the same message. Not true! While the author has a message he or she wants to share, the reader—that's you!—has at least three jobs to do:

My Job

1 → **First,** enjoy what you are reading.

2 → **Second,** figure out the message the author wanted to share. Authors write for a reason (no, not to make a lot of money!), and part of that reason is to share something important. That's the author's message, and this year we'll be showing you some ways to really focus in on that.

3 → **Third,** you need to figure out the message that matters most to **YOU.** (YES, WE SAVED THE BEST FOR LAST!!!) Sometimes the author's message and what matters most to you will be the same; sometimes not. For instance, it's obvious that J.K. Rowling wrote the Harry Potter series to show us all the sustaining power of love.

From Dr. Beers:
" But when I read these books, what really touched my heart was the importance of standing up to our fears. "

From Dr. Probst:
" And what mattered most to me was the idea that one person, one small person, can make a huge difference in the world. I think that's a critically important point. "

Understanding the author's message requires you to do some work while you read, work that requires you to read the text closely. No. You don't need a magnifying glass. But you do need to learn how to notice some things in the text we call SIGNPOSTS.

A signpost is simply something the author says in the text that helps you understand how characters are changing, how conflicts are being resolved, and, ultimately, what theme—or lesson—the author is trying to convey.

You can also use signposts to help you figure out the author's purpose when you are reading nonfiction. If you can identify the author's purpose—why she or he wrote that particular piece of nonfiction—then you'll be better able to decide whether or not you agree, and whether you need more information.

We do want you thinking about signposts, but first, as you read, we want you to remember three letters: BHH.

B	Book	As you read, we want you to remember that you have to pay attention to what's in the book (or article).
H	Head	And, you need to think about what you are reading as you read—so you have to think about what's in your head.
H	Heart	And sometimes, maybe as you finish what you're reading, you'll ask yourself what you have taken to heart.

To think carefully about what's in the book and what's in your head, you need to become an alert reader, one who notices things. If you're reading fiction, for instance, you ought to pay attention to how characters act. When a character starts acting in a way you don't expect, something is up! That's as if the author has put up a blinking sign that says "Pay attention here!" Or, if you are reading nonfiction, and the author starts using a lot of numbers, that's the same as the author waving a huge flag that says "Slow down! Pay attention! I'm trying to show you something!"

How do I find the author's message?

So, as I read, I have to think about something called signposts?

Pay attention HERE!

FM27

Beers and Probst introduce the concept of **signposts** which will be used throughout *Into Literature*. Ask students to underline this definition in their copy.

Ask students why the term *signpost*, which is used in other contexts, is also a good one for reading. **Possible answer:** *Writers give us direction, clues, and insight with their words just as drivers are given vital information with stop signs, yield signs, and school zone warnings.*

Ask students to bracket in their consumable the reference to "BHH." Review each. Provide an example and ask students for additional examples.

Example:

B I read an article in the local newspaper discussing five ways to get involved in my community. One suggestion was to begin volunteering.

H I thought about my personal interests: teaching, animals, and the environment.

H I decided to sign up for a volunteers' orientation at the local animal shelter.

Featured Essays **T41**

Read aloud the four signposts listed here as examples. Explain that these are only four of the signposts they will be learning while using *Into Literature*. Refer students to the entire list of signposts on Student Edition page FM 29. Ask them to mark this page with a sticky note for easy reference.

Review the "keep reading" challenge. Ask students to discuss if this challenge is one they can accept.

Direct students to complete a three-minute quick write in the margin of their book responding to the quote:

"... reading is something that can help you become the person you most want to be."

Ask a few volunteers to share.

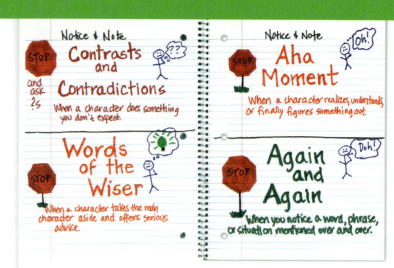

Don't worry about memorizing all the signposts. You'll learn them this year. Your teacher will probably have you make some notes—perhaps as the student above did.

Some of the things you'll read this year, you might not like. (OK—just being honest!) But most of the things we bet you will. What we hope you'll do, throughout this year, is keep reading.

Keep Reading
- » Read every day.
- » Read something hard.
- » Read something easy.
- » Read something you choose.
- » Read what your teachers ask you to read.
- » Read something that makes you laugh.
- » And it's OK if sometimes what you read makes you cry.

One of us LOVES to read scary books while the other much prefers survival books, so don't worry if you like something your best friend doesn't. Read joke books and how-to books and love stories and mysteries and absolutely be sure you read about people who aren't like you. That's the best way to learn about the world around you, about other people, about other ways of thinking. The best way to become a more open person is to live for a while, in the pages of a book, the life of someone you are not.

We hope you have a great year. Stay alert for signposts that you'll be learning throughout this book.

And remember . . .

. . . reading is something that can help you become the person you most want to be.

FM28

NOTICE & NOTE SIGNPOSTS

Signpost	Definition	Anchor Question(s)
FICTION		
Contrasts and Contradictions	A sharp contrast between what we would expect and what we observe the character doing; behavior that contradicts previous behavior or well-established patterns	Why would the character act (feel) this way?
Aha Moment	A character's realization of something that shifts his actions or understanding of himself, others, or the world around him	How might this change things?
Tough Questions	Questions a character raises that reveal his or her inner struggles	What does this question make me wonder about?
Words of the Wiser	The advice or insight about life that a wiser character, who is usually older, offers to the main character	What is the life lesson, and how might this affect the character?
Again and Again	Events, images, or particular words that recur over a portion of the story	Why might the author bring this up again and again?
Memory Moment	A recollection by a character that interrupts the forward progress of the story	Why might this memory be important?
NONFICTION		
Contrasts and Contradictions	A sharp contrast between what we would expect and what we observe happening. A difference between two or more elements in the text.	What is the difference, and why does it matter?
Extreme or Absolute Language	Language that leaves no doubt about a situation or an event, allows no compromise, or seems to exaggerate or overstate a case.	Why did the author use this language?
Numbers and Stats	Specific quantities or comparisons to depict the amount, size, or scale. Or, the writer is vague and imprecise about numbers when we would expect more precision.	Why did the author use these numbers or amounts?
Quoted Words	Opinions or conclusions of someone who is an expert on the subject, or someone who might be a participant in or a witness to an event. Or, the author might cite other people to provide support for a point.	Why was this person quoted or cited, and what did this add?
Word Gaps	Vocabulary that is unfamiliar to the reader—for example, a word with multiple meanings, a rare or technical word, a discipline-specific word, or one with a far-removed antecedent.	Do I know this word from someplace else? Does it seem like technical talk for this topic? Can I find clues in the sentence to help me understand the word?

Read the chart on this page noting that it is divided into **Fiction** and **Nonfiction** signposts and includes a definition and an anchor question for each. An **anchor question** helps students identify the signposts as they read by "questioning" the text.

The essay by program consultant Carol Jago is an accessible explanation of **genre** and its importance. Genre has an elevated role in the new standards—both in reading and writing.

Ask students to read the first paragraph and then to write their own definition of genre in the margin of their book.

Ask students to turn to a partner and provide examples of their favorite genre.

If your students need an analogy to better understand **genre**, explain that genre refers to different categories or kinds of texts we read. This is similar to vehicles that we use for transportation. Vehicles transport people and goods but may be trucks, vans, sedans or sports cars—different categories for vehicles—different genres for texts.

READING AND WRITING ACROSS GENRES

by Carol Jago

Reading is a first-class ticket around the world. Not only can you explore other lands and cultures, but you can also travel to the past and future. That journey is sometimes a wild ride. Other books can feel like comfort food, enveloping you in an imaginative landscape full of friends and good times. Making time for reading is making time for life.

Genre

One of the first things readers do when we pick up something to read is notice its genre. You might not think of it exactly in those terms, but consider how you approach a word problem in math class compared to how you read a science fiction story. Readers go to different kinds of text for different purposes. When you need to know how to do or make something, you want a reliable, trusted source of information. When you're in the mood to spend some time in a world of fantasy, you happily suspend your normal disbelief in dragons.

In every unit of *Into Literature,* you'll find a diverse mix of genres all connected by a common theme, allowing you to explore a topic from many different angles.

Writer's Craft

Learning how writers use genre to inform, to explain, to entertain, or to surprise readers will help you better understand—as well as enjoy—your reading. Imitating how professional writers employ the tools of their craft—descriptive language, repetition, sensory images, sentence structure, and a variety of other features—will give you many ideas for making your own writing more lively.

GENRE ELEMENTS: SHORT STORY
- is a work of short fiction that centers on a single idea and can be read in one sitting
- usually includes one main conflict that involves the characters and keeps moving
- includes the basic elements of fiction—plot, character, setting, and theme
- may be based on real and historical events

GENRE ELEMENTS: INFORMATIONAL TEXT
- provides factual information
- includes evidence to support ideas
- contains text features
- includes many forms, such as news articles and essays

GENRE ELEMENTS: HISTORICAL FICTION
- includes the basic elements of fiction: setting, character, plot, conflict, and theme
- is set in the past and includes real places and real events of historical importance
- is a type of realistic fiction in which fictional characters behave like real people and use human abilities to deal with life's challenges

GENRE ELEMENTS: POETRY
- may use figurative language, including personification
- often includes imagery that appeals to the five senses
- expresses a theme, or a "big idea" message about life

Into Literature provides you with the tools you need to understand the elements of all the critical genres and advice on how to learn from professional texts to improve your own writing in those genres.

Reading with Independence

Finding a good book can sometimes be a challenge. Like every other reader, you have probably experienced "book desert" when nothing you pick up seems to have what you are looking for (not that it's easy to explain exactly what you are looking for, but whatever it is, "this" isn't it). If you find yourself in this kind of reading funk, bored by everything you pick up, give yourself permission to range more widely, exploring graphic novels, contemporary biographies, books of poetry, historical fiction. And remember that long doesn't necessarily mean boring. My favorite kind of book is one that I never want to end.

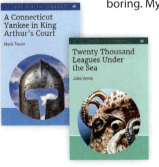

Take control over your own reading with *Into Literature's* Reader's Choice selections and the HMH Digital Library. And don't forget: your teacher, librarian, and friends can offer you many more suggestions.

SHORT STORY
Vanquishing the Hungry Chinese Zombie
Claudine Gueh
A girl faces terror to protect her parents and the family store.

POEM
Horrors
Lewis Carroll
What are those terrible things that go bump in the night?

NARRATIVE NONFICTION
Running into Danger on an Alaskan Trail
Cinthia Ritchie
A long-distance runner has a terrifying encounter with a bear.

Direct students to read the paragraph under the heading "writer's craft." Ask students to write their own definition of writer's craft in the margin of *Into Literature*. Discuss.

Encourage students to find the Genre Elements chart with each selection in *Into Literature*.

Call students' attention to the **Reader's Choice** selections listed at the end of each unit and show students how to find the **HMH Digital Library** in the **Reading Studio**.

TEACHER'S EDITION

GRADE 7

Program Consultants:
Kylene Beers
Martha Hougen
Elena Izquierdo
Carol Jago
Erik Palmer
Robert E. Probst

UNIT 1

Instructional Overview and Resources

		Instructional Focus	Online Ed Resources
	Unit Instruction **Taking Action**	**Unit 1 Essential Question** **Unit 1 Academic Vocabulary**	**Stream to Start:** Taking Action **Unit 1 Response Log**

ANALYZE & APPLY

	"Rogue Wave" Short Story by Theodore Taylor **Lexile 980L** **NOTICE & NOTE** READING MODEL **Signposts** • Again and Again • Memory Moment • Aha Moment	**Reading** • Analyze Plot • Make Inferences **Writing:** Adapt as a Film **Speaking and Listening:** Share and Discuss Plot Details **Vocabulary:** Latin Roots **Language Conventions:** Sentence Structure	**Audio** **Text in Focus:** Building Background **Close Read Screencast:** Modeled Discussions **Reading Studio:** Notice & Note **Writing Studio:** Writing Informative Texts **Speaking and Listening Studio:** Participating in Collaborative Discussions **Grammar Studio:** Module 7: Sentence Structure
	"The Flight of Icarus" Greek Myth retold by Sally Benson **Lexile 1110L**	**Reading** • Analyze Genre: Myth • Determine Themes **Writing:** Write an Explanation **Speaking and Listening:** Discuss with a Small Group **Vocabulary:** Latin Roots **Language Conventions:** Commas and Coordinate Adjectives	**Audio** **Text in Focus:** Analyzing Language **Close Read Screencast:** Modeled Discussions **Speaking and Listening Studio:** Participating in Collaborative Discussions **Reading Studio:** Notice & Note **Writing Studio:** Using Textual Evidence **Vocabulary Studio:** Latin Roots **Grammar Studio:** Module 14: Lesson 2–6: Using Commas
	"Icarus's Flight" Poem by Stephen Dobyns p_body-bold-orange	**Reading** • Analyze Form in Poetry • Analyze Punctuation and Tone **Writing:** Write a Poem **Speaking and Listening:** Critique a Poem Orally	**Audio** **Reading Studio:** Notice & Note **Writing Studio:** Analyzing and Evaluating Presentations
	MENTOR TEXT **"Women in Aviation"** Informational Writing by Patricia and Frederick McKissack **Lexile 1150L**	**Reading** • Determine Author's Purpose • Cite Evidence and Draw Conclusions **Writing:** Write an Informational Essay **Speaking and Listening:** Discuss with a Small Group **Vocabulary:** Connotations and Denotations **Language Conventions:** Consistent Verb Tenses	**Audio** **Reading Studio:** Notice & Note **Writing Studio:** Writing Informative Texts **Speaking and Listening Studio:** Participating in Collaborative Discussions **Grammar Studio:** Module 9: Using Verbs Correctly

SUGGESTED PACING: 30 DAYS

Unit Introduction	Rogue Wave	The Flight of Icarus	Icarus's Flight	Women in Aviation
1	2 3 4 5 6	7 8 9 10	11 12 13	14 15 16

1A Unit 1

PLAN

English Learner Support		Differentiated Instruction	Assessment
• Learn Vocabulary • Learning Strategies			
• Text X-Ray • Use Cognates • Learning Strategies • Monitor Comprehension • Confirm Understanding • Read and Share • Develop Fluency • Reinforce Meaning • Oral Assessment	• Discuss with Small Group • Latin Roots • Language Conventions	**When Students Struggle** • Use Strategies **To Challenge Students** • Learning Strategy	**Selection Test**
• Text X-Ray • Use Prior Knowledge • Use Cognates • Learning Strategies • Language Conventions • Reinforce Meaning • Oral Assessment	• Discuss with a Small Group • Latin Roots	**When Students Struggle** • Learning Strategy **To Challenge Students** • Conduct Research	**Selection Test**
• Text X-Ray • Question of Punctuation • Reading Comprehension • Punctuation	• Sentence Structures • Recognizing Patterns • Reading Comprehension • Critique a Poem Orally	**When Students Struggle** • Think-Pair-Share	**Selection Test**
• Text X-Ray • Understand Author's Purpose • Understand Critical Vocabulary • Analyze Language • Draw Conclusions • Contextual Support • Use Cognates	• Monitor Comprehension • Understanding Verb Tense • Oral Assessment • Discuss with a Small Group • Understand Connotations and Denotations • Understand Verb Tenses	**When Students Struggle** • Identify Supporting Details • Understanding Plagiarism	**Selection Test**

Women in Aviation 15 16
Thank You M'am / Police Stop 19 20 21 22 23 24 25 26
Independent Reading 27 28
End of Unit 29 30 31

Taking Action 1B

PLAN

UNIT 1 Continued

	Instructional Focus	Online Ed Resources

COLLABORATE & COMPARE

"Thank You, Ma'am"
Short Story by Langston Hughes
Lexile 660L

Reading
• Analyze Character Traits
• Analyze Internal and External Conflict
Writing: Write a Letter of Request
Speaking and Listening: Discuss with a Small Group
Vocabulary: Suffixes –able and -ible
Language Conventions: Capitalization

🔊 **Audio**
Reading Studio: Notice & Note
Speaking and Listening Studio: Participating in Group Discussion
Vocabulary Studio: Suffixes
Grammar Studio: Capital Letters

"A Police Stop Changed This Teenager's Life"
Article by Amy B. Wang
Lexile 890L

Reading
• Analyze Structure
Writing: Write an Objective Summary
Speaking and Listening: Share and Discuss Opinions
Vocabulary: Context Clues
Language Conventions: Quotation Marks in Dialogue

🔊 **Audio**
Reading Studio: Notice & Note
Writing Studio: Using Textual Evidence
Writing Studio: Conducting Research
Speaking and Listening Studio: Participating in Collaborative Discussions
Vocabulary Studio: Context Clues
Grammar Studio: Module 3: Lesson 6: Conjunctions and Interjections

---

Collaborate and Compare

Reading: Compare Characters and People
Speaking and Listening: Research and Share

Speaking and Listening Studio: Having a Debate

INDEPENDENT READING

The independent Reading selections are only available in the eBook.

📖 Go to the Reading Studio for more information on **NOTICE & NOTE.**

"Chemistry 101"
Poem by Marilyn Nelson

"It Couldn't Be Done"
Poem by Edgar Albert Guest

END OF UNIT

Writing Task: Write an Informational Essay

Speaking and Listening Task: Present a Film Critique

Reflect on the Unit

Writing: Writing an Informational Essay
Language Conventions: Consistent Verb Tenses
Speaking and Listening: Present a Film Critique of an Action Movie

Unit 1 Response Log
Mentor Text: "Women in Aviation"
Writing Studio: Writing Informative Texts
Grammar Studio: Module 9: Using Verbs Correctly
Speaking and Listening Studio: Giving a Presentation

PLAN

English Learner Support	Differentiated Instruction	Online Ed Assessment
• Text X-Ray • Learning Strategies • Demonstrate Comprehension • Comprehend Language Structures • Monitor Comprehension • Understand Critical Vocabulary	**When Students Struggle** • Character Traits **To Challenge Students** • Characterization in Fiction	**Selection Tests**
• Text X-Ray • Learning Strategies • Cognates • Confirm Understanding • Understand Language Structures • Oral Assessment • Share and Discuss Opinions • Vocabulary Strategy • Language Conventions	**When Students Struggle** • Make Inferences **When Students Struggle** • Compare Texts	**Selection Tests**
from Young Arthur Legend by Robert D. San Souci **Lexile 830L**	"Perseus and the Gorgon's Head" Myth by Ann Turnbull **Lexile 890L**	**Selection Tests**
• Language Text X-Ray • Understand Academic Language • Write a Group Essay • Use the Mentor Text • Use Connecting Words • Consistent Verb Tenses • Adapt the Essay	**When Students Struggle** • Draft the Essay • Use Consistent Verb Tenses • Take Notes **To Challenge Students** • Conduct Research	**Unit Test**

Reality Check **1D**

TEACH

? Connect to the ESSENTIAL QUESTION

Ask a volunteer to read aloud the Essential Question. What are some of the common characteristics of people who face obstacles and overcome them? How do the images on the page relate to the Essential Question? Ask students to think of real-life situations in which people persevere when confronted with challenges.

■ English Learner Support

Learn Vocabulary Make sure students understand the Essential Question. If necessary, explain the following terms:

- *Rise up to face* means "to confront, or deal with, a challenge."
- *Difficulties* means "things that are hard to do or deal with."
- *Effective* (from the quotation) means "successful."

Help students paraphrase the question: for example, ask *What helps people do things that are hard to do?*
SUBSTANTIAL/MODERATE

DISCUSS THE QUOTATION

Tell students that Amelia Earhart (1897-1937?) was an American aviation pioneer, the first woman to fly solo across the Atlantic Ocean. She wrote best-selling books about her flying experiences and founded the Ninety-Nines, a groundbreaking organization of female pilots. Ask students to read the quotation. Then discuss how Earhart's advice might apply to almost any situation in which people have obstacles to overcome. Discuss how the quotation relates to the Essential Question. What might "it" refer to in Amelia Earhart's quote? Ask students: *Where and how do people find it in themselves to "just do it?"*

UNIT

TAKING ACTION

? ESSENTIAL QUESTION

What helps people rise up to face difficulties?

> " The most effective way to do it, is to do it. "
>
> — Amelia Earhart

 LEARNING MINDSET

Growth Mindset Explain that students who believe they can learn and improve at their skills are more successful than students who believe they're "just not good at" certain subjects. But in order to grow their brain, students must be willing to put forth effort and accept challenges, even if it means making mistakes. This is called having a *growth mindset*. It is essential to embrace this kind of mindset so students can break out of their comfort zone and reach their full potential.

UNIT 1

ACADEMIC VOCABULARY

Academic Vocabulary words are words you use when you discuss and write about texts. In this unit you will practice and learn five words.

☑ aspect   ☐ cultural   ☐ evaluate   ☐ resource   ☐ text

Study the Word Network to learn more about the word **aspect.**

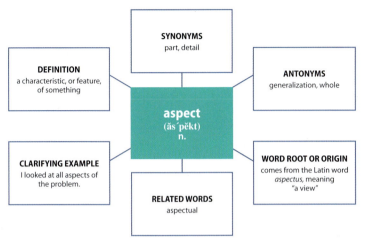

Write and Discuss Discuss the completed Word Network with a partner, making sure to talk through all of the boxes until you both understand the word, its synonyms, antonyms, and related forms. Then, fill out Word Networks for the remaining four words. Use a dictionary or online resource to help you complete the activity.

 Go online to access the Word Networks.

RESPOND TO THE ESSENTIAL QUESTION

In this unit, you will explore how different people take action to overcome difficulties. As you read, you will revisit the **Essential Question** and gather your ideas about it in the **Response Log** that appears on page R1. At the end of the unit, you will have the opportunity to write an **informational essay** about the qualities used by people to overcome obstacles. Filling out the Response Log will help you prepare for this writing task.

 You can also go online to access the Response Log.

Taking Action   1

TEACH

ACADEMIC VOCABULARY

As students complete Word Networks for the remaining four vocabulary words, encourage them to include all the categories shown in the completed network if possible, but point out that some words do not have clear synonyms or antonyms. Some words may also function as different parts of speech—for example, *text* may be a noun or a verb.

aspect (ăs´pĕkt) *n.* a characteristic or feature of something (Spanish cognate: *aspecto*)

cultural (kŭl´chər-əl) *adj.* relating to the ideas, customs, and social behavior of a society (Spanish cognate: *cultural*)

evaluate (ĭ-văl´yōō-āt´) *tr. v.* to determine the importance, effectiveness, or value of (Spanish cognate: *evaluar*)

resource (rē´sôrs) *n.* something that can be used for support or help

text (tĕkst) *n.* written or printed words (Spanish cognate: *texto*)

RESPOND TO THE ESSENTIAL QUESTION

Direct students to the Unit 1 Response Log. Explain that students will use it to record ideas and details from the selections that help answer the Essential Question. When they work on the writing task at the end of the unit, their Response Logs will help them think about what they have read and make connections between texts.

ENGLISH LEARNER SUPPORT

Learning Strategies Use a simple Concept Map organizer with "*aspect*" on the top and boxes for "Synonyms", "Things that are like this," and "Antonyms" below. Use the word in sentences so that students can understand the different ways the word is used: *An aspect of lunchtime that I do not like is that we do not get enough time to eat and talk to our friends.* Or, *The cloudy, dark sky makes a scary aspect.*

Use this strategy with different Academic Vocabulary words or with any difficult words in the unit.   **SUBSTANTIAL**

Taking Action   1

READING MODEL
ROGUE WAVE
Short Story by Theodore Taylor

GENRE ELEMENTS
SHORT STORY

Remind students that the aim of a **short story** is to interest and entertain readers. Authors achieve this aim by crafting compelling characters who experience events and situations that readers want to follow until the conclusion. Short stories may be based on real-life, everyday situations or on imaginary and unusual ones. They can be funny or serious, and they usually have something meaningful to say about life. In an **adventure story**, the characters usually face extremely dangerous situations in exciting settings.

LEARNING OBJECTIVES

- Cite evidence to support inferences drawn from the text.
- Analyze plot elements, including plot stages, conflict, and setting.
- Conduct research about rogue waves.
- Write a description of how to adapt the story as a movie.
- Discuss plot details in "Rogue Wave."
- Use Latin roots to determine the meaning of unfamiliar words.
- Analyze and write simple, compound, and complex sentences.
- **Language** Understand sentence structure.

TEXT COMPLEXITY

Lexile: 980L

	Rogue Wave
Quantitative Measures	
Qualitative Measures	**Ideas Presented** Mostly explicit, but moves to some implied meaning.
	Structure Used Ideas presented sequentially; several points of view.
	Language Used Mostly explicit; some difficult vocabulary.
	Knowledge Required Requires no special knowledge; situations easily envisioned.

PLAN

RESOURCES

- Unit 1 Response Log
- Selection Audio
- Building Background
- Close Read Screencasts: Modeled Discussions
- Reading Studio: Notice & Note
- Writing Studio: Writing Informative Texts
- Speaking and Listening Studio: Participating in Collaborative Discussions
- Grammar Studio: Module 7: Sentence Structure
- "Rogue Wave" Selection Test

SUMMARIES

English

A nineteen-year-old boy and his fourteen-year-old sister are sailing on a cutter-rigged sailboat off the coast of Southern California. A giant wave suddenly appears behind them. The "rogue" wave turns their boat upside down. The boy is outside: he's on the bottom of the boat; his sister is trapped inside the cabin, and water is pouring in fast. What follows is their dramatic story of survival. As the boy experiences terror and frustration because he cannot help her, the girl realizes that only she can save herself. She must keep calm, remember what she's learned about the boat, and use her analytical skills and instincts.

Spanish

Un chico de diecinueve años y su hermana de catorce navegan en un velero por la costa sur de California. Una ola gigante aparece súbitamente detrás de ellos. La ola "forajida" pone el bote de cabeza. El chico queda afuera: está sobre el casco del bote; su hermana está atrapada dentro de la cabina y el agua entra rápidamente. Lo que sigue es su dramática historia de supervivencia. Mientras el chico siente terror y frustración por no poder ayudarla, la chica se da cuenta de que solo ella puede salvarse a sí misma. Debe conservar la calma, recordar lo que ha aprendido del bote y utilizar sus capacidades analíticas e instintos.

SMALL-GROUP OPTIONS

Have students work in small groups to read and discuss the selection.

Jigsaw with Experts

- Divide the last three pages of the story into six parts, beginning at paragraph 47.
- Have students count off, or assign each student a numbered section.
- After they read the text, have students form groups with other students who read the same section. Each expert group should discuss its section.
- Then, have students form new groups with a representative for each section. These groups should discuss all the sections as a whole.

Think-Pair-Share

- After students have read and discussed "Rogue Wave," pose this question: *What qualities did Scoot have that helped her save herself?*
- Have students think about the question individually and write down their ideas.
- Then, have pairs discuss their ideas about the question.
- Finally, ask pairs to share their responses with the class.

Rogue Wave   2B

PLAN

Text X-Ray: English Learner Support
for "Rogue Wave"

Use the Text X-Ray and the supports and scaffolds in the Teacher's Edition to help guide students at different proficiency levels through the selection.

INTRODUCE THE SELECTION
DISCUSS TENSION AND SUSPENSE

In this lesson, students will need to be able to analyze and discuss how elements of an adventure story work together to create tension and suspense. Distinguish these two concepts by explaining:

- Tension is the uncomfortable feeling readers feel because the main characters haven't been able to solve their problem yet.
- Suspense is the excitement and anxiety readers feel because they don't know what is going to happen next.

For example, a reader may feel tense because a character can't make up his mind about how to handle a problem. A reader may be in suspense about what will happen to the character if he or she doesn't make a decision fast.

Have volunteers share stories about experiences that made them feel tense and suspenseful. Supply the following sentence frames:

- *I felt tense when I couldn't figure out how to.*
- *I was filled with a feeling of suspense because I didn't know.*

CULTURAL REFERENCES

The following words and phrases may be unfamiliar to the students:

- *split second* (paragraph 8): a very small amount of time: less than a second
- *lapping at Scoot's chin* (paragraph 11): the water coming into the cabin is moving: it touches and then moves away from Scoot's chin like waves at a shoreline.
- *seawater has no heart* (paragraph 20): to have no heart means to have no feelings
- *broke down* (paragraph 22): gave up, started to cry
- *willing to take the gamble* (paragraph 25) willing to take a big risk
- *mantra* (paragraph 49) a word or phrase people repeat to calm themselves down

LISTENING

Understand the Conflict

Direct students' attention to the conflict that the character is facing in paragraphs 26 and 27. Remind students that conflict means the problem that the character must overcome. Explain that understanding conflict helps readers better understand a story.

Have students listen as you read aloud paragraphs 26 and 27. Use the following supports with students at varying proficiency levels. Display images of a cutter rigged boat and big waves to begin:

- Model that students should give a thumbs up if the answer is yes, a thumbs down for no to your questions. Ask: *Did the boat go down?* (Make a downward motion) (*yes*) Have students choral read the fragment: "*Vaguely . . . body going up.*" **SUBSTANTIAL**
- Have students identify the conflict. Ask: *What does the character remember?* (*The boat going down*) *Why does she feel around herself?* (Make motion of feeling around)(*She's in the dark and must find everything by touch.*) **MODERATE**
- Pair students and ask them to work together to list details from the text that explain how the character figures out what happened. (*She remembers the boat slanting steeply downward, feeling her body going up, trapped in the Sea Dog's cabin*) **LIGHT**

2C   Unit 1

PLAN

SPEAKING

Discuss Plot Details in "Rogue Wave"

Have students discuss how the story builds tension and creates suspenseful moments. Circulate around the room to make sure that they are using the terms tension and suspense correctly.

Use the following supports with students at varying proficiency levels. Provide images to go with the selection illustrations for students in need of extra support.

- Read paragraph 20 aloud to students, pausing frequently to answer any questions they may have. Ask them to quietly say "tension" if the sentence creates tension: "And he knew what would happen down there." (*students say "Tension"*) "The water would torture her." (*Tension*) **SUBSTANTIAL**
- Have students of different abilities work in pairs to read paragraphs 20 and 21 aloud to each other. Have them pick out the sentences that create the most tension. (*Answers will vary.*) **MODERATE**
- Have students discuss paragraph 30 with a partner. What specific event in this paragraph creates suspense? (*Scoot comes out of shock and knows that she has to find a way out.*) **LIGHT**

READING

Analyze the Setting

Remind students that the setting is an important part of the story's plot. Remind students that the story has two settings: inside and outside the boat. Ask students to identify how changes in the settings affect the characters and the plot.

Work with students to read paragraphs 8, 9, and 10. Use the following supports with students at varying proficiency levels. Provide images of the inside of a cutter-rigged boat, and of a sailboat upside down in the ocean to clarify that there are two settings.

- Choral read the paragraphs. Ask students to stop anytime they see or hear a word or a phrase that identifies or describes the setting. Encourage students to decode independently or with assistance. **SUBSTANTIAL**
- Guide student pairs to search the text for evidence of how changes in the setting affect Scoot. **MODERATE**
- Ask students to work in pairs to find two problems in each setting that create suspense. Ask students to use at least two important words such as *mast* or *galley* to describe both settings. **LIGHT**

WRITING

Write a Description of a Film Adaptation

Work with students to read the writing assignment on p. 25. Clarify any parts of the four story elements outlined in the assignment that might be unclear.

Use the following supports with students at varying proficiency levels: Encourage students in need of extra support to make storyboards using appropriate images gathered on online.

- Work with students to create a written list of phrases with images that identify four events from the story (plot) that they would like to include in their movie. Have them make storyboards to show cause and effect in action. **SUBSTANTIAL**
- Work with students to decide on an opening scene that establishes the characters, setting, and conflict. Have students use graphic organizers showing cause and effect in action. **MODERATE**
- Help students craft a controlling idea that will guide them to say what they want to express through characters, plot, and setting. A controlling idea could be: "Use prior knowledge about dangerous settings to survive." What you learn today could save you tomorrow." or "Don't give up. Believe that you can find a solution, even in the worst situation." **LIGHT**

TEACH

EXPLAIN THE SIGNPOSTS

Explain that **NOTICE & NOTE Signposts** are significant moments in the text that help readers understand and analyze works of fiction or nonfiction. Use the instruction on these pages to introduce students to the signposts **Memory Moment**, **Again and Again**, and **Aha Moment**. Then use the selection that follows to have students apply the signposts to a text.

For a full list of the fiction and nonfiction signposts, see p. 84.

MEMORY MOMENT

Explain that some **Memory Moments** are obvious. The character might start a sentence by saying, "Back in my day…" Other Memory Moments, like the one in the example passage, can be more subtle and easy to miss.

Read aloud the example passage and pause at the phrase "last night's meal." Model for students how to determine that the phrase is a signpost for a Memory Moment. Point out that this is a subtle cue pointing to Scoot's recollection, and that it also provides important information about **setting** and **character**.

Tell students that when they spot a Memory Moment, they should pause, mark it in their consumable texts, and ask the anchor question: *Why might this memory be important?*

Notice Note
READING MODEL

For more information on these and other signposts to Notice & Note, visit the **Reading Studio**.

When you read and encounter phrases like these, pause to see if a phrase indicates a **Memory Moment** signpost:

"She remembered that . . ."
"He'd heard of . . ."
"It was just like when . . ."
"Earlier that week . . ."
"as a baby, she'd . . ."

Anchor Question
When you notice this signpost, ask: Why might this memory be important?

ROGUE WAVE

You are about to read the short story "Rogue Wave." In it, you will notice and note signposts that will give you clues about the story's characters and themes. Here are three key signposts to look for as you read this short story and other works of fiction.

Memory Moment You're sitting on the bench waiting for the coach to post the names of the kids who made the team. As you wait, your mind drifts back to when you started shooting hoops at the neighborhood courts. You were just eight. Others would laugh every time you missed. Not anymore. The coach comes out and you run over to read the list.

Our brains are linking the present to the past almost all of the time. Something—an image, a sound, a smell, an event—will trigger a memory of an earlier time. When an author introduces a memory, it's usually for a good reason. Paying attention to a **Memory Moment** can:

- provide background that relates to the current situation
- reveal details about characters' histories or relationships
- show what motivates or drives a character's actions
- show what leads a character to an "aha moment"

The paragraph below of "Rogue Wave" illustrates a student's annotation of a Memory Moment:

> 5 Below deck Scoot was listening to Big Sandy & His Fly-Rite Boys doing "Swingin' West," and singing along with them while slicing leftover steak from last night's meal. <u>They'd grilled it on a small charcoal ring that was mounted outboard on the starboard side at the stern, trailing sparks into the water.</u> The *Sea Dog* had every blessed thing, including a barbecue pit, she marveled.

What memory is introduced?	the memory of grilling steak the previous night
Why do you think this memory is important to the story?	The memory shows that Scoot is impressed by how well equipped the *Sea Dog* is. It also shows that she and her brother are enjoying this trip.

▶ **Again and Again** Have you ever noticed how soft drink ads use certain words over and over—like *cool* and *refreshing*? They do this to create a certain image in your mind. When images, events, or words appear in a story **Again and Again**, they can also create or reinforce a certain image, idea, or feeling. Here a student marked an "Again and Again" example:

> 1   A killer wave, known to mariners as a "rogue wave," was approaching a <u>desolate area of Baja California below Ensenada</u>. . . .
> 4   Sullivan Atkins, Scoot's oldest brother, was steering the cutter-rigged boat on a northerly course about fifteen miles off <u>desolate Cabo Colnett, south of Ensenada.</u>

Anchor Question
When you notice this signpost, ask: Why might the author keep bringing this up?

What images or words appear again and again?	the word <u>desolate</u>; the location close to Ensenada
What effect does this have?	It makes clear that no other boats or people are around.

▶ **Aha Moment** It's your birthday and you're mad because your mom has again put off getting you new running shoes. Then you open her present. Just the shoes you wanted! Now you have to reconsider what happened and why.

A character experiencing an **Aha Moment** may suddenly realize he or she faces a serious problem, discover the pathway to resolving the conflict or solving the problem, or reach a broader understanding about life. Here's an example of an Aha Moment a student discovered:

> 8   But a split second before it lifted the boat like a carpenter's chip, he sensed something behind him and glanced backward, toward the towering wall of shining water.

When you see phrases like these, pause to see if it's an **Aha Moment**:
"It took a little longer to realize . . ."
"That had to be the reason . . ."
"he sensed something . . ."

Anchor Question
When you notice this signpost, ask: How might this change things?

What does Sully suddenly realize in paragraph 8?	A huge wave is about to hit the boat.
How do we know Sully realizes this?	Sully glances backward and sees the wall of water.

Notice & Note   3

WHEN STUDENTS STRUGGLE . . .

Use Strategies Visualizing is important in identifying signposts, especially Aha Moments. If students are struggling to recognize signposts, have them use the Sketch to Stretch strategy to visualize what is happening in a text. Ask students to identify the Aha Moment in the Reading Model. Then, tell them to sketch what they see happening. Explain that it's acceptable to use stick figures. Finally, have students turn to a partner and share their drawings. Ask: *What might your drawing of Sully's situation look like, five minutes after his Aha Moment?*

TEACH

▶ **AGAIN AND AGAIN**

Explain that repetition, or saying things **Again and Again**, stresses details a writer wants an audience to remember, in the chorus of a popular song or the context of fiction and nonfiction.

Read the example passage aloud and pause at the words *desolate* and *Ensenada* each time. Model for students that the repeated words refer to the same geographic area, described with the same adjective. Point out that the rogue wave and the boat are in the same area, and that the coastline is deserted or desolate. Ask students to consider how this signpost may indicate something about the **plot**. What seems likely to happen?

Tell students when they spot repetition, they should pause, mark it in their consumable texts, and ask themselves the anchor question: *Why is this element repeated?*

▶ **AHA MOMENT**

Explain that **Aha Moments** almost always point to a change in circumstances for a story **character.** Point out that some Aha Moments will not be as sudden and dramatic as a rogue wave; they may involve a gradual realization over time.

Read aloud the example passage and stress the phrases *But a split second before* and *he sensed something behind him*. These clue words strongly suggest that something is just about to happen to Sully.

Tell students that when they spot an Aha Moment, they should pause, mark it in their consumable texts, and ask themselves the anchor question: *How might this change things in the story?*

APPLY THE SIGNPOSTS

Have students use the selection that follows as a model text to apply the signposts. As students encounter signposts, prompt them to stop, reread, and ask themselves the anchor questions that will help them understand the story's characters and themes.

Notice & Note   3

TEACH

? Connect to the ESSENTIAL QUESTION

"Rogue Wave" tells the story of a brother and a sister who rise up to face difficulty when their small sailboat is upended by a killer wave. They must draw on their strength, quick thinking and survival instincts to find each other and stay alive.

ANALYZE & APPLY

ROGUE WAVE

Short Story by **Theodore Taylor**

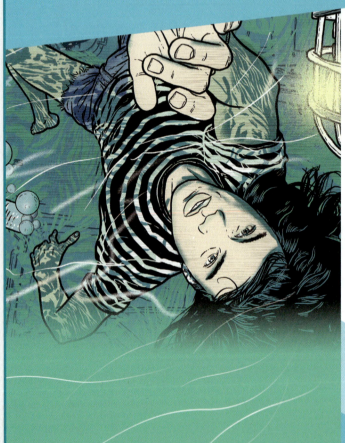

? ESSENTIAL QUESTION:

What helps people rise up to face difficulties?

 LEARNING MINDSET

Growth Mindset Remind students that even if they don't yet quite understand a text or a particular concept, if they keep trying they will eventually understand it. Stress to students that learning takes effort and that the important thing is not to give up.

GET READY

QUICK START

Do you panic or do you keep a clear head in a crisis? Make a list of the qualities needed to deal with a crisis. Discuss your ideas with a partner.

ANALYZE PLOT

The power of an adventure story, such as "Rogue Wave," comes from its action and events. Most stories recount a series of events, also known as a **plot**. An important part of the plot is the setting, or the time and place of the action. The setting influences the characters and the **conflict**, the struggle between opposing forces. As the characters try to resolve the conflict, the plot builds **suspense**, the growing tension felt by the reader. Writers also use **foreshadowing,** or hints that suggest future events, to create suspense and increase readers' interest in what will happen. Most plots have five stages:

- The **exposition** introduces characters, setting, and conflict.
- The **rising action** presents complications that intensify the conflict.
- The **climax** is the story's moment of greatest interest—and the point where the conflict is resolved.
- In the **falling action**, the story begins to draw to a close.
- The **resolution** reveals the final outcome of the conflict.

As you read "Rogue Wave," make notes about how the characters, setting, and plot work together to create suspense and excitement.

MAKE INFERENCES

Authors do not always describe every aspect of a story, character, or setting. Instead, they provide clues to help you make **inferences**, logical guesses based on story details and your own knowledge and experience. Making these connections helps you understand the plot.

To support inferences, you can **cite textual evidence** that provides specific information from the text. For example, you can identify story details that show how the setting influences the plot. As you read "Rogue Wave," notice details and use them to make inferences about the characters, events, and setting. Note them in a chart like this.

TEXT EVIDENCE	MY EXPERIENCE	INFERENCE
The title of the story is "Rogue Wave." The setting is a small sailboat.	Big waves can be dangerous.	The characters may be in danger on their small boat.

GENRE ELEMENTS: SHORT STORY
- includes one or more characters
- provides a setting
- develops a plot
- may be realistic or imaginary
- often conveys a theme or lesson about life
- characters in most realistic fiction stories face everyday problems; characters in adventure stories face extreme dangers

Rogue Wave 5

TEACH

QUICK START

Have students read the Quick Start question, and invite them to share real-life crises they have faced and whether they reacted calmly or panicked. Then ask them which positive qualities aided them in handling the crisis and which negative qualities got in their way.

ANALYZE PLOT

Help students understand the difference between the elements of a plot (events, setting, characters, conflict, resolution of the conflict, foreshadowing) and the five stages of a plot (exposition, rising action, climax, falling action, resolution) that are defined on page 5. Have students make a word-web organizer to show that a plot is made of elements that relate to one another. Then, have students make a line-graph organizer to show that the stages occur in time.

MAKE INFERENCES

Remind students that inferences are logical guesses based on specific details in a story, and a reader's prior knowledge and experience. It's important that the knowledge readers use to make inferences is based on facts. Inferences have to make sense; just as a good detective uses facts, evidence, and experience to get at the truth. Inferences help readers to be more involved in understanding the characters, setting, and plot of a story. Suggest that students use these questions to make their inferences when filling out the chart on page 5:

- *What evidence is clearly stated in the story?*
- *What does their personal knowledge tell them about that evidence?*
- *What logical guesses can they make based on that evidence?*

ENGLISH LEARNER SUPPORT

Use Prereading Supports

Have students examine the illustrations and use words or phrases they know about dangers of the overall setting, e.g., *small boat, big waves, shark, storm, lost.* **SUBSTANTIAL**

Have students work in pairs and write phrases that describe the dangers of the setting in the illustrations. **MODERATE**

Have students look up "rogue waves." Ask: Why is this important information to the setting? What other settings might be good for adventure stories? **LIGHT**

Rogue Wave 5

TEACH

CRITICAL VOCABULARY

Encourage students to read all the sentences before deciding which word best completes each one. Remind them to look for context clues that help them determine the meaning of each word.

Answers:

1. *porthole*
2. *navigation*
3. *deck*
4. *swell*
5. *submerge*

LANGUAGE CONVENTIONS

Reinforce the differences between simple, compound, and complex sentences. Remind students that a compound sentence always uses a coordinating conjunction preceded by a comma, and a complex sentence always uses a subordinating conjunction. Supply students with a list of conjunctions. Model dividing the list by type: and use them in sentences. Then, have students identify each of the following sentences: *The election results are in. Jose will be president because he won by a clear majority. Sara will be vice president and Carla will serve as secretary/treasurer.* (The first sentence is simple, the second is complex, and the third is compound.)

ANNOTATION MODEL

Students can review the Reading Model introduction if they have questions about any of the signposts. Suggest that they underline important phrases or circle key words that help them identify signposts. They may want to color-code their annotation by using a different color highlighter for each signpost. Point out that they may follow this suggestion or use their own system for marking up the selections in their write-in texts.

 GET READY

CRITICAL VOCABULARY

swell   deck   navigation   submerge   porthole

To see how many Critical Vocabulary words you already know, use them to complete the sentences.

1. Our room on the ship had a small _____ that let light in.
2. _____, especially over long distances, was much more difficult before the invention of detailed maps and GPS.
3. I leapt from the dock and onto the _____ of the boat.
4. Each _____ gently rocked the boat.
5. Standing on the shore, we watched the submarine _____ .

LANGUAGE CONVENTIONS

Sentence Structure In this lesson, you will learn about types of sentences and how to use punctuation between clauses. A **simple sentence** contains one main clause, as in "She was still inside." A **compound sentence** has two independent clauses. An example of this is, "The doors were jammed, and he returned to the surface for air." A **complex sentence** combines an independent clause with a subordinate clause. The sentence "In the blackness, water continued to lap at Scoot's chin." is an example of a complex sentence.

As you read "Rogue Wave," note the types of sentences the author uses to express ideas and how the punctuation makes the meanings clear.

ANNOTATION MODEL   NOTICE & NOTE

As you read, notice and note signposts, including Memory Moments, Again and Again, and Aha Moments. Here is an example of how one reader responded to the opening of "Rogue Wave."

> 1 A killer wave, known to mariners as a "rogue wave," was approaching a desolate area of Baja California below Ensenada. It had been born off the east coast of Australia during a violent storm; it had traveled about 7,000 miles at a speed of 20.83 miles an hour. Driven by an unusual pattern of easterly winds, it was a little over 800 feet in length and measured about 48 feet from the bottom of its trough to its crest. On its passage across the Pacific, <u>it had already killed thirteen people, mostly fishermen in small boats, but also an entire French family of five aboard a 48-foot schooner</u> . . .

This sets a suspenseful tone and reminds me of reading a newspaper article about a dangerous situation in my city.

BACKGROUND

This adventure story features a cutter-rigged sailboat. Cutter-rigged boats are small sailing yachts, each with a single mast for the main sail and smaller sails up front. Cutters can be equipped with a cabin that usually includes a small kitchen, called a galley. Author **Theodore Taylor** (1921–2006) wrote many stories about self-reliant characters who face great challenges. His best-known book, The Cay, depicts the struggles and revelations of a boy shipwrecked during World War II.

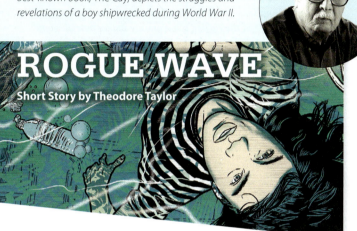

ROGUE WAVE
Short Story by Theodore Taylor

SETTING A PURPOSE

Pay attention to the details and events that make this story an adventure. As you read, think about the setting and how the author builds excitement and anticipation throughout the short story.

1   A killer wave, known to mariners as a "rogue wave," was approaching a desolate area of Baja California below Ensenada. It had been born off the east coast of Australia during a violent storm; it had traveled almost 7,000 miles at a speed of 20.83 miles an hour. Driven by an unusual pattern of easterly winds, it was a little over 800 feet in length and measured about 48 feet from the bottom of its trough to its crest. On its passage across the Pacific, it had already killed thirteen people, mostly fishermen in small boats, but also an entire French family of five aboard a 48-foot schooner . . .

Notice & Note

Use the side margins to notice and note signposts in the text.

MAKE INFERENCES

Annotate: In paragraph 1, mark details that describe rogue waves.

Interpret: What do these details suggest about the conflict of this story?

TEACH

 TEXT IN FOCUS

Building Background Have students view the **Text in Focus** video in their eBook to learn how to use background information to inform their reading. Then have students use **Text in Focus Practice** to apply what they have learned.

 ANALYZE PLOT

Remind students that the **setting** of a story, meaning the time and place of action, is an important part of this story. The setting influences the **characters** and the **conflict**. (**Answer:** *Scoot and Sully are in different parts of the boat, so if a wave strikes, they may get separated and won't be able to help each other.*)

CRITICAL VOCABULARY

swell: By the time waves reach the shore, they break. Out at sea, waves can roll for a while without ever breaking.

ASK STUDENTS what happens to a boat when it is on a swell in the middle of the ocean. (*A boat is lifted by the swell, rides its crest, and lowers as the crest recedes.*)

deck: In "Rogue Wave," Sullivan and Scoot are on different levels of the boat. Sullivan is on the deck and Scoot is below the deck.

ASK STUDENTS which activities are done on deck and which activities are done below. (*On-deck activities include steering the boat, handling the sails, and viewing the ocean. Below-deck activities include cooking, sleeping, and using the bathrooms.*)

8 Unit 1

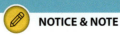 **NOTICE & NOTE**

2   Melissa "Scoot" Atkins went below into the *Old Sea Dog's* tiny galley, moving down the three steps of the companionway, closing the two solid entry doors behind her, always a good idea in offshore sailing. The three horizontal hatch boards that were on top of the doors were also firmly in place, securing the thirty-foot Baba type against sudden invasion of seawater.

ANALYZE PLOT
Annotate In paragraphs 2 and 4, circle the names of the main characters. Underline details that describe where each is on the boat.
Predict: Why might it be important to the plot that these characters are in two different settings?

3   Rogues and sneakers have been around since the beginning of the oceans, and the earliest sea literature makes note of "giant" waves. The U.S. Navy manual *Practical Methods for Observing and Forecasting Ocean Waves* says, "In any wave system, after a long enough time, an exceptional high one will occur. These monstrous out-sized waves are improbable but still possible and the exact time of occurrence can never be predicted." Naval hydrography[1] studies indicate that waves 15 to 25 feet high qualify for "sneaker" or "sleeper" status; the freak rogue is up to 100 feet or over. As waters slowly warm they seem to be occurring more frequently. In 1995 the *Queen Elizabeth 2* (the *QE2*), the great British passenger liner, encountered a 95-foot rogue south of Newfoundland. More than 900 feet long, the *QE2* rode over it, but her captain said it looked like they were sailing into the White Cliffs of Dover.

swell
(swĕl) *n.* A *swell* is a long, unbroken wave.

deck
(dĕk) *n.* The *deck* is the platform on a ship or boat where people stand.

4   Sullivan Atkins, Scoot's oldest brother, was steering the cutter-rigged boat on a northerly course about fifteen miles off desolate Cabo Colnett, south of Ensenada. Under a brilliant sun, the glittering blue Pacific rose and fell in long, slick **swells**, a cold light breeze holding steady.

5   Below **deck** Scoot was listening to Big Sandy & His Fly-Rite Boys doing "Swingin' West," and singing along with them while slicing leftover steak from last night's meal. They'd grilled it on a small charcoal ring that was mounted outboard on the starboard side[2] at the stern, trailing sparks into the water. The *Sea Dog* had every blessed thing, including a barbecue pit, she marveled.

---
[1] **hydrography:** the scientific description and analysis of the earth's surface waters.
[2] **outboard on the starboard side:** positioned outside and on the right side of the boat.

8 Unit 1

APPLYING ACADEMIC VOCABULARY

☐ aspect   ☐ cultural   ☑ evaluate   ☑ resource   ☑ text

Write and Discuss Have students turn to a partner to discuss the following questions. Guide students to include the Academic Vocabulary words *resource* and *evaluate* in their responses. Ask volunteers to share their responses with the class.

- What inner **resource** do people in frightening situations rely on and why? Bravery? Inventiveness?
- How would you **evaluate** Scoot and Sully's chances for survival?

6   Scoot was learning how to be a deep-water sailor. She was fourteen years old and pretty, with dark hair. Though small in size, not even five feet, she was strong. She'd started off with eight-foot Sabots. On this trip, her first aboard the *Sea Dog*, she'd manned the wheel for most of the three days they'd been under way. She'd stood four-hour watches at night. Sully was a good teacher.

7   It was one of those perfect days to be out, Sully thought: the three Dacron sails belayed and whispering, white bow waves singing pleasant songs as the fiberglass hull, tilting to starboard, sliced through the ocean. It was a day filled with goodness, peace, and beauty. They'd come south as far as Cabo Colnett, turning back north only an hour ago. They'd sailed from Catalina Island's Avalon Harbor, the *Sea Dog's* home port, out in the channel off Los Angeles. Sully had borrowed the boat from a family friend, Beau Tucker, a stockbroker with enough money to outfit it and maintain it properly. Built by Ta-Shing, of Taiwan, she was heavy and sturdy, with a teakwood deck and handsome teakwood interior, and the latest in **navigation** equipment. Sully had sailed her at least a dozen times. He'd been around boats, motor and sail, for many of his nineteen years. He thought the *Old Sea Dog* was the best, in her category, that he'd ever piloted.

8   As he was about to complete a northeast tack, Sully's attention was drawn to a squadron of seagulls diving on small fish about a hundred yards off the port bow, and he did not see the giant wave that had crept up silently behind the *Sea Dog*. But a split second before it lifted the boat like a carpenter's chip, he sensed something behind him and glanced backward, toward the towering wall of shining water.

9   It was already too late to shout a warning to Scoot so she could escape from the cabin; too late to do anything except hang on to the wheel with both hands; too late even to pray. He did manage a yell as the *Sea Dog* became vertical. She rose up the surface of the wall stern first and then pitch-poled violently, end over end, the bow **submerging** and the boat going upside down, taking Sully and Scoot with it, the forty-foot mast, sails intact, now pointing toward the bottom.

navigation
(năv´ĭ-gā´shən) *n.* The *navigation* of a ship or boat is the act of guiding it along a planned course.

▶ **AGAIN AND AGAIN**

Notice & Note: Mark words that are repeated in paragraph 9.

Predict: Why might the author have chosen to repeat these words?

submerge
(səb-mûrj´) *v.* To *submerge* is to descend beneath the surface of the water.

Rogue Wave   9

TEACH

ENGLISH LEARNER SUPPORT

Monitor Comprehension Use the following supports to help students at varying proficiency levels.

- While reading aloud, work with students to create physical visual representations of what is happening in paragraph 8. Use materials at hand or ask students to visualize what you are reading. **SUBSTANTIAL**

- Pair students of different abilities. Have students read paragraph 8 to each other and circle any unfamiliar words. Working with their partners, have students use context clues to determine the meaning of unfamiliar words. Then ask them to write down the meaning of those words. **MODERATE**

- Have students read paragraph 8 to themselves and circle any unfamiliar words. Have students use context clues to determine the meaning of unfamiliar words. Then ask them to write sentences using those words. **LIGHT**

▶ **NOTICE & NOTE**

Explain to students that artists often repeat images, sounds, and words for a reason; compare word repetition with repeated notes in music.

(Answer: *The words are repeated to create greater suspense in the story and greater tension for the reader.)*

CLOSE READ SCREENCAST

Modeled Discussion Have students click the Close-Read icon in their eBook to access a screencast in which readers discuss and annotate paragraphs 9 and 20 of the story.

As a class, view and discuss the video. Then have students pair up to do an close read of paragraph 59. Students can record their answers on the Close Read Practice PDF.

 Close Read Practice PDF

CRITICAL VOCABULARY

navigation: Sully is the captain, so safe navigation of the boat through the ocean waters is his responsibility.

submerge: The *cabin, decks, mast,* and *sails* of the boat are submerged; they are all underwater. The bottom of the boat—called the *hull*—is above the water.

ASK STUDENTS what navigation skills are necessary in order to be a captain of a ship. *(Navigation skills include steering the boat, handling the sails, reading a map, riding large waves, and dealing with bad weather conditions.)*

Rogue Wave   9

TEACH

✏️ ANALYZE PLOT

Ask students what **conflict** the characters are trying to resolve. Explain that the conflict often emerges in a story when the main characters have to contend with unexpected events like a rogue wave. **(Answer:** *To resolve this conflict, Scoot needs to get out of the cabin before she drowns, and she and Sully need to turn the boat right side up or get rescued somehow.)*

■ ENGLISH LEARNER SUPPORT

Language Conventions Help students identify, define, and understand unfamiliar phrases and vocabulary in paragraphs 10 and 11.

ASK STUDENTS to work in pairs. Have them look up unfamiliar words in expressions, such as *hurled upward, instantly blacked out,* and *dogged securely.* Next, ask students to add what they already know from paragraph 9 to what they have just learned. Ask: *What is getting filled with water? (the boat's cabin) Why is water pouring in? (The boat's cabin is upside down and underwater.)* **MODERATE/LIGHT**

CRITICAL VOCABULARY

ASK STUDENTS what has prevented the entire boat from becoming submerged? *(The boat has not yet filled with enough water so that its weight would pull it completely under. An air-pocket is keeping it afloat.)*

porthole: is a small round window that can be shut so tightly that water can't get in. The author identifies the open porthole as one place through which water poured into the cabin.

ASK STUDENTS to make an inferences about why all the entrances to the cabin weren't tightly shut. Ask whether the author states exactly why they weren't shut. *(No)*

10   Unit 1

✏️ NOTICE & NOTE

ANALYZE PLOT
Annotate: In paragraphs 9–15, mark details that describe the conflict.

Predict: How do you think the characters will resolve this conflict?

porthole
(pôrt´hōl´) *n.* A *porthole* is a circular window on a boat or ship.

10   Scoot was hurled upward, legs and arms flying, her head striking the after galley bulkhead and then the companionway steps and the interior deck, which was now the ceiling. She instantly blacked out.

11   Everything loose in the cabin was scattered around what had been the overhead. Water was pouring in and was soon lapping at Scoot's chin. It was coming from a four-inch **porthole** that had not been dogged securely and a few other smaller points of entry.

12   Sully's feet were caught under forestay sailcloth, plastered around his face, but then he managed to shove clear and swim upward, breaking water. He looked at the mound of upside-down hull, bottom to the sky, unable to believe that the fine, sturdy *Sea Dog* had been flipped like a cork, perhaps trapping Scoot inside. Treading water, trying to collect his thoughts, he yelled, "Scoot," but there was no answer. Heart pounding, unable to see over the mound of the hull, he circled it, thinking she might have been thrown clear. But there was no sign of her.

13   He swam back to the point of cabin entry, took several deep breaths, and dove. He felt along the hatch boards and then opened his eyes briefly to see that the doors were still closed. She *was* still inside. Maneuvering his body, he pulled on the handles. The doors were jammed, and he returned to the surface for air.

10   Unit 1

NOTICE & NOTE

14   He knew by the way the boat had already settled that there was water inside her. Under usual circumstances, the hull being upright, there would be four feet, nine inches of hull below the waterline. There would be about the same to the cabin overhead, enabling a six-foot-person to walk about down there.

15   Panting, blowing, Sully figured there was at least a three-foot air pocket holding the *Sea Dog* on the surface, and if Scoot hadn't been knocked unconscious and drowned, <u>she could live for quite a while in the dark chamber. How long, he didn't know.</u>

16   In the blackness, water continued to lap at Scoot's chin. She had settled against what had been the deck of the galley alcove, her body in an upright position on debris. Everything not tied down or in a locker was now between the overhead ribs. Wooden hatch covers[3] from the bilges were floating in the water and the naked bilges were exposed. Just aft of her body, and now above it, was the small diesel engine as well as the batteries. Under the water were cans of oil, one of them leaking. Battery acid might leak, too. Few sailors could imagine the nightmare that existed inside the *Sea Dog*. Scoot's pretty face was splashed with engine oil.

17   Over the next five or six minutes, <u>Sully dove repeatedly, using his feet as a fulcrum, and using all the strength that he had in his arms, legs, and back, in an effort to open the doors.</u> The pressure of the water defeated him. Then he thought about

---

[3] **Wooden hatch covers:** door-like coverings made of wood that fit over openings on the deck or hull of a boat.

AGAIN AND AGAIN

Notice & Note: Mark the action that is repeated in paragraph 17 and explain why Sully does something over and over.

Infer: How does this add to the story's suspense?

Rogue Wave 11

TEACH

▶ AGAIN AND AGAIN

Explain to students that actions which a character does **Again and Again** may indicate something important about that character's central **conflict**. Remind students that **suspense** is the tension readers feel until the conflict is resolved. **(Answer:** *Sully repeatedly dives into the water to try to open the cabin doors. This adds to the suspense because it is clear that Sully will not be able to open the doors this way—and time is running out!)*

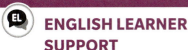

ENGLISH LEARNER SUPPORT

Confirm Understanding Use the following supports with students at varying proficiency levels:

Write *maneuvering* on the board, and draw lines to separate the syllables. Pronounce the word several times, with students repeating after you. Then, act out what Sully is doing to try to reach Scoot. Place two chairs or other objects close together, and then maneuver between them. **SUBSTANTIAL**

Have students pronounce *maneuvering* and help them understand what it means (*moving carefully*) by acting it out. Prompt them to explain why Sully had to maneuver. (*He had to get his body in just the right position to allow him to open the door.*) **MODERATE**

Ask students to pronounce *maneuvering*, correcting them as needed. Then ask them to summarize in their own words why Sully needed to maneuver his body. **LIGHT**

WHEN STUDENTS STRUGGLE...

Use Strategies Visualizing is important in understanding fast-moving, complicated sequences of events, such as the boat overturning. If students are struggling to understand what happened to the boat and where the characters are situated once it overturns, have them use the Sketch to Stretch strategy to visualize what is happening. Tell students to reread the page they are confused about and underline what they find confusing. Then, tell them to sketch what they see happening. Explain that it's acceptable if their drawings are simple. Finally, have students turn to a partner and share their drawings. To help students understand the importance of visualizing, have them consider how their sketches help them better understand the passage.

Rogue Wave 11

TEACH

ENGLISH LEARNER SUPPORT

Read and Share Ask students to reread paragraphs 19 and 20 in pairs. Then ask them to work together and create a list of the different thoughts that were going through Sully's head as he planned his next step. (*There was no way to reach Scoot, the water would soon fill up the air pocket, the water would drown her.*)
MODERATE/LIGHT

 **NOTICE & NOTE**

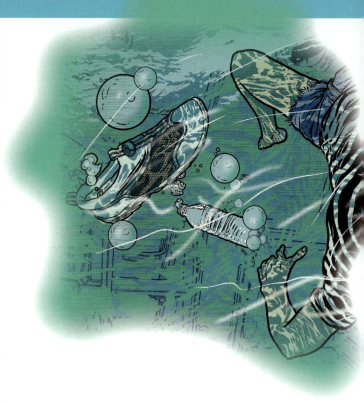

trying to pry the doors open with the wooden handle of the scrub brush. Too late for that, he immediately discovered. It had drifted away, along with Scoot's nylon jacket, her canvas boat shoes—anything that could float.

18   Finally he climbed on top of the keel, catching his breath, resting a moment, trying desperately to think of a way to enter the hull. Boats of the Baba class, built for deep-water sailing, quite capable of reaching Honolulu and beyond, were almost sea-tight unless the sailors made a mistake or unless the sea became angry. The side ports were supposed to be dogged securely in open ocean. Aside from the cabin doors, there was no entry into that cabin without tools. He couldn't very well claw a hole through the inch of tough fiberglass.

19   He thought about the hatch on the foredeck, but it could only be opened from inside the cabin. Then there was the skylight on the top of the seventeen-foot cabin, used for ventilation as well as a sun source; that butterfly window, hinged in the middle, could be opened only from the inside. Even with scuba gear, he couldn't open that skylight unless he had tools.

20   He fought back tears of frustration. There was no way to reach Scoot. And he knew what would happen down there. The water would slowly and inevitably rise until the air pocket was only six inches; her head would be trapped between the surface of the water and the dirty bilge. The water would torture her, then it would drown her. Seawater has no heart, no brain. The *Sea Dog* would then drop to the ocean floor, thousands of feet down, entombing her forever.

21   Maybe the best hope for poor Scoot was that she was already dead, but he had to determine whether she was still alive. He began pounding on the hull with the bottom of his fist, waiting for a return knock. At the same time, he shouted her name over and over. Nothing but silence from inside there. He wished he'd hung on to the silly scrub brush. The wooden handle would make more noise than the flesh of his fist.

22   Almost half an hour passed, and he finally broke down and sobbed. His right fist was bloody from the constant pounding. Why hadn't *he* gone below to make the stupid sandwiches? Scoot would have been at the wheel when the wave grasped the *Sea Dog*. His young sister, with all her life to live, would be alive now.

23   They'd had a good brother-sister relationship. He'd teased her a lot about being pint-sized and she'd teased back, holding her nose when he brought one girl or another home for display. She'd always been spunky. He'd taken her sailing locally, in the channel, but she'd wanted an offshore cruise for her fourteenth birthday. Now she'd had one, unfortunately.

24   Their father had nicknamed her Scoot because, as a baby, she'd crawled so fast. It was still a fitting name for her as a teenager. With a wiry body, she was fast in tennis and swimming and already the school's champion in the hundred-yard dash.

25   Eyes closed, teeth clenched, he kept pounding away with the bloody fist. Finally he went back into the ocean to try once more to open the doors. He sucked air, taking a half-dozen deep breaths, and then dove again. Bracing his feet against the companionway frames, he felt every muscle straining, but the doors remained jammed. He was also now aware that if they did open, more water would rush in and he might not have time to find Scoot in the blackness and pull her out. But he was willing to take the gamble.

26   Scoot awakened as water seeped into her mouth and nose. For a moment she could not understand where she was, how she got there, what had happened . . . Vaguely, she remembered the

LANGUAGE CONVENTIONS

Annotate: Writers use a mix of sentence types to convey ideas. Read the first two sentences in paragraph 22. Mark the simple sentence and circle the compound sentence.

Summarize: Explain how you were able to identify which sentence was simple and which was compound.

MEMORY MOMENT

Notice & Note: In paragraphs 23 and 24, underline memories Sully has about Scoot.

Infer: What do the memories suggest about how Sully is feeling about Scoot's chances of escape?

Rogue Wave   13

TEACH

LANGUAGE CONVENTIONS

Review information about simple, compound, and complex sentences. If necessary, review coordinating and subordinating conjunctions and appropriate comma usage. (**Answer:** *The first sentence is a compound sentence because there are two clauses, each with a complete subject and a complete predicate, and the clauses are joined by a comma and the coordinating conjunction* and. *The second sentence is a simple sentence: there is only one clause.*)

MEMORY MOMENT

Remind students that Memory Moments may provide useful information about how a **character** will act in the present. (**Answer:** *Sully remembers Scoot as being a fast, agile, athletic child. These qualities may lead Sully to believe that Scoot has a good chance of survival.*)

 For **listening support** for students at varying proficiency levels, see the **Text X-Ray** on page 2C.

ENGLISH LEARNER SUPPORT

Express Feelings Provide students with a three-column graphic organizer with labels for paragraphs 20, 21, and 22 at the head of each column. After reading, guide students to see that Sully is feeling different emotions in each paragraph. Have students record the emotions while rereading, using text evidence. Then, have small groups compare their organizers, and ask each other how they felt while reading about Sully. **LIGHT**

TEACH

 MAKE INFERENCES

Remind students that the **setting** influences the characters and their conflict. As the characters try to resolve their conflict, the plot builds suspense, which is the growing tension that the reader experiences. (**Answer:** *The details show that night is falling. This adds tension because it is unlikely that a ship will be able to see them in the darkness. And the "eerie silence" underscores how alone they are and heightens the danger.*)

ENGLISH LEARNER SUPPORT

Monitor Comprehension Use the following supports for students at varying proficiency levels:

- Read aloud paragraph 32. Pair students of different abilities. Ask them to find text evidence of what Scoot finds that might help her. (a knife) Have them discuss or show how/why it might help her.
  SUBSTANTIAL

- Have student pairs read paragraph 32 to each other. Then, ask them to explain what they think Scoot will do next. Have them discuss what *they* would do.
  MODERATE

- Have students read paragraph 32 to themselves. Then, ask them to use text evidence to explain how the author creates suspense in this paragraph.
  LIGHT

 **NOTICE & NOTE**

MAKE INFERENCES
Annotate: In paragraph 28, mark details that describe the setting.

Interpret: How do these details add tension to the central conflict?

---

boat slanting steeply downward, as if it were suddenly diving, and she remembered feeling her body going up.

27 That's all she remembered, and all she knew at the moment was that she had a fierce headache and was in chill water in total darkness. It took a little longer to realize she was trapped in the *Sea Dog's* cabin, by the galley alcove. She began to feel around herself and to touch floating things. The air was thick with an oil smell. Then she ran her hand over the nearest solid thing—a bulkhead. *That's strange,* she thought—her feet were touching a pot. She lifted her right arm and felt above her—the galley range. The galley range above her? *The boat was upside down.* She felt for the companionway steps and found the entry doors and pushed on them; that was the way she'd come in. The doors didn't move.

28 Sully crawled up on the wide hull again, clinging to a faint hope that a boat or ship would soon come by; but the sun was already in descent, and with night coming on, chances of rescue lessened with each long minute. It was maddening to have her a few feet away and be helpless to do anything. Meanwhile the hull swayed gently, in eerie silence.

29 Scoot said tentatively, "Sully?" Maybe he'd been drowned. Maybe she was alone and would die here in the foul water.

30 She repeated his name, but much more loudly. No answer. She was coming out of shock now and fear icier than the water was replacing her confusion. To die completely alone? It went that way for a few desperate moments, and then she said to herself, *Scoot, you've got to get out of here! There has to be some way to get out . . .*

31 Sully clung to the keel with one hand, his body flat against the smooth surface of the hull. There was ample room on either side of the keel before the dead-rise, the upward slope of the hull. The *Sea Dog* had a beam of ten feet. Unless a wind and waves came up, he was safe enough in his wet perch.

32 Scoot again wondered if her brother had survived and if he was still around the boat or on it. With her right foot she began to probe around the space beneath her. The pot had drifted away, but her toes felt what seemed to be flatware. That made sense. The drawer with the knives and forks and spoons had popped out, spilling its contents. She took a deep breath and ducked under to pick out a knife. Coming up, she held the knife blade, reaching skyward with the handle . . .

33 Eyes closed, brain mushy, exhausted, Sully heard a faint tapping and raised up on his elbows to make sure he wasn't dreaming. No, there was a tapping from below. He crawled back toward what he thought was the source area, the galley area, and put an ear to the hull. *She was tapping!* He pounded the fiberglass, yelling, "Scoot, Scooot, Scooot . . ."

34 Scoot heard the pounding and called out, "Sully, I'm here, I'm here!" Her voice seemed to thunder in the air pocket.

35 Sully yelled, "Can you hear me?"

36 Scoot could only hear the pounding.

37 "Help me out of here . . ."

38 Ear still to the hull, Sully shouted again, "Scoot, can you hear me?" No answer. He pounded again and repeated, "Scoot, can you hear me?" No answer. The hull was too thick and the slop of the sea, the moan of the afternoon breeze, didn't help.

39 Though she couldn't hear his voice, the mere fact that he was up there told her she'd escape. Sully had gotten her out of jams before. There was no one on earth that she'd rather have as a rescue man than her oldest brother. She absolutely knew she'd survive.

40 Though it might be fruitless, Sully yelled down to the galley alcove, "Listen to me, Scoot. You'll have to get out by yourself. I can't help you. I can't break in. Listen to me, I know you're in water, and the best way out is through the skylight. You've got to dive down and open it. You're small enough to go through it . . ." She could go through either section of the butterfly window. "Tap twice if you heard me!"

41 She did not respond, and he repeated what he'd just said, word for word.

42 No response. No taps from below.

43 Scoot couldn't understand why he didn't just swim down and open the doors to the cabin, release her. That's all he needed to do, and she'd be free.

44 Sully looked up at the sky. "Please, God, help me, help us." It was almost unbearable to know she was alive and he was unable to do anything for her. Then he made the decision to keep repeating: "Listen to me, Scoot. You'll have to get out by yourself. I can't break in. Listen to me, the best way out is through the skylight. You've got to dive down and open it. You're small enough to go through it . . ."

NOTICE & NOTE

AHA MOMENT

Notice & Note: Mark what Sully realizes in paragraph 33.

Infer: What effect might this realization have on him?

AGAIN AND AGAIN

Notice & Note: In paragraphs 38–45, underline words and phrases that Sully repeats.

Infer: What does the repetition reveal about Sully?

Rogue Wave   15

TEACH

▶ **AHA MOMENT**

Explain that an **Aha Moment** may reveal a dramatic change in the **character** and **plot**. Point out that the Aha Moment in paragraph 33 is a powerful one because it provides Sully with some important information.

Tell students that when they spot an Aha Moment, they should pause, mark it in their consumable texts, and ask themselves the anchor question: *How might this change things?*

(Answer: *The realization that Scoot is still alive greatly relieves Sully and gives him hope that she will be able to escape even if he is unable to help her.)*

▶ **AGAIN AND AGAIN**

Explain that when a **character** repeats certain words and phrases **Again and Again**, it may indicate a variety of important feelings and wishes that the character has.

Point out to students that the manner in which a **character** repeats word and phrases is also important to recognize. In the example passage, Sully is yelling, which reveals a great deal about the situation and his state of mind. **(Answer:** *Sully cares deeply about his sister and wants to help her escape. He is powerless to help her directly, so he does whatever he can—in this case, explaining to her what she needs to do to escape. He repeats the same words over and over in the wild hope that she will somehow sense what he is saying.)*

 ENGLISH LEARNER SUPPORT

Develop Fluency Select a passage from the story that matches students' reading abilities. Read the passage aloud as the students follow along silently. Tell students they will have a set amount of time to do the following:

- Echo read the passage by reading aloud one sentence at a time and then having students repeat the sentence back to you, checking for comprehension by asking yes-and-no questions. Break down the longer sentences into appropriate chunks to better support the students. **SUBSTANTIAL**

- Have student pairs take turns reading the passage to each other one paragraph at a time. Have them make a list of things they don't understand or want to know more about that they can share. **MODERATE**

- Allow more fluent readers to select their own passage, giving them a specific amount of time to read it silently. Then, check their comprehension by asking them to summarize what they've read orally or in writing. Ask for volunteers to share with the class. **LIGHT**

Rogue Wave   15

TEACH

AHA MOMENT

Explain to students that in a dramatic story such as "Rogue Wave," an **Aha Moment** can make the difference between life and death, as it does for Scoot at this crucial moment.

As always, tell students that they should ask themselves how an Aha Moment will change the **character** and the **plot** moving forward.

(Answer: These two realizations—"I'll have to get out on my own" and that Scoot "should first try the butterfly windows of the skylight"— coincide exactly with the words and phrases Sully kept yelling over and over again. Sully's repetition **foreshadows** the steps that Scoot must take to survive. Knowing that Scoot has figured this out gives the reader hope that Scoot will make it out alive.)

MEMORY MOMENT

Explain to students that during certain **Memory Moments**, a **character** may recall some important information that will prove invaluable to resolving the **conflict** and advancing the **plot**.

Point out that the Memory Moment in the example passage marks an important discovery that will probably help the character overcome her conflict.

(Answer: Scoot's memories about the location of the flashlight and the quality of boat owner's emergency equipment give her hope that she will figure out her escape route.)

NOTICE & NOTE

AHA MOMENT

Notice & Note: Mark two related realizations that Scoot has in paragraphs 47 and 48.

Connect: How do these realizations tie in with the words that Sully keeps repeating?

MEMORY MOMENT

Notice & Note: Underline what Scoot remembers in paragraph 50.

Infer: How do these memories help Scoot think through her situation?

---

45 He decided to keep saying it the rest of the day and into the night or for as long as it took to penetrate the hull with words. *Skylight! Skylight!* Over and over.

46 He'd heard of mental telepathy but had not thought much about it before. Now it was the only way to reach her.

47 Scoot finally thought that maybe Sully was hurt, maybe helpless up on that bottom, so that was why he couldn't open the doors and let her out. That had to be the reason—Sully up there with broken legs. *So I'll have to get out on my own*, she thought.

48 Over the last two days, when she wasn't on the wheel she had been exploring the *Sea Dog*, and she thought she knew all the exits. Besides the companionway doors, which she knew she couldn't open, there was the hatch on the foredeck for access to the sails; then there was the skylight, almost in the middle of the long cabin. Sully had opened it, she remembered, to air out the boat before they sailed. As she clung to a light fixture by the alcove, in water up to her shoulders, something kept telling her she should first try the butterfly windows of the skylight. The unheard message was compelling—*Try the skylight*.

49 Sully's voice was almost like a recording, a mantra, saying the same thing again and again, directed down to the position of the galley.

50 Scoot remembered that an emergency flashlight was bracketed on the bulkhead above the starboard settee, and she assumed it was waterproof. From what Sully had said, Beau Tucker took great care in selecting emergency equipment. It might help to actually see the dogs on the metal skylight frame. She knew she wouldn't have much time to spin them loose. Maybe thirty or forty seconds before she'd have to surface for breath. Trying to think of the exact position of the upside-down flashlight, she again tapped on the hull to let her brother know she was very much alive.

51 He pounded back.

52 Sully looked at his watch. Almost four-thirty. About three hours to sundown. Of course, it didn't make much difference to Scoot. She was already in dank night. But it might make a difference if she got out after nightfall. He didn't know what kind of shape she was in. Injured, she might surface and drift away.

53 The mantra kept on.

54 Scoot dove twice for the boxy flashlight, found it, and turned it on, suddenly splitting the darkness and immediately feeling

NOTICE & NOTE

hopeful. But it was odd to see the *Sea Dog's* unusual overhead, the open hatchways into the bilge and the debris floating on the shining water, all streaked with lubricants; odd to see the toilet upside down. She held the light underwater and it continued to operate.

55 Every so often, Sully lifted his face to survey the horizon, looking for traffic. He knew they were still within sixteen or seventeen miles of the coast, though the drift was west. There was usually small-boat activity within twenty miles of the shore—fishermen or pleasure boats.

56 Scoot worked herself forward a few feet, guessing where the skylight might be, and then went down to find the butterfly windows, the flashlight beam cutting through the murk. It took a few seconds to locate them and put a hand on one brass dog. She tried to turn it, but it was too tight for her muscles and she rose up to breathe again.

57 Not knowing what was happening below or whether Scoot was trying to escape, Sully was getting more anxious by the moment. He didn't know whether or not the crazy telepathy was working. He wished she would tap again to let him know she was still alive. It had been more than twenty minutes since she'd last tapped.

58 Scoot had seen a toolbox under the companionway steps and went back to try to find it. She guessed there'd be wrenches inside it, unless they'd spilled out. Using the flashlight again, she found the metal box and opened it. Back to the surface to breathe again, and then back to the toolbox to extract a wrench. With each move she was becoming more and more confident.

MAKE INFERENCES
Annotate: In paragraph 55, mark details that describe the setting.
Interpret: What effect do these details have on the plot?

ANALYZE PLOT
Annotate: In paragraphs 56–61, mark the parts of the story that keep you anxious about what will happen.
Draw Conclusions: How does the action in these paragraphs help the plot advance?

Rogue Wave   17

TEACH

✏️ MAKE INFERENCES

Tell students that making inferences about the **setting** of a story can give the reader an idea about where the **plot** may be going and what the **characters** might be thinking in order to resolve their conflict. **(Answer:** *Sully knows roughly their location on the ocean. He also knows that small boats might be in the area. This information indicates that Sully and Scoot may be rescued.)*

✏️ ANALYZE PLOT

Remind students that a **plot** is made up of a series of events and actions that keep building on each other until the conflict is resolved. These actions can create suspense as they advance the plot. **(Answer:** *The action in these paragraphs keeps the reader anxious about the outcome of the situation. At the same time, the action makes it clear that Scoot is making progress toward resolving her conflict by escaping the sinking boat. Sully's anxiety about his sister adds to the overall tension.)*

 ENGLISH LEARNER SUPPORT

Reinforce Meaning Read aloud paragraph 56 accompanied by appropriate images from the Internet of a *butterfly window* and a *brass dog*. Pause for students to ask for clarification. Then, confirm their understanding by asking students: *What did Scoot try to turn?* (brass dog) *What is she trying to do?* (Get out of the cabin) *Why couldn't she turn it?* (too tight to turn)

Have students read paragraphs 55 and 56. Suggest that they pause after each sentence and use context clues to clarify the meaning of unfamiliar words. Then confirm students' understanding of those words by asking students to use them conversationally. **LIGHT**

Rogue Wave   17

TEACH

✏️ ANALYZE PLOT

Remind students that the **climax** is the story's moment of greatest interest and the point in which the conflict is resolved, that the **falling action** begins to draw the story to a close, and that the **resolution** reveals the final outcome of the conflict. It may be helpful to review the earlier stages of the plot—**exposition** (the background information) and **rising action** (the mounting complications) so students can answer the question. **(Answer:** *The exposition and rising action are much longer because it takes time to introduce the characters and the setting, and to present the series of events that cause the conflict. The remaining three stages take up only eight paragraphs because once Scoot frees herself from the galley, the rest of the story takes far less time to tell.***)**

 **NOTICE & NOTE**

ANALYZE PLOT

Annotate: Mark and label the climax, the falling action, and the resolution.

Infer: Why are these three plot stages shorter than the rest of the story?

59 A big sailboat, beating south, came into Sully's view; but it was more than two miles away and the occupants—unless he was very lucky—would not be able to spot the *Sea Dog's* mound and the man standing on it, waving frantically.

60 Four times Scoot needed to dive, once for each dog; and working underwater was at least five times as difficult as trying to turn them in usual circumstances. She'd aim the light and rest it to illuminate the windows. Finally, all the dogs were loose and she rose once again. This time, after filling her lungs to bursting, she went down and pushed on the starboard window. It cracked a little, but the outside sea pressure resisted and she had to surface again.

61 Sully sat down, almost giving up hope. How long the air pocket would hold up was anybody's guess. The boat had settled at least six inches in the last two hours. It might not last into the night.

climax

62 On her sixth dive Scoot found a way to brace her feet against the ceiling ribs. She pushed with all her strength, and this time the window opened. Almost out of breath, she quickly pushed her body through and the *Old Sea Dog* released her. Treading water beside the hull, she sucked in fresh air and finally called out, "Sully . . ."

falling action

63 He looked her way, saw the grin of triumph on the oil-stained imp face, and dived in to help her aboard the derelict.

64 Shivering, holding each other for warmth all night, they rode and rocked, knowing that the boat was sinking lower each hour.

resolution

65 Just after dawn, the *Red Rooster,* a long-range sports fishing boat out of San Diego bound south to fish for wahoo and tuna off the Revilla Gigedo Islands, came within a hundred yards of the upside-down sailboat and stopped to pick up its two chattering survivors.

66 The *Red Rooster's* captain, Mark Stevens, asked, "What happened?"

67 "Rogue wave," said Sully. That's what he planned to say to Beau Tucker as well.

68 Stevens winced and nodded that he understood.

69 The *Old Sea Dog* stayed on the surface for a little while longer, having delivered her survivors to safety; then her air pocket breathed its last and she slipped beneath the water, headed for the bottom.

18 Unit 1

TO CHALLENGE STUDENTS...

Use A Graphic Organizer Provide students with a five-column graphic organizer. Have them label the columns with the different stages of the plot (exposition, rising action, climax, falling action, resolution). Then ask students to review the story, noting pertinent details about each stage on the organizer. Have students use the organizer as a guide to help them make an outline of an adventure story they would like to write.

NOTICE & NOTE

CHECK YOUR UNDERSTANDING

Answer these questions before moving on to the **Analyze the Text** section on the following page.

1. The setting is important to the story because —
   A rogue waves are common south of Ensenada
   B the characters wouldn't face as much danger anywhere else
   C it is an essential part of the plot's central conflict
   D Sully has never sailed so far off coast before

2. The details about Scoot's attempts to open the skylight serve to —
   F slow the action down so that readers can relax
   G show that Scoot isn't as experienced a sailor as Sully
   H underscore how strong and well-built the boat is
   J heighten suspense by emphasizing the difficulty of the task

3. Which of these is an important idea suggested by the story?
   A People can solve problems with clear thinking and effort.
   B Fear can cloud people's judgment and increase their danger.
   C People who enjoy adventure are strong and resourceful.
   D The ocean is the strongest force of nature.

Rogue Wave   19

TEACH

CHECK YOUR UNDERSTANDING

Have students answer the questions independently.

Answers:
1. C
2. J
3. A

If they answer any questions incorrectly, have them reread the text to confirm their understanding. Then they may proceed to ANALYZE THE TEXT on p. 20.

 ENGLISH LEARNER SUPPORT

Oral Assessment Use the following questions to assess students' listening, comprehension, and speaking skills.

1. Where does the story take place? *(on a boat at sea)* What problem do Sully and Scoot face that can only happen at sea? *(A rogue wave sinks the boat and traps Scoot inside.)*

2. Is it easy or hard for Scoot to escape the boat? *(hard)* How does the author show that it is hard? *(The author gives a lot of details.)*

3. How does Scoot escape the boat? *(She thinks about how to get out and then tries very hard to open the skylight.)* What do Scoot's actions tell the reader about the best way to solve a problem? *(It's important to stay calm, think clearly, and try very hard.)* **SUBSTANTIAL/MODERATE**

Rogue Wave   **19**

APPLY

ANALYZE THE TEXT

Possible answers:

1. **DOK 2:** *Scoot has scary thoughts about whether Sully is okay. Fear takes over her, but only for a few moments. Then she turns her attention to getting out. People who act like this in the face of disaster are resilient.*

2. **DOK 2**: *The details about the dangers of rogue waves underscore the threat to Scoot and Sully, and suggest the conflict that they will soon face—surviving a strike by a rogue wave.*

3. **DOK 4:** *The two settings are on the outside of the Sea Dog's upturned hull and below in the upturned cabin. Shifting between these settings builds suspense by alternating between the obstacles each character encounters.*

4. **DOK 3:** *Scoot's complications: 1. the flooding, upturned dark cabin; 2. a headache; 3. concern about Sully and her inability to hear him; 4. dwindling air; 5. the locked skylight. Sully's complications: 1. his inability to see or hear Scoot; 2. his inability to get inside the capsized cabin; 3. fears of what could happen to Scoot; 4. guilt about putting Scoot in danger; 5. the sinking hull and the oncoming sunset.*

5. **DOK 4:** *"He began pounding on the hull with the bottom of his fist." (par. 21); "His right fist was bloody from the constant pounding." (par. 22); "he kept pounding away with the bloody fist." (par. 25)*

RESEARCH

Remind students they should confirm any information they find by checking multiple websites and assessing the credibility of each one.

Connect Students will find that rogue waves are as tall and powerful as the one described in the story. They may note that rogue waves are typically twice the height of any of the other waves surrounding them, with the biggest ones being as tall as 100 feet.

 RESPOND

ANALYZE THE TEXT

Support your responses with evidence from the text. 📓 **NOTEBOOK**

1. **Infer** Reread paragraphs 29–30. What inference can you make about Scoot's personality, based on those paragraphs?

2. **Connect** How does the information in paragraph 3 help foreshadow the conflict?

3. **Analyze** Identify two settings on the boat in this story. How does the shifting between these settings influence the plot and build suspense?

4. **Compare** What complications or conflicts do Scoot and Sully encounter in the story? Fill out a chart like this one to trace the conflicts or complications Scoot and Sully encounter in the story.

COMPLICATION	1	2	3	4	5
Scoot's					
Sully's					

5. **Notice & Note** Reread paragraphs 21–22 and 25. What words are repeated again and again to show how hard Sully tries to save Scoot?

RESEARCH TIP
Focused questions can help you research a topic more quickly and successfully. For example, to find a description of a rogue wave, you could ask, "How tall is a rogue wave?" To learn how dangerous a rogue wave is, you might ask, "Can a rogue wave sink a sailboat?"

RESEARCH

"Rogue Wave" is a fiction story that presents facts about rogue waves. How accurate are they? With a partner, research rogue waves. Begin by generating several questions to guide your research. Record your questions and the answers you learn in the chart.

QUESTION	ANSWER
How big is a rogue wave?	They vary in height, but are about twice the height of any of the other waves surrounding them.
Does a rogue wave look like a "wall of water?"	The captain of a ship hit by a rogue wave in 1995 described it as a "great wall of water"
Can a rogue wave turn a sailboat upside down?	A rogue wave capsized a boat off the shore of New Jersey in 2017

Connect How accurately does the story depict the phenomenon of rogue waves? In a small group, share your research and discuss whether the author described rogue waves in a realistic and accurate way.

 LEARNING MINDSET

Belonging Remind students that a belonging mindset means that each student can experience being a valuable member of a learning community. Remind students that part of the learning process is asking teachers and fellow students for help when needed. One of the greatest gifts of belonging is the ability to help others.

RESPOND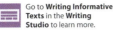

CREATE AND DISCUSS

Adapt as a Film How would you change "Rogue Wave" if you wanted to turn it into an action movie? Write a three-to-four-paragraph description of how this short story could be adapted as a film. Include each of the following:

❏ a clear controlling idea or thesis statement
❏ a description of the opening scene that establishes the characters, setting, and conflict
❏ a description of each important scene in the plot
❏ suggestions for how to shoot each scene to convey the suspense

Share and Discuss Plot Details In a small group, evaluate the plot of "Rogue Wave." Dissect the ways it builds tension and delivers suspenseful moments. Consider details about characters, setting, and events in each stage of the plot. Use text evidence to support your views. Remember to participate in the discussion using an appropriate tone and vocabulary in your responses. These are some of the things you might talk about:

❏ how story events build rising tension
❏ how characters' traits, thoughts, feelings, or actions affect the plot
❏ the role setting plays in heightening suspense

Go to **Writing Informative Texts** in the **Writing Studio** to learn more.

Go to **Participating in Collaborative Discussions** in the **Speaking and Listening Studio** for help.

RESPOND TO THE ESSENTIAL QUESTION

? **What helps people rise up to face difficulties?**

Gather Information Review your annotations and notes on "Rogue Wave." Then, add relevant details to your Response Log. As you determine which information to include, think about:

- the kinds of difficulties the characters faced
- what happens to people when they face difficulties
- how people can overcome those difficulties

At the end of the collection, use your notes to write an informational essay.

ACADEMIC VOCABULARY

As you write and discuss what you learned from the short story, be sure to use the Academic Vocabulary words. Check off each of the words that you use.

❏ aspect
❏ cultural
❏ evaluate
❏ resource
❏ text

Rogue Wave 21

APPLY

CREATE AND DISCUSS

Adapt as a Film Point out that information on page 21 can help them create an outline for a film adaptation of the story. Use the **Writing Activities** on **Text X-Ray** page 2D to help scaffold instruction.

Share and Discuss Plot Details Remind students that they should not interrupt when other members of the group are presenting their ideas. Encourage students to ask questions to clarify meaning if they do not understand the ideas that are being presented.

RESPOND TO THE ESSENTIAL QUESTION

Allow time for students to add details from "Rogue Wave" to their Unit 1 Response Logs.

For **speaking** and **writing** support for students at varying proficiency levels, see the Text X-Ray on page 2D.

ENGLISH LEARNER SUPPORT

Share and Discuss Plot Details Have partners use text evidence to discuss plot details that make "Rogue Wave" a suspenseful story. Provide these sentence frames to begin the discussion. Explain that *sequence of events* means "events that happen in order: one after another": *This sequence of events made the story suspenseful:*_____. *These are things I learned about Scoot's character:*_____. *I felt most tense when*_____. *I felt sorry for*_____ *when*_____. *An unexpected event was*_____, *because*_____.
MODERATE/LIGHT

Rogue Wave 21

APPLY

CRITICAL VOCABULARY

Make inferences and use text evidence.

Possible Answers::

1. *rises and falls on the ocean.*
2. *to operate the steering wheel or rudder.*
3. *powerful waves can throw the boat off course.*
4. *all of the sandcastles near the water.*
5. *could see the other ships in the harbor.*

VOCABULARY STRATEGY:
Latin Roots

Answers:

1. navy: *fleet of ships;* submarines: *sea vessels that travel underwater*
2. Mariners: *sea sailors;* navigated: *directed a ship's course*

 RESPOND

CRITICAL VOCABULARY

| swell | deck | navigation | submerge | porthole |

Practice and Apply Complete each sentence to show that you understand the meaning of the boldfaced vocabulary word.

1. I can see the water's motion by watching how a **swell** . . .
   _____

2. One reason to be on the **deck** of a boat is . . .
   _____

3. **Navigation** becomes more difficult in bad weather because . . .
   _____

4. When the tide comes in on that beach, it could **submerge** . . .
   _____

5. There was a **porthole** in our room on the ship, so we . . .
   _____

VOCABULARY STRATEGY: Latin Roots

A **root** is a word part—such as *nav* in the word *navigation*—that came into English from an older language. Roots from the ancient language of Latin appear in many English words. For example, the chart shows two words from "Rogue Wave" that have Latin roots.

WORD	LATIN ROOT	ROOT'S MEANING
navigation	nav	ship or sail
mariner	mar	sea

Often, by identifying Latin roots, you can figure out the meanings of words that seem unfamiliar. Using a resource such as a print or online dictionary can help you confirm your ideas.

Practice and Apply Identify the words in each sentence with the Latin roots *mar* and *nav*. Tell what each word means. Then use a print or online dictionary to check your ideas.

1. Sailors in the navy may spend time in submarines.
   _____

2. Mariners long ago navigated using the stars.
   _____

 Go to the **Vocabulary Studio** for more on Latin roots.

22 Unit 1

 ENGLISH LEARNER SUPPORT

Latin Roots Explain to students that some words in the English language have Latin roots, or word parts that come from the Latin language. Tell them that Latin roots can be found in other languages as well and can help them identify a word's meaning. Write the Latin root *mar* on the board. Guide Spanish speaking students to connect the meaning of the Latin root with the Spanish word for *sea (el mar)*. Have student pairs of varying proficiencies locate words in the text that include the Latin root *mar*, such as *maritime, submarine,* and *marlin*. Point out that these words have meanings that are associated with the sea. Then, have pairs work together to write definitions for each word. **ALL LEVELS**

LANGUAGE CONVENTIONS:
Sentence Structure

A **clause** is a group of words that includes a complete subject and a complete predicate. Every sentence includes at least one clause. A **complete subject** includes all the words that identify the person, place, thing, or idea that the clause is about. The **complete predicate** includes all the words that tell or ask something about the subject.

COMPLETE SUBJECT	COMPLETE PREDICATE
"The *Sea Dog*	had every blessed thing...."
"Sully	was a good teacher."

As in "Rogue Wave," authors use different types of sentences to convey meaning.

- A **simple sentence** contains only one clause, as in the sentence, "Sully looked at his watch."
- A **compound sentence** contains two or more clauses that are joined either by a comma and a **coordinating conjunction,** such as *and, but, or, for, so, yet,* and *nor;* or by a semicolon.

Independent Clauses	She pushed with all her strength. This time the window opened.
Compound Sentence	"She pushed with all her strength, and this time the window opened."

- A **complex sentence** is a combination of a subordinate clause an independent clause. A subordinate clause begins with a **subordinating conjunction,** such as *after, although, as, because, before, even though, if, since, so that, though, unless, until, when, where,* and *while*.

Complex Sentence	Although sailing can be dangerous, Sully was an experienced sailor.

Practice and Apply Write two pairs of related simple sentences. Then, for one set of sentences, use a comma and coordinating conjunction or semicolon to create a compound sentence. Use a subordinating conjunction to connect the other set of sentences to make a complex sentence. When you have finished, share your sentences with a partner and discuss the structure of each sentence.

RESPOND

Go to **Simple Sentences and Compound Sentences** in the **Grammar Studio** to learn more.

Rogue Wave 23

APPLY

LANGUAGE CONVENTIONS:

Sentence Structure Review the information about sentence structure with students. Explain that clauses contain complete subjects and predicates. Then explain the differences between simple, compound, and complex sentences, indicating the kinds of clauses and conjunctions each sentence requires.

- "The *Sea Dog* had every blessed thing" and "Sully was a good teacher" are simple sentences because they contain one complete subject and predicate and are only one clause.
- "She pushed with all her strength, and this time the window opened" is a compound sentence because it has two independent clauses that are joined by the conjunction *and,* and it has a comma before the conjunction.
- "Although sailing can be dangerous, Sully was an experienced sailor" is a complex sentence because it has one dependent clause (at the beginning of the sentence) and one independent clause.

Practice and Apply Have partners evaluate whether they wrote the appropriate sentence types, using the correct conjunctions and punctuation. *(Students' sentences will vary.)*

ENGLISH LEARNER SUPPORT

Language Conventions Use the following supports with students at varying proficiency levels:

- Have students complete the following simple and compound sentences based on information from the text. *Before the wave struck, the weather was _____.* (calm, beautiful, peaceful) *Scoot was enjoying herself on the _____,* (boat) *and she was learning a lot about sailing.* **SUBSTANTIAL**
- Have partners work together to find simple, compound, and complex sentences in "Rogue Wave." Ask them to refer to their lists of conjunctions to help them identify the sentences. **MODERATE**
- Have students work with partners to write their own original simple, compound, and complex sentences. Then have them meet with another pair to compare their sentences. **LIGHT**
- Optional Game: Have students create simple, compound, and complex sentences, and then pass them on to other students who must 1) Identify subject(s) and verb(s), and 2) explain how that helps them identify the sentence type.

Rogue Wave 23

PLAN

THE FLIGHT OF ICARUS
Greek Myth retold by Sally Benson

GENRE ELEMENTS

MYTH

Remind students that a myth is a traditional story that usually explains a belief, custom, or natural occurrence. The myth of Icarus and his father, Daedalus, is unusual in that it does not involve the actions of the gods, nor does the hero of the story, Daedalus, possess superhuman physical qualities. His most notable attribute is his incredible intelligence. This myth presents events that occur the first time human beings break the laws of nature and defies the limits of gravity

LEARNING OBJECTIVES

- Analyze elements of a myth.
- Determine multiple themes.
- Understand characters' traits and behavior.
- Comprehend academic vocabulary
- Understand and use the Latin root *struct*.
- Discuss themes in small groups.
- Write an explanation.
- **Language** Understand and use commas.

TEXT COMPLEXITY

Qualitative Measures	The Flight of Icarus	Lexile: 1110L
Qualitative Measure	**Ideas Presented** Much is explicit, but moves to multiple levels of meaning.	
	Structure Used Primarily explicit but some complex story concepts.	
	Language Used Some figurative language and difficult vocabulary.	
	Knowledge Required Some complexity in theme with cultural and literary knowledge useful.	

24A Unit 1

PLAN

RESOURCES
Online Ed

- Unit 1 Response Log
- Selection Audio
- Analyzing Language
- Close Read Screencasts: Modeled Discussions
- Reading Studio: Notice and Note
- Writing Studio: Using Textual Evidence
- Speaking and Listening Studio: Participating in Collaborative Discussions
- Vocabulary Studio: Latin Roots
- Grammar Studio: Module 14: Lesson 2–6: Using Commas
- "The Flight of Icarus" Selection Test

SUMMARIES

Daedalus and his son Icarus are imprisoned on an island, unable to escape by land or by sea. Daedalus creates huge wings from feathers and wax, and he and his son fly off. Icarus is overcome with excitement and flies too close to the sun despite having been warned of the danger. The sun melts the wax in his wings, and he plunges to his death. Daedalus is heartbroken and mourns the loss of his son.

Spanish

Dédalo y su hijo Ícaro son prisioneros en una isla, incapaces de escapar por tierra o mar. Dédalo crea unas alas inmensas de plumas y cera, y él y su hijo huyen volando. Ícaro se llena de entusiasmo y vuela muy cerca del sol aunque le habían advertido del peligro. El sol le derrite la cera de las alas e Ícaro cae hacia su muerte. Dédalo está desconsolado y lamenta la pérdida de su hijo.

SMALL-GROUP OPTIONS

Have students work in small groups to read and discuss the selection.

Sense It

- Tell students to take notes while they are reading "The Flight of Icarus" that reflect what Icarus and Daedalus see, hear, and feel during the story.
- Ask students to take notes about sensory experiences the author does not describe but which they think the characters are likely to have experienced.
- After reading the myth, have students form small groups and discuss their notes, concentrating on where they agree and disagree.

Numbered Heads Together

- After students have read "The Flight of Icarus," have them form groups of four and number off 1 – 2 – 3 – 4 within the group.
- Pose this question to the groups: *What is the most important lesson readers can learn from this myth?*
- Have students discuss the question and record an answer that reflects the group's opinion-- either a consensus or an answer that reflects differing ideas.
- Call a number from 1 to 4 and have the student with that number from each group respond for the group.

The Flight of Icarus **24B**

PLAN

 Text X-Ray: English Learner Support
for "The Flight of Icarus"

Use the Text X-Ray and the supports and scaffolds in the Teacher's Edition to help guide students at different proficiency levels through the selection.

INTRODUCE THE SELECTION

DISCUSS CAUTION AND RISKS

In this lesson, students will need to understand the danger of "throwing caution to the winds," that is, being overcome by excitement or the thrill of an experience to the point of ignoring warnings and getting into a risky situation. Provide the following explanations:

- Explain that people show caution when they are careful to avoid danger.
- Point out that a risk is a dangerous chance that a person takes.
- Make sure that students understand what a thrill is—a feeling of extreme pleasure that often results from an adventure.

Explain that when people are excited about doing something, they may take a risk that they wouldn't take if they were thinking clearly. They may also ignore a warning they have been given because they are feeling a thrill.

Have students give examples of risks a person might take and why these risks could be dangerous.

CULTURAL REFERENCES

The following words and phrases may be unfamiliar to students:

- *labyrinth* (paragraph 1): a maze
- *bade* (paragraph 5): commanded or asked
- *misgivings* (paragraph 5): serious doubts
- *bewitched* (paragraph 7): to be controlled and tempted by something
- *an offering to the god* (paragraph 9) a gift Greeks gave to please the gods
- *thrown caution to the winds* (paragraph 9) was reckless

LISTENING

Understand a Character's Actions

Draw students' attention to Icarus's feelings and actions in paragraph 7. Tell students that these elements help explain a character's behavior.

Have students listen as you read aloud paragraph 7. Use the following supports with students at varying proficiency levels:

- Tell students that you will ask them questions about what they just heard and they should be answered by signaling yes or no by nodding or shaking their heads. For example, ask: *Did Icarus enjoy being able to fly?* (yes) **SUBSTANTIAL**
- Have students identify specific words in paragraph 7 that indicate Icarus's feelings and actions. Ask: *What words tell you what Icarus was feeling as he flew higher and higher?* (thrill, soared, bewitched) **MODERATE**
- Challenge students to determine why Icarus kept flying higher and higher. Ask: *Why did Icarus fly in a way he had been told would be very dangerous?* (He was excited by the thrill of flying.) **LIGHT**

PLAN

SPEAKING

Discuss Themes

Draw students' attention to the themes, or messages, in this myth. Point out that the themes of myths often involve lessons about what people should or should not do and that myths may contain more than theme.

Use the following supports with students at varying proficiency levels:
- Display and read aloud this sentence: *Children should always obey their parents*. Have students take turns saying the sentence aloud in a way that shows that they agree with it and then in a way that shows they disagree with it. **SUBSTANTIAL**
- Ask: *Was Daedalus being a responsible parent when he put wings on his young son?* Have students volunteer an answer. **MODERATE**
- Ask: *What might the gods have said to Daedalus about doing something humans weren't intended to do?* Have students discuss their answers in small groups. **LIGHT**

READING

Discuss Foreshadowing

Draw students' attention to the ways in which the author uses characters' behavior and feelings to foreshadow events in the myth.

Work with students to reread paragraphs 5–7. Use the following supports with students at varying proficiency levels:
- Read paragraph 6 with students, checking for proper pronunciation and understanding. Ask: *Why does Daedalus look back at Icarus from time to time?* Allow one-word answers. (*afraid, nervous*) **SUBSTANTIAL**
- Ask: *Why do you think Daedalus's eyes fill with tears as he looks at Icarus before they begin their flight?* Encourage volunteers to respond. **MODERATE**
- Ask: *How does Daedalus's alarm as he sees Icarus fly into the clouds suggest that something bad will happen?* (He realizes that Icarus is ignoring his advice and is in danger.) **LIGHT**

WRITING

Write an Explanation

Work with students to read the writing assignment on p. 33. Help students to use commas correctly in their work.

Use the following supports with students at varying proficiency levels:
- Help students compile lists of the kinds of behavior that they found in the story such as: bravery, foolishness, disobedience, etc. Then, have them use the lists to write a paragraph on the board. Have students copy the paragraph in their notebooks. Ask them to pay special attention to comma usage when listing kinds of behavior in their paragraph. Work with them to complete it. **SUBSTANTIAL**
- Provide sentence frames such as the following that students can use to craft their essays: *An example of Daedalus's/Icarus's behavior is ____. This behavior would be acceptable/unacceptable in ancient Greece because____.* (Have students give a number of reasons. Ask them to pay attention to comma usage.) **MODERATE**
- Remind students to use transitions to link their evidence to their explanations, such as *therefore, another reason, as a result, furthermore*. Have pairs find three places in their essays where they can use a transition. **LIGHT**

TEACH

? **Connect to the ESSENTIAL QUESTION**

"The Flight of Icarus" is the story of a man and his son who are held captive on an island. They literally rise up to face their problem by learning how to fly like birds.

ANALYZE & APPLY

THE FLIGHT OF ICARUS

Myth retold by **Sally Benson**

? **ESSENTIAL QUESTION:**

What helps people rise up to face difficulties?

GET READY

QUICK START

In a journal entry, describe an experience in which you wish you had acted differently. What should you have done instead? What did you learn from that experience?

ANALYZE GENRE: MYTH

"The Flight of Icarus" is a **myth**, an old and traditional story that tries to answer basic questions about the origins of the world, events in nature, human life, and social customs. Most myths share these elements:

- gods and other supernatural beings with special powers
- unrealistic or supernatural events and settings
- a lesson about life or human behavior

Myths can tell exciting, action-packed stories. Many myths also suggest values—for example, honesty, cleverness, or moderation (acting within reasonable limits)—that are important to a culture. In the past, in fact, myths often were used to encourage people to act in a way that reflected these values and helped society to function properly.

DETERMINE THEMES

A **theme** is a message about life or human nature that a writer shares with the reader. An example of a theme might be "greed can lead to ruined lives" or "simple things in life are the most meaningful." Writers sometimes state a theme directly. More often, you must analyze story events and characters' actions to infer, or make logical guesses about, the theme of a story.

Myths often contain more than one theme. These themes reflect the cultural values of the society in which the myth was told. By analyzing the behavior of mythic characters in unusual situations, you can learn lessons about the traits that mattered to a culture. Think about these questions as you determine the life lessons or other big ideas— that is, the themes—in a myth.

GENRE ELEMENTS: MYTH
- has characters who have special abilities or are gods
- is set in ancient times
- includes events that could not happen in real life
- often tells a story that teaches a lesson relating to a cultural value

The Flight of Icarus 25

TEACH

QUICK START

Have students read the Quick Start question, and invite them to share their responses with a partner before writing their journal entries. To guide them, ask them to think about a decision they made, an action they took, or a reaction they had—planned or spontaneous—that turned out to be a big mistake. Did they ever make that same mistake again?

ANALYZE GENRE: MYTH

Help students understand common elements of myths. Remind students that myths are not simply fanciful stories involving gods and goddesses with special powers. Myths teach lessons about life. To figure out these life lessons, advise students to ask themselves what is the moral of the story.

DETERMINE THEMES

Tell students that a theme is not a one-word topic like greed or bravery. A theme expresses an idea across a topic. Explain that a tip on its own in the graphic organizer is just a piece of the theme--it needs to be combined with others makes up a theme. Tell students that themes are related to the life lesson being taught in the myth.

Suggest that students use these questions to help them determine the theme or themes in a myth.
- What is the moral of the story?
- Can the moral be restated as a theme?
- Is there more than one moral or lesson?

 ENGLISH LEARNER SUPPORT

Use Prior Knowledge

Tell students that even if they are not familiar with the myth "The Flight of Icarus," they probably know other myths. Students may name myths from their own cultures.

- Ask students whether a myth or story is literally, actually, true. If it is not actually true, can it still have something true to say? **SUBSTANTIAL**
- If a myth is not literally true, why do people still read myths? What can an ancient myth relate that is still important to us today? **MODERATE**
- What are some myths (urban legends, stories) that we tell today? Is there value in these modern stories? **LIGHT**

The Flight of Icarus 25

TEACH

CRITICAL VOCABULARY

Encourage students to read all the sentences before deciding which word best completes each one. Remind them to look for context clues that match the meaning of each word.

Answers:

1. *moderate*
2. *frantic*
3. *prowess*
4. *anxiety*

■ **English Learner Support**

Use Cognates Tell students that several of the Critical Vocabulary words have Spanish cognates *(moderate/ moderado/a, frantic/frenético, anxiety/ansiedad).*
ALL LEVELS

LANGUAGE CONVENTIONS

Remind students that the word *coordinate* means "equal in importance," when it refers to adjectives in a sentence. Tell students to test sentences to see whether they need commas. Ask: *Does a sentence make sense if the order of the adjectives is reversed? Can the word* and *go between the adjectives?* The commas are clues that these are coordinate adjectives. Give correct and incorrect examples such as: *She is a strong, purposeful, woman.* (coordinate) *Ann has a blue cotton sweater.* (*This sentence cannot use* and *or a comma; it is not coordinate.* Cotton *is a noun, but here it modifies* sweater)

 ANNOTATION MODEL

Remind students of the kinds of evidence they are seeking and why. Point out that they may circle relevant qualities and traits and underline supernatural actions and events, or they may devise a color-coding system of their own to indicate these elements.

 GET READY

CRITICAL VOCABULARY

moderate   prowess   frantic   anxiety

To see how many Critical Vocabulary words you already know, choose one to complete each sentence.

1. _____ politicians from both countries favored the treaty.
2. The young children became _____ and started crying when the earthquake began.
3. The _____ of the athletes during the tournament helped them win the championship.
4. The citizens' fear and _____ increased as food became scarce.

LANGUAGE CONVENTIONS

Commas and Coordinate Adjectives In this lesson, you will learn about the effective use of commas and coordinate adjectives in writing. Coordinate adjectives are describing words that equally modify the same noun:

Daedalus was a smart, purposeful man.

Notice that *smart* and *purposeful* appear before the noun *man* and are separated by a comma.

ANNOTATION MODEL NOTICE & NOTE

As you read, note elements of myths that you can identify. You also can mark details that show aspects of the myth's theme. This model shows one reader's notes about "The Flight of Icarus."

> 2   Daedalus was an (ingenious) artist and was not (discouraged) by his failures. "Minos may control the land and sea," he said, "but he does not control the air. I will try that way."

Daedalus seems to have important values. Part of the theme, or not?

"control the air" = something special or even supernatural in a time before airplanes

26   Unit 1

APPLYING ACADEMIC VOCABULARY

Write and Discuss Have students turn to a partner to discuss the following questions. Guide students to include Academic Vocabulary words *aspect* and *resource* in their responses with the class.

- What **aspect** of Greek mythology do you find interesting?
- What **resource** should you use to find other Greek myths?
- What color is the **text** on this page?

26   Unit 1

BACKGROUND

Today we think of myths as stories that have been passed down through countless generations. In the ancient civilization of Greece, myths were the basis of an elaborate system of beliefs. Myths explained their mystifying world and offered wisdom on how to live in it. The myth of Daedalus and his son Icarus is one example.

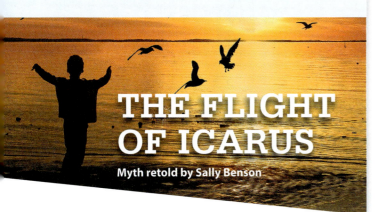

THE FLIGHT OF ICARUS

Myth retold by Sally Benson

SETTING A PURPOSE

As you read, pay close attention to the choices Icarus and his father make. What do these choices reveal? Write down any questions you may have while reading.

1 When Theseus escaped from the labyrinth, King Minos flew into a rage with its builder, Daedalus, and ordered him shut up in a high tower that faced the lonely sea. In time, with the help of his young son, Icarus, <u>Daedalus managed to escape from the tower, only to find himself a prisoner on the island.</u> Several times he tried by bribery to stow away on one of the vessels sailing from Crete, but King Minos kept strict watch over them, and no ships were allowed to sail without being carefully searched.

2 Daedalus was an ingenious artist and was not discouraged by his failures. "Minos may control the land and sea," he said, "but he does not control the air. I will try that way."

NOTICE & NOTE

Notice & Note

Use the side margins to notice and note signposts in the text.

ANALYZE GENRE: MYTH

Annotate: Mark the detail in paragraphs 1–2 that states the problem Daedalus and Icarus face.

Draw Conclusions: How do you think Daedalus plans to solve the problem? Why do you think so?

The Flight of Icarus 27

TEACH

BACKGROUND

Have students read the background information about myths and their role in ancient Greek civilization. Tell students that Greek myths, literature, art, and ideas play an important part in many cultures. Students are likely to come across references to mythological characters like Icarus in a wide variety of media. To introduce the story, point out that Theseus, the character mentioned in the first paragraph, escaped from a fierce monster in King Minos's labyrinth. Explain the a labyrinth is like a maze. Show students pictures of famous mazes and labyrinths. The escape of Theseus creates a problem for Daedalus that he must use all of his genius to overcome.

SETTING A PURPOSE

Direct students to use the Setting a Purpose prompt to focus their reading.

ANALYZE GENRE: MYTH

Remind students that events occur in myths that cannot happen in real life. Explain that some mythological characters have supernatural powers. Others have exaggerated human characteristics like enormous physical strength or very high intelligence. The most unusual characters have a little bit of all these qualities; for example, Theseus was unusually strong, highly intelligent, and had a god for a father. Daedalus has no supernatural powers, but he has a genius for making things. **(Answer:** *Daedalus has failed to escape by sea, so he will have to find another way to get off the island, probably by flying. Daedalus says that Minos "does not control the air. I will try that way."*

 ENGLISH LEARNER SUPPORT

Support Understanding of Sequence Provide students with cause-and-effect graphic organizers. Read paragraphs 1 and 2 aloud. Define unfamiliar vocabulary and expressions, such as *flew into a rage*, *labyrinth*, and *stow away*. Circulate among students working in small groups as they fill in the organizers with the key events in the correct sequence. Encourage students to draw illustrations to accompany their recording of events. **ALL LEVELS**

The Flight of Icarus 27

TEACH

ANALYZE GENRE: MYTH

Remind students that Greek myths usually teach important lessons about life and human behavior. They also reveal the attitudes and values that were important in ancient Greek culture. **(Answer:** *Their interaction suggests that fathers were responsible for the well-being of their children and that children were obedient and followed their father's instructions.)*

▶ WORDS OF THE WISER

Remind students that this signpost indicates that a character who is wiser and usually older is offering some important advice or insight to the main character. **(Answer:** *One theme suggested by Daedalus's warning is that extremes can be dangerous: it is safer to follow a more moderate course. Another theme is that you should listen to people who are older and wiser than you.)*

NOTICE & NOTE

ANALYZE GENRE: MYTH

Annotate: Reread paragraphs 3 and 4. Mark words and phrases that show that Daedals is happy about the work he and his son are doing.

Infer: What do these paragraphs suggest about the kind of family interactions that the Greek culture valued?

WORDS OF THE WISER

Notice & Note: In paragraph 5, mark the warning that Daedalus gives Icarus.

Connect: What might Daedalus's warning suggest about one theme of this myth?

3   He called his son, Icarus, to him and told the boy to gather up all the feathers he could find on the rocky shore. As thousands of gulls soared over the island, Icarus soon collected a huge pile of feathers. Daedalus then melted some wax and made a skeleton in the shape of a bird's wing. The smallest feathers he pressed into the soft wax and the large ones he tied on with thread. Icarus played about on the beach happily while his father worked, chasing the feathers that blew away in the strong wind that swept the island and sometimes taking bits of the wax and working it into strange shapes with his fingers.

4   It was fun making the wings. The sun shone on the bright feathers; the breezes ruffled them. When they were finished, Daedalus fastened them to his shoulders and found himself lifted upwards, where he hung poised in the air. Filled with excitement, he made another pair for his son. They were smaller than his own, but strong and beautiful.

5   Finally, one clear, wind-swept morning, the wings were finished, and Daedalus fastened them to Icarus's shoulders and taught him how to fly. He bade him watch the movements of the birds, how they soared and glided overhead. He pointed out the slow, graceful sweep of their wings as they beat the air steadily, without fluttering. Soon Icarus was sure that he, too, could fly and, raising his arms up and down, skirted over the white sand and even out over the waves, letting his feet touch the snowy foam as the water thundered and broke over the sharp rocks. Daedalus watched him proudly but with

28   Unit 1

CLOSE READ SCREENCAST

Have students click the Close Read icons in their eBooks to access a screencast in which readers discuss and annotate the passage about Icarus's first flight and Daedalus's warning to him (paragraph 5).

[paragraph break] "As a class, view and discuss this video. Then have students pair up to do an independent close read of an additional passage—Icarus flies too high and begins to lose his feathers (paragraph 7).

 Close Read Practice PDF

NOTICE & NOTE

misgivings. He called Icarus to his side and, putting his arm round the boy's shoulders, said, "Icarus, my son, we are about to make our flight. No human being has ever traveled through the air before, and I want you to listen carefully to my instructions. Keep at a **moderate** height, for if you fly too low, the fog and spray will clog your wings, and if you fly too high, the heat will melt the wax that holds them together. Keep near me and you will be safe."

6   He kissed Icarus and fastened the wings more securely to his son's shoulders. Icarus, standing in the bright sun, the shining wings dropping gracefully from his shoulders, his golden hair wet with spray, and his eyes bright and dark with excitement, looked like a lovely bird. Daedalus's eyes filled with tears, and turning away, he soared into the sky, calling to Icarus to follow. From time to time, he looked back to see that the boy was safe and to note how he managed his wings in his flight. As they flew across the land to test their **prowess** before setting out across the dark wild sea, plowmen below stopped their work and shepherds gazed in wonder, thinking Daedalus and Icarus were gods.

7   Father and son flew over Samos and Delos, which lay on their left, and Lebinthus,¹ which lay on their right. Icarus, beating his wings in joy, felt the thrill of the cool wind on his face and the clear air above and below him. He flew higher

---

¹ **Samos . . . Delos . . . Lebinthus** (sāˊmŏsˊ . . . dēˊlŏsˊ . . . lu bĭnˊthusˊ): small Greek islands in the eastern Aegean Sea.

moderate
(mŏdˊər-ĭt) *adj.* When something is kept *moderate*, it is kept within a certain limit.

prowess
(prouˊĭs) *n.* *Prowess* is the strength and courage someone has.

LANGUAGE CONVENTIONS
Annotate: Mark the example of coordinate adjectives that appears in paragraph 7.
Interpret: What does the comma in that example tell you about those adjectives?

The Flight of Icarus   29

TEACH

 LANGUAGE CONVENTIONS

Review the meaning of coordinate adjectives with students, and remind them that the comma takes the place of the word *and*. (**Answer:** *The comma tells you that* soft *and* moist *both modify* the clouds *equally*.)

■ **English Learner Support**

Language Conventions   Point out the phrase *his eyes bright and dark* in the middle of paragraph 6. Ask for volunteers to restate the phrase so that it has coordinate adjectives. Write the correct restated phrase on the board, and then ask students to identify where the comma goes and why. (*His bright, dark eyes—the comma takes the place of the word* and.) Emphasize that in both variations, *eyes bright and dark*, and, *bright, dark eyes*, the adjectives carry equal weight and modify *eyes*.

For **listening and reading support** for students at varying proficiency levels, see the **Text X-Ray** on page 24C.

CRITICAL VOCABULARY

moderate: Daedalus warned his son to keep at a moderate height, neither too high nor too low.

ASK STUDENTS why Daedalus gave his son this warning to be moderate. (*Daedalus and Icarus were about to try something dangerous, so it was important to be safe and careful.*)

prowess: Icarus and Daedalus tested their flying prowess, or ability, before setting out across the sea.

ASK STUDENTS to describe the prowess that this flight required. (*The flight required physical strength and navigation skills.*)

TO CHALLENGE STUDENTS...

Conduct Research   Challenge students to research another famous character from Greek mythology, like Narcissus, Pandora, or Pygmalion. Ask them to identify the problems these characters face, the supernatural or unrealistic aspects of the story, and as many distinct themes as they can identify. Students may present their findings as either a written or an oral report.

The Flight of Icarus   29

TEACH

TEXT IN FOCUS

Previewing the Text Have students view the **Text in Focus** video on this page of their eBook to learn how to preview a text. Then have students use **Text In Focus Practice** to apply what they have learned.

DETERMINE THEMES

Remind students that asking themselves what the moral of the story is will help them determine the theme. **(Answer:** *The placement of this sentence at the very end of the myth emphasizes the theme: lack of moderation can lead to disaster and heartbreak. This is the final thought the reader is left with, so it drives home the main life lesson that the myth teaches.)*

ENGLISH LEARNER SUPPORT

Reinforce Meaning Read aloud paragraph 7, pausing after each sentence to allow students to ask for clarification of any unfamiliar words or phrases. Confirm their understanding of those words and phrases by asking students to use them conversationally. Ask for volunteers to rephrase the second sentence or the second to last sentence in their own words.

MODERATE

CRITICAL VOCABULARY

frantic: Icarus beat his wings frantically because he wanted more power to fly higher.

ASK STUDENTS how the author's use of the word *frantically* helps us picture the scene. *(It helps us visualize Icarus moving his arms or wings with great speed and excitement.)*

anxiety: Daedalus is "crazed by anxiety" because he hears his son crying but doesn't know where he is.

ASK STUDENTS what Daedalus's anxiety says about his feelings for Icarus. *(Daedalus's anxiety makes it clear how much he loves his son and is concerned for his well-being.)*

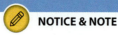 **NOTICE & NOTE**

frantic
(frăn´tĭk) *adj.* If you do something in a *frantic* way, you do it quickly and nervously.

anxiety
(ăng-zī´ĭ-tē) *n.* Anxiety is an uneasy, worried feeling.

DETERMINE THEMES
Annotate: Mark the sentence in paragraph 9 that relates directly to the main theme of this myth.

Critique: Why is the placement of this sentence effective in emphasizing the theme?

and higher up into the blue sky until he reached the clouds. His father saw him and called out in alarm. He tried to follow him, but he was heavier and his wings would not carry him. Up and up Icarus soared, through the soft, moist clouds and out again toward the glorious sun. He was bewitched by a sense of freedom and beat his wings **frantically** so that they would carry him higher and higher to heaven itself. The blazing sun beat down on the wings and softened the wax. Small feathers fell from the wings and floated softly down, warning Icarus to stay his flight and glide to earth. But the enchanted boy did not notice them until the sun became so hot that the largest feathers dropped off and he began to sink. Frantically he fluttered his arms, but no feathers remained to hold the air. He cried out to his father, but his voice was submerged in the blue waters of the sea, which has forever after been called by his name.

8   Daedalus, crazed by **anxiety**, called back to him, "Icarus! Icarus, my son, where are you?" At last he saw the feathers floating from the sky, and soon his son plunged through the clouds into the sea. Daedalus hurried to save him, but it was too late. He gathered the boy in his arms and flew to land, the tips of his wings dragging in the water from the double burden they bore. Weeping bitterly, he buried his small son and called the land Icaria in his memory.

9   Then, with a flutter of wings, he once more took to the air, but the joy of his flight was gone and his victory over the air was bitter to him. He arrived safely in Sicily, where he built a temple to Apollo and hung up his wings as an offering to the god, and in the wings he pressed a few bright feathers he had found floating on the water where Icarus fell. And he mourned for the birdlike son who had thrown caution to the winds in the exaltation of his freedom from the earth.

WHEN STUDENTS STRUGGLE...

Analyze the Concept Some students may have difficulty understanding the concept of moderation that is integral to the myth. To illustrate the concept, distribute a three-column graphic organizer with the headings "Moderate," "Extreme," and "Result of Extreme Behavior." In the rows, list several topics, like "Desserts," "Exercise," "Sleep," "Parties," etc. Then ask students to write or discuss their idea of moderate and extreme amounts of these activities and the results of extreme amounts.

 For additional support, go to the **Reading Studio** and assign the following Level Up tutorial: Specific Skill TK here.

NOTICE & NOTE

CHECK YOUR UNDERSTANDING

Answer these questions before moving on to the **Analyze the Text** section on the following page.

1 The detail <u>He bade him watch the movements of the birds, how they soared and glided overhead</u> emphasizes that —

   A birds were worshipped as gods in ancient Greece
   B flying by your own power was possible but dangerous
   C nature was highly respected by ancient Greeks
   D Daedalus wanted to make wings from birds' feathers

2 Against his father's advice, Icarus flew higher and higher because he —

   F was eager to prove that he was stronger than his father
   G often disobeyed his father's commands
   H became lost when the sun blinded him
   J was overtaken by the thrill that came from flying freely

3 Which sentence states an important theme in this myth?

   A Only true heroes can perform superhuman acts.
   B People must know their place in the universe.
   C Being able to live in freedom is worth any cost.
   D Doing things with family members is always fun.

The Flight of Icarus 31

TEACH

CHECK YOUR UNDERSTANDING

Have students answer the questions independently.

Answers:

1. C
2. J
3. B

If they answer any questions incorrectly, have them reread the text to confirm their understanding. Then they may proceed to ANALYZE THE TEXT on p. 32.

 ENGLISH LEARNER SUPPORT

Oral Assessment Use the following questions to assess students' comprehension and speaking skills.

1. Based on "The Flight of Icarus," what attitudes did the ancient Greeks have about nature? *(The ancient Greeks respected nature, and in the case of Daedalus, he turned to nature to find the inspiration for his escape.)*

2. Why did Icarus keep flying higher and higher? *(Icarus got so excited about flying that he forgot his father's instructions.)*

3. Do you think Daedalus ever flew again after he escaped from the island and King Minos? *(No, the text says he "hung up his wings as an offering to the god." And flying would have reminded him of his lost son.)*

4. What is the theme of "The Flight of Icarus"? *(One theme of the story is moderation is the safest way to live life. Another theme is people should not attempt to do what they are not intended do.)* **MODERATE**

APPLY

ANALYZE THE TEXT
Possible answers

1. **DOK 2:** *Daedalus makes two sets of wings from melted wax and feathers. He intends that he and his son Icarus will use the wings to fly away from the island.*

2. **DOK 3:** *Textual evidence includes the following: "Daedalus watched him proudly but with misgivings"; "No human being has ever traveled through the air before"; "if you fly too low, the fog and spray will clog your wings, and if you fly too high, the heat will melt the wax that holds them together."*

3. **DOK 3:** *Both Daedalus and Icarus ignore their limitations and seek to be more than human. Daedalus is mature and careful, but Icarus is impulsive and caught up in the thrill of the moment. If you are going to do something that has never been tried before, you must be especially moderate.*

4. **DOK 4:** *Daedalus's original plan was to escape from the island. He succeeded at that goal, but "his victory over the air was bitter to him" because he had lost his son. This outcome suggests the theme "know your place"—don't soar too high or try to be like the gods.*

5. **DOK 4:** *The myth emphasizes the ideas of acting in moderation and of listening to someone who has authority over you. The "wiser" person could be the storyteller or the society that supports the story. Either way, the "words" encourage the audience to avoid extremes and to live in harmony with the culture's values.*

RESEARCH
Remind students that they should confirm any information they find by checking multiple websites and assessing the credibility of each one. It may be helpful to bring in books on Greek mythology, so students can look up the myth of Theseus and the labyrinth.

 RESPOND

ANALYZE THE TEXT
Support your responses with evidence from the text. NOTEBOOK

1. **Summarize** Reread paragraphs 3–4. Summarize in a few sentences what Daedalus does to help himself and his son escape from the island.

2. **Cite Evidence** What specific evidence in paragraph 5 suggests that Daedalus's plan will not go well?

3. **Compare** How are the actions of Daedalus and Icarus related to the idea of moderation in this myth? Explain how their actions are based on similarities and differences in their personalities and experiences.

4. **Synthesize** Reread paragraph 9. Keeping in mind Daedalus's original goal, do you think that he succeeded, or failed? What does your answer suggest about the Greeks' beliefs concerning their place in the world in relation to their gods?

5. **Notice & Note** "The Flight of Icarus" includes some specific wise words from a father to his son. How does this myth, as a whole, illustrate the idea of "Words of the Wiser"?

RESEARCH TIP
When you conduct online research, use several search terms that are specific. Include key words that reflect what you are looking for, such as a character's name, the setting of the story, a key event, and the genre of the selection.

RESEARCH
The character of Daedalus appears in another famous Greek myth. In that story, he designed and constructed a labyrinth, or maze, in which a monster was kept as a prisoner. The monster would find and kill people who were sent into the labyrinth as a form of punishment. Use the questions below to analyze the themes of this myth.

QUESTION	ANSWER
Who are the characters in the myth about Daedalus and the labyrinth?	*Daedalus, King Minos, Ariadne, Theseus, and the Minotaur*
What problem must the main character solve?	*Theseus must enter the labyrinth, kill the Minotaur, and then find his way out of the labyrinth*
How does the main character's solution reflect some of the same themes that appear in "The Flight of Icarus"?	*Theseus, like Daedalus, is smart and brave. His ingenious solution involves simple materials.*

Extend Find out how the design of the labyrinth inspired actual maze-like structures or how it was used in other stories.

RESPOND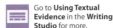

WRITE AND DISCUSS

Write an Explanation People today may refer to someone "who flew too close to the sun" as a cautionary tale. Write a two- to three-paragraph explanation of what this expression means and what it has to do with the myth of Icarus. Base your explanation on evidence from "The Flight of Icarus."

- ❏ Clearly state the topic in a strong thesis statement—a clear controlling idea.
- ❏ Support your thesis with evidence. Cite relevant examples from the myth.
- ❏ Use appropriate transitions to link ideas.
- ❏ Provide a conclusion that follows from and supports the information that you have presented.

Discuss with a Small Group Share your explanation with other students in a small group. Then discuss the following questions.

- ❏ How well does each explanation meet the criteria listed above?
- ❏ Which examples provide the strongest evidence? Why?
- ❏ What suggestions would improve the explanation?
- ❏ Have you listened closely and respectfully to all ideas?

 Go to **Using Textual Evidence** in the **Writing Studio** for more.

 Go to **Participating in Collaborative Discussions** in the **Speaking and Listening Studio** for help.

RESPOND TO THE ESSENTIAL QUESTION

 What helps people rise up to face difficulties?

Gather Information Review your annotations and notes on "The Flight of Icarus." Then, add relevant details to your Response Log. As you determine which information to include, think about:

- what kinds of difficulties people face
- what motivates people to want to rise above their difficulties
- what it means to overcome difficulties successfully

At the end of the unit, use your notes to write an informational essay.

ACADEMIC VOCABULARY

As you write and discuss what you learned from the myth, be sure to use the Academic Vocabulary words. Check off each of the words that you use.

- ❏ aspect
- ❏ cultural
- ❏ evaluate
- ❏ resource
- ❏ text

The Flight of Icarus 33

APPLY

WRITE AND DISCUSS

Write an Explanation Point out that the list on page 33 can serve as an outline for the students' essays. Each item can be one paragraph. Remind students that their explanations must be based on evidence from the myth.

For **writing support** for students at varying proficiency levels, see the **Text X-Ray** on page 24D.

Discuss with a Small Group Remind students that when they do not understand a comment made by another group member, they should ask questions to clarify meaning. The process of asking and answering questions can help everyone understand an issue more clearly and can lead to new ideas. Note that they should wait until the group member has finished speaking, and not interrupt.

RESPOND TO THE ESSENTIAL QUESTION

Allow time for students to add details from "The Flight of Icarus" to their Unit 1 Response Logs.

 ENGLISH LEARNER SUPPORT

Discuss with a Small Group Restate the writing topic as a question: What kinds of behavior did the ancient Greeks find acceptable? Allow students to work with partners to form opinions that answer the question. Provide these sentence frames to help them develop their ideas for the discussion: *The ancient Greeks felt that freedom _____. (can be dangerous, involves responsibility)* The ancient Greeks believed that when a parent gives a child an order the child should _____. *(follow the order)* The ancient Greeks found this kind of behavior acceptable because in the Icarus myth_____. *(We see the dangers of not listening to wise advice.)* Do you think that Daedalus is a good example of the kind of behavior that the ancient Greeks find acceptable or even praiseworthy? If you know anything else about Daedalus from other Greek myths, such as Theseus and the labyrinth, you can use this knowledge to help answer the question. What about Icarus? *(Answers will vary.)*
MODERATE/LIGHT

The Flight of Icarus 33

APPLY

CRITICAL VOCABULARY

Answers::

1. *b*
2. *b*
3. *b*
4. *a*

VOCABULARY STRATEGY:
Latin Roots

Answers:

1. instructive: *informative, useful*
2. destruction: *ruin, wreckage*
3. structure: *building, arena*
4. reconstructed: *rebuilt, constructed again*

 RESPOND

WORD BANK
moderate
prowess
frantic
anxiety

CRITICAL VOCABULARY

Practice and Apply Circle the letter of the better answer to each question. Be prepared to explain your response.

1. Which of the following is an example of **moderate** behavior?
   a. yelling at a parent about a disagreement
   b. explaining the cause of a disagreement to a friend

2. Which of the following is more likely to cause **anxiety**?
   a. winning first prize in a contest or game
   b. not having a way to leave a bad situation

3. Which of the following involves **prowess**?
   a. the ability to accept failure when challenged
   b. the ability to solve a difficult problem successfully

4. Which of the following is an example of **frantic** behavior?
   a. a group of people running away from an out-of-control vehicle
   b. a crowd of sports fans cheering about a strong showing on the field

 Go to the **Vocabulary Studio** for more on Latin roots.

VOCABULARY STRATEGY: Latin Roots

A **root** is a word part that came into English from an older language such as ancient Latin. Roots can help you figure out the meanings of some unfamiliar words. In paragraph 5, Daedalus tells Icarus "to listen carefully to my *instructions*." The Latin root *struct* means "to build or create a pile." *Instructions* means "a set [pile] of directions telling someone what to do."

Practice and Apply In your own words, write the meaning of the boldface word in each sentence that uses the Latin root *struct*. You may use print or online resources to check your answers.

1. The astronomer's presentation was **instructive** to all of us.
   _____

2. The ocean waves caused widespread **destruction** in the area.
   _____

3. The new labyrinth, a magnificent **structure** made of wood and stone, cost a great deal to build.
   _____

4. The historic building had been damaged during a conflict, but it was **reconstructed** within a decade.
   _____

🗨 ENGLISH LEARNER SUPPORT

Latin Roots Give students additional practice in determining the meaning of unfamiliar words by applying their knowledge of Latin root *struct*. Write the following words on the board: *destructive, constructive, substructure, obstruct,* and *instructional, reconstruct*. Have pairs of students copy the words, underline the Latin roots, and write definitions. Tell them to confirm their definitions by looking up each word in a dictionary. Note that many Spanish words also have their roots in Latin and may be similar to English words. For example, *destructive=destructivo*.

LANGUAGE CONVENTIONS: Commas and Coordinate Adjectives

Writers often include **coordinate adjectives** to make their descriptions more interesting and precise. In "The Flight of Icarus," the author occasionally includes coordinate adjectives.

In the two examples below, note that both adjectives appear before the noun that they describe. They have distinct meanings, but they have an equal effect in describing the noun.

> one clear, wind-swept morning
> the slow, graceful sweep of their wings

The fact that two adjectives appear just before a noun doesn't necessarily mean they are coordinate adjectives. In this example, dark modifies wild sea. The adjectives do not have an equal effect, so no comma is needed.

> the dark wild sea

Do you need a comma? You can test by substituting the word and for the comma and by switching the order of the adjectives. If the new phrase makes sense, then the words are very likely coordinate adjectives, and a comma is needed.

> the slow and graceful sweep of their wings
> the graceful and slow sweep of their wings

Practice and Apply Write your own sentences using coordinate adjectives. Your sentences may be based on the selection or another myth you know. When you have finished, share your sentences with a partner and compare your use of coordinate adjectives.

RESPOND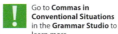

Go to **Commas in Conventional Situations** in the **Grammar Studio** to learn more.

The Flight of Icarus 35

APPLY

LANGUAGE CONVENTIONS: Commas and Coordinate Adjectives

Review the information about coordinate adjectives with students. Remind students that authors use coordinate adjectives to add specific and descriptive language to a text.

Emphasize that coordinate adjectives have an equal effect on the noun they are modifiying and should always have a comma between them. Remind students to reverse the adjectives or replace the comma with the word when they are unsure if a sentence uses coordinate adjectives.

- Up and up Icarus soared, through the soft moist clouds and out again toward the glorious sun. *(Up and up Icarus soared, through the soft, moist clouds and out again toward the glorious sun.)*

Explain to students that some sentences use more than two coordinate adjectives and provide the following example: *The dragon gave a loud, fiery, ferocious roar.* Challenge students to use three coordinate adjectives when writing their sentences.

Practice and Apply Have partners discuss whether coordinate adjectives are used correctly in their sentences. *(Students' sentences will vary.)*

 ENGLISH LEARNER SUPPORT

Language Conventions Ask students to think of a prominent person or celebrity and use adjectives to describe him or her. Then use the following supports with students at varying proficiency levels:

- Have students work in groups to circle five adjectives that appear in "The Flight of Icarus." Then ask them to discuss with each other why those words are adjectives.

- Have students work with partners to write original sentences that contain properly punctuated coordinate adjectives. Then have them meet with another pair to compare their sentences.

- Ask students to write a brief paragraph that contains at least four sets of properly punctuated coordinate adjectives. Then ask them to justify their use of a comma between the adjectives.

PLAN

READING MODEL
ICARUS'S FLIGHT
Poem by Stephen Dobyns

GENRE ELEMENTS
POETRY

Remind students that one of the purposes of a **poem** is to experiment with story form, language, rhythm, and even punctuation. Related genres like **song lyrics** work in a similar way, but poems are not regularly put to music; the "rhythm" of a poem has to do with the sound of its language, not music. In this lesson, students will use the poetic form to explore topics of form in addition to conceptions of knowledge, wisdom, and what it takes to push yourself to the limits of your abilities.

LEARNING OBJECTIVES

- Analyze form in poetry.
- Analyze punctuation and tone in poetry.
- Research poems about a myth.
- Present and critique a poem orally
- **Language** Understand how the sounds of poetry read aloud can help you recognize ideas or patterns in poetry.

TEXT COMPLEXITY

Quantitative Measures	Icarus's Flight	Lexile: 1080L
Quantitative Measures	**Ideas Presented** Multiple levels, with greater demand for inference.	
	Structure Used More complex, though a familiar poetic form.	
	Language Used Meanings are implied, more inference is demanded.	
	Knowledge Required More complexity in theme, experiences may be less familiar to many.	

36A Unit 1

PLAN

RESOURCES

Online

- Unit 1 Response Log
- 🔊 Selection Audio
- 📖 Reading Studio: Notice & Note
- 💬 Speaking and Listening Studio: Analyzing and Evaluating Presentations
- ✓ "Icarus's Flight" Selection Test

SUMMARIES

English

For centuries, the story of Icarus has been a cautionary tale about the dangers of arrogance and overconfidence. But poet Stephen Dobyns has a perspective that's a little different. Through verse, Dobyns portrays Icarus as a daring hero who seeks a higher wisdom through investigating and understanding his own limitations. In this way, his failure becomes an inspiration to others who seek self-knowledge, his fall a flight of its own.

Spanish

Por siglos, la historia de Ícaro ha sido una moraleja sobre los peligros de la arrogancia y el exceso de confianza. Pero el poeta Stephen Dobyns tiene una perspectiva un poco distinta. A través del verso, Dobyns representa a Ícaro como un héroe osado quien busca una sabiduría mayor a través de la investigación y el entendimiento de sus propias limitaciones. De esta manera, su fracaso se convierte en inspiración para otros que buscan el autoconocimiento: su caída fue en sí misma un vuelo.

SMALL-GROUP OPTIONS

Have students work in small groups to read and discuss the selection.

Sticky Note Peer Review

- Break students into groups or pairs.
- Provide each group with pads of sticky notes.
- Ask the groups to reread the poem and to jot down one of each of the following: one positive comment, one critical comment, and one question about the text.
- Students then exchange the sticky notes, marking the notes they agree with or have questions or answers to add.
- Students discuss and exchange ideas.

Jigsaw with Experts

- Divide the poem into two to six numbered parts.
- Students are assigned to a numbered part.
- Students read and take notes on their part.
- Students join small groups who share the same part and discuss their part.
- Students then form new groups that include one representative for each part of the poem.
- Students discuss their respective parts and the whole poem for a designated amount of time.

Icarus's Flight **36B**

PLAN

Text X-Ray: English Learner Support
for "Icarus's Flight"

Use the Text X-Ray and the supports and scaffolds in the Teacher's Edition to help guide students at different proficiency levels through the selection.

INTRODUCE THE SELECTION
DISCUSS FORM

Start the discussion by asking the students whether they are familiar with poetry. Can they identify poems from books they've read or from popular culture, such as rapping or even commercials? What does poetry mean to them? Gradually lead them to the idea that poetry can have rules and structure, or form. The poetry they're going to encounter will have content that is strengthened by particular sounds, beats, and rhythms.

Inform students that poetry tells a story much in the way prose does, but it does so with "style"—that is, with incredibly close attention paid to form and detail. In poetry, the *way* a poem is read and heard is often equally as important as what it means. In this lesson, *how* the poem is composed will be examined as closely as ideas of pursuit, flight, and failure.

CULTURAL REFERENCES

The following words and phrases may be unfamiliar to students:

- *dissolved the wax* (line 6): Icarus's wings were made of feathers and wax
- *plummeting* (line 7): falling, tumbling, descending
- *to flutter ignorantly from petal to petal within some garden* (lines 12—13): suggests a butterfly flying from flower to flower in a confined space.
- *disintegrating* (line 16): coming apart, breaking up into pieces
- *plunge* (line 19): a rapid jump, dive, or thrust inward or downward

LISTENING

Understand Poetic Form

Draw students' attention to the way "Icarus's Flight" sounds by reading the short poem aloud to the class.

Have students listen as you read the poem, pausing briefly after each stanza. Use the following supports with students at varying proficiency levels:

- Ask simple questions about the form of the poem you just read. Students can nod or shake their heads for yes or no. For example, ask: *Is the poem written in sections, stanzas? Could you tell when the different stanzas began?* **SUBSTANTIAL**
- Ask students to identify some of the central forms of the poem. (*stanzas, lines, rhythm etc.*) **MODERATE**
- Put students small groups and have them read the poem to each other. Have them identify lines, stanzas, and complete sentences in the poem Ask: *Why does the poem break up the complete sentences into different lines and stanzas?* (See page 40.) **LIGHT**

36C   Unit 1

PLAN

SPEAKING

Discuss Alliteration

Have students review the concept of alliteration on p. 37. This task is aligned with the Language Objective for all proficiencies.

Use the following supports with students at varying proficiency levels:

- Display or present to students a list of words that begin with the same initial letter (bug, bed, buddy, buy). Ask them to pronounce the words and identify what the words share. **SUBSTANTIAL**
- Ask students to read aloud the first stanza of the poem. Ask students to identify which words are *alliterated*. (Answers: *what, wasn't; boy, both*). **MODERATE**
- Pair students and ask them to find lines with alliteration in the poem and read them aloud to each other. *(Answers will vary.)* **MODERATE**

READING

Read a Poem

Explain to students that poets use rhyme, meter, alliteration, lines, and stanzas to produce a feeling in the reader that builds upon the poem's content.

Use the following supports with students at varying proficiency levels:

- Have pairs reread the poem to each other. Ask them to listen for when they stopped and to mark in their consumables where natural pauses occur. (*at the end of sentences; at the end of lines.*) **SUBSTANTIAL**
- Ask students if they can identify a rhythm, or pattern, that repeats in the poem. It can be as simple as noting how the tone repeatedly changes at the end of a question. What effect does this repetition have on the reader? *(Answers will vary.)* **MODERATE**
- The poem presents Icarus as admirable. How do the elements of poetry, the rhythm, alliteration and lines, support this view? *(Answers will vary.)* **MODERATE**

WRITING

Write a Poem

Work with students to read the writing assignment on p. 43.

Use the following supports with students at varying proficiency levels:

- Provide students with rhyming words. For example, *pie, sky, high, why, lie;* and *go, low, row, throw, so,* etc. Put students in pairs, and ask them to match the rhyming words and put them in separate piles or lists. **SUBSTANTIAL**
- Have students write two original lines or sentences in which the ending words rhyme. Work with students to make the two lines about the same length. When done, congratulate them for writing their first *rhyming couplet!* **LIGHT**
- Group students and have them brainstorm story or idea concepts for their poems. What kind of words would they like to use in their short poems? Circulate and help groups create their own lists of words, ideas, and poetic forms and tools they may like to use. **MODERATE**

TEACH

? **Connect to the ESSENTIAL QUESTION**

In "Icarus's Flight," the poet takes a unique view of the tragic story of the mythological boy, Icarus, who flew too close to the sun and fell to Earth. Although he technically failed in his goal, Icarus gained important wisdom on his brief flight. His yearning for knowledge helped him overcome his fears, his eagerness to learn brought him to the limits of his capabilities, and so his failure to stay in flight can be seen as a kind of triumph in the face of difficulty.

ANALYZE & APPLY

ICARUS'S FLIGHT

Poem by **Stephen Dobyns**

? **ESSENTIAL QUESTION:**

What helps people rise up to face difficulties?

GET READY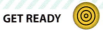

QUICK START

The poem you are about to read explores the myth of Icarus flying toward the sun and the thoughts that may have run through his head as he fell to earth. What is it about an unfortunate incident that causes people to want to review it in their minds and question what happened? List reasons why you think people review such events in this way. Is it better to think about these events, or to forget them?

ANALYZE FORM IN POETRY

Poetry is a type of literature in which words are carefully chosen to create certain effects. A poem's **form** is its structure, which includes the way its words and lines are arranged. This is linked to its meaning, which makes the poem's form important to its message. Here are some elements of form in poetry:

- The **line** is the main unit of all poems. The poet's thoughts can flow from one line to another. Poets also play with line length and words to establish meaning and to create rhythm.
- **Rhythm** is a pattern of stressed and unstressed syllables in a line of poetry, similar to the rhythmic beats in music. A repeated pattern of rhythm is called **meter**. The meter of a poem emphasizes the musical quality of a poem.
- Another element of poetry is the way the lines are presented in groups, called **stanzas**. It is important to pay attention to how lines are presented within a stanza and how punctuation may be used within and across stanzas.

Crafting a poem's form includes choices of words, rhythms, and sounds. Like songs, poems are meant to be heard. **Sound devices** are the use of certain words for their connection to the sense of hearing. Poets often choose different words for their sounds. **Alliteration** is a the repetition of consonant sounds at the beginning of words. It can establish rhythms in a poem that emphasize ideas and images.

Read aloud the following lines from "Icarus's Flight." Listen for the alliterative sounds. What do the repeated sounds suggest to you? How do they create rhythm and add emphasis to ideas or images in text?

> from petal to petal within some garden
> forever? As a result, flight for him was not
> upward escape, but descent, with his wings
> disintegrating around him. Should it matter

Notice how the alliterative words of *descent* and *disintegrating* emphasize similar sounds and create a sense of falling downward. As you read "Icarus's Flight," make notes about how the form, rhythm, and alliteration give you a better sense of the feeling the poet intended.

GENRE ELEMENTS: POETRY
- includes many forms, such as sonnets, haikus, and limericks
- conveys a poet's meaning through carefully selected words and structure (stanzas, line length, punctuation)
- uses imagery and a variety of sound devices and types of figurative language to express emotions and ideas

Icarus's Flight 37

TEACH

QUICK START

Have students read the Quick Start question and do the writing assignment. Then invite them to share their sentences. Ask some students to describe a difficult experience that in the end made them stronger, wiser, or more informed in some way. If students are uncomfortable doing this, tell them they can talk about a friend or family member's experience.

ANALYZE FORM IN POETRY

Remind students that form in poetry is the way that words are arranged on the page and that this arrangement involves the poetic tools described (line, stanza, rhythm, meter, sound device, and alliteration). Examine each tool with the class and answer questions as necessary.

Tell students that a poet can create rhythm in a poem by using lines of different length, alternating or inventing new rhyme schemes, or by ending sentences in different places. Part of what makes poetry interesting is that the possibilities are endless. To get students thinking about poetic form, ask some of the following questions about the provided lines from "Icarus's Flight" below.

- *What emotion are these lines trying to express?*
- *Which words make use of alliteration?*
- *How many syllables are in each line? Why might there be more syllables in some lines than others?*
- *Why does the stanza end with the fragment, "Should it matter," that is incomplete until the next stanza?*

 ENGLISH LEARNER SUPPORT

Reading Comprehension Ask students to silently read the title of the poem and the first stanza. Then ask three basic questions about the content: *Who is the poem about? (Icarus) What is he doing? (Flying) What are you struggling to understand in this stanza?* If the student cannot answer the first two questions, provide the answers and help the student fill in knowledge gaps anywhere they arise. Then have the student continue the silent reading, inquiring about his/her understanding with similarly basic questions. How does continued reading of the poem make the first stanza more clear? **LIGHT**

Icarus's Flight **37**

TEACH

ANALYZE PUNCTUATION AND TONE

Tell students that understanding the relationship between punctuation and tone will make it easier for them to comprehend and enjoy poetry. Discuss what type of tone the questions used by the author create.

Tell the students that punctuation tells readers when to pause and think about what they've read. Exclamation marks can be used to express a range of emotion (anger, excitement, passion). As we see in the reading, a question mark can be used to suggest to the reader that there is more than one way of interpreting the myth of Icarus.

■ English Learner Support

Punctuation Tell students that poets make use of all kinds of punctuation. Have students identify and count all commas (3), periods (8), and question marks (5) in this short poem. What does the amount (or scarcity) of certain types of punctuation tell you about the poem? **ALL LEVELS**

ANNOTATION MODEL

Tell students to jot down any note they want to remember about the poem in the margins. Ask them also to follow the instructions in the Analyze Punctuation and Tone and underline any questions they find in the poem. Also tell students to write possible answers to the questions in the margin as well. Tell them that they may also want to write down their own questions and ideas. Is there any idea in the poem that they disagree with? Remind them that notes are personal and do not have to follow any rules except that they help the reader.

GET READY

ANALYZE PUNCTUATION AND TONE

Poets use structure and poetic elements to create mood and reinforce meaning. A key element of poetry is **tone**, or the writer's attitude toward his or her subject. Tone can convey emotions that suggest how readers should react to the poem. Poets also use certain kinds of **punctuation** to show tone. In "Icarus's Flight," the tone is shown through questions asked by the author to show his thoughts about Icarus's fall. The poet wonders if Icarus was aware of the consequences of his disobedience.

Read aloud the following lines from "Icarus's Flight." Notice how the punctuation helps you understand the tone.

> disintegrating around him. Should it matter
>
> that neither shepherd nor farmer with his plow
> watched him fall? He now had his answer,
> laws to uphold him in his downward plunge.

Pay attention to details as you dig deeper into the poem. Use text clues and punctuation to determine the poet's attitude and to analyze how the poet's meaning is developed.

ANNOTATION MODEL   NOTICE & NOTE

As you read, consider how the poem's punctuation helps to convey tone and emotion. You can also make notes about the poem's structure. This model shows one reader's notes about the first few lines of "Icarus's Flight."

> What else could the boy have done? Wasn't flight both an escape and a great uplifting? And so he flew. <u>But how could he appreciate his freedom without knowing the exact point</u>
> 5 <u>where freedom stopped?</u> So he flew upward and the sun dissolved the wax and he fell. But at last in his anticipated plummeting he grasped the confines of what had been

The poem uses questions to justify Icarus's actions.

This question isn't answered here. Maybe I'll find the answer in a later stanza of the poem.

38   Unit 1

BACKGROUND

Writers have been fascinated by the characters of myths for centuries. They have featured famous mythic characters in such forms as dramas, stories, and poetry. "Icarus's Flight" reflects the poet's fascination with the myth of Icarus, the son of Daedalus, who flew too close to the sun. The author of "Icarus's Flight," **Stephen Dobyns** (b. 1941), is the author of popular works of fiction, but he considers himself primarily a poet.

NOTICE & NOTE

ICARUS'S FLIGHT

Poem by Stephen Dobyns

SETTING A PURPOSE

As you read this poem, think about the way the poet portrays Icarus and his true intention.

What else could the boy have done? Wasn't
flight both an escape and a great uplifting?
And so he flew. But how could he appreciate
his freedom without knowing the exact point

> **Notice & Note**
>
> Use the side margins to notice and note signposts in the text.
>
> **ANALYZE PUNCTUATION AND TONE**
> **Annotate:** Underline the instances where the poet asks questions.
>
> **Infer:** Based on the questions asked, what can you determine about the author's opinion of Icarus?

Icarus's Flight 39

TEACH

BACKGROUND

In this version of the ancient Greek myth, Icarus and his father, Daedalus, are imprisoned in a tower on an island. Daedalus is a great builder; he makes two sets of wings so that he and Icarus can escape the tower by flight. Daedalus warns Icarus not to fly too close to the sun; the wax that holds the wings together will melt and the wings will fall apart. Icarus ignores his father's warning. He cannot resist the urge to experience the greatest possible sense of freedom by flying too high. The wax melts. The wings fall apart; Icarus falls into the sea and drowns. This anonymous story (myth) has been told for thousands of years. Poets, musicians, writers, and painters have created many different interpretations. Most versions focus on Icarus falling because he did not obey his father; "Icarus's Flight" offers another reason for Icarus flying too close to the sun.

SETTING A PURPOSE

Direct students to use the Setting a Purpose prompt to focus their reading.

ANALYZE PUNCTUATION AND TONE

Remind students that **punctuation** can help the reader understand the poet's tone and point of view. **(Answer:** *The author is sympathetic towards Icarus and believes his actions were justified.***)**

> For **listening support** for students at varying proficiency levels, see the **Text X-Ray** on page 36C.

 ENGLISH LEARNER SUPPORT

Examine a Sentence Read the entire poem aloud. Have students complete the frame sentence: *Icarus flew _____ and the _____ on his wings. He _____ into the sea.*
MODERATE

Display this sentence from the poem: "But how could he appreciate his freedom without knowing the exact point where freedom stopped?" Ask students to discuss the main ideas contained in the sentence, and how those ideas relate to the overall theme of the poem.
LIGHT

Icarus's Flight 39

TEACH

ENGLISH LEARNER SUPPORT

Recognizing Patterns Have students identify and highlight any repeated words or sounds in the third stanza (*flew, far, flutter*).

ASK STUDENTS to work with a partner to come to a conclusion about why the author may have emphasized this word and made use of alliteration. (*The word* flew *is repeated to emphasize Icarus's plight, and also to emphasize the poet's tone and viewpoint on Icarus' story. It's as if the poet is confronting an imaginary critic who is continually pointing out the mistake of Icarus.*)

ANALYZE FORM

Remind students that poetic **form** refers to the arrangement of words, lines, and stanzas. (**Answer:** *Allowing sentences to flow from one stanza to the next pulls the reader along and gives a strong sense of Icarus's inevitable downward descent. Also, an idea in a sentence may change, or take on an additional meaning, when it is continued in the following stanza.*)

NOTICE & NOTE

ANALYZE FORM
Annotate: Mark where the sentences in lines 5–8 begin and end.

Infer: What does the poet achieve by allowing ideas in the form of questions and sentences to flow from one stanza to the next?

> 5 where freedom stopped? So he flew upward
>   and the sun dissolved the wax and he fell.
>   But at last in his anticipated plummeting
>   he grasped the confines of what had been
>
>   his liberty. You say he flew too far?
> 10 He flew just far enough. He flew precisely
>   to the point of wisdom. Would it
>   have been better to flutter ignorantly
>
>   from petal to petal within some garden
>   forever? As a result, flight for him was not
> 15 upward escape, but descent, with his wings
>   disintegrating around him. Should it matter
>
>   that neither shepherd nor farmer with his plow
>   watched him fall? He now had his answer,
>   laws to uphold him in his downward plunge.
> 20 Cushion enough for what he wanted.

IMPROVE READING FLUENCY

Targeted Passage While you read the entire poem aloud, have pairs pay close attention to the passage that begins on line 10 and ends with the last complete sentence on line 16. Reread lines 10–16 aloud. Discuss the meaning with students and check for comprehension. Have pairs take turns reciting the passage (10–16) to each other. Have each listener take notes about his or her partner's reading. Tell students to be respectful of their partners and to try to help them build fluency with comments such as, "There is a question mark after *forever* but I didn't hear it." Have students find at least one positive thing about their partner's reading.

Go to the **Reading Studio** for additional support in developing fluency.

NOTICE & NOTE

CHECK YOUR UNDERSTANDING

Answer these questions before moving on to the **Analyze the Text** section on the following page.

1. Why does the author ask questions in "Icarus's Flight"?
   - **A** To offer insight into his opinion of Icarus's actions
   - **B** To express that he understands Icarus
   - **C** To show that Icarus never acknowledged his mistake
   - **D** To prove that Icarus was reckless in his actions

2. What does the author argue about Icarus?
   - **F** His decision to fly toward the sun was ignorant.
   - **G** He deserved to fall from the sky.
   - **H** Daedalus should have kept a closer eye on him.
   - **J** Icarus was aware of the consequences of his flight.

3. In the sentences <u>He flew just far enough. He flew precisely to the point of wisdom.</u>, what tone does the poet express?
   - **A** Irritation
   - **B** Surprise
   - **C** Disappointment
   - **D** Admiration

Icarus's Flight 41

TEACH

CHECK YOUR UNDERSTANDING

Have students answer the questions independently.

Answers
1. *A*
2. *J*
3. *D*

If they answer any questions incorrectly, have them reread the text to confirm their understanding. Then they may proceed to ANALYZE THE TEXT on p.42.

ENGLISH LEARNER SUPPORT

Oral Assessment Use the following questions to assess student reading comprehension skills.

1. What does Icarus do? (*He flies; he flies too close to the sun.*)
2. Why does Icarus fly so close to the sun, according to the author? (*He had to see what freedom meant.*)
3. The poet says Icarus flew "just far enough" and "to the point of wisdom." Does the poet admire or disapprove of how high Icarus flew? (*admires*)
   ALL LEVELS

Icarus's Flight **41**

APPLY

ANALYZE THE TEXT
Possible answers:

1. **DOK 1:** *It pulls the reader along and gives the poem an almost vertical motion downward, suggesting the descent of Icarus.*

2. **DOK 4:** *The questions lead us to identify with Icarus. Dobyns believes that if you could suddenly escape and fly, wouldn't you want to see how high you could go?*

3. **DOK 4:** *The tone is triumphant. The poet suggests that though Icarus falls, the "answer" (wisdom) provides him with a "cushion."*

4. **DOK 2:** *The speaker believes Icarus succeeded because by flying to that point, he learned what freedom was. He achieved "precisely" the "wisdom" of understanding both freedom and mortality at the same time.*

5. **DOK 3:** *This poem changed my perception of Icarus. I thought of him before as a young boy who did not heed his father's warning, and now I think of him as someone who became fully aware of his actions. In failure, he gained wisdom and freedom.*

RESEARCH
Remind students that they should confirm any information they find by checking multiple websites and books and assessing credibility of sources.

Extend Inform students that the Poetry Foundation has a useful website for researching poets and poems (poetry foundation.org). Point out how interesting it is that many poets have used a vast range of forms and themes all based on the same idea of Icarus. No two poems are exactly alike, although many include similar themes of flight and failure.

 RESPOND

ANALYZE THE TEXT
Support your responses with evidence from the text. 📓 NOTEBOOK

1. **Identify** Look closely at how certain sentences of "Icarus's Flight" extend from one stanza into the next one. What effect is created by extending a sentence into the next line or the next stanza?

2. **Analyze** Examine the questions in lines 1–2. What is the purpose of these questions in the poem? What do they show about Dobyns's beliefs about Icarus?

3. **Analyze** Look at the last stanza in "Icarus's Flight." What tone is conveyed here, and how does the poet achieve it?

4. **Interpret** In poems, the speaker is the voice that expresses feelings and emotions. The speaker in "Icarus's Flight" uses the poem to show opinions of Icarus. What do lines 10–11 show about the speaker's attitude towards Icarus?

5. **Compare** Consider what you already knew about the mythological character of Icarus before reading this poem. How does this poem cause your perception of Icarus to change? Explain.

RESEARCH

RESEARCH TIP
When you are looking for specific information about the works of an author or publisher, make sure that you check the resources at the author's or publisher's official website.

Research other poems about the myth of Daedalus and Icarus. Discover what themes or other details are common across these poems. Record what you learn in the chart.

POEMS	THEMES
"Landscape with Fall of Icarus" by William Carlos Williams	Flight, falling, painting, drowning, seasons, indifference
"Musee des Beaux Arts" by WH Auden	Flight, falling, painting, martyrdom, loss
"Failing and Flying" by Jack Gilbert	Flying, failure, love

Extend Find another poem by Stephen Dobyns. Compare the form of the poem with the "Icarus's Flight" and the poems you researched. Discuss with your partner what effects the forms of the poems create and what emotions the poems make you feel.

42   Unit 1

WHEN STUDENTS STRUGGLE...

Analyze Punctuation and Tone Remind students that the tone of the poem is revealed in the details and emphasized through punctuation. Have students reread lines 9–11 and identify the question: *You say he flew too far?* Point out that the poet answers his own question in the next lines. Ask: *How does the poet feel about what Icarus did? How do you know?* Have student pairs make a list of feelings the poet has about Icarus. Guide them to understand what the feelings have in common and how these details add to the tone of admiration.

RESPOND

CREATE AND CRITIQUE

Write a Poem Write a poem in which an observer comments on witnessing a compelling event.

- ❏ Decide whether you want your poem to be humorous or serious.
- ❏ Choose examples of situations that create the most vivid picture in your mind or evoke the strongest feelings.
- ❏ Focus on form, punctuation, and rhythm to emphasize the meaning of the poem and express a tone about the subject.

Critique a Poem Orally Review "Icarus's Flight" and think about its conversational tone. Then work with a partner to read the poem aloud and analyze the content.

- ❏ Take turns reading the poem aloud.
- ❏ As your partner reads, take notes on the questions the poet asks throughout the poem. What is the purpose of these questions? Can you relate to Icarus's struggle and goals?
- ❏ With your partner, review your notes and think about the questions and the views the poet presents. Be sure to come up with examples to support your views.
- ❏ Share your views with the class in an oral critique. Make sure your points are clear and convincing.

 Go to **Analyzing and Evaluating Presentations** in the **Speaking and Listening Studio** for more help.

RESPOND TO THE ESSENTIAL QUESTION

 What helps people rise up to face difficulties?

Gather Information Review your annotations and notes on "Icarus's Flight." Then, add relevant details to your Response Log. As you determine which information to include, think about:

- how poets use form and punctuation to create meaning and express tone
- the use of questions to show Stephen Dobyns's opinion of Icarus's actions

At the end of the unit, use your notes to help you write an informational essay.

ACADEMIC VOCABULARY

As you write and discuss what you learned from the poem, be sure to use the Academic Vocabulary words. Check off each of the words that you use.

- ❏ aspect
- ❏ cultural
- ❏ evaluate
- ❏ resource
- ❏ text

Icarus's Flight 43

APPLY

CREATE AND CRITIQUE

Write a Poem Remind students of the poetic tools reviewed on pp. 37–40, including line, form, rhythm, meter, sound devices, alliteration, and punctuation. They should take advantage of the great range of means and methods they have for expressing themselves through poetry. The poem may be *based* on something very simple, but have complex meanings. For example, a student could describe a very humorous situation in which a guest wore the wrong clothes to a wedding. However, the poem could also suggest how the guest felt at the wedding.

 For **writing support** for students at varying proficiency levels, see the **Text X-Ray** on page 36D.

Critique a Poem Orally Remember to encourage students to listen to each other's critical points and consider them seriously. A critique is no time to say whether a poem is "good" or "bad," but rather a thoughtful investigation into the meaning, scope, and success of the poetic endeavor. What does the poem communicate?

RESPOND TO THE ESSENTIAL QUESTION

Allow students time to add details from "Icarus's Flight " to their Unit 1 Response Logs.

 ENGLISH LEARNER SUPPORT

Critique a Poem Conduct an informal assessment. Have students get into pairs and read another short poem that you know well and have chosen for them. At the end of their readings, have each student restate or orally recap the story or main idea of the poem. If necessary, use the following sentence frame: *This poem was about _____ as seen from the point of view of _____.* **MODERATE**

Icarus's Flight 43

PLAN

MENTOR TEXT

WOMEN IN AVIATION
Informational Writing by Patricia and Frederick McKissack

This article serves as a **mentor text**, a model for students to follow when they come to the Unit 1 Writing Task: Writing an Informational Essay.

GENRE ELEMENTS
INFORMATIONAL TEXT

Remind students that the purpose of an **informational text** is to provide readers with factual information. Types of informational texts include biographies, news articles, how-to instructions, or excerpts from nonfiction books. To support its ideas, a text will use evidence, such as quotes from historical figures, text from newspaper articles, and photographs. In this lesson, students will cite evidence to draw conclusions about the topic of the text "Women in Aviation."

LEARNING OBJECTIVES

- Determine an author's purpose in writing a text.
- Cite evidence from a text in order to draw conclusions.
- Use consistent verb tenses.
- Research the achievements of a female aviator.
- Write an informative essay about a female aviator.
- Discuss the challenges faced by women in the early 20th century.
- Understand the difference between the denotation and connotation of words.
- **Language** Tell stories using past, present, and future tenses.

TEXT COMPLEXITY

	Women in Aviation	Lexile 1050L
Quantitative Measures		
Quantitative Measures	**Ideas Presented** Mostly explicit, but moves into some implied meaning.	
	Structure Used May vary from simple chronological order	
	Language Used Mostly explicit; Tier II and Tier III words are for the most part illuminated by context clues.	
	Knowledge Required Some references to events or other texts; most of the text deals with common or easily imagined experience.	

PLAN

RESONICES

- Unit 1 Response Log
- Selection Audio
- Reading Studio: Notice & Note
- Writing Studio: Writing Informative Texts
- Speaking and Listening Studio: Participating in Collaborative Discussions
- Grammar Studio: Module 9: Using Verbs Correctly
- "Women in Aviation" Selection Test

SUMMARIES

English
While this informational text features the accomplishments of many prominent women in early aviation (Sophie Blanchard, Katherine Wright, Raymonde de la Roche, Harriet Quimby, and Amelia Earhart), it zeroes in on Bessie Coleman, an African American woman from Texas who moved to France to become the first black woman to earn her pilot's license. Coleman's and other's stories from the time will open up discussion about this period when women were considered inferior to men in most avenues of life.

Spanish
Aunque este texto informativo destaca los logros de muchas mujeres prominentes en la era inicial de la aviación (Sophie Blanchard, Katherine Wright, Raymonde de la Roche, Harriet Quimby y Amelia Earhart), hace hincapié en Bessie Coleman, una afroamericana de Texas, quien se mudó a Francia para convertirse en la primera mujer negra en obtener una licencia de piloto. Con la historia de Bessie Coleman y otras de la época se inicia la discusión con respecto a este período en que las mujeres eran consideradas inferiores a los hombres en casi todos los caminos de la vida.

SMALL-GROUP OPTIONS

Have students work in small groups to read and discuss the selection.

Pinwheel Discussion
- In groups of eight, four students are seated facing in; four students are seated facing out.
- Students in inner circle remain stationary throughout discussion.
- Students in outer circle move clockwise after discussing each question.
- Control the discussion by asking a guiding question for each round. Examples:
  - *Would it be harder for a man or a woman to obtain a piloting license in the early 1900s? Explain.*
  - *Would it be harder for a white woman or an African American woman to obtain a piloting license in the early 1900s? Explain.*

Think-Pair-Share
- After students have read and analyzed "Women in Aviation," pose this question: *What would be the most difficult part of being a woman trying to learn how to fly in the early 1900s?*
- Have students think about the question individually and take notes.
- Then, have pairs discuss their ideas about the question.
- Finally, ask pairs to share their responses with the class.

PLAN

Text X-Ray: English Learner Support
for "Women in Aviation"

Use the Text X-Ray and the supports and scaffolds in the Teacher's Edition to help guide students at different proficiency levels through the selection.

INTRODUCE THE SELECTION
DISCUSS SELECTION-RELATED VOCABULARY

In this lesson, students will need to understand and discuss aviation as well as discrimination. Read paragraph 1 with students, and point out the words *aviation*, *sexist*, and *racist*. Provide the following explanations, and have students discuss the terms.

- *Aviation* is the technical word (noun) used for all the knowledge, engineering, science, skill, and craft that go into flying.
- *Sexist* is the term (adjective or noun) given to any behavior or opinion that assumes one gender is better than the other. It can also be used as a noun for a person who has sexist opinions.
- *Racist* is the term (adjective or noun) given to any behavior or opinion that assumes one race is better than the other. It can also be used as a noun for a person who has racist opinions.

Ask students whether other readings or media they have encountered have helped them understand these concepts. Explain they will be discussing these concepts in the following text, "Women in Aviation."

CULTURAL REFERENCES

The following words and phrases may be unfamiliar to students:

- *taken for granted* (paragraph 1): assumed to be true
- *Katharine Wright* (paragraph 3): sister of Orville and Wilbur Wright, who built the first successful airplane
- *fired back* (paragraph 5): answers a question in a quick or angry way
- *Woman's Suffrage Amendment* (paragraph 5): gave women the right to vote in the United States, the 19th Amendment to the U.S. Constitution.
- *manicurist* (paragraph 12): someone who styles and shapes a person's fingernails and toenails

LISTENING

Determine Author's Purpose

Draw students' attention to the Get Ready text under the heading Determine Author's Purpose on p. 45. Review the four types of purposes and how to determine an author's purpose.

Use the following supports with students at varying proficiency levels:

- Tell students that you will read aloud paragraph 1 and then ask questions about the paragraph. Ask: *What do you think this text will be about?* (women aviators) Then, Have students answer the following questions, giving a thumbs up for yes and a thumbs down for no. *Will the author probably give facts about women aviators?* (thumbs up) *Will the author probably tell an adventure story about women aviators?* (thumbs down) **SUBSTANTIAL**

- Read aloud paragraph 2 to students. Ask: *What kinds of things does the author tell you in paragraph 2?* Have students use this sentence frame: *In paragraph 2 the author tells readers about_____.* (Sophie Blanchard and other women who piloted hot air balloons.) Ask: *Do you think this text will mostly inform, persuade, entertain, or express thoughts and feelings?* (inform) **MODERATE**

- Read aloud paragraphs 2 and 3 to students. Ask: *Why do the authors mention Katherine Wright? What is their purpose?* (to show that women could understand aviation) **LIGHT**

PLAN

SPEAKING

Understand Verb Tense

Have students discuss the importance of keeping verb tenses consistent. Ask: *How does using verb tenses correctly prevent the reader from becoming confused?* Circulate around the room to make sure students grasp the importance of consistent verb tense.

Use the following supports with students at varying proficiency levels:

- Pair students of differing abilities. Display and read aloud this sentence: *Early aviators risked many dangers when they flew*. Explain that the sentence tells about past events. Have students complete this sentence using a verb in the past tense. *In 1812, Harriet Quimby ____ while flying her plane.* (died) **SUBSTANTIAL**
- Pair students. Display and read aloud this sentence: *Sophie Blanchard made her first solo flight in 1805*. Ask: *What does the verb in the sentence tell readers?* (that it describes an event that took place in the past) **MODERATE**
- Display and read aloud this sentence: *Sophie Blanchard made her first solo flight in 1805*. Have students explain how this sentence tells them the text will be in the past tense. **LIGHT**

READING

Find Text Evidence

Tell students that authors of informational text provide evidence in the form of facts, examples, explanations, definitions, direct quotations, and other details to help readers understand the central idea, or most important idea.

Work with students to read paragraph 15. Use the following supports with students at varying proficiency levels:

- Help students locate the quotation in paragraph 15. Explain how they can identify where the quotation begins and ends. Have them practice writing the quotation, beginning with "I was . . . " **SUBSTANTIAL**
- Have students discuss how hearing a person's exact words helps them better understand the person. Have them write their thoughts using the sentence frame: *The quotation helps me understand that Bessie Coleman ____.* **MODERATE**
- Have students discuss the main idea of paragraph 15. Then, have them write about how the quotation helps support the main idea. **LIGHT**

WRITING

Write an Informational Essay

Work with students to help them use the four bulleted items on p. 45 to think about and organize their informational essay.

Work with students to help them create questions they would like to answer in their essays. Use the following supports with students at varying proficiency levels:

- Use sentence frames, such as this to help students think of ideas about women aviators: *How did Bessie Coleman develop such a strong ____? What did ____ think about women being aviators?* **SUBSTANTIAL**
- Help students use their questions to write their controlling idea. Remind students that their controlling idea states the direction of their essays and what they intend to emphasize. Provide sentence frames such as this for ideas: *Even though other people thought she was ____, Bessie Coleman never lost faith in herself and her abilities.* **MODERATE**
- Working in pairs or small groups, have students put the information they gathered during their research in chronological order or some other order that makes sense. **LIGHT**

Women in Aviation **44D**

TEACH

? Connect to the ESSENTIAL QUESTION

"Women in Aviation," recounts the stories of several pioneering women in the field of aviation. The primary subject is Bessie Coleman, an African American who not only had to overcome gender exclusion, but also racial prejudice. Hers and the stories of other female aviators exemplify the lives of people who had to overcome great obstacles.

MENTOR TEXT

At the end of this unit, students will be asked to write an informational essay. "Women in Aviation" is an example of a historical, partially biographical, informational text that makes use of narrative features as well as citations.

ANALYZE & APPLY

WOMEN IN AVIATION

History Writing by **Patricia and Fredrick McKissack**

? ESSENTIAL QUESTION:

What helps people rise up to face difficulties?

GET READY

QUICK START

Make a web of the traits that you think can help a person who is pursuing a dream. Discuss your choices with the class.

DETERMINE AUTHOR'S PURPOSE

An **author's purpose** is the reason the author wrote a work. Usually an author writes for one or more purposes, as shown in this chart.

AUTHOR'S PURPOSE	EXAMPLES OF WRITTEN WORKS
To inform or explain	encyclopedia entries, informational articles, how-to articles, biographies
To persuade	editorials, opinion essays and blogs, advertisements
To entertain	short stories, novels, plays, humorous essays
To express thoughts or feelings	poems, personal essays, journals

To determine an author's purpose, consider how the details and evidence in a text fit together to lead to a main idea or message for readers. Consider, too, how you feel about the topic (for example, informed, entertained, or challenged) after reading the text.

**GENRE ELEMENTS:
INFORMATIONAL TEXT**

- provides factual information
- presents evidence to support ideas
- includes biographies, news articles, how-to instructions, and many other forms
- may focus on historical events or trends

CITE EVIDENCE AND EVALUATE DETAILS

After reading informational text, you will often be asked to **cite evidence** to support your own ideas. Before you can do that, you must first **evaluate details**—make judgments about the facts, quotations, examples, and other details in the text. In order to evaluate details, ask: How do these details support the author's purpose and main idea or message of the selection? Next, consider your own knowledge about or experience with the topic. Based on your evaluation of the details, cite the evidence that best supports your ideas.

If you were asked whether women were pioneers in aviation, you might evaluate details from paragraph 2 of the selection, which is about women who piloted hot-air balloons in the early 1800s. Even if you have never piloted a hot-air ballon yourself, you may know that it takes great skill and courage. Now, you could cite evidence to support the idea that women were pioneers in aviation in the early 1800s.

Women in Aviation 45

TEACH

QUICK START

Have students read the Quick Start question, and invite them to share their web of traits with the class. On the whiteboard, build a classroom web of traits for success. Then have the class name people they know or have read about who exhibit some or all of these traits.

DETERMINE AUTHOR'S PURPOSE

Review the four main reasons authors have for writing: to inform or explain, to persuade, to entertain, and to express thoughts or feelings. Have students discuss purpose of each type of work. Then go through each of the examples of written works and explain their purposes. It would also be helpful to compare and contrast the types of writings. (*The purpose of a novel about women in aviation would primarily be to entertain the reader, whereas the following selection is meant to inform.*) Tell students that often the title of a piece is a clue to the author's purpose. Finally, remind them that monitoring how they feel or respond when reading a text is a good way to determine the author's purpose.

CITE EVIDENCE AND DRAW CONCLUSIONS

Tell students that when they draw conclusions, they need to cite text evidence to support their conclusions. Explain that as they read they should be looking for quotations, ideas, and examples that jump out at them. These can help them support their conclusions. The example provided about paragraph 2 of "Women in Aviation" uses the specific dates and events listed in that paragraph to draw the conclusion that, yes, women were involved in aviation as far back as the early 1800s.

ENGLISH LEARNER SUPPORT

Understand Author's Purpose Present students with two to four types of text written about the same topic. (For example, a comic strip about a dog, a pamphlet from a dog shelter, an opinion piece about dogs, and a poem about a dog.) Split students into pairs or groups.

- Ask students to identify which of the four types of writing each text represents, and explain why. Ask students to point to the different types and use one-word or multi-word responses. **MODERATE**
- Ask students to identify which of the four types of writing each text represents, and explain why, pointing to specific details. Then, have them speculate how one of the authors could have written his or her text differently to change its purpose. **LIGHT**

LEARNING MINDSET

Seeking Challenges Explain that taking worthwhile risks and losing fear of failure is a habit of mind that everyone can develop. It takes practice to lose fear of the unknown—and fear of failure. By trying to accomplish difficult things over and over, everyone can be inspired to create, invent, and learn.

Women in Aviation 45

TEACH

CRITICAL VOCABULARY

Encourage students to read all the sentences before deciding which word best completes each one. Remind them to look for context clues that match the precise meaning of each word.

Answers:

1. exhibition
2. restrictive
3. precaution
4. inundate

ENGLISH LEARNER SUPPORT

Understand Critical Vocabulary The four vocabulary words can be split into three categories: nouns (*exhibition* and *precaution*) adjectives (*restrictive*) and verbs (*inundate*). Divide students into pairs, and after giving them the definitions, have them put the words into the correct categories. **SUBSTANTIAL/MODERATE**

LANGUAGE CONVENTIONS

Review with students the three basic verb tenses: present, past, and future. In writing, authors should use the same verb tense when describing actions that happen at the same time. They should only make a change in verb tense if actions are happening at different times. Go over the example provided on p. 46.

Here is another example:

Original: Ian is bringing over his video games. I was glad that he brought them. (Bringing is in present tense, and was and brought are in the past tense.)

Revised: Ian is bringing over his video games. I am glad he is bringing them. (Both sentences now agree and are in the present tense.)

 ANNOTATION MODEL

Remind students of the annotation ideas on p. 46, which suggest underlining details and circling words that signal important ideas. Point out that they may follow this suggestion or use their own system for marking up the selection in their write-in text. They may want to color-code their annotations by using highlighters. Their notes in the margin may include questions about ideas that are unclear or topics they want to learn more about.

46 Unit 1

 GET READY

CRITICAL VOCABULARY

inundate   restrictive   exhibition   precaution

To see how many Critical Vocabulary words you already know, use them to complete the sentences.

1. The pilot's photographs appeared in a(n) _____ at the library.
2. A 20-pound weight limit for suitcases seems a little _____.
3. Airline passengers must take the _____ of wearing seatbelts.
4. The hurricane may _____ the coast with a heavy storm surge.

LANGUAGE CONVENTIONS

Consistent Verb Tenses In this lesson, you will learn about the importance of using the correct verb tense to clarify meaning and of using a single tense unless you have a good reason to switch:

[Coleman's] mother, who had been a slave, . . . encouraged all of her children to attend school in order to better themselves.

Encouraged is in the past tense; *had been* is in the past perfect tense. The switch shows that the mother's time as a slave came earlier. As you read "Women in Aviation," note how the authors consistently use the past tense and switch only when necessary to make the meaning clear.

ANNOTATION MODEL **NOTICE & NOTE**

As you read, note clues about the authors' purpose in writing. You can also mark up evidence and note how you are evaluating it. In the model, you can see one reader's notes about "Women in Aviation."

> 2   The story of women in aviation actually goes back to the time of the hot-air balloons. A number of women in Europe and America gained fame for their skill and daring. Sophie Blanchard made her first solo balloon flight in 1805. She grew in fame and was eventually named official aeronaut of the empire by Napoleon. By 1834, at least twenty women in Europe were piloting their own balloons.

aviation came before airplanes

women aviators of the era

These details support the idea that women flew long before there were airplanes.

46   Unit 1

 ENGLISH LEARNER SUPPORT

Language Transfer Issues Speakers of Vietnamese may struggle to use the correct verb tense. Students may use present tense in place of past tense. For example: *I walk to school yesterday.* Point out the past tense verb *encouraged* in the example sentence. Have students copy the sentence, and underline the *-ed* in *encouraged.* Guide students to understand that this action happened in the past. Explain that many regular verbs in the English language add *-ed* to the end to signify an action has already happened. Then, have students conjugate the following sentence in the past tense: *I ____ (played) baseball last Saturday.* Have student pairs check each others' work. Monitor language production as students complete the activity, correcting their use of verb tense as necessary.

BACKGROUND

In the early 1900s, flying in "aeroplanes"—fixed-winged, self-propelled flying machines—was a bold undertaking. Male pilots were dashing heroes. However, female aviators—especially African American women—had to struggle for acceptance. **Patricia and Fredrick McKissack** (1944–2017; 1939–2013) wrote more than 100 biographies and other nonfiction books, most focusing on the achievements of African Americans.

WOMEN IN AVIATION

History Writing by Patricia and Fredrick McKissack

SETTING A PURPOSE

As you read, pay attention to the details that describe what it was like for a woman to become a pilot during the early 1900s. What obstacles did each pilot face? Write down any questions you have while reading.

1   American aviation was from its very beginnings marred with sexist and racist assumptions. It was taken for granted that women were generally inferior to men and that white men were superior to all others. Flying, it was said, required a level of skill and courage that women and blacks lacked. Yet despite these prevailing prejudices, the dream and the desire to fly stayed alive among women and African-Americans.

2   The story of women in aviation actually goes back to the time of the hot-air balloons. A number of women in Europe and America gained fame for their skill and daring. Sophie Blanchard made her first solo balloon flight in 1805. She grew in fame and was eventually named official aeronaut of the empire by Napoleon. By 1834, at least twenty women in Europe were piloting their own balloons.

Notice & Note

Use the side margins to notice and note signposts in the text.

DETERMINE AUTHORS' PURPOSE

Annotate: Mark groups of words in paragraph 1 that signal details about the topic—women in aviation.

Draw Conclusions: Based on these details, what seems to be the authors' purpose in writing "Women in Aviation"? Be specific.

Women in Aviation 47

TEACH

BACKGROUND

Have students read the background and author information. Explain that aviation—the operation of aircraft—dates back to the first balloon flights in the late 1700s. In the 1890s, the first gliders, airplane-like aircraft without engines, were flown. But it was not until 1903 that the Wright brothers made the first successful flight in an engine-powered aircraft, the airplane. Airplane flight really "took off" during and after World War I (1914–1918), which saw a more widespread use of airplanes for military purposes.

SETTING A PURPOSE

Direct students to use the Setting a Purpose question to focus their reading. Remind them to generate questions as they read.

DETERMINE AUTHORS' PURPOSE

Tell students to either mark or write down phrases from paragraph 1 that will help them draw conclusions about the author's purpose. Also, remind them that often the first paragraph of a text will lay out the authors' purpose. (**Answer:** The purpose is to inform—specifically, to explain American aviation's past unfairness to women and African Americans and the way those groups kept their dream of flying alive.)

For **listening support** for students at varying proficiency levels, see the **Text X-Ray** on page 44C.

 ENGLISH LEARNER SUPPORT

Analyze Language Read paragraph 2 aloud as students follow. Highlight *aviation, flight, aeronaut,* and *piloting*.

- After clarifying the definition of each word, ask students how these words are related. Allow them to use visual clues on the page to determine that the words relate to flying aircraft.
- Would an aeronaut pilot an airplane? Have students work in pairs to explain why or why not.
  SUBSTANTIAL/MODERATE

Women in Aviation 47

TEACH

NOTICE & NOTE

Inform students that **quoted words** are very important in any informational text and that they should always pay close attention to them. Quoted words are a direct source of information about what someone sees or believes. Have students compare that attitude toward women described in paragraph 1 with the quoted words by Orville Wright in paragraph 3. (**Answer:** *Paragraph 1 describes the attitude that women were inferior to men and could not be competent pilots. In contrast, Orville Wright's comment recognizes that a woman—his sister—was of great help to the Wrights' efforts.*)

CITE EVIDENCE AND DRAW CONCLUSIONS

Remind students that in order to draw a valid **conclusion** they need to be able to **cite evidence to support** their conclusion. (**Answer:** *The words that describe Coleman might include* confident *and* brave. *An example from the text is that she made a life-altering decision, without knowing how things were going to work out.*)

ENGLISH LEARNER SUPPORT

Draw Conclusions Have students re-read paragraph 8. Then have them draw a story map of the events of Coleman's life described in the paragraph.

Have students identify the point(s) in their story maps that show the major change in Coleman's thinking. Ask: *What words would you use to describe Bessie Coleman, based on this evidence?* (*They should identify the point when she changed her goal to becoming a pilot; She was brave and had big dreams.*) **SUBSTANTIAL**

CRITICAL VOCABULARY

inundate: The author uses the verb *inundate* to describe how Harriet Quimby felt when surrounded by male reporters who found her both attractive and entertaining.

ASK STUDENTS how a woman aviator might feel inundated by large groups of reporters. (*She might feel crowded or overwhelmed, or confused by several people asking her questions at the same time.*)

48   Unit 1

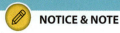 **NOTICE & NOTE**

QUOTED WORDS

Notice & Note: In paragraph 3, mark the comment that Orville Wright made about Katherine, his sister.

Compare: How is his attitude different from the attitude described in paragraph 1?

inundate
(ĭn´ŭn-dāt´) *v.* To *inundate* is to overpower with a huge amount of something.

CITE EVIDENCE AND EVALUATE DETAILS
Annotate: Mark the information in paragraphs 8 and 9 that reveal a major change in Coleman's thinking.

Evaluate: How effective are these text details in explaining why Bessie Coleman decided to become a pilot?

3   Though she did not fly, Katherine Wright was a major supporter of her brothers' efforts. Orville so appreciated his sister's help that he said, "When the world speaks of the Wrights, it must include my sister. . . . She inspired much of our effort."

4   Although Raymonde de la Roche of France was the first woman in the world to earn her pilot's license, Harriet Quimby held the distinction of being the first American woman to become a licensed pilot.

5   On August 1, 1911, Quimby, who was described as a "real beauty" with "haunting blue-green eyes," strolled off the field after passing her pilot's test easily. To the male reporters who **inundated** her with questions, Quimby fired back answers with self-confidence. Walking past a group of women who had come to witness the historic event, Quimby was overheard to quip with a smile and a wink: "Flying is easier than voting." (The Woman's Suffrage Amendment wasn't passed until 1920.)

6   As difficult as it was for women to become pilots in significant numbers, it was doubly hard for African-Americans, especially black women. That's why Bessie Coleman, the first African-American to earn her pilot's license, is such an exciting and important figure in aviation.

7   Bessie Coleman was born in 1893 in Atlanta, Texas, the twelfth of thirteen children. Her mother, who had been a slave, valued education and encouraged all of her children to attend school in order to better themselves. The encouragement paid off, because Coleman graduated from high school, a feat not too many black women were able to accomplish in the early 1900s.

8   Bessie Coleman refused to accept the limitations others tried to place on her. She attended an Oklahoma college for one semester but ran out of money. Accepting the offer of one of her brothers to come live with him and his family in Chicago, Coleman found a job as a manicurist. She fully intended to return to school after saving enough money. But she never did. While in Chicago she learned about flying and made a new set of goals for herself. She wanted to be a pilot.

9   Coleman learned about flying from reading newspaper accounts of air battles during World War I. She tried to find a school that would accept her as a trainee. But no American instructor or flying school was willing to teach her.

10   When the war ended, a friend, Robert S. Abbott, the founder of the *Chicago Defender*, one of the most popular

48   Unit 1

TO CHALLENGE STUDENTS. . .

Explore Intention Direct students' attention to paragraphs 10 and 11. Have students conjecture why Coleman sought the suggestions and experiences of other black Americans in her quest to become a pilot. As needed, explore the lives of Robert S. Abbott, Eugene Jacques Ballard, and other successful black Americans of the period.

NOTICE & NOTE

The image above shows Bessie Coleman's pilot's license. Regarded as the world's first female African American aviator, Bessie receives a bouquet at an appearance at Curtiss Field in Garden City, Long Island.

black-owned and -operated newspapers in the country, suggested that Coleman go to France, where racial prejudice was not as **restrictive** as it was in America. Even though the United States was the birthplace of flight, it was slower than other countries to develop an organized aviation program. European leaders immediately saw the commercial and military advantages of a strong national aviation program. Bessie knew from her reading that both French and German aircraft were among the best in the world.

restrictive
(rĭ-strĭk´tĭv) *adj.* When something is *restrictive*, it is limiting in some way.

Women in Aviation 49

APPLYING ACADEMIC VOCABULARY

☐ aspect   ☑ cultural   ☑ evaluate   ☐ resource   ☑ text

THINK-PAIR-SHARE Have partners discuss the questions below. Guide students to include the Academic Vocabulary words **cultural**, **evaluate**, and **text** in their responses.

- What does this **text** say were **cultural** obstacles in America for women who wanted to become pilots?
- **Evaluate** the **cultural** challenges faced by the first women aviators.

TEACH

🇪🇱 ENGLISH LEARNER SUPPORT

Contextual Support Have students choral read paragraph 11 together, without stopping. Read again, in groups of 2 or 3 this time so students can help each other determine the meaning of unfamiliar words through context clues.

Ask students to use context to arrive at the meaning of the unknown words. **SUBSTANTIAL**

Have students to explain how they used context to arrive at the meaning of the unknown words. **MODERATE**

CRITICAL VOCABULARY

restrictive: The authors use the word *restrictive* to compare racial prejudice in the United States with racial prejudice in France.

ASK STUDENTS to describe how restrictive policies in the United States affected Bessie Coleman. *(The restrictive policies of American instructors and flying schools prevented Coleman from pursuing her dream of becoming a pilot.)*

Women in Aviation 49

TEACH

CITE EVIDENCE AND DRAW CONCLUSIONS

Remind students that in order to draw a valid **conclusion** they need to be able to **cite evidence** to support it. (**Answer:** *You can conclude that Coleman dreamed of a challenging goal—going to France to learn to fly—and that she was willing to work hard to achieve her goal by taking two jobs to fund her trip and by studying French.*)

ENGLISH LEARNER SUPPORT

Use Cognates Tell students there are many Spanish cognates in paragraphs 12 and 13. Ask them to write them down, along with their Spanish equivalents—server–*servidor*, time–*tiempo*, France–*Francia*, famous–*famoso*, history–*historia*. Also direct them to the words that are the same in English as they are in Spanish: chili, instructors, natural.

Ask Students to fill in the blanks using the cognates.

One _____ when my mother was working as a _____ at a cafe in Paris, _____, she met a singer who was very _____. My mother met someone who will go down in _____! **SUBSTANTIAL/MODERATE**

ASK STUDENTS to write a paragraph using each of the five cognates listed above. **LIGHT**

DETERMINE AUTHORS' PURPOSE

Tell students that using different ways of marking (highlighter/red pen, underlining/circling) can be a useful way to distinguish important points and can help them when returning to a text to **critique** it. (**Answer:** *These facts—that Coleman recognized a problem and tried to solve it—are effective support for the authors' purpose because they show a woman aviator who faced and at least attempted to overcome an obstacle to her dream.*)

CRITICAL VOCABULARY

exhibition: The authors use the word *exhibitions* to explain how Bessie Coleman became well known by performing as an aviator and public speaker.

ASK STUDENTS to describe what they might have seen at one of Bessie Coleman's exhibitions. (**Sample answer:** *Coleman might have been flying upside down in her airplane above a large crowd on the ground.*)

50   Unit 1

NOTICE & NOTE

CITE EVIDENCE AND EVALUATE DETAILS

Annotate: In paragraph 11, mark details that describe Coleman's dream at this point in her life. Then, in paragraph 12, mark her plans for making that dream a reality.

Draw Conclusions: Based on this evidence, what can you conclude about Coleman and her dream? Which text detail would you cite as being most important to your conclusion?

DETERMINE AUTHORS' PURPOSE

Annotate: Underline the problem that the authors introduce in paragraph 14. Then circle the way that Coleman tried to solve it.

Critique: Are these facts effective in supporting the authors' purpose? Explain.

exhibition
(ĕk′sə-bĭsh′ən) *n.* An *exhibition* is an organized presentation or show.

11   Coleman had also read about Eugene Jacques Bullard, the well-decorated[1] and highly honored native of Georgia who had become the first African-American to fly an airplane in combat as a member of the French Lafayette Flying Corps during World War I. Other blacks had gone to Europe to get their training, too. Coleman realized that if she were ever going to get a chance to fly, she, too, would have to go to France. But she didn't have any money to get there, and besides, she couldn't speak a word of French.

12   For almost two years, Coleman worked part-time as a manicurist and as a server in a Chicago chili parlor and saved every penny to finance her trip to France. Meanwhile she learned to speak French, so when the time came, she'd be able to understand her instructors.

13   In 1921, Coleman made it to France, where she found an instructor who was one of Tony Fokker's chief pilots. Fokker, the famous aircraft manufacturer, said Coleman was a "natural talent." On June 15, 1921, Coleman made history by becoming the first black woman to earn her wings, thus joining the ranks of the handful of American women fliers.

14   Returning to the United States determined to start a flying school where other African-American pilots could be trained, Coleman looked for ways to finance her dream. There were very few jobs in the aviation industry for women or blacks. She soon learned that there was little or no support for a black woman who wanted to start a flying school. To call attention to aviation and to encourage other women and African-Americans to take part in the new and growing field, Coleman gave flying exhibitions and lectured on aviation. She thrilled audiences with daredevil maneuvers, just as Quimby had done before her.

15   Along with racism, Coleman encountered the burden of sexism, but she made believers out of those who doubted her skill. "The color of my skin," she said, "[was] a drawback at first. . . . I was a curiosity, but soon the public discovered I could really fly. Then they came to see *Brave Bessie*, as they called me."

---
[1] **well-decorated:** term used to describe a person in the military who has received many awards.

50   Unit 1

IMPROVE READING FLUENCY

Targeted Passage Read paragraph 15 aloud to the class once. Then, have students echo along in their books as you read the text. Next, have individual students take turns reading aloud the paragraph to see whether they use the right emphases. Encourage students to ask questions about why you place emphasis in certain places and why you take pauses in others.

Go to the **Reading Studio** for additional support in developing fluency.

NOTICE & NOTE

16   The strict rules and regulations that govern aviation today didn't exist during the first three decades of flying. For example, it wasn't uncommon for aviators to ignore safety belts and fly without parachutes. One of these simple safety **precautions** might have saved the lives of both Harriet Quimby and Bessie Coleman.

precaution
(prĭ-kô′shən) *n.* A *precaution* is an action taken to avoid possible danger.

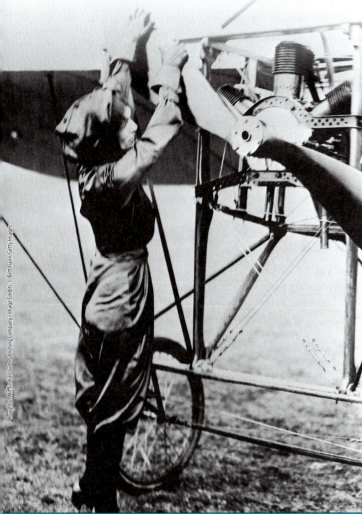

In 1912, Harriet Quimby (shown holding the propeller to start the engine of her monoplane) became the first woman to fly across the English Channel.

Women in Aviation   51

TEACH

ENGLISH LEARNER SUPPORT

Monitor Comprehension Treat paragraph 17 as its own short story. Print off or project it onto a whiteboard for students to mark up and take notes on. Students will break into groups to create their own comic strips of the tragic tale.

Ask Students to draw out the events detailed in paragraph 17. Students should caption their pictures and present their comic strips, retelling the tale.
SUBSTANTIAL

Take away the projection of paragraph 17. **Ask Students** to draw the events detailed in paragraph 17 from what they have in their notes. Have students should caption their pictures and present their storyboards, retelling the tale. **MODERATE**

Take away the projection of paragraph 17. **Ask Students** to put away their notes and draw the events detailed in paragraph 17 from what they remember. Have students caption their pictures and present their comic strips, retelling the tale.
LIGHT

 For **speaking support** for students at varying proficiency levels, see the **Text X-Ray** on page 44D.

WHEN STUDENTS STRUGGLE...

Identify Supporting Details   Have students use a chart to evaluate details and draw conclusions.

Detail	Conclusion
Coleman realized that if she were ever going to get a chance to fly, she, too, would have to go to France.	. . .there was little or no support for a black woman who wanted to start a flying school. .

 For additional support, go to the **Reading Studio** and assign the following Level Up tutorial: Drawing Conclusions.

CRITICAL VOCABULARY

precaution: The authors explain that safety *precautions* had to be taken because early aviation was a particularly dangerous as pilots flew in relatively unstable aircraft, sitting in open-air cockpits.

ASK STUDENTS to describe why a safety belt would be a good precaution for an aviator in an open-air cockpit. (**Sample answer:** *It would prevent them from falling out of the aircraft.*)

Women in Aviation   51

TEACH

LANGUAGE CONVENTIONS

Note that when several sentences are quoted they are put into an idented free-standing block of text (block quote) which does not require quotations marks. (**Answer:** *The present tense is appropriate because the authors are quoting a source [commentary from a newspaper] that was written in the present tense. What the source is saying was current at that time.*)

DETERMINE AUTHORS' PURPOSE

Ask students whether they think accidents involving male pilots got the same attention as Miss Quimby's. (**Answer:** *The quotation comes from Amelia Earhart, another pioneer of aviation and an authority on the topic of women in aviation. Her quotation shows that the problem of discrimination was widespread. It underscores the authors' purpose—to provide information about how women aviators of that era had to overcome cultural obstacles to pursue their dreams.*)

NOTICE & NOTE

17   On a July morning in 1912, Quimby, and a passenger named William P. Willard, set out to break an over-water speed record. When Quimby climbed to five thousand feet, the French-made Blériot monoplane[2] suddenly nosed down. Both Quimby and Willard were thrown from the plane and plunged to their deaths in the Boston Harbor.

18   The *New York Sun* used the opportunity to speak out against women fliers:

LANGUAGE CONVENTIONS
Annotate: Mark the present-tense verbs in this quotation from the *New York Sun*.

Critique: We usually use past-tense verbs to talk about past events. Why is the present tense appropriate here?

> Miss Quimby is the fifth woman in the world killed while operating an aeroplane (three were students) and their number thus far is five too many. The sport is not one for which women are physically qualified. As a rule they lack strength and presence of mind and the courage to excel as aviators. It is essentially a man's sport and pastime.

19   Fourteen years later, Bessie Coleman died in a similar accident. With almost enough savings to start her school, Coleman agreed to do an air show in Florida on May Day for the Negro Welfare League of Jacksonville. At 7:30 p.m. the night before, Coleman, accompanied by her publicity agent, William Wills, took her plane up for a test flight. When she reached an altitude of about five thousand feet, her plane flipped over. Coleman was thrown from the plane and plunged to her death April 30, 1926. Wills died seconds later when the plane crashed.

DETERMINE AUTHORS' PURPOSE
Annotate: Mark the text that gives the name and description of the person whom the authors quote in paragraph 20.

Connect: What purpose does this quotation serve in the paragraph? How does it relate to the overall purpose of the selection?

20   Once again critics used the tragedy to assert that neither women nor blacks were mentally or physically able to be good pilots. "Women are often penalized by publicity for their every mishap," said Amelia Earhart, the most famous female pilot in aviation history. "The result is that such emphasis sometimes directly affects [a woman's] chances for a flying job," Earhart continued. "I had one manufacturer tell me that he couldn't risk hiring women pilots because of the way accidents, even minor ones, became headlines in the newspapers."

21   Although Bessie Coleman died tragically, her plans to open a flight training school for blacks were continued by those she had inspired.

---

[2] **monoplane:** an airplane with only one pair of wings.

52   Unit 1

ENGLISH LEARNER SUPPORT

Understand Verb Tense Use the block newspaper quote in paragraph 18 as a jumping off point for verb tense. Point out how the article is written in present tense, but when it mentions events that have already happened, it switches over to past tense. Break students into pairs of mixed abilities to engage in collaborative dialogues. Beginning level students will tell a story in present tense. Then, the intermediate or advanced student will repeat the same story, only they will convert it to past tense. Finally, the beginning student will repeat the story as it was told to them by the intermediary or advanced student, in the converted past tense.

NOTICE & NOTE

CHECK YOUR UNDERSTANDING

Answer these questions before moving on to the **Analyze the Text** section on the following page.

1 The authors include information about women hot-air balloonists in order to —

   A prove that women tend to avoid careers in aviation

   B give examples that help readers know what an "aeronaut" is

   C explain that women have been interested in aviation for a long time

   D entertain readers with amusing stories about women who inspired pilots

2 Which fact from the selection most clearly explains why Harriet Quimby and Bessie Coleman died?

   F Both pilots performed daredevil maneuvers in the air.

   G They did not take safety precautions that are standard today.

   H Their planes suddenly malfunctioned during test flights.

   J Both women were victims of racial and gender prejudice.

3 The authors' main purpose for ending the selection by mentioning Bessie Coleman's flight training school is to —

   A show one effect of her inspiring example

   B remind readers that she died doing something she loved

   C explain how women today learn to become pilots

   D persuade readers to consider a career in aviation

Women in Aviation 53

TEACH

CHECK YOUR UNDERSTANDING

Have students answer the questions independently.

Answers:

1. C
2. G
3. A

If they answer any questions incorrectly, have them reread the text to confirm their understanding. Then they may proceed to ANALYZE THE TEXT on page 54.

ENGLISH LEARNER SUPPORT

Oral Assessment Use the following questions to assess students' comprehension and speaking skills:

1. What did women enjoy flying before airplanes? *(hot air baloons)* Does the author include these details to claim that women have always been interested in flying? *(yes)*

2. What safety equipment can save a pilot during a plane crash? *(a parachute)* Did Harrient Quimby and Bessie Coleman have parachutes? *(No)*

3. Why does the author tell readers that Bessie Coleman's flight school opened after she passed away? *(to show that people belived in her dream)* **MODERATE**

Women in Aviation 53

TEACH

ANALYZE THE TEXT

Possible answers:

1. **DOK 2:** *Harriet Quimby was an attractive, self-confident woman with a sense of humor.*
2. **DOK 3:** *Answers on chart, page 54.*
3. **DOK 2:** *Both were pioneers in aviation; both were courageous risk-takers. They had the self-confidence to overcome male prejudice.*
4. **DOK 4:** *The authors chose facts and used language to emphasize Coleman's inspirational qualities, but also emphasize the hardships that she faced. They indicate that Coleman's death was due, in part, to her failure to take safety precautions.*
5. **DOK 4:** *The authors' purpose is to explain that women pilots had to overcome "sexist and racist assumptions." Quimby's comment takes the assumption that women were not competent to fly and translates it into a larger social issue of the time.*

RESEARCH

Students may choose from Sophie Blanchard, Katherine Wright, Raymonde de la Roche, Harriet Quimby, or Amelia Earhart. Remind students to fact-check their information by consulting multiple sources and making sure their sources are well respected.

CONNECT Students will most likely find their subject was driven to overcome the odds against them, like Coleman. Have students pair up with someone who did not choose the same aviator. Have students compare their organizers and check each other's work. Students should draw the conclusion that these women were driven to prove that people were wrong about their presumptions about gender back then.

RESPOND

ANALYZE THE TEXT

Support your responses with evidence from the text. 📓 **NOTEBOOK**

1. **Interpret** Reread paragraph 5. What impression of Harriet Quimby do the authors create by using facts and quotations?
2. **Cite Evidence** Reread paragraphs 11 and 12. Based on your evaluation of the text details in these paragraphs, what conclusion can you draw about Bessie Coleman's personality? Fill out a chart like this one to show support for your conclusion.

TEXTUAL EVIDENCE	MY EXPERIENCE	CONCLUSION

3. **Compare** In what ways were Harriet Quimby and Bessie Coleman probably most alike? Explain.
4. **Evaluate** Do you think the authors presented Bessie Coleman's life in an overly positive way? Why or why not?
5. **Notice & Note** Think about Harriet Quimby's statement, "Flying is easier than voting." What situation does her comment highlight? How does the quote help the authors achieve their purpose?

RESEARCH TIP
The best search terms are very specific. Along with the person's name, you will want to include a word such as *aviator* or *achievements* to make sure that you get the information you need.

RESEARCH

Bessie Coleman is the main focus of "Women in Aviation," but other female aviators are mentioned in the text. Do some in-depth research into the achievements and importance of one of these aviators. Use question words such as *who, what, why,* and *how* to form questions. In the chart below, record what you learned in your research.

QUESTION	ANSWER
Who?	*Sophie Blanchard*
What?	*First professional woman baloonist*
Where?	*Europe (especially France and Italy)*
When?	*Early 1800s*

Connect Consider how the aviator you chose seems similar to Bessie Coleman. Compare your thoughts with those of a classmate who chose another aviator. What conclusions can you draw about these aviators?

WHEN STUDENTS STRUGGLE . . .

Cite Evidence Remind students to look for sepcific details about women aviators as they conduct their research. Provide them with targeted questions that expand on *who, what, why* and *how* questions, such as: *What type of aircraft did Sophie Blanchard fly? When did Raymonde de la Roche get her pilot's license? How did Harriet Quimby learn to fly?* Have student pairs work together to fill in the chart for the Research activity.

📖 For additional support, go to the **Reading Studio** and assign the following **Level Up tutorial: Evidence**.

CREATE AND DISCUSS

Write an Informational Essay Write a three- to four-paragraph essay in which you present research on a female aviator other than Bessie Coleman—either one mentioned in the selection or someone else.

- Review the information you gathered in the Research activity, or conduct research on another female aviator.
- Write an introduction in which you introduce the topic and express your controlling idea about the aviator you chose.
- Then, provide information about this aviator's life and work. Be specific with your facts, details, and examples. Arrange information in a way that makes sense (perhaps chronological order) and remember to use transitions to connect ideas.
- In your final paragraph, sum up the aviator's achievements.

Discuss with a Small Group Have a meaningful discussion about how information in "Women in Aviation" helps readers understand the challenges faced by women in the early 20th century as they struggled to gain acceptance in male-dominated fields.

- As a group, review the text and decide which information is relevant to the discussion topic.
- Have the group prepare ideas and details that relate to the topic.
- Review the ideas and decide which can help someone overcome obstacles. Listen closely and respectfully to all ideas. Provide constructive feedback and accept the feedback you receive.

 Go to **Writing Informative Texts** in the **Writing Studio** to learn more.

 Go to **Participating in Collaborative Discussions** in the **Speaking and Listening Studio** for more.

RESPOND TO THE ESSENTIAL QUESTION

 What helps people rise up to face difficulties?

Gather Information Review your annotations and notes on "Women in Aviation." Then, add relevant details to your Response Log. As you determine which information to include, think about:

- the attitudes that keep people from pursuing their dreams
- the traits that help people pursue a dream and overcome challenges

At the end of the unit, use your notes to write an informational essay.

ACADEMIC VOCABULARY

As you write and discuss what you learned from the informational text, be sure to use the Academic Vocabulary words. Check off each of the words that you use.

- ❏ aspect
- ❏ cultural
- ❏ evaluate
- ❏ resource
- ❏ text

Women in Aviation 55

TEACH

CREATE AND DISCUSS

Write an Informational Essay Tell students they should look to the selection for inspiration on how to model their essays. "Women in Aviation" includes an engaging narrative about Bessie Coleman that interweaves the stories of other, tangentially connected, female aviators of her time period.

For **writing support** for students at varying proficiency levels, see the **Text X-Ray** on page 44D.

Discuss with a Small Group You might aid in the discussion by interjecting any knowledge you may have about women local to your school who overcame gender inequality during the same time period as the subjects of "Women in Aviation." Then, bring the discussion up to date by asking how far women have come in a hundred years, as well as also how they may still be not seen as totally equal.

RESPOND TO THE ESSENTIAL QUESTION

Allow time for students to add details from "Women in Aviation" to their Unit 1 Response Logs.

ENGLISH LEARNER SUPPORT

Discuss with a Small Group Rephrase the small discussion prompt as a question: *What helped women in aviation rise up to face difficulties?* Allow students to work with partners to review the text for details that answer the question. Provide these sentence frames to help them formulate their ideas for the discussion: *I now know that... I learned... I was surprised that... I feel... I agree/disagree with...* **SUBSTANTIAL/MODERATE**

TEACH

CRITICAL VOCABULARY

Answers:

1. *a*
2. *a*
3. *b*
4. *b*

VOCABULARY STRATEGY:
Connotations and Denotations

Possible Answers:

1. **determined;** Determined *has the positive connotation of working toward a goal;* serious *is more neutral and does not suggest the sacrifices Coleman made.*

2. **foolhardy;** Risky *connotes some degree of danger, but* foolhardy *is more strongly negative because it suggests that some fliers were careless about the dangers involved.*

3. **pursued;** Pursued *has a slightly stronger positive connotation of striving toward a goal than* followed *does.*

4. **inspiration;** Inspiration *connotes that Coleman did more than just help—she actually motivated others.*

 **RESPOND**

WORD BANK
inundate
restrictive
exhibition
precaution

CRITICAL VOCABULARY

Practice and Apply Mark the letter of the situation that better shows the meaning of the Critical Vocabulary word. Explain your choice.

1. **inundate**
   a. More than 400 people came to the airshow.
   b. One or two visitors came to the museum.

2. **restrictive**
   a. The gate at the airport is locked at six o'clock.
   b. The gate at the airport has a rusty lock.

3. **exhibition**
   a. A crowd gathered at a school to hear an astronaut speak.
   b. The crowd watched a kite-making demonstration.

4. **precaution**
   a. The state lets people apply for licenses online.
   b. The government requires pilots to follow safety checks.

Go to the **Vocabulary Studio** for more on connotations and denotations.

VOCABULARY STRATEGY: Connotations and Denotations

A word's **denotation** is its literal, "dictionary" meaning. A word's **connotation** comes from the ideas and feelings, either positive or negative, associated with the word. For example, the authors of "Women in Aviation" state that Harriet Quimby "strolled off the field." The denotation of *strolled* is "took an unhurried walk," but the connotation suggests that Quimby was relaxed and assured.

Practice and Apply In each of the following sentences, the words in parentheses have similar denotations. Complete each sentence with the word that has the strongest positive or negative connotation.

1. Bessie Coleman refused to give up because she was (**serious, determined**) _____.

2. Early pilots sometimes performed (**foolhardy, risky**) _____ stunts—stunts that proved to be fatal.

3. Despite barriers, women pilots (**pursued, followed**) _____ their dreams.

4. Coleman died as a pioneer, but she has been a great (**help, inspiration**) _____ to the generations that came after her.

56 Unit 1

 ENGLISH LEARNER SUPPORT

Understand Connotations and Denotations Give students some extra practice with this vocabulary strategy by discussing the denotations and connotations of the following words: *cold, cool, heated, soft.* In front of the students, demonstrate the denotations and connotations of each word using total physical response (i.e. *cool* can mean a refreshing beverage you drink and go "ah" after gulping it, or it can describe what you look like when you style your hair and strut across the room). After demonstrating, have students act out the denotations and connotations themselves until they understand the differences. **MODERATE**

LANGUAGE CONVENTIONS:
Consistent Verb Tenses

The **tense** of a verb indicates the time of an action or a state of being. An action or state of being can occur in the present, the past, or the future—or at times "in between" (the "perfect" tenses). Notice some of the ways that tenses are used in "Women in Aviation."

- **Present tense** is used to make general statements that are true now:

    The story of women in aviation actually <u>goes</u> back to the time of the hot-air balloons.

- **Past tense** is used to provide information about events in the past:

    . . . Coleman <u>gave</u> flying exhibitions and <u>lectured</u> on aviation.

- **Past perfect tense** is used to show that certain events happened before other events in the past.

    [Coleman] thrilled audiences with daredevil maneuvers, just as Quimby <u>had done</u> before her.

Usually, it's important to be consistent, but you sometimes need to change tenses to be clear, as you can see in the third example above.

INCORRECT: While in Chicago she **learned** about flying and **makes** a new set of goals for herself. [mix of past tense and present tense]

CORRECT: While in Chicago she **learned** about flying and **made** a new set of goals for herself. [consistent past tense]

Practice and Apply Rewrite these sentences so that the tenses are correct and consistent. Shift tenses only if necessary to make the meaning clear.

1. In the 1920s, stunt pilots called "barnstormers" attract crowds around the United States.

2. Their colorful name comes from the fact that barnstormers often perform their air shows at rural farms.

3. Some fliers were military pilots before they took up barnstorming.

4. People from small towns gasped in amazement as barnstormers dove, looped-the-loop, and even fly upside-down.

RESPOND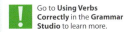

Go to **Using Verbs Correctly** in the **Grammar Studio** to learn more.

Women in Aviation 57

ENGLISH LEARNER SUPPORT

Understand Verb Tenses Present students with pictures of the morning (past), the daytime (present), and the night (future). Together, make up a separate story for each picture, keeping them all in present tense. Next, assign students to three groups, each assigned a picture. Have each group tell their part of the story in the correct tense: present, past, or future. **SUBSTANTIAL/MODERATE**

Ask Students to write their stories including sentences in the past- and future-perfect tenses. **LIGHT**

TEACH

LANGUAGE CONVENTIONS:
Consistent Verb Tenses

Ask students to think about how the same information can take on a very different meaning if the tenses are changed. (It would be surprising if barnstormers were performing today.)

1. *In the 1920s, stunt pilots called "barnstormers"* attracted *crowds around the United States.*

2. *Their colorful name comes from the fact that barnstormers often* performed *their air shows at rural farms.*

3. *Some fliers* had been *military pilots before they took up barnstorming.*

4. *People from small towns gasped in amazement as barnstormers dove, looped-the-loop, and even* flew *upside-down.*

Women in Aviation 57

PLAN

THANK YOU, M'AM
Short story by Langston Hughes

GENRE ELEMENTS
SHORT STORY

Remind students that the purpose of a **short story** is to depict fictional characters in circumstances that force them to deal with internal and external conflicts. Related genres like **novels** and **plays** work in a similar way, but short stories are notable because they are meant to be read and digested in a single sitting. The texts of short stories make creative use of characterization and language conventions, such as capitalization. In this lesson, students will use the short story genre to explore these topics as well as broader issues of belonging, community, and encouragement.

LEARNING OBJECTIVES

- Cite textual evidence to support analysis of character and conflict in fiction writing.
- Conduct research about the history and cultural importance of Harlem.
- Write a formal letter of request to a leadership organization.
- Discuss information that can help encourage other community members to overcome difficulties in life.
- Use suffixes –*able* and –*ible* to identify and define new words.
- Analyze how writers use capitalization.
- **Language** Write sentences using correct capitalization.

TEXT COMPLEXITY

Quantitative Measures	Thank You, M'am	Lexile: 660L
Qualitative Measures	**Ideas Presented** Much is explicit, but moves to some implied meaning	
	Structure Used Largely conventional with clear chronology	
	Language Used Much is explicit, but uses figurative language and colloquialisms	
	Knowledge Required Requires no special knowledge, but uses some unique cultural references	

58A Unit 1

PLAN

Online Ed

RESOURCES

- Unit 1 Response Log
- 🔊 Selection Audio
- 📖 Reading Studio: Notice and Note
- 💬 Speaking and Listening Studio: Participating in Group Discussion
- ⚙️ Vocabulary Studio: Suffixes
- ❗ Grammar Studio: Capital Letters
- ✅ "Thank You, Ma'am" Selection Test

SUMMARIES

English

Roger is a teen boy in need of a new pair of shoes—specifically a stylish new pair of *blue suede* shoes. To get the cash he'll need, he decides to snatch a woman's purse and, hopefully, get away before getting caught. Unfortunately, his chosen victim is one Mrs. Luella Bates Washington Jones, a rough, tough, no-nonsense local character with some words of wisdom for Roger that he won't soon forget. The two come together in unexpected ways—leaving Roger with a life experience worth far more than a mere pair of shoes.

Spanish

Roger es un adolescente que necesita un par de zapatos, específicamente un nuevo par de zapatos elegantes de gamuza azul. Para obtener el dinero que necesita, decide robar el bolso de una mujer y, con suerte, escapar antes de ser atrapado. Desafortunadamente, la víctima que consiguió fue una tal Sra. Luella Bates Washington Jones, un personaje local con una actitud fuerte y de carácter decidido, quien tiene unas palabras de sabiduría que Roger nunca olvidará. Los dos se reúnen de maneras inesperadas, dejando a Roger con una vivencia mucho más valiosa que un simple par de zapatos.

👥 SMALL-GROUP OPTIONS

Have students work in small groups to read and discuss the selection.

Pinwheel Discussion
- Break students into groups of six.
- Seat three students at center, back-to-back, facing outward.
- Place the other three students in front of the seated students, facing in.
- Students in the inner circle remain stationary while the out circle rotates to the right.
- For each rotation, provide one discussion question based on the class study of "Thank You, M'am" (For example: Name and discuss one character trait shared by Roger and Mrs. Jones).

Three-Minute Review
- Pause the classwork or lesson at any time.
- Direct students to study independently for three minutes, rereading and reviewing class notes. Ask them to write clarifying questions as they conduct their review.
- Set a timer for three minutes.
- When time is up, ask, *What did you notice in your review?* and conduct a brief class discussion on student findings.

PLAN

Text X-Ray: English Learner Support
for "Thank You, M'am"

Use the Text X-Ray and the supports and scaffolds in the Teacher's Edition to help guide students at different proficiency levels through the selection.

INTRODUCE THE SELECTION
DISCUSS CONFLICT

In this lesson, students will need to understand the concepts of conflict and encouragement. Conflict is defined as "the struggle between opposing forces." Encouragement from others is what helps us get through conflict to find resolution. In fiction, conflict is portrayed through character and setting:

- Character traits are how characters appear, speak, think, and behave in general.
- Setting is the specific time and place of an action or event.

Inform students that conflict happens in fiction much in the way it happens in real life: between two opposing forces and in a specific time and place. Ask students to think of a *setting* in which they experienced a conflict—either an external conflict (something or someone opposing them) or an internal conflict (like finding courage to do the right thing even if there are consequences). Ask: *Think of a conflict you have experienced. What or who helped you to resolve your conflict?* Have students share their experiences.

CULTURAL REFERENCES

The following words and phrases may be unfamiliar to students:

- *blue-jeaned sitter* (paragraph 1): Roger is wearing blue jeans in the story, and "sitter" refers to his behind.
- *pocketbook* (paragraph 2): a handbag.
- *blue suede shoes* (paragraph 26): shoes that were popular in America in the 1950s; the original blue suede shoes were military-issue shoes for U.S. airmen.
- *icebox* (paragraph 33): an old word for refrigerator
- *ten-cent cake* (paragraph 37): inexpensive sweets popularized during the Great Depression in the 20s.

LISTENING

Understand Character and Conflict

Draw students' attention to the setting of the story (in paragraph 1) and the names of the two characters, "Mrs. Luella Bates Washington Jones" (paragraph 16) and "Roger" (paragraph 19).

Have students listen as you read aloud paragraphs 1–20. Use the following supports with students at varying proficiency levels:

- Ask simple questions about what you just read aloud, instructing students to give a thumbs up or down as an answer. For example, ask: *Will Roger run if Mrs. Jones lets him go?* (yes) **SUBSTANTIAL**
- Have students identify the relationship between Roger and Mrs. Jones. Ask: *Is Mrs. Jones older than Roger?* (yes). *Is she pleased or upset by Roger's actions?* (upset) **MODERATE**
- Put students in pairs or small groups and have the groups list character traits of Roger and Mrs. Jones. **LIGHT**

58C Unit 1

PLAN

SPEAKING

Discuss Capitalization

Have students review the difference between upper- and lower-case letters. Ask them to point out a few capital letters in the first paragraph and circulate to ensure they understand the concept.

Use the following supports with students at varying proficiency levels:
- Display and/or have students read aloud the first sentence of the short story, noting which letter is capitalized. Have students read the sentence back to you or practice saying it to a partner. **SUBSTANTIAL**
- Ask students to read aloud paragraphs 16 and 19 and identify the main characters in the text. Ask: *How do you know those words are the characters' names? (because the words* Roger *and* Mrs. Luella Bates Washington Jones *are capitalized).* **MODERATE**
- Pair students. Have them take turns locating and speaking aloud *any* word that is capitalized in the text. Have them explain why the words are capitalized to each other. **LIGHT**

READING

Identify Internal and External Conflict

Explain to students that authors of fiction use character, setting, and description to convey internal and external conflict in a story.

Work with students to read paragraphs 22–34. Use the following supports with students at varying proficiency levels:
- Read paragraphs 22–26 aloud to students, pausing frequently for any questions that may arise. Use these sentence frames to help students explain what happens. *Roger is afraid that Mrs. Jones will _____. Mrs. Jones wants Roger to _____ before they have supper.* **SUBSTANTIAL**
- Guide students to identify a main conflict between Roger and Mrs. Jones in paragraphs 22–29. Ask simple questions, such as *Why did Roger snatch Mrs. Jones's purse? What is Mrs. Jones's response to his explanation?* **MODERATE**
- Ask students to identify Roger's internal conflict, using the frame: *Inside, Roger can't decide whether to _____ or to _____.* **LIGHT**

WRITING

Write a Letter of Request

Work with students to read the writing assignment on page 67.

Use the following supports with students at varying proficiency levels:
- Provide students with a list of some possible opening salutations to a formal letter *(Dear Sir, Dear Madam, Dear [name])* and possible endings *(Sincerely; Best; Regards)*. Explain the meanings of the endings as needed. Have students practice writing both the openings and the endings. **SUBSTANTIAL**
- Have students write words that list of all the information they need to include in their letters *(their own names, the name of the organization, a greeting, an ending, and their reason for writing)*. **MODERATE**
- Have students write the first paragraph of their letter, in which they introduce themselves and identify their reason for writing. Use the frame: *My name is _____ and I am writing because/to/for _____.* **LIGHT**

TEACH

? Connect to the ESSENTIAL QUESTION

In "Thank You, M'am," a poor young man attempts to snatch a woman's purse, but his victim turns out to be far tougher and far kinder than expected. The two strangers bond in a way that changes the young man. Ask students to think about a time when they faced up to difficulties in their own lives, and whether they had someone like Mrs. Jones who helped, encouraged, or mentored them during that hard time.

COMPARE ACROSS GENRES

Point out that "A Police Stop Changed This Teenager's Life" is a piece of journalism, whereas "Thank You, M'am" is a piece of fiction. Ask students to consider the differences in the way each text deals with the ideas of encouragement and facing up to life's difficulties. Where do the texts overlap conceptually, and how do they differ in their resolutions? Which story is more likely to have an impact on readers and why?

COLLABORATE & COMPARE

SHORT STORY

THANK YOU, M'AM

by **Langston Hughes**
pages 61–65

COMPARE ACROSS GENRES

As you read, notice how the ideas in both texts relate to your own experiences, as well as how they relate to the experiences of other teens. Then, look for ways that the ideas in the two texts relate to each other. After you read both selections, you will collaborate with a small group on a final project.

 ESSENTIAL QUESTION:

What helps people rise up to face difficulties?

ARTICLE

A POLICE STOP CHANGED THIS TEENAGER'S LIFE

by **Amy B Wang**
pages 73–77

58 Unit 1

 LEARNING MINDSET

Setting Goals Remind students that setting goals and tracking progress is an important element of learning. Setting a goal can be as simple as deciding to read a few paragraphs or pages in one sitting or deciding to focus on a text for a specific period of time. Learning how to spread out work into small goals can reduce stress and make any reading or learning assignment—small or large—more manageable and fun. Because every student learns at his or her own pace, stress to students the importance of setting their own goals.

Thank You, M'am

QUICK START

Make a list of the people who have encouraged you in the past. Think about what you were able to do as a result of this support.

ANALYZE CHARACTERS' QUALITIES

The characters in a short story are the people, animals, or imaginary creatures that take part in the action. **Characterization** is the way that the author develops the characters by

- making comments about the character through the voice of the narrator
- describing the character's physical appearance
- presenting the character's speech, thoughts, and actions
- conveying ideas through the character's speech, thought, and actions

An author uses these methods of characterization to help readers identify **character traits,** which are the qualities of appearance and personality that make a character seem real. As you read "Thank You, M'am," analyze how the characters' traits influence events and affect the resolution of conflict by thinking about the characters' words, actions, thoughts, appearance, and interactions with other characters.

GENRE ELEMENTS: SHORT STORY
- short work of fiction
- centered around a single idea
- usually has one main conflict
- character interactions with the conflict keep the story moving

ANALYZE SETTING AND CONFLICT

The plot of a story centers on conflict, or the struggle between opposing forces. An **external conflict** is a character's struggle against an outside force, while an **internal conflict** takes place inside the character. Stories can have more than one type of conflict. Often the plot of a story is influenced by the setting, or the time and place of the action. As you read "Thank You, M'am," use a chart like this to analyze how setting and conflict affect the ending of the story.

Setting:	Where:	When:
Major Characters:		Minor Characters:
Problem/Conflict:	Events: (List important events in story.)	
Outcome/Resolution:		

TEACH

QUICK START

Have students read the Quick Start question and invite them to take a few minutes to compose a list of people who have personally encouraged them. If some students struggle with this task, remind them to consider people in their lives outside of school or family, such as coaches, babysitters, neighbors, or leaders in their local religious or civic communities. Call on a few students to describe one of the people on their list, the encouragement that was offered, and what difficulty it helped the student overcome.

ANALYZE CHARACTERS' QUALITIES

Help students identify character qualities, such as physical appearance, actions, interactions, and speech patterns, by asking them to underline character descriptions that appear in the first paragraph of the text. Discuss how these character qualities might contribute to the plot and how they make the characters more realistic. Suggest students contrast the character qualities of Roger and Mrs. Jones as they read.

ANALYZE SETTING AND CONFLICT

Discuss how the setting of a story influences the external conflict, using familiar examples such as the setting of a popular film or TV show to make the point. (*For example, could* Star Wars *be set in a hotel? The Wild West?*).

Suggest that students use these questions to help them analyze conflict in this story:

- *What kinds of people, other than these characters, might be found in this setting?*
- *What kinds of dangers does the setting pose?*

Thank You, M'am 59

WHEN STUDENTS STRUGGLE . . .

Note Character Qualities Have individuals or partners use a chart to list Mrs. Jones's and Roger's character qualities.

	Mrs. Jones	Roger
Physical Characteristics		
Behavior		

 For additional support, go to the **Reading Studio.**

Thank You, M'am **59**

TEACH

CRITICAL VOCABULARY

Encourage students to read all the sentences before deciding which word best completes each one. Remind them to look for context clues that match the precise meaning of each word.

Answers:

1. *embarrassed*
2. *suede*
3. *latches*
4. *mistrust*
5. *barren*

LANGUAGE CONVENTIONS

Review the information about capitalization with students. Remind them that nearly all nouns naming a particular person, place, or thing get capital letters, such as days of the week, months, time periods, people, titles, and specific geographic locations. Capitalization also occurs at the beginning of all sentences.

Read the sentences in paragraph 16 aloud and have students make note of the capital letters in the character's name. Write the name on the board if needed, and ask students to explain why "Mrs. Luella Bates Washington Jones" is capitalized. (*It is capitalized because* Mrs. Luella Bates Washington Jones *is Mrs. Jones's entire name and names of particular persons are capitalized.*)

ANNOTATION MODEL

Remind students of the annotation ideas in Analyze Character on p. 65, which suggests marking details that show that Mrs. Jones is a strong person and underlining words and phrases that signal character traits. Point out that students may follow this suggestion or use their own system for marking up the selections in their write-in texts. They may want to color-code their annotations by using highlighters. Their notes in the margins may include questions about ideas that are unclear or topics they want to learn more about.

 GET READY

CRITICAL VOCABULARY

suede   mistrust   embarrass   latch   barren

To preview the Critical Vocabulary words, complete each sentence with a word from the list.

1. Sometimes a person may feel self-conscious, or _____.
2. The shoes were _____, which is soft and fuzzy leather.
3. When someone _____ on to you, it's hard to free yourself.
4. It is easy to _____ a person who has done you harm.
5. An empty room looks uninteresting, or _____.

LANGUAGE CONVENTIONS

Capitalization In this lesson, you will learn about the use of capital letters for the first words of sentences and quotations. Proper nouns, such as names and titles, and time periods, such as days and months (but not seasons), are also capitalized. As you read the selection, note the author's use of capitalization and think about how you use correct capitalization in your own writing.

ANNOTATION MODEL   **NOTICE & NOTE**

As you read, note the author's use of characterization to create realistic characters and move the plot along. You can also mark up details about the setting and conflict. In the model, you can see one reader's notes about "Thank You, M'am."

> 1 She was a large woman with a large purse that had everything in it but hammer and nails. It had a long strap and she carried it slung across her shoulder. It was about eleven o'clock at night, and she was walking alone, when a boy ran up behind her and tried to snatch her purse.... But the boy's weight, and the weight of the purse combined caused him to lose his balance so, instead of taking off full blast as he had hoped, the boy fell on his back on the sidewalk, and his legs flew up. The large woman simply turned around and kicked him....

author gives details about the physical appearance of the woman

setting is in evening—it is dark—I wonder how the setting is part of the plot?

The details show the woman is strong and not intimidated.

BACKGROUND

Langston Hughes *(1902–1967) was raised by his grandmother in Lawrence, Kansas. As a child, he began a lifelong exploration of literature and blues music. He went to Columbia University in New York City and eventually was recognized for his talent for writing poems. He went on to write novels, short stories, and plays as well as poems. Hughes's work shows a special understanding of everyday people—people who may not be famous or rich but whose lives are inspiring and valuable nonetheless.*

THANK YOU, M'AM

Short Story by Langston Hughes

PREPARE TO COMPARE

As you read, pay attention to how characters' traits affect events and influence how conflicts are resolved. This will help you compare this short story with the news article "A Police Stop Changed This Teenager's Life."

Notice & Note

Use the side margins to notice and note signposts in the text.

ANALYZE SETTING AND CONFLICT

Annotate: Review paragraph 1 and mark evidence of the setting of the story.

Analyze: How does the setting influence the woman's external conflict with the boy?

ANALYZE CHARACTER

Annotate: In paragraphs 1–11, mark text details that show that Mrs. Jones is a strong person.

Interpret: What character qualities do these text details tell readers about Mrs. Jones?

1   She was a large woman with a large purse that had everything in it but hammer and nails. It had a long strap and she carried it slung across her shoulder. It was about eleven o'clock at night, and she was walking alone, when a boy ran up behind her and tried to snatch her purse. The strap broke with the single tug the boy gave it from behind. But the boy's weight, and the weight of the purse combined caused him to lose his balance so, instead of taking off full blast as he had hoped, the boy fell on his back on the sidewalk, and his legs flew up. The large woman simply turned around and kicked him right square in his blue jeaned sitter. Then she reached down, picked the boy up by his shirt front, and shook him until his teeth rattled.

Thank You, M'am   61

ENGLISH LEARNER SUPPORT

Demonstrate Comprehension To help students understand conflict, have them form pairs comprised of two different learner levels. Have one partner be Roger and the other Mrs. Jones. Then have them write a few words that explain what their character is doing in paragraphs 1–20. After they describe their characters' actions, have partners write a sentence together that describes the conflict. **MODERATE**

TEACH

BACKGROUND

After students read the Background note, explain that a fiction writer's work will often reflect his or her origins or worldview. In this note, we learn that Hughes wanted to portray the experiences of ordinary people. In this short story, a teenage boy has a run-in with a local woman. His experience has the power to change his view of the world around him, and of himself. He has the opportunity to see things differently because of a single encounter.

PREPARE TO COMPARE

Direct students to use the Prepare to Compare prompt to focus their reading.

ANALYZE SETTING AND CONFLICT

Remind students that conflicts are often conveyed to the reader through details of events in the **setting**. Highlighting descriptive words or phrases related to setting, plot events, and characters will help reveal the nature of the conflict.

(**Answer:** *The setting is a sidewalk late at night. The words "late at night" will have an ominous or threatening sound for some readers. The fact that she's "walking alone" tells that the setting is probably empty. The sidewalk could be in a small town, a city— or anywhere that has sidewalks. The absence of other details about the setting is supplemented by the fast-paced action and the characterization of the woman.*)

ANALYZE CHARACTER

Remind students that **characterization** consists of details in the text related to the physical appearance, speech, and actions of the character. (**Answer:** *She is a strong woman because she is physically large; she can hold the boy so he can't get away. Even though she has almost been robbed, she acts decisively and shows that she wants him to understand the consequences of his actions. She shows no fear at all.*)

 For **listening support** for students at varying proficiency levels, see the **Text X-Ray** on page 58C.

Thank You, M'am   **61**

TEACH

✏️ ANALYZE CHARACTER

Tell students that what a character says or does reveals their traits, or what they are like. Remind students to pay careful attention to characters' actions and behaviors.
(Answer: *Her statements indicate that she is angry, but that she is also caring. A frightened, resentful, or rigid person might scream for help or attempt to turn him in to the police and have him prosecuted. She is concerned that the boy is dirty and hungry. The boy's responses show that he is feeling frightened and doesn't know what to say.)*

✏️ LANGUAGE CONVENTIONS

Remind students of the grammatical rules of **capitalization:** to start a sentence, for proper nouns, titles, and acronyms. Briefly review use of capitals for style or emphasis in comic books, advertising, and other media.

(Answer: *By having the character state her entire name, the author is emphasizing that Mrs. Jones is strong, proud, and forceful. Her name is like her: impressive, memorable, and as long as she is big.)*

✏️ NOTICE & NOTE

2   After that the woman said, "Pick up my pocketbook, boy, and give it here."

3   She still held him. But she bent down enough to permit him to stoop and pick up her purse. Then she said, "Now ain't you ashamed of yourself?"

4   Firmly gripped by his shirt front, the boy said, "Yes'm."

5   The woman said, "What did you want to do it for?"

6   The boy said, "I didn't aim to."

7   She said, "You a lie!"

8   By that time two or three people passed, stopped, turned to look, and some stood watching.

9   "If I turn you loose, will you run?" asked the woman.

10 "Yes'm," said the boy.

11 "Then I won't turn you loose," said the woman. She did not release him.

12 "I'm very sorry, lady, I'm sorry," whispered the boy.

13 "Um-hum! And your face is dirty. I got a great mind to wash your face for you. Ain't you got nobody home to tell you to wash your face?"

14 "No'm," said the boy.

15 "Then it will get washed this evening," said the large woman starting up the street, dragging the frightened boy behind her.

16 He looked as if he were fourteen or fifteen, frail and willow-wild, in tennis shoes and blue jeans.

17 The woman said, "You ought to be my son. I would teach you right from wrong. Least I can do right now is to wash your face. Are you hungry?"

18 "No'm," said the being-dragged boy. "I just want you to turn me loose."

19 "Was I bothering *you* when I turned that corner?" asked the woman.

20 "No'm."

21 "But you put yourself in contact with me," said the woman. "If you think that that contact is not going to last awhile, you got another thought coming. When I get through with you, sir, you are going to remember Mrs. Luella Bates Washington Jones."

22 Sweat popped out on the boy's face and he began to struggle. Mrs. Jones stopped, jerked him around in front of her, put a half nelson about his neck, and continued to drag him up the street. When she got to her door, she dragged the boy inside, down a hall, and into a large kitchenette-furnished room at the rear of the house. She switched on the light and left the door open. The boy could hear other roomers laughing and talking in the large house. Some of their doors were open, too,

ANALYZE CHARACTER
Annotate: Review paragraphs 15–21 and mark evidence that Mrs. Jones is explaining how Roger should behave with people.
Analyze: How have the characters' words, actions, and interactions with each other so far affected the events in the story? Would the events be the same with other characters?

LANGUAGE CONVENTIONS
Capitalization is useful in distinguishing titles and people. It can also be used for emphasis. Circle the capital letters in the woman's name in paragraph 21.
Infer: What is the author emphasizing by having the character state her entire name?

62 Unit 1

🗨️ ENGLISH LEARNER SUPPORT

Comprehend Language Structures Use the following supports to teach and/or review capitalization. Supply groups with samples of letters that correctly use capitalization.

- Supply pairs with short, simple letters written to Mrs. Jones that express feelings and opinions about how she confronted the boy. All characters in the letters should be lower case. Have students correct the letters using the samples. **SUBSTANTIAL**
- Working in pairs, have students write short emails to people they admire. Tell them to use the samples to follow rules of capitalization. **MODERATE**

so he knew he and the woman were not alone. The woman still had him by the neck in the middle of her room.

23   She said, "What is your name?"

24   "Roger," answered the boy.

25   "Then, Roger, you go to that sink and wash your face," said the woman, whereupon she turned him loose—at last. Roger looked at the door—looked at the woman—looked at the door—and went to the sink.

26   "Let the water run until it gets warm," she said. "Here's a clean towel."

27   "You gonna take me to jail?" asked the boy, bending over the sink.

28   "Not with that face, I would not take you nowhere," said the woman. "Here I am trying to get home to cook me a bite to eat and you snatch my pocketbook! Maybe you ain't been to your supper either, late as it be. Have you?"

29   "There's nobody home at my house," said the boy.

30   "Then we'll eat," said the woman. "I believe you're hungry—or been hungry—to try to snatch my pocketbook."

31   "I wanted a pair of blue **suede** shoes," said the boy.

32   "Well, you didn't have to snatch *my* pocketbook to get some suede shoes," said Mrs. Luella Bates Washington Jones, "You could of asked me."

33   "M'am?"

NOTICE & NOTE

ANALYZE SETTING AND CONFLICT
Annotate: Review paragraph 25 and mark the text that shows that Roger is conflicted about how to behave with Mrs. Rogers in this unfamiliar place.

Infer: What does Roger's decision tell you about his internal conflict and his relationship with adults?

suede
(swād) *n. Suede* is leather that is treated to be fuzzy and soft.

ANALYZE CHARACTER
Annotate: In paragraphs 32–35, mark the text that shows that Roger is unsure about what to do and confused by Mrs. Jones's behavior toward him.

Draw Conclusions: Do Mrs. Jones's statements and actions cause Roger to think about what he has done? Why?

Thank You, M'am   63

APPLY

ANALYZE SETTING AND CONFLICT

Remind students that conflicts can be external or internal. An internal conflict, such as the one shown in paragraphs 19 and 20, takes place inside a character as he or she battles opposing internal forces.
(Answer: *Roger is ashamed of the way he has behaved, and his decision to obey the woman shows that he respects her.***)**

EL ENGLISH LEARNER SUPPORT

Monitor Comprehension Review paragraphs 13–17 and 25. Have students consider why it is so important to Mrs. Jones that Roger washes his face before eating supper.

ASK STUDENTS to work in pairs and fill in these sentence frames to answer the question. *Mrs. Jones notices that Roger's face is _____.* (dirty, needs to be washed) *She wants him to wash his face because _____.* (Answers will vary, including: wants him to feel cared for, learn self-respect, develop self-care.) **SUBSTANTIAL**

ANALYZE CHARACTER

Tell students that characters show confusion in different ways. Confusion occurs when characters don't understand what's happening. Suggest that students think about how they react when they are confused or puzzled by someone's actions. **(Answer:** *Mrs. Jones's statements and actions confuse Roger, but they also make him think. He's trying to figure out if Mrs. Jones wants to punish him; it doesn't occur to him that someone would want to help him or be kind to him.***)**

CRITICAL VOCABULARY

suede: Suede (soft leather) shoes became very popular in the late 1950s. The story was written in 1958.

ASK STUDENTS hat might be appealing about suede? Why might someone not want a suede product? *(What might be appealing about suede is its soft feel. Someone might not want suede because it can be hard to keep clean.)*

Thank You, M'am   **63**

TO CHALLENGE STUDENTS

Characterization in Fiction Mrs. Jones is an astute observer. She very quickly understands that Roger is not cared for. Have students write an essay analyzing what Mrs. Jones observes, what she concludes, based on those observations, and how those observations affect her behavior. *(Students' analyses might include that Mrs. Jones notices that Roger is skinny and concludes that he is probably hungry; that probably no one is home to take care of Roger and teach him common personal hygiene, such as washing before a meal; and that Roger is used to not being trusted. This affects her behavior. She feeds him, teaches him, trusts him, and warns him to behave himself.)*

APPLY

MEMORY MOMENT

Explain that this **Memory Moment** sheds light on the **character** of Mrs. Jones and explains her dealings with Roger. Mrs. Jones tells Roger that she is not that dissimilar to him and that she too has wanted things she couldn't have. (**Answer**: *Mrs. Jones is perhaps treating Roger as she would have liked to have been treated when she was his age.*)

ENGLISH LEARNER SUPPORT

Monitor Comprehension Working in pairs of different abilities, have students discuss this question: *In paragraphs 35–37, what is Mrs. Jones trying to make Roger understand?* (*She doesn't think that she's morally better than he is; she admits that she has done things that she regrets. She tries to make him feel comfortable: she is not judging him.*) **SUBSTANTIAL**

CRITICAL VOCABULARY

mistrust: Roger doesn't want to be "mistrusted now." He wants Mrs. Jones to believe in him. He wants to prove that he can be trusted.

ASK STUDENTS to discuss what kinds of events might cause people to mistrust others. (*being lied to, being abandoned, being hurt*)

embarrass: The narrator makes it clear that Mrs. Jones does not ask him questions that might make him feel uncomfortable or ashamed.

ASK STUDENTS Why might Roger be embarrassed about his home and family? (*Roger may have neglectful parents, or feel embarrassed to think of home after what he has done.*)

64 Unit 1

NOTICE & NOTE

MEMORY MOMENT

Notice & Note: What is the woman telling the boy about her past?

Analyze: How does this help you understand how the woman is treating the boy?

mistrust
(mĭs-trŭst´) *v.* To *mistrust* is to be without confidence or trust.

embarrass
(ĕm-băr´əs) *v.* To *embarrass* is to cause to feel uncomfortable or self-conscious.

34 The water dripping from his face, the boy looked at her. There was a long pause. A very long pause. After he had dried his face and not knowing what else to do dried it again, the boy turned around, wondering what next. The door was open. He could make a dash for it down the hall. He could run, run, run, run, *run!*

35 The woman was sitting on the day-bed.[1] After awhile she said, "I were young once and I wanted things I could not get."

36 There was another long pause. The boy's mouth opened. Then he frowned, but not knowing he frowned.

37 The woman said, "Um-hum! You thought I was going to say *but*, didn't you? You thought I was going to say, *but I didn't snatch people's pocketbooks.* Well, I wasn't going to say that." Pause. Silence. "I have done things, too, which I would not tell you, son —neither tell God, if he didn't already know. So you set down while I fix us something to eat. You might run that comb through your hair so you will look presentable."

38 In another corner of the room behind a screen was a gas plate and an icebox. Mrs. Jones got up and went behind the screen. The woman did not watch the boy to see if he was going to run now, nor did she watch her purse which she left behind her on the day-bed. But the boy took care to sit on the far side of the room where he thought she could easily see him out of the corner of her eye, if she wanted to. He did not trust the woman *not* to trust him. And he did not want to be **mistrusted** now.

39 "Do you need somebody to go to the store," asked the boy, "maybe to get some milk or something?"

40 "Don't believe I do," said the woman, "unless you just want sweet milk yourself. I was going to make cocoa out of this canned milk I got here."

41 "That will be fine," said the boy.

42 She heated some lima beans and ham she had in the icebox, made the cocoa, and set the table. The woman did not ask the boy anything about where he lived, or his folks, or anything else that would **embarrass** him. Instead, as they ate, she told him about her job in a hotel beauty-shop that stayed open late, what the work was like, and how all kinds of women came in and out, blondes, red-heads, and Spanish. Then she cut him a half of her ten-cent cake.

43 "Eat some more, son," she said.

44 When they were finished eating she got up and said, "Now, here, take this ten dollars and buy yourself some blue suede

---
[1] **day-bed** (dā´bĕd´): a sofa or couch that is used as a bed.

64 Unit 1

shoes. And next time, do not make the mistake of **latching onto** *my* **pocketbook** *nor nobody else's*—because shoes come by devilish like that will burn your feet. I got to get my rest now. But I wish you would behave yourself, son, from here on in."

45   She led him down the hall to the front door and opened it. "Goodnight! *Behave yourself, boy!*" she said, looking out into the street.

46   The boy wanted to say something else other than, "Thank you, m'am," to Mrs. Luella Bates Washington Jones, but he couldn't do so as he turned at the **barren** stoop and looked back at the large woman in the door. He barely managed to say, "Thank you," before she shut the door. And he never saw her again.

NOTICE & NOTE

latch
(lăch) *v.* To *latch* means to hold on to or get hold of.

ANALYZE CHARACTER
Annotate: In paragraphs 44–45, mark instances where Mrs. Jones gives Roger advice.

Analyze: How do Mrs. Jones's advice and actions affect the resolution of the conflict?

barren
(băr´ən) *adj.* Something that is empty and lacking interest or charm is *barren*.

CHECK YOUR UNDERSTANDING

Answer these questions before moving on to the **Analyze the Text** section on the following page.

1 How does the author's use of setting advance the plot of the story?
   A It causes the characters to be embarrassed.
   B It allows the characters to witness an unusual event.
   C It offers the characters a chance to learn about each other.
   D It provides the solution to the characters' problems.

2 In paragraph 39, Roger wants to go to the store for Mrs. Jones in order to —
   F get sweet milk to drink with dinner
   G take the money for the milk and run away
   H show Mrs. Jones he is trustworthy
   J buy the blue suede shoes he wants

3 Based on the details in paragraphs 35–37, the reader can conclude that Mrs. Jones most likely —
   A thinks that hunger has driven Roger to snatch her purse
   B expects Roger to try to steal things from other people
   C regrets things she has done in the past to get what she wanted
   D knows that Roger's parents are looking for him in the neighborhood

Thank You, M'am   65

 ENGLISH LEARNER SUPPORT

Oral Assessment Use the following questions to assess students' comprehension and speaking skills.

1 Why does Mrs. Jones take Roger home? *(to give him dinner and talk to him)* Does Mrs. Jones teach Roger that it is wrong to steal? *(yes)*

2 In paragraph 39, do you think Roger wants to keep the money or buy Mrs. Roger milk? *(yes)*

3 Why does Mrs. Jones tell Roger she has also done things that were wrong? *(to teach him to do the right thing)*

APPLY

ANALYZE CHARACTER
Reminds students that Mrs. Jones's **character traits** are revealed in everything she says and does, as here where she urgently but politely gives Roger her final advice before she bids him goodnight. **(Answer:** *She gives him the money to show that she understands what it is to want something, but she also warns him that if he had succeeded in robbing her, there would have been consequences. She speaks as though she has experienced these consequences in her past and wants to help him avoid them.)*

CHECK YOUR UNDERSTANDING
Have students answer the questions independently.
Answers:
1. C
2. G
3. C

If they answer any questions incorrectly, have them reread the text to confirm their understanding. Then they may proceed to ANALYZE THE TEXT on page 66.

CRITICAL VOCABULARY

latch: Mrs. Jones warns Roger not to try to latch onto, or grab hold of, someone's purse again.

ASK STUDENTS to consider how this sentence would be different if Mrs. Jones had said that Roger "taken" her pocketbook. *(The sentence would sound out of character; it wouldn't sound like Mrs. Jones, who likes bold, descriptive words.)*

barren: In this context, the *barren* (empty, lifeless) stoop contrasts with the door, where the "large woman," a "life" stands.

ASK STUDENTS to think of other things that might be described as barren. *(a lifeless tree, a desert, a place where nothing grows)*

Thank You, M'am   **65**

APPLY

ANALYZE THE TEXT
Possible answers:

1. **DOK 2:** *In paragraph 29, Roger considers running away, but in paragraph 33, he thinks, "He did not trust the woman not to trust him. And he did not want to be mistrusted now." Roger wants the shoes enough to have tried to steal money for them, but he doesn't want to be mistrusted. He doesn't know how to behave with Mrs. Jones because she is nice even though he tried to rob her.*

2. **DOK 2:** *Mrs. Jones works hard and lives simply in a small room in a boarding house. She works late at her job and eats simple food like cocoa, lima beans, and ham.*

3. **DOK 3:** *Roger is a very slight and small person, while Mrs. Jones is described as large. Roger isn't able to break free because she is stronger and larger.*

4. **DOK 2:** *Roger, an aspiring thief, is treated kindly and given money. However, his encounter with Mrs. Jones has made him think about how his behavior affected her and how such behavior might affect him. He will probably not try to rob someone again.*

5. **DOK 4:** *As Mrs. Jones talks about her work life, Roger is able to relax. He doesn't have to explain what made him try to rob Mrs. Jones.*

RESEARCH

Remind students they should confirm any information they find by checking multiple websites and assessing the credibility of each one.

Connect Students may note that Harlem was both an inexpensive place to live and a location in New York City that was separated from the other white communities in Manhattan. These two factors led to a dense and thriving community of African Americans in Harlem, which included people of different backgrounds, laborers, managers, rich, poor, teachers, students, and artists. In small groups, students can note how Mrs. Jones's doors being open suggests a community of familiars, like a large family, or how her inviting in Roger, who is a stranger, suggests an environment that is open to newcomers and welcoming to different kinds of people.

RESPOND

ANALYZE THE TEXT
Support your responses with evidence from the text. 📓 **NOTEBOOK**

1. **Infer** What details does the author provide to show the relationship between how Roger behaves with Mrs. Jones and how he deals with his internal conflict?

2. **Interpret** What does the setting of the story tell you about Mrs. Jones's life? Cite details from the text that support your answer.

3. **Draw Conclusions** Reread the descriptions the author provides of Mrs. Jones and Roger in paragraphs 1 and 22. Explain why Roger isn't able to break free from Mrs. Jones.

4. **Predict** How is Roger's external conflict resolved and why might Mrs. Jones's involvement in the resolution affect Roger's actions in the future?

5. **Notice & Note** Review paragraph 42. What role do Mrs. Jones's memories of her beauty-shop job play in making Roger feel more comfortable?

RESEARCH TIP
Research terms can be specific, but also general. Along with a topic such as *Harlem*, you will want to include a description of the dates that you are interested in learning about. For example, you might include *early 1900s* in your initial search to make sure you get listings for websites that have the information you seek.

RESEARCH
Investigate Harlem, an area of New York City that became a vibrant African American community in the early 1900s. Find out why people moved to Harlem and how its social and cultural environment nurtured writers and artists. Note what you learn in the chart.

RESEARCH TOPICS	DETAILS ABOUT LIFE IN HARLEM
Reasons people moved to the area	Inexpensive lifestyle; proximity to central New York City; includes people of different backgrounds
Social organizations that helped create a community in Harlem	Apollo Theater; Cotton Club; Sylvia's restaurant; night life; jazz clubs; labor unions
Cultural organizations that supported artists	Local churches; city universities; National Black Theater; Works Works Progress Administration

Connect In paragraph 22, the writer describes the house where Mrs. Jones lives and mentions that Roger could hear "other roomers laughing and talking in the large house. Some of their doors were open, too, so he knew he and the woman were not alone." With a small group, discuss how the setting points to a vibrant and supportive community.

LEARNING MINDSET

Setting Goals Have students share and celebrate their success with setting and achieving goals. Remind them that sometimes we do not achieve all of our goals. The important thing is to set goals and try to meet those goals. Have students share goals they have recently met, and goals they would like to meet.

RESPOND

CREATE AND DISCUSS

Write a Letter of Request Conduct research to find an organization that promotes intergenerational leadership or mentorship. Then write a letter of request asking for more information about the advantages such partnerships hold for young people.

- ❏ Start your letter with a heading that includes your school address, the date, and the inside address of the organization. Finally, give a salutation, or greeting, such as "Dear Sir/Madam."
- ❏ In the body of the letter, explain why you are writing, what you already know about the organization, and what information you are requesting about leadership or mentorship.
- ❏ Finish your letter with a closing such as "Sincerely, (your name)."

Discuss with a Small Group Now that you've read "Thank You, M'am," think about how Roger and Mrs. Jones both took action. Discuss the consequences of these actions and as a group decide whether the brief mentorship that Mrs. Jones offered could make a difference in Roger's life. To prepare for your discussion, review the text and think about the characters' actions at the beginning and end of the story.

- ❏ What clues does the text provide to support the idea that Roger has been positively influenced by Mrs. Jones's reaction to his attempt to steal from her?
- ❏ Could just a few minutes with a supportive person change someone's life? Support your ideas with details from the text and your general knowledge about how people react.

 Go to **Participating in a Group Discussion** in the **Speaking and Listening Studio** for help.

RESPOND TO THE ESSENTIAL QUESTION

 What helps people rise up to face difficulties?

Gather Information Review your annotations and notes on "Thank You, M'am." Then, add relevant details to your Response Log. As you determine which information to include, think about:

- the difference in how people react to challenges
- how people can support each other in big and small ways
- the best way to take action to improve a challenging situation

At the end of the unit, use your notes to write an informational essay.

ACADEMIC VOCABULARY

As you write and discuss what you learned from the short story, be sure to use the Academic Vocabulary words. Check off each of the words that you use.

- ❏ aspect
- ❏ cultural
- ❏ evaluate
- ❏ resource
- ❏ text

Thank You, M'am 67

APPLY

WRITE AND DISCUSS

Write a Letter of Request Tell students to closely follow the outline on page 67 for writing their request letters. Remind them that this is formal writing, which requires brevity, politeness, respect, and clear articulation of the reason for the letter.

Discuss with a Small Group Remind students that not everyone will have the same interpretation of the characters and that discussing different ideas is something that should be encouraged. Groups should answer the questions provided and be respectful of one another's contributions to the discussion.

RESPOND TO THE ESSENTIAL QUESTION

Allow time for students to add details from "Thank You, Ma'am" to their Unit 1 Response Logs.

For **writing support** for students at varying proficiency levels, see the **Text X-Ray** on page 58D.

ENGLISH LEARNER SUPPORT

Discuss with a Small Group Point out examples of the informal language used by Mrs. Jones and Roger. Have students list words or phrases used by Mrs. Jones. Discuss why her way of speaking is effective (or not). Then, pair students at different proficiency levels. Have them work together to create an alternate ending to the story. Tell students the dialogue between Mrs. Jones and Roger should take place one year after their first meeting; students may use informal and/or informal language. **LIGHT**

APPLY

CRITICAL VOCABULARY

Answers:

1. **embarrass:** When people feel embarrassed, they are uncomfortable about a situation, event, or interaction.
2. **barren:** A place that is barren doesn't have anything in it.
3. **suede:** Suede is a soft material that is used for shoes and clothing.
4. **mistrust:** When a person mistrusts another person, they are often suspicious of their actions.
5. **latch:** When a person latches onto something, they are gripping the person or object tightly.

VOCABULARY STRATEGY:
Suffixes –able and –ible

Answers:

1. Chang**eable** means "capable of change."
2. Regrett**able** refers to behavior or an action that someone regrets; capable of regret.
3. Digest**ible** means "something that can be, or is capable of being eaten or digested."
4. revers**ible** means "an action that can be reversed, or is capable of being reversed."

 RESPOND

WORD BANK
suede
mistrust
embarrass
latch
barren

CRITICAL VOCABULARY

Practice and Apply Identify the vocabulary word that is tied in meaning to the italicized word in each question. Provide reasons for your choices.

1. Which word goes with *uncomfortable*? Why?
2. Which word goes with *empty*? Why?
3. Which word goes with *soft*? Why?
4. Which word goes with *suspicious*? Why?
5. Which word goes with *grip*? Why?

 Go to the **Vocabulary Studio** for more on suffixes.

VOCABULARY STRATEGY:
Suffixes –able and –ible

A **suffix** is a word part that appears at the end of a root or base word to form a new word. You can use your knowledge of suffixes to figure out word meanings. For example, look for a word with a suffix in this sentence from "Thank You, M'am."

> You might run that comb through your hair so you will look presentable.

Note that the word *presentable* is made of the base word *present* and the suffix *–able*. The suffixes *–able* and *–ible* mean "capable of or worthy of." Therefore, the meaning of *presentable* is "worthy of being introduced to others."

Practice and Apply Underline the suffix in each boldface word. Then, state the meaning of the boldface word in your own words.

1. People's behavior is often **changeable** because life experiences can influence thoughts, feelings, and actions.

   _____

2. It is **regrettable** when one friend lies to another friend.

   _____

3. The meal was **digestible**, but it was not very tasty.

   _____

4. The consequences of committing a crime are not easily **reversible**.

   _____

 ENGLISH LEARNER SUPPORT

Understand Critical Vocabulary The five vocabulary words can be split into two categories: words with a negative meaning (*embarrass, barren, mistrust*) and words with a neutral meaning (*suede* and *latch*). Divide students into pairs. Explain the categories and after giving students definitions of the words, have them put the words into the correct categories.
SUBSTANTIAL/MODERATE

LANGUAGE CONVENTIONS: Capitalization

It is important for writers to capitalize words correctly so that readers do not get confused. Writers use capital letters to distinguish people and titles, geographical names, organizations or events, proper adjectives, first words in sentences or titles, and the pronoun *I*.

Here are some examples of capitalization in "Thank You, M'am."

- Starting sentences:

    Firmly gripped by his shirt front, the boy said, "Yes'm."

- Distinguishing the pronoun *I* and identifying a person:

    When I get through with you, sir, you are going to remember Mrs. Luella Bates Washington Jones.

Here are some other examples of capitalization.

CATEGORY	EXAMPLE
People and Titles	Langston Hughes, Professor Du Bois
Geographical Names	Brooklyn, Central Park
Organizations, Events, etc.	Thursday, March, Labor Day
Proper Adjectives	Hispanic restaurant, American colonies

Practice and Apply Using the examples above as a guide, rewrite each of the following sentences and correct the capitalization.

1. Tourists in new york City visit the empire state building.
2. The Boy in "Thank You, M'am" was named roger.
3. none of the other people in the House spoke to mrs. Jones.
4. The Story takes place in an urban area that could be harlem.
5. It is clear that the setting of the story is An american city.

_____

_____

_____

_____

RESPOND

Go to the **Grammar Studio** for more on capitalization.

Thank You, M'am 69

APPLY

LANGUAGE CONVENTIONS: Capitalization

Review the information about capitalization with students. Remind students that capital letters are used in a variety of grammatical situations, such as for proper nouns, given names, sentence beginnings, and titles. Ask students to identify where words should or should not be capitalized.

Practice and Apply Have students discuss their use of capital letters and in what situations they are appropriate in writing.

Answers:

1. *People visiting a city often visit structures like the Empire State Building.*
2. *The boy in "Thank You, M'am" was named Roger.*
3. *None of the other people in the house spoke to Mrs. Jones.*
4. *The story takes place in an urban area that could be New York City.*
5. *It is clear that the setting of the story is an American city.*

 ENGLISH LEARNER SUPPORT

Demonstrate Comprehension Make use of the following supports to help students understand the rules of capitalization:

- Have students of different abilities pair up and read sentences from the text. The listener should identify the words that are capitalized, while the reader can confirm whether the answers are correct. **SUBSTANTIAL**
- In pairs, students create three to five new sentences, write them down, and exchange them with their partners. Partners correct for capitalization, pass back, and discuss. **MODERATE**
- In pairs, have students use the Internet to find an article in which they can find examples of all the different types of capitalization (proper nouns, beginning sentences, titles, given names, time periods). Then, have students discuss why the author(s) capitalized those words. **LIGHT**

Thank You, M'am **69**

PLAN

A POLICE STOP CHANGED THIS TEENAGER'S LIFE

Article by Amy B. Wang

GENRE ELEMENTS
ARTICLE

Remind students that the purpose of a non-fiction **article** is to present facts and information. A **human-interest story** is a type of article; it presents facts and information about a person or people in order to create an emotional and intellectual response. Articles use time order and calendar words and phrases to give the reader a clear picture of the chronological sequence in which the events occurred. In this lesson, students will use time order words to help them recognize the order in which particular events in the story occurred.

LEARNING OBJECTIVES

- Identify the chronological order of events in an informational text.
- Conduct research about crowdfunding.
- Write an objective summary of the article.
- Discuss opinions on a human-interest story.
- Use context clues to define unfamiliar words.
- Analyze how writers use quotation marks.
- **Language** Identify, discuss, and use time-order words.

TEXT COMPLEXITY

Quantitative Measures	A Police Stop Changed This Teenger's Life	Lexile: 890L
Qualitative Measures	**Ideas Presented** Mostly explicit, but moves to some implied meaning	
	Structure Used Sequence language guides reading.	
	Language Used Mostly Tier II and III words used	
	Knowledge Required Most of the text deals with easily imagined experiences.	

70A Unit 2

PLAN

RESOURCES

Online

- Unit 1 Response Log
- 🔊 Selection Audio
- 📖 Reading Studio: Notice & Note
- 📝 Writing Studio: Using Textual Evidence
- 📝 Writing Studio: Conducting Research
- 💬 Speaking and Listening Studio: Participating in Collaborative Discussions
- ⚪ Vocabulary Studio: Context Clues
- ❗ Grammar Studio: Module 3: Lesson 6: Conjunctions and Interjections
- ✓ "A Police Stop Changed One Teenager's Life" Selection Test

SUMMARIES

English

When Jourdan Duncan was stopped by a police officer on his walk home from work, he never imagined the events that would happen next. The officer, Cpl. Keffer, gave him a ride. After hearing that Jourdan was walking nearly five hours a day to get to his job, Cpl. Keffer, was impressed with his work ethic and determination. Jourdan made such an impression that Cpl. Keffer shared his story with the department and resolved to help him get a bike. The unexpected gift would change Jourdan's life for good.

Spanish

Cuando Jourdan Duncan fue detenido por un oficial de policía de camino a su casa, nunca imaginó lo que sucedería luego. El oficial, Col. Keffer, le dio un aventón. Después de escuchar que Jourdan caminaba casi cinco horas al día para llegar a su trabajo, el Col. Keffer quedó impresionado por su determinación y ética laboral. Jourdan dejó tal impresión, que el Col. Keffer compartió su historia con el departamento y decidió ayudarle a conseguir una bicicleta. Ese regalo inesperado habría de cambiar la vida de Jourdan para siempre.

SMALL-GROUP OPTIONS

Have students work in small groups to read and discuss the selection.

Think-Pair Share

- After students have read and analyzed "A Police Stop Changed This Teenager's Life," pose this question: *Why is it important to take action when you face a challenge?* An action can have immediate consequences (Keffer getting Duncan a bicycle) or be a continuous decision (Duncan commutes to work by walking after his car breaks down).
- Have students think about the question individually and take notes.
- Then, have pairs discuss their ideas about the question.
- Finally, ask pairs to share their responses with the class.

Three Before Me

- After students have completed their summaries on page 79, have them ask three classmates to edit their writing.
- Provide students with a list of errors to look for as they edit each others' work: clear topic sentences, key details included, correct usage of quotations marks, and correct spelling and usage of vocabulary words.
- Finally, have students apply the edits their peers have identified before turning them in.

A Police Stop Changed This Teenager's Life   **70B**

PLAN

Text X-Ray: English Learner Support
for "A Police Stop Changed This Teenager's Life"

Use the Text X-Ray and the supports and scaffolds in the Teacher's Edition to help guide students at different proficiency levels through the selection.

INTRODUCE THE SELECTION
DISCUSS FACING CHALLENGES

In this lesson, students will need to be able to discuss how different people respond to challenges. Tell students that the teenager in the story is facing a challenge. Point out the words dedication and work ethic in paragraph 7. Provide the following explanations:

- *Dedication* is time and effort a person puts towards a task.
- A *work ethic* is the importance a person places on working hard.

Explain that a person who is dedicated has a good *work ethic*. A dedicated person will show up on time and work very hard to makes sure to get their work done. Have volunteers discuss people they know who have *dedication* and a *good work ethic*. Supply sentence frames if necessary:

- I know _____ works very hard. He/She works as a _____. He/She has a good _____.
- When I grow up I want to work as a _____.

CULTURAL REFERENCES

The following words and phrases may be unfamiliar to students:

- *industrial area* (paragraph 2): a place where there are factories and warehouses but not residences; a place where things are made, usually not a place to live.
- *foot traffic* (paragraph 2): traffic: cars and trucks moving on roads; foot traffic is: people moving on paths, sidewalks, and other places.
- *follow in the footsteps* (paragraph 5): do something similar to someone you admire
- *dialed* (paragraph 10): called by phone

LISTENING

Understand Dialogue

Draw students' attention to the events in paragraphs 11-13. Point out the words that are spoken by Jourdan, his supervisor, and the police. Tell students to look for quotation marks to know when a person in a text is speaking.

Have students listen as you read aloud paragraphs 11–13. Use the following supports with students at varying proficiency levels:

- Tell students that you will ask questions about what you just read aloud. Ask questions about the dialogue. Accept one-word responses or gestures. For example, ask: *Who says "Is this some kind of trick?"* (Jourdan) **SUBSTANTIAL**
- Have students identify each person who is speaking the paragraphs. Ask: *Who is speaking in paragraph 11?* (Jourdan) *Who is speaking in paragraph 12?* (the officers, Cpl. Keffer) *Paragraph 13?* (Jourdan) **MODERATE**
- Place students in groups of three. Have them take turns reading the dialogue to each other. Have students take turns reading what Jourdan says, what the police say, and what Cpl. Keffer says. **LIGHT**

PLAN

SPEAKING

Discuss Events

Draw students' attention to the events that occur in paragraphs 11–13. Point out that action words tell the reader what is happening in an article.

Use the following supports with students at varying proficiency levels:

- Point out the clause *pulling the bicycle out from behind a car* in paragraph 11. Ask: *What action word tells what the police are doing.* (*pulling*) **SUBSTANTIAL**
- Have students identify the action words in paragraphs 11–13. Supply sentence frames to guide students' discussion of the events. *Jourdan's supervisor _____ him to go outside. The police _____ a bicycle out. Jourdan _____ he is bowled over by the gift.* **MODERATE**
- Have student pairs work together to summarize what happens in paragraphs 11–13. Students should ask and answer the following questions with a partner: *What does Jourdan's supervisor do? What do the police do? How does Jourdan respond?* **LIGHT**

READING

Discuss Time-Order Words

Draw students' attention to the time order and calendar words in paragraphs 5–6. The author has included these details so the reader will know when events took place.

Work with students to read paragraphs 5–6. Use the following supports with students at varying proficiency levels:

- Tell students that you will ask questions about what you just read aloud. For example, ask: *Does Jourdan's car break down* before *or* after *he graduates high school?* (*after*) **SUBSTANTIAL**
- Have students place the following events in the correct order: *Jourdan's car breaks down* (2), *Jourdan graduates high school* (1), *Jourdan starts to walk to work* (3) **MODERATE**
- Have students describe three events in the paragraph, using the words *first, next,* and *last*. For example, *First, Jourdan starts working at Pro-Form, Next; Jourdan's car breaks down; Last, he begins walking to work.* **LIGHT**

WRITING

Write a Summary

Draw students' attention to the section on summary writing on page 79. Review with them that a summary should include key details, be brief and in their own words, and not include any opinions.

Use the following supports with students at varying proficiency levels:

- Provide students with sample sentences for summarizing the article. Also provide a list of vocabulary and definitions to help them fill in the sentences: *Jourdan meets Cpl. Keffer on his* _____ (*walk*) *home. Cpl. Keffer think Jourdan is* _____ (*dedicated*) *and hard* _____ (*working*). *He and his friends buy Jourdan a* _____ (*bike*). *Jourdan does not have to* _____ (*walk*) *anymore.* **SUBSTANTIAL**
- Provide some sample sentence frames that students can use to craft their summaries: *The most important detail in paragraph 1 is* _____. *Jourdan is facing a* _____ *because he does not have a way to* _____. **MODERATE**
- Have pairs find at least one important event in each paragraph. Then, have them select the most important details and delete the others. Students should use their final list to write their summaries. **LIGHT**

TEACH

 Connect to the
ESSENTIAL QUESTION

The article "A Police Stop Changed This Teenager's Life" tells the true story of a young man who finds himself without transportation to get to his job. The article explores the exceptional way he rises up to meet the challenge, and the effect his strength of character has on those he meets along the way.

COMPARE ACROSS GENRES

Point out that "Police Stop" is an informational text, while "Thank You Ma'am" is a fictional story. Tell students to think about the common themes included in each story. Remind students that fiction is often based on real-life situations and circumstances. Ask: *How is the character of Mrs. Jones similar to the real life police officer Kirk Keffer? How is she different?* Have students compare and contrast Roger's character with Jourdan Duncan, as well as the events that occur in each text.

COLLABORATE & COMPARE

ARTICLE

A POLICE STOP CHANGED THIS TEENAGER'S LIFE

by **Amy B Wang**
pages 73–77

COMPARE ACROSS GENRES

Now that you've read "Thank You, M'am," read "A Police Stop Changed This Teenager's Life." Explore how this news article connects to the ideas in "Thank You, M'am." As you read, think about the similarities and differences between the teenager in the news article and the boy in "Thank You, M'am." After you are finished, you will collaborate with a small group on a final project that involves an analysis of both texts.

 ESSENTIAL QUESTION:

What helps people rise up to face difficulties?

SHORT STORY

THANK YOU, M'AM

by **Langston Hughes**
pages 61–65

70 Unit 1

A Police Stop Changed This Teenager's Life

QUICK START

Think about an everyday person in your school or community who reaches out to others in positive ways. Describe some examples of how this person helps others.

ANALYZE STRUCTURE

Every piece of writing has an organization, or a structure. An author will arrange ideas and information in ways that will help readers understand how they are related. Recognizing how a text is organized, or its **structural pattern,** makes the text easier to read and understand. One common structural pattern is chronological order.

Chronological order, or time order, is the arrangement of events in the order in which they occur. There are often clues to the order of events in a text. Look for:

- calendar dates, such as Wednesday, September 30, 2020
- clock time, such as *after 11 P.M.* and *around midnight*
- words and phrases that show time order, such as *at first, soon,* or *graveyard shift.*

You can use the sequence chain below to gather time order clues and track events in "A Police Stop Changed This Teenager's Life."

GENRE ELEMENTS: INFORMATIONAL TEXT
- reports on recent events
- presents the most important information first, followed by details
- remains brief and to the point

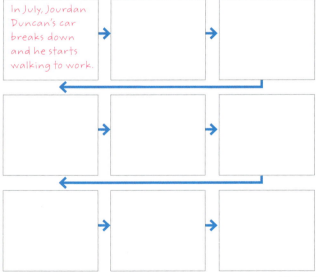

In July, Jourdan Duncan's car breaks down and he starts walking to work.

TEACH

QUICK START

Have students read the Quick Start question, and ask them to write the name of the person they've selected on a sheet of paper. Ask them to list at least three characteristics that describe the person they've selected. Call on students to list some of the characteristics they've written down. Discuss what traits people who help others in their community tend to have in common. Then have volunteers share the person they've selected with the class.

ANALYZE STRUCTURE

Tell students that the details that tell time order will help them better understand the pacing of events the article is describing. Point out the first event in the sequence chart is not revealed in the first paragraph, but later on in the article. Underlining important details and circling words that indicate time order are good ways to understand the correct sequence of events in an informational text.

Suggest that students use these questions to help them analyze understand when each event in the story occurred.

- *In what month and year did this event occur?*
- *Did this event happen before or after another event in the article?*
- *Is there a time order word or phrase in the sentence or sentences that is describing the event?*

ENGLISH LEARNER SUPPORT

Understand Sequence Provide students with a simple sequence of events graphic organizer. Title the boxes "First," "Next," and "Last." Guide students to understand the sequence words using gestures. Have partners of mixed proficiencies work together to complete the organizer for paragraph 1, including time-order words or dates that they see in the text. More fluent students should guide beginning students in locating the time words and writing them down. **ALL LEVELS**

TEACH

CRITICAL VOCABULARY

Encourage students to read all the sentences before deciding which word best completes each one. Remind them to look for context clues that match the precise meaning of each word.

Answers:
1. *meeting; complete*
2. *travel; consistent*
3. *conversation; trouble*
4. *give; symbol*

■ **English Learner Support**

Cognates Tell students that several of the Critical Vocabulary words have Spanish cognates: *encounter/ encuentro, absolute/absoluto, interaction/interación, donate/ donar.* **ALL LEVELS**

LANGUAGE CONVENTIONS

Point out that dialogue gets special punctuation; quotation marks show that a person or people are speaking. Explain that dialogue has beginning *and* end punctuation. Note that the example sentence has the dialogue tag "Keffer told" after the quotation ends, to show who is speaking. Writers often, but not always, include dialogue tags for clarity; sometimes who spoke can be inferred through context.

Point out the example sentence. Ask students to identify the speaker, and the speaker's exact words. (**Speaker:** *Keffer;* **Exact words:** *Usually in the industrial area, there's no foot traffic, so it was kind of weird to see someone walking around on foot.*)

 ANNOTATION MODEL

Remind students of the annotation ideas in Analyze Structure on page 71, which suggest underlining important details and circling words that signal how the text is organized. Point out that they may follow this suggestion or use their own system for marking up the selection in their write-in text. They may want to color-code their annotations by using highlighters. Their notes in the margin may include questions about ideas that are unclear or topics they want to learn more about.

 GET READY

CRITICAL VOCABULARY

absolute	interaction	encounter
burden	reliable	token
commute	donate	

To preview the Critical Vocabulary words, replace each boldface word with a different word or words that have the same meaning.

1. The (**encounter**) _____ between the walkers was a(n) (**absolute**) _____ surprise because it was early in the day.

2. The daily (**commute**) _____ to work or school requires (**reliable**) _____ and safe transportation.

3. An (**interaction**) _____ with another person can (**burden**) _____ you if that person is unfriendly.

4. Many families (**donate**) _____ their help in schools as a (**token**) _____ of gratitude for educating their children.

LANGUAGE CONVENTIONS

Conjunctive Adverbs In this lesson, you will learn how to use conjunctive adverbs in writing. With conjunctive adverbs, two independent clauses can be connected to form a sentence. Notice how the clauses are connected in this sentence about a person featured in "A Police Stop Changed This Teenager's Life."

Jourdan estimated his walk to work would be long one; therefore, he prepared himself.

ANNOTATION MODEL **NOTICE & NOTE**

As you read, mark up words and phrases that help you understand how the text is organized. In the model, you can see one reader's notes about "A Police Stop Changed This Teenager's Life."

> 1 As its name might suggest, Industrial Way is <u>not known for being pedestrian-friendly</u>. . . . So when Corporal Kirk Keffer of the Benicia Police Department spotted a lone, lanky teenager walking on Industrial Way during the <u>graveyard shift</u> a few Saturdays ago, he was curious. It was <u>after 11 P.M.</u> and <u>dark outside</u>, and the boy was just nearing the highway overpass.

These first details show why the policeman was surprised to see a teenager there.

The author describes the setting early on; it is late at night and dark. Is it safe?

BACKGROUND

Amy B Wang *has been reporting the news since 2009. She is a general assignment reporter at* The Washington Post. *During her career, she has covered economic development, aviation, education, state politics, breaking news, and human-interest stories.*

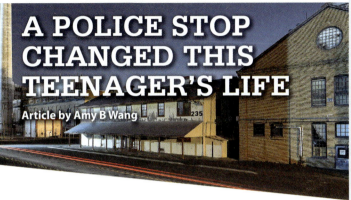

A POLICE STOP CHANGED THIS TEENAGER'S LIFE

Article by Amy B Wang

PREPARE TO COMPARE

As you read, notice how the author indicates the sequence of events and highlights the actions of the people involved in these events.

1   As its name might suggest, Industrial Way is not known for being pedestrian-friendly. The road in the Northern California city of Benicia is lined with trucking companies, warehouses and metal-finishing factories. As it curves north, before it turns into Channel Road, the street cuts under busy Interstate 680. So when Corporal Kirk Keffer of the Benicia Police Department spotted a lone, lanky teenager walking on Industrial Way during the graveyard shift a few Saturdays ago, he was curious. It was after 11 P.M. and dark outside, and the boy was just nearing the highway overpass.

2   "Usually in the industrial area, there's no foot traffic, so it was kind of weird to see someone walking around on foot," Keffer told *The Washington Post*. He stopped his patrol car, got out and called out to the pedestrian. Was he okay? What was he doing out there by himself?

NOTICE & NOTE

Notice & Note

Use the side margins to notice and note signposts in the text.

ANALYZE STRUCTURE

Annotate: Review the first paragraph and mark details that show when the events began.

Infer: What effect might the time of day have had on the actions of Corporal Kirk Keffer?

ANALYZE STRUCTURE

Annotate: In paragraph 2, mark how the author indicates what Keffer remembers seeing.

Analyze: How does including Keffer's memory help achieve the author's purpose? Why is it important to know what Keffer remembered?

TEACH

BACKGROUND

After students read the background note, explain that Amy B. Wang self-describes herself as a "fan of all kinds of storytelling" and that some journalists write about a wide range of topics. One kind is a human-interest story, which connects the reader to a person, people, or even animals in an emotional way.

PREPARE TO COMPARE

Direct students to use the Prepare to Compare prompt to focus their reading

ANALYZE STRUCTURE

Remind students to look for time-order words and phrases to determine when the events began. Tell them that sometimes an author will include time-order details to give the reader a clear picture of the events in their mind. Point out that the time of day and the place where the events take place make up the setting. (**Answer:** *Because it was so late at night, Cpl. Kirk Keffer was probably curious and concerned about why a young man was walking by himself in an isolated area.*)

ANALYZE STRUCTURE

Tell students that reporters often include details about the thoughts or words of the people they are interviewing to help the reader better understand the qualities of the real people they are reading about. (**Answer:** *The reason the author includes the details about what Keffer remembers is to show that the police officer was concerned about the young man's safety. It tells the reader he is the kind of person who cares about others.*)

ENGLISH LEARNER SUPPORT

Confirm Understanding Read aloud paragraphs 1-2 to students. Use gestures to show students what *foot traffic* is, and display a surprised expression to indicate that Keffer was surprised to see Jourdan Duncan walking. Ask questions to confirm their understanding, allowing students to provide one to two word or yes/no responses. For example, ask: *Who is walking?* (Jourdan Duncan) *Is it late at night or early in the morning?* (late at night) *Is Cpl. Keffer surprised to see Jourdan?* (yes) **SUBSTANTIAL/MODERATE**

TEACH

CONTRASTS AND CONTRADICTIONS

Explain to students that this signpost is often used to set up a **compare-and-contrast** pattern of organization. Here, the text compares Jourdan Duncan's behavior to what most other people would do. Have students identify how Keffer's response shows that he is surprised by Duncan's decision to walk to work. (**Answer:** *Keffer shows his surprise by asking a lot of questions. The author describes him as "agog." This shows that it is unlikely that most people would commute by walking so far every day.*)

ANALYZE STRUCTURE

Remind students that calendar dates, as well as time order words such as *first* and *soon* can help them understand the chronological order of events in the article. (**Answer:** *Duncan is telling Keffer about the events that led to his walking commute so Keffer will understand why Duncan is out walking in a surprising place so late at night. He wants Keffer to know that he is not doing anything that might get him into trouble.*)

CRITICAL VOCABULARY

absolute: A synonym for the way the author uses *absolutely* is *definitely*. *Absolute* has the same meaning, but is an adjective instead of an adverb.

ASK STUDENTS to use the word *absolute* in a sentence, and share their sentences with a partner. (**Possible responses:** *The article is the absolute truth. It is absolute proof that Jourdan has a good work ethic.*)

burden: In the article, *to burden* means "to inconvenience others."

ASK STUDENTS how Duncan Jourdan thinks he would be a burden to others by asking for rides. (*He thinks it would take up a lot of their time, and that wouldn't be fair to them.*)

commute: Most people commute to and from work or school each day. A commute can impact a person's quality of life in a positive or negative way.

ASK STUDENTS how a long commute can negatively impact someone's life. (*A long commute can mean that a person does not get to do other things or relax when they are not working.*)

74 Unit 1

 **NOTICE & NOTE**

CONTRASTS AND CONTRADICTIONS

Notice & Note: How is Duncan getting to and from work?

Infer: What does Keffer's surprise about Duncan's actions indicate what most people would do instead in a similar situation?

absolute
(ăb′sə-lo͞ot′) *adj.* Something that is without qualifications or exceptions is *absolute*.

ANALYZE STRUCTURE
Annotate: Review paragraphs 5–6. Mark words and phrases that show the sequence of events.

Infer: Why is Duncan telling Keffer about the events that led up to his walking to and from work?

burden
(bûr′dn) *v.* If you *burden* someone, you create a situation that is difficult or stressful for him or her.

commute
(kə-myo͞ot′) *n.* A *commute* is a person's travel to and from work or school.

74 Unit 1

3   The teenager, 18-year-old Jourdan Duncan, was equally startled at first. "I was **absolutely** nervous," he said. "I thought, okay, um, did I do anything wrong? Is he going to put me in cuffs? I didn't do anything bad." Duncan told Keffer he was walking back to his parents' home in Vallejo. He had just gotten off from his job, where the teen worked on the packaging line from 3 P.M. until around midnight.

4   "Vallejo? That's like seven miles away," Keffer said he remembered saying to Duncan. Soon, he had cleared out the passenger seat in his patrol car and offered Duncan a ride home. On the drive, Keffer asked the teen more questions. *Why Benicia? Why not drive to work?* He was agog[1] that anybody would walk more than two hours each way, every day.

5   Duncan explained that he had just graduated from Jesse Bethel High School the year before. He had gotten a job in May, and enjoyed being around his co-workers. He was saving money for college, he said—but really wanted to be an officer with the California Highway Patrol, to follow in the footsteps of some relatives who were in law enforcement.

6   When the timing belt and an engine valve on his 2001 Volvo broke in July, Duncan got a few rides from friends and co-workers, but soon decided he would try to walk to avoid **burdening** others. "I didn't want to always call somebody and be like, 'Hey, can you pick me up?'" he said. "That would have took a lot of people's time." Duncan never told his parents he started walking. ("They thought I was getting rides every day," he admits.) The first time he plotted out a walkable route on Google Maps, it spit out an estimated **commute** time of 2 hours and 15 minutes. "This is going to be a long walk," Duncan thought. On his first day going to work by foot, he didn't know

---
[1] **agog** (ə-gŏg′): full of surprise or astonishment.

what to expect. "The whole way there I just had my earphones in, kept quiet and I just power-walked[2] the whole way." That was in July. Gradually, the foot commute grew easier for him. "The walk now, it's not a problem for me," he said.

7 By the time Keffer pulled up to Duncan's parents' house that night—all of 15 minutes later, by car—the police officer was impressed. Most people won't even walk down to the store, he joked. "I was just like, wow, Jourdan, that's really impressive, your dedication and your hard work," Keffer said. "At age 18, that's a good work ethic to have, and I said, you know, I admire that. Just keep doing what you're doing."

8 They parted ways and Keffer returned to the police department in Benicia. Still, he couldn't get Duncan's commute out of his head. He mentioned his **interaction** to his shift supervisor, who, like Keffer, happened to be a board member of the Benicia Police Officers' Association. "So I hit him up and say, 'I just had this contact with this young man,'" Keffer said. "'He's walking five hours a day, and I think it should be rewarded. What if we help him out?'"

9 They e-mailed the rest of the board to seek approval to buy a bicycle. It was, he said, one of the fastest votes they've ever taken: Within an hour, enough board members wrote back in agreement. And so, the following day, Keffer visited a local bike shop. He was looking for a good mountain bike, Keffer explained to the owner. Something with a **reliable** gearing system that could handle Benicia's steep hills. The longtime shop owner, Greg Andrade, helped him pick out a $500 bicycle—and loved the teen's story so much that he also **donated** a lighting system, brake light and helmet.

10 The only matter left was how to surprise Duncan. Keffer looked up and dialed Duncan's company, asking for Duncan's

---

[2] **power-walk:** to walk quickly with a definite purpose.

NOTICE & NOTE

LANGUAGE CONVENTIONS
Annotate: Review paragraph 6 and mark *gradually*, which is acting as a conjunctive adverb.

Analyze: What does *gradually* show about how long it took for Jourdan's commute to get easier?

interaction
(ĭn′tər-ăk′shən) *n.* An *interaction* occurs when people speak or otherwise are in contact with one another.

reliable
(rĭ-lī′ə-bəl) *adj.* A person or object that can be trusted, or depended on, is *reliable*.

donate
(dō′nāt′) *v.* To *donate* is to give, or contribute, something to a person, cause, or fund.

APPLY

ENGLISH LEARNER SUPPORT

Confirm Understanding Use the following supports with students at varying proficiency levels:

Point out the phrase *within an hour* in paragraph 9. Use an analog clock to help students visualize how much time has passed. Ask: *Did the board members write back quickly or slowly?* (quickly) **SUBSTANTIAL**

Have students locate the time-order words in paragraph 9. Prompt them to state the order of events in the paragraph using words like *first, then,* and *next.* **MODERATE**

Ask students to list the most important events in paragraph 9. Then ask them to write the events out in a four-box sequence chart, using arrows to indicate chronological sequence. **LIGHT**

For **listening, speaking** and **reading support** for students at varying proficiency levels, see the **Text X-Ray** on pages 70C–70D.

CRITICAL VOCABULARY

interaction: When a person meets and talks to another person, the situation is often called an interaction.

ASK STUDENTS what interaction is Keffer is referring to when he talks to his supervisor. *(Keffer is referring to meeting Duncan and talking with him as he drives him home.)*

reliable: When an object is constructed well, it will not easily break, needs minimal repairs, and last a long time.

ASK STUDENTS why Keffer thinks it's important to give Duncan a *reliable* bike. *(He wants to make sure Jourdan has a safe and consistent way to get to work that won't cost him money.)*

donate: Giving money or items to those in need is a good way to contribute to society in a meaningful way.

ASK STUDENTS why Greg Andrade donates items he would usually sell to Duncan. *(He is impressed by Duncan's work ethic and knows his donation will go to a good cause.)*

WHEN STUDENTS STRUGGLE . . .

Make Inferences Model making inferences: Read paragraph 2 aloud. Reread the italicized text and offer *inferences* to explain why Corporal Keffer does not think that the teenager is walking home. Ask students to make inferences about the following questions: Why does Jourdan think the police might handcuff him? What are some reasons Keffer might have for believing Jourdan's story? What can the reader infer is the overall theme of the article?

For additional support, go to the **Reading Studio** and assign the following Level Up tutorial: **Making Inferences.**

TEACH

✏️ ANALYZE STRUCTURE

Remind students that quotation marks are used to indicate the exact words someone says. However, people don't always remember exactly what they said in conversations that happened in the past. **(Answer:** *The lack of quotation marks and italics shows that the text is not a direct quote, but it is a description by Keller of what he said to Duncan's boss.)*

🔵 ENGLISH LEARNER SUPPORT

Understand Language Structures Explain that in English, the text that tells exactly what someone says is shown in quotation marks, instead of dashes or brackets.

ASK STUDENTS to locate the quotations in paragraph 12. *("We would like to acknowledge your hard work and dedication for what you do and setting the example for kids your age . . . Hopefully this'll make your trip easier.")*
MODERATE

▸ CONTRASTS AND CONTRADICTIONS

Remind students that this signpost is often used to set up a **compare-and-contrast** pattern of organization. How does the author show that Duncan is different? **(Answer:** *Keller goes out of his way to help Duncan, and tells Duncan that his hard work and dedication is impressive.)*

CRITICAL VOCABULARY

encounter: The short, unexpected meeting between Keffer and Duncan has a special impact on both men.

ASK STUDENTS How does the first encounter between Keffer and Duncan lead to a second one? *(Keffer is so impressed with Duncan that he seeks him out again.)*

token: The bike is a gift that represents how much the police respect and admire the positive example Duncan sets for others his age.

ASK STUDENTS Why do people give gifts when they're not expected? *(to reward them, show gratitude, respect, love, or loyalty)*

76   Unit 1

✏️ NOTICE & NOTE

encounter
(ĕn-koun′tər) *n.* An *encounter* is a short meeting that is unplanned or unexpected.

ANALYZE STRUCTURE

Annotate: In paragraph 10, mark the words that Keffer says to Duncan's boss.

Analyze: What does the lack of quotation marks around Keffer's words indicate?

token
(tō′kən) *n.* A *token* serves as an expression or a sign of something else.

▸ CONTRASTS AND CONTRADICTIONS

Notice & Note: What is Duncan's reaction to the attention of the police, and what philosophy does he have about his walking commute?

Infer: What do Keffer's actions show about how Duncan differs from other teenagers Keffer encounters?

---

boss. Then, he explained their **encounter** the night before. *Was Jourdan scheduled to work Monday? Would they mind if a few officers stopped by the warehouse to surprise him with something?*

11   That Monday night, September 19, Duncan's supervisor called him out and told him to go outside. Some policemen were waiting for him. Once again, Duncan was taken aback. His boss assured him he was not in trouble. Outside, he spotted Keffer, along with some other Benicia police officers. "We have something for you," he said they told him, pulling the bicycle out from behind a car. "'This is your bike' . . . I was like, wait, what? Is this some kind of trick?"

12   The bike was a **token** of their gratitude, the officers said. "We would like to acknowledge your hard work and dedication for what you do and setting the example for kids your age," Keffer said they told him. "Hopefully this'll make your trip easier."

13   Duncan said he was bowled over by the gift, but also stymied by the attention. Several local news stations wanted him on their shows. Normally reserved, he shyly agreed to talk to all of them—"I was so nervous; I've never been on TV"—but couldn't help but think: They want to interview me for *walking?* "The walk isn't hard," he said. "It's like a challenge. To me, it was like a challenge to see if I was willing to do whatever it takes to get to work."

14   Keffer said that was precisely what moved him to do something for Duncan. And Duncan said the bicycle has made him "feel more at ease" with his commute, which has now been cut down to an hour. Duncan said he and Keffer are keeping in

76   Unit 1

touch, and that *Keffer has offered to take him on a ride-along³ so he can get a better idea of what being a police officer is all about.* "It's something I've been interested in since high school. A lot of my family members, they're in law enforcement," Duncan said. "It's like, what they do and, due to a lot of people thinking that there are bad cops out there, I want to prove that all cops aren't bad—which is true, due to what just happened to me."

---

³ **ride-along:** to accompany a professional, such as a police officer, on a ride in their vehicle to experience how the person works.

NOTICE & NOTE

ANALYZE STRUCTURE
Annotate: Review paragraphs 12–14. Mark words and phrases that express the actions of the police.

Infer: What does the quote from Duncan in the concluding paragraph indicate about the author's purpose in writing the article?

CHECK YOUR UNDERSTANDING

Answer these questions before moving on to the **Analyze the Text** section on the following page.

1. How does the author's organization of the news story contribute to the author's purpose?
   - A It entertains readers with details of events.
   - B It informs readers of the sequence of events.
   - C It persuades readers that Duncan needs a bike.
   - D It allows readers to draw conclusions about events.

2. In paragraph 3, Jourdan Duncan has just gotten off his job and is nervous about being stopped because —
   - F he knows there is a curfew for teenagers in Benicia
   - G his parents told him not to walk home from work
   - H he isn't sure what the policeman wants
   - J his friends didn't pick him up on time

3. Based on the details in paragraphs 7–8 and 12, which statement best expresses Corporal Keffer's opinion about Jourdan's situation?
   - A Corporal Keffer thinks that Jourdan should be getting rides.
   - B Corporal Keffer thinks that all teenagers should work at night.
   - C Corporal Keffer thinks the police should patrol the industrial area more often.
   - D Corporal Keffer thinks that keeping commitments and working hard can help someone succeed.

TEACH

ANALYZE STRUCTURE

Tell students that they should look for important details about the police department's actions in paragraphs 12–14. Then ask: *Why do the police do all these things for Duncan? How does he feel about it? Do these actions explain why Duncan feels the way he does about the police?* (Answer: *The author wants readers to understand that there are positive relations between community members and their police officers.*)

CHECK YOUR UNDERSTANDING

Have students answer the questions independently.

Answers:
1. B
2. H
3. D

If they answer any questions incorrectly, have them reread the text to confirm their understanding. Then they may proceed to ANALYZE THE TEXT on page 78.

ENGLISH LEARNER SUPPORT

Oral Assessment Use the following questions to assess students' comprehension and speaking skills:

1. Why does the author use time-order words and calendar dates in the article? *(to show the order of events that happened)*

2. Does Jourdan think he is in trouble when he is stopped? *(He does not know.)* Does this make him feel nervous? *(yes)*

3. What is the last thing Cpl. Keffer says in paragraph 8? Does this mean he wants to help Jourdan? *(He says he thinks Jourdan should be rewarded for walking so much. He wants to help him.)*
   SUBSTANTIAL/MODERATE

APPLY

ANALYZE THE TEXT
Possible answers:

1. **DOK 1:** *In paragraph 6, Jourdan Duncan says that he hadn't told his parents that he was walking and that they thought he was getting rides to work. This shows that they would have been concerned to know he was walking long distances at night.*

2. **DOK 3:** *The author uses words such as after in paragraph 1 or first in paragraphs 3 and 6, different type faces, as in paragraphs 2, 4, 10, 14, and verb tenses to show the sequence of events and indicate when the people are remembering something that happened in the past.*

3. **DOK 2:** *A negative effect was that Duncan no longer had a way to get to work, something he solved by starting to walk. A positive effect is that through his walking he met and impressed a large number of people.*

4. **DOK 4:** *It seems likely that he will reach his goal because he showed that he is determined to succeed even though things might be difficult. In addition, he made contacts within the police force who might be able to help him achieve his goal.*

5. **DOK 4:** *Cpl. Keffer is surprised to see Duncan walking on his own late at night. Keffer is surprised again to find out why Duncan is walking and what a great work ethic he has. Another surprise is that the police department raises money to buy Jourdan a bike and brought it to him at his job. It surprised me the most that so many people wanted to help Duncan, even though they'd never met him.*

RESEARCH

Remind students they should confirm any information they find by checking multiple websites and assessing the credibility of each one.

Connect Encourage students to research Jourdan Duncan's story further. Cpl. Keffer's funding for Duncan started with people he knew personally. The online crowdfunding efforts followed the initial funds raised by the police association. People who didn't know Keffer or Duncan donated money online. Enough funds were raised for Duncan to purchase a new car and to pay for his continued education.

78 Unit 1

RESPOND

ANALYZE THE TEXT
Support your responses with evidence from the text. NOTEBOOK

1. **Identify** What details does the author provide to show that Jourdan Duncan and his parents have a caring relationship?

2. **Cite Evidence** How does the structure of the news story help inform the reader about the sequence of events? Cite details from the text that support your answer.

3. **Cause/Effect** What positive and negative effects resulted after the timing belt and engine valve broke on Jourdan's car?

4. **Connect** What parts of the news story point to Jourdan Duncan achieving his goal of working in law enforcement?

5. **Notice & Note** Review the many surprises that took place in this news story. Which one most surprised you, and why?

RESEARCH

Crowdfunding is an online fundraising method in which people seek contributions from a huge pool of donors. Crowdfunding sites typically allow people to propose ideas for new businesses or for social-service projects. Visitors to a crowdfunding site review the proposals and can support them by contributing money. Sometimes people seeking funds also promise to give goods or services to any donors. Search the Internet to find case studies, or examples, of people and organizations that have received support through crowdfunding. Record notes about two case studies in the chart.

CROWDFUNDING	
Example 1	Example 2

RESEARCH TIP
Because the information on the Internet is not always verified for accuracy by website creators, a search on a general topic such as *crowdfunding* may produce results that are too broad or unreliable. Look for independent sites, not advertised ones, that list the top crowdfunding sites. These sites describe the major, legitimate crowdfunding sites and provide links to those sites for information about projects they funded and guidelines for seeking funding of new projects.

Connect Paragraphs 8–9 of the news story describe how Corporal Keffer gets funding to buy Jourdan a new bike for his commute. With a small group, discuss how the process Keffer uses to raise money is similar to and different from crowdfunding a project.

78 Unit 1

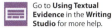 **RESPOND**

CREATE AND DISCUSS

Write an Objective Summary A summary is a brief retelling, in your own words, of the main ideas and key supporting details of a text. When you summarize, you should be objective, or unbiased, and not include your own opinions or judgments about the text.

❏ Start by reviewing the news article. Mark main ideas and key supporting details in each paragraph.
❏ Summarize the news article by briefly restating in your own words the main ideas and key details you noted. Add a sentence to sum up the controlling idea of the news article.

Share and Discuss Opinions A human-interest story is a news article that focuses on a person or people. This type of article is intended to bring out an emotional response from readers. Review your notes and think about your response to "A Police Stop Changed This Teenager's Life."

❏ In a small group, share your opinions about the news article. What makes it an example of a human-interest story?
❏ Make sure to provide examples from the news article to support your opinions. In addition, listen to others' ideas and respond with appropriate register and tone to their opinions.

 Go to **Using Textual Evidence** in the **Writing Studio** for more help.

 Go to **Participating in Collaborative Discussions** in the **Speaking and Listening Studio** to learn more.

RESPOND TO THE ESSENTIAL QUESTION

 What helps people rise up to face difficulties?

Gather Information Review your annotations and notes on "A Police Stop Changed This Teenager's Life." Then, add details to your Response Log. Think about:

- how people show determination
- why people are surprised by others' actions
- what people can do to help each other succeed

At the end of the unit, use your notes to write an informational essay.

ACADEMIC VOCABULARY
As you write and discuss what you learned from the news article, be sure to use the Academic Vocabulary words. Check off each of the words that you use.

❏ aspect
❏ cultural
❏ evaluate
❏ resource
❏ text

APPLY

CREATE AND DISCUSS

Write an Objective Summary Tell students to use *who, what, when, where, why* and *how* questions to help them identify the most important details to include in their summary. Remind them that their summaries should be brief and in their own words. Remind them to keep opinions out of the Objective Summary, for example "unlike most lazy teens, Jourdan was a hard worker."

 For **writing support** for students at varying proficiency levels, see the **Text X-Ray** on page 70D.

Share and Discuss Opinions Tell students to consider details from the article as they form their opinions; they will need to support their opinions with details when sharing them with the group. Remind them that an emotional response may be related to the surprises, the unexpected events in the article. Encourage students to take turns and to listen to their peers respectfully as the group discusses the article.

RESPOND TO THE ESSENTIAL QUESTION

Allow time for students to add details from "A Police Stop Changed This Teenager's Life" to their Unit 1 Response Logs.

ENGLISH LEARNER SUPPORT

Share and Discuss Opinions Restate the discussion prompt as a question: *What emotions does the article "A Police Stop Changed This Teenager's Life" make you feel?* Allow students to work with partners to list feelings they had as they read and to review the text for details that support their answers. Provide these sentence frames to help them formulate their ideas for the discussion: *The article made me feel ___. The article says that the police ___ Jourdan get a bike. This was a ___ thing to do.* **SUBSTANTIAL/MODERATE**

APPLY

CRITICAL VOCABULARY

Answers:

1. d. quarrel
2. c. keep
3. a. ease
4. d. stop
5. c. evasion
6. d. untrustworthy
7. c. unimportant
8. c. limited

VOCABULARY STRATEGY:
Context Clues

Answers:

1. *nervous means "troubled or anxious"*
2. *plot means to "map or plan"*
3. *stymied means "confused or surprised"*

 RESPOND

WORD BANK
- absolute
- burden
- commute
- interaction
- reliable
- donate
- encounter
- token

CRITICAL VOCABULARY

Practice and Apply For each item, mark the letter of the word that differs most in meaning from the other words.

1. a. interaction   b. discussion   c. conversation   d. quarrel
2. a. give   b. contribute   c. keep   d. donate
3. a. ease   b. burden   c. encumber   d. hamper
4. a. commute   b. travel   c. journey   d. stop
5. a. meeting   b. encounter   c. evasion   d. interview
6. a. reliable   b. quality   c. dependable   d. untrustworthy
7. a. sign   b. proof   c. unimportant   d. token
8. a. complete   b. absolute   c. limited   d. pure

Go to the **Vocabulary Studio** for more on context clues.

VOCABULARY STRATEGY: Context Clues

When you encounter an unfamiliar word, examine its **context**—or the surrounding words, phrases, or sentences—for clues to its meaning. Look at the following example from the news article:

> Industrial Way is not known for being *pedestrian-friendly*. The road . . . is lined with trucking companies, warehouses and metal-finishing factories. . . . So when Corporal Kirk Keffer of the Benicia Police Department spotted a lone, lanky teenager walking on Industrial Way . . . he was curious. . . .

The writer has included **contrast clues** to help readers understand the term *pedestrian-friendly*. This type of context clue occurs when a term is contrasted with something familiar. In this case, "trucking companies, warehouses and metal finishing factories" contrasts with something friendly. The context clue "walking" also helps readers understand that *pedestrian-friendly* means "welcoming for walkers."

Practice and Apply Use contrast clues in each sentence to figure out the boldfaced word's meaning. Write its definition below the sentence.

1. Unlike the calm officer, Jourdan was **anxious** when he was stopped.
   _____

2. Although Jourdan was uncertain how to get to work, he was able to **plot** out a walking route.
   _____

3. Instead of being overjoyed, Jourdan was **stymied** by the attention.
   _____

80   Unit 1

 ENGLISH LEARNER SUPPORT

Vocabulary Strategy Give students additional practice in determining the meanings of unfamiliar words and phrases. Write the following words on the board with their locations in the text: *warehouses, graveyard shift, avoid, approval, taken aback*. Have pairs of students at different proficiency levels work together to use context clues to determine meaning. Have them confirm their definitions by looking up each word in a dictionary. Have pairs use at least two of the words in oral sentences of their own construction. Have Advanced High students focus on using the words in written sentences of their own. **ALL LEVELS**

LANGUAGE CONVENTIONS: Conjunctive Adverbs

Writers rely on conjunctions to link ideas smoothly. A **conjunctive adverb** can connect two independent clauses, in effect, to combine two sentences into one. It can also link ideas in two sentences.

Here is a list of some commonly used conjunctive adverbs by type. Notice that some consist of more than one word.

Comparison	similarly, besides, alternatively
Contrast	by contrast, nevertheless, instead, otherwise
Examples	for example, specifically, for instance, namely
Result	therefore, consequently, thus, so
Time	meanwhile, then, now, at last, gradually

When a conjunctive adverb joins two independent clauses, it functions as a coordinating conjunction. In this case, a semicolon must be used before the conjunction, as in this example about "A Police Stop Changed This Teenager's Life." A comma should follow the conjunctive adverb.

> Corporal Keffer couldn't stop thinking of Jourdan's tough commute; consequently, he took action.

A conjunctive adverb can also link ideas in two sentences. Again, a comma always follows the conjunctive adverb.

> Jourdan's car had broken down. Nevertheless, he was determined to get to work.

Practice and Apply Combine the two sentences in each item using a conjunctive adverb from the list.

1. Jourdan didn't want to burden others to give him rides. He walked to work.
2. Jourdan worked on a packaging line. He planned for a career in law enforcement.
3. Corporal Keffer was impressed with Jourdan's personal qualities. He liked his work ethic.
4. The officer phoned Jourdan's company. He learned details about Jourdan's work schedule.

RESPOND

Go to **Conjunctions and Interjections** in the **Grammar Studio** for more.

APPLY

LANGUAGE CONVENTIONS: Conjunctive Adverbs

Review the information about conjunctive adverbs marks with students. Explain that one reason authors use conjunctive adverbs to link independent clauses is to vary sentences in a text for stylistic effect. Another reason is to emphasize the relationship of two separate ideas. Direct students' attention to the list of conjunctive adverbs on page 81. Tell students that in addition to these words, they should pay attention to the punctuation in a sentence when identifying conjunctive adverbs. Remind students that a complete clause can stand alone as a complete sentence. Explain that semicolons are only used to link complete clauses, while commas can be used to link various clauses.

Provide students with examples sentences and have volunteers connect the ideas using conjunctive adverbs.

- The blizzard created perfect packing snow. It was perfect for snowball fight. *(The blizzard created perfect packing snow; therefore, it was perfect for snowball fight.)*
- Ava studied all night for her algebra test. Anthony stayed up late watching television. *(Ava studied all night for her algebra test; meanwhile Anthony stayed up late watching television.)*
- The Grey Wolf Soccer team practiced harder than ay other team in the league. The team won the championship. *(The Grey Wolf Soccer team practiced harder than ay other team in the league; consequently, they won the championship.)*
- Some of the tallest building in the world are in New York City. The Freedom Tower is 1,792 feet tall. *(Some of the tallest building in the world are in New York City; for example, the Freedom Tower is 1,792 feet tall.)*

Practice and Apply Have partners discuss whether conjunctive adverbs are used correctly to link their sentences. *(Students' sentences will vary.)*

ENGLISH LEARNER SUPPORT

Language Conventions Use the following supports with students at varying proficiency levels:

- Have students find other examples of conjunctive adverbs in the article and copy them into their notebooks. **SUBSTANTIAL**
- Have students work with partners to write a sentence using a conjunctive adverb from the list on page 81. Then have them meet with another pair to check they have used conjunctive adverbs correctly. **MODERATE**
- Ask students to write a sentence using conjunctive adverbs independently. Then have them check their work with a partner. **LIGHT**

APPLY

COMPARE CHARACTERS AND PEOPLE

Before students begin their charts, point out that they are comparing not only what they have learned in the two texts, but also how similar information is presented in each genre. How does "Thank You, M'am" present character motivations and internal and external conflicts? How does "A Police Stop Changed This Teenager's Life" convey similar concepts, or how does it add to the ideas covered in the short story?

ANALYZE THE TEXTS

Possible answers:

1. **DOK 4** *Mrs. Jones and Cpl. Keffer care about people and try to help them. Although the circumstances differ, they both give the boys encouragement.*

2. **DOK 3** *Roger is wild and willing to steal to get what he wants, while Jourdan is hardworking and willing to challenge himself. Both boys are shy and seem to be looking for ways to achieve something better. Jourdan wants to be in law enforcement. Roger doesn't know what he wants, but his interaction with Mrs. Jones has made him thoughtful about how he should behave.*

3. **DOK 2** *Jourdan feels grateful and surprised at the attention he receives. Roger would probably have wanted to say that he was grateful that Mrs. Jones had helped him. He might have hoped to see her again.*

4. **DOK 4 Possible answer:** *Even small acts of kindness can make a difference in another person's life. Doing these kinds of things not only helps the person, but makes society better.*

 RESPOND

Collaborate & Compare

THANK YOU, M'AM
Short Story by Langston Hughes

A POLICE STOP CHANGED THIS TEENAGER'S LIFE
Article by Amy B Wang

COMPARE CHARACTERS AND PEOPLE

Comparing texts from different genres—such as an article and a short story—can lead to revelations about how characters and people are similar and different in what motivates them. The author may provide a direct motivation, or reason, for a character's actions, or the author may imply the character's motivation.

With a partner, complete the chart with information about the traits and motivations of the characters and people in the texts. Then use your notes to discuss similarities and differences in how Mrs. Jones supports Roger and how Corporal Keffer supports Jourdan.

Character/Person	Traits/Motivations	Textual Evidence
Mrs. Jones	*Strong both physically and mentally, kind, caring*	*"large women" "shook him until his teeth rattled" "Then it will get washed"*
Roger	*Lonely, shy, in need of care, frightened*	*"frail and willow-wild" "You gonna take me to jail?"*
Corporal Keffer	*Strong and caring, willing to go out of his way to help*	*"he was curious" "Was he okay? What was he doing out there by himself?"*
Jourdan Duncan	*Determined and hardworking, shy*	*"The walk now, it's not a problem for me" "Normally reserved, he shyly agreed"*

ANALYZE THE TEXTS

Discuss these questions in your group.

1. **Connect** What similarities do you see between the actions of Mrs. Jones in the short story and Corporal Keffer in the article?

2. **Compare** Consider how Roger and Jourdan each solve problems. How are they alike and how do they differ in solving problems?

3. **Infer** Based on what Jourdan said at the end of the article, what else might Roger have said at the end of the short story?

4. **Synthesize** What have you learned from these texts about how people can take positive action to make their own lives and the lives of others better?

82 Unit 1

 ENGLISH LEARNER SUPPORT

Ask Questions Use the following questions to help students compare the selections.

1. What qualities do Mrs. Jones and Cpl. Keffer share? (*They both care about the teenagers they meet.*)

2. How do you think Roger's and Jourdan's lives differ? (**Possible response:** *Roger may not have a family that cares about him, while Jourdan probably does.*)

3. What do you think each teenager probably learned from his experience? (**Possible answer:** *Roger probably learned that adults can be both understanding and firm; Jourdan probably learned that adults notice and support hard work.*) **MODERATE/LIGHT**

RESEARCH AND SHARE

Now, your group can continue exploring the idea of taking positive action to help others presented in both texts by researching an organization that supports young people in your community and then writing a news bulletin about it. Follow these steps:

1. **Brainstorm Organizations** In your group, share ideas about local organizations that help young children or students. Some examples might be a public library, parks and recreation department, and teen or community center. Brainstorm and list these organizations and then choose several to research.

2. **Research the Organizations** Decide which group member will research each organization. Since these are community organizations, sources might include the organization's own **website** for information about its mission or goals and how it operates. Other sources may include local **newspapers.**

You can use a **5Ws and H Chart** to record information about each organization you research. Then use the chart as a framework for synthesizing your information into a news bulletin.

What is the organization's mission, or key goals?
Who is involved with the organization?
Why is the organization supporting young people?
When did the organization start its work with young people?
Where is the organization located?
How does the organization support young people?

3. **Share What You Learn** Everyone in your group is now an expert on an organization. Listen carefully as group members present their news bulletins. Ask questions to request and clarify information, and build on each other's ideas when you discuss how these organizations help young people in your community.

RESPOND

Go to **Conducting Research** in the **Writing Studio** to learn more.

RESEARCH TIP

To find reliable sources, begin by searching for specific organizations in your community. You may also learn more about these organizations by interviewing people at your school who know or are affiliated with the organization.

Collaborate & Compare   83

APPLY

RESEARCH AND SHARE

Explain that the student groups will have to listen carefully to the results of each other's brainstorming in order to decide which organization to research. Model using the 5Ws chart so students who need it will have a template to work from. Explain the thinking process and logic behind every answer. Explain any unfamiliar vocabulary in the chart.

Brainstorm Organizations Circulate among the student groups, making suggestions or adjustments where needed. The groups chosen should be civic or humanitarian organizations, not clubs or sports teams. Allow students to brainstorm, but if groups cannot settle on a choice, pick one from their list for them.

Research the Organizations The Internet is an obvious tool for researching organizations. However, not every classroom has multiple computers for all students to do research. Other options for research include newspapers, telephone calls, in-person interviews, personal experience, and library books. If the teacher has had experience working at such an organization, offer that information to groups. Ensure that each group fills in the graphic organizer clearly and that all members understand the *what, who, why, when, where,* and *how* of the chosen organization.

Share What You Learn Continue to circulate and ensure that students carefully listen to one another as they present new information. Encourage students to ask questions and even get involved with the various organizations outside of class.

WHEN STUDENTS STRUGGLE . . .

Comparing Texts Some students may have difficulty comparing and contrasting texts written in different genres. To help these students, remind them that even texts written in different genres (in this case fiction text and informative text) can have similar themes, or messages. Suggest that students focus first on how the two texts are alike, and then examine how they differ. Students might ask themselves:

- How are the themes—or messages about life—of these two texts alike? (**Possible answer:** *They both emphasize the importance of kindness.*)
- How are the endings—or resolutions of the conflicts—in these two texts alike? (**Possible answer:** *Both Roger and Jourdan, because of the kindness of strangers, have their problems solved.*)
- How are Roger's and Jourdan's problems different? (**Possible answer:** *Roger's problem is avoiding arrest; Jourdan's problem is finding an easier way to get to work.*)

INDEPENDENT READING

READER'S CHOICE

Setting a Purpose Have students review their Unit 1 Response Log and think about what they've already learned about overcoming difficulties. As they select their Independent Reading titles, encourage them to consider what more they want to know.

NOTICE NOTE

Explain that some selections may contain multiple signposts; others may contain only one. Close reading rewards the search for signposts, which are sometimes subtle.

LEARNING MINDSET

Setting Goals Encourage students to use graphic organizers to track their progress by breaking down their overall goals into smaller goals. Show them how to spread out their work for greater efficiency. Tell them to encourage themselves after each small goal is met.

 INDEPENDENT READING

 ESSENTIAL QUESTION:

What helps people rise up to face difficulties?

Reader's Choice

Setting a Purpose Select one or more of these options from your eBook to continue your exploration of the Essential Question.
- Read the descriptions to see which text grabs your interest.
- Think about which genres you enjoy reading.

Notice & Note

In this unit, you practiced noticing and noting three signposts: **Memory Moment, Again and Again,** and **Aha Moment.** As you read independently, these signposts and others will aid your understanding. Below are the anchor questions to ask when you read literature and nonfiction.

Reading Literature: Stories, Poems, and Plays		
Signpost	Anchor Question	Lesson
Contrasts and Contradictions	Why did the character act that way?	p. 99
Aha Moment	How might this change things?	p. 3
Tough Questions	What does this make me wonder about?	p. 362
Words of the Wiser	What's the lesson for the character?	p. 363
Again and Again	Why might the author keep bringing this up?	p. 3
Memory Moment	Why is this memory important?	p. 2

Reading Nonfiction: Essays, Articles, and Arguments		
Signpost	Anchor Question(s)	Lesson
Big Questions	What surprised me? What did the author think I already knew? What challenged, changed, or confirmed what I already knew?	p. 265 p. 183 p. 437
Contrasts and Contradictions	What is the difference, and why does it matter?	p. 183
Extreme or Absolute Language	Why did the author use this language?	p. 182
Numbers and Stats	Why did the author use these numbers or amounts?	p. 264
Quoted Words	Why was this person quoted or cited, and what did this add?	p. 437
Word Gaps	Do I know this word from someplace else? Does it seem like technical talk for this topic? Do clues in the sentence help me understand the word?	p. 265

 ENGLISH LEARNER SUPPORT

Develop Vocabulary Review key terms from Unit 1 for comprehension and correct usage.

- Recite key unit vocabulary words such as *obstacle, challenge,* and *overcome* and then have students repeat them back to you. Display the words and direct students to write them in their notebooks. Point out Spanish cognates or synonyms: *obstáculo; dificultad; triunfo.* **SUBSTANTIAL**

- Ask students to write basic sentences using key unit vocabulary words. Ask partners to exchange papers and review sentences for correct usage. **MODERATE**

- Ask students to write paragraphs using key unit vocabulary. Challenge them to use synonyms for each word where applicable. (*barrier; difficulty; triumph*) **LIGHT**

INDEPENDENT READING

You can preview these texts in Unit 1 of your eBook.

Then, check off the text or texts that you select to read on your own.

LEGEND

from **Young Arthur**
Robert D. San Souci

Find out what obstacles King Arthur overcame in his youth to become king.

MYTH

Perseus and the Gorgon's Head
Ann Turnbull

Perseus faces unimaginable and mysterious dangers as he embarks on a unique quest.

POEM

It Couldn't Be Done
Edgar Albert Guest

What would you do if someone said you couldn't do something?

POEM

Chemistry 101
Marilyn Nelson

Discover the wonders of learning through the eyes of a teacher.

Collaborate and Share With a partner, discuss what you learned from at least one of your independent readings.

- Give a brief synopsis or summary of the text.
- Describe any signposts that you noticed in the text and explain what they revealed to you.
- Describe what you most enjoyed or found most challenging about the text. Give specific examples.
- Decide if you would recommend the text to others. Why or why not?

Go to the **Reading Studio** for more resources on **Notice & Note**.

Independent Reading

INDEPENDENT READING

MATCHING STUDENTS TO TEXTS

Use the following information to guide students in choosing their texts.

Chemistry 101
  Genre: poem
  Overall Rating: Accessible

It Couldn't Be Done
  Genre: Poem
  Overall Rating: Challenging

from **Young Arthur**   Lexile: 830L
  Genre: Legend
  Overall Rating: Accessible

Perseus and the Gorgon's Head   Lexile: 890L
  Genre: Myth
  Overall Rating: Accessible/Challenging

Collaborate and Share To assess how well students read the selections, walk around the room and listen to their conversations. Encourage students to be focused and specific in their comments.

Ed for Assessment

- Independent Reading Selection Tests

Encourage students to visit the **Reading Studio** to download a handy bookmark of **NOTICE & NOTE** signposts.

WHEN STUDENT STRUGGLE...

Keep a Reading Log As students read their selected texts, have them keep a reading log for each selection to note signposts and their thoughts about them. Use their logs to assess how well they are noticing and reflecting on elements of the texts.

Reading Log for (title)		
Location	Signpost I Noticed	My Notes about It

Independent Reading

PLAN

UNIT 1 Tasks

- **WRITE AN INFORMATIONAL ESSAY**
- **PRESENT A FILM CRITIQUE**

MENTOR TEXT
WOMEN IN AVIATION
Informational Text by PATRICIA and FREDRICK McKISSACK

LEARNING OBJECTIVES

Writing Task
- Write an informational essay about overcoming obstacles.
- Employ and practice skills for planning, preparing, and organizing text.
- Use the Mentor Text as a model for style and structure.
- Revise drafts, incorporating feedback from peers.
- Edit drafts for consistent verb tenses.
- Use a rubric to evaluate writing.
- Apply skills developed crafting informational essays to write a film critique.
- Publish writing to share it with an audience.
- **Language** Write with and revise connecting words.

Speaking Task
- Present a film critique to an audience.
- Practice presentation skills in less structured settings.
- Use appropriate verbal and nonverbal techniques.
- Listen actively to a presentation.
- **Language** Share information using the sentence stem *She proved them wrong when* _____ .

RESOURCES

- Writing Studio: Writing Informative Texts
- Writing Studio: Writing Informative Texts: Developing a Topic
- Writing Studio: Writing Informative Texts: Organizing Ideas
- Writing Studio: Writing Informative Texts: Introductions and Conclusions
- Speaking and Listening Studio: Giving a Presentation
- Grammar Studio: Module 9: Using Verbs Correctly

PLAN

Language X-Ray: English Learner Support

Use the instruction below and the supports and scaffolds in the Teacher's Edition to help you guide students of different proficiency levels.

INTRODUCE THE WRITING TASK

Explain that an informational essay is a type of writing that presents or explains information about a topic. Point out that the word *informative* is related to the Spanish adjective *informativo*, which means "providing information." Most news articles, how-to features, and factual human interest stories would be considered informational essays.

Remind students that the selections in this unit deal with overcoming difficulties. Work with students to select a subject that illustrates the qualities needed for triumphing over an obstacle and achieving a goal. Remind students that some obstacles can be overcome with the right attitude. Use sentence frames to help them articulate their ideas. _____ overcame difficulties by _____. Brainstorm words and phrases related to the topic and write them on the board. Then have students write a sentence about individual struggle and triumph against adversity. Tell students to use their sentences to begin their essays.

WRITING

Use Connecting Words

Tell students that one way to connect ideas in their essays is to combine related points or ideas with a connecting word, such as *and, but, next,* or *finally*.

- Work individually with students on connecting words and phrases. Ask them to define such terms as *and* or *but* and to write down other connecting words they might know. **SUBSTANTIAL**
- Use sentence frames to help students practice using connecting words. For example: *She became an astronaut in 2013, _____ it took years of hard work.* **MODERATE**
- After students have completed their drafts, have partners exchange papers and suggest places where a connecting word or phrase should be inserted, or could be improved upon. Encourage partners to suggest alternative connecting words or phrases. **LIGHT**

SPEAKING

Present Information

Tell students that public speaking is a challenge for almost everyone. Congratulate them for their courage, and encourage them to be supportive of one another for an honest effort.

- Provide students with a sample sentence such as *I learn new words every day*. Ask them to repeat the sentence and expand on it with a follow-up statement, as if speaking to a group. Encourage them to use a new word in their next statement. **SUBSTANTIAL**
- Offer students the sentence stem *She learned to rock climb although _____.* Have them orally complete the stem and use a connecting word to add a supporting detail in another sentence. (*She learned to rock climb although she was scared. At first, she went slowly.*) **MODERATE**
- Have partners build on the sentence stem using the connecting words *first, next,* and *finally* to write a paragraph. Have them read their work to each other as if before a group. **LIGHT**

WRITING

WRITE AN INFORMATIONAL ESSAY

Introduce students to the Writing Task by reading the introductory paragraph with them. Remind students to refer to the notes they recorded in the Unit 1 Response Log as they plan and draft their essays. The Response Log should contain ideas about overcoming difficulties from a variety of perspectives. Drawing on these different perspectives will make their own writing more interesting and well informed.

 For **writing support** for students at varying proficiency levels, see the **Language X-Ray** on page 86B.

USE THE MENTOR TEXT

Point out that their essays will be similar to the informational article "Women in Aviation" in that they will present facts and examples related to a topic. However, their essays will be shorter than the article and will focus on a more specific aspect of the topic of achievement under adversity.

WRITING PROMPT

Review the prompt with students. Encourage them to ask questions about any part of the assignment that is unclear. Make sure they understand that the purpose of their essay is to answer the question using facts and examples from the texts they have read.

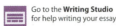 **WRITING TASK**

Write an Informational Essay

Go to the **Writing Studio** for help writing your essay.

Either quite suddenly or with deliberate care, the characters and people in this unit take decisive action. For this writing task, you will write a short informational essay about the qualities needed for overcoming an obstacle and achieving a goal. For an example of a well-written informational text you can use as a mentor text, review "Women in Aviation."

As you write your essay, use the notes from your Response Log, which you filled out after reading the texts in this unit.

Writing Prompt

Read the information in the box below.

> Consider stories you have read or heard about people who worked hard to start a new business or who conquered their fears to climb mountains or soar into space. While the goals may differ, the qualities that help people overcome challenges and obstacles are often the same.

This is the topic or context for your essay.

This is the Essential Question for the unit. How would you answer this question based on the texts in this unit?

Think carefully about the following question.

> What helps people rise up to face difficulties?

Now mark the words that identify exactly what you are being asked to produce.

Write an essay explaining the qualities that are most important for overcoming obstacles and achieving a goal.

Review these points as you write and again when you finish. Make any needed changes or edits.

Be sure to—
- ❑ provide an introduction that grabs the reader's attention, clearly states the topic, and has a clear controlling idea or thesis statement
- ❑ develop the topic using facts, definitions, examples, and quotations
- ❑ organize information in a logical way
- ❑ use verb tenses consistently and switch tenses only if necessary
- ❑ use appropriate word choice and sentence variety
- ❑ end by summarizing ideas or drawing an overall conclusion

---

 LEARNING MINDSET

Belonging Remind students that they are together for a common purpose: to learn, grow, and take on challenges. In this shared endeavor, everyone will hit snags occasionally. Encourage students to seek help from a friend or teacher if they are struggling with the planning or drafting of their essays. Reassure them that they should not feel "silly" or "less than" about asking for support. Every member of the group belongs and has value.

1 Plan

Planning the form and content of your informational essay is the first step in writing. When planning your draft, choose a genre that is appropriate for your topic, purpose, and audience. For this writing task, the topic is about overcoming obstacles, and the genre is an informational essay. On the previous page, you identified your purpose for writing. Now you must identify your audience. Is it an audience of your peers, or an audience of adults? Your audience helps determine word choice and tone. Additional strategies you can use in planning include brainstorming ideas with classmates, thinking about personal experiences and stories related to the topic, and listing questions about the topic. Use the table below to help you plan your draft.

Informational Essay Planning Table	
Genre	Informational essay
Topic	Qualities necessary for overcoming challenges and obstacles
Purpose	
Audience	
Ideas from brainstorming with classmates	
Experiences and stories related to the topic	
Questions about the topic	

Background Reading Review the notes you have taken in your Response Log after reading the texts in this unit. These texts provide background reading that will help you formulate the key ideas you will include in your essay.

WRITING TASK

Go to **Writing Informative Texts: Developing a Topic** for help in planning your essay.

Notice & Note

As you plan your essay, apply what you've learned about signposts to your own writing. Remember that writers use common features, called signposts, to help convey their message to readers.

Think about how you can incorporate evidence of **Quoted Words** into your essay.

Go to **Reading Studio** for more resources on **Notice & Note**.

Use the notes from your Response Log as you plan your essay.

Write an Informational Essay 87

TO CHALLENGE STUDENTS . . .

Conduct Research Have students conduct online or library research about women who have risen up to overcome challenges in their fields. Then, ask students to decide on a woman or a group of women they want to write about. Have students use the mentor text, primary sources, Response Logs, and Planning Tables to research and write an informational essay. Have them to add details from their research texts to the Response Log while exploring the Essential Question as it applies here: *What did these women do to face difficulties?*

WRITING

1 PLAN

Allow time for students to discuss the topic with partners or in small groups and then to complete the planning table independently.

NOTICE AND NOTE

Remind students that they can use **Quoted Words** to incorporate the findings, conclusions, or opinions of an expert on the topic of their informative essay. Students should remember that using **Quoted Words** in this way can support or explain a point they are trying to make in their essay. Remind them to format direct quotations correctly and to cite the source of each quotation.

English Learner Support

Understand Academic Language Make sure students understand words and phrases used in the chart, such as *genre, purpose,* and *audience.* Work with them to fill in the blank sections, providing text that they can copy into their charts as needed. **SUBSTANTIAL/MODERATE**

Background Reading As they plan their essays, remind students to refer to the notes they took in the Response Log. They may also review the selections to find additional facts and examples to support ideas they want to include in their writing.

Write An Informational Essay 87

WRITING

Organize Your Ideas Tell students that their outlines may have one main section for each paragraph of the essay. Provide the following sample based on the chart:

I. Introduction

II. Kinds of Adversity

III. Qualities that Help People Deal with Adversity

IV. How People Rise Up to Face Adversity

V. Conclusion

Then point out that they may also outline the body paragraphs by reading the chart from left to right, with one paragraph for each row. Under this structure, each paragraph would introduce a specific difficulty or challenge, describe how people respond to it, and explain how they can overcome it. By thinking about the details and examples they have gathered, students can select the best ways to structure their essays.

❷ DEVELOP A DRAFT

Remind students to follow their outlines as they draft their essays, but point out that they can still make changes to their writing plan during this stage. As they write, they may discover that they need a different example to support an idea, or that a particular detail belongs in a different paragraph.

■ English Learner Support

Write a Group Essay Simplify the writing task and provide direct support by working together to write an informative paragraph that answers the Essential Question.
SUBSTANTIAL/MODERATE

WRITING TASK

Go to **Writing Informative Texts: Organizing Ideas** for more help.

Organize Your Ideas The next step in planning your essay is to organize ideas and information in a way that will help you draft your essay. You can use the chart below to make a list of the topics you will cover. You can also use the chart to plan how you will support your ideas with supporting details and evidence.

Main Topic: Qualities for Overcoming Obstacles & Achieving a Goal

Kinds of difficulties that people face	Qualities that help people deal with difficulties	Ways that people rise up to face difficulties

You may prefer to draft your essay online.

❷ Develop a Draft

Once you have completed your planning activities, you will be ready to draft your informational essay. Refer to your Informational Essay Planning Table and the chart above, as well as any notes you took as you studied the texts in this unit. These will be like a road map for you to follow as you write. Using a computer program for writing or an online writing application can make it easier to rework sentences or move them around later when you are ready to revise your first draft.

88   Unit 1

WHEN STUDENTS STRUGGLE...

Draft the Essay Even when working from an outline, students may struggle to get started on their drafts. Encourage them to begin with a simple sentence that relates directly to one of the items in the sample chart: For example, the sentence stem *She proved them wrong when* ____ briefly sums up a "Kind (or type) of Adversity" (Item II). Ask students to build on that stem with a story a volunteer might tell aloud, from memory, experience, or imagination. Suggest that other students should take notes, to gain a sense of how a story develops through detail, aloud and into text. Invite other students to present similar stories to a group, using that stem or a similar introduction.

WRITING

WRITING TASK

Use the Mentor Text

Author's Craft
Your introduction is your first chance to grab the reader's attention. In addition to your controlling idea or thesis statement, your introduction should include something that makes readers want to keep reading your essay. Note how the writers of "Women in Aviation" introduce the topic and then transition to a concise thesis statement.

> American aviation was from its very beginnings marred with sexist and racist assumptions. It was taken for granted that women were generally inferior to men and that white men were superior to all others. Flying, it was said, required a level of skill and courage that women and blacks lacked. Yet despite these prevailing prejudices, the dream and the desire to fly stayed alive among women and African-Americans.

The writers capture the reader's interest by making an assertion about prejudices in early aviation. They conclude the introductory paragraph with a thesis statement that is then supported throughout the text.

Apply What You've Learned Consider including a bold assertion or question, personal anecdote, or quotation that will interest your reader.

Genre Characteristics
Supporting details provide evidence to support a central idea and give readers more information about the topic. Note how this quotation from "Women in Aviation" supports a key idea about obstacles that women aviators faced.

> Along with racism, Coleman encountered the burden of sexism, but she made believers out of those who doubted her skill. "The color of my skin," she said, "[was] a drawback at first. . . . I was a curiosity, but soon the public discovered I could really fly. Then they came to see *Brave Bessie*, as they called me."

The writers provide a quotation to help support the idea that black women aviators had to overcome discrimination to fly.

Apply What You've Learned The supporting details you include in your essay should relate directly to your key ideas. These details might be facts, examples, and quotations.

Write an Informational Essay 89

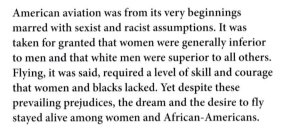

WHY THIS MENTOR TEXT?
"Women in Aviation" provides a good example of informative writing. Use the instruction below to help students review the mentor text as a model for writing strong introductions and selecting relevant details to develop their informational essays.

USE THE MENTOR TEXT

Author's Craft Ask a volunteer to read aloud the introduction to "Women in Aviation." Discuss words and details that make this paragraph a dramatic example of adversity under "racist and sexist assumptions." Then ask students to offer examples outside of aviation in which people had to overcome racism or sexism, or contend with disability or disadvantage in order to pursue a dream. Discuss strategies students might use to search for such inspiring personal narratives at a library or online.

Genre Characteristics To help students understand how the example functions in the article, have them locate paragraphs 7 and 8 in the text. Note that those paragraphs also provide supporting details as to the kinds of difficulties Bessie Coleman faced from birth. Paragraph 8 also furnishes detail corresponding to item IV in their outlines: She showed extraordinary determination in refusing "to accept the limitations others placed on her."

 ENGLISH LEARNER SUPPORT

Use the Mentor Text Use the following supports with students at varying proficiency levels:

- Draw a mountain and point to the peak. Engage students in a discussion about mountain climbing, in terms of overcoming an obstacle. Read the first sentence of the text, and compare mountain climbing to the story's premise, of overcoming "racist and sexist assumptions." **SUBSTANTIAL**

- Review the fundamental terms for the theme of their essay: *overcome* and *obstacle*, and ask students to write down synonyms. **MODERATE**

- Refer students to paragraphs 8 and 9 of the text. Ask them to identify obstacles Bessie Coleman overcame as she grew up. (*She was the daughter of a former slave, from a large family.*) **LIGHT**

Write An Informational Essay 89

WRITING

3 REVISE

Have students answer each question in the chart to determine how they can improve their drafts. Invite volunteers to model their revision techniques.

With a Partner Have students ask peer reviewers to evaluate their supporting evidence by answering the following questions:

- Is my thesis statement clear? What might be unclear about it?
- Which pieces of evidence are unclear? Why?
- What questions do you have about my main points?

Students should use the reviewer's feedback to add relevant facts, details, examples, or quotations that further develop their main points.

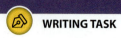

WRITING TASK

3 Revise

On Your Own Once you've written a first draft of your essay, you'll want to go back and look for ways to improve it. As you reread and revise your essay, think about whether you have achieved your purpose. The Revision Guide will help you focus on specific elements to make your writing stronger.

Go to **Writing Informative Texts: Introductions and Conclusions** for help in revising your essay.

Revision Guide

Ask Yourself	Tips	Revision Techniques
1. Does my introduction grab readers' attention?	**Highlight** the introduction.	**Add** an interesting fact, a question, an anecdote, or a famous quotation that illustrates the topic.
2. Does my introduction have a clear thesis statement?	**Underline** the thesis statement, or controlling idea.	**Add** a sentence that clearly states the idea you will develop in your essay.
3. Are ideas organized logically? Is there coherence within and across paragraphs? Do transitions connect ideas?	**Highlight** the main point or key idea in each paragraph that supports your thesis. **Underline** transitions that connect ideas.	**Rearrange** paragraphs to organize ideas logically and create coherence. **Add** transitions to connect ideas and clarify the organization.
4. Do I support each key idea with evidence?	**Underline** each supporting fact, definition, example, or quotation.	**Add** facts, specific details, examples, or quotations to support key ideas.
5. Do I use a variety of sentences?	**Underline** each compound and complex sentence.	**Combine** some simple sentences to form compound and complex sentences.
6. Does my conclusion support the topic?	**Highlight** the conclusion.	**Add** a statement that restates the thesis and summarizes the key ideas.

ACADEMIC VOCABULARY
As you conduct your **peer review**, be sure to use these words.

- ❏ aspect
- ❏ cultural
- ❏ evaluate
- ❏ resource
- ❏ text

With a Partner Once you have worked through the Revision Guide on your own, exchange essays with a partner and evaluate each other's draft in a **peer review**. Focus on suggesting revisions for at least three items mentioned in the Revision Guide. Explain why you think your partner's draft should be revised and what your suggestions are.

When receiving feedback from your partner, listen attentively and ask questions to make sure you fully understand the revision suggestions.

 ENGLISH LEARNER SUPPORT

Use Connecting Words Model connecting words that can be used to combine sentences, and encourage students to use these words as they edit their essays. Remind students that they have practiced using the conjunctions *and* and *because* to form compound and complex sentences. Model ways that the subordinating conjunction *because* can be used effectively in sentences that offer explanations. Have students work in pairs to practice using *and* and *because* in oral and written sentences. Then, have them apply what they have learned in their essays. **MODERATE/LIGHT**

4 Edit

Once you have made necessary revisions to your essay, one important task remains. Don't let simple mistakes distract or confuse your readers. Edit your final draft for the proper use of standard English conventions and make sure to correct any misspellings, punctuation errors, and grammatical errors.

Language Conventions

Consistent Verb Tenses Shifting from one verb tense to another can be confusing for the reader. When writers shift verb tenses, it is usually because they want to show a change in the timing of events.

- Use a consistent verb tense within a **sentence**, unless there is a shift in the time frame.
- Use a consistent verb tense within a **paragraph**, unless it is necessary to refer to events that occurred in the past or to events that will occur in the future.

Go to **Using Verbs Correctly** in the **Grammar Studio** to learn more.

The chart below contains examples from "Women in Aviation." The first example is a sentence that consistently uses the past tense. The second is a paragraph that correctly shifts from the past tense to the present.

	Example
Consistent Verb Tense	But she <u>didn't</u> have any money to get there, and besides, she <u>couldn't</u> speak a word of French.
Correct Shift in Verb Tense	As difficult as it <u>was</u> for women to become pilots in significant numbers, it <u>was</u> doubly hard for African-Americans, especially black women. That's why Bessie Coleman, the first African-American to earn her pilot's license, <u>is</u> such an exciting and important figure in aviation.

5 Publish

Finalize your essay and choose a way to share it with your audience. Consider these options:

- Present your essay as a speech to a small group of students.
- Post your essay as a blog on a classroom or school website.

WHEN STUDENTS STRUGGLE...

Use Consistent Verb Tenses Remind students that a verb describes an action, and a verb tense indicates when the action occurred: in the past, present, or future. When multiple verbs describe one event, or a chain of events, the tenses must be consistent: I *left* around 1:15 and *arrived* at 3 p.m. An informational essay such as "Women in Aviation" tends to be set in the past; the text reverts to the present tense to describe Bessie Coleman's enduring status as an aviator.

4 EDIT

Suggest that students read their drafts aloud to assess how clearly and smoothly they have presented their ideas. Remind them of the fundamentals of informational essays: a clear thesis statement, logical organization of ideas or subtopics, and supporting detail for each key idea. Encourage students to listen for text that "rings true" and correct flaws as noticed.

LANGUAGE CONVENTIONS

Consistent Verb Tenses Review the information about consistent verb tenses with students. Then discuss the sample sentences in the chart, asking students to identify consistency and appropriate shifts in verb tenses. Rewrite the sample sentences as follows to illustrate the way details are recast when verb tenses change.

- But she doesn't have any money to get there, and besides, she can't speak a word of French. (*Consistent verb tenses in a shift to the present, describing a current state of affairs.*)
- As difficult as it was for women to become pilots in significant numbers, it is doubly hard for African-Americans, especially black women. (*Inconsistent verb tenses muddle meaning.*)

■ English Learner Support

Consistent Verb Tenses Explain that writers should be consistent in their use of verb tenses to describe action. Have students identify the consistent verb tenses in this passage:

"Bessie Coleman refused to accept the limitations others tried to place on her. She attended an Oklahoma college for one semester but ran out of money."

5 PUBLISH

Students can present their essays as blog posts on a classroom or school website. Encourage others to read the essays and write constructive comments about them. The authors can then respond to the comments.

WRITING

USE THE SCORING GUIDE

Allow students time to read the scoring guide and to ask questions about any words, phrases, or ideas that are unclear. Then have partners exchange final drafts of their informational essays. Ask them to score their partner's essay using the scoring guide. Each student should write a paragraph explaining the reasons for the score he or she awarded in each category.

WRITING TASK

Use the scoring guide to evaluate your essay.

Writing Task Scoring Guide: Informational Essay

	Organization/Progression	Development of Ideas	Use of Language and Conventions
4	• The organization is effective and appropriate to the purpose. • All ideas are focused on the topic specified in the prompt. • Transitions clearly show the relationship among ideas.	• The introduction catches the reader's attention and clearly identifies the topic. • The essay contains a clear, concise, and well-defined thesis statement. • The topic is well developed with clear key ideas that are supported by specific, well-chosen details, facts, examples, and quotations. • The conclusion effectively summarizes the information presented.	• Language and word choice is purposeful and precise. • A variety of simple, compound, and complex sentences is used; the sentences effectively show how ideas are related. • Spelling, capitalization, and punctuation are correct. • Grammar and usage are correct.
3	• The organization is, for the most part, effective and appropriate to the purpose. • Most ideas are focused on the topic specified in the prompt. • A few more transitions are needed to show the relationship among ideas.	• The introduction could be more engaging. The topic is identified. • The essay contains a clear thesis statement. • The development of ideas is clear because the writer uses specific and appropriate details, facts, examples, and quotations. • The conclusion summarizes the information presented.	• Language and word choice could be more purposeful and precise. • A greater variety of simple, compound, and complex sentences could be used; the sentences could more effectively show how ideas are related. • Spelling, capitalization, and punctuation are mostly correct. • Grammar and usage are mostly correct.
2	• The organization is evident but is not always appropriate to the purpose. • Only some ideas are focused on the topic specified in the prompt. • More transitions are needed to show the relationship among ideas.	• The introduction is not engaging; the topic is unclear. • The thesis statement does not express a clear idea. • The development of ideas is minimal. The writer uses details, facts, examples, and quotations that are inappropriate or ineffectively presented. • The conclusion is only partially effective.	• Language is often vague and general. • There is little sentence variety. • Spelling, capitalization, and punctuation are often incorrect but do not make reading difficult. • Grammar and usage are incorrect in many places.
1	• The organization is not appropriate to the purpose. • Ideas are not focused on the topic specified in the prompt. • No transitions are used, making the essay difficult to understand.	• The introduction is missing or confusing. • The thesis statement is missing. • The development of ideas is weak. Supporting details, facts, examples, and quotations are unreliable, vague, or missing. • The conclusion is missing.	• Language is vague, confusing, or inappropriate for the text. • There is no sentence variety. • Many spelling, capitalization, and punctuation errors are present. • Many grammatical and usage errors are present, making the writer's ideas difficult to understand.

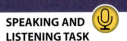

SPEAKING AND LISTENING TASK

Present a Film Critique

You have written an informational essay about people in the real world overcoming obstacles. Now think about movies that also tell stories of people overcoming obstacles. For example, consider movies from genres such as action, drama, and biography that portray strong characters and have event-filled plots—but are not rated beyond PG. Then choose a movie and watch it carefully, with a critical eye. Next you will plan and present a critique of the film, or movie review, to your classmates. You also will listen and respond to their presentations.

Go to **Giving a Presentation** in the **Speaking and Listening Studio** to learn more.

① Plan Your Presentation

As you view the movie, take careful notes. Also think about the following questions to guide you in creating your film critique.

- How will you grab your audience's attention? Do you clearly state the central idea of your critique in the introduction to your presentation?
- Have any classmates already seen the movie? Will your review make them want to see it again? Will it make classmates who have not seen the movie want to see it for the first time?
- Do you clearly describe which obstacles the movie characters face, how they overcome the obstacles, and how they achieve their goals?
- Does your conclusion restate your central idea about the movie?

You can use this chart to take notes as you watch the movie and to record specific details for your presentation.

Main Character(s) and Goals	Obstacles and Challenges	How They Reach Their Goals

Present a Film Critique   93

SPEAKING AND LISTENING

PRESENT A FILM CRITIQUE OF AN ACTION MOVIE

Introduce students to the Speaking and Listening Task by noting that a film critique is also an informational essay, in this case about a movie. Encourage them to think about conflict (or difficulties) as fundamental to storytelling across a range of forms: informational essays, novels, movies, or TV shows. Then suggest that students rehearse their critiques before a friendly audience, striving to employ eye contact and manage speaking rate, volume, enunciation, and gestures to share ideas effectively.

① PLAN YOUR PRESENTATION

Have students review the note-taking chart. Then encourage them to structure critiques along the same lines as their informational essays: with an arresting opener; a clear thesis statement; logically arranged supporting detail; and a conclusion that supports the topic. Next, work with the class to list some general principles for presenting information orally. (*Examples: Use short sentences. Repeat important ideas. Use humor or interesting examples to keep the audience engaged.*)

 For **speaking support** for students at varying proficiency levels, see the **Language X-Ray** on page 86B.

 ENGLISH LEARNER SUPPORT

Adapt the Essay Use the following supports with students at varying proficiency levels:
- Work individually with students on vocabulary appropriate to a movie review. Ask them to define such terms as *colorful, heroic,* and *surprising* and to write down analogous words and phrases of their own. **SUBSTANTIAL/MODERATE**
- Review the chart to ensure students' understanding. Then have students work in pairs or small groups to write from memory elements of movies they liked that correspond to the headings in the chart. Ask them to record these elements in sentence form. **LIGHT**

Write An Informational Essay   93

SPEAKING AND LISTENING

② PRACTICE WITH A PARTNER OR GROUP

Review the information and tips with the class, ensuring that all the terms and ideas are clear. Remind students that the practice exercise is intended to solicit useful feedback from their peers. Emphasize that speaking before a group makes most people feel nervous, so everyone should be as supportive and helpful as possible.

③ DELIVER YOUR PRESENTATION

Set aside time for all students to give their presentations. When everyone has finished, ask students to share their thoughts on how their classmates' feedback helped them improve their performance.

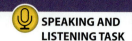 **SPEAKING AND LISTENING TASK**

As you work to improve your presentations, be sure to follow discussion rules:
- ❏ listen closely to each other
- ❏ don't interrupt
- ❏ stay on topic
- ❏ ask helpful, relevant, and thoughtful questions
- ❏ provide only clear, direct, and appropriate answers

② Practice with a Partner or Group

Once you've completed a draft of your film critique, practice presenting it with a partner or group. Focus on ways to improve your presentation and delivery.

Practice Effective Verbal Techniques
- ❏ **Enunciation** Replace words that you stumble over and rearrange sentences so that your words and ideas are clear.
- ❏ **Voice Modulation and Pitch** Use your voice to sound enthusiastic and to give emphasis to your key points.
- ❏ **Speaking Rate** Speak at a steady pace so that listeners can follow along. Pause now and then after making a key point.
- ❏ **Volume** Speak loudly enough so that everyone in the room can hear you clearly, but avoid shouting.

Practice Effective Nonverbal Techniques
- ❏ **Eye Contact** Try to let your eyes rest on each member of the audience at least once.
- ❏ **Facial Expressions** Use natural facial expressions—smiling, frowning, or raising an eyebrow—to emphasize key points.
- ❏ **Gestures** Stand tall and relaxed. Gesture with your hands to add meaning and interest to your presentation.

Provide and Consider Advice for Improvement

As a listener, pay close attention to the other presenters. Take notes about ways they can improve their presentations and more effectively use verbal and nonverbal techniques. Paraphrase and summarize each presenter's key ideas to confirm your understanding. Remember to ask questions to clarify any confusing ideas or details.

As a presenter, listen closely to the audience's questions and give thoughtful consideration to ideas for improving your presentation. Remember to ask for suggestions about how you could make your presentation clearer and more interesting.

③ Deliver Your Presentation

Use the advice you received during practice to make final changes to your presentation. Then, using effective verbal and nonverbal techniques, present your film critique to your classmates.

WHEN STUDENTS STRUGGLE . . .

Take Notes If students find it challenging to take notes during their classmates' presentations, divide the task between several students. One student may focus on the list of verbal techniques, checking off effective approaches and making brief notes about potential improvements. Another student may do the same for the list of effective nonverbal techniques. A third may listen for key ideas and write those down. This student may choose to listen with eyes closed to tune out distractions.

REFLECT

Reflect on the Unit

The informational essay you wrote enabled you to pull together and express some of your thoughts about the reading you have done in this unit. Now is a good time to reflect on what you have learned.

Reflect on the Essential Question

- How do people rise up to face difficulties? How has your thinking about this question changed since the beginning of the unit?

- What are some examples from the texts you've read that show how people overcome obstacles and take decisive action? Explain.

Reflect on Your Reading

- Which selections were the most interesting or surprising to you? Why?

- From which selection did you learn the most about how people face challenges and take decisive action? Explain.

Reflect on the Writing Task

- What obstacles did you encounter while working on your informational essay? How might you avoid them next time?

- What parts of the essay were the easiest and the hardest to write? Why?

Reflect on the Speaking and Listening Task

- What aspects of verbal and nonverbal communication did you find most challenging as you delivered your presentation?

- What did you learn from the other presenters? How can this help you the next time you create and deliver a presentation?

UNIT 1 SELECTIONS
- "Rogue Wave"
- "The Flight of Icarus"
- "Icarus's Flight"
- "Women in Aviation"
- "Thank You, M'am"
- "A Police Stop Changed This Teenager's Life"

Reflect on the Unit 95

SPEAKING AND LISTENING

REFLECT ON THE UNIT

Have students reflect on the questions independently and write some notes in response to each one. Then have students meet with partners or in small groups to discuss their reflections. Circulate during these discussions to identify the questions that are generating the liveliest conversations. Wrap up with a whole-class discussion focused on these questions.

 LEARNING MINDSET

Self Reflection Explain to students that an important part of developing a learning mindset is the ability to overcome obstacles. As students reflect on the unit, encourage them to ask themselves these questions: *Did I ask questions if I needed help? Did I persist when faced with challenges in writing my essay? Was I supportive of my classmates? Am I proud of the work I turned in?*

Write An Informational Essay 95

UNIT 2

Instructional Overview and Resources

		Instructional Focus	Online Ed Resources
	Unit Introduction **Reality Check**	Unit 2 Essential Question Unit 2 Academic Vocabulary	**Stream to Start:** Reality Check **Unit 2 Response Log**

ANALYZE & APPLY

		Instructional Focus	Resources
	"Heartbeat" Short Story by David Yoo **Lexile 840L** **NOTICE & NOTE** READING MODEL **Signposts** • Aha Moment • Contrasts and Contradictions • Again and Again	**Reading** • Analyze Character • Analyze Conflict **Writing:** Write Text for an Infographic **Speaking and Listening:** Devise an Infographic **Vocabulary:** Context Clues **Language Conventions:** Subject-Verb Agreement and Prepositional Phrases	🔊 **Audio** **Reading Studio:** Notice & Note **Level Up Tutorial:** Characters and Conflict **Writing Studio:** Writing an Informative Text **Speaking and Listening Studio:** Using Media in a Presentation **Vocabulary Studio:** Context Clues **Grammar Studio:** Module 8: Lessons 1 & 2: Agreement of Subject and Verb
	MENTOR TEXT **"The Camera Does Lie"** Magazine Article by Meg Ross **Lexile 990L**	**Reading** • Determine Author's Purpose • Cite Evidence and Draw Conclusions **Writing:** Write an Opinion Essay **Speaking and Listening:** Create a Multimodal Presentation **Vocabulary:** Reference Aids **Language Conventions:** Semicolons	🔊 **Audio** **Text in Focus:** Interpreting Numbers/Drawing Conclusions **Reading Studio:** Notice & Note **Speaking and Listening Studio:** Usiing Media in a Presentation **Vocabulary Studio:** Using Reference Resources **Grammar Studio:** Conjunctions and Interjections
	"Two Legs or One?" Folk Tale by Josepha Sherman **Lexile 600L**	**Reading** • Analyze Folk Tales • Analyze Humor **Writing:** Write a Friendly Letter **Speaking and Listening:** Direct a Retelling **Vocabulary:** Glossary **Language Conventions:** Commas	🔊 **Audio** **Reading Studio:** Notice & Note **Speaking and Listening Studio:** Giving a Presentation **Vocabulary Studio:** Using a Glossary **Grammar Studio:** Module 14: Lessons 2–6: Using Commas Correctly

COLLABORATE & COMPARE

"The Song of Wandering Aengus" Poem by W.B. Yeats **"Eldorado"** Poem by Edgar Allen Poe	**Reading** • Analyze Rhyme • Analyze Rhyme Schemes • Analyze Sound Devices and Mood **Writing:** Write a Poem **Speaking and Listening:** Present Your Poem	🔊 **Audio** **Reading Studio:** Notice & Note **Writing Studio:** Writing as a Process

SUGGESTED PACING: 30 DAYS

Unit Introduction	Heartbeat	The Camera Does Lie	Two Legs or One?	Aengus/Eldorado
1	2 3 4 5	6 7 8 9	10 11 12	13 14 15 16 17

96A Unit 2

PLAN

English Learner Support		Differentiated Instruction	Assessment
• Learn Vocabulary • Learning Strategies			
• Text X-Ray • Academic Language • Cognates • Language Acquisition • Idioms	• Oral Assessment • Discuss With a Small Group • Use Context Clues • Understand Subject-Verb Agreement	**When Students Struggle** • Make Inferences • Reteach Character	**Selection Test**
• Text X-Ray • Understand Directionality • Use Cognates • Learning Strategies • Understand Contrast • Support Comprehension • Use Semicolons	• Oral Assessment • Discuss with a Small Group • Vocabulary Strategy • Language Conventions	**When Students Struggle** • Cite Evidence	**Selection Test**
• Text X-Ray • Understand Humor • Use Cognates • Understand Main Idea • Understand Commas • Oral Assessment	• Write a Friendly Letter • Vocabulary Strategy: Glossary • Language Conventions: Commas	**To Challenge Students** • Write a Friendly Letter	
• Text X-Ray • Distinguish Sounds • Understand Sound Devices • Present Your Poem	• Learning Strategies • Confirm Understanding • Oral Assessment	**When Students Struggle** • Identify Mood	**Selection Test**

Governess/Photos
18 › 19 › 20 › 21 › 22 › 23 › 24 › 25

Independent Reading
26 › 27

End of Unit
28 › 29 › 30

Reality Check **96B**

PLAN

UNIT 2 Continued

		Instructional Focus	Resources

COLLABORATE & COMPARE

	Collaborate and Compare	**Reading:** • Compare Mood **Speaking and Listening:** Collaborate and Present	**Speaking and Listening Studio:** Giving a Presentation
The Governess Drama by Neil Simon		**Reading:** • Analyze Drama • Analyze Humor **Writing:** Write a Personal Narrative **Speaking and Listening:** Adapt Stage Directions **Vocabulary:** Word Origins **Language Conventions:** Complex Sentences: Subordinating Conjunctions	🔊 Audio **Reading Studio:** Notice & Note **Writing Studio:** Writing Narratives **Vocabulary Studio:** Word Origins **Grammar Studio:** Module 3: Lesson 6: Conjunctions and Interjections
	from *The Governess* Production Images	**Reading:** • Analyze Media • Identify Rhetorical Devices **Writing:** Write a Dialogue **Speaking and Listening:** Stage the Scene	🔊 Audio **Reading Studio:** Notice & Note **Writing Studio:** Writing Narratives
	Collaborate and Compare	**Reading:** • Compare Characterizations • Analyze the Versions **Speaking and Listening:** Create and Share	

INDEPENDENT READING

The independent Reading selections are only available in the eBook.

📖 Go to the Reading Studio for more information on **NOTICE & NOTE**.

 "A Priceless Lesson in Humility"
Personal Essay by Felipe Morales
Lexile 930

 "H–ey, Come On Ou–t!"
Short Story by Shinichi Hoshi
Lexile 860L

END OF UNIT

Writing Task: Create a Multimodal Presentation **Reflect on the Unit**	**Writing:** Create a Multimodal Presentation	**Unit 2 Response Log** **Mentor Text:** "The Camera Does Lie" **Writing Studio:** Writing Informative Text **Speaking and Listening Studio:** Giving a Presentation

96C Unit 2

PLAN

English Learner Support		Differentiated Instruction	Online Ed Assessment
• Ask Questions • Identify Supporting Details			
• Text X-Ray • Understand Drama • Pronunciation • Understand Directionality • Understand Drama • Monitor Comprehension • Analyze Humor	• Analyze Drama • Oral Assessment • Write a Personal Narrative • Practice Cognates • Understand Subordinating Conjunctions	**When Students Struggle** • Analyze Drama **To Challenge Students** • What If?	**Selection Tests**
• Text X-Ray • Reinforce Meaning • Discuss with a Small Group • Monitor Understanding • Write a Dialogue		**When Students Struggle** • Teamwork	**Selection Tests**
• Ask Questions		**To Challenge Students** • Analyze Special Techniques	

| "Way Too Cool"
Short Story by Brenda Woods
Lexile 610L | "Forever Now"
Informational Text by Dan Risch
Lexile 1030L | | **Selection Tests** |

| • Language X-Ray
• Understand Academic Language
• Write a Collaborative Script
• Use the Mentor Text
• Subject-Verb Agreement
• Assess Comprehension | | **When Students Struggle**
• Develop a Draft
• Take Notes
To Challenge Students
• Genre Characteristics | **Unit Test** |

Reality Check **96D**

TEACH

Connect to the
ESSENTIAL QUESTION

Ask a volunteer to read aloud the Essential Question. Discuss the quote in terms of the question: *How can a change in focus change our sense of what is real? How do we know for sure what is "real" and what isn't? How are we tricked sometimes, and why do we like it?* Ask students to furnish examples of illusion that bedevils, intrigues, and entertains them.

■ **English Learner Support**

Learn Vocabulary Make sure students understand the Essential Question. If necessary, explain the following terms:
- *Reality* means "things as they really are."
- *Illusion* means " "something that appears to be what it is not."
- *Blur* means "to make unclear or hard to see."

Help students reframe the question in simple language: *What things can make it hard to tell what is real and what is not?* **SUBSTANTIAL/MODERATE**

DISCUSS THE QUOTATION

Tell students that George Lucas (1944-) is an accomplished American filmmaker and entrepreneur, best known as the creator of the *Star Wars* and *Indiana Jones* movie franchises. He also established Industrial Light and Magic, a pioneering enterprise specializing in the use of CGI (computer-generated imagery) and other special effects. Ask students: *How does a sci-fi movie use illusions to captivate audiences? Why is it important that the effects seem real?*

UNIT 2

REALITY CHECK

ESSENTIAL QUESTION

What can blur the lines between what's real and what's not?

"Always remember: Your focus determines your reality."

— George Lucas

 LEARNING MINDSET

Curiosity Mindset Encourage students to pay attention to the things they are curious about. Explain that maintaining a curious mind makes it possible to embrace new skills, tasks, and ideas that might seem too difficult to approach. Share things that you have learned that you didn't think you could learn. Explain the part curiosity played in helping you be free of the illusion that you could not do something. Have partners share things that they would like to know more about, but that they think might be hard to learn, like speaking another language, or becoming an artist or scientist.

UNIT 2

ACADEMIC VOCABULARY

Academic Vocabulary words are words you use when you discuss and write about texts. In this unit you will practice and learn five words.

☑ abnormal ☐ feature ☐ focus ☐ perceive ☐ task

Study the Word Network to learn more about the word **abnormal**.

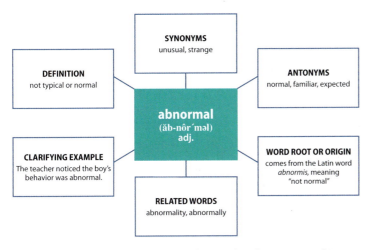

Write and Discuss Discuss the completed Word Network with a partner, making sure to talk through all of the boxes until you both understand the word, its synonyms, antonyms, and related forms. Then, fill out Word Networks for the remaining four words. Use a dictionary or online resource to help you complete the activity.

 Go online to access the **Word Networks**.

RESPOND TO THE ESSENTIAL QUESTION

In this unit, you will explore how different people distinguish between reality and fiction. As you read, you will revisit the **Essential Question** and gather your ideas about it in the **Response Log** that appears on page R2. At the end of the unit, you will have the opportunity to create a **multimodal presentation** to demonstrate how things are not always as they seem. Filling out the Response Log will help you prepare for this writing task.

 You can also go online to access the **Response Log**.

Reality Check 97

TEACH

ACADEMIC VOCABULARY

As students complete Word Networks for the remaining four vocabulary words, encourage them to include all the categories shown in the completed network if possible, but point out that some words do not have clear synonyms or antonyms. Some words may also function as different parts of speech—for example, *feature* may be a noun or a verb.

abnormal (ăb-nôr´məl) *adj.* Not typical, usual, or regular (Spanish cognate: *abnormal*)

feature (fē´chər) *n.* A prominent or distinctive part, quality, or characteristic

focus (fō´kəs) *n.* A center of interest or activity (Spanish cognate: *foco*)

perceive (pər-sēv´) *tr. v.* To become aware (of something) through the senses (Spanish cognate: *percibir*)

task (tăsk) *n.* A piece of work assigned or done as part of one's duties; a function to be performed

RESPOND TO THE ESSENTIAL QUESTION

Direct students to the Unit 2 Response Log. Explain that students will use it to record ideas and details from the selections that help answer the Essential Question. When they work on the writing task at the end of the unit, their Response Logs will help them think about what they have read and make connections between texts.

 ENGLISH LEARNER SUPPORT

Learning Strategies Use this strategy to help students learn essential language and encourage collaborative discussion:

- Have students make concept-map organizers with "Things I Like" in the center.
- In the extensions, have them draw pictures or write about things they've seen in movies, read in books, or experienced that are either real or illusions. Have them label the extensions "real" or "illusion."
- For example, a student might draw a picture of herself flying with a cape and label it: "Me, flying in a dream," another student might write about seeing a movie with special effects that were impressive.
- Pair students and have them share their organizers. Guide students to talk about illusions people enjoy *because* they are not real, real events people have to face that might be difficult, and illusions people might have about themselves. **ALL LEVELS**

Reality Check **97**

PLAN

HEARTBEAT
Short Story by David Yoo

GENRE ELEMENTS
SHORT STORY

Remind students that **short stories** are fictional stories that have a single idea and can be read in one sitting. Short stories develop one or more characters as they present a plot with one main conflict, with the action taking place in a particular setting or settings. Short stories can be realistic or imaginary, and often convey a theme or lesson about life.

LEARNING OBJECTIVES

- Analyze character and conflict.
- Conduct research about improving self-esteem.
- Write and devise an infographic about the benefits of rejecting negative thinking.
- Discuss strategies that can help boost self-esteem.
- Use context clues to define unfamiliar words.
- Identify and understand subject-verb agreement.
- **Language** Use selection-specific vocabulary: *self-esteem, confidence, perceive, motivation,* and *qualities.*

TEXT COMPLEXITY

Quantitative Measures	**HEARTBEAT**	Lexile: 840L
Qualitative Measures	**Ideas Presented** Text is explicit, but moves to some implied meaning and requires inferential reasoning.	
	Structure Used Text is written in first person point of view in chronological order.	
	Language Used Mostly explicit; some figurative and allusive language as well as colloquial language	
	Knowledge Requires Situations and subjects familiar or easily envisioned	

PLAN

RESOURCES

- Unit 2 Response Log
- 🔊 Selection Audio
- 📖 Reading Studio: Notice & Note
- Level Up Tutorial: Characters and Conflict
- Writing Studio: Writing Informative Texts
- Speaking and Listening Studio: Using Media in a Presentation
- Vocabulary Studio: Context Clues
- Grammar Studio: Module 8: Lessons 1 and 2: Agreement of Subject and Verb.
- "Heartbeat" Selection Test

SUMMARIES

"Heartbeat" is a short story about Dave, a sixteen-year-old high school student. Dave is obsessed by the belief that he is too thin to be considered manly and attractive by his peers. The story is told from the first-person point of view. The title comes from the nickname his friends have given him; they call him *Heartbeat* because they can "see the pulse on my bare chest." Dave attempts to change how he thinks people see him through intense exercise, overeating, and wearing multiple layers of clothing. He learns valuable lessons about developing a positive self-image, and the importance of not giving in to negative self-talk.

Spanish

"El latido" es un cuento acerca de Dave, un estudiante de secundaria de dieciséis años a quien sus amigos llaman latido, debido a que pueden "verme el pulso en el pecho". Mientras Dave trata de deshacerse del sobrenombre a través de intensos ejercicios y ropa incómoda e impráctica, aprende una valiosa lección acerca de la importancia de ser uno mismo y de crear una autoimagen positiva.

SMALL-GROUP OPTIONS

Have students work in small groups to read and discuss the selection.

Think-Pair Share

- After students have read and analyzed "Heartbeat," pose this question: Why is having good self-esteem important?
- Have students think about the question individually and take notes.
- Then, have pairs discuss their ideas about the question.
- Finally, ask pairs to share their responses with the class.

Three Before Me

- After students have completed the text for their infographics, have them ask three classmates to edit their writing.
- Provide students with a list of issues to look for as they edit each others' work: clear topic sentences at the beginning of each paragraph, correct subject-verb agreement in sentences, and correct spelling and usage of vocabulary words.
- Finally, have students apply the edits their peers have identified before presenting their infographics to the class.

Heartbeat 98B

PLAN

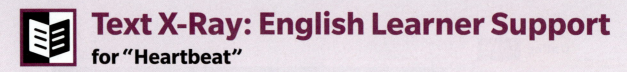

Text X-Ray: English Learner Support
for "Heartbeat"

Use the Text X-Ray and the supports and scaffolds in the Teacher's Edition to help guide students at different proficiency levels through the selection.

INTRODUCE THE SELECTION
DISCUSS SELF-ESTEEM AND CONFIDENCE

In this lesson, students will need to be able to discuss self-esteem and confidence. Provide the following explanations:

- *self-esteem*: the level of self-respect, pride, or faith one has in oneself.
- *confidence*: trust, belief in one's worth, abilities, and judgment.

Explain to students that self-talk is what people say to themselves in their minds. Sometimes self-talk is unkind. It also may be untrue. The way Dave talks to himself in the story shows how he feels about himself; it tells the reader about his self-esteem and self-confidence. Reread paragraph 1. Have volunteers pick words or phrases from it to finish the sentence frames.

- *Dave thinks everyone sees him as _____ . (a weakling, skinny, thin)*
- *He believes that Sarah is _____ when she looks at him. Another word for what he thinks Sarah feels is _____ .*
- *Dave's nickname is _____ because _____ .*

CULTURAL REFERENCES

The following words and phrases may be unfamiliar to students:

- *become the "after" picture* (paragraph 1): references the way advertisers use "before" and "after" pictures to promote products they claim will improve the quality or appearance of someone or something.
- *NBA* (paragraph 5): National Basketball Association
- *noogie* (paragraph 7): poking someone with knuckles, especially on the head
- *Abandon ship* (paragraph 12): to leave a bad situation
- *puffball* (paragraph 12): a puffy, soft-looking mushroom
- *sheared sheep* (paragraph 13): a sheep that has just had its wool taken off.

LISTENING

Understand the Character

Draw students' attention to the way the main character, Dave, describes himself. Point out the other information Dave shares, such as how he believes his peers view him.

Have students listen as you read aloud paragraphs 1–2. Use the following supports with students at varying proficiency levels:

- Tell students that you will ask questions about what you just read aloud. Model using thumbs up for yes, and thumbs down for no. Ask: *Does Dave like the way he looks?* (no) Tell students to answer verbally: *Does Dave want to be bigger or smaller?* (bigger). **SUBSTANTIAL**
- Have students identify how Dave feels about his appearance. Ask: *Is Dave happy about his body?* (no) *How would he like to look?* (thicker, bigger) *Who is the girl Dave likes?* (Sarah) **MODERATE**
- Have students in pairs share their written answers to the following questions: *Why does Dave lift weights and eat a lot?* (He wants to look thicker.) *Why does he think that Sarah does not like the way he looks?* (She says that he's "so skinny" he thinks she looks "repulsed" by him.) **LIGHT**

98C   Unit 2

PLAN

SPEAKING

Discuss Conflict

Model identifying the source(s) of conflict in the story: Who has a problem? Where is the conflict coming from? Is there a conflict between characters? What does the text evidence tell the reader about the conflict? Who is telling the story?

Use the following supports with students at varying proficiency levels:

- Read the following sentence from paragraph 2 aloud: *I didn't care about getting stronger if nobody could tell.* Explain that *tell* means "see" in the sentence. Have students respond by saying yes or no: *Dave does not care what people think?* (no) *Dave cares if people see that he getting stronger.* (yes) **SUBSTANTIAL**
- Have pairs work together to complete the following sentences, taking turns to read each one aloud. *Dave cares less about getting ____ (strong) than he does about ____ (looking strong/good).* **MODERATE**
- Have students read paragraphs 1–3: Ask: *What is Dave's larger problem—his thinking, or his weight? Why?* Have them use text evidence to discuss their answers with a partner. Have each pair share their answer with the rest of the group. **LIGHT**

READING

Understand a Character's Motivation

Looking for details in what a character thinks, says, and does, helps readers identify a character's qualities, or traits. Identifying qualities such as "honesty" can help readers discover a character's motivation.

Work with students to read paragraphs 3–5. Use the following supports with students at varying proficiency levels:

- Remind students that what a character does can explain why they do things (motivations). Ask: *Why does Dave wear so many shirts at the same time?* Accept single words or phrases. **SUBSTANTIAL**
- Guide students to discuss why Dave reacts the way does after Sarah asks if he's been working out. Provide sentence frames as necessary: *Dave wears ____ (extra layers) to school because he wants to ____ (look bigger) and ____ (impress Sarah).* **MODERATE**
- Have students identify why Dave wears extra shirts to school. Ask the following question and have them share their response with a partner: *Identify some of Dave's qualities. for example: Is he an anxious, worried boy? Why does he want to look bigger? Find details in the text that support your answers.* (He's very anxious. He's motivated by wanting to belong, and to be attractive.) **LIGHT**

WRITING

Write an Infographic

Work with students to read the writing assignment on page 121.

Use the following supports with students at varying proficiency levels:

- Provide students with a list of vocabulary and definitions to guide the writing portion of their infographics: *self-esteem, confidence, perceive, motivation,* and *qualities*. Have pairs work together to find an image that matches each definition. Students should label each definition with the appropriate vocabulary term. **SUBSTANTIAL**
- Provide some sample sentence frames that students can use to craft their paragraphs: *Self-esteem is how you ____ (perceive) yourself. Being kind to yourself can give you ____ (confidence).* **MODERATE**
- Remind students to use the following words and their definitions in their paragraphs: *self-esteem, confidence, perceive, motivation,* and *qualities*. Have pairs identify the terms and definitions in each other's paragraphs. **LIGHT**

TEACH

EXPLAIN THE SIGNPOSTS

Explain that Notice & Note Signposts are significant moments in the text that help readers understand and analyze works of fiction or nonfiction. Use the instruction on these pages to introduce students to the signposts **Aha Moment**, **Contrasts and Contradictions**, and **Again and Again**. Then use the selection that follows to have students apply the signposts to a text.

For a full list of the fiction and nonfiction signposts, see p. 170.

AHA MOMENT

The **Aha Moment** arrives when a character realizes something he or she had previously not known. Words like *suddenly* or *all at once* signal to an Aha Moment. But sometimes the cues about an Aha Moment are more subtle.

Read the example passage aloud. Ask the students to identify the two verbs that signal Dave's Aha Moment: *realized, stumbled (onto)*. Note that this Aha Moment was a delayed reaction, coming well after the compliment that prompts him to look in a mirror.

Tell students that when they spot an Aha Moment, they should pause, mark it in their consumable texts, and ask themselves the anchor question: *How might this change things in the story?*

Notice Note
READING MODEL

HEARTBEAT

You are about to read the short story "Heartbeat." In it, you will notice and note signposts that will give you clues about the story's characters and themes. Here are three key signposts to look for as you read this short story and other works of fiction.

For more information on these and other signposts to Notice & Note, visit the **Reading Studio**.

Aha Moment Have you ever searched for something only to suddenly remember where you left it? A story character can also have an **Aha Moment**—a moment in which the character suddenly sees things differently or understands something. A character experiencing an Aha Moment may view something in a new way, suddenly solve a problem, or reach a deeper understanding about herself or himself.

When you see a phrase like one of these in a text, pause to see whether it may be an **Aha Moment** signpost:

"I finally realized . . ."
"That must be why . . ."
"and all of a sudden . . ."
"I decided to . . ."

In this example from "Heartbeat," a student found and underlined an Aha Moment:

> 3   . . . I was sitting in study hall two weeks ago when Sarah said the magic words: "Have you been working out, Dave? You look bigger." I couldn't tell if she was being sarcastic. I went home and inspected myself in the mirror. <u>I did look bigger!</u>
>
> 4   <u>But then I realized the reason: I'd accidentally worn two T-shirts</u> under my rugby shirt that day. It was just an illusion. I was futilely stuffing my face and religiously <u>pumping iron and failing to alter my appearance, and now I'd stumbled on the simplest solution to looking bigger. I felt like I was reborn.</u>

Anchor Question
When you notice this signpost, ask: How might this change things?

What does Dave suddenly realize?	He realizes that wearing extra layers is the easiest way for him to look bigger.
What does this realization tell you about Dave?	He will go to any lengths—even "disguising" himself—to look bigger and less skinny.

Contrasts and Contradictions Have you ever ignored someone when you actually *liked* that person? People often act in contradictory ways. Just as in real life, **Contrasts and Contradictions** in stories can give you insight into a character. Here a student underlined an example in "Heartbeat" of Contrasts and Contradictions:

> 2   For the rest of fall, I did countless push-ups and curled free weights until I couldn't bend my arms. I got ridiculously strong and defined, but I wasn't gaining weight. I wanted to be *thicker*. I didn't care about getting stronger if nobody could tell. . . .

Anchor Question
When you notice this signpost, ask: Why would the character feel this way?

What contradiction is expressed here?	The character wants to be thicker but doesn't care about being stronger.
Why do you think the character isn't gaining weight?	The student may be naturally thin.

Again and Again In a movie, you see a character having trouble writing. He scribbles words on paper and then wads it up and throws it into the trash. By showing balls of paper falling into the trash again and again, the director indicates that the character can't find the right words. When images, events, or words appear in a story **Again and Again**, they can create or emphasize a certain image, idea, or feeling. Here's an example of a student noting how Dave in "Heartbeat" does something Again and Again:

> 3   . . . I constantly weighed myself. At least once an hour, no matter where I was, I'd find a bathroom so I could take off my shirt and flex in the mirror for a couple of minutes. . . .

Anchor Question
When you notice this signpost, ask: Why might the author keep bringing this up?

What does Dave do again and again?	He weighs himself constantly, and he flexes his muscles in the mirror.
What do these repeated actions tell you about Dave?	Dave has become too concerned about getting bigger.

Notice & Note   99

WHEN STUDENTS STRUGGLE . . .

Use Strategies   Sometimes repeated story elements are widely spaced within a page or from one page to another. If students struggle to recognize the **Again and Again** signpost, have them use the Syntax Surgery strategy. In their consumable texts, ask them to circle and number the first reference to Dave looking into a mirror. Then ask them to find and mark the next instance when Dave looks in the mirror. Ask: *What can you infer about a character who is always checking his reflection?*

TEACH

▶ CONTRASTS AND CONTRADICTIONS

Explain that Contrasts and Contradictions call attention to story elements by highlighting noteworthy differences or contradictions.

Read the example passage aloud. Ask: *What insight does this contradiction give you into the character?* (He contradicts the assumption that people lift weights to become strong and fit. All he cares about is his appearance.)

Tell students when they spot Contrasts and Contradictions, they should pause, make a note in their consumable text, and ask themselves the anchor question: *Why would the character feel this way?*

▶ AGAIN AND AGAIN

Repetition adds emphasis. Emphasis draws attention. A speaker or a writer says something Again and Again to indicate that this something is of special significance.

Read the example passage aloud. Ask: *How would the meaning change if Dave did not weigh himself repeatedly?* (The repetition underscores the character's obsession with acquiring bulk and his discomfort with his natural physique.)

Tell students when they spot **repetition**, they should pause, make a note in their consumable text, and ask themselves the anchor question: *Why does this happen again and again?*

APPLY THE SIGNPOSTS

Have students use the selection that follows as a model text to apply the signposts. As students encounter signposts, prompt them to stop, reread, and ask themselves the anchor questions that will help them understand the story's characters and themes.

Tell students to continue to look for these and other signposts as they read the other selections in the unit.

Notice & Note   99

TEACH

? Connect to the ESSENTIAL QUESTION

The short story "Heartbeat" follows the struggles of a character named Dave—a high school athlete who becomes concerned with his appearance after receiving a nickname he dislikes. His perceptions about what his peers think of him, as well as his perception of his own looks drive his thoughts and actions throughout the story.

ANALYZE & APPLY

HEARTBEAT

Short Story by **David Yoo**

? ESSENTIAL QUESTION:

What can blur the lines between what's real and what's not?

 LEARNING MINDSET

Effort Tell students that part of making one's best effort is developing a balance between thought and action. Sometimes it is important to reflect on whether it makes sense to put forth a great deal of effort on a particular task. For example, it does not make sense to spend too much time on one question in a timed test. Have students come up with examples of times they focused their thinking, prioritized their efforts, and got better results.

QUICK START

Do you have friends who sometimes seem unsure of themselves? How do you think they could become more positive and brave? Make a list of some ways in which you think an individual can build confidence.

ANALYZE CHARACTER

Characters are the people who take part in a story. By analyzing a character's traits and motivations, you can understand the character—and the story—better.

Character traits are the qualities shown by characters or the expressions of their personality.	The writer may state the character's traits, or you may need to infer traits based on the character's words, thoughts, actions, appearance, or relationships.
Character motivations are the reasons why characters act the way they do.	To understand motivations, think about how the setting and other characters influence a character's actions.

GENRE ELEMENTS: SHORT STORY

- has a single idea and can be read in one sitting
- develops one or more characters
- presents a plot with one main conflict
- includes a setting
- may be realistic or imaginary
- often conveys a theme or lesson about life

As you read "Heartbeat," think about what the thoughts, words, and actions of Dave, the main character, reveal about him. Copy and complete this diagram to help you analyze his traits and motivations.

ANALYZE CONFLICT

Every story is built upon a **conflict**, a struggle between opposing forces. Two types of conflicts often appear in stories:

- An **external conflict** is a struggle against an outside force, such as nature, a physical obstacle, or another character.
- An **internal conflict** is a struggle that occurs in a character's mind, often due to a clash in feelings, thoughts, or values.

Authors may also use the **setting**—the time and place of the action—to shape the conflict and its **resolution** (how the conflict is resolved).

As you read "Heartbeat," look closely at the struggle that Dave faces. Infer whether it reveals a primarily external or internal conflict. Think, too, about why the conflict is important and how it is resolved.

Heartbeat 101

GET READY

TEACH

QUICK START

Have students read the Quick Start questions, and invite them to brainstorm strategies for confidence building. For example, a student who struggles with a subject in school might need to ask for help. Sometimes asking for help can be the bravest thing to do. Ask students to give examples of people have overcome illusions about their abilities by asking for help.

ANALYZE CHARACTER

Help students understand that evaluating the traits an author reveals about a character allows the reader to analyze that character's motivations. A character's words and thoughts can be positive, negative, or neutral, which reveals how the character feels about himself or herself, other characters, events occurring in the plot, and the setting.

ANALYZE CONFLICT

Tell students that all stories use some form of conflict to drive the plot forward. Conflict makes a story interesting and keeps the attention of the reader. Review the differences between external and internal conflict, then ask students to consider the following questions as they read to help them determine whether the conflict in "Heartbeat" is mostly external or mostly internal.

- What do the main character's thoughts and feelings reveal about him?
- Does the main character have a problem with another character in the story?
- Is the main character struggling to prove something to himself or to others?

ENGLISH LEARNER SUPPORT

Use Academic Language Introduce students to the academic language they need to discuss characters in a story. Direct students to the character chart on page 101. After reading the definitions for *character traits* and *character motivations*, read aloud the information in the right column of the chart, creating a list of key terms as you go along: *thoughts, actions, appearance, relationships, take action, avoid action*. Have students stop to note any unfamiliar words, and provide scaffolded definitions as necessary. **MODERATE**

Heartbeat 101

TEACH

CRITICAL VOCABULARY

Encourage students to read all the sentences before deciding which word best completes each one. Remind them to look for context clues that match the precise meaning of each word.

Answers:

1. *delirious, futile*
2. *repulse*
3. *moot, metabolism*

■ English Learner Support

Cognates Tell students that two of the Critical Vocabulary words have Spanish cognates: *delirious/delirante, metabolism/metabolismo.* **ALL LEVELS**

LANGUAGE CONVENTIONS

Review the information about subject-verb agreement and prepositional phrases. Explain that the reason the verb agrees with the subject is because the subject is taking the action in the sentence. Tell students a good way to check for subject-verb agreement is to remove the prepositional phrase from the sentence. If the subject and verb agree without the prepositional phrase, it is grammatically correct. Have students remove the prepositional phrase from the example sentence to check for subject verb-agreement. *(The kids are waving. The subject and verb agree even without the prepositional phrase.)*

ANNOTATION MODEL

Students can review the Reading Model introduction if they have questions about any of the signposts. Suggest that they underline important phrases or circle key words that help them identify signposts. They may want to color-code their annotation by using a different color highlighter for each signpost. Point out that they may follow this suggestion or use their own system for marking up the selections in their write-in texts.

 GET READY

CRITICAL VOCABULARY

repulse   metabolism   moot   futile   delirious

Use the Critical Vocabularly words to complete each sentence.

1. The flu made her feel _____ , so she knew it was _____ to try to go to work.

2. He was not a good cook and feared that he might _____ his guests with his cooking.

3. Was it a _____ point to argue that his fast _____ prevented him from gaining weight?

LANGUAGE CONVENTIONS

Subject–Verb Agreement and Prepositional Phrases Verbs must agree (or match) their subjects in number. Look at this sentence:

The <u>kids</u> on the bus <u>are waving</u>.

Are waving (the verb) agrees with *kids* (the subject). Notice the prepositional phrase *on the bus* does not change the subject-verb agreement. As you read "Heartbeat," notice subject–verb agreement.

ANNOTATION MODEL   **NOTICE & NOTE**

As you read, pay attention to signposts, including **Aha Moments**, **Contrasts and Contradictions**, and **Again and Again**. Here is an example of how one reader responded to the opening of "Heartbeat."

> 1   My nickname's ⟨Heartbeat,⟩ because my friends swear that you can actually see the pulse on my bare chest. I've always been skinny. Everyone assumes I'm a weakling because I'm so thin (I prefer "lean and mean" or "wiry"), despite being a three-sport athlete. <u>I decided to do something about it this fall when Sarah, the girl I have a crush on, said, "Oh my gosh . . . you are so skinny."</u> She was visibly repulsed by my sunken chest as I stepped off the soccer bus after practice. <u>I silently vowed to do everything within my power to become the "after" picture.</u> I was sixteen years old, but looked like I was eleven.

This nickname explains the title of the story.

Aha! Sarah's words push him into a sudden decision.

I wonder if this story is going to show how he wins the girl?

BACKGROUND

Born in 1974, **David Yoo** has often felt like an outsider. While attending an international school in Korea, he was the only Korean American student among German and Saudi Arabian classmates. When his family moved to Connecticut, he again encountered few Asian peers. He published his first book, *Girls for Breakfast*, when he was twenty-nine. The book is a humorous account of a Korean American teenage hero's efforts to fit in at a suburban American high school.

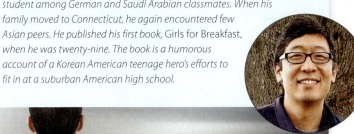

HEARTBEAT
Short Story by David Yoo

SETTING A PURPOSE

As you read, pay attention to the way that the main character talks about himself and to the things that he decides to do. Note details that help you understand what he is like—his traits and motivations—and why he has a conflict.

1   My nickname's "Heartbeat," because my friends swear that you can actually see the pulse on my bare chest. I've always been skinny. Everyone assumes I'm a weakling because I'm so thin (I prefer "lean and mean" or "wiry"), despite being a three-sport athlete. I decided to do something about it this fall when Sarah, the girl I have a crush on, said, "Oh my gosh . . . you are so skinny." She was visibly **repulsed** by my sunken chest as I stepped off the soccer bus after practice. I silently vowed to do everything within my power to become the "after" picture. I was sixteen years old, but looked like I was eleven.

2   For the rest of fall, I did countless push-ups and curled free weights until I couldn't bend my arms. I got ridiculously strong and defined, but I wasn't gaining weight.

NOTICE & NOTE

Notice & Note
Use the side margins to notice and note signposts in the text.

ANALYZE CHARACTER
Annotate: In paragraph 1, mark three things that Dave says other people say to him or think about him.

Infer: What does beginning the story with this information suggest about the kind of person Dave is?

repulse
(rĭ-pŭls´) v. Something that *repulses* you makes you want to reject it because you find it disgusting.

Heartbeat   103

ENGLISH LEARNER SUPPORT

Acquire Language Point out the title of the selection. Have students highlight the words *nickname* and *heartbeat* in the text as you read the first paragraph aloud. Explain that when the title is in a story, that means it is important

Have pairs work together to find clues to the meaning of *nickname* and *heartbeat*. Provide the cognate *pulse/pulso* if students struggle defining *heartbeat* on their own. Have pairs work together to answer the following question: Why is the title of the story "Heartbeat"? *(It is about a skinny boy nicknamed Heartbeat.)* **ALL LEVELS**

TEACH

BACKGROUND
Have students read the background and the biographical information about the author. Introduce the selection by telling students that David Yoo is a Korean American writer known for his true-to-life stories and young-adult novels that mix humor with brutal honesty about being different. Yoo's writing is known for its endearing self-deprecation, revealing the insecurities we all feel, but hate to admit.

SETTING A PURPOSE
Direct students to use the Setting a Purpose prompt to focus their reading.

ANALYZE CHARACTER
Remind students that a **character's traits** and **motivations** are revealed by what he or she says, thinks, or does. (**Answer:** *Dave describes himself in a humorous way; but because he begins by sharing negative views of himself, he seems like a person who is rather down on himself, who is not very confident, and who cares a lot about what others think of him.*)

> For **listening support** for students at varying proficiency levels, see the **Text X-Ray** on page 100C.

CRITICAL VOCABULARY

repulse: The author uses the word *repulsed* to show the reader that Sarah's look conveys rejection to Dave.

ASK STUDENTS why the author chose *repulsed* instead of *grossed out*. *(Repulsed is a stronger description. It helps illustrate that Dave is affected by Sarah's expression.)*

TEACH

ANALYZE CONFLICT

Remind students that **external conflict** in a story is between a character and an outside force or other character, while **internal conflict** is a struggle the character grapples with within his or her own mind. (**Answer:** *Dave seems to struggle mostly with his thoughts and feelings about not looking very athletic, despite being an athlete. This indicates an internal conflict: His main problem is caused by the way he thinks and by his desire to impress other people.*)

 For **reading support** for students at varying proficiency levels, see the **Text X-Ray** on page 100C

CRITICAL VOCABULARY

metabolism: The human body turns food into energy in a process called metabolism. The food we eat can turn into muscle or fat or can be burned off with physical activity.

ASK STUDENTS why Dave is complaining about having a fast metabolism. (*Dave is trying to gain weight, but his body burns all the calories he eats.*)

moot: Dave views eating a Snickers as pointless to his goals since he burns more calories eating it than he takes in from it.

ASK STUDENTS to identify the context clue in the sentence where *moot* appears that supports the definition on page 112. (*"waste 90 chewing it"*)

futile: Dave ultimately realizes that all his efforts to gain weight have been ineffectual when he notices an extra shirt makes him appear bigger.

ASK STUDENTS to identify what Dave has been doing taht was *futile* up until paragraph 3 in the story. (*Dave has been lifting weights and eating a lot, but it hasn't helped him gain weight.*)

104 Unit 2

 NOTICE & NOTE

ANALYZE CONFLICT

Annotate: In paragraph 2, mark Dave's motivation for exercising.

Draw Conclusions: Does Dave struggle mostly with an external conflict or an internal conflict? Explain.

metabolism
(mĭ-tăb′ə-lĭz′əm) *n.* A living thing's *metabolism* is the chemical processes that give it energy and produce growth.

moot
(mo͞ot) *adj.* Something that is *moot* is unimportant or irrelevant.

futile
(fyo͞ot′l) *adj.* When something is *futile*, it has no useful or meaningful result.

I wanted to be *thicker*. I didn't care about getting stronger if nobody could tell. I did research, and started lifting heavier weights at lower reps and supplemented my meals with weight-gainer shakes, egg whites, boiled yams, and tubs of cottage cheese. I forced myself to swallow the daily caloric intake equivalent of three overweight men and still wasn't able to increase my mass. (I have a ridiculously fast **metabolism**.) Over Christmas break I cut out all useless movement, like Ping-Pong and staircases, because I'm like a sieve—the 83 calories in a mini-Snickers bar is **moot** because I waste 90 chewing it.

3   I returned to school in January depressed, because I was still Heartbeat in everyone's eyes. I constantly weighed myself. At least once an hour, no matter where I was, I'd find a bathroom so I could take off my shirt and flex in the mirror for a couple of minutes. I was so frustrated that nothing was working—but the frustration didn't last. I was sitting in study hall two weeks ago when Sarah said the magic words: "Have you been working out, Dave? You look bigger." I couldn't tell if she was being sarcastic. I went home and inspected myself in the mirror. I did look bigger!

4   But then I realized the reason: I'd accidentally worn *two* T-shirts under my rugby shirt that day. It was just an illusion. I was **futilely** stuffing my face and religiously pumping iron and failing to alter my appearance, and now I'd stumbled on the simplest solution to looking bigger. I felt like I was reborn.

5   I went to school the next day wearing two T-shirts under my turtleneck. I felt solid. By the end of last week, I was wearing three T-shirts under my rugby shirt. This Monday I tucked four T-shirts under my plaid button-down. It gave me traps that didn't exist. My Q-tip-sized shoulders transformed

104 Unit 2

 ENGLISH LEARNER SUPPORT

Understand Idioms Explain to students that an idiom is an expression or saying that has a figurative meaning instead of a literal one. Read paragraph 3 aloud and point out the idiom *the magic words*. Ask: *What 'magic words' does Sarah say to Dave in paragraph 3?* ("Have you been working out? You look bigger.") *Are Sarah's words actually magical? How do you know?* (*No. The story is realistic and is not about magic.*) Guide students to understand that in the text, *the magic words* means special, important, or significant. Have student pairs identify why Dave thinks what Sarah says are *the magic words*. Then ask volunteers share their answer with the group. (*Dave realizes the way to look bigger is to wear extra clothes.*) **LIGHT**

into NBA-grapefruit deltoids.[1] I could tell my classmates subtly regarded me differently. It was respect. Sarah gave me a look I'd never seen before, as if she felt . . . *safer* around me. I was walking down the hallway at the end of the day and must have twisted awkwardly because suddenly my zipper literally exploded, and all my T-shirts spilled out of my pants. Luckily, the hallway was empty and I was wearing a belt.

6   I realized I had artificially outgrown my clothes. My buttondowns were so tight that a few seconds after jamming the extra layers into my pants, the pressure would suddenly bunch the cloth up in random places so it looked like I had a goiter[2] on my shoulder or something. I complained to my parents over dinner last night. "I don't fit into anything anymore," I said. "It reflects poorly on you guys. You could get arrested."

7   "What are you talking about? You look the same as always. You're still my little boy," my dad replied, putting me in a headlock and giving me a noogie. I glared at him.

8   "I need a new ski jacket," I said. It was true. I could barely clap my hands with all the layers I was wearing. I was getting out of control at this point. The four T-shirts under my wool sweater were smushing my lungs together like a male girdle. It was a small price to pay; nobody called me Heartbeat anymore, I reminded myself.

9   After dinner I went to a party. Even though it was winter, I opted to hang out on the back porch as much as possible because it was so hot inside. Being indoors was like a sauna, but Sarah was in the basement so I headed that way. We were talking and she noticed that I was dripping with perspiration. "You're trembling," she said, touching my shoulder. She thought I was nervous talking to her and probably thought it was cute, but in reality I was on the verge of passing out because I was wearing four tight T-shirts and two long-sleeves under my wool sweater, not to mention the sweatpants tucked into my tube socks to add heft to my (formerly chicken-legs) quads. She squeezed my biceps.[3]

10 "Jeez, Dave, how many layers are you wearing?"
11 I couldn't even feel her squeezing them.
12 "I have to go," I said, excusing myself to another corner of the basement. Everyone was smushed together. It was so hot

---
[1] **traps . . . deltoids:** traps (short for trapezius) are large, flat upper-back muscles; deltoids are triangular muscles that connect the top of the shoulder to the arm.
[2] **goiter:** swollen thyroid gland often visible at the bottom of the neck.
[3] **quads . . . biceps:** quads (short for quadriceps) are long muscles in the front of the thigh; biceps are the large muscles in the front of the upper arm.

NOTICE & NOTE

AGAIN AND AGAIN

Notice & Note: In paragraph 5, mark each phrase that includes the word *T-shirts*.

Analyze: What does the growing number of T-shirts tell you about Dave's state of mind?

LANGUAGE CONVENTIONS

Annotate: In paragraph 8, mark the prepositional phrase that separates a subject and predicate in a sentence.

Analyze: How might the prepositional phrase in this sentence confuse subject-verb agreement?

CONTRASTS AND CONTRADICTIONS

Notice & Note: In paragraph 9, mark the sentence that shows a contrast between what Sarah believes and Dave knows to be true.

Interpret: How does the contrast add to your understanding of Dave?

Heartbeat 105

TEACH

AGAIN AND AGAIN

Explain to students that this signpost is used when a word or a phrase appears over and over in a story. Sometimes the word or phrase has an unusual meaning, and other times an author uses repetitious language to draw attention to an important element of the story, such as the **character's development** or the story's central conflict. (**Answer:** *Dave is losing sight of reality. He's become attached to the illusion that he appears much bigger. As a result, he believes that he's winning more respect from his friends and attention from Sarah. He's hooked on the illusion, so he tries to maintain it.*)

LANGUAGE CONVENTIONS

Guide students to identify the sentence in paragraph 8 that includes a prepositional phrase between the subject and the predicate. Remind students that removing a prepositional phrase from a sentence is a good way to check for subject-verb agreement. (**Answer:** *The prepositional phrase "under my wool sweater" includes the singular noun sweater, which could confuse subject-verb agreement because the subject of the sentence is the plural word* t-shirts.)

CONTRASTS AND CONTRADICTIONS

Explain to students that this signpost is often used when a character behaves in a way that contradicts past behavior, or in a way the reader wouldn't expect. By contrasting what Dave believes Sarah is thinking with the reality of why Dave is trembling, the author is revealing important information about Dave's **character development**. It also shows that Dave may not know what Sarah is thinking. (**Answer:** *The contrast shows that Dave is still interested in Sarah but that he also is starting to realize that his plan for looking "thicker" is failing.*)

APPLYING ACADEMIC VOCABULARY

 abnormal   feature   focus   perceive   task

Write and Discuss Have students turn to a partner to discuss the following questions. Guide students to include the Academic Vocabulary words *feature* and *perceive* in their responses. Ask volunteers to share their responses with the class

- Which of Dave's physical **features** are altered by the way he is dressed?
- What does Dave think Sarah **perceives** about why he is trembling at the party?

Heartbeat 105

TEACH

AHA MOMENT

Explain to students that this signpost is often used when a character has a sudden realization that creates a change in the character's behavior, or propels the character's development, allowing for the character to come to a significant realization. (**Answer:** Dave suddenly understands how crazy it was for him to try to pretend to be someone he isn't. He was making himself miserable all because of how he thinks people perceive him. He relies on new self-talk: I'm not disgustingly thin. I am wiry. I'm lean and mean.)

ANALYZE CONFLICT

Remind students to analyze Dave's thoughts and actions in order to understand the conflict he is experiencing. (**Answer:** Dave is now seeing himself more clearly, and he has more realistic expectations of how others see him. He has changed from the beginning of the story, when he didn't care about getting stronger "if nobody could tell.")

CRITICAL VOCABULARY

delirious The layers Dave is wearing causes him to overheat and become confused and disoriented at the party.

ASK STUDENTS what details the author includes in paragraph 12 to illustrate that Dave begins to feel delirious at the party. ("felt claustrophobic," "lurched into the bathroom," "stop midway and take a rest," "gasping")

106   Unit 2

 **NOTICE & NOTE**

delirious
(dĭ-lîr′ē-əs) *adj.* Someone who is *delirious* is temporarily confused, often because of fever or shock.

AHA MOMENT

Notice & Note: Mark what Dave suddenly realizes in paragraph 12.

Infer: What can you infer from that evidence, along with the question at the end of paragraph 12?

ANALYZE CONFLICT

Annotate: In paragraph 13, mark two reasons why Dave decides to stop wearing extra layers. Number them 1 and 2.

Interpret: Has Dave resolved his conflict? Explain.

---

everyone except me was hanging out in T-shirts and tank tops. I was sopping and **delirious** and felt claustrophobic. My chest was cold because I had four drenched T-shirts underneath my sweater. It looked like I was breaking out with Ebola[4] or something. When I coughed people turned away from me in fear. *Abandon ship, abandon ship!* I had no choice but to take some layers off. I lurched to the bathroom. My arms were ponderously heavy as I pulled off the sweater. Just lifting my arms exhausted me, and I had to stop midway and take a rest by sitting on the edge of the tub, gasping. I slowly peeled off the layers, one at a time. I took off my pants and peeled off my sweatpants, too, down to my undies. I dried myself off with a wash cloth. My red T-shirt had bled onto the three white Ts because of the sweat, so they now were faded pink tie-dyes. I hoisted the bundle of clothes and was shocked at the weight. I jammed them into the closet. I'd retrieve them later, before I left. I put my sweater back on without anything underneath. After two weeks of constricting my air supply and range of motion by wearing upwards of six layers, I was amazed at how much freedom I had with my arms. I felt like dancing for the first time in my life. I suddenly realized what I really looked like at this party: a padded, miserable, and frustrated puffball, burning up in all my layers. All this because I hated my nickname?

13   I got home and realized I'd left my bundle of wet clothes back at the party. I took this as a sign. My days of wearing extra layers was officially over.(1) Had Sarah fallen for the padded me, she'd be falling for someone else. Besides,(2) winter wasn't going to last forever, and I couldn't just revert back to wearing just one set of clothes like a normal human being come spring. The

---

[4] **Ebola:** deadly virus that causes high fever and bleeding.

106   Unit 2

WHEN STUDENTS STRUGGLE...

Make Inferences Have partners work together to complete the inferences chart.

Dave's thoughts/actions	Inference
"Had Sarah fallen for the padded me, she'd be falling for someone else."	(He doesn't want to look silly when he can't wear layers any longer.)
"The change in my outward appearance would be the equivalent of a sheared sheep."	(He doesn't want to look silly when he can't wear layers any longer.)

 For additional support, go to the **Reading Studio** and assign the following Level Up tutorial: **Characters and Conflict.**

NOTICE & NOTE

change in my outward appearance would be the equivalent of a sheared sheep. From now on, I was going to just be me.

14   That was last night. *I'm not disgustingly thin*, I constantly remind myself. I am wiry. I'm lean and mean.

15   Outside it's snowing again. There's a party tonight, and my friends are on their way to pick me up. I don't know what to wear, so I lay out four different outfits on the floor as if they're chalk outlines of people. A car horn honks ten minutes later and I still haven't decided on an outfit. Maybe I'll just wear all of them.

ANALYZE CHARACTER
Annotate: Mark the sentences in paragraph 15 that show Dave's indecision.

Draw Conclusions: Has Dave's essential personality changed?

TEACH

 ANALYZE CHARACTER

Remind students that characters reveal their traits and motivations through thoughts, words, and actions. Examine the way Dave thinks at the beginning of the story compared to way he thinks at the end. (**Answer:** *Dave hasn't really changed. He uses the same humor as he has throughout the story, but seems to still be uncertain of exactly how he wants to present himself despite his resolution to only be himself from now on.*)

CHECK YOUR UNDERSTANDING

Answer these questions before moving on to the **Analyze the Text** section on the following page.

1. In paragraph 2, the details about Dave's attempts to gain body mass suggest that he —
   A. wants to get quick results without making an effort
   B. is disciplined and determined to reach his goal
   C. is strong and healthy but not very athletic
   D. cares about his health as much as his image

2. Why is the party scene important to the story's plot?
   F. At the party, Dave realizes that looking thicker isn't really important.
   G. Dave loses his extra clothing, and his deception is revealed.
   H. While dancing with Sarah, Dave is able to say how he feels about her.
   J. Dave's friends finally express their appreciation of him there.

3. Which of these best sums up the conflict in the story?
   A. Dave struggles to get the respect of his classmates.
   B. Dave struggles to gain control of his metabolism.
   C. Dave struggles to think correctly about his body image.
   D. Dave struggles to persuade Sarah to accept him as he is.

CHECK YOUR UNDERSTANDING

Have students answer the questions independently.

Answers:
1. B
2. F
3. C

If they answer any questions incorrectly, have them reread the text to confirm their understanding. Then they may proceed to ANALYZE THE TEXT on page 108.

Heartbeat 107

ENGLISH LEARNER SUPPORT

Oral Assessment Use the following questions to assess students' comprehension and speaking skills.

1. What details tell about what Dave does to look bigger? What do the details tell the reader about Dave? (*He exercises a lot and eats a lot of food. The details shows that he works hard.*)

2. What does Dave realize at the party after wearing too many clothes makes him feel ill? (*He realizes that it is more important to be happy and comfortable than to look bigger.*)

3. What does Dave struggle with throughout the story? (*Accepting the way he looks.*)

Heartbeat 107

APPLY

ANALYZE THE TEXT

Possible answers:

1. **DOK 3** Dave says, "I didn't care about getting stronger if nobody could tell."

2. **DOK 4** When Dave's father says, "You're still my little boy," he sees the "real Dave," the boy he loves. He isn't fooled by Dave's attempt to look "thicker," nor does he seem to care what Dave looks like on the outside. Likewise, Dave's friends probably don't view him differently just because he's wearing more layers. They like him just the way he is.

3. **DOK 3** Before he takes off the layers, Dave feels "sopping and delirious" and "claustrophobic." His arms are "ponderously heavy," and just lifting them exhausts him. After he takes off the layers, he is amazed at how free he feels—free enough to dance.

4. **DOK 2** Dave realizes that if Sarah had fallen for him with the padding, it wouldn't have been the "real" Dave.

5. **DOK 4** Dave has resolved his conflict by accepting himself as he is. For example, he calls himself "wiry" and "lean and mean" rather than "disgustingly thin."

RESEARCH

Remind students to asses the credibility of each website they use in their research.

CONNECT Students should come up with questions and answers about self-esteem, such as: 1. *What is self-esteem? 2. What can cause low self-esteem? 3. What can raise a person's confidence?* Students should understand that self-esteem is how we see ourselves and how we view our value as a person. Students should identify that difficult life circumstances, negative thoughts, perfectionism, and comparisons all lead to low self-esteem, while being positive, taking care of yourself, and getting support can improve circumstances.

108 Unit 2

 RESPOND

ANALYZE THE TEXT

Support your responses with evidence from the text. 📓 **NOTEBOOK**

1. **Cite Evidence** Reread paragraph 2. How can you tell that Dave is motivated by other people's feelings rather than by his own?

2. **Analyze** Dave thinks his friends view him with more respect now that he's wearing the layers. How does what Dave's father says in paragraph 7 bring that idea into question?

3. **Compare and Contrast** How does being at the party affect Dave's actions? Contrast how Dave feels before and after he takes off his extra layers of clothing at the party. Cite details from paragraph 12 to support your answer.

4. **Interpret** According to paragraph 13, how has Dave's thinking about Sarah changed? Explain.

5. **Notice & Note** As the story ends, what do Dave's thoughts suggest about how he has resolved his conflict?

RESEARCH TIP
Focused questions can help you research a topic more quickly and successfully. For example, to get a better understanding of the term *self-esteem*, you might ask, "What is the definition of *self-esteem*?" or "What are the characteristics of *self-esteem*?"

RESEARCH

Dave, the main character in "Heartbeat," thinks that he looks too skinny. Would he feel so self-conscious if he had healthy self-esteem? Research behaviors that can help boost self-esteem and self-confidence. Begin by generating several questions to guide your research. Record your questions and the answers you learn in the chart.

QUESTION	ANSWER
What is self-esteem?	How we see ourselves and how we view our value as a person.
What can cause low self-esteem?	Difficult life circumstances Having negative thoughts Comparing yourself with others
What can raise a person's self-esteem?	Change your ways of thinking Set realistic expectations and accept successes and failures. Get support from friends and family.

Connect Do you think it would have helped Dave to know some of the information that you gathered in your research? With a small group, discuss the information you uncovered and how it might have boosted Dave's self-confidence.

108 Unit 2

WHEN STUDENTS STRUGGLE . . .

Reteach Character Have partners work together to identify details that describe Dave's characteristics. Reread paragraphs 2, 7, 12, and 13. Have students underline the details that describe what Dave is saying, thinking, or doing in these paragraphs, then share the details with their partner. Tell students to make a list of words that describe Dave as a character based on the details they've underlined.

 For additional support, go to the **Reading Studio** and assign the following 🔼 **Level Up tutorial: Characters.**

CREATE AND PRESENT

Write Text for an Infographic An **infographic** is a visual representation of information, such as a chart, that's made up of text and images. Using your research on boosting self-esteem, write several paragraphs about the benefits of rejecting negative thinking.

- ❏ Think about the members of your audience. What questions about this topic do you think they have? What message do you want your answers to convey to them?
- ❏ Draft several paragraphs that are brief and to the point. Make sure that each one has a clear, concise topic sentence that is supported by text evidence from your research.
- ❏ Think about how you might show this information visually for greatest effect.

Devise an Infographic Devise an infographic to illustrate the benefits of rejecting negative thinking. Then, prepare to present your infographic to the class.

- ❏ Sketch out visual elements you might include in the infographic.
- ❏ Create illustrations or other images to convey information visually.
- ❏ Incorporate the text that you wrote earlier into the infographic.

RESPOND

Go to **Writing Informative Texts** in the **Writing Studio** to learn more.

Go to **Using Media in a Presentation** in the **Speaking and Listening Studio** for help.

RESPOND TO THE ESSENTIAL QUESTION

? What can blur the lines between what's real and what's not?

Gather Information Review your annotations and notes on "Heartbeat." Then, add relevant details to your Response Log. As you determine which information to include, think about:

- the difference between how we see ourselves and how others see us
- what affects how people see themselves and the world around them
- how people can lose a sense of what's "real" about themselves when trying to "fit in"

At the end of the unit, use your notes to help you create a multimodal presentation.

ACADEMIC VOCABULARY

As you write and discuss what you learned from the short story, be sure to use the Academic Vocabulary words. Check off each of the words that you use.

- ❏ abnormal
- ❏ feature
- ❏ focus
- ❏ perceive
- ❏ task

APPLY

CREATE AND PRESENT

Write Text for an Infographic Tell students they should revisit their research from page 108 when writing text and selecting images for their self-esteem infographic.

 For writing support for students at varying proficiency levels, see the **Text X-Ray** on page 100D.

Devise an Infographic Remind students that they should use rulers and circular items to make their infographics, so that the lines and circles are neat. Tell them to leave plenty of space in the boxes and the circles for the text. They should revise and edit their texts for clarity and brevity before adding them to their infographics. In an infographic, only the most important text needs to be included.

RESPOND TO THE ESSENTIAL QUESTION

Allow time for students to add details from "Heartbeat" to their Unit 2 Response Logs.

 ENGLISH LEARNER SUPPORT

Use Key Vocabulary Give students lists of key vocabulary words and phrases. Help them internalize words such as *self-esteem, confidence, self-talk, focus,* and *perceive* by giving them infographic templates they can illustrate and fill in with vocabulary words. Have them choose a title for their infograpics. Beginning students may populate the template with single words and illustrations. Create frame sentences for intermediate students such as: *Positive_____ helps me_____.* **SUBSTANTIAL/MODERATE**

APPLY

CRITICAL VOCABULARY

Possible Answers:

1. we saw all the half-eaten food that had been thrown out.
2. he does not seem to burn calories very quickly.
3. even after a loss, it is important for the team to work on improving its performance for the next season.
4. washed the car now, when the sky is filled with rain clouds.
5. hear that all the trains have stopped running.

VOCABULARY STRATEGY:
Context Clues

Possible Answers:

1. *regarded*: **Context Clue:** "I could tell my classmates subtly regarded me differently. It was respect. Sarah gave me a look I'd never seen before, as if she felt . . . safer around me."; **My Guessed Definition:** looked at or had a different opinion about? **Dictionary Definition:** "to think of (someone) in a particular way"; "to look at"

2. *lurched*: **Context Clue:** "I lurched to the bathroom."; **Possible Definition:** ran or hurried, maybe unsteadily?; **Dictionary Definition:** "to make a sudden movement, to stagger"

3. *hoisted*: **Context Clue:** "I hoisted the bundle of clothes and was shocked at the weight."; **Possible Definition:** lifted; **Dictionary Definition:** "to lift or pick up (something heavy)"

 RESPOND

CRITICAL VOCABULARY

WORD BANK
repulse
metabolism
moot
delirious
futile

Practice and Apply Complete each sentence in a way that shows the meaning of the Critical Vocabulary words.

1. When we cleaned up after the party, we were **repulsed** when _____.
2. He knows that he has a slow **metabolism** because _____.
3. It would not be **moot** for a baseball team to practice because _____.
4. I would probably be **delirious** if I _____.
5. It is **futile** to try to be on time when you _____.

 Go to the **Vocabulary Studio** for more on context clues.

VOCABULARY STRATEGY: Context Clues

The **context** of a word includes words, sentences, and paragraphs that surround the word. Context may provide clues to the meaning of an unfamiliar word. Look at the following example:

> After two weeks of constricting my air supply and range of motion by wearing upwards of six layers, I was amazed at how much freedom I had with my arms.

Context clues suggest that *constricting* is part of the effect of Dave's wearing many layers. Because Dave wore upwards of six layers of clothes, he limited his air supply and range of motion. Therefore, *constricting* probably means "limiting."

Practice and Apply Review "Heartbeat" to find the following words. Complete a chart like the one shown to determine their meaning.

WORD	CONTEXT CLUES	MY GUESSED DEFINITION	DICTIONARY DEFINITION
regarded (paragraph 5)	"I could tell my classmates subtly regarded me differently. It was respect. Sarah gave me a look I'd never seen before, as if she felt . . . safer around me."	looked at or had a different opinion about?	"to think of (someone) in a particular way"; "to look at"
lurched (paragraph 12)	"I lurched to the bathroom."	ran or hurried, maybe unsteadily?	"to make a sudden movement"; "to stagger"
hoisted (paragraph 12)	"I hoisted the bundle of clothes and was shocked at the weight."	lifted?	"to lift or pick up (something heavy)"

110 Unit 2

 ENGLISH LEARNER SUPPORT

Use Context Clues Provide students with extra support as they identify the definitions for *regarded, lurched,* and *hoisted*. Remind students to look for sentences in the paragraphs that start with I statements, and that the surrounding words will help them identify the definitions. (Regarded: "Sarah gave me a look I'd never seen before"; Lurched: "I was sopping and delirious; I had no choice but to take some layers off"; Hoisted: "was shocked at the weight") Use gestures to demonstrate the meaning of each word and have students repeat your motions as you say each one aloud.

LANGUAGE CONVENTIONS: Subject–Verb Agreement and Prepositional Phrases

The subject and verb in a clause must agree in number. (A **clause** is a group of words that includes a complete subject and predicate.) **Agreement** means if the subject is singular, the verb takes the singular form, and if the subject is plural, the verb takes the plural form.

SINGULAR: <u>David Yoo</u> <u>tells</u> the story of "Heartbeat."

PLURAL: His <u>characters</u> <u>seem</u> very true to life.

In the examples above, the subject and verb are right next to each other. Sometimes, however, a **prepositional phrase** comes between the subject and the verb. As a general rule, ignore the prepositional phrase or phrases. Focus only on the subject.

The <u>opinion</u> of his classmates <u>is</u> very important to Dave.

<u>People</u> at Dave's school <u>call</u> him "Heartbeat."

A few <u>words</u> from Sarah after soccer practice <u>propel</u> Dave into an important decision.

<u>Exercise</u> and <u>shakes</u> for gaining weight <u>are</u> not enough.

Occasionally, the prepositional phrase can influence subject-verb agreement. Note these rules for certain pronoun subjects.

- Pronouns such as *each*, *either*, *everyone*, *nobody*, *someone*, and *something* are always considered to be singular.

  <u>Nobody</u> in Dave's classes <u>knows</u> about Dave's plan.

- Pronouns such as *both*, *few*, *many*, and *several* are considered plural.

  <u>Many</u> of Dave's exercises <u>make</u> him stronger but not "thicker."

- For the pronouns *all*, *any*, *most*, *none*, and *some*, however, look at the object of the preposition.

  <u>Most</u> of his food <u>metabolizes</u> way too quickly.

  <u>None</u> of his meals <u>gave</u> Dave his desired "look."

Practice and Apply Choose and write the verb that agrees with the subject.

1. T-shirts under his rugby shirt (**transforms**, **transform**) _____ Dave's appearance.
2. The use of extra garments (**makes**, **make**) _____ a big difference.
3. Almost everyone around Dave (**senses**, **sense**) _____ a change in him.
4. All of his regular clothes (**were**, **was**) _____ too tight.

RESPOND

Go to **Phrases Between Subject and Verb** in the **Grammar Studio** for more on subject-verb agreement.

Heartbeat 111

APPLY

LANGUAGE CONVENTIONS: Subject–Verb Agreement and Prepositional Phrases

Review the information about subject-verb agreement and prepositional phrases with students. Remind them that a sentence is made up of several parts and that separating words into these parts is a good strategy to use to ensure correct grammar in their writing.

Guide students through each aspect of identifying prepositional phrases and checking subject-verb agreement.

- If the subject is singular, verbs take on the singular form, while verbs that agree with plural subjects take on the plural form. For example, *The knitted* stocking is *a gift*; *The knitted* stockings are *a gift*.

- Remind students to look for prepositions in a sentence to identify where the prepositional phrase begins. It's often right after the subject, which can cause subject-verb agreement confusion.

- When in doubt about which form the verb should take, students should remove the prepositional phrase from the sentence and read it aloud.

- Subjects that appear singular, but use a plural verb form (*both, few, many,* and *several*) can be decoded by their meaning. *Both* means two, *few* means more than two, *many* means a large amount, and *several* more than two, but fewer than many.

PRACTICE AND APPLY

1. transform
2. makes
3. senses
4. were

ENGLISH LEARNER SUPPORT

Understand Subject-Verb Agreement Provide students with example sentences and have them choose the correctly formed verb: *The football team ___ (practice/practices) every day. Our sister ___ (swim/swims) very well.* **MODERATE**

Have students use the word bank to fill in the correctly formed words.

calls   put   make   puts

Jacinta ___ her dishes away before her brothers ___ a mess. **LIGHT**

Heartbeat 111

PLAN

MENTOR TEXT

THE CAMERA DOES LIE

Magazine Article by Meg Ross

This article serves as a **mentor text**, a model for students to follow when they come to the Unit 2 Task: Create a Multimodal Presentation.

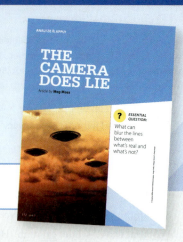

GENRE ELEMENTS
MAGAZINE ARTICLE

Remind students that a **magazine article** is another form of informational text. Its purpose is to present readers with facts and information about a specific topic in order to inform, entertain, or persuade. Writers frequently express their opinions in magazine articles, using facts, details, and examples to support their beliefs.

The words writers choose for their articles also suggest what their attitudes are about the topic.

LEARNING OBJECTIVES

- Determine an author's purpose.
- Cite evidence and draw conclusions.
- Write an opinion essay about fake images or videos.
- Conduct research about a photographic or video hoax.
- Use a dictionary to expand vocabulary.
- Analyze and write sentences that use semicolons properly.
- **Language** Discuss with a partner how to do a multimodal presentation.

TEXT COMPLEXITY

Quantitative Measures	The Camera Does Lie	Lexile: 990L
Qualitative Measures	**Ideas Presented** Literal and direct with a clear purpose	
	Structure Used Clear, conventional, with subheads	
	Language Used Explicit, literal, contemporary with mostly Tier 1 words	
	Knowledge Required Requires no special knowledge and subjects are familiar	

112A Unit 2

PLAN

RESOURCES

- Unit 2 Response Log
- 🔊 Selection Audio
- [Text in Focus] Interpreting Numbers/ Drawing Conclusions
- 📖 Reading Studio: Notice & Note
- 💬 Speaking and Listening Studio: Using Media in a Presentation
- ⚪ Vocabulary Studio: Using Reference Resources
- ❗ Grammar Studio: Module 3: Lesson 6: Conjunctions and Interjections
- ✅ "The Camera Does Lie" Selection Test

SUMMARIES

English

"The Camera Does Lie" provides information about how digital technology enables video artists, pranksters, and advertisers to create fake images and videos. Their purpose is to entertain, fool, or persuade people to buy products. The article presents a sampling of fake images and offers scientific ways to analyze them to determine whether they are real. The author expresses the belief that viewers should learn to call out the fakes.

Spanish

En "La cámara sí miente" se da información acerca de cómo la tecnología digital permite a los artistas de video, los bromistas y los anunciantes crear imágenes y videos falsos. Su propósito es entretener, engañar o persuadir para que la gente compre productos. El artículo presenta muestras de imágenes falsas y ofrece formas científicas de analizarlas para determinar si son reales o no. El autor expresa su convicción de que el espectador debe aprender a identificar las que son falsas.

SMALL-GROUP OPTIONS

Have students work in small groups to read and discuss the selection.

Jigsaw with Experts

- Divide the article into five sections, based on the five subheadings.
- Have students count off, or assign each student a numbered section.
- After they read the text, have students form groups with other students who read the same section. Each expert group should discuss its section.
- Then, have students form new groups with a representative for each section. These groups should discuss all the sections as a whole.

Think-Pair-Share

- After students have read and discussed "The Camera Does Lie," pose this question: *When are fake images and videos acceptable and when are they unacceptable or even illegal?*
- Have students think about the question individually and write down their ideas.
- Then, have pairs discuss their ideas about the question.
- Finally, ask pairs to share their responses with the class.

The Camera Does Lie **112B**

PLAN

Text X-Ray: English Learner Support
for Mentor Text "The Camera Does Lie"

Use the instruction below and the supports and scaffolds in the Teacher's Edition to help you guide students of different proficiency levels.

INTRODUCE THE SELECTION
DISCUSS PURPOSE

In this lesson, students will need to be able to discuss what the writer's purpose is in writing an article. Provide the following explanation:

- A purpose is the reason writers choose to write about the specific topics that they do. A writer may want to publicize a wrongdoing or make readers laugh or provide information about an interesting subject.

Have volunteers share purposes writers might have. Use the following sentence frames: *A writer's purpose in writing an article about a new law might be _____. A writer's purpose in writing about a famous historical figure might be _____.*

CULTURAL REFERENCES

The following words and phrases may be unfamiliar to students:

- *prankster* (paragraph 2): someone who enjoys playing tricks on people
- *UFOs* (paragraph 4): a mysterious object in the sky for which there is no scientific explanation
- *smacks down* (paragraph 9): criticizes harshly
- *fishy* (paragraph 10) suspicious
- *common sense* (paragraph 16) sound judgment
- *debunk* (paragraph 19) prove something is false

LISTENING

Understand the Central Idea

Draw students' attention to the expert that the author introduces in the "Fooled You Once" section of the article. Explain that understanding what an expert says will help students understand the author's main point in the article.

Have students listen as you read aloud paragraphs 7–10. Use the following supports with students at varying proficiency levels:

- Tell students that you will ask questions about what they just heard. Model that they should give a thumbs up if the answer is yes and a thumbs down for no. For example, ask: *Is the video of the pig saving the drowning goat faked?* (yes) **SUBSTANTIAL**
- Use sentence frames to check understanding. *What kind of track was used to help the pig?* (elaborate) *How does the Bigfoot film look to us today?* (bogus) **MODERATE**
- Ask students to work in pairs and explain why the author included the testimony from this expert in her article. **LIGHT**

PLAN

SPEAKING

Create a Multimodal Presentation

Draw students' attention to the multimodal presentation outlined at the end of the unit.

To assist students with their multimodal presentation assignment at the end of the unit, use the following supports at varying proficiency levels:

- Pronounce key technical terms that would have to be used in the multimodal presentation, and have students echo the pronunciation. **SUBSTANTIAL**
- Have student partners explain to each other why they selected the image they did and why the image is a fake. **MODERATE**
- Have students form small groups to compare and contrast the different images they brought in and the different technical gimmickry involved in each. **LIGHT**

READING

Determine the Central Idea

Draw students' attention to the "Fake Shake" section of the article. Tell students that authors of informational texts provide evidence in the form of facts, examples, and explanations to help readers understand the central idea.

Work with students to reread paragraphs 14–17. Use the following supports with students at varying proficiency levels:

- Ask students to answer yes or no questions: *If a person is wearing different clothes at the end of a short video from what they were wearing in the beginning, does this mean the video is fake?* (yes) **SUBSTANTIAL**
- Guide students to identify a central idea. Then, have students find evidence to support that idea. Supply sentence frames, such as *According to the text, video pranksters use fake shakes in order to _____.* **MODERATE**
- Do you think that some elements of a fake video are easier to spot than others? (A video with fake shake is hard to spot without special software but continuity errors can be spotted by just looking) **LIGHT**

WRITING

Give a Multimodal Presentation

Work with students to read the writing assignment on p. 121.

Use the following supports with students at varying proficiency levels:

- Create a word web on the board with the word *multimodal* in the center. Add the following terms to circles below: *writing, speech, visual*. Have students copy the word web into their notebooks. Then, have student pairs create or find images for each category, such as a student making a speech, an image of a written report, a timeline, and a map. **SUBSTANTIAL**
- Provide sentence frames that students can use to create the written portion of their multimodal presenation: *This image of a _____ is fake. This video of _____ is not real.* **MODERATE**
- Encourage students to include a bulleted or numbered how-to guide that explains how to identify forgeries in the written portion of their multimodal presentation. **LIGHT**

Mentor Text Title **112D**

TEACH

? Connect to the ESSENTIAL QUESTION

"The Camera Does Lie" explains how modern digital technology enables video artists, pranksters, and advertisers to create images that are so convincing, they blur the line between what's real and what's not.

MENTOR TEXT

At the end of the unit, students will be asked to create a multimodal presentation. "The Camera Does Lie" provides a model for incorporating text and visuals into an informational text.

ANALYZE & APPLY

THE CAMERA DOES LIE

Article by **Meg Moss**

? ESSENTIAL QUESTION:

What can blur the lines between what's real and what's not?

QUICK START

Can you always trust what you see with your own eyes? Does seeing mean believing? Describe to a partner the last time you saw something that made you think that seeing *isn't* always believing.

DETERMINE AUTHOR'S PURPOSE

An author's **purpose** is the reason the author wrote a particular work. In other words, it's what the author wants to do for you, the reader. This chart shows common purposes for writing different types of texts.

Author's Purpose			
Inform or Explain	Persuade	Entertain	Express Thoughts or Feelings
Examples			
• encyclopedia entries • informational articles • how-to articles • biographies	• editorials • opinion essays/blogs • advertisements	• stories • novels • some essays	• poems • personal essays • journals

To determine an author's purpose in an informational text, examine the kinds of facts and examples the author presents. Realize, too, that an author may have not only a main purpose for writing but also some additional purposes.

CITE EVIDENCE

When you **draw conclusions**, you make judgments or take a position. To reach a conclusion, you must evaluate details in a text to determine the key ideas. You can then combine this evidence with your own experience. Consider this example from "The Camera Does Lie."

> While some people still debate whether the Bigfoot film is real, it looks plenty bogus compared to today's slick videos. The best modern fakers spare no expense or sleight of hand.

The author makes a comparison to older, "bogus" videos, and she uses the terms *spare no expense* and *sleight of hand*. In addition, you probably have seen many recent videos—perhaps including some fake ones. You can conclude that today's fake videos are made to look so real that it is hard to tell that they are not real.

GET READY

GENRE ELEMENTS: INFORMATIONAL TEXT
- provides factual information
- includes evidence to support ideas
- includes many forms, such as magazine articles
- often contains text features such as headings, photographs, and captions

TEACH

QUICK START

Have students read the Quick Start question, and invite them to share their responses with a partner. Ask them to think about an image they might have seen in an advertisement, a commercial, a TV show, or a movie that tricked them into thinking it was real. Ask them to explain why the image fooled them and why it couldn't have been real in the first place.

DETERMINE AUTHOR'S PURPOSE

Help students understand the terms and concepts related to determining an author's purpose when reading or discussing an informational text. Remind them that authors of informational texts present facts and details to help explain, persuade, entertain, or express thoughts and feelings about a topic. Some authors set out to do more than one of these things. Encourage students to think about how an author presents information and what this tells the reader about the author's purpose.

CITE EVIDENCE

Inform students that when they write about or discuss an informational text, it isn't enough just to have an opinion about what they've read. They need to back up those opinions with evidence from the text. Advise students to ask themselves three important questions as they evaluate evidence:

- Do I agree or disagree with what the author is saying?
- Do the author's facts and details seem logical and truthful?
- Does my personal knowledge or experience make me agree or disagree?

ENGLISH LEARNER SUPPORT

Understand Directionality Reinforce the directionality of English by reviewing how to read the Author's Purpose chart. Explain that each heading applies to the text in the column beneath it. To read the chart, students should begin at the top left of the first row and track to the right to read the different purposes authors have for writing. Then students should go back to the first column and track down to see examples of the first author's purpose. Have them continue this way until they read the entire chart. Ask a volunteer to trace with a finger the order a reader would read the information in the chart. **SUBSTANTIAL**

TEACH

CRITICAL VOCABULARY

Encourage students to read all the sentences before deciding which word best completes each one. Remind them to look for context clues that match the precise meaning of each word.

Answers:

1. *bogus, hoax*
2. *elaborate, ruse*
3. *obsess*
4. *continuity, accelerate*

■ **English Learner Support**

Use Cognates Tell students that several of the Critical Vocabulary words have Spanish cognates: *elaborate/elaborar, obsess/obsesionar, continuity/continuidad, accelerate/acelerar*. **ALL LEVELS**

LANGUAGE CONVENTIONS

Review the information about semicolons. Explain that a semicolon can replace the coordinating conjunction (*and, but, or, nor, yet, so, for*) in a compound sentence. Read aloud the example sentence, replacing the semicolon with the word *and* to illustrate the point.

Discuss why a writer might choose to use a semicolon in a sentence. *(Using a semicolon is an excellent way to achieve sentence variety in a paragraph. It can join two simple sentences in a paragraph with many simple sentences or provide an alternative to coordinating conjunctions.)*

ANNOTATION MODEL

Remind students of the annotation ideas in Cite Evidence on page 113, which suggest evaluating details in a text to determine key ideas. Point out that students may choose to underline important details and facts in the text and write their observations and conclusions in the margins, or create their own annotation methods. For example, students may choose to color-code evidence as being "funny" or "serious," "believable" or "questionable," "supported by my own experience" or not and write their judgments in the margin.

 GET READY

CRITICAL VOCABULARY

bogus	elaborate	accelerate	hoax
obsess	continuity	ruse	

To see how many Critical Vocabulary words you already know, use them to complete the sentences.

1. At first, I trusted the "UFO expert," but he was totally _____. His UFO video wasn't real; it was a complete _____.

2. My family made up a(n) _____ plan to throw me a party. I saw through their _____, but I acted surprised anyway.

3. It's lucky that my sister likes to _____ over camera equipment.

4. The actor wore a different shirt in the second take, which caused _____ problems. Also, a falling object in the film did not _____ at a constant rate between the takes.

LANGUAGE CONVENTIONS

Correlative Conjunctions In this lesson, you will learn how to use correlative conjunctions in writing. A **correlative conjunction** is a pair of conjunctions that connects words used in the same way. Correlative conjunction word pairs must be used together. See how two subjects are connected in this sentence based on "The Camera Does Lie."

Both young **and** old have been fooled by fake videos.

ANNOTATION MODEL **NOTICE & NOTE**

As you read, note how the author expresses her purpose or purposes for writing. You can also mark up evidence that supports your conclusions. In the model, you can see one reader's notes about "The Camera Does Lie."

1   Let's face it: the Internet is a wonderful place. Where else can you read all the works of Shakespeare without leaving home? Or catch up on the news around the world with only a few clicks? <u>See eagles snatching children! Witness men flying with homemade bird wings! Cheer for pigs saving goats!</u>

2   Whoa. If you think those last three sound sketchy, you should. . . .

These examples are funny but untrue. I wonder if they help explain the title "The Camera Does Lie."

114 Unit 2

BACKGROUND

"The camera doesn't lie" is an old saying from the time when photos were shot on film and were hard to alter. Digital technology has changed all that—and altered images can be posted online and go viral in a few hours! The author of this magazine article, **Meg Moss**, writes on a variety of topics, and she especially enjoys making complicated topics easy to understand. Here, she shares information to help readers understand why we can't always believe what we see.

NOTICE & NOTE

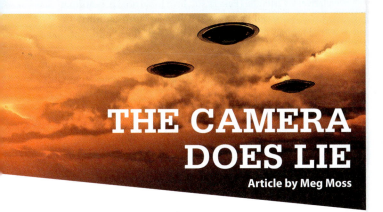

THE CAMERA DOES LIE
Article by Meg Moss

SETTING A PURPOSE

As you read, think about what the author means by the term video conartistry *(paragraph 2). Look for facts and examples that give you more information about that term.*

1   Let's face it: the Internet is a wonderful place. Where else can you read all the works of Shakespeare without leaving home? Or catch up on the news around the world with only a few clicks? See eagles snatching children! Witness men flying with homemade bird wings! Cheer for pigs saving goats!

2   Whoa. If you think those last three sound sketchy, you should. There's a whole world of video conartistry out there, and the Internet loves it. Besides ordinary pranksters and video artists, there are even corporations getting into the act, faking videos to sell products.

3   What's a trusting person to do? Learn to call out the fakes.

Notice & Note
Use the side margins to notice and note signposts in the text.

DETERMINE AUTHOR'S PURPOSE
Annotate: In paragraph 2, mark words and phrases that relate to the title of the article—that is, the idea of a "lying camera."

Predict: You already know that the author's main purpose is to inform or explain. What, specifically, do you think the author will provide information or explanations about?

The Camera Does Lie   115

ENGLISH LEARNER SUPPORT

Learning Strategies Provide students with a main-idea-and-details organizer. Ask them to work individually to complete the organizer for paragraphs 1–3. Then have small groups compare their organizers, decide on the best main idea statements and most important details, and create a revised version that reflects their decisions. They may repeat this process for the four remaining sections of the article.   **ALL LEVELS**

TEACH

BACKGROUND

After students read the Background note, explain that because of the Internet and social media, people see more altered images than ever before, so it is more important than ever to distinguish real from fake—and the same is true of information.

SETTING A PURPOSE

Direct students to use the Setting a Purpose prompt to focus their reading.

DETERMINE AUTHOR'S PURPOSE

Remind students that the author's purpose is the reason the author wrote a particular work, whether it is to inform, explain, entertain, or persuade. (**Answer:** *The author will probably provide information about the world of video conartistry, including the kinds of videos being made and how to determine that they're fake.*)

CRITICAL VOCABULARY

sketchy: Really good con artists never act as if they're up to something *sketchy*.

ASK STUDENTS why the three videos the author mentions sound sketchy. (*The videos sound sketchy because eagles snatching children, men flying with homemade wings, and pigs saving goats are impossibilities.*)

The Camera Does Lie   115

TEACH

CONTRASTS AND CONTRADICTIONS

Explain to students that this signpost is often used to set up a **compare-and-contrast** pattern of organization. In paragraph 4–6, several famous fake images from three different centuries are identified to make the point that fake images have been around for a long time. (**Answer:** *Students may suggest that fake images can be fun or funny but that they also may scare people or cause them to believe in things that are not true. People who are fooled in that way also may be fooled about more serious matters.*)

ENGLISH LEARNER SUPPORT

Understand Contrast Help students understand the descriptions of the different images in paragraphs 4–6. Remind them that the images are from different centuries.

ASK STUDENTS to work in partners and discuss how these fake images from previous centuries are similar and different to images from modern times.

(**Answer:** *Students may suggest that the fake images are similar because they have similar subjects, like ghosts and monsters, and they fooled people. They are different because they were made using completely different kinds of technology.*) **MODERATE**

CRITICAL VOCABULARY

bogus: The Bigfoot film looks bogus compared to today's videos because technology has improved since 1967.

ASK STUDENTS what would look bogus in a homemade horror movie from 1967. (*The monster might not look real by today's standards, and the special effects might not look so special.*)

elaborate: The elaborate track that the pig was walking on must have had many curves and turns.

ASK STUDENTS what the track looked like. (*The track must have looked like an underwater road.*)

obsess: If the professor obsesses about those videos, he must spend all his time thinking about them.

ASK STUDENTS what the professor is thinking about when he obsesses about those films. (*The professor might be trying to figure out how those videos were made.*)

116 Unit 2

 **NOTICE & NOTE**

CONTRASTS AND CONTRADICTIONS

Notice & Note: In paragraphs 4–6, mark the examples of fake images the author provides.

Evaluate: What difference does it make if these images are fake? Does it really do any harm? Explain.

bogus
(bō´gəs) *adj.* Something that is *bogus* is fake or not genuine.

elaborate
(ĭ-lăb´ər-ĭt) *adj.* Something that is *elaborate* has been carefully planned and constructed with great attention to detail.

obsess
(əb-sĕs´) *v.* If you *obsess* over something, your mind is filled with thinking about a single topic, idea, or feeling.

Ye Olde Fakeroo

4   There's nothing new about faking images. Falsified pictures of ghosts, unidentified flying objects (UFOs), and monsters have been around for years.

5   In the 19th century, "spirit photography" captured the public's imagination. Clever photographers created portraits of living people alongside ghostly versions of their deceased relatives or friends. (Fakers still love to record "paranormal activity" with cell phones and handheld video recorders.) "Photographing" UFOs became popular after World War II and remains so today.

6   Perhaps the most famous fake photograph ever was taken in 1934 at Loch Ness in Scotland. Gray and grainy, it supposedly shows the head and neck of Nessie, the dinosaur-like monster of the lake. And you can still view the first moving images of "Bigfoot," shot in 1967, on YouTube.

Fooled You Once

7   While some people still debate whether the Bigfoot film is real, it looks plenty **bogus** compared to today's slick videos. The best modern fakers spare no expense or sleight of hand.[1]

8   A few years back, you may have watched a video of a pig saving a drowning goat (all together now: awwww!). That 30-second scene took days to make. Legions of animal trainers participated (and were sworn to secrecy). An **elaborate** track was built for the pig to follow in the water. With millions of hits, the really good videos—like this one—go viral, spreading like wildfire and keeping the whole world guessing.

9   One person who'd rather not guess is Rhett Allain, an associate professor of physics at Southeastern Louisiana University and author of the Wired Science blog *Dot Physics*. Allain enjoys analyzing online videos. He smacks down those that don't live up to the rigors of physics and **obsesses** about those he suspects but can't pin down.

10 Allain explains that when he looks at fishy videos, he asks, "Is this video physically possible?" Then he uses "known physics models to see if I could come up with a way to get the video to be real."

---

[1] **sleight of hand** (slīt ŭv hănd): a trick, such as a magic trick or card trick, performed so quickly and skillfully that no one notices it.

116   Unit 2

Fooled You Twice

11 A viral video in 2012 showed an eagle snatching a small child in its claws, then dropping the kid safely on the ground. Very convincing—until you do the math.

12 The best way to start your analysis is to ask questions like, "Could an eagle lift and carry a child that size?" The larger the bird is, the larger its wingspan must be to get it off the ground and keep it airborne. Doing a little research, Allain discovered that the golden eagle needs a 7.5-foot (2.3-meter) wingspan just to lift its own body weight of about 14 pounds (6.4 kilograms)—and perhaps some small prey. Estimating the size of the child in the video at about 28 pounds (13 kilograms) means the eagle is lifting almost twice its own weight. This would take a wingspan of about 33 feet (10 meters)!

13 In a video like this one, Allain also measures the way things move, **accelerate**, and fall to see if they obey natural laws. He asks more questions: At what angle does the child fall? How does the child move through the air as the eagle lifts him or her up? Does the child accelerate constantly through the fall like a falling object should? In the eagle video, none of these adds up.

Fake Shake

14 One of Allain's favorite techniques is to analyze camera shake—you know, that quaking picture people get from holding a camera in their hand instead of using a tripod.

15 Allain explains, "To make editing easier and the video more realistic, some people use a tripod for their camera to record the video. They then add fake shake to make it look like the camera was handheld." Voilà—the jerking and unsteady motion of a camera in the hands of someone walking. There's software that lets you graph camera shake by analyzing the movement of the background. If there's a pattern to the jumpiness, it's a fake. Real shake is random.

16 Of course, there are also some simple, common-sense ways to spot an imposter just by looking.

NOTICE & NOTE

CITE EVIDENCE
Annotate: In paragraph 12, mark the facts about golden eagles that Rhett Allain uncovered during his research.

Draw Conclusions: Could the video be real? Why or why not?

accelerate
(ăk-sĕl′ə-rāt′) *v.* When something *accelerates*, its speed increases.

DETERMINE AUTHOR'S PURPOSE
Annotate: Mark the sentence in Allain's quotation that tells one way in which camera shake is analyzed.

Critique: How does this information help the author achieve her purpose for writing this article?

The Camera Does Lie 117

TEACH

CITE EVIDENCE

Remind students that any conclusions they make about what a text is saying must be based on details, facts, and their own judgment and experience. (**Answer:** *The video cannot be real because the eagle did not have a wingspan large enough to lift a child of that weight.*)

DETERMINE AUTHOR'S PURPOSE

Remind students that examining the facts and examples in an informational text will help them determine the author's purpose in writing that text (**Answer:** *The information helps authors explain one method [software] by which an image can be checked to determine whether it is real or fake.*)

TEXT IN FOCUS

Interpreting Numbers/Drawing Conclusions Have students view the **Text in Focus** video on this page of their ebook to learn how evaluating numbers can help them determine the credibility of a piece of information. Then have students use **Text in Focus Practice** to apply what they have learned.

For **listening and reading support** for students at varying proficiency levels, see the **Text X-Ray** on page 112C.

CRITICAL VOCABULARY

accelerate: If an eagle suddenly accelerates to a hundred miles an hour, the image is a hoax.

ASK STUDENTS aside from eagles, what else can accelerate. (**Answer:** *Cars, jets, motor boats, people, and animals can all accelerate.*)

continuity: If a man is wearing a green tie at the beginning of a scene and a red one at the end of the scene, there is a continuity problem.

ASK STUDENTS what filmmakers can do to make sure that there are no continuity problems in their movies. (**Answer:** *They can hire someone to watch for these kinds of mistakes.*)

The Camera Does Lie **117**

APPLYING ACADEMIC VOCABULARY

 abnormal   feature   ☑ focus   perceive   ☑ task

Write and Discuss Have students turn to a partner to discuss the following questions. Guide students to include the Academic Vocabulary words *focus* and *task* in their responses with the class.

- What should people **focus** on in an image to determine if it is a fake?
- Why is it a harder **task** to spot a fake image nowadays than in the past?

TEACH

CITE EVIDENCE

Remind students that any conclusions they draw from the text must be based on evidence from the text. (**Answer:** *The evidence suggests that as technology improves, it may become harder and harder to detect forged photos and videos scientifically. We may need to use other investigative tools, such as background checks, to determine if an image is faked.*)

EL
ENGLISH LEARNER SUPPORT

Use Strategic Learning Techniques to demonstrate the vocabulary in paragraph 14: *camera, shake* and *tripod.*

ASK STUDENTS to identify the words as you pantomime a camera shaking, to demonstrate "camera shake." Pantomime, or use props, to show a camera resting on a tripod. **SUBSTANTIAL**

CRITICAL VOCABULARY

hoax: The missing helmet proved that the video was a hoax even though it looked realistic.

ASK STUDENTS what kind of hoaxes can get pranksters in trouble with the law. (**Answer:** *Hoaxes, like fooling people into buying bogus products, can get pranksters in trouble.*)

ruse: The seller painted over the moldy spots in the house she was selling, and the buyer fell for her ruse.

ASK STUDENTS what kind of ruse would be innocent. (**Answer:** *Telling a friend that you didn't get him a present for his birthday, when you did actually get him something.*)

118   Unit 2

NOTICE & NOTE

continuity
(kŏn´tə-nōō´ĭ-tē) *n.* In the movies, *continuity* refers to making sure that things that were filmed at different times or out of sequence look as if they were filmed at the same time or in the intended sequence.

hoax
(hōks) *n.* A *hoax* is something that is meant to trick or fool someone.

CITE EVIDENCE
Annotate: In paragraph 19, circle what happened when Allain used scientific analysis on the "birdman" film. Then underline how journalists proved the video to be a fake.

Draw Conclusions: What does this example suggest about the future of digital image analysis?

118   Unit 2

17   One factor to check is "**continuity**." Is everybody wearing the same thing throughout a video that is supposedly a single take? In a 2009 slip-and-slide video called "Megawoosh," a daredevil barrels down a giant water slide, off a launch pad, and into a tiny kiddie pool over 100 feet away. Amazing! . . . Until someone noticed that as he flies through the air, the jumper's helmet seems to be missing. The video was actually made in three segments and edited together; the middle section is an animation. The elaborate **hoax** turned out to be an ad for Microsoft Germany.

Faux Flight

18   As technology improves and fakers become more determined (with bigger budgets), it gets harder to weed out the hoaxes. Sometimes, a little old-fashioned research goes a long way.

19   When he watched the video of the Dutch "birdman" flying like a bird with gigantic artificial wings, Rhett Allain was on the fence. The fake was so good, even his scientific analysis couldn't

---

WHEN STUDENTS STRUGGLE . . .

Cite Evidence Point out the main idea of section *Faux Flight* is included in the first sentence of paragraph 18. Restate the main idea for students: *Today, it's harder to tell what is a hoax because technology is more advanced.* Then, have partners work together to identify 2–3 details in the section that support this idea.

 For additional support, go to the **Reading Studio** and assign the following  Level Up tutorial: Evidence

debunk it But when journalists began looking into the résumé of the supposed birdman, nothing checked out. He didn't exist.

20   Finally, the person behind the hoax confessed. Dutch filmmaker Floris Kaayk admitted that it took eight months to achieve his near-perfect **ruse**.

21   People love to be entertained—and fooled. We are drawn to amazing feats and want to believe that they're real. With a willing audience, and social media making it easier all the time to reach us, there's no reason to think the fakers will quit anytime soon.

NOTICE & NOTE

ruse
(rōōz) *n.* A *ruse* is a plan meant to deceive someone.

CHECK YOUR UNDERSTANDING

Answer these questions before moving on to the **Analyze the Text** section on the following page.

1 The author included the section Ye Olde Fakeroo in order to —

  A entertain readers with stories of the Loch Ness monster

  B explain that faking images is not a recent development

  C persuade readers that images of Bigfoot and UFOs are fake

  D share her opinion of people who create fake images

2 In paragraph 17, the writer describes the "Megawoosh" video in order to —

  F provide a specific example of a continuity problem

  G explain how different film segments can be edited together

  H entertain readers with a funny story about a daredevil

  J show how video continuity problems can be avoided

3 Which evidence most strongly supports the conclusion that the video of the eagle snatching the child was forged?

  A A golden eagle weighs only about 14 pounds.

  B A falling child would accelerate at a constant rate.

  C The child probably weighs roughly 28 pounds.

  D Lifting 28 pounds would require a 33-foot wingspan.

The Camera Does Lie   119

TEACH

CHECK YOUR UNDERSTANDING

Have students answer the questions independently.

Answers:

1. B
2. F
3. D

If they answer any questions incorrectly, have them reread the text to confirm their understanding. Then they may proceed to **ANALYZE THE TEXT** on p.120.

ENGLISH LEARNER SUPPORT

Oral Assessment Use the following questions to assess students' comprehension and speaking skills. Make sure they use words from the questions, e.g. "Fakeroo" and "ruse" in their answers to check their pronunciation.

1. What is the connection between something bogus and a sleight of hand in paragraph 7? *(Something bogus is done with a sleight of hand.)*

2. Why did the author include the section "Ye Old Fakeroo"? *(The section is included to explain that faking images is not a recent development.)*

3. Why does the writer describe the Megawoosh video in paragraph 17? *(The writer describes the Megawoosh video in order to provide a specific example of a continuity problem.)*

4. How long did it take Floris Kaayk to achieve his "birdman" ruse? *(It took him 8 months to achieve his ruse.)* **SUBSTANTIAL/MODERATE**

The Camera Does Lie   **119**

APPLY

ANALYZE THE TEXT
Possible answers

1. **DOK 2:** The headings "Ye Olde Fakeroo" and "Fooled You Twice" are informal and rather funny. They suggest that the author wants the article to be entertaining as well as informative.

2. **DOK 3:** When people film without a tripod, the camera shakes a little bit. Scientists can look at film and use software to graph the shaking of the camera. If there is a regular pattern to the shake, scientists know the shake is fake, because actual camera shake is random.

3. **DOK 4:** Videos are made to entertain people—people love to watch amazing feats, and they love to be fooled into thinking that what they see is real. The more amazing the feat is and the more realistic it looks, the more likely it is to become viral. Corporations also make videos to sell people products.

4. **DOK 2:** The author probably figures that fake videos aren't going away; in fact, they are getting better and better. Therefore, the more that people know about how to identify fake videos, the better—they will be less likely to fooled or taken advantage of.

5. **DOK 4:** The author writes, "Whoa. If you think those last three sound sketchy, you should." She uses the word *whoa*, which means "stop," to draw readers' attention to the last three examples and point out that they are suspicious.

RESEARCH

Remind students that standard research guidelines do not apply to this assignment—they are free to use the most bogus, unreliable images they can find. However, the images must relate to the ideas and concepts presented in the article.

Connect Two excellent choices for the purposes of this assignment are the 2005 magazine photo of a shark swimming in a flooded street in Houston and a "live" video of a tornadic supercell. A software program was used to make the shark photo, which was sent around again after Hurricane Harvey struck in 2017. The tornadic cell video began as a weather GIF; it was manipulated into a video and a sound loop of a thunderstorm was added. The video was aired live for four hours.

 RESPOND

ANALYZE THE TEXT
Support your responses with evidence from the text. 📓 NOTEBOOK

1. **Infer** Reread each of the section headings. What do they suggest about one of the author's purposes for writing?

2. **Cite Evidence** How does graphing camera shake reveal fake videos? Cite evidence from the text in your answer.

3. **Synthesize** Review paragraphs 2 and 21. What reasons does the author provide for why fake videos are made and why some become viral?

4. **Interpret** Reread the last sentence of "The Camera Does Lie." Why might the author have spent time talking about ways to tell whether a video is real? Cite evidence to support your response.

5. **Notice & Note** In paragraph 2, how does the author highlight the contrast or contradiction between two examples of reliable information found on the Internet and three sketchy examples?

RESEARCH

Uncover another example or two of a photographic or video hoax. Also find an explanation of any techniques used to create such a deceptive image. In the following chart, record what you learn in your research.

HOAX	DECEPTIVE TECHNIQUES
Photo of a shark swimming in a flooded street in Houston, Texas	The shark image appeared in a magazine in 2005. Someone used a software program to copy and paste the image into a photo of a street
Live video of a tornadic supercell	The creators began with a weather GIF. They manipulated it and turned it into a video and added as sound loop of a thunderstorm.

RESEARCH TIP
When you are doing research, be sure to stay on topic. With a topic such as photographic or video hoaxes, it would be easy to get distracted and to spend your time looking at example after example. Remember that your topic is not just the hoax itself but also how it was made.

Connect In paragraphs 11–20, the author describes several ways that people analyze videos to determine whether they are authentic—that is, if the videos depict things that actually could happen. With a small group, take turns describing the video hoaxes you researched. Discuss ways that you could analyze those videos to expose them as hoaxes.

RESPOND

CREATE AND DISCUSS

Write an Opinion Essay Write a three- to four-paragraph essay in which you express your opinion about why fake images or videos fascinate people.

- Introduce the topic and state your opinion clearly.
- Provide reasons that support your opinion. Support each reason with facts, examples, and other details from the text and from additional research. Use transitions to connect ideas.
- In your final paragraph, state your conclusion about the topic.

Create a Multimodal Presentation A multimodal presentation is one that includes different modes of communication, such as writing, speech, and visuals (such as time lines, maps, or photos). With a partner or group, create a storyboard make a brief multimodal presentation about forged images and video.

- each As a group, locate examples of images and video that seemed designed to be authentic but are not.
- Review the article for ways to detect fakery. Use those methods (and others, as appropriate) to analyze the images or video you located.
- Consider the information you discover and then work together to plan and organize your presentation.
- Present your findings to the class. Speak clearly and use eye contact and hand gestures to hold the audience's attention.

Go to **Using Media in a Presentation** in the **Speaking and Listening Studio** for tips.

RESPOND TO THE ESSENTIAL QUESTION

 What can blur the lines between what's real and what's not?

Gather Information Review your annotations and notes on "The Camera Does Lie." Then, add relevant details to your Response Log. As you determine which information to include, think about:

- the seeming "realness" of faked images
- how knowing about faked images might affect the way we think about all images, real or not

At the end of the unit, you can use your notes to help you create a multimodal presentation.

ACADEMIC VOCABULARY

As you write and discuss what you learned from the magazine article, be sure to use the Academic Vocabulary words. Check off each of the words that you use.

- abnormal
- feature
- focus
- perceive
- task

The Camera Does Lie 121

APPLY

CREATE AND DISCUSS

Write an Opinion Essay Point out that the first list on page 121 can be used as the outline for the three-to-four paragraph description of why fake images and images fascinate people.

For **writing support** for students at varying proficiency levels, see the **Text X-Ray** on page 112D.

Create a Multimodal Presentation Remind students that the second list on page 121 can be used as a step-by-step guide to creating their presentations. Inform students that one of best ways to overcome fear of public speaking is to make sure that they are prepared.

RESPOND TO THE ESSENTIAL QUESTION

Allow time for students to add details from "The Camera Does Lie" to their Unit 2 Response Logs.

 ENGLISH LEARNER SUPPORT

Discuss with a Small Group Restate the writing topic as a question: Why do fake images or videos fascinate people? Allow students to work with partners to form opinions that answer the question. Provide these sentence frames to help them develop their ideas for the discussion: *One reason fake images or videos fascinate people is because _____. People like to be fooled because _____. Fake images and videos fascinate me because_____. Another reason why fake images and videos fascinate people is because _____.* **MODERATE/LIGHT**

The Camera Does Lie **121**

APPLY

CRITICAL VOCABULARY

Answers:

1. applying the laws of physics to analyze the video.
2. no research studies supported the ad's claims.
3. at the same rate they do in the real world.
4. people enjoy fooling other people.
5. they hired animal handlers to train the "actors."
6. I glued a dollar to the ground and filmed people trying to pick it up.
7. examine each scene for details that changed but shouldn't have.

VOCABULARY STRATEGY:
Reference Resources

Answers:

1. rigors: n. harsh inflexibility in opinion, temper, or judgment; strict precision. From the Latin *rigor*, literally meaning "stiff," from *rigere*, "to be stiff."
2. physics: n. a science dealing with matter and energy and their interaction. From the Latin *physica*, meaning "natural science," from the Greek *physikos*, meaning "nature," *physis*, meaning "growth," *phyein*, meaning "to bring forth."

"The rigors of science" means the strict rules and concepts that govern the science of physics.

 RESPOND

WORD BANK
bogus
elaborate
obsess
accelerate
continuity
hoax
ruse

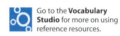 Go to the **Vocabulary Studio** for more on using reference resources.

CRITICAL VOCABULARY

Practice and Apply On separate paper, complete each sentence in a way that shows the meaning of the Critical Vocabulary word.

1. People who analyze fake videos **obsess** over . . .
2. I knew that the advertiser's claims were **bogus** because . . .
3. Filmed objects should **accelerate** . . .
4. There are many **hoaxes** on the Internet because . . .
5. They made an **elaborate** plan for the animal video; in fact, . . .
6. To create a funny video, I arranged a **ruse** in which . . .
7. To check the **continuity** of a film, you can . . .

VOCABULARY STRATEGY:
Reference Resources

A **dictionary** is a valuable resource for those who want to check definitions and expand their vocabulary. The searching and browsing methods differ for print and digital dictionaries, but users can find the same basic information about each entry word.

- pronunciation
- part of speech label
- one or more definitions
- etymology (word origin or history)

> **a·nal·y·sis** (ə-năl′ĭ-sĭs) *n.* **1.** The separation of an intellectual or material whole into its constituent parts for individual study. **2.** *Chemistry* The separation of a substance into its constituent elelments to determine their nature. **3.** *Mathematics* A branch of mathematics principally involving differential and integral calculus, sequences, and series and concerned with limits and convergence.
>
> [Medieval Latin, from Greek *analusis*, a dissolving < *analūein*, to undo]

Practice and Apply Review paragraph 9 of "The Camera Does Lie" and locate the sentence that contains the phrase *rigors of physics*. Look up the words *rigors* and *physics* in a print or digital dictionary. Note word meanings and parts of speech. Think about the origin of each word, too. Then, use your own words to tell what the sentence means.

 ENGLISH LEARNER SUPPORT

Vocabulary Strategy Give students additional practice with using an online or print dictionary to check definitions and expand their vocabulary. Ask students to look up other words and phrases from the article, like *paranormal, natural law, sleight of hand, daredevil,* and *viral*. Have them check for pronunciation, multiple definitions, etymology, and parts of speech. Then have students use the words and phrases conversationally. **MODERATE/LIGHT**

LANGUAGE CONVENTIONS:
Correlative Conjunctions

Writers rely on such single-word conjunctions as *and, but,* and *if* to link ideas. **Correlative conjunctions** are pairs of words that connect words, phrases, and clauses.

Here is a list of commonly used correlative conjunctions:

either / or	neither / nor	both / and
no sooner / than		whether / or

In using correlative conjunctions to construct sentences, be aware the two parts of the conjunction need to connect similar parts of speech, phrases, or clauses. The connected elements must be grammatically equal. For example, nouns must connect to nouns, a prepositional phrase must connect to a prepositional phrase, and so on. Using the word pairs in this way helps to maintain a **parallel structure**.

Notice how in the example below, two nouns are connected by the correlative conjunction *either . . . or*.

> It was either a trick or a fake photograph.

It is also important to maintain pronoun-antecedent agreement when using correlative conjunctions, as shown in these examples.

> **INCORRECT:** Neither Kenzo nor his friends understood how he had been fooled.

> **CORRECT:** Neither Kenzo nor his friends understood how they had been fooled.

In the incorrect sentence, the word *friends* is plural. Therefore, the singular pronoun *he* is not in agreement with the second antecedent *friends*. Replacing the singular pronoun *he* with the plural *they* is correct. Similarly, subject-verb agreement must be maintained when using correlative conjunctions. In the correct sentence, the verb *understood* agrees with the subject nearer to it—the word *friends*.

Practice and Apply Work with a partner to write sentences using correlative conjunctions. Use the examples above as models. Your sentences can be about funny videos or photographs you've seen, or they can be on another topic. When you have finished, share your sentences with another pair and review whether the sentences maintain pronoun-antecedent and subject-verb agreement. Apply what you have learned the next time you proofread your writing.

RESPOND

Go to **Using Conjunctions and Interjections** in the **Grammar Studio** to learn more.

APPLY

LANGUAGE CONVENTIONS:
Correlative Conjunctions

Tell students that when writing a sentence with correlative conjunctions, the verb must agree with the subject *nearest* to it.

For example: *Either gorillas or a panda* **is** *the top attraction in the zoo.*

Point out that the above example, though correct, may sound unnatural and for this reason most writers place the plural subject nearest the verb.

For example: *Either a panda or gorillas* **are** *the top attraction in the zoo.*

Practice and Apply Have partners discuss whether correlative cinjunctions are used correctly in their sentences.

(Students' sentences will vary.)

ENGLISH LEARNER SUPPORT

Language Conventions Use these supports with students at varying proficiency levels:

- Write the following sentences on the board: *It is snowing out. It is also cold.* Combine the sentences with a semicolon. Have students copy the sentences into their notebooks. **SUBSTANTIAL**
- Have students work with partners to write original sentences that require a semicolon. Then have them meet with another pair to compare their sentences. **MODERATE**
- Ask students to write a brief paragraph with at least two semicolons. **LIGHT**

PLAN

TWO LEGS OR ONE?
Folk Tale by Josepha Sherman

GENRE ELEMENTS
FOLK TALES

Remind students that **folk tales** began as an oral tradition, passed down from generation to generation; they have entertained and instructed people for thousands of years. It is important to remember that for the majority of time that folk tales have been in existence, most people could not read. Folk tales were an important way of passing along information about the perils and uncertainty of daily life; they had to be entertaining—and sometimes very frightening or funny—to keep the attention of listeners.

LEARNING OBJECTIVES

- Be able to identify the elements of a folk tale.
- Analyze uses of humor such as **exaggeration** and **irony**.
- Analyze how **mood** and **tone** set the stage for humor to be used.
- Learn how to use commas to create pauses.
- Write a friendly letter that expresses opinions and ideas about the uses of humor in folktales.
- Direct a retelling of this folk tale, or another story.
- Understand how to use a glossary.
- **Language:** Identify humorous language.

TEXT COMPLEXITY

Quantitative Measures	Two Legs or One?	Lexile: 600L
Qualitative Measures	**Ideas Presented** Much is explicit but moves to some implied meaning.	
	Structure Used Clear, chronological, conventional.	
	Language Used Some dialect or other unconventional language	
	Knowledge Required Situations and subjects are familiar or easily envisioned	

PLAN

Online

RESOURCES

- Unit 2 Response Log
- 🔊 Selection Audio
- 📖 Reading Studio: Notice & Note
- 💬 Speaking and Listening Studio: Giving a Presentation
- 🔵 Vocabulary Studio: Using a Glossary
- ❗ Grammar Studio: Module 14: Lessons 2-6: Using Commas Correctly
- ✅ "Two Legs or One?" Selection Test

SUMMARIES

English
This Middle Eastern folk tale has been recounted by Josepha Sherman. The well-known trickster, Goha, brings home two calf legs from a butcher for his wife to prepare for dinner. While he is away, his wife eats one of the legs. Upon his return, Goha's wife tries to convince him that he only brought one leg home. But Goha the trickster, is not one to be easily tricked!

Spanish
Este cuento folklórico del Oriente Medio ha sido recontado por Josepha Sherman. El famoso embaucador, Goha, trae a casa dos piernas de ternero de la carnicería para que su esposa las prepare. Mientras él no está, su esposa se come una de las piernas. A su regreso, la esposa de Goha trata de convencerlo de que solo había traído una pierna a casa. Pero ¡nadie embauca a Goha, el embaucador!

SMALL-GROUP OPTIONS

Have students work in small groups to read and discuss the selection.

Triple-Entry Journal

- Students divide a sheet of notebook paper down the middle with headings: "Questions About the Text" and "My Guesses."
- Ask students to come up with their own questions.
- They write their own interpretations in the right column, leaving space for more notes.
- Students then exchange their journals and write their own answers to the original students' questions.
- Pass them back and discuss.

Sticky Note Peer Review

This activity can be used for the "Friendly Letter" writing exercise at the end of the selection.

- In pairs or small groups, as each student in turn reads his or her paper, the other students listen, recording specific feedback on sticky notes.
- It is important for students to keep each purpose separate by writing positive comments on one sticky note, suggestions on another note, and questions on a third note.
- Students initial their sticky notes, giving them to the writer to use for revision.

PLAN

 Text X-Ray: English Learner Support
for "Two Legs Or One?"

Use the Text X-Ray and the supports and scaffolds in the Teacher's Edition to help guide students at different proficiency levels through the selection.

INTRODUCE THE SELECTION
DISCUSS UNIT THEME-RELATED IDEA

In this lesson, students will need to understand aspects of folktale humor as it relates to a character type that finds its roots in mythology: the trickster.

- Humor is anything that makes people laugh.
- Some tricksters are known as "wise fools." They play pranks that teach a lesson, but they are often unaware that a lesson has been taught.

Explain the difference between the word *joke* and *tricks*, or *pranks*. A joke is usually told or written as a very short story that is meant to make the listener laugh. A prank is when someone tries to trick someone else into believing something. In this selection, the character of Goha is a known prankster. Tell students that trickster characters are as old as storytelling. Some are gods and shape-shifters (like the Norse god *Loki*). Ask students to make lists of tricksters; they can be figures in contemporary culture or from another era. Have them share about their tricksters and the lessons the tricksters teach.

CULTURAL REFERENCES

The following words and phrases may be unfamiliar to students:

- "Goha" is a Middle Eastern name, although "Gohan" is more common
- a *butcher* (paragraph 1) is someone who sells meat
- a *leg of lamb* (paragraph 1) is a part of traditional Middle Eastern cuisine
- *funeral procession* (paragraph 18) is when the body of a dead person is transported by mourners to its grave site
- a *marketplace* (paragraph 18) is place where a variety of goods are sold in stores, stalls, or from vehicles that are gathered together in a single space: often outdoors, and often on specific days, at specific times.

LISTENING

Analyze Folktales

Draw students' attention to the conflict, or problem, that creates the framework for the story. Point out that folktales often address human weaknesses such as greed, laziness, pride, and overly strict, or tyrannical, behavior. Characters may do exaggerated things to try to fix their problems.

Have students listen as you read aloud paragraphs 3–5. Use the following supports with students at varying proficiency levels:

- Ask students to raise their hands when they hear the problem created by a character. Reread, "She had eaten the entire calf's leg." Ask: *Is it the Wife who created the problem?* (yes, raised hands) *Is Goha her husband?* (yes) *Is it a funny or serious story?* (funny) **SUBSTANTIAL**
- Reread "the smell of them was sweeter to her than any rose." Ask: *What is the narrator talking about?* (the calf's leg) *Why does the wife say, "But what am I to tell him?* (She has greedily eaten one whole calf's leg and she doesn't know what to do.) *Who is Goha?* (Her husband) *Is it a funny or serious story?* (funny) **MODERATE**
- Ask: *Which sentence explains why the wife is worried?* (She had eaten the entire calf's leg!) **LIGHT**

124C Unit 2

PLAN

SPEAKING

Analyze Humorous Language

Guide students in a discussion of the language of humor. Review parts of the folktale to help them identify how word patterns (repetition) and exaggerated intonation creates humor that is specific to the story.

Use the following supports with students at varying proficiency levels:

- Have two of the most advanced students read the argument between Goha and the Wife aloud (paragraphs 7–17). Have them focus on lines 8–14: make sure the readers emphasize the rhythmic quality of this exchange. **SUBSTANTIAL**
- Have the students taking the parts of Goha and the Wife reread the exchange. This time, split the rest of the class in half and have half of them chorally repeat Goha's lines, and the other half chorally repeat the Wife's lines. Repeat. Stress the humor in the "One-Two" exchange. **MODERATE**
- Extract the lines of dialogue from paragraphs 20–23, and distribute them among three groups according to difficulty. Point to each group when they should say their lines. **LIGHT**

READING

Identify Illusions

Remind students that folk tales are passed down orally over many generations. They are often set in the past, and feature a trickster who creates an illusion that is meant to teach, explain, distract, and entertain. Folk tales also display elements of the cultures they come from.

Work with students to read paragraphs 18–23. Use the following supports with students at varying proficiency levels:

- Have students identify the illusion that Goha is creating. Ask: *Is Goha dead? (no) Is Goha trying to trick his wife? (yes) Does "bolt upright" mean that he is sitting up after lying down? (yes)* Write *upright* on the board. Underline the silent letters *gh* and have the class repeat after you when you say: *These are silent letters. They make no sound. The word is* upright. Repeat for the words: *high, might*, and *light*. **SUBSTANTIAL**
- Ask: *What is Goha pretending to do? (be dead) Is he doing this to fool everyone, but mostly his wife? (his wife) What does he want to win? (the argument) An argument is when we agree? (no)* Model the argument by having students read lines 7-17 aloud again. *Is this an argument? (yes)* **MODERATE**
- Ask students why they believe this particular folktale has been passed down from generation to generation. How does it does it use humorous language to teach? Tell students to use text evidence when writing a two-paragraph answer. **LIGHT**

WRITING

Write a Friendly Letter

Work with students to read the writing assignment on p. 131. Point out the use of commas in letters. Provide students with templates for letters.

Use the following supports with students at varying proficiency levels:

- Provide a short letter made up of frame sentences and an answer key students can use to complete the sentences. Read the letter aloud as students follow along. Allow time for them to write. For example, *One of the main characters is a trickster named_____. (Answer Key: Goha).* **SUBSTANTIAL**
- Provide students with stems to help them write a short retelling of the folktale. The retelling should take the form of a friendly letter to a friend. Have students be sure to use text evidence. **MODERATE**
- Have students write a short retelling of the folktale to a student who has not read it. Tell students to be sure to include examples of how the story uses humor. **LIGHT**

Two Legs Or One? **124D**

TEACH

? Connect to the
ESSENTIAL QUESTION

The folk tale "Two Legs or One?" plays on the characters' perceptions. Goha's wife tries to play a trick on him, insisting he brought home one leg, not two. Goha then plays the ultimate trick on his wife by playing dead and convincing everyone in their village that he is deceased.

ANALYZE & APPLY

TWO LEGS OR ONE?

Folk Tale by **Josepha Sherman**

? ESSENTIAL QUESTION:

What can blur the lines between what's real and what's not?

QUICK START

What can motivate someone to trick or fool someone else? Write down your thoughts in response to this question.

ANALYZE FOLK TALES

Folk tales are stories passed along by word of mouth from generation to generation. "Two Legs or One?" is a folk tale that would have been shared as an oral tradition for a long time before it was written down.

Folk tales vary among cultures, but many teach life lessons about values (such as honesty) or behaviors (such as helping the poor) that are central to the culture of origin (the culture in which the folk tale was first told). As you read, think about what life lessons this folk tale is trying to teach about values and behavior.

In a folk tale, the main character may be a **trickster**—a character who goes against acceptable behavior and fools someone. The trickster's motive may be selfish, or it may come from a desire to help others. The trickster may succeed, or it may fail. The trickery may be discovered, or it may not. In any case, there is a life lesson to be learned. When you meet a trickster in a folk tale, ask yourself, "What can we learn from this trickster?"

ANALYZE HUMOR

Like many folk tales, "Two Legs or One?" features humor. **Humor** is what causes us to laugh or be amused. Humor may come from plot events, characters' words, or the language a writer uses to tell a story.

These are some techniques writers use to add humor to a story:

- They include surprising characters or events.
- They use **exaggeration**, or extreme overstatements.
- They use **irony**, a contrast in which the reality is the opposite of what it seems to be.
- They choose words that create amusing mental images.
- They include clever and insightful dialogue.

Humor can influence the mood and tone of a story. **Mood** is the feeling or atmosphere that a writer creates through the use of descriptive words, imagery, and figurative language. The **tone** of a literary work expresses the writer's attitude toward his or her subject.

As you read "Two Legs or One?" look for humor in the folk tale. Analyze the techniques used to create that humor. Then think about how those techniques influence the mood and tone of the story.

GET READY

GENRE ELEMENTS: FOLK TALES
- are usually set in the past and are based on an oral tradition
- often show the importance of a cultural value or behavior
- often focus on a problem that needs to be solved
- may feature supernatural characters or events
- sometimes feature a "trickster"

Two Legs or One? 125

TEACH

QUICK START

Have students read the Quick Start and write down their answers. Invite them to share their thoughts on tricking and fooling people. Are there times tricks are considered rude? Can they also bring people closer together? Expand the conversation by asking whether there are times when tricking people or joking are not acceptable. Give examples. Conversely, be sure to list times when tricks are acceptable.

ANALYZE FOLK TALES

Help students understand that many folk tales have been passed down through oral traditions over hundreds—or even thousands—of years. Ask students to imagine living in a time with no electronic devices, no electric lights, and when large numbers of people did not read. Have them think about how important it would have been for parents to tell their children stories on long winter nights. The stories functioned as more than entertainment; they served to teach children—and others—how to live happy, prosperous lives. Folk tales also warn against indulging in forbidden behavior.

ANALYZE HUMOR

Ask the class for examples of things they think are funny, such as a scene from a television show, movie, or book. They may include memes and videos they have seen on the Internet. Have students examine the definitions on p. 125 and come with examples of:

- scenes with clever dialogue
- dialogue with effective use of exaggeration
- surprising events that create a comic effect

Ask about other comic effects: *How do actors use gestures and expressions? How can settings be used? Music? Sound effects? In the case of a meme, was it the font used?* These questions will get them thinking about **mood** and **tone.**

ENGLISH LEARNER SUPPORT

Humor and Hyperbole An important part of humor is exaggeration. Supply students with lists of common exaggerations that are intended to be humorous. If they have trouble with this activity, offer sentence starters.

- Read sentences aloud and ask students to raise their hands if the sentence uses exaggeration for effect: "I would like to help, but I would have to move about a million muscles." *(yes)* "I only have about 10,000 pages to read; I'm almost done!" *(yes)* "I will do my best to answer all the questions." *(no)* **SUBSTANTIAL/MODERATE**

- Have students work in small groups to come up with exaggerated statements about their lives. Remind them to be respectful of others and to themselves; beware of students using humor to say harmful things about themselves and others. Ask volunteers to share their statements with the class. **LIGHT**

- Ask students to create their own exaggerated phrases and use them in three-paragraph descriptions of trying to leave their homes on a busy morning.

Two Legs or One? **125**

TEACH

CRITICAL VOCABULARY

Encourage students to read all the sentences before deciding which word best completes each one. Remind them to look for context clues that match the precise meaning of each word.

Answers:
1. *dash*
2. *parade*
3. *formal or serious*
4. *straight up*

■ English Learner Support

Use Cognates Tell students that two of the Critical Vocabulary words are Spanish cognates. (procession/procesión, dignified/digno) **SUBSTANTIAL/MODERATE**

LANGUAGE CONVENTIONS

Review the information about commas. Explain that commas are used for more than just creating lists and combining sentences. The examples provided help the author emphasize important details in the story.

Read aloud the example sentences, using appropriate pauses to indicate the use of commas. Then read them aloud again as though the commas were not there. Discuss what the commas add to the sentence. Construct a sentence that needs commas and read it aloud for students, e.g., *A few months ago a friend allowed me to use his boat car ATV house and other things. Thank you I said That is so generous I would like to ask you one more thing will you take a picture of my fish fishing rod the sunset and the deer?* Have students guide you in punctuating the sentence.

✏ ANNOTATION MODEL

Remind students that for this selection they should be looking for elements that make the story a folk tale—elements of humor, mood, and tone—in addition to the author's use of commas. Point out that they may follow this suggestion or use their own system for marking up the selection in their write-in text. For instance, marking commas with a highlighter or a caret (^) might be best.

126   Unit 2

🎯 GET READY

CRITICAL VOCABULARY

scurry   procession   dignified   upright

To preview the Critical Vocabulary words, replace each boldfaced word with a different word or words that have the same meaning.

1. When I returned home, I saw a mouse (**scurry**) _____ away.
2. The people marched proudly in a grand (**procession**) _____.
3. The judge was sworn in during a (**dignified**) _____ ceremony.
4. After the lamp fell, she set it (**upright**) _____ on the table.

LANGUAGE CONVENTIONS

Commas Writers can use commas to control the **pace** of a story, or how fast it is read or told. A comma after introductory words or phrases lets readers pause, as in these examples from "Two Legs or One?":

- Ah, but the meat was tender and perfectly cooked.
  The pause after *Ah* helps you appreciate how good the meat must have been.

- To his surprise, the dish his wife brought from the kitchen held one leg, and one leg alone.
  The pause after *To his surprise* prepares you for a change in the plot.

As you read, think about how the author uses commas for pacing.

ANNOTATION MODEL   NOTICE & NOTE ✏

As you read, note clues about characteristics of folk tales that you identify and mark examples of humor. In the model, you can see one reader's notes about "Two Legs or One?"

> 1 One day, a hungry man named Goha was walking in the marketplace, his mind on the dinner to come, when he chanced to pass a butcher's shop. There, hanging right in front of Goha's eyes, were two nice, meaty calf legs, every bit as tasty-looking to him as a good leg of lamb might be. He grew more hungry with every moment of looking, and at last bought them and scurried home.

The opening is like "Once upon a time."

Calf legs seem important—"legs" in title.

"Scurried" is funny to visualize.

126   Unit 2

BACKGROUND

Josepha Sherman (1946–2012) wrote fantasy and science fiction tales as well as many biographies. Partly inspired by author J.R.R. Tolkien (who had a great love of folklore), Sherman studied folklore from cultures around the world, and she published several collections of her retellings of folk tales. In this story, Sherman shares one of the many Middle Eastern folk tales that feature a character named Goha.

TWO LEGS OR ONE?

Folk Tale by Josepha Sherman

SETTING A PURPOSE

As you read, think about the characters in this story. Do they act as you might expect? Write down any "surprises" you encounter along the way. Also note what you think someone might learn from hearing or reading this tale.

1 One day, a hungry man named Goha was walking in the marketplace, his mind on the dinner to come, when he chanced to pass a butcher's shop. There, hanging right in front of Goha's eyes, were two nice, meaty calf legs, every bit as tasty-looking to him as a good leg of lamb might be. He grew more hungry with every moment of looking, and at last bought them and **scurried** home.

2 "Wife, come, cook these as quickly as you can, and I'll go back to the market and buy some rice to go with them."

3 The calf legs cooked quickly indeed, and when Goha's wife took the lid off the pot, she saw that they were done wonderfully well—so wonderfully well that <u>the smell of them was sweeter to her than any rose</u>.

NOTICE & NOTE

Notice & Note

Use the side margins to notice and note signposts in the text.

scurry
(skûr´ē) *v.* To *scurry* means to hurry along with light footsteps.

ANALYZE HUMOR
Annotate: Mark the example of exaggeration that appears in paragraph 3.

Predict: What do you think will happen next? Explain.

Two Legs or One? 127

 ENGLISH LEARNER SUPPORT

Understand Events in Sequence The first paragraph of "Two Legs or One?" contains complex sentence structures and may be difficult for English Language Learners to follow. Choral read paragraph 1 with the students, stopping at any confusing words or phrases. Provide sequence graphic organizers; have students write key words and phrases from the text in sequentially oriented boxes, then draw or paste images that match the words and phrases in the boxes (e.g., images of open markets). Repeat for paragraphs 2-4. **SUBSTANTIAL**

TEACH

BACKGROUND
Explain that folklore exists in every culture; many folk tales have a great deal in common across cultures. Trickster characters—like one of the main characters in this story—occur again and again throughout recorded history. Josepha Sherman studied folklore and retold a number of folktales in print. If students are curious about more tales about Goha, they can look for more online.

SETTING A PURPOSE
Direct students to use the Setting a Purpose prompt to focus their reading.

ANALYZE HUMOR
Remind students that **exaggeration** is an extreme overstatement of a description, plot event, or idea. (**Answer:** *The exaggeration helps show that the meat is a powerful temptation. That temptation will probably create a problem that the characters in the folk tale will need to solve.*)

> For **speaking support** for students at varying proficiency levels, see the **Text X-Ray** on page 124C

CRITICAL VOCABULARY

scurry: Here, Goha is anxious to take the legs home to eat, so he *scurries*.

ASK STUDENTS How the sentence would have read differently if the word *walked* or *tiptoed* had been used. (*"Walked" does not suggest a sense of urgency; "tiptoed" means he walked cautiously—it does not fit the tone at all.*)

Two Legs or One? **127**

TEACH

ANALYZE FOLK TALES

Annotate: Remind students that folk tales focus on a problem that needs to be solved. Even though Goha is supposed to be the trickster, it is his wife who is trying to trick him this time. (**Answer:** *Students might suggest running to the butcher and trying to replace the calf leg—or just confessing and apologizing to Goha.*)

LANGUAGE CONVENTIONS

Remind students that commas can be used to add dramatic pauses and emphasis. This "dramatic moment" contrasts with what follows. The sheer ridiculousness of Goha pretending to die takes the tale to a new level of humor through exaggeration. (**Answer:** *The pause created by the comma leaves the audience with a moment of suspense. "WHAT HAPPENS in the next moment?" everyone wonders. Creating suspense is part of effective storytelling.*)

CRITICAL VOCABULARY

procession: This sentence gives the reader an idea of how important the funeral is.

ASK STUDENTS how the sentence would change if *procession* is taken out. (*It would just say "funeral" and we would have less of an idea how big it was.*)

dignified: This word works as an exaggeration, tying into the humor component of this lesson. Goha is a trickster, therefore calling his funeral procession "dignified" is ironic.

ASK STUDENTS whether using another word like *sad* or *strange* would change the effect. (*Both would go against the story's tone. The funeral is not described in "sad" terms, so we are prepared for a surprise. "Strange" would be disrespectful.*)

128   Unit 2

NOTICE & NOTE

ANALYZE FOLK TALES
Annotate: Mark the detail in paragraph 5 that presents a problem to be solved.

Connect: Put yourself in the wife's situation. How would you solve the problem?

LANGUAGE CONVENTIONS
Annotate: In paragraph 17, underline an introductory phrase that signals a sudden, surprising event, and circle the comma that follows it.

Interpret: How does this comma add to the storytelling "feel" of the selection?

procession
(prə-sĕsh´ən) *n.* In a *procession,* people or things move along in an orderly and serious way.

dignified
(dĭg´nə-fīd´) *adj.* Someone or something that is *dignified* has or shows honor and respect.

128   Unit 2

4   "I'd better taste one," she told herself. "Just to be sure they're done, of course. Just a taste."

5   Ah, but the meat was tender and perfectly cooked. She took a second taste, a third. And suddenly there was nothing more to taste. She had eaten the entire calf's leg! The wife worried, "I can't tell Goha how greedy I was! But what *am* I to tell him?"

6   Just then Goha returned. "I have the rice here, wife. Come, bring the calf's legs, and let us eat!"

7   To his surprise, the dish his wife brought from the kitchen held one leg, and one leg alone. "Where is the second leg?" Goha asked.

8   "What second leg?" his wife replied. "Here is the only one!"

9   "There were two legs!"

10 "There is only one!"

11 "There were two!"

12 "One!"

13 "Two!"

14 "One!"

15 So there they were, arguing so loudly it frightened the pigeons off the roof. "I will prove to you that there were two legs!" Goha shrieked. "I'll win this argument even if it means my very life!"

16 "There was one leg!" his wife shrieked back. "One leg!"

17 "There were two!" Goha shouted. But in the next moment, he clutched at his chest, gasping, "My heart, oh, my heart . . ."

18 With that, Goha fell to the floor and pretended to be dead. His wife at first thought this must surely be another of her husband's tricks. But when he remained so very still, she burst into tears and called the undertaker. Goha was carried from his house with great care. The funeral **procession** wound its slow, **dignified** way through the marketplace on its way to the cemetery, and everyone came running to see if the great and tricky Goha was, indeed, finally dead.

WHEN STUDENTS STRUGGLE . . .

Analyze Humor Remind students that one way to identify humor in a story is to look for surprising or exaggerated events or details. Have student pairs work together to identify the surprising detail in paragraph 23. Ask: Why does Goha pretend to be dead? (*to win the argument with his wife*) What about this detail makes it humorous? (*Goha plays a very big trick when he pretends to be dead. This is an exaggeration and would not happen in real life.*)

19 At last the procession passed the butcher shop. The butcher came out to see who had died, but by now such a crowd had gathered that he could see nothing.
20 "Who has died?" he asked loudly.
21 "Goha," came the answer from several mouths.
22 "Goha!" the butcher exclaimed. "But how can he be dead? He only just bought a pair of calf legs from me!"
23 On hearing this, Goha sat bolt **upright**. "You see?" he cried to his wife in triumph. "There *were* two legs. I win our argument!"

NOTICE & NOTE

AHA MOMENT

Notice & Note: Mark the plot detail that could be called an "Aha Moment."

Infer: What does this moment help you understand about Goha's personality?

upright
(ŭp′rīt′) *adv.* Someone or something that sits or stands *upright* is in a strictly vertical position.

CHECK YOUR UNDERSTANDING

Answer these questions before moving on to the **Analyze the Text** section on the following page.

1 The author mentions that the calf legs <u>were done wonderfully well</u> in order to —

   A introduce the problem that will shape the rest of the tale
   B reveal that Goha appreciates his wife's good cooking
   C explain why Goha needs to return to the marketplace
   D show that this story could not happen in real life

2 The action that Goha takes after his wife brings one calf leg to the table indicates that he —

   F cannot take the stress of arguing any longer
   G does not understand why his wife seems so upset
   H is tired of arguing and wants to make up with his wife
   J is willing to take an extreme measure to be proven right

3 The butcher's words when the procession passes by his shop are important because they —

   A show that Goha is loved by the townspeople
   B summarize the lesson that the folk tale teaches
   C prove that Goha's wife has been lying to Goha
   D express the butcher's hope that Goha will come back to life

Two Legs or One? 129

ENGLISH LEARNER SUPPORT

Oral Assessment Use the following questions to assess students' comprehension and speaking skills:

1. How many legs did Goha buy? *(2)* How many legs did Goha's wife bring to the table? *(1)* Why does Goha pretend to be dead? *(to win the argument)* **SUBSTANTIAL/MODERATE**

2. What does the last sentence of paragraph 18 tell the reader? *(that Goha has played many tricks before the one in this tale)* **SUBSTANTIAL/MODERATE**

TEACH

AHA MOMENT

Remind students that an **Aha Moment** is when a character realizes something. (**Answer:** *This moment reinforces the idea that Goha is obsessed with being "right." The trickster always wins! It also indicates that he is willing to humiliate himself and his wife to do so.*)

CHECK YOUR UNDERSTANDING

Have students answer the questions independently.

Answers:

1. *A*
2. *J*
3. *C*

If students answer any questions incorrectly, have them reread the text to confirm their understanding. Then they may proceed to ANALYZE THE TEXT on page 130.

CRITICAL VOCABULARY

upright: The word, in conjunction with the adjective *bolt* describes a sudden shooting up from his coffin. The language effectively conveys the surprise.

ASK STUDENTS Whether *up* or *upwards* would have the same effect here. (*"Up" and "upwards" don't have the same effect as "upright." "Up" is too simple a word to pair with "bolt" and upwards doesn't suggest how lifelike Goha now is.*)

Two Legs or One? 129

APPLY

ANALYZE THE TEXT

Possible answers:

1. **DOK 2**: *In these opening paragraphs, the author introduces the characters (Goha and his wife), as well as the source of the conflict by vividly describing the high quality of the meat.*

2. **DOK 3:** *As the argument reaches its conclusion, Goha shrieks that he will be proven right "even if it means my very life!" This statement hints at his method of getting to the truth—by faking his death.*

3. **DOK 3:** *The townspeople "came running to see if the great and tricky Goha was, indeed, finally dead." This suggests that Goha is famous throughout the area for being a trickster and that people may have reason to doubt that he is, in fact, dead.*

4. **DOK 4:** *Because of the argument and the nature of Goha's trick, the clearest lesson seems to be one about the value of truthfulness. When Goha's wife fails to be truthful, the result is a bitter argument and a trick that exposes her lie to the public. A lesson that is not quite as obvious is that people should treat each other with openness and respect.*

5. **DOK 4:** *Goha's wife fears that Goha will see her as greedy for eating the first calf's leg. So she quickly attempts a deception.*

RESEARCH

To jumpstart students' research, mention that many stories in popular culture have been adapted from folk tales. If they pick one, they may be able to trace it back to its folklore roots. Students may be surprised to discover that the tale of "Little Red Riding Hood" is more than one thousand years old. "The Story of Cam and Tam" is a Vietnamese folk tale that resembles "Cinderella" in many ways. Complex stories to come out of the oral tradition include the *Epic of Sundiata* from 13th-century Africa.

Extend Students may suggest that people enjoy trickster tales because they identify with the characters, or that they enjoy such stories because they wish they themselves could outwit others or do the outrageous things that tricksters do.

 RESPOND

ANALYZE THE TEXT

Support your responses with evidence from the text. 📓 NOTEBOOK

1. **Interpret** In paragraphs 1–3, how does the author prepare readers for the conflict that will shape the rest of the folk tale?

2. **Analyze** Reread the couple's argument in paragraphs 6–17. What technique or techniques does the author use to make this a humorous moment in the story?

3. **Draw Conclusions** In paragraph 18, what description explains why people came running to see the procession? What can you conclude from that description?

4. **Evaluate** Identify two life lessons suggested by this folk tale. Explain which lesson is expressed more clearly and which lesson is expressed less clearly or directly.

5. **Notice & Note** What "Aha Moment" does Goha's wife have in paragraph 5 that causes her to lie to Goha about the calf's legs? Explain.

RESEARCH

RESEARCH TIP
Whether you conduct a search online or at the library, the first source you locate may or may not contain exactly what you need. Be patient! Look at a few more sources before you decide which one or ones contain the most helpful information.

Trickster tales appear in the oral traditions of many cultures. Research some trickster tales from around the world. Compare the central characters and humorous twists in the stories, as well as the cultural values that the tales reveal. Record your notes in this chart, and be prepared to share your results.

"TWO LEGS OR ONE?"	OTHER TALE: _____
Character(s): Goha, his wife	**Character(s):** Anansi, an unnamed boy
Humorous twist(s): Goha pretends to die and then "comes back to life" during the funeral procession when the butcher verifies that there were two calf legs	**Humorous twist(s):** Anansi discovers that he does not have all of the common sense in the world—and, as a result, he loses the common sense that he has hoarded
Cultural value(s): the value of common sense, the dangers of selfish pride and jealousy	**Cultural value(s):** telling the truth, not being greedy

Extend Explain why you think a "trickster" is often the main character in many cultures' folk tales. What is it about such characters that makes people want to hear about their adventures?

TO CHALLENGE STUDENTS . . .

Write a Friendly Letter Instead of writing about humor, ask students to use the folk tale "Two Legs or One?" or another story of their choosing, and then write a letter from the perspective of a character in the story. This letter should include:

- an address to someone, whether another character in the story, or a new character
- a summary of one or more major events from the story
- how the character felt during the experience, as well as his or her opinion
- a wrap-up or resolution to how the character or characters have changed

RESPOND

CREATE AND ADAPT

Write a Friendly Letter In a two-page letter to a friend, express your opinions about humorous writing or another form of entertainment that's designed to appeal to people's sense of humor.

- Begin by expressing a clear opinion about humor—such as what kind of humor you enjoy, or why you are writing about humor.
- Then, share specific facts and examples that support your opinion. You might mention the techniques in "Analyze Humor" (p. 125) or give examples from stories or shows you know.
- Keep the tone of your letter light. Aim for a friendly, conversational style and tone.
- In your conclusion, restate your opinion using other words. Leave your friend with something to think about.

Direct a Retelling With a partner, review "Two Legs or One?" or another trickster tale of your choice. Then prepare to take turns as director and reteller as you adapt the story for an oral retelling.

- As the director, listen carefully to your partner's retelling. Give constructive feedback and helpful tips for improvement.
- As the reteller, listen to your director about ways to convey the humorous or dramatic moments of the tale. If your director suggests different ways of speaking, give them a try. Work together to make the retelling the best it can be!

 Go to in **Giving a Presentation** in the **Speaking and Listening Studio** for presentational style tips.

RESPOND TO THE ESSENTIAL QUESTION

 What can blur the lines between what's real and what's not?

Gather Information Review your annotations and notes on "Two Legs or One?" Then, add relevant details to your Response Log. As you determine which information to include, think about:

- the humor that can result when "surprises" happen in life
- the qualities that give folk tales their "staying power"

At the end of the unit, refer to your notes to help you create a multimodal presentation.

ACADEMIC VOCABULARY

As you write and discuss what you learned from the folk tale, be sure to use the Academic Vocabulary words. Check off each of the words that you use.

- ❏ abnormal
- ❏ feature
- ❏ focus
- ❏ perceive
- ❏ task

APPLY

CREATE AND ADAPT

Write a Friendly Letter Remind students that although the assignment is to write a letter to a friend, they are only *pretending*. Their letters should demonstrate proper grammar, punctuation, and spelling, the same as any other paper they would turn in for a grade.

For **writing support** for students at varying proficiency levels, see the **Text X-Ray** on page 124D.

Direct a Retelling Remind student pairs to make sure they both understand the events as well as the themes of the folk tale, "Two Legs Or One?" before they begin their retelling.

RESPOND TO THE ESSENTIAL QUESTION

Allow time for students to add details from "Two Legs Or One?" to their Unit 2 Response Logs.

 ENGLISH LEARNER SUPPORT

Retell the Tale Have student pairs of varying proficiencies work together to complete the Direct a Retelling Activity. Provide students with sentence frames to use during their retelling: Goha asks his wife to ____ two calf legs. Goha's ____ one of the calf legs. Then, Goha's wife says there was only ____ leg! After, Goha ____ his wife by ____ to be dead. Goha wins the ____ he has with his wife. Monitor language production as students speak, correcting pronunciation and word choice as necessary. **ALL LEVELS**

APPLY

CRITICAL VOCABULARY

Possible Answers:

1. *I might scurry if I needed to get inside quickly because of a sudden rainstorm.*
2. *As a bridesmaid, my sister was part of the wedding procession.*
3. *She answered all questions in a way that lead us to believe that she is an intelligent and dignified woman.*
4. *After many days of lying in bed, the patient was able to sit upright and read a book.*

VOCABULARY STRATEGY:
Glossary

Answers:

1. *Glossary of Critical Vocabulary*
2. *Glossary of Literary and Informational Terms*
3. feature *is a noun and* upright *is an adverb*
4. *A* feature *is an important part, quality, or characteristic of something.*

RESPOND

WORD BANK
scurry
procession
dignified
upright

Go to the **Vocabulary Studio** for more on using a glossary.

CRITICAL VOCABULARY

Practice and Apply Answer each question using the Critical Vocabulary word in a complete sentence.

1. What kind of situation might cause you to *scurry*?
2. When have you seen (or been part of) a *procession*? What was the purpose of that *procession*?
3. How are you expected to react to a *dignified* person or event?
4. When might you need to remain *upright* for a long time?

VOCABULARY STRATEGY: Glossary

A **glossary** is a list of specialized terms and their definitions. A text may have more than one glossary if it refers to multiple types of specialized terms that a reader is not assumed to know.

- When a printed book contains a glossary, words are listed in the back of the book in alphabetical order.
- A digital, or electronic, glossary allows readers to click on a word in the text to see its definition and hear its pronunciation.

Notice the parts of this glossary entry for the word *procession*.

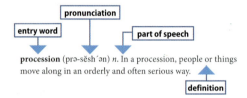

Practice and Apply This literature program contains multiple glossaries. Use the table of contents and the glossaries in this book to answer the following questions.

1. In which glossary would you expect to find a listing for the Critical Vocabulary words that are highlighted in each selection?
2. Use the Glossary of Academic Vocabulary to look up the words *feature* and *perceive*. What part of speech is given for each word? What is the glossary definition of *feature*?

 ENGLISH LEARNER SUPPORT

Vocabulary Strategy: Glossary Give students additional practice using glossaries. Have them look up each of the academic vocabulary words for this unit in the glossary of this book. (*abnormal, feature, focus, perceive, task*) Have students write out their definitions as well as the part of speech. Choral read the words aloud with students. Guide them in using the words in oral sentences. **SUBSTANTIAL/MODERATE**

RESPOND

LANGUAGE CONVENTIONS: Commas

Writers often use a **comma** when they want to indicate a very brief pause following an introductory word or phrase. By using a comma in this way, they can emphasize a plot event or signal a change in the plot. They can also help create the storytelling "feel" of a text.

The following examples from "Two Legs or One?" show how writers use commas after introductory words and phrases.

- Following an introductory noun of direct address:

    Wife, come, cook these as quickly as you can. . . .

- Following an introductory prepositional phrase (especially if there is more than one introductory prepositional phrase):

    With that, Goha fell to the floor and pretended to be dead.

    On hearing this, Goha sat bolt upright.

- Following an introductory interjection, adverb, or adverbial phrase that expresses time:

    One day, a hungry man named Goha was walking. . . .

Practice and Apply Write your own sentences with commas following introductory words and phrases. Use the examples above as models. Your sentences can be about an experience that you or someone you know had with a "trickster," or they can be about another topic related to folk tales or humor writing. When you have finished, share your sentences with a partner and compare your use of commas.

Go to **Using Commas Correctly** in the **Grammar Studio** for more on comma usage.

APPLY

LANGUAGE CONVENTIONS: Commas

Review the information about commas with students. Explain that commas in the examples below indicate a brief pause when following an introductory word or preposition. Commas can also be used as a stylistic choice to create pauses and give the text a rhythm. When students compose their own writing, they should ask themselves where they can place commas to create rhythm and tone in their sentences.

Discuss the use of commas below.

"Wife, come, cook these as quickly as you can, . . ."

Here, Goha is directly addressing his wife, ordering her to do something. The use of commas in this sentence emphasizes the tone of command Goha is using with his wife. The structure of the sentence also exemplifies a tone men have used with women in the past. Imagine how some women would react if thier husbands spoke that way now.

With that, Goha fell to the floor and pretended to be dead.

The prepositional phrase, "With that," adds to the dramatic effect of the sentence.

On hearing this, Goha sat bolt upright.

The prepositional phrase, "On hearing this" introduces the comic climax of the folk tale.

One day, a hungry man named Goha was walking. . . .

This is an example of an introductory adverbial phrase that marks time.

 ENGLISH LEARNER SUPPORT

Language Conventions: Commas Use the following supports with students at varying proficiency levels:

- Provide students with introductory phrases such as "If you want to do well on the test." Give them main clauses that will best match the introductory phrases, e.g., "you must get enough sleep." Do not punctuate the introductory clauses. Read aloud all text you provide as necessary. Have students choose the correct combinations. **SUBSTANTIAL**

- Supply students with a list of introductory clauses (without commas) and have them add their own independent clauses to form complete sentences. **MODERATE**

- Have students write comic and/or dramatic paragraphs in which they are tricksters. Have them transform text from the story if they wish to, e.g., "One day, I asked my neighbor if I could use his hang-glider to get to school. On hearing this, he sat bolt upright and said, "Are you okay?" **LIGHT**

PLAN

THE SONG OF WANDERING AENGUS and ELDORADO

Poems by W.B. Yeats and Edgar Allen Poe

GENRE ELEMENTS
POETRY

Remind students that a **poem** tells a story or conveys a message using figurative language. Poems often utilize rhyme schemes and include different sound devices, such as alliteration, assonance, consonance, and repetition. These poetic elements help to create a mood and central theme, or message.

LEARNING OBJECTIVES

- Identify and analyze rhyme and rhyme schemes.
- Analyze sound devices (such as alliteration, assonance, consonance, and repetition) and mood in poetry.
- Conduct research about the legend of Eldorado.
- Discuss and compare and contrast the mood of two poems.
- **Language** Identify rhyming devices in text read aloud.

TEXT COMPLEXITY

Quantitative Measures	"The Song of Wandering Aengus" and "Eldorado"	Lexile: N/A
Qualitative Measures	**Ideas Presented** Multiple levels, use of symbolism, imagery, figurative language and demand for inference	
	Structure Used Conventionally structured stanzas, includes rhyme scheme and one speaker	
	Language Used Meanings are implied; more figurative and metaphorical language	
	Knowledge Requires More complex themes; necessitates more cultural and historical references	

134A Unit 2

PLAN

Online

RESOURCES

- Unit 2 Response Log
- Selection Audio
- Reading Studio: Notice & Note
- Writing Studio: Writing as a Process
- Speaking and Listening Studio: Giving a Presentation
- "The Song of Wandering Aengus" and "Eldorado" Selection Test

SUMMARIES

English
"The Song of Wandering Aengus" is a poem by Irish poet W.B. Yeats. It presents the mythological quest of the Irish god Aengus as a way to convey a message of love and loss. "Eldorado" is a poem written by Edgar Allan Poe. Similarly, it deals with the theme of a quest, but its message is more melancholic and focuses in disappointment and despair over a fruitless search.

Spanish
"La canción Aengus el Errante" es un poema del irlandés W.B. Yeats, que presenta la búsqueda mitológica de Aengus, el dios irlandés, como una manera sencilla de transmitir un mensaje de amor y pérdida. "Eldorado" es un poema escrito por Edgar Allan Poe. Trata del mismo tema de una búsqueda, pero su mensaje es de mayor melancolía y se enfoca en la decepción y desesperación de una búsqueda infructuosa.

SMALL-GROUP OPTIONS

Have students work in small groups to read and discuss the selection.

Numbered Heads Together

- Divide students into equally numbered groups. Assign each student a number. They will later respond to a question when their number is called.
- Ask students: *Why do people go on quests? If you went on a quest, what would you search for?* Have students share their responses with their group, and give each other feedback on their ideas.
- Call on each number. Each student should respond to the question when his or her number is called.

Think-Pair Share

- After students have read and analyzed each poem, pose these questions: *How are the quests similar to each other? How are they different from each other?*
- Have students think about these questions individually and take notes.
- Then, have pairs discuss their ideas about the comparison.
- Guide students to discuss the ideas, concepts, and emotions the poems evoke.
- Finally, ask pairs to share their responses with the class.

"The Song of Wandering Aengus" and "Eldorado"

PLAN

Text X-Ray: English Learner Support
for "The Song of Wandering Aengus" and "Eldorado"

Use the instruction below and the supports and scaffolds in the Teacher's Edition to help you guide students of different proficiency levels.

INTRODUCE THE SELECTION
DISCUSS TYPES OF QUESTS

In this lesson, students will need to be able to talk about why a person might go on a quest, or journey. They should be able to recognize the mood created by each poem and how it relates to the quests of each narrator. Define mood and tone for students.

Mood tells the feeling of a poem. The reader can understand the mood by examining the word choice and sound devices used by the poet.

Tone is how the author feels about his or her subject. The author may feel angry, sad, understanding, empathic, or curious about the subject.

Explain to students that mood and tone are closely related. Students should use the tone of a poem along with the author's use language and sound devices to determine the mood.

CULTURAL REFERENCES

The following words, phrases, and idioms may be unfamiliar to students:

- "hazel wood" (Aengus): forest of hazel trees
- "fire was in my head" (Aengus): the narrator feels intense emotion
- "gaily bedight" (Eldorado): brightly dressed

LISTENING

Understand Sound Devices

Draw students' attention to the annotation model on page 136. Point out the different types of sound devices students may encounter when reading poetry: *alliteration, repetition rhyme, end rhyme,* and *meter*.

Have students listen as you read aloud the first stanza of "The Song of Wandering Aengus" on page 137. Use the following supports with students at varying proficiency levels:

- Tell students that you will ask questions about what you just read aloud. For example, ask: *What word in the poem rhymes with head?* (threads) Review short vowel digraphs that rhyme, e.g., bread and dead; distinguish between short and long *ea* words: *dead, bread, great, beach.* **SUBSTANTIAL**
- Have students identify the sound device in line 5. Give examples before asking. Ask: *Do you see alliteration, repetition, consonance or assonance in this line?* (alliteration: when white...were...wing) **MODERATE**
- Pair students up to identify two examples of end rhyme in the stanza. Ask: *What lines include end rhyme?* (head/thread, out/trout) **LIGHT**

134C Unit 2

PLAN

SPEAKING

Discuss Mood

Draw students' attention to the instruction about mood on page 138. Tell students that sound devices, rhythm, and word choice all help to set the mood, or atmosphere of the poem. Another way to figure out the mood is to ask: How does this poem make you feel?

Use the following supports with students at varying proficiency levels:

- Tell students that you will ask questions about what you just read aloud. Use images of peaceful and wild places as necessary. Ask: *Is the mood of the first stanza peaceful or wild?* (peaceful) **SUBSTANTIAL**
- Have students identify the mood of the stanza. Ask: *What feeling do you get when you read the first stanza?* Provide students with sample sentences to respond: *I feel ____ (peaceful/curious/calm) when I read the first stanza.* **MODERATE**
- Pair students up to identify the events and sound devices in the stanza and describe what mood they create. Ask: *What is the mood of this stanza? What parts of the poem support your answer?* (The mood is calm and peaceful as Aengus goes fishing in the woods. The poet repeats words like *hazel* to create a musical rhythm.) **LIGHT**

READING

Identify Imagery

Draw students' attention to the imagery created in stanza two of "The Song of Wandering Aengus" on page 138. Point out that poetry can create images in the reader's mind, which, along with sound devices, can help create a particular mood.

Work with students to read stanza two on page 138. Use the following supports with students at varying proficiency levels:

- Tell students that you will ask questions about what you just read aloud. Point out the words *glimmering girl*. Tell students that *glimmering* means "sparkling." Stars and diamonds are examples of *glimmering*. Ask: *Is the glimmering girl bright or dark?* (bright) **SUBSTANTIAL**
- Have students identify the phrase *glimmering girl*. Ask: *What do you see in your mind when you read* glimmering girl? (a girl with light around her) **MODERATE**
- Pair students up to identify examples of imagery in the stanza. Ask: *What mood do these images create?* (Imagery: fire aflame, glimmering girl, brightening air. Mood: bright, exciting, mysterious) **LIGHT**

WRITING

Write a Poem

Draw students' attention to the elements of poetry on 135. Remind them that they should include these elements in their own poems.

Use the following supports with students at varying proficiency levels:

- Tell students that you will ask questions about what you just read aloud. For example, ask: *What will your poem be about?* Allow students to write one-word responses. Provide ideas if students need more guidance. Allow students to use images. Display collages or photo essays as examples. **SUBSTANTIAL**
- Have students identify two sound devices they will include in their poems. Provide sample sentences for students to fill in to demonstrate understanding of sound devices. For example: *"The wet water"* is an example of ____ (alliteration). **MODERATE**
- Have student pairs write short poems that include at least two sound devices. Partners should switch poems and identify each other's sound devices and mood. **LIGHT**

TEACH

 Connect to the ESSENTIAL QUESTION

The narrators in the poems, "The Song of Wandering Aengus" by W.B. Yeats and "Eldorado" by Edgar Allan Poe explore two different but elusive quests. Both poems leave it up to the reader to decide whether the object of each of the narrators' quests is real or only a product of the narrator's imagination.

COMPARE MOODS

Point out that each poem uses language and sounds to express a different mood. Ask students to note the similarities and differences in the way the writers use word choice, rhyme, and sound devices to create a certain mood. How are the moods of the two poems similar? How are they different?

COLLABORATE & COMPARE

POEM

THE SONG OF WANDERING AENGUS

by **W. B. Yeats**
pages 137–139

COMPARE MOODS

As you read, notice the words and sounds that help shape each poem's mood, or the feeling the poem creates for the reader. Then, think about what is similar about the mood of the two poems. After you read both poems, you will collaborate with a small group on a final project.

 ESSENTIAL QUESTION:

What can blur the lines between what's real and what's not?

POEM

ELDORADO

by **Edgar Allan Poe**
pages 140–141

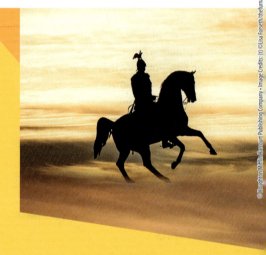

 LEARNING MINDSET

Effort Remind students that effort is necessary for growth, emphasizing that hard work leads to success. When students demonstrate growth through hard work, offer praise and feedback on the specific way students have demonstrated effort. Be sure to focus praise on student effort and progress rather than natural ability.

QUICK START

Has a friend ever told you a story about a strange or unexplained occurrence? Did it make you wonder what really happened? What reactions did the event stir in you? Discuss your reaction with the class.

ANALYZE RHYME

A poem's effect is created through sound and meaning. Poets choose their words carefully, since word choice, or **diction,** affects a poem's meaning and the way it sounds.

Rhyme is the repetition of sounds at the ends of words. Words rhyme when their accented vowels and the letters that follow them create identical or similar sounds.

dreary / weary   more / roar   chair / stare

Poets use rhyme for a number of purposes:

- to create a musical quality
- to emphasize sounds that suggest particular feelings, such as surprise or sadness
- to create rhythms, or patterns of stressed and unstressed syllables, that help convey sensory feelings, such as a sense of motion

ANALYZE RHYME SCHEME

End rhyme refers to words that rhyme at the ends of lines of poetry. A **rhyme scheme** is a pattern of end rhymes in a poem. A rhyme scheme is noted by assigning a letter of the alphabet, starting with *a*, to each end rhyme.

FROM "ELDORADO"	RHYME SCHEME
Gaily bedight,	Gaily bedight, *a*
A gallant knight,	A gallant knight, *a*
In sunshine and in shadow,	In sunshine and in shadow, *b*
Had journeyed long,	Had journeyed long, *c*
5 Singing a song,	5 Singing a song, *c*
In search of Eldorado.	In search of Eldorado. *b*

As you read "The Song of Wandering Aengus" and "Eldorado," think about how each authors' use of rhyme and rhyme scheme contributes to the poem's **mood**—the feeling the poem creates for the reader; its **voice**—the unique way the author uses language and expresses a human personality in the text; and its **tone**—the author's attitude toward the subject presented.

GET READY

GENRE ELEMENTS: POETRY
- includes imagery that appeals to the senses
- includes sound devices such as rhyme, alliteration, assonance, consonance, and repetition
- creates a mood
- expresses a theme, or message, about life

The Song of Wandering Aengus / Eldorado 135

ENGLISH LEARNER SUPPORT

Distinguish Sounds Read aloud the rhyming words in the excerpt from "Eldorado": *shadow/Eldorado, song/long.* Read each word pair slowly, pausing after each pair to have students repeat the words.

- Confirm students' understanding of sound and rhyme by asking yes-or-no questions such as the following: *Do the words* song *and* long *sound alike?* (yes) *Do these words rhyme?* (yes) **SUBSTANTIAL/MODERATE**
- Have students find another example of end-line rhyming words in the excerpt. (*bedight/knight*) **LIGHT**

TEACH

QUICK START

After students choose their experience of a strange or unexplained event and have listed their reactions to the event, have them share their reactions with a partner. Compile a list of possible reactions (for example, *curious, happy, confused, etc.*), and encourage students to explore whether any other reactions could apply to their experience as well.

ANALYZE RHYME

Help students understand that rhyme is often an important part of a poem. Point out the examples of rhyme pairs on page 135. Have students look at each pair, define each word, and then describe the feeling those words evoke when used together. Remind students that because poets choose their words very carefully, they should pay attention to word choice and rhyme as they read each poem.

ANALYZE RHYME SCHEME

Explain that rhyme is used in poems to create a musical quality, introduce a beat or rhythm, or emphasize a feeling.

Have students choral read the rhyming words that occur at the end of each line in the excerpt from "Eldorado": *bedight/night, shadow/Eldorado, long/song.* Explain that each of these rhyming word pairs contributes to the mood, voice, and tone of the poem. Ask volunteers to describe what they think, based on the excerpt, will be the mood, voice, and tone of the entire poem, "Eldorado".

"The Song of Wandering Aengus" and "Eldorado" 135

TEACH

ANALYZE SOUND DEVICES AND MOOD

Explain that **sound devices** are another way poets convey meaning and mood. Poets use four main kinds of sound devices: alliteration, assonance, consonance, and repetition. Have students explain the difference between assonance/consonance and alliteration/repetition to a partner to help them more easily identify sound devices as they read. (**Answer:** *Assonance repeats a vowel, while consonance repeats a consonant; alliteration repeats the sound at the beginning of a word, while repetition repeats an entire word.*)

■ English Learner Support

Understand Sound Devices Help students locate the phrase *with wandering* in the annotation model. Say the phrase aloud to students. Have students repeat it several times, emphasizing the initial *w* consonant sound. Point out that this repetition is called alliteration. **SUBSTANTIAL**

Have students work in pairs to find another example of alliteration in the sample. (*hollow lands, hilly lands; her hands*) **MODERATE**

ANNOTATION MODEL

Remind students to use the strategies in Analyze Rhyme on page 135 to identify the mood created by the poem's rhyme. Point out that they may follow this suggestion or use their own system for marking up the selection in their write-in text. They may want to color-code their annotations by using highlighters. Their notes in the margin may include questions about ideas that are unclear or topics they want to learn more about.

 GET READY

ANALYZE SOUND DEVICES AND MOOD

Poets use **sound devices** to convey a poem's meaning and mood. **Rhythm** is the pattern of stressed and unstressed syllables in a line of poetry. Rhythm brings out a poem's musical qualities and helps create its mood, the feeling or atmosphere that the poet wishes to create.

Sound Device	Definition	Example
alliteration	repetition of beginning consonant sounds in words	"And when white moths…"
assonance	repetition of vowel sounds in non-rhyming words	"Though I am old…"
consonance	repetition of consonant sounds within and at ends of words	"When I had laid…"
repetition	restating the same words or phrases, or the same grammatical constructions	"apple blossom" "apples of the moon" "apples of the sun"

ANNOTATION MODEL   NOTICE & NOTE

As you read, note each poet's use of rhyme and sound devices. Explain how these sound devices help create the mood of the poem. In the model, you can see one reader's notes about "The Song of Wandering Aengus."

> Though I am old (with wandering)
> Through (hollow lands) and (hilly lands)
> I will find out where she has gone,
> 20 And kiss her lips and take her hands;

First line: alliteration

Second line: alliteration and repetition

Second and fourth lines: end rhyme

The rhymes, the sound devices, and the rhythm remind me of a simple song.

136 Unit 2

BACKGROUND

"The Song of Wandering Aengus" was inspired by Aengus, the god of love and beauty in Irish mythology. In the original myth, Aengus falls in love with a girl he has dreamed about and has lost. **W. B. Yeats** (1865–1939) was an Irish poet, a playwright, and a notable literary figure of the twentieth century. As a boy, Yeats visited a rural part of Ireland called Sligo where he heard stories about heroes, heroines, and magic. In Yeats's later life, this folklore influenced his poetry and drama. "The Song of Wandering Aengus" reflects this influence.

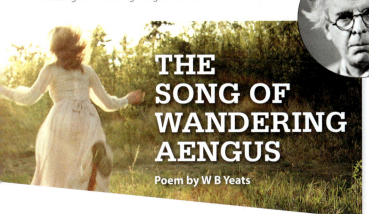

THE SONG OF WANDERING AENGUS
Poem by W B Yeats

PREPARE TO COMPARE
As you read, look for examples of rhyme, repetition, and other devices. Think about how the poet uses these devices to help create the poem's mood.

NOTICE & NOTE

Notice & Note

Use the side margins to notice and note signposts in the text.

I went out to the hazel wood,
Because a fire was in my head,
And cut and peeled a hazel wand,
And hooked a berry to a thread;
5 And when white moths were on the wing,
And moth-like stars were flickering out,
I dropped the berry in a stream
And caught a little silver trout.

TEACH

BACKGROUND
After students read the background of the poem and the information about Yeats, explain that many poems are inspired by the experience of love and loss. Yeats used his knowledge of Irish mythology to expand on the theme of loss in "The Story of Wandering Aengus," which tells about a man in search of a loved one and his hope that he will spend the rest of his life in happiness with her.

PREPARE TO COMPARE
Direct students to the Prepare to Compare prompt to focus their reading on page 137.

 ENGLISH LEARNER SUPPORT

Use Learning Strategies Tell students they will be reading a poem that is inspired in part by a myth. Provide cognates to help students understand the topics that will be covered in this lesson: *poem/poema, inspire/inspirer, myth/mito*. Provide sentence frames for students to talk about what they are about to read: *I know that this _____ (poem) is inspired by a _____ (myth)*.
SUBSTANTIAL

TEACH

ENGLISH LEARNER SUPPORT

Understand Sound Devices Provide students with the cognate: *rhyme/rima*. Then, help students locate the rhyming end words *aflame/name* and *hair/air*. Use visuals and gestures to help students understand the meaning of these words, such as a drawing of a flame and pointing to your hair as you say the words aloud. Have students repeat the rhyming sounds after you.
SUBSTANTIAL

ANALYZE RHYME SCHEME/ANALYZE SOUND DEVICES AND MOOD

Remind students that they should pay attention to the end rhyme of each line to determine the poem's rhyme scheme and examples of alliteration. To determine mood, students should consider the effect of rhyme scheme and sound devices. Have partners read the poem aloud, listening carefully. Then ask them to answer the following questions: *What mood—or feeling—do the sounds in the poem create?* (reflective, nostalgic, sad) *What tone—or attitude on the part of the author to his subject—do the sounds in the poem create?* (that the author understands the narrator's sadness) (**Answer:** *The end rhymes are aflame/name and hair/air; alliteration occurs in the words floor/fire/aflame and in "glimmering girl." The sounds create a musical rhythm. They also create images of glowing fire, suggesting a feeling of burning love and the sudden disappearance of this love almost into thin air.*)

For **speaking and reading support** for students at varying proficiency levels, see the **Text X-Ray** on page 134D.

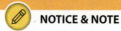 **NOTICE & NOTE**

ANALYZE RHYME SCHEME/ANALYZE SOUND DEVICES AND MOOD

Annotate: Reread lines 9–16 aloud. Mark examples of end rhymes and alliteration.

Interpret: What effects do these rhymes and sound devices have in understanding the poet's intended meaning?

> When I had laid it on the floor
> 10 I went to blow the fire aflame,
> But something rustled on the floor,
> And someone called me by my name:
> It had become a glimmering girl
> With apple blossom in her hair
> 15 Who called me by my name and ran
> And faded through the brightening air.
>
> Though I am old with wandering
> Through hollow lands and hilly lands,
> I will find out where she has gone,
> 20 And kiss her lips and take her hands;
> And walk among long dappled[1] grass,
> And pluck till time and times are done,
> The silver apples of the moon,
> The golden apples of the sun.

---
[1] **dappled:** marked with many spotted colors or light.

IMPROVE READING FLUENCY

Targeted Passage Model how to read poetry with appropriate rate and expression as students follow along in their books. Begin by reading lines 1–4 aloud to the class. Then, have students work with a partner to read lines 1–8 aloud, alternating reading every other line. Encourage students to provide feedback and support for reading with appropriate rate, reminding them to pause briefly at the end of each line and to emphasize rhyming words.

 Go to the **Reading Studio** for additional support in developing fluency.

NOTICE & NOTE

CHECK YOUR UNDERSTANDING

Answer these questions before moving on to the next selection.

1 Which word best describes the story told in the poem?

   A Incident

   B Quest

   C Hallucination

   D Mystery

2 Which event was most surprising to Aengus?

   F He sleepwalked into the forest.

   G Moths were all around him.

   H The fish he caught became a girl.

   J He found silver and golden apples.

3 In the line <u>I went out to the hazel wood</u>, the sound device used is called —

   A rhyme

   B alliteration

   C assonance

   D consonance

TEACH

CHECK YOUR UNDERSTANDING

Have students answer the questions independently.

Answers:

1. *B*
2. *H*
3. *B*

If they answer any questions incorrectly, have them reread the poem to confirm their understanding. Then they may proceed to ANALYZE THE TEXT on page 140.

ENGLISH LEARNER SUPPORT

Confirm Understanding Use the following supports with students at varying proficiency levels:

Read lines 17–18 aloud, and have students echo-read after you. Use images to illustrate that the speaker has grown older and gestures to help them understand the word *wandering*. Accept one-word responses to the following questions: *Is the poet old or young now? (old) Is the speaker still wandering? (yes)* **SUBSTANTIAL**

Have students read lines 17–19 with a partner. Ask them to tell their partner who is telling the story in the poem and what he is doing. Provide the following sentence frames to facilitate their discussion: *An ___ (old) man is telling the story in the poem. He is ____ (looking) for a girl.* **MODERATE**

Have students read lines 17–20 independently and take notes to respond to the following questions: *Who is wandering in the poem? (the narrator) What is the man in the poem looking for? (lost love) Why? (He loves the woman.)* **LIGHT**

For **listening support** for students at varying proficiency levels, see the **Text X-Ray** on page 134C.

TEACH

BACKGROUND

After students read the background note, explain that Poe's writing and poems often dealt with mysterious as well as gloomy topics. When "Eldorado" was first published, the California Gold Rush of the 1840s was drawing many people west in search of fortune. However, like the search for El Dorado–the mythical city of gold that drew many early explorers to the Americas–not everyone who searched for gold in California had a happy or successful quest.

PREPARE TO COMPARE

Direct students to the Prepare to Compare prompt to focus their reading.

ANALYZE RHYME AND MOOD

Remind students to consider the message of the poem when trying to determine mood. What feelings does the language of the poem evoke in the reader? Have students pause after reading pairs of lines to consider the feeling the poet is trying to convey. How do the feelings and ideas in the poem build on each other to connect to a central theme, or message?

Have students listen to the rhyming words *old* and *bold* in the second stanza. Ask them why the poet is drawing the reader's attention to these words. (**Answer:** *The opening lines in the second and third stanzas indicate the passage of time and the growing realization of the knight that he will never find Eldorado. He was bold [and younger] when he started out. Now that he is old, his mood shifts—as does the mood and tone of the poem—from his youthful excitement to growing disappointment and despair at the end.*)

NOTICE & NOTE

BACKGROUND

Edgar Allan Poe *(1809–1849) was an American poet, short story writer, and literary critic. Orphaned at the age of three, he was raised by friends of his family. As a young man, Poe worked as a journalist while writing short stories and poems. Widely known for his short stories, Poe also was an influential poet. He focused a great deal on construction and style, using devices such as rhyme, alliteration, assonance, and repetition. He employs some of these devices in the poem "Eldorado."*

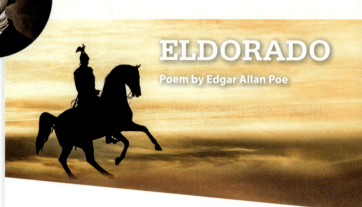

ELDORADO
Poem by Edgar Allan Poe

Notice & Note

Use the side margins to notice and note signposts in the text.

PREPARE TO COMPARE
As you read, think about the story the poem tells. Consider how the poet's use of rhyme and repetition affects the mood of the story and helps make it more enjoyable

Gaily bedight,
A gallant knight,
In sunshine and in shadow,
Had journeyed long,
5 Singing a song,
In search of Eldorado.

But he grew old—
This knight so bold—
And o'er his heart a shadow
10 Fell as he found
No spot of ground
That looked like Eldorado.

ANALYZE RHYME AND MOOD

Annotate: Reread lines 7–18 aloud. Mark examples of rhyme and lines that indicate the passage of time.

Interpret: What effect do these lines—and the rhyme within these lines—have on the mood of the poem?

140 Unit 2

WHEN STUDENTS STRUGGLE . . .

Identify Mood Have students use the chart to determine mood and meaning in the poem.

Words/ Images	What They Suggest	Mood Created
Had journeyed long/Singing a song.	a happy journey	optimistic, eager
Down the Valley of the Shadow	an end to the quest, despair	melancholy, despairing

  For additional support, go to the **Reading Studio** and apply the following **Level Up Tutorial: Tone**

And, as his strength
Failed him at length,
15 He met a pilgrim shadow—
"Shadow," said he,
"Where can it be—
This land of Eldorado?"

"Over the Mountains
20 Of the Moon,
Down the Valley of the Shadow,
Ride, boldly ride,"
The shade replied—
"If you seek for Eldorado!"

NOTICE & NOTE

CHECK YOUR UNDERSTANDING

Answer these questions before moving on to the **Analyze the Text** section on the following page.

1. What is the knight's goal?
   - A To travel the world
   - B To please his love
   - C To find Eldorado
   - D To become famous

2. What sound device does the poet use in the last line of each stanza?
   - F Repetition
   - G Assonance
   - H Consonance
   - J Mood

3. What is the meaning of <u>shadow</u> as used in line 15?
   - A Traveler
   - B Knight
   - C Ghost
   - D Cloud

The Song of Wandering Aengus / Eldorado 141

TEACH

CHECK YOUR UNDERSTANDING

Have students answer the questions independently.

Answers:

1. C
2. F
3. C

If they answer any questions incorrectly, have them reread the poem to confirm their understanding. Then they may proceed to Analyze the Text on page 142.

ENGLISH LEARNER SUPPORT

Oral Assessment Use the following questions to assess students' comprehension and speaking skills:

1. Does the poem tell about a journey? *(yes)* What is another word for journey? *(trip, quest)* Who goes on the journey? *(the knight)* What is the knight looking for? *(Eldorado; the city of gold)*

2. Look at the end of each stanza. What word do you see? *(Eldorado)* What is it called when a poet uses the same word over and over again? *(repetition)*

3. What is a shadow? *(a dark shape)* The knight asks the shadow a question. Can you talk to shadows? *(no)* Is the shadow real or is it meant to be figurative language? *(figurative language)* What does the shadow represent? *(a ghost)*

"The Song of Wandering Aengus" and "Eldorado" **141**

APPLY

ANALYZE THE TEXT

Possible answers:

1. **DOK 1:** *Stanza 1: Aengus makes a fishing rod and catches a silver trout. Stanza 2: The trout turns into a girl who calls his name and runs away Stanza 3: He is old and dreams of finding the girl.*

2. **DOK 2:** *The speaker is Aengus. The speaker is telling the story about searching for the girl, and poem is titled, "The Song of Wandering Aengus."*

3. **DOK 2:** *The knight represents many good people who try to achieve their goals in the life, no matter how difficult. It also represents the illusions that often motivate people to continue hopeless quests. Eldorado represents the unattainable goal.*

4. **DOK 3:** *Poe uses repetition in the last two lines of each stanza, which refer to the search for Eldorado. At first, the knight is singing a song, which indicates that he is joyful in his quest. By the second stanza, the knight continues his search though he has grown old. In the third stanza, he meets a "shadow" or ghost indicating that he is near death. In the final stanza, the ghost tells the knight he must continue his quest "Over the mountains / Of the Moon," indicating that reaching Eldorado is a futile goal.*

5. **DOK 3:** *The shadow is a reference to death. In stanza one it hints the knight's travel is not all happy. But the references become ominous: a shadow moves over his heart in stanza two, refers to a ghost in stanza three, and refers to death in stanza four.*

RESEARCH

Point out that students should be sure to assess the credibility of each website they use in their research.

Connect Students may note that the knight is looking for gold in a mythical place. Research shows that historically the quest for treasure in mythical places is most often futile.

RESPOND

ANALYZE THE TEXT

Support your responses with evidence from the text.   NOTEBOOK

1. **Summarize** What are the primary actions that take place in the three stanzas of "The Song of Wandering Aengus"?

2. **Infer** Who is the speaker—the person telling the story—in "The Song of Wandering Aengus"? How do you know?

3. **Interpret** Whom does the knight in "Eldorado" represent? What does Eldorado itself represent?

4. **Critique** Think about the words that appear at the end of each stanza of "Eldorado." How effectively do they connect to the changing mood of the poem?

5. **Analyze** The poet references a shadow in each of the four stanzas of "Eldorado." Why do you think the poet repeatedly refers to a shadow? How does the reference to the shadow change from the first stanza to the last?

RESEARCH TIP
The legend of El Dorado has long been featured in literature and popular entertainment. Because a search for "El Dorado" on the Internet will yield a range of results, look for sources that suggest content that deals with the history behind the legend. *National Geographic* and the BBC are both good sources, as are sites ending in *.org* and *.edu*.

RESEARCH

Over the centuries, the legend of El Dorado, the "city of gold," inspired adventurers, rulers, and others. Research where the legend of El Dorado comes from. Use what you learn to answer these questions.

QUESTION	ANSWER
Where was the lost "city of gold" supposedly located?	Somewhere in Central or South America
Who was El Dorado, or "the golden one"?	He was a king or chieftain who covered himself in gold dust
Why were the Spanish and other Europeans convinced that a city of gold actually existed?	They had heard stories about a city where the ruler covered himself in gold and where gold was so plentiful that it was thrown into a lake to appease the gods.
Did Europeans ever find El Dorado?	No; they searched but never found the city of gold.

Connect In the final stanza, the pilgrim shadow tells the knight that Eldorado is located "Over the Mountains/Of the Moon." With a small group, discuss how your research helps you understand the knight's quest and the pilgrim shadow's response.

LEARNING MINDSET

Curiosity Ask students to think about the mythical city of El Dorado. Is there anything about the city that makes them feel curious? Explain that curiosity and the habit of asking questions enhances learning. Tell students that setting a purpose by asking a question before reading can help them approach a topic with curiosity. Suggest that students think of a time they learned something in school that helped them outside of the classroom. Encourage students to use reading to explore their interests both inside and outside of the classroom.

RESPOND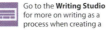

CREATE AND PRESENT

Write a Poem Write a poem about a mysterious event and its effects. Think about the following questions.

- ❏ Who will be the speaker in your poem?
- ❏ What will be the theme of your poem?
- ❏ What structure will you use in your poem?
- ❏ Will your poem have rhyme and a rhyme scheme?
- ❏ What sound devices will you use?

Present Your Poem The way a poem is read aloud can help convey its meaning. Prepare a dramatic reading of your poem and present it to your group.

- ❏ Practice reading the poem, adjusting the rhythm of your reading according to different line lengths in the poem.
- ❏ Read in a strong, confident voice, but do not yell.
- ❏ Think about words that you want to emphasize and places where you might want to pause for effect.
- ❏ Use facial expressions and natural gestures to help convey the meaning of the poem.

 Go to the **Writing Studio** for more on writing as a process when creating a poem.

 Go to the **Speaking and Listening Studio** for help with presenting your poem.

RESPOND TO THE ESSENTIAL QUESTION

 What can blur the lines between what's real and what's not?

Gather Information Review your annotations and notes on "The Song of Wandering Aengus" and "Eldorado." Then, add relevant details to your Response Log. As you determine which information to include, think about how:

- people react to unexplainable events
- each person's experience of reality is unique
- people's reactions to events change over time

At the end of the unit, use your notes to help you create a multimodal presentation.

ACADEMIC VOCABULARY
As you write and discuss what you learned from the poems, be sure to use the Academic Vocabulary words. Check off each of the words that you use.

- ❏ abnormal
- ❏ feature
- ❏ focus
- ❏ perceive
- ❏ task

The Song of Wandering Aengus / Eldorado 143

APPLY

CREATE AND PRESENT

Write a Poem Point out that students should use their answers to the questions in the list on page 143 as they write their poems. Students should review the checklist when they are finished to be sure they have included each element in their poems.

For **writing support** for students at varying proficiency levels, see the **Text X-Ray** on page 134D.

Present Your Poem Remind students that they should read their poems at an appropriate rate and with the intended expression. Tell them to be mindful of rhythm and meter. Have students practice with a partner, going over the checklist after they complete reading their poems aloud.

RESPOND TO THE ESSENTIAL QUESTION

Allow time for students to add details from "The Song of Wandering Aengus" and "Eldorado" to their Unit 2 Response Logs.

 ENGLISH LEARNER SUPPORT

Present Your Poem Pair students with different levels of proficiency to present their poems. Have students practice reading their poems aloud or presenting their words and images. Encourage students to advise their partners about pacing (too fast, too slow) and about emphasizing important words or phrases in their poems. Encourage more proficient students to provide feedback to partners who are presenting their poems as images or gestures.

APPLY

COMPARE MOODS

Before groups work on the comparison chart, emphasize that they should choose details about each element in the poems that relate to the message, or theme, of the poem.

ANALYZE THE TEXTS

Possible answers:

1. **DOK 1:** Aengus: the speaker is in search of the fish-turned-girl from his dream. The fish-girl symbolizes love. Eldorado: the knight seeks the fabled city of gold. Eldorado symbolizes unattainable life goals.

2. **DOK 3:** Aengus: though the speaker is old, he keeps searching for the girl, giving it a mood of love and determination. Eldorado: the speaker's age has cast a shadow "over his heart." He keeps searching, but there is a sense of sadness and impending death.

3. **DOK 3:** Answers will vary. Students' responses should mention examples of some of these sound devices: end rhyme, rhyme scheme, alliteration, assonance/consonance, and repetition.

4. **DOK 4:** Aengus: The image of the "apple blossom in her hair" in lines 13–14 represents new or blossoming love. In lines 22–24, the poet indicates that he will enjoy full-blown love as they pluck "The silver apples of the moon,/the golden apples of the sun." The mood is magical, loving, and hopeful. Eldorado: in the first stanza the knight is happy as he sets out, "In sunshine and in shadow." In the second stanza, the knight has grown old and "over high heart [fell] a shadow." In the third and fourth stanzas, the knight is approaching death when he meets a shadow who advises him to travel, "Down the Valley of the Shadow" or to death itself. The mood shifts throughout, from excitement, to disappointment, to despair, and to disappointment or resignation. Both poems reflect the changes that come as youthful dreams, loves, and aspirations disappear; in both poems, the seekers persevere in their searches.

144   Unit 2

RESPOND

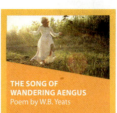

THE SONG OF WANDERING AENGUS
Poem by W.B. Yeats

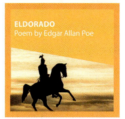

ELDORADO
Poem by Edgar Allan Poe

Collaborate & Compare

COMPARE MOODS

Both "The Song of Wandering Aengus" and "Eldorado" are poems that describe a quest, a journey in which someone searches for something desired. Although the poems share this idea, each poem creates a distinctly different mood. **Mood** is the general feeling, or emotional atmosphere, that a poem produces in readers. Mood in a poem is developed in several ways.

- **Setting/Events**—what happens and where
- **Speaker**—the person speaking the words to the reader
- **Diction**—the choice of words and images
- **Sound devices**—rhyme, rhythm, alliteration, assonance, consonance, and repetition

With your group, complete the chart with details from both poems.

	THE SONG OF WANDERING AENGUS	ELDORADO
Setting/Events	Woods; Aengus dreams; fish turns into girl; search for girl	Varied landscape; knight travels; search for fabled city
Speaker	First person; Aengus	Third person; unknown
Diction	Fire in head; fish-girl; apples	Knight; different types of shadow
Sound Devices	End rhymes (*head/thread, out/trout*); even rhythm; alliteration (*glimmering girl*)	End rhymes (*bedight/night, long/song*); quick rhythm; alliteration (*singing a song*)

ANALYZE THE TEXTS

Discuss these questions in your group.

1. **Compare** With your group, discuss the goals of the quest in each poem. What do these goals symbolize?

2. **Interpret** In both poems, the speaker notes that the person on the quest has grown old. How does age affect the quest differently in the two poems? How does it affect the mood of each poem?

3. **Evaluate** Both poems use several sound devices to develop mood. Which poem do you think does this more effectively? Why?

4. **Critique** In "The Song of Wandering Aengus," Yeats uses the image of "apples" to develop mood. In "Eldorado," Poe uses "shadow." How do these words reflect the development of mood in each poem?

144   Unit 2

ENGLISH LEARNER SUPPORT

Ask Questions Use the following questions to help students compare the poems:

1. Who is Aengus looking for? (*a girl*) What is the knight looking for? (*Eldorado*)

2. Does time pass in each poem? (*yes*) What lines tell you that time passes? (*"Though am old with wandering" and "But he grew old"*)

3. What is one example of repetition in each poem? (*floor, lands; Eldorado*)

MODERATE/LIGHT

RESPOND

COLLABORATE AND PRESENT

Now, your group can continue exploring the ideas in these texts by identifying and comparing the mood of the poems. Follow these steps:

1. **Determine the Most Important Details** With your group, review the most important details about each poem. Identify points you agree on and resolve disagreements through collaborative discussion. Try to reach a consensus about how you would express the mood of each poem based on evidence from the texts.

2. **Create Mood Word Webs** Prepare a word web for each poem. In the center of each web, write a key word or phrase that describes the poem's basic mood. Then, add quotations from the poem or descriptive phrases that provide evidence about the poem's mood.

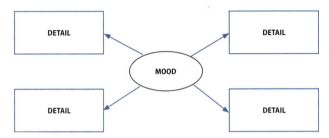

3. **Present to the Class** As a group, prepare a presentation of your ideas about the mood of each poem, using your word webs as visuals. For each poem, write a complete sentence stating your main idea about the poem's mood. Then, use your details to support your main idea, taking care that you cite specific evidence from both poems. Share your presentations with the class.

4. **Discuss Presentations** When all the groups have made presentations, discuss how the ideas presented were similar and different. Listen actively to the members of other groups and ask them to clarify any points you do not understand.

 Go to the **Speaking and Listening Studio** for help with giving a presentation.

APPLY

COLLABORATE AND PRESENT

1. **Determine the Most Important Details** As students select the most important details, circulate among the groups to make sure that each student is contributing. Remind students that they need to be able to explain why the details they are selecting are important. Encourage students to pause and listen to each other as they present their ideas, and to respond to ideas with respect and curiosity.

2. **Create Mood Word Webs** Remind students that the supporting details in their word webs should be text from the poems. Encourage each student in the group to contribute at least one detail to the mood word web.

3. **Present to the Class** Before students present their mood webs, have students decide which detail they will each be presenting to the class. Groups may also select a leader to present the mood and describe why they have determined a certain mood best describes the poem.

4. **Discuss Presentations** Guide the classroom discussion by addressing each group's mood chart individually. Many of the groups may come to similar conclusions about the mood of each poem. On the board, list all the moods students have identified. Guide students to recognize which ideas were similar and compare the details each group has compiled for that mood. Allow the class to suggest additional details for the charts where appropriate.

 ENGLISH LEARNER SUPPORT

Identify Supporting Details Divide students into groups of mixed proficiency levels. Provide students with a word bank for identifying the mood of each poem: *hopeful, excited, loving, sad, disappointed*. Have students select one mood to develop their mood word webs around. Provide beginning students with vocabulary support through gestures and visuals as necessary. Advanced students may suggest their own description for the mood of the poem.
ALL LEVELS

PLAN

THE GOVERNESS
Drama by Neil Simon

GENRE ELEMENTS
DRAMA
Remind students that **drama** is one of the first forms of written entertainment. Dramas are written by playwrights. In the initial script, the playwright imagines what the play will look like by describing the **setting** and the **characters** in the play. The playwright then writes the **dialogue** and **stage directions** for the characters and lists the **cast of characters**. Eventually, the play will be put on by a group of actors.

LEARNING OBJECTIVES
- Analyze drama, including cast of characters, dialogue, and stage directions.
- Conduct research about class structures in 19th-century Europe.
- Write a personal narrative about overcoming expectations.
- Direct a scene from the play, "The Governess."
- Use a dictionary to find the word origins of vocabulary words.
- Identify subordinating conjunctions, independent clauses, and dependent clauses in complex sentences.
- **Language** Understand and use complex sentences.

TEXT COMPLEXITY

Quantitative Measures	The Governess	Lexile: N/A
Qualitative Measures	**Ideas Presented** Much is explicit but moves to some implied meaning	
	Structure Used Clear, chronological, conventional	
	Language Used Some unconventional period-specific language	
	Knowledge Required Begins to rely on outside knowledge	

146A Unit 2

PLAN

RESOURCES

Online

- Unit 2 Response Log
- Selection Audio
- Reading Studio: Notice & Note
- Writing Studio: Writing Narratives
- Vocabulary Studio: Word Origins
- Grammar Studio: Module 3: Lesson 6: Conjunctions and Interjections
- "The Governess" Selection Test

SUMMARIES

English

In 19th-century Russia, the mistress of a house summons her new governess to discuss her first two months' wages. Throughout their dialogue, the mistress reminds the young woman to keep her head up and be more confident. Meanwhile, she lists off many reasons, in detail, for docking her pay, until her final payment is a small fraction of what she was owed. Finally, the mistress tells the young governess the whole meeting was a lesson to teach her the meaning of standing up for herself.

Spanish

Estas fotografías de una producción universitaria de la obra "La Institutriz" muestran a una joven institutriz y a su empleadora en varios momentos de la obra. Es una escena independiente de la dramatización El buen doctor, realizada por Neil Simon sobre la base de los cuentos del siglo XIX de Antón Chéjov. Las imágenes de la producción muestran la iluminación, el vestuario y la puesta en escena, capturando los momentos de conflicto en que una empleadora se propone estafar a su institutriz para evitar que ésta reciba el salario que merece.

 SMALL GROUP OPTIONS

Have students work in small groups to read and discuss the selection.

Think-Pair-Share
- After students have read and analyzed "The Governess," pose this question: *Did the Mistress's lesson work?*
- Have students think about the question individually and take notes.
- Then, have pairs discuss their ideas about the question.
- Finally, ask pairs to share their responses with the class.

Three-Minute Review
- Have students get into pairs, gathering their notes on "The Governess," but without the text.
- Tell students that they have three minutes to come up with an answer to a question you will ask them.
- Ask a series of questions, varying in difficulty (such as *What does Mistress keep reminding Julia to do with her head?* or *What is the Mistress's son's name?*)
- Afterwards, discuss the answers, but also how well they remembered the text and how thorough their notes were.

The Governess **146B**

PLAN

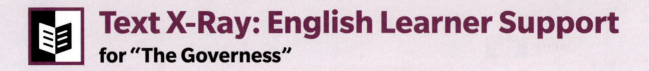

Text X-Ray: English Learner Support
for "The Governess"

INTRODUCE THE SELECTION
DISCUSS DRAMA AND STAGE PRODUCTIONS

In this lesson, students will be studying and discussing drama. Discuss features of a drama with students: character, dialogue, and stage directions. Provide the following explanations:

- *characters:* point out the cast of characters (Writer, Julia, Mistress) and explain that when students read each characters' name at the beginning of a line, this shows that this character is speaking.
- *dialogue:* explain that what a character says in a play comes after that character's name and is called dialogue.
- *stage directions:* point to the stage directions and explain that these notes describe what a character is doing during the drama.

Tell students that dramas, just like other kinds of fiction, include conflict and themes that are revealed by paying attention to what characters do and say.

CULTURAL REFERENCES

The following words and phrases may be unfamiliar to students:

- *uplifting* (paragraph 1): inspiring
- *coming along* (paragraph 11): how something is going
- *financial matters* (paragraph 45): dealing with money
- *let it go* (paragraph 61): choosing to forget about something
- *taking losses* (paragraph 61): suffering minor setbacks
- *head in the clouds* (paragraphs 67 and 69): not paying attention; being impractical
- *playing a little joke* (paragraph 91): tricking someone to make him or her appear foolish

LISTENING

Understand Complex Sentences

Remind students that complex sentences are sentences that combine two or more clauses. Students may know that compound sentences use the conjunctions *and*, *but*, and *or*, but in this lesson they will learn about subordinating conjunctions.

Use the following supports with students at varying proficiency levels:

- Read aloud the following sentences: *Julia was surprised when Mistress would not pay her the full amount. Mistress was not a kind person.* Re-read the sentences again, instructing students to raise one hand when they hear a simple sentence and two hands when they hear a complex sentence. When you read the sentences for a second time emphasize the coordinating conjunction *when*. **SUBSTANTIAL**
- Read aloud the same two sentences, instructing students to say whether each sentence is complex or simple. Then, ask students to identify the subordinating conjunction. **MODERATE**
- Read aloud paragraph 8. Have students identify the simple sentences, the complex sentence, and the subordinating conjunction. **LIGHT**

PLAN

SPEAKING

Discuss Humor

Lead classroom discussions on the literary techniques of **mood** (the feeling created by the play), **voice** (the playwright's unique use of language), and **tone** (the writer's attitude toward his or her subject) and how these elements create humor in "The Governess."

Use the following supports with students at varying proficiency levels:

- Say the word tone aloud and have students repeat after you. Say: *The tone is how the writer feels about the topic.* Provide students with the following sentence frames: *The _____ of the drama is humorous.* **SUBSTANTIAL**
- Ask students: Do you think the drama is serious or humorous? (humorous) Explain that this is the tone of the drama. Have student pairs use sentence frames to discuss the tone. *The tone of the drama is _____. It is funny when _____.* **MODERATE**
- Lead a discussion on the drama's use of mood, voice, and tone, and how the playwright creates humor. Definte irony for students: the difference between what a character says and what a character does. Then, have student pairs locate an example of irony in the drama. **LIGHT**

READING

Read Drama

Tell students that writing **drama** requires the playwright to focus on just a few basic elements: **dialogue**, **characters**, and **stage directions**. The script provides the blueprints for a theater company to then make and produce a play.

Work with students to read paragraphs 7–9. Use the following supports with students at varying proficiency levels:

- Have students run their fingers underneath the names of the characters as you read them aloud. Provide sentence frames. *Julia is a _____. Mistress is also a _____.* **SUBSTANTIAL**
- Have student pairs take turns reading a line of dialogue aloud to each other. Encourage students to act out the stage directions as they take turns. **MODERATE**
- Have students explain what is happening in the passage. Provide sentence frames: *I know Mistress is bossy because she says in the dialogue _____. I know Julia is timid because the stage directions say _____.* **LIGHT**

WRITING

Write a Personal Narrative

Work with students to read and understand the writing assignment on p. 159.

Use the following supports with students at varying proficiency levels:

- Suggest that students begin their narratives by drawing pictures and adding single words or captions. **SUBSTANTIAL**
- Have students write words, phrases, and/or sentences that tell the major parts of their narratives. **MODERATE**
- Encourage students to use transitional words and phrases to connect and clarify the major parts of their narratives. **LIGHT**

TEACH

Connect to the ESSENTIAL QUESTION

In this semi-serious, semi-comedic short play by Neil Simon, a young woman in 19th-century Russia is the victim of a cruel prank by her employer whose motive is to teach the young woman an important life lesson. Is it ever right to be cruel to another person in order to teach him or her a lesson?

COMPARE VERSIONS

Prompt students to keep in mind as they read, that the humor may not immediately come across to them. Some students may not think the written play is funny at all until they have seen the video—and hear the laughs from the audience. What does this say about how humor comes across in different media?

COLLABORATE & COMPARE

DRAMA

THE GOVERNESS
from The Good Doctor

by **Neil Simon**

pages 149–157

COMPARE VERSIONS

As you read the drama and view the production images, notice how each version conveys humor. Think about how the effect is different when you are reading the lines compared to viewing how one group staged the production. After going through both versions, you will collaborate with a small group on a final project.

ESSENTIAL QUESTION:

What can blur the lines between what's real and what's not?

PRODUCTION IMAGES

from

THE GOVERNESS

presented by the
Theater Arts Department, Clackamas Community College

page 165

146   Unit 2

⚙ LEARNING MINDSET

Persistence Students may have trouble reading "The Governess" because it is set in a time they are not familiar with. Tell them that many people will have trouble reading texts that take place in a long-ago period. Remind students that if they keep at it, they will be able to find similarities between the character and the situation she faces with situations they have faced themselves. Remind students that dealing with a difficult text may be hard the first time but that it gets easier with practice.

The Governess *from* The Good Doctor

QUICK START

We have all been in situations where we had to stand up for ourselves. With a group, discuss what it means to "stand up for yourself."

ANALYZE DRAMA

The play you are about to read is a **drama**, a form of literature intended to be performed. Like other literature, a drama presents events, called the **plot**, and conveys the time and place of those events, called the **setting**. The plot centers on a **conflict**, or a struggle between opposing forces, and unfolds through the characters' words and actions. Unlike other literature, a drama usually includes the following:

- **cast of characters**—a list of all the characters in the drama; the cast appears at the beginning of the drama.
- **dialogue**—the words that the characters say; the character's name precedes his or her lines of dialogue.
- **stage directions**—instructions for how the drama is to be performed; these instructions are often set in parentheses.

Because dramas are meant to be performed, reading the script requires you to focus on the dialogue and stage directions to picture the action and understand the drama's meaning.

ANALYZE HUMOR

Playwrights create humor by using certain literary techniques. The **mood** of a play is the feeling that the playwright creates, such as happy or somber. **Voice** refers to the playwright's unique style of expression. **Tone** is the playwright's attitude toward the play, which might be playful or ironic. In this play, Neil Simon uses **irony**, in which characters say the opposite of what is expected, to create humor.

LINES FROM "THE GOVERNESS"	ANALYSIS
Julia. Only once since I've been here have I ever been given any money and that was by your husband. On my birthday he gave me three rubles. **Mistress.** Really? There's no note of it in my book. I'll put it down now. *(She writes in the book.)* Three rubles. Thank you for telling me. Sometimes I'm a little lax with my accounts . . .	Mistress's sharp voice helps to create a humorous mood. The difference between her point of view and that of the audience (and Julia) creates humor through irony.

As you read "The Governess," think about how the dialogue and stage directions help you understand the characters of Julia and Mistress.

GENRE ELEMENTS: DRAMA

- written by a playwright
- includes a cast of characters
- relies on dialogue and stage directions to tell a story

GET READY

TEACH

QUICK START

After student groups have discussed what it means to "stand up for yourself," ask them to explain the factors that might in certain situations prevent people from standing up for themselves.

ANALYZE DRAMA

Go over with students the essentials of drama, by distinguishing what separates it from the other genres, such as fiction and poetry.

- **cast of characters**—neither poetry nor fiction provides a list of characters
- **dialogue**—neither poetry nor fiction requires anyone to talk. A novel, for instance, could be made up entirely of exposition without including the words of any of its characters.
- **stage directions**—as drama is specifically written for the stage, plays come with stage directions. This is unique to the genre.

ANALYZE HUMOR

In the case of "The Governess," the **mood** and **tone** are both very stiff. The action centers around an uncomfortable scenario—an employer and employee going over the subject of money due. While the setting is formal and the characters serious, the **voice** of the play is actually rather humorous. This is not the broad humor students may be used to; instead, it is more subtle. Evidence for this is that many of the laughs come from how increasingly uncomfortable and ridiculous the situation becomes for the governess.

ENGLISH LEARNER SUPPORT

Understand Drama Explain that to analyze drama it is important to understand **characters, dialogue,** and **stage directions**.

Have students preview the text by reading the title and noting how the text is set up. Have students complete the following sentences: *I know who is talking because the character's name is _____.* (in bold print) *The text that is in italics and set in parentheses gives information about _____.* (*lighting, props, or what the actors should be doing*)

SUBSTANTIAL/MODERATE

Have students read lines 3–15 of the text. What is the Mistress's attitude toward Julia? How do you know? (*She has an aloof, superior attitude. Evidence of this is that she keeps telling Julia how to hold her head and assumes that Vanya's math abilities are because of her.*)

LIGHT

TEACH

CRITICAL VOCABULARY

Encourage students to read all the sentences before deciding which word best completes each one. Remind them to look for context clues that match the meaning of each word.

Answers:

1. *discrepancy*
2. *madame*
3. *heirloom*
4. *inferior*

■ **English Learner Support**

Pronunciation Help students sound out the Critical Vocabulary words. Make sure that they can distinguish sounds and intonation patterns. Explain that *discrepancy* has both a prefix as well as a suffix, *madame* comes from the French, *heirloom* has a silent *h*, and *inferior* is a Spanish cognate. **SUBSTANTIAL/MODERATE**

LANGUAGE CONVENTIONS

Complex Sentences: Subordinating Conjunctions
Explain that **subordinating conjunctions** are words that are commonly used to connect two clauses to make a complex sentence. Read the example out loud. Then, break it into two clauses. *(I like to see your eyes. When I speak to you.)* Have students identify the independent and dependent clause as well as the subordinating conjunction

ANNOTATION MODEL

Remind students of the annotation ideas in Analyze Drama on page 147, which suggest underlining stage directions. Point out that students may follow this suggestion or use their own system for marking up the selection in their write-in text. They may want to color-code their annotations by using highlighters. Their notes in the margins may include questions about ideas that are unclear or about topics they may want to learn more about.

 GET READY

CRITICAL VOCABULARY

madame   inferior   discrepancy   heirloom

To see how many Critical Vocabulary words you already know, use them to complete the sentences.

1. Few trusted the young man because of the _____ between what he said in public and what he said in private.
2. Lena's employer had asked the young maid to call her _____, though the term was rarely used these days.
3. The vase that her grandmother gave her was an expensive family _____.
4. The staff at the newspaper treated the new hire as a(n) _____.

LANGUAGE CONVENTIONS

Complex Sentences: Subordinating Conjunctions   In this lesson, you will learn about forming **complex sentences** by using **subordinating conjunctions** to connect ideas. Common subordinating conjunctions include *as*, *while*, *although*, *when*, *until*, *unless*, and *because*.

Example from "The Governess":

| 1st Idea | 2nd Idea |

I didn't bother making a note of it (because) I always do it.

As you read "The Governess," note the playwright's use of subordinating conjunctions to link ideas.

ANNOTATION MODEL   **NOTICE & NOTE**

As you read, note dialogue and stage directions to help you understand how the playwright develops characters and creates humor through mood, tone, and voice. In the model, you can see one reader's notes about "The Governess."

> 17   **Mistress.** Head up . . . *(She lifts head up.)* That's it. Don't be afraid to look people in the eyes, my dear. If you think of yourself as inferior, that's exactly how people will treat you.
>
> 18   **Julia.** Yes, ma'am.

Why does Mistress keep saying this?

This is ironic, because Mistress treats Julia as inferior. But Mistress's words may reveal that she really is trying to help Julia.

148   Unit 2

BACKGROUND

Neil Simon (b. 1927) has written many popular plays, movies, and television shows. Simon's collection of skits, The Good Doctor, which features "The Governess," was inspired by the Russian writer Anton Chekhov. Chekov, like Simon, uses humor to explore class and human nature. Simon acknowledges Chekhov's influence by including a Chekhov-inspired character, the Writer.

NOTICE & NOTE

THE GOVERNESS
from The Good Doctor
Drama by Neil Simon

PREPARE TO COMPARE

As you read, make note of the dialogue and stage directions that help to shape the characters. This information will help you compare the drama with the production images that follow it.

1 **Writer.** *(Appears in a spot and addresses the audience).* Wait! For those who are offended by life's cruelty, there is an alternate ending . . . "Ivan Ilyitch Cherdyakov went home, took off his coat, lay down on the sofa . . . and inherited five million rubles." There's not much point to it, but it *is* uplifting. I assure you it is not my intention to paint life any harsher than it is. But some of us are, indeed, trapped. Witness the predicament of a young governess who cares for and educates the children of a well-to-do family.

2 *(Lights up on the MISTRESS of the house at her desk. She has an account book in front of her.)*

3 **Mistress.** Julia!

4 **Writer.** Trapped, indeed . . .

5 **Mistress** *(Calls again).* Julia!

Notice & Note

Use the side margins to notice and note signposts in the text.

ANALYZE DRAMA

Annotate: Mark the stage directions on this page.

Analyze: How do some of the stage directions help you understand the relationship between Mistress and Julia?

The Governess 149

TEACH

BACKGROUND

Although Neil Simon was born after Anton Checkov's death, his play takes place during the era in which Checkov lived and set his plays. Explain to students that in order to write this period piece—a work set in the past—with any authority, Simon would have had to have thoroughly researched the period, Checkov himself, and his works.

SETTING A PURPOSE

Direct students to use the Setting a Purpose prompt to focus their reading.

✎ ANALYZE DRAMA

The stage directions are set off in parentheses with italic font. Point out to students that sometimes the stage directions appear before the characters' dialogue, but at other times, they appear between blocks of dialogue. Having Mistress at her desk with her account book, helps "set the stage" of her being the one in charge. (**Answer:** *Julia rushes in and curtsies, so she is used to doing what she's told. She also keeps her head down, so this suggests that she may be fearful or passive around Mistress.*)

🗨 ENGLISH LEARNER SUPPORT

Understand Directionality Guide students as they read the first page of "The Governess." Point out that a play is laid out differently from other types of writing, such as prose and poetry. Explain that there are three characters: the Writer, Julia, and Mistress. Before each character speaks, their name is listed in boldface. The text that follows is what they are saying. Show the students that what the characters do and the props they need are set out in stage directions (in parentheses and italics). **MODERATE/LIGHT**

The Governess 149

TEACH

For **listening support** for students at varying proficiency levels, see the **Text X-Ray** on page 146C.

ANALYZE DRAMA

Use this guided reading question to explain that in drama, often things are intentionally repeated or reiterated in an effort to be sure the audience understands the characters, conflict, and themes. (**Answer:** *She is bossy and controlling.*)

LANGUAGE CONVENTIONS

If students need help identifying subordinate conjunctions, refer them back to the list on page 148. (*The second idea, "you never ask me for it yourself" gives more information about the first idea, "I imagine you must need money."*)

ANALYZE HUMOR

Explain to students that sometimes italics or other ways of distinguishing words and phrases are often a cue for humor. (**Answer:** *She is speaking to Julia as if she is speaking to a child. It is condescending.*)

CRITICAL VOCABULARY

madame: Julia uses the formal word *madame* to address Mistress. This word was commonly used in the period depicted, but people rarely use the word today.

ASK STUDENTS how replacing the word *madame* with "ma'am" or "boss" would change the tone. ("*Ma'am*" *is less formal; "boss" is much less formal and more contemporary.*)

inferior: The definition refers to objects and ideas that are lower in quality, but it can be applied to people as well.

ASK STUDENTS what the antonym for *inferior* is, and who in this scene that word applies to. (*Superior; the term applies to Mistress in the scene.*)

150   Unit 2

 NOTICE & NOTE

madame
(mə-dăm´) *n. Madame* is a form of polite address for a woman.

ANALYZE DRAMA
Annotate: Mark the dialogue in which Mistress tells Julia to lift her head.
Infer: What do Mistress's constant reminders suggest about her?

inferior
(ĭn-fîr´ē-ər) *adj.* If something is *inferior*, it is lower in value and quality.

LANGUAGE CONVENTIONS
Annotate: In paragraph 19, circle the subordinating conjunction *although*. Then underline the two ideas it connects.
Analyze: How are the two ideas you underlined related?

ANALYZE HUMOR
Annotate: Mark Mistress's explanation in paragraph 23 for how Julia may have been confused about her salary.
Analyze: How would you describe Mistress's voice here?

6   (*A young governess,* JULIA, *comes rushing in. She stops before the desk and curtsies.*)
7   **Julia** (*Head down*). Yes, **madame?**
8   **Mistress.** Look at me, child. Pick your head up. I like to see your eyes when I speak to you.
9   **Julia** (*Lifts her head up*). Yes, madame.
10 (*But her head has a habit of slowly drifting down again.*)
11 **Mistress.** And how are the children coming along with their French lessons?
12 **Julia.** They're very bright children, madame.
13 **Mistress.** Eyes up . . . They're bright, you say. Well, why not? And mathematics? They're doing well in mathematics, I assume?
14 **Julia.** Yes, madame. Especially Vanya.
15 **Mistress.** Certainly. I knew it. I excelled in mathematics. He gets that from his mother, wouldn't you say?
16 **Julia.** Yes, madame.
17 **Mistress.** Head up . . . (*She lifts head up.*) That's it. Don't be afraid to look people in the eyes, my dear. If you think of yourself as **inferior**, that's exactly how people will treat you.
18 **Julia.** Yes, ma'am.
19 **Mistress.** A quiet girl, aren't you? . . . Now then, let's settle our accounts.[1] I imagine you must need money, although you never ask me for it yourself. Let's see now, we agreed on thirty rubles a month, did we not?
20 **Julia** (*Surprised*). Forty, ma'am.
21 **Mistress.** No, no, thirty. I made a note of it. (*Points to the book.*) I always pay my governesses thirty . . . Who told you forty?
22 **Julia.** You did, ma'am. I spoke to no one else concerning money . . .
23 **Mistress.** Impossible. Maybe you *thought* you heard forty when I said thirty. If you kept your head up, that would never happen. Look at me again and I'll say it clearly. *Thirty rubles a month.*

---
[1] **Settle our accounts:** pay a debt or receive payment for a debt.

150   Unit 2

 ENGLISH LEARNER SUPPORT

Understand Drama Using gestures and mannerisms, show students what Mistress keeps asking Julia to do: "Pick your head up," "Eyes up," "Head up," etc. Then, using stage directions, show by imitating Julia's gestures and words her reaction to Mistress. Have students suggest other gestures and body language Julia might use.

ASK STUDENTS to look for and describe the stage directions that show Julia's physical responses to Mistress. (*Lifts her head up; But her head has a habit of slowly drifting down again; She lifts her head up.*) **SUBSTANTIAL**

24 **Julia.** If you say so, ma'am.

25 **Mistress.** Settled. Thirty a month it is . . . Now then, you've been here two months exactly.

26 **Julia.** Two months and five days.

27 **Mistress.** No, no. Exactly two months. I made a note of it. You should keep books the way I do so there wouldn't be these **discrepancies**. So—we have two months at thirty rubles a month . . . comes to sixty rubles. Correct?

28 **Julia** (*Curtsies*). Yes, ma'am. Thank you, ma'am.

29 **Mistress.** Subtract nine Sundays . . . We did agree to subtract Sundays, didn't we?

30 **Julia.** No, ma'am.

31 **Mistress.** Eyes! Eyes! . . . Certainly we did. I've always subtracted Sundays. I didn't bother making a note of it because I always do it. Don't you recall when I said we will subtract Sundays?

32 **Julia.** No, ma'am.

33 **Mistress.** Think.

34 **Julia** (*Thinks*). No, ma'am.

35 **Mistress.** You weren't thinking. Your eyes were wandering. Look straight at my face and look hard . . . Do you remember now?

36 **Julia** (*Softly*). Yes, ma'am.

37 **Mistress.** I didn't hear you, Julia.

38 **Julia** (*Louder*). Yes, ma'am.

39 **Mistress.** Good. I was sure you'd remember . . . Plus three holidays. Correct?

40 **Julia.** Two, ma'am. Christmas and New Year's.

41 **Mistress.** And your birthday. That's three.

42 **Julia.** I worked on my birthday, ma'am.

43 **Mistress.** You did? There was no need to. My governesses never worked on their birthdays . . .

NOTICE & NOTE

discrepancy
(dĭ-skrĕp´ən-sē) *n*. When there is a *discrepancy* between two things, there is a difference or disagreement.

ANALYZE DRAMA
Annotate: In paragraphs 31–38, mark Julia's response to Mistress as well as the stage directions that tell how Julia responds.

Draw Conclusions: Why do you think Julia changes her mind about remembering?

ANALYZE HUMOR
Annotate: In paragraphs 39–43, mark the reasons Mistress is deducting from Julia's pay.

Infer: What tone does the playwright create with these reasons?

The Governess   151

TEACH

ANALYZE DRAMA

Even though the dialogue in these lines is very short, it tells the readers a great deal about the characters and their relationship to each other. (**Answer:** *She knows it will do no good to argue with Mistress.*)

English Learner Support

Understand Drama Choral read lines 29–38. Using total body response when applicable (i.e. shaking your head "no," demonstrating the idiom Mistress uses: "your eyes were wandering.") When finished, discuss with students for comprehension. **SUBSTANTIAL/MODERATE**

ANALYZE HUMOR

If students struggle, suggest that they think about how they would feel if someone talked to them the way Mistress talks to Julia. (**Answer:** *scornful and abusive.*)

CRITICAL VOCABULARY

discrepancy: In the text, Mistress uses the word *discrepancy* deliberately to humiliate Julia, suggesting that if Julia were smarter she would keep her own records the way the Mistress keeps her own. This reinforces the idea that Mistress considers herself thoroughly superior to Julia.

ASK STUDENTS how they would have figured out what *discrepancies* meant without having the definition given to them? (**Possible answers:** *Use context clues, or look it up in a dictionary.*)

The Governess   151

TEACH

ENGLISH LEARNER SUPPORT

Monitor Comprehension Tell students that active readers notice and take action when they come across text they don't understand. Have students practice monitoring comprehension verbally.

- Have student pairs of differing abilities read lines 42–54 to each other. Instruct listeners to stop readers when they don't understand something. Tell readers to reread the confusing part slowly. Read the sentence before and after the confusing part for clues to meaning. Have reader pairs discuss how to rephrase any confusing details. This may help students understand the confusing part. **MODERATE**

- Have pairs read lines 42–54 to each other. Instruct the listeners to take notes on anything they don't understand. Have pairs then go back through the notes, discuss why those details were difficult, and decide how to use the text to better understand them. **LIGHT**

NOTICE & NOTE

44 **Julia.** But I did work, ma'am.

45 **Mistress.** But that's not the question, Julia. We're discussing financial matters now. I will, however, only count two holidays if you insist . . . Do you insist?

46 **Julia.** I did work, ma'am.

47 **Mistress.** Then you *do* insist.

48 **Julia.** No, ma'am.

49 **Mistress.** Very well. That's three holidays, therefore we take off twelve rubles. Now then, four days little Kolya was sick, and there were no lessons.

50 **Julia.** But I gave lessons to Vanya.

51 **Mistress.** True. But I engaged you to teach two children, not one. Shall I pay you in full for doing only half the work?

52 **Julia.** No, ma'am.

53 **Mistress.** So we'll deduct it. . . Now, three days you had a toothache and my husband gave you permission not to work after lunch. Correct?

54 **Julia.** After four. I worked until four.

55 **Mistress** (*Looks in the book*). I have here: "Did not work after lunch." We have lunch at one and are finished at two, not at four, correct?

152 Unit 2

APPLYING ACADEMIC VOCABULARY

 abnormal   feature ☐ focus   perceive ☐ task

Write and Discuss Have students turn to a partner to discuss the following questions. Guide students to include the Academic Vocabulary words *abnormal, feature,* and *perceive* in their responses. Ask volunteers to share their responses with the class:

- What is **abnormal** about Mistress's record keeping?
- What **feature** does Mistress keep noticing about Julia?
- How do you **perceive** Julia at this point in the play?

NOTICE & NOTE

56 **Julia.** Yes, ma'am. But I—

57 **Mistress.** That's another seven rubles . . . Seven and twelve is nineteen . . . Subtract . . . that leaves . . . forty-one rubles . . . Correct?

58 **Julia.** Yes, ma'am. Thank you, ma'am.

59 **Mistress.** Now then, on January fourth you broke a teacup and saucer, is that true?

60 **Julia.** Just the saucer, ma'am.

61 **Mistress.** What good is a teacup without a saucer, eh? . . . That's two rubles. The saucer was an **heirloom**. It cost much more, but let it go. I'm used to taking losses.

62 **Julia.** Thank you, ma'am.

63 **Mistress.** Now then, January ninth, Kolya climbed a tree and tore his jacket.

64 **Julia.** I forbid him to do so, ma'am.

65 **Mistress.** But he didn't listen, did he? . . . Ten rubles . . . January fourteenth, Vanya's shoes were stolen . . .

66 **Julia.** By the maid, ma'am. You discharged her yourself.

67 **Mistress.** But you get paid good money to watch everything. I explained that in our first meeting. Perhaps you weren't listening. Were you listening that day, Julia, or was your head in the clouds?

68 **Julia.** Yes, ma'am.

69 **Mistress.** Yes, your head was in the clouds?

70 **Julia.** No, ma'am. I was listening.

71 **Mistress.** Good girl. So that means another five rubles off. *(Looks in the book.)* . . . Ah, yes . . . The sixteenth of January I gave you ten rubles.

72 **Julia.** You didn't.

73 **Mistress.** But I made a note of it. Why would I make a note of it if I didn't give it to you?

74 **Julia.** I don't know, ma'am.

ANALYZE DRAMA
Annotate: Review paragraphs 59–65 and mark the questions that Mistress asks Julia.
Analyze: What do you notice about these questions? Do you think Mistress really wants to know the answer?

heirloom
(âr´lo͞om´) *n.* An *heirloom* is a valued possession that was passed down in a family.

ANALYZE HUMOR
Annotate: Mark the questions Mistress asks Julia in paragraphs 67–73.
Infer: What is the tone in these paragraphs?

The Governess 153

IMPROVE READING FLUENCY

Targeted Passage Have students work with partners to read lines 59–70. First, read lines 49–58 aloud for them. Have students follow along in their books as you read the text with appropriate phrasing and emphasis. Then, have partners each take a character and read aloud lines 59–70. Remind students to pay special attention to commas and ellipses, at which points they should break for pauses to add emphasis and tension to the performance. After completing their reading, have students switch roles. Encourage students to provide feedback and support for each other's readings.

 Go to the **Reading Studio** for additional support in developing fluency.

TEACH

ANALYZE DRAMA

Briefly discuss how people sometimes ask questions to which the answers are known. Ask students to give an example of a question meant to point out something they may have done wrong. *(Responses will vary.)* Then discuss how the criticism that Mistress levels at Julia with these questions heightens the conflict between the two characters. (**Answer:** *They are not questions that are intended to be answered--they are rhetorical questions. Mistress just wants Julia to confirm what Mistress already believes to be true.*)

ANALYZE HUMOR

Be sure students understand that Simon is aiming for humor by having Julia reflexively answer "Yes, ma'am" to the question in line 67. Ask students why Julia may be so quick to answer "yes." *(Possible response: Because of her inferior position as a servant, Julia is used to answering "yes" to Mistress.)* Discuss with students how this reflex to agree leaves Julia open to Mistress's further interrogation about whether Julia's head was indeed "in the clouds." (**Answer:** *insulting*)

CRITICAL VOCABULARY

heirloom: This word almost always connotes something that is old and has monetary or sentimental value.

ASK STUDENTS how the meaning would have changed if Mistress said the saucer was a "something I got from my grandmother" or "secondhand." ("Heirloom" has a connotation of worth, while the other two similar terms do not necessarily suggest monetary value.)

The Governess 153

TEACH

✏️ ANALYZE HUMOR

Remind students that character traits are behavior patterns; character flaws are behaviors that not desirable.(**Answer:** *Mistress doesn't seem to care about insulting Julia, so it seems odd that it would pain her to see Julia in tears. Because Mistress has essentially cheated Julia of money, it is ironic that she congratulates herself on her bookkeeping skills, which is essentially what she has used to cheat Julia out of her rightful pay.*)

■ English Learner Support

Analyze Humor In this selection, you can define *irony* as a type of humor that occurs when what a person says doesn't match what they do. Divide students into pairs to discuss, first, the use of irony in paragraph 80. Then discuss the use of irony throughout the text. (*In paragraph 80, Mistress claims it pains her to see Julia in tears, even though she has been insulting and cheating Julia throughout their entire meeting. Earlier, Mistress claimed she was "lax" in her bookkeeping, even though she is painstakingly detailed in her accounts of Julia's many infringements of her rules.*)
LIGHT

✏️ NOTICE & NOTE

ANALYZE HUMOR
Annotate: In paragraph 80, mark the character traits and flaws that Mistress admits to having.

Analyze: What is ironic about these admissions?

75 **Mistress.** That's not a satisfactory answer, Julia . . . Why would I make a note of giving you ten rubles if I did not in fact give it to you, eh? . . . No answer? . . . Then I must have given it to you, mustn't I?

76 **Julia.** Yes, ma'am. If you say so, ma'am.

77 **Mistress.** Well, certainly I say so. That's the point of this little talk. To clear these matters up . . . Take twenty-seven from forty-one, that leaves . . . fourteen, correct?

78 **Julia.** Yes, ma'am.

79 (*She turns away, softly crying.*)

80 **Mistress.** What's this? Tears? Are you crying? Has something made you unhappy, Julia? Please tell me. It pains me to see you like this. I'm so sensitive to tears. What is it?

81 **Julia.** Only once since I've been here have I ever been given any money and that was by your husband. On my birthday he gave me three rubles.

154   Unit 2

WHEN STUDENTS STRUGGLE . . .

Analyze Drama To help students grasp the conflict in the scene, have them reread sections 75-81 with a partner. Have students note what Julia does as she speaks. (*Julia turns away, and is crying.*) Ask guided reading questions to help students understand how the structure of the drama helps the reader to understand the conflict: How do you know Julia is crying? (*the stage directions and dialogue tell she is crying.*) Why is Julia crying (*She is told she is not owed any money.*)

NOTICE & NOTE

82 **Mistress.** Really? There's no note of it in my book. I'll put it down now. *(She writes in the book.)* Three rubles. Thank you for telling me. Sometimes I'm a little lax with my accounts . . . Always shortchanging[2] myself. So then, we take three more from fourteen . . . leaves eleven . . . Do you wish to check my figures?

83 **Julia.** There's no need to, ma'am.

84 **Mistress.** Then we're all settled. Here's your salary for two months, dear. Eleven rubles. *(She puts the pile of coins on the desk.)* Count it.

85 **Julia.** It's not necessary, ma'am.

86 **Mistress.** Come, come. Let's keep the records straight. Count it.

87 **Julia** *(Reluctantly counts it).* One, two, three, four, five, six, seven, eight, nine, ten . . . ? There's only ten, ma'am.

88 **Mistress.** Are you sure? Possibly you dropped one . . . Look on the floor, see if there's a coin there.

89 **Julia.** I didn't drop any, ma'am. I'm quite sure.

90 **Mistress.** Well, it's not here on my desk, and I *know* I gave you eleven rubles. Look on the floor.

91 **Julia.** It's all right, ma'am. Ten rubles will be fine.

92 **Mistress.** Well, keep the ten for now. And if we don't find it on the floor later, we'll discuss it again next month.

93 **Julia.** Yes, ma'am. Thank you, ma'am. You're very kind, ma'am.

94 *(She curtsies and then starts to leave.)*

95 **Mistress.** Julia! (JULIA *stops, turns.*) Come back here. *(She goes back to the desk and curtsies again.)* Why did you thank me?

96 **Julia.** For the money, ma'am.

97 **Mistress.** For the money? . . . But don't you realize what I've done? I've cheated you . . . *Robbed* you! I have no such notes in my book. I made up whatever came into my mind. Instead of the eighty rubles which I owe you, I gave you only ten. I have actually stolen from you and still you thank me . . . Why?

98 **Julia.** In the other places that I've worked, they didn't give me anything at all.

---

[2] **Shortchanging:** treating unfairly; cheating.

ANALYZE DRAMA

Annotate: In paragraph 97, mark the details that show that Mistress was playing a trick on Julia.

Analyze: What does this dialogue suggest about Mistress?

The Governess 155

TEACH

ENGLISH LEARNER SUPPORT

Analyze Drama Explain that very often plays and other forms of popular entertainment end with a surprise.

ASK STUDENTS Ask students to explain, in their own words, the surprise at the ending of the play. (*Mistress gives Julia her full pay. She explains that all along she was never serious about taking away deductions.*)

MODERATE

ANALYZE DRAMA

(**Answer:** *It was a surprise to learn that Mistress was trying to "help" Julia rather than cheat her. Julia is actually much wiser than Mistress because her smile says that she understands that in order to survive she must continue to play along with Mistress's cruel games.*)

WORDS OF THE WISER

Words of the Wiser usually point to genuine advice from a wiser person. In this case, the advice Mistress gives to Julia is neither genuine nor practical. If Julia were to take Mistress's words to heart she would most likely be fired, and Julia knows this. (**Answer:** *Although Mistress is very clear in her statements about how Julia's lack of protest against her unfair treatment shows that Julia is passive and not very bright, the stage directions imply that it may actually be Julia who has played a trick on Mistress. Julia has received her money, but at the same time has allowed Mistress to think she is the one in control.*)

 **NOTICE & NOTE**

ANALYZE DRAMA

Annotate: Mark the details in paragraph 99 that explain why Mistress cheated Julia.

Analyze: Are you surprised by Mistress's admission? Do you think she was right to try to teach Julia a lesson?

WORDS OF THE WISER

Notice & Note: In paragraph 102, mark where Mistress is asking how Julia can act the way she does.

Draw Conclusions: Read the stage directions and Julia's final response to Mistress. Is Mistress actually the wise one?

99 **Mistress.** Then they cheated you even worse than I did . . . I was playing a little joke on you, a cruel lesson just to teach you. You're much too trusting, and in this world that's very dangerous . . . I'm going to give you the entire eighty rubles. (*Hands her an envelope.*) It's all ready for you. The rest is in this envelope. Here, take it.

100 **Julia.** As you wish, ma'am.

101 (*She curtsies and starts to go again.*)

102 **Mistress.** Julia! (JULIA *stops.*) Is it possible to be so spineless? Why don't you protest? Why don't you speak up? Why don't you cry out against this cruel and unjust treatment? Is it really possible to be so guileless, so innocent, such a—pardon me for being so blunt—such a simpleton?

TO CHALLENGE STUDENTS. . .

What If? In "The Governess," Mistress goes to a lot of trouble to prove a point to Julia. But what if her plan had backfired? For students who need a little more challenge, prompt them to ask "What if" Mistress's little ruse didn't work out the way she had planned? What if Julia had actually confronted Mistress about her scheme to cheat Julia? Then, ask students to write a brief, three to five page alternate ending to "The Governess."

NOTICE & NOTE

103 **Julia** *(The faintest trace of a smile on her lips).* Yes, ma'am . . . it's possible.

104 *(She curtsies again and runs off. The* MISTRESS *looks after her a moment, a look of complete bafflement on her face. The lights fade.)*

CHECK YOUR UNDERSTANDING

Answer these questions before moving on to the **Analyze the Text** section on the following page.

1 In Neil Simon's "The Governess," an upper-class woman tries to teach her children's nanny to —

   A care for the children better

   B speak up for herself

   C listen to instructions

   D curtsy like a servant

2 When Julia says to Mistress in paragraph 93, <u>Yes, ma'am. Thank you, ma'am. You're very kind, ma'am</u>, it reinforces the idea that Julia is —

   F passive

   G polite

   H repetitive

   J simple

3 At the end of the play, Julia is —

   A fired for speaking out

   B cheated by her employer

   C paid what she deserves

   D unhappy with her job

The Governess 157

TEACH

CHECK YOUR UNDERSTANDING

Have students answer the questions independently.

Answers:

1. *B*
2. *F*
3. *C*

If they answer any questions incorrectly, have them reread the text to confirm their understanding. Then they may proceed to ANALYZE THE TEXT on page 158.

ENGLISH LEARNER SUPPORT

Oral Assessment Use the following questions to assess students' comprehension and speaking skills:

1. Is the Mistress kind to Julia? *(no)* Why does she treat Julia unkindly? *(to teach her how to stand up for herself)*

2. Why does Julia repeat herself in paragraph 93? *(She is not good at standing up for herself.)* Is Julia a strong character or a passive character? *(passive)*

3. Does Mistress treat Julia fairly at the end of the play? How do you know? *(Yes. She pays Julia what she is owed.)* **MODERATE**

APPLY

ANALYZE THE TEXT
Possible answers:

1. **DOK 3:** At first Julia seems to be trapped and at the mercy of her employer. But in the end, she is paid what she deserves. Her smile at the end of the play suggests that she does not feel trapped.

2. **DOK 2:** She was trying to get Julia to insist, to stand up for herself. It shows that Mistress is trying to show that she cares about Julia.

3. **DOK 3:** Up to that point, Mistress has not taken any losses. She has accounted for every penny.

4. **DOK 4:** Julia is passive and polite because she has been trained to be so. She is a governess and is of the working class, so she is expected to be passive.

5. **DOK 4:** Julia is paid what she deserves and smiles as she leaves. Her answer to Mistress's question about whether it is possible to be such a simpleton reveals that she knows more than she's letting on. The fact that Mistress is baffled also shows that she isn't quite certain that Julia is a "simpleton."

RESEARCH

Remind students they may have read other novels or short stories about class differences in the 19th-century Europe. Although these sources may not contain the factual detail of an encyclopedia article, they can be a useful resource for gathering impressions about class during this time period.

Connect Mistress fits the description of someone from either the middle or upper class. She seems educated, entitled, and aware of her privilege and power.

 RESPOND

ANALYZE THE TEXT
Support your responses with evidence from the text. **NOTEBOOK**

1. **Draw Conclusions** Examine the Writer's lines at the beginning of the play. What conclusion can you draw about the meaning of the Writer's line "Trapped, indeed . . ."? Is Julia really trapped? Cite details from the play in your response.

2. **Infer** Reread paragraphs 45–49, when Mistress asks Julia if she insists that Mistress only count two holidays. Why is Mistress most likely asking Julia if she insists? What does this reveal about Mistress?

3. **Evaluate** Review paragraphs 59–61 when Mistress points out that the saucer was an heirloom but that she's used to taking losses. What makes this line funny?

4. **Analyze** Use Julia's actions and dialogue to analyze her character. In your own words, describe how her actions may be shaped as much by class as by her personality.

5. **Notice & Note** Reread the last few paragraphs of the play. What details suggest that Julia is not a simpleton?

RESEARCH TIP
Use as many specific search terms as possible in locating information online. Then scan the descriptions of the results and note the source of the website (.gov, .edu, .org, .com) before choosing the results that can best answer your research question with reliable information.

RESEARCH

"The Governess" is set in nineteenth-century Europe. Sociologists generally separate the society of that period into three distinct classes—upper, middle, and working (or lower) classes. Explore these distinctions as defined by sociologists and historians. Focus on the common characteristics and attitudes of each class.

CLASS	CHARACTERISTICS/ATTITUDES
Upper Class	wealthy, aristocratic, no manual labor, privileged, controlling of politics
Middle Class	bankers, lawyers, shopkeepers, merchants, striving to establish society based on merit, diverse
Working Class	laborers, factory workers, etc., shut out of economy and politics, no power, increasingly hostile to middle and upper classes

Connect Does Mistress fit the description of someone from the upper or middle class? Explain.

 LEARNING MINDSET

Problem Solving The Analyze the Text questions are meant to challenge us to think and exercise our problem-solving skills. The following tips may help answer the questions:

- Go back to the text. Some questions prompt students to do some re-reading. No one is expected to remember everything from the first reading.
- Look things up. If terms or phrases are confusing, check a dictionary or online resource.
- Ask questions. Don't be afraid to ask a teacher or another student for help. This is part of learning, too.

RESPOND

CREATE AND ADAPT

Write a Personal Narrative Write about a situation in which someone was underestimating your efforts or bargaining unfairly with you. Describe what you said and did to change the situation in a positive way to improve your position.

- Introduce the topic with an engaging idea and include a conclusion that sums up the narrative in a satisfying way.
- Use details in your description of the situation and in explaining the actions you took to improve the situation for yourself.
- Use transitions to clarify the sequence of events and subordinating conjunctions to link ideas.

Adapt Stage Directions Suppose you are staging the interaction between Mistress and Julia in the opening of the play. With your group, take turns as the play's director and giving instructions to the actors for performing the play's opening.

- Explain exactly how the actors should be positioned in relation to each other and to the audience.
- Guide the actors in how to convey emotion through their tone of voice and their gestures.

Go to **Writing Narratives** in the **Writing Studio** for more help.

RESPOND TO THE ESSENTIAL QUESTION

 What can blur the lines between what's real and what's not?

Gather Information Review your annotations and notes on "The Governess." Then, add relevant details to your Response Log. As you determine which information to include, think about:

- how your opinion of Mistress changed by the end of the play, and why
- how your opinion of Julia changed by the end of the play, and why

At the end of the unit, use your notes to create a multimodal presentation.

ACADEMIC VOCABULARY
As you write and discuss what you learned from the play, be sure to use the Academic Vocabulary words. Check off each of the words that you use.

- ❏ abnormal
- ❏ feature
- ❏ focus
- ❏ perceive
- ❏ task

The Governess 159

APPLY

CREATE AND ADAPT

Write a Personal Narrative Some students may have trouble coming up with a personal story to fit this situation. As a variation, suggest they instead write about a time they wish they had stood up for themselves and what they would have done differently.

 For **writing support** for students at varying proficiency levels, see the **Text X-Ray** on page 146D.

Adapt Stage Directions Remind students to keep the audience in mind when staging the scene. The actors should be standing where the majority of the audience can see their expressions. If they want, students can also vary the stage directions to create more action.

RESPOND TO THE ESSENTIAL QUESTION

Allow time for students to add details from "The Governess" to their Unit 2 Response Logs.

 ENGLISH LEARNER SUPPORT

Write a Personal Narrative and Adapt Stage Directions Give students time to brainstorm a time from their life when someone didn't believe they could do something, but they overcame it. Then, have them write the story in their own words, or have them draw it with captions. Use the following sentence frames to guide them: *I now know that...I learned...I discovered...I was surprised that...* Next, have them break into groups. Have groups each help each other perform their own stories. Go through the steps of staging a play with them. Finally, have them present their stories to the class. **SUBSTANTIAL/MODERATE**

The Governess **159**

APPLY

CRITICAL VOCABULARY

Answers:

1. *discrepancy* because *discrepancy* means difference or disagreement.
2. *heirloom* because *heirloom* and *inheritance* both suggest something of monetary value.
3. *inferior* because *inferior* suggests something or something of lesser value.
4. *Madame* because *madame* is a formal way of saying M'am or Mrs.

VOCABULARY STRATEGY:
Word Origins

Answers:

1. **Middle English/Latin:** lower or under
2. **Late Middle English/Latin:** to sound discordant or to crack
3. **Old French/Latin and Middle English:** bereaved instrument

---

 **RESPOND**

WORD BANK
madame
inferior
discrepancy
heirloom

CRITICAL VOCABULARY

Practice and Apply With a partner, discuss and write an answer to each of the following questions. Then work together to write sentences using each Critical Vocabulary word.

1. Which vocabulary word goes with *difference* and *conflict*? Why?
   discrepancy
2. Which vocabulary word goes with *inheritance*? Why?
   heirloom
3. Which vocabulary word goes with *lesser*? Why?
   inferior
4. Which vocabulary word goes with *ma'am* and *Mrs.*? Why?
   madame

Go to the **Vocabulary Studio** for more on word origins.

VOCABULARY STRATEGY: Word Origins

An **etymology** shows the origin and historical development of a word. Studying a word's history and origin can help you clarify its precise meaning. Look at this example of an etymology for the Critical Vocabulary word *madame*.

> [French, from Old French *ma dame* : *ma,* my (from Latin *mea;* see **me-**¹ in the Appendix of Indo-European roots) + *dame,* lady (from Latin *domina,* feminine of *dominus,* lord, master of a household; see **dem-** in the Appendix of Indo-European roots).]

The etymology for *madame* shows that the word is French but has its roots in Latin words that mean "my lady."

Practice and Apply Use a dictionary to find the etymology or word origin of each of the other Critical Vocabulary words below.

WORD	ROOT LANGUAGE(S)	MEANING
inferior	Middle English/Latin	Lower/under
discrepancy	Late Middle English/Latin	To sound discordant/to crack
heirloom	Old French/Latin + Middle/Old English	Bereaved implement

160 Unit 2

 ENGLISH LEARNER SUPPORT

Practice Cognates Many words in the English language have nearly the same spelling and definition as they do in other languages. These are called cognates. Direct students' attention to these Spanish cognates from the text: necessary–necesario, impossible–imposible, lesson–lección. Instruct them to go back into the text in search of other cognates as well.
SUBSTANTIAL/MODERATE

RESPOND

LANGUAGE CONVENTIONS: Complex Sentences: Subordinating Conjunctions

A **complex sentence** consists of an independent clause and at least one subordinate clause. **Subordinate clauses** are clauses that contain subjects and verbs, but do not form complete sentences. **Subordinating conjunctions** are conjunctions that are used to introduce subordinate clauses.

Subordinating conjunctions provide links or transitions between ideas in a sentence. These conjunctions show place, time, or cause and effect relationships between ideas. A subordinate conjunction can also show that one idea in a sentence is more important than another idea.

In a line of dialogue from "The Governess," the playwright uses the complex sentence below to link two complete thoughts. The subordinating conjunction *when* is used at the beginning of a subordinate clause.

> I like to see your eyes **when** I speak to you.

The example sentence contains two complete thoughts:

1. *I like to see your eyes.*
2. *I speak to you.*

The playwright tells you how these two complete thoughts are related to each other by using the subordinating conjunction *when*. The word *when* indicates a time relationship between the ideas.

The chart below lists common subordinating conjunctions you can use when writing your own complex sentences:

after	before	since	until
although	even though	so that	when
as	if	though	where
because	once	unless	while

Practice and Apply Write three or four complex sentences summarizing what happens in "The Governess." Use a different subordinating conjunction in each sentence.

Go to **Conjunctions and Interjections** in the **Grammar Studio** to learn more.

APPLY

LANGUAGE CONVENTIONS: Complex Sentences: Subordinating Conjunctions

Review the information about subordinating conjunctions with students. Explain that using subordinating conjunctions will allow them to vary their sentence structure by creating complex sentences, which join two or more clauses.

Practice and Apply For additional practice, write the following sentence frames on the board. Point out the coordinating conjunction and dependent clause in each sentence frame. Have students add an independent clause to each sentence frame to form a complex sentence.

As the governess waits to be paid, her employer . . .

After the governess fails to stand up for herself, Mistress lectures her about . . .

Although Mistress criticizes her behavior, she gives Julia . . .

Possible sentences: As a governess waits to be paid, her employer lists reason after reason why her pay should be less. After the governess fails to stand up for herself, Mistress lectures her about demanding fair treatment. Although Mistress criticizes her behavior, she gives Julia her full pay.

PLAN

THE GOVERNESS
Production Images

GENRE ELEMENTS
MEDIA

Tell students that they will examine still photographs of a stage production of "The Governess." These images will help them understand the elements of **stagecraft** that are essential for creating a theatrical production from a written work. Reinforce the elements of drama students learned about in the previous selection as they learn new technical terms. Point out that the photographs show the importance of scenery, costume design, makeup, lighting, composition, and stage directions. Have students note the importance of details such as facial expressions.

LEARNING OBJECTIVES

- Analyze drama, including cast of characters, dialogue, and stagecraft.
- Research the role of the governess in 19th-century Europe.
- Write a personal narrative about the experience of someone underestimating your abilities.
- Direct and stage a scene.
- Compare stagecraft to the written text from which it was adapted.
- Write and share a critique.
- **Language** Write dialogue.

TEXT COMPLEXITY

Quantitative Measures	The Governess	Lexile: N/A
Qualitative Measure	**Ideas Presented** Much is explicit but moves to some implied meaning	
	Structure Used Clear, chronological, conventional	
	Language Used Some period-specific or other unconventional language	
	Knowledge Required Begins to rely on outside knowledge	

162A Unit 2

PLAN

RESOURCES

- Unit 2 Response Log
- 🔊 Selection Audio
- 📖 Reading Studio: Notice & Note
- ▭ Writing Studio: Writing Narratives
- ✓ "The Governess" Selection Test

SUMMARIES

English

These images from a community college production of the play show a young governess and her employer at various points in "The Governess"– a stand-alone scene in *The Good Doctor*, Neil Simon's dramatization of Anton Chekhov's nineteenth-century short stories. The production images show the lighting, costumes, and staging of the scene. The images also capture moments in the conflict between the two characters: Mistress and her employee, Julia. Mistress appears to be in complete control of achieving her aim. The question is: who really wins in the end?

Spanish

En la Rusia del Siglo XIX, la dueña de una casa convoca a su nueva institutriz para discutir el salario de sus primeros dos meses. En su diálogo, la dueña le recuerda a la joven mujer que mantenga su cabeza en alto y confíe más en sí misma. Mientras tanto, enumera muchas razones, en detalle, para bajarle el sueldo; hasta que el pago final es una pequeña fracción de lo que se le debía. Finalmente, la dueña le dice a la joven institutriz que la reunión fue una lección para enseñarle el significado de defenderse por sí misma.

SMALL GROUP OPTIONS

Have students work in small groups to read and discuss the selection.

Think-Pair-Share

- After students have watched the production images from "The Governess," pose this question: Did it look the way you imagined it?
- Have students think about the question individually and take notes with specific details.
- Then, have pairs discuss their impressions of the images.
- Finally, ask pairs to share their responses with the class.

Sticky Note Peer Review

This activity can be used for the "Write a Dialogue" writing exercise at the end of the selection.

- In pairs or small groups, as each student in turn reads his or her paper, the other students listen, recording specific feedback on sticky notes.
- It is important for students to keep each purpose separate by writing positive comments on one sticky note, suggestions on another note, and questions on a third note.
- Students initial their sticky notes, giving them to the writer to use for revision.

PLAN

 Text X-Ray: English Learner Support
for "The Governess"

Use the Text X-Ray and the supports and scaffolds in the Teacher's Edition to help guide students at different proficiency levels through the selection.

INTRODUCE THE SELECTION
DISCUSS STAGECRAFT AND DRAMA

In this lesson, students will examine how the elements of stagecraft and drama work together to create a unified work of art for the stage. Students will examine how directors, actors, and technicians collaborate to interpret what the author of a play has written. They will need to be able to discuss

- how lighting, composition, and stage directions help create tone and mood according to the author's and director's artistic aims
- how scenery, costumes, and makeup frame settings and characters
- how direction and acting transform the dialogue of a written work

Ask students how they might adapt the play as a contemporary work for the stage. Use frame sentences such as: *The lighting would be_____. (e.g., soft, like a spring morning, dark and frightening)* Help students find images that express how they might interpret the scene. *(e.g., costumes and makeup)*

CULTURAL REFERENCES

The following words and phrases may be unfamiliar to students:

- *well-to-do* (the Writer): wealthy
- *coming along* (Mistress): how something is going
- *he gets that from his mother* (Mistress): implying the quality of a child is inherited from the parent
- *wouldn't you say?* (Mistress): common idiom, asking someone if they believe the same thing you believe (usually with the implication they are expected to agree with you).
- The actors' mannerisms are characteristic of 19th Century European society—they were much more formal and guarded than we are today.

LISTENING

Analyze Media

Monitor students' understanding of new words and phrases. Read aloud the Analyze Media section on pp 163–164. Use images to help define the stagecraft techniques discussed on these pages. Help students build a word bank supported by labeled images.

Use the following supports with students at varying proficiency levels:

- After reading, ask students questions such as, *What do actors put on their faces and bodies to make them look like the characters?* (Use gestures for putting on makeup.) Do the same for costumes, lighting, and other stagecraft terms. Encourage students to hold up labeled images to answer questions. Help students with the pronunciation of new words such as *lighting*. Help students pronounce other silent *gh* words + *ing* such as *frightening*. **SUBSTANTIAL**
- Ask students questions, e.g., *What is used to create the setting? (scenery)* Encourage students to elaborate on the purpose of each stagecraft technique. Before listening, have students use word-web graphic organizers or charts to keep track of the terms. Have them illustrate their organizers with drawings or images to reinforce definitions. **MODERATE**
- Ask partners to take notes and then engage in retells of pp 163–164. **LIGHT**

PLAN

SPEAKING

Discuss Research

Guide students in conducting research on the role of the governess in 19th-century society (see p.166). Help students gather images and words for their word banks to build vocabulary and aid in proper speech.

Use the following supports with students at varying proficiency levels:

- Guide students in completing frame sentences with words from their word banks, e.g., *The role of the governess was to _____ children. (teach, or educate)* Make sure that students understand each word in the sentences. Help them read their sentences aloud with correct pronunciation. **SUBSTANTIAL**
- Ask: *Were governesses men or women? (women) Did governesses have a good education or were they uneducated? (educated)* Have students help you compose and pronounce each word in a list of what governesses taught *(e.g., languages, mathematics, geography, piano)* **MODERATE**
- Have partners research and discuss the role of the nineteenth-century governesses with each other. Ask volunteers to share their findings with the class. **LIGHT**

READING

Use Visual Media

Tell students that the production images can help them understand the text of the play. They can also show how the elements of stagecraft have been used to interpret the play and stage the production.

Use the following supports with students at varying proficiency levels:

- Display the following sentences and choral read them with students. Point to the words and the photographs. Use gestures: *Mistress is wearing an expensive red, gold, and green dress. Julia is wearing a skirt, white shirt, and a shawl. These are costumes. Costumes are elements of stagecraft.* **SUBSTANTIAL**
- Display the following sentences and have students choral read them with limited support while using the photographs for reference: *Mistress is sitting in a chair. Julia is standing up. Mistress is the employer. The chair is a prop. The setting is a room in Mistress's house.* **MODERATE**
- Have students reread paragraphs 95–98. Ask them to refer to the photographs to determine how elements of stagecraft might help contribute to the climax in the play. **LIGHT**

WRITING

Write Dialogue

Work with students to read the writing assignment on p. 167. Explain that you will help them construct dialogue for the scene they want to create. Point out the necessity of using stage directions. Pre-teach beginning and intermediate students the vocabulary they will need.

Use the following supports with students at varying proficiency levels:

- Read the assignment aloud. Supply frame lines of dialogue and word lists that include pre-taught words: Mistress *(Looks in her account____. (book). I have paid you all the____ you have earned. (money)* Julia *(Smiles). Thank you. Beginning next week, I would like you to pay me____(more) money, because I believe I am _____(earning) it.* Have students draw storyboards for their own dialogue. **SUBSTANTIAL**
- Pre-teach and then help students use the following words and phrases in dialogue for the assignment: *raise in pay, earn, earned, earning, money, work hard, good results, speak up for myself.* **MODERATE**
- Tell partners to each take a role (either as Mistress or Julia). Provide them with storyboard organizers to help them construct a scene with a beginning, rising action, climax, and resolution. Tell them to read aloud the lines of dialogue so that they hear how the words sound. **LIGHT**

The Governess **162D**

TEACH

 Connect to the
ESSENTIAL QUESTION

In the "The Governess," Mistress at first appears to have complete control over Julia, but this turns out to be an illusion. The reality is that Mistress is baffled and Julia exhibits a greater measure of control than expected at the end. By examining production images of "The Governess," students can explore how elements of stagecraft were used by the director to reveal and interpret his ideas about the characters in the play.

COMPARE VERSIONS

Point out that these photographs show things directly that the written version alone does not show, such as setting, facial gestures and expressions, body stance, and physical reactions.

COLLABORATE & COMPARE

PRODUCTION IMAGES

from
THE GOVERNESS

presented by the
**Theater Arts Department,
Clackamas Community College**
page 165

COMPARE VERSIONS

Now that you've read "The Governess," examine some production images from a staging of the play. Think about how the sets and costuming reflect how the actors and director have interpreted the play and stage directions. Afterward, you will work with a small group on a final project that involves an analysis of both selections.

 ESSENTIAL QUESTION:

What can blur the lines between what's real and what's not?

DRAMA
THE GOVERNESS
from **The Good Doctor**

by **Neil Simon**
pages 149–157

from The Governess

QUICK START

Think about a scene in a play where a character is standing up for himself or herself. How was the drama (or the humor) of the situation shown? Describe the scene and discuss your reactions with a partner.

ANALYZE MEDIA

The production images of "The Governess" show the staging of a written work. Writers, directors, and theater technicians use various techniques to create humor, express irony, and tell a story.

- Writers of dramas create a cast of characters to add a dynamic element and use dialogue to drive the action forward.
- Directors instruct actors to use energetic facial expressions and movements to make things dramatic or humorous.

The technical aspects of producing a play are called **stagecraft**. Directors and other people involved in the staging may use scenery to convey the setting or costume design to highlight character traits and details. In the production images from "The Governess," look for these stagecraft techniques.

GENRE ELEMENTS: MEDIA
- shared for a specific purpose, or reason
- combines visual and sound techniques
- play productions are a popular media format
- stagecraft includes scenery, lighting, costumes, makeup, props, music and sound effects

TECHNIQUE	WHAT IT IS	WHY IT IS USED
Scenery/Sets	Two- and three-dimensional backgrounds or elements on stage	To show setting, time period, or mood
Costume Design	Clothes, masks, or headdresses worn by actors	To convey information about setting, character, and status
Props	Furniture and objects on the stage or handled by actors.	To illustrate the story and help actors show emotions and ideas
Makeup	Painting or changing the body of an actor	To allow actors' expressions and bodies to be seen

Stagecraft is all about the effect on the audience. Makeup can make a young person look old; scenery can transport the audience to another city or country. Other techniques that help convey meaning in a play are voice, sound, and music. Actors talk, laugh, or murmur. Sounds, such as city noises, support the setting, and music conveys emotions. All of these draw the audience into the story being told on stage.

QUICK START

If students struggle to think of a scene, suggest something students have viewed or read as a class. If they struggle to remember how the scene played out, suggest that they close their eyes to remember it in their minds.

ANALYZE MEDIA

Go over the Analyze Media section with students. Remind them that there are different types of visual media that can be used to document the staging of plays—including photographs, drawing, and moving images captured on video. The images they are examining are photographs of a production of a play. Use the following prompts to get students thinking about their comparisons.

1. How does the character of The Writer appear in the images? What information was given about him in the text?

2. Why might a director or set designer choose colorful backgrounds that evoke Russia in the 19th-century? Does the costuming fit the written version? Were there any notes on costuming in the original text? How did the director decide on these costumes?

3. How do the production images help the viewer understand the importance of lighting in setting the mood of the scene?

4. Why might the photographer choose to have both close-up and more distant shots of an actor or actors? (In the first case, to show how deeply the character feels about something, in the second case to show the effect of the character's speech on the other listener(s) on the stage.)

 ENGLISH LEARNER SUPPORT

Reinforce Meaning Review the Analyze Media section with students, making sure they understand the terms *writer, director, actors, characters,* and *dialogue*. Allow students time to ask for clarification of these terms. Use gestures and pantomime as needed to help convey meaning. Then confirm students' understanding by asking yes-or-no questions such as the following: *Is the writer the person who wrote the words being said by actors?* (yes) *Do the actors choose the words they are saying?* (no) *Does the director tell the actors how to act?* (yes)

ALL-STANDARDS

TEACH

ANALYZE MEDIA

Use the following information to help students think about their comparisons.

- **Lighting** The lighting in the images may be different than how students pictured it would be when reading the text. Point out that the artificial lighting is meant to give the audience a clear look at the actors' faces.
- **Composition** The stage is set to accommodate different parts of the play, but the staging will often draw attention to the actors involved. In the images, as in the text version, the readers and/or viewers must fill in the details they cannot see.
- **Facial expressions and posture** Actors use their faces and bodies to suggest emotion, thought, and mood. Sometimes they do this subtly; other times they might exaggerate their expressions to stress a feeling or to create a comic or tragic effect.

ENGLISH LEARNER SUPPORT

Discuss with a Small Group After viewing the images, have students discuss which parts of the play they think these images portray. Encourage them to share ideas, and remind them that they are only making educated guesses.

ASK STUDENTS How many close-ups were there in the scene, and who did they show? *(There are three: One on the Writer, one on both Julia and the Mistress, and one on Julia.)* **SUBSTANTIAL**

 GET READY

ANALYZE MEDIA (continued)

Directors may also use other techniques to convey mood, express humor, and focus viewers' attention on certain characters and events.

- **Lighting** is usually used to direct viewers' eyes to what is most important on the stage. Lighting can also be used to create a mood that is funny, confusing, or scary. Plays that express subtle humor might use a spotlight to highlight the expression on an actor's face.
- **Composition,** like a painting, can show the deliberate way characters or objects are arranged on stage. Viewers can learn much about how a scene is unfolding just by being aware of how the director is framing the characters and setting.
- **Motions and facial expressions** work together to convey meaning. These elements are often planned, or choreographed, as the play is rehearsed. Some directors also allow actors to improvise, or develop their own movements and expressions. For example, a director has to consider how close the actors stand to each other. In a play, actors needs to stand farther apart to allow the audience to see the action and to distinguish expressions. Another important "rule" is that actors shouldn't turn their back to other actors or the audience.

Use this chart to help you analyze the stagecraft techniques that are evident in the production images.

TECHNIQUE	EFFECT
1.	
2.	
3.	

When a director crafts a production of a drama, he or she has to make choices about how closely to follow the written work. Will the play:

- include all of the same characters?
- have the same setting?
- add or cut a scene?

As you examine these production images, think about how the director's choices are conveyed and how the images of the play production compare to your earlier reading of it.

WHEN STUDENTS STRUGGLE . . .

Analyze Media To help students clarify media terms, have them form small groups.

Using a graphic organizer split into two columns (Term and Definition). Have the student groups write down media terms they are not familiar with. Then, have them divide the terms, with each group member looking up definitions for their assigned terms and reporting back to the group to fill out the organizer.

GET READY

BACKGROUND

These production images convey one interpretation of the dialogue and stage directions in the script. The images include a man talking to the audience. In the script for "The Governess," this man is the Writer. Look at his facial expression and the background scenery to analyze how the director and the actors are expressing the story and the mood of the play. Think about how the costumes convey class differences.

PREPARE TO COMPARE

As you view the production images, consider how the actors reflect the stage directions that you read in the script. Notice facial expressions that help you understand how the actors develop the characters of Julia and Mistress.

For more online resources log in to your dashboard and click on **"The Governess"** from the selection menu.

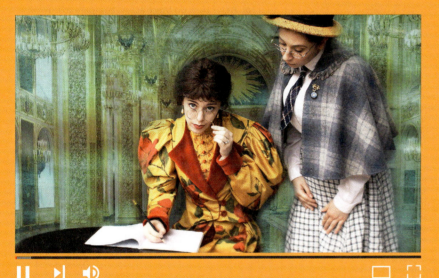

As needed, pause and look carefully at the production images to make notes about what impresses you or to jot down ideas you might want to discuss later.

from The Governess   165

TEACH

BACKGROUND

The Writer is the narrator of "The Governess" and all of the other scenes in the original play, *The Good Doctor*. A narrator is a character who is "telling" the story to the audience, but often the narrator's role is to simply introduce the action and the themes at play and then step away once the action begins.

PREPARE TO COMPARE

Ask students to not look at their text or follow along during their first viewing of the production images. Looking at something besides the photographs will detract from their viewing experience.

 ENGLISH LEARNER SUPPORT

Monitor Understanding To make sure students understood the images, ask a series of simple questions that also refer back to the original text. Ask:

- Who is the man pictured in the image? *(the Writer)*
- Which character wore the gold dress with red trimming? *(Mistress)*
- Did she wear a gold dress in the text? *(can't know because the color of costumes is not mentioned in the text)*

SUBSTANTIAL/MODERATE

The Governess   **165**

APPLY

ANALYZE MEDIA

Possible answers:

1. **DOK 3:** *The scenery is lively and colorful seeming to indicate this might be a comedy. The writer's costume is also interesting and mismatched. His expression expresses the idea that he is telling the audience something funny, but at the same time, it is almost as if he is telling a secret or something more than a joke.*

1. **DOK 3:** *Mistress is wearing a gown of nice cloth, with velvet trimming. She has a ring, gold earrings, and gold glasses. Her costume expresses that she is wealthy. Julia is wearing a nice, but practical outfit. She has only a pin, no other jewelry. Her costume expresses that she is less wealthy than Mistress.*

2. **DOK 3:** *Julia is curious, concerned, and worried. Her facial expression shows that, as well as the way she is holding her hands in the images.*

3. **DOK 4:** *The mood is serious. The darker lighting and the way that the actors are looking at each other express that they are discussing something that is important and worrying.*

4. **DOK 3: Possible answer:** *I think the actors were chosen appropriately, but I would have expected Mistress to be older and Julia to be younger.*

RESEARCH

Remind students that they may have read novels or short stories that deal with class differences in the nineteenth century and/or the traditional role of a governess at that time. Although novels and short stories do not contain the facts an encyclopedia would give, they can be a valuable source for impressions about class during the time period.

Connect *Yes, the author portrays the role of the governess accurately, in that Julia had no power and was completely dependent of the whims of her mistress.*

RESPOND

ANALYZE MEDIA

Support your responses with evidence from the production images.

📓 NOTEBOOK

1. **Evaluate** Examine the photograph of the Writer. What does the scenery, props, costuming, and the Writer's expression convey about his attitude toward what he is telling the audience? Explain.

2. **Synthesize** How do the actors' costumes in the production images help to reinforce the idea of class?

3. **Interpret** Review the images of the Mistress and Julia together. How does Mistress's advice affect Julia? How can you tell?

4. **Analyze** Look at the image that shows Mistress holding Julia around her shoulders. What mood does the lighting and the actors' expressions convey? Explain.

5. **Critique** Think about the characters of Julia and Mistress in the production images. Do you think the actors who played them were chosen appropriately? How do these actors compare to how you imagined the characters as you read the play?

RESEARCH

RESEARCH TIP
Searching for the role of the governess in 19th-century society might give you results for literature that features governesses. Look closely at the description and the source of the information as you scan your results. You want to make sure that you find historical information that comes from multiple reliable sites and is factually accurate.

The governess performed a specific role in 19th-century society. Research the role of the governess and record what you learn in the chart. Answer the two questions in the chart and add your own.

THE GOVERNESS	19TH-CENTURY ROLE
Who employed a governess?	At first only upper class families employed a governess, but later, middle-class families also employed a governess.
What duties did a governess have?	A governess was in charge of providing an education for children and also being a moral guide. She was supposed to look after them and teach them how to function in high society

Connect Given what you have learned about governesses in 19th-century society, do you think "The Governess" portrays the role of the governess accurately? Explain.

LEARNING MINDSET

Problem Solving Remind students that almost everyone sometimes has problems understanding and answering difficult questions, such as the ones in the Analyze Media section. These questions are difficult because they are meant to challenge us to think and exercise our problem solving skills. Remind students that every problem they stick with and solve will make them smarter.

CREATE AND PRESENT

Write Dialogue Imagine that a year has passed since the scene portrayed in the production images. Julia and Mistress are now meeting to discuss a raise in pay. Create at least 15 lines of dialogue that portray this conversation.

- ❏ Determine who will bring up the topic: Julia, or Mistress.
- ❏ Maintain each character's traits through speaking style and gestures. Include stage directions with your lines.
- ❏ Make sure there is a clear ending to the conversation.

Stage the Scene Set up the scene in "The Governess" by using the front of the classroom as a stage.

- ❏ As a group, review the stage directions of the play and review the scenery, costuming, and props in the production images.
- ❏ Provide simple props. Then, using the front of the classroom as the stage, instruct two classmates representing the main characters to take positions facing the audience.
- ❏ Have the actors act out the first few lines of the play, using the script and stage directions to guide them. Then invite other students to take turns playing Julia or Mistress.

 Go to **Writing Narratives** in the **Writing Studio** for more on point of view and characters.

RESPOND TO THE ESSENTIAL QUESTION

 What can blur the lines between what's real and what's not?

Gather Information Review your notes on the production images of "The Governess." Then, add relevant details to your Response Log. As you determine which information to include, think about:

- what you learned about each character from facial expressions, and gestures
- the staging used and how effective it was

At the end of the unit, use your notes to help create a multimodal presentation.

ACADEMIC VOCABULARY

As you write and discuss what you learned from the production images, be sure to use the Academic Vocabulary words. Check off each of the words that you use.

- ❏ abnormal
- ❏ feature
- ❏ focus
- ❏ perceive
- ❏ task

from The Governess 167

APPLY

CREATE AND PRESENT

Write a Dialogue Some of the questions students might want to consider before they write their dialogue are: *Has the relationship between Julia and Mistress changed? Why or why not? Has Julia developed more confidence in herself? Why or why not?*

For **writing support** for students at varying proficiency levels, see the **Text X-Ray** on page 162D.

Stage the Scene Remind students to keep the audience in mind when staging their scene. The actors should be standing where the majority of the audience can see their expressions. If they want, students can also vary the stage directions to create more action.

RESPOND TO THE ESSENTIAL QUESTION

Allow time for students to add details from "The Governess" to their Unit 2 Response Logs.

🗨 ENGLISH LEARNER SUPPORT

Write a Dialogue Give students time to brainstorm how things have changed or not changed in the lives of Julia and Mistress. Then, have them write their dialogue in single words or phrases, or have them draw it and add captions. Use the following sentence frames to guide them: (Julie) *Mistress, I know you're busy but I would like ___.* (Mistress) *Now Julie, you know that ___.* Next, have students form small groups. The groups will read each other's dialogues and offer suggestions about how they might be improved. **SUBSTANTIAL/MODERATE**

APPLY

COMPARE CHARACTERIZATIONS

As students review and compare the two versions of "The Governess," suggest that they focus on the actors' interpretations—or understanding—of their characters in the photographs. How did the actress who played Mistress seem to have interpreted her character? What qualities and/or character flaws did she see in Mistress? How did the actress who played Julia seem to have interpret her character? Remind students to pay attention to gestures, facial expressions, and bodily stance to determine the actress's interpretation of their character.

ANALYZE THE VERSIONS

Possible answers:

1. **DOK 3:** *The depiction of Mistress is most surprising. She is younger and friendlier looking than I expected, although her costume does match my expectations.*

2. **DOK 3:** *She seems more gullible and awed in the text. In the production images, she seems more confident, but in the text, her lines of dialogue show that she is following the orders of her mistress.*

3. **DOK 3:** *The production image of the Writer seems to reflect the lines of the Writer. The image shows a person who is telling something that is humorous, but serious at the same time.*

4. **DOK 3:** *The text was more humorous because the lines of dialogue help develop the characters, the setting, and the plot.*

 RESPOND

THE GOVERNESS
from The Good Doctor
Drama
by Neil Simon

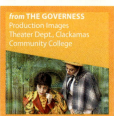

from **THE GOVERNESS**
Production Images
Theater Dept., Clackamas
Community College

Collaborate & Compare

COMPARE CHARACTERIZATION

Both the text of the play and the production images of "The Governess" feature characters: the Writer, the governess, Julia, and her employer, Mistress. While the scene is the same, how you imagined the characterization while reading the drama probably differs from the depiction in the production images.

A playwright develops characters through dialogue and stage directions, but directors and actors may interpret those directions differently. Work in a small group to review the text and production images. As you compare and contrast characterization in the two versions, consider:

❏ the stage directions in the drama versus the actors' gestures and facial expressions in the production images
❏ stage directions versus the costuming of the actors
❏ stage directions versus the sets in the production images

	Stage Directions	Production Images
Gestures/Facial Expressions	Julia has a surprised expression when Mistress tells her she only owes her 30 rubles	Julia sometimes shows on her face what she is really thinking, but then quickly assumes the expression she thinks Mistress wants her to have.
Costuming	Julia curtsies before approaching Mistress; Mistress lifts Julia's head up, but Julia's head goes slowly down again; Julia cries when Mistress tells her she will only pay her 14 rubles.	Mistress's voice is loud and authoritative.
Stage/Set Details		Julia curtsies and can't keep her head up. Mistress carries herself with great authority.

ANALYZE THE VERSIONS

Discuss these questions in your group.

1. **Compare** With your group, review your chart. Which character depiction in the production images surprises you more: Julia, or Mistress? Explain.

2. **Analyze** In the text, Mistress calls Julia a simpleton. Where does Julia seem more gullible and awed by Mistress: in the text, or in the production images? Explain.

3. **Critique** Compare the lines of the Writer at the beginning of the script with the actor who plays the Writer in the production image. Is his depiction an effective interpretation of the stage directions and script? Why?

4. **Evaluate** Which version, the text or the production images, was more humorous? Why?

168 Unit 2

 ENGLISH LEARNER SUPPORT

Ask Questions Use sentence frames and questions to help students compare the selections:

Mistress seemed *(domineering, cruel, mean)* in the images. In the written play, Mistress seemed *(superior, cold, clever)*. **SUBSTANTIAL**

Which helped you best to understand the character, Julia, the images or the written play? Why? **MODERATE**

Did being able to see how the play was staged help you understand it better? Explain why or why not. Cite specific examples to prove your point. **LIGHT**

RESPOND

CRITIQUE AND SHARE

Now, your group can continue exploring the two versions of the play by taking turns presenting an oral critique of how the production images compare to the written play. Follow these steps:

1. **Develop Criteria** Brainstorm the criteria, or measures of what makes a drama and production of a drama interesting. Consider ideas such as how closely a production should follow the text of the script or play, how effectively the versions portray characters, and how stagecraft affects how a production conveys the story. Then, identify the four or five most important criteria.

2. **Record Your Thoughts** Use the criteria you developed to record your thoughts about the two versions, using this chart.

CRITERIA	MY THOUGHTS
1.	
2.	
3.	
4.	
5.	

3. **Write a Short Critique** Use your chart to write a brief critique about the script and production images. Begin with a clear controlling idea, or thesis, that states whether you think the production images compare favorably or unfavorably to the written version. You can support your thesis by noting how well the production images met the criteria you established in your chart. Remember to include specific details as evidence.

4. **Present the Critique** Now it is time to present your opinion to your group. As you speak, make eye contact with each group member and speak clearly, enunciating words carefully. Speak loudly enough so that everyone in the group can hear you. Use natural gestures and facial expressions.

RESEARCH TIP
To help you develop and write your critique, search online newspapers, journals, and magazines for examples of film and theater reviews.

Collaborate & Compare   169

APPLY

CRITIQUE AND SHARE

Write an Oral Critique Explain that to critique means to analyze or assess a literary work or works. Suggest that students follow the steps on p. 169 and the suggestions below to write and present their critiques.

1. **Develop Criteria** As students develop their criteria about what makes a play worth watching, circulate among groups and check that the criteria are appropriate for the task of evaluating a play. Have students consider the play's script, its character portrayal, and its entertainment/informational value.

2. **Record Your Thoughts** Have students list four or five of their most important criteria in the chart provided.

3. **Write a Short Critique** Remind students to include a controlling idea, the idea that states the direction in which they want their critique to go. Have them support their ideas with specific references to the photographs.

4. **Present the Critique** Suggest that students practice presenting their critique with a partner. Remind them to speak loudly and clearly, make eye contact with their audience, and use gestures and expression to draw in their audience.

 For **listening support** for students at varying proficiency levels, see the **Text X-Ray** on page 162C.

 ENGLISH LEARNER SUPPORT

Ask Questions Use the following questions to help students compare the text to the production images.

1. Did you prefer the written text or the photographs? Why?

2. How were the images different than what you pictured when reading the text?

3. Overall, what are the differences between analyzing a text and a stage production?

MODERATE/LIGHT

TO CHALLENGE STUDENTS

Analyze Special Techniques Have students add to their play critique an analysis of elements of staging—including performance style, set design, lighting, costumes, and makeup—as captured in the images of this community college production of the play. Ask them what conclusions they can draw about how the director and producer may have interpreted Neil Simon's work.

The Governess   169

INDEPENDENT READING

READER'S CHOICE

Setting a Purpose Have students review their Unit 2 Response Log and think about what they've already learned regarding reality and illusion. As they make their Independent Reading selections, encourage them to consider what more they want to know.

NOTICE & NOTE

Explain that some selections may contain multiple signposts; others may contain only one. And the same type of signpost can occur many times in the same text.

LEARNING MINDSET

Curiosity Reinforce the attitude that curiosity is about being open to new ideas and trying new things. Every answer will not be obvious; everyone's approach to problem solving will vary. The desire to find out what you don't know is vital to discovery and learning. Encourage students to always feel comfortable asking questions, and to mutually support curiosity whenever possible.

 INDEPENDENT READING

 ESSENTIAL QUESTION:

What can blur the lines between what's real and what's not?

Reader's Choice

Setting a Purpose Select one or more of these options from your eBook to continue your exploration of the Essential Question.

- Read the descriptions to see which text grabs your interest.
- Think about which genres you enjoy reading.

Notice & Note

In this unit, you practiced noticing and noting three signposts: **Aha Moment, Again and Again,** and **Contrasts and Contradictions.** As you read independently, these signposts and others will aid your understanding. Below are the anchor questions to ask when you read literature and nonfiction.

Reading Literature: Stories, Poems, and Plays		
Signpost	Anchor Question	Lesson
Contrasts and Contradictions	Why did the character act that way?	p. 99
Aha Moment	How might this change things?	p. 3
Tough Questions	What does this make me wonder about?	p. 362
Words of the Wiser	What's the lesson for the character?	p. 363
Again and Again	Why might the author keep bringing this up?	p. 3
Memory Moment	Why is this memory important?	p. 2

Reading Nonfiction: Essays, Articles, and Arguments		
Signpost	Anchor Question(s)	Lesson
Big Questions	What surprised me? What did the author think I already knew? What challenged, changed, or confirmed what I already knew?	p. 265 p. 183 p. 437
Contrasts and Contradictions	What is the difference, and why does it matter?	p. 183
Extreme or Absolute Language	Why did the author use this language?	p. 182
Numbers and Stats	Why did the author use these numbers or amounts?	p. 264
Quoted Words	Why was this person quoted or cited, and what did this add?	p. 437
Word Gaps	Do I know this word from someplace else? Does it seem like technical talk for this topic? Do clues in the sentence help me understand the word?	p. 265

ENGLISH LEARNER SUPPORT

Note-Taking Sharpen listening and comprehension skills with note-taking exercises.

- Model note-taking by saying words like *car* and *bar* aloud as you write them for display. Then say *cat* and *bat* aloud, emphasizing the final consonant. Ask students to write *cat* and *bat*. **SUBSTANTIAL**
- Read a sample text aloud, and ask students to make note of the main idea. Invite pairs to exchange papers and discuss their notes. **MODERATE**
- Read a sample text aloud, and challenge students to make note of the main idea and supporting details. Ask them to rank supporting details in order of importance. **LIGHT**

INDEPENDENT READING

You can preview these texts in Unit 2 of your eBook.
Then, check off the text or texts that you select to read on your own.

SHORT STORY
Way Too Cool
Brenda Woods

A boy with asthma struggles to uphold his high social status at school.

INFORMATIONAL TEXT
Forever New
Dan Risch

What is life like for those whose reality is affected by severe memory loss?

SHORT STORY
He–y, Come On Ou–t!
Shinichi Hoshi

A mysterious hole appears in a small fishing village.

PERSONAL ESSAY
A Priceless Lesson in Humility
Felipe Morales

Sometimes we have to be reminded of who we are and what we most value.

Collaborate and Share With a partner, discuss what you learned from at least one of your independent readings.

 Go to the **Reading Studio** for more resources on **Notice & Note.**

- Give a brief synopsis or summary of the text.
- Describe any signposts that you noticed in the text and explain what they revealed to you.
- Describe what you most enjoyed or found most challenging about the text. Give specific examples.
- Decide if you would recommend the text to others. Why or why not?

Independent Reading 171

INDEPENDENT READING

MATCHING STUDENTS TO TEXTS

Use the following information to guide students in choosing their texts.

A Priceless Lesson in Humility   Lexile: 930L
  Genre: personal essay
  Overall Rating: Challenging

He-y, Come On Ou-t!   Lexile: 860L
  Genre: short story
  Overall Rating: <Accessible/Challenging>

Way Too Cool   Lexile: 610L
  Genre: short story
  Overall Rating: <Accessible/Challenging>

Forever Now   Lexile: 1030L
  Genre: myth
  Overall Rating: Challenging

Collaborate and Share To assess how well students read the selections, walk around the room and listen to their conversations. Encourage students to be focused and specific in their comments.

 for Assessment

- Independent Reading Selection Tests

 Encourage students to visit the **Reading Studio** to download a handy bookmark of **NOTICE & NOTE** signposts.

WHEN STUDENTS STRUGGLE...

Keep a Reading Log As students read their selected texts, have them keep a reading log for each selection to note signposts and their thoughts about them. Use their logs to assess how well they are noticing and reflecting on elements of the texts.

Reading Log for (title)		
Location	**Signpost I Noticed**	**My Notes about It**

Independent Reading 171

PLAN

UNIT 2 Tasks

- **CREATE A MULTIMODAL PRESENTATION**

MENTOR TEXT

THE CAMERA DOES LIE
Magazine Article by MEG MOSS

LEARNING OBJECTIVES

Writing Task

- Write a script for a multimodal presentation on the art and craft of illusion.
- Employ and practice skills for planning, preparing, and organizing ideas and text.
- Craft text that supports and expands on audiovisual presentation elements.
- Develop a focused, structured draft.
- Use the Mentor Text as a model for form and content in examining the theme.
- Use guidelines to develop text, with an introduction, a thesis statement, supporting detail, and conclusion.
- Revise drafts, incorporating feedback from peers.
- Use a rubric to evaluate writing.
- Publish writing to share it with an audience.
- **Language** Write about illusion using evidence.

Speaking Task

- Present a multimodal project to an audience.
- Practice presentation skills with peers.
- Use appropriate verbal and nonverbal techniques.
- Listen actively to a presentation.
- **Language** Share information using the sentence stem *I learned _____*.

Assign the Writing Task in **Ed.**

OBJECTIVES

- Unit 2 Response Log
- Writing Studio: Writing Informative Text: Using Graphics and Multimedia
- Writing Studio: Writing Informative Text: Organizing Ideas
- Writing Studio: Writing Informative Text: Introductions and Conclusions
- Speaking and Listening Studio: Giving a Presentation

172A Unit 2

PLAN

Language X-Ray: English Learner Support

Use the instruction below and the supports and scaffolds in the Teacher's Edition to help you guide students of different proficiency levels.

INTRODUCE THE WRITING TASK

Explain that a **script** is a form of text that is generally written to be read and heard aloud. Script-based media include political speeches, newscasts, movies, and TV shows. Point out that *guion* is the Spanish word for *script*.

Remind students that the selections in this unit deal with reality and illusion. Work with students to narrow their search for content that illustrates the nature of illusion, in forms they can incorporate into a multimodal presentation.

To introduce the topic, provide students with a graphic organizer they can use for note taking. Review the Mentor Text, and direct students to note *Types of Illusion* and the paragraph number for each example. Then have students gather into small groups and pool their notes to create a single list, based on collective discussion about which notes are most accurate, thorough, and likely to be useful.

WRITING

Use Supporting Details

Tell students that supporting details often appear after the first sentence in a paragraph, which should start with a general statement about the information to be presented. Topic sentences and supporting details will form the main part of most informative text.

- Read the following sentence, and ask students to point out the topic sentence, details and conclusion. *A new house was built in the neighborhood. It took many months to build. It has two floors, a basement and an attic. It is made of bricks and has large windows. It is a complete house with plenty of space for a new family.* **SUBSTANTIAL**
- Provide students with a sample paragraph, and ask them to underline the details that support the topic sentence. Work with them to craft basic paragraphs that have a topic sentence and supporting detail. **MODERATE**
- After students have completed their script drafts, have partners exchange papers and suggest places where additional supporting detail might be useful. Encourage partners to make detailed notes in sentence form using content-based vocabulary. **LIGHT**

SPEAKING

Present Information

Encourage students to rehearse their presentations in front of supportive audiences. Practice can ease some of the anxieties that commonly attend public speaking,

- Write a sentence, such as *The magician showed five rabbits, but then the rabbits vanished.* Ask them to read it aloud. Point out that *vanished* is a synonym for *disappeared*. **SUBSTANTIAL**
- Offer students the sentence stem *An illusion is _____.* Ask them to complete the sentence aloud. Invite them to continue if they have more to add. **MODERATE**
- Working in pairs, have students practice using verbal and non-verbal techniques to present a brief sample text to one another. Encourage each student to make notes on the strengths and weaknesses of their partner's presentation. **LIGHT**

Unit 2 Tasks **172B**

WRITING

CREATE A MULTIMODAL PRESENTATION

Introduce students to the writing task by reading the introductory paragraph with them. Remind students to refer to the notes they recorded in the Unit 2 Response Log as they develop their scripts. The Response Log should contain ideas from a variety of perspectives about reality and illusion. Drawing on these different perspectives will make the students' writing more interesting and well informed.

 For **writing support** for students at varying proficiency levels, see the **Language X-Ray** on page 172B.

USE THE MENTOR TEXT

Point out that their scripts will follow the form of the magazine article "The Camera Does Lie" in citing facts and examples related to the theme of illusion. However, their scripts may not feature as much detail as the Mentor Text, and students' work should be crafted to integrate with multimedia.

WRITING PROMPT

Review the prompt with students. Encourage them to ask questions about any part of the assignment that is unclear. Make sure they understand that the purpose of their script is to illuminate the Essential Question with facts and examples from the texts they have read and other media used in their research.

 **WRITING TASK**

Create a Multimodal Presentation

 Go to the **Writing Studio** for help creating the script for your multimodal presentation.

This unit features many instances in which things are not as they seem. For this task, you will create a multimodal presentation that can include images, videos, music, and other elements of media. Review the article "The Camera Does Lie," which can help you think about how to create an interesting presentation. You might also refer to the notes from your Response Log, which you filled out after reading the texts in this unit.

Writing Prompt

Read the information in the box below.

This is the topic or context for your presentation.

> We often take what we see at face value, believing that what we see is real and that our first impression is correct. A closer look, however, may change our mind.

Think carefully about the following question.

This is the Essential Question for the unit. How would you answer this question based on the texts in this unit?

> What can blur the lines between what's real and what's not?

Now circle the word or words that identify exactly what you are being asked to produce.

Create and deliver a multimodal presentation to demonstrate and explain certain illusions and the techniques used to create them. Combine various media to illustrate your ideas. You may work alone or with a partner.

Be sure to—

Review these points as you develop your presentation and again when you finish. Make any needed changes.

- ☐ provide an intriguing opening that states your purpose
- ☐ include a thesis statement or controlling idea
- ☐ research examples of illusions
- ☐ devise an interactive activity for audience participation
- ☐ end with a summary and explain why illusions are interesting

 LEARNING MINDSET

Asking for Help Encourage students to always feel comfortable asking questions. Explain that asking for help from others can help students get past difficult situations. Having the courage to admit what you don't know is an important part of learning.

WRITING TASK

1 Plan

The first step in planning your presentation is to do some research and gather materials. You can find examples of illusions online at various websites, including government and social media sites. You might also explore the methods of the artist M.C. Escher, whose mathematical prints and impossible constructions are compelling examples of the power of illusions.

Once you have gathered your materials, you can plan the elements of your presentation—both the script and the media components. If you are working with a partner, discuss ideas about how to structure your presentation. Use the table below to guide you as you create a script and identify various media that you will include.

Go to **Writing Informative Texts: Organizing Ideas** for help.

Presentation Planning Table	
Introduction: How will you capture your audience's attention in the opening of your presentation? What is the main point you want to convey?	
Audience: What will your audience already know about illusions? How can you include the audience in your presentation?	
Visuals and other media: What images, videos, and music can you use in your presentation? What would add interest or help clarify ideas?	
Script: What information will you include in your script? How will you connect it to the media you will present?	

Use the notes from your Response Log as you plan your presentation.

Background Reading Review the notes you have taken in your Response Log after reading the texts in this unit. These texts provide background reading that can support the key ideas you will include in your presentation.

Create a Multimodal Presentation 173

WRITING

1 PLAN

Allow time for students to discuss the topic with partners or in small groups and then to complete the planning chart independently.

■ English Learner Support

Understand Academic Language Make sure students understand words and phrases used in the chart, such as *audience, media,* and *script*. Work with them to fill in the blank sections, providing text that they can copy into their charts as needed. **SUBSTANTIAL/MODERATE**

Background Reading As they plan their presentations, remind students to refer to the notes they took in the Response Log. They may also review the selections to find additional facts and examples to support ideas they want to include in their writing.

TO CHALLENGE STUDENTS...

Genre Characteristics Challenge students to learn more about the finer points of illusions in movie making. They might start by considering movies they liked in which makeup, audio, set design, and/or CGI contributed to illusions that engaged the audience. Encourage them to search online or at the library for more information on a given movie or movies. They may add details from their research to the Response Log and think about how these details support their answer to the Essential Question.

Create a Multimodal Presentation 173

WRITING

Organize Your Ideas Encourage students to select examples that represent a range of illusions, in terms of particularly deft "tricks" that fool the eye and ear. They may expand the chart to include more than three examples, making notes on a chart of their own devising. With as many examples as possible, they can hone their lists to feature the illusions that tell their stories most effectively.

Then point out that the splashiest or strongest illusions may be preferable for the opener and closer of their presentations. As they organize they scripts, ask them to consider: *What effect does this illusion have on an audience? Is it meant to scare people? To make them laugh? To convey hope or hopelessness? How does this illusion serve the story it is part of? How did the creators manufacture the illusion?*

② DEVELOP A DRAFT

Remind students to follow their charts as they draft their scripts, but point out that they can still make changes to their writing plans during this stage. As they write, they may decide to move script elements closer to the beginning or end, change emphasis for a given element, and add or subtract detail as warranted.

■ English Learner Support

Write a Collaborative Script Simplify the writing task and provide direct support by working together to write a skeletal script that answers the Essential Question.
SUBSTANTIAL/MODERATE

174   Unit 2

 WRITING TASK

Go to **Writing Informative Texts: Using Graphics and Multimedia** for help in preparing your presentation.

Organize Your Ideas After you have gathered ideas and information from your planning activities, you need to organize the information in a way that will help you make your presentation effective. You can use the chart below to identify illusions you will display during the presentation. You can also use the chart to plan how you will demonstrate and explain how each illusion is created.

Main Topic: Illusions and How They Are Created

Illusion: _____	Illusion: _____	Illusion: _____
Description	Description	Description
How it is created	How it is created	How it is created

② Develop a Draft

 You might prefer to draft your script online.

Once you have completed your planning activities, you will be ready to begin drafting a script for your presentation. Refer to the chart above and the Presentation Planning Table you completed, as well as any notes you took as you studied the texts in the unit. These will provide a kind of map for you to follow as you develop your presentation. Using a word processor or online writing application makes it easier to make changes or move sentences around later when you are ready to revise the first draft of your script.

174   Unit 2

WHEN STUDENTS STRUGGLE...

Develop a Draft Script writing will be an unfamiliar form to many students, who may encounter difficulty getting started. Remind them that a script is meant to be read aloud, "live" or as an audio recording. Ask them to complete the following sentence: *Text meant to be read aloud should be ____.* (**Possible answers:** brief, direct, "punchy" or arresting, tightly connected to visual elements.) Suggest that students take notes, to be pooled and shared to help establish guidelines for writing a first draft.

WRITING TASK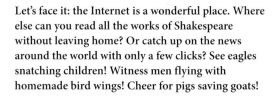

Use the Mentor Text

▶ **Author's Craft**
Your introduction is your first chance to capture the audience's attention. In addition to your controlling idea or thesis statement, your introduction should include something that gets your audience interested in following your presentation. Note how the introduction to "The Camera Does Lie" captures your attention.

> Let's face it: the Internet is a wonderful place. Where else can you read all the works of Shakespeare without leaving home? Or catch up on the news around the world with only a few clicks? See eagles snatching children! Witness men flying with homemade bird wings! Cheer for pigs saving goats!

The author begins with questions and some amazing "facts" that she will explore in the article.

Apply What You've Learned To capture your audience's attention, you have several options. You might open with a question that will make your audience curious. Or begin your presentation with a nonverbal demonstration of an illusion. Another option is to include a surprising fact, a famous quotation, or a personal anecdote related to the topic.

▶ **Genre Characteristics**
Supporting details are words, phrases, or sentences that tell more about a central idea. Notice how the author of "The Camera Does Lie" uses details in the close analysis of a video.

> . . . [T]he golden eagle needs a 7.5-foot (2.3-meter) wingspan just to lift its own body weight of about 14 pounds (6.4 kilograms). . . . Estimating the size of the child in the video at about 28 pounds (13 kilograms) means the eagle is lifting almost twice its own weight. This would take a wingspan of about 33 feet . . . !

The author provides details to explain why a video of an eagle snatching a child has to be fake.

Apply What You've Learned The details you include in your own presentation should clearly explain how the illusions work. Facts, examples, and quotations are some of the types of details you can use to support your ideas. some small prey. Estimating the size of the child in the video at about 28 pounds means the eagle is lifting almost twice its own weight. This would take a wingspan of about 33 feet!

Create a Multimodal Presentation 175

WRITING

WHY THIS MENTOR TEXT?
"The Camera Does Lie" provides a solid introduction into the mechanics of illusory images. Use the instruction below to help students review the mentor text as a model for selecting material to be used in their scripts and describing the finer points of deception in various media.

USE THE MENTOR TEXT

Author's Craft Ask a volunteer to read aloud the first paragraph of "The Camera Does Lie." Discuss words and details that "jump out" as sensational, highly unusual, or unlikely. Then ask students to identify the author's shift from one broad category of Internet material (*the works of Shakespeare* and *news*) to another (*eagles snatching children, pigs saving goats*). Ask: *What is the effect of such a shift?* (*The author grabs the reader's attention with a series of outrageous examples, which she juxtaposes with relatively standard Internet fare.*) Discuss strategies students might use to search for analogous examples of illusions.

Genre Characteristics To demonstrate consistent form in the presentation of supporting detail, refer students to paragraph 17 of the Mentor Text. Note that paragraph 17 is similar in structure to paragraph 12, which is given in the example. Ask: *How are these paragraphs alike?* (*Both begin with topic sentences regarding scrutiny of incredible images, or "ways you can tell something's fishy." Each paragraph then provides supporting details laying out the physical impossibility that the images could be real as represented: that they must therefore be fakes.*)

 ENGLISH LEARNER SUPPORT

Use the Mentor Text Use the following supports with students at varying proficiency levels:

- Ask volunteers to give examples of things that are false. Work with students to develop a definition of the term: *not true*. Ask students to offer synonyms in their native language. (Spanish cognate: *falso*)
  SUBSTANTIAL

- Read the introduction aloud, and invite students to ask about any words or phrases that are unclear. Review the fundamental terms around the Essential Question: *reality, illusion, conartistry, faker*. Ask students to come up with synonyms. (*the real world; make-believe; trickery; pretender*) **MODERATE**

- Refer students to the Mentor Text and ask them to identify two types of fakery cited in the text after the introduction.
  LIGHT

Create a Multimodal Presentation 175

WRITING

3 REVISE

Have students answer each question in the chart to determine how they can improve their drafts. Invite volunteers to model their revision techniques.

With a Partner Have students ask peer reviewers to evaluate their supporting evidence by answering the following questions:

- How strong is my introduction? How might it be improved?
- Are my main ideas well supported with evidence? Is the connection clear between main ideas and supporting details?
- How well have I connected my script to multimedia elements: video, audio, or other modes of media?
- In general, what do you see as the strong points of my draft? In what areas might it need more work?

Students should use the reviewer's feedback in revising the introduction, thesis statement, supporting details, and conclusion of their drafts.

4 EDIT

Suggest that students read their drafts aloud to assess how clearly and smoothly they have presented their ideas. Remind them of the fundamentals of script writing: a compelling introduction; a strong thesis statement; a logical arrangement of ideas, well supported by details; and a conclusion that summarizes the main ideas. Encourage them to work on the flow of text that is written to be read aloud, and to tighten the synergy between script and proposed visuals as they edit.

176   Unit 2

WRITING TASK

Go to **Writing Informative Texts: Introductions and Conclusions** in the Writing Studio for help.

3 Revise

Improving Your First Draft Once your draft is complete, you'll want to go back and look for ways to improve your script for the presentation. As you reread and revise, think about whether you have achieved your purpose. The Revision Guide will help you focus on specific elements to make the presentation stronger.

Revision Guide		
Ask Yourself	**Tips**	**Revision Techniques**
1. Does my introduction grab the audience's attention?	**Highlight** the introduction.	**Add** an interesting fact, example, or quotation about the topic.
2. Is my thesis statement clear?	**Underline** the thesis statement.	**Reword** the thesis statement using action verbs and specific nouns and adjectives.
3. Are ideas and examples organized logically? Do transitions connect ideas?	**Highlight** transitional words and phrases.	**Rearrange** sentences to organize ideas logically. **Add** transitions.
4. Do I support each main idea with evidence?	**Underline** each supporting fact, definition, example, or quotation.	**Add** more facts, details, examples, or quotations to support ideas.
5. Does my conclusion summarize the main ideas? Do I speculate about why illusions intrigue people?	**Underline** the summary. **Highlight** sentences that speculate about illusions.	**Add** a statement that summarizes the main ideas. **Insert** supporting sentences and speculations.

ACADEMIC VOCABULARY
As you conduct your **peer review**, be sure to use these words.

☐ abnormal
☐ feature
☐ focus
☐ perceive
☐ task

With a Partner If you have been working on your own, exchange scripts with another classmate and evaluate each other's drafts in a **peer review**. Provide revision suggestions for at least three of the items mentioned in the Revision Guide. When receiving feedback from your partner, listen attentively. If necessary, ask for clarification.

4 Edit

Once you have addressed the organization, development, and flow of ideas in your presentation, you can look to improve the finer points of your script. Edit for the proper use of standard English conventions and make sure to correct any misspellings or grammatical errors.

176   Unit 2

ENGLISH LEARNER SUPPORT

Subject-Verb Agreement Explain that a verb must agree with the singular or plural subject.

Have students work in pairs of differing abilities to identify the subject and verb in this sample sentence from the Mentor Text: *The Internet is a wonderful place.* (Subject: *Internet*. Verb: *is*.) Ask students to complete this sentence stem, which includes a plural subject and is based on the sample sentence: *Internet users _____ pleased with the wealth of information available.* (*are*)
SUBSTANTIAL

Direct students to edit their drafts for subject-verb agreement.   **LIGHT**

5 Practice Your Presentation

After completing your draft, practice with a partner or in a small group to improve both the presentation and your delivery.

Practice Timing
Use notes or cues in your script to ensure that you incorporate video, images, and sound at the appropriate time.

Practice Effective Verbal Techniques
- ❏ **Enunciation** Replace words that you stumble over. Rearrange sentences so that your delivery is smooth.
- ❏ **Voice Modulation and Pitch** Use your voice to show enthusiasm and emphasis.
- ❏ **Speaking Rate** Speak a little slowly. Pause frequently to let the audience consider important points.
- ❏ **Volume** Speak so that everyone can hear you.

Practice Effective Nonverbal Techniques
- ❏ **Eye Contact** Look at each member of the audience at least once.
- ❏ **Facial Expression** Smile, frown, or raise an eyebrow to show your feelings or to emphasize points.
- ❏ **Gestures** Stand tall and relaxed, and use natural gestures (for example, shrugs, nods, or shakes of your head) to add meaning and interest to your presentation.

Provide and Consider Advice for Improvement
As a listener, pay close attention. Take notes about how presenters can improve their presentations. Summarize each presenter's main points to check your understanding, and ask questions if you need clarification.

As a presenter, listen closely to questions. Consider how to make your presentation clearer or better organized. Ask for suggestions about changing onscreen text or images to improve your presentation.

6 Deliver Your Presentation

Use the advice you received to make final changes in your presentation. Then, using effective verbal and nonverbal techniques, present it to your classmates.

WRITING TASK

Go to **Giving a Presentation** in the **Speaking and Listening Studio** to learn more.

As you work to improve your presentations, be sure to follow discussion rules:
- ❏ listen closely to each other
- ❏ don't interrupt
- ❏ ask helpful, relevant, and thoughtful questions
- ❏ provide only clear, direct, and appropriate answers

Create a Multimodal Presentation 177

WHEN STUDENTS STRUGGLE...

Take Notes If students find it challenging to take notes during their classmates' presentations, divide the task between several students. One student may focus on the list of verbal techniques, checking off effective approaches and making brief notes about potential improvements. Another student may do the same for the list of effective nonverbal techniques. A third may listen for key ideas and write those down. This student may choose to listen with eyes closed to tune out distractions.

WRITING

5 PRACTICE YOUR PRESENTATION

Invite volunteers to model elements of presentation and delivery in reading their script drafts or a sample text aloud. Encourage students to constructively evaluate peers according to the guidelines for verbal and nonverbal techniques. Invite listeners to take notes, which they should reference in honing their own presentation skills.

With a Partner Have students ask peer reviewers to evaluate their practice presentations by answering the following questions:
- Were my points clear and logically arranged?
- Was my delivery smooth? Could you understand everything I said?
- Did I convey enthusiasm and appropriate emphasis? Were there moments when I went too fast?
- How would you assess my nonverbal techniques: eye contact, facial expression, and gestures?

Remind students that almost everyone gets anxious about addressing a group and that practice makes public speaking a little less stressful. Students should use the reviewer's feedback to improve elements of their presentation and delivery. Encourage students to rehearse their presentations informally in front of small groups of supportive listeners.

■ English Learner Support

Assess Comprehension Have students form two straight lines parallel to each other, so each student is facing a partner. Ask partners to start a discussion using the following sentence stem: *This lesson about illusions taught me* ____ . Signal the line to shift so each student has a new partner. Ask partners to continue the discussion using the stem: *To give a good presentation, I should* ____ . Challenge students to take brief notes as their partner speaks, while maintaining a fluid discussion. **ALL LEVELS**

6 DELIVER YOUR PRESENTATION

Set aside time for all students to give their presentations. When everyone has finished, ask students to share their thoughts on how their classmates' feedback helped them improve their performance.

WRITING

USE THE SCORING GUIDE

Allow students time to read the scoring guide and invite questions about any words, phrases, or ideas that are unclear. Then have partners exchange copies of the current draft of their script. Ask them to mark up their partner's script according to the benchmarks enumerated in the scoring guide, citing areas of strength and room for improvement. Then ask them to score their partner's essay according to their assessments in each category of the guide, giving reasons for the score they have awarded in each category.

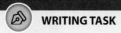

WRITING TASK

Use the scoring guide to evaluate your presentation.

Task Scoring Guide: Multimodal Presentation

	Organization/Progression	Development of Ideas	Use of Language and Conventions
4	• The organization is effective and appropriate to the purpose. • All ideas are focused on the topic specified in the prompt. • Transitions clearly show the relationship between ideas.	• The introduction catches the audience's attention and clearly identifies the topic. • The script contains a clear, concise, and well-defined thesis statement. • The topic is well developed with clear main ideas supported by facts, details, examples, and appropriate media elements. • The conclusion effectively summarizes the information presented.	• Language and word choice are purposeful and precise. • There is a variety of simple, compound, and complex sentences; they show how ideas are related. • Spelling, capitalization, and punctuation are correct. • Grammar and usage are correct.
3	• The organization is, for the most part, effective and appropriate to the purpose. • Most ideas are focused on the topic specified in the prompt. • A few more transitions are needed to show the relationship between ideas.	• The introduction could be more engaging. The topic is identified. • The script contains a clear thesis statement. • The development of ideas is clear because the writer uses facts, details, examples, and mostly appropriate media elements. • The conclusion summarizes the information presented.	• Language is, for the most part, specific and clear. • Sentences vary somewhat in structure. • Some spelling, capitalization, and punctuation mistakes are present. • Some grammar and usage errors occur.
2	• The organization is evident but is not always appropriate to the purpose. • Only some ideas are focused on the topic specified in the prompt. • More transitions are needed to show the relationship between ideas.	• The introduction is not engaging; the topic is unclear. • The thesis statement does not express a clear point. • The development of ideas is minimal. The writer uses inappropriate facts, details, examples, as well as some ineffective media elements. • The conclusion is only partially effective.	• Language is often vague and general. • Compound and complex sentences are rarely used. • Spelling, capitalization, and punctuation are often incorrect but do not make reading difficult. • Grammar and usage are often incorrect, but the writer's ideas are still clear.
1	• The organization is not appropriate to the purpose. • Ideas are not focused on the topic specified in the prompt. • No transitions are used, making the relationship among ideas difficult to understand.	• The introduction is missing or confusing. • The thesis statement is missing. • The development of ideas is weak. Supporting facts, details, examples, and media elements are unreliable, vague, or missing. • The conclusion is missing.	• Language is vague, confusing, or inappropriate for the presentation. • There is no sentence variety. • Many spelling, capitalization, and punctuation errors are present. • Many grammatical and usage errors confuse the writer's ideas.

Reflect on the Unit

By completing your multimodal presentation, you have created a product that pulls together and expresses your thoughts about the reading you have done in this unit. Now is a good time to reflect on what you have learned.

Reflect on the Essential Question

- What can blur the lines between what's real and what's not? How has your answer to this question changed since you first considered it when you started this unit?

- What are some examples from the texts you've read that show how illusions are created?

Reflect on Your Reading

- Which selections were the most interesting or surprising to you?

- From which selection did you learn the most about how people respond to illusions?

Reflect on the Task

- What difficulties did you encounter while working on your multimodal presentation? How might you avoid them next time?

- What parts of the presentation were the easiest and hardest to complete? Why?

- What improvements did you make to your presentation as you were revising?

REFLECT

UNIT 2 SELECTIONS
- "Heartbeat"
- "The Camera Does Lie"
- "Two Legs or One?"
- "The Song of Wandering Aengus"
- "Eldorado"
- "The Governess" (drama)
- "The Governess" (production images)

SPEAKING AND LISTENING

REFLECT ON THE UNIT

Have students reflect on the questions independently and write some notes in response to each one. Then have students meet with partners or in small groups to discuss their reflections. Circulate during these discussions to identify the questions that are generating the liveliest conversations. Wrap up with a whole-class discussion focused on these questions.

 LEARNING MINDSET

Problem Solving Encourage students not to get stuck on any one issue. Sometimes when you aren't immediately able to solve a problem, it's better to move on and try something else. Then circle back and try to solve the problem later. In the course of working on something else, you might have across the solution to your original problem!

UNIT 3

Instructional Overview and Resources

	Instructional Focus	Online Ed Resources
Unit Introduction Inspired By Nature	**Unit 3 Essential Question** **Unit 3 Academic Vocabulary**	**Stream to Start:** Inspired By Nature **Unit 3 Response Log**

ANALYZE & APPLY

	Instructional Focus	Resources
"Never Retreat" from *Eyes Wide Open* Argument by Paul Fleischman **Lexile 1010L** **NOTICE & NOTE** READING MODEL **Signposts** • Extreme or Absolute Language • Contrasts and Contradictions • Big Questions	**Reading** • Analyze an Argument • Analyze Subjective and Objective Point of View **Writing:** Write a Letter **Speaking and Listening:** Group Discussion **Vocabulary:** Context Clues **Language Conventions:** Conjunctions and Complex Sentences	🔊 **Audio** **Reading Studio:** Notice & Note **Writing Studio:** Writing as a Process: Planning and Drafting **Level Up Tutorial:** Analyzing Arguments **Speaking and Listening Studio:** Participating in Collaborative Discussions **Vocabulary Studio:** Context Clues **Grammar Studio:** Module 3: Lesson 6: Conjunctions and Interjections
MENTOR TEXT **from *Mississippi Solo*** Memoir by Eddy Harris **Lexile 830L**	**Reading** • Analyze Memoir • Analyze Figurative Language **Writing:** Write a Literary Analysis **Speaking and Listening:** Produce a Podcast **Vocabulary:** Reference Aids **Language Conventions:** Consistent Verb Tenses	🔊 **Audio** **Text in Focus:** Visualizing **Close Read Screencast:** Modeled Discussion **Reading Studio:** Notice & Note **Writing Studio:** Writing Informative Texts **Speaking and Listening Studio:** Using Media in a Presentation **Vocabulary Studio:** Reference Resources **Grammar Studio:** Module 9: Lesson 4: Using Verb Tenses Consistently
"The Drought" Poem by Amy Helfrich	**Reading** • Analyze Sonnet • Analyze Rhyme Scheme **Writing:** Write a Sonnet **Speaking and Listening:** Listen to the Sonnet	🔊 **Audio** **Reading Studio:** Notice & Note **Level Up Tutorial:** Symbol **Speaking and Listening Studio:** Giving a Presentation
"Allied with Green" Short Story by Naomi Shihab Nye **Lexile 900L**	**Reading** • Analyze Theme • Monitor Comprehension **Writing:** Write a Poem **Speaking and Listening:** Share and Discuss Opinions **Vocabulary:** Context Clues **Language Conventions:** Complex Sentences	🔊 **Audio** **Reading Studio:** Notice & Note **Level Up Tutorial:** Theme **Speaking and Listening Studio:** Participating in Collaborative Discussions **Vocabulary Studio:** Context Clues

SUGGESTED PACING: 30 DAYS

Unit Introduction: 1 | *from* Never Retreat: 2 3 4 5 6 | Mississippi Solo: 7 8 9 10 | The Drought: 11 12 13 13

PLAN

English Learner Support		Differentiated Instruction	Assessment
• Learn Vocabulary • Learning Strategies		**When Students Struggle** • Discuss Big Questions	
• Text X-Ray • Comprehend Academic Terms • Use Cognates • Learning Strategies • Understand Point of View • Oral Assessment • Discuss with a Small Group	• Vocabulary Strategy • Language Conventions	**When Students Struggle** • Learning Strategy	**Selection Test**
• Text X-Ray • Ad-Lib Similes • Reference Aids • Who is You? • Similar Simile • Past Tense Skills	• First, Second, and Third Person • Oral Assessment • Produce a Podcast • Vocabulary Strategy • Language Conventions	**When Students Struggle** • Genre Reformulation	**Selection Test**
• Text X-Ray • Demonstrate Rhythm • Understand Sound Devices • Use Background Knowledge	• Understand Poetry Elements • Oral Assessment • Listen to the Sonnet	**When Students Struggle** • Read Aloud • Draw Inferences **To Challenge Students** • Conduct Research	**Selection Test**
• Text X-Ray • Reinforce Strategy • Use Cognates • Learning Strategy • Figurative Language • Oral Assessment • Share and Discuss	• Vocabulary Strategy • Language Conventions	**When Students Struggle** • Read Closely **To Challenge Students** • Explore Terminology	**Selection Test**

Allied With Green 14 15 16 17

Ode to Enchanted Light / Sleeping in the Forest 18 19 20 21

Trash Talk / You're Part of the Solution 22 23 24 25

Independent Reading 26 27

End of Unit 28 29 30

Inspired By Nature 180B

PLAN

UNIT 3 Continued

COLLABORATE & COMPARE

		Instructional Focus	Online Ed Resources
	**"Ode to Enchanted Light"** Poem by Pablo Neruda	**Reading** • Analyze Form: Ode • Analyze Form: Lyric Poem **Writing:** Write an Ode **Speaking and Listening:** Listen for a Poem's Message	🔊 **Audio** **Close Read Screencast:** Modeled Discussion **Text in Focus:** Understanding Form **Reading Studio:** Notice & Note **Speaking and Listening Studio:** Analyzing and Evaluating Presentations
	"Sleeping in the Forest" Poem by Mary Oliver	**Writing:** Write a Lyric Poem **Speaking and Listening:** Listen for a Poem's Rhythm and Melody	
	Collaborate and Compare	**Reading:** Forms and Elements **Speaking and Listening:** Explore and Present	**Speaking and Listening Studio:** Giving a Presentation
	Trash Talk Video by the National Oceanic and Atmospheric Administration **"You're Part of the Solution"** Poster	**Media:** • Analyze Persuasive Media • Analyze Digital Texts **Writing:** Write a Letter **Speaking and Listening:** Present a Critique	**Reading Studio:** Notice & Note **Writing Studio:** Persuasive Techniques **Speaking and Listening Studio:** Introduction: Using Media in a Presentation
	Collaborate and Compare	**Media:** Compare Persuasive Media **Speaking and Listening:** Research and Share	

INDEPENDENT READING

The independent Reading selections are only available in the eBook.

 Go to the Reading Studio for more information on **NOTICE & NOTE.**

 from *Unbowed*
Memoir by Wangari Muta Maathal
Lexile 1020L

 "Problems With Hurricanes"
Poem by Victor Hernández Cruz

END OF UNIT

	Instructional Focus	Online Ed Resources
Writing Task: Personal Narrative **Reflect on the Unit**	**Writing:** Write a Personal Narrative **Language Conventions:** Correctly Spell Commonly Confused Words	**Unit 3 Response Log** **Mentor Text:** from *Mississippi Solo* **Reading Studio:** Notice & Note **Writing Studio:** Writing Narratives **Writing Studio:** Narrative Structures **Writing Studio:** Writing as a Process

180C Unit 3

PLAN

English Learner Support	Differentiated Instruction	Assessment (Online Ed)
• TUnderstand Figurative Language • Oral Assessment • Listen for a Poem's Rhythm and Melody • Listen for a Poem's Message	**When Students Struggle** • Take Notes	**Selection Tests**
	When Students Struggle • Understand Figurative Language	**Selection Tests**
• Ask Questions	**To Challenge Students** • Compare Odes	
• Text X-Ray • Understand Academic Terms • Understand Video Elements • Understand Idioms • Comprehend the Text • Oral Assessment	**To Challenge Students** • Analyze Media	**Selection Tests**
• Ask Questions	**When Students Struggle** • Work Collaboratively	
"Living Large Off the Grid" Magazine Article by Kristen Mascia **Lexile L/k**	"Haiku" Poem by Issa, Bahso, and Buson, translated by Richard Haas	**Selection Tests**
• Language X-Ray • Understand Academic Language • Write a Collaborative Personal Narrative • Use the Mentor Text • Use Synonyms • Commonly Confused Words	**When Students Struggle** • Develop a Draft • Descriptive Langauage **To Challenge Students** • Use Advanced Sources	**Unit Test**

Inspired By Nature 180D

TEACH

? Connect to the ESSENTIAL QUESTION

Ask a volunteer to read the Essential Question aloud. Discuss how the images on page 180 relate to the question. Ask: *How does a butterfly pollinating a flower illustrate nature in harmony? How does the image below the butterfly suggest nature's bounty?* Ask students to think of real-life situations when nature inspired them.

■ English Learner Support

Learn Vocabulary Make sure students understand the Essential Question. If necessary, explain the following terms:
- *nature* means "everything in the world not made by people"
- *harmony* means that separate parts of something cooperate or work together for the good of the whole; e.g., musicians who play different instruments play together to create a pleasing piece of music.

Help students reframe the question: *How does nature inspire you?* **SUBSTANTIAL/MODERATE**

DISCUSS THE QUOTATION

Tell students that Rachel Carson (1907—1964) was a well-known American biologist, professor, and writer. Her 1962 best seller, *Silent Spring*, alerted America to the dangers of pesticides and other pollutants. The book was praised for its style and scientific details.

Ask students: *How is nature affected by pollutants? How would Carson's background have helped her inform the public about pesticides?*

UNIT 3

INSPIRED BY NATURE

? **ESSENTIAL QUESTION**

What does it mean to be in harmony with nature?

" Here again we are reminded that in nature nothing exists alone. "

— Rachel Carson

180 Unit 3

LEARNING MINDSET

Setting Goals Tell students that setting goals is an important part of having a learning mindset. Encourage students to set a goal for reading self-selected texts outside of class, for example, reading for a set time or number of pages per day. Consider setting up a class progress report for students to track their goals.

UNIT 3

ACADEMIC VOCABULARY

Academic Vocabulary words are words you use when you discuss and write about texts. In this unit you will practice and learn five words.

 ☑ affect ☐ element ☐ ensure ☐ participate ☐ specify

Study the Word Network to learn more about the word **affect**.

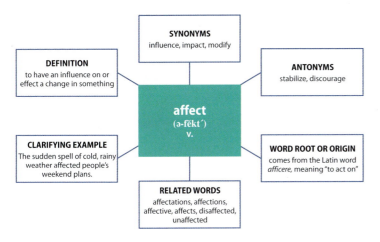

Write and Discuss Discuss the completed Word Network with a partner, making sure to talk through all of the boxes until you both understand the word, its synonyms, antonyms, and related forms. Then, fill out Word Networks for the remaining four words. Use a dictionary or online resource to help you complete the activity.

*Go online to access the **Word Networks**.*

RESPOND TO THE ESSENTIAL QUESTION

In this unit, you will explore how different people find—or are challenged to find—harmony in nature. As you read, you will revisit the **Essential Question** and gather your ideas about it in the **Response Log** that appears on page R3. At the end of the unit, you will have the opportunity to write a **personal narrative** about an experience you had in nature or a lesson learned from nature. Filling out the Response Log will help you prepare for this writing task.

*You can also go online to access the **Response Log**.*

Inspired by Nature 181

TEACH

ACADEMIC VOCABULARY

As students complete Word Networks for the remaining four vocabulary words, encourage them to include all the categories shown in the completed network if possible, but point out that some words do not have clear synonyms or antonyms. Note that some words can be confusing to make use of—for example, *affect* is a verb that means "to influence something," and *effect* is a noun that means "something brought about by a cause or agent." To wit: "The relentless cold had begun to *affect* us. Its *effect* was to numb our weary souls."

affect (ə-fĕkt´) *tr. v.* To have an influence on or effect a change in (Spanish cognate: *afectar*)

element (ĕl´ə-mənt) *n.* A fundamental, essential, or irreducible constituent of a composite entity (Spanish cognate: *elemento*)

ensure (ĭn-shŏŏr´) *tr. v.* To make sure, certain, or secure

participate (pär-tĭs´ə-pāt´) in*tr. v.* To be active or involved in something; take part (Spanish cognate: *participar*)

specify (spĕs´ə-fī´) *tr. v.* To state explicitly or in detail (Spanish cognate: *especificar*)

RESPOND TO THE ESSENTIAL QUESTION

Direct students to the Unit 3 Response Log. Explain that students will use it to record ideas and details from the selections that help answer the Essential Question. When they work on the writing task at the end of the unit, their Response Logs will help them think about what they have read and make connections between texts.

Inspired by Nature 181

PLAN

NEVER RETREAT
ARGUMENT by Paul Fleischman

GENRE ELEMENTS
ARGUMENT
Reading Model

Inform students that the purpose of an **argument** is to convince readers of the importance of an idea or a course of action. Authors usually write arguments because they feel strongly about a particular issue. As with all **informational texts**, an argument presents facts and evidence, but it does so in order to support the author's position on a topic. Authors of arguments will also include contrary opinions in order to prove them wrong or less important than their own opinions.

LEARNING OBJECTIVES
- Analyze an argument.
- Analyze subjective and objective points of view.
- Conduct research about the Transition movement.
- Write a letter.
- Discuss efforts to attain sustainability.
- Use subordinating conjunctions to form complex sentences.
- Use context clues to determine the meaning.
- **Language** Discuss evidence that supports an author's claim.

TEXT COMPLEXITY

Quantitative Measures	Never Retreat	Lexile: 1010L
Qualitative Measures	**Ideas Presented** Mostly explicit; require some inferential reasoning	
	Structure Used Primarily explicit; primarily one perspective	
	Language Used Mostly explicit; Tier II and III words defined in context	
	Knowledge Required Some references to events; deals mostly with common experience	

PLAN

Online

RESOURCES

- Unit 3 Response Log
- Selection Audio
- Reading Studio: Notice & Note
- Level Up Tutorial: Analyzing Arguments
- Writing Studio: Writing as a Process: Planning and Drafting
- Speaking and Listening Studio: Participating in Collaborative Discussions
- Vocabulary Studio: Context Cues
- Grammar Studio: Module 3: Lesson 6: Conjunctions and Interjections
- "Never Retreat" Selection Test

SUMMARIES

English

According to the author of "Never Retreat," fossil fuels are hard to give up because of the many products that rely on them provide convenience and comfort, which are addictive. Using less energy, consuming less, and switching to renewable energy would help the environment, of course, but making these changes would mean a lifestyle change that Americans traditionally refuse to undertake. Nonetheless, the author concludes by expressing his faith in human adaptability.

Spanish

De acuerdo con el autor de "Nunca retirarse", es difícil renunciar a los combustibles fósiles debido a que muchos de los productos que dependen de ellos proveen conveniencia y confort, que son cualidades adictivas. Al usar menos energía consumimos menos, y cambiarse a energías renovables ayudaría al ambiente. Claro, hacer estos cambios significaría un cambio de estilo de vida que los americanos se rehúsan hacer. Sin embargo, el autor concluye expresando su fe en la adaptabilidad humana.

SMALL-GROUP OPTIONS

Have students work in small groups to read and discuss the selection.

Pinwheel Discussion

- After students have read "Never Retreat," ask them to create pinwheel formations of six per group.
- For the first rotation, ask students to discuss the author's claim that convenience is addictive.
- For the second rotation, ask students to discuss the author's claim that fossil fuel usage is hard to give up.
- For the third rotation, ask students to discuss the author's claim that human adaptability will help people change their lifestyles.

Think-Pair-Share

- After students have read and discussed "Never Retreat," pose this question: *Which lifestyle changes would you be willing to make for the environment, which ones would you be unwilling to make, and why?*
- Have students think about the question individually and write down their ideas.
- Then, have pairs discuss their ideas about the question.
- Finally, ask pairs to share their responses with the class.

Never Retreat **182B**

PLAN

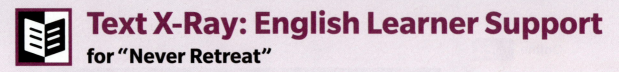

Text X-Ray: English Learner Support
for "Never Retreat"

Use the Text X-Ray and the supports and scaffolds in the Teacher's Edition to help guide students at different proficiency levels through the selection.

INTRODUCE THE SELECTION
DISCUSS NECESSITIES AND NONESSENTIALS

In this lesson, students will need to be able to distinguish between necessities and nonessentials, a distinction that "Never Retreat" claims is very difficult for Americans to make. Provide the following explanations of terms:

- A necessity is something people need in order to stay alive. These include food, water, shelter, clothing, and medical care.
- A nonessential is a luxury, something that might make life easier and more comfortable, but is not needed to stay alive.

Explain that nutrients from vegetables and fruits are needed in order for people to stay alive. Explain that rich desserts are not.

Have volunteers share what they consider to be necessities and nonessentials. Use the following sentence frames: Something I use every day that is a necessity is _____. Something I use every day that is a nonessential is _____.

CULTURAL REFERENCES

The following words and phrases may be unfamiliar to students:

- *every corner of our lives* (paragraph 3): all parts of our lives
- *lifestyle* (paragraph 3): the way a person or group lives
- *crunch* (paragraph 5): an important point or situation
- *standard of living* (paragraph 6): level of wealth and material comfort a person or group has
- *breadwinners* (paragraph 8): people who earn money
- *sustainable* (paragraph 9): involving methods that do not completely use up or destroy natural resources

LISTENING

Understand a Claim
Draw students' attention to the claim the author makes in paragraphs 13 and 14 about the human ability to adapt to change. Remind students that the word "claim" refers to what the author believes to be true; he is offering his opinion based on his interpretation of scientific facts and history.

Have students listen as you read aloud paragraphs 12--14. Use the following supports with students at varying proficiency levels:

- Tell students that you will ask questions about what they just heard. Model that they should say yes if the answer is yes and no for no. For example, ask: *Does the author believe we can change the way we live? (Yes)* **SUBSTANTIAL**
- Have students discuss examples of adaptability in their lives. For example, *How would your family get to work, stores, or school if a car wasn't available?* **MODERATE**
- The author talks about how Americans experienced a "downshift" in World War II. Discuss what a downshift would be like today. **LIGHT**

182C   Unit 3

PLAN

SPEAKING

Discuss Evidence that Supports a Claim

Have students discuss the evidence the author presents in paragraph 8. Circulate around the room, checking that they are expressing key ideas clearly.

Use the following supports with students at varying proficiency levels:
- Echo read the paragraph with students, listening for proper pronunciation. Encourage students to ask clarifying questions about the ideas being presented in the paragraph and the words and phrases being used. **SUBSTANTIAL**
- Ask students to choose a partner to discuss the pros and cons of buying less stuff, as explained by the author. **MODERATE**
- Pair students to discuss why the author mentions bacon-flavored dental floss and Elvis Presley mouse pads in the paragraph. **LIGHT**

READING

Evaluate Evidence

Tell students that it is up to the reader to evaluate the strength of arguments by judging how well authors support their claims.

Work with students to reread paragraphs 4 and 5. Use the following supports with students at varying proficiency levels:
- Ask students to circle words in the text that explain why fossil fuels are hard to give up. **SUBSTANTIAL**
- Pair students to explain what is easy and what is difficult about giving up fossil fuel usage. **MODERATE**
- Pair students to explain how the author backs up his claims about fossil fuel usage. **LIGHT**

WRITING

Write a Letter

Work with students to read the writing assignment on p. 193

Use the following supports with students at varying proficiency levels:
- Help students find words that express their feelings or opinions about "Never Retreat." Write a brief letter to the author on the board using the words students suggested. Have students copy the letter in their notebooks. **SUBSTANTIAL**
- Provide sentence frames such as the following that students can use to craft their letters: *What events inspired you to _____? What kinds of things do you think ordinary people should do to _____.* **LIGHT**
- Remind students to use evidence to support their opinions. Have pairs find places in their letters where they can use evidence. **MODERATE**

TEACH

EXPLAIN THE SIGNPOSTS

Explain that Notice & Note Signposts are significant moments in the text that help readers understand and analyze works of fiction or nonfiction. Use the instruction on these pages to introduce students to the signposts **Extreme or Absolute Language**, **Contrasts and Contradictions**, and **Big Questions**. Then use the selection that follows to have students apply the signposts to a text.

For a full list of the fiction and nonfiction signposts, see p. 252.

EXTREME OR ABSOLUTE LANGUAGE

Extreme or Absolute Language is written to ring out like the crack of bat on ball, or the ping and clatter of dropped silverware on tile. Exaggerated prose emphasizes a point of importance to authors of nonfiction, and sometimes the strongly held convictions of fictional characters.

Display the following sentence, which recasts the topic sentence in the sample paragraph: *With fossil fuels new uses began to multiply until we wove them into different corners of our lives.* Underline the altered language. Then ask: *How is this sentence different in tone from the sample text?* (*The sample text is emphatic. The alternative sentence is closer to a neutral or businesslike tone.*)

Tell students that when they spot **Extreme or Absolute Language**, they should pause, mark it in their consumable texts, and ask themselves the anchor question: *Why did the author choose such strong terms?*

Notice & Note
READING MODEL

NEVER RETREAT

You are about to read "Never Retreat," an argument presented in a book about environmental issues. In it, you will notice and note signposts for clues about the author's opinions and the techniques he uses to make his argument convincing. Here are three key signposts to look for as you read this argument and the other texts in this unit.

 For more information on these and other signposts to Notice & Note, visit the **Reading Studio**.

When you encounter words or phrases like these in a text, pause to see whether you have discovered an **Extreme or Absolute Language** signpost:

"It always happens that . . ."

"and the saddest part of all . . ."

"Of course, you have to realize that . . ."

"but few could doubt that . . ."

Extreme or Absolute Language While talking with a friend, you comment that your favorite basketball team lost because a key player was hurt. Your friend says, "Give me a break! That player is the worst in the league!" You reply, "No way! You couldn't tell a good player from a broken shoelace!" Both speakers have used exaggerated language to indicate that they are sure their opinion is correct. An author who uses **Extreme or Absolute Language** in an argument does so for a specific reason. For example, such language can:

- get other people's attention and force them to rethink their position
- introduce new and engaging details to support a claim
- emphasize the author's true feelings about a subject
- reveal an author's biases toward a subject

The paragraph below illustrates a student's annotation within "Never Retreat" and a response to a Notice and Note signpost.

> 3   With fossil fuels, new uses (multiplied madly) until we wove them into (every corner) of our lives. What used to be luxuries—garage-door openers, dishwashers, cell phones— came to feel like necessities. It's easy to go up the lifestyle ladder but painful climbing down. <u>This is important.</u>

Anchor Question
When you notice this signpost, ask: Why did the author use this language?

What absolute or extreme language is used?	Extreme language: "multiplied madly" and "every corner" Absolute language: "This is important"
Why do you think this language is important to the argument?	The extreme language catches the reader's attention and emphasizes the author's feeling about the convenience items that grew from the expanded use of fossil fuels. "This is important" is an absolute statement that does not allow the reader to disagree.

▶ **Contrasts and Contradictions** Have you ever had a situation turn out in an unexpected way? In nonfiction, **Contrasts and Contradictions** often point to a difference between what people generally think is true and what the author claims is actually true. That difference can surprise readers. It can cause them to wonder about their own views and be more willing to consider the author's argument and evidence. Here a student marked a Contrast and Contradiction.

> 6   When our standard of living is threatened by scarcity and side effects, you'd think we'd cut back. Instead, the common response is to maintain it at any cost. . . . <u>We know our freshwater aquifers are limited, but we're draining them faster rather than slower.</u> . . .

Anchor Question
When you notice this signpost, ask: What is the difference, and why does it matter?

Which statement does the underlined sentence contradict?	It contradicts the first sentence: "When our standard of living is threatened by scarcity and side effects, you'd think we'd cut back."
What effect does this have?	The author thought I knew about the many different strains of humans.

▶ **Big Questions** If a person assumes you know something when you actually don't—such as how to use an app or define a new term—you might feel a bit awkward or confused. If you feel a bit lost while reading a nonfiction text, ask yourself one of the **Big Questions**—"What did the author think I already knew?" The answer can help you better grasp the point the author is making. (Other Big Questions include "What surprised me?" and "What changed, challenged, or confirmed what I already knew?") In this example, a student underlined details that relate to a Big Question.

> 13   Adaptability is one of humankind's hallmarks. We evolved during difficult climatic times . . . times so challenging that <u>the twenty or so other strains of humans who weren't as flexible all died out.</u> Is that ability to adapt still within us?

Which words or details are confusing?	The detail "the twenty or so other strains of humans who weren't as flexible all died out" seems a little confusing.
What did the author think I already knew?	The author thought I already knew about the many different strains of humans.

Notice & Note 183

WHEN STUDENTS STRUGGLE . . .

Discuss Big Questions Model applying signposts. Display text from the article that asks a big question about fossil fuels, e.g., "Can we run this film in reverse? Only once have we replaced an energy source so central to our economy and lifestyle: when slave labor was abolished, a change so jarring that its threat brought on war." Clarify the sentence as necessary, then model a think aloud: *I want to know more about how abolishing slavery can be compared to giving up fossil fuels.* Have student pairs mark statements that offer a perspective that may be new to them. Circulate around the class to offer clarification and suggestions.

TEACH

▶ CONTRASTS AND CONTRADICTIONS

Contrasts and Contradictions call attention to juxtaposed elements. The contrast is sharp between the racing speed of tortoises and hares; the victory of the former becomes a resonant lesson as it challenges (or contradicts) expectations.

Review the sample paragraph. Ask: *What is the author's argument, and how does the contradiction strengthen it?* (The author believes water should be conserved. His contradiction dramatizes that argument: faced with "scarcity and side effects," people drain underground reserves "faster rather than slower.")

Tell students that when they spot **Contrasts and Contradictions**, they should pause, mark them in their consumable texts, and ask themselves the anchor question: *Why is the author calling attention to this?*

▶ BIG QUESTIONS

Big Questions assume common knowledge that may not be universal. A **Big Question** might be seen as a significant claim on the part of the author, about something the author seems to know and the reader may or may not.

Big Questions invite the curious to "look it up." Otherwise, careful readers should decide whether the author's claim that "twenty or so other strains of humans" have become extinct seems solid.

Tell students that when they spot **Big Questions**, they should stop, mark them in their consumable texts, and ask themselves the anchor question: *What just surprised me?*

APPLY THE SIGNPOSTS

Have students use the selection that follows as a model text to apply the signposts. As students encounter signposts, prompt them to stop, reread, and ask themselves the anchor questions that will help them understand the story's characters and themes.

Never Retreat **183**

TEACH

? **Connect to the ESSENTIAL QUESTION**

"Never Retreat" proposes harmony with nature by asking Americans to choose more eco-friendly ways of living—using renewable fuels, reducing energy consumption, growing our own food, and buying fewer unnecessary consumer items.

ANALYZE & APPLY

NEVER RETREAT
from Eyes Wide Open

Argument by **Paul Fleischman**

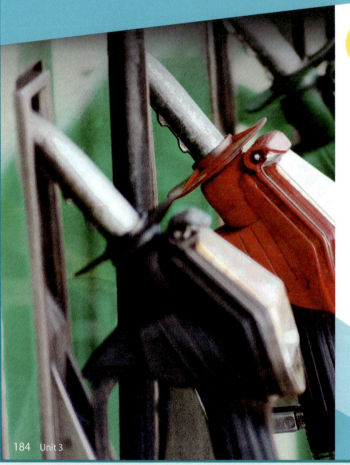

? **ESSENTIAL QUESTION:**

What does it mean to be in harmony with nature?

 LEARNING MINDSET

Curiosity Remind students that a curiosity mindset means curiosity leads to learning, so ask questions. Explore new ideas and skills. Use reading to find out more about the things that interest you. Set a purpose for yourself in reading and writing.

QUICK START

Think about what it might mean to live a "simple" life. If you had to live more simply, what would you find easy—and difficult—to give up?

ANALYZE AN ARGUMENT

In an **argument,** the author expresses a position—an opinion—on an issue or a problem and provides supporting evidence for it. Strong arguments have the following key elements:

- a **claim,** which is the writer's position on the issue or problem
- **support,** which includes reasons and evidence the writer provides to back up the claim
- **counterarguments,** which are the writer's responses to opposing opinions—responses that show that the writer's position is stronger

Use a chart like the one below to help you analyze "Never Retreat."

ELEMENT	EXAMPLE FROM ARGUMENT
Claim	
Support	
Counterarguments	

ANALYZE SUBJECTIVE AND OBJECTIVE POINT OF VIEW

In arguments and other nonfiction texts, authors convey a **point of view,** or perspective, about their topic. How authors view a topic is often shaped by their ideas, feelings, and beliefs. In nonfiction writing, an author's point of view may be subjective, objective, or both.

- When writing from a **subjective point of view,** the author includes personal opinions, feelings, and beliefs.
- When writing from an **objective point of view,** the author leaves out personal opinions and instead presents information in a straightforward, unbiased way.

Many elements in an argument can suggest the author's point of view. Word choices such as *easy* or *threatened,* for example, can signal a subjective point of view—if not for the entire selection, at least for that part of it. In addition, an author sometimes will include a rhetorical question. A **rhetorical question** either has no answer or an answer that is so obvious that the author doesn't need to state it. In either case, a rhetorical question can emphasize a key point or just make readers think. As you read "Never Retreat," consider the author's point of view and the questions he asks. Consider why he asks each one.

GET READY

GENRE ELEMENTS: ARGUMENT

- purpose is to share the author's claim and persuade readers to agree with it—and, sometimes, to take action because they agree
- presents reasons to support the author's claim
- supports reasons with statistics, examples, and other factual evidence
- may anticipate and respond to counterarguments, questions, and other points of view

Never Retreat 185

TEACH

QUICK START

Have students read the Quick Start question, and invite them to share their responses with a partner. Ask them to think of electronic gadgets, everyday conveniences, and recreational activities they would be willing to give up to live a simpler life. Remind them that they would be making these sacrifices for the sake of the environment.

ANALYZE AN ARGUMENT

Help students understand the terms and concepts related to analyzing an argument. Tell them than analyzing an argument means identifying the claim the author is making, evaluating the evidence supporting the claim, and seeing if the argument stands up to the counterarguments. Encourage students to come up with counterarguments of their own.

ANALYZE SUBJECTIVE AND OBJECTIVE POINT OF VIEW

Tell students that the main difference between the two points of view is that in subjective writing, the authors talk about themselves and their personal experiences; in objective writing, they don't. Remind students that both points of view can be used to present an argument and require evidence.

Suggest that students use these questions to determine point of view:

- Are there any first-person (*I, me, we, us*) pronouns?
- Does the author tell any personal stories?
- Is the evidence of a personal nature?

Never Retreat **185**

TEACH

CRITICAL VOCABULARY

Encourage students to read the entire sentence first before answering the question. Remind them to look for context clues to help them with their answers.

Answers:

1. *Combustion could cause fire to spread rapidly.*
2. *No; scarcity means a shortage.*
3. *They might use the aquifer if there was a drought or a water shortage.*
4. *Yes; they are able to adapt to new situations.*

■ English Learner Support

Use Cognates Tell students that several of the Critical Vocabulary words have Spanish cognates (*combustion/combustión, aquifer/acuífero, adaptability/adaptabilidad*).
ALL LEVELS

LANGUAGE CONVENTIONS

Review information about compound and complex sentences, the different kinds of conjunctions they require, and whether they need commas. Ask students to identify coordinating conjunctions (*and, but, or, so,* etc.) and subordinating conjunctions (*because, if, unless,* etc.)

ANNOTATION MODEL

Tell students that the signposts they encounter in the reading selection will help them better understand the claims, evidence, and counterarguments the author presents in the article, as described in Analyze an Argument on p. 185. Remind students that it will also be useful for them to color-code these elements or devise a system of their own.

 GET READY

CRITICAL VOCABULARY

combustion   scarcity   aquifer   adaptability

To see how many Critical Vocabulary words you already know, answer these questions.

1. Why is the **combustion** of dried brush in a forest so dangerous?
2. If there were a **scarcity** of food, would people be eating well? Why?
3. Why would a city's government decide to tap into an **aquifer**?
4. Do people known for their **adaptability** react well to change? Why?

LANGUAGE CONVENTIONS

Conjunctions and Complex Sentences In sentences, conjunctions join words and word groups. **Correlative conjunctions** such as *either / or* or *neither / nor* are used as a pair to join words or word groups used in the same way. In a complex sentence, however, ideas may be connected in a way that shows which idea is stronger and which ideas are less important, or subordinate. Words such as *after, although, because, if,* and *when* signal the subordinate ideas. These words are called **subordinating conjunctions.** In the following complex sentences, the subordinate idea is underlined once and the subordinating conjunction twice.

> With fossil fuels, new uses multiplied madly <u>until</u> <u>we wove them into every corner of our lives.</u>

> <u>When</u> <u>a job is lost in the family,</u> we cut budgets.

As you read "Never Retreat," note the use of conjunctions. Decide what relationship it signals between ideas in the sentence.

ANNOTATION MODEL   NOTICE & NOTE

As you read, notice and note signposts, including **Extreme or Absolute Language, Contrasts and Contradictions,** and **Big Questions.** Here is an example of how one reader responded to the opening of "Never Retreat."

1 Our dependence on fossil fuels didn't arise from an (evil plot) but through our curiosity and ingenuity. Coal was seen only as a heat source until we found it could power (steam engines). Later we discovered that the gas it gave off when heated could light homes and streets. Gasoline was considered a useless by-product of petroleum—and (then came the internal combustion engine).

Evil plot is extreme language. It's part of a sentence that contrasts two ideas about why we depend on fossil fuels.

I'll read on to learn why the author felt it was important to talk about engines.

BACKGROUND

Paul Fleischman (b. 1952) grew up in Santa Monica, California, and lives in Santa Cruz today. He is the award-winning author of more than forty novels, short story and poetry collections, and nonfiction books for children and young adults. His *Joyful Noise: Poems for Two Voices*, which celebrates the insect world, received the Newbery Medal in 1989. Many of Fleischman's other books explore carefully researched historical settings and social issues.

NEVER RETREAT
from Eyes Wide Open
Argument by Paul Fleischman

SETTING A PURPOSE

As you read, identify the author's opinions about modern environmental problems and about the way many people live today. In addition, pay attention to the historical and present-day evidence that he offers to support his argument.

1   Our dependence on fossil fuels didn't arise from an evil plot but through our curiosity and ingenuity. Coal was seen only as a heat source until we found it could power steam engines. Later we discovered that the gas it gave off when heated could light homes and streets. Gasoline was considered a useless by-product of petroleum—and then came the internal **combustion** engine.

2   Necessity is said to be the mother of invention, but the reverse is also true. We tinker and probe, then see if our discovery fills any need, including needs we didn't know we had.

3   With fossil fuels, new uses multiplied madly until we wove them into every corner of our lives. What used to be luxuries—garage-door openers, dishwashers, cell phones—

Notice & Note

Use the side margins to notice and note signposts in the text.

CONTRASTS AND CONTRADICTIONS

Notice & Note: In paragraph 1, mark the energy sources about which people's attitudes changed.

Cause/Effect: According to the author, why did people later contradict their original opinion of these sources?

combustion
(kəm-bŭs´chən) *n. Combustion is the process of burning, which produces heat and light.*

Never Retreat   187

ENGLISH LEARNER SUPPORT

Expand Learning Strategies Discuss fossil fuels as non-renewable energy. Provide students with a three-row graphic organizer that has "Coal" and "Gasoline" as its headings. The rows should read: "Original Use," "Unexpected Use," "Results." Fill out part of the organizer with the class, then have small groups complete the graphic organizer based on the information presented in paragraphs 1—3 of "Never Retreat."
MODERATE/LIGHT

TEACH

BACKGROUND

Provide students with background information about fossil fuels and renewable energy so they understand the claim being made in the argument. Tell them that when fossil fuels are burned, they emit carbon dioxide and other toxic pollutants that are harmful to the environment. Extracting fossil fuels also causes pollution and may result in environmental disasters like oil spills. Explain that renewable energy (solar, wind, water) does not pose these threats.

SETTING A PURPOSE

Direct students to use the Setting a Purpose prompt to focus their reading.

CONTRASTS AND CONTRADICTIONS

Explain to students that this signpost is used to indicate the sharp contrast between what was expected and what actually happened. Have students identify the words in paragraph 1 that signal this contrast ("Later we discovered" and "then came"). Then have students answer the question to explain the contrast. (**Answer:** *People later contradicted their original opinion when they discovered they had become so dependent on fossil fuels.*)

CRITICAL VOCABULARY

combustion: The author uses the word *combustion* to describe the way a car engine burns gasoline. An internal combustion engine burns gasoline, which, in turn, powers a car.

ASK STUDENTS to identify other kinds of combustion in everyday life. (*burning wood in a fireplace, fireworks, charcoal in a barbecue grill*).

Never Retreat   **187**

TEACH

ANALYZE ARGUMENT

Remind students that the **claim** is the author's opinion on the problem or issue that is being discussed in the argument. (**Answer:** *Students should identify an object [cell phones] or service [cable TV] that is not absolutely necessary for their daily existence but which they feel they could not do without.*)

ANALYZE SUBJECTIVE AND OBJECTIVE POINT OF VIEW

Remind students that when authors write from a **subjective point of view**, they are expressing personal opinions, feelings, and beliefs. (**Answer:** *These details relate to the argument by making the point that once we have gotten used to some new convenience, it is very difficult to give it up.*)

▶ EXTREME OR ABSOLUTE LANGUAGE

Explain to students that this signpost is used to indicate when an author wishes to make a point or express an opinion in strong, dramatic terms. Have students identify the words in paragraph 5 ("we don't need," "only once," "slavery") that indicate the author's extreme or absolute language. (**Answer:** *The author's use of the words "only once" makes the statement seem absolute.*)

 For **reading support** for students at varying proficiency levels, see the **Text X-Ray** on page 182D.

CRITICAL VOCABULARY

scarcity: A scarcity of oranges occurs if the orange trees freeze in extremely cold winters.

ASK STUDENTS what would cause a scarcity of water. (*There's a drought; a dam breaks; a reservoir runs out of water.*)

aquifer: An aquifer contains water even if there is a drought aboveground.

ASK STUDENTS how people reach the water in an aquifer. (*People dig wells or use water pumps.*)

188   Unit 3

 **NOTICE & NOTE**

ANALYZE ARGUMENT
Annotate: In paragraph 3, mark the author's claim about learning to live without the things we consider "necessary."

Connect: What would be an example of a change that would make this claim true in your life?

ANALYZE SUBJECTIVE AND OBJECTIVE POINT OF VIEW
Annotate: In paragraph 4, mark two details that show that the author is expressing a subjective point of view.

Critique: How do these details relate to the author's argument?

EXTREME OR ABSOLUTE LANGUAGE
Notice & Note: In paragraph 5, mark what the author says is the only time that Americans made a radical change in an energy source.

Analyze: What is it about his statement that makes it seem absolute? Explain.

scarcity
(skâr´sĭ-tē) *n.* When you experience a *scarcity*, you have a shortage or lack of something.

aquifer
(ăk´wə-fər) *n.* An *aquifer* is an underground layer of rock that contains water.

188   Unit 3

came to feel like necessities. It's easy to go up the lifestyle ladder but painful climbing down. This is important.

4   It's not hard to understand. The windfall of cheap fossil fuels that's fueled the West for two centuries got us used to ever-rising living standards. Energy buys convenience. And convenience is addictive—highly so. Each increased dosage quickly becomes our new minimum requirement. You see this whenever gas prices rise and endanger our freedom to drive as much as we want—causing politicians to leap into action on our behalf. They know that whatever level of comfort we're at feels like a must.

5   To escape from the environmental crunch, we don't need to throw out our entire lifestyle but simply to power it on something other than fossil fuels. We're on the way. Switching to renewables for electricity is probably the easy part. Harder will be getting oil out of transportation and agriculture and the military, as well as all the products it's currently in: the asphalt in your street, the carpet on your floor, the clothes in your closet, and all the plastic around you in furniture, appliances, cars, and packaging. Can we run this film in reverse? Only once have we replaced an energy source so central to our economy and lifestyle: when slave labor was abolished, a change so jarring that its threat brought on war.

6   When our standard of living is threatened by **scarcity** and side effects, you'd think we'd cut back. Instead, the common response is to maintain it at any cost. Bluefin tuna is in steep decline, but the tuna-loving Japanese are catching all they can. We know our freshwater **aquifers** are limited, but we're draining them faster rather than slower. Scarcity was humankind's enemy for so long that resistance to a downshift in lifestyle is

strong. At the first international climate summit in 1992, the U.S. delegation's attitude was that America's standard of living wasn't up for negotiation. Every U.S. administration since then has followed the same path.

7   Developing countries feel the same. People getting their first paved roads, safe water, electric lights, and refrigerators don't want to march backward any more than the West does.

8   Using less energy and consuming less—taking a step down the ladder—would make the West's transition to renewables that much easier. What would happen if we cut the amount of stuff we bought in half? We'd save hugely on resources as well as on the energy needed to make them into products. We'd also lose large numbers of jobs. To keep employment up, we need people to keep buying <u>bacon-flavored dental floss</u> and <u>Elvis Presley mouse pads</u> and other nonessentials. The call "Never retreat" comes from us both as consumers and breadwinners.

9   Many have sketched a sustainable economy that doesn't rest on unnecessary consumption. These proposals often favor decentralization—a more dispersed and rural society, with people growing more of their own food and generating more of their own power. This would give us an economy with greater resilience than our current highly connected one.

NOTICE & NOTE

ANALYZE SUBJECTIVE AND OBJECTIVE POINT OF VIEW

Annotate: In paragraph 8, mark the two examples of "nonessentials" that the author mentions.

Analyze: Is the author presenting an objective point of view, or a subjective point of view? Why do you think so?

Never Retreat 189

TEACH

✏️ ANALYZE SUBJECTIVE AND OBJECTIVE POINT OF VIEW

Remind students that when writers use first-person pronouns like *I* or *we* in an argument, they are usually writing from a subjective point of view because they are writing about themselves and their personal experience. Then have students look for these pronouns. (**Analyze:** *The author is presenting a subjective point of view. I know this because he uses the pronoun "we" and because he presents silly examples, probably meant to be humorous.*)

■ English Learner Support

Understand Point of View Explain that in order to determine point of view, students have to be able to identify subjective (based on personal opinions) and objective (evidence based) writing. Have students work in pairs of varying proficiencies and circle the pronoun *we* in paragraph 8. Remind students that the use of the pronoun *I* or *we* indicates subjective point of view.
SUBSTANTIAL/MODERATE

 For **speaking support** for students at varying proficiency levels, see the **Text X-Ray** on page 182D.

APPLYING ACADEMIC VOCABULARY

 affect    element   ☐ ensure   ☐ participate   ☐ specify

Write and Discuss Have students turn to a partner to discuss the following questions. Guide students to include Academic Vocabulary words *affect* and *element* in their responses with the class.

- How does buying nonessential products **affect** the environment?
- What **element** of the author's argument is the most convincing?

Never Retreat 189

TEACH

ANALYZE ARGUMENT

Remind students that authors frequently ask **rhetorical questions** in their writing so they can answer them. (*Answer: Previously, the author states that we have to decentralize. By asking what's wrong with a centralized system, the author makes it clear that he is about to offer another viewpoint.*)

LANGUAGE CONVENTIONS

Remind students that subordinating conjunctions connect a **dependent clause** with an **independent clause** to form a complete thought. (*Answer: The subordinating conjunction "if" indicates a condition that would affect the topic of the sentence—integrated systems.*)

BIG QUESTIONS

Remind students that this signpost is used to indicate questions that are important to understanding the overall text. Have students explain the importance of the question asked in the paragraph. (*The author is advocating that Americans downshift their lifestyle. He asks what that downshift might feel like and gives two historical examples of when Americans had to downshift their lifestyle.*) (*Answer: Both examples required that Americans do without things.*)

EXTREME OR ABSOLUTE LANGUAGE

Have students locate the paragraph in which the extreme language was first used (paragraph 5) and to review its context. (*Answer: Many people considered slavery indispensable to the U.S. economy. As it turns out they were wrong; the United States did abolish slavery without ending in financial ruin.*)

 For **listening support** for students at varying proficiency levels, see the **Text X-Ray** on page 182C.

CRITICAL VOCABULARY

adaptability: Human beings show their adaptability when they adjust to new situations and circumstances.

ASK STUDENTS how they have shown adaptability to new circumstances in their own lives. (*Answers will vary.*)

190   Unit 3

NOTICE & NOTE

ANALYZE ARGUMENT
Annotate: Mark the question that begins paragraph 10.
Infer: How does that question suggest a point of view that the author is going to challenge?

LANGUAGE CONVENTIONS
Annotate: Mark the two subordinating conjunctions in paragraph 10.
Interpret: What do the ideas introduced by these words add to the rest of each sentence?

BIG QUESTIONS
Notice & Note: In paragraph 12, mark two topics that the author thinks you may already know about.
Compare: What do these topics have in common?

adaptability
(ə-dăp′tə-bĭl′ĭ-tē) *n.* People who have *adaptability* can change to survive and fit in with new circumstances.

EXTREME OR ABSOLUTE LANGUAGE
Notice & Note: In the final paragraph, mark two word choices that recall some absolute/extreme language from earlier in the selection.
Interpret: What point does the author make by repeating this reference?

10   What's the problem with highly integrated systems? They're efficient and low cost, but brittle. Ours brings us fruit from South America and computer parts from China but leaves us in the lurch if anything interrupts trade. We're so connected that a single power outage or oil shortage affects millions. Sicknesses can more easily become epidemics. The American housing collapse of 2008 quickly brought on a worldwide recession.

11   Life used to be much more decentralized. The Transition movement, beginning in Britain, guides communities toward a lower energy, more self-sufficient future, with hundreds of branches active in the United States and elsewhere. The Slow Food movement, back-to-the-landers reviving rural skills, and those pursuing voluntary simplicity are pointed in the same direction.

12   What might a major lifestyle downshift feel like? Real-world Americans experienced a downshift during World War II. The U.S. auto industry stopped making cars and switched to building tanks and planes. Gasoline, milk, meat, coffee, cheese, sugar, heating oil, and shoes were strictly rationed. Could we do it again?

13   **Adaptability** is one of humankind's hallmarks. We evolved during difficult climatic times, when temperatures swung between ice ages and warmer interglacial periods, times so challenging that the twenty or so other strains of humans who weren't as flexible all died out. Is that ability to adapt still within us?

14   Consider a power outage's frustrations, then the gradual adaptation the longer it goes on until dining by lantern light feels almost normal. Use of mass transit goes up when gas prices rise. We adjust to water rationing. When a job is lost in the family, we cut budgets. People think they can't go backward, then find out that they can. We ended up succeeding in getting rid of slavery, after all. Stranger still to a time-traveling slave owner: we no longer even notice its absence.

190   Unit 3

WHEN STUDENTS STRUGGLE...

Evaluate Claims   If students have difficulty identifying the claims, supporting evidence, and counterargument presented in "Never Retreat," choose one paragraph (for example, paragraph 8) and review it carefully with students, guiding them to identify the claim, evidence, and counterargument the author makes in that paragraph. Then select another paragraph and have students do the same, individually or with a partner.

 For additional support, go to the **Reading Studio** and assign the following Level Up tutorial: Analyzing Arguments

CHECK YOUR UNDERSTANDING

Answer these questions before moving on to the **Analyze the Text** section on the following page.

1 In paragraphs 1–3, the author argues that —

   A our dependence on coal is the result of a plot by energy companies

   B we invent only those things that we know will be useful to everyone

   C sometimes we unexpectedly find new uses for a discovery or invention

   D fossil fuels have always been useful for powering machines

2 In paragraph 6, the author mentions the fishing of Bluefin tuna and the 1992 climate summit in order to support the idea that —

   F the world's nations are interconnected in ways that eventually will harm their economies

   G when facing a common problem, nations will work together to find a solution

   H people want to maintain their current way of life, even when cutting back would be wise

   J individuals, not governments, must lead the way in switching to renewable sources of energy

3 What evidence does the author offer to support the idea that we have become addicted to the convenience of fossil fuels?

   A The greater amount of coal, the more nonessential products are manufactured.

   B Developing countries require fewer roads and less electricity than industrialized nations.

   C It's easier to go down the lifestyle ladder than up it.

   D When gas prices rise, politicians take action to limit the increase.

Never Retreat 191

TEACH

CHECK YOUR UNDERSTANDING

Have students answer the questions independently.

Answers:

1. C
2. H
3. D

If they answer any questions incorrectly, have them reread the text to confirm their understanding. Then they may proceed to ANALYZE THE TEXT on page 192.

ENGLISH LEARNER SUPPORT

1. **Oral Assessment** Use the following questions to assess students' comprehension and speaking skills:

   1. What evidence does the author provide in paragraphs 1–3 to support his claim that a discovery can fill a "need we didn't know we had?" *(Coal was originally used only for heat, but it was discovered that the gas it gave off could be used for lighting.)*

   2. In paragraph 6, why does the author mention fishing for Bluefin tuna and the 1992 climate summit? *(The author mentions them to support the claim that people want to maintain their current lifestyle when, in fact, it would be wise for them to change.)*

   3. In paragraph 14, what evidence does the author provide to support his claim that humans can make great adjustments and not even notice the change? *(We do not notice the absence of slavery in modern-day society.)*
   MODERATE/LIGHT

Never Retreat **191**

APPLY

ANALYZE THE TEXT

Possible answers:

1. **DOK 2:** *The author's position is that inventions are not always created to meet current needs. He states that many inventions that run on fossil fuels, like steam engines and internal combustion engines—came after coal and gasoline were already being used.*

2. **DOK 3:** *The author clearly states the main reason in paragraph 3: "We wove [uses of fossil fuels] into our lives. What used to be luxuries...came to feel like necessities. It's easy to go up the lifestyle ladder but painful coming down."*

3. **DOK 3:** *The author calls our dependence on fossil fuels "addictive," as if it is like a drug addiction. Here again the author uses extreme language, as he did by referencing slavery, to support his argument.*

4. **DOK 4:** *The author presents both subjective and objective points of view in the paragraph. He says that "we're so connected," which includes him, but he also cites objective information such as "The American housing collapse of 2008 quickly brought on a worldwide recession."*

5. **DOK 4:** *The author feels that his readers already know that fossil fuels harm the environment, that people depend greatly on fossil fuels, and that people own a lot of unnecessary products. This prior knowledge is important because it allows the author to make a claim that readers know is based on truth.*

RESEARCH

Remind students that they should confirm any information they find by checking multiple websites and assessing the credibility of each one.

Connect Students may note that one of the main goals of the Transition movement is to increase the self-sufficiency of communities through helping them to become independent of large, wasteful, agricultural systems. This can be accomplished through community members discovering how to use less energy while working in harmony with local, sustainable ecosystems; some food cooperatives will not sell anything that is grown further than one day's drive away. Students may discover that one problem the movement tries to address is waste. According to the United Nations Food and Agriculture Organization, one third of all food on the planet is wasted. Finding ways to inspire people to change how they live is a big problem. Student's research may lead them to discover "Zero Waste" classrooms in which students, teachers, and community members work together to limit their output of trash.

RESPOND

ANALYZE THE TEXT

Support your responses with evidence from the text. NOTEBOOK

1. **Summarize** Reread paragraphs 1–2. Summarize the author's position on whether inventions are created to meet current needs.

2. **Cite Evidence** According to the author, what is the main difficulty in ending our dependence on fossil fuels? Cite text evidence in your response.

3. **Compare** In paragraph 4, to what does the author compare our dependence upon fossil fuels? How does this comparison relate to other instances of the author's use of extreme language?

4. **Analyze** In paragraph 10, do you think the author is presenting an objective point of view, a subjective one, or both? Explain.

5. **Notice & Note** Consider "Never Retreat" as a whole. What do you think the author feels his readers already know before they start reading? Why is that prior knowledge important to his argument?

RESEARCH TIP
When you conduct online research, be sure to evaluate the credibility of websites. Web addresses ending in *.gov*, *.edu*, or *.org* are often more reliable than other sites. Other reliable sources may include major news outlets. It's always a good idea to confirm information using multiple, reliable sites.

RESEARCH

In paragraph 11, the author mentions the Transition movement, which began in Great Britain and spread to the United States. Use the chart to find out more about this movement and then share what you learn.

RESEARCH QUESTIONS	WHAT YOU LEARNED
What are the main goals of the Transition movement?	*To increase the self-sufficiency and resilience of local communities*
What problems does the Transition movement try to address?	*Challenges causes by fossil fuel use, climate change, and resulting economic instability*
What types of activities does the Transition movement engage in?	*Creating community gardens and recycling centers; promoting masstransportation*

Extend Find out about another group concerned with the long-term sustainability of the environment. What is the major focus of the group? What activities does it engage in to promote its cause? Share your findings with some of your classmates.

 LEARNING MINDSET

Try Again Remind students that a try again mindset means learn from your mistakes and try again in a different way. It's okay to make mistakes. Everyone does. It's how we learn. With a partner, share a mistake you made and what you learned from it.

WRITE AND DISCUSS

Write a Letter Paul Fleischman began his writing career as a poet and then a novelist. Write a letter to the author requesting information about his decision to write about the environment.

- ❏ Start by explaining how you learned about his writing.
- ❏ Ask about event(s) in his life that inspired him to write *Eyes Wide Open*, especially the chapter entitled "Never Retreat."
- ❏ Discuss details from "Never Retreat" that you especially liked or that you had questions about. Mention issues about the environment that you have been involved in or that interest you.
- ❏ Write with a friendly, respectful tone, and follow the correct form for a friendly letter.

Group Discussion In a small group, discuss how your school or community promotes sustainability of the environment. How well do their approaches to sustainability seem to be working? What other ways to improve or expand those efforts would you suggest?

- ❏ Remember to stay focused on the discussion topic.
- ❏ Be prepared to share your thoughts with others in the group.
- ❏ Encourage all group members to participate in the discussion.
- ❏ Respect the ideas and feelings of other group members.
- ❏ Ask clarifying questions that build on others' ideas.

RESPOND TO THE ESSENTIAL QUESTION

What does it mean to be in harmony with nature?

Gather Information Review your annotations and notes on "Never Retreat." Then, add relevant details to your Response Log. As you determine which information to include, think about:

- how trying to rely on easy solutions can affect long-term problems
- how individual needs might conflict with social goals
- why people's behavior might not change when facing new problems

At the end of the unit, use your notes to write a personal narrative.

RESPOND

Go to the **Writing Studio** for more help with planning and drafting what you write.

Go to **Participating in Collaborative Discussions** in the **Speaking and Listening Studio** for more help.

ACADEMIC VOCABULARY
As you write and discuss what you learned from the argument, be sure to use the Academic Vocabulary words. Check off each of the words that you use.

- ❏ affect
- ❏ element
- ❏ ensure
- ❏ participate
- ❏ specify

Never Retreat   193

APPLY

WRITE AND DISCUSS

Write a Letter Point out that the list on p. 193 can serve as an outline for the students' letters. Each of the first three items can be one paragraph. Advise students to select events and details from "Never Retreat" before they begin to write their letters.

For **reading support** for students at varying proficiency levels, see the **Text X-Ray** on page 182D.

Group Discussion Remind students that when they do not understand a comment made by another group member, they should ask questions to clarify meaning. The process of asking and answering questions can help everyone understand a topic more clearly and can lead to new ideas.

RESPOND TO THE ESSENTIAL QUESTION

Allow time for students to add details from "Never Retreat" to their Unit 3 Response Logs.

Never Retreat   193

APPLY

CRITICAL VOCABULARY

answers:

1. *riding in a gasoline-powered vehicle, because gasoline fuels combustion, which powers the car*
2. *store shelves are empty, because scarcity means a shortage of something*
3. *irrigating crops, because aquifers contain water*
4. *changing your decision, because adaptability suggests the ability to change*

VOCABULARY STRATEGY:
Context Clues

Answers:

1. *make easy*
2. *future generations*
3. *withdrawn, silent*
4. *nauseated, developed headaches*

194   Unit 3

 RESPOND

WORD BANK
combustion
scarcity
aquifer
adaptability

CRITICAL VOCABULARY

Practice and Apply Choose the letter of the best answer to each question. Then, explain your response.

1. Which of the following involves **combustion**?
   a. squeezing into an over-crowded room
   b. riding in a gasoline-powered vehicle

2. Which of the following is an example of **scarcity**?
   a. store shelves filled with fruits and vegetables
   b. store shelves empty of fruits and vegetables

3. Which of the following would be the most likely use of an **aquifer**?
   a. irrigating crops
   b. heating homes

4. Which of the following is an example of **adaptability**?
   a. changing your decision after listening to a friend
   b. sticking with your decision no matter what

 Go to the **Vocabulary Studio** for more on context clues.

VOCABULARY STRATEGY: Context Clues

When you come across an unfamiliar word in your reading, look for **context clues.** These clues—found in surrounding words, phrases, or sentences—can help you figure out the word's meaning. In this example, the author provided a definition within the sentence itself.

> These proposals often favor *decentralization*—a more dispersed and rural society, with people growing more of their own food and generating more of their own power.

Practice and Apply Mark the word or phrase in each sentence that defines the boldfaced word. Then, use the boldfaced word in a sentence of your own.

1. The state set up a new website to **facilitate,** or make easy, the registration of first-time voters before Election Day.

2. The victims' names are inscribed on the wall so that they will be remembered by **posterity**—that is, by future generations.

3. At her new school, Riya was **reticent,** withdrawn, and silent even when classmates invited her to join in their activities.

4. The leaks from the gas tanks spread **noxious** fumes that caused residents to become nauseated and develop headaches.

194   Unit 3

 ENGLISH LEARNER SUPPORT

Vocabulary Strategy Give students additional practice in determining the meaning of unfamiliar words by using context clues. Direct students to the following words in "Never Retreat: *windfall* (paragraph 4), *dispersed* (paragraph 9), *rationed* (paragraph 12), and *interglacial* (paragraph 13). Have pairs of students use context clues to determine the meaning of these words. Tell them to confirm their definitions by looking up each word in a dictionary.
MODERATE/LIGHT

LANGUAGE CONVENTIONS: Conjunctions and Complex Sentences

A **conjunction** is a word that joins words or word groups. **Correlative conjunctions** are used as a pair to join words or word groups used the same way in a sentence. Common correlative conjunctions are *either / or*, *neither / nor*, and *both / and*, as in this example from the selection:

> The call "Never retreat" comes from us <u>both</u> as consumers <u>and</u> [as] breadwinners.

Subordinating conjunctions, such as *although*, *after*, and *because*, are used in complex sentences to introduce clauses that cannot stand by themselves as complete sentences. A **complex sentence** expresses two or more related ideas and shows that one idea is more important than the others. The more important idea in a complex sentence appears in an **independent clause,** which can stand alone as a sentence. The other clause (or clauses) in a complex sentence is the **subordinate clause.** It is less important and cannot stand alone as a sentence. These type of clause is a **sentence fragments,** or group of words that is only part of a sentence because it does not express a complete thought and may be confusing to a reader or listener. However, a subordinate clause still adds key information to a sentence.

Subordinate clauses often answer questions such as *How? When? Where? Why? To what degree? Under what condition?* In the example sentence below, the subordinating conjunction *because* joins the independent clause and the subordinate clause:

Question: *Why did coal become a popular fuel?*
Answer: <u>Coal became popular</u> **because** <u>it was plentiful and cheap.</u>
   independent clause   subordinate clause

In the following example, notice that because the subordinate clause comes before the independent clause, it is set off by a comma.

Question: *When did gasoline become useful?*
Answer: **After** <u>the combustion engine was invented</u>, <u>gasoline became very useful.</u>

Practice and Apply Write your own sentences using subordinating conjunctions to create complex sentences and correlative conjunctions to join words that are used the same way. Base your sentences on "Never Retreat" or another topic. Share your sentences with a partner. Make sure that you have avoided writing confusing sentence fragments that do not express complete thoughts. Discuss how different sentence constructions help readers and listeners understand your ideas and add interest to your writing.

Go to **Conjunctions and Interjections** in the **Grammar Studio** for more help.

Never Retreat 195

APPLY

LANGUAGE CONVENTIONS: Conjunctions and Complex Sentences

Review the information about subordinating and correlative conjunctions with students. Explain that in contrast to subordinating conjunctions, correlative conjunctions are pairs of conjunctions that connect words, phrases, or clauses. Emphasize that correlative conjunctions link two ideas of similar weight, while subordinating conjunctives link two ideas of different weight (one idea is central, the other is lesser). Discuss the example of correlative conjunctions excerpted from the text.

Explain to students that using subordinating conjunctions to create complex sentences will help them clarify ideas and vary their sentence structure.

Practice and Apply Have partners discuss how the complex sentences clarify meaning. *(Students' sentences will vary.)*

ENGLISH LEARNER SUPPORT

Language Conventions Tell students that an easy way of remembering the seven coordinating conjunctions is the acronym FANBOYS: *for, and, nor, but, or, yet, so*. Use the supports with students at varying proficiency levels:

- Have students work in groups to find subordinating conjunctions in "Never Retreat."
  SUBSTANTIAL
- Have students work with partners to write five original sentences using the FANBOYS.
  MODERATE
- Ask students to write a brief paragraph about their own energy consumption, using at least three properly punctuated complex sentences. **LIGHT**

PLAN

MENTOR TEXT
MISSISSIPPI SOLO
Memoir by Eddy Harris

This memoir serves as a **mentor text**, a model for students to follow when they come to the Unit 3 Writing Task: Write a Personal Narrative.

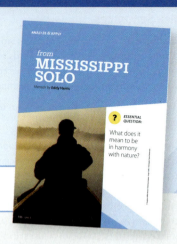

GENRE ELEMENTS
MEMOIR

Explain to students that a **memoir** is a historical narrative derived from the personal experiences and unique knowledge of the author. Memoirs often have a conversational, even confidential style. They have become more common and popular than **biographies** and **autobiographies**. An autobiography is the story of a person's life by that person. Biographies tell the story of an individual based on verifiable facts, tend to rely heavily on research, and usually stick to a chronology of events. Memoirs can rely on the author's diaries, notes, recordings, memories, and outside sources; they can include the author's opinions, and impressions of the events discussed.

LEARNING OBJECTIVES

- Read and analyze the memoir literary form.
- Research the Mississippi River.
- Write a literary analysis and create a podcast.
- Analyze the text: cite evidence, interpret information, evaluate literary devices, and author's craft.
- Use consistent verb tenses when writing.
- Make good use of reference aids, such as dictionaries.
- **Language** Discuss a passage that uses figurative language.

TEXT COMPLEXITY

Quantitative Measures	Mississippi Solo	Lexile: 830L
Qualitative Measures	**Ideas Presented** Mostly explicit, but moves into some implied meaning	
	Structure Used Clear, chronological, and conventional	
	Language Used Mostly explicit, with some figurative language	
	Knowledge Required Requires no special knowledge	

PLAN

Online Ed

RESOURCES

- Unit 3 Response Log
- 🔊 Selection Audio
- Text in FOCUS: Visualizing
- Close Read Screencasts: Modeled Discussions
- Reading Studio: Notice & Note
- Writing Studio: Writing Informative Texts
- Speaking and Listening Studio: Using Media in a Presentation
- Vocabulary Studio: Reference Resources
- Grammar Studio: Module 9: Lesson 4: Using Verb Tenses Consistently
- "Mississippi Solo" Selection Test

SUMMARIES

English

In *Mississippi Solo*, Eddy Harris experiences the natural world in a way that most urban people never do. Exploring the Mississippi River alone in a canoe, Harris finds himself communing with nature in a way that changes his perspective on the world. In this short excerpt, he confronts both the quiet beauty and the volatile unpredictability of the waterway he travels. After battling a passing storm, he's left with a strange serenity that represents a renewed closeness with nature, and a deeper understanding of himself.

Spanish

En *Mississippi Solo*, Eddy Harris experimenta el mundo natural de una manera en que la mayoría de las personas urbanas nunca pueden. Explorando el Río Mississippi cuando joven y por sí solo, en una canoa, Harris se encuentra a sí mismo comunicándose con las tierras salvajes americanas de una manera que cambia su perspectiva del mundo. En este corto pasaje, confronta la tranquila belleza y la imprevisibilidad volátil de las aguas que surca. Después de batallar con una tormenta pasajera, se queda con la extraña serenidad que parece representar una nueva cercanía con la naturaleza.

SMALL-GROUP OPTIONS

Have students work in small groups to read and discuss the selection.

Send a Problem

- Present a question about Eddy Harris's trip on the Mississippi. For example: Is this a trip that most people could do alone? Why or why not?
- Call upon partners to respond. Partners may confer for up to ten seconds before responding.
- If the students do not know the answer within ten seconds, they "send" it by repeating the full question to another pair.
- Monitor the routine and call on partners or change the question at any time. (For example: *What would you like to you learn about before going on a trip on a powerful unpredictable river like the Mississippi?*)

Think-Pair-Share

- After students have read and analyzed "Mississippi Solo," pose this question: What would be the most challenging thing about taking a solo trip down the Mississippi? Why? (If necessary give examples, e.g., fear, loneliness, and danger)
- Have students think about the question individually and take notes.
- Then, have pairs discuss their ideas about the question.
- Finally, ask pairs to share their responses with the class.

from Mississippi Solo

PLAN

 Text X-Ray: English Learner Support
for *Mississippi Solo*

Use the Text X-Ray and the supports and scaffolds in the Teacher's Edition to help guide students at different proficiency levels through the selection.

INTRODUCE THE SELECTION
DISCUSS DESCRIPTIVE LANGUAGE

Tell students that a good way to learn and understand figurative language is to practice using it themselves. Similes, metaphors, and personification all transform ordinary language to make it more interesting.

- Similes compare two ideas, objects, or experiences using the words *like* or *as*, e.g., *The tree hit our car* like *a hammer. The boat is big* as *a house.*
- Metaphors use words or phrases that ordinarily identify one thing, but are used to identify something else: the result is a comparison or symbol. Metaphors do not use *like* or *as*, e.g., "All the world's a stage."
- Personification gives human characteristics to an animal or object, e.g., *The tree's thick branches said, "Don't be afraid, I will hold you."*

Model using sentence frames to complete a few similes. Then, have small groups use "like a" and "as a" frames to compete with one another in creating the most amusing, dramatic, or the greatest number of similes. For example: _ like a/as____. *She sang* like a *bird. His explanation was clear* as *mud*.

CULTURAL REFERENCES

The following words and phrases may be unfamiliar to students:

- *If you only get sunshine ... desert.* (paragraph 1): a way of saying that too much of a good thing can be harmful
- *idle chatter* (paragraph 2): casual, empty talk
- *jabbers away* (paragraph 2): nonstop talking
- *swirls like batter in a bowl* (paragraph 5): clouds can look very much like thick batter that has recently been mixed; clouds and batter can both have the same spiral shape.
- *army scouts* (paragraph 6): soldiers who move ahead of their army to find out about anything important
- *fishing rods* (paragraph 8): long poles used to catch fish
- *stern (paragraph 10):* the back of a boat

LISTENING

Understand Figurative Language

Draw students' attention to the similes in paragraph 8. Explain that memoirs generally make use of figurative language. If they are not overused, similes and metaphors can communicate the unique qualities of remembered thoughts and events.

Have students listen as you read aloud paragraph 8. Use the following supports with students at varying proficiency levels. Explain the meaning of "sky split open," and lightning.

- Display images and use gestures to indicate trees bent in high winds, and bent fishing rods. Have students echo read the sentences with you. Point out the simile in "The tips . . . big one." Have students identify what is happening in this paragraph. Ask: *Is this a dangerous storm? (yes)* Have them repeat the simile "like the tide" with you. Display images of an ocean's tide coming in, and have them compare it to the picture on page 210. **SUBSTANTIAL/MODERATE**
- Pair students and have them each identify the two similes and the dramatic, descriptive language (words such as *splintery* and *swooshed*). Ask students to discuss the ways in which the figurative language works to heighten the dramatic tension. **LIGHT**

196C Unit 3

PLAN

SPEAKING

Speak Expressively

Draw attention to paragraphs 8–10. Explain to students that speaking with expressive intonation, proper pacing, and fluency is especially important when using figurative language.

Use the following supports with students at varying proficiency levels:

- Reread paragraph 8 aloud. Display an image (from online or elsewhere) of a *splintery* flash of lightning. Reread the sentence that features lightning. Have students repeat it and then the word *splintery* after you. Emphasize the short vowel *i*. Say: Splintery means, "thin, small." Repeat for *crackle, swooshed,* and *bucketfuls*. **SUBSTANTIAL/MODERATE**
- Pair students and have them read paragraph 11 to each other. Ask them to take note of each other's rate, pronunciation, and expressiveness as they read. Have students politely give each other feedback. Circulate among them to help with words, such as *ethereal*. **LIGHT**

READING

Identify Verb Tenses and Unfamiliar Vocabulary

Remind students that verb tenses (e.g., past, and future) must remain consistent. If tenses change in the middle of a sentence, there must be a clear stylistic reason for doing so or readers will be confused.

Use the following supports with students at varying proficiency levels:

- Read paragraph 11 aloud once, then have students echo read with you. Repeat what you did with paragraph 8 for paragraph 11; guide students to internalize vocabulary in context through decoding and defining unfamiliar words, such as *ethereal*. Then, say: *This is a memoir. It comes from the author's memory.* Ask: *Is this happening now, or did it happen in the past?* (the past) **SUBSTANTIAL**
- Ask: *What verb tense is used throughout most of paragraph 11?* (mostly past tense) *Why is it in the past tense?* (It's a memoir.) *Would it make sense to change tenses?* (no) *Why?* **MODERATE**
- Have students work in pairs or small groups to read paragraphs 10-12, and then answer the following questions: *Why does the author use the past tense? How is it useful and/or effective to use (mostly) the past tense in a story like this one?* Have them share their answers with the class. **LIGHT**

WRITING

Write a Literary Analysis of Figurative Language

Work with students to begin a response to the writing assignment on page 205.

Use the following supports with students at varying proficiency levels:

- Decode and define *personification* using paragraph 4 as an example. Guide students in finding more examples of figurative language. Help them combine words and images they've gathered to create a response to the assignment. **SUBSTANTIAL/MODERATE**
- Put students in groups, and have them discuss the ways in which the personification of the river in paragraph 4 affects the story. Ask: *How would the story be different if the river had not "spoken" to Eddy Harris?* Have them write a short analysis of how the story would be different if the author didn't treat the river as a living companion on his journey. *(Answers will vary.)* **LIGHT**

from Mississippi Solo

TEACH

? Connect to the ESSENTIAL QUESTION

Mississippi Solo tells the story of a man's encounter with the natural world. The excerpt examines the mental and emotional connection the author feels with the beauty and volatility of the Mississippi River, and how this experience changes his worldview.

MENTOR TEXT

At the end of the unit, students will be asked to write a personal narrative. *Mississippi Solo* will serve as an example of writing about a personal experience.

ANALYZE & APPLY

from MISSISSIPPI SOLO

Memoir by **Eddy Harris**

? ESSENTIAL QUESTION:

What does it mean to be in harmony with nature?

LEARNING MINDSET

Effort Remind students that effort can be as important as achievement and is necessary for growth, even when we don't get the result we want. We may also end up with a different—even more valuable--result than the one we expected. Hard work, regardless of whether we struggle or stumble along the way, will lead to success. Engaging with challenges in life, such as reading difficult books or newspapers, is a deeply fulfilling experience.

GET READY

QUICK START

How connected to nature do you feel? Mark this scale with an X to indicate your connection. Compare your response with the response of at least one classmate.

ANALYZE MEMOIR

A **memoir** is a form of autobiographical writing in which the author shares his or her personal experiences and observations related to significant events and people. Memoirs are often written in the first person. Authors of memoirs often do the following:

- "talk" to readers, using informal language and sharing personal feelings
- recall actual events and emphasize their reactions to them
- show how the experiences affected their attitudes and lives

GENRE ELEMENTS: MEMOIR
- focuses on past events that are meaningful to the author
- reveals the author's thoughts and feelings about past events
- is told from the first-person point of view, with pronouns such as *I*, *me*, and *my*
- may address readers as "you," as if conversing with them

ANALYZE FIGURATIVE LANGUAGE

Figurative language is an imaginative use of words to express ideas that are not literally true but that convey meaningful and sometimes emotional ideas. Compare these common kinds of figurative language.

TYPE OF FIGURATIVE LANGUAGE	EXAMPLE	EFFECT
simile: a comparison of two unlike things using the words *like* or *as*	"Clouds rolled overhead in wild swirls like batter in a bowl." (paragraph 5)	vivid image of a changing sky
metaphor: a comparison of two unlike things that have qualities in common, without using *like* or *as*	". . . the far curtain of the insulated air, . . ." (paragraph 5)	warmth that is trapped inside a barrier
personification: the giving of human qualities to an animal, an object, or an idea	"The river was talking to me, . . ." (paragraph 2)	a feeling of connectedness

Analyzing figurative language can help you understand the author's experiences and feelings. This use of language can convey a mood or feeling, the author's voice and personality, and the tone, or the attitude that the author has about the events described in the memoir. Look for examples of figurative language as you read the excerpt from *Mississippi Solo*.

Mississippi Solo 197

TEACH

QUICK START

Take a moment to have students list and discuss fun or interesting outdoor activities with a partner. Get a discussion going between student pairs about hiking, skiing, camping, swimming, or going to parks in cities. Have them discuss any experience they've had outdoors that drew them closer to nature. Ask students to consider what effect this experience has had on their connections with nature. Urge students who have not had many outdoor experiences to be curious and ask questions of others.

ANALYZE MEMOIR

Assist students in grasping the basic elements of a memoir: first-person narrative, personal or conversational tone, and a focus on a personal experience and unique point of view.. Remind them that these elements can be used in a great range of other literary genres, but that the three together tend to appear in memoir. Discuss the differences between memoirs, autobiographies, and biographies. Encourage students to discuss problematic aspects of the memoir form. Readers often wonder: *How reliable is the narrator?*

ANALYZE FIGURATIVE LANGUAGE

Help students identify figurative language in any text by encouraging them to look for these details:
- the words *like* or *as*
- the use of unusual adjectives and adverbs
- language that induces very strong imagery in the mind
- comparisons of two disparate objects or ideas
- objects or animals that behave like human beings

from Mississippi Solo 197

TEACH

CRITICAL VOCABULARY

Encourage students to read all the sentences before deciding which word best completes each one. Remind them to look for context clues that match the meaning of each word.

Answers:

1. *insulate*
2. *ethereal*
3. *avalanche*
4. *splinter*

■ English Learner Support

Use Reference Resources Ask students to look up one Critical Vocabulary word in a dictionary, then use a thesaurus to find one of its synonyms. Challenge students to write one sentence for each word: two sentences in all. **LIGHT**

LANGUAGE CONVENTIONS

Discuss why it's important keep verb tenses consistent. Provide students with sentences that use inconsistent tenses, and then have them correct the tenses.

Read aloud the example sentences. Ask the class which statement sounds like something a person would more likely say in real life. Ask students why the verb tense in the second sentence is correct. (*It's correct because the tense makes it clear that the event has already happened, whereas the first sentence makes it unclear by implying present and past.*)

✏ ANNOTATION MODEL

Point out that students may follow this suggestion or use their own system for marking up the selection in their write-in text. They may want to color-code their annotations with highlighters. Notes in the margin may include questions about the text or topics they want to learn more about.

 GET READY

CRITICAL VOCABULARY

| avalanche | insulate | splinter | ethereal |

To see how many Critical Vocabulary words you already know, use them to complete the sentences.

1. You can stay warm in cold weather if you _____ yourself.
2. She has a(n) _____ voice, but the song she sang was powerful.
3. A(n) _____ can bury people under many feet of snow.
4. The mirror will _____ into many pieces if you drop it on the floor.

LANGUAGE CONVENTIONS

Consistent Verb Tenses In this lesson, you will learn why it is important to maintain the consistency of verb tenses in your writing. When writing about events, be careful not to change needlessly from one tense to another. (Sometimes there is a need—but the change has to make sense.)

INCONSISTENT: Rains **come** [present tense] and **poured** [past tense] down bucketfuls.

CONSISTENT: Rains **came** [past tense] and **poured** [past tense] down bucketfuls.

As you read the excerpt from *Mississippi Solo*, note the author's use of consistent verb tenses.

ANNOTATION MODEL   NOTICE & NOTE

As you read, note the author's use of figurative language. You also can mark up details that show characteristics of a memoir. In the model, you can see one reader's notes about the excerpt from *Mississippi Solo*.

3   . . . I didn't care about anything. The river kept me company and kept me satisfied. Nothing else mattered.

4   Then the river whispered, "Get ready. Get ready."

5   The day turned gray and strange. Clouds rolled overhead in wild swirls like batter in a bowl. I could see the rainstorm forming off in the distance but swirling rapidly to me like a dark gray avalanche.

The author is sharing his thoughts, not just facts about the event.

These comparisons are similes. They tell me that the storm probably will be fierce, powerful, and maybe even deadly.

198   Unit 3

BACKGROUND

Eddy Harris (b. 1956) is a writer, adventurer, and seeker who spent his early years in New York City before moving to St. Louis. His first published book, Mississippi Solo, chronicles the canoe trip he took down the entire length of the Mississippi River in the 1980s—a risky trip for which this city dweller was unprepared. Harris also has written about adventurous journeys in other southern regions and in Africa.

from MISSISSIPPI SOLO
Memoir by Eddy Harris

SETTING A PURPOSE

As you read, focus on how the author recounts a special moment from his life while he canoed by himself down the Mississippi River. What makes his experience so meaningful for him?

1   Too many marvelous days in a row and you begin to get used to it, to think that's the way it's supposed to be. Too many good days, too many bad days—you need some break in the monotony of one to appreciate the other. If you only get sunshine, someone said, you end up in a desert.

2   I guess I'd had enough hard days to last me for a while, enough scary times to be able to appreciate the peaceful, easy, glorious days. On the way to Natchez,[1] I had another one, and I took full advantage of it to do absolutely nothing. No singing, no thinking, no talking to myself. Just feeling. Watching the river, noticing the changes in color, seeing the way it rises and falls depending on the wind and on what lies on the river bed. Each change had something to say, and I listened to the river. The river was talking to me,

---
[1] **Natchez** (năch´ĭz): a city in southwest Mississippi on the Mississippi River.

Notice & Note

Use the side margins to notice and note signposts in the text.

ANALYZE MEMOIR
Annotate: Mark four places in paragraph 1 where the author seems to address readers.

Critique: How do you think this paragraph is meant to affect readers?

TEACH

ENGLISH LEARNER SUPPORT

Identify Similes Tell students to reread the two uses of the word *like* that appear at the very end of paragraph 2 ("and he feels **like** it" and "The river was **like** that to me. A comfortable buddy").

ASK STUDENTS to discuss which of the two uses of *like* is a simile. Have students get into pairs to discuss the reasons for their choice. *(The second use is a simile because it compares two things, a river and a comfortable buddy; the first is not a simile because even though it uses the word like it does not actually compare two people or things.)* **LIGHT**

ANALYZE FIGURATIVE LANGUAGE

Remind students that **personification** is the attribution of *any* human quality—not just voice—to *any* nonhuman entity—not just rivers or animals. (**Answer:** *By comparing it to a "favorite niece or nephew" and "a comfortable buddy," he emphasizes the close connection he feels to the Mississippi River.*)

CRITICAL VOCABULARY

avalanche: This word gives the reader both an image and a feeling of what the storm was like—sudden and intimidating.

ASK STUDENTS to describe what they think the writer felt at this time. *(Harris probably felt fear, insecurity, and helplessness in the face of such a sudden threat.)*

insulate: The air in this part of the river is oddly warmer than elsewhere, signaling to Harris that something is going on.

ASK STUDENTS why "insulated air" would make Harris rethink his strategy. *(The weather appears to be volatile and quickly changing, so Harris got the impression that he should prepare for the worst.)*

200 Unit 3

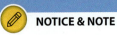

NOTICE & NOTE

ANALYZE FIGURATIVE LANGUAGE

Annotate: Mark examples of personification in paragraph 2.

Analyze: What point does the author make by comparing the river to these particular human beings?

avalanche
(ăv′ə-lănch′) *n.* An *avalanche* is a large mass of snow, ice, dirt, or rocks falling quickly down the side of a mountain.

insulate
(ĭn′sə-lāt′) *v.* When you *insulate* something, you prevent the passage of heat through it.

changing colors from puce[2] to brown to thick, murky green. Saying nothing. The idle chatter you get when you walk with your favorite niece or nephew going no place in particular with nothing special on your minds and the little kid just jabbers away because it's comfortable and he feels like it. The river was like that to me. A comfortable buddy sharing a lazy day.

3   Nothing else mattered then. Going someplace or not. Arriving in New Orleans or shooting past and landing in Brazil. I didn't care about anything. The river kept me company and kept me satisfied. Nothing else mattered.

4   Then the river whispered, "Get ready. Get ready."

5   The day turned gray and strange. Clouds rolled overhead in wild swirls like batter in a bowl. I could see the rainstorm forming off in the distance but swirling rapidly toward me like a dark gray **avalanche**. I felt the river dip down and up—a shallow dale[3] in the water. I passed from the cool moisture surrounding me and into a pocket of thin air hot and dry. It was as though a gap had opened in the clouds and the sun streamed through to boil the water and heat up this isolated patch of river a scant[4] thirty yards long. My first thought was to shed a shirt and stay cool, but when I passed through the far curtain of the **insulated** air, I knew I had better do just the opposite. I drifted and donned my yellow rain suit and hood. The sky above grew serious and advanced in my direction with the speed of a hurricane. Looking for a place to land, I scanned the shore. There was no shore. Only trees. Because of the heavy rains and high water, the shore had disappeared, and the new shoreline of solid earth had been pushed back through the trees and beyond the woods. How far beyond, I couldn't tell. I looked across to the other side of the river half a mile away. No way could I have made it over there. Halfway across and the wind would have kicked up and trapped me in the middle.

6   The leading edge of the storm came, and the first sprinkles passed over like army scouts. The wooded area lasted only another hundred yards or so, and I thought I could easily get there before the rains arrived. I could then turn left and find ground to pull out and wait out the storm. But the voice of the river came out and spoke to me teasingly but with a chill of seriousness down my spine. I could have ignored it, but as if reading my thoughts and not wanting me to fight it, the river

---

[2] **puce** (pyo͞os): purplish brown.
[3] **dale:** valley.
[4] **scant:** just short of.

200 Unit 3

CLOSE READ SCREENCAST

Modeled Discussion Have students click the Close-Read icon in their eBook to access a screencast in which readers discuss and annotate the following key passage:

"The river was like that to me . . . like batter in a bowl" (paragraph 2)

As a class, view and discuss the video. Then have students pair up to do an independent close read of paragraph 11. Students can record their answers on the Close Read Practice PDF.

 Close Read Practice PDF

NOTICE & NOTE

grabbed the end of the canoe and turned me toward the trees. I thought I was looking for land. I wasn't. I was looking for shelter.

7   The urge to get into the trees came on me quite suddenly and really without thought or effort on my part. Almost an instinct.

8   No sooner had I ducked into the trees than the sky split open with a loud crash and a **splintery** crackle of lightning. I was not going to make it through the trees. The wind came in at hurricane strength. The tips of the trees bent way over and aimed toward the ground, like fishing rods hooked on a big one. Water flooded like the tide rushing upstream. The trees swooshed loudly as the leaves and branches brushed hard together. Branches fell. Rains came and poured down bucketfuls.

9   The trees were tall and no more than three feet around. I maneuvered the canoe as best I could in the wind and rushing water, turned it to face upstream, and kept my back to the rain,

splinter
(splĭn´tər) v. To *splinter* means to break up into sharp, thin pieces.

LANGUAGE CONVENTIONS
Annotate: Mark the past-tense verbs in the final three sentences of paragraph 8.
Evaluate: Why is it important for all of these verbs to be in the past tense?

Mississippi Solo   201

TEACH

✏️ LANGUAGE CONVENTIONS

Remind students that **verb tense** will change according to what the author is saying. For sentences that describe events that occur in the same time frame, tense should remain consistent; if you say, *I will be tired if I didn't go home*, people will be confused. (**Answer:** *It is consistent for these verbs to be past tense because they describe details of an event that happened in the past.*)

English Learner Support

Identify the Past Tense Help students find the verbs *were, maneuvered, slanted,* and *reached* in paragraph 9. Ask when they believe the action is taking place—in past, present, or future? (*The words are all past tense so the action must take place in the past.*) Ask students to change the verb tense to make it sound as though a reporter is on the scene describing what is going on in the present tense. (*The trees are tall and no more than three feet around. I am maneuvering the canoe as best I can in the wind and rushing water, turning it to face upstream, and keeping my back to the rain, which is slanting in at a sharp angle. I am reaching out for the sturdiest tree I can get my arms around and I am holding on.*)
MODERATE

📖 For **listening, reading,** and **support** for students at varying proficiency levels, see the **Text X-Ray** on pages 196C–196D.

APPLYING ACADEMIC VOCABULARY

❑ affect   ❑ element   ☑ ensure   ☑ participate   ☑ specify

Write and Discuss Have students turn to a partner to discuss the following questions. Guide students to include the Academic Vocabulary words *ensure, participate,* and *specify* in their responses. Ask volunteers to share their responses with the class.

- Does Harris try to **ensure** his safety in the dangerous situation he's in?
- Is a long canoe ride on the Mississippi a trip something you would like to **participate** in?
- In this passage, does Harris **specify** exactly where he is going?

CRITICAL VOCABULARY

splinter: Sometimes turning a verb or noun—*splinter*—into an adjective—*splintery*—is a creative way of producing striking images.

ASK STUDENTS whether "splintery crackle of lightning" is a metaphor and whether the wording is effective. (*Yes it is a metaphor that likens the sound of lightning to the sound of wood splitting apart. It is effective because it produces a strong and memorable image in the mind.*)

from Mississippi Solo   **201**

TEACH

✏️ ANALYZE MEMOIR

Remind students that the use of **I-me-my pronouns** indicate who is speaking and when the focus has shifted. (**Answer:** *The comment is not about the storm itself but about his personal observations and feelings at that moment. It is one of the signs that this selection is a memoir.*)

🎬 TEXT IN FOCUS

Visualizing Have students view the **Text in Focus** video on this page of their ebook to learn how to visualize elements of a story. Then have students use **Text in Focus Practice** to apply what they have learned.

▶ CONTRASTS AND CONTRADICTIONS

Explain that **contrasts and contradictions** are a major part of the **memoir** genre. In fact, authors will often decide to compose a memoir in order to help themselves understand their own choices and behavior. To do this they will present their own contradictions honestly to the reader as a way of exploring their own identity and as a way of understanding human behavior.

Direct student attention to the use of the word *But* in the sixth sentence of the eleventh paragraph, which marks the moment when the contrast-and-contradiction turn begins. (Other words that may indicate a contrast and contradiction in a text include *yet, however, on the other hand,* and *by contrast.*) (**Answer:** *The author decides to stay out in the storm instead of continuing to try to find shelter.*)

Interpret: As he stays out in the storm, he feels "one with this river." The experience strengthens his bond with nature.

CRITICAL VOCABULARY

ethereal: Harris is unsure where the river's message came from, or even what the message was.

ASK STUDENTS whether they believe *ethereal* refers more to material things or to spiritual matters, like feelings and beliefs. (*It's clear from the passage that "ethereal" refers more to spiritual matters, at least for Harris, although ethereal could easily refer to "light and airy" materials like silk or cotton.*)

202 Unit 3

NOTICE & NOTE

ANALYZE MEMOIR

Annotate: In paragraph 11, mark what the author says he enjoyed.

Compare: How is this information different from details about the storm itself?

CONTRASTS AND CONTRADICTIONS

Notice & Note: Mark the author's action at the end of paragraph 11. How does the author's action contrast with what he had planned to do?

Interpret: How does his action affect his feelings about the river?

ethereal
(ĭ-thîr´ē-əl) *adj.* If something is *ethereal*, it is light and airy.

which slanted in at a sharp angle. I reached out for the sturdiest tree I could get my arms around and I held on.

10   Water everywhere.[5] The river sloshed over the side and into the canoe. I tried to keep the stern pointed right into the flow so the canoe could ride the waves, but it didn't work. The canoe was twisted about, and water poured over the side. The rain was heavier than any I had ever been in or seen before. It really was more like a tropical storm. The heavy winds, the amount of water, the warmth of the air, and the cold rain. Only my neck was exposed to the rain. When the rain hit my neck, it ran under the rain suit and very cold down my back.

11   The wind shifted as the storm came directly overhead. Water streamed straight down. I was drenched, and the canoe was filling up quickly. Anything in the canoe that could float was floating. If the rain continued for long or if the wind kept up strong and the rain kept spilling into the canoe, I would sink. But I was not worried, hardly more than concerned. In fact I enjoyed the feeling of the water all around me and on me, enveloping me like a cocoon, and despite the drama I felt no real threat. I was more amazed than anything, trying to analyze the voice I had heard or whatever instinct or intuition it was that urged me to park in these trees. It had been something so very definite that I could feel it and yet so **ethereal** that I could not put my finger on it. So I stopped trying and just sat there patiently waiting and hugging my tree. I was one with this river, and nothing could happen to me.

12   The storm slid forward, and the rain slanted in on my face. Then it moved on farther up the river to drench someone else. It was gone as suddenly as it had arisen. Only the trailing edge was left, a light rain that lasted almost until I reached Natchez.

---

[5] **Water everywhere:** The author is referring to the line "water, water, everywhere" from *The Rime of the Ancient Mariner,* a widely known poem about a sailor recounting supernatural events at sea.

202   Unit 3

WHEN STUDENTS STRUGGLE . . .

Genre Reformulation If students struggle to understand the story in the memoir genre, break it down with the genre reformulation strategy.

When students have finished reading, make a list on the board of the main events, ideas, and elements in the story. Then get student groups to cast those story elements into a new form—a rap song, poem, or song lyric. Urge students to be creative yet simple, and retell the story of *Mississippi Solo* in a fun, memorable way that anyone can understand and remember.

NOTICE & NOTE

TEACH

CHECK YOUR UNDERSTANDING

Have students answer the questions independently.

Answers:

1. A
2. H
3. D

If they answer any questions incorrectly, have them reread the text to confirm their understanding. Then they may proceed to ANALYZE THE TEXT on p. 204.

CHECK YOUR UNDERSTANDING

Answer these questions before moving on to the **Analyze the Text** section on the following page.

1. The simile used at the beginning of paragraph 6, which compares the first sprinkles of rain to army scouts, conveys the idea that —

   A something powerful is about to happen
   B the author will be safe during the storm
   C the storm may be less severe than expected
   D it is too late for the author to seek shelter

2. Which idea is supported most strongly by details throughout the selection?

   F People who do not prepare for every situation are liable to get into trouble.
   G Survival during natural disasters depends on having both experience and good equipment.
   H A connection with nature can help someone make good decisions in a dangerous situation.
   J Traveling alone is risky but rarely results in a bad outcome.

3. Why is the author no longer afraid as he hugs a tree during the most intense part of the storm?

   A He feels sure that he will be rescued after the storm has passed.
   B He has accepted that he probably will be stranded on the shore.
   C He believes that his knowledge of the river has kept him safe.
   D He trusts that listening to the river is always the right decision.

Mississippi Solo 203

ENGLISH LEARNER SUPPORT

Oral Assessment Use the following questions to assess students' comprehension and speaking skills:

1. Read the following from paragraph 11: "I was drenched, and the canoe was filling up quickly. Anything in the canoe that could float was floating." What is filling up the canoe? *(water)*

2. Do you think the author feels a connection with the river? Why? *("I was one with this river, and nothing could happen to me." This sentence exemplifies the author's connection with the river.)*

3. How can you change the following sentence from paragraph 5 into a clear simile: I felt the river dip down and up—a shallow dale in the water. Hint: a dale is a valley on land—the opposite of water. Similes compare, using like or as. *(I felt the river dip down and up like a shallow dale in the water)* **MODERATE/LIGHT**

from Mississippi Solo **203**

APPLY

ANALYZE THE TEXT

Possible answers:

1. **DOK 3:** *The author presents himself as friendly. He shares observations and feelings, not just the facts. He addresses readers as "you" as he makes remarks about having talkative young family members. His mix of complete sentences and fragments suggests the conversational style associated with memoirs.*

2. **DOK 2:** *The paragraphs suggest that the author looks for opportunities to be in nature. Supporting details include "able to appreciate the peaceful, easy, glorious days," references to watching and listening to the river, and calling the river "a comfortable buddy."*

3. **DOK 2:** *In paragraph 4, the river's whispering of "Get ready" signals a turning point. Up till then, the author is enjoying a lazy day on the river. Paragraph 5 begins with "The day turned gray and strange," a definite and dramatic change that drives the rest of the selection.*

4. **DOK 4:** *Answers will vary, but students will find examples that effectively create a mood of suspense. These include a rainstorm "swirling rapidly toward me like a dark gray avalanche" (paragraph 5) and "trees bent way over and aimed toward the ground, like fishing rods hooked on a big one" (paragraph 8).*

5. **DOK 4:** *Most people would be very frightened in that situation. The author expresses a lack of worry, an actual sense of enjoyment of the storm, and patience as he waits for the storm to move away.*

RESEARCH

Point out to students that they should confirm any information they find online by cross-checking with other reputable websites and with books from the library.

Connect Students will find that the Mississippi River serves more than one community or one country, and runs longer than the length of the United States, north to south. Encourage them to appreciate the great risk that Eddy Harris took in traveling the entire distance in a canoe.

RESPOND

ANALYZE THE TEXT

Support your responses with evidence from the text. NOTEBOOK

1. **Cite Evidence** Reread paragraph 2. What is it about the author's way of writing that identifies the text as a memoir?

2. **Interpret** What does the author reveal about himself in paragraphs 1–3? What details support the ideas the author is trying to express?

3. **Interpret** Why could paragraph 4 be said to be a turning point in this selection?

4. **Evaluate** How effectively does the author use figures of speech to convey the mood of suspense connected to his experience during the storm? Explain.

5. **Notice & Note** Reread paragraphs 10–11. How do the author's thoughts and feelings during this experience contradict what you think most people would think and feel if they faced the same?

RESEARCH TIP
The most effective search terms are very specific. Along with the river's name, you will want to include a word such as *history* or *characteristics* to make sure that you locate the most relevant information.

RESEARCH

The Mississippi River has inspired many American writers and travelers, including Eddy Harris. With a partner, research why the river has been important to so many people. Use these questions and develop your own; then record what you learn in the chart.

QUESTION	ANSWER
Why is the Mississippi River important to people living along its banks?	Many settlements along the Mississippi River's banks depend on the river for their livelihood. The river provides the water supply for more than 50 cities.
Why do people around the world depend on the Mississippi River?	Most of the U.S. exports in agricultural products and livestock are produced in the Mississippi River basin. People in the United States and around the world depend on the river to bring goods to ports in the US and the Gulf of Mexico
How does the Mississippi River compare to other rivers in the US and around the world?	The Mississippi River is the fourth-largest river in the world, and the longest river in the United States, flowing for 2,350 miles through the continent. At its widest point, it is 11 miles from one bank to the other

Extend How would you present the information you've learned about the Mississippi River in a video? With a partner, discuss ways you could use maps, other visuals, and perhaps filmed interviews to share what you have found most interesting during your research.

LEARNING MINDSET

Try Again Everyone makes mistakes. Make it a goal for students to embrace and learn from mistakes rather than trying to avoid them. The classroom should be risk free for students, a place where they can always try again in a different way. Remind students that no person ever achieved anything important without first making mistakes along the way. Falling down and getting up to try again is what helps students learn and strengthen their confidence for future challenges.

RESPOND

CREATE AND PRESENT

Write a Literary Analysis Look back through the excerpt from *Mississippi Solo* to list examples of how Eddy Harris uses similes and personifies the river. Focusing on examples from your list, write a two- to four-paragraph literary analysis that explains how Harris uses figurative language in this memoir.

- ❏ Introduce the topic and express a controlling idea about the use of figurative language in the memoir.
- ❏ Then, identify specific examples of each type of figurative language.
- ❏ Explain the meaning of each example and the way in which the example contributes to key ideas in the memoir.
- ❏ In your final paragraph, draw a general conclusion about the topic.

Produce a Podcast Work with a partner to create a podcast critique of this excerpt from *Mississippi Solo*.

- ❏ With your partner, review your literary analyses. Decide which parts you wish to record in the form of a conversation about the selection.
- ❏ Decide when each of you will speak and how you will connect your thoughts. Demonstrate that you understand the selection.
- ❏ Before you record your podcast, practice. You and your partner should consider your speaking rate, volume, and enunciation—but make it sound like a conversation, too.

 Go to **Writing Informative Texts** in the **Writing Studio** to learn more.

 Go to **Using Media in a Presentation** in the **Speaking and Listening Studio** for help.

RESPOND TO THE ESSENTIAL QUESTION

 What does it mean to be in harmony with nature?

Gather Information Review your annotations and notes on the excerpt from *Mississippi Solo*. Then, add relevant details to your Response Log. As you determine which information to include, think about:

- experiences—both good and bad—that can occur in nature
- how we can learn from experiences in nature
- how being connected to nature influences the way we live.

At the end of the unit, use your notes to write a personal narrative.

ACADEMIC VOCABULARY

As you write and discuss what you learned from the memoir, be sure to use the Academic Vocabulary words. Check off each of the words that you use.

- ❏ affect
- ❏ element
- ❏ ensure
- ❏ participate
- ❏ specify

Mississippi Solo   205

APPLY

CREATE AND PRESENT

Write a Literary Analysis Point out to students that they may make use of the metaphors, similes, or personifications already discussed in this lesson (paragraphs 2 and 5).

 For **writing support** for students at varying proficiency levels, see the **Text X-Ray** on page 196D.

Produce a Podcast Podcasts are audio or video episodes that exist in a series and often address a particular subject. People create podcasts that are as personal as memoirs or as impersonal as news delivered on technical subjects. In the planning stages, make sure students find strong controlling ideas and edit their scripts carefully for the time limit they have set for their podcasts. Remind them that what sounds good on paper, doesn't always sound good when spoken aloud. Have them practice reciting their lines enough times to feel comfortable before recording. The recording will then sound more natural and less "rehearsed." If they do get stage fright, tell them that even celebrities sometimes feel nervous before performing and that it's perfectly normal.

RESPOND TO THE ESSENTIAL QUESTION

Allow time for students to add details from *Mississippi Solo* to their Unit 3 Response Logs.

from *Mississippi Solo*   205

APPLY

CRITICAL VOCABULARY

Answers:

1. . . . *an earthquake shook the mountain.*
2. . . . *cold temperatures.*
3. . . . *the wind or perhaps lightning causes the tree to break into pieces.*
4. . . . *the person has a delicate, otherworldly "look."*

VOCABULARY STRATEGY:
Reference Resources

Answers:

Related forms of *maneuvered* are *maneuvers, maneuvering,* and *maneuverability.* Synonyms for the verb *maneuver* include *move, turn,* and *steer.* In the sentence, the author is trying to change the direction of the canoe so it will face upstream. Rewrite: *I steered the canoe as best I could in the wind and rushing water, turned it to face upstream, and kept my back to the rain.* . . .

 **RESPOND**

WORD BANK
avalanche
insulate
splinter
ethereal

 Go to the **Vocabulary Stud**io for more on reference resources.

CRITICAL VOCABULARY

Practice and Apply Complete each sentence to show that you understand the meaning of the Critical Vocabulary word.

1. An **avalanche** was triggered when . . .
2. A layer of down helps **insulate** birds from . . .
3. A tree can **splinter** during a storm because . . .
4. A person's appearance can be called **ethereal** when . . .

VOCABULARY STRATEGY:
Reference Resources

A **dictionary** is a resource for those who are checking word meanings and expanding their vocabulary. The searching and browsing methods differ for print and digital dictionaries, but users can find the same basic information about each entry word.

- pronunciation and syllabication
- part of speech label
- one or more definitions
- word origins

Dictionary Entry
mo·not·o·ny (mə-nŏt′n-ē) *n.* **1.** Uniformity or lack of variation in pitch, intonation, or inflection. **2.** Tedious sameness or repetitiousness. [Greek *monotonos,* monotonous; see MONOTONOUS.]

Synonyms are words with similar meanings. The dictionary entry for *monotony* includes some synonyms within the definitions: *uniformity, sameness,* and *repetitiveness.* Some dictionaries provide a list of synonyms after an entry. A **thesaurus** is a reference aid that lists synonyms. Writers can use a print or digital thesaurus to help find the exact word they need.

Thesaurus Entry
monotony, *n.* boredom, tedium, uniformity, sameness, unchangeableness, dullness, repetitiveness

Practice and Apply Find the sentence with the word *maneuvered* in paragraph 9 of the excerpt from *Mississippi Solo*. Look up the word in a dictionary and a thesaurus. Check its meaning and look for synonyms and related forms of the word. Use your own words to tell what the sentence containing *maneuvered* means. Then revise the sentence using an appropriate synonym.

206 Unit 3

ENGLISH LEARNER SUPPORT

Use Vocabulary Strategies Encourage students to keep personal dictionaries where they can record the definitions of new words. If possible, have some students make audio books and/or videos to help with pronunciation. Have students enter new or interesting words in their books as they learn them. Model noting the context, i.e., where the word is located in a text, its definition, and examples of how to use the word in sentences. **LIGHT**

RESPOND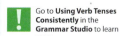

APPLY

LANGUAGE CONVENTIONS: Consistent Verb Tenses

In your writing, use **consistent verb tenses** to express your meaning exactly. The tense of a verb indicates the time of an action or a state of being. In general, use the past tense to tell about events in the past and the present tense to tell about current events.

INCORRECT: The sky above me **grew** [past tense] serious and **advances** [present tense] in my direction with the speed of a hurricane.
CORRECT: The sky above me **grew** serious and **advanced** in my direction with the speed of a hurricane. [consistent past tense]

Note the exceptions in these examples from "Mississippi Solo":

- You may use the present tense to set the scene for a "past" story as you talk to readers in the present.

  Too many good days, too many bad days—you <u>need</u> some break in the monotony. . . .

- You may use the present tense to state things that are always true.

  Watching the river, . . . seeing the way it <u>rises</u> and <u>falls</u> depending on the wind and on what <u>lies</u> on the river bed.

- You should use the past perfect tense (with *had* as the helping verb) to show that some events happened before other past-tense events.

  The rain was heavier than any I <u>had</u> ever <u>been</u> in or [had] <u>seen</u> before.

Practice and Apply Six of the boldfaced verbs in the following paragraph show errors in consistent verb tense. Think about what the writer probably means:
- Does the writer set a scene?
- Does the writer mention something that is always true?
- Does the writer refer to an event that happened before a past-tense event?

Also look for places where both verbs need to be in the past tense but are not. Then revise the paragraph, correcting the errors in verb tense.

    If you **are** like me, you **knew** how hard it **is** to watch a movie when the person with you **kept** talking. Just last week, my cousin and I **watch** an exciting wilderness adventure movie together. I would like to say that I **enjoy** that movie, but my cousin's chatter **made** it impossible. He **kept** talking about what **happened** in an earlier scene. I **survived** the experience, but I **think** that it will be some time before I **invited** him to watch with me again.

Go to **Using Verb Tenses Consistently** in the **Grammar Studio** to learn more.

Mississippi Solo 207

LANGUAGE CONVENTIONS: Consistent Verb Tenses

Review what students have learned about verb tense and consistency. Remind them that tense generally remains consistent throughout a single sentence, although there are important exceptions to this rule. Tenses need to be used with a keen eye for meaning and intent. Remind students that many adults and professional writers still make mistakes when it comes to verb tense, so no one should feel embarrassed about making a mistake.

Have students share why using consistent tenses is important. Present a sentence that shows inconsistent use of tense and have students guide you in correcting it. Start a game in which small groups create sentences with incorrect use of tenses and pass them on to other groups to correct.

Practice and Apply Before giving the answers, put students into groups to discuss their verb changes in the test paragraph:

If you **are** like me, you <u>**know**</u> how hard it **is** to watch a movie when the person with you <u>**keeps**</u> talking. Just last week, my cousin and I <u>**watched**</u> an exciting wilderness adventure movie together. I would like to say that I <u>**enjoyed**</u> that movie, but my cousin's chatter **made** it impossible. He **kept** talking about what <u>**had happened**</u> in an earlier scene. I **survived** the experience, but I **think** that it will be some time before I <u>**invite**</u> him to watch with me again.

Transfer Note Verbs do not change form in the past tense in Hmong, Korean, and Vietnamese. Help Vietnamese students and others practice using the past tense by supplying sentences to convert to the simple past (verb + *ed*). For example, I walk. (*I walked.*), They play. (*They played.*) After students gain mastery, move on to more challenging sentence types.

 ENGLISH LEARNER SUPPORT

Reinforce Language Conventions Use the following supports with students at varying proficiency levels:

- Read the following frame sentences aloud and ask students to pick the verb in the correct tense. I *(watch/watched)* the game yesterday. I *(see/saw)* that the river was dangerous. I *(was/am)* going to school tomorrow. **SUBSTANTIAL**

- Have students compose past-tense sentences about being in the wilderness using the appropriate conjugations of the verbs *walk, look, touch,* and *climb*. **MODERATE**

- Pair students of varied English proficiency, and have them work together to compose the first paragraph of a memoir about visiting a new place. Have them make use of past and present tenses. Circulate to assist where needed. **LIGHT**

from *Mississippi Solo* 207

PLAN

THE DROUGHT
Poem by Amy Helfrich

GENRE ELEMENTS
POETRY
Remind students that **poetry** conveys emotions, ideas, and stories using particular styles and rhythms. The **sonnet** is a form of poetry that always has 14 lines and expresses an idea in four parts. In "The Drought," a farmer is described in the first four lines, his land in the next four lines, and their common problem—drought—occupies the four lines that follow. The two lines at the end offer a sharp insight into the farmer's struggle with nature.

LEARNING OBJECTIVES
- Identify and analyze an idea or problem in a sonnet.
- Identify the form of a sonnet.
- Identify and analyze a sonnet's parts.
- Identify and analyze a sonnet's rhyme scheme.
- Research the nature of droughts.
- Write about an aspect of nature.
- **Language Objective** Understand rhyme, meter, and meaning.

TEXT COMPLEXITY

	The Drought	Lexile: N/A
Quantitative Measures		
Qualitative Measures	**Ideas Presented** Multiple levels, use of symbolism, imagery, figurative language and demand for inference	
	Structures Used Conventionally structured stanzas, includes rhyme scheme and one speaker	
	Language Used Meanings are implied, more figurative and metaphorical language	
	Knowledge Required More complex themes, necessitates more cultural and historical references	

208A Unit 3

PLAN

RESOURCES

- Unit 3 Response Log
- Selection Audio
- Reading Studio: Notice & Note
- Level Up Tutorial: Symbol
- Speaking and Listening Studio: Giving a Presentation
- "The Drought" Selection Test

SUMMARIES

English

Sonnets often deal with nature in order to convey an idea or explore a problem. A drought is a particularly emotional and threatening experience for those who must live through one. Sonnets, such as "The Drought," provide an expressive way to share one of the most terrible things that can happen to individuals and communities. Loss, uncertainty, and hope are all explored through the metaphor of a natural disaster and human courage in this poem

Spanish

Los sonetos generalmente tratan la naturaleza como tema, para expresar una idea o para explorar un problema. Una sequía es una experiencia particularmente emocional para aquellos que deben vivirla. Los sonetos tales como "La sequía" ofrecen una manera expresiva de compartir esa experiencia universal. La pérdida, la incertidumbre y la esperanza son explorados a través de la metáfora de un desastre natural en este poema.

 ## SMALL-GROUP OPTIONS

Have students work in small groups to read and discuss the selection.

Numbered Heads Together

- Divide students into equally numbered groups. Assign each student a number. They will later respond to a question when their number is called.
- Ask students: *Why are droughts dangerous?* Have students share their responses with their group, and give each other feedback on their ideas.
- Call on each number. Each student should respond to the question when his or her number is called.

Think-Pair Share

- After students have read and analyzed "The Drought," pose this question: How does the farmer feel about the drought?
- Have students think about the question individually and take notes.
- Then, have pairs discuss their ideas about the question.
- Finally, ask pairs to share their responses with the class.

The Drought **208B**

PLAN

 Text X-Ray: English Learner Support
for "The Drought"

Use the Text X-Ray and the supports and scaffolds in the Teacher's Edition to help guide students at different proficiency levels through the selection.

INTRODUCE THE SELECTION
DISCUSS NATURE AND HUMAN SURVIVAL

In this lesson, students will need to be able to talk about how poetry can illuminate the human struggle to live in harmony with nature. Display appropriate images of farmers in areas affected by extreme drought. Label the images with key words from "The Drought," such as *field* and *dust*. Display the images in sequence like frames in a graphic novel. Explain the following:

A rhyme scheme is the pattern of rhyming words that helps the reader feel, understand, and visualize what the poem means. (Point out rhyming words.)

The form of the sonnet develops the problem in the first three parts and ends with a resolution. (Use gestures to show the build-up of the problem.)

Read the first four lines aloud. Tap the surface of an object as you would a drum when you reach the last word in each line. Repeat the words: *plains, pace, veins, face*. Have the students repeat the process with you. Have the most proficient students lead an echo-read as you point to the images.

CULTURAL REFERENCES

The following words and phrases may be unfamiliar to students:

- *sharpened pace* (line 2): to walk quickly, fast
- *stretch the life that's puddled in his veins* (line 3): refers to the need to move in order to increase the circulation of blood in the body.
- *muster up* (line 4): to gather, to bring together
- *salvage* (line 5): to rescue or save
- *tilled* (line 10): land that has been prepared for crops; land sewn with seeds

LISTENING

Understand Rhyme and Meaning

Review the first stanza of the poem. Point to the images already displayed. Explain that in sonnets, **rhyming words** are arranged in a specific way; they help create meaning. Rhyme schemes help readers understand the poem. The word *sonnet* comes from a word that means "little song."

Have students listen as you read aloud the first stanza of the poem. Use the following supports with students at varying proficiency levels:

- Allow students to use home language words. Ask while gesturing: *What is in your veins?* (blood) Model a "sharpened pace." Use gestures and images to show that movement quickens circulation (*circulación*) in the human body. Show an image of a dying plant. Ask students what the plant needs to survive. (water) Show images of human and plant circulatory systems. Point to the rhyming words: *plains, pace, veins,* and *face,* then make connections between the words and images. **SUBSTANTIAL/MODERATE**

- Have student pairs alternate reading every other line for the first 8 lines in "The Drought." Have them work together to identify the rhyme scheme in the first 8 lines. Then, have them retell what is happening in the poem; help them identify the meaning of the third line. **LIGHT**

208C Unit 3

PLAN

SPEAKING

Read Aloud

Tell students that reading poetry aloud can help them to enjoy and understand the author's message. Reading with expression is crucial to the poem's meaning. Discussing meaning with peers is also important.

Use the following supports with students at varying proficiency levels:

- Provide students with images and cards with words from the poem such as *plains, veins, rain,* and *grain*. Have students take turns matching the images to the words and clearly enunciating as they take turns reading the words aloud and holding up the images and word cards. **SUBSTANTIAL**
- Repeat the definition of *salvage*. Point to images with labels and use gestures while reading lines 5–8 aloud with students. Repeat the following with students while pointing to the words: *dust/grain/trust/rain.* Ask: What rhymes with grain? (rain) What does the grain need?(rain) **MODERATE**
- Have pairs read the entire poem aloud to each other. Then, have them write at least two encouraging notes to each other about the quality of their readings. Ask them to discuss and take notes about what they need to clarify for understanding. Have them save their notes. **LIGHT**

READING

Read for Form and Content

Tell students to try to be aware that the poem's **formal** elements like **rhyme** can help them understand the deeper meanings in the poem.

Work with students to read lines 9–12 of the "The Drought." Use the following supports with students at varying proficiency levels:

- Review that the poem has three parts and a final couplet. Ask: *Who is the beginning about?* (the farmer) *Is the second part about the land and the drought?* (yes) *Which word rhymes with hands?* (Lands) *What is he looking for inside "the broken lands" at the end?* Prompt as necessary. *(breath, hope, life)* **SUBSTANTIAL**
- Ask students what the author means by, *"And, yet, because in years he's learned that, often times, there's something left to save."* Prompt students to infer that the farmer may rely on past experience to give him hope for the future. **MODERATE**
- Have students reread the sonnet. Have them take out their notes from the Speaking activity. Work with them to clarify anything they don't understand about the form and content of the poem. **LIGHT**

WRITING

Write a Sonnet

Draw students' attention to the writing activity on p. 215. Ask them to use "The Drought" as a model for their own sonnets. Model writing the first four lines of a sonnet you have written, or use a sonnet that you like that has the same form and rhyme scheme as "The Drought."

Use the following supports with students at varying proficiency levels:

- Provide students with a list of words and images that relate to nature topics, e.g., animals, forests, and mountains. Be sure to include many rhyming words in their lists. **SUBSTANTIAL**
- Have students work with a partner to brainstorm nature topics for their sonnets. Then, have them work independently to create a list of rhyming words to use in their sonnets. Provide support as students write the first four lines of their sonnet, suggesting rhyming words and ideas as necessary. **MODERATE**
- Have students write the first eight lines of a sonnet and then share it with a partner. Have partners identify the topic of the sonnet their partner has written about and the rhyme scheme. **LIGHT**

The Drought **208D**

TEACH

? Connect to the ESSENTIAL QUESTION

The sonnet "The Drought" provides moving insight into the importance of being in harmony with nature. Farmers rely on the weather to grow healthy crops. Plants thrive under the careful tending of farmers. However, even the most careful farmer cannot control the weather, and farmers must rely on their knowledge and experience of nature to survive.

ANALYZE & APPLY

THE DROUGHT

Poem by **Amy Helfrich**

? ESSENTIAL QUESTION:

What does it mean to be in harmony with nature?

QUICK START

The poem you are about to read explores a farmer's response to a drought—a long time without rain. Think about how a drought might affect a farmer. Jot down ideas and then discuss them with your group.

ANALYZE SONNETS

The **form** of a poem is the arrangement of its words and lines. One form of poetry is a 14-line poem called a **sonnet.** The sonnet originated in Italy but was altered by English poets, especially William Shakespeare. As a result, the following two traditional styles of sonnets emerged: Italian sonnets and English or Shakespearean sonnets. Here are some characteristics of each.

SHAKESPEAREAN SONNET	ITALIAN SONNET
• develops a single idea • idea is developed in three parts, each made up of four lines • final pair of lines, called a **couplet,** offers a sharp, insightful conclusion and shift in emotion	• develops a single idea or problem • idea or problem is laid out in the first eight lines • resolution appears in last six lines

GENRE ELEMENTS: POETRY

- includes a core unit called a line that can be a complete sentence or part of a sentence
- uses carefully chosen words and sounds to express an idea and create a mood
- may include rhyme and meter

The two kinds of sonnets also differ in their use of rhyme, as you will see on the next page.

A traditional sonnet has a specific **meter,** or pattern of stressed and unstressed syllables. Often, the pattern is this: da-DUM da-DUM da-DUM da-DUM da-DUM. The rhythm or pace of the poem is influenced by meter. Because meaning in poetry is expressed as much by sound and rhythm as by word choice, any variation in meter can impact meaning. Rhythm and meaning are also affected by **graphical elements,** such as punctuation and capitalization.

Notice the rhythm, word choice, and use of graphical elements in these lines from "The Drought." What idea is developed in these lines?

> 5   and see what he can salvage from the dust:
> this season's bitterness has starved his grain
> and left the soil with nothing but a trust
> that time will make a friend out of the rain.

As you read "The Drought," note how the poet uses graphical elements, word choice, and rhythm to express emotions and develop ideas.

The Drought   209

TEACH

ANALYZE RHYME SCHEME

Remind students that identifying the **rhyme scheme** of a sonnet can help them differentiate between Shakespearean and Italian sonnets. Point out that identifying the rhyme scheme shows how many line groups exist in a sonnet, which is one way to quickly tell which type of sonnet they are reading.

- Shakespearean sonnet: four parts, made up of three 4-line groups and one couplet, rhyme scheme is *abab cdcd efef gg*.
- Italian sonnet: two parts, one group of eight lines followed by a group of six lines, rhyme scheme is *abbaabba cdcdcd* or *cdecde*.

■ English Learner Support

Understand Rhyme and Meaning Provide students with the Spanish cognate: *rhyme/rima*. Then, help students locate the rhyming end words *high/sky* and *away/array* on page 210. Emphasize that in English endings of words can be spelled very differently, but still rhyme, e.g., *plough* and *how*. Use visuals and gestures to help students understand the meaning of these words, such as pointing to the *sky* and placing something *high* on a shelf as you say them aloud, having students repeat the rhyming sounds after you.
SUBSTANTIAL

 ## ANNOTATION MODEL

Remind students of the annotation lettering used to mark rhyme scheme in a poem. Point out that they should follow this model in their write-in text. Students should also make notes in the margins about connecting ideas throughout the sonnet. They may want to color-code their annotations by using highlighters. Their notes in the margin may include questions about ideas that are unclear or topics they want to learn more about.

 GET READY

ANALYZE RHYME SCHEME

Rhyme occurs when two or more words end with the same (or similar) sound. It is the sound, not the spelling, that matters; for example, *write*, *height*, and *megabyte* rhyme. In poems, rhyming words usually appear at the ends of lines, so they are called end rhymes.

A **rhyme scheme** is a pattern of end rhymes in a poem. You can keep a record of the rhyme scheme in a poem by assigning a letter of the alphabet (*a, b, c,* and so on) to each end rhyme. Lines with the same end rhyme get the same letter, as shown in this example of the first four lines of a sonnet:

At night I stand and watch the stars on high	a
And think of how they twinkle, far away.	b
I wonder if somewhere in that array	b
There stands another watcher of the sky....	a

The rhyme scheme of these lines, then, is *abba*. That rhyme scheme helps identify it as an Italian sonnet, which has a rhyme scheme of *abbaabba* for the first eight lines and either *cdcdcd* or *cdecde* for the last six lines. A Shakespearean sonnet has a rhyme scheme of *abab cdcd efef gg*.

As you read "The Drought," determine the rhyme scheme. Also consider how rhyme may connect details and ideas.

ANNOTATION MODEL NOTICE & NOTE

As you read, consider how the poet uses the sonnet form to develop an idea. You also can mark the rhyme scheme and other details that catch your attention. In the model, you can see one reader's notes about the beginning of "The Drought."

> At dusk, he moves among the dying (plains)
> of winter wheat and walks a sharpened pace
> to stretch the life that's puddled in his (veins),
> muster up some color in his face, . . .

The idea seems to be about a farmer and his dying crop of wheat.

Veins rhymes with plains. Is there a connection—maybe that the farmer's life is tied up in his land?

WHEN STUDENTS STRUGGLE . . .

Read Aloud Have partners work together to read the excerpt from the poem aloud and identify the rhyme scheme.

Partners should alternate reading each line to each other, and then switch lines for a second reading. After students have read the excerpt aloud twice, have pairs write down the rhyming words at the end of each line. *(plains/veins and pace/face)*

 For additional support, go to the **Reading Studio** and assign the following Level Up tutorial: **Rhyme**.

BACKGROUND

The word **drought** refers to a time of unusually dry weather. A drought is not merely a day or two without rain or snow. Instead, it is a dry time that lasts long enough to cause shortages in the water supply. Drought is a particular concern to farmers. In "The Drought," poet **Amy Helfrich** explores the impact of drought on one farmer and how he responds to the toll it takes on him and his land.

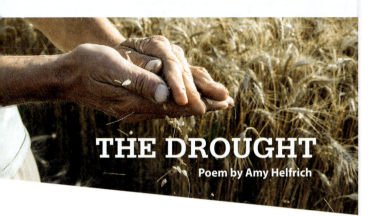

THE DROUGHT
Poem by Amy Helfrich

SETTING A PURPOSE

Read "The Drought" several times. Start by reading it at least once to get a general idea of what it's about. Consider what the farmer thinks of his present situation and of the future. Next, reread the poem, focusing on its structure as a sonnet. How are the lines grouped? How does each group of lines add to the meaning of the sonnet as a whole? Be sure to read the sonnet aloud to appreciate its rhythm and rhyme scheme. Finally, think about the sonnet's overall effect on readers.

NOTICE & NOTE

Notice & Note

Use the side margins to notice and note signposts in the text.

TEACH

BACKGROUND

Explain to students that poets often write about how humans interact with nature. Natural disasters, such as droughts, wildfires, earthquakes, hurricanes, tornadoes, and floods, all create hazardous conditions for farms and farmers; all people rely on land to provide food for survival. Throughout history and up until the present day, droughts are a worrisome issue for farmers, and for all people. As you read the sonnet, pay attention to the emotions the farmer is experiencing and the way the poet chooses to express them.

SETTING A PURPOSE

Direct students to use the Setting a Purpose prompt to focus their reading.

For **listening, speaking,** and **reading support** for students at varying proficiency levels, see the **Text X-Ray** on page 208C–208D.

ENGLISH LEARNER SUPPORT

Use Background Knowledge Create a K-W-L chart titled "Droughts" that students can fill in together. Provide questions to students to guide their discussion: *What does a drought feel like? A drought feels ___ (dry) because there is not enough water. Have you ever lived in a place that is dry? What do plants need to live? Do farmers worry about rain? What does the background note tell you?* Allow Beginning students to answer with single-word responses or gestures. Have intermediate and advanced volunteers fill in the chart as the group discusses droughts. **ALL LEVELS**

TEACH

ANALYZE RHYME SCHEME

Have students analyze the end rhyme in each line to determine the rhyme scheme. Have pairs compare their answers to be sure they have correctly marked the rhyme scheme in the sonnet. (**Answer:** Annotate: abab cdcd efef gg **Analyze:** The rhyme scheme shows that this is a Shakespearean sonnet. The idea contained in each group of four lines is of the devastating effects of drought on crops and the people who rely on them to survive.)

ANALYZE SONNET

Point out that the word *couplet* contains the word *couple*, which means a group of two. One way to remember that a couplet is two specific lines is to think about the word part *couple*. (**Answer:** Annotate: Students should mark the last two lines of the sonnet. **Analyze:** The emotion in the couplet is different from the rest of the sonnet because it conveys a kind of hopefulness that something can still grow in the future, despite the drought.)

ENGLISH LEARNER SUPPORT

Understand Poetry Elements Guide students to understand how to identify the idea of a sonnet, and how it shifts in the last few lines. Point out that lines 5 and 13 use the words *dust* and *dusty*. The repetition of this word links the ideas, but also conveys a very different idea at the end.

ASK STUDENTS Have pairs discuss what the mood of the poem is in line 5 compared to line 13. How has the mood changed? *(In line 5, the farmer is very sad that his land is dust, but in line 13 he puts it in his hands because he hopes it can be saved.)* **LIGHT**

NOTICE & NOTE

ANALYZE RHYME SCHEME
Annotate: Use letters to mark the rhyme scheme.
Interpret: What kind of sonnet is this? What idea is expressed within each group of four lines?

ANALYZE SONNETS
Annotate: Mark the couplet.
Analyze: How does the mood, or feeling, expressed in the couplet differ from that in the lines above it?

At dusk, he moves among the dying plains
of winter wheat and walks a sharpened pace
to stretch the life that's puddled in his veins,
muster up some color in his face,
5 and see what he can salvage from the dust:
this season's bitterness has starved his grain
and left the soil with nothing but a trust
that time will make a friend out of the rain.
So now he wanders through the field he's turned
10 and tilled with care, a twenty acre grave
it seems. And, yet, because in years he's learned
that, often times, there's something left to save,
he stops to sift the dusty earth in hands
that look for breath inside the broken lands.

WHEN STUDENTS STRUGGLE . . .

Draw Inferences Guide students to draw inferences about the couplet at the end of the sonnet by providing them with the following cloze sentences.

The poet says the earth in the farmer's hands is ___ *(dusty) The farmer is looking for* ___ *(breath) in the broken lands. (Breath)* ___ *is a symbol for life. This shows the farmer has* ___ *(hope).*

For additional support, go to the **Reading Studio** and assign the following **Level Up tutorial: Symbol**.

NOTICE & NOTE

CHECK YOUR UNDERSTANDING

Answer these questions before moving on to the **Analyze the Text** section on the following page.

1. Why does the farmer walk quickly—at <u>a sharpened pace</u>—in line 2?

    A He wants to feel more alive and hopeful.

    B He is eager to get inside, out of the cold.

    C He wants to escape from the dust quickly.

    D He is hurrying to harvest his wheat crop.

2. The phrase <u>this season's bitterness</u> in line 6 is most likely a reference to —

    F the soil

    G the drought

    H the wheat

    J the farm

3. In lines 7 and 8, the use of personification, or giving human qualities to an animal, object, or idea, is intended to show that —

    A the soil will be washed away in the first rain

    B the farmer does not think that rain will come soon

    C the soil will become healthy when the rain returns

    D the farmer has waited too long for the rain

The Drought 213

TEACH

CHECK YOUR UNDERSTANDING

Have students answer the questions independently.

Answers:

1. *a*
2. *g*
3. *c*

If they answer any questions incorrectly, have them reread the test to confirm their understanding. Then they may proceed to ANALYZE THE TEXT on page 214.

 ENGLISH LEARNER SUPPORT

Oral Assessment Use the following questions to assess students' comprehension and speaking skills.

1. What does *sharpened* mean in line 2? Think of another word that means almost the same thing. *(quickly, briskly)* Why does the farmer walk this way? *(He walks this way to see what is happening to the wheat, to aid his circulation, to get warm, to feel alive)* Why might the poet have used *sharpened* instead of a more common word? *(it suggests determination)*

   Why is the season bitter? *The season is bitter because it has not ____ (rained). There is a ____ (drought).*

2. The farmer hopes *"...that time will make a friend out of the rain."* Does this mean time and rain are friends? *(No)* What do you think the author means? *(after some time has passed, rain will come and plants—probably wheat—will grow in the soil again.)* **ALL LEVELS**

The Drought **213**

APPLY

ANALYZE THE TEXT

Possible answers:

1. **DOK 2:** *The poet means that the "twenty acre grave" is where his wheat is growing, but it is more like a graveyard than a field because the wheat has died.*

2. **DOK 4:** *Dust rhymes with trust (line 7). This word pairing may suggest that although the field seems doomed at the moment (the "dust"), there is hope (the "trust") that rain may yet arrive.*

3. **DOK 4:** *Answers will vary. Students may at first feel that the lack of capitalization is odd, but get used to it quickly. They also may feel that the lack of capitalization helps readers follow each thought as it goes from one line to the next, as opposed to having the separation of ideas marked by capital letters.*

4. **DOK 4:** *The poet's use of commas in lines 11 and 12 slows down the rhythm of the poem. It changes the meaning by giving the reader a sense that the farmer is pausing to reconsider the land, and suggests there may be a shift in meaning.*

5. **DOK 4:** *Accept all reasonable responses. Students should note that the first groups of lines indicate a measure of sadness, but the sonnet does end on a hopeful note that there might be breath left in the land.*

RESEARCH

Remind students to use quotes around specific terms when they conduct research on the Internet. They can also check reputable sites, such as the Smithsonian or NASA Earth Observatory.

Connect *Answers will vary, but students should note that the effects of the drought for the farmer is mainly economic, while the effect on the land is environmental.*

RESPOND

ANALYZE THE TEXT

Support your responses with evidence from the text. **NOTEBOOK**

1. **Infer** What does the poet mean by the phrase "a twenty acre grave" in line 10?

2. **Critique** Which word is meant to rhyme with *dust* at the end of line 5? How does the relationship between these two rhyming words help develop the idea of the poem?

3. **Connect** "The Drought" has an unusual graphical element—almost every line begins with a lowercase letter. What does this tell you about how the lines are structured? How does this structure help convey the poet's message or purpose?

4. **Analyze** How does the poet's use of commas in lines 11 and 12 change the rhythm of the poem? How does the use of commas affect the poem's meaning?

5. **Draw Conclusions** Is this ultimately a sad poem, or a hopeful one? Explain.

RESEARCH

RESEARCH TIP
To help narrow the focus of an Internet search, use quotes around a specific phrase—for example, "environmental effects of drought." To quickly find the online definition of a technical word or phrase you're not familiar with, try this tip: Search for "define [word]" (for example, "define drought").

In the Background note, you learned a little about droughts. With a partner, do research to find out the effects a drought can have on the environment and the economy. Use questions such as "How do droughts affect wheat crops?" to guide your research. Record your findings in the graphic organizer.

EFFECTS OF DROUGHT	
Environmental	**Economic**
Plants and animals that may die due to a lack of water.	*Loss of money in providing water to crops or in losing the crops altogether*

Connect Based on your research, identify what kind of effect(s) a drought like the one in the poem would have on a farm. Compare your answers with those of a classmate. Do you agree? Why or why not?

TO CHALLENGE STUDENTS...

Conduct Research Challenge students to research a different sonnet that discusses some aspect of nature. They might start by using the research tips they learned to locate sonnets on the Internet. Guide students to analyze the sonnet as thoroughly as they have analyzed "The Drought." Students should identify the type of sonnet, annotate the rhyme scheme, and recognize what idea or problem is being developed in the sonnet. Encourage them think about how the sonnet relates to the Essential Question.

RESPOND

CREATE AND PRESENT

Write a Sonnet Write a sonnet about some aspect of nature.

❏ Choose an aspect of nature that interests you—for example, something about plants, animals, rivers, oceans, or a weather event. Spend a few minutes making notes about your topic. Choose the idea that you want to develop and decide which sonnet form you will use: Italian, or Shakespearean.

❏ Think about a rhyme scheme. Try using a rhyming dictionary to list pairs of rhyming words that you might include. Think about the meter, too. See whether your lines make the pattern da-DUM da-DUM da-DUM da-DUM da-DUM or another meter.

❏ Don't be afraid to rewrite or replace lines to make the idea clearer or to make the poem fit the sonnet form more closely.

Listen to the Sonnet In pairs, take turns reading "The Drought" aloud and listening to it as it is read to you.

❏ As the reader, notice how the lines are structured. There are only three sentences in "The Drought." Read the sonnet as sentences instead of stopping at the end of each line.

❏ Plan how you will be expressive. Where should your voice be louder or softer? Where should you speed up, slow down, or pause? Which words should you emphasize or express with certain emotion?

❏ As the listener, pay attention to the speaker's words, pace, and tone. Listen closely to see whether you can interpret the sonnet's message. Does hearing the poem in addition to reading it make a difference to your understanding of its message?

 Go to **Giving a Presentation** in the **Speaking and Listening Studio** to learn more.

RESPOND TO THE ESSENTIAL QUESTION

 What does it mean to be in harmony with nature?

Gather Information Review your annotations and notes on "The Drought." Then, add relevant details to your Response Log. As you determine which information to include, think about:

- how nature challenges us and how we challenge nature
- how resilient or tough people and nature can be
- how we depend on nature and how nature depends on us

At the end of the unit, use your notes to write a personal narrative.

ACADEMIC VOCABULARY

As you write and discuss what you learned from the poem, be sure to use the Academic Vocabulary words. Check off each of the words that you use.

❏ affect
❏ element
❏ ensure
❏ participate
❏ specify

The Drought 215

APPLY

CREATE AND PRESENT

Write a Sonnet Point out that students should use the list on the page as a checklist to be completed as they create their sonnets. To help students decide which type of sonnet to choose, ask them to think about whether they want to shift the emotion in the couplet at the end, or whether their topic would work better if the resolution could be presented in the last six lines, instead of the last two.

For **writing support** for students at varying proficiency levels, see the **Text X-Ray** on page 208D.

Listen to the Sonnet Remind students that their use of graphical elements can impact the meter of the sonnet. Readers should be sure to adjust their rhythm according the structure of the poem, and listeners should read along as the poem is read aloud to see how these elements impact the meter and meaning of the sonnet.

RESPOND TO THE ESSENTIAL QUESTION

Allow time for students to add details from "The Drought" to their Unit 3 Response Logs.

 ENGLISH LEARNER SUPPORT

Listen to the Sonnet Remind students that they have practiced recognizing meter, i.e., the patterns created by stressed syllable. Have Advanced students read their sonnets aloud twice while tapping the beat out. Beginning and Intermediate students should quietly tap the beat along with the reader during the second reading. Have Advanced students take notes on the rhyming words at the end of each line and then share their answers with the class after each reader has finished. **ALL LEVELS**

The Drought 215

PLAN

ALLIED WITH GREEN
Short Story by Naomi Shihab Nye

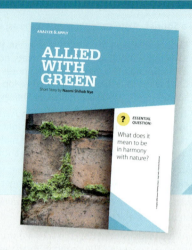

GENRE ELEMENTS
SHORT STORY

Remind students that the purpose of a **short story** is to entertain, inspire, and present ideas. "Allied With Green" is a work of fiction that centers on a single idea and can be read in one sitting. Generally, a short story has one main conflict that involves the characters, keeps the story moving, and stimulates readers' interest.

LEARNING OBJECTIVES

- Analyze the theme of a short story.
- Monitor comprehension of fictional text.
- Conduct research about the environmental movement.
- Write a poem about a short story character.
- Form and punctuate complex sentences.
- Use context clues to determine word meaning.
- **Language** Discuss with a group a character's motivations and character traits.

TEXT COMPLEXITY

Quantitative Measures	Allied With Green	Lexile: 900L
Qualitative Measures	**Ideas Presented** Single level of complex meaning	
	Structure Used Some unconventional story structure elements	
	Language Used More complex sentence structure	
	Knowledge Required Single perspective with unfamiliar aspects	

216A Unit 3

PLAN

Online

RESOURCES

- Unit 3 Response Log
- 🔊 Selection Audio
- 📖 Reading Studio: Notice & Note
- Level Up Tutorial: Theme
- 💬 Speaking and Listening Studio: Participating in Collaborative Discussions
- Vocabulary Studio: Context Clues
- ✓ "Allied with Green" Selection Test

SUMMARIES

English

Lucy's assignment is to write a paper about "What I Believe In." She begins thinking about it as the phrase "the color green" echos in her mind. She goes about her day, noticing the green of the city, thinking about what green things mean to her and to other people, and exploring what you can learn if you devote yourself to the color green.

Spanish

La tarea de Lucy es escribir un ensayo acerca de "Lo que creo", así que empieza a pensar en ello. Con la frase "el color verde" haciendo eco en su mente, continúa su día, notando el verde en la ciudad, pensando acerca de qué significan las cosas verdes para ella y para otros, y explorando qué se puede aprender si le dedicas la vida al color verde.

SMALL-GROUP OPTIONS

Have students work in small groups to read and discuss the selection.

Pinwheel Discussion

- In groups of eight, four students are seated in a square, facing out. Four other students are seated facing in towards the first four.
- Students in the inner square remain stationary throughout the discussion.
- Students in the outer square move to their right after discussing each question.
- Control the discussion by providing a question for each rotation. For example, *Why does Lucy like trimming? What is important about tending things?*

Numbered Heads Together

- Form groups of four students and then number off 1 – 2 – 3 – 4 within the group.
- Ask students, *Why do you think cities don't treat green things and green spaces better?*
- Have students discuss their responses in their groups.
- Call a number from 1 to 4. That "numbered" student will then respond for the group.
- If you like, groups may adopt names, such as "Wildcats," to identify their groups. You will then call on Wildcat number 4.

Allied With Green **216B**

PLAN

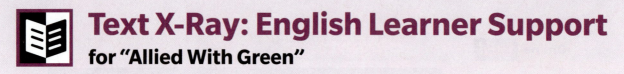

Text X-Ray: English Learner Support
for "Allied With Green"

Use the Text X-Ray and the supports and scaffolds in the Teacher's Edition to help guide students at different proficiency levels through the selection.

INTRODUCE THE SELECTION
DISCUSS UNIT THEME-RELATED IDEA

In this lesson, students will need to be able to think about the value of green spaces in our lives. Discuss the different meanings of *green*. What does it mean to be in harmony with nature? What does nature do to help us be happier, healthier people? How do city places differ from places in rural areas?

Have students generate a list of urban places and things and natural places and things. Write these words on the board: *high-rise, forests, mountains, streets, lakes, cars, parks, shopping malls, gardens,* and *alleys*. Then write these adjectives: *peaceful, exciting, beautiful, fun, challenging, spiritual, dangerous, joyful, refreshing, healthy,* and *busy*.

Ask volunteers to connect places with adjectives. Have the class discuss whether they agree with each connection.

CULTURAL REFERENCES

The following words and phrases may be unfamiliar to students:

- *recorded history* (paragraph 5): the period of time when people noted events, in this case of weather
- *Queen's crown germander, plumbago* (paragraph 8): flowers
- *demonstrated* (paragraph 10): publicly marched to protest something
- *population* issues (paragraph 10): worries about too many people in the world
- *took green for granted* (paragraph 21): thought that growing things would always be there and didn't worry

LISTENING

Understand the Theme

Draw students' attention to details in lines 11–16 that will help them understand what the theme is. Remind students that the theme is the overall message of a story. For example, the theme of a story about a woman who happily works many hours to feed her children might be "love of family conquers all," or "with gratitude comes strength."

Have students listen as you read aloud lines 11-16. Use the following supports with students at varying proficiency levels:

- Tell students that you will ask questions about what you just read aloud. Model that they should give a thumbs up if the answer is yes, and a thumbs down for no. For example, ask: *Is a parking lot a green place? (no)* **SUBSTANTIAL**
- Have students identify the main idea of the excerpt. Ask: *What is the main idea of these paragraphs? (Green spaces make people feel better.)* **MODERATE**
- Pair students to list details that support the main idea of the excerpt. Ask: *What examples does Lucy give of how green spaces affect people?* **LIGHT**

216C Unit 3

PLAN

SPEAKING

Discuss the Title

Draw students' attention to the title of the story. Then help students discuss the idea expressed in "Allied with Green."

Discuss what *allied* and *green* mean. Use the following supports with students at varying proficiency levels:

- Divide the students into two teams. *Say, You are allied with the people on your team.* Then ask individual students, *Marcie, are you allied with Jonah? Will, are you allied with Suzette?* Have students say yes or no. **SUBSTANTIAL**
- Tell students that you will ask questions about what the title means. Begin by defining the word *allied*. Explain that, if you are allied with someone, you are on their side. You have the same goal. Ask: *Are you allied with people who are on your sports team? Why?* (Yes, because we have the same goal.) **MODERATE**
- Pair students to discuss what it means to be "allied with green." **LIGHT**

READING

Identify Supporting Details

Draw students' attention to Lucy's thoughts and feelings about the good that green spaces and green plants do in the world. Look at how those thoughts and feelings support the theme of the story.

Work with students to reread paragraph 3. Use the following supports with students at varying proficiency levels:

- Have students circle each instance of *green* in paragraph 3. Tell students that you will ask questions about what they just read. For example, ask: *What word do you see repeated the most? Does Lucy believe that people need to see green?* (green; yes) **SUBSTANTIAL**
- Have students explain what Lucy's feelings are about green spaces. Ask: *What does she believe would happen to the hospital without green?* (It might fall down.) **MODERATE**
- Pair students to analyze the excerpt. Ask: *What specific things does Lucy name that "seem to keep everything else going"?* (plants between buildings, on the side of the road, in pots, in handing baskets, along the river, etc.) **LIGHT**

WRITING

Write a Poem

Help students understand the structure of a poem as they work through the assignment on page 225.

Use the following supports with students at varying proficiency levels:

- Give students pairs of words and ask whether they rhyme. Model that they should give a thumbs up if the answer is yes, and a thumbs down for no. For example: *green/queen, plant/ant, garden/hard* **SUBSTANTIAL**
- Provide students with this poem frame. *Lucy likes ____. Lucy looks ____. Lucy loves ____.* **MODERATE**
- Pair students and have them work together on a poem about Lucy, with each student writing every other line. Begin with "Lucy likes things green." **LIGHT**

Allied With Green **216D**

TEACH

? Connect to the ESSENTIAL QUESTION

This selection explores being in harmony with nature by trying to preserve it in an increasingly urban world. Students will encounter a girl whose love of all green things is challenged by her environment.

ANALYZE & APPLY

ALLIED WITH GREEN

Short Story by **Naomi Shihab Nye**

? ESSENTIAL QUESTION:

What does it mean to be in harmony with nature?

GET READY

QUICK START

Imagine that your community has announced an environmental program called "Changing Our Ways for Greener Days." Make a list of projects that you think might be part of such a program.

ANALYZE THEME

Authors often use the characters in short stories to share a theme with readers. A **theme** is a message about life or human nature. "Show kindness" and "We might not appreciate what we have until it's gone" are just two of the many themes that stories might convey.

The theme of a story is usually implied rather than stated directly. To infer a theme, it is helpful to do the following:

- Look at the title to see if it suggests a significant idea.
- Analyze the characters' words and actions.
- Consider whether the setting has special meaning to a character.
- Look for important statements by the narrator or a character.

As you read "Allied with Green," look for clues that suggest a theme.

GENRE ELEMENTS: SHORT STORY

- a fictional work that centers on a single idea and that can be read in one sitting
- has a limited number of characters and settings
- often presents a conflict, or challenge, that the main character or characters must try to overcome
- sometimes makes a point more through vivid language and powerful images than through a traditional plot

MONITOR COMPREHENSION

One way to be an effective reader, regardless of the kind of text you are reading, is to **monitor** your **comprehension**—that is, to check and adjust your understanding while you are reading. By monitoring your comprehension, you can clear up any confusion about the writer's intent and make sure that you understand the text.

Several strategies can help you monitor your comprehension. Each one has its benefits. The strategy or strategies you use will depend on the sentence or passage from the text that you are considering.

MONITORING STRATEGY	BENEFIT
Rereading	Reread text that you don't understand. You may need to reread slowly, aloud, or more than once—but repeated readings will help.
Connecting	Use what you already know, plus any background information provided with the text (such as an introduction or footnotes) to connect with the text.
Questioning	Develop and ask questions about the text as you read. Questions that start with *who*, *what*, *where*, *when*, *why*, and *how* will take you far!
Annotating	Mark words, phrases, and details that will help you understand the text. When reading a story, for example, mark details about characters, setting, and plot events.

Allied with Green   217

TEACH

QUICK START

To help students think about what might be part of a "Changing Our Ways for Greener Days" program, quickly explain to them the 5 *Rs* of environmental responsibility:

- Refuse (disposable products)
- Reduce (use of earth's resources)
- Reuse (anything you can)
- Repair (instead of throwing away)
- Recycle (everything you can)

ANALYZE THEME

Remind students that the theme of a story is often not stated directly anywhere in the story. When this happens, readers must infer, or make a good guess about, the theme from evidence in the text. Explain that authors sometimes reveal the theme in the story's title, as well as in the words and actions of characters.

MONITOR COMPREHENSION

Explain to students that monitoring comprehension is something that good readers do, whether they know they are doing it or not. Give students these tips about monitoring comprehension:

- Practice the strategies listed on p. 217 until they become a natural part of reading.
- Use the strategies together. For example, ask yourself questions and then reread if you can't answer them.

TEACH

CRITICAL VOCABULARY

Encourage students to read all the questions before answering each one. Remind them to look for context clues that help them understand the meaning of each word.

Answers:
1. yes
2. no
3. no
4. yes
5. yes

■ English Learner Support

Use Cognates Tell students that several of the Critical Vocabulary words have Spanish cognates: *addiction/ adicción, median/mediana, arboretum/arboreto, obituary/ obituario.* **ALL LEVELS**

LANGUAGE CONVENTIONS

Point out to students that a subordinate clause is separated by a comma from an independent clause only when the subordinate clause comes before the independent clause.
- When I finished dinner, I had dessert.
- I had dessert when I finished dinner.

ANNOTATION MODEL

The model suggests underlining important details and circling words that signal how the text is organized. Point out that students may follow this suggestion or use their own system for marking up the selection in their write-in text. They may want to color-code their annotations by using highlighters. Their notes in the margin may include questions about ideas that are unclear or topics they want to learn more about.

 GET READY

CRITICAL VOCABULARY

addiction   remorseful   median   arboretum   obituary

To see how many Critical Vocabulary words you already know, answer each question with **yes** or **no**. In a small group, explain your answers.

1. Could someone have an **addiction** to chocolate?
2. Do **remorseful** people usually feel happy about their actions?
3. Would you expect to see a **median** on a single-lane road?
4. Is an **arboretum** like a garden?
5. Is an **obituary** like a biography?

LANGUAGE CONVENTIONS

Complex Sentences In this lesson, you will learn more about complex sentences. A **complex sentence** consists of one independent clause (which can stand on its own as a sentence) and one or more subordinate clauses (which need the independent clause to complete their meaning). In this example, the subordinate clause begins with *when*. It follows an independent clause, so it does not need a comma. (If the subordinate clause came first, a comma would need to follow it.)

> The boulevard wakes up when a strip of green is planted down its center.

Notice that in each clause, the subject and its verb agree (*boulevard + wakes up*; *strip + is planted*). As you read "Allied with Green," note how the author uses correctly written complex sentences to express ideas.

ANNOTATION MODEL   NOTICE & NOTE

As you read, note clues about the theme of the story. You also can mark up anything that will help you monitor your comprehension. In the model, you can see one reader's notes about "Allied with Green."

| 1 | For her paper on "What I Believe In," Lucy writes first "the color green." | The theme may involve the word green. |
| 2 | That's how everything starts. A tiny shoot of phrase prickling the mind . . . | Here's my question: Why is the author comparing language to a growing plant? |

BACKGROUND

Naomi Shihab Nye *(b. 1952) was born to a Palestinian father and an American mother. During her adolescence, she lived in St. Louis, Missouri; Jerusalem, Israel; and San Antonio, Texas. She has traveled extensively as an adult, as well. Influenced by her heritage and the cultural diversity of the places she has known, Nye has written books of poetry as well as fiction for younger audiences.*

ALLIED WITH GREEN

Short Story by Naomi Shihab Nye

SETTING A PURPOSE

As you read, consider the author's use of the word green. *How is she using the term to describe something that Lucy, the story's main character, feels very strongly about?*

1 For her paper on "What I Believe In," Lucy writes first "the color green."

2 That's how everything starts. A tiny shoot of phrase prickling the mind . . .

3 Then she runs around for a few days doing other things but noticing the green poking up between buildings, on sides of roads, in front of even the poorest homes, how pots of green lined on rickety front porches, hanging baskets of green on light posts downtown, the new meticulous xeriscape[1] beds of puffy green grasses and plants alongside the river, are what seem to keep everything else going. If

---
[1] **xeriscape** (zîr´ĭ-skāp´): landscaping that is designed to save water and protect the environment.

Notice & Note

Use the side margins to notice and note signposts in the text.

MONITOR COMPREHENSION

Annotate: Mark the sentence that makes up most of paragraph 3.

Interpret: What does the author emphasize with the details in that sentence? Why might you need to reread that sentence before answering?

Allied with Green 219

TEACH

LANGUAGE CONVENTIONS

Explain to students that a subordinate clause acts as one of the parts of speech. It can act as a noun, an adjective, or an adverb. Subordinate clauses that act as adverbs always answer the questions when, where, why, how, and to what extent? So, the word *when* is a clue that the sentence might include a subordinating conjunction. (**Answer:** *The complex sentence in paragraph 6 is the second sentence. The subordinate clause "When she and her mother wash lettuce, blueberries, peaches . . ."*)

ANALYZE THEME

Explain that ideas that are repeated or emphasized often point toward the theme. Noting repeated phrases or images as well as ideas or events that are described in detail can help to identify the theme. In other words, the theme of a story is often revealed in the **supporting details** of the story. Those details may include a character's actions, the development of the plot, or even just a thought in passing. (**Answer:** *The names suggest growing plants, especially trees and relate to the message about caring for growing things.*)

MONITOR COMPREHENSION

Explain to students that writers sometimes refer to things outside their stories. These are called **allusions**, and it may be important part of understanding to find out what they mean. (**Answer:** *Look up Joni Mitchell on the Internet.*)

CRITICAL VOCABULARY

addiction: Lucy was supposed to write a paper about addiction, and she wrote about trimming plants.

ASK STUDENTS why Lucy considers trimming plants to be an addiction. (*Lucy feels that she is addicted to plants, or "green," because she loves plants and feels we are all dependent on them, in much the same way an addict is dependent on a substance.*)

remorseful: Lucy thinks cities name places for "green" because they feel remorseful.

ASK STUDENTS why the cities might feel remorseful. (*They might feel remorseful for destroying green places.*)

220 Unit 3

NOTICE & NOTE

LANGUAGE CONVENTIONS
Annotate: Underline the complex sentence that appears in paragraph 6.
Analyze: In that sentence, what are the subjects and the verbs that agree with them? Where is a comma placed to set the subordinate clause apart from the independent clause?

addiction
(ə-dĭk′shən) *n.* An *addiction* is a habit upon which a person becomes physically or emotionally dependent.

ANALYZE THEME
Annotate: In paragraph 9, mark the new names that people create for places in cities.
Connect: How do these names relate to the message conveyed through Lucy's story?

remorseful
(rĭ-môrs′fəl) *adj.* If you are *remorseful*, you feel very sorry about something that you have done.

median
(mē′dē-ən) *n.* A *median* is a dividing area between opposing lanes of traffic on a highway or road.

MONITOR COMPREHENSION
Annotate: Mark the name of the singer mentioned in paragraph 10.
Identify: How would you find information about the singer so that you can clarify this reference?

220 Unit 3

people could not see green from the windows of the hospital, the hospital might fall down. She believes this.

4 Once she starts making a list, it will not stop.

5 Green has had a terrible summer. Threatened by the longest drought and highest heat in recorded history, green has had many second thoughts.

6 Lucy's family could only water with a sprinkler on Wednesday evenings between eight and ten. When she and her mom wash lettuce, blueberries, peaches, they carry the plastic tubs of fruit water outside to pour onto a plant. It's ritual now. It's holy water. The city had a water waster hotline. It made the national news. You could turn people in for excessive watering.

7 Last semester, when asked to write a paper on **addictions,** Lucy wrote about trimming and got a C. Her teacher scrawled across the top of the paper, "What is this?" But Lucy often feels happiest with pruning shears in her hand, heading toward an overgrown jasmine vine.

8 It's a clear task, trimming. The longer you've done it, the more you know how it encourages green, in the long run. Also, you can have fine ideas while trimming. Queen's crown, germander, plumbago. *Snip, snip, snip*.

9 She knew it had been mentioned before, but thought she ought to include how cities assault their green for two reasons: money and greed. Later, feeling **remorseful,** or sickened by the new view, they name everything for green—Oak Meadows, Lone Pine. You could find it almost anywhere now.

10 Lucy's father demonstrated against developments when he was in college. She had a faded black and white picture of him holding a NO! sign, his hair bushy and wild. Highways slashing through green space—he now drives one of those highways almost every day, feeling guilty. He plants free trees in scrappy **medians,** as an apology. Sometimes people steal them. When he planted four little palms in pots as a gift to Freddy's Mexican Restaurant, they got plucked from the soil overnight. Obviously some people were desperate for green. And surely, with all the population issues now, some developments were necessary, but look at what happened before you knew it—hills sheared, meadows plucked, fields erased, the world turns into an endless series of strip centers—yo, Joni Mitchell! Joni sang about parking lots when the world had probably half the number it has now. Her dad told her that. She likes Joni Mitchell.

11 The boulevard wakes up when a strip of green is planted down its center.

median: The author says that Lucy's father plants trees on medians as an apology.

ASK STUDENTS to explain what he is apologizing for and why he chooses medians for his planting. (*He is apologizing for driving on the highway every day. Because the median runs down the middle of the highway, he is trying to at least make the space a bit more beautiful.*)

NOTICE & NOTE

12   The sad room smiles again when a pot of green is placed on a white tablecloth.
13   No one goes to Seattle to see the concrete.
14   An exhausted kid says, I'm going outside—sick of her mother's voice, she knows she will feel better with bamboo.
15   In Dallas people run around the lake or refresh themselves at the **arboretum**.
16   San Antonians send their kids to summer digging classes at the botanical gardens. The kids come home with broccoli. After a while.
17   Patience is deeply involved with green.

arboretum
(är′bə-rē′təm) *n.* An *arboretum* is a place where many trees are grown for educational or viewing purposes.

TEACH

ENGLISH LEARNER SUPPORT

Figurative Language Remind students that figurative language describes things not as they actually, literally are, but in an imaginative way. One form of figurative language is personification, which occurs when humans give an object, animal, or idea human-like qualities.

ASK STUDENTS to reread paragraph 12. Ask, *What is personified in this sentence and in what way?* (*The room. It is given the human quality of being sad and then of smiling.*) **SUBSTANTIAL/MODERATE**

 For **listening support** for students at varying proficiency levels, see the **Text X-Ray** on page 216C.

WHEN STUDENTS STRUGGLE . . .

Read Closely Display lines 5-13, focusing on the word *green*.
- Note that in line 10, *green* is an adjective. Other times, it is a noun. Ask what the noun *green* means. (*anything that grows*)
- Ask why green "Seems to keep everything else growing." (*People depend on plants.*)
- Ask why Nye repeats the word *green*. (*to emphasize the story's theme.*)

 For additional support, go to the **Reading Studio** and assign the following **Level Up** tutorial: Theme.

CRITICAL VOCABULARY

arboretum: The author says that in Dallas people refresh themselves in the arboretum.

ASK STUDENTS why an arboretum is refreshing. (*An arboretum provides a green place that is very different most of city life.*)

TEACH

 ANALYZE THEME

Explain to students that a theme may imply how a person should live but should not be confused with a **moral**. **(Answer:** *The first question reflects Lucy's attitude about respecting growing things; the second question reflects the thinking of people who don't see how important respecting growing things is.)*

 AGAIN AND AGAIN

Remind students that, when a word, phrase, or other text element is repeated, this is often a sign that the writer wants the reader to pay attention to something important. **(Answer:** *The repetition emphasizes Lucy's strong feelings about the effort to make things green.)*

 ANALYZE THEME

Encourage students to talk about what they think of when they hear the word tend. Say, *A shepherd tends sheep, a gardener tends a gardener, and on a camping trip someone has to tend the campfire.* Talk about what these people are doing and what they have in common. **(Answer:** *If you tend something, you take care of it. The author's choice to focus on that idea at the end of the story helps the reader remember the story's theme.)*

CRITICAL VOCABULARY

obituary: The author tells us that Lucy clipped Robert Isabell's obituary, or death notice, from the newspaper and kept it on her desk.

ASK STUDENTS what Lucy might have learned from Isabell's obituary, and why she kept it on her desk. (*She might have learned facts about his life and accomplishments. She kept it because she admired him and felt inspired by him.*)

222   Unit 3

 **NOTICE & NOTE**

ANALYZE THEME
Annotate: Mark the two questions that appear in paragraphs 18 through 20.
Analyze: How do the different points of view in the questions help show a theme of the story?

AGAIN AND AGAIN
Notice & Note: In paragraphs 22–25, mark the things that Lucy loved.
Critique: How do you think the repetition of *loved* is meant to affect the reader?

obituary
(ō-bĭch´ōō-ĕr´ē) *n.* An *obituary* is a public notice of a person's death.

ANALYZE THEME
Annotate: Reread paragraphs 26–28. Mark the verb that Lucy found especially important.
Interpret: Why do you think the story ends by focusing on this verb? What idea does it leave readers thinking about?

18   It's required.
19   So, why don't people respect green as much as they should?
20   This was the serious question growing small fronds and tendrils at the heart of Lucy's paper. She knew her teacher might turn a snide nose up at it. *Oh, blah blah, isn't this rather a repeat of what you wrote last semester?*
21   People took green for granted. They assumed it would always be skirting their ugly office buildings and residences and so they didn't give it the attention it deserved. Somewhat like air. Air and green, close cousins.
22   Lucy truly loved the words *pocket park*.[2]
23   She loved community gardeners with purple bandannas tied around their heads. She loved their wild projects—rosemary grown so big you could hide in it.
24   She loved roofs paved with grass.
25   She loved the man in New York City—Robert Isabell—who planted pink impatiens on the metal overhang of his building. He had started out as a florist, at seventeen, in Minnesota—green state in the summer, not so green in December. Then he moved to New York City and became a major party planner, incorporating flowers, lighting, tents, fabrics, to create magical worlds of festivity. He didn't attend his own parties. He disappeared once he got everything set up. Sometimes he hid behind a giant potted plant to see what people liked. Lucy found his obituary in the newspaper, clipped it out, and placed it on her desk. She wished she could have worked for him just to learn how he put flowers together on tables, how he clipped giant green stalks and placed them effectively around a tent to make Morocco, Italy, the French Riviera. Transporting. Green could take you away.
26   Save you. But you had to care for it, stroke it, devote yourself to it, pray to it, organize crews for it, bow down to it. You had to say the simple holy prayer, rearranging the words any way you liked best—"Dig, Grow, Deep, Roots, Light, Air, Water, Tend."
27   *Tend* was a more important verb than most people realized.
28   You had to carry a bucket.

---
[2] **pocket park:** a small park accessible to the general public.

222   Unit 3

IMPROVE READING FLUENCY

Model read paragraph 25. Explain to students that unlike the shorter paragraphs in this selection that are concerned with simpler subjects, this paragraph, like paragraph 10, is longer than the other paragraphs and is also about someone who is important to Lucy. Have volunteers read aloud this paragraph or paragraph 10. There is a humorous element in paragraph 25, try to make sure it comes across to the audience. Remind them that reading aloud longer paragraphs requires extra care with pacing and emphasis—they must hold listeners' attention throughout the reading.

NOTICE & NOTE

TEACH

CHECK YOUR UNDERSTANDING

Have students answer the questions independently.

Answers:

1. A
2. J
3. B

If they answer any questions incorrectly, have them reread the text to confirm their understanding. Then they may proceed to ANALYZE THE TEXT on page 224.

CHECK YOUR UNDERSTANDING

Answer these questions before moving on to the **Analyze the Text** section on the following page.

1 Early in the story, the statement <u>That's how everything starts</u> is meant to show that —

   A being "green" is essential to the character of Lucy

   B belief in "the color green" should begin in childhood

   C the world could not survive without its plant life

   D talking about the environment leads to arguments

2 The author mentions Seattle, Dallas, and San Antonio to suggest that —

   F only a few cities are taking steps to care for the environment

   G cities are in great danger of having developers take over green spaces

   H places have different ideas about how to care for the environment

   J people in many places appreciate green spaces

3 Robert Isabell is important to Lucy because —

   A he was a party planner known throughout New York

   B his life represented a skill that she would like to have

   C his beliefs about the environment are similar to her own

   D he traveled the world in search of interesting plants

Allied with Green 223

 ENGLISH LEARNER SUPPORT

Oral Assessment Use the following questions to assess students' comprehension and speaking skills:

1. In paragraph 12, review the sentence "The sad room smiles again when a pot of green is placed on a white tablecloth." Does this mean that the someone is smiling or that the room looks like a happier place because there is a green plant on the table? *(The room looks like a happier place with a green plant on the table.)*

2. "Why does the author mention Seattle, Dallas, and San Antonio? *(to show that people in many places appreciate green spaces)*
   SUBSTANTIAL/MODERATE

3. Why is Robert Isabell important to Lucy? *(His beliefs about the environment are similar to her own.)*

Allied With Green **223**

APPLY

ANALYZE THE TEXT

Possible answers:

1. **DOK 2:** *It shows that Lucy is a sensitive, perceptive person who cares very much about the importance of green plants.*

2. **DOK 4:** *The main theme of the story is that green spaces are a necessary part of human life. The author develops this theme through examples of the negative impact of development and descriptions of Lucy's appreciation for green and growing things.*

3. **DOK 4:** *Lucy's father demonstrated against land urban development when he was in college and plants trees today. The information about him helps readers understand how Lucy came to her opinions about environmentalism.*

4. **DOK 4:** *Answers will vary, depending on the life experience of the student.*

5. **DOK 4:** *Prayer. The simple prayer is really a list of things we need to do to take care of the earth.*

RESEARCH

Explain to students that many not-for-profit groups have large websites with a great deal of reliable information.

Connect Help students connect their research findings with what Lucy is most concerned about; the human need for green, growing things. From Lucy's point of view, urbanization and growth threaten plant life because people take it for granted; but having it as a part of daily life is not an option: it's a necessity. She complains that "...they didn't give it [green] the attention it deserved. Somewhat like air. Air and green, close cousins." Information about cultivating more green space while curtailing unnecessary development would probably be the issues Lucy feels most strongly about.

224   Unit 3

RESPOND

ANALYZE THE TEXT

Support your responses with evidence from the text. 📓 NOTEBOOK

1. **Infer** Once Lucy decides on the topic for her writing assignment, she can't help but notice the green around her. What does this tell you about her character and how she feels about her topic?

2. **Analyze** What is the theme of "Allied with Green"? Give examples of how the author develops the theme.

3. **Critique** What do you know about Lucy's father? Why does he matter to the story?

4. **Connect** Reread paragraphs 9 and 10. How might what you know about your own community, or other communities, help you connect with what the author is saying about Lucy?

5. **Notice & Note** Paragraph 6 mentions "holy water." At the end of the story, what else is called "holy"? How do those "holy" things help express the theme of "Allied with Green"?

RESEARCH

RESEARCH TIP
Before you start your research, make sure that you know just what kind of information you're looking for. To complete this activity, for example, you are asked to find out a little about the environmental movement in general, but you also are asked to learn about "green-focused" living. Make sure that you gather information about both topics.

As you have seen, the word *green* in "Allied with Green" means more than a color. It relates to the beliefs and goals of the environmental movement. Research the environmental movement and what it means to lead a green-focused lifestyle. Use what you learn to answer the questions in the chart.

QUESTION	ANSWER
What beliefs do many environmentalists share?	*Most environmentalists respect the world's plant and animal life, and they believe in protecting the environment. They are concerned about climate change.*
What are some goals of the environmental movement?	*The movement's goals include persuading the world's governments and businesses to become more energy efficient, including limiting carbon emissions and using alternative sources of energy.*
What does it mean to be "green"?	*Being "green" means that people and communities take action to protect the environment.*
What are some ways to lead a "green-focused" lifestyle?	*You can have a "green-focused lifestyle" if you use natural cleaners, take public transportation instead of driving a car, and plant an organic garden, for example.*

Connect Review your findings and share them with a small group. Then, think about how Lucy in "Allied with Green" is focused on "green" living. Which information from your research do you think Lucy would feel most strongly about? Why?

224   Unit 3

TO CHALLENGE STUDENTS . . .

Explore Terminology Point out the footnotes on page 219. Explain that *xeriscape* comes from the Greek word for "dry," *xeros*. This type of landscaping saves water and reduces the use of chemicals. Plants used in xeriscaping thrive in local conditions and so need less "tending." Have groups of students look up the word *permaculture* and then give a presentation to the class explaining its principles and how it might include xeriscaping in some areas.

CREATE AND DISCUSS

Write a Poem Write a poem about the character Lucy in "Allied with Green" and what you think matters most to her.

- ❏ Use story details to make inferences about Lucy's character.
- ❏ Choose a poetic form. For example, you might follow a pattern of alternating end rhyme. Or you may prefer free verse, which does not contain regular patterns of rhythm or rhyme.
- ❏ Experiment with word choice and with figurative language.

Share and Discuss Opinions With a small group, discuss your opinions about Lucy in "Allied with Green." Is she an idealist, who dreams about a world that will never happen? Is she an activist, who has the will and the power to make changes in the world? How would you characterize her?

- ❏ Review the story with your group. Together, look for details about Lucy's actions, thoughts, and feelings.
- ❏ Then, discuss what the details in the story reveal about Lucy's character. Listen closely to each other. Ask each other questions to help clarify ideas.
- ❏ End your discussion by identifying each group member's characterization of Lucy. Then, work together to combine those responses into a sentence or two. Share your response with the class and see whether your classmates agree.

RESPOND TO THE ESSENTIAL QUESTION

? What does it mean to be in harmony with nature?

Gather Information Review your annotations and notes on "Allied with Green." Then, add relevant details to your Response Log. As you determine which information to include, think about:

- the ways that people sometimes ignore or even harm the natural world
- the things that Lucy does to show that she cares about the environment

At the end of the unit, use your notes to write a personal narrative.

RESPOND

Go to **Participating in a Collaborative Discussion** in the **Speaking and Listening Studio** for help.

ACADEMIC VOCABULARY
As you write and discuss what you learned from the short story, be sure to use the Academic Vocabulary words. Check off each of the words that you use.

- ❏ affect
- ❏ element
- ❏ ensure
- ❏ participate
- ❏ specify

Allied with Green 225

APPLY

CREATE AND DISCUSS

Write a Poem Suggest to students that they create their own Lucy. She should have all the character traits that they can infer from the Lucy in the story. Besides these traits, students should feel free to add others. For example, they can decide whether their Lucy is twelve or fourteen, what she looks like, and where she lives: Brooklyn, Denver, or wherever they choose. When their own idea of Lucy is complete, they can begin writing about her. They do not have to include all the information they imagined, just what the poem needs.

For **writing support** for students at varying proficiency levels, see the **Text X-Ray** on page 216D.

Share and Discuss Opinions Remind students that group discussions should include contributions from all members of the group. If full participation does not happen naturally, use the token method. Give the group an object such as a book or a hat. Explain that the token should be passed around the group and that a student must be holding the token in order to speak.

RESPOND TO THE ESSENTIAL QUESTION

Allow time for students to add details from "Allied with Green" to their Unit 3 Response Logs.

Allied With Green **225**

APPLY

CRITICAL VOCABULARY

Answers:

1. Someone with an **addiction** might seek the help of a therapist or doctor who could help them break their dependency.

2. If you are **remorseful**, apologize and you will feel less guilty.

3. **Medians** are more common in areas with heavy traffic because they control traffic flow.

4. People visit an **arboretum** to see trees and be in nature.

5. In an **obituary**, I would expect to see information about someone's life.

VOCABULARY STRATEGY:
Context Clues

Answers:

1. sheared: plucked, erased; had the greenery taken away; removed through the use of a cutting tool

2. snide: nose up, blah, blah; scornful; mocking in an indirect way

3. transporting: take you away; making you feel like you are in another place; move someone or something or overwhelm with emotion.

226   Unit 3

 RESPOND

WORD BANK
addiction
remorseful
median
arboretum
obituary

CRITICAL VOCABULARY

Practice and Apply Answer each question using the Critical Vocabulary word in a complete sentence.

1. What help might people who have an **addiction** seek? Why?
2. What advice would you give to a **remorseful** person, and why?
3. Are **medians** more common in areas with light traffic, or with heavy traffic? Why?
4. Why would people visit an **arboretum**?
5. What information would you expect to see in an **obituary**?

 Go to the **Vocabulary Studio** for more on context clues.

VOCABULARY STRATEGY: Context Clues

When you encounter an unfamiliar word or phrase in your reading, one way to figure out the meaning is to use **context clues.** Context clues are hints about meaning that may appear in the words, phrases, sentences, and paragraphs that surround that unknown word or phrase.

In the example below from "Allied with Green," the word *sickened* provides a clue to the meaning of *remorseful*. Both words describe the negative feeling that Lucy thinks causes cities to "name everything for green" after the natural landscape has been destroyed.

> She knew it had been mentioned before, but thought she ought to include how cities assault their green for two reasons: money and greed. Later, (feeling remorseful) or (sickened) by the new view, they (name everything for green)—Oak Meadows, Lone Pine.

Practice and Apply Use context clues in "Allied with Green" to help you define the meaning of the words in the chart. Then look up each word's precise meaning in a dictionary.

WORD	CONTEXT CLUES	MY GUESSED DEFINITION	DICTIONARY DEFINITION
sheared (paragraph 10)			
snide (paragraph 20)			
transporting (paragraph 25)			

226   Unit 3

 ENGLISH LEARNER SUPPORT

Vocabulary Strategy Give students additional practice in determining the meanings of unfamiliar words by using context clues or synonyms. Display the following sentences:

- Many new farming <u>methods</u> are plans or ways of using modern techniques to grow food.
- These methods do less damage to soil and use fewer things, or <u>supplies</u>, such as insect poisons.

Have students look for clues in the sentences to help them determine the meanings of the underlined words. Then have them look up the words to confirm those meanings.
SUBSTANTIAL/MODERATE

RESPOND

APPLY

LANGUAGE CONVENTIONS:
Complex Sentences

When you add a subordinate clause to an independent (main) clause, you create a **complex sentence,** as in this example:

(Because I have told my friends about conservation,) they care more about the environment.

A clause is built on a subject and verb working together. Therefore, no matter how many clauses are in a sentence, the subject and verb in each clause must agree. In the example above, *I* agrees with *have told,* and *they* agrees with *care*.

Now, notice that the first clause in the example is a subordinate clause. It needs the rest of the sentence for it to make sense. If it were written with a period after *conservation,* it would be a sentence fragment. A **sentence fragment** is a group of words that is only part of a sentence. It does not express a complete thought. A sentence fragment may be lacking a subject, a predicate, or both. Be alert to errors like these and two other kinds of errors as you write:

- In a **comma splice,** two independent clauses are joined with only a comma. You can correct a comma splice by making the clauses separate sentences, by changing the comma into a semicolon, by adding a coordinating conjunction, or by rephrasing the sentence as a complex sentence (as in the example above).

    INCORRECT: I have told my friends about conservation, they care more about the environment.

    REVISION: I have told my friends about conservation. They care more about the environment.

    REVISION: I have told my friends about conservation; they care more about the environment.

    REVISION: I have told my friends about conservation, so they care more about the environment.

- In a **run-on sentence,** there is no punctuation or conjunction between clauses: *I have told my friends about conservation they care more about the environment.* You can correct run-on sentences in the same ways that you correct comma splices.

Practice and Apply Write a paragraph about conservation and use complex sentences for most of your sentences. With a partner, make sure that all subjects and verbs agree and that you have avoided sentence fragments, comma splices, and run-on sentences.

Allied with Green 227

LANGUAGE CONVENTIONS:
Complex Sentences

Explain to students that one way to think of complex sentences is to imagine taking a complete sentence and adding a fragment of a sentence to it to make what they say more interesting. Tell students to think of how boring it would be to read one simple sentence after another:

I like to walk in the park. I like to look at flowering plants. I like to look at birds.

Forming a complex sentence is one way to allow writers to say more with fewer words:

When I go to the park, I like to look at birds and green plants.

Tell students to notice that *When I go to the park* is not a complete sentence because it does not express a complete thought: it begins with the subordinating conjunction *when*. If one person said to another person "*When I go to the park*" and nothing else, the person hearing it would want to know what happens when the speaker goes to the park.

If students struggle, have them practice forming dependent clauses beginning with the subordinating conjunctions *because*, and *after*. Have their partners add a comma and an independent clause to form a complex sentence, e.g., *After I went to the movies + comma + I realized that I didn't finish my homework.*

Practice and Apply

Possible answers:

1. *Before I started my garden, I planned the placement of flowers very carefully.*
2. *If a sun-loving flower is planted in the shade, it will not survive.*
3. *I chose this type because it grows well in the shade.*
4. *When the season is over, I will enjoy a break from gardening.*

ENGLISH LEARNER SUPPORT

Language Conventions Use the following supports with students at varying proficiency levels.

- Work with students to identify the subordinate clause in each of these sentences. Remind them to look for commas or words that separate 2 different subjects: *When I saw her, I smiled. I was happy because she brought lunch.* **SUBSTANTIAL**

- Have students identify the subordinate clause in this sentence: *Lucy's father demonstrated against developments when he was in college.*

- Ask: *Why does this sentence not need a comma?* (*The subordinating clause is after the main, independent clause.*) **MODERATE**

- Ask students to write two complex sentences, punctuating them correctly. **LIGHT**

Allied With Green **227**

PLAN

ODE TO ENCHANTED LIGHT / SLEEPING IN THE FOREST
Poems by Pablo Neruda/Mary Oliver

GENRE ELEMENTS
POETRY: ODE/LYRIC POEM

Remind students that modern **lyric poems** are often written in the first person. They express personal thoughts and feelings. Lyric poems are characterized by strong sound to meaning relationships. An **ode** is a complex lyric poem that develops a serious and dignified theme. Odes appeal to both the imagination and the intellect, and many commemorate events or praise people or elements of nature.

LEARNING OBJECTIVES

- Analyze an ode and a lyric poem.
- Research famous nature poems.
- Write an ode and a lyric poem.
- Compare the organization, sound devices, and figurative language in two poems.
- Prepare and present a comparison of two poems.
- **Language** Understand sound and meaning in lyric poetry.

TEXT COMPLEXITY

Quantitative Measures	Ode to Enchanted Light / Sleeping in the Forest	Lexile: N/A
Qualitative Measures	**Ideas Presented** Multiple levels of meaning, use of symbolism and ambiguity	
	Structure Used Complex, leading to intentional multiple interpretations	
	Language Used Accessible vocabulary, but considerable figurative language	
	Knowledge Required Requires no special knowledge, some experience of nature	

228A Unit 3

PLAN

Online Ed

RESOURCES

- Unit 3 Response Log
- 🔊 Selection Audio
- Text in FOCUS Understanding Form
- Close Read Close Read Screencasts: Modeled Discussions
- 📖 Reading Studio: Notice & Note
- 💬 Speaking and Listening Studio: Analyzing and Evaluating Presentations
- 💬 Speaking and Listening Studio: Giving a Presentation
- ✓ "Ode to Enchanted " and "Sleeping in the Forest" Selection Test

SUMMARIES

English
"Ode to Enchanted Light" describes light as it falls through the tree canopy in a forest or jungle, creating a sense of enchantment. "Sleeping in the Forest" explores the speaker's sense of belonging to and being embraced by nature as she sleeps under the stars in a forest.

Spanish
"Oda a la luz encantada" describe la luz mientras cae del dosel de un árbol en un bosque o jungla, creando una sensación de encantamiento. "Durmiendo en el bosque" explora la sensación de pertenencia de la voz narrativa, además de la sensación de ser abrazada por la naturaleza mientras se duerme bajo las estrellas en un bosque.

 ## SMALL-GROUP OPTIONS

Have students work in small groups to read and discuss the selection.

Pinwheel Discussion
- In groups of eight, four students are seated in a square, facing out. Four other students are seated facing in towards the first four.
- Students in the inner square remain stationary throughout the discussion.
- Students in the outer square move to their right after discussing each question.
- Control the discussion by providing a question for each rotation, such as, *Which poem is closer to your sense of nature? Which poem tells you more about the speaker's feelings?*

Send a Problem
- Pose questions about the ideas or actions described in one of the two poems. Call on a student to respond.
- Wait up to 11 seconds.
- If the student does not have a response, student must call on another student by name to answer the same question.
- The sending student repeats the question as he or she calls on another for assistance.
- Monitor responses and redirect or ask another question as needed.

Ode to Enchanted Light;/Sleeping in the Forest **228B**

PLAN

Text X-Ray: English Learner Support
for "Ode to Enchanted Light/Sleeping in the Forest"

Use the Text X-Ray and the supports and scaffolds in the Teacher's Edition to help guide students at different proficiency levels through the selection.

INTRODUCE THE SELECTION
DISCUSS NATURE IN POETRY

In this lesson, students will need to discuss how nature can inspire poets. For example, a poet might be surprised to discover that leafcutter ants build complex underground gardens that can feed over eight million ants. This knowledge could fill the poet with the urge to compare ants to humans— to use personification to change, or transform ants in order to say something about nature in a way that will interest people.

An *inspiration* is an urge to do something inventive or creative.

A *transformation* is a big change in the form of something; caterpillars are transformed when they become butterflies

Model cluster word-web graphic organizers. Label the extensions to help students get ideas: 1) reminds me of . . . 2) is like . . . Give students lists and images of living and non-living things. Model using the organizer, e.g., put an image of ant in the center circle; write: *An ant is like a tiny gardener in armor*.

CULTURAL REFERENCES

The following words and phrases may be unfamiliar to students:

- Neruda: *latticework* (line 5): crossed strips of wood that a vine climbs up
- Neruda: *cicada sends its sawing sound* (line 10): a cicada is a large, flying insect that makes a sound a little like a saw going through wood
- Oliver: *luminous doom* (line 16) luminous: bright, shining. doom: death, destruction

LISTENING

Understand Sound and Meaning in Poetry

Draw students' attention to the sounds in the introductory lines of the poem "Sleeping in the Forest." Explore the way the words express the softness and warmth of the image.

Have students listen as you read aloud the title and first sentence of "Sleeping in the Forest" with expression, paying particular attention to the words with r-controlled vowels (*earth, remembered, tenderly, arranging, her, dark, skirts*). Use the following supports with students at varying proficiency levels:

- Point out the soft "ur" sounds, as in *purr*. Ask students to listen for *r* sounds as you reread the sentences. Have them signal with thumbs up when they hear an r-controlled word. **SUBSTANTIAL**
- Have students listen for r-controlled vowel sounds as you reread the sentence. Then, have them use single words or sentences to describe the feelings the sounds create. (*soft, warm, comforting, dreamlike, frightening; answers may vary.*) **MODERATE**
- Pair students and have them identify words or phrases, such as *her dark skirts*. Ask them to talk about how the sounds in those words relate to the meaning of the first sentence. **LIGHT**

PLAN

SPEAKING

Discuss the Purpose of an Ode

Draw students' attention to the title of Pablo Neruda's "Ode to Enchanted Light." Explain that an ode expresses appreciation for its subject.

Read "Ode to Enchanted Light." Use the following supports with students at varying proficiency levels:

- Tell students that you will ask questions about what you just read aloud. For example, ask: *What does the speaker talk about in the first stanza of the poem? (light)* Have students use single words and phrases while looking at images that match the words. Have them label the images. **SUBSTANTIAL**
- Have students identify what Neruda is expressing appreciation for in the poem. Ask: *What does the title suggest the poem is about? (light) Does the rest of the poem support this idea? (yes)* Have them echo-read the poem with you. **MODERATE**
- Have partners read the poem aloud to each other. Pair students to discuss what Neruda appreciates about light. Ask: *How does Neruda talk about light in the poem? (It's beautiful and magical.)* **LIGHT**

READING

Read for Understanding

Draw students' attention to how Pablo Neruda and Mary Oliver use certain words and images in their poems. Focus on descriptive language and figurative language.

Read the title and first five lines of "Ode to Enchanted Light" and the title and the first sentence of "Sleeping in the Forest." Use the following supports with students at varying proficiency levels:

- After you read the title and selected lines of each poem, ask students where the speaker of the poem is. Help them to understand that each speaker is in a forest. **SUBSTANTIAL**
- Have groups of students choose one of the poems and read the title and opening lines from the poem. Then ask them to match words and phrases from a word list that can be substituted for words in the poem *(e.g., from Neruda: light/sunlight, dropped/fell, drifting/floating)* review word meanings such as *latticework*. Have students practice asking for clarification. **MODERATE**
- Pair students and have each pair choose one of the poems. Help them identify the kind of figurative language used in the poem's first image and then describe the effect of the image. *(Neruda: simile, light, clear; Oliver: personification, warm, caring)* **LIGHT**

WRITING

Write an Ode

Work with students to read the writing assignment on p. 235.

Use the following supports with students at varying proficiency levels:

- Tell students that *appreciate* (cognate: *apreciar*) means "to value or admire." Ask, *What do you like about trees?* Help them find words and images of and about trees. Repeat for other things in nature. Have them use words and images to answer the questions and begin to create an ode. **SUBSTANTIAL**
- Provide sentence frames for beginning an ode. *A _____ is a wonderful thing. It looks like _____. It makes me feel _____.* **MODERATE**
- Pair students to talk about possible topics for an ode. Remind students that nature includes gardens, pets, and even weeds in sidewalk cracks. Have them brainstorm ideas, take notes, and write a first stanza or sentence. **LIGHT**

TEACH

? **Connect to the**
ESSENTIAL QUESTION

Poetry can capture the beauty and peculiarities of nature in a unique way, allowing the reader to see aspects of the world they might not have thought about. This selection focuses on two forms of poetry and the different ways poets express personal thoughts and feelings.

COMPARE FORMS AND ELEMENTS

Have students read the background and information about the poets. Tell students that, although Mary Oliver and Pablo Neruda use different poetic forms and styles to write about nature, both express an appreciation for it. Their insights can help the reader reexamine his or her thoughts, feelings, beliefs, and ideas about the natural world.

COLLABORATE & COMPARE

POEM

ODE TO ENCHANTED LIGHT

by **Pablo Neruda**

pages 231–233

COMPARE FORMS AND ELEMENTS

As you read, notice the form of each poem by focusing on the way words and lines are arranged on the page. Think about how each poem's structure—along with its use of rhythm, rhyme, and figurative language—deepens your understanding of its meaning and helps you make comparisons.

 ESSENTIAL QUESTION:

What does it mean to be in harmony with nature?

POEM

SLEEPING IN THE FOREST

by **Mary Oliver**

pages 236–237

228 Unit 3

GET READY

QUICK START

Think about a time when something in nature took you by surprise and caused you to pause and reflect for a moment. What did you experience in that moment—and what made it meaningful to you?

ANALYZE FORM: ODE

An **ode** is a type of lyric poetry (see next page) that deals with serious themes, such as justice, truth, or beauty. An ode celebrates or praises its subject, which is usually a person, event, thing, or element in nature.

The word *ode* comes from the Greek word *aeidein*, which means "sing" or "chant." A traditional ode is a long poem with a formal structure—often with patterns in its **meter**, or use of stressed and unstressed syllables, and its **rhyme**, its repetition of sounds at the end of words. Many modern poets experiment with the ode form to make it fresh and interesting for readers.

An ode and other types of poems reflect the poet's **style**, a manner of writing that involves *how* something is said rather than *what* is said. A poet can share ideas by using stylistic elements such as these:

GENRE ELEMENTS: POETRY

Form in poetry includes:
- how the poem's words and lines are presented on a page
- how the poem's sounds and rhythms are organized
- how the poem is structured with stanzas, line length, meter, and rhyme scheme

POETIC ELEMENT	WHAT IT DOES
Word choice poet's use of words	• A poet's word choice can be formal or informal, serious or humorous. • Well-chosen words and phrases help a poet express ideas precisely and creatively. They also help readers "see" what the poet is describing and better understand what she or he is feeling. • Through descriptive words, imagery, and **figurative language** (such as similes, metaphors, and personification), poets create a **mood**, or feeling or atmosphere.
Tone poet's attitude toward a subject	• Like word choice, a poet's tone can convey different feelings. • A feeling can often be described in one word—for example, playful, serious, or determined.
Voice poet's unique style of expression	• The poet's language lets a reader "hear" a personality in the poem. • The use of voice can reveal a poet's traits, beliefs, and attitudes.

As you read "Ode to enchanted light" and "Sleeping in the Forest," note how each poet uses these elements. Consider how they shape your experience of reading the poem.

Ode to enchanted light / Sleeping in the Forest 229

WHEN STUDENTS STRUGGLE . . .

Understand Figurative Language Review the basics of figurative language, using the following supports for students at varying proficiency levels"

- Give students a simple simile. Say, *Her smile is like the sun*. Use gestures/and or pantomime to explain the simile as needed. Ask, *How could a smile and the sun be alike?* (both are bright; both make you happy). How are they different? (a smile is an expression, the sun is a huge ball of fiery gas) What do you think I meant when I said her smile is like the sun? (Her smile is bright and makes you happy.)

TEACH

QUICK START

Remind students that nature does not refer only to places that are uninhabited by people— like forests, mountains, and oceans. Nature exists everywhere, including in cities. Nature is that which was not made by humans. Students may have had experiences in parks or zoos, or may think of nature as places they wouldn't ordinarily go. It's important to help students see that they are part of nature and that they are always interacting with nature in some way.

ANALYZE FORM: ODE

Remind students that an ode appeals to the intellect, or mind, as well as the emotions. Suggest that students use these questions to help them analyze the intellectual appeal of the poem

- Tell students to think about how specific combinations of words can help readers to visualize what is going on in a poem. Have them think of some images they would use for something they appreciate.
- Ask students to think about how the form of the ode can be used to express appreciation for big and small things. Tell students that Pablo Neruda wrote a poem titled "Ode to Salt."
- Tell students to talk about how authors use metaphors and similes in odes. Remember that similes compare two or more things that are unalike (the tiny *leaves* fell like *rain*). Metaphors are words and phrases that identify things with language that would normally be used to identify something else. Try to think of your own similes and metaphors: The world is…/ The world is like…
- Ask: Do you like language that makes you see an image easily or more complex language that you have to figure out, like a riddle? Why?

Ode to Enchanted Light   229

TEACH

ANALYZE LYRIC POETRY

Explain to students that an ode is one kind of lyric poem. Many lyric poems are less serious and less formal than an ode. Lyric poems can even be humorous. However, each lyric poem creates one particular mood or impression. That is one of the things that make a lyric poem different from other forms of poetry, such as **narrative poems** and **dramatic poems**. As you read each of the poems, think about these questions:

- Can I feel a particular mood in this poem?
- What words can describe that mood?
- What word choices or literary devices has the poet used to create that mood?

ANNOTATION MODEL

Remind students of the annotation ideas on p. 230, which suggest underlining poetic elements that create meaning for the reader. Point out that they may follow this suggestion or use their own system for marking up the selection in their write-in text. They may want to color-code their annotations by using highlighters. Their notes in the margin may include questions about ideas that are unclear or topics they want to learn more about.

 GET READY

ANALYZE LYRIC POETRY

A **lyric poem** is a short poem in which a single speaker expresses personal thoughts and feelings. Lyric poetry is a broad category that includes traditional forms such as odes and sonnets. Lyric poetry also includes **free verse,** a form that does not use a formal structure or rhyme scheme. In ancient times, lyric poems were meant to be sung and were often accompanied by a lyre, a simple stringed instrument like a harp.

- Lyric poems have some elements in common with songs, including the following:
  - rhythm and **melody,** a pleasing arrangement of sounds
  - the use of a **refrain,** one or more phrases or lines repeated in each stanza of a poem
  - imaginative word choice, or **diction**
  - the creation of a single, unified impression

As you analyze "Ode to enchanted light" and "Sleeping in the Forest," think about the images of nature presented in each poem. What do these images suggest about each speaker's relationship to nature? How does the poets' use of language affect the mood, voice, and tone that each poem conveys?

ANNOTATION MODEL   NOTICE & NOTE

As you read, think about the poetic elements that each poet uses and how these create meaning for the reader. In the model, you can see one reader's notes about "Ode to enchanted light."

> Under the trees <u>light</u>
> has dropped from the top of the sky,
> <u>light</u>
> like a green
> 5 latticework of branches, . . .

It is interesting how the poet chooses to repeat the word <u>light</u>. I think this is done to show how important the effect of light is in nature.

I think these lines have a mood of playfulness even though this ode is about a more serious topic.

230   Unit 3

 ENGLISH LEARNER SUPPORT

Use Cognates The Spanish term for a lyric poem is *poema lírico*.

Transfer Issues Speakers of Vietnamese may have some difficulty pronouncing and hearing r-controlled vowels and certain consonants. This can present a challenge when listening to lyric poetry in English. Encourage Vietnamese students to practice r-controlled short vowels in sentences like these: The *birds* in the *birch* trees *chirp*. *Purple fur* covered *her shirt*. Invite students to write and recite their own sentences with r-controlled words.
ALL LEVELS

BACKGROUND

Nature has been a popular subject for poets throughout history. Two of the 20th century's most important poets, Pablo Neruda and Mary Oliver, continue this tradition. **Pablo Neruda** (1904–1973) was the pen name of Ricardo Eliecer Neftalí Reyes Basoalto, who was born in Chile. Over his lifetime, he wrote hundreds of poems and was awarded the Nobel Prize for Literature in 1971 for his body of work. Neruda's poem "Ode to enchanted light" was written in Spanish. Its Spanish title is "Oda a la luz encantada."

ODE TO ENCHANTED LIGHT

Poem by Pablo Neruda
translated by Ken Krabbenhoft

PREPARE TO COMPARE

As you read, note the different word choices and the structural and stylistic elements of an ode used in the poem.

Under the trees light
has dropped from the top of the sky,
light
like a green
5 latticework of branches,
shining
on every leaf,
drifting down like clean
white sand.

Notice & Note

Use the side margins to notice and note signposts in the text.

AGAIN AND AGAIN

Notice & Note: Mark instances where the poet is expressing how things look in the light.

Analyze: How does repeated use of similes (comparisons using *like* or *as*) create a mood or emotional effect?

TEACH

BACKGROUND

Born in a small town in 1904, Pablo Neruda began writing poetry as a child. When he was still in his early teens, he changed his name to Neruda to honor a Czech poet named Jan Neruda. While a student, he met Gabriela Mistral, a famous poet who had received the Nobel Prize in Literature. She encouraged Neruda to continue writing and, years later, Neruda also won the Nobel Prize.

PREPARE TO COMPARE

Direct students to use the Prepare to Compare prompt to focus their reading.

▶ AGAIN AND AGAIN

Neruda uses **repetition** in "Ode to Enchanted Light" by adding several examples of **figurative language,** from **similes** in the first stanza to **imagery** in the second to **metaphor** in the third. Together, they create a **mood** of wonder and, as the title suggests, enchantment. (**Answer:** *The repeated use of similes adds to the enchanted mood of the poem by comparing the light to latticework and clean sand.*)

IMPROVE READING FLUENCY

Targeted Passage   Reread lines 1-5. Model reading with expression and using the poem's rhythm and sound devices to emphasize the melody of the lines. Then have a volunteer read the same lines. Remind students that they should not stop at the ends of lines unless there is punctuation. Suggest that they choose certain words to emphasize before they begin reading aloud.

  Go to the **Reading Studio** for additional support in developing fluency.

TEACH

■ English Learner Support

Analyze Figurative Language Remind students to look for comparisons that use *like* and *as*: they are similes. Point out that the poet does not say the world is *like* a glass of water; the world *is* a glass of water. Discuss the difference in word choice.

ASK STUDENTS how the light the speaker is talking about is like water overflowing from a glass. *(Both seem to be falling or flowing down.)* **LIGHT**

 ANALYZE FORM: ODE

Explain to students that poets use line breaks to guide readers and, sometimes, to make them pay attention. When reading a poem, students may be surprised and feel that a line is not finished. For example, "A cicada sends" is only the beginning of a description. The poet breaks the line to make us think, to ask ourselves, for an instant, what a cicada might send. Then, as the next line becomes an answer, we pay more attention to it. In the final stanza, what question does the line "a glass overflowing" raise. *(What is the glass overflowing with?)* **(Answer:** Interpret: The line length and arrangement of the lines creates a slow and comforting rhythm.*)*

 TEXT IN FOCUS

Understanding Form Have students view the **Text in Focus** video on this page of their ebook for help in understanding form in poetry. Then have students use **Text in Focus Practice** to apply what they have learned.

For **listening** and **reading support** for students at varying proficiency levels, see the **Text X-Ray** on page 228C–228D.

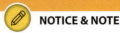 **NOTICE & NOTE**

ANALYZE FORM: ODE
Annotate: Observe the difference in line lengths in the poem. Circle lines that stand out and underline shorter lines.

Interpret: How does the length and arrangement of lines in Neruda's poem impact its meaning?

10 A cicada sends
    its sawing song
    high into the empty air.

    The world is
    a glass overflowing
15 with water.

232   Unit 3

CLOSE READ SCREENCAST

Modeled Discussion Have students click the Close-Read icon in their eBook to access a screencast in which readers discuss and annotate the following key lines from each poem:

- "A cicada sends . . ." ("Ode to Enchanted Light" lines 10–12)
- "I though the earth . . ." ("Sleeping in the Forest" lines 1–5)

As a class, view and discuss the video. Then have students pair up to do an independent close read of the last lines of each poem. Students can record their answers on the Close Read Practice PDF.

 Close Read Practice PDF

232   Unit 3

NOTICE & NOTE

TEACH

CHECK YOUR UNDERSTANDING

Have students answer the questions independently.

Answers:

1. C
2. G
3. A

If they answer any questions incorrectly, have them reread the test to confirm their understanding. Then they may proceed to ANALYZE THE TEXT on page 234.

CHECK YOUR UNDERSTANDING

Answer these questions before moving on to the **Analyze the Text** section on the following page.

1 Which best expresses where the speaker in the poem is located?

   A In a meadow where cicadas sing

   B Near a river that is overflowing

   C Under the branches of some trees

   D In an airplane high in the air

2 Toward what does the poet express an appreciative tone, or attitude?

   F Cicadas

   G Natural light

   H Leaves

   J Empty air

3 Which word best describes the mood of the third stanza: <u>A cicada sends / its sawing song / high into the empty air</u>?

   A Happy

   B Ominous

   C Eager

   D Lonely

Ode to enchanted light 233

ENGLISH LEARNER SUPPORT

Oral Assessment Use the following questions to assess students' comprehension and speaking skills:

1. Where is the speaker in the poem located? *(under the branches of some trees.)*

2. What is the poet expressing appreciation for in this ode? *(the forest)*

3. How could the mood of the third stanza be described? *(happy, joyful, delighted)*
   SUBSTANTIAL/MODERATE

Ode to Enchanted Light **233**

APPLY

ANALYZE THE TEXT

Possible answers:

1. **DOK 4:** *In lines 6–9, Neruda uses a simile in which he compares the light to white sand falling. The image is effective because it describes a peaceful, calm motion.*

2. **DOK 4:** *The comparisons convey the sense of light as something that is almost magical as it moves, shines, drifts, and transforms.*

3. **DOK 4:** *The /s/ sounds in "cicada sends / its sawing song" suggest the repetitious, raspy voice of a cicada itself.*

4. **DOK 4:** *Yes. The poem expresses an appreciation for how light enhances the beauty of sights and sounds in nature.*

5. **DOK 4:** *The /w/ sound is repeated again and again in the final stanza. The author's repeated use of alliteration reveals the lyrical or song-like style of his writing.*

RESEARCH

Point out to students that there are a number of sites dedicated to poetry and poets. Help students locate good places to look for reliable information.

Connect The research results will vary greatly, depending on the poem and the poet students have chosen. Other types of the nature experience students might suggest are storms, floods, or extremely hot or cold temperatures. Students should find at least one poem to analyze and should be encouraged to find some information about the poet and his or her world.

RESPOND

ANALYZE THE TEXT

Support your responses with evidence from the text. **NOTEBOOK**

1. **Interpret and Evaluate** What type of comparison does the poet make in lines 6–9 of "Ode to enchanted light"? Do you think this comparison is effective? Explain.

2. **Analyze** How do the comparisons made in lines 1–9 of "Ode to enchanted light" relate to the title of the poem? How is the light "enchanted"?

3. **Analyze** A cicada is an insect that makes a high-pitched, continual sound, usually in summer. Reread lines 10–12. What repeated first sounds, or **alliteration,** do you hear, and how are the sounds connected to the poem's meaning?

4. **Evaluate** Does this poem meet the requirements of an ode? Why or why not?

5. **Notice & Note** How is alliteration used in the final stanza of this poem? What does the repeated use of alliteration tell you about the author's style of writing?

RESEARCH TIP
Once you select a poem for analysis, consider doing some further research about the historical, literary, social, or even geographical context in which the poet was writing.

RESEARCH

Throughout history, poets have celebrated the beauty and power of nature. Research a few poets known for their nature poems—perhaps a poet you've read before and one you're curious about reading for the first time. Then select one poem that appeals to you and use the graphic organizer below to analyze its key elements.

QUESTION	ANSWER
What is the form of the poem?	
What is the mood of the poem?	
What memorable images does the poem contain?	
What tone, or attitude, does the poet have toward the subject?	
What is the theme of the poem?	

Connect With a small group, discuss whether nature poetry must always be about pleasant or positive experiences of nature. What other types of nature experience might be appropriate for a poem?

WHEN STUDENTS STRUGGLE . . .

Take Notes Explain to students that they should always take notes when they are doing research. Their notes do not have to be written in complete sentences, but they should write down the sources for all of their important information.

Suggest that students create a simple two-column graphic organizer, noting information on one side and the source of the information on the other.

RESPOND

CREATE AND DISCUSS

Write an Ode Write an ode about a memorable experience that you have had in a natural setting, or perhaps something that you observed in nature and want to share. Think about the following questions.

- ❏ Who will be the speaker in your ode?
- ❏ How will you set up your lines and stanzas?
- ❏ How will you describe your experience or observation?
- ❏ What images or sound devices, such as alliteration, will you use?
- ❏ What will be the theme, or message, of your ode?

Listen for a Poem's Message In a group, take turns reading aloud and listening to your poems. Use the questions below to guide your listening and follow-up discussion.

- ❏ What is the poem about?
- ❏ What does the poem make me think about?
- ❏ How does the poem make me feel?
- ❏ What images and sounds in the poem do I like best?
- ❏ How can I state the message in the poem in a sentence?

Go to **Analyzing and Evaluating Presentations** in the **Speaking and Listening Studio** for help.

RESPOND TO THE ESSENTIAL QUESTION

 What does it mean to be in harmony with nature?

Gather Information Review your annotations and notes on "Ode to enchanted light." Then, add relevant details to your Response Log. As you determine which information to include, think about how:

- people react to different types of experiences in nature
- your past experiences affect new ones
- your past experiences shape your views about yourself and the world around you

At the end of the unit, use your notes to write a personal narrative.

ACADEMIC VOCABULARY

As you write and discuss what you learned from the poem, be sure to use the Academic Vocabulary words. Check off each of the words that you use.

- ❏ affect
- ❏ element
- ❏ ensure
- ❏ participate
- ❏ specify

Ode to enchanted light 235

APPLY

CREATE AND DISCUSS

Write an Ode Remind students that an ode expresses appreciation and therefore should have a positive tone. The images and themes students use should communicate approval and other positive feelings for the subject of their ode.

For **writing support** for students at varying proficiency levels, see the **Text X-Ray** on page 228D.

Listen for a Poem's Message Explain to students that listening to a poem is a little like listening to a song. The message is important, but so is the sound. Suggest that students listen to each poem with their eyes closed so they can focus their complete attention on the sounds and what they add to the meaning of the poem.

RESPOND TO THE ESSENTIAL QUESTION

Allow time for students to add details from "Ode to Enchanted Light" to their Unit 3 Response Logs.

ENGLISH LEARNER SUPPORT

Listen for a Poem's Message Provide these sentence frames to help students express their ideas about each other's poems. *The poem is about _____. The poem makes me think about _____. The poem makes me feel _____. The images and sounds in the poem I like best are _____. I think the poem means that _____.* **SUBSTANTIAL/MODERATE**

TEACH

BACKGROUND

Explain to students that Mary Oliver once described herself as married to amazement. In her poetry, she approaches nature with this amazement. She seems continually surprised by the wonders of the natural world and beautifully crafts poems that communicate her awe.

PREPARE TO COMPARE

Direct students to use the Prepare to Compare prompt to focus their reading.

▶ MEMORY MOMENT

Point out that, in order for the earth to remember the speaker, the speaker must have been close to the earth in this way before. The words "took me back" confirm this inference and reveal something about the speaker's relationship to nature. (**Answer:** *The speaker has often spent time close to nature.*)

ENGLISH LEARNER SUPPORT

Understand Figurative Language. Read aloud the first five lines of the poem using gestures/pantomime to help students understand the comparison between the earth and a comforting woman. Have students draw the earth and what the author compares the earth to.
SUBSTANTIAL

Have students read the first five lines of the poem and complete this sentence frame: *The author thinks the earth is like a ___.* **MODERATE**

Ask students these questions:
- *What are the two things being compared?*
- *What is the quality they share?* **MODERATE**

 For **listening support** for students at varying proficiency levels, see the **Text X-Ray** on page 228C.

 **NOTICE & NOTE**

BACKGROUND

Mary Oliver (b. 1935) is an American poet who was born in Maple Heights, Ohio. In her youth, she was an avid reader and writer. She also spent a lot of time walking through nearby woods and fields. Today, Oliver is regarded by many as a poetic guide to the natural world and an heir to the Romantic nature tradition in American poetry begun by Ralph Waldo Emerson and Henry David Thoreau. Oliver has published more than two dozen books and is the winner of many prestigious awards for her poetry.

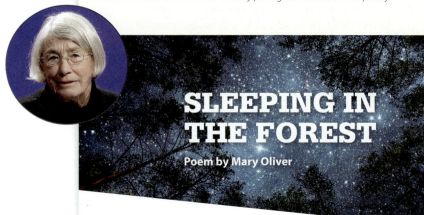

SLEEPING IN THE FOREST
Poem by Mary Oliver

Notice & Note

Use the side margins to notice and note signposts in the text.

MEMORY MOMENT

Notice & Note: Mark the place in the poem where the speaker mentions a memory.

Analyze: What does the memory mentioned in the poem say about the speaker's relationship to nature?

PREPARE TO COMPARE

As you read, note the different structural and stylistic elements of a lyric poem that the author uses. How is the poem similar to or different from an ode?

> I thought the earth
> remembered me, she
> took me back so tenderly, arranging
> her dark skirts, her pockets
> 5   full of lichens[1] and seeds. I slept
> as never before, a stone
> on the riverbed, nothing
> between me and the white fire of the stars
> but my thoughts, and they floated
> 10 light as moths among the branches
> of the perfect trees. All night

---
[1] **lichens** (līˊkənz): fungi that grow together with algae and form a crust-like growth on rocks or tree trunks.

236   Unit 3

WHEN STUDENTS STRUGGLE . . .

Understand Figurative Language Review the basics of figurative language, using the following supports:

- Give students a simple simile. Say, *Her smile is like the sun.* Use gestures/and or pantomime to explain the simile as needed. Ask, *How could a smile and the sun be alike?* (both bright; both make you happy) *How are they different?* (smile is an expression, sun is a huge ball of fiery gas, etc.) *What do you think I meant when I said her smile is like the sun?* (Her smile is bright and makes you happy.)

I heard the small kingdoms breathing
around me, the insects, and the birds
who do their work in the darkness. All night
15   I rose and fell, as if in water, grappling²
with a luminous doom. By morning
I had vanished at least a dozen times
into something better.

---

² **grappling:** struggling.

NOTICE & NOTE

ANALYZE LYRIC POETRY
Annotate: Mark personal thoughts and feelings that the speaker expresses in lines 9–14.

Interpret: Is the speaker comfortable in the natural world? What text evidence supports your answer?

CHECK YOUR UNDERSTANDING

Answer these questions before moving on to the **Analyze the Text** section on the following page.

1 In lines 1–5, how does the speaker think of the forest?

  A As an uncomfortable bed

  B As a skirt with pockets

  C As a comforting friend

  D As a riverbed with rushing water

2 In lines 9–10, what is compared to <u>light as moths among the branches</u>?

  F Thoughts

  G Stones

  H Lights

  J Branches

3 How does the use of **personification**—the giving of human qualities to an animal, object, or idea—help achieve the poet's purpose?

  A It downplays the importance of Earth.

  B It downplays the importance of the speaker.

  C It highlights the importance of Earth.

  D It highlights the importance of the speaker.

TEACH

ANALYZE LYRIC POETRY

Remind students that a lyric poem is a poem that expresses the personal thoughts and feelings of a speaker. The speaker, or the person who is talking in the poem, can be the poet or an invented character telling about an experience that he or she is responding to. *(Answer: The speaker is comfortable with the natural world and conveys the idea that, in the forest, there is no real separation between nature and the speaker. The speaker's thoughts are expressed with "my thoughts," "they floated," "I heard"—each of which shows a connection to what is happening in the forest.)*

CHECK YOUR UNDERSTANDING

Have students answer the questions independently.

Answers:

1. C
2. F
3. C

If they answer any questions incorrectly, have them reread the text to confirm their understanding. Then they may proceed to ANALYZE THE TEXT on page 238.

 ENGLISH LEARNER SUPPORT

Oral Assessment Use the following questions to assess students' comprehension and speaking skills:

1. *Does the speaker feel that she is cared for and protected by the earth and the forest?* (yes) Have students match images of the forest with words and phrases from the poem they have written on cards. Have them say the words and arrange the cards in sequence to show that they understand the poem.

2. In lines 9-10, what is being compared to moths in the description "light as moths among the branches?" (The speaker's thoughts are compared to moths.)

3. What are the small kingdoms? *(the insects and birds)* Does the speaker in the poem really hear the insects and birds *breathing* or is that a form of figurative language? *(it's figurative language; birds and insects make many noises, but not the sounds of breathing.)* **ALL LEVELS**

APPLY

ANALYZE THE TEXT

Possible answers:

1. **DOK 4:** *The sleeping speaker is compared to a stone on the riverbed; both lie still. The image of being in water is repeated by the words "rose and fell, as if in water."*

2. **DOK 4:** *The poem expresses the speaker's thoughts and feelings about nature and life. The poem has a steady rhythm, and the word choices such as "the white fire of the stars" and "small kingdoms breathing" are imaginative. It does give a unified impression of nature as a mother and the speaker sleeping in her arms.*

3. **DOK 3:** *The poet compares two unlike things: her thoughts to moths, floating lightly in the air above her. There is a sense of perfect comfort and sweetness.*

4. **DOK 2:** *Perhaps sleeping in the forest enriches the speaker so she is a better person, at one with nature. Perhaps spending a night in the forest has sent the speaker into another realm, better than the world of daylight.*

5. **DOK 4:** *The poet uses the phrases, "All night" and "By morning" to indicate when these events occurred. During the night, she remembered hearing insects and birds "do their work in the darkness;" At night, she "rose and fell, as if in water." These phrases reinforce the idea of sleeping.*

RESEARCH

Point out to students that there are many good sites that contain poetry and biographical information about poets. Those are good places to look for reliable information.

Connect The research results will vary greatly, depending on the poem and the poet students have chosen.

RESPOND

ANALYZE THE TEXT

Support your responses with evidence from the text. 📓 **NOTEBOOK**

1. **Analyze** Reread lines 5–7. What is compared to "a stone / on the riverbed"? Where else does this image appear in the poem?

2. **Evaluate** Identify examples of each of the elements of a lyric poem that appear in "Sleeping in the Forest." Is Oliver's poem a good example of a lyric poem? Why or why not?

3. **Critique** In lines 9–11, how does the **simile,** or comparison of unlike things using *like* or *as*, affect the meaning of the poem?

4. **Interpret** In the last sentence, the speaker says, "By morning / I had vanished at least a dozen times / into something better." What might the speaker mean by the phrase "something better"?

5. **Notice & Note** What transitional phrases does the poet use in lines 11–18 to indicate the time during which the events are being remembered? How do these time-related transitional phrases help convey the theme of the poem?

RESEARCH

Look for more examples of lyric poetry. Choose two poems that you find interesting and then answer the questions below about the speaker in each poem. Remember, in a lyric poem, the speaker can be the poet but doesn't have to be. (Note: You need to write the title of each poem only once.)

Questions About Speakers	Answers
Is there just one speaker?	Title of Poem: Answer:
	Title of Poem: Answer:
What words and details suggest who the speaker is?	
What are the thoughts and feelings of the speaker?	
Is the speaker's experience similar to any that you have had? How?	

Connect With a small group, discuss the speakers in each of your poems. How does thinking about the speaker give you clues about the main message, or theme, of the poems? Read aloud the parts of the poems that support your ideas.

RESEARCH TIP
When you need to research a general topic to find examples, search first for the broadest category, such as "lyric poetry." Scan a few websites to find specific poems, poets, and topics that interest you and then jot down words that you can use to further pinpoint your search.

CREATE AND DISCUSS

Write a Lyric Poem Remember that a lyric poem has a sense of rhythm and melody, is imaginative in word use, and gives a unified impression. Think of a moment in which you have felt connected to nature. Then use the idea web to organize your ideas before you begin writing your poem.

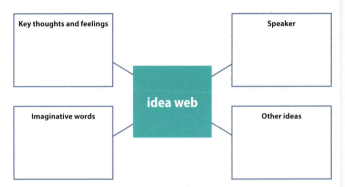

Listen for a Poem's Rhythm and Melody Find a partner and read your poems to each other. Do the following on your copy of the poem.

❏ Mark imaginative word choices.
❏ Write notes about how the arrangement of lines creates rhythm.
❏ Put an arrow at lines where the rhythm changes.
❏ Note the strongest impression the poem leaves in your mind.

Afterward, discuss ideas for revising word choice and other elements in each poem to strengthen the impression it conveys.

RESPOND TO THE ESSENTIAL QUESTION

? **What does it mean to be in harmony with nature?**

Gather Information Review your annotations and notes on "Sleeping in the Forest." Then, add relevant details to your Response Log. As you determine which information to include, think about how:

- people make connections to nature
- rhythm can affect the mood of a poem

At the end of the unit, use your notes to write a personal narrative.

RESPOND

Go to **Giving a Presentation** in the **Speaking and Listening Studio** to learn more.

ACADEMIC VOCABULARY
As you write and discuss what you learned from the poem, be sure to use the Academic Vocabulary words. Check off each of the words that you use.

❏ affect
❏ element
❏ ensure
❏ participate
❏ specify

Sleeping in the Forest 239

APPLY

CREATE AND DISCUSS

Write a Lyric Poem Remind students that a lyric poem is strongest when it expresses one feeling. Have students think about the experience or moment they want to write about and explore what they felt or now feel about the experience. Ask them to find a word that describes the feeling and keep it in their thoughts as they write, even if they never use it in the poem.

 For **writing support** for students at varying proficiency levels, see the **Text X-Ray** on page 228D.

Listen for a Poem's Rhythm and Melody Remind students that really listening to a poem requires concentration and focus. Before they mark anything on their partner's poem, they should listen to the poem all the way through and pay attention to the sounds.

RESPOND TO THE ESSENTIAL QUESTION

Allow time for students to add details from "Sleeping in the Forest" to their Unit 3 Response Logs.

🇪🇱 ENGLISH LEARNER SUPPORT

Listen for a Poem's Sound and Meaning Choose one or two of the students' poems to read to the class. Emphasize the sounds and give full expression to the emotions expressed. Model how to comment on people's poems. Be sure to include praising words and phrases that refer to specific features. Then give students sentence frames to help them critique their partner's poem. *I like the way you _____. I notice that you _____. The poem gives me a strong impression of _____.* Provide copies of all the poems to the students.
SUBSTANTIAL/MODERATE

Sleeping in the Forest 239

APPLY

COMPARE FORMS AND ELEMENTS

Before groups work on the chart, remind them that they are comparing, not the content of the poems, but the forms and the elements that make them up.

ANALYZE THE TEXTS

Possible answers:

1. **DOK 4:** "*Ode to Enchanted Light*" *has three stanzas, with a mix of long and short lines. The first stanza creates a cascading tumbling feeling—as if words are falling down the page in the same ways that light is tumbling through the trees. "Sleeping in the Forest" is free verse. The uninterrupted flow fits with the poet's experience of spending a long, peaceful night sleeping on the forest floor.*

2. **DOK 3:** *Neruda uses a simile comparing the light dropping through the trees to drifting sand. Oliver uses a simile comparing the speaker's thoughts to floating moths. One image conveys downward motion; the other conveys a feeling of floating upward, but they both communicate a sense of lightness, almost weightlessness.*

3. **DOK 2:** *The central image of the Neruda poem is sparkling, full of light and magic. Oliver's central image is darker, warm, and comforting. Both poets view nature positively, but Oliver directly expresses a personal link with nature, whereas Neruda describes an observation of nature.*

4. **DOK 4:** *Neruda effectively uses similes and metaphors to create a feeling of magic. Oliver uses personification to create a feeling of connection and comfort.*

 RESPOND

Collaborate & Compare

COMPARE FORMS AND ELEMENTS

Both "Ode to enchanted light" and "Sleeping in the Forest" describe the speakers' responses to experiences they have had in nature. Despite the poems' thematic similarities, the poets use different poetic forms and styles to create unique visions. These include:

- **Organization**—length of lines, stanzas, punctuation
- **Sound Devices**—rhyme, rhythm, alliteration, repetition
- **Figurative Language**—such as the following:
  - metaphor: comparing two things that are unlike but have some qualities in common
  - simile: comparing two unlike things using the word *like* or *as*
  - personification: giving human qualities to an animal, object, or idea

With your group, complete the chart with details from both poems.

ODE TO ENCHANTED LIGHT
Poem by Pablo Neruda
translated by Ken Krabbenhoft

SLEEPING IN THE FOREST
Poem by Mary Oliver

POETIC ELEMENTS	"ODE TO ENCHANTED LIGHT"	"SLEEPING IN THE FOREST"
Organization	Divided into three stanzas	One long continuous text
Sound Devices	Alliteration, simile, metaphor	Consonance and assonance
Figurative Language	Simile and metaphor	Personification and metaphor

ANALYZE THE TEXTS

Discuss these questions in your group.

1. **Evaluate** With your group, discuss the organization of each poem. How does it differ? Is the organization of each poem appropriate to its content? Explain.

2. **Compare** Reread lines 8–9 of "Ode to enchanted light" and lines 9–11 of "Sleeping in the Forest." What similarities do you observe in each poet's use of figurative language?

3. **Interpret** How would you describe the central image presented in each poem? How does the speaker's central image relate to each poem's theme?

4. **Critique** How effectively does each poem use figurative language to convey its theme? Explain.

240   Unit 3

 ENGLISH LEARNER SUPPORT

Ask Questions Use the following questions to help students compare the selections.

1. Which poem has a song-like first line with words that rhyme?
2. Which poem has a stanza that uses alliteration to describe the sound made by an insect?
3. Does the "Sleeping in the Forest" or "Ode to Enchanted Light" describe a feeling of being taken care of and made better by nature? **MODERATE/LIGHT**

RESPOND

EXPLORE AND PRESENT

Now, your group can continue exploring ideas about nature by comparing the different poetic forms and elements in these poems. Follow these steps:

1. **Choose a Focus for Your Comparison** As a group, review your completed charts. Identify the most important ways the poems are alike and different. Discuss the significance of these key points and how they relate to nature. Then, reach a consensus about what to focus on in your presentation. For example, think about comparing the figurative language in each poem and the way that it impacts the reader's thoughts and feelings about nature.

2. **Create a Venn Diagram** After selecting a focus for your comparison, use the Venn diagram below to organize the similarities and differences you identified. Then, add words and phrases from the poem as supporting evidence.

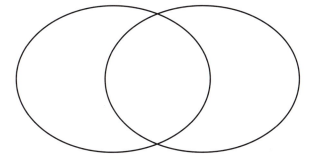

"Ode to enchanted light"   "Sleeping in the Forest"

3. **Share What You Have Learned** As a group, prepare a presentation of your comparison. Consider using your Venn diagram, drawings, and other images as visual aids in your presentation. While other groups make their presentations, remember to listen actively and note any questions you have. After each group has presented, discuss what you learned about people's relationship to nature by analyzing and comparing the two poems.

Go to **Delivering Your Presentation** in the **Speaking and Listening Studio** to learn more.

Collaborate & Compare 241

APPLY

EXPLORE AND PRESENT

The charts you and your students completed comparing the organization, sound devices, and figurative language in the two poems should be very useful as students make their final comparisons. Suggest that the student groups keep those charts available for reference during this activity. They should also refer to any notes they may have made while discussing the Analyze the Texts questions.

1. **Choose a Focus for Your Comparison** This is particularly important. One of the most serious problems students have with discussions, essays, and presentations is too wide a topic. As students work together to decide on a focus, circulate among the groups and help students with the process of narrowing their focus to something they can handle productively.

2. **Create a Venn Diagram** The Venn Diagram is a good tool for organizing information as students work on drawing conclusions about the two poems. Help students to use the diagram without getting too caught up in its technicalities. If students aren't sure where a certain piece of information goes on the diagram, point out that such a difficulty is in itself useful information that can lead to productive insights.

3. **Share What You Have Learned** As they create their presentations, groups should make sure to make use of the skills and talents of all of its members. If someone in a group is particularly good at making or researching images, for example, that group may present more visuals in their presentation than do other groups.

TO CHALLENGE STUDENTS...

Compare Odes If students need a challenge, suggest that they read John Keats's ode, "To Autumn" and analyze it using what they have learned after studying "Ode to Enchanted Light." Then have them compare the two odes, noting similarities and differences in theme, tone, use of figurative language, and form. Finally, have them evaluate the relative effectiveness of the two poems and defend their assessment.

PLAN

MEDIA
TRASH TALK/YOU'RE PART OF THE SOLUTION

GENRE ELEMENTS
MEDIA

Explain to students that the aim of all visual **media** is to be viewed, like movies, television programs, videos and posters. **Persuasive media**—like all persuasive messages—aim to persuade viewers to buy something or to support a person, group, cause, or idea. Tell students that makers of persuasive media use many of the same approaches and techniques that writers of persuasive messages use in their texts. Conclude by saying that visual media also involve the written word.

LEARNING OBJECTIVES

- Analyze and compare persuasive media.
- Analyze digital texts and video.
- Research environmental problems and solutions.
- Write an opinion letter.
- Create a media campaign.
- **Language** Discuss video elements.

TEXT COMPLEXITY

Quantitative Measures	Trash Talk/You're Part of the Solution	Lexile: N/A
Qualitative Measure	**Ideas Presented** Offers basic information	
	Structure Used Easily identified text structure	
	Language Used Explicit, literal, simple	
	Knowledge Required Requires no special knowledge or experience	

PLAN

RESOURCES

- Unit 3 Response Log
- Writing Studio: Persuasive Techniques
- Speaking and Listening Studio: Introduction: Using Media in a Presentation
- "Trash Talk" and "You're Part of the Solution" Selection Test

Online

SUMMARIES

English
"Trash Talk" is a video produced by the National Oceanic and Atmospheric Administration. Its aim is to inform viewers about different kinds of marine debris. "You're Part of the Solution" is a poster aimed at persuading young people to get involved with marine debris clean-up projects at government agencies. Both deal with the same topic, but they do so in different ways and with different purposes.

Spanish
"Trash Talk" es un video producido por la Administración Nacional Oceánica y Atmosférica. Su objetivo es informar a los espectadores acerca de los diferentes tipos de desperdicios marinos. "Eres parte de la solución" es un cartel dirigido a persuadir a los jóvenes de que se involucren con proyectos de limpieza de desperdicios marinos en oficinas del gobierno. Ambos tratan el mismo tema, pero lo hacen de maneras distintas y con diferentes propósitos.

SMALL-GROUP OPTIONS

Have students work in small groups to read and discuss the selection.

Think-Pair-Share
- After students have viewed the video, have them work with a partner to evaluate it critically.
- Have students discuss what they would do differently if they were to make their own video about marine debris.
- Tell students to consider such elements as the visuals and the narration.
- Ask students to keep notes of their discussion.
- Ask for volunteers to share their ideas with the class.

Pinwheel Discussion
- After students have viewed the video, ask them to create pinwheel formations of six per group.
- For the first rotation, ask students to discuss the video's aim.
- For the second rotation, ask students to discuss the video's visuals.
- For the third rotation, ask students to discuss the performance of the narrator in the video.

Trash Talk/You're Part of the Solution **242B**

PLAN

 # Text X-Ray: English Learner Support
for "Trash Talk" / "You're Part of the Solution"

Use the Text X-Ray and the supports and scaffolds in the Teacher's Edition to help guide students at different proficiency levels through the selection.

INTRODUCE THE SELECTION
DISCUSS WATCHING AND EXAMINING

In this lesson, students will be asked to view different forms of visual media analytically and critically in order to compare them. To help them understand the active role they must play in achieving this end, provide students with the following explanations:

- Watching is looking at something without thinking critically about it.
- Examining means thinking about what you are looking at.

Explain that watching a television program means following a story and waiting to see what happens next. Examining a television program means judging it like a critic and evaluating its quality and meaning.

Have volunteers share what they look for when they are examining visual media. Use the following sentence frames: *When I examine a photograph, I look at how the photographer_____. When I examine a movie, I judge the quality of the _____.*

CULTURAL REFERENCES

The following words and phrases may be unfamiliar to students:

- *man-made* (video): made by humans, not occurring naturally
- *derelict* (video): in bad condition because of neglect
- *tackle* (poster) to deal with a problem
- *trashes* (poster) damages
- *conservation group* (poster) a group devoted to protecting and saving some aspect of the environment

LISTENING

Listen for Details

Explain to students that one of the important elements to focus on in an informative or persuasive video is the information provided by the narrator.

Have students view the video, paying particular attention to the narration. Use the following supports with students at varying proficiency levels:

- Tell students that you will ask questions about the narration. Ask questions that require a one- or two-word answer. For example, ask: *Does the narrator believe marine debris is bad for the ocean?* **SUBSTANTIAL**
- Ask students to identify items mentioned by the narrator that are marine debris. **MODERATE**
- Ask students to explain how things become marine debris. **LIGHT**

PLAN

SPEAKING

Present a Critique

Draw students' attention to the presentation assignment on p. 249. Remind them that a *critique* is a detailed examination, or analysis that reviews the merits (good points) and defects (problems or faults) of something.

Discuss the elements of the poster. Use the following supports with students at varying proficiency levels:
- Ask students what they liked or disliked about the poster. Allow for one-word answers or gestures. **SUBSTANTIAL**
- Have students work in pairs, delivering their critiques to each other. Ask the listeners to identify areas in which the speakers excel and areas where they need improvement. **MODERATE**
- Have students read their critiques aloud, asking them to deliver it like a professional voice-over artist. **LIGHT**

READING

Understand Text in Media

Draw students' attention to the text on the "You're Part of the Solution" poster. Tell them that understanding the text in a visual medium is as important as understanding the images.

Use the following supports with students at varying proficiency levels:
- Ask students to underline words in the poster that tell them what the poster wants them to do. Point out that the exclamation points signal that something needs to be done. **SUBSTANTIAL**
- Ask students to read the poster, analyzing the different purposes achieved in each of the different parts of the text. (*What* the poster says must be done, and *how* it must be done.) **MODERATE**
- Ask students to read the poster, explaining why the text is an example of persuasive writing. **LIGHT**

WRITING

Write a Letter

Work with students to read the writing assignment on p. 249.

Use the following supports with students at varying proficiency levels:
- Help students find words that express what they felt as they viewed "Talking Trash." Write a brief letter to the NOAA on the board using students' words, and have students copy the letter in their notebooks. **SUBSTANTIAL**
- Provide sentence frames such as the following that students can use to craft their essays: *I felt that the narration was _____. I thought that the visual elements were_____.* **MODERATE**
- Remind students to use transitions to link their details to their opinions. Have pairs find three places in their essays where they can use a transition. **LIGHT**

TEACH

 Connect to the
ESSENTIAL QUESTION

The "Trash Talk" video and the "You're Part of the Solution" poster both advocate harmony with nature by addressing the serious problem of marine debris in our oceans and waterways and by proposing solutions.

COMPARE ACROSS MEDIA

Point out the distinguishing characteristic of each medium: the video presents many different images in quick succession whereas the digital photograph is one static image. Ask students to keep this in mind as they evaluate and compare the purpose and message of each. Tell students that although each one addresses the same topic, they both have different capabilities and intentions.

COLLABORATE & COMPARE

VIDEO
from
TRASH TALK
by the **National Oceanic and Atmospheric Administration**
page 245

COMPARE ACROSS MEDIA
As you view the video and poster, notice how each medium presents information. Consider the purpose and message of the video and the poster. Think, too, about how the purpose and message may have influenced the way each was designed. After you view both media, you will collaborate with a small group on a final project.

 ESSENTIAL QUESTION:

What does it mean to be in harmony with nature?

POSTER
YOU'RE PART OF THE SOLUTION
pages 246–247

QUICK START

Think of a cause you care about. How could you persuade others to share your views about that cause? Write down your thoughts.

ANALYZE PERSUASIVE MEDIA

Creators of persuasive media use many techniques to communicate meaning and to influence you to adopt a position or take an action. Recognizing these techniques will help you analyze persuasive media.

TECHNIQUE	DESCRIPTION
Glittering generalization	Broad statement that includes words with a **positive connotation**—suggesting something pleasant—to influence an audience
Rhetorical question	Asks an obvious or unanswerable question to make a point or keep the audience thinking
Appeal to logic	Persuades through reason and evidence
Appeal to emotion	Persuades by appealing to strong feelings
Appeal by association	**Bandwagon** appeals urge you to do something because "everyone else" is doing it. **Testimonials** are endorsements or approvals from famous people or researchers.
Appeal to loyalty	Relies on people's connection to a particular group

Along with these techniques, look for signs of bias. **Bias** is an inclination for or against a particular opinion. A media piece may reveal bias by overlooking key facts, by stacking evidence on one side of an argument, by using unfairly weighted evidence, or by using loaded language (words with emotionally charged connotations). Asking questions like these will help you evaluate media pieces:

- Who is presenting the information? What motives or goals does that individual or organization have?
- Who is the intended audience?
- Is the evidence factual, accurate, relevant, current, and sufficient?

As you examine the media selections, analyze how ideas are presented. Decide whether each selection persuades you—and why or why not.

GET READY

GENRE ELEMENTS: MEDIA
- created for a specific purpose
- convey a message
- target a specific audience
- come in many forms, including videos, posters, podcasts, and other digital texts

Trash Talk / You're Part of the Solution 243

TEACH

ANALYZE DIGITAL TEXTS

Explain to students that posters and other fixed images can be viewed quickly, as people do when they see magazine advertisements or billboards, and they can also be examined slowly and carefully. Encourage students to try both approaches as they analyze the "You're Part of the Solution" poster.

Videos Help students understand the terms and concepts related to the elements of video. Tell students that the different elements can be used in any combination in a single video or even a single scene. Ask students for examples of animation and computer-generated imagery in movies and on television.

Posters Explain to students that there are different kinds of posters—commercial ones, artistic ones, and ones aimed at sharing important information like public service announcements. Remind students that the text and images in posters share the same goal: to communicate something. Some posters communicate information or a feeling; others try to persuade. If the poster advertises a product or service or promotes a cause, the text and image will have the goal of trying to persuade.

GET READY

ANALYZE DIGITAL TEXTS

When you view a video or a digital text such as a downloadable poster, think about the message and the intended purpose of the text. Is its goal to inform, to entertain, to persuade, or to express the feelings or thoughts of those who created it? Analyzing the elements of a digital text can help you understand and evaluate its message, purpose, reliability, and effectiveness.

Videos Producers of videos use words as well as visual and sound elements to convey information and encourage you to think or feel a certain way. Through effective use of these elements, a video can communicate a message, convince viewers that something is true and important, or persuade viewers to do something. These are some of the visual and sound elements that often appear in videos:

FILM FOOTAGE	Film shot with a video camera and then edited by cutting and pasting sections together
ANIMATION	Images created through drawings, computer graphics, or photographs that appear to move
COMPUTER-GENERATED IMAGERY (CGI)	Computer-created or manipulated images and animations; may combine elements of actual film footage with computer imagery
NARRATION	Words spoken by the narrator, which are carefully chosen to deliver facts and/or to persuade; quality of the narrator's voice and the way he or she expresses the words to convey a message
MUSIC	Singing, playing instruments, or using computer-generated tones; can create a mood or emphasize key moments in the video

As you watch *Trash Talk*, note how the producers use a variety of visual and sound elements to convey a message and persuade viewers.

Posters A poster combines text and visual elements to make a strong visual impact on viewers.

- **Text (print) elements** are the letters, words, and sentences on the poster. To analyze text elements, think about how language is used to communicate information and stir your emotions. Also think about the fonts (type styles) and sizes used to make text stand out.

- **Visual (graphic) elements** include all other visual information—images (photographs, designs, illustrations), colors, lines, and so on. To analyze visual elements, consider how the images and visual design help communicate information and express a message.

244   Unit 3

ENGLISH LEARNER SUPPORT

Understand Video Elements Clarify the differences between *film footage, animation, and computer-generated imagery*. Use stills or pictures to illustrate the different media. Then use the frames to determine understanding. For example, *A home movie of Americans landing in Europe during World War II is an example of ___. A cartoon of two rabbits in parachutes is an example of ___. A lifelike scene of a million soldiers marching during the Roman Empire is an example of ___.*
MODERATE

GET READY

BACKGROUND

The video clip you're about to see was produced by the National Oceanic and Atmospheric Administration (NOAA) for World Ocean Day 2016. NOAA scientists and researchers monitor changes in the environment—from the very bottom of the ocean all the way to the surface of the sun. Then they communicate the information they gather to private citizens, emergency managers, and key government and business decision-makers. Marine debris—the topic of this video—is just one of the many areas that NOAA studies.

PREPARE TO COMPARE

As you view the video, make note of how the narrators define marine debris. Also consider how the various visual and sound elements used to convey information in the video might or might not work in print.

For more online resources, log in to your dashboard and click on "TRASH TALK" from the selection menu.

As needed, pause the video to make notes about what impresses you or about ideas you might want to talk about later. Replay or rewind so that you can clarify anything you do not understand.

Trash Talk / You're Part of the Solution   245

TEACH

BACKGROUND

After students read the Background note, tell them that NOAA's World Ocean Day is a global day of ocean celebration. It is part of an annual month-long effort to present public events focused on ocean science and conservation.

PREPARE TO COMPARE

Direct students to use the Prepare to Compare prompt to focus their viewing.

 ENGLISH LEARNER SUPPORT

Understand Idioms Discuss the title of the video. Explain that the phrase *trash talk* has two meanings. As an idiom, *trash talk* means gossip or rumors or saying bad things about people behind their backs. As the title of the video, trash talk refers to the topic of the video—talking about marine trash, or debris. Tell students that titles, headlines, and captions of photographs frequently use idioms this way. Provide students with other idioms that could have served as the title of this video, like *taking out the trash* or *cleanup time*. Invite students to search for other titles that use idioms this way and to bring them into class. **MODERATE**

Trash Talk/You're Part of the Solution   **245**

TEACH

BACKGROUND

After students read the Background note, explain that before the computer age, posters were typically made by professional artists and photographers and were printed at commercial presses. Tell students that in addition to digital photography and computer applications, the availability of free online images, designs, patterns, and fonts has also made it easier for people to make their own professional-looking posters.

PREPARE TO COMPARE

Direct students to use the Prepare to Compare prompt to focus their viewing.

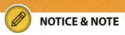

NOTICE & NOTE

BACKGROUND

For more than 200 years, posters have been a popular way to convey information and share messages with the public. They have been used to proclaim laws, publicize events, advertise products, and communicate ideas. The earliest posters were simply words printed on paper in black ink. As printing and poster art techniques developed, posters became more sophisticated. Now, digital photography and computer applications have made it possible for almost anyone to combine text and graphics to make a poster.

PREPARE TO COMPARE

As you view the poster, consider the message that it conveys. Think of the responses the creator of the poster might be trying to inspire. Consider that as much deliberate design can go into the creation of a still image as in moving ones. Think about the ways in which persuasion is at work in the carefully chosen wording in the text and in how the visual elements have been deliberately chosen to catch the eye and capture attention. Be aware of the effectiveness of techniques that help to communicate messages in different types of media.

246   Unit 3

TO CHALLENGE STUDENTS...

Analyze Media   Have students find online examples of 19th- and 20-century posters that aimed to persuade or promote, such as circus posters or ads asking Americans to buy war bonds. Have students compare and contrast these posters to the "You're Part of the Solution" poster. Suggest that students evaluate such things as message, interplay between image and text, and overall effectiveness. Have students write essays about their findings or present them in oral reports.

Trash Talk / You're Part of the Solution 247

TEACH

ENGLISH LEARNER SUPPORT

Comprehend Environmental Print Point out to students that not all words appear in books. Words and numbers appear in the world around them. Display and read aloud printed matter on signs, posters, and online advertisements. Explain that they warn of danger, supply directions (as on highway signs), or tell people about something they should do or buy. Point out key words and phrases in the poster on p. 247: *Problem, Help, Take action now!* Then, point out the contraction *You're* in the selection title. Ask: Is this poster trying to get us to do something? (*Yes*) Have students of varying proficiencies design their own posters with words supplied from a word bank. Help them match words with images and then use them in a poster. Use gestures, cognates, and pre-labeled images to get students started. **SUBSTANTIAL/MODERATE**

For reading support for students at varying proficiency levels, see the Text X-Ray on page 242D.

Trash Talk/You're Part of the Solution **247**

APPLY

ANALYZE MEDIA

Possible answers:

1. **DOK 3:** *The items most often found in marine cleanups are made out of plastic, meaning that people buy many plastic products but do not dispose of them properly.*

2. **DOK 3:** *The video includes footage of actual marine debris as well as basic two-dimensional animations. These images convey the problem and suggest possible solutions.*

3. **DOK 4:** *The narration includes a string of rhetorical questions ("Have you ever seen . . . ?"). It appeals to the viewer's logic because of all the factual data it presents, and it appeals to the viewer's emotions because of the many unsightly images of debris.*

4. **DOK 2:** *The image of the marine debris clearly depicts the problem. It might sadden some viewers, make others feel guilty for contributing to the problem, or inspire others to help solve the problem.*

5. **DOK 4:** *Breaking up the text into separate chunks with different fonts and sizes makes each idea stand out. The variable text grabs viewers' attention ("You're part of the solution!") and makes clear what readers should do ("Take action now! Get involved").*

RESEARCH

Review the Research Tip with students. Remind them to use reliable sources of information, like government websites that are independent of political affiliation, and sites published by respected news organizations, universities, and environmental organizations that present factual evidence.

Extend To guide students, suggest that students think about their audience and which media—a poster, a video, or another type— would work the best and reach the largest number of people.

 RESPOND

ANALYZE MEDIA

Support your responses with evidence from the video and poster.

 NOTEBOOK

1. **Draw Conclusions** According to the video, what items are found most often in marine cleanups? What can you conclude from that information?

2. **Evaluate** Describe the visuals used in the video. How do they work together to convey information?

3. **Analyze** Which persuasive techniques are used in the video? Provide examples to support your answer.

4. **Interpret** How do the visual elements in the poster help support the text elements?

5. **Critique** Look at how the text in the poster is presented. Why do you think the creators of the poster broke up the text and used different font styles and sizes?

RESEARCH TIP
To research a problem and its possible solutions, try using phrases that you would expect to find in a piece of writing about the topic—for example, you could search for phrases such as *problems and solutions*, *solve the problem*, or *what you can do*, combined with a topic such as *trash in the ocean* or *plastic soda can rings*.

RESEARCH

Choose two problems that you learned about in this lesson. Then do some research to find one or two possible solutions to each problem. Record what you learn in the chart.

PROBLEM	SOLUTION(S)

Extend If you wanted to share information about marine debris problems and solutions with a wider audience, would you use a poster, a video, or another type of media? Why?

248   Unit 3

ENGLISH LEARNER SUPPORT

Oral Assessment To gauge comprehension and speaking skills, conduct an informal assessment. Walk around the class asking the following questions:

- Which item is found the most often in marine debris? *(plastic)* **SUBSTANTIAL**
- Which medium—the poster or the video—appeals more to your emotions and why? *(Answers will vary.)* **MODERATE**
- Which medium most makes you want to volunteer for a cleanup squad and why? *(Answers will vary.)* **LIGHT**

RESPOND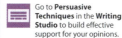

CREATE AND PRESENT

Write a Letter to NOAA Write a letter to the National Oceanic and Atmospheric Administration to express your opinion about the effectiveness of their *Trash Talk* video.

- ❏ Introduce the topic and express your overall opinion about the video. Be truthful but tactful.
- ❏ Include details from the video to support your views. Describe particular visual or sound elements that you feel were very effective or that you think would be more effective if they were changed.
- ❏ In your final paragraph, state your conclusion about the video and your purpose for writing the letter—or whether you would like NOAA to take a particular action.

Present a Critique Examine the poster once more. Consider the effect created by the combination of text and visual elements. Write a critique that explains your ideas and then present it to your classmates.

- ❏ Identify which text and visual elements work well and why.
- ❏ Identify text or visual elements that do not work or that you think could be improved. Offer suggestions for improving the poster to make it more effective.
- ❏ Present your ideas clearly and persuasively. Include an opinion statement at the end of your presentation that summarizes your response to the poster.

RESPOND TO THE ESSENTIAL QUESTION

 What does it mean to be in harmony with nature?

Gather Information Review your notes on the poster and the video. Then, add relevant details to your Response Log. As you determine which information to include, consider what these persuasive media suggest about how people can live in harmony with nature.

At the end of the unit, use your notes to write a personal narrative.

 Go to **Persuasive Techniques** in the **Writing Studio** to build effective support for your opinions.

 Go to **Introduction: Using Media in a Presentation** in the **Speaking and Listening Studio** for help.

ACADEMIC VOCABULARY
As you write and discuss what you learned from the video and poster, be sure to use the Academic Vocabulary words. Check off each of the words that you use.

- ❏ affect
- ❏ element
- ❏ ensure
- ❏ participate
- ❏ specify

Trash Talk / You're Part of the Solution 249

APPLY

CREATE AND PRESENT

Write a Letter Point out that the list on p. 249 can serve as an outline for the students' letters. Each item can be one paragraph. Advise students to select their details from the video before they begin to write their letters.

Present a Critique Suggest that students use the list on p. 249 to serve as an outline for their critiques. Each item can be one paragraph. Advise students to practice their presentation with a partner before delivering it to the class.

> For **writing** and **speaking support** for students at varying proficiency levels, see the **Text X-Ray** on page 242D.

RESPOND TO THE ESSENTIAL QUESTION

Allow time for students to add details from "Trash Talk/You're Part of the Solution" to their Unit 3 Response Logs.

APPLY

COMPARE PERSUASIVE MEDIA

Before groups complete their Venn diagrams, emphasize that they are comparing not only what they learned from the video and the poster but *how* they learned it. Also, ask students to keep in mind that the video and the poster have slightly different purposes that they will need to address.

ANALYZE THE MEDIA

Possible answers:

1. **DOK 3:** *Both the video and the poster are targeted at young audiences. The video has a young narrator, and the narration is casual and conversational. Much of the footage includes images of young people. The 2D animations are lively and colorful, suggesting an appeal to a younger audience. The text of the poster speaks to "young people like you."*

2. **DOK 3:** *The video is more informational than persuasive, although its images persuade the viewer that marine debris is a problem. The poster is more persuasive than informational. It aims at getting its audience to take action to solve the problem rather than explaining causes and effects of the problem.*

3. **DOK 4:** *The poster primarily shows trash and litter, especially plastics. Marine debris also includes derelict vessels and fishing equipment, but that type of debris doesn't appear in the poster—only in the video.*

4. **DOK 4:** *Students may feel that the video is more effective because it provides more information about marine debris and what causes it. It is also livelier and more engaging. However, it does not include a call to action. The poster clearly shows that there's a problem and encourages people to join cleanups, but students may feel that it's not as motivating as the video.*

 RESPOND

from **TRASH TALK**
Video

YOU'RE PART OF THE SOLUTION
Poster

Collaborate & Compare

COMPARE PERSUASIVE MEDIA

The video clip from *Trash Talk* and the "You're Part of the Solution" poster both focus on the issue of marine debris. Their form and the way in which they present information is different, however. When you compare two or more media on the same topic, you analyze the information, making connections and expanding on key ideas in one medium by studying the other.

In a small group, complete the Venn diagram with similarities and differences in how you learned about marine debris in the two types of media you viewed.

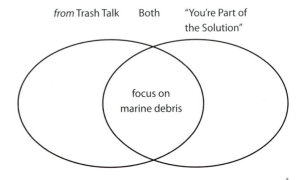

from Trash Talk   Both   "You're Part of the Solution"

focus on marine debris

ANALYZE THE MEDIA

Discuss these questions in your group.

1. **Draw Conclusions** Are both the video and the poster targeted at the same audience? What evidence supports your conclusion?

2. **Compare** How does the purpose of the video differ slightly from the purpose of the poster?

3. **Connect** Examine the trash shown along the shore in the poster and think about what you learned in the video. What type of common debris is pictured in the poster, and what other type of marine debris is not pictured?

4. **Critique** Which is more effective at conveying its message: the video or the poster? Why do you think so?

250   Unit 3

 ENGLISH LEARNER SUPPORT

Ask Questions Use the following questions to help students compare the selections:

1. The poster says "young people like you." Do you think the video also is intended for people your age? *(yes)*

2. What problem do you think both the poster and the video are targeting. *(marine debris)*

3. Is the poster mostly intended to inform you or encourage you to take action? *(take action)* What about the video? *(inform)*   **SUBSTANTIAL**

RESPOND

RESEARCH AND SHARE

Imagine that the National Oceanic and Atmospheric Administration has asked you for help with its marine debris media campaign. A media campaign is a group of different media that work together to achieve a common purpose. As a team, collaborate to research, design, and pitch to NOAA a media campaign that builds on the ideas presented in the video and the poster. Follow these steps:

1. **Identify a Problem** In your group, brainstorm to choose a particular type of marine debris to focus on in your campaign. You may want to focus on one of the problems you already researched and expand that research. Come to an agreement about one problem to address.

2. **Gather Information** As you research the problem your group identified, make sure that your sources are reliable and credible.

3. **Synthesize Information** In your group, share the facts you learned about your problem and one or more possible solutions. Choose the most persuasive facts to include in your messaging.

4. **Develop a Message** As a group, decide who your target audience is. What message will you communicate to that audience?

5. **Plan a Video or Poster** Half the members of your group will plan a video and the other half will plan a poster. Talk about how the message will be conveyed in each form of media. Remember: The audience and message should remain the same; only the type of media will change. Each medium should include some of the persuasive techniques you learned about. Use an organizer like this one to capture your notes:

Problem:	Possible Solutions:
Target audience:	Message:
Type of media:	
Description:	
Persuasive techniques:	

Pitch Your Media Campaign With your group, present your ideas for a video and poster to a larger group. Include information about how and where the video and poster will be distributed. Be prepared to answer questions that your audience may have.

RESEARCH TIP

When searching for information online, a specific question can sometimes help you find information more quickly. For example, you might search for *How does plastic harm the environment?* or *How many plastic water bottles are saved each year by using reusable bottles?*

APPLY

RESEARCH AND SHARE

Explain that a full media campaign may include the creation of a poster and video as well as written materials like brochures and mailings. People who plan media campaigns also determine where their materials will appear: on television, in print, and/or online.

1. **Identify a Problem** As students identify a problem, circulate among the groups, and check that the problem is suitable for the level of research you want them to conduct. The problem should not be too broad or too narrow.

2. **Gather Information** Review information about credible sources. Remind students to be on the lookout for bias and exaggeration and explain why these characteristics make a source less credible. Point out the Research Tip.

3. **Synthesize Information** Remind students to give all members of the group an opportunity to share their facts and solutions. Recommend that as a group they seek consensus about which facts to include in the media messaging.

4. **Develop a Message** Encourage students to come up with appropriate catchphrases, rhetorical questions, and glittering generalizations. Remind them to consider logical and emotional appeals in their messaging.

5. **Plan a Video or Poster** As students plan their videos and posters, circulate among the groups and check that everyone is participating in one of the planning committees. Remind students that the message they come up with must be conveyed both in images as well as text and that these two elements should have a clear relationship to each other.

WHEN STUDENTS STRUGGLE . . .

Work Collaboratively If students are having difficulty developing both a video and a poster simultaneously, divide the task into two separate activities. Have students start with the easier task of creating the poster. Let each group work on the overall message. Then divide the group into two planning committees. Have one group work on the text and the other group work on the selection of the image. Use the same approach for creating the video.

INDEPENDENT READING

READER'S CHOICE

Setting a Purpose Have students review their Unit 3 Response Log and think about what they've already learned about how nature can inspire. As they select their Independent Reading selections, encourage them to consider what more they want to know.

NOTICE & NOTE

Explain that some selections may contain multiple signposts; others may contain only one. And the same type of signpost can occur many times in the same text.

LEARNING MINDSET

Plan Remind students to keep up with their reading so challenging assignments don't overwhelm them at the last minute. Planning is essential to doing work they can be proud of. Encourage students to budget time and have a quiet space in which to engage with academic material.

 INDEPENDENT READING

ESSENTIAL QUESTION:

What does it mean to be in harmony with nature?

Reader's Choice

Setting a Purpose Select one or more of these options from your eBook to continue your exploration of the Essential Question.

- Read the descriptions to see which text grabs your interest.
- Think about which genres you enjoy reading.

Notice & Note

In this unit, you practiced asking **Big Questions** and noticing and noting two signposts: **Extreme or Absolute Language** and **Contrasts and Contradictions**. As you read independently, these signposts and others will aid your understanding. Below are the anchor questions to ask when you read literature and nonfiction.

Reading Literature: Stories, Poems, and Plays		
Signpost	Anchor Question	Lesson
Contrasts and Contradictions	Why did the character act that way?	p. 99
Aha Moment	How might this change things?	p. 3
Tough Questions	What does this make me wonder about?	p. 362
Words of the Wiser	What's the lesson for the character?	p. 363
Again and Again	Why might the author keep bringing this up?	p. 3
Memory Moment	Why is this memory important?	p. 2

Reading Nonfiction: Essays, Articles, and Arguments		
Signpost	Anchor Question(s)	Lesson
Big Questions	What surprised me? What did the author think I already knew? What challenged, changed, or confirmed what I already knew?	p. 265 p. 183 p. 437
Contrasts and Contradictions	What is the difference, and why does it matter?	p. 183
Extreme or Absolute Language	Why did the author use this language?	p. 182
Numbers and Stats	Why did the author use these numbers or amounts?	p. 264
Quoted Words	Why was this person quoted or cited, and what did this add?	p. 437
Word Gaps	Do I know this word from someplace else? Does it seem like technical talk for this topic? Do clues in the sentence help me understand the word?	p. 265

ENGLISH LEARNER SUPPORT

Develop Inferential Skills Use the following supports with students at varying proficiency levels:

- Show students a photo from which an inference can be readily drawn: For example, a child about to blow out candles on a cake. Ask: *What day is it for that child? How do you know?* **SUBSTANTIAL**

- Provide students the following sentence stem: *I knew it would be a tough afternoon when ___.* Point out that they must draw inferences from the stem to complete the exercise. **MODERATE**

- Provide students with a sample story title, such as "Almost Too Late" or "A Houseful of Bees." Challenge them to write a paragraph or two of a story making inferences based on the title.
LIGHT

INDEPENDENT READING

You can preview these texts in Unit 3 of your eBook.
Then, check off the text or texts that you select to read on your own.

☐ **MEMOIR**
from **Unbowed**
Wangari Muta Maathai

A woman reflects on her childhood impressions of the natural world around her home.

☐ **POEM**
Problems with Hurricanes
Victor Hernández Cruz

This poem asks and answers the question: What is the greatest danger for people during a hurricane?

☐ **ARTICLE**
Living Large Off the Grid
Kristen Mascia

Discover how one family lives sustainably in a house that was built from straw in 2009.

☐ **POETRY**
Haiku
Issa, Basho, and Buson, translated by Richard Haas

This selection of haiku poetry describes observations of people and nature.

Collaborate and Share With a partner, discuss what you learned from at least one of your independent readings.

 Go to the **Reading Studio** for more resources on **Notice & Note.**

- Give a brief synopsis or summary of the text.
- Describe any signposts that you noticed in the text and explain what they revealed to you.
- Describe what you most enjoyed or found most challenging about the text. Give specific examples.
- Decide if you would recommend the text to others. Why or why not?

Independent Reading 253

INDEPENDENT READING

MATCHING STUDENTS TO TEXTS

Use the following information to guide students in choosing their texts.

***from* Unbowed** **Lexile: 1020L**
 Genre: Memoir
 Overall Rating: Challenging

Problems with Hurricanes
 Genre: Poem
 Overall Rating: Accessible

Living Large Off the Grid
 Genre: Magazine Article
 Overall Rating: Accessible

Haiku
 Genre: Poetry
 Overall Rating: Accessible

Collaborate and Share To assess how well students read the selections, walk around the room and listen to their conversations. Encourage students to be focused and specific in their comments.

 for Assessment

- Independent Reading Selection Tests

 Encourage students to visit the **Reading Studio** to download a handy bookmark of **NOTICE & NOTE** signposts.

WHEN STUDENT STRUGGLE...

Keep a Reading Log As students read their selected texts, have them keep a reading log for each selection to note signposts and their thoughts about them. Use their logs to assess how well they are noticing and reflecting on elements of the texts.

Reading Log for (title)		
Location	**Signpost I Noticed**	**My Notes about It**

Independent Reading 253

PLAN

UNIT 3 Tasks

- **WRITE A PERSONAL NARRATIVE**

MENTOR TEXT
MISSISSIPPI SOLO
Memoir by EDDY HARRIS

LEARNING OBJECTIVES

Writing Task
- Write a personal narrative about an experience with nature.
- Employ and practice skills for planning, preparing, and organizing ideas and text.
- Develop a focused, structured draft.
- Use the Mentor Text as a model for form and content in developing narratives.
- Follow structural guidelines for narrative form, with an engaging introduction, a thesis statement, supporting detail, and conclusion.
- Craft a story around a chronology of events that inspired insight or self-reflection.
- Use vivid and specific sensory detail to engage a reading audience.
- Revise drafts, incorporating feedback from peers.
- Use a rubric to evaluate writing.
- Publish writing to share it with an audience.
- **Language** Write a personal narrative using vivid specific sensory detail.

Assign the Writing Task in *Ed.*

OBJECTIVES

- Unit 3 Response Log
- Writing Studio: Writing Narratives
- Writing Studio: Narrative Structures
- Writing Studio: Writing as a Process
- Grammar Studio: Module 16: Spelling

PLAN

 # Language X-Ray: English Learner Support

Use the instruction below and the supports and scaffolds in the Teacher's Edition to help you guide students of different proficiency levels.

INTRODUCE THE WRITING TASK

Explain that a **personal narrative** is the most common form of storytelling: a kitchen-table summary of a loved one's lively day is a personal narrative. Or a description of an event, a special time in one's life, or a description of how a problem was solved. The Unit 3 Writing Task is a variation on this common form. Point out that narrative can be a synonym for story. The Spanish cognate for *story* is *historia*.

Remind students that the selections in this unit address human *harmony* with nature. Discuss individual experiences with nature that made a lasting impression on each student. Invite them to read their stories aloud to help them discover if what they've written makes sense and if they like the mood and tone they've created. Encourage partners or small groups to take careful notes as they review each other's work. These notes may later be exchanged to use as a reference for each writer in planning and drafting their personal narratives.

WRITING

Use Descriptive Language

Tell students that vivid descriptive language draws on human senses. Ask them to frame their work in these terms: What did it look like? Sound like? Feel like? How else could you describe it?

Use the following supports with students at varying proficiency levels:

- Move an object quickly in front of students. Display the word *fast* and ask them to write it down. Move the same object slowly. Display the word *slow* and ask them to write it down. **SUBSTANTIAL**
- Give students the sentence stem *It was so hot* _____. Ask them to complete the sentence using descriptive language. **MODERATE**
- Give students the sentence stem *It rained so hard* _____. Ask students to write a paragraph based on the completed stem using descriptive language. **LIGHT**

WRITING

Write a Personal Narrative

Ask students to share personal stories of their experiences with nature. Ask them to think of times they felt happy or peaceful because they were near trees, water, or the desert. Have them think of times when they struggled with elements of nature (as in a storm.) Ask them to pick the clearest memory to write about.

Use the following supports with students at varying proficiency levels:

- Ask students to use images found online, drawings, home language words, and cognates to describe a personal experience with nature. Offer frame sentences that stress sensory language: I felt hot in the _____ (desert/forest/park), then I saw _____ . (a storm coming) **SUBSTANTIAL**
- Ask students to write about a personal experience with nature that uses sensory details to describe what happened. (what did they see, hear, smell, taste, touch) Encourage students to use cognates and to ask for help in forming clear sentences about their experiences. **MODERATE**
- Ask students to write a personal narrative that includes sensory language to describe nature. **LIGHT**

WRITING

WRITE A PERSONAL NARRATIVE

Introduce students to the Writing Task by reading the introductory paragraph with them. Remind students to refer to the notes they recorded in the Unit 3 Response Log as they plan and draft their personal narratives. The Response Log should contain ideas about experiences with nature from a variety of perspectives. Drawing on these different perspectives will make their own writing more interesting and well informed.

 For **writing support** for students at varying proficiency levels, see the **Language X-Ray** on page 254B.

USE THE MENTOR TEXT

Have students review the excerpt from *Mississippi Solo* to help them understand why they should focus on experiences they have had that were important to them. Remind them that their personal narratives will come from their unique knowledge; only they have experienced what they are going to write about. It is their job to remember and then describe the details of their experiences to make their narratives interest the reader. Point out that when Eddy Harris writes about being caught in a storm, he uses descriptive language such as "splintery crackle of lightening" to help the reader feel what it was like to be there.

WRITING PROMPT

Review the prompt with students. Encourage them to ask questions about any part of the assignment that is unclear. Make sure they understand the purpose of their narrative: to answer the question by describing a personal experience with nature.

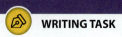 **WRITING TASK**

Write a Personal Narrative

 Go to the **Writing Studio** for help writing a personal narrative.

This unit focuses on ways in which people interact with nature. For this writing task, you will write a short personal narrative about an experience you had in nature or a lesson you learned from observing the natural world. For an example of a well-written personal narrative you can use as a mentor text, review the excerpt from the memoir *Mississippi Solo*.

As you write your personal narrative, you can use the notes from your Response Log, which you filled out after reading the texts in this unit.

Writing Prompt

Read the information in the box below.

> We all can remember experiences that changed our thinking or even our life. Events that took place in natural settings—in places either close to home or more remote—often create such memories. Some experiences were simple; others were dramatic. Because they were important to us, however, most of us enjoy remembering them and telling others about them.

This is the topic or context for your personal narrative.

Think carefully about the following question.

> What does it mean to be in harmony with nature?

This is the Essential Question for the unit. How would you answer this question, based on the texts in this unit?

Write a personal narrative in which you share an experience in nature or a lesson you learned by observing some part of the natural world.

Now mark the words that identify exactly what you are being asked to produce.

Be sure to—

- ❑ provide an introduction that catches the reader's attention, indicates the topic, and sets the scene
- ❑ focus on a single experience
- ❑ describe events (parts of the experience) in chronological order, with transitions that make the sequence of events clear
- ❑ include vivid, specific, and sensory details that make people, places, and events seem real
- ❑ include your thoughts and feelings
- ❑ conclude by explaining why the experience was meaningful to you

Review these points as you write and again when you finish. Make any needed changes.

254 Unit 3

 LEARNING MINDSET

SEEKING CHALLENGES Remind students that having a growth mindset means that it is important to seek out things that are hard to do. Sometimes writing down every detail, thought, and feeling of an experience so that you can use it later can seem difficult or even boring at first. You might only use one out of ten details in a story. But it might be a great detail! The reader may think, "That's incredible. Now I really *know* what the author is writing about."

254 Unit 3

WRITING TASK

1 Plan

Before you start writing, you need to plan your narrative. When you plan a draft, you often start by selecting a genre that is appropriate for a particular topic, purpose, and audience. For this writing task, you already know that the topic is related to experiences in nature, and you know that the genre is a personal narrative. Next, you should consider your purpose and audience. What key idea and details do you want to convey? Who might enjoy hearing about your experience? Try using a range of strategies in planning your draft. These might include discussing the topic with your classmates, doing some background reading, and thinking about personal interests you have that relate to the topic. Use the table below to assist you in planning your draft.

Personal Narrative Planning Table	
Genre	Personal narrative
Topic	An experience in nature
Purpose	
Audience	
Ideas from discussion with classmates	
Ideas from background reading	
Personal interests related to topic	

Background Reading Review the notes you have taken in your Response Log after reading the texts in this unit. These texts provide background reading that will help you formulate the key ideas you will include in your narrative.

Notice & Note
From Reading to Writing

As you plan your personal narrative, apply what you've learned about signposts to your own writing. Remember that writers use common features, called signposts, to help convey their message to readers.

Think about how you can incorporate **Aha Moment** into your essay.

Go to the **Reading Studio** for more resources on Notice & Note.

Use the notes from your Response Log as you plan your narrative.

Write a Personal Narrative 255

WRITING

1 PLAN

Allow time for students to discuss the topic with partners or in small groups and then to complete the planning chart independently.

■ **English Learner Support**

Understand Academic Language Make sure students understand words and phrases used in the chart, such as *genre*, *topic*, and *purpose*. Work with them to fill in the blank sections, providing text that they can copy into their charts as needed. **SUBSTANTIAL/MODERATE**

▶ **NOTICE AND NOTE**

Ask students to think of a moment when they suddenly or gradually realized something important during the period they are writing about. Model an Aha Moment: *I was thinking about how to do a better job on my personal narrative while I was driving home. I realized that I had taken a wrong turn and pulled over to a safe spot by the side of the road. I suddenly realized that I had taken a wrong turn in my writing, too! I was using too many fancy words that didn't describe anything very interesting instead of using details that might interest the reader. I also realized that I should have paid more attention to driving.*

Background Reading As they plan their narratives, remind students to refer to the notes they took in the Response Log. They may also review the selections to find additional facts and examples to support ideas they want to include in their writing.

TO CHALLENGE STUDENTS . . .

Use Advanced Sources Challenge students to seek out other personal narratives for inspiration, e.g., Chapter 1 of *My Bondage and My Freedom* by Frederick Douglass. Encourage them to search online or at the library for memoirs that they can use as guides to dig deeper into their own experiences. Have them pay particular attention to descriptions of settings, people, and moments when the writer is suddenly to forced by circumstances to confront or understand something important.

Write a Personal Narrative 255

WRITING

Organize Your Ideas Encourage students to draw on an experience they recall in some detail, that lends itself to narrative form. They need not manufacture epiphanies or consider life and death struggles. However, a story will be easier to plan and develop if it is built around a memory in which a number of things happened in sequence. Guide them to consider experiences that made enduring impressions on them, that in some fundamental way changed the way they perceive and respond to the natural world.

Suggest to students that they consider each vertical row in the chart as a paragraph or grouping of paragraphs. As they move to the next row, a story is unfolding through the chart in chronological order. Point out that their narratives may be centered around the first event: the thing and the moment that set the spark. Encourage them to develop the chart by considering what happened next, and after that, in the course of the experience they are writing about.

❷ DEVELOP A DRAFT

Remind students to follow their charts as they draft their narratives, but point out that they can still make changes to their writing plan during this stage. As they write, they may decide to consider other experiences, change emphasis on a given event, or modify language to enhance color or verisimilitude.

■ English Learner Support

Use Informal English Simplify the Writing Task. Point out the effective use of descriptive informal English in *Mississippi Solo* on page 201, "...the sky split open with a loud crash and a splintery crackle of lightning." Ask students to use the kind of informal English words and phrases they would use to describe something to a friend. Tell them to choose words that will help their friends see and feel what they are describing. As needed, supply frame sentences: I was in _____. (describe a place) Suddenly, I saw _____. I felt _____. I knew that I would have to _____. I said _____.

ALL LEVELS

256 Unit 3

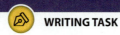

WRITING TASK

 Go to **Writing Narratives: Narrative Structure** for help organizing your ideas.

Organize Your Ideas After you have gathered ideas and information from your planning activities, you need to organize your material in a way that will help you draft your narrative. You can use the chart below to record each part of the experience in chronological order. You also can use the chart to record how you thought and felt about the events then or how you think and feel about them now.

Main Topic: An Experience in Nature		
First Event	**Second Event**	**Third Event**
Key Details	**Key Details**	**Key Details**
Thoughts and Feelings	**Thoughts and Feelings**	**Thoughts and Feelings**

❸ Develop a Draft

 You may prefer to draft your narrative online.

Once you have completed your planning activities, you will be ready to begin drafting your personal narrative. Refer to your planning table and the completed chart above, as well as any notes you took as you studied the texts in the unit. These will provide a kind of map for you to follow as you write. Using a word processor or online writing application makes it easier to make changes or move sentences around later when you are ready to revise your first draft.

256 Unit 3

WHEN STUDENTS STRUGGLE . . .

Develop a Draft It may be a challenge to recall in detail an experience of inspiration in nature. But even a park can provide inspiration. Remind them to consider everyday experiences. Remembering one thing leads to remembering other things. Ask them to complete the sentence stem *Nature made a strong impression on me when* _____. Or *I never noticed before how beautiful a (tree, landscape, river, etc.)* _____. Students can begin writing narratives building on that stem, in a form to be modified as warranted in developing their drafts.

WRITING

WRITING TASK

Use the Mentor Text

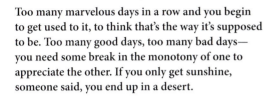

Author's Craft
Your introduction is your first chance to capture the reader's attention. Note how the author of *Mississippi Solo* does so.

> Too many marvelous days in a row and you begin to get used to it, to think that's the way it's supposed to be. Too many good days, too many bad days—you need some break in the monotony of one to appreciate the other. If you only get sunshine, someone said, you end up in a desert.

By suggesting that bad days are as important as good ones, the author hints that he will share his memories of a difficult experience.

Apply What You've Learned To capture your reader's attention in your personal narrative, you might include a compelling hint of upcoming events or a thought-provoking question related to the topic.

Genre Characteristics
In a personal narrative, sensory details—details that appeal to our senses of sight, hearing, touch, smell, and taste—can help the reader picture the events. Notice how the author of *Mississippi Solo* uses vivid sensory details to help his readers picture the events and understand his feelings.

> No sooner had I ducked into the trees than the sky split open with a loud crash and a splintery crackle of lightning. I was not going to make it through the trees. The wind came in at hurricane strength. The tips of the trees bent way over and aimed toward the ground, like fishing rods hooked on a big one. Water flooded like the tide rushing upstream. . . .

The author provides vivid details that appeal to the senses of sight and hearing. They help the reader understand how frightened he was when the storm began.

Apply What You've Learned The details you include in your personal narrative should be clearly related to your experience in nature and the lesson you learned from the experience. They should help readers imagine themselves in your place and understand why you think and feel the way you do about what you experienced.

Write a Personal Narrative 257

WHY THIS MENTOR TEXT?
The excerpt describes Eddy Harris's deep communion with nature and his encounter with wild weather on the Big River. Use the instruction below to help students review the mentor text as a model for narrative form and vivid descriptive language in the personal stories they choose to write about.

USE THE MENTOR TEXT

Author's Craft Ask a volunteer to read aloud the first paragraph of *Mississippi Solo*. Note that the paragraph contains a "teaser": a hint at something interesting just ahead in a narrative. Then ask: *How does a reader get the sense that trouble is just ahead?* (*The paragraph gently mocks "too many marvelous days in a row" as "monotony," We can be all but certain that at least one day of trouble is looming.*) Point toward the use of teasers in movie previews and news broadcasts, and discuss the effect of such hints on an audience.

Genre Characteristics Ask a volunteer to read the sample paragraph aloud. Then ask: *What is some of the vivid sensory detail used in this example?* (*Lightning comes "with a loud crash and splintery crackle." Winds at hurricane strength bent the tips of trees "like fishing rods hooked on a big one."*) Note that the best nature writing uses language like glitter to add spark and color to physical description. Point out that the sample text paints a memorable word picture using everyday language, through verbs like *ducked* and *flooded*, and nouns like *crash* and *crackle*.

 ENGLISH LEARNER SUPPORT

Use the Mentor Text Use the following supports with students at varying proficiency levels:

- Ask a volunteer to define the word *nature*: "the physical world, not created by people." Solicit synonyms in the students' native language. (Spanish cognate: *naturaleza*) Discuss elements and forces of nature, using terms such as *wind*, *storm*, *lightning*, and *hail*. **SUBSTANTIAL**

- Review the fundamental terms around the Essential Question: *inspired*, *harmony*, *element*. Ask students to come up with synonyms. **MODERATE**

- Refer students to the Mentor Text and ask them to identify sensory language used in the sample paragraphs. (**Possible examples:** "loud crash" and "splintery crackle.") **LIGHT**

Write a Personal Narrative 257

WRITING

3 REVISE

Have students answer each question in the chart to determine how they can improve their drafts. Invite volunteers to model their revision techniques.

With a Partner Have students ask peer reviewers to evaluate the form and content of their narratives by answering the following questions:

- Does my narrative include a clear thesis statement, followed by a tight chronology of events? If not, where is revision warranted?
- Have I made good use of transitional words and phrases? Is there variety in my sentence structure?
- How might I improve my representation of sensory detail? Have I chosen strong, colorful verbs, nouns, and adjectives?
- How well do I connect my observations of nature to the feelings they inspired?

Students should use the reviewer's feedback to add relevant facts, details, examples, or quotations that further develop their main points.

 **WRITING TASK**

 Go to the **Writing as a Process** for help revising your narrative.

3 Revise

On Your Own Once you have written the draft of your personal narrative, you'll want to go back and look for ways to improve your writing. As you reread and revise, think about whether you have achieved your purpose. The Revision Guide will help you focus on specific elements to make your writing stronger.

Revision Guide

Ask Yourself	Tips	Revision Techniques
1. Does my introduction grab readers' attention and set the scene?	**Underline** interesting or surprising statements. **Circle** details that show when and where the experience happened.	**Add** an attention-getting statement. **Add** details about where and when the event took place.
2. Are events in chronological order?	**Number** the events in the narrative. **Check** to make sure that they are in the correct order.	**Rearrange** events in the order in which they occurred, if necessary. **Add** transitions to link events.
3. Do vivid and specific sensory details make people, places, and events seem real?	**Highlight** vivid, specific, and sensory details.	**Add** more sensory details. **Delete** irrelevant details.
4. Have I included my thoughts and feelings?	**Put a check mark** next to statements of feelings or thoughts.	**Add** specific details about feelings and thoughts, if necessary.
5. Does my conclusion reveal why the experience was meaningful to me and/or what lesson I learned?	**Underline** the statement about why the experience is meaningful to you or what lesson you learned from it.	**Add** a statement that explains why the experience is important.

ACADEMIC VOCABULARY

As you conduct your **peer review,** be sure to use these words.

❏ affect
❏ element
❏ ensure
❏ participate
❏ specify

With a Partner Once you and your partner have worked through the Revision Guide on your own, exchange papers and evaluate each other's draft in a **peer review.** Focus on providing suggestions for at least three of the items mentioned in the Revision Guide. Explain why you think your partner's draft should be revised and what specific suggestions you have.

When receiving feedback from your partner, listen attentively and ask questions to make sure you fully understand the revision suggestions.

258 Unit 3

 ENGLISH LEARNER SUPPORT

Use Synonyms Explain that writers use synonyms to convey shades of meaning and add variety to text. Have students identify the pair of synonyms in this passage:

> The spider *struggled* to climb its web in the stiff, wet, stormy breeze. It *labored* against the elements, and against the clock as the warm September rain intensified.

Encourage students to look for places in their narratives where synonyms might improve their work. **LIGHT**

WRITING TASK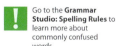

4 Edit

Once you have addressed the organization, development, and flow of ideas in your narrative, you can look to improve the finer points of your draft. Edit for the proper use of standard English conventions and be sure to correct any misspellings or grammatical errors.

Language Conventions

Commonly Confused Words Words that sound alike are often confused in writing. Some of these words are *its/it's, your/you're, two/too/to,* and *there/they're/their.*

> Go to the **Grammar Studio: Spelling Rules** to learn more about commonly confused words.

To make sure that you are using the right word and spelling it correctly, ask yourself what it means and how you are using it in the sentence. Note the examples that appear in the excerpt from *Mississippi Solo*.

Commonly Confused Words	Example of Correct Spelling
two: one plus one **too:** excess, also **to:** part of a verb, preposition of direction	<u>Too</u> many marvelous days in a row and you begin <u>to</u> get used <u>to</u> it, <u>to</u> think that's the way it's supposed <u>to</u> be.
your: belonging to you **you're:** "you are"	The idle chatter you get when you walk with <u>your</u> favorite niece or nephew going no place in particular with nothing special on <u>your</u> minds . . .
its: belonging to something **it's:** "it is"	. . . the little kid just jabbers away because <u>it's</u> comfortable and he feels like it.
their: belonging to them **they're:** "they are" **there:** a place	The wooded area lasted only another hundred yards or so, and I thought I could easily get <u>there</u> before the rains arrived.

5 Publish

Finalize your personal narrative and choose a way to share it with your audience. Consider these options:

- Present your narrative as a speech to the class.
- Post your narrative as a blog on a classroom or school website.

WRITING

4 EDIT

Suggest that students read their drafts aloud to assess how clearly and smoothly they have presented their ideas. Review the fundamentals of the assignment: an introduction that commands attention; a chronological sequence of events; vivid sensory detail, and a tight connection between observations and the thoughts or feelings they elicited. Encourage them to recast sensory detail as warranted with an eye and ear toward enhanced color and specificity.

LANGUAGE CONVENTIONS

Correctly Spell Commonly Confused Words Review the information about commonly confused words with students. Then discuss the samples in the chart, asking students to consider the definition of each commonly confused word before using it in their own work. Encourage students to use a dictionary if they have any doubts about spelling or meaning.

> **ENGLISH LEARNER SUPPORT**
>
> **Spell Homophones Correctly** Read aloud and display the words *to, two,* and *too.* Explain that the word *to* is a preposition that has a number of meanings, such as moving toward something. Model walking *to* an object. *Two* with a *w* always means the number *2*. *Too* means "also" or "overly." Write the three spellings on the board and number them 1, 2, and 3. Display and read the sentences below aloud. Have students hold up the correct number of fingers to indicate which word to use. You might want to repeat this activity with similar sentences.
>
> I am going _____ (to) the store to buy a birthday cake.
> My daughter is _____ (two) years-old. My parents called, and they want to come to come _____ (too).
> **SUBSTANTIAL/MODERATE**

WHEN STUDENTS STRUGGLE . . .

Use Descriptive Language Some students may find it difficult to render word pictures with artfully chosen descriptors. Suggest that a thesaurus and a will to experiment can help recast a given textual image. Ask: *What other words could you use for "tall, thin grass" bending in a breeze? (slim; slender; wispy; pliant; reeds; shoots; threads; wisps.)* Encourage students to craft basic sentences such as *The cat crawled under the fence* and expand upon them using descriptive language.

5 PUBLISH

Students can present their work as blog posts on a school website. Encourage others to read the narratives and to write constructive comments about them. The authors can then respond to the comments.

Write a Personal Narrative **259**

WRITING

USE THE SCORING GUIDE

Allow students time to read the scoring guide and ask questions about any words, phrases, or ideas that are unclear. Then have partners exchange final drafts of their personal narratives. Ask them to assess their partner's work using the scoring guide, based on reviewer's notes they make in the margins of their partner's draft.

Those notes should address the strengths and weaknesses of key elements: organization; development of ideas; use of language and conventions. In their review, ask students to pay special attention to their partner's use of descriptive language, and to make notes to that effect as warranted.

 **WRITING TASK**

Use the scoring guide to evaluate your personal narrative.

	Writing Task Scoring Guide: Personal Narrative		
	Organization/Progression	**Development of Ideas**	**Use of Language and Conventions**
4	• The narrative is clearly focused on the events related to a single experience. • All events are presented in a clear and logical order. • Transitions clearly show the sequence of events.	• The introduction catches the reader's attention and sets the scene. • The narrative is well developed with key details and the writer's thoughts and feelings. • The conclusion of the narrative makes clear the significance of the experience to the writer.	• Precise words and vivid, sensory language are used throughout to bring people, places, and events to life. • Commonly confused words are used correctly. • Spelling, capitalization, and punctuation are correct. • Grammar and usage are correct.
3	• The narrative focuses primarily on events relating to a single experience but may include one or two unrelated events. • Most events are presented in chronological order, but some are not. • A few more transitions are needed to clarify the sequence of events and other details.	• The introduction could be more engaging. The scene is set adequately. • The narrative is somewhat well developed with key details and the writer's thoughts and feelings. • The conclusion of the narrative suggests but doesn't make clear the significance of the event to the writer.	• Precise words and vivid, sensory details are often used to describe people, places, and events. • Commonly confused words are generally used correctly. • Spelling, capitalization, and punctuation are mostly correct, with only a few errors. • Grammar and usage are mostly correct, with only a few errors.
2	• The narrative explores a number of events, with only a vague focus on one main experience. • The sequence of events is confusing. • More transitions are needed to show the sequence of events.	• The introduction is not very engaging or clear. • The narrative is missing key details or doesn't include enough of the writer's thoughts and feelings. • The conclusion of the narrative offers conflicting interpretations of the significance of the event to the writer.	• Precise words and vivid details are used only occasionally; descriptions are often vague and general. • There are several errors in the use of commonly confused words. • Spelling, capitalization, and punctuation are often incorrect but do not make reading difficult. • Grammar and usage are often incorrect, but the writer's ideas are still clear.
1	• The narrative wanders from event to event, with little or no focus. • Events are presented in random order, with no logical connections. • No transitions are used, making the narrative difficult to follow.	• The introduction is missing or very confusing. • The narrative is not well developed. There are no key details and the writer's thoughts and feelings are unclear. • The conclusion is missing or fails to convey the significance of the experience to the writer.	• Language is vague and confusing. • There are enough errors in the use of commonly confused words to cause confusion. • Many spelling, capitalization, and punctuation errors are present. • Many grammatical and usage errors confuse the writer's ideas.

Reflect on the Unit

By completing your personal narrative, you have created a writing product that helps pull together and express your thoughts about the reading you have done in this unit. Now is a good time to reflect on what you have learned.

Reflect on the Essential Question

- What does it mean to be in harmony with nature? How has your answer to this question changed since you first considered it when you started this unit?

- What are some examples from the texts you've read that show how people experience being in harmony with nature?

Reflect on Your Reading

- Which selections were the most interesting or surprising to you?

- From which selection did you learn the most about what it means to be in harmony with nature?

Reflect on the Writing Task

- What difficulties did you encounter while working on your personal narrative? How might you avoid them next time?

- What parts of the narrative were the easiest and hardest to write? Why?

- What improvements did you make to your narrative as you were revising?

REFLECT

UNIT 3 SELECTIONS

- "Never Retreat" from *Eyes Wide Open*
- *Mississippi Solo*
- "The Drought"
- "Allied with Green"
- "Ode to enchanted light"
- "Sleeping in the Forest"
- from *Trash Talk* (video)
- "You're Part of the Solution" (poster)

REFLECT ON THE UNIT

Have students reflect on the questions independently and write some notes in response to each one. Then have students meet with partners or in small groups to discuss their reflections. Circulate during these discussions to identify the questions that are generating the liveliest conversations. Wrap up with a whole-class discussion focused on these questions.

LEARNING MINDSET

Self Reflection Explain to students that reflecting on struggles or shortcomings will help them grow as learners. *Everyone* will be challenged by some element of a curriculum or new experience. Encourage persistence as a habit of mind and spirit; the will to try, risk failure, and try again will be rewarded in any endeavor. As students reflect on the unit, encourage them to ask themselves these questions: *Did I request help when I needed it? Did I try Plan B when Plan A didn't work? Am I proud of the work I turned in?*

UNIT 4

Instructional Overview and Resources

	Instructional Focus	Ed Resources
Unit Instruction **The Terror and Wonder of Space**	Unit 4 Essential Question Unit 4 Academic Vocabulary	**Stream to Start:** The Terror and Wonder of Space **Unit 4 Response Log**

ANALYZE & APPLY

	Instructional Focus	Resources
"Martian Metropolis" Science Writing by Meg Thatcher **Lexile 930L** **NOTICE & NOTE** READING MODEL **Signposts** • Numbers and Stats • Word Gaps • Big Questions	**Reading** • Analyze Structural Elements • Analyze Organizational Patterns **Writing:** Write an Informative Report **Speaking and Listening:** Create a Timeline **Vocabulary:** Greek Roots *atmos* and *sphere* **Language Conventions:** Capitalization	**Audio** **Reading Studio:** Notice & Note **Writing Studio:** Writing Informative Texts **Speaking and Listening Studio:** Participating in Collaborative Discussions **Vocabulary Studio:** Roots **Grammar Studio:** Module 13: Lesson 1: Capitalizing the Names of Heavenly Bodies
"Dark They Were, and Golden-Eyed" Science Fiction by Ray Bradbury **Lexile 540L**	**Reading** • Analyze Science Fiction • Analyze Mood **Writing:** Write a Letter **Speaking and Listening:** Make a Graphic **Vocabulary:** Latin Root *pend* **Language Conventions:** Consistent Verb Tenses	**Audio** **Close Read Screencast:** Modeled Discussion **Reading Studio:** Notice & Note **Writing Studio:** Writing as a Process **Speaking and Listening Studio:** Participating in Collaborative Discussions **Vocabulary Studio:** Roots **Grammar Studio:** Module 9: Lesson 4: Using Verb Tense Consistently
MENTOR TEXT **"Challenges for Space Exploration"** Argument by Ann Leckie **Lexile 880L**	**Reading** • Analyze Author's Purpose • Analyze Repetition **Writing:** Write a Poem **Speaking and Listening:** Listen for a Poem's Message **Vocabulary:** Etymology **Language Conventions:** Commas After Introductory Phrases	**Audio** **Text in Focus:** Analyzing an Argument **Reading Studio:** Notice & Note **Writing Studio:** Writing a Poem **Vocabulary Studio:** Etymology **Speaking and Listening Studio:** Participating in a Discussion **Grammar Studio:** Module 7: Lesson 2: Using Commas
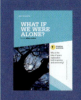 **"What if We Were Alone?"** Poem by William Stafford	**Reading** • Analyze Graphical Elements • Analyze Theme **Writing:** Write a Poem **Speaking and Listening:** Listen for the Theme	**Audio** **Reading Studio:** Notice & Note **Writing Studio:** Planning and Drafting a Poem **Speaking and Listening Studio:** Analyzing and Evaluating Presentations

SUGGESTED PACING: 30 DAYS

Unit Introduction	Martian Metropolis	Dark They Were, and Golded-Eyed	Challenges for Space Exploration
1	2 3 4 5	6 7 8 9 10 11 12	13 14 15 16

PLAN

English Learner Support		Differentiated Instruction	Assessment
• Learn Vocabulary • Discussion Web			
• Text X-Ray • Understand Organizational Patterns • Conjugate • Monitor Comprehension • Understand Capitalization • Oral Assessment	• Write an Informal Report • Understand Greek Roots	**When Students Struggle** • Graphic Organizer **To Challenge Students** • Create Diagrams	**Selection Test**
• Text X-Ray • Understand Mood • Practice Critical Vocabulary • Monitor Comprehension • Understand Science Fiction • Understand Consistent Verb Tenses	• Oral Assessment • Write a Letter • Understand Latin Roots	**When Students Struggle** • Possible Sentences • Storyboard **To Challenge Students** • Analyze Mood	**Selection Test**
• Text X-Ray • Understanding Word Choice • Use Cognates • Using Images • Oral Assessment	• Listen for a Poem's Message • Etymology	**When Students Struggle** • Reteach Repetition	**Selection Test**
• Text X-Ray • Understand Concepts • Understand Academic Language • Analyze Graphical Elements	• Comprehend Structure • Listen for the Theme	**When Students Struggle** • Reteach Theme	**Selection Test**

What if We Were Alone? 17 18

Seven Minutes of Terror 19 20

Space Exploration Should Be More Than Science Fiction / Humans Should Stay Home and Let Robots Take to the Stars 21 22 23 24 25

Independent Reading 26 27

End of Unit 28 29 30

The Terror and Wonder of Space **262B**

PLAN

UNIT 4 Continued | **Instructional Focus** | **Online Ed** Resources

ANALYZE & APPLY

"Seven Minutes of Terror"
Video by the National Aeronautics and Space Administration

Media
• Analyze Video

Writing: Write a Personal Narrative

Speaking and Listening: Present the Techniques

🔊 **Audio**

Reading Studio: Notice & Note

Writing Studio: Writing Narratives

Speaking and Listening Studio: Participating in Collaborative Discussions

COLLABORATE & COMPARE

"Space Exploration Should Be More Than Science Fiction"
Argument by Claudia Alarcon
Lexile 1060L

Reading
• Analyze Argument
• Analyze Rhetorical Devices

Writing: Write a Letter

Speaking and Listening: Create a Loaded Language Chart

Vocabulary: Connotations and Denotations

Language Conventions: Subordinating Conjunctions to Form Complex Sentences

🔊 **Audio**

Reading Studio: Notice & Note

Writing Studio: Writing as a Process

Speaking and Listening Studio: Participating in Collaborative Discussions

Grammar Studio: Module 10: Lesson 5: Who and Whom

"Humans Should Stay Home and Let Robots Take to the Stars"
Argument by Eiren Caffall
Lexile 1060L

Reading
• Analyze Argument
• Analyze Rhetorical Devices

Writing: Write a Short Story

Speaking and Listening: Describe a Process

Vocabulary: Dictionary/Glossary Entries

Language Conventions: Complete Complex Sentences

🔊 **Audio**

Writing Studio: Writing Narratives

Speaking and Listening Studio: Giving a Presentation

Vocabulary Studio: Using a Dictionary or Glossary

Grammar Studio: Module 6: Lesson 2: Subject-Verb Agreement

Collaborate and Compare

Reading:
• Compare Arguments
• Analyze the Texts

Speaking and Listening: Research and Share

Speaking and Listening Studio: Having a Debate

INDEPENDENT READING

 The independent Reading selections are only available in the eBook.

Go to the Reading Studio for more information on **NOTICE & NOTE**.

"Let's Aim for Mars"
Argument by Buzz Aldrin
Lexile 1140L

"An Optimistic View of the World"
Personal Essay by Dan Tani
Lexile 970L

END OF UNIT

Writing Task: Write an Argument

Speaking and Listening Task: Present a Podcast

Reflect on the Unit

Writing: Write an Argument

Language Conventions: Pronoun-Antecedent Agreement

Speaking and Listening: Prepare a Podcast

Unit 4 Response Log

Mentor Text: "Challenges for Space Exploration"

Writing Studio: Writing an Argument

Writing Studio: Introduction: Argument

Writing Studio: Support: Reasons

PLAN

English Learner Support		Differentiated Instruction	Online Ed Assessment
• Text X-Ray • Use Cognates • Confirm Understanding • Understand Questions • Discuss with a Small Group		**When Students Struggle** • Analyze the Video	**Selection Tests**
• Text X-Ray • Internalize New Terms • Practice • Oral Critique • Seek Clarification and Express Opinions • Evidence	• Verbal Response • Create a Chart • Cute Connotations • Language Conventions	**When Students Struggle** • Pros and Cons	**Selection Tests**
• Text X-Ray • Use Prereading Strategies • Oral Assessment • Describe a Process • Vocabulary Strategy • Language Conventions		**When Students Struggle** • Sketch to Stretch **To Challenge Student** • Write an Argument	**Selection Tests**
• Think About It		**When Students Struggle** • Analyze an Example	
"Your World" Poem by Georgia Douglas Johnson		"Sally Ride" from *Headstrong* Biograph by Rachel Swaby **Lexile 1140L**	Selection Tests
• Language X-Ray • Understand Academic Language • Write a Collaborative Argument • Use the Mentor Text	• Use a Variety of Sentence Types • Pronoun-Antecedent Agreement • Prepare a Podcast	**When Students Struggle** • Develop a Draft • Transitional Words and Phrases • Belonging **To Challenge Students** • Explore Multimedia	**Unit Test**

The Terror and Wonder of Space

TEACH

? Connect to the ESSENTIAL QUESTION

Ask a volunteer to read aloud the Essential Question. Discuss how the images on p. 262 relate to the question. Ask: *What is inspiring about space travel? How might it be frightening?* Encourage students to picture themselves exploring space, and ask them to reflect on the hazards and limits of exploration.

■ **English Learner Support**

Learn Vocabulary Make sure students understand the Essential Question. If necessary, explain the following terms:
- *inspiring* means "exciting"
- *unnerving* means "scary"

Help students reframe the question: *Why do people want to explore outer space?* **SUBSTANTIAL/MODERATE**

DISCUSS THE QUOTATION

Tell students that space exploration excited the world when Neil Armstrong, commander of *Apollo 11*, became the first human to set foot on the moon in 1969. More recently, Sally Ride became the first woman to fly in space. Advances in technology have extended human understanding of the scope, form, and mechanics of the cosmos. We have compelling new information about the birth and death of stars like the sun; far-flung indications of what may be water-bearing planets, like Earth; a sense of the outermost edges of a vast universe, and the nature of its expansion. Ask: *What is scary about ventures into space? If it's scary, why do so many people want to go "out there" anyway?*

UNIT 4

THE TERROR AND WONDER OF SPACE

? ESSENTIAL QUESTION

Why is the idea of space exploration both inspiring and unnerving?

> "All adventures, especially into new territory, are scary."
>
> — Sally Ride

🧠 LEARNING MINDSET

Growth Mindset Remind students that mistakes are a sign of progress, and give them opportunities to think about how to improve. With repeated effort comes progress. On every learning journey, everyone advances at her or his own pace. Encourage them to take pride in their work, and to look at every selection as an opportunity to set higher goals and stretch past their comfort zone.

UNIT 4

ACADEMIC VOCABULARY

Academic Vocabulary words are words you use when you discuss and write about texts. In this unit you will practice and learn five words.

- ✓ **complex**
- ☐ **potential**
- ☐ **rely**
- ☐ **stress**
- ☐ **valid**

Study the Word Network to learn more about the word **complex**.

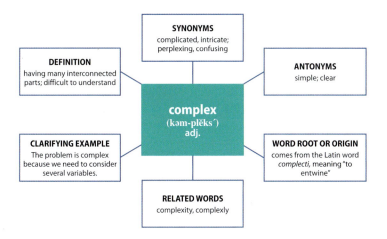

Write and Discuss Discuss the completed Word Network with a partner, making sure to talk through all of the boxes until you both understand the word, its synonyms, antonyms, and related words. Then, fill out Word Networks for the remaining four words. Use a dictionary or online resource to help you complete the activity.

 *Go online to access the **Word Networks**.*

RESPOND TO THE ESSENTIAL QUESTION

In this unit, you will explore how space exploration has affected our world. As you read, you will revisit the **Essential Question** and gather your ideas about it in the **Response Log** that appears on page R4. At the end of the unit, you will have the opportunity to write an **argument** in which you present and support your opinion about the necessity of human space travel. Filling out the Response Log will help you prepare for this writing task.

 *You can also go online to access the **Response Log**.*

The Terror and Wonder of Space 263

PLAN

READING MODEL
MARTIAN METROPOLIS
Science Writing by Meg Thatcher

GENRE ELEMENTS
INFORMATIONAL TEXT

Review the elements of informational text with students. Remind them that informational texts give facts and do not set out to convince or persuade. Writers of informational texts support their information with direct quotes from experts and footnotes citing their sources. They also often use text features such as headings to organize the information. In this lesson, students will examine three types of organization that informational texts might use: classification, cause and effect, and advantages and disadvantages.

LEARNING OBJECTIVES

- Analyze structural elements, such as references and acknowledgments.
- Analyze organizational patterns.
- Conduct research about past missions to Mars.
- Write an informative report on the current status of Mars exploration.
- Create a timeline depicting Mars missions.
- Study the Greek roots *atmos* and *sphere*.
- Review capitalization of proper nouns and abbreviations.
- **Language** Identify proper nouns based on capitalization.

TEXT COMPLEXITY

Quantitative Measures	Martian Metropolis	Lexile: 930L
Quantitative Measure	**Ideas Presented** Literal, explicit, and direct, purpose or stance clear	
	Structure Used May support through subheads, definitions, glossary	
	Language Used Meanings are implied but support is offered	
	Knowledge Required Begins to rely more on outside knowledge	

264A Unit 4

PLAN

RESOURCES

Online Ed

- Unit 4 Response Log
- 🔊 Selection Audio
- 📖 Reading Studio: Notice & Note
- 📝 Writing Studio: Writing Informative Texts
- 💬 Speaking and Listening Studio: Participating in Collaborative Discussions
- 🔬 Vocabulary Studio: Roots
- ❗ Grammar Studio: Module 13: Lesson 1: Capitalizing the Names of Heavenly Bodies
- ✅ "Martian Metropolis" Selection Test

SUMMARIES

English

Meg Thacher, a professor of astronomy, discusses point-by-point what living on Mars would be like for humans. Because its environment is so different from that of Earth, life on Mars would contrast sharply from what humans are used to. According to Thatcher, recent discoveries and technological innovations make human colonization of Mars is a very real (and fast-approaching) possibility.

Spanish

Meg Thacher, una profesora de astronomía, discute punto por punto cómo sería para los humanos vivir en Marte. Debido a que tiene un ambiente tan diferente al de la Tierra, la vida en el planeta rojo vecino sería un contraste fuerte a la vida a la que estamos acostumbrados. Pero con la combinación del ingenio humano y las innovaciones tecnológicas, la colonización humana de Marte es una posibilidad (próxima) muy real.

SMALL-GROUP OPTIONS

Have students work in small groups to read and discuss the selection.

Pinwheel Discussion

- In groups of eight, four students are seated facing in; four students are seated facing out.
- Students in the inner circle remain stationary throughout the discussion.
- Students in the outer circle move clockwise after discussing each question.
- Guide the discussion by asking a question for each round. Examples:
    - *Would you move to Mars? Why or why not?*
    - *What would be the hardest part about living on Mars? Explain.*
    - *What would you miss the most about living on Earth?*

Three-Minute Review

- Have student pairs gather their notes and materials on "Martian Metropolis" (texts remain closed).
- Tell them they have three minutes to come up with answers to each question you will ask.
- Ask a series of questions, varying in difficulty, such as:
    - *What is the greatest danger to humans living on Mars?* (radiation)
    - *How long would the journey from Earth to Mars take?* (6–8 months)

Afterwards, discuss the answers. Have students analyze how well they remembered the text versus how thorough their notes were.

Martian Metropolis **264B**

PLAN

Text X-Ray: English Learner Support
for "Martian Metropolis"

Use the Text X-Ray and the supports and scaffolds in the Teacher's Edition to help guide students at different proficiency levels through the selection.

INTRODUCE THE SELECTION
DISCUSS THE COLONIZATION OF MARS

In this lesson, students will need to discuss the science and technology required for humans to live on Mars. Read paragraph 3 with students, and point out the word *atmosphere*. Provide the following explanations:

- *Atmosphere is the air that is around a planet. It is made up of gases. The gases around Earth are easy for people to breathe. But people cannot breathe the gases around Mars.*

Explain to students that Mars's atmosphere makes it impossible for people to live there without special technology. Have volunteers tell whether they think people will ever live on Mars. Supply the following sentence frames:

I think people will live on Mars because ____.

I do not think people will live on Mars because ____.

CULTURAL REFERENCES

The following words and phrases may be unfamiliar to students:

- *life raft* (paragraph 2): a small boat or vehicle that is used to help people escape during an emergency
- *cool* (paragraph 2): great, fantastic, awesome
- *Fourth Rock from the Sun* (paragraph 4): creative way of saying Mars is four planets away from the sun
- *Living Off the Land* (paragraph 7): meeting needs for food and shelter by farming or hunting where you live
- *wear and tear* (paragraph 14): normal damage that happens when an item is used regularly

LISTENING

Understand Organizational Patterns

Draw students' attention to the subheading "Living Off the Land" on p. 270. Tell them that they can use subheadings to find details about a topic in a text more easily when rereading. In this section, they will find details about how settlers might survive on Mars.

Have students listen as you read aloud the subheading "Living Off the Land" followed by paragraphs 7 and 8. Use the following supports with students at varying proficiency levels:

- Tell students you will ask some questions about what they just heard. Allow students to answer using thumbs up or thumbs down responses. For example, ask: *Does Mars have metals and rock? Does Mars have wood or soil? Does Mars have animals?* **SUBSTANTIAL**
- Have students identify which resources Mars does and does not have. Supply these sentence frames: *Mars has ____, ____, and ____. Mars does not have ____, ____ or ____.* **MODERATE**
- After listening to the excerpt read aloud, have pairs work together to tell which resources people would need to bring with them to Mars. **LIGHT**

264C Unit 4

PLAN

SPEAKING

Pronounce Challenging Words

Have students practice pronouncing challenging words from the text. Circulate around the room to make sure students are pronouncing words correctly.

Use the following supports with students at varying proficiency levels:

- Point to the words *organisms* and *fertilizer* in paragraph 8, and model how to sound them out. Provide students with definitions. Then have them repeat the words after you. **SUBSTANTIAL**
- Have students identify the words *organisms*, *fertilizer*, and *sewage* in paragraph 8. Have student pairs take turns sounding out and pronouncing the words. Correct pronunciation as necessary. **MODERATE**
- Instruct partners to read this sentence from paragraph 8 aloud: *Poop makes excellent fertilizer, so the sewage treatment plant will be near the greenhouses.* Have students correct each other's pronunciation, providing support as necessary. Then, have them reread the sentence using correct pronunciation. **LIGHT**

READING

Read with Image Support

Provide students with labeled images of Mars to help them connect with the descriptions in the section "Fourth Rock From the Sun." Reinforce content-area vocabulary.

Work with students to read paragraphs 4–6. Provide students with images of Mars that clearly depict craters, dunes, mountains, dust, rocks, red soil, and pink sky. Use the following supports with students at varying proficiency levels:

- Point to geographic features and have students identify them with words from a word bank. Allow students to answer with single word responses or in their home language. If students struggle, provide the word and have them chorally repeat it. **SUBSTANTIAL**
- Guide students to complete sentence frames with words from a word bank; the sentences should describe provided images. For example: *I see _____ and _____ in the image of Mars.* **MODERATE**
- Have pairs work together to read the descriptions from the text that match the images. **LIGHT**

WRITING

Capitalize Proper Nouns

Work with students to understand the writing assignment on p. 279. Emphasize the importance of correctly capitalizing proper nouns when writing an informative report.

Use the following supports with students at varying proficiency levels:

- Work with students to identify proper nouns they would include in their informative report. Use these proper nouns to write 2–3 sentences about current Mars exploration on the board. Have students copy the sentences into their notebooks. **SUBSTANTIAL**
- Guide students to write short sentences about Mars exploration. Make sure students use correct capitalization of proper nouns. Supply this sentence frame: *It takes a long time to get from ____ to ____.* **MODERATE**
- Have student pairs generate a list of proper nouns they wish to include in their informative reports. Then have students write their informative reports, using each proper noun from their lists in their writing. **LIGHT**

TEACH

EXPLAIN THE SIGNPOSTS

Explain that **Notice & Note Signposts** are significant moments in the text that help readers understand and analyze works of fiction or nonfiction. Use the instruction on these pages to introduce students to the signposts **Numbers and Stats**, **Word Gaps**, and **Big Questions**. Then use the selection that follows to have students apply the signposts to a text.

For a full list of the fiction and nonfiction signposts, see p. 348.

NUMBERS AND STATS

If you argue about how warm it was three winters ago, your case will be stronger if you can cite dates and temperatures. **Numbers and Stats** support an **argument** with data, a form of **evidence** or proof that is difficult to refute.

Display the following sentence: *Because Earth and Mars are so far apart, signals are delayed for a little while.* Underline the clause *for a little while.* Ask: *How is the example text more convincing?* (*The sentence in the example defines the short signal delay. Vague language leaves room for doubt in an argument.*)

Tell students that when they see **Numbers and Stats**, they should pause, mark them in their consumable texts, and ask the anchor question: *How does this affect the argument?*

Notice & Note
READING MODEL

For more information on these and other signposts to Notice & Note, visit the **Reading Studio**.

When you read and encounter quantities or a comparison with numbers, pause to see if it's a **Numbers and Stats** signpost:

Numerals such as eight, 98%, and 1,001

Numerals and stats used in a comparison: three out of ten, five times as many

Indefinite quantities, such as *most, some, many, bigger than, younger than*

Anchor Question
When you notice this signpost, ask: Why did the author use these numbers or amounts?

MARTIAN METROPOLIS

You are about to read the informational text "Martian Metropolis." In it, you will notice and note signposts that will help you identify important details and make inferences about the text. Here are three key signposts to look for as you read this article and other works of nonfiction.

Numbers and Stats Have you ever seen a commercial that promised that a product was 99% fat free? Or maybe you heard a sportscaster fire off a series of statistics about a basketball game. How did the use of numbers and statistics help you understand the information?

Authors use specific quantities and statistics to help support an idea or argument. Paying attention to **Numbers and Stats** can:

- help reveal the key points the author is making
- hint at the author's bias or purpose for writing
- show comparisons between two things

Here, a student underlined evidence of a Numbers and Stats instance in "Martian Metropolis":

> 15   But people on Mars will communicate with Earth pretty often. Because Earth and Mars are so far apart, <u>signals are delayed by up to 24 minutes</u>. Communication will mostly resemble email. Jay Dickson, a planetary geologist at Brown University, has lived at Antarctica's isolated McMurdo Station. "Just being able to send pictures back and forth is great for morale," Dickson explains.

What statistic is used?	. . . signals [between Earth and Mars] are delayed by up to 24 minutes.
Why do you think the author included this statistic?	It supports the author's point that people on Mars will communicate often with Earth because there is only a 24-minute delay. It also helps show how far away Mars is.

Word Gaps Have you ever come across a word or phrase in a textbook that you didn't recognize? What did you do? Did you read on, or did you go back to look for clues in the text?

Noting **Word Gaps**, or unfamiliar words and phrases, can guide you to use context clues and a dictionary or other resources to determine meanings. Doing this can then help you understand important details and ideas in the text. Here's how a student marked the text to indicate an example of Word Gaps:

> 8   Settlers will need to grow food. Mars has dirt, but it doesn't have soil. Soil contains <u>microbes</u> that help plants grow. Fortunately, humans will take those organisms along with them! Poop makes excellent fertilizer, so the sewage treatment plant will be near the greenhouses. . . .

What context clues helped you determine the meaning of *microbes*?	"that help plants grow," "those organisms"
How does understanding the word *microbes* help clarify how settlers can overcome the challenges of living on Mars?	Knowing the meaning of the word helps me understand that even though settling Mars will be difficult, there are solutions to problems.

Big Questions As you read nonfiction texts, you will likely encounter information that is new to you. It's time to think about this **Big Question**: **What surprised you?** Doing this can help you think more critically about the author's claims. A student marked what appeared to be a surprising detail in this way:

> 6   . . . On Mars, cosmic radiation is much higher than it is on Earth. This can cause serious damage to DNA, which increases the risk of cancer. <u>The danger decreases if you burrow 16 feet (5 meters) under the surface of the Red Planet</u>. The soil overhead would provide about the same amount of protection as Earth's atmosphere.

What surprised you in this passage?	The danger of cosmic radiation decreases if you burrow 16 feet under the surface of Mars.
Why might the author have included this information?	The author probably included the information to show that even though cosmic radiation is dangerous, there is a way to protect settlers.

When you see the following, pause to see if it's a **Word Gaps** signpost:

- a boldfaced or highlighted word
- an unfamiliar word, phrase, or concept
- an unclear or confusing word, phrase, or concept

Anchor Question
When you notice this signpost, ask, "Do I know this word from someplace else?"

Notice & Note   265

TEACH

WORD GAPS

A **Word Gap** is the textual equivalent of a stubbed toe: a moment that brings a reader up short when he or she bumps into unfamiliar words or phrases.

Point out that context offers clues to language and concepts that may at first be unfamiliar. Sometimes those clues may come multiple paragraphs before and after an obscure reference. (And remind students to refer to a dictionary or thesaurus for clarification.)

Tell students that when they encounter **Word Gaps**, they should pause, mark them in their consumable texts, and ask the anchor question: *Can I find clues to help me understand this?*

BIG QUESTIONS

Explain that readers can use **Big Questions** to guide their reading or to deepen understanding of a text. Tell students that they should think about the **Big Question** as they read.

Authors often make claims or present facts and information that a reader may never have encountered before. When students are surprised by a particular detail in the text, they should ask the following questions to understand what makes a particular detail intriguing: *Why does this detail surprise me? Why did the author include this detail? Is the author presenting facts or stating an opinion?*

Tell students that when they spot a **Big Question** they should stop, mark them in their consumable texts, and ask themselves the anchor question: *What just surprised me?*

APPLY THE SIGNPOSTS

Have students use the selection that follows as a model text to apply the signposts. As students encounter signposts, prompt them to stop, reread, and ask themselves the anchor questions that will help them understand the author's argument.

WHEN STUDENTS STRUGGLE . . .

Syntax Surgery If students are struggling with **Big Questions**, model the Syntax Surgery strategy for them. Display text that features words or phrases that may be unfamiliar. Circle those terms. Then draw arrows that connect them to underlined words and phrases that provide context clues. Ask: *How does this circled item relate to the underlined ones? How does this help answer a Big Question?* Encourage students to use Syntax Surgery in their consumable texts when they encounter new information.

Notice & Note   **265**

TEACH

? Connect to the
ESSENTIAL QUESTION

This informational essay explains what living on Mars would be like for humans. While it may dispel some fears about living in space, it also makes it clear that living on the red planet would come with some great obstacles.

ANALYZE & APPLY

MARTIAN METROPOLIS

Science Writing by **Meg Thacher**

? ESSENTIAL QUESTION:

Why is the idea of space exploration both inspiring and unnerving?

LEARNING MINDSET

Seeking Challenges This informational text focuses on seeking challenges. Use it to show students that with hard work and perseverance, humans can overcome anything. We all are capable of achieving great things provided we establish a goal and set our minds to achieving that goal. Most goals involve overcoming challenges. Remind students that when they set their goals they should include some challenges. Meeting these challenges will improve their self-confidence and inspire them to face future challenges.

GET READY

QUICK START

Maybe you've seen amazing photographs of Mars. But have you ever thought about what it would be like to live there? Discuss with your class the likely challenges of humans living on Mars.

ANALYZE STRUCTURAL ELEMENTS

Text features are elements of a text that help organize and call attention to important information. Science writing—such as "Martian Metropolis"—and other informational texts often contain multiple text features, including **references** and **acknowledgments.**

- **References** include footnotes and endnotes. Footnotes appear at the bottom of the page and provide additional information about terms or ideas in the text, including sources. Endnotes appear at the end of the text and include the same information as footnotes.
- The **acknowledgments** is a list of statements that recognize the contributions made by people or organizations to the creation of the text. This might include research or image contributions, or other help that was given to the author.

ANALYZE ORGANIZATIONAL PATTERNS

To ensure that informational texts are clear to readers, writers choose a **pattern of organization,** or a particular arrangement of ideas and information. Facts and details can be organized in a variety of ways. This chart shows a few common patterns of organization. As you read "Martian Metropolis," note the organizational patterns the author uses.

PATTERN	EXAMPLE FROM THE SELECTION
A **classification** pattern presents objects, ideas, and information in groups, or classes, based on common characteristics.	The city will need energy for heat and electricity. The best sources will be solar, geothermal, and wind, as there's no oil or gas on Mars. Settlers will also want to make fuel for trips back home. They'll likely use carbon dioxide from the Martian atmosphere to make methane gas. . . .
A **cause and effect** pattern shows the relationship between events and their causes.	Because it has to produce its own air, the Martian city will be small.
An **advantages and disadvantages** pattern divides ideas about a topic into the positive and negative points, or advantages and disadvantages.	Of all the planets in the solar system, Mars is the most Earth-like. It's made of rock and has a thin atmosphere. . . . The biggest danger on Mars, though, is radiation.

GENRE ELEMENTS: INFORMATIONAL TEXT
- provides factual information
- includes evidence to support ideas
- contains text features to convey information
- can be presented in many forms, such as science writing, news articles, and essays

TEACH

QUICK START

Have students read the Quick Start question, and invite them to share any information they know about Mars. Create a "What is Mars like?" graphic organizer on the board. Invite volunteers to add details to the chart. Then, have the class discuss what these details help them understand about what life might be like for humans on Mars.

ANALYZE STRUCTURAL ELEMENTS

Ask students whether they think references such as footnotes and endnotes are important. Explain that footnotes clarify details and add additional information that is not included in the text. For instance, anyone reading "Martian Metropolis" who wants to know more about any of the topics discussed need only look up the sources listed in the references.

This selection ends with an acknowledgment. Point out that acknowledgments provide authors with the opportunity to thank the people who helped them in the preparation of a text. Acknowledgements usually appear at the beginning of a text.

ANALYZE ORGANIZATIONAL PATTERNS

- **Classification** Explain to students that authors of informational texts often classify, or categorize, details based on common ideas. This helps readers understand how facts and information relate to one another. In "Martian Metropolis," the author classifies solar, geothermal, and wind as types of energy.
- **Cause and Effect** Point out the word *because* in the example sentence. Remind students to look for cause-and-effect signal words and phrases as they read, such as *for, because, since, so, as a result, due to, cause, effect, therefore, thus,* and *consequently*. Signal words are not always present, but can help readers more easily identify cause and effect in a text.
- **Advantages and Disadvantages** Explain that authors present both positive and negative aspects of a topic so readers can assess the good and bad points and then use these points to form an opinion. Point out that a vernacular phrase for this organizational pattern is *pros and cons*.

TEACH

CRITICAL VOCABULARY

Encourage students to read all the sentences before deciding which word best completes each one. Remind them to look for context clues that match the meaning of each word.

Answers:

1. *geothermal*
2. *radiation*
3. *atmosphere*
4. *colonize*

■ English Learner Support

Use Cognates Tell students that all the Critical Vocabulary words have Spanish cognates: *geothermal/ geotérmica, radiation/ radiación, atmosphere/atmósfera, colony/colonia, colonize/colonizar.* **LIGHT**

LANGUAGE CONVENTIONS

Explain to students that with today's technology, many people do not take the time to capitalize in their text messages, social media posts, and e-mails. Some software even automatically capitalizes words for us. Point out that it is still important to know correct capitalization when writing for formal occasions, such as college application essays, resumes, school or college essays, and job applications. Explain that in many of these cases, students will not be able to rely on autocorrect and will need know the rules of capitalization.

Provide students with a brief, sample e-mail that includes incorrectly capitalized proper nouns. Have them work individually to identify the proper nouns. Then, have student pairs check each other's work.

ANNOTATION MODEL

Students can review the Reading Model if they have questions about any of the signposts. Suggest that they underline important phrases or circle key words that help them identify signposts. They may want to color-code their annotation by using a different color highlighter for each signpost. Point out that they may follow this suggestion or use their own system for marking up the selections in their write-in texts.

268   Unit 4

 GET READY

CRITICAL VOCABULARY

atmosphere   radiation   colonize   geothermal

To see how many Critical Vocabulary words you already know, use them to complete the sentences.

1. The large volcanic island got much of its energy from _____ resources.
2. _____ from the sun and other sources in space can pose a danger to humans.
3. Earth's _____ is thicker and more protective than that of Mars.
4. In order to _____ Antarctica, people would have to cope with the cold temperatures and lack of resources.

LANGUAGE CONVENTIONS

Capitalization In this lesson, you will learn about capitalization. Proper nouns—the names of specific people, places, and things—are always capitalized, as in this example from "Martian Metropolis":

"This could be our life raft," says Darby Dyar, an astronomy professor at Mount Holyoke College and a member of the Mars Curiosity rover team.

As you read, note the capitalization of proper nouns.

ANNOTATION MODEL NOTICE & NOTE

As you read, notice and note signposts, including **Numbers and Stats, Word Gaps,** and **Big Questions.** Here is an example of how one reader responded to this paragraph from "Martian Metropolis."

> 5   It's farther from the sun than Earth, so Mars is much colder. On average, it's <u>a bone-chilling -80° F / -62° C</u>. The Martian day (called a "sol") is <u>about 40 minutes longer than an Earth day</u>; a Martian year is <u>668.6 sols</u>. Its atmosphere is <u>about 100 times thinner than Earth's</u>[1] and it's <u>95 percent carbon dioxide</u>. Even if Mars' atmosphere were thicker, we wouldn't be able to breathe it. Earth's atmosphere is <u>mostly nitrogen and oxygen, with 0.04 percent carbon dioxide</u>—a combination that's friendlier to our planet's life forms.

The statistics in this paragraph help me see how different Mars is from Earth.

There is a footnote. It will tell me more about what I'm reading.

Stats about Earth and Mars show that life there won't be easy.

268   Unit 4

WHEN STUDENTS STRUGGLE . . .

Organizational Patterns To help students understand the information the author presents about life on Mars, have students fill in an advantages and disadvantages graphic organizer.

Life on Mars	Advantages	Disadvantages
Atmosphere		
Food		
Work		
Play		

 For additional support, go to the **Reading Studio** and assign the following **Level Up** tutorial: Reading for Details.

BACKGROUND

Meg Thacher is an astronomy instructor at Smith College in western Massachusetts. In addition, she serves as the academic director for the college's Summer Science and Engineering Program, offered to high school girls who are interested in science, engineering, and medicine. Thacher explains her passion for science writing by saying, "I love all things science, and I love explaining it in terms that kids can understand."

MARTIAN METROPOLIS

Science Writing by Meg Thacher

SETTING A PURPOSE

As you read, pay attention to the information about the Red Planet that surprised you. What do you think would be most challenging about living on Mars?

1   NASA plans to send humans to Mars in the 2030s, and several private entities aim to send settlers to live on Mars permanently.

2   There are several reasons to create an off-planet colony. One is survival of our species. "We never know what will happen to threaten the habitat. This could be our <u>life raft</u>," says Darby Dyar, an astronomy professor at Mount Holyoke College and a member of the Mars Curiosity rover team. "There's also the cool factor," she says. "<u>Who would *not* want to live on Mars?</u>"

3   Scientists living on Mars can study the planet up close better than rovers can. They can compare it to Earth and other planets. They can study its **atmosphere**—and humans'

NOTICE & NOTE

Notice & Note

Use the side margins to notice and note signposts in the text.

WORD GAPS

Notice & Note: Mark the clues in paragraph 2 that help you understand the word *colony*.

Infer: Why did the author introduce this term so early in the text?

atmosphere
(ăt´mə-sfîr´) *n.* An *atmosphere* is the gaseous mass or envelope that surrounds a planet.

ENGLISH LEARNER SUPPORT

Monitor Comprehension Tell students that active readers notice and take action when they come across text they don't understand. Have students practice monitoring comprehension verbally.

Supply sentence frames to help students take action when part of a text is unclear or confusing: *I do not understand ___. What does the word ___ mean?* **SUBSTANTIAL/MODERATE**

Have student pairs of varying proficiency take turns reading paragraph 1. Instruct listeners to stop readers when they don't understand something. Then, have them reread the text slowly. **LIGHT**

TEACH

BACKGROUND

Students may not be aware that Mars is barely habitable because of the lack of oxygen in the atmosphere and its lack of protection from harmful radiation. Make sure students understand these facts, but also let them know that humans can use technology to overcome these difficulties.

SETTING A PURPOSE

Direct students to use the Setting a Purpose prompt to focus their reading.

▶ **WORD GAPS**

Students may recognize the word *colony* from their history studies, but may it may not occur to them to apply it to the concept of moving to another planet. (**Answer:** *The author introduced the term early because the article is about establishing a colony on Mars.*)

CRITICAL VOCABULARY

atmosphere: Earth's atmosphere is a mixture of nitrogen, oxygen, and other gases.

ASK STUDENTS why it is important for scientists to study Mars's atmosphere. (*It is important for scientists to study Mars's atmosphere in order to understand how humans might survive on the planet one day.*)

TEACH

NUMBERS AND STATS

Provide students with background information to help them understand the numbers cited in paragraph 5. *C* and *F* refer to Celsius and Fahrenheit, which are measurements for temperature. The difference between Mars's 95% carbon dioxide atmosphere and Earth's 0.04% is staggering. (**Answer:** *It helps illustrate how difficult it would be to live on Mars, especially because it is so cold and has such a thin atmosphere.*)

 ANALYZE STRUCTURAL ELEMENTS

The footnote number (2) refers to the text it is referencing and its position at the bottom of the page. Be sure to show students that the page contains three footnotes and their corresponding sources. (**Answer:** *It tells the source of the information that explains why radiation on Mars is an important concern.*)

ANALYZE ORGANIZATIONAL PATTERNS

Explain to students that organizational patterns help with the flow of information in the text. The author uses these patterns to jump from category to category without having to use transitions. (**Answer:** *Classification: This section focuses on how colonists would use resources found on Mars, as opposed to another section that focuses on entertainment in the colony.*)

CRITICAL VOCABULARY

radiation: The particles and waves that are transmitted through radiation can cause serious illness in humans.

ASK STUDENTS how people protect their skin from the sun's radiation on Earth (**Possible answers:** *sunscreen, limiting exposure to the sun, long clothes.*)

colonize: When settlers create a home in an unfamiliar place, they are colonizing it, whether it is inhabited or not.

ASK STUDENTS whether they think colonists on Mars will be the first people to live there. (**Possible answer:** *Yes because it is too hard for life to thrive in Mars's atmosphere.*)

270   Unit 4

 **NOTICE & NOTE**

NUMBERS AND STATS

Notice & Note: In paragraph 5, mark the statistics the author provides about Mars.

Analyze: What does this information help you understand about what it would be like to live on Mars?

radiation
(rā′dē-ā′shən) *n.* Radiation is energy transmitted in the form of waves or particles.

ANALYZE STRUCTURAL ELEMENTS

Annotate: Circle the footnote number in paragraph 6 and underline its footnote at the bottom of the page.

Analyze: What information does this footnote provide?

colonize
(kŏl′ə-nīz′) *v.* When you *colonize* a place, you send a group of people to a new place to establish a colony or settlement.

ANALYZE ORGANIZATIONAL PATTERNS

Annotate: Mark the subheads on these pages.

Analyze: Which main organizational pattern is the author using? How can you tell?

---

effect on that atmosphere. If they find evidence for life on Mars, whether past or present, that will tell humans we're not alone in the universe.

Fourth Rock from the Sun

4   Of all the planets in the solar system, Mars is the most Earth-like. It's made of rock and has a thin atmosphere. The scenery is beautiful but also strange, with craters and sand dunes, dust and scattered rocks. It has massive landforms—the tallest mountains and deepest canyons in the solar system—all under a pink sky.

5   It's farther from the sun than Earth, so Mars is much colder. On average, it's a bone-chilling -80° F/-62° C. The Martian day (called a "sol") is about 40 minutes longer than an Earth day; a Martian year is 668.6 sols. Its atmosphere is about 100 times thinner than Earth's,[1] and it's 95 percent carbon dioxide. Even if Mars' atmosphere were thicker, we wouldn't be able to breathe it. Earth's atmosphere is mostly nitrogen and oxygen, with 0.04 percent carbon dioxide—a combination that's friendlier to our planet's life forms.

6   The biggest danger on Mars, though, is **radiation.** Mars has no magnetic field to protect humans from high-energy particles from the sun and other sources, called cosmic rays. On Mars, cosmic radiation is much higher than it is on Earth. This can cause serious damage to DNA, which increases the risk of cancer. The danger decreases if you burrow 16 feet (5 meters) under the surface of the Red Planet.[2] The soil overhead would provide about the same amount of protection as Earth's atmosphere.

Living Off the Land

7   Sending stuff to Mars is very expensive. The cheapest way to **colonize** will be to make everything there. "It's really all about the resources," says Dyar. "If we find things there that allow us to sustain human life, then we can settle there." Mars has plenty of metals and rock, and probably lots of water, but no wood or petroleum (which is used to make gasoline, plastic, and many other useful products). The settlers could make bricks from local dirt. Mars has plenty of silicon and iron, elements that will allow people to produce glass and steel.[3] And of course,

---

[1] "The Terrestrial Planets," National Oceanic and Atmospheric Administration, https://www.esrl.noaa.gov/gmd/outreach/info_activities/pdfs/TBI_terrestrial_planets.pdf

[2] "Mission to Mars Would Double Astronauts' Cancer Risk," U.S. National Library of Medicine, https://medlineplus.gov/news/fullstory_166629.html

[3] "Oxygen in the Martian Atmosphere: Regulation of PO2 by the deposition of iron formations on Mars", NASA Technical Reports Server, Nov 7, 1995, https://ntrs.nasa.gov/search.jsp?R=19920019239

270   Unit 4

everything sent to Mars will stay on Mars. Martian citizens will be really good at recycling.

8   Settlers will need to grow food. Mars has dirt, but it doesn't have soil. Soil contains microbes that help plants grow. Fortunately, humans will take those organisms along with them! Poop makes excellent fertilizer, so the sewage treatment plant will be near the greenhouses. Martians will most likely eat a vegan diet. Animals are hard to transport, and it takes much less energy to grow plants than to raise animals. Plants also use up carbon dioxide and produce oxygen, which people need to breathe.

9   The city will need energy for heat and electricity. The best sources will be solar, **geothermal**, and wind, as there's no oil or gas on Mars. Settlers will also want to make fuel for trips back home. They'll likely use carbon dioxide from the Martian atmosphere to make methane gas. To do this, they'll need hydrogen. They could bring it from Earth, or get it from water found on Mars.

Smaller Is Better

10 Because it has to produce its own air, the Martian city will be small. At first, residents will probably live underground to protect against cosmic radiation. They'll work to develop radiation-blocking glass or plastic. Once that's in place, settlers can live above ground in brick buildings with windows, or even under a dome or tent.

11 To limit exposure to radiation, scientists will send rovers and drones out exploring and will use the information to decide where to send human explorers. Temporary shelters and labs will pop up all over the planet for short-term science projects.

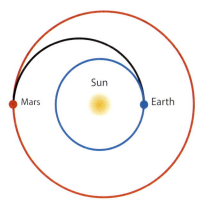

The black line traces the most efficient path from Earth to Mars. Space travelers will need to wait as long as two years for the planets' orbits to align.

NOTICE & NOTE

BIG QUESTIONS

Notice & Note: Mark the information in paragraph 8 that most surprised you.

Infer: Why do you think the author included this information?

geothermal
(jē´ō-thûr´məl) *adj.* Geothermal relates to the internal heat of the earth.

WORD GAPS

Notice & Note: Mark the word *cosmic* in paragraph 10 and then use a dictionary or context clues in the article to determine its meaning.

Infer: Why might the author have used this term to describe the radiation?

Martian Metropolis   271

TO CHALLENGE STUDENTS...

Create a Diagram Challenge students to come up with their own diagrams for a Mars colony. Have them research NASA.gov and other science websites that include information on Mars colonization for ideas. Students may accompany their diagrams with a written explanation. Encourage students to make their diagrams as detailed as possible by adding captions that explain the functions of each part of the colony.

TEACH

BIG QUESTIONS

Explain to students that this signpost is used to help students connect details to the most important ideas in a text. Have students list details from the text that most surprised them. Then, have student pairs discuss what detail most surprised them and why. (**Possible Answer:** *I think using human poop as fertilizer is the most surprising detail. I didn't know that poop could be recycled that way.*)

EL ENGLISH LEARNER SUPPORT

Monitor Comprehension Use a Think Aloud routine with students as you reread paragraph 10: *I read that the Martian City might be in a dome. I can use context clues to understand that a dome is a kind of tent. I wonder how big the dome will be? I can reread to see that a Martian city will be small, so the dome will only fit a small city.*

Have student pairs of varying proficiencies reread together to understand the terms *underground* and *above ground,* using the Think Aloud strategy as a model. Provide support as needed. **ALL LEVELS**

For **listening support** for students at varying proficiency levels, see the **Text X-Ray** on page 264C.

WORD GAPS

Notice & Note: Remind students that in some cases context clues are not sufficient, and they will need to use a dictionary to find the meaning of unknown words, such as the word *cosmic,* which means "coming from space." (**Answer:** *The author may have decided to note this specific kind of radiation to distinguish it from radiation coming from another source.*)

CRITICAL VOCABULARY

geothermal: The article explains that geothermal heat is a type of energy that comes from within a planet. Scientists may be able use Mars's internal heat to create electricity to power a colony.

ASK STUDENTS why geothermal energy is a good option for creating power on Mars. (*Possible response: Geothermal energy is a natural resource on Mars. It doesn't have oil or gas.*)

Martian Metropolis   271

TEACH

LANGUAGE CONVENTIONS

Earth can be used as a proper or common noun. When referring to the planet itself, we capitalize it. When referring to the ground or soil, we do not capitalize it. (**Answer:** *Earth* and *Mars* are specific planets, but the other nouns are not specific.)

■ English Learner Support

Understand Capitalization Ask students how they know the words *Earth* and *Mars* are proper nouns. *(because they are capitalized)* Remind students that words that begin a sentence are also capitalized. **SUBSTANTIAL**

 **NOTICE & NOTE**

12   Wealthy tourists might visit the Red Planet, but you won't have to be rich or a scientist to live on Mars. The city will need farmers to grow crops, cooks, people to run the spaceport and sewage plant, trash collectors, doctors and nurses—the list goes on. Some jobs can be done by machines, which use fewer resources than human workers. So add robot mechanic to that list of careers!

All Work and No Play?

13   Colonists will keep busy with work, but they'll want entertainment too. They can venture outside for short sightseeing trips. They'll have television, radio, and movies—some transmitted from (Earth,) some made right on (Mars.) They can read and do crafts. Colonists will probably make up new sports that take advantage of (Mars') low gravity. Zip lines, rock climbing, and trampolines will be popular.

14   But travel will be hard. The most fuel-efficient trip back to Earth (using gravity to do most of the work) will take around six to eight months. Earth and Mars are properly aligned for this trip for about 20 days every 26 months. Travelers in a spaceship will experience more radiation than people get

LANGUAGE CONVENTIONS

Annotate: In paragraph 13, mark the proper nouns.

Analyze: Why are these words capitalized, but nouns such as *television*, *radio*, and *movies* are not?

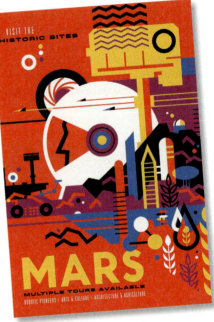

Artists at NASA's Jet Propulsion Laboratory collaborated with space scientists to create this poster. It imagines a time when human visitors celebrate the robot pioneers of Mars.

on Earth. Our muscles will weaken unless engineers create "artificial gravity" by spinning the ships. It adds up to a lot of wear and tear; humans will keep trips to a minimum.

15 But people on Mars will communicate with Earth pretty often. Because Earth and Mars are so far apart, signals are delayed by up to 24 minutes. Communication will mostly resemble email. Jay Dickson, a planetary geologist at Brown University, has lived at Antarctica's isolated McMurdo Station. "Just being able to send pictures back and forth is great for morale," Dickson explains.

16 A colony on Mars will be humankind's first steps in expanding our reach within the solar system and beyond.

The author wishes to acknowledge the factual contributions of the space exploration experts consulted for this article.

NOTICE & NOTE

ANALYZE STRUCTURAL ELEMENTS
Annotate: Mark the acknowledgments.
Analyze: What experts is the author likely referring to?

CHECK YOUR UNDERSTANDING

Answer these questions before moving on to the **Analyze the Text** section on the following page.

1 The author mainly supports her ideas by —
  A citing opinions of multiple experts
  B providing amusing anecdotes
  C using scientific evidence
  D providing diagrams

2 Why does the author include the section <u>Living Off the Land</u>?
  F To prove that colonizing another planet is possible
  G To show that it will be expensive to live on Mars
  H To convince readers that people should not farm on Mars
  J To explain that colonists will need to make what they need

3 In paragraph 12, the author includes a list of jobs that will be available in a Mars colony to show that —
  A there will be a need for people with many different skills
  B running the colony will require too many people and resources
  C there will be many opportunities for science and tourism
  D many jobs in the colony will be done by machines

Martian Metropolis 273

TEACH

ANALYZE STRUCTURAL ELEMENTS

Point out to students that the author lists acknowledgments at the end of the text. In this case of this article, the acknowledgments list a team of people all working together to convey accurate information. (**Answer:** *people mentioned in the article, such as Jay Dickson and Darby Dyar*)

CHECK YOUR UNDERSTANDING

Have students answer the questions independently.

Answers:
1. C
2. J
3. A

If they answer any questions incorrectly, have them reread the text to confirm their understanding. Then they may proceed to ANALYZE THE TEXT on p. 274.

 ENGLISH LEARNER SUPPORT

Oral Assessment Use the following questions to assess students' comprehension and speaking skills.

1. The author supports her ideas with _____. *(scientific evidence)*
2. What does the section "Living Off the Land" tell readers? *(to explain that colonists will have to make and grow what they need)*
3. What kinds of workers will a Martian colony need? *(farmers, people to run machinery, trash collectors, doctors, and nurses)*
SUBSTANTIAL/MODERATE

Martian Metropolis **273**

APPLY

ANALYZE THE TEXT

Possible answers:

1. **DOK 2:** *Mars is the most Earth-like planet.*

2. **DOK 3:** *Settlers could make bricks from local dirt. Mars has plenty of silicon and iron, elements that will allow people to produce glass and steel.*

3. **DOK 2:** *It supports the idea that because Mars is so far away, it would be too costly to transport items from Earth.*

4. **DOK 3:** *Each section in the article compares life on Earth to life on Mars. For example, Mars has dirt but no soil. Earth has soil, which contains microbes that help plants grow.*

5. **DOK 4:** *The author uses numbers and statistics to support her points about the challenges of traveling to and living on Mars.*

RESEARCH

Remind students it's important to always keep a list of their sources in case they have to go back and check their facts again.

Connect *Mars Curiosity* and *Opportunity* would be models because both involve using rovers to explore the surface of the planet and send back data about rocks and soil, as well as the landscape of different parts of the planet. Students might also explore the current use of drones and the additional information they might give scientists.

RESPOND

ANALYZE THE TEXT

Support your responses with evidence from the text. NOTEBOOK

1. **Explain** Why does the author propose that humans colonize Mars rather than another planet?

2. **Cite Evidence** What natural resources does Mars have? Use evidence from the text to explain how settlers could use the natural resources of Mars to build a colony.

3. **Infer** Review paragraph 7. How does the use of a footnote help the author explain why colonists will have to make things?

4. **Compare** How does the organization of the text help you understand Earth and Mars? Review the text and explain how the atmosphere and soil of Mars differ from those of Earth.

5. **Notice & Note** Why did the author use numbers and stats?

RESEARCH

RESEARCH TIP
Remember that information about Mars research may change over time. One reliable source for updates is www.nasa.gov. However, always check to make sure the information you have is dated within the last year or so, whether it comes from a *.gov* site, an *.edu* site, or a news site.

What other questions do you have about Mars? Brainstorm some questions and find the answers by researching some Mars missions, including key events and their dates, to learn what's been discovered.

MISSION	DISCOVERIES
MAVEN	Obtain information on Mars's atmosphere to understand dramatic climate change in Mars's history.
Mars Reconnaissance Orbiter	Camera obtains information on geology and structure of Mars.
Mars Science Laboratory—Curiosity	Rover sent to find out if Mars was or is suitable for life.
Mars Rovers Spirit and Opportunity	Search and characterize rocks and soil, take photographs to determine Mars's past and to understand geology of Mars.
2001 Mars Odyssey	Orbiter's mission includes making map of distribution of chemicals and minerals, identifying areas with buried ice, and identifying potential landing sites for rovers.

Connect In paragraph 11, the writer states that "scientists will send rovers and drones out exploring and will use the information to decide where to send human explorers." How could your Mars research help you decide where—and what—humans should explore there?

274 Unit 4

 LEARNING MINDSET

Asking For Help No one should be embarrassed about asking for help. In fact, students will find that most people, whether they are older or their same age, enjoy answering each other's questions. If a student can't think of anyone to ask for help, then help them brainstorm a list of people they can reach out to. First, list someone who is the best person to ask help, second should be the person they can ask if the first person is too busy, and so on. Also, you can break the list into categories, such as who to ask for help on reading, writing, or math. This way, students will have a list of contacts for whenever they stumble. Finally, suggest that they keep updating the list as time goes on.

WRITE AND PRESENT

Write an Informative Report Use your research to write a two- to three-page report about the current status of Mars exploration.

- ❏ Introduce the topic and state your controlling idea, or thesis statement, about the current Mars missions you researched.
- ❏ In the body of your report, briefly describe each mission you researched and what we've learned about Mars from it. Remember to include references for the sources you used.
- ❏ In your final paragraph, restate your controlling idea and summarize the current status of Mars exploration.

Create a Timeline With a partner, use your combined research to create an annotated timeline for Mars missions.

- ❏ Review the research you both conducted on Mars explorations. Work together to determine key events that are most important to include in your timeline.
- ❏ Create your timeline on a computer or poster board. List the key dates for each event along with a brief description. To enhance your timeline, consider including diagrams and other visuals that you create or download from the NASA website.
- ❏ Share your timeline with a small group. Discuss the similarities and differences in the timelines—and what most surprised you.

RESPOND TO THE ESSENTIAL QUESTION

 Why is the idea of space exploration both inspiring and unnerving?

Gather Information Review your annotations and notes on "Martian Metropolis." Then, add relevant details to your Response Log. As you determine what information to include, think about:

- the reasons for colonizing Mars
- the challenges of living on Mars
- the benefits of Mars exploration

At the end of the unit, use your notes to write an argument.

RESPOND

Go to **Writing Informative Texts** in the **Writing Studio** to learn more.

Go to **Participating in Collaborative Discussions** in the **Speaking and Listening Studio** for help.

ACADEMIC VOCABULARY

As you write and discuss what you learned from the article, be sure to use the Academic Vocabulary words. Check off each of the words that you use.

- ❏ complex
- ❏ potential
- ❏ rely
- ❏ stress
- ❏ valid

APPLY

WRITE AND DISCUSS

Write an Informative Report Remind students that they can use the text they just read, "Martian Metropolis," as a resource. Even better, they can look up the works cited in the footnotes and use them as resources.

 For **writing support** for students at varying proficiency levels, see the **Text X-Ray** on page 264D.

Create a Timeline Review how to make a timeline. Timelines should show the same increments of time, such as months, years, or decades. Timelines can also have sections that split off from the basic timeline and zoom in to a short period of time that merits closer examination.

RESPOND TO THE ESSENTIAL QUESTION

Allow time for students to add details from "Martian Metropolis" to their Unit 4 Response Logs.

 ENGLISH LEARNER SUPPORT

Create a Timeline Have student pairs create a timeline of Mars missions based on their informative reports.

- Provide student pairs with a Mars timeline that includes important Mars exploration dates and a list of content-based vocabulary they can use to complete the timelines. Allow Beginning students to add illustrations to the timeline that demonstrate understanding of content-based vocabulary, such as *dunes* and *rock*.
  SUBSTANTIAL/MODERATE

- Have student pairs follow the instructions on p. 275 for completing their timelines. Remind students to use content-based vocabulary from their informative reports in their timelines as well.
  LIGHT

APPLY

CRITICAL VOCABULARY

Answers:

1. *fluids and rock found deep in the earth* because *geothermal* relates to the internal heat of Earth.

2. *Antarctica,* because "colonize" means "to establish a settlement in a new, uninhabited place"

3. *A mixture of nitrogen, oxygen, and other gases* because *atmosphere* relates to the gaseous envelope that surrounds our planet

4. *in outer space,* because planets like Mars emit intense radiation

VOCABULARY STRATEGY:
Greek Roots *atmos* and *sphere*

Answers:

1. **hemisphere:** *half of Earth*

2. **stratosphere:** *a layer of Earth's atmosphere*

3. **hydrosphere:** *the waters of Earth's surface*

4. **biosphere:** *the part of Earth that can support life*

 RESPOND

WORD BANK
atmosphere
radiation
colonize
geothermal

CRITICAL VOCABULARY

Practice and Apply Mark the letter of the answer to each question. Then, explain your response.

1. Which of the following is a source of **geothermal** energy?
   a. fluids and rock found deep in the earth
   b. rushing rivers, streams, and ocean waves

2. Which place could people still **colonize**?
   a. Antarctica
   b. Australia

3. Which of the following would you find in Earth's **atmosphere**?
   a. a mixture of rock, fluids, and minerals
   b. a mixture of nitrogen, oxygen, and other gases

4. Where would you more likely be exposed to intense **radiation**?
   a. in outer space
   b. in a desert

 Go to the **Vocabulary Studio** for more on roots.

VOCABULARY STRATEGY: Greek Roots *atmos* and *sphere*

A **root** is a word part that came into English from an older language, such as ancient Latin or Greek. The word *atmosphere* in "Martian Metropolis" comes from two Greek roots: *atmos* (Greek for "steam or vapor") and *sphaira* (Greek for "globe or ball"). The root *sphere* also appears in other English words related to the earth. One example is *troposphere,* which is a layer of Earth's atmosphere.

Practice and Apply Use context clues and your knowledge of the root *sphere* to write a likely meaning for each bold word. Use a print or online dictionary to confirm your word meanings.

1. For people in the southern **hemisphere,** winter falls in the months of June, July, and August.
   _____

2. To avoid turbulence, jets often fly in the lower part of the **stratosphere.**
   _____

3. The **hydrosphere** is made up of ocean waters, rivers, lakes, and streams.
   _____

4. Life on Earth can exist only in the **biosphere.**
   _____

 ENGLISH LEARNER SUPPORT

Pronounce Consonant Clusters Write the word *geothermal* on the board. Underline the consonant cluster *th,* and model how to make the sound by pushing your tongue against your two front teeth while expelling air. Read the word aloud, and have students chorally repeat. Have student pairs repeat the activity with the word *atmosphere*. Model how to make produce the *sph* sound before allowing students to work together independently.
SUBSTANTIAL/MODERATE

RESPOND

LANGUAGE CONVENTIONS: Capitalization

In your writing, you need to apply the rules of capitalization to proper nouns—the names of specific people, places, and things—including organizations and places for specialized research. In this example from "Martian Metropolis," note which proper nouns are capitalized.

> But people on Mars will communicate with Earth pretty often. Because Earth and Mars are so far apart, signals are delayed by up to 24 minutes. Communication will mostly resemble email. Jay Dickson, a planetary geologist at Brown University, has lived at Antarctica's isolated McMurdo Station. "Just being able to send pictures back and forth is great for morale," Dickson explains.

The chart below shows four types of proper nouns that require capitalization. When organizations are abbreviated, their abbreviations are also capitalized.

CAPITALIZATION OF PROPER NOUNS		ABBREVIATIONS
Organizations	National Aeronautics and Space Administration	NASA
	Jet Propulsion Laboratory	JPL
Places	McMurdo Station Antarctica	
Planets	Venus Earth Mars	
Spacecraft	Mars rovers Spirit and Opportunity	

Practice and Apply The following sentences include proper nouns that lack correct capitalization. In each sentence, indicate which proper nouns should be capitalized. Consult reference materials for terms or titles that are unfamiliar to you.

1. The united nations (un) headquarters is in new york city.
2. In January 2006, NASA launched the spacecraft new horizons on a mission to explore pluto.
3. The space shuttle was launched from the kennedy space center at cape canaveral, florida.
4. Astronauts routinely conduct spacewalks from the international space station.

> Go to **Capitalizing the Names of Heavenly Bodies** in the **Grammar Studio** for more.

Martian Metropolis 277

APPLY

LANGUAGE CONVENTIONS: Capitalization

Review the information about capitalization of proper nouns with students. Explain that capitalization is often forgotten or ignored in informal communication, but it is important in that It helps us highlight someone's or something's importance. Furthermore, it's a sign of respect for a person, place, or institution.

For additional practice, make a list of things in students' lives they know require capitalization, such as:

- the name of your school
- their last names
- the name of their favorite restaurant
- their favorite movie

Discuss why these things should or should not be capitalized. If needed, demonstrate how not using capital letters can be confusing, such as when using the title of a movie or film in a sentence. Capital letters help set the title apart from the rest of the text.

Practice and Apply

1. *The United Nations (UN) headquarters is in New York City.*
2. *In January 2006, NASA launched the spacecraft New Horizons on a mission to explore Pluto.*
3. *The space shuttle was launched from the Kennedy Space Center at Cape Canaveral, Florida.*
4. *Astronauts routinely conduct spacewalks from the International Space Station.*

ENGLISH LEARNER SUPPORT

Understand Capitalization Remind students that proper names are capitalized in the English language. Guide students to identify the types of proper nouns that are included in the graphic organizer on page 277.

Guide students to understand that proper nouns help readers understand that they are reading about a particular person, place, or thing. Provide the following sentence frame: *I know Mars, Venus, and Earth are proper nouns because they are _____.* (planets/places).
SUBSTANTIAL/MODERATE

Martian Metropolis 277

PLAN

DARK THEY WERE, AND GOLDEN-EYED
Science Fiction by Ray Bradbury

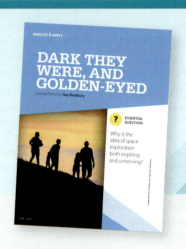

GENRE ELEMENTS
SCIENCE FICTION

Remind students that **science fiction** is a genre in which characters, settings, and events are not bound by an era's contemporary conceptions of reality; science and technology defeat limitations set by time and distance; characters can change from human form to other forms; the only limits are set by the author's ability to make a story understandable. Stories often reflect or comment on important contemporary issues that interest and excite readers.

LEARNING OBJECTIVES

- Identify and analyze elements of science fiction.
- Identify ways in which authors create mood.
- Conduct research about the dangers of space exploration.
- Write a friendly letter to someone speculating about alien life forms.
- Create a graphic story of "Dark They Were, and Golden-Eyed."
- Use the Latin root *pend*.
- **Language** Understand complex language structures.

TEXT COMPLEXITY

Quantitative Measures	Dark They Were, and Golden-Eyed	Lexile: 540L
Qualitative Measures	**Ideas Presented** Multiple levels, use of symbolism, greater demand for inference	
	Structure Used Clear, chronological, conventional	
	Language Used Allusive, figurative language, complex sentence structures.	
	Knowledge Required More complexity in theme, experiences may be less familiar to many	

278A Unit 4

PLAN

Online Ed

RESOURCES

- Unit 4 Response Log
- 🔊 Selection Audio
- Close Read Screencasts: Modeled Discussions
- Reading Studio: Notice & Note
- Writing Studio: Writing as a Process
- Speaking and Listening Studio: Participating in Collaborative Discussions
- Vocabulary Studio: Roots
- Grammar Studio: Module 9: Lesson 4: Using Verb Tense Consistently
- "Dark They Were, and Golden-Eyed" Selection Test

SUMMARIES

English

The Bittering family arrives on Mars as part of a small colony. Within moments of their arrival, Mr. Bittering becomes obsessed by the idea of returning to Earth. He senses that he will be changed in some way and becomes fearful of losing his identity. Mr. Bittering begins building a rocket in order to return to Earth. In time, he notices slight but significant changes in his family. Gradually, all of the colonists attain Martian characteristics and begin to use the Martian language. Finally, the family is transformed into a Martian family. Another rocket arrives on Mars and finds no Earthlings.

Spanish

Una familia llega a Marte como parte de una pequeña colonia. Inmediatamente, el padre expresa su deseo de volver a la Tierra. Y empieza a construir un cohete para regresar a la Tierra. Al tiempo, nota pequeños pero significativos cambios en su familia y en los otros colonizadores después de comer la comida cultivada en el nuevo planeta. Gradualmente, el padre y su familia se acostumbran a Marte y se hacen más marcianos. Finalmente, la familia se transforma en una familia marciana. Otro cohete llega a su colonia y no encuentra a ningún terrícola.

 SMALL-GROUP OPTIONS

Have students work in small groups to read and discuss the selection.

Think-Pair-Share

- After students have read and analyzed "Dark They Were, And Golden-Eyed," Ask: *What mysteries are left unexplained at the end of the story?*
- How does the story's theme apply to real life?
- Have students think about the questions individually and take notes.
- Have pairs discuss their ideas about the question.
- Ask pairs to share their responses with the class.

Sticky Note Peer Review

This activity can be used for the "Write a Letter" writing exercise at the end of the selection.

- Have each student read his or her paper to a partner or small group.
- Have the students who listen, record specific feedback on sticky notes.
- Have students categorize their notes: positive comments, suggestions, and questions are three categories and should go on three separate notes.
- Have students initial their sticky notes and present them to the writer.

PLAN

Text X-Ray: English Learner Support
for "Dark They Were, And Golden-Eyed"

Use the Text X-Ray and the supports and scaffolds in the Teacher's Edition to help guide students at different proficiency levels through the selection.

INTRODUCE THE SELECTION
DISCUSS ESCAPE AND FEAR OF CHANGE

In this selection, students will need to be able to discuss the changing nature of reality in an imagined world. Point out that the story was published at a time when people began to realize that the entire world could be destroyed by nuclear weapons. Ask students to think about how tempting it is to search for ways to escape danger—if only in imagination. Ask what it might be like to escape danger at home only to find one's self marooned in a strange new place; talk about the fear of losing one's identity. Explain key concepts.

The need to escape is a common starting point in many science fiction stories.

Fear of change or loss of identity through alien forces is a common theme.

Help students make lists of things they would do if marooned on an island (e.g., build a boat to escape, test the safety of food, hold on to their core values). Have them save their lists to refer to after they have read the story. Ask them to compare what they would do with what Mr. Bittering did.

CULTURAL REFERENCES

The following words and phrases may be unfamiliar to students:

- *clock interior* (paragraph 1): the intricate interior of a mechanical clock, also known as clockwork
- *whispered away* (paragraph 1): quietly walk away;
- *mind* (paragraph 22): to be concerned or annoyed by; care
- *In spite of* (paragraph 42): to do something and not let something else affect it
- *never mind* (paragraph 164): used to tell someone to forget something
- *hadn't the foggiest notion* (paragraph 269): expression for not knowing something

LISTENING

Understand Complex Language

Monitor students' understanding of the story's content and figurative language after they listen to the selection audio. Use a variety of media to create appropriate scaffolds for interpreting form and meaning in the story.

Have students listen to the selection audio for paragraphs 1–8. Use the following supports with students at varying proficiency levels:

- Play paragraphs 1–6 of the selection audio while holding up images inspired by science fiction stories, e.g., people leaving a rocket ship. Use gestures and the images to indicate what the events and dialogue mean. Ask: *Where does the father want to go? (He wants to get back on the rocket and return to Earth.)* Accept single word answers such as "Earth." **SUBSTANTIAL**
- After listening to the selection audio, reread paragraph 8 aloud. (Point out the cognates *disolver*, and *intelecto*.) Ask: *What is the father afraid of losing? (his intellect)* **MODERATE**
- Have partners each listen to the selection audio and then retell the events in paragraphs 1–8. Have them listen for unfamiliar words and seek clarification as needed. **LIGHT**

278C Unit 4

PLAN

SPEAKING

Retell for Understanding

Help students to retell events and important concepts in the text. Explain that the story they are reading contains many words, images, and expressions that may be unfamiliar. Encourage students to seek clarification.

Use the following supports with students at varying proficiency levels:

- Read paragraphs 9–12 aloud. Have students chorally repeat after you: *This is a science fiction story*. Have students retell what they visualize is happening in paragraph 9. Encourage them to use their home language, cognates, drawings, and found images to retell events in paragraphs 9–12. **SUBSTANTIAL**
- Have students work in small groups. Ask them to identify unfamiliar words and phrases from paragraphs 9–12. Circulate among them to clarify meaning. Listen to individual students retell the events in the text. Encourage use of cognates, images, and gestures. **MODERATE**
- Have students in pairs read paragraphs 9–12 to each other. Have them seek clarification as needed. Ask students to summarize the events and predict what they think may happen. **LIGHT**

READING

Read for Main Ideas and Concepts

Guide students through paragraphs 196-200. Encourage some learners to use gestures, images, and single words to demonstrate understanding of the main ideas.

Read paragraphs 196–199 aloud. Use the following supports with students at varying proficiency levels:

- Have students read the summary of the story in Spanish or a summary in their home language. Play the selection audio. Have students use cognates, home language words, drawings, and images to demonstrate comprehension of paragraph 196. (*piscina = swimming pool, mural = mural, villa = villa*) **SUBSTANTIAL**
- Have students read paragraphs 196–199. Ask: *Is the father more or less afraid than in the beginning?* (*less afraid*) Ask students to use single words to describe the setting. **MODERATE**
- After they silently read paragraphs 196–200, have pairs discuss the ways that the Bitterings have changed. Have them make inferences about what is happening to Mr. Bittering. **LIGHT**

WRITING

Write a Letter

Work with students to read the writing assignment on p. 301. Help them do the necessary research to form and express opinions.

Use the following supports with students at varying proficiency levels. Have students go to the Writing Studio for help:

- Model finding images of Mars as it actually exists; label them with words students can use in a graphic letter or infographic; encourage students to do research on reputable astrobiological research sites in their home languages. Have students use graphic organizers to put together a succession of images and words in English that support their opinions. Tell students that they do not have to have fully formed opinions about the possibility of alien life in space, but they should try to express their thoughts clearly. **SUBSTANTIAL**
- Ask students to follow the same guidelines that students at the Beginning proficiency level are using. Have them use a greater number of words, phrases, and sentences in their letters. **MODERATE**
- Ask students to do research on reputable sites to support their opinions. Have them create outlines of their ideas using the four bulleted points on the student page. Then, ask them to write two paragraphs about what they discovered in their research; have them concentrate on what they are most curious about. **LIGHT**

TEACH

? **Connect to the ESSENTIAL QUESTION**

For the characters in "Dark They Were and Golden-Eyed," space travel and exploration is an unnerving necessity brought about by imminent war. There are only hints that an inspirational spirit of investigation may have prevailed in earlier expeditions. Even the natural monuments are named after corporations and the wealthiest men in the early twentieth century. Discovery occurs in an unexpected way.

ANALYZE & APPLY

DARK THEY WERE, AND GOLDEN-EYED

Science Fiction by **Ray Bradbury**

? **ESSENTIAL QUESTION:**

Why is the idea of space exploration both inspiring and unnerving?

LEARNING MINDSET

Asking for Help Explain to students that they will often encounter texts that offer new challenges which they may find hard to meet. Tell them that it's almost never too soon to ask for help—especially when negative feelings toward work are present. It is important to identify the real sources of frustration; there are times when engaging in positive self-talk and self-monitoring will help students discover how to ask for the help they need. Practicing self-questioning of the sort found in small group activities like reciprocal teaching can help students to clarify their needs before throwing up their hands and saying "I can't do it!"

GET READY

QUICK START

Films and TV shows often focus on characters who find themselves in predicaments—that is, difficult situations. What types of predicaments fascinate you? What is it about them that draws you in and holds your attention? Record your thoughts in your journal.

ANALYZE SCIENCE FICTION

Writers of science fiction often present readers with fantastical settings, characters, and events set in the future. At the same time, they often tell stories that in some way comment upon new and emerging science and technology, contemporary society, and human nature in general. As you read Ray Bradbury's story, use the chart to note characteristics of science fiction.

GENRE ELEMENTS: SCIENCE FICTION

- explores unexpected possibilities of the past, present, or future
- mixes scientific facts and theories with imaginative settings and plots
- usually includes familiar elements and conflicts found in real life

CHARACTERISTICS OF SCIENCE FICTION	EXAMPLES IN THE STORY
Scientific/Technological Information	
Familiar Elements of Life Today	
Imaginary Locations and Situations	

ANALYZE MOOD

Mood is the feeling or atmosphere that a writer creates for a reader. A writer creates mood by

- carefully choosing words to describe the plot, setting, and characters
- revealing what characters think and how they speak

Identifying mood helps you understand a story. As you read, think about how the story makes you feel and the effect that particular words have on you. Use the graphic organizer below to record your notes.

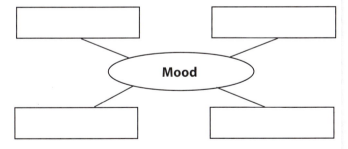

Dark They Were, and Golden-Eyed 279

TEACH

QUICK START

Have students read the Quick Start question. Encourage students to write in their journals about why they think people find entertainment value in the predicaments of others. Is it to relieve one's own stress? Do people identify or empathize with those in trouble? Is it because they expect to find solutions in art that they don't find in life? Ask students to use their personal experience as readers to write about this question.

ANALYZE SCIENCE FICTION

Have students examine the text for examples they can use in the chart on p. 279. Model filling in a cell for "Examples In The Story." For example: The Hormel Valley is named after a food company. (*Many students may know that in the present era, large stadiums that were once named after teams and geographical areas are now named after corporations.*)

ANALYZE MOOD

Model using a graphic organizer like the one shown on p. 279. Explain to students that mood can be thought of as the overall atmosphere in a work of fiction. As an example, choose "comedic" for the center elipse of the organizer; explain that *comedic* is an adjective that describes things that are characteristic of comedy. Have the class guide you in filling in examples of setting, plot, character, and dialogue that would add to the overall mood of a comedic book or film, e.g., *The setting is a mechanical house that keeps falling apart at unexpected moments during a wedding.*

TEACH

CRITICAL VOCABULARY

Encourage students to read all the sentences before deciding which word best completes each one.

1. recede
2. pendulum
3. muse
4. subtly
5. convivial
6. forlorn
7. idle

■ English Learner Support

Practice Critical Vocabulary Have student pairs practice pronouncing and using the Critical Vocabulary words in sentences. Then have them think of synonyms for each of the words. If after several minutes they're still struggling, they can use a dictionary or thesaurus.   **LIGHT**

LANGUAGE CONVENTIONS

Sounding out verb tenses can be helpful. Practice these examples:

Last summer we swim in the pool. *(swam)*

Kyle turn his paper in late. *(turned or turns)*

The teacher was upset with Kyle right now. *(is)*

The teacher is upset with Kyle earlier today. *(was)*

Tell students if they are ever unsure about verb tense agreement, they can simply read it aloud, or sound it out in their head, to check if verb tense agreement is correct.

✎ ANNOTATION MODEL

Inform students that marking up a text can get messy. Encourage them to come up with a system that won't mark up too much of the page, such as the graphic organizer on page 279.

Tell them that in this text they are to look for examples of science fiction elements as well as mood. Finally, remind them to be on the lookout for instances of changing verb tenses, such as when characters are speaking.

280   Unit 4

⊙ GET READY

CRITICAL VOCABULARY

convivial   subtly   idle   forlorn   recede   pendulum   muse

To see how many Critical Vocabulary words you already know, use them to complete the sentences.

1. As we drove away, the city's skyline began to _____ .
2. Visitors could hear the regular swish of the old _____ clock.
3. I just want to _____ about the strange things I saw today.
4. People's opinions have shifted _____ during the past year.
5. The _____ host moved with ease from guest to guest.
6. The abandoned garden seems _____ , sad, and empty.
7. It's too hot to work today; let's just _____ here in the shade.

LANGUAGE CONVENTIONS

Consistent Verb Tenses The **tense** of a verb tells the time of the action or the state of being. In writing, it is important to use the same tense to describe actions that take place at the same time. Unnecessarily shifting, or inconsistent, verb tenses can confuse the reader.

INCORRECT: Ms. Sherman **coaches** us as we **practiced** our songs.
CORRECT: Ms. Sherman **coached** us as we **practiced** our songs.

ANNOTATION MODEL   NOTICE & NOTE

As you read, note the author's use of the elements of science fiction and the choice of words to create mood. In the model, you can see one reader's notes about "Dark They Were, and Golden-Eyed."

> 2   The man felt his hair flutter and the tissues of his body draw tight as if he were standing at the center of a vacuum. His wife, before him, seemed almost to whirl away in smoke. The children, small seeds, might at any instant be sown to all the Martian climes.

This description makes me feel scared for the man.

The man's family is with him.

The setting is Mars.

280   Unit 4

BACKGROUND

Ray Bradbury (1920–2012) grew up in Los Angeles, California, and began writing stories as a young teenager. Over the course of his adult life, he wrote science fiction, mysteries, and screenplays, including more than two dozen novels and hundreds of short stories. Several of his works, such as *The Illustrated Man* and *Fahrenheit 451*, became major motion pictures. Bradbury received dozens of awards, including a special Pulitzer Prize in 2007 for his distinguished literary career.

DARK THEY WERE, AND GOLDEN-EYED

Science Fiction by Ray Bradbury

SETTING A PURPOSE

Pay attention to the elements of science fiction that appear in the story and the references to personal and social issues. Notice the author's choice of words and consider how they contribute to the mood of the story.

1 The rocket metal cooled in the meadow winds. Its lid gave a bulging *pop*. From its clock interior stepped a man, a woman, and three children. The other passengers whispered away across the Martian meadow, leaving the man alone among his family.

2 The man felt his hair flutter and the tissues of his body draw tight as if he were standing at the center of a vacuum. His wife, before him, seemed almost to whirl away in smoke. The children, small seeds, might at any instant be sown to all the Martian climes.

3 The children looked up at him, as people look to the sun to tell what time of their life it is. His face was cold.

4 "What's wrong?" asked his wife.

5 "Let's get back on the rocket."

6 "Go back to Earth?"

Notice & Note

Use the side margins to notice and note signposts in the text.

ANALYZE MOOD

Annotate: In paragraphs 1–6, mark details that reveal the man's first response to Mars.

Interpret: How would you describe the man's first impression of Mars? How might his feelings affect the mood of the story?

Dark They Were, and Golden-Eyed 281

TEACH

ANALYZE MOOD

Guide students to consider the descriptive language, "old cities," racing hiss of wind," stiff grass," that the author is using here. (**Answer:** *The initial descriptions of the setting use words and phrases to create a feeling that the Martian landscape is forgotten and lonely.*)

 For **listening and speaking support** for students at varying proficiency levels, see the **Text X-Ray** on pages 278C-D.

ANALYZE SCIENCE FICTION

Some terms may require explanation. *Voice-clock* will sound familiar, but students should know that the addition of the word *voice* to the alarm is to make the alarm clock sound like something futuristic to 1949 readers. A *hearth* is part of a fireplace, the *blood-geraniums* are simply plants the Bitterings have in their home, and the *morning paper*, in this context, would have been a printed newspaper, a staple of people's morning routines in 1949. (**Answer:** *Familiar elements of everyday life include: being awakened by an alarm clock, a home with a hearth and potted geraniums, and the morning newspaper. These details make it clear that life on Mars is supposed to be as "normal" as life on Earth.*)

CRITICAL VOCABULARY

convivial: A convivial person is friendly and at ease with other people.

ASK STUDENTS given what they've learned so far about Harry Bittering, why do they think he has to force himself to be convivial? *(He is forcing himself to be pleasant in front of his wife and children in their new, unearthly surroundings.)*

282 Unit 4

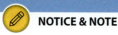 **NOTICE & NOTE**

ANALYZE MOOD
Annotate: Mark details in paragraphs 8–13 that the author uses to create a feeling about the setting of the story.

Analyze: Does the author create a positive feeling or a negative feeling about the setting? What words help create this feeling?

ANALYZE SCIENCE FICTION
Annotate: Mark details that the author uses in paragraphs 18–19 to refer to familiar elements of life on Earth.

Interpret: Why do you think the author includes these details in the story?

convivial
(kən-vĭv´ē-əl) *adj.* A person who is *convivial* enjoys the company of others in a sociable manner.

7   "Yes! Listen!"

8   The wind blew as if to flake away their identities. At any moment the Martian air might draw his soul from him, as marrow comes from a white bone. He felt submerged in a chemical that could dissolve his intellect and burn away his past.

9   They looked at Martian hills that time had worn with a crushing pressure of years. They saw the old cities, lost in their meadows, lying like children's delicate bones among the blowing lakes of grass.

10 "Chin up, Harry," said his wife. "It's too late. We've come over sixty million miles."

11 The children with their yellow hair hollered at the deep dome of Martian sky. There was no answer but the racing hiss of wind through the stiff grass.

12 He picked up the luggage in his cold hands. "Here we go," he said—a man standing on the edge of a sea, ready to wade in and be drowned.

13 They walked into town.

14 Their name was Bittering. Harry and his wife Cora; Dan, Laura, and David. They built a small white cottage and ate good breakfasts there, but the fear was never gone. It lay with Mr. Bittering and Mrs. Bittering, a third unbidden partner at every midnight talk, at every dawn awakening.

15 "I feel like a salt crystal," he said, "in a mountain stream, being washed away. We don't belong here. We're Earth people. This is Mars. It was meant for Martians. For heaven's sake, Cora, let's buy tickets for home!"

16 But she only shook her head. "One day the atom bomb[1] will fix Earth. Then we'll be safe here."

17 "Safe and insane!"

18 *Tick-tock, seven o'clock* sang the voice-clock; *time to get up.* And they did.

19 Something made him check everything each morning— warm hearth, potted blood-geraniums—precisely as if he expected something to be amiss. The morning paper was toast-warm from the 6 A.M. Earth rocket. He broke its seal and tilted it at his breakfast place. He forced himself to be **convivial**.

---

[1] **atom bomb:** In 1945, in an attempt to end World War II, the United States dropped atomic bombs over the Japanese cities of Hiroshima and Nagasaki. The bombs killed more than 100,000 people and injured many thousands more.

282 Unit 4

NOTICE & NOTE

20 "Colonial days all over again," he declared. "Why, in ten years there'll be a million Earthmen on Mars. Big cities, everything! They said we'd fail. Said the Martians would resent our invasion. But did we find any Martians? Not a living soul! Oh, we found their empty cities, but no one in them. Right?"

21 A river of wind submerged the house. When the windows ceased rattling Mr. Bittering swallowed and looked at the children.

22 "I don't know," said David. "Maybe there're Martians around we don't see. Sometimes nights I think I hear 'em. I hear the wind. The sand hits my window. I get scared. And I see those towns way up in the mountains where the Martians lived a long time ago. And I think I see things moving around those towns, Papa. And I wonder if those Martians *mind* us living here. I wonder if they won't do something to us for coming here."

23 "Nonsense!" Mr. Bittering looked out the windows. "We're clean, decent people." He looked at his children. "All dead cities have some kind of ghosts in them. Memories, I mean." He stared at the hills. "You see a staircase and you wonder what Martians looked like climbing it. You see Martian paintings and you wonder what the painter was like. You make a little ghost in your mind, a memory. It's quite natural. Imagination." He stopped. "You haven't been prowling up in those ruins, have you?"

24 "No, Papa." David looked at his shoes.

25 "See that you stay away from them. Pass the jam."

26 "Just the same," said little David, "I bet something happens."

27 Something happened that afternoon. Laura stumbled through the settlement, crying. She dashed blindly onto the porch.

28 "Mother, Father—the war, Earth!" she sobbed. "A radio flash just came. Atom bombs hit New York! All the space rockets blown up. No more rockets to Mars, ever!"

29 "Oh, Harry!" The mother held onto her husband and daughter.

30 "Are you sure, Laura?" asked the father quietly.

31 Laura wept. "We're stranded on Mars, forever and ever!"

32 For a long time there was only the sound of the wind in the late afternoon.

Dark They Were, and Golden-Eyed 283

TEACH

ENGLISH LEARNER SUPPORT

Monitor Comprehension Tell students that active readers notice and take action when they come across text they don't understand. Have them practice monitoring comprehension verbally.

Have pairs read paragraphs 20–26 to each other. Instruct listeners to stop readers when they don't understand a detail. Tell students to reread the confusing part slowly. Read the sentence before and after the detail for clues. Discuss how you might rephrase the detail. **SUBSTANTIAL/MODERATE**

Have pairs read paragraphs 20–26 to each other. Instruct the listeners to take notes on details they don't understand. Have pairs then go back through the notes, discuss why those details were difficult, and decide how to use the text to better understand them.

LIGHT

WHEN STUDENTS STRUGGLE...

Storyboard For students who have trouble following along through this long text, encourage them to keep track of the events of the story in a graphic organizer. Then, have them draw each event in a storyboard to help them visualize the flow of the narrative.

Key Event	Significance

 For additional support, go to the **Reading Studio** and assign the following Level Up tutorial: **Plot Stages.**

Dark They Were, And Golden-Eyed 283

TEACH

 ANALYZE MOOD

The sentence fragments are used to give us a realistic picture of a mind that can only think in quick, panicked, repetitive bursts. (**Answer:** *The repetition and short, sharp, shock of the fragments reveal a mind dominated by a few simple and terrifying thoughts: They are alone with no way to get home! The mood is tense.*)

■ **English Learner Support**

Understand Mood Have students reread paragraph 33. Ask them to explain how the short sentences create the mood of panic and intensity. **MODERATE**

▶ CONTRASTS AND CONTRADICTIONS

Explain to students that **Contrasts and Contradictions** refers to anything that is being compared. This may not be obvious upon first reading paragraph 42, but a clue is the listing technique the narrator uses. If students struggle, ask them to brainstorm different ways of comparing two things. (**Answer:** *Both Martians and human civilizations built cities, named places, climbed mountains, and sailed seas. The fact that Martians did these things, but that their cities, mountains, and seas are gone, may suggest that present-day human civilization could also come to an end and disappear.*)

284 Unit 4

 **NOTICE & NOTE**

ANALYZE MOOD
Annotate: Mark examples of sentence fragments in paragraph 33.

Interpret: What do these sentence fragments reveal about Bittering's state of mind? How do they help create a mood?

33 Alone, thought Bittering. Only a thousand of us here. No way back. No way. No way. Sweat poured from his face and his hands and his body; he was drenched in the hotness of his fear. He wanted to strike Laura, cry, "No, you're lying! The rockets will come back!" Instead, he stroked Laura's head against him and said, "The rockets will get through someday."

34 "Father, what will we do?"

35 "Go about our business, of course. Raise crops and children. Wait. Keep things going until the war ends and the rockets come again."

36 The two boys stepped out onto the porch.

37 "Children," he said, sitting there, looking beyond them, "I've something to tell you."

38 "We know," they said.

39 In the following days, Bittering wandered often through the garden to stand alone in his fear. As long as the rockets had spun a silver web across space, he had been able to accept Mars. For he had always told himself: Tomorrow, if I want, I can buy a ticket and go back to Earth.

40 But now: The web gone, the rockets lying in jigsaw heaps of molten girder and unsnaked wire. Earth people left to the strangeness of Mars, the cinnamon dusts and wine airs, to be baked like gingerbread shapes in Martian summers, put into harvested storage by Martian winters. What would happen to him, the others? This was the moment Mars had waited for. Now it would eat them.

41 He got down on his knees in the flower bed, a spade in his nervous hands. Work, he thought, work and forget.

CONTRASTS AND CONTRADICTIONS

Notice & Note: In paragraph 42, mark text that comments on the similarities between Martian and human civilizations.

Infer: What comment about present-day human civilization might Bradbury be making by having Bittering think about Martian civilizations?

42 He glanced up from the garden to the Martian mountains. He thought of the proud old Martian names that had once been on those peaks. Earthmen, dropping from the sky, had gazed upon hills, rivers, Martian seats left nameless in spite of names. Once Martians had built cities, named cities; climbed mountains, named mountains; sailed seas, named seas. Mountains melted, seas drained, cities tumbled. In spite of this, the Earthmen had felt a silent guilt at putting new names to these ancient hills and valleys.

43 Nevertheless, man lives by symbol and label. The names were given.

284 Unit 4

WHEN STUDENTS STRUGGLE...

Rewrite Sentences Some students will struggle with Bradbury's lyrical use of language. Have student pairs examine paragraphs 39–40. Have them look up synonyms for confusing words and rewrite sentences in a graphic organizer. Ask them why the author chooses complexity over simplicity.

Original Sentence	New Sentence

 For additional support, go to the **Reading Studio** and assign the following Level Up tutorial: **Author's Style.**

44 Mr. Bittering felt very alone in his garden under the Martian sun, anachronism[2] bent here, planting Earth flowers in a wild soil.

45 Think. Keep thinking. Different things. Keep your mind free of Earth, the atom war, the lost rockets.

46 He perspired. He glanced about. No one watching. He removed his tie. Pretty bold, he thought. First your coat off, now your tie. He hung it neatly on a peach tree he had imported as a sapling from Massachusetts.

47 He returned to his philosophy of names and mountains. The Earthmen had changed names. Now there were Hormel Valleys, Roosevelt[3] Seas, Ford Hills, Vanderbilt Plateaus, Rockefeller[4] Rivers, on Mars. It wasn't right. The American settlers had shown wisdom, using old Indian prairie names: Wisconsin, Minnesota, Idaho, Ohio, Utah, Milwaukee, Waukegan, Osseo. The old names, the old meanings.

48 Staring at the mountains wildly, he thought: Are you up there? All the dead ones, you Martians? Well, here we are, alone, cut off! Come down, move us out! We're helpless!

49 The wind blew a shower of peach blossoms.

50 He put out his sun-browned hand and gave a small cry. He touched the blossoms and picked them up. He turned them, he touched them again and again. Then he shouted for his wife.

51 "Cora!"

52 She appeared at a window. He ran to her.

53 "Cora, these blossoms!"

54 She handled them.

55 "Do you see? They're different. They've changed! They're not peach blossoms any more!"

56 "Look all right to me," she said.

57 "They're not. They're wrong! I can't tell how. An extra petal, a leaf, something, the color, the smell!"

58 The children ran out in time to see their father hurrying about the garden, pulling up radishes, onions, and carrots from their beds.

59 "Cora, come look!"

60 They handled the onions, the radishes, the carrots among them.

---

[2] **anachronism** (ə-năk′rə-nĭz′əm): something placed outside of its proper time period.
[3] **Roosevelt:** most likely refers to Franklin Delano Roosevelt, the 32nd president of the United States.
[4] **Hormel ... Ford ... Vanderbilt ... Rockefeller:** names of industrial and financial "giants" in American history.

ANALYZE SCIENCE FICTION
Annotate: In paragraphs 53–63, mark the text that describes how the plants are changing.

Analyze: Is Bittering's concern about the changing plants realistic? Why do you think the author introduces this detail?

TEACH

ANALYZE MOOD

Inform students that events in the story have made Bittering more and more fearful. The demanding, panicked statements and questions show a man in a fearful and defiant mood. **(Answer:** Bittering's new fear—that he and his family will change, will become more "Martian"—makes the mood of the story more threatening. He fears that they are threatened by strange new forces they do not understand and cannot control. But Bittering will do his best to resist.**)**

■ English Learner Support

Understand Sentence Fragments Explain to students that in everyday speech, people do not always speak in complete sentences. In paragraphs 73-74, Bittering uses sentence fragments to explain his concerns to his family. Have students use the information from paragraphs 71-74 to change the following fragments into complete sentences by adding a verb and/or a noun: *(The food was changed.)* Subtly, very subtly. *(The food was changed.)* A very little bit. Even the house *(is different)*. The fog at night *(changed the house)*. The boards *(are)* all warped out of shape. **MODERATE**

CRITICAL VOCABULARY

subtly: A subtle change is one that a person only notices if he or she is carefully paying attention.

ASK STUDENTS to replace the word *subtly* with the word *slightly*, and discuss how the effect of the paragraph changes. *(Student answers will vary. It can be a matter of preference.)*

286 Unit 4

 **NOTICE & NOTE**

61 "Do they look like carrots?"
62 "Yes . . . no." She hesitated. "I don't know."
63 "They're changed."
64 "Perhaps."
65 "You know they have! Onions but not onions, carrots but not carrots. Taste: the same but different. Smell: not like it used to be." He felt his heart pounding, and he was afraid. He dug his fingers into the earth. "Cora, what's happening? What is it? We've got to get away from this." He ran across the garden. Each tree felt his touch. "The roses. The roses. They're turning green!"
66 And they stood looking at the green roses.
67 And two days later Dan came running. "Come see the cow. I was milking her and I saw it. Come on!"
68 They stood in the shed and looked at their one cow.
69 It was growing a third horn.
70 And the lawn in front of their house very quietly and slowly was coloring itself like spring violets. Seed from Earth but growing up a soft purple.
71 "We must get away," said Bittering. "We'll eat this stuff and then we'll change—who knows to what? I can't let it happen. There's only one thing to do. Burn this food!"
72 "It's not poisoned."
73 "But it is. **Subtly,** very subtly. A little bit. A very little bit. We mustn't touch it."
74 He looked with dismay at their house. "Even the house. The wind's done something to it. The air's burned it. The fog at night. The boards, all warped out of shape. It's not an Earthman's house any more."

ANALYZE MOOD

Annotate: In paragraphs 70–73, mark the sentence that identifies Bittering's latest fear.

Infer: What impact does this new plot turn have on the mood of the story?

subtly
(sŭt´lē) *adv.* To do something *subtly* means to do it in a manner hard to notice or perceive—that is, not obviously.

286 Unit 4

75 "Oh, your imagination!"

76 He put on his coat and tie. "I'm going into town. We've got to do something now. I'll be back."

77 "Wait, Harry!" his wife cried. But he was gone.

78 In town, on the shadowy step of the grocery store, the men sat with their hands on their knees, conversing with great leisure and ease.

79 Mr. Bittering wanted to fire a pistol in the air.

80 *What are you doing, you fools!* he thought. *Sitting here! You've heard the news—we're stranded on this planet. Well, move! Aren't you frightened? Aren't you afraid? What are you going to do?*

81 "Hello, Harry," said everyone.

82 "Look," he said to them. "You did hear the news, the other day, didn't you?"

83 They nodded and laughed. "Sure. Sure, Harry."

84 "What are you going to do about it?"

85 "Do, Harry, do? What *can* we do?"

86 "Build a rocket, that's what!"

87 "A rocket, Harry? To go back to all that trouble? Oh, Harry!"

88 "But you *must* want to go back. Have you noticed the peach blossoms, the onions, the grass?"

89 "Why, yes, Harry, seems we did," said one of the men.

90 "Doesn't it scare you?"

91 "Can't recall that it did much, Harry."

92 "Idiots!"

93 "Now, Harry."

94 Bittering wanted to cry. "You've got to work with me. If we stay here, we'll all change. The air. Don't you smell it? Something in the air. A Martian virus, maybe; some seed, or a pollen. Listen to me!"

95 They stared at him.

96 "Sam," he said to one of them.

97 "Yes, Harry?"

98 "Will you help me build a rocket?"

99 "Harry, I got a whole load of metal and some blueprints. You want to work in my metal shop on a rocket, you're welcome. I'll sell you that metal for five hundred dollars. You should be able to construct a right pretty rocket, if you work alone, in about thirty years."

ANALYZE MOOD

Annotate: In paragraphs 78–93, mark words that describe how the other men respond to Bittering's observation about changes in the plants.

Interpret: What feeling do the characters' reactions to Bittering suggest?

Dark They Were, and Golden-Eyed   287

TEACH

✏️ ANALYZE MOOD

Ask students to note how the author describes the men; contrast this with how Bittering has been described. (**Possible response:** *The fact that the other characters are so easygoing about the changes is odd; that might mean they are turning into Martians. On the other hand, readers may wonder if Bittering is really overreacting or going crazy.*)

TO CHALLENGE STUDENTS...

Analyze Mood For students interested in creative writing, ask them to take a section from the story, "Dark They Were, and Golden-Eyed" and rewrite it using a light or comedic mood. Tell students to first analyze how Bradbury uses language to create the mood of the scene they are rewriting. From there, they should be able to pull out certain words, phrases, and imagery, and redo them in their own ways to create a different mood. Finally, ask them how their stories will end. Does mood affect the outcome of the story an author tells?

TEACH

ANALYZE SCIENCE FICTION

Inform students that sometimes science fiction borders on the fantastical. The fact that *some* of it is based on science allows for its name, but much of it is speculative about space, extraterrestrial settings, aliens, and the future. In this case, Bradbury would have been aware that people could not undergo such mutations in a few weeks unless fundamental laws and theories about cellular mutation were changed. (**Answer:** *Possible response: The changes are purely imaginative. Eye color in adults does not change, and people do not grow taller so quickly.*)

NOTICE & NOTE

ANALYZE SCIENCE FICTION

Annotate: In paragraphs 102–113, mark the sentences that describe changes in Sam's appearance, according to Bittering.

Analyze: Do you think the changes in Sam's appearance are real, or is Bittering imagining them?

100   Everyone laughed.
101   "Don't laugh."
102   Sam looked at him with quiet good humor.
103   "Sam," Bittering said. "Your eyes—"
104   "What about them, Harry?"
105   "Didn't they used to be gray?"
106   "Well now, I don't remember."
107   "They were, weren't they?"
108   "Why do you ask, Harry?"
109   "Because now they're kind of yellow-colored."
110   "Is that so, Harry?" Sam said, casually.
111   "And you're taller and thinner—"
112   "You might be right, Harry."
113   "Sam, you shouldn't have yellow eyes."

IMPROVE READING FLUENCY

Targeted Passage With students, read paragraphs 95–118. Bittering is speaking to one of the men, Sam. Many of these paragraphs contain dialogue with no attribution. Walk through the dialogue and narration in the paragraphs to help students understand how they can tell who is speaking when there is no attribution listed (when only two characters are speaking, the lines will alternate between the two of them, with an attribute added every few lines to remind the reader who is speaking).

Go to the **Reading Studio** for additional support in developing fluency.

114 "Harry, what color eyes have *you* got?" Sam said.
115 "My eyes? They're blue, of course."
116 "Here you are, Harry." Sam handed him a pocket mirror. "Take a look at yourself."
117 Mr. Bittering hesitated, and then raised the mirror to his face. There were little, very dim flecks of new gold captured in the blue of his eyes.
118 "Now look what you've done," said Sam a moment later. "You've broken my mirror."

119 Harry Bittering moved into the metal shop and began to build the rocket. Men stood in the open door and talked and joked without raising their voices. Once in a while they gave him a hand on lifting something. But mostly they just **idled** and watched him with their yellowing eyes.
120 "It's suppertime, Harry," they said.
121 His wife appeared with his supper in a wicker basket.
122 "I won't touch it," he said. "I'll eat only food from our Deepfreeze. Food that came from Earth. Nothing from our garden."
123 His wife stood watching him. "You can't build a rocket."
124 "I worked in a shop once, when I was twenty. I know metal. Once I get it started, the others will help," he said, not looking at her, laying out the blueprints.
125 "Harry, Harry," she said, helplessly.
126 "We've *got* to get away, Cora. We've got to!"

127 The nights were full of wind that blew down the empty moonlit sea meadows past the little white chess cities lying for their twelve-thousandth year in the shallows. In the Earthmen's settlement, the Bittering house shook with a feeling of change.
128 Lying abed, Mr. Bittering felt his bones shifted, shaped, melted like gold.
129 His wife, lying beside him, was dark from many sunny afternoons. Dark she was, and golden-eyed, burnt almost black by the sun, sleeping, and the children metallic in their beds, and the wind roaring **forlorn** and changing through the old peach trees, the violet grass, shaking out green rose petals.
130 The fear would not be stopped. It had his throat and heart. It dripped in a wetness of the arm and the temple and the trembling palm.

idle
(īd´l) *v.* When you *idle*, you pass time without doing anything purposeful.

ANALYZE MOOD
Annotate: In paragraph 129, mark two examples of unusual sentence structure or word choice.

Interpret: What word would you use to describe the feeling this paragraph conveys?

forlorn
(fər-lôrn´) *adj.* Something that is *forlorn* appears lonely or sad.

TEACH

AHA MOMENT

Inform students that an **Aha Moment** signals a point where a character has an important realization.

In paragraphs 132—134, students may mark "strange word– It was a Martian word. He knew no Martian." (**Answer:** Mr. Bittering suddenly realizes that what he has feared is actually happening to him. He is changing as he is seeing others change.)

LANGUAGE CONVENTIONS

If students have trouble, first have them identify all of the verbs. Then have them look up the different tenses for each. (**Answer:** The rest of the verbs are contained within quotation marks, denoting that they are part of Cora's dialogue, which is given in the present tense, unlike the rest of the paragraph. Putting verbs in the past tense makes the actions described sound more passive. This is a contrast to Cora's immediate and direct statements.)

■ English Learner Support

Understand Consistent Verb Tenses Have students mark the past-tense verbs in paragraph 155. Draw a picture of quotation marks, and explain that the words inside the marks are what the characters actually say.

ASK STUDENTS why the verbs on the inside of the quotations are in present tense. (*The dialogue between characters happens in present tense. People do not talk in past tense unless they are talking about something that happened in the past.*) **MODERATE**

290 Unit 4

 **NOTICE & NOTE**

AHA MOMENT

Notice & Note: Mark the place in paragraphs 132–137 where Mr. Bittering is surprised.

Infer: What does Mr. Bittering suddenly realize?

131 A green star rose in the east.
132 A strange word emerged from Mr. Bittering's lips.
133 "*Iorrt. Iorrt.*" He repeated it.
134 It was a Martian word. He knew no Martian.
135 In the middle of the night he arose and dialed a call through to Simpson, the archaeologist.
136 "Simpson, what does the word *Iorrt* mean?"
137 "Why that's the old Martian word for our planet Earth. Why?"
138 "No special reason."
139 The telephone slipped from his hand.
140 "Hello, hello, hello, hello," it kept saying while he sat gazing out at the green star. "Bittering? Harry, are you there?"
141 The days were full of metal sound. He laid the frame of the rocket with the reluctant help of three indifferent men. He grew very tired in an hour or so and had to sit down.
142 "The altitude," laughed a man.
143 "Are you *eating*, Harry?" asked another.
144 "I'm eating," he said, angrily.
145 "From your Deepfreeze?"
146 "Yes!"
147 "You're getting thinner, Harry."
148 "I'm not!"
149 "And taller."
150 "Liar!"

151 His wife took him aside a few days later. "Harry, I've used up all the food in the Deepfreeze. There's nothing left. I'll have to make sandwiches using food grown on Mars."
152 He sat down heavily.
153 "You must eat," she said. "You're weak."
154 "Yes," he said.

LANGUAGE CONVENTIONS

Annotate: Mark the past-tense verbs in paragraph 155.

Analyze: Why aren't all of the verbs in the paragraph in the past tense?

155 He <u>took</u> a sandwich, <u>opened</u> it, <u>looked</u> at it, and <u>began</u> to nibble at it. "And take the rest of the day off," she <u>said</u>. "It's hot. The children want to swim in the canals and hike. Please come <u>along</u>."
156 "I can't waste time. This is a crisis!"
157 "Just for an hour," she urged. "A swim'll do you good."
158 He rose, sweating. "All right, all right. Leave me alone. I'll come."
159 "Good for you, Harry."

290 Unit 4

160 The sun was hot, the day quiet. There was only an immense staring burn upon the land. They moved along the canal, the father, the mother, the racing children in their swimsuits. They stopped and ate meat sandwiches. He saw their skin baking brown. And he saw the yellow eyes of his wife and his children, their eyes that were never yellow before. A few tremblings shook him, but were carried off in waves of pleasant heat as he lay in the sun. He was too tired to be afraid.

161 "Cora, how long have your eyes been yellow?"
162 She was bewildered. "Always, I guess."
163 "They didn't change from brown in the last three months?"
164 She bit her lips. "No. Why do you ask?"
165 "Never mind."

ANALYZE MOOD

Annotate: In paragraph 160, mark the sentences that suggest a change in Bittering's thinking.

Draw Conclusions: How does this change affect the mood of the story and suggest what may happen next?

Dark They Were, and Golden-Eyed 291

ANALYZE MOOD

Inform students that Bittering's acceptance of the "pleasant heat" shows that he no longer has the same resistance to Mars.

(**Answer: Possible response:** *Bittering is becoming less resistant to the forces of Mars. The reader may feel sorry for Bittering's plight and worry that if he—the most vocal opponent of change—stops resisting Mars, more dramatic changes are yet to come.*)

APPLYING ACADEMIC VOCABULARY

☑ **complex**   ☐ potential   ☑ **rely**   ☐ stress   ☑ **valid**

Write and Discuss Have students turn to a partner to discuss the following questions. Guide students to include the Academic Vocabulary words *complex*, *rely*, and *valid* in their responses. Ask volunteers to share their responses with the class.

- Which character in this story has the most **complex** emotions?
- Upon what do the Bitterings learn to **rely** and to not rely in this story?
- Why do the others consider Harry Bittering's concerns not **valid**?

Dark They Were, And Golden-Eyed 291

TEACH

ENGLISH LEARNER SUPPORT

Understand Mood Use paragraphs 174–193 for discussion.

What does the word *Utha* mean? *(father)* Why does the boy call his father the Martian word *Utha*? *(He's becoming Martian.)* **SUBSTANTIAL**

Why does Bittering not seem to mind his son changing his name to *Linnl*? How is the mood different? **MODERATE**

Have students discuss the change in Bittering. How is Bittering's mood different? How is the mood in the story different? Encourage students to use their notes and the marks they have made in the text. **LIGHT**

NOTICE & NOTE

166 They sat there.
167 "The children's eyes," he said. "They're yellow, too."
168 "Sometimes growing children's eyes change color."
169 "Maybe *we're* children, too. At least to Mars. That's a thought." He laughed. "Think I'll swim."
170 They leaped into the canal water, and he let himself sink down and down to the bottom like a golden statue and lie there in green silence. All was water-quiet and deep, all was peace. He felt the steady, slow current drift him easily.
171 If I lie here long enough, he thought, the water will work and eat away my flesh until the bones show like coral. Just my skeleton left. And then the water can build on that skeleton—green things, deep water things, red things, yellow things. Change. Change. Slow, deep, silent change. And isn't that what it is up *there*?
172 He saw the sky submerged above him, the sun made Martian by atmosphere and time and space.
173 Up there, a big river, he thought, a Martian river; all of us lying deep in it, in our pebble houses, in our sunken boulder houses, like crayfish hidden, and the water washing away our old bodies and lengthening the bones and—
174 He let himself drift up through the soft light.
175 Dan sat on the edge of the canal, regarding his father seriously.
176 "*Utha*" he said.

292 Unit 4

177 "What?" asked his father.
178 The boy smiled. "You know. *Utha's* the Martian word for 'father.'"
179 "Where did you learn it?"
180 "I don't know. Around. *Utha!*"
181 "What do you want?"
182 The boy hesitated. "I—I want to change my name."
183 "Change it?"
184 "Yes."
185 His mother swam over. "What's wrong with Dan for a name?"
186 Dan fidgeted. "The other day you called Dan, Dan, Dan. I didn't even hear. I said to myself, That's not my name. I've a new name I want to use."
187 Mr. Bittering held to the side of the canal, his body cold and his heart pounding slowly. "What is this new name?"
188 "Linnl. Isn't that a good name? Can I use it? Can't I, please?"
189 Mr. Bittering put his hand to his head. He thought of the silly rocket, himself working alone, himself alone even among his family, so alone.
190 He heard his wife say, "Why not?"
191 He heard himself say, "Yes, you can use it."
192 "Yaaa!" screamed the boy. "I'm Linnl, Linnl!"
193 Racing down the meadowlands, he danced and shouted.
194 Mr. Bittering looked at his wife. "Why did we do that?"
195 "I don't know," she said. "It just seemed like a good idea." They walked into the hills. They strolled on old mosaic paths, beside still pumping fountains. The paths were covered with a thin film of cool water all summer long. You kept your bare feet cool all the day, splashing as in a creek, wading.
196 They came to a small deserted Martian villa with a good view of the valley. It was on top of a hill. Blue marble halls, large murals, a swimming pool. It was refreshing in this hot summertime. The Martians hadn't believed in large cities.
197 "How nice," said Mrs. Bittering, "if we could move up here to this villa for the summer."
198 "Come on," he said. "We're going back to town. There's work to be done on the rocket."

NOTICE & NOTE

ANALYZE MOOD

Annotate: Reread paragraphs 175–194. Mark the words that express Dan's request.

Infer: Why do you think Dan wants to make this change? How does his father's reaction show a change in the story's mood?

AGAIN AND AGAIN

Notice & Note: Mark the details in paragraphs 189–200 that describe Bittering's changing attitude toward the rocket he is building.

Infer: Why does the author keep bringing up the rocket and Bittering's attitude toward the work?

Dark They Were, and Golden-Eyed 293

TEACH

ANALYZE MOOD

Inform students that sometimes the mood of a story can change from the beginning to the end. (**Infer:** *Dan is becoming a Martian. He feels that his old name no longer fits him and he wants a Martian name instead. His father's response shows a change from a mood of fear to that of acceptance and calm about how things are changing.*)

AGAIN AND AGAIN

Cue students to look for words, phrases, and imagery that the author repeats within a text. Remind them that repetition calls attention to details in the text.

Tell students to look for repetitions, either in the passage itself, or for things that have been repeated from earlier in the story. Possible responses:

- Bittering has begun to accept, at least in part that he and his family are changing. Life on Mars doesn't seem too bad anymore.
- No one is helping Bittering build the rocket, and it is difficult to build it alone.
- The summer heat makes it difficult for Bittering to focus on his work.
- Building the rocket doesn't seem so urgent.

The author uses the rocket as a measure of Bittering's acceptance of what is happening. It is a way for the reader to understand Bittering's change in his person and attitude.

Dark They Were, And Golden-Eyed 293

TEACH

NOTICE & NOTE

199 But as he worked that night, the thought of the cool blue marble villa entered his mind. As the hours passed, the rocket seemed less important.

200 In the flow of days and weeks, the rocket **receded** and dwindled. The old fever was gone. It frightened him to think he had let it slip this way. But somehow the heat, the air, the working conditions—

recede
(rĭ-sēd′) v. To recede means to become fainter or more distant.

201 He heard the men murmuring on the porch of his metal shop.

202 "Everyone's going. You heard?"

203 "All going. That's right."

204 Bittering came out. "Going where?" He saw a couple of trucks, loaded with children and furniture, drive down the dusty street.

205 "Up to the villas," said the man.

206 "Yeah, Harry. I'm going. So is Sam. Aren't you Sam?"

207 "That's right, Harry. What about you?"

208 "I've got work to do here."

209 "Work! You can finish that rocket in the autumn, when it's cooler."

210 He took a breath. "I got the frame all set up."

211 "In the autumn is better." Their voices were lazy in the heat.

212 "Got to work," he said.

213 "Autumn," they reasoned. And they sounded so sensible, so right.

214 "Autumn would be best," he thought. "Plenty of time, then."

215 No! cried part of himself, deep down, put away, locked tight, suffocating. No! No!

216 "In the autumn," he said.

217 "Come on, Harry," they all said.

218 "Yes," he said, feeling his flesh melt in the hot liquid air. "Yes, in the autumn. I'll begin work again then."

219 "I got a villa near the Tirra Canal," said someone.

220 "You mean the Roosevelt Canal, don't you?"

221 "Tirra. The old Martian name."

222 "But on the map—"

223 "Forget the map. It's Tirra now. Now I found a place in the Pillan Mountains—"

224 "You mean the Rockefeller Range," said Bittering.

225 "I mean the Pillan Mountains," said Sam.

226 "Yes," said Bittering, buried in the hot, swarming air. "The Pillan Mountains."

294 Unit 4

CRITICAL VOCABULARY

recede: The word *receded* is used to let the reader know that the rocket is moving away.

ASK STUDENTS whether by knowing the meaning of *receded*, they can infer the meaning of *dwindled*. ("Dwindle" means "to become gradually less until little remains," which is similar, but not the same, as receded.)

WHEN STUDENTS STRUGGLE...

Understand Science Fiction Inform students that science fiction often features characters doing things that most normal people would not be capable of doing in our times (or world). But the students should still be able to identify with the characters' actions. Instead of making a rocket, is it possible to make a car? What other technological things could they imagine making? Ask students to identify the science fiction elements in paragraphs 198–200. Then ask them to swap out the science fiction elements for modern-day elements. Does the story still make sense? (*Bittering is building a rocket. But I can substitute car for "rocket," garage for "metal shop."*)

227   Everyone worked at loading the truck in the hot, still afternoon of the next day.

228   Laura, Dan, and David carried packages. Or, as they preferred to be known, Ttil, Linnl, and Werr carried packages.

229   The furniture was abandoned in the little white cottage.

230   "It looked just fine in Boston," said the mother. "And here in the cottage. But up at the villa? No. We'll get it when we come back in the autumn."

231   Bittering himself was quiet.

232   "I've some ideas on furniture for the villa," he said after a time. "Big, lazy furniture."

233   "What about your encyclopedia? You're taking it along, surely?"

234   Mr. Bittering glanced away. "I'll come and get it next week."

235   They turned to their daughter. "What about your New York dresses?"

236   The bewildered girl stared. "Why, I don't want them any more."

237   They shut off the gas, the water, they locked the doors and walked away. Father peered into the truck.

238   "Gosh, we're not taking much," he said. "Considering all we brought to Mars, this is only a handful!"

239   He started the truck.

240   Looking at the small white cottage for a long moment, he was filled with a desire to rush to it, touch it, say good-bye to it, for he felt as if he were going away on a long journey, leaving something to which he could never quite return, never understand again.

241   Just then Sam and his family drove by in another truck.

242   "Hi, Bittering! Here we go!"

243   The truck swung down the ancient highway out of town. There were sixty others traveling in the same direction. The town filled with a silent, heavy dust from their passage. The canal waters lay blue in the sun, and a quiet wind moved in the strange trees.

244   "Good-bye, town!" said Mr. Bittering.

245   "Good-bye, good-bye," said the family, waving to it.

246   They did not look back again.

NOTICE & NOTE

ANALYZE MOOD

Annotate: In paragraphs 227–239, mark the text that shows Bittering's feelings about what the family is taking to the villa.

Analyze: What effect does Bittering's response have on the overall mood of the story?

TEACH

✏️ ANALYZE MOOD

Have students read the paragraphs. Explain to them that mood does not have to come from the descriptions, it can come from dialogue, too. (**Answer: Possible response:** Earlier in the story, an anxious mood characterized the Bitterings' feelings about Mars. However, when the Bitterings admit to each other that they are leaving behind their Earth belongings, the mood becomes strangely calm. They seem to be accepting that Mars has changed them.)

TO CHALLENGE STUDENTS...

Express Opinions Although this short story may be science fiction, Bradbury makes reference to very real-world matters. Have students discuss what life on another planet would be like for future colonists from Earth. Do they think that the colonists would try to make the new planet as much like Earth as possible? Or would they try to adapt themselves to the new planet?

TEACH

ANALYZE SCIENCE FICTION

Remind students that science fiction may have some fantastical aspects. This includes characters undergoing transformations, as in fantasy and horror stories. (**Answer: Possible response:** *The Bitterings may no longer be human. The dialogue shows only their perspective, but they do not seem to think of themselves as human—they have started to use the Martian language and they refer to Earth people as "ugly."*)

CRITICAL VOCABULARY

pendulum: The rubber tires, which are compared to pendulums, no longer swing because the children are no longer interested in playing on them—that's an Earth game or activity.

ASK STUDENTS what affect *pendulum* has in the sentence. (By comparing the image of the rubber tire swings to the pendulums of stopped clocks, the narrator is painting an image of a place that has been untouched by people, as though time has stopped.)

296   Unit 4

NOTICE & NOTE

pendulum
(pĕn´jə-ləm) *n.* A *pendulum* is a weight that is hung so that it can swing freely. Sometimes it is used in timing the workings of certain clocks.

ANALYZE SCIENCE FICTION
Annotate: Mark details in paragraphs 249–259 that describe how the Bitterings have physically changed since their arrival on Mars.

Analyze: Do you think the Bitterings are still human? Explain.

247 Summer burned the canals dry. Summer moved like flame upon the meadows. In the empty Earth settlement, the painted houses flaked and peeled. Rubber tires upon which children had swung in back yards hung suspended like stopped clock **pendulums** in the blazing air.

248 At the metal shop, the rocket frame began to rust.

249 In the quiet autumn Mr. Bittering stood, very dark now, very golden-eyed, upon the slope above his villa, looking at the valley.

250 "It's time to go back," said Cora.

251 "Yes, but we're not going," he said quietly. "There's nothing there any more."

252 "Your books," she said. "Your fine clothes."

253 "Your *Illes* and your fine *ior uele rre*" she said.

254 "The town's empty. No one's going back," he said. "There's no reason to, none at all."

255 The daughter wove tapestries and the sons played songs on ancient flutes and pipes, their laughter echoing in the marble villa.

256 Mr. Bittering gazed at the Earth settlement far away in the low valley. "Such odd, such ridiculous houses the Earth people built."

296   Unit 4

257 "They didn't know any better," his wife **mused.** "Such ugly people. I'm glad they've gone."

258 They both looked at each other, startled by all they had just finished saying. They laughed.

259 "Where did they go?" he wondered. He glanced at his wife. She was golden and slender as his daughter. She looked at him, and he seemed almost as young as their eldest son.

260 "I don't know," she said.

261 "We'll go back to town maybe next year, or the year after, or the year after that," he said, calmly. "Now—I'm warm. How about taking a swim?"

262 They turned their backs to the valley. Arm in arm they walked silently down a path of clear-running spring water.

263 Five years later a rocket fell out of the sky. It lay steaming in the valley. Men leaped out of it, shouting.

"We won the war on Earth! We're here to rescue you! Hey!"

264 But the American-built town of cottages, peach trees, and theaters was silent. They found a flimsy rocket frame rusting in an empty shop.

muse
(myōōz) v. When you *muse*, you say something thoughtfully.

CRITICAL VOCABULARY

muse: When we muse, we're being reflective and unexcited.

ASK STUDENTS wow the paragraph would be different had the author used the word *said* in place of *mused*. *("Said" would not emphasize her surprising lack of excitement over the transformation of her family.)*

TEACH

ANALYZE SCIENCE FICTION

For students who do not realize that the Bitterings have transformed into Martians, read aloud paragraphs 249-255, which emphasize key points: their physical changes, their use of the Martian language, their move away from their original settlement, and their adoption of Martian customs and practices. Then move onto paragraphs 263-274.
(**Answer: Possible response:** *Like the Bitterings, in time the captain and lieutenant will turn into Martians. Or the captain and lieutenant may be threatened by the "Martians" and try to destroy them.*)

NOTICE & NOTE

265 The rocket men searched the hills. The captain established headquarters in an abandoned bar. His lieutenant came back to report.

266 "The town's empty, but we found native life in the hills, sir. Dark people. Yellow eyes. Martians. Very friendly. We talked a bit, not much. They learn English fast. I'm sure our relations will be most friendly with them, sir."

267 "Dark, eh?" mused the captain. "How many?"

268 "Six, eight hundred, I'd say, living in those marble ruins in the hills, sir. Tall, healthy. Beautiful women."

269 "Did they tell you what became of the men and women who built this Earth settlement, Lieutenant?"

270 "They hadn't the foggiest notion of what happened to this town or its people."

271 "Strange. You think those Martians killed them?"

272 "They look surprisingly peaceful. Chances are a plague did this town in, sir."

273 "Perhaps. I suppose this is one of those mysteries we'll never solve. One of those mysteries you read about."

274 The captain looked at the room, the dusty windows, the blue mountains rising beyond, the canals moving in the light, and he heard the soft wind in the air. He shivered. Then, recovering, he tapped a large fresh map he had thumbtacked to the top of an empty table.

ANALYZE SCIENCE FICTION
Annotate: Reread paragraphs 263–274. Mark the sentences that describe what the rocket men found.

Predict: What do you think will happen to the captain and the lieutenant?

275 "Lots to be done, Lieutenant." His voice droned on and quietly on as the sun sank behind the blue hills. "New settlements. Mining sites, minerals to be looked for. Bacteriological specimens[5] taken. The work, all the work. And the old records were lost. We'll have a job of remapping to do, renaming the mountains and rivers and such. Calls for a little imagination.

276 "What do you think of naming those mountains the Lincoln Mountains, this canal the Washington Canal, those hills—we can name those hills for you, Lieutenant. Diplomacy. And you, for a favor, might name a town for me. Polishing the apple.[6] And why not make this the Einstein Valley, and farther over . . . are you *listening*, Lieutenant?"

277 The lieutenant snapped his gaze from the blue color and the quiet mist of the hills far beyond the town.

278 "What? Oh, *yes*, sir!"

---

[5] **bacteriological specimens:** samples of different kinds of single-celled living things.
[6] **Polishing the apple:** acting in a way to get on the good side of another person.

298 Unit 4

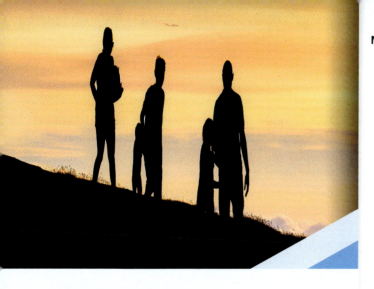

NOTICE & NOTE

TEACH

CHECK YOUR UNDERSTANDING

Have students answer the questions independently.

Answers:

1. B
2. H
3. D

If they answer any questions incorrectly, have them reread the text to confirm their understanding. Then they may proceed to ANALYZE THE TEXT on page 300.

CHECK YOUR UNDERSTANDING

Answer these questions before moving on to the **Analyze the Text** section on the following page.

1 Why is paragraph 8 important to the story?

   A It introduces a familiar setting.

   B It helps establish a foreboding mood.

   C It describes realistically what will happen.

   D It describes the most important characters.

2 Rockets stopped coming to Mars because —

   F fuel to power them had run out

   G everyone was dying of a strange illness

   H war had broken out on Earth

   J people no longer wanted to live there

3 Based on the details provided in the selection about the lieutenant's reaction to Mars, he will most likely —

   A leave Mars and forget about what he has seen

   B try to continue building the old rocket

   C move into a cottage in the American-built town

   D continue visiting the Martians in the hills

Dark They Were, and Golden-Eyed 299

 ENGLISH LEARNER SUPPORT

Oral Assessment Use the following questions to assess students' comprehension and speaking skills:

1. Reread paragraph 8 and ask if Mars sounds like a nice place to live. *(No, "At any moment the Martian air might draw his soul from him.")*

2. Why did the rockets stop coming to Mars? *(The rockets stopped coming to Mars because there was a war on Earth)*

3. What do you think will happen to the lieutenant who visited the Martians in the hills? *(He will continue to visit the Martians and will probably change into a Martian himself.)*

SUBSTANTIAL/MODERATE

Dark They Were, And Golden-Eyed **299**

APPLY

ANALYZE THE TEXT
Possible answers

1. **DOK 4:** *Students may say that the mood is tense, eerie, scary, or suspenseful. Supporting examples will vary.*

2. **DOK 2:** *They are becoming permanent residents of Mars and consider themselves Martians. Naming is a way of taking possession of a new location.*

3. **DOK 3:** *Cora is a wife and a mother. Her role seems to be that of a traditional nurturer, whose primary work is to care for her family.*

4. **DOK 2:** *The captain is more likely to resist the changes because he wants to bring Earth culture to Mars. This is indicated by his desire and effort to rename places.*

5. **DOK 4:** *The changing eye color of residents indicates that they are being physically transformed by their new location. It also is a metaphor for their changing psychological perspective: they now "see" Mars as Martians, not Earthlings. The title of the story reflects the physical and psychological changes the settlers have undergone. The use of the phrase "golden-eyed" indicates that their new view on life is positive.*

RESEARCH
When researching this specific topic, students are very likely to run into sites with unfounded information on space. Do not discourage them from seeking out this information, but rather encourage them to check the information they find against scientific sources. Then ask, which sources are more reliable.

Connect: *Responses will vary.*

RESPOND

ANALYZE THE TEXT
Support your responses with evidence from the text. 📓 NOTEBOOK

1. **Analyze** What words would you use to describe the overall mood of the story? Cite examples of Bradbury's use of language.

2. **Interpret** Why is it significant that the settlers are using the old Martian names of local landmarks and changing their own names?

3. **Compare** Why might Cora be more accepting of life on Mars than her husband Harry? What practical matters might affect her behavior?

4. **Predict** Who do you think will resist change more: the captain, or the lieutenant? Which details from the story best support your prediction?

5. **Notice & Note** How does the author's contrasting the eye color among the settlers at various points in the text connect to a main theme of the story? Explain how this connection relates to the title of the story.

RESEARCH

RESEARCH TIP
When researching to find examples of a particular genre, you can look for information using the genre name and/or particular author names. You can also narrow your search by looking for books recommended for a particular age group.

What is science fiction? Are science fiction stories always about space travel or colonization of other worlds? Find out more about science fiction. Look for two examples science fiction to read and compare. You can either look for short stories or consider reading chapters in longer works. As you read, ask yourself why each text is an example of science fiction. What makes each one unique? Record what you learn about the characters, setting, and plot of each text in the chart below. Then discuss your impressions of science fiction with a partner.

SELECTION 1	SELECTION 2

Extend With a small group, discuss science fiction and how it expresses ideas about people, cultures, and the social and political challenges that societies face.

300 Unit 4

LEARNING MINDSET

Asking For Help Some students will be too shy to ask a neighbor for help. You might want to share a personal anecdote with them about a time you weren't sure about asking someone for help, but did it anyway, and it turned out all right. Tell students that asking for help does not equal failure. If they were with an adult and their car got stuck in the mud, wouldn't they ask someone for help? Or would they keep trying to get themselves out of the mud? Asking for help is just another way of getting unstuck.

CREATE AND DISCUSS

Write a Letter Write a letter to a friend in which you express your opinions about the possibility of alien life forms in space.

- ❑ Be sure to use correct letter form, including the date, greeting, body of the letter, and signature.
- ❑ In your introductory paragraph, state your opinion.
- ❑ In the paragraphs that follow, offer support for your opinion.
- ❑ In your final paragraph, restate your opinion. Encourage your friend to write back with his or her thoughts on the subject.

Make a Graphic Track the gradual but important ways that Harry Bittering's attitude changes as the story unfolds.

- ❑ Review the text of "Dark They Were, and Golden-Eyed." Look for details about the changes in Bittering's thoughts about Mars.
- ❑ Record your findings, including quotations from the story, in a graphic organizer like the one shown.

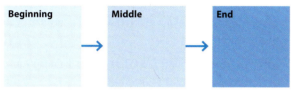

- ❑ Use your graphic organizer as the basis for discussion with other members of a small group.

RESPOND

Go to **Writing as a Process** in the **Writing Studio** for help.

Go to **Participating in Collaborative Discussions** in the **Speaking and Listening Studio** to learn more.

RESPOND TO THE ESSENTIAL QUESTION

 Why is the idea of space exploration both inspiring and unnerving?

Gather Information Review your annotations on "Dark They Were, and Golden-Eyed." Then, add details to your Response Log. As you determine which information to include, think about:

- why people might want to settle on another planet
- how people might respond to having limited contact with Earth

At the end of the unit, use your notes to help you write an argument.

ACADEMIC VOCABULARY

As you write and discuss what you learned from the story, be sure to use the Academic Vocabulary words. Check off each of the words that you use.

- ❑ complex
- ❑ potential
- ❑ rely
- ❑ stress
- ❑ valid

APPLY

CREATE AND DISCUSS

Write a Letter Students should integrate their research into the letters in natural, conversational ways. This is not the same as writing quotes and citations for a formal essay. Instead, they can slip their research into the flow of the letter, such as:

Have you heard of this new idea for colonizing Mars? I read on [science website] the other day that a billionaire is going to start sending people there by 2030. So, are you coming with me?

 For **writing support** for students at varying proficiency levels, see the **Text X-Ray** on page 278D.

Make a Graphic Because their graphic organizers will lead to a small group discussion, encourage students to look for things in the text that not everyone else will bring to the discussion. That way, the discussion will be more rich and unpredictable.

RESPOND TO THE ESSENTIAL QUESTION

Allow time for students to add details from "Dark They Were, and Golden-Eyed" to their Unit 4 Response Logs.

WHEN STUDENTS STRUGGLE...

Understand How to Write a Letter Instruct students to imagine a conversation in which they will not hear back from the other person for a long time. This will not be like a text, or even an email. They will have to cover their topic without getting prompt feedback from the other person. They will need to anticipate what the other person might think or question. Tell them to take the information from their research and put it into this letter, sometimes in their own words, and sometimes in quotations. Encourage students to use English idioms and slang, possibly in quotation marks.

APPLY

CRITICAL VOCABULARY

1. b, a grandfather clock
2. a, a plane landing on a runway
3. c, a lonely child
4. b, striking workers with nothing to do
5. a, a person considering choices
6. b, a friendly crowd of people
7. c, a dimming light

VOCABULARY STRATEGY:
Latin Root *pend*

1. pendant
2. dependent
3. suspenseful
4. suspenders
5. impending

 RESPOND

WORD BANK
convivial
subtly
idle
forlorn
recede
pendulum
muse

CRITICAL VOCABULARY

Practice and Apply In each item, mark the phrase that has a connection to each Critical Vocabulary word.

1. **pendulum:** a writing instrument / a grandfather clock / a racing motorcycle

2. **recede:** a plane flying off into the distance / a plane landing on a runway / a plane parked at the gate

3. **forlorn:** a bitter quarrel / a heavy snowfall / a lonely child

4. **idle:** singers in a contest / striking workers with nothing to do / a parking lot filling with cars

5. **muse:** a person considering choices / a windy, rainy afternoon / a noisy rock band

6. **convivial:** a dog chasing a squirrel / a friendly crowd of people / a curving staircase

7. **subtly:** a fireworks show / a long bus ride / a dimming light

 Go to the **Vocabulary Studio** for more on roots.

VOCABULARY STRATEGY: Latin Root *pend*

The vocabulary word *pendulum* contains the Latin root *pend*, which means "hang." This root, sometimes spelled *pens*, is found in many English words. Use context clues and your knowledge of the root's meaning to help you understand unfamiliar words with *pend* or *pens*.

Practice and Apply Choose the word that best completes each sentence. Then explain to a partner how the root *pend* or *pens* relates to the meaning of the word.

| pendulum | suspenseful | dependent |
| suspenders | impending | pendant |

1. She wears that _____ around her neck every day.
2. My choice is _____ on what you decide to do.
3. The book was so _____ that he could not put it down.
4. To hold up his pants, Dad prefers _____ to belts.
5. They could not shake off their feeling of _____ trouble.

302 Unit 4

 ENGLISH LEARNER SUPPORT

Understand Latin Roots Write the following Spanish cognates on the board and underline the Latin roots *pend/pens* in each word: *pendulum/péndulo, dependent/dependiente, suspense/suspenso*. Point out that both Spanish and English have Latin roots. Tell students that they can use their knowledge of Latin roots to help them understand the meaning of unfamiliar words in English. Use gestures to define the Latin roots *pend/pens*. Then have student pairs of varying proficiency create definitions for the remaining vocabulary words: *suspenders, impending,* and *pendant*. Allow students to use gestures or images in their definitions. Encourage students at higher levels of proficiency to create written definitions.

LANGUAGE CONVENTIONS: Consistent Verb Tenses

English verbs express the time of an action or state of being—past, present, or future—through verb tense. To keep the time of the verb clear in the readers' minds, writers usually are consistent. In these examples from "Dark They Were, and Golden-Eyed," Ray Bradbury uses consistent verb tenses:

- To express actions that happened in the past
  Mr. Bittering *hesitated*, **and then** *raised* **the mirror to his face.** (*Both verbs end in -ed and are in the past tense.*)

- To express actions that happen in the present
  Sometimes nights I *think* **I** *hear* **'em. I** *hear* **the wind. The sand** *hits* **my window.** (*All three verbs—*think, hear, *and* hits—*are in the present tense. Notice how* hits *ends in -s because the subject—*sand—*is singular.*)

- To express actions that will happen in the future
  One day the atom bomb *will fix* **Earth. Then** *we'll be* **safe here.** (*Both verbs use the helping verb* will *to show the future tense.* We'll be *means "we will be."*)

Unexpected or inconsistent use of verb tenses can lead to confusion. On the other hand, sometimes tenses need to shift to show changes in time. What's important is to use the same tense to describe actions that take place at the same time. Change tenses only when you intend to shift from one time period to another.

Practice and Apply Write your own sentences based on the models from the story. You may write sentences about the story or about a topic of your own choosing. When you have finished, share your sentences with a partner and compare your use of verb tenses.

RESPOND

Go to **Using Verb Tense Consistently** in the **Grammar Studio** for more help.

APPLY

LANGUAGE CONVENTIONS: Consistent Verb Tenses

Review the information about consistent verb tenses with students. Explain that an author must always determine which tense he or she will use. In the case of "Dark They Were, and Golden-Eyed," Bradbury chose to tell the story as if the events had already occurred.

Illustrate how inconsistent verb tenses can confuse readers. Read these sample sentences with altered tenses.

- Mr. Bittering hesitates, and then raising the mirror to his face.
- Sometimes nights I think I heard 'em. I am hearing the wind. The sand hits my window.
- One day the atom bomb fixed Earth. Then we'll be safe here.

Ask students why a writer of nonfiction would choose past, present, or future tenses in their articles or books about real-life subjects. Remind them that when working on their own writing, whether creative or for school, they should always keep consistent verb tense in mind. If an author does use an inconsistent tense deliberately, it may be to draw attention to an important detail.

Practice and Apply: *Responses will vary.*

ENGLISH LEARNER SUPPORT

Understand Consistent Verb Tenses Have students read the sample sentences on the student page. Write the different tenses of the verbs on the board. Then, have them think about how the verbs relate to the subjects and reflect when the actions are taking place. Pair students up to practice saying the sentences, changing the verb tense. Finally, have them share with the group how the sentences change meaning when they use different verb tenses.
SUBSTANTIAL/MODERATE

PLAN

MENTOR TEXT
CHALLENGES FOR SPACE EXPLORATION
Argument by Ann Leckie

This argument serves as a **Mentor Text**, a model for students to follow when they come to the Unit 4 Writing Task, Write an Argument

GENRE ELEMENTS
ARGUMENT

Remind students that the purpose of an **argument** is to persuade the reader to accept the author's viewpoint on an issue. An author uses information—facts, and sometimes images and graphics—to support his or her argument. In addition, the author often uses language and literary devices that draw attention to the main point and engage the reader's attention.

LEARNING OBJECTIVES

- Analyze author's purpose.
- Recognize the use of rhetorical devices in argument.
- Conduct research on space exploration.
- Write a poem from the point of view of an astronaut.
- Listen to and discuss a poem's message.
- Use commas in introductory phrases.
- Use a print or online dictionary to study the history and origins of critical vocabulary.
- **Language** Discuss visuals.

TEXT COMPLEXITY

Quantitative Measures	Challenges for Space Exploration	Lexile: 880L
Qualitative Measures	**Ideas Presented** Mostly implied with explicit statement at end	
	Structures Used Primarily one perspective	
	Language Used Mostly Tier 1 and Tier II words	
	Knowledge Required Most factual content is common knowledge	

PLAN

RESOURCES

Online

- Unit 4 Response Log
- Selection Audio
- Previewing the Text
- Previewing the Text
- 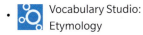 Reading Studio: Notice & Note
- Writing Studio: Planning and Drafting
- Speaking and Listening Studio: Participating in Collaborative Discussions
- Vocabulary Studio: Etymology
- Grammar Studio: Module 14: Lesson 2-6: Using Commas
- "Challenges for Space Exploration" Selection Test

SUMMARIES

English

Humans explored Earth for thousands of years in spite of the dangers of the unknown. Space travel is even more dangerous, yet it has yielded great rewards. The author argues that our planet needs a peaceful and necessary project that will enable us to find new planets to live on when Earth is no longer habitable. Seeking a new habitat for humans will be dangerous, perhaps impossible, but it is human nature to attempt it anyway.

Spanish

Una familia llega a Marte como parte de una pequeña colonia. Inmediatamente, el padre expresa su deseo de volver a la Tierra. Y empieza a construir un cohete para regresar a la Tierra. Al tiempo, nota pequeños pero significativos cambios en su familia y en los otros colonizadores después de comer la comida cultivada en el nuevo planeta. Gradualmente, el padre y su familia se acostumbran a Marte y se hacen más marcianos. Finalmente, la familia se transforma en una familia marciana. Otro cohete llega a su colonia y no encuentra a ningún terrícola.

SMALL-GROUP OPTIONS

Have students work in small groups to read and discuss the selection.

Numbered Heads Together

- After students have read the argument, arrange them in groups of four, assigning each student a number from 1 to 4.
- Ask each group: *Do the benefits of space exploration outweigh the risks. Why or why not?*
- Allow students time to discuss their opinions among themselves and formulate a group response.
- Call upon a "numbered head" in the group to explain the group's opinion and the reasoning behind it.

Think-Pair-Share

- Assign partners to each student. Ask students to consider the following question: *What would be the greatest benefits of working with other nations to look for other planets on which humans can live?*
- Have partners discuss the question and formulate an opinion.
- Then call on a member of each pair of students to share the result of their discussion with the class.

Challenges for Space Exploration **304B**

PLAN

Text X-Ray: English Learner Support
for "Challenges for Space Exploration"

Use the Text X-Ray and the supports and scaffolds in the Teacher's Edition to help guide students at different proficiency levels through the selection.

INTRODUCE THE SELECTION
DISCUSS THE TERROR AND WONDER OF SPACE

In this lesson, students will need to be able to discuss ideas about exploration, danger, and technology, and how all these ideas are connected. Read the first four paragraphs with students. Provide the following explanations

- Exploration is about finding out what is out there.
- It can be dangerous to explore space.
- New technology makes it possible to discover new worlds.

Explain to students that the challenges of space exploration can be related to the challenges they face in their own lives. Just as the human race must take on new challenges in order to survive, they must take on new challenges if they want to grow. Have volunteers share their beliefs about space exploration. Supply the following sentence frames.

One benefit of space explorations is _____. The dangers of exploration are acceptable because _____. One major difference between exploration of Earth and exploration of space is the use of _____.

CULTURAL REFERENCES

The following words and phrases may be unfamiliar to students:

- *cutting-edge technology* (paragraph 3): the most advanced technology
- *beyond the horizon* (paragraph 3): beyond what we can guess or anticipate
- *keep all our eggs in this . . . basket* (paragraph 5): rely on a single way for success
- *join the non-avian dinosaurs* (paragraph 5): become extinct.

LISTENING

Understand Consonant Blends

Explaing that consonant blends are groups of consonants that are without vowels and make a distinct, blended sound. A very common one is *cr* found in the word *crucial*.

Have students listen as you read aloud paragraph 6. Draw students' attention to the word *crucial*, and explain that if something is "kroo-shul," it means it is something important to survival. Use the following supports with students at varying proficiency levels:

- Have students repeat the word crucial, stressing the *cr* and the *shul* sound in *-cial*. **SUBSTANTIAL**
- Model the pronunciation of other *cr* blends, in addition to *crucial*, such as *cross, crumb, crazy,* and *crow*, and have students repeat them back. **MODERATE**
- Have students in small groups make up sentences using the word *crucial* and other words with the *cr* blend. **LIGHT**

304C Unit 4

PLAN

SPEAKING

Discuss the Visual

Draw students' attention to the image of the person in the spacesuit. Ask students to examine the image carefully. Then ask individual students about the relationship between the image and the argument in the author's article.

Use the following supports with students at varying proficiency levels:

- Call students' attention to the visual of the person in a spacesuit. Have students repeat after you as you make statements about the poster. For example: *The person in the spacesuit is floating in space.* **SUBSTANTIAL**
- Ask students questions about the poster. Ask: *Why is this visual next to the article? (It shows what the article is about.)* **MODERATE**
- Pair students to discuss the visual. Ask: *What does the image tell you about the problems that are part of space exploration? (Space explorers need protection from the environment of space.)* **LIGHT**

READING

Understand an Argument

Tell students that authors of arguments often use repetition to support their claims.

Work with students to read paragraphs 4–8. Use the following supports with students at varying proficiency levels:

- Point out that at the beginning of each of these paragraphs is the phrase, "I could tell you," and have students repeat the phrase. **SUBSTANTIAL**
- Have students take turns reading the paragraphs with special emphasis on the phrase, "I could tell you." **MODERATE**
- Put students in small groups, and ask them whether the phrase "I could tell you" helps the author make her argument strong. **LIGHT**

WRITING

Write a Poem

Work with students to read the writing assignment on p. 311.

Use the following supports with students at varying proficiency levels:

- Work with students to create a word web about space travel. Help them identify words from the text that might be used in a poem. Help them sound out the letters and words they have chosen. **SUBSTANTIAL**
- Guide students to identify the words that will be important in the poem. Provide sentence frames, such as "The text says *Could we go there?* _____. **MODERATE**
- Remind students that poems do not have to rhyme. Tell them to think of how they would feel if they were an astronaut. Would they feel brave? Excited? Scared? Tell them to write about the feelings they would have. **LIGHT**

TEACH

? Connect to the ESSENTIAL QUESTION

"Challenges for Space Exploration" invites readers to consider similarities between the motives for the early exploration of Earth and the current motives for space exploration. The argument for exploring space emphasizes our common human aspirations--and the dangers inherent in leaving the safety of our home planet.

MENTOR TEXT

At the end of the unit, students will be asked to write a poem in which an astronaut discusses the risks and sacrifices of space exploration. "Challenges for Space Exploration" provides an introspective look at why humans have always explored new frontiers, and the importance of continuing to do so today. Students can use this information to add details to their poems about how an astronaut might feel when exploring humanity's final frontier—outer space.

ANALYZE & APPLY

CHALLENGES FOR SPACE EXPLORATION

Argument by **Ann Leckie**

? ESSENTIAL QUESTION:

Why is the idea of space exploration both inspiring and unnerving?

QUICK START

The possibility of humans exploring space is exciting—but dangerous, too. What do you think are the main challenges of space exploration? Make a list; then compare lists with two or three classmates.

ANALYZE AUTHOR'S PURPOSE

Purpose is an author's reason for writing a text. In an argument, the purpose is to persuade. The author presents a **claim**—a viewpoint or position on an issue—and then supports it with reasons and evidence.

Some arguments begin with a clear statement of the author's claim. Others imply a claim through the presentation of information and through **rhetoric,** the art of using language effectively to appeal to an audience. One aspect of rhetoric is **word choice.** Word choice helps to shape both tone and voice in a text.

SHAPED BY WORD CHOICE	EXAMPLE FROM SELECTION
Tone is the author's attitude toward a subject—for example, serious, lighthearted, or (as in this example) inspirational.	It's a huge, dangerous, maybe impossible project. But that's never stopped humans from trying anyway.
Voice is an author's unique use of language that allows a reader to "hear" a human personality in the author's work.	. . . one good meteor strike and we all join the non-avian dinosaurs. And have you noticed the weather lately?

GENRE ELEMENTS: ARGUMENT

- presents and defends a claim
- provides reasons to support the claim and factual evidence to support the reasons
- uses persuasive language
- can be formal or informal

ANALYZE REPETITION

One way to make a point in an argument is through **repetition.** Repetition is the use of the same word, phrase, clause, or sentence more than once for emphasis. Repetition is one of the **rhetorical devices**—specific ways of using language—authors use to emphasize key ideas, convey tone, and sometimes to encourage an emotional response in readers. In this example from "Challenges for Space Exploration," repetition of the word *there* emphasizes the idea of going into space. It also captures the curiosity and excitement that people have felt about exploring space:

> What's up <u>there</u>? Could we go <u>there</u>? Maybe we could go <u>there</u>.

As you read "Challenges for Space Exploration," look for other examples of repetition that the author uses as she develops her argument.

Challenges for Space Exploration 305

TEACH

QUICK START

Have students read the Quick Start question and give them a few minutes to write their lists. Call on groups of two or three to identify the challenges they have identified. Have a volunteer list the challenges on the board.

ANALYZE AUTHOR'S PURPOSE

Help students understand the idea of writing with a purpose. Explain that writers are artists who use words to describe, inform, entertain, or persuade. Have students read the explanation of tone and the examples from the essay. Ask: *What are some other words that might affect tone?* (*terrifying, monstrous, comical, peaceful*) Next, ask students to read the definition of *voice* in the text. Explain that the author's voice can make his or her words more persuasive by creating a personal bond between the writer and the reader. Addressing readers by writing in the second person (as "you") can make readers feel as though the writer is conducting a conversation with them in person.

ANALYZE REPETITION

Repetition is a commonly used rhetorical technique in music, literature, and speeches. For example, the repetition of the line "Follow the yellow brick road" in the song "We're Off to see the Wizard" from *The Wizard of Oz.* In poems, for example, Poe's "The Raven" the word *Nevermore,* is continuously repeated to create a sense of doom. Repetition is often a feature of speeches. (Martin Luther King, Jr. repeated the phrase "I have a dream" in his famous speech.) Discuss the effect of repetition in each of these instances. (*optimism, sorrow, inspiration*). Explain that writers use repetition to stir emotions in order to drive home a point or establish a mood. Repetition is also used in daily speech: The father told his child: I love you because you're kind, I love you because you're good to Grandma, I love you because you take care of the dog, I love you because you are you!

TEACH

CRITICAL VOCABULARY

Encourage students to read all the sentences before deciding which word best completes each one. Remind them to look for context clues that match the meaning of each word.

Answers:

1. entail
2. habitat
3. crucial
4. infinitely

■ **English Learner Support**

Use Cognates Tell students that several of the Critical Vocabulary words have Spanish cognates: *habitat/habitación, infinitely/infinidad.* **LIGHT**

LANGUAGE CONVENTIONS

Review the instructions about commas. Read the sample sentences aloud leaving out the pause for the comma. Then read them again, demonstrating the pause created by the comma. Point out that the comma makes the sentences easier to understand, whether they have been written or spoken.

ANNOTATION MODEL

Point out the annotation ideas on this page, which suggest underlining persuasive phrases and indicating repetition of words by circling or drawing a box around them. Tell them that they can use this suggestion or create their own system for marking up the selection in their write-in text. They may want to color code their annotations by using highlighters. Their notes in the margin may include questions about ideas or topics they want to learn more about.

306   Unit 4

 GET READY

CRITICAL VOCABULARY

infinitely   entail   crucial   habitat

To see how many Critical Vocabulary words you already know, use them to complete these sentences.

1. Exploring another solar system would _____ many years of research and preparation.
2. If the _____ of a species is destroyed, the species must find a new environment that's suitable.
3. Protection from radiation is _____ if humans are to survive travel in space.
4. There are _____ more places to explore in space than people can imagine.

LANGUAGE CONVENTIONS

Commas After Introductory Phrases   In "Challenges for Space Exploration," you will learn to use a comma after an introductory phrase. The comma gives the reader a moment to pause before moving on to the main part of the sentence. Note these examples:

> Without a doubt, human beings have long had a thirst for exploring the unknown.

> Centuries before the first telescope, people studied the night sky and wondered what might be "out there."

Look for comma usage as you read and write about the text.

ANNOTATION MODEL   NOTICE & NOTE

As you read, note how the author reveals her purpose for writing. You can also mark up examples of repetition and other rhetorical devices that make her argument effective. In the model, you can see one reader's notes about one paragraph in "Challenges for Space Exploration."

> 6   I could tell you that it might be good for us to unite behind a project that (doesn't involve) killing one another, that (does involve) understanding our home planet and the ways we |survive on it| and what things are crucial to our continuing to |survive on it|.

Author addresses readers directly to persuade them to accept her claim.

Repetition and contrast make the statement memorable.

I need to keep reading to figure out the point of this repetition.

306   Unit 4

BACKGROUND

Ann Leckie (b. 1966) *is an award-winning science fiction author. She has published many short stories but perhaps is best known for her novel* Ancillary Justice, *the first volume in the highly praised* Imperial Radch *series. The selection you are about to read, however, is persuasive nonfiction—an argument. It is Leckie's introduction to a feature in* Wired *magazine that explains problems humans face when they leave the relative safety of Earth.*

CHALLENGES FOR SPACE EXPLORATION

Argument by Ann Leckie

SETTING A PURPOSE

As you read, remember that this selection is an introduction to a longer piece, filled with specific challenges. Think about what Leckie says here about the challenges of space exploration in general and how she feels about facing those challenges.

1 Thousands of years ago, when our ancestors came to the sea, they built boats and sailed tremendous distances to islands they could not have known were there. Why?

2 Probably for the same reason we look up at the moon and the stars and say, "What's up there? Could we go there? Maybe we could go there." Because it's something human beings do.

3 Space is, of course, **infinitely** more hostile to human life than the surface of the sea; escaping Earth's gravity **entails** a good deal more work and expense than shoving off from the shore. But those boats were the cutting-edge technology of their time. Voyagers carefully planned their expensive, dangerous journeys, and many of them died trying to find out what was beyond the horizon. So why keep doing it?

Notice & Note

Use the side margins to notice and note signposts in the text.

LANGUAGE CONVENTIONS

Annotate: In paragraph 1, mark the introductory phrase that is set off by a comma.

Analyze: Why is it helpful to have a comma there?

infinitely
(ĭn´fə-nĭt-lē) *adv. Infinitely* means to a great extent, or with no limits.

entail
(ĕn-tāl´) *v.* To *entail* means to have or require.

Challenges for Space Exploration 307

TEACH

 For **listening support** for students at varying proficiency levels, see the **Text X-Ray** on page 304C.

ANALYZE REPETITION

Remind students that repetition is a rhetorical device, one of many that authors use to draw attention to their ideas. (**Answer:** *The repetition draws readers to the idea that there are many strong reasons for humans to explore space, especially to find places other than Earth where humans can live.*)

ANALYZE AUTHOR'S PURPOSE

The paragraph begins with the final repetition of the phrase "I could tell you," and continues with a summing up of the reasons the author gives for her conclusion: "Maybe we could go there." The words and the tone together make up her argument. (**Answer:** *The tone is hopeful, positive, perhaps inspirational.*)

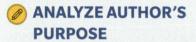 TEXT IN FOCUS

Previewing the Text Have students view the Text in Focus video on this page of their eBook to learn how to preview a nonfiction text. Then have students use Text In Focus Practice to apply what they have learned.

CRITICAL VOCABULARY

crucial: There are some things that are so important that they must be done if we are to keep existing.

ASK STUDENTS what might be crucial to our surviving on the planet. (*uniting behind a project that doesn't involve killing one another*)

habitat: The article emphasizes that we must find places in space where people can live.

ASK STUDENTS why a habitat would be necessary on Mars or the moons of Jupiter. (*Humans would need a safe home to survive in hostile environments.*)

NOTICE & NOTE

ANALYZE REPETITION
Annotate: Mark the clause that is repeated in paragraphs 4–8.
Analyze: How does the author's use of repetition help her support her claim?

crucial
(krōō´shəl) *adj.* Something that is *crucial* is extremely important or significant.

habitat
(hăb´ĭ-tăt´) *n.* In this instance, a *habitat* is a structure that provides a controlled environment for living in very hostile or even deadly locations.

ANALYZE AUTHOR'S PURPOSE
Annotate: Mark the words and phrases in paragraph 8 that help shape the tone of the paragraph.
Interpret: What tone, or attitude toward the subject, does the writing convey?

---

4 I could tell you about spinoff technologies, ranging from small products of convenience to discoveries that might feed millions or prevent deadly accidents or save the lives of the sick and injured.

5 I could tell you that we shouldn't keep all our eggs in this increasingly fragile basket—one good meteor strike and we all join the non-avian dinosaurs. And have you noticed the weather lately?

6 I could tell you that it might be good for us to unite behind a project that doesn't involve killing one another, that does involve understanding our home planet and the ways we survive on it and what things are **crucial** to our continuing to survive on it.

7 I could tell you that moving farther out into the solar system might be a good plan, if humanity is lucky enough to survive the next 5.5 billion years and the sun expands enough to fry the Earth.

8 I could tell you all those things: all the reasons we should find some way to live away from this planet, to build space stations and moon bases and cities on Mars and **habitats** on the moons of Jupiter. All the reasons we should, if we manage that, look out at the stars beyond our sun and say, "Could we go there? Maybe we could go there."

9 It's a huge, dangerous, maybe impossible project. But that's never stopped humans from trying anyway.

10 Humanity was born on Earth. Are we going to stay here? I suspect—I hope—the answer is no.

Inset image: An interplanetary vehicle orbits Mars.
Background image: a supernova

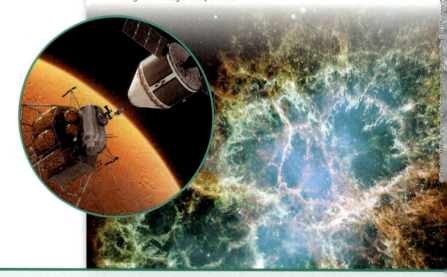

NOTICE & NOTE

CHECK YOUR UNDERSTANDING

Answer these questions before moving on to the **Analyze the Text** section on the following page.

1 The author points out that our ancestors sailed great distances to unknown places in order to —

  A express that it is important to go to new places

  B suggest that it is human nature to be explorers

  C warn about the risks of going to unknown places

  D describe what might have happened to our ancestors

2 In paragraph 5, the author states that <u>we shouldn't keep our eggs in this increasingly fragile basket</u>. What does she mean?

  F We need to create a safer environment on Earth.

  G We must focus on the threat of meteor strikes.

  H We must increase food production on Earth.

  J We need to find other suitable planets to live on.

3 Which of the following is an example of repetition?

  A *And have you noticed the weather lately?* (paragraph 5)

  B *"Could we go there? Maybe we could go there."* (paragraph 8)

  C *But that's never stopped humans from trying anyway.* (paragraph 9)

  D *Humanity was born on Earth. Are we going to stay here?* (paragraph 10)

Challenges for Space Exploration 309

TEACH

CHECK YOUR UNDERSTANDING

Have students answer the questions independently.

Answers:

1. B
2. J
3. B

If students answer any questions incorrectly, have them reread the text to confirm their understanding. Then they may proceed to ANALYZE THE TEXT on p. 310.

 ENGLISH LEARNER SUPPORT

Oral Assessment Use the following questions to assess students' comprehension and speaking skills:

1. Why did the author say that our ancestors sailed great distances to unknown places? *(The author wanted to suggest that it is human nature to be explorers.)*

2. Does the author think humans should live only on Earth? *(No)* Where does the author think humans should go? *(other planets)*

APPLY

ANALYZE THE TEXT
Possible answers:

1. **DOK 4:** *The central claim is that humans should look beyond Earth for other planets to live on. The claim is hinted at throughout but is not clearly stated until the end.*

2. **DOK 2:** *The author explains that there would be spinoff benefits—for example, technologies to feed millions or prevent accidents; we should have a back-up plan in case Earth is threatened with destruction; a common mission would unite humanity and help us understand our planet.*

3. **DOK 3:** *Both are examples of cutting-edge technology (for their times) that allow humans to explore unknown places.*

4. **DOK 2:** *The author's use of repetition gives the argument a tone of urgency. The author expresses the attitude that space exploration is a matter of survival for humanity.*

5. **DOK 4:** *The author contrasts the seeming impossibility of sending human explorers into space with humanity's history of accepting challenges that seem impossible. It ties in well with the overall argument that there are strong reasons for having humans explore space.*

RESEARCH

Suggest to students that they look online for reliable sources of information about space exploration. Remind them that sources like NASA and the Smithsonian are often helpful for this kind of research.

Extend Scientists track weather and make sure conditions are good before take-off. Engineers and scientists try to make sure that there are no problems associated with the spacecraft. Spacecraft are coated with materials that help protect astronauts from radiation.

310   Unit 4

 RESPOND

ANALYZE THE TEXT
Support your responses with evidence from the text.   **NOTEBOOK**

1. **Analyze** What is the claim of the author's argument? Where is that claim stated most clearly?

2. **Summarize** Describe some of the reasons the author gives in support of her claim.

3. **Compare** According to the author, how were boats that set sail thousands of years ago like modern spaceships?

4. **Infer** How does the author's use of repetition convey tone, or her attitude toward space exploration? How does it help her achieve her purpose?

5. **Evaluate** Does the author's voice, or unique use of language, make her argument more or less effective? Explain.

RESEARCH

RESEARCH TIP
Remember to evaluate the websites to determine if they provide up-to-date and reliable information. Comparing information from several sites can be helpful.

Humans have been traveling into space for decades. They have orbited Earth and landed on the moon. Some have even lived for months at a time in space. However, space exploration is not without risk. Research some of the risks involved with going into space. Use several sources and record the information you find in the chart below.

RISK	PROBLEMS ASSOCIATED WITH RISK
Take-off	*A spacecraft must reach high speeds to escape Earth's gravity. A problem with the spacecraft can cause it to break apart.*
Radiation	*Exposure to radiation is much higher in space. Radiation can damage cells and lead to cancer.*
Zero Gravity	*Circulation changes; blood pools in head and chest, causing high blood pressure. Muscles waste and fat develops. Bones lose calcium.*

Extend Work with a partner to research and explain what scientists and engineers do to reduce one particular risk. Share your information with another pair of students.

310   Unit 4

WHEN STUDENTS STRUGGLE . . .

Reteach Repetition Point out that the author begins paragraphs 4-8 with the phrase "I could tell you . . ." Have students locate each sentence in their text and take turns reading each aloud with a partner. Remind students that authors use repetition to stir emotions in readers. Have students work with a partner to answer the questions: What does the author want you to feel when she repeats the phrase "I could tell you..."? Then have pairs work together with another group to compare their answers.

CREATE AND DISCUSS

Write a Poem Write a poem in which an astronaut speaker considers the risks and sacrifices that she or he would face on a space mission.

- ❏ Make a list of feelings and ideas you have about the topic.
- ❏ Think about the main idea or message you want your speaker to express, even if she or he does not state it directly.
- ❏ Choose concrete words and phrases related to the topic that create strong images and appeal to the five senses.
- ❏ Include repetition, which is an effective rhetorical device in poetry as well as in nonfiction writing.

Listen for a Poem's Message Read your astronaut poem to a partner and listen to your partner's poem. Compare and discuss the poems.

- ❏ Take turns reading your poems aloud. Read with expression.
- ❏ As your partner reads, listen carefully to interpret the poem's message. Pay particular attention to specific words and phrases that stand out to you. (You may want to write them down or ask your partner to read the poem a second time.)
- ❏ Discuss which words and phrases convey each poem's message and what makes those words so powerful.

RESPOND TO THE ESSENTIAL QUESTION

? Why is the idea of space exploration both inspiring and unnerving?

Gather Information Review your annotations and notes on "Challenges for Space Exploration." Then, add relevant details to your Response Log. As you determine which information to include, think about:

- why space exploration is important
- the risks involved in space exploration

At the end of the unit, you may want to refer to your notes when you write an argument.

RESPOND

 Go to the **Writing Studio** for more on planning and drafting text.

 Go to the **Speaking and Listening Studio** for help with listening to literature, reading it aloud, and having a partner discussion.

ACADEMIC VOCABULARY

As you write and discuss what you learned from the argument, be sure to use the Academic Vocabulary words. Check off each of the words that you use.

- ❏ complex
- ❏ potential
- ❏ rely
- ❏ stress
- ❏ valid

Challenges for Space Exploration 311

APPLY

CREATE AND DISCUSS

Write a Poem Point out to students that the research they did to complete the chart on page 310 can be a source of ideas for their poem. Remind students that they should use what they have learned about tone and voice to express their ideas in a way that will engage their readers.

For **writing support** for students at varying proficiency levels, see the **Text X-Ray** on page 304D.

Listen for a Poem's Message Remind students to pay close attention to their partner's reading of the poem. Tell students to listen for the key point made in the poem. Is it about danger? Does it express joy at being in space? What is the writer saying about his or her personal feelings? Emphasize that students are to find positive aspects of the poem to comment on. Point out that many poets write several drafts of a poem and continue to polish their work until they find it acceptable. As students compare their poems, remind them that a poem is a personal expression and that poems on the same subject can be very different in form and content.

RESPOND TO THE ESSENTIAL QUESTION

Allow time for students to add details from "Challenges for Space Exploration" to their Unit 4 Response Logs.

APPLY

CRITICAL VOCABULARY

Answers:

1. habitat
2. infinitely
3. entail
4. crucial

VOCABULARY STRATEGY: Etymology

Answers:

infinite: Latin, from in- ("not") + fīnīre ("to limit"); It corresponds to the current meaning of the word, "limitless."

entail: Middle English, from en- ("make") + taile ("legal limitation"); One current meaning of the word corresponds with this meaning.

crucial: Latin, from crucis ("crossroads"); This meaning is somewhat related to the current meaning, "important to the determination of an outcome."

habitat: Latin, from habitāre ("to dwell"); This is closely related to the current definition, "an environment suitable for living in."

 RESPOND

WORD BANK
infinitely
entail
crucial
habitat

 Go to the **Vocabulary Studio** for more on etymology.

CRITICAL VOCABULARY

Practice and Apply Write the Critical Vocabulary word asked for in each question. Be prepared to explain your response.

1. Which word goes with *environment*? _____
2. Which word goes with *limitless*? _____
3. Which word goes with *require* and *involve*? _____
4. Which word goes with *important*? _____

VOCABULARY STRATEGY: Etymology

Etymology is the origin and historical development of a word. When you study a word's history and origin, you can find out when, where, and how the word came to be used. For example, a dictionary entry for *solar* will tell you that the word comes from Middle English but that it can be traced back to the Latin word *sōlāris*, from *sōl*, which means "sun." *Solar* means "of or relating to the sun."

Practice and Apply Follow these steps to record the etymology of each Critical Vocabulary word in the chart below.

- Look up the word in a print or digital dictionary.
- Find the etymology of the word after the definition(s). If you are not sure about how to read the etymology, you can check the front or the back of a print dictionary. There should be a section that explains how the etymology is noted and what the abbreviations mean.
- Write the origin of the word and its original meaning in the chart below. Is the word's current meaning related to its original meaning? If so, explain how.

WORD	ETYMOLOGY/MEANING
infinitely	
entail	
crucial	
habitat	

 ENGLISH LEARNER SUPPORT

Practice Vocabulary Spell out the parts of the words in the vocabulary: in-fin-ite, en-tail, cru-cial, hab-i-tat. Have students copy the parts of the words, sound out the parts, and then sound out the word altogether. Make sure that the pronunciations of the parts match how they should sound, not how students may think they should sound, e.g., *ite* should be pronounced "it," not "iteuh." **SUBSTANTIAL/MODERATE**

LANGUAGE CONVENTIONS: Commas After Introductory Phrases

Writers place a comma after most introductory phrases to signal the reader to pause and to avoid confusion. (Sometimes you will see a very short introductory phrase without a comma, but a comma there is not incorrect.) When you write, read your sentences aloud, noticing where you pause in the early part of a sentence. The places where you pause probably need to be punctuated by a comma. Study these examples based on "Challenges for Space Exploration":

> <u>Without a doubt</u>, the long-term effects of zero gravity are a health risk for astronauts.
>
> <u>Working in space</u>, robots and other machines can perform tasks that are too dangerous for humans.

Read the two sentences aloud, noticing where you pause. The comma after *doubt* in the first sentence signals the reader to pause. The comma after *space* in the second sentence signals the reader to pause and also avoids confusion. Without the comma, the reader might think at first that the writer is referring to space robots. Additional examples are shown in the following chart.

PURPOSE OF COMMA	EXAMPLE
To signal the reader to pause	<u>To understand the health risks of living in space</u>, scientists have studied astronauts living on the International Space Station.
To avoid confusion	<u>Under the rules of NASA</u>, astronauts must meet certain health requirements.

Practice and Apply These sentences include introductory phrases that need to be punctuated with commas. Read each sentence and insert the comma where necessary.

1. Having performed the experiments Anita recorded her findings.
2. Without better protection from radiation people could not possibly live on Mars.
3. Outside the laboratory five rockets blasted off and flew for about a mile.
4. On the other hand there is no reason to doubt that humans will eventually land on the moons of Jupiter.
5. To travel to other planets all I need to do is read my favorite science fiction stories.

RESPOND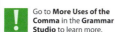

Go to **More Uses of the Comma** in the **Grammar Studio** to learn more.

APPLY

LANGUAGE CONVENTIONS: Commas After Introductory Phrases

Tell students that it is sometimes helpful to look for the subject of the sentence first, and then place the comma before the subject. For example, in the first sentence, "Anita" is the subject, the comma is placed right before "Anita."

1. Having performed the experiments, Anita carefully recorded her findings.
2. Without better protection from radiation, people could not possibly live on Mars.
3. Outside the laboratory, five rockets blasted off and flew for about a mile.
4. On the other hand, there is no reason to doubt that humans will eventually land on the moons of Jupiter.
5. To travel to other planets, all I need to do is read science fiction stories.

PLAN

WHAT IF WE WERE ALONE?
Poem by William Stafford

GENRE ELEMENTS
POETRY
Remind students that **poetry** is a literary form structured in relatively short lines, grouped into stanzas or sentences. Much poetry is built around images, feelings, and impressions. Poetic detail is written to resonate in frames of sound and meaning that use graphical elements to express ideas and themes.

LEARNING OBJECTIVES
- Read and demonstrate comprehension of poetry.
- Infer multiple themes using text evidence.
- Analyze the effects of graphical elements such as capitalization, punctuation, and line length in poetry.
- Write a poem that conforms to basic poetic structure.
- Discuss with a partner the features of the text using the key term *theme*.
- **Language** Discuss the features of the text using the term *graphical elements*.

TEXT COMPLEXITY

Quantitative Measures	What If We Were Alone?	Lexile: N/A
Qualitative Measures	**Ideas Presented** Multiple levels, use of symbolism, greater demand for inference	
	Structures Used Complex, does not follow chronology or sequence	
	Language Used Implied meanings; allusive, figurative language; complex sentence structures	
	Knowledge Required Explores complex ideas	

314A Unit 4

PLAN

RESOURCES

Online

- Unit 4 Response Log
- 🔊 Selection Audio
- 📖 Reading Studio: Notice & Note
- 📝 Writing Studio: Writing as a Process
- 💬 Speaking and Listening Studio: Analyzing and Evaluating Presentations
- ✓ "What If We Were Alone?" Selection Test

SUMMARIES

English

William Stafford's poem "What If We Were Alone" begins with the question "What if there weren't any stars?" Stafford then tells us that the existence of stars demonstrates that "There is something beyond," hinting that humans are not alone in the universe. One way to look at the poem is to read it as saying that if people did not impose limits on their thinking, then it would be easier to "look outward," to see that there are many things to be discovered. The figurative language of lines 15-21 speak of an almost mystical form harmony in nature.

Spanish

La exploración espacial comienza en la imaginación: cuando miramos extasiados las noches despejadas resplandecientes con "brillantes (puntos) luminosos". Por milenios, los astrónomos se han inspirado a preguntarse acerca del alcance, forma y magnitud del espacio. Especialmente en años recientes, las investigaciones refinadas han nutrido la nueva visión de la naturaleza y los orígenes de nuestra "compañía" cósmica. Pero las nuevas respuestas engendran aún más preguntas, mientras los misterios permanecen en los cielos para ser explorados y reflexionados por poetas.

 ## SMALL-GROUP OPTIONS

Have students work in small groups to read and discuss the selection.

Numbered Heads Together

- Have students read the selection. Then form them into groups of four, designating each member as number 1, 2, 3, or 4.
- Ask: *What are the major themes or messages of "What If We Were Alone?"*
- Have students discuss their responses in groups.
- Call a number from 1 to 4. Ask that "numbered" student to respond for the group.

Think-Pair-Share

- Have students read and analyze "What If We Were Alone?" Then ask: *How does the poem make the argument that we are not alone?*
- Have students think about the question individually and take notes.
- Have pairs discuss their ideas about the question.
- Finally, ask pairs to share their responses with the class.

PLAN

Text X-Ray: English Learner Support
for "What if We Were Alone?"

Use the Text X-Ray and the supports and scaffolds in the Teacher's Edition to help guide students at different proficiency levels through the selection.

INTRODUCE THE SELECTION

DISCUSS POETRY AND THEME

In this lesson, students will need to be able to discuss **poetry** and **theme**. Provide the following definitions:

- "What If We Were Alone?" is a *poem* written in free-verse; it doesn't have a traditional rhyme scheme or consistent meter.
- A *theme* is a central idea in a literary work. (Spanish cognates: *poema, tema*)

Explain to students that poetry takes many forms: free verse allows the author to create sentences (or lines) that are almost like everyday language. Ask students to observe that short poems can be powerful: important or playful themes can be created with very few words. Model the following line frame for a poem: Ask students to come up with their own "What if" beginnings for poems.

What if Earth had no _____? (oceans, trees, people, nighttime)

CULTURAL REFERENCES

The following words and phrases may be unfamiliar to students:

- *Galileo* (line 4): invented a type of telescope; his observations helped change scientific theories.
- *cold space* (lines 8 and 9) outer space beyond Earth's atmosphere
- *beckons* (paragraph 11): to call to; to use gestures to come nearer, to offer an invitation
- *each glittering point of light* (line 13) the stars
- *moon rolls through the trees* (line 15): a description of the moon rising as seen through the branches of trees
- *voice floats from rock to sandbar, to log:* (line 17): the personification of the sound of water

LISTENING

Understand the Theme

Explain to students that the theme of a poem is the message of the poem, or the poem's most important idea. Tell students to pay attention to details that seem important and ask what these details have in common in order to determine the theme of the poem.

Have students listen as you play the selection audio once. Then, read the first two stanzas aloud. Use the following supports with students at varying proficiency levels:

- Tell students that a poem's theme might also be seen as its "big idea." Display the word *idea* in large type, and gesture to indicate "big." Note that *idea* is the same in English and Spanish. Ask students to give a thumbs-up signal for *yes* and a thumbs-down for *no* after you ask a question. Say, *The author says that "something is out there." Does that mean that there is something beyond the stars? (thumbs-up) Is that a big idea? (thumbs-up)* **SUBSTANTIAL**
- Have intermediate students join beginners at first, and then ask them an additional question: *What do these words mean: "Each glittering point of light"? (They are all stars.)* **MODERATE**
- Have students listen to the audio selection. Allow them to play it twice. Ask them to take notes about what they think the main idea is in the poem. **LIGHT**

PLAN

SPEAKING

Discuss Graphical Elements

Have students discuss the features of the text using the key term *graphical elements*. Circulate around the room to make sure students understand the key term.

Use the following supports with students at varying proficiency levels:

- Display two large white cards: one with a comma and one with a dash. Model walking, pausing, and resuming. Pause for shorter and longer intervals to represent each punctuation mark. Ask students to take turns holding up the correct card. Have each student read one line of the poem aloud to a classmate and then listen to his or her classmate. **SUBSTANTIAL**
- Display two large white cards: one with a comma and one with a dash. Read the poem aloud. Ask students to take turns holding up the correct card when you pause. Have each student read one line of the poem aloud to a classmate and then listen to his or her classmate. **MODERATE**
- Invite students in groups to discuss the use of graphical elements in "What If We Were Alone?," identifying dramatic line breaks, capitalization, and punctuation. **LIGHT**

READING

Read for Understanding

Tell students that poets play with ideas and images, sound and meaning to develop theme through complex language.

Read the poem with students. Use the following supports with students at varying proficiency levels:

- Review concept vocabulary for the poem, including the terms *connection* and *nature*. (Spanish cognates: *conexión, naturaleza*) Display both words. Ask: *Are we all part of nature?* (yes) **SUBSTANTIAL**
- Have students read this sentence with you: *The moon rolls through the trees, rises from them, and waits*. Explain that this means that the moon is rising as seen through the trees. Ask: *Does the moon really roll?* (no) *What is the moon is shaped like?* (a circle, disk, ball) **MODERATE**
- Ask students to read the poem. Then invite them to form groups to discuss its theme or themes, or "big ideas." **LIGHT**

WRITING

Write a Poem

Work with students to read the writing assignment on p. 321.

Use the following supports with students at varying proficiency levels:

- Review basic vocabulary for the poem: *curious, frightened, angry*. (Spanish cognates/synonyms: *curioso, asustado, enojado*) Invite students to come up with synonyms. (*wondering, scared, mad*) Ask students to record the words in their notebooks. **SUBSTANTIAL**
- Provide sentence frames such as the following that students can use to draft their poems: *The humans scare us when they _____*. Remind students to complete the frames from the perspective of aliens observing humans. **MODERATE**
- Working in pairs or small groups, invite students to review drafts of each other's poems. Encourage students to make suggestions regarding theme and structure, including graphical elements. **LIGHT**

TEACH

? **Connect to the ESSENTIAL QUESTION**

"What If We Were Alone" inspires readers to consider that we are almost certainly *not* by ourselves, we are not "everything" in the vast cosmos. The poem suggests "we are led outward" by our natures, or by nature itself, to consider "something beyond;" to hear the voice of nature in different forms. Exploration starts in the imagination. The poet begins the journey with a sense of certainty that "something is out there."

ANALYZE & APPLY

WHAT IF WE WERE ALONE?

Poem by **William Stafford**

? **ESSENTIAL QUESTION:**

Why is the idea of space exploration both inspiring and unnerving?

GET READY

QUICK START

The poem you are about to read challenges the reader to consider the idea of Earth's being alone in the universe. Think about your feelings when you are lonely and what makes you feel connected to the world around you. With a partner, create a web like this one, describing activities or people that help you feel connected. An example is given.

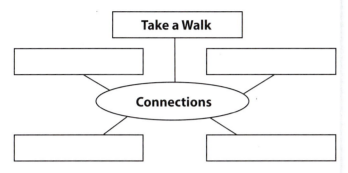

ANALYZE GRAPHICAL ELEMENTS

"What If We Were Alone?" is an example of **free verse**, a poem without regular rhyme or rhythm. The lines in the poem don't rhyme and it has strong rhythm in only a few places. Even without rhyme or rhythm, the poem has ways to affect the reader. Among these are **graphical elements**—the visual ways the poem is represented on the page. Here are a few common graphical elements:

CAPITALIZATION	We expect each line of a poem to start with a capital letter. When that doesn't happen, a thought probably runs from one line to the next.
PUNCTUATION	A dash signals a break in thought. Periods, question marks, and exclamation points in the middle of lines indicate pauses and changes in ideas. A comma signals a shorter pause, especially in the middle of a line. When you find these kinds of pauses, stop and think carefully about what you are reading.
LINE LENGTH	If you see lines in a poem that are much longer or shorter than usual, consider what effects they have on the poem's meaning.

All three kinds of graphical elements appear in "What If We Were Alone?" When you encounter one of them, stop and think about what the poet wants you to remember at that moment.

GENRE ELEMENTS: POETRY

- a form of literature structured into relatively short lines, often arranged into groups (stanzas)
- often focuses on feelings and impressions, and presented in ways that create images in the reader's mind
- often features sound devices that help create meaning
- includes graphical elements, such as capitalization, punctuation, and line length to help express ideas and themes

What If We Were Alone?   315

TEACH

QUICK START

Have students read the Quick Start prompt, and invite them to share the things (or people) that give them a sense of connectedness. Then, ask them to expand on that web by considering connections on a broader scale. Ask: *How are we all connected to the things William Stafford writes about? What is the "company" we glimpse when we look at the stars, the "something" that is out there in cold space? How might our perspective change if the skies were empty of the moon and stars?*

ANALYZE GRAPHICAL ELEMENTS

Tell students to find meaning in verse by reading it according to the cues on the typeset page to *start, pause,* and *stop*. Remind students that verse is better grasped when read aloud, speed is changed, and points of emphasis are followed for capitalization, punctuation, and line breaks.

Have students turn for a moment to the poem on p. 349 and follow along as you read lines 1–7. Ask these questions to help them analyze graphical elements:

- Why might the poet lowercase the word earth *in line 2?* (to show it is just another heavenly body). Why might he break the line after "earth"? (Possible response: to leave the meaning hanging.)
- How do the dashes change how you read lines 5–7? (The first dash makes me stress the phrase "no Galileo." The second dash makes me stress the word Look. Read this way, both the phrase and the word might be part of an urgent argument.)
- How is understanding of verse enhanced by reading it aloud? (Responses will vary.)

What if We Were Alone?   **315**

TEACH

ANALYZE THEME

Remind students of the difference between **theme** and its subject: The subject of "A Christmas Carol" is a struggle between three spirits and an old British miser. One of its themes, or messages, is that "people can change."

Review the bulleted items with students, asking them to take notes in responding to the questions. Then, have them use their notes to determine themes of the poem.

Suggest that students use these questions to help them analyze theme:

- How can a theme be "between the lines?" How does the poet's message develop and take shape over the course of lines and stanzas?
- What ideas or images stay with you from the poem? Do these things suggest a theme?
- Why would theme be treated differently in a poem than in an argument?

■ English Learner Support

Understand Academic Language Make sure students understand words and terms used in the lesson, such as *poem*, *theme*, and *graphic*. (Spanish cognates: *poema*, *tema*.)
SUBSTANTIAL/MODERATE

✏ ANNOTATION MODEL

Suggest that students use a highlighter and arrows to annotate the poem so as to direct attention to supporting notes about theme. Point out that they may follow this suggestion or use their own system for marking up the selections in their write-in texts.

 GET READY

ANALYZE THEME

Poems like "What If We Were Alone?" often have a **theme,** or a lesson about life or human nature that the poet shares with the reader. Examples of themes include statements such as "We must face challenges with courage" or "Friends are a positive part of life."

A theme is rarely stated directly at the beginning or end of a poem. Instead, the poet usually develops the message over the course of a poem. It is up to you, the reader, to read closely (several times, if possible, and maybe aloud as well as silently) and think carefully about questions such as these:

- Does the title of the poem hint at an important idea?
- What seems to be the main subject of the poem?
- If the poem has several **stanzas** (groups of lines), how does the main idea of each stanza relate to the main idea of the other stanzas?
- Is there a change of setting or focus in the poem? If so, why does the change happen?
- Are there words or phrases that are repeated or that stand out in other ways?
- What images come to mind as you read the poem?
- What do you know about the speaker of the poem? What seems to be important to the speaker?

As you think about answers to these questions, ask yourself, "What big message about life, or about human nature, is the poem trying to tell me?" Your response probably will be a theme—and possibly the main theme—of the poem.

ANNOTATION MODEL   NOTICE & NOTE

As you read, consider how the poet develops a theme. You also can mark graphical elements and other details that stand out to you. This model shows one reader's notes about the first stanza of "What If We Were Alone?"

> What if there weren't any stars?
> What if only the sun and the earth
> circled alone in the sky? What if
> no one ever found anything outside
> 5 this world right here?—no Galileo
> could say, "Look—it is out there,
> a hint of whether we are everything."

Three question marks = three questions. Why does the poet want me to think about these questions?

The poet includes a made-up quotation about space. The theme may have something to do with a lesson we can learn from space.

316   Unit 4

BACKGROUND

William Stafford (1914–1993) was born in Hutchinson, Kansas. He attended the University of Kansas and earned a BA and MA. He later earned a PhD from the University of Iowa. *Traveling Through the Dark,* his first major collection of poems, was published in 1962 and won the National Book Award in 1963. Many of Stafford's poems have roots in the nature that he experienced in the West, and they focus on the lessons that nature can teach.

WHAT IF WE WERE ALONE?

Poem by William Stafford

SETTING A PURPOSE

As you read, pay attention to the effect of graphical elements and to the words and phrases that catch your attention. How do these aspects of the poem work together to suggest one or more themes for the poem?

What if there weren't any stars?
What if only the sun and the earth
circled alone in the sky? What if
no one ever found anything outside
5   this world right here?—no Galileo
could say, "Look—it is out there,
a hint of whether we are everything."

NOTICE & NOTE

Notice & Note

Use the side margins to notice and note signposts in the text.

WORDS OF THE WISER

Notice & Note: Mark the words that the speaker imagines Galileo saying.

Interpret: How are Galileo's words a response to the title of the poem?

What If We Were Alone?   317

TEACH

BACKGROUND

After reading the background note, tell students that William Stafford was a person who followed his principles with action. He was a pacifist: a person who does not believe in using violence for any reason. Rather than go to World War II as a soldier, he registered with the government as a conscientious objector. Stafford was allowed to work conserving and repairing forests in Arkansas and California. He spent four years in work camps living close to nature. It was there that he formed the habit of waking early to write—a practice he continued for the rest of his life. William Stafford did not publish his first book of poetry until he was forty-six years old.

SETTING A PURPOSE

Direct students to use the Setting a Purpose prompt to focus their reading. Point out the graphical features in the poem. Tell them to take note of any word, phrase, or idea that captures their attention or interests them. Tell them that keeping track of their first impressions may be a valuable way to begin examining and enjoying the poem. Challenge students to try to use some of the graphical elements in their own poems.

▶ WORDS OF THE WISER

Explain to students that **Words of the Wiser** cite a definitive source: often an insightful, mature fictional character, or in this case the legendary astronomer and polymath Galileo.

(**Answer**: *The question the title poses is answered by the words Stafford gives to Galileo: No, we are not alone. There is something beyond us. It is important to remember that for thousands of years, many people thought that the universe simply ended.*)

 For **listening support** for students at varying proficiency levels, see the **Text X-Ray** on page 314C.

🗨 ENGLISH LEARNER SUPPORT

Analyze Theme   Have students gather in small groups. Invite one group member to read the Analyze Theme Question on p. 318 aloud. Then, have the group engage in reciprocal teaching techniques to identify the poem's themes while rereading the poem. Ask all group members to offer answers, with one or two students in each group taking notes.
LIGHT

What if We Were Alone?   **317**

TEACH

ANALYZE GRAPHICAL ELEMENTS

Remind students that a line break tends to emphasize the word or words that precede it and that a dash signals a pause that also modifies inflection. (**Answer:** *Both dashes encourage the reader to slow down and think about what the poet is saying. In line 6, it calls attention to the idea that space may have the answer to the questions being asked. In line 8, in emphasizes that space is cold and so does not seem a likely place for answers—but that is where the answers may be, just the same.*)

ANALYZE THEME

Note that a theme may develop through shifts in perspective, as the poet makes at line 15. Remind students that the author remains close to his essential theme, even as his focus and style varies from the second stanza to the third. (**Answer:** *No; in line 15, the poem connects the moon to the earth and then gives details only about the earth. The theme of the poem, therefore, must be a lesson that includes both what is in space and what is on the earth.*)

NOTICE & NOTE

ANALYZE GRAPHICAL ELEMENTS

Annotate: Mark the dashes in lines 5–8.

Compare: Are the dashes used the same way in each line? Explain.

ANALYZE THEME

Annotate: In line 15, mark something found in space and something found on Earth.

Draw Conclusions: Does the poem's theme only relate to space? Explain.

Look out at the stars. Yes—cold
space. Yes, we are so distant that
10 the mind goes hollow to think it.
But something is out there. Whatever
our limits, we are led outward. We glimpse
company. Each glittering point of light
beckons: "There is something beyond."

15 The moon rolls through the trees, rises
from them, and waits. In the river all
night a voice floats from rock
to sandbar, to log. What kind of listening
can follow quietly enough? We bow, and
20 the voice that falls through the rapids
calls all the rocks by their secret names.

NOTICE & NOTE

TEACH

CHECK YOUR UNDERSTANDING

Answer these questions before moving on to the **Analyze the Text** section on the following page.

1. The poet uses questions in the first stanza in order to —
   A prove that everyone thinks about these questions
   B emphasize the seriousness of the question in the title
   C suggest that the universe really is an empty place
   D indicate that people think about space too much

2. According to the poem's speaker, what is the main purpose of the stars?
   F They encourage us to seek answers by looking beyond what we find familiar.
   G They urge us not to think about space because the universe is impossible to understand.
   H They remind us that we are limited and that human life is short.
   J They give us hope for a future in which we will travel among them.

3. In the third stanza, the voice that the speaker describes is a —
   A message from Galileo
   B message from the moon
   C power that exists throughout nature
   D listener that unites all human beings

What If We Were Alone? 319

CHECK YOUR UNDERSTANDING

Have students answer the questions independently.

Answers:
1. B
2. F
3. C

If they answer any questions incorrectly, have them reread the text to confirm their understanding. Then they may proceed to ANALYZE THE TEXT on p. 320.

 ENGLISH LEARNER SUPPORT

Oral Assessment To gauge comprehension and speaking skills, conduct an informal assessment. Walk around the class, talking with students and asking these questions:

- *Does the poem say that we are we alone, or not alone?* (not alone) **SUBSTANTIAL**
- *Does the poet say that there is "something beyond"?* (yes) *What are glittering points of light?* (stars) **MODERATE**
- *Is being "connected" to nature one of the main themes? How do you know?* (Answers will vary.) **LIGHT**
- *Discuss what the poet means by: "Look—it is out there, a hint of whether we are everything."* (Answers will vary.)

APPLY

ANALYZE THE TEXT

Possible answers

1. **DOK 2:** *The phrase "What if" is repeated, which may indicate that the speaker is anxious about this issue. Also, the three successive questions are essentially asking the same thing, which suggests urgency.*

2. **DOK 2:** *A dash can indicate a break in someone's thinking, and that may be what is happening here: After asking the questions, the speaker suddenly thinks about Galileo (someone who indeed has "found anything outside / this world right here").*

3. **DOK 3:** *In the second stanza, the poet says that when one considers the distance of the stars, "the mind goes hollow." In the same stanza, he refers to being "led outward;" to a sense that we "glimpse company;" and to the call of starlight toward "something beyond." In the final stanza, he describes a "voice" that floats through nature that knows the "secret names" of rocks.*

4. **DOK 3:** *The theme may be that humans are not alone—we are connected to nature, a force everywhere. The thought appears in the reference to "company" beyond our own planet; in the connection between the moon and the trees; and in the suggestion that we attend to the "voice" that speaks through "the rapids."*

5. **DOK 4:** *The "words" belong to the "voice" that floats through nature. The poet suggests they are "wise" words by referring to following the voice quietly, even bowing to it.*

RESEARCH

Remind students they should confirm information they find by checking multiple websites and assessing the credibility of each one.

Connect Students may note that telescopes are a relatively modern invention: prior to the 17th century, humans tracked the movement of planets and satellites by eye. Students may discover that Galileo Galilei (1564-1642) has been called "the father of observational geometry." His study of the planets suggested *heliocentrism*, or planetary orbits around the sun.

320 Unit 4

RESPOND

ANALYZE THE TEXT

Support your responses with evidence from the text. NOTEBOOK

1. **Infer** What phrase is repeated in the title and the questions in the first stanza? What does this repetition indicate about the poem's speaker?

2. **Interpret** In line 5, why do you think a dash appears at the end of the third question?

3. **Compare** How does the poet suggest that both space and the earth itself are mysterious?

4. **Draw Conclusions** What do you think is the theme of "What If We Were Alone?" Why do you think so?

5. **Notice & Note** In the first stanza, you read some "words of the wiser" as spoken by Galileo. Whose "words" are described in the final stanza? What makes these "wise" words, too?

RESEARCH

RESEARCH TIP
When a topic is broad, such as astronomy, create a list of subtopics to use as key words in Internet searches. In this activity, you are given the subtopics. At other times, however, you will need to choose them. In that case, it can be helpful to start by reading an encyclopedia entry about the topic. Doing this can help you identify interesting subtopics.

People have been wondering about space for thousands of years. Astronomy is the scientific study of things that exist beyond Earth's atmosphere. With a partner, research these aspects of astronomy. You can use this graphic organizer to record your findings.

METHODS USED TO STUDY THE UNIVERSE	
In ancient times:	Today:

THREE TOPICS THAT ASTRONOMERS STUDY

TWO QUESTIONS THAT ASTRONOMERS TRY TO ANSWER

Connect In a small group, compare your findings. Discuss how you think astronomers view their work. How do you see that view addressed in "What If We Were Alone?"

320 Unit 4

WHEN STUDENTS STRUGGLE . . .

Reteach Theme If students struggle to grasp theme, suggest a well-known fairytale to them, such as Snow White. Invite students to tell the story aloud, and look up further details in a guided discussion. Ask: *What life lessons are conveyed in this story? What might be one or two of its themes?* (Vanity is self-destructive; jealousy is likewise; beauty does not equate with blessed lives, nor does wealth and power.) Ask students to review other fairy tales or fables and reference theories as to their themes.

For additional support, go to the **Reading Studio** and assign the following Level Up tutorial: **Theme**.

RESPOND

CREATE AND LISTEN

Write a Poem Imagine that an intelligent life form witnesses the arrival of a group of human space explorers who plan to start a colony. Create a poem written from the life form's point of view about the newcomers' arrival. The poem may use rhyme and rhythm, or it may be in free verse (like "What If We Were Alone?").

❏ Decide whether the life form is curious, frightened, or angry about the newcomers. Brainstorm words that express emotions.

❏ Consider how to include descriptions of what the life form is observing about the humans.

❏ Write a draft of your poem. Use graphical elements to help you express the message, or theme, that you want to convey.

❏ Revise your poem. Consider the specific effects the words, phrases, and graphical elements have.

Listen for the Theme Now share your poem with a partner. Take turns reading your poems aloud to each other with expression.

❏ Listen carefully as the poem is read. If you would like to hear it again, ask your partner to read it a second time.

❏ After the poems have been read, discuss your interpretation of each one's message, or theme.

❏ Give each other positive feedback about what works best in the poem or about how to revise the poem to strengthen its theme.

RESPOND TO THE ESSENTIAL QUESTION

 Why is the idea of space exploration both inspiring and unnerving?

Gather Information Review your annotations and notes on "What If We Were Alone?" Then, add relevant details to your Response Log. As you determine which information to include, think about:

- why people are fascinated by the stars
- whether exploring space would be wonderful or terrible
- how interactions with nature inform our interest in space

At the end of the unit, you can use your notes when you write an argument.

Go to **Writing as a Process** in the **Writing Studio** to learn more.

Go to **Analyzing and Evaluating Presentations** in the **Speaking and Listening Studio** for more details.

ACADEMIC VOCABULARY

As you write and discuss what you learned from the poem, be sure to use the Academic Vocabulary words. Check off each of the words that you use.

❏ complex
❏ potential
❏ rely
❏ stress
❏ valid

APPLY

CREATE AND LISTEN

Write a Poem After students have completed a draft, encourage them to read their poems aloud, either to themselves or to a partner. This should guide them to consider their use of sensory detail and language that expresses emotion in their work. Remind students to use graphical elements for poetic effect, including well-chosen line breaks, punctuation, and capitalization.

For **writing support** for students at varying proficiency levels, see the **Text X-Ray** on page 314D.

Listen for the Theme Have students form peer groups to critique each other's poems before presenting them to the class.

- Students should give concrete, specific ideas for how their peers might improve their work.
- Pairs should review the suggestions and decide which ones to incorporate into their poems, with a critical eye toward sharpening themes.

RESPOND TO THE ESSENTIAL QUESTION

Allow time for students to add details from "What If We Were Alone?" to their Unit 4 Response Logs.

PLAN

SEVEN MINUTES OF TERROR
Video

GENRE ELEMENTS
VIDEO

Remind students that the aim of all visual **media** is to interest the viewer through its choice of images and sound elements. **Informational videos**, like informational text, aim to provide viewers with facts and details that explain a particular topic. Successful informational videos provide this information in an exciting and interesting way, using a variety of visual and sound techniques.

LEARNING OBJECTIVES

- Analyze video elements.
- Conduct research about the rover *Curiosity*.
- Write a personal narrative about encountering a being from another planet.
- Deliver a presentation about video techniques.
- **Language** Identify the main idea in an informational video.

TEXT COMPLEXITY

Quantitative Measures	Seven Minutes of Terror	
Qualitative Measures	**Ideas Presented**	Literal, explicit, and direct with some difficult ideas
	Structure Used	Clear and chronological
	Language Used	Explicit with some complicated technical terms
	Knowledge Required	Some complex ideas beyond students' experiences

PLAN

RESOURCES

- Unit 4 Response Log
- Writing Studio: Writing Narratives
- Speaking and Listening Studio: Participating in Collaborative Discussions
- "Seven Minutes of Terror" Selection Test

SUMMARIES

English

"Seven Minutes of Terror" details the intricate procedures that the spacecraft carrying *Curiosity*, the NASA space rover, follows as it descends from the top of the atmosphere of Mars to a landing on the planet's surface. The "terror" refers to the extreme anxiety NASA engineers feel because they cannot control or even communicate with the rover during a procedure that is fraught with dangers. Several NASA engineers guide viewers through their remarkable technological feat in this exciting video.

Spanish

"Siete minutos de terror" detalla los intrincados procesos que *Curiosity*, el vehículo espacial de la NASA, sigue mientras desciende desde la parte superior de la atmósfera de Marte para aterrizar en la superficie del planeta. El terror se refiere a la ansiedad extrema que sienten los ingenieros de la NASA al no poder controlar o siquiera comunicarse con el vehículo durante el peligroso proceso. Varios ingenieros de la NASA guían a los espectadores a través de su impresionante hazaña tecnológica en este emocionante video.

SMALL-GROUP OPTIONS

Have students work in small groups to read and discuss the video.

Think-Pair-Share

- After students have viewed the video, have them work with a partner to discuss the problems *Curiosity* faced during each stage addressed in the video.
- Ask students to discuss its problems upon entering Martian atmosphere.
- Ask students to discuss the problems it faced during its descent to Mars.
- Ask students to discuss the problems it faced during its landing.

Pinwheel Discussion

- After students have viewed the video, ask them to create pinwheel formations of six per group.
- For the first rotation, ask students to discuss the video's aim.
- For the second rotation, ask students to discuss the video's visuals.
- For the third rotation, ask students to discuss the video's sound and narration.

PLAN

 Text X-Ray: English Learner Support
for "Seven Minutes of Terror"

Use the Text X-Ray and the supports and scaffolds in the Teacher's Edition to help guide students at different proficiency levels through the selection.

INTRODUCE THE SELECTION
DISCUSS ENGINEERING

Explain to students that this video describes how engineers built a spacecraft that could safely transport a vehicle to the surface of Mars. Give students the following background information:

- Engineers are people who create complex machines and systems.
- The Mars rover *Curiosity* is a vehicle that was designed to detect whether people could live on Mars.
- Informational videos rely on visual, sound, and story elements—such as animation, music, and scripts—to accurately describe their subjects.

Explain the title of the video and how it relates to the fear experienced by the engineers.

CULTURAL REFERENCES

The following words and phrases may be unfamiliar to students:

- *emotional reaction*: feeling
- *time pressure*: the anxious feeling that time is running out
- *aerodynamic drag*: a powerful force
- *zero margin of error*: no mistakes allowed
- *to get word*: to find out
- *collision course*: path that will lead to a crash

LISTENING

Identify the Main Idea

Tell students that informational videos, like informational texts, present ideas that are supported by facts and details. Viewers must listen carefully to the narration if they are to understand the point of the video.

Have students listen to the first 90 seconds of the video without watching it. Instruct students to focus on the narration. Use the following supports with students at varying proficiency levels:

- Tell students that you will ask questions about the narration. Ask questions that require signaling with thumbs-up or thumbs-down or single word answers. For example, ask: *Do the engineers know right away if everything went okay? (thumbs down) How long do they have to wait? 10 minutes? Seven minutes? (seven minutes)* **SUBSTANTIAL**
- Ask students to identify one main idea that is expressed in this portion of the video. (e.g., landing on Mars is difficult) **MODERATE**
- Ask students to identify two main ideas that are expressed in this portion of the video. (e.g., landing on Mars is difficult, computers do all the work of landing the spacecraft). **LIGHT**

PLAN

SPEAKING

Present Film Techniques

Direct students' attention to the oral presentation on p. 325. Use this practice to help them prepare for the larger-group summary. Circulate around the room to make sure students are using terms correctly.

Use the following supports with students at varying proficiency levels:

- Ask students: *What emotions do the visual/sound elements of the video make you feel?* Model a response. Supply students with a word bank. Encourage one-word answers and gestures. Write students' response words on the board. Then, have students pronounce the words properly, and ask for volunteers to define the terms. **SUBSTANTIAL**
- Supply pairs with word banks. Help them fill in sentence frames such as: *The most effective element in the video was the_____.* Have them read the sentences aloud to their partners. Listeners take notes on the presentation of the sentences to give to their partners. **MODERATE**
- Have students create an outline for presentation based on their notes from the small-group discussion. Then have them share it with a larger group. **LIGHT**

READING

Read for Information

Direct students' attention to the Background note on p. 323.

Use the following supports with students at varying proficiency levels:

- Have students echo-read the paragraph. Ask them to raise their hands if they need clarification of a word or phrase. Provide clarification by word or gesture. Then ask a yes-or-no question to see if they understand the word or phrase. Ask students for one-word responses when appropriate. **SUBSTANTIAL**
- Ask students to read the paragraph and identify two of NASA's most significant achievements. Encourage students to seek clarification when needed. **MODERATE**
- Ask students to read the paragraph and to provide evidence that NASA cooperates with other nations and improves the quality of life here on Earth. **LIGHT**

WRITING

Write a Personal Narrative

Work with students to read the writing assignment on p. 325.

Use the following supports with students at varying proficiency levels:

- Ask students for the details they would like to include in their narratives (where the being comes from, if it's a boy or a girl, etc.). Allow one- or two-word answers or gestures. Write sentences on the board using those words and have students copy the sentences into their notebooks. **SUBSTANTIAL**
- Provide sentence frames such as the following that students can use to craft their essays: *The being I met is from _____. The being looks like _____. The being and I met when I was _____.* **MODERATE**
- Remind students that details are especially important in creative writing like science fiction. Have students read each other's narratives to see if there are enough details. **LIGHT**

TEACH

 Connect to the ESSENTIAL QUESTION

"Seven Minutes of Terror" vividly depicts what is inspirational and unnerving about space travel by showing what it takes to get a rover to the surface of Mars and what can go terribly wrong.

QUICK START

Have students read the Quick Start question and think about it by themselves for a moment before they form groups. Explain that space missions undergo many different stages and face many technological and atmospheric challenges from takeoff to touchdown.

ANALYZE VIDEO

Help students understand the purpose of informational videos and the different visual and sound elements they employ. Tell them that "Seven Minutes of Terror" is a particularly dramatic example of an informational video not only because of its exciting subject matter but also because of the way the video tells its story.

Suggest that students keep these questions in mind as they analyze the video:

- How do the visual elements make the video exciting?
- How do the sound elements make the video even more dramatic?
- How do the visual and sound elements work together to make the video exciting?

■ **English Learner Support**

Use Cognates Tell students that all of the video elements and many of the words in the descriptions have Spanish cognates: *animation/animación, graphics/gráficos, film footage/filmaciones, narration/narración, music/musica, image/imagen, visual/visual, maps/mapas.*

ANALYZE & APPLY

MEDIA

SEVEN MINUTES OF TERROR

Video by the **National Aeronautics and Space Administration**

 **ESSENTIAL QUESTION:**

Why is the idea of space exploration both inspiring and unnerving?

QUICK START

As NASA scientists and engineers plan missions, what challenges might they face? Talk about your ideas with a partner or a small group.

ANALYZE VIDEO

The **purpose**, or intent, of an informational video is to explain a topic. The video's creator combines visual and sound elements to meet this purpose. An informational video may also use these elements to express the feelings and thoughts of the creator.

Visual elements include the images, the style of the images, and the ways in which the elements work together.

GENRE ELEMENTS: MEDIA
- often conveys information
- may target a general or specific audience
- frequently includes experts or eyewitnesses who provide explanations and key insights
- examples include television broadcasts, newspapers, videos, magazines, and the Internet

ANIMATION	images that appear to move; created through drawings, computer graphics, or photographs
FILM FOOTAGE	visual images captured on film or digitally; edited to deliver information clearly
GRAPHICS	drawings (maps, charts, diagrams, and so on) used to represent ideas or data

Sound elements include what you hear in a video.

MUSIC	instrumental and/or singing; emphasizes the emotional mood; may signal shifts in topic
NARRATION	words spoken over the images; carefully worded to present key facts

322 Unit 4

 ENGLISH LEARNER SUPPORT

Identify Video Elements Have students echo-read the visual and sound elements in the charts on p. 322. Use the beginning of the video for visual and sound reference to help students understand and define the items in the chart. Provide clarification accordingly, using words or gestures. To confirm comprehension, ask students to identify elements as you continue to play the video. For example, point to an animated sequence and say: *This is _____. (animation)* Continue until all of the elements in the video charts have been covered.
SUBSTANTIAL/MODERATE

GET READY

BACKGROUND

The people of the National Aeronautics and Space Administration (NASA) have always felt pressure, including the pressure of time. NASA had to detemine whether humans could survive in space before it sent anyone to the moon. It took NASA about a decade; but in 1969, American astronauts Neil Armstrong and Buzz Aldrin became the first humans to set foot on the moon. NASA went on to establish the space shuttle program, partner with space agencies from multiple countries on the International Space Station, and explore our solar system with orbital spacecraft telescopes. NASA's technological innovations continue to lead the world in space exploration and to improve life on Earth, especially in air travel and weather forecasting.

SETTING A PURPOSE

As you view the informational video, consider how it communicates a sense of time pressure. Pay attention to how experts explain a difficult process and the time pressures they feel as they try to ensure its success. **NOTEBOOK**

For more online resources, log in to your dashboard and click on **"SEVEN MINUTES OF TERROR"** from the selection menu.

As needed, pause the video to make notes about what impresses you or about ideas you might want to talk about later. Replay or rewind so that you can clarify anything you do not understand.

Seven Minutes of Terror   323

WHEN STUDENTS STRUGGLE . . .

Analyze the Video Use this organizer while playing the video repeatedly.

The Challenge	What Can Go Wrong
Entry:	Entry:
Descent:	Descent:
Landing:	Landing:

TEACH

BACKGROUND

After students read the Background note, provide them with more information about NASA's missions, particularly to Mars. Explain that unlike lunar missions, the Mars missions so far have been unmanned. Point out that many of the missions experienced technological problems, that their purpose has been to study the planet up close, and that some have ventured to the moons of Mars as well.

SETTING A PURPOSE

Direct students to keep in mind the sense of time pressures they sometimes feel in their own lives or that they observe others in their lives going through. You might also have them think of the plot of a favorite movie or book that generates suspense by conveying the tension and pressure of elapsing time.

APPLY

ANALYZE THE MEDIA
Possible answers

1. **DOK 2:** *The title refers to the time it takes Curiosity to travel from the top of the Martian atmosphere to touchdown and to the dread the engineers feel because they can't do anything to help. The intensity of the music, the fast-paced editing, and the experts' seriousness all convey the drama and tension.*

2. **DOK 2:** *The engineers explained that the weak atmosphere of Mars couldn't slow Curiosity down sufficiently. The parachute solves this problem.*

3. **DOK 3:** *The graphics and animation clearly and effectively show the risks posed by the surface dust and how the skycrane maneuver solves this problem, enabling Curiosity to land safely. The experts provide a concise, step-by-step explanation.*

4. **DOK 3:** *The graphics and animation show that the EDL sequence is incredibly tricky, with many different challenges requiring immediate and intricate solutions that must work in quick succession.*

5. **DOK 4:** *Students should address the excellent quality of the visual and sound elements and the clear explanations provided by the experts. On the negative side, the pacing of the video moves too quickly for viewers to fully understand such a technical subject.*

RESEARCH

Review the Research Tip with students. Remind them to use reliable sources, like the NASA website and sites published by respected organizations and universities.

Connect Students may include information about Curiosity's various discoveries, such as the fact that there was once water on Mars and that Mars's atmosphere has changed over time. Students may also explain that Curiosity's power source is a nuclear generator that allows it to move from place to place, collect data and information, and communicate its findings to a teach of scientists on Earth.

RESPOND

ANALYZE MEDIA

Support your responses with evidence from the video. 📓 NOTEBOOK

1. **Interpret** Explain the title of *Seven Minutes of Terror*. How do the music, pacing of the video, and the experts' tone of voice suggest a sense of danger or even terror?

2. **Cause/Effect** Review the animation and the experts' narration about the parachute used in this mission. What problems did the NASA engineers identify that the parachute could solve?

3. **Evaluate** How effective was the video in explaining NASA's plan to prevent a dust cloud when Curiosity landed? Explain which visual and sound elements support your evaluation, and why.

4. **Draw Conclusions** Review the graphics and animation that show the EDL (entry, descent, and landing) sequence for Curiosity. What do they tell you about the complexity of landing safely on Mars?

5. **Critique** Think about the purpose of the video. Consider the techniques that are used to support the information presented. Do you think *Seven Minutes of Terror* is an effective informational video? Why or why not?

RESEARCH

As you've learned from the video, NASA engineers had to figure out how to meet several significant challenges in planning how to land Curiosity safely on Mars. With a partner, do some research to learn more about Curiosity beyond the account in the video.

QUESTION	ANSWER
What did Curiosity discover about water on Mars?	*Curiosity analyzed rock and mineral samples it collected, which provided evidence that Mars once had water as part of its environment.*
What did Curiosity discover about the atmospheric conditions on Mars?	*Curiosity found evidence that Mars has lost most of its original atmosphere by analyzing current atmospheric conditions on Mars and monitoring its local clouds.*
How does Curiosity generate the power it needs to explore Mars?	*A specially designed, self-contained nuclear generator produces the electricity that Curiosity needs for running its computers, moving on Mars' surface, communicating with NASA, and other functions.*

Connect How would you present your information about Curiosity in a video? With your partner, sketch out the sound and visual elements you would include to convey this information.

RESEARCH TIP
Understanding complex technical information found on the Internet can be a challenge. It's often helpful to search specific technical terms using a reputable online encyclopedia, such as *Encyclopædia Britannica*, or dictionary, such as the *American Heritage Dictionary*.

ENGLISH LEARNER SUPPORT

Oral Assessment Use the following questions to assess students' comprehension and speaking skills:

1. What is one of the main ideas of the video? (*It is very difficult to land a rover on the surface of Mars.*)

2. Name some of the visual and sound elements in the video. (*music, narration, animation*)

3. What is the purpose of an informational video? (*The purpose of an informational video is to explain a topic.*) **SUBSTANTIAL/MODERATE**

RESPOND

CREATE AND PRESENT

Write a Personal Narrative Write a personal narrative to tell what it might be like for you to encounter a being from another planet.

- ❏ Choose a setting (Earth? Another planet? In space?) and outline the beginning, middle, and end of the narrative.
- ❏ Decide whether your narrative will have a "lesson"—and, if so, how you will show it through events in the plot.
- ❏ Tell the events in a logical order, using a first-person point of view.
- ❏ Choose words and details that appeal to the senses.

Present the Techniques With a small group, talk about the visual and sound elements of the video. Which elements most effectively communicate the "terror" suggested by the video's title? Discuss how each element delivers a particular emotional effect.

- ❏ Make notes about visual and sound elements in the video that particularly impressed you, both positively and negatively.
- ❏ Using examples from the video, explain how each element you have chosen delivers an emotional effect. Present ideas for ways to improve the video, or note elements that you might use in a video of your own.
- ❏ Take notes on your group's discussion. Use your notes to present a summary of the discussion for a larger group.

Go to **Writing Narratives** in the **Writing Studio** to learn more.

Go to **Participating in Collaborative Discussions** in the **Speaking and Listening Studio** for help.

RESPOND TO THE ESSENTIAL QUESTION

Why is the idea of space exploration both inspiring and unnerving?

Gather Information Review your annotations and notes on *Seven Minutes of Terror*. Then, add relevant details to your Response Log. As you determine which information to include, think about:

- the planning that went into the Curiosity mission
- the unique features of Mars that made landing Curiosity a challenge

At the end of the unit, use your notes to help you write an argument.

ACADEMIC VOCABULARY

As you write and discuss what you learned from the video, be sure to use the Academic Vocabulary words. Check off each of the words that you use.

- ❏ complex
- ❏ potential
- ❏ rely
- ❏ stress
- ❏ valid

Seven Minutes of Terror 325

APPLY

CREATE AND PRESENT

Write a Personal Narrative Point out that the checklist on p. 325 can serve as a guide to planning the structure and content of their narratives. Remind students that narratives, like all writing, depend on interesting details. Help students outline their stories and how they plan to tell them. Encourage creativity.

Present the Techniques Point out to students that the checklist can guide their discussions. As they take notes, they can share observations, opinions, evaluations. Remind students to allow everyone in the small group to participate. Advise students to run through their presentations in the small group before delivering them to the large group.

 For **writing support** for students at varying proficiency levels, see the **Text X-Ray** on page 322D.

RESPOND TO THE ESSENTIAL QUESTION

Allow time for students to add details from "Seven Minutes of Terror" to their Unit 4 Response Logs.

ENGLISH LEARNER SUPPORT

Discuss with a Small Group Restate the discussion topic as a question: *What emotions do the visual/sound elements of the video make you feel?* Make sure that students understand the terms *impressed* (admired), *suggested* (meant), and *delivers an emotional effect* (made you feel something). Give/show examples as needed. Then have students complete this sentence frame: *The visual/sound element that impressed me the most was the _____.*
SUBSTANTIAL/MODERATE

Have students work with a partner to form opinions that answer the questions before starting the discussion. Provide these sentence frames to help them develop their ideas for the discussion: *The most dramatic sound effect was_____. The most exciting visual element was the_____. One thing I didn't like bout the video was_____.* **LIGHT**

Seven Minutes of Terror **325**

PLAN

SPACE EXPLORATION SHOULD BE MORE THAN SCIENCE FICTION
Argument by Claudia Alarcon

HUMANS SHOULD STAY HOME AND LET ROBOTS TAKE TO THE STARS
Argument by Eiren Cafall

GENRE ELEMENTS
ARGUMENT

Remind students that the purpose of an **argument** is to present facts and information regarding a specific claim. Although ordinary people make or have arguments every day in many different forms, an **article** or **essay** presents claims that are rooted in deep research and include convincing evidence and support in order to persuade readers. Paying close attention to argumentation, rhetorical devices, and evidentiary support when reading will help them produce and improve their own arguments and also help them navigate the arguments of others.

LEARNING OBJECTIVES

- Analyze the claims, evidence, and counter arguments in an argument.
- Conduct research on the Cassini orbiter and the International Space Station.
- Write a formal letter to Congress about space exploration to a member of Congress and a short story about a space mission.
- Use subordinating conjunctions, relative pronouns, complex sentences, and complete complex sentences
- Analyze the denotations and connotations of words.
- Use dictionaries and glossaries.
- **Language** Use the consonant blend *str*.

TEXT COMPLEXITY

Quantitative Measures	Space Exploration Should Be More Than Science Fiction/ Humans Should Stay Home and Let Robots Take to the Stars **Lexile 1060L/1060L**
Qualitative Measures	**Ideas Presented** Explicit and direct with clear purpose
	Structure Used Easily identified text structure
	Language Used Sentence structure more complex
	Knowledge Required More complex problems, experiences will be less familiar

326A Unit 4

PLAN

Online

RESOURCES

- Unit 4 Response Log
- Selection Audio
- Reading Studio: Notice & Note
- Writing Studio: Writing as a Process/ Writing Narratives
- Speaking and Listening Studio: Participating in Collaborative Discussions/ Giving a Presentation
- Vocabulary Studio: Connotations and Denotations/ Using a Dictionary or Glossary
- Grammar Studio: Module 10: Lesson 5: Who and Whom/ Module 8: Agreement
- "Space Exploration Should Be More Than Science Fiction" Selection Test/ "Humans Should Stay Home and Let Robots Take to the Stars" Selection Test

SUMMARIES

English

Space exploration comes with a host of critical implications for human society on Earth. "Space Exploration Should Be More Than Science Fiction" makes the argument that although the prospect may be unnerving or even dangerous, continued deep space exploration by humans offers major benefits and infinite possibilities that will be critical for the future of science, technology, and even human survival. "Humans Should Stay Home and Let Robots take to the Stars" adopts a different viewpoint, arguing that robots are better suited to the task of space exploration than human beings. Both authors provide reasons and details to support their arguments, leaving it up to the reader to decide whether or not their cases are persuasive.

Spanish

La exploración espacial viene con una multitud de implicaciones críticas para la sociedad humana en la Tierra. En "La exploración espacial debería ser más que ciencia ficción" se argumenta que, a pesar de que el prospecto pueda ser desconcertante o incluso peligroso, la exploración espacial continua y profunda por parte de los humanos ofrece beneficios mayores y posibilidades infinitas que serán cruciales para el futuro de la ciencia, la tecnología e incluso la supervivencia humana. En "Los humanos deberían quedarse en casa y dejar que los robots se vayan a las estrellas" se adopta un punto de vista distinto. Se afirma que los robots son más adecuados para la exploración espacial que los seres humanos. Ambos autores dan razonamientos y detalles que apoyan sus argumentos, dejándole al lector la decisión sobre si sus casos son persuasivos.

SMALL-GROUP OPTIONS

Have students work in small groups to read and discuss the selection.

Numbered Heads

- Break class into groups of four.
- Give each student in a group a number: 1–2–3–4.
- Ask students: *Is the idea of space exploration exciting, unnerving, or both? Why?*
- Groups must settle on their response to the question as a collective.
- Call on any of the four numbers, and that number from each group must respond with the group's answer.

Wheel Discussion

- Break students into groups of six.
- Seat three students at center, back-to-back, facing outward.
- Place the other three students in front of the seated students, facing in.
- Students in the inner circle remain stationary while the outer circle rotates to the right.
- For each rotation, provide one discussion question based on wither "Space Exploration..." or "Humans Should Stay Home..."

PLAN

Text X-Ray: English Learner Support

for "Space Exploration Should Be More Than Science Fiction" / "Humans Should Stay Home and Let Robots Take to the Stars"

Use the Text X-Ray and the supports and scaffolds in the Teacher's Edition to help guide students at different proficiency levels through the selection.

INTRODUCE THE SELECTION
DISCUSS SPACE TRAVEL

Explain to students that there are many different opinions about space exploration and they do not all have to think the same way. Give students a moment to think about what space travel means and compose a response using the following frames:

- I would <u>like/not like</u> to travel in space.
- Some form of life does/does not exist on Mars.
- In the future, space travel might look like ___.
- Travelling in space is too dangerous/worth the risk.

CULTURAL REFERENCES

The following words and phrases may be unfamiliar to students:

- *Cold War* (paragraph 2): poor relations between the US and the Soviet Union (Russia) after WWII
- *New Space* (paragraph 3): the budding commercial space flight industry
- *rare-earth metals* (paragraph 6): uncommon metals used in technology, such as coltan (used in cell phones)
- *reality television show* (paragraph 3): a television show that follows the everyday lives of people or celebrities
- *geoengineering* (paragraph 5): the science of stopping carbon from harming the environment in the upper atmosphere, or in space

LISTENING

Identify Author's Point of View

Draw students' attention to the titles of each selection. Have them identify each author's position on space travel based on each article's title.

Have students listen as you read aloud each title and author name. Use the following supports with students at varying proficiency levels:

- Help students understand the terms *science fiction* and *to the stars*. Provide these sentence frames: *People want to travel to the stars, or to ____. Today, humans cannot travel very far in ____, but robots can travel to ____. We can watch ____ adventures on TV and in movies.* **SUBSTANTIAL**
- Ask students to identify each author's position on space travel. Provide these sentence frames: *Claudia Alarcon wants ____ to explore space. Eiren Caffall wants ____ to explore space.* **MODERATE**
- Ask students to identify a word that is repeated in each title (should). Have partners discuss how the word *should* helps them identify the position each author will take in her article. **LIGHT**

326C Unit 4

PLAN

SPEAKING

Understand Consonant Blends

Consonant blends are groups of consonants that are without vowels and make a distinct, blended sound, such as *str* found inside the word *administration*. Note that consonant blends usually appear at the beginning of words.

Have students listen as you read aloud paragraphs 1-3. Draw students' attention to the words *construction* and *administrations*. Use the following supports with students at varying proficiency levels:

- Ask students to repeat the words *construction* and *administration*, stressing the *str* sounds.
- Model the pronunciation of other *str* blends from the selection, such as *astronaut* and *strategy*, and have student repeat them.
- Have students in small groups make up sentences using the words, *construction*, *administration*, *astronaut* and *strategy*.

READING

Compare and Contrast Details

Draw students' attention to the first paragraph in each selection. Have them read each paragraph and compare and contrast the details that support each author's position on space travel.

Use the following supports with students at varying proficiency levels:

- Guide students to understand that each author has a different opinion about space travel. *Ask: Which article argues that space travel is important? Which article says that humans should not travel to space?* Allow students to point to the correct title or rephrase the title using short phrases.
- Have students identify one detail both paragraphs have in common. Provide these sentence frames: *Both articles use _____ to show that many people are interested in space exploration.*
- Ask students identify one similar detail in each paragraph. Then have them identify a sentence in each that represents the opposing viewpoints of each author.

WRITING

Write Complex Sentences

Have students practice deconstructing and writing complex sentences. Provide students with the following complex sentence to use during the activity: *After it rains, the sun sometimes shines, making a beautiful rainbow in the sky.*

Use the following supports with students at varying proficiency levels:

- Have students copy the sentence into their notebooks. Point out the subject verb agreement in each clause and have them underline it.
- Have students write down their responses to the following questions: *What subject is in the second clause?* (the sun) *What verb agrees with it?* (shines)
- Provide student pairs with the clauses in the complex sentence, but out of order (*After it rains,/ making a beautiful rainbow in the sky./the sun sometimes shines,*). Have student pairs work together to place the clauses in the correct order to form a complex sentence.

TEACH

Connect to the ESSENTIAL QUESTION

Claudia Alarcon examines the benefits and dangers of continuing humanity's exploration of deep space. As a rapidly expanding industry, the prospect of commercial space travel introduces a host of complicated and difficult issues for humankind to consider.

COMPARE ARGUMENTS

Remind students that Claudia Alarcon's and Erien Caffall's articles are nonfiction accounts of space exploration history, both of which put forward convincing yet opposed arguments about humankind's destiny in space. Parsing the different ideas in the articles—weighing the arguments, considering the evidence—will help readers to decide or even reverse how they feel about the very important issue of space travel.

COLLABORATE & COMPARE

ARGUMENT

SPACE EXPLORATION SHOULD BE MORE SCIENCE THAN FICTION

by **Claudia Alarcón**

pages 329–333

COMPARE ARGUMENTS

As you read, notice the persuasive techniques and main points contained in each argument. Then think about each argument's central claim. After you read both arguments, you will collaborate with a small group on a project.

 ESSENTIAL QUESTION:

Why is the idea of space exploration both inspiring and unnerving?

ARGUMENT

HUMANS SHOULD STAY HOME AND LET ROBOTS TAKE TO THE STARS

by **Eiren Caffall**

pages 338–341

GET READY

QUICK START

An important debate has been taking place about the costs and risks of space exploration. How important is space exploration for our future? Is space travel too risky for humans? Discuss your ideas with the class.

ANALYZE ARGUMENT

In an **argument,** a speaker states a claim and supports it with reasons and evidence. A **claim** is the speaker's position on a problem or issue. The strength of an argument relies not on the claim itself but on the support. **Support** consists of reasons and evidence used to prove the claim. **Reasons** are declarations made to explain an action or belief. **Evidence** includes specific facts, statistics, or examples. To **trace,** or follow the reasoning of, an argument:

- Identify the claim, which may be stated directly or implied.
- Look for reasons and evidence that support the claim.
- Note how author connects the claim, reasons, and evidence.
- Identify **counterarguments,** statements that address opposing viewpoints. A good argument anticipates opposing viewpoints and provides counterarguments to disprove the opposing views.

GENRE ELEMENTS: ARGUMENT
- includes a claim and counterarguments
- includes reasons and evidence to support the claim
- may contain rhetorical devices
- may be formal or informal

ANALYZE RHETORICAL DEVICES

Rhetorical devices are techniques that writers use to enhance their arguments and communicate more effectively. A few rhetorical devices are described below, along with examples of each from the selections.

RHETORICAL DEVICE	EXAMPLE
Addressing readers using the pronouns *you* or *yourself* is a device called **direct address.** Direct address gets readers' attention and connects them to the topic.	Imagine yourself as an astronaut, a part of the first manned mission to Mars.
Rhetorical questions are those that do not need a reply. Writers use them to engage the reader or to suggest that their arguments make the answer obvious.	Would you want to trust a scientific mission to the people who run reality TV?
Sweeping generalizations are those that are too broad. Sweeping generalizations often include words such as *all, everyone, every time, anything, no one,* and *none.*	Obviously, no single government would want to take on that kind of funding.
Loaded language consists of words with strongly positive or negative connotations intended to influence a reader or listener.	This form of mining, therefore, would be incredibly beneficial for our survival and advancement.

TEACH

QUICK START

After students discuss the topic, ask the groups or pairs to make a list of pros and cons regarding commercial space travel. The items on their lists can be anything from personal preferences—many people find space terrifying and refuse to travel there—to issues of funding, infrastructure, risk, the environment, and global poverty. Allow them to briefly look issues up online if needed.

ANALYZE ARGUMENT

Remind students that an "argument" is not always a "disagreement," but can also be a reasoned presentation of claims and evidence. Assist students in understanding the terms and concepts regarding claims, arguments, and evidence. Remind them that ordinary people, including students, make claims and examine evidence every day, presenting arguments all the time. Good journalists and essayists simply use these skills to research a topic thoroughly and present the best possible argument.

ANALYZE RHETORICAL DEVICES

Help students to familiarize themselves with rhetorical devices. After examining the different devices, ask them to try to think of examples of each from their own lives. Remind them that making note of the devices in the reading will help them understand the argument and come to their own conclusions more effectively. Ask students:

- *How effective is the direct address that appears in the reading?*
- *What purpose does a rhetorical question serve?*
- *Why do authors use sweeping generalizations and loaded language in argument texts?*

TEACH

CRITICAL VOCABULARY

Encourage students to read all the sentences before deciding which word best completes each one. Remind them to look for context clues that match the meaning of each word.

Answers:

1. *prominent/administration*
2. *erupted*
3. *plague/beneficial*
4. *advancement/dubious*

■ English Learner Support

Practice Put students in pairs and ask them to speak the Critical Vocabulary words aloud, paying close attention to pronunciation, especially vowels and consonant blends.
SUBSTANTIAL

LANGUAGE CONVENTIONS

Have students review the information about subordinating conjunctions and complex sentences. Explain that the example sentence demonstrates both.

Read the example sentence aloud and ask students to consider the first idea, second idea, and the subordinating conjunction. What kind of sentence is this? *(It's a complex sentence with one subordinating conjunction and one subordinate clause.)*

ANNOTATION MODEL

Point out that students may follow the suggestions or use their own system for marking up the selection. They may want to color-code their annotations with highlighters. Their notes in the margin may include questions and topics they want to learn more about.

GET READY

CRITICAL VOCABULARY

| administration | beneficial | plague | erupt |
| prominent | advancement | dubious | |

To see how many Critical Vocabulary words you already know, use them to complete the sentences.

1. One _____ official in the presidential _____ voiced concern about the expense of the Mars mission.
2. The crowd will _____ in cheers when the astronauts land.
3. Although problems continue to _____ the project, the results will be _____ .
4. Some officials claim that the technology will lead to an _____ for society, but most are _____ about such claims.

LANGUAGE CONVENTIONS

Subordinating Conjunctions A subordinate clause begins with a **subordinating conjunction,** such as *after, although, as, because, before, even though, if, since, so that, though, unless, until, when, where,* and *while.* A subordinate clause may also begin with a **relative pronoun,** such as *which, that, who,* and *whose.* As you read, watch for subordinating conjunctions and relative pronouns that are used to form **complex sentences,** those with one main clause and one or more subordinate clauses.

ANNOTATION MODEL   NOTICE & NOTE

As you read, note the author's use of rhetorical devices. You can also mark reasons and evidence that support the argument. In the model, you can see one reader's notes about "Humans Should Stay Home and Let Robots Take to the Stars."

> 4 The risks of space exploration could be (grave) for a planet already (plagued) by pollution. There is an extra result of space travel: black carbon from rocket exhaust that's deposited in the outer atmosphere. . . . <u>With no weather to wash it into the oceans, black carbon can stay put for up to ten years.</u>

The negative connotation of these words suggests that the author is against space exploration.

The author is using this statistic to support her argument.

328 Unit 4

BACKGROUND

Exploring the outer reaches of our solar system and sending humans to Mars is no longer the stuff of science fiction. NASA has sent orbiters and rovers to the Red Planet for decades. But now the goal is to send humans to orbit Mars by the 2030s. Many scientists and politicians are rallying around this goal, as well as around other missions that will allow humans to probe the mysteries of space.

SPACE EXPLORATION SHOULD BE MORE SCIENCE THAN FICTION

Argument by Claudia Alarcón

PREPARE TO COMPARE

As you read, pay attention to the persuasive language and to the reasons and evidence this author uses to support her argument. Consider how forms of persuasion can differ.

1 What is out there? Are we alone in the universe? Are there inhabitable planets in our galaxy and beyond? For decades, science-fiction novels, movies, and TV shows fired our curiosity. After the real-life Apollo 11's moon mission in 1969, enthusiasm for new discoveries soared. Now, well into the twenty-first century, we must face the fact that these same questions are still unanswered. <u>With so much human investment made, we must go forward, fully embracing space exploration as an important priority.</u> Our future in space depends on science.

2 Space exploration in the 1960s was fueled by the Cold War space race between the United States and Russia. The twenty-first century has brought a universal spirit of collaboration among scientists from around the globe.

NOTICE & NOTE

Notice & Note

Use the side margins to notice and note signposts in the text.

ANALYZE ARGUMENT

Annotate: Underline the author's central claim in paragraph 1.

Interpret: What does the author think we should do?

Space Exploration Should Be More Science Than Fiction 329

TEACH

BACKGROUND

After students read the Background note, explain that everyone on Earth, not just in America, has a stake in space exploration. If commercial space travel becomes a reality, many people may one day get to experience it, and the minerals and resources that are extracted in space will benefit all humankind.

PREPARE TO COMPARE

Direct students to use the Prepare to Compare prompt to focus their reading.

ANALYZE ARGUMENT

Remind students that a **claim** is a central idea or argument that the author will pursue. **(Answer:** *We must continue to explore and prioritize space exploration.)*

 For **speaking support** for students at varying proficiency levels, see the **Text X-Ray** on page 326D.

ENGLISH LEARNER SUPPORT

Preteach Vocabulary Display the words *galaxy* and *inhabitable* on the board. Explain that these words will appear in the article they are about to read. Provide students with images of the *galaxy*. Have them chorally repeat the word *galaxy* after you. Say: *There are many planets in the galaxy. Earth is one.* Discuss the word *inhabitable* with students. Say: *The Earth is inhabitable. Many people, animals, and plants live on Earth.* Explain that there may be other planets like Earth in the galaxy. Have student pairs discuss if they think there are other inhabitable planets in the galaxy. Supply the following sentence frame: *I think there are other _____ planets in the _____.* **SUBSTANTIAL/MODERATE**

Space Exploration Should Be More Than Science Fiction **329**

TEACH

ANALYZE RHETORICAL DEVICES

Remind students that **loaded language** is the use of words with strong connotations meant to influence the reader towards the author's view. (**Answer:** *They are words with positive connotations; they help enhance the argument by suggesting that exploring is exciting.*)

This section of the immense Carina Nebula was captured by the Hubble Telescope. Inset at right: a view of the Hubble Telescope

NOTICE & NOTE

An excellent example is the International Space Station. This orbiting laboratory and construction site combines the scientific expertise of 16 nations. It allows for a permanent human outpost in space. The hope is that the station can serve as a launching platform for further space exploration.

3   But space travel is not without risk. NASA's Space Shuttle Program, which was the main connection to the International Space Station, suffered two terrible losses. After the explosions of the *Challenger* in 1986 and *Columbia* in 2003, the program was shut down in 2011. Recent presidential **administrations** supported putting priority on the commercial space flight industry. A program was put into place to help private companies pursue work on human space flight. There are dozens of private companies in the industry known informally as "New Space." These companies have set their sights on what seem to be impossible goals. These range from tourist trips to the moon to the colonization of Mars. Space travel has its documented dangers; however, direct human involvement, aided by technological innovation, could likely boost the potential for discovery.

4   Technological innovations are developing to allow us to venture even farther into space. Such advances are <u>opening windows into worlds we previously could not have imagined.</u>

administration
(ăd-mĭn´ĭ-strā´shən) *n.* A president's *administration* is his or her term of office.

ANALYZE RHETORICAL DEVICES
Annotate: Mark examples of loaded language in paragraph 4.

Analyze: Why do you think the author chose these words? How do they enhance her argument?

330   Unit 4

CRITICAL VOCABULARY

administration: The fact that successive U.S. government executive officials have supported continued space exploration gives the practice credence.

ASK STUDENTS which administration is presently in office in the White House and which was the previous administration. (*The current president is Donald J. Trump and the previous was Barack Obama.*)

NOTICE & NOTE

Robotic spacecraft have conducted some of NASA's most exciting and productive missions. A **prominent** example is the Hubble Space Telescope, which has made more than 1.3 million observations since its mission began in 1990. It has traveled more than 4 billion miles, sending back stunning photos of faraway stars and galaxies.

5 NASA has also conducted robotic missions within our solar system. The *Cassini*'s mission to Saturn was one of the most ambitious efforts in planetary space exploration. This robotic spacecraft carried the Huygens probe, which parachuted to the surface of Titan, Saturn's largest moon. The Juno spacecraft orbited around Jupiter, sending observations that can help scientists understand the beginnings of the solar system. The New Horizons spacecraft flew by Pluto in 2015 after an almost ten-year flight. According to the National Academy of Sciences, the exploration of Pluto and the Kuiper belt is the highest priority for solar system exploration. The asteroids in the Kuiper belt offer a great opportunity for mining. Space mining presents an important step for finding resources necessary for interstellar travel and exploration. In addition, icy asteroids may provide a cost-effective solution to space travel. Space entrepreneurs are looking into using hydrogen and oxygen from asteroid ice to

prominent
(prŏm´ə-nənt) *adj.* If something is *prominent*, it stands out.

LANGUAGE CONVENTIONS
Annotate: Underline the two complex sentences in paragraph 5 and circle the relative pronouns.

Interpret: What two ideas do the relative pronouns connect in each sentence?

Space Exploration Should Be More Science Than Fiction 331

APPLYING ACADEMIC VOCABULARY

☐ **complex** ☑ **potential** ☐ **rely** ☑ **stress** ☐ **valid**

Write and Discuss Pair students, and ask them to discuss the following questions. Guide them to include the Academic Vocabulary words *potential* and *stress* in their responses. Ask volunteers to share their responses with the class:
- What future **potential** does space exploration offer humanity?
- What factors about commercial space travel does Alarcon **stress** in her article?

TEACH

LANGUAGE CONVENTIONS

Remind students that a **complex sentence** includes one main idea and at least one other idea, or subordinate clause. (*Answer:* First sentence: The robotic spacecraft carried the Huygens probe. The Huygens probe parachuted to the surface of Titan. Second sentence: The Juno spacecraft orbited around Jupiter and sent observations.)

ENGLISH LEARNER SUPPORT

Evidence Point out specific details identified in paragraph 5, including probe names, space mission titles, and the names of spacecraft and orbiters. Ask students why the author included this information and where she got it from. (*She included it to support her argument that space exploration is important and exciting. She got the information from her research.*)

MODERATE

CRITICAL VOCABULARY

prominent: The Hubble telescope is one of the most important and well-known accomplishments of NASA and is still used today.

ASK STUDENTS who the most prominent figures in commercial space travel are today. (*Answers will vary but will likely include Elon Musk, Richard Branson, or Jeff Bezos.*)

Space Exploration Should Be More Than Science Fiction **331**

TEACH

ANALYZE ARGUMENT

Remind students that a **reason** is a declaration made to explain an event, action, or belief. (**Answer:** *The reason is relevant because discovering a new home for humanity is important, and it supports the claim that we must embrace space travel.*)

ANALYZE RHETORICAL DEVICES

Remind students that a **rhetorical question** needs no answer but should make readers think or consider something in a new way. (**Answer:** *It engages the readers and makes them think about what space exploration could accomplish.*)

▶ EXTREME OR ABSOLUTE LANGUAGE

Remind students that authors will loosely link this signpost to **claims** and **evidence** in order to make an argument seem factual or incontrovertible, even if it's not. Have students point out the words in paragraph 11 that signal the signpost. (*"the human race and Earth itself is at stake"*). Then have them answer the question to determine the purpose of this extreme language. (**Answer:** *They suggest the importance and urgency of exploring space.*)

CRITICAL VOCABULARY

beneficial: Space exploration isn't only for science, but would produce raw materials for goods on Earth.

ASK STUDENTS who benefits most when outer space is mined for minerals. (*Large corporations benefit but so do tech producers and consumers.*)

advancement: Because Earth has been fully mapped and explored, space remains the last frontier for human cultural colonization.

ASK STUDENTS how *survival* differs from *advancement*. (*Survival means only the most basic needs are met, whereas advancement means there are sufficient resources for growth and expansion.*)

332 Unit 4

✏ NOTICE & NOTE

beneficial
(bĕn′ə-fĭsh′əl) *adj.* When something is *beneficial*, it is good or favorable.

advancement
(ăd-văns′mənt) *n.* Something that is an *advancement* is an improvement or step forward.

ANALYZE ARGUMENT
Annotate: In paragraph 7, mark a reason that the author uses to support her claim that we must continue to explore space.

Evaluate: Is the reason relevant? Does it make sense? Explain.

ANALYZE RHETORICAL DEVICES
Annotate: Mark the rhetorical question in paragraph 9.

Analyze: What purpose does the rhetorical question serve?

EXTREME OR ABSOLUTE LANGUAGE
Notice & Note: Mark the words in paragraph 11 that seem to exaggerate or overstate a case.

Analyze: How does the use of these words help the author's argument?

332 Unit 4

---

manufacture rocket fuel. This space-made fuel can be used to launch expeditions farther out into space at considerably less cost.

6 Our moon contains helium-3, an element that could be useful on Earth for energy developments such as nuclear fusion research. Mining there can also yield rare-earth metals (REMs) that are used in electronics and in the construction of solar panels. This form of mining, therefore, would be incredibly **beneficial** for our survival and **advancement**. In recent years, geological surveys have indicated the presence of water on the moon, which can serve to sustain a human-inhabited lunar base.

7 Scientists are also looking toward Mars as a potential new home for humankind. New discoveries keep emerging that raise more questions. It is imperative that we use all our available resources to continue research on Mars.

8 Early missions to Mars such as that of Mars Odyssey were designed to make discoveries under the theme of "Follow the Water." These missions showed the possibility of liquid water below the surface of Mars. With the Curiosity rover, the Mars Exploration Program is following a next-step strategy known as "Seek Signs of Life." This exploration phase aims to discover the possibilities for past or present life on the Red Planet. Curiosity is seeking evidence of organic materials, the chemical building blocks of life. Future Mars missions would likely be designed to search for life itself in places identified as potential past or present habitats.

9 With all these advances and technologies in place and in development, will we see a human colony on the moon or on Mars in our lifetime? The best-case scenario will involve a partnership between NASA and international space travel companies.

10 Some New Space pioneers have tested supersonic retropropulsion technology, landing rocket boosters on floating platforms and on land. This technique could be important for future Mars landings. NASA's rovers, weighing up to a ton, have successfully landed on Mars. However, they have dropped to the planet's surface in air bags, using rockets, and with the assistance of cables extended from a "sky crane." A human mission would weigh much more, making landing more problematic. The previous solutions would not work for spacecraft carrying humans.

11 On the other hand, the future of the human race and Earth itself is at stake. We are close to surpassing our planet's carrying capacity and exhausting our natural resources. Yet scientists and space entrepreneurs remain hopeful. Private companies seeking

---

WHEN STUDENTS STRUGGLE . . .

Pros and Cons Have student pairs create a list of pros and cons regarding space exploration.

Space Travel	Pros	Cons
Humankind	To live on other planets; find aliens	Space travel is dangerous.
Industry	Business opportunities	Expensive; lots of unknowns
Resources	Rare metals in space	Difficult to bring to Earth

📖 For additional support, go to the **Reading Studio** and assign the following Level Up tutorial: Analyzing Arguments.

to colonize Mars believe the risk of space flight is similar to that of climbing Mount Everest. As we all know, this is a risky, but not impossible, proposition.

12   The final frontier is a vast and dangerous place, difficult and expensive to explore. But it offers infinite possibilities for expanding our scientific knowledge of our planet and its origins. Exploring outer space can yield new sources for precious natural resources and perhaps even find a home for future generations. We live in times where space travel and exploration should be more science than fiction. Let's keep pursuing the compelling questions that have driven us to these times. Space exploration may very well hold the key to humanity's future.

NOTICE & NOTE

CHECK YOUR UNDERSTANDING

Answer these questions before moving on to the **Analyze the Text** section on the following page.

1 The author opens the text with questions most likely to —
   A introduce the topics that she will cover in the selection
   B suggest that her essay will attempt to answer the questions
   C note that science fiction fuels our interest in science
   D remind readers that there is much we still don't know

2 In paragraph 2, the author brings up the example of the International Space Station to make the point that space exploration —
   F has come a long way since the 1960s
   G encourages cooperation among scientists
   H has led to a permanent human outpost
   J requires a great deal of human investment

3 The author mostly supports her ideas with —
   A expert opinions
   B interesting anecdotes
   C scientific evidence
   D references to other texts

TEACH

CHECK YOUR UNDERSTANDING

Have students answer the questions independently.

Answers:
1. D
2. G
3. C

If they answer any questions incorrectly, have them reread the text to confirm their understanding. Then they may proceed to ANALYZE THE TEXT on p. 334.

ENGLISH LEARNER SUPPORT

Oral Assessment Use the following prompts to assist students with their comprehension and verbal skills. Pair students of varying proficiencies to complete the prompts.

1. Put students into pairs and have them ask each other yes-or-no questions. Ask: *Should humans explore space? Is it dangerous for humans to be in space?*

2. Point out to students the rhetorical questions that begin the article. Have them read the questions aloud to each other and discuss what they mean.

3. Pair students and have them test each other with simple questions about the article topic. For instance, they can ask: *Who wrote this article? (Claudia Alarcon) What is it about? (space exploration).*

ALL LEVELS

APPLY

ANALYZE THE TEXT

Possible answers:

1. **DOK 2:** *The government has shifted the focus because of the people who are interested in space travel. Space travel involves risks, as evidenced by the Challenger and Columbia explosions. Private industry sets bigger goals, like colonization of Mars and tourist trips to the moon.*

2. **DOK 3:** *The moon contains helium-3, which could be used in nuclear fusion research.*

3. **DOK 3:** *You can conclude that water is a necessary component for life, because the early missions were under the theme of "Follow the water." Once they found the potential for water, the next step was missions under the theme "Seek signs of life." This suggests a connection.*

4. **DOK 4:** *The retropropulsion technology being tested to land humans safely on Mars supports the author's claim that science will make it possible for Mars colonization.*

5. **DOK 4:** *The use of absolute or extreme language is alarming and is meant to frighten the reader into agreeing, but it often makes the reader doubt the author's claims.*

RESEARCH

Point out to students that they should double check their information with multiple vetted websites and books.

Connect Point out to students that although much work is left to be done regarding space travel, humankind has been exploring space since before the 1960s—more than half a century. Scientists did enormous work in the 1940s and 1950s to figure out how to send rockets into space. Today, orbiters and spacecraft like Cassini send to NASA data and imagery of far-away moons and planets every day. Students should think about what obstacles need to be overcome now to allow sustained human space flight and resource exploration.

RESPOND

ANALYZE THE TEXT

Support your responses with evidence from the text. 📓 NOTEBOOK

1. **Infer** Why might the government have shifted from supporting space travel through NASA to prioritizing commercial travel?

2. **Cite Evidence** How could space mining aid in scientific research? Cite evidence from the text that explains the importance of space mining.

3. **Draw Conclusions** Review paragraph 8. What can you conclude from the support provided by the author about the connection between water and the possibility of life on Mars? Explain.

4. **Explain** Why does the fact that New Space pioneers are testing supersonic retropropulsion technology support the author's claim? How does it add to your understanding of the argument?

5. **Notice & Note** Explain the overall effect that the author's use of extreme or absolute language has on the reader. Does it make you more persuaded by the argument, or less so? Why?

RESEARCH TIP
Remember that the *Cassini* mission has been in the news since its launch. To get an overview of its findings, scan search results that are dated 2017 and later.

RESEARCH

The *Cassini* orbiter ended its journey in 2017. Research the details of its contributions. Record what you learn in the chart.

QUESTION	ANSWER
What were the goals of the *Cassini* orbiter mission?	*to find out more about the universe, and Saturn and its moons, especially Titan*
What important discoveries did *Cassini* make?	*an ocean beneath the surface of Saturn's moon Enceladus, seven new moons, hurricanes at Saturn's poles; Saturn's rings are made up of massive and tiny particles*
What discoveries did *Cassini*'s probe Huygens make?	*Titan has river systems, shorelines and lakes; its rivers and seas are filled with liquid ethane and methane; it has clouds and maybe volcanoes.*

Connect In paragraph 5, the author states, "The *Cassini*'s mission to Saturn was one of the most ambitious efforts in planetary space exploration." With a small group, discuss what made the *Cassini* mission so ambitious.

RESPOND

CREATE AND DISCUSS

Write a Letter Write to your representative in Congress to find out his or her views on space exploration.

- ❏ Determine who your representative is by going online to the U.S. House of Representatives website.
- ❏ Include a heading and a formal greeting. Then, begin the body of the letter by introducing the topic. Be clear in stating your reasons for writing.
- ❏ Close your letter by thanking your representative. Provide contact information so that he or she can send you the information you are seeking. Remember to end with a signature.

Create a Loaded Language Chart Create a chart of the loaded language used in the text.

- ❏ As a group, review the selection and make a list of the loaded language that you find.
- ❏ Categorize the words in your chart according to whether each word has a positive connotation or a negative connotation.
- ❏ Review the words with positive connotations and those with negative ones. Discuss the author's purpose for using them.

Go to the **Writing as a Process** in the **Writing Studio** to learn more.

Go to **Participating in Collaborative Discussions** in the **Speaking and Listening Studio** for help.

RESPOND TO THE ESSENTIAL QUESTION

? Why is the idea of space exploration both inspiring and unnerving?

Gather Information Review your annotations and notes on "Space Exploration Should Be More Science Than Fiction." Then, add relevant details to your Response Log. As you determine which information to include, think about the:

- reasons for sending humans into space
- risks associated with space travel
- benefits of robotic missions for space exploration

At the end of the unit, use your notes to help you write an argument.

ACADEMIC VOCABULARY

As you write and discuss what you learned from the argument, be sure to use the Academic Vocabulary words. Check off each of the words that you use.

- ❏ complex
- ❏ potential
- ❏ rely
- ❏ stress
- ❏ valid

Space Exploration Should Be More Science Than Fiction 335

APPLY

CREATE AND DISCUSS

Write a Letter Point out that getting the details correct is critical. Make sure students find the proper representative in their district/city, spell the representative's name correctly, and use the correct address or email. Make sure students' own contact information is accurate.

 For **writing support** for students at varying proficiency levels, see the **Text X-Ray** on page 326D.

Create a Loaded Language Chart Remind students that certain words are commonly used in loaded language, such as *all*, *none*, *never*, *always*, *everyone*, *totally*, and *nothing*. They should pay close attention to extreme phrasing, such as *We must all agree that*.

RESPOND TO THE ESSENTIAL QUESTION

Allow time for students to add details from "Space Exploration Should be More Science than Fiction" to their Unit 4 Response Logs.

APPLY

CRITICAL VOCABULARY

Possible answers:

1. *The current presidential* administration *is that of Donald J. Trump.*
2. *The principal is a* prominent *person in the school.*
3. *Studying would be* beneficial *to my grades.*
4. *Advancements in science improve medicine, technology, and communication for everyone.*

VOCABULARY STRATEGY: Connotations and Denotations

Answers:

1. **Inquisitive** *(Prying is not appropriate because it connotes nosiness or rudeness.)*
2. **Cooperate** *(Conspire is not appropriate because it connotes bad intentions.)*
3. **Hazardous** *(Menacing is not appropriate because it has the denotation of being personally threatening.)*
4. *Students may answer either interesting or useful. Explanations will vary for their choices.*

 RESPOND

WORD BANK
administration
prominent
beneficial
advancement

 Go to the **Vocabulary Studio** for more on connotations and denotations.

CRITICAL VOCABULARY

Practice and Apply Answer each question using the Critical Vocabulary word in a complete sentence.

1. Which presidential **administration** is in the White House?
2. Who is a **prominent** person in your school?
3. What is one thing that would be **beneficial** for your grades?
4. Why would someone work toward **advancements** in science?

VOCABULARY STRATEGY: Connotations and Denotations

A word's **denotation** is its literal dictionary definition. A word's **connotation** comes from the ideas and feelings associated with the word. Words can have positive or negative connotations. The author of "Space Exploration Should Be More Science Than Fiction" chose many words based on their connotation as well as their denotation.

> **Technological innovations are developing to allow us to venture even farther into space.**

Notice how the specific word choice of *venture*, rather than *go*, suggests daring. The word *venture* conjures up an adventure that requires courage. The context of a phrase, sentence, or paragraph can help you determine the connotation of a word.

Practice and Apply For each item, mark the word that better fits the meaning of the sentence. Use a print or online dictionary to help you with unfamiliar words. Then write the reason for your choice.

1. NASA scientists want to find out more about Mars. The scientists are (**inquisitive, prying**).
   _____

2. Astronauts on the International Space Station must work with each other for months at a time. The work requires them to (**conspire, cooperate**).
   _____

3. Radiation is a serious risk for astronauts working in space. It can be (**hazardous, menacing**) to their health.
   _____

4. The space program has enabled us to learn about our solar system and universe. It has provided (**interesting, useful**) information.
   _____

336 Unit 4

 ENGLISH LEARNER SUPPORT

Cute Connotations If students struggle with the idea of connotations, flip the concept. Put them in groups and give them a few definite categories: *cute, funny, sad, boring, mean, gross*. Now ask them to brainstorm as a group and come up with at least five matching verbs and adjectives for each category. For instance, for the category of *cute* they might write the words *small, adorable, tickle*. When done, ask each member of the group to choose a category and write a complex sentence that includes all of the words, including the category name. For example: *The cute bunny, which I tickled, was small and adorable.* **LIGHT**

LANGUAGE CONVENTIONS: Subordinating Conjunctions to Form Complex Sentences

A **clause** is a group of related words that contains a subject and a verb. A **subordinate clause** cannot stand alone as a sentence because it does not express a complete thought. It is subordinate to—that is, it depends on—an **independent clause** (the main clause that can stand alone as a sentence). A sentence that contains at least one subordinate clause and an independent clause is called a **complex sentence.**

Consider these examples of complex sentences from "Space Exploration Should Be More Science Than Fiction."

> **As we all know, this is a risky, but not impossible, proposition.**

> **NASA's Space Shuttle Program, which was the main connection to the International Space Station, suffered two terrible losses.**

In the first example, the subordinate clause begins with a **subordinating conjunction** (*as*). The conjunction reveals a relationship between the two clauses. In fact, the subordinate clause introduces the independent clause. In the second example, the subordinate clause begins with a **relative pronoun** (*which*). Relative pronouns introduce a relative clause, a type of subordinate clause.

This chart shows some common subordinating conjunctions and relative pronouns.

SUBORDINATING CONJUNCTIONS	RELATIVE PRONOUNS
as, although, as much as, after, as long as, as soon as, before, since, until, when, whenever, while, because, so	who, whom, whomever, whoever, whose, that, which,

Practice and Apply Write your own complex sentences using a subordinating conjunction or a relative pronoun.

RESPOND

Go to *Who* and *Whom* in the **Grammar Studio** to learn more.

Space Exploration Should Be More Science Than Fiction 337

APPLY

LANGUAGE CONVENTIONS: Subordinating Conjunctions to Form Complex Sentences

Review the information about subordinating conjunctions and complex sentences with students. Remind them that even though we may speak using sentence fragments and isolated clauses, in writing it is necessary to carefully use grammar rules with complex sentences, otherwise readers will struggle to understand.

Have students look at the first example sentence and see whether they can identify the subordinate clause ("As we all know"). Ask them how they identified it. (*It begins with a subordinating conjunction.*) Point out that subordinate clauses don't always appear in the middle of a sentence, sometimes they begin a sentence, too.

Move on to the second sentence, and ask the same questions. (The subordinate clause here is "which was the main connection to the International Space Station.") Ask students to rewrite the clause and make it into a main or independent clause. (*e.g., It was the main connection to the International Space Station.*) Ask them what they added to make it a main clause and why. (*A subject is added because that is what is missing in the subordinate clause and is also what the relative pronoun replaces.*)

Practice and Apply Have student partners work together to write both the longest and the shortest complex sentences they can think of. Circulate to ensure students have a clear understanding of independent clauses, subordinate clauses, subordinate conjunctions, and relative pronouns.

TEACH

 ANALYZE ARGUMENT

Point out that this text presents an argument and is intended to persuade the reader. In this type of text, the argument an author is making can often be found in the title. Authors presenting an argument will give their opinion on a topic as well as facts or information that support the main idea. Point out that the very first line is a sweeping generalization, and is used to engage the reader. What the authors says may be true for many people, but it is also possible that not everyone finds space travel alluring. (**Answer:** *The author's argument will be that we should let robots explore space rather than humans. The title helps clarifies that the author isn't arguing against space exploration, just against sending humans into space.*)

 ENGLISH LEARNER SUPPORT

Use Prereading Strategies Before students start the selection, point to the title and the headings on each page. Point to the tile of the selection, and read it aloud. Explain the word *should* is used to express the author's belief that it is better for humans to stay home instead of traveling to space.

ASK STUDENTS to discuss each heading in the selection with a partner. *Why does the author include these sections?* (*Each section tells a different reason why humans should stay home instead of going to space.*)

LIGHT

 **NOTICE & NOTE**

BACKGROUND
While space travel and exploration have been widely celebrated since the first humans walked on the moon, not everyone is in favor of space travel. A short search on the Internet reveals blogs, editorials, and opinion essays expressing an opposing view. For these writers, there are other ways to find out about our solar system.

HUMANS SHOULD STAY HOME AND LET ROBOTS TAKE TO THE STARS
Argument by Eiren Caffall

PREPARE TO COMPARE
As you read, notice the way this author outlines her argument. Think about how she uses evidence to support her argument and whether that evidence makes the argument effective.

Notice & Note

Use the side margins to notice and note signposts in the text.

ANALYZE ARGUMENT
Annotate: In paragraph 1, underline the author's central claim and circle the reasons the author will use to support the claim.

Interpret: What will the author's argument be? How does the title of the selection help clarify the author's argument?

1   The lure of human space travel is undeniable. We've all grown up on endless types of entertainment set in the future that portray adventures on distant planets. Imagine yourself as an astronaut, a part of the first manned mission to Mars. Beyond that, there are generations of people who have been working to make space and space travel look cool, even inevitable. But high aspirations and romance aside, we need to face the harsh realities. Our notions about the inevitability and wonder of human space travel need to be checked, and any plans need to be reconsidered. Some of the best reasons to curtail space exploration come down to economics, human cost, and technology.

Space Travel Is Expensive

2   Space travel is extremely expensive. To get humans to Mars, it would take $1 trillion over a 25-year period. Obviously, no single government would want to take on that kind

of funding. A Mars mission would require international cooperation at a significant cost to each partner nation. A Mars mission might foster international cooperation, but it would consume funds that could be used for other things.

3   Some people suggest that the only way to get to Mars would be with the help of private companies. Because of this, the space exploration industry is made up not only of government agencies but also private companies headed by dreamers and people interested in profits over practicality. But these organizations are often badly managed. They don't work for the government, so accountability could be a problem. Even well-run companies are unlikely to have enough money to launch a Mars mission on their own. There are some experts who say that it wouldn't be possible to launch a mission to Mars without funding from commercials that would run during coverage of the project. That would turn a scientific mission into a reality television show. Would you want to trust a scientific mission to the people who run reality TV?

Space Travel Could Harm Our Polluted World

4   The risks of space exploration could be grave for a planet already **plagued** by pollution. There is an extra result of space travel: black carbon from rocket exhaust that's deposited in the outer atmosphere. The launch of a suborbital tourist craft is said to produce less carbon emissions than a standard flight from New York to London. However, once the rocket is above the atmosphere, the black carbon it releases can be pretty damaging. Try to imagine the black smoke from a diesel truck sitting above the sky. With no weather to wash it into the oceans, black carbon can stay put for up to ten years.

5   Many space boosters are suggesting that being able to leave our planet once it's exhausted of resources is a priority. They seem to be proposing that we have some sort of Planet B. Somehow they think that a colony on Mars or the moon could take the pressure off our world. Many of these people planning to profit from two things at once are also fans of the **dubious** technology of geoengineering.

6   As covered earlier, the essential ingredients for space exploration are international cooperation, vast investments of money, technological advances, global regulations, and the buy-in of the general population. Yet those ingredients may well be what's needed to tackle the problem of Earth's pollution.

NOTICE & NOTE

LANGUAGE CONVENTIONS
Annotate: In paragraph 3, circle the relative pronoun in the first sentence and underline the two ideas it connects.

Analyze: How are the two ideas related?

plague
(plāg) v. To *plague* something is to cause hardship or suffering for it.

ANALYZE ARGUMENT
Annotate: In paragraph 5, mark an opposing viewpoint.

Analyze: What are the author's counterarguments to this viewpoint, as explained in paragraphs 5 and 6?

dubious
(do͞o′bē-əs) adj. If something is *dubious*, it is questionable or not to be relied upon.

WHEN STUDENTS STRUGGLE...

Sketch to Stretch   To help students understand the argument being made by the author in paragraph 3, provide a Sketch to Stretch Activity. Have students reread the paragraph and underline words or sentences they find confusing or unclear. As students reread, have them draw what they think the author is describing in the margin. Then, have students label their drawing with terms from the text. Model the activity by rereading the last sentence aloud while drawing a reality TV personality on the board and labeling it accordingly.

TEACH

LANGUAGE CONVENTIONS

Ask a volunteer to explain what a coordinating conjunction is. Invite the class to provide examples. (*a word that connects two clauses: and, but, for, nor, or, so, yet*) Then have them read the paragraph independently to answer the prompt. (**Answer:** *The conjunction "so" connects the ideas that companies might not be accountable because they don't work for the government.*)

ANALYZE ARGUMENT

Tell students that to identify the counterargument the author addresses, they must first identify the argument the author is making. Ask students to identify the text feature on p. 339 that helps them know the author's point of view. (*heading*) Then have them identify the opposing viewpoint in paragraph 5. (**Answer:** *The author argues against the idea that finding a Planet B should be a priority by asserting that people who promote the idea of setting up a colony on another planet are actually hoping to profit from the idea and that the very skills and resources needed to set up a colony elsewhere are the ones that would allow us to tackle Earth's pollution and keep Earth habitable.*)

CRITICAL VOCABULARY

plague: The text explains that our planet is harmed by pollution.

ASK STUDENTS what kinds of pollution the author is worried will continue to plague the planet. (*black carbon in the atmosphere*)

dubious: The science of geoengineering is still quite young, and many are skeptical about it.

ASK STUDENTS who supports the dubious technology of geoengineering. (*People who want to profit off a Planet B initiative.*)

TEACH

NOTICE AND NOTE

Have students identify the three numbers in paragraph 7. Then have them work with a partner to understand why the author included these details. Provide sample questions to guide the discussion: What do these figures tell you about the effects of space travel on the human body? Do you think these details are important? (**Answer:** *The specific numbers are strong evidence that help support the argument and make it seem more valid.*)

 ANALYZE RHETORICAL DEVICES

Point out that authors often use certain types of language when making generalizations. *All, entire, absolutely,* and *total* are some examples of language used to make generalizations. Pay attention to this kind of language as you read paragraph 9. (**Answer:** *The author is making the idea of robots, as opposed to astronauts, seem more appealing by suggesting that everyone loves the photos the robotic explorers send back. However, this rhetorical device depends on the reader's familiarity with the images from the robots. Readers who are unfamiliar may either gloss over the statement or become annoyed that the author assumes they know something about this.*)

ANALYZE RHETORICAL DEVICES

Remind students that direct address occurs when an author speaks straight to the reader. Often, an author will use a generic you in a direct address. (**Answer:** *The clause "As you might guess" is a suggestion that the author has presented so much evidence that the reader must conclude that robots will be better for space exploration than humans. It's a way of bringing the reader into the discussion.*)

CRITICAL VOCABULARY

erupt: At NASA there was a loud burst of enthusiastic cheering when *Opportunity* landed on Mars.

ASK STUDENTS Why did the author include the detail that the Mission Control Center erupted in cheers? (*to show that the people who worked there were extremely excited and their reactions were just as enthusiastic as they would have been for a human mission*)

 **NOTICE & NOTE**

NUMBERS AND STATS

Notice & Note: In paragraph 7, mark specific numbers that identify amounts.

Analyze: What purpose does the use of specific numbers serve?

ANALYZE RHETORICAL DEVICES

Annotate: Mark an example of a sweeping generalization in paragraph 9.

Evaluate: How effective is this statement in convincing readers of the benefit of robots over astronauts?

erupt
(ĭ-rŭpt´) *v.* When something *erupts,* it develops suddenly.

ANALYZE RHETORICAL DEVICES

Annotate: Mark an example of direct address in paragraph 10.

Infer: Why does the author use direct address here?

Space Travel Is More Suited to Robots

7 NASA recently collected data from the Mars Curiosity rover. The data were used to estimate the radiation impact on an astronaut traveling to and from Mars for 365 days and spending 500 days on the surface. It was determined that during that trip an astronaut would get a radiation dose that was about five percent of what he or she would get over a lifetime on Earth. That significantly increases the risk of cancer.

8 There is also the danger of running low on supplies. Once on the Red Planet, humans would eventually run out of food and materials. A Massachusetts Institute of Technology study guessed that agriculture would make too much oxygen for the small colony to support inside its dome. Without enough carbon dioxide, the colony would not be able to grow what it needed. Earth would constantly be sending supplies to the colonists. It's obvious that without that resupply, there would be no hope of agriculture supporting a manned station on Mars.

9 Considering the extreme risks for humans, some scientists assert space exploration should be strictly robotic. Think about the achievements of the Hubble Space Telescope and the Mars Pathfinder and Opportunity. Their exploratory missions have captured the public imagination, and all of us love to see images from those robot explorers. When Opportunity landed safely on the surface of Mars, NASA's Mission Control Center **erupted** in as loud a cheer as greeted any human mission.

10 There are scientists who say that robots can't accomplish space travel as cheaply or efficiently as humans. But, as is often the case, those ideas are based on data from the distant history of space travel. As you might guess, the future of space exploration presents a very different picture, one where robots will replace humans as the better pilots and researchers.

TO CHALLENGE STUDENTS. . .

Write an Argument Challenge students to write an argument paragraph that includes sweeping generalizations, modeling the style of the author, Eiren Caffall. Provide students with the following topic: Are people today too dependent on technology? Allow students to research the topic if necessary. Remind them that they should include factual information in their paragraphs, along with their opinions.

Space Travel Isn't Inevitable or Even Necessary

11 There are many solid arguments against spending money, time, and energy on manned space exploration. There is no solid reason to think of space as the only hope of our bright technological future. There are as many ways to innovate as there are human ideas. Just because the idea of space travel has been with us for decades doesn't mean that it's the best way to direct our dreams. Let's plot a course that doesn't involve humans. Without space travel as the default idea for our future, what new ideas might lead to amazing discoveries and inventions?

CHECK YOUR UNDERSTANDING

Answer these questions before moving on to the **Analyze the Text** section on the following page.

1 The author included the section Space Travel Is Expensive to —

   A offer an opposing argument for sending robots
   B support the claim that space travel should be reduced
   C convince readers that space travel could be cheaper
   D suggest that space travel requires international cooperation

2 The author refers to a Massachusetts Institute of Technology study in paragraph 8 to support the idea that —

   F humans are not suited to live on Mars
   G the Mars Curiosity rover has had great success
   H agriculture on Mars would be possible
   J a colony on Mars would require a lot of food

3 In paragraph 10, the author offers the counterargument that —

   A robotic missions are as exciting as any human missions
   B the future of space travel is dependent on scientific data
   C data for space travel is often out of date or not trustworthy
   D robotic missions are at least as efficient as human missions

Humans Should Stay Home and Let Robots Take to the Stars 341

TEACH

CHECK YOUR UNDERSTANDING

Have students answer the questions independently.

Answers:

1. B
2. F
3. D

If they answer any questions incorrectly, have them reread the test to confirm their understanding. Then they may proceed to ANALYZE THE TEXT on p. 342.

ENGLISH LEARNER SUPPORT

Oral Assessment Use the following questions to assess students' comprehension and speaking skills.

1. Remember that the author is making an argument. Why does the author want the reader to know space travel is expensive? *(to show that humans should not do it)*

2. What details in paragraph 8 tell about life on Mars? Is it easy for humans to live on Mars? *(It is not easy for humans to live on Mars. It is impossible to grow food there. People would always need supplies to survive.)*

3. Do some scientists think robots are not good for space travel? What does the author think? *(Yes. Some scientists think humans are better at space travel. The author does not agree.)* **ALL LEVELS**

APPLY

ANALYZE THE TEXT

Possible answers:

1. **DOK 4:** The author does not think it's a good idea to let private companies fund Mars missions because they would not be accountable to government. She ends the paragraph with a rhetorical question to show the reader that it's not a good idea to let inexperienced people who have no background in a highly specialized field be in charge of something so important; such people or entities might not consider the welfare of society or know how to solve important problems.

2. **DOK 4:** The author presents an effective argument by explaining that black carbon can stay in the atmosphere for 10 years. The argument might be stronger if she explained how serious of an effect black carbon could have on the environment.

3. **DOK 3:** Possible response: I agree with the author that robots will, if not replace humans, then greatly outnumber them for space travel. Based on the data that describes the dangers of radiation, the unsustainability of a colony on another planet, and the successful robot missions that have already happened, it makes more sense to use robots.

4. **DOK 4:** The author's main reasons for claiming robots are better suited for space travel relate directly to each heading in the text. First, she explains that it is costly. Next she explains that too much space exploration would further pollute the planet. After that she explains that space exploration is dangerous to humans. Last, she includes a heading that restates her argument that space travel isn't inevitable or necessary. By concluding with a strong statement that summarizes her argument, she is making the argument more effective since it will likely stick in readers' minds.

5. **DOK 4:** The specific numbers make the author sound as if research backs her up. The argument would be less effective without the specific numbers, as they provide the real evidence and support for her argument.

RESEARCH

Point out that while the NASA website has a wealth of information, students should also look for interviews and news articles about the astronauts they've chosen for their charts.

Extend Remind students that many countries contributed to the creation of the ISS. More information can be found on the European Space Agency website as well.

RESPOND

ANALYZE THE TEXT

Support your responses with evidence from the text. 📓 **NOTEBOOK**

1. **Interpret and Analyze** Review paragraph 3. What is the author's position on using private companies for Mars missions? What rhetorical devices does the author use to support her position, and why?

2. **Evaluate** Review paragraphs 4–6. Does the author present an effective argument about why space travel could end up harming Earth? Explain.

3. **Critique** In paragraph 10, the author predicts robots will replace humans for space travel. Do you agree with the author? Why? Be sure to use reasons and supporting evidence in your response.

4. **Summarize and Analyze** Examine the headings and then summarize the reasons the author provides to support her claim. Explain why you think she put the reasons in the order that she did. Which reason is last? Why do you think she saved it for last?

5. **Notice & Note** How does the author use specific numbers and statistics to support her claim? Would her argument be as effective without specific numbers—for example, dollar amounts? Explain.

RESEARCH TIP
You may need to follow several leads for your research, but you likely may find much of it on the NASA website. Begin with a specific search for International Space Station crew members. Then look for research information and updates that involve the crew members you have identified.

RESEARCH

Explore the International Space Station (ISS). Find out about three crew members—past or present—including their length of time on the ISS and their research efforts. Record your findings in a chart like this one.

CREW MEMBER	TIME ON ISS/RESEARCH
Mark Vande Hel	Sept 2017-Feb 2018: investigations in biology, Earth science, human research, physical sciences. Exploring ability of synthetic bone material to help bone repair.
Joe Acaba	Sept 2017-Feb 2018: reasearch in slowing or reversing muscle atrophy in astronauts.
Alexander Misurkin	Sept 2017-Feb 2018: experiments in biology, biotechnology, physical science, and Earth science.

Extend The International Space Station is exactly that—international. Find out which countries collaborate to support the International Space Station and how they work together.

WRITE AND PRESENT

Write a Short Story Write about an astronaut who is about to embark on a space mission but suddenly changes his or her mind.

- ❏ Introduce your characters and setting, and establish a point of view through your narrator.
- ❏ Then, establish and develop the conflict and sequence of events. Remember to use dialogue, pacing, and descriptive details.
- ❏ To conclude your story, resolve the conflict and leave readers with a message to consider.

Describe a Process Become familiar with the resources on NASA's website. Then, with a partner, demonstrate how to use the resources.

- ❏ With your partner, go to NASA.gov and explore the website. Notice the specific mission and project links on the home page, as well as recent NASA news.
- ❏ Note the pathways you must take to access various kinds of information (for example, to find recent crew members on the International Space Station or to view images).
- ❏ With your partner, demonstrate how to navigate the NASA site to access the site's resources. Walk your audience through the steps, noting the range of information and how to find specific items.

RESPOND TO THE ESSENTIAL QUESTION

 Why is the idea of space exploration both inspiring and unnerving?

Gather Information Review your annotations and notes on "Humans Should Stay Home and Let Robots Take to the Stars." Then, add relevant details to your Response Log. As you determine which information to include, think about:

- the roles humans and robots each play in space research
- the risks and benefits of space exploration
- your own position on space exploration

At the end of the unit, use your notes to help you write an argument.

RESPOND

Go to **Writing Narratives** in the **Writing Studio** to help develop a point of view.

Go to **Giving a Presentation** in the **Speaking and Listening Studio** to learn more.

ACADEMIC VOCABULARY

As you write and discuss what you learned from the argument, be sure to use the Academic Vocabulary words. Check off each of the words that you use.

- ❏ complex
- ❏ potential
- ❏ rely
- ❏ stress
- ❏ valid

APPLY

WRITE AND PRESENT

Write a Short Story Tell students to create reference materials, such as an outline or plot diagram before they begin writing. Guide students to reference these documents as they write their short stories. Point out that their reference documents are only a guide. If an element from their outlines no longer works, such as the point of view or the main conflict, they can swap those details out for something that works better for their story.

Describe a Process Remind students that they can keep a record of the steps they take to find different information on the NASA website by writing the steps on a sheet of paper, typing the steps out, or saving digital documents from the website that they can refer to later. Numbering the steps will help them retrace their process the next time they need to reference a particular piece of information

RESPOND TO THE ESSENTIAL QUESTION

Allow time for students to add details from "Humans Should Stay Home and Let Robots Take to the Stars" to their Unit 4 Response Logs.

APPLY

CRITICAL VOCABULARY

Answers:

1. *a report on an alien spaceship in Central Park because most people would be skeptical about aliens visiting New York City, while heat waves in California are quite common.*

2. *traffic jams and litter because those things are unpleasant, while warm weather and sunshine are likely to be welcomed by people living in a city.*

3. *a guitarist playing a solo because people usually react enthusiastically to a good musician, but a lecture on hygiene would likely not be very exciting.*

VOCABULARY STRATEGY:
Dictionary/Glossary Entries

Answers:

1. **plague** (plăg) *n.*

   Something that causes persistent hardship, trouble, or annoyance

   [Middle English plage, "blow, calamity, plague," from Late Latin plāga, from Latin, "blow, wound"; Middle English plaghen, from Middle Dutch, from plaghe, "plague," from Late Latin plāga.]

2. **dubious** (d(y)ü-bē-əs) *adj.*

   Uncertain or doubtful

   [Latin dubiosis, doubtful, from dubium, to doubt.]

 RESPOND

WORD BANK
plague
dubious
erupt

CRITICAL VOCABULARY

Practice and Apply Mark the letter of the better answer to each question. Be prepared to explain your responses.

1. Which of these Internet articles is more likely to be **dubious**?
   a. a report on a heat wave in California
   b. a report on an alien spaceship in Central Park

2. Which pair of factors is more likely to **plague** a city?
   a. traffic jams and litter
   b. warm weather and sunshine

3. Which situation is more likely to make an audience **erupt** in applause?
   a. a guitarist playing a solo
   b. a lecture on hygiene

VOCABULARY STRATEGY:
Dictionary/Glossary Entries

Print or digital dictionaries and glossaries are a great first step for checking the correct **spelling** and **definition** of a word. They can also give you information about the **syllabication, pronunciation, part of speech, alternate meanings,** and **word history** of entries.

Here is an example of a dictionary entry for the Critical Vocabulary word *erupt*:

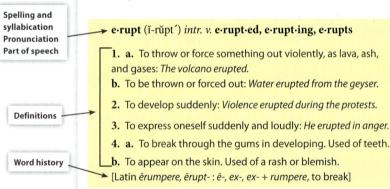

Go to the **Vocabulary Studio** for help using a dictionary or glossary.

Practice and Apply Use a print or digital dictionary to look up the Critical Vocabulary words *plague* and *dubious*. On a separate sheet of paper, write the syllabication, pronunciation, word history, and definition of each word as it is used in the selection. Then write a complete sentence using a Critical Vocabulary word of your choice.

344 Unit 4

 ENGLISH LEARNER SUPPORT

Vocabulary Strategy Point out that English, unlike other languages such as Spanish, does not always spell words the way they sound. When you read a word that you're unsure how to pronounce, check how the word is pronounced in a dictionary or ask a teacher or other expert for help. Write the word *plague* on the board and then write *play—guh* under it. Sound out the parts of the word, and then pronounce the word altogether. Have the students repeat after you. Do the same with the word *dubious. Dew—b—us.* **ALL LEVELS**

RESPOND

LANGUAGE CONVENTIONS: Complete Complex Sentences

In this lesson, you learned that a **complex sentence** contains an independent, or main, clause and at least one subordinate clause. You also learned that a clause is a group of related words that includes both a subject and a verb.

In complex sentences, the subject and verb must agree in number in both kinds of clauses. Study this example from "Humans Should Stay Home and Let Robots Take to the Stars."

> As you might guess, the future of space exploration presents a very different picture, one where robots will replace humans as the better pilots and researchers.

Note that there are two subordinate clauses in the sentence. In the first one, the subject *you* agrees with the verb *might guess*. In the second one, the subject *robots* agrees with the verb *will replace*. The subject and verb of the independent clause (*future* and *presents*) also agree.

A complex sentence that is **complete** must contain a subject and a verb in each clause. A **sentence fragment,** or a sentence that is not complete, lacks either a subject or a verb. To avoid sentence fragments, make sure that each clause contains both a subject and a verb.

Other types of errors to avoid as you create complete complex sentences include run-on sentences and comma splices. A **run-on sentence** is made up of two or more sentences written as though they were one. Sometimes a run-on sentence will have no punctuation. Other times, a comma will be used instead of a conjunction or a semicolon. You can often fix a run-on by adding a semicolon or conjunction.

A **comma splice** occurs when two independent clauses are joined with only a comma. One way to correct a comma splice is to split the clauses into separate sentences, but you can also replace the comma with a semicolon, add a coordinating conjunction, or rephrase the sentence as a complex sentence with the use of a subordinating conjunction or relative pronoun.

Practice and Apply Write your own complex sentences. Your sentences can be about space travel or about the arguments that you just read. Underline the subject and verb in each clause. Then, check that every sentence is complete and uses correct subject-verb agreement.

Go to **Agreement of Subject and Verb** in the **Grammar Studio** for more help.

APPLY

LANGUAGE CONVENTIONS: Complete Complex Sentences

Review the information about complex sentences with students. Explain that authors often include complex sentences to add sentence variety, to link related ideas, to contrast different ideas, or to expand on one idea with more information.

Guide students to deconstruct the complex sentence as they check for subject-verb agreement.

Identify subordinate clauses Remind students that like a sentence fragment, a subordinate clause cannot stand on its own because it is not a complete thought. The two subordinate clauses in the sample sentence are "As you might guess," and "one where robots will replace humans as the better pilots"

Evaluate subject and verb Have a volunteer remind the class of the definition for *subject* and *verb*. Explain that when subject and verb *agree in number*, that means students should identify whether the subject is plural or singular in order to use the correct form of the verb it agrees with. Point out the subject-verb agreement in *robots will replace*. Have students identify what form the verb would take if *robots* were singular. *(would replace)*

Practice and Apply Tell students to include at least one subordinate clause in their complex sentences. Then have partners work together to review each other's sentences and check that they have correct subject-verb agreement in their sentences.

ENGLISH LEARNER SUPPORT

Language Conventions Use the following supports with students at varying proficiency levels:

- Provide pairs of students with this complex sentence: *As the scientist predicted, the robot was able to explore Mars*. Have students underline each clause. Assist them in identifying the subject and verb. Then, read the subject and verb aloud with correct agreement, and have students chorally repeat. **MODERATE**

- Ask students to write a complex sentence independently that is connected to the subject of the article. Have pairs exchange sentences, identify the clauses in the sentences, and check for correct subject-verb agreement. **LIGHT**

APPLY

COMPARE ARGUMENTS

Encourage students to cite claims and evidence from both Alarcon's and Caffall's articles in completing the Venn diagram. Remind the class that the goal is not only to contrast the two opposed viewpoints, but to assess the strengths and similarities of the specific arguments made in each text.

ANALYZE THE TEXTS

Possible answers:

1. **DOK 2:** *In Alarcon's article the author argues that space exploration is important and essential for our survival. In Caffall's article, the author argues that space exploration is important but that human travel is unnecessary. While the first article presents the idea of a Mars colony as a possible home for humankind, the second article suggests that a Mars colony would not be self-sufficient. The author argues instead that the time, money, and effort should be spent solving the problems on Earth.*

2. **DOK 2:** *Both authors are in favor of robotic space exploration. Both cited robotic missions to Mars and their findings.*

3. **DOK 4:** *Both use loaded language, such phrases as "key to humanity's future" and "face the harsh realities." But the first article by Alarcon uses more incidences of loaded language, noting that "the future of the human race and Earth itself is at stake." The second article relies on numbers and statistics. Statistics like costs of space missions help lend the argument credibility.*

4. **DOK 4: Possible answer:** *The article by Caffall was more convincing because it outlined the reasons for the argument and included compelling evidence to support each reason, including numbers and statistics.*

 RESPOND

SPACE EXPLORATION SHOULD BE MORE SCIENCE THAN FICTION
Argument by Claudia Alarcón

HUMANS SHOULD STAY HOME AND LET ROBOTS TAKE TO THE STARS
Argument by Eiren Caffall

Collaborate & Compare

COMPARE ARGUMENTS

When you compare two or more texts on the same topic, you synthesize the information, making connections and expanding upon key ideas.

In a small group, complete the Venn diagram with similarities and differences in the two arguments you read. Consider the subjects being compared, claims made, reasons and evidence given, and rhetorical devices and persuasive techniques used by each author.

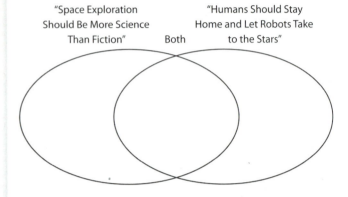

ANALYZE THE TEXTS

Discuss these questions in your group.

1. **Compare** With your group, study your Venn diagram. How do the claims in the two arguments differ? How are the ways each author presents their reasons and supporting evidence similar? How do they differ?

2. **Analyze** What similarities do you see between the authors' ideas about space exploration? Explain.

3. **Evaluate** What rhetorical devices and persuasive techniques does each author use? How effective is each author's use of these devices and techniques? Why?

4. **Critique** Which argument is more convincing? Why?

 ENGLISH LEARNER SUPPORT

Think About It Ask students a few simple questions to get them thinking about the ways the two articles compare and contrast.

1. What did you learn from Alarcon's article about the good things in space exploration?
2. What did you learn in Caffall's article about the bad things in space travel?
3. What ideas did the two articles share?

Put students into pairs of varying proficiency and encourage them to discuss the issues presented in both articles. **MODERATE**

RESPOND

RESEARCH AND SHARE

Your group can continue exploring the ideas in these texts by working together to research and write a job description for being an astronaut. Then you will research specific astronauts and determine how well these candidates meet your job description. Follow these steps:

1. **Choose a Focus** In your group, decide who will research the requirements for becoming an astronaut and who will research specific astronaut candidates.

2. **Gather Information** As you research your specific focus, check that your sources are **reliable** (reputable and up to date) and **credible** (presenting ideas fairly and accurately). Take notes from at least one source, paraphrasing and summarizing key information. You can use this framework to record your findings.

Focus:
Source(s):
Information:

3. **Write a Job Description or Profile** Use your research notes to write either a job description for being an astronaut or a profile of the astronaut candidate you researched. Your profile should include information about the astronaut's education, work experiences, and training.

4. **Share What You Learn** Each person in your group now has a general idea of what it takes to become an astronaut. Listen as each group member presents a job description or profile. Then, discuss how well each astronaut candidate meets the job description. As a group, discuss what most surprised you about the astronauts' backgrounds and about specific job requirements. Talk about whether the research made you more or less interested in becoming an astronaut.

RESEARCH TIP
For help in writing a job description, look at the "help wanted" section in newspapers or the "careers" or "jobs" page on company or employment websites.

Collaborate & Compare 347

APPLY

RESEARCH AND SHARE

Explain that a job description is a list of duties and responsibilities for any job in a company or agency and that candidates apply for these roles based on how well they believe they can perform the tasks. Help students conduct their research by first encouraging them to brainstorm about what an astronaut's training might look like. Then suggest a few websites and books they can mine for information, such as the NASA website and www.space.com.

1. **Choose a Focus** Remind students that these tasks can be delegated with fairness, giving every student the same amount of responsibility for the research.

2. **Gather Information** Encourage students to fill out their charts thoroughly. Ask them to vet their resources by checking the primary resources of things like online encyclopedia entries and blogs.

3. **Write a Job Description or Profile** The NASA website will be helpful for these tasks (www.nasa.gov) or www.science.howstuffworks.com.

4. **Share What You Learn** Decide on the discussion format before students share, for instance allowing one group member to facilitate while the others take turns presenting their work. Alternatively, the groups could play a role-playing game in which some students are the employers at NASA while others are the potential astronauts. Allow students the time to test their ideas and research, and have a little bit of fun with the scenario.

WHEN STUDENTS STRUGGLE . . .

Analyze an Example Have students get into pairs and view one former astronaut biography online at www.nasa.gov.

Encourage students to discuss the individual and to take notes. Have them ask one another simple questions: *What education did this astronaut have? What kind of skills does she or he have? How long did the astronaut work before she or he was sent into out space?*

Astronaut Name	Education	Skills	Training

Space Exploration Should Be More Than Science Fiction/Humans Should Stay Home 347

INDEPENDENT READING

READER'S CHOICE

Setting a Purpose Have students review their Unit 4 Response Log and think about what they've already learned about the possibilities and dangers of space exploration. As they select their Independent Reading selections, encourage them to consider what more they want to know.

NOTICE & NOTE

Explain that some selections may contain multiple signposts; others may contain only one. And the same type of signpost can occur many times in the same text.

LEARNING MINDSET

Persistence Grit is good stuff: Sparks eventually fly when we grind away at work, as we begin to "get the idea." Remind students that the will to bear down and keep trying is rewarded in every endeavor. Encourage them to ask questions and share information freely in an environment where persistent curiosity is warmly supported.

 INDEPENDENT READING

 ESSENTIAL QUESTION:

Why is the idea of space exploration both inspiring and unnerving?

Reader's Choice

Setting a Purpose Select one or more of these options from your eBook to continue your exploration of the Essential Question.

- Read the descriptions to see which text grabs your interest.
- Think about which genres you enjoy reading.

Notice & Note

In this unit, you practiced asking **Big Questions** and noticing and noting two signposts: **Numbers and Stats** and **Word Gaps**. As you read independently, these signposts and others will aid your understanding. Below are the anchor questions to ask when you read literature and nonfiction.

Reading Literature: Stories, Poems, and Plays		
Signpost	Anchor Question	Lesson
Contrasts and Contradictions	Why did the character act that way?	p. 99
Aha Moment	How might this change things?	p. 3
Tough Questions	What does this make me wonder about?	p. 362
Words of the Wiser	What's the lesson for the character?	p. 363
Again and Again	Why might the author keep bringing this up?	p. 3
Memory Moment	Why is this memory important?	p. 2

Reading Nonfiction: Essays, Articles, and Arguments		
Signpost	Anchor Question(s)	Lesson
Big Questions	What surprised me? What did the author think I already knew? What challenged, changed, or confirmed what I already knew?	p. 265 p. 183 p. 437
Contrasts and Contradictions	What is the difference, and why does it matter?	p. 183
Extreme or Absolute Language	Why did the author use this language?	p. 182
Numbers and Stats	Why did the author use these numbers or amounts?	p. 264
Quoted Words	Why was this person quoted or cited, and what did this add?	p. 437
Word Gaps	Do I know this word from someplace else? Does it seem like technical talk for this topic? Do clues in the sentence help me understand the word?	p. 265

ENGLISH LEARNER SUPPORT

Enhance Fluency Select appropriate passages for the levels below.

- Display the passage on the board. Echo read it aloud with students and guide decoding as necessary. Provide images with labels and cognates to assist students' understanding of new vocabulary. Use gestures to support comprehension. Transition to choral reading the passage; stress proper intonation to reinforce fluency. Check comprehension by asking simple questions that require students to use vocabulary from the passage. **SUBSTANTIAL**

- Provide partners with two short passages. Have one partner read the first passage aloud while the other notes words or phrases that were pronounced with difficulty. Partners then reread the passage silently to reinforce comprehension. The partner who read aloud then tells his or her partner what the passage was about. Repeat for the second passage; have partners switch roles. **MODERATE**

- Have each student pick a passage, read it silently for a fixed period of time, and then write a summary. **LIGHT**

INDEPENDENT READING

You can preview these texts in Unit 4 of your eBook.
Then, check off the text or texts that you select to read on your own.

☐

ARGUMENT
Let's Aim for Mars
Buzz Aldrin

A former astronaut proposes "opening space to the average person," by exploring and colonizing Mars.

☐

PERSONAL ESSAY
An Optimistic View of the World
Dan Tani

Based on his experiences in space, Dan Tani provides us with a uniquely optimistic perspective on life.

☐

POEM
Your World
Georgia Douglas Johnson

Discover inspiration in these well-crafted words about the importance of taking risks.

☐

BIOGRAPHY
Sally Ride *from* Headstrong
Rachel Swaby

Learn how America's first female astronaut launched into space and changed our approach to its exploration.

Collaborate and Share With a partner discuss what you learned from at least one of your independent readings.

- Give a brief synopsis or summary of the text.
- Describe any signposts that you noticed in the text and explain what they revealed to you.
- Describe what you most enjoyed or found most challenging about the text. Give specific examples.
- Decide if you would recommend the text to others. Why or why not?

 Go to the **Reading Studio** for more resources on **Notice & Note.**

Independent Reading 349

INDEPENDENT READING

MATCHING STUDENTS TO TEXTS

Use the following information to guide students in choosing their texts.

Let's Aim for Mars **Lexile: 1140L**
  Genre: Argument
  Overall Rating: Challenging

An Optimistic View of the World **Lexile: 970L**
  Genre: Personal Essay
  Overall Rating: Accessible

Your World
  Genre: Poetry
  Overall Rating: Accessible

Sally Ride *from* Headstrong **Lexile: 1140L**
  Genre: Biography
  Overall Rating: Challenging

Collaborate and Share To assess how well students read the selections, walk around the room and listen to their conversations. Encourage students to be focused and specific in their comments.

 for Assessment

- Independent Reading Selection Tests

 Encourage students to visit the **Reading Studio** to download a handy handbook of **NOTICE & NOTE** signposts.

WHEN STUDENTS STRUGGLE . . .

Keep a Reading Log As students read their selected texts, have them keep a reading log for each selection to note signposts and their thoughts about them. Use their logs to assess how well they are noticing and reflecting on elements of the texts.

Reading Log for (title)		
Location	**Signpost I Noticed**	**My Notes About It**

Independent Reading **349**

PLAN

UNIT 4 Tasks

- **WRITE AN ARGUMENT**
- **PRESENT A PODCAST**

MENTOR TEXT
CHALLENGES FOR SPACE EXPLORATION
Argument by ANN LECKIE

LEARNING OBJECTIVES

Writing Task
- Write an argument supporting or opposing human space exploration.
- Use strategies to plan and organize information.
- Develop a focused, structured draft.
- Use the Mentor Text as a model for writing a persuasive argument with supporting reasons and evidence.
- Recognize and use transitional words and phrases.
- Use a rubric to evaluate writing.
- Write a script for a podcast, working in groups to explain aspects of a complex task.
- Publish writing to share it with an audience.

Speaking Task
- Present a podcast to an audience.
- Use appropriate verbal and nonverbal techniques.
- Listen actively to a presentation.
- **Language** Share information using the sentence stem *I learned _____* .

Assign the writing Task in Ed.

RESOURCES

- Unit 4 Response Log
- Writing Studio: Writing an Argument
- Speaking and Listening Studio: Using Media in a Presentation
- Grammar Studio: Module 8: Lesson 8: Pronoun-Antecedent Agreement

350A Unit 4

Language X-Ray: English Language Support

Use the instruction below and the supports and scaffolds in the Teacher's Edition to help you guide students of different proficiency levels.

INTRODUCE THE WRITING TASK

Explain that an **argument** is a form of writing that tries to convince readers of something: the wisdom of human space travel, maybe, or the best candidate for governor. An argument in this definition is not "a heated exchange of opposing views," the usual meaning of the term. Instead, it is an organized summary of a persuasive opinion, based on reasons and evidence in support of a claim. In groups, invite students to work on paragraphs that begin with the sentence stem *The best day of the week is _____*. Ask groups to pick different days, and group members to come up with reasons or arguments as to why that day is best. Have the groups choose one student to structure the argument in written form, taking notes from other members. Invite the students to collaborate on revisions to this written argument, which may later be read aloud by a member of each group.

WRITING

Use Transitional Words and Phrases

Tell students that ideas in text are connected with transitional words and phrases such as *for example*, *on the other hand* or *in conclusion*.

Use the following supports with students at varying proficiency levels:

- Draw three suns: on the rise, high in the sky, and setting behind a hill. Label the drawing as follows: *First it goes up. Later it comes down.* Review the use of the transitional word to connect sunrise and sunset. **SUBSTANTIAL**
- Present sentence frames for practice in using transitional words. For example: *It is heavier to launch, _____ it is cheaper to build.* (but) **MODERATE**
- Have students work with a partner to identify transitional words and phrases in a sample text and make note of possible synonyms. **LIGHT**

SPEAKING

Present Information

Provide students with the sentence stem *Human space travel is _____*. Circulate around the room to make sure students are using the sentence stem correctly.

Use the following supports with students at varying proficiency levels:

- Work with students to complete the sentence stem. Ask them to practice reciting the completed sentence to a partner. **SUBSTANTIAL**
- Have students build on the sentence stem using two reasons from their arguments. Ask them to cite those reasons aloud, to a partner or in a group. **MODERATE**
- Have the students build on the sentence stem using the following transitional words and phrases: *also*, *however*, and *finally*. Then have students practice their presentations with a partner. **LIGHT**

WRITING

WRITE AN ARGUMENT

Introduce students to the writing task by reading the introductory paragraph with them. Remind students to refer to the notes they recorded in the Unit 4 Response Log as they develop their textual arguments. The Response Log should contain ideas from a variety of perspectives about human space exploration. Drawing on these different perspectives will make the students' writing more interesting and well informed.

 For **writing support** for students at varying proficiency levels, see the **Language X-Ray** on page 350B.

USE THE MENTOR TEXT

Point out that their work will follow the form of "Challenges for Space Exploration" in presenting an argument addressing human space travel. However, caution students against adopting the first well-reasoned argument they read on this or any subject. Remind them to review varying perspectives on the topic before reaching an opinion on which to base their arguments.

WRITING PROMPT

Review the prompt with students. Encourage them to ask questions about any part of the assignment that is unclear. Make sure they understand the purpose of their narrative: to frame and present an argument for or against human space exploration.

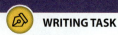 **WRITING TASK**

Go to the **Writing Studio** for help writing your argument.

Write an Argument

What are the short- and long-term consequences of space exploration? Are the risks worth the effort and the cost? For this writing task, you will write an argument about whether human space travel is necessary. For an example of a well-written argument you can use as a mentor text, review "Challenges for Space Exploration."

As you write your argument, you can use the notes from your Response Log, which you filled out after reading the texts in this unit.

Writing Prompt

Read the information in the box below.

> *This is the topic or context for your argument.*
>
> For more than half a century, we humans have reached farther and farther into space—not only walking on the moon, but exploring deep into our solar system. What more might we find out in space, if we keep exploring?

Think carefully about the following question.

> *This is the Essential Question for the unit. How would you answer this question, based on the texts in this unit?*
>
> Why is the idea of space exploration both inspiring and unnerving?

Write an argument in which you support a claim, or position, about whether or not human space travel is necessary.

Now mark the words that identify exactly what you are being asked to produce.

Be sure to—

Review these points as you write and again when you finish. Make any needed changes.

- ☐ provide an introduction with a claim that clearly states your position on the issue and reflects your depth of thought
- ☐ present at least two strong reasons to support your position
- ☐ support each reason with logical arguments and with various types of evidence from several reliable sources
- ☐ arrange reasons from least to most important
- ☐ group related ideas and organize ideas logically to create coherence within and across paragraphs
- ☐ use transitions to make the relationship between ideas clear
- ☐ use appropriate word choices and pronoun-antecedent agreement
- ☐ conclude by restating your position and summarizing your reasons

350 Unit 4

 LEARNING MINDSET

Belonging Encourage students to feel comfortable asking teachers or one another for help. Encourage those who can help to share knowledge and insight freely. Students who teach others will find that this is an excellent way of improving their own understanding of the topic. Learning is a collective endeavor that allows everyone to grow and make progress.

1 Plan

Before you start writing, you need to plan your argument. When you plan a draft, you begin by selecting a genre that is appropriate for the topic, purpose, and audience. For this writing task, you know that the topic is related to human space travel and that the genre is an argument. Next, consider your purpose and audience. Will you write to an audience of classmates, or to an audience of adults? Your audience helps determine the focus of your argument. In addition, you can use other helpful strategies to plan your draft. These might include discussing the topic with your classmates, doing some background reading, or thinking about personal interests related to the topic. Use the table below to assist you in planning your draft.

Argument Essay Planning Table	
Genre	Argument
Topic	The necessity for human space travel
Purpose	
Audience	
Ideas from discussions with classmates	
Ideas from background reading	
Personal interests related to topic	

Background Reading Review the notes you have taken in your Response Log after reading the texts in this unit. These texts provide background reading that can help you formulate the key ideas to include in your argument.

WRITING TASK

Go to **Introduction: Argument** for help planning your argument.

Notice & Note
From Reading to Writing

As you plan your argument, apply what you've learned about signposts to your own writing. Remember that writers use common features, called signposts, to help convey their message to readers.

Think about how you can incorporate evidence of **Contrasts and Contradictions** into your argument.

Go to the **Reading Studio** for more resources on Notice & Note.

Use the notes from your Response Log as you plan your argument.

Write an Argument 351

WRITING

1 PLAN

Allow time for students to discuss the topic with partners or in small groups and then to complete the planning chart independently.

■ **English Learner Support**

Understand Academic Language Make sure students understand words and phrases used in the chart, such as *genre*, *topic*, and *purpose*. Work with them to fill in the blank sections, providing text that they can copy into their charts as needed. **SUBSTANTIAL/MODERATE**

▸ **CONTRASTS AND CONTRADICTIONS**

From Reading to Writing Remind students that they can refer back to the signposts in the texts to look for common features. Have students list the different signposts they read aout in Unit 4. (**Answer**: numbers and stats, word gaps, big questions, contrasts and contradictions, ah ha moments, again and again, language conventions, words of the wiser, extreme or absolute language.)

Background Reading As they plan their arguments, remind students to refer to the notes they took in the Response Log. They may also review the selections to find additional facts and examples to support ideas they want to include in their writing.

TO CHALLENGE STUDENTS . . .

Explore Multimedia Challenge students to look for books, stories, movies, and documentaries that address human space exploration, including the history of lunar missions under the Apollo space program and the imagined odysseys of science fiction. Ask them to consider the persuasive argument woven into many of these stories: the allure of travel into unknown realms, as shared through select human eyes. Encourage them to search online or at the library and to add details from their research to the arguments they develop regarding human space exploration.

Write an Informative Essay 351

WRITING

Organize Your Ideas Remind students that their reasons will form the bulk of their arguments, to be delivered more or less as follows:

I. Introduction

II. First Reason to Support Your Position

III. Second Reason to Support Your Position

IV. Third Reason to Support Your Position

V. Conclusion

Remind students that each reason must be supported by evidence, which they should uncover as they do their research. The chart can serve as a guideline for structuring paragraphs, in which reasons and evidence are logically sequenced according to their importance. Point out that reasons supporting an argument may change as new evidence is encountered, and remind students to cite multiple authoritative sources in compiling their arguments.

2 DEVELOP A DRAFT

Remind students to follow their charts as they draft their arguments, but point out that they can still make changes to their writing plan during this stage. As they write, they may decide to consider other reasons, include other evidence, or modify language to hone their work.

■ English Learner Support

Write a Collaborative Argument Simplify the writing task and provide direct support by working in groups to write an argument that addresses the Essential Question.
SUBSTANTIAL/MODERATE

352   Unit 4

 WRITING TASK

Go to **Writing Arguments: Support: Reasons and Evidence** for help organizing your ideas.

Organize Your Ideas After you have gathered ideas from your planning activities, organize your material in a way that will help you draft your argument. You can use the chart below to outline the reasons you will use to support your position and to choose the order of importance in which you will present them. You can also use the chart to gather relevant information and to plan how you will support your reasons with specific facts, details, and examples.

Main Topic: Human Space Travel

IS HUMAN SPACE TRAVEL NECESSARY?

First reason to support your position	Second reason to support your position	Third reason to support your position
Evidence	Evidence	Evidence

 You may prefer to draft your argument online.

2 Develop a Draft

Once you have completed your planning activities, you will be ready to begin drafting your argument. Refer to your planning table and the completed chart above, as well as any notes you took as you studied the texts in this unit. These will provide a kind of road map for you to follow as you write. Using a computer program for writing or an online writing application makes it easier to rework sentences or move them around later when you are ready to revise your first draft.

352   Unit 4

WHEN STUDENTS STRUGGLE . . .

Develop a Draft Some students may need to have a stake in a given debate before they can take it on. An argument at home or with peers is reflexively framed this way. Students may be more comfortable developing their drafts using this framework. Ask them to complete the following sentence stem: *I think human space exploration is a _____ idea because _____ .* Point out to them that the parts they filled in are the beginnings of an argument their draft can develop from.

WRITING

WRITING TASK

Use the Mentor Text

Author's Craft
The introduction to your argument should grab the reader's attention and introduce your claim, or position. In her multi-paragraph introduction to "Challenges for Space Exploration," the author engages readers by presenting an interesting fact and asking a question about it. Her answer suggests the claim she will support.

> Thousands of years ago, when our ancestors came to the sea, they built boats and sailed enormous distances to islands they could not have known were there. Why?
> Probably for the same reason we look up at the moon and the stars and say, "What's up there? Could we go there? Maybe we could go there." Because it's something human beings do.

The author grabs the reader's attention with an interesting fact followed by a question. Her answer allows her to introduce the topic of space exploration and suggest her claim: humans should continue exploring space.

Apply What You've Learned To introduce your argument, you might provide an interesting detail or example to capture your reader's attention and provide context for your claim, or position.

Genre Characteristics
Writers of argumentative texts use reasons to support their position. Notice how the author of "Challenges for Space Exploration" gives a reason to support her opinion about humans' exploration of space.

> I could tell you that it might be good for us to unite behind a project that doesn't involve killing one another, that does involve understanding our home planet and the ways we survive on it and what things are crucial to our continuing to survive on it.

One reason the author gives to support her claim is that space exploration will help people be more successful living on Earth and surviving as a species.

Apply What You've Learned The reasons you give should clearly support the position you stated in the introduction. Remember, too, to supply facts, examples, and other evidence to support your reasons.

Write an Argument 353

WHY THIS MENTOR TEXT?
In form and content, "Challenges for Space Exploration" is good example of a text argument. Use the instruction below to help students review the mentor text as a model for developing an argument. Student work should reflect the structure of the mentor text: a strong thesis statement, reasons that support the argument, and a concise persuasive conclusion.

USE THE MENTOR TEXT

Author's Craft Note that an author's claim can be as plain as *I climbed that mountain* or as layered as the introduction to "Challenges for Space Exploration." Have students review the example paragraph. Ask: *What do ancient mariners and space explorers have in common?* (The author implies that all humans possess the same restless curiosity that pushes and drives us into uncharted territory.) Ask: *Does the author's claim appeal to logic or emotion?* (It appeals to emotion, through the romance of discovery and bold ventures into the unknown.)

Genre Characteristics Ask a volunteer to read the sample paragraph aloud. Ask: *In her argument supporting human space exploration, how many reasons does the author cite in a single sentence?* (three) Invite students to identify each reason. (Non-violent unity; better understanding of Earth; long-term survivability here.) Ask: *How would you search for evidence to support the reasons the author gives?* (Internet searches should yield evidence of benefits to science from modern space-based endeavors. "The benefits of space science" may point students to facts and figures that support the author's argument.)

ENGLISH LEARNER SUPPORT

Use the Mentor Text Use the following supports with students at varying proficiency levels:

- Draw a boat on water and a rocket flying through space. Then read the introduction aloud, referring back to the drawing. Ask: *How would* <u>exploring</u> *be the same, on a boat or in a rocket?* (Spanish cognate: *explorar*) **SUBSTANTIAL**

- Read the introduction aloud, and invite students to ask about any words or phrases that are unclear. Ask students to work in pairs, with one helping the other review unfamiliar terms. **MODERATE**

- Have students review the Mentor Text to identify reasons the author gives in favor of human space exploration. **LIGHT**

Write an Informative Essay **353**

WRITING

3 REVISE

Have students answer each question in the chart to determine how they can improve their drafts. Invite volunteers to model their revision techniques.

With a Partner Have students ask peer reviewers to evaluate the form and content of their arguments by answering the following questions:

- Is my argument (or claim) clearly stated in my introduction? How might I improve on it?
- Does my argument follow logical order, citing the strongest reasons first? Are my reasons strong enough, or could I come up with others? If so, how?
- Are my reasons supported with evidence, including facts and examples?
- Have I made good use of transitional words and phrases? Is there variety in my sentence structure?
- Does my conclusion summarize and restate my opening claim?

Students should use the reviewer's feedback to add relevant facts, details, examples, or quotations that further develop their main points.

 WRITING TASK

Go to the **Writing Studio: Concluding Your Argument** for revision help.

3 Revise

On Your Own Once you have written the draft of your argument, you'll want to go back and look for ways to improve your writing. As you reread and revise it, think about whether you have achieved your purpose. The Revision Guide will help you focus on specific elements to make your writing stronger.

Revision Guide

Ask Yourself	Tips	Revision Techniques
1. Does my introduction contain a clear claim?	**Highlight** the introduction. **Underline** the claim.	**Add** a claim—the point your argument makes—or **revise** the claim to clarify or strengthen your position on the issue.
2. Are paragraphs arranged in order of importance?	**Number** the paragraphs and identify whether they are presented so that the most important reason comes last.	**Rearrange** paragraphs in order of importance.
4. Do I include at least two reasons to support my argument? Do I support my reasons with evidence?	**Put a star** next to each reason. **Highlight** the supporting evidence for each reason.	**Add** reasons, and/or **include** another specific fact, example, or comparison to further support each reason.
5. Do transitions connect ideas?	**Circle** transitions that connect ideas.	**Add** transitions to connect ideas and clarify the organization.
6. Does my conclusion restate my position and summarize my reasons?	**Underline** the restatement of the claim. **Highlight** the summary of reasons.	**Add** or **revise** a restatement of the claim and a summary of the reasons.

ACADEMIC VOCABULARY
As you conduct your **peer review**, be sure to use these words.

- ☐ complex
- ☐ potential
- ☐ rely
- ☐ stress
- ☐ valid

With a Partner Once you and your partner have each worked through the Revision Guide on your own, exchange papers and evaluate each other's draft in a **peer review**. Focus on suggesting revisions for at least three of the items mentioned in the chart. Explain why you think your partner's draft should be revised and what specific suggestions you have.

When receiving feedback from your partner, listen attentively and ask questions to make sure you fully understand the revision suggestions.

 ENGLISH LEARNER SUPPORT

Use a Variety of Sentence Types Explain that text reads better when writers use a variety of sentence types. Share the following sample to model such variations:

"Big dumb boosters" have been considered. They are heavier rockets of a simpler design, built at a lower cost, than the smaller, more **complex** launch vehicles NASA traditionally favors.

Encourage students to revise their arguments to vary sentence length and structure.
LIGHT

WRITING TASK

4 Edit

Once you have addressed the organization, development, and flow of ideas in your argument, look to improve the finer points of your draft. Edit your final draft to check for proper use of standard English conventions and to correct any misspellings or grammatical errors.

Language Conventions

Pronoun-Antecedent Agreement Effective writers make sure that pronouns agree with their antecedents in number, gender, and person. A **pronoun** (such as *I*, *you*, *he*, *she*, *we*, and *they*) usually refers to a noun or another pronoun, called its **antecedent.** An **indefinite pronoun** refers to a person, place, or thing that is not specifically named. Examples include *all*, *both*, *many*, *each*, *none*, *several*, and *any*. Both kinds of pronouns agree in number—singular or plural—with their antecedents. Some indefinite pronouns, like *each*, are always singular. Others, like *both*, are always plural. And some, like *all* and *none*, can be either singular or plural, depending on the noun they refer to.

 Go to **Pronoun-Antecedent Agreement** in the **Grammar Studio** to learn more.

- The astronaut put on **her** spacesuit. [singular antecedent; **singular pronoun**]
- The astronauts put on **their** spacesuits. [plural antecedent; **plural pronoun**]
- All of them put on **their** spacesuits. [indefinite pronoun antecedent, in this case plural because of "them"; plural pronoun; **plural pronoun**]

Consider these examples based on "Challenges for Space Exploration."

Pronoun-Antecedent Agreement	Example
Agreement with an antecedent that is a noun	Voyagers [plural antecedent] to the stars will face dangers unimaginable to their [plural pronoun] ancestors.
Agreement with an antecedent that is an indefinite pronoun	Few [plural indefinite pronoun antecedent], however, would give up their [plural pronoun] chance to explore the universe.

5 Publish

Finalize your argument and choose a way to share it with your audience. Consider these options:

- Present your argument as a speech to the class.
- Post your argument as a blog on a classroom or school website.

Write an Argument   355

WHEN STUDENTS STRUGGLE . . .

Transitional Words and Phrases Some students struggle with transitions, the sinews that connect the elements (or ideas) of text together. Ask: *If your teacher asks you to do this but not that, where has she used a transition?* Working in pairs, ask students to describe out loud the route they take to school each morning until arrival. Ask the other student to make note of the speaker's transitional words and phrases. (**Possible examples:** *first, so, after that, then, because, finally*) Invite students to share notes and come up with more examples of transitional words and phrases.

WRITING

4 EDIT

Suggest that students read their drafts aloud to assess how clearly and smoothly they have presented their ideas. Guide them to edit for transitional words and phrases to develop continuity and cohesion in their texts. Remind them of examples such as *likewise, on the other hand, in general, for example*, and *finally* or *ultimately*. Encourage them to search the Internet or other resources for catalogues of transitional words and phrases.

LANGUAGE CONVENTIONS

Pronoun-Antecedent Agreement Review the information about pronoun-antecedent agreement with students. Then discuss the example sentence in the chart, asking students to identify the pronoun and antecedent in each one. Remind students that pronouns refer to people, places, or things:

- *their* space suits are bulky or
- *Its* density is largely unknown.

Note that pronouns "reach backwards" to agree with antecedents, which means "existing or coming before." For example:

- Astronauts (antecedent) walk slowly because *their* (pronoun) space suits are bulky.

Encourage students to edit their arguments for pronoun-antecedent agreement.

■ English Learner Support

Pronoun-Antecedent Agreement Review a short list of commonly used pronouns. Ask students to offer examples. (*I, you, he, she, his, hers, its, our, their*) Remind students that *singular* means "one" and *plural* means "more than one." Ask students to identify each pronoun cited as singular or plural. Encourage students to edit their arguments for pronoun-antecedent agreement.

MODERATE/LIGHT

5 PUBLISH

Students can present their arguments as blog posts on a school website. Encourage others to read the texts and write constructive comments about them. The authors can then respond to the comments.

Write an Informative Essay   355

WRITING

USE THE SCORING GUIDE

Allow students time to read the scoring guide and to ask questions about any words, phrases, or ideas that are unclear. Then have partners exchange final drafts of their arguments. Ask them to score their partner's work using the scoring guide, according to an assessment log they create by making notes on the strengths and weaknesses in each other's text. Those notes should be based on the criteria established in the chart: organization and progression; development of ideas; and use of language and conventions.

ENGLISH LEARNER SUPPORT

Use Formal English Help students with the Writing Task. Tell them to think of themselves as powerful lawyers who are trying to convince a jury or government panel to accept their claims about human space travel and exploration. Tell students that their listeners will expect them to use formal English in their arguments. Use the following categories from the Writing Task Scoring Guide to create frame sentences for students to use: Introduction, Claim, Supporting Ideas, and Conclusion. For example: *Claim: Some people think that human space travel is not as important as _____.* (Possible responses: using telescopes, global warming.) *This is not true because _____.* (Responses will vary.) **ALL LEVELS**

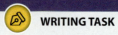 **WRITING TASK**

Use the scoring guide to evaluate your argument.

	Writing Task Scoring Guide: Argument		
	Organization/Progression	Development of Ideas	Use of Language and Conventions
4	• The organization is effective and appropriate to the purpose. • All ideas are focused on the topic specified in the prompt. • Reasons are clearly ordered from least to most important. • Transitions clearly show the relationship among ideas.	• The introduction catches the reader's attention. • The argument contains a clear, concise, and well-defined claim, or position. • The argument is very well developed, with reasons supported by convincing evidence. • The conclusion effectively restates the position and summarizes all the supporting reasons.	• Language and word choice are purposeful and precise. • Pronoun-antecedent agreement is correct. • Spelling, capitalization, and punctuation are correct. • Grammar and usage are correct.
3	• The organization is mostly effective and appropriate to the purpose. • Most ideas are focused on the topic specified in the prompt. • Reasons are ordered from least to most important. • A few more transitions are needed to show the relationship among ideas.	• The introduction could be more engaging. • The argument contains a clear claim, or position. • The argument is well developed, but not every reason is supported by convincing evidence. • The conclusion restates the position but may not summarize all the supporting reasons.	• Language and word choice show some thought but sometimes are ineffective. • Pronoun-antecedent agreement is mostly correct. • Spelling, capitalization, and punctuation are mostly correct, with only a few errors. • Grammar and usage are mostly correct, with only a few errors.
2	• The organization is evident but is not always appropriate to the purpose. • Only some ideas are focused on the topic specified in the prompt. • The order of importance of the reasons is not clear. • More transitions are needed to show the relationship among ideas.	• The introduction is not compelling. • The claim does not express a clear position. • The argument is not well developed and contains only one or two reasons, with evidence that is often unconvincing. • The conclusion does not restate the claim or summarize all the reasons.	• Language and word choice are often vague and general. • There are multiple errors in pronoun-antecedent agreement. • Spelling, capitalization, and punctuation are often incorrect but do not make reading difficult. • Grammar and usage are often incorrect, but the writer's ideas are still clear.
1	• The organization is not appropriate to the purpose. • Ideas are not focused on the topic specified in the prompt. • Reasons do not appear in order of importance. • No transitions are used, making the argument difficult to understand.	• The introduction is missing or confusing. • The claim is missing. • The argument is not well developed, lacking sufficient reasons and evidence. • The conclusion is missing or incomplete.	• Language and word choice are vague and confusing. • There are many errors in pronoun-antecedent agreement. • Many spelling, capitalization, and punctuation errors are present. • Many grammatical and usage errors are present, making the writer's ideas confusing.

Prepare a Podcast

SPEAKING AND LISTENING TASK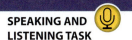

You have written an argument about the necessity of human space travel. Now you will consider one aspect of space travel: the spacewalk. With a group of your classmates, you will plan and present a 10-minute podcast explaining how this challenging task is accomplished. Each of you will research one aspect of the topic. Then, together, you will create a script for the podcast, practice it with your group, and record it so that you will have a permanent account of your work.

Go to **Using Media in a Presentation** in the **Speaking and Listening Studio** for help.

1 Plan Your Podcast Presentation

With your group, divide up the different aspects of a spacewalk that you will research for the podcast. Each group member should choose one of the following topics and become an "expert" in that topic:

- Purposes of spacewalks
- Training that prepares astronauts for a spacewalk
- Spacesuits and other equipment astronauts use on a spacewalk
- The procedure, or steps, for a safe, successful spacewalk

To research spacewalks, you can consult NASA's website and other reliable sources for information. In the chart below, you can answer the questions and take notes on the most important information you find. Then use the completed chart to create a draft of a script for your part of the podcast. Also consider visuals you might use to illustrate your topic.

Questions	Answers and Notes
What is the best way to introduce my part of the podcast? How can I grab the audience's attention?	
What information will my audience already know? What information should I leave out or add?	
Which parts of my presentation should I simplify? Where can I add transitions such as *first, second, in addition,* and *finally*? Is my pronoun-antecedent agreement correct?	
What images or graphics might help clarify ideas or add interest? When I present them, how will I explain them so that listeners to the recorded podcast (who won't be able to see the visuals) will understand what they show?	

Prepare a Podcast 357

ENGLISH LEARNER SUPPORT

Prepare a Podcast Use the following supports with students at varying proficiency levels:

- I enjoy listening to the ____. *(podcast)* The astronauts went out of the spaceship on a ___. *(spacewalk)* **SUBSTANTIAL**
- Review the questions in the chart to ensure students' understanding. Then have students work in pairs to apply the questions to their scripts. **MODERATE**
- Have students discuss the questions in the chart with partners before writing their answers independently. **LIGHT**

SPEAKING AND LISTENING

PREPARE A PODCAST

Introduce students to the Speaking and Listening Task by discussing distinctions between an argument, which is read silently, and a script, which they will write to be read aloud. Point out that readers can adjust their reading rate when the text presents difficult or complicated information. They can also reread passages they didn't understand the first time. Have students consider what a speaker can do to make sure everyone in the audience understands the information.

1 PLAN YOUR PODCAST PRESENTATION

Have students read the questions in the chart. Then work with the class to list some general principles for presenting information orally. (**Examples:** *Use short sentences. Repeat important ideas. Use humor or interesting examples to keep the audience engaged.*) Encourage students to use sensory detail in their scripts, to help listeners visualize subject matter. Point out the importance of transitions in moving the podcast from one "expert" voice to the next.

Write an Informative Essay **357**

WRITING

2 PRACTICE WITH A PARTNER OR GROUP

Review the information and tips with the class, ensuring that all the terms and ideas are clear. Remind students that they can all gain useful feedback from peers through practicing their presentations aloud. Encourage them to be mutually supportive in this process, noting that almost everyone has some anxieties about public speaking.

3 DELIVER YOUR PRESENTATION

Set aside time for all students to deliver their presentations. When everyone has finished, ask students to share their thoughts on how their classmates' feedback improved their performance.

 **SPEAKING AND LISTENING TASK**

As you work to improve your podcast presentation, be sure to follow discussion rules:

- ☐ Listen closely to one another.
- ☐ Don't interrupt.
- ☐ Stay on topic.
- ☐ Ask only helpful, relevant questions.
- ☐ Provide only clear, thoughtful, and direct answers.

2 Practice with a Partner or Group

Once you've completed the draft of your script, practice with the other "experts" in your group. Work collaboratively to improve one another's section of the podcast and delivery. Make note cards or an outline to guide you as you speak.

Practice Effective Verbal Techniques

- ☐ **Enunciation** Practice words that you stumble over and rearrange sentences so that your delivery is smooth.
- ☐ **Voice Modulation and Pitch** Use your voice to display enthusiasm and to emphasize key details and points.
- ☐ **Speaking Rate** Speak at a pace that allows listeners to understand you. Pause now and then after making a key point.
- ☐ **Volume** Speak loudly enough so that everyone can hear you, but avoid shouting.

Practice Effective Nonverbal Techniques

- ☐ **Eye Contact** Even for a podcast, letting your eyes rest briefly on audience members helps make the delivery feel more natural.
- ☐ **Facial Expressions** Use natural facial expressions, such as smiling, frowning, or nodding, to add emphasis to key points.
- ☐ **Gestures** Stand tall and relaxed. Gesture with your hands to add interest to your delivery and keep it feeling more natural.

Provide and Consider Advice for Improvement

As a presenter, listen closely to questions. Consider ways to revise your section of the podcast so that your key points are clear and logically sequenced. Remember to ask for suggestions about how you might make your presentation more interesting.

As a listener, pay close attention to each presenter. Take notes about ways that presenters can improve their delivery and more effectively use verbal and nonverbal techniques. Paraphrase and summarize each presenter's key points to confirm your understanding, and ask questions to clarify any confusing parts.

3 Record Your Podcast

With your teacher, plan how to record your presentation and share it as a podcast. After everyone in your group has practiced, record your podcast presentation. Then, as a group, review the recording and edit as needed. Share the final version—or just enjoy listening to it on your own!

FOR STRUGGLING STUDENTS

Belonging A group brings together individuals with a range of personal strengths and struggles. Encourage students to see their class as a unit, a team that gets more wins when every member's contribution is valued. That includes those who need to ask questions, and those who may be able to answer them. Remind them that asking questions may feel more difficult than answering questions. Education is a positive group activity in which everyone can grow and make progress. Everyone learns, every day.

Reflect on the Unit

By completing your argument, you have created a writing product that helps pull together and express your thoughts about the reading you have done in this unit. Now is a good time to reflect on all that you have learned.

Reflect on the Essential Question

- Why is the idea of space exploration both inspiring and unnerving? How has your response to this question changed since you first considered it when you started this unit?

- What are some examples from the texts you've read that show how people are inspired or unnerved by the idea of space exploration?

Reflect on Your Reading

- Which selections were the most interesting or surprising to you?

- From which selection did you learn the most about the challenges of space exploration, and from which one did you learn the most about its benefits?

Reflect on the Writing Task

- What challenges did you encounter while working on your argument? How might you avoid or overcome them next time?

- What parts of the argument were the easiest and hardest to write? Why?

- As you were revising, how did you decide what improvements to make to strengthen your argument?

Reflect on the Speaking and Listening Task

- What did you find most interesting about preparing the podcast on spacewalking?

- What aspects of verbal and nonverbal communication did you find most challenging as you delivered your presentation—first to your group, and then when you recorded your podcast?

- What did you learn from planning and presenting this podcast that you can use when developing your next presentation?

REFLECT

UNIT 4 SELECTIONS
- "Martian Metropolis"
- "Dark They Were, and Golden-Eyed"
- "Challenges for Space Exploration"
- "What If We Were Alone?"
- Seven Minutes of Terror (video)
- "Space Exploration Should Be More Science Than Fiction"
- "Humans Should Stay Home and Let Robots Take to the Stars"

REFLECT ON THE UNIT

Have students reflect on the questions independently and write some notes in response to each one. Then have students meet with partners or in small groups to discuss their reflections. Circulate during these discussions to identify the questions that are generating the liveliest conversations. Wrap up with a whole-class discussion focused on these questions.

LEARNING MINDSET

Self Reflection An argument is a reasoned presentation of an opinion that aims to convince readers (listeners, or viewers) that something is right or wrong. Is it possible for students to use this skill in their own lives? All of us hold views that we never challenge. Suggest that students reflect on these views and see whether they stand up to scrutiny. *Is it true that educational videos help me learn better than books do? And, is using a smartphone or tablet better than taking notes by hand in the classroom?*

UNIT 5

Instructional Overview and Resources

		Instructional Focus	Online Ed Resources
	Unit Instruction **More Than a Game**	Unit 5 Essential Question Unit 5 Academic Vocabulary	**Stream to Start:** Taking Action **Unit 5 Response Log**

ANALYZE & APPLY

	"Ball Hawk" Short Story by Joseph Bruchac **Lexile 830L** **NOTICE & NOTE** READING MODEL **Signposts** • Tough Questions • Words of the Wiser • Aha Moment	**Reading** • Analyze Point of View • Set a Purpose **Writing:** Write an Epilogue **Speaking and Listening:** Create a Baseball Card **Vocabulary:** Spelling Commonly Confused Words **Language Conventions:** Capitalization	**Audio** **Reading Studio:** Notice & Note **Writing Studio:** Writing Narratives **Speaking and Listening Studio:** Participating in a Collaborative Discussion **Vocabulary Studio:** Word Origins **Grammar Studio:** Module 10: Glossary of Usage
	"Get in the Zone: The Psychology of Video Game Design" Informational Text by Aaron Millar **Lexile 800L**	**Reading** • Predict • Analyze Subjective and Objective Point of View **Writing:** Write an Objective Summary **Speaking and Listening:** Discuss a Video Game **Vocabulary:** Use Context **Language Conventions:** Semicolons	**Audio** **Reading Studio:** Notice & Note **Writing Studio:** Using Textual Evidence **Speaking and Listening Studio:** Participating in a Collaborative Discussion **Vocabulary Studio:** Context Clues **Grammar Studio:** Module 14: Lesson 6: Semicolons
	"It's Not Just a Game!" Informational Text by Lori Calabrese **Lexile 990L**	**Reading** • Set a Purpose • Analyze Organizational Patterns **Writing:** Write a Poem **Speaking and Listening:** Present an Infographic **Vocabulary:** Reference Aids **Language Conventions:** Complex Sentences and Subject-Verb Agreement	**Audio** **Close Read Screencasts:** Modeled Discussions **Reading Studio:** Notice & Note **Writing Studio:** Writing as a Process **Speaking and Listening Studio:** Using Media in a Presentation **Grammar Studio:** Module 8: Lesson 1: Agreement of Subject and Verb

SUGGESTED PACING: 30 DAYS

Unit Introduction: 1 | Ball Hawk: 2 3 4 5 6 | Get in the Zone: 7 8 9 10 11 | It's Not Just a Game!: 12 13 14 15 16

360A Unit 5

PLAN

English Learner Support		Differentiated Instruction	Assessment
• Learn New Expressions			
• Text X-Ray • Vocabulary Pronunciation • Think Out Loud • Characterization • Choral Reading • Point of View	• Oral Assessment • Vocabulary Strategy	**When Students Struggle** • Gallery Walk **To Challenge Students** • Write It Your Way	**Selection Test**
• Text X-Ray • Use Cognates • Understand First-Person Point of View • Understand Quotations • Language Conventions • Confirm Understanding • Oral Assessment	• Discuss a Presentation • Vocabulary Strategy	**When Students Struggle** • Use Graphic Organizers **To Challenge Students** • Consult Multiple Sources	**Selection Test**
• Text X-Ray • Use Cognates • Getting Organized • Understand Word Play • Confirm Understanding • Identify Quotations • Oral Assessment • Using Articles		**When Students Struggle** • Using Graphic Organizers	**Selection Test**

The Crossover/ Double Doubles
17 › 18 › 19 › 20 › 21 › 22 › 23 › 24 › 25

Independent Reading
26 › 27

End of Unit
28 › 29 › 30

More Than a Game **360B**

PLAN

UNIT 5 Continued

	Instructional Focus	Online Ed Resources

COLLABORATE & COMPARE

"The Crossover"
Novel in Verse by Kwame Alexander
Lexile 660L

Reading
- Analyze Novel in Verse
- Analyze Metaphor and Personification

Writing: Write a Letter

Speaking and Listening: Create a Podcast

 Audio

Text in Focus: Interpreting Graphic Elements
Reading Studio : Notice & Note
Writing Studio: Writing as a Process
Speaking and Listening Studio: Participating in Collaborative Discussions; Using Media in a Presentation

"Double Doubles"
Poem by J. Patrick Lewis

Reading
- Analyze a Two-Voice Poem
- Make Inferences

Writing: Write a Two-Voice Poem

Speaking and Listening: Critique a Poem

 Audio

Reading Studio: Notice & Note
Writing Studio: Writing as a Process
Speaking and Listening Studio: Participating in a Collaborative Discussion

Collaborate and Compare

Reading:
- Compare Theme
- Analyze the Texts

Speaking and Listening: Collaborate and Present

Speaking and Listening Studio: Giving a Presentation

INDEPENDENT READING

 The independent Reading selections are only available in the eBook.
Go to the Reading Studio for more information on Notice & Note.

"Batting After Sophie"
Short Story by Sue Macy
Lexile 760L

"Bridging the Generational Divide Between a Football Father and Soccer Son
Blog by John McCormick
Lexile 1040L

END OF UNIT

Writing Task: Write a Short Story

Reflect on the Unit

Writing: Write a Short Story
Language Conventions: Correct Punctuation of Dialogue

Unit 5 Response Log
Reading Studio: Notice & Note
Writing Studio: Writing Narratives
Grammar Studio: Module 15: Lesson 1: Quotation Marks

PLAN

English Learner Support	Differentiated Instruction	Online Ed Assessment
• Text X-Ray • Comprehend Academic Terms • Language Conventions • Confirm Understanding • Oral Assessment • Discuss with a Small Group	**When Students Struggle** • Learning Strategy **To Challenge Students** • Historical Research	**Selection Tests**
• Text X-Ray • Understand Directionality • Making Inferences • Confirm Understanding • Repeated Language • Oral Assessment • Discuss with Partners	**When Students Struggle** • Adjust for Graphic Elements	**Selection Tests**
• Ask Questions	**When Students Struggle** • Identify Themes	

"Arc of Triumph"
Short Story by Nick D'Alto
Lexile 830L

"Amigo Brothers"
Short Story by Piri Thomas
Lexile 910L

English Learner Support	Differentiated Instruction	Assessment
• Language X-Ray • Understand Academic Language • Create a Collaborative Short Story • Use the Mentor Text • Use Modifiers • Correct Punctuation of Dialogue	**When Students Struggle** • Develop a Draft • Correct Punctuation of Dialogue **To Challenge Students** • Expand Themes	**Unit Test**

More Than a Game **360D**

TEACH

? Connect to the ESSENTIAL QUESTION

Ask a volunteer to read aloud the Essential Question. Discuss how the images on page 360 relate to the question. What makes a given sport "more than a game?" What life lessons can sports teach? Ask students to consider sports as a unifying force among the participants and the fans in the stands.

■ **English Learner Support**

Learn New Expressions Make sure students understand the Essential Question. If necessary, explain the following idiomatic expressions:

- *sports* refers to any number of American games, such as football, soccer, baseball, and golf. As needed, pantomime or demonstrate examples.
- *bring together* means "to unite people around an issue, idea, or goal." If needed, in order to convey the concept, show students an image of fans, united and cheering for their team.

Help students restate the question in simpler language: *How do sports, like soccer, unite* (cognate: *unir*) *people?*
SUBSTANTIAL/MODERATE

DISCUSS THE QUOTATION

Tell students that Phiona Mutesi (b. 1996) is an extraordinary chess player whose gifts at the game lifted her up and out of dire poverty in Kampala, Uganda. She began playing the game as a nine-year-old girl when she visited a Sports Outreach Missionary program hoping to get a free cup of porridge. She stayed to play and went on to excel, representing Uganda in international chess tournaments and earning worldwide recognition. Phiona's story has inspired millions, especially girls in places and circumstances that make them feel less privileged than boys.

UNIT 5

MORE THAN A GAME

? ESSENTIAL QUESTION:

How do sports bring together friends, families, and communities?

> " I watched them play the game and get happy . . . and I wanted a chance to be that happy. "
>
> — Phiona Mutesi

360 Unit 5

 LEARNING MINDSET

Plan/Predict Suggest that students plan their work in practical terms by sorting and labeling tasks and placing them in *do now*, *do soon*, and *do later* categories. Encourage them to make a plan for completing an assignment, then map out the steps. Recommend that they commit to specific times when they will work on the *do now*, *do soon*, and *do later* parts of their plan.

UNIT 5

ACADEMIC VOCABULARY

Academic Vocabulary words are words you use when you discuss and write about texts. In this unit you will practice and learn five words.

✓ attitude ☐ consume ☐ goal ☐ purchase ☐ style

Study the Word Network to learn more about the word **attitude**.

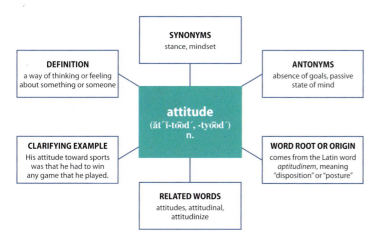

Write and Discuss Discuss the completed Word Network with a partner, making sure to talk through all of the boxes until you both understand the word, its synonyms, antonyms, and related forms. Then, fill out Word Networks for the remaining four words. Use a dictionary or online resource to help you complete the activity.

 Go online to access the Word Networks.

RESPOND TO THE ESSENTIAL QUESTION

In this unit, you will explore how people participate in and respond to games. As you read, you will revisit the **Essential Question** and gather your ideas about it in the **Response Log** that appears on page R5. At the end of the unit, you will have the opportunity to write a **short story** related to sports and games. Filling out the Response Log will help you prepare for this writing task.

 You can also go online to access the Response Log.

More Than a Game 361

TEACH

ACADEMIC VOCABULARY

As students complete Word Networks for the remaining four vocabulary words, encourage them to include all the categories shown in the completed network if possible, but point out that some words do not have clear synonyms or antonyms. Some words may also function as different parts of speech—for example, *factor* may be a noun or a verb.

attitude (ăt´-ĭ-tōōd´) *n.* A manner of thinking, feeling, or behaving that reflects a state of mind or disposition (Spanish cognate: *actitud*)

consume (kən-sōōm´) *tr. v.* To eat or drink up; to expend or use up (Spanish cognate: *consumir*)

goal (gōl) *n.* The object of an endeavor; an end (Spanish cognate: *gol*)

purchase (pûr´chĭs) *tr. v.* To obtain or acquire, by money or effort

style (stīl) *n.* The way in which something is said, done, expressed, or performed (Spanish cognate: *estilo*)

RESPOND TO THE ESSENTIAL QUESTION

Direct students to the Unit 4 Response Log. Explain that students will use it to record ideas and details from the selections that help answer the Essential Question. When they work on the writing task at the end of the unit, their Response Logs will help them think about what they have read and make connections among texts.

PLAN

MENTOR TEXT

BALL HAWK

Short Story by Joseph Bruchac

This story serves as a **mentor text**, a model for students to follow when they come to the Unit Writing Task: Writing a Short Story.

GENRE ELEMENTS
SHORT STORY

Explain to students that the purpose of a **short story** is not only to stimulate a reader's imagination, but also to allow an author to experiment with character, perspective, and craft. All storytelling, including **film, novels,** and **plays**, involves some amount of experimentation with people and conflict, but short stories tend to be a perfect platform for playing with narration, perspective, and characterization. In this lesson, students will examine these formal concepts, as well as the ideas of struggle and perseverance in life.

LEARNING OBJECTIVES

- Examine narration and perspectives in fiction writing.
- Conduct research on Native American baseball players.
- Write their own epilogue to the story "Ball Hawk."
- Create a baseball card for a character.
- Learn how to set a purpose before reading.
- Use capitalization appropriately for proper nouns and proper adjectives.
- **Language** Work with a partner to capitalize words correctly.

TEXT COMPLEXITY

Quantitative Measures	Ball Hawk	Lexile: 830L
Qualitative Measures	**Ideas Presented** Mostly explicit, with some implied meaning	
	Structure Used Largely conventional with clear chronology	
	Language Used Much is explicit, but uses figurative language	
	Knowledge Required Requires no special knowledge, but uses some unique cultural references	

362A Unit 5

PLAN

Online Ed

RESOURCES

- Unit 5 Response Log
- 🔊 Selection Audio
- 📖 Reading Studio: Notice & Note
- ✏️ Writing Studio: Writing Narratives
- 💬 Speaking and Listening Studio: Participating in a Collaborative Discussion
- 🔵 Vocabulary Studio: Word Origins
- ❗ Grammar Studio: Module 10: Glossary of Usage
- ✓ "Ball Hawk" Selection Test

SUMMARIES

English
Mitchell's late father was a great baseball player; Mitchell is the worst player on his high school team. Just when he's decided to drop out, his uncle shows up to remind him of what it means uphold the traditions of his Indian tribe, even when it seems hopeless. Uncle Tommy is there to persuade him that something as simple as a small-town sport can reconnect his spirit to his community, his father, and to his heritage.

Spanish
El difunto padre de Mitchell era un gran jugador de béisbol; Mitchell es el peor jugador del equipo de su secundaria. Justo cuando decide renunciar, su tío le recuerda lo que significa conservar las tradiciones de su tribu indígena, incluso cuando parece imposible. El tío Tommy está ahí para persuadirle de que algo tan sencillo como un deporte en un pueblito le servirá para reconectar su espíritu con su comunidad, su padre y su herencia.

SMALL-GROUP OPTIONS

Have students work in small groups to read and discuss the selection.

Think-Pair-Share

- After students have read and digested "Ball Hawk," ask the class a question such as: *How do sports and sporting events help individuals and communities?*
- Have students think about the question individually, and take notes on their thoughts.
- Ask students to get into pairs and discuss their answers.
- Finally, ask students to share their answers with the class.

Send a Problem

- Present a question about the material to the class, such as: *Who is the narrator in "Ball Hawk"?*
- Call upon a student to respond, giving him or her ten seconds to respond.
- If the student does not know the answer within that timeframe, the student has the option to "send" it by repeating the full question to another student.
- Monitor the routine and call on a student or change the question at any time.

Ball Hawk   **362B**

PLAN

Text X-Ray: English Learner Support
for "Mentor Text Ball Hawk"

INTRODUCE THE SELECTION
DISCUSS ANXIETY AND STRUGGLE

In this lesson, students will read about a young man who struggles playing baseball.

Put students into small groups and have them discuss what group or communal activities make them happy. These group activities can be sports, or they can be family holidays, religious ceremonies, or games with friends. Then ask the groups to write a sentence or two about *why* group or community activities make them better people—what do they get from group activities like sports that they can't get alone?

Use the following frames:

A sport or group/community activity that I enjoy is _____.

Group activities like sports are important because _____.

CULTURAL REFERENCES

The following words and phrases may be unfamiliar to students:

- *goth* (paragraph 2): a style of dress and music, related to punk-rock, that is a teen subculture
- *buffaloed* (paragraph 6): a verb meaning intimidated and/or baffled
- *tight and D-end* (paragraph 20): tight-end and defensive-end, two field positions in football
- *beater* (paragraph 56): an old junk car that still functions
- *Louisville Slugger* (paragraph 58): a famous brand of baseball bat
- *doe* (paragraph 71): a female deer

LISTENING

Describe the Narrator

Tell students that you're going to read them the opening to the short story "Ball Hawk." Ask that they pay close attention to details about the narrator, taking notes if necessary.

Have students listen as you read aloud paragraphs 1–3. Use the following supports with students at varying proficiency levels:

- Ask students simple questions, such as: *Does the story involve family?* (yes) *Native Americans?* (yes) *Tennis?* (no, baseball) **SUBSTANTIAL**
- Guide students to describe the narrator, Mitchell. Supply the following sentence frames: The story is about a high school ____ (*student*). He plays ____ (*baseball*) but he is not ____ (*good*) at it. He learns that ____ (*Indians/Native Americans*) invented baseball. **MODERATE**
- Now read the first few paragraphs, and ask students to take notes on the narrator. Pair students with varying English proficiencies and have them compare their notes. Ask what conclusions they can draw about the narrator. **LIGHT**

362C Unit 5

PLAN

Ball Hawk 362D

SPEAKING

Discuss Point of View

Have students talk about the different forms of narrative perspective discussed on p. 365. Circulate to ensure they understand the different points of view.

Use the following supports with students at varying proficiency levels:

- Display and read aloud the following sentences while modeling the actions that occur in them: (Point to yourself while walking) *"I walk to the door" is first person.* (Indicate a student) *"He sits in the chair" is third person.* Read sentences that indicate point of view on p. 365. Have students use a thumbs-up signal when they hear a first or third person pronoun. **SUBSTANTIAL**
- Ask students to fill in the following frames orally: *"I lived in New York City" is _____ person. She lived in Chicago" is _____ person.* **MODERATE**
- Pair students and ask them to find a first-person sentence from the text of "Ball Hawk" (using I). Now have them work together to reformulate it and say it as a third-person sentence. **LIGHT**

READING

Describe a Character

Inform students that they can learn about the narrator's character through his own words and by analyzing the *way* or *style* he describes other people and things around him.

Work with students to read paragraphs 6–7. Use the following supports with students at varying proficiency levels:

- After reading, ask students some simple yes-no questions about the text: *Is Uncle Tommy Indian?* (yes) *Is Mitchell related to Uncle Tommy?* (yes) **SUBSTANTIAL**
- Present students with the idea that the narrator Mitchell is upset and depressed. Then have students read and underline any descriptions in the text that might indicate that this is true of Mitchell's character. **MODERATE**
- Pair students and ask them to read and discuss both paragraphs. Then have them write one sentence that describes the central idea(s) of each paragraph. Use the frame: *In paragraph _____, the author is telling us that _____.* **LIGHT**

WRITING

Write an Epilogue

Work with students to read the writing assignment on p. 377.

Use the following supports with students at varying proficiency levels:

- Have students complete the Create a Baseball Card activity on page 377. Provide the following sentence frames to help students create their baseball cards: *Mitchell plays baseball at _____ High School. Mitchell's mother is from _____.* **SUBSTANTIAL**
- Have students work together to write epilogues. Have pairs fill in a few experimental frames in first-person, past-tense narrative: *One year later, I _____ and Uncle Tommy _____.* **MODERATE**
- Have students brainstorm a few ideas about how Mitchell's life might have continued after the story ended. Did he still play baseball? Did he move away? Make lists on the board and encourage students to use their imaginations and experiment with sentences in the first person. **LIGHT**

TEACH

EXPLAIN THE SIGNPOSTS

Explain that Notice & Note signposts are significant moments in the text that help readers understand and analyze works of fiction or nonfiction. Use the instruction on these pages to introduce students to the signposts **Tough Questions, Words of the Wiser,** and **Aha Moment.** Then use the selection that follows to have students apply the signposts to a text.

For a full list of the fiction and nonfiction signposts, see p. 424.

TOUGH QUESTIONS

Conflict drives narratives in much the same way as people drive cars: a problem for the main character becomes the vehicle for telling a story—for taking it from here to there. **Tough Questions** identify the vehicle, almost as if naming make, model, and color. With a **Tough Question,** the protagonist puts into words the struggle he or she is facing.

Review the sample passage. Ask: *What is the conflict that the tough questions suggests?* (Mitchell plays baseball because he is expected to, even though he doesn't like the game that much.)

Tell students that when they spot a **Tough Question,** they should pause, mark it in their consumable texts, and ask the anchor question: *What makes this moment important to the story?*

Notice & Note
READING MODEL

BALL HAWK

 For more information on these and other signposts to Notice & Note, visit the **Reading Studio.**

You are about to read the short story "Ball Hawk." In it, you will notice and note signposts that will give you clues about the story's characters and ideas that are expressed from the narrator's point of view. Here are three key signposts to look for as you read this short story and other works of fiction.

When you read or infer questions like these—questions that express a challenge or, sometimes, serious confusion—pause and ask yourself whether you have found a **Tough Questions** signpost:

"What in the world did you think you were doing?"

"Is this really what you want to do?"

"What could I possibly do?"

"How could I ever understand?"

"Why did this happen?"

Tough Questions You may have been there—in an argument with a friend or a relative. You find yourself asking or answering some tough questions about your feelings or maybe about your relationship.

Authors of fiction often present situations in which a character asks **Tough Questions** that reveal inner struggles. The struggles may be within that character, or they may reveal a struggle that another character is facing. When you come across Tough Questions in a story, ask yourself what they make you wonder about. They usually point to some inner conflict that helps reveal an important idea in the story. The paragraphs below illustrate a student's annotation within "Ball Hawk" and a response to a Notice & Note signpost.

> 43 "I hate this game!"
> 44 Uncle Tommy shook his head. "Why did you keep playing it so long?"
> 45 "Because the other guys won't let me quit. No . . . because my mom wants so bad for me to play baseball."
> 46 "And why is that?"
> 47 "Because she's got some idea that Indians should play baseball."
> 48 "Why?"
> 49 "Because there are teams with Indian names. Right?"
> 50 I looked over at Uncle Tommy and he shook his head.

Anchor Question
When you notice this signpost, ask: What does this make me wonder about?

What tough questions does Uncle Tommy ask Mitchell?	"Why did you keep playing it [baseball] so long?" Why does his mom want him to play baseball? Why does she think Indians should play baseball?
What inner struggle do these questions reveal? Whose struggle is it?	This is Mitchell's struggle. The questions show that he is struggling to understand why he plays a game that his father was very good at but that he himself is not.

▶ **Words of the Wiser** To whom do you turn for encouragement or advice? Just as in real life, a story character may offer **Words of the Wiser** to the main character. These words of wisdom or advice often help the main character with a problem. Paying attention to these moments in a story can help readers understand the story's theme or life lesson and how it relates to the main character. In the following example, a student underlined and responded to Words of the Wiser.

28	Sometimes Uncle Tommy made it all seem so easy.
29	"Mitchell," he said, "things that are supposed to come easy aren't always that easy to do."
30	Uncle Tommy, the mind-reading Zen master.

Anchor Question
When you notice this signpost, ask: What's the lesson for the character?

What words of wisdom or advice does the older character give?	"Mitchell, . . . things that are supposed to come easy aren't always that easy to do."
What is Uncle Tommy referring to? Why might this be helpful advice for Mitchell?	He is referring to baseball. He is encouraging Mitchell to believe that he can improve his game if he works harder at it.

▶ **Aha Moment** Have you ever worked for what seemed like hours on a homework problem, only to have the answer come to you all at once, as a "surprise"? These **Aha Moments** happen in fiction, too. For example, a character may realize a problem or its solution, or may suddenly reach a broader understanding about life. Here, a student marked and responded to an Aha Moment.

When you see phrases like these, pause to see if it's an **Aha Moment**:
"All of a sudden . . ."
"for the first time . . ."
"and just like that . . ."
"I realized . . ."

67	"How can this hawk catch a bird in flight at ninety miles an hour?" Uncle Tommy said.
68	"Because he sees it?" I asked.
69	Uncle Tommy shook his head. He wanted me to think.
70	"Because he sees where it's going to be," I said.

Anchor Question
When you notice this signpost, ask: How might this change things?

What word(s) tell you that Mitchell has realized something about baseball?	"Because he sees where it's going to be."
How might this realization help Mitchell with his conflict?	It might help him change his focus, enabling him to hit the ball more accurately.

WHEN STUDENTS STRUGGLE . . .

Use Strategies If students struggle to recognize **Aha Moments**, have them use the Syntax Surgery strategy. In their consumable texts, ask students to underline details that define characters or the conflict, with arrows to brief notes such as *He seems overconfident* or *She doesn't like him*. Then ask them to likewise note a moment when a character trait or element of the conflict may have changed. (*She is talking to him now.*) Encourage students to patiently review the text and their notes, looking for a moment of insight or action in that changes a character or the nature of the conflict.

TEACH

▶ WORDS OF THE WISER

Explain that **Words of the Wiser** is a literary device that helps the writer convey the story's theme or message. When this device is used, an individual, often an older mature person, offers insights or shares a life lesson with another character.

Read the example passage. Ask: *If this is a teaching moment, what are the wise words meant to teach?* (that Mitchell shouldn't quit because a given thing is not easy)

Tell students that when they spot **Words of the Wiser**, they should pause, mark them in their consumable texts, and ask the anchor question: *What's the life lesson here?*

▶ AHA MOMENT

Aha Moments are like the familiar light bulb going on above a cartoon character's head: in literature, a solution of some kind is suddenly illuminated in the **Aha Moment**.

Read the example passage. Ask: *What makes line 70 a clever Aha Moment?* (It has two meanings, applying to a hawk tracking a bird and a player tracking a baseball.)

Tell students that when they spot an **Aha Moment**, they should pause, mark them in their consumable texts, and ask the anchor question: *How might this change things?*

APPLY THE SIGNPOSTS

Have students use the selection that follows as a model text to apply the signposts. As students encounter signposts, prompt them to stop, reread, and ask themselves the anchor questions that will help them understand characters and themes.

TEACH

ANALYZE & APPLY

BALL HAWK

Short Story by **Joseph Bruchac**

 Connect to the ESSENTIAL QUESTION

"Ball Hawk" tells the story of a young Native American boy, Mitchell, living on an Indian reservation with his mother. At a time in his young life when nothing seems to go right—including baseball practice—Uncle Tommy Fox shows up to show Mitchell how playing the game well can make life worthwhile, reaffirm his place in his Indian tribe, and keep the memory of his father alive.

MENTOR TEXT

At the end of the unit, students will be asked to compose a short story. "Ball Hawk" provides a model for how to incorporate plot, character, point of view, and dialogue into a story.

ESSENTIAL QUESTION:

How do sports bring together friends, families, and communities?

 LEARNING MINDSET

Grit Remind students that good work depends on a strong, flexible way of thinking. A person's intellectual strategy is as important as the results, since good strategies can be applied to a range of difficult problems in life. Encourage students to view problems and setbacks as opportunities, and to value the experiences of struggle and failure as much as success. Working hard is its own reward, and ultimate success in the end will come not as a result of a single achievement but from a lifetime of applying reliable strategies, grit, and integrity to life's difficulties.

GET READY

QUICK START

Have you ever struggled to do something that you thought would be easy? Discuss how anxiety might affect how you play a sport.

ANALYZE POINT OF VIEW

In a work of fiction, the **narrator** is the voice that tells the story. The author's choice of narrator becomes a story's **point of view.** Authors choose a point of view in order to give readers a certain perspective on the story. The three types of point of view are shown in this chart.

POINT OF VIEW IN NARRATIVES		
First Person	**Third-Person Limited**	**Third-Person Omniscient ("All-Knowing")**
• Narrator is a story character. • Narrator uses first-person pronouns such as *I, me, mine, we, us,* and *our.* • Reader sees events and characters through the narrator's eyes.	• Narrator is not a story character and is outside the story. • Narrator uses third-person pronouns such as *he, she, him, her,* and *their.* • Reader sees events and characters through one character's eyes.	• Narrator is not a story character and is outside the story. • Narrator uses third-person pronouns such as *he, she, him, her,* and *their.* • Reader is shown different characters' thoughts and feelings.

As you read "Ball Hawk," consider how the point of view affects the way you understand the story.

SET A PURPOSE

When you **set a purpose** for reading, you choose one or more specific reasons to read a text. For example, in reading a short story, you might set a purpose of following how an author uses **characterization,** the methods that help develop each character. These methods can include presenting (and commenting about) the character's thoughts, words, and actions, and looking at how the setting influences the characters. An author can also develop a character through other characters' thoughts, words, and actions towards that character.

As you read "Ball Hawk," set the purpose of noticing which methods the author uses to develop the character of Mitchell. Consider how Mitchell responds to the story events, to the setting, and to the other characters—and how other characters respond to him.

GENRE ELEMENTS: SHORT STORY

- includes the basic elements of fiction—setting, characters, plot (including conflict), and theme
- centers on one particular moment or event in life
- can be read in one sitting

TEACH

QUICK START

Have students respond to the Quick Start question in small groups. As they listen to each other's stories, encourage other group members to ask questions about what strategy the student used or could have used to help in a time when they were struggling. Then call on students to recount the most interesting story they heard.

ANALYZE POINT OF VIEW

Help students understand the terms and concepts related on this page. Point out that narrators and points of view are used in novels, plays, and films as well, but that the short story makes use of these by focusing on a single moment in an individual character's life and giving a brief snapshot of that experience. Remind students to keep an eye on the narrator (the voice that tells the story) and point of view (first person, past tense) throughout the story, making notes on how the narrator's worldview changes over the course of the tale.

SET A PURPOSE

Inform students that setting a purpose for their reading will help them in comprehension and retention. To follow the changes that Mitchell's character undergoes, they may simply make marginal notes or notes in a log as they read. Questions they might ask themselves are:

- At this point in the story, how has Mitchell changed?
- What is different about the choice he makes or the language he uses here?
- How is Mitchell the same or different at the beginning and end of this story?

TEACH

CRITICAL VOCABULARY

Encourage students to read all the sentences before deciding which word best completes each one. Remind them to look for context clues that match the meaning of each word.

Answers:

1. *clique*
2. *talons*
3. *mascot*
4. *consecutive*
5. *federal*

■ English Learner Support

Vocabulary Pronunciation Put students into pairs and ask them to pronounce the Critical Vocabulary terms clearly and articulately. Have Spanish speakers pay special attention to pronouncing the two consecutive voiceless consonants *sc* in *mascot* and the two consecutive voiced consonants in *ns* in *talons*. Then have them write and say aloud their own simple sentences using each. **LIGHT**

LANGUAGE CONVENTIONS

Review the capitalization instruction with students, and ask them to make note of when words are capitalized in "Ball Hawk." Ask students what the purpose of capitalization is. *(The purpose of capitalization is to mark off important words, such as words that begin a sentence or identify important people, places, and things.)*

ANNOTATION MODEL

Point out to students that they may follow this annotation suggestion or use their own system for marking up the selection in their write-in text. They may want to color-code their annotations by using highlighters. Their notes in the margin may include questions about ideas that are unclear or topics they want to learn more about.

366 Unit 5

 GET READY

CRITICAL VOCABULARY

| clique | consecutive | mascot | federal | talon |

To see how many Critical Vocabulary words you already know, use them to complete the sentences.

1. In school, he was never part of any particular _____.
2. The owl swooped down and snatched up the field mouse in its _____.
3. Union High School's _____ is a roaring tiger.
4. Because of the blizzard, school was canceled for three _____ days.
5. The _____ budget is approved by the U.S. Congress.

LANGUAGE CONVENTIONS

Commonly Confused Words Many words challenge writers because they look similar and sound alike. Because each word of this kind is actually a word, electronic spell-checkers can't tell if the wrong word is being used. Here are some examples of commonly confused words.

accept / except   affect / effect   than / then   to / two / too

As you read "Ball Hawk," note the spellings of words that are similar, such as *its* and *it* in this example from the text:

A very big bird, the circle of <u>its</u> soaring flight carrying <u>it</u> closer to us.

ANNOTATION MODEL **NOTICE & NOTE**

As you read, notice and note signposts, including **Tough Questions, Words of the Wiser,** and **Aha Moments.** In the model, you can see one reader's notes about the opening paragraphs of "Ball Hawk."

1 "Indians invented baseball."
2   That's what Uncle Tommy Fox said on the day <u>I was ready to throw in my glove and quit the Long Pond High School team for</u> good. It was one of his (typically cryptic remarks) and, (as usual, it started me thinking.)

The narrator is a player on a school baseball team.

Uncle Tommy has helped the narrator's thinking in the past. Maybe he will be a wise voice in this story.

366 Unit 5

BACKGROUND

Joseph Bruchac (b. 1942) lives in Greenfield Center, New York, where he grew up. While he was a student at Cornell University, he began to consider a career as a writer. Today, as a professional storyteller and the author of more than 120 books for adults and young people, Bruchac creates works that often are rooted in the traditions of his Abenaki heritage. He also writes poetry and music that reflect his Native American ancestry.

BALL HAWK
Short Story by Joseph Bruchac

SETTING A PURPOSE

As you read, pay attention to how Mitchell tries to connect to his late father. Note details that help you understand Mitchell's personality, his feelings and motivations, and the conflict he faces.

1 "Indians invented baseball."

2 That's what Uncle Tommy Fox said on the day I was ready to throw in my glove and quit the Long Pond High School team for good. It was one of his typically cryptic remarks and, as usual, it started me thinking.

3 Quite frankly, if Uncle Tommy hadn't come into my life when he did, I probably would have ended up dyeing my hair purple and going goth.[1] (I would, I might add, have been the first to do that in Long Pond High School, which is barely big enough to have **cliques.** My high school's size is one of the reasons why I was still, pathetic as I was with a glove and a bat, a regular member of the varsity nine. There just weren't that many eligible candidates.)

---
[1] **going goth:** adopting the thinking and appearance of those who are attracted to things that most people find dark, gloomy, and mysterious.

NOTICE & NOTE

Notice & Note

Use the side margins to notice and note signposts in the text.

ANALYZE POINT OF VIEW
Annotate: In paragraph 3, mark the words that tell you what point of view the author is using in this story.

Identify: What is that point of view, and what does Mitchell reveal about himself in this paragraph?

clique
(klĭk) *n.* If you are part of a *clique,* you belong to a small group of friends that doesn't allow outsiders.

Ball Hawk 367

TEACH

BACKGROUND

After students read the Background note, explain that authors often draw characters, experiences, and settings from their own lives. In this note, we learn that Joseph Bruchac is Native American (Abenaki) and that he bases much of his storytelling on his heritage.

SETTING A PURPOSE

Direct students to use the Setting a Purpose prompt to focus their reading.

ANALYZE POINT OF VIEW

Remind students that **point of view** is not the identity of the voice telling the story, but the *perspective* from which the story is told (first person, third person). **(Answer:** *Using first-person point of view, Mitchell shows that his Uncle Tommy had a profound influence on him, he attends a small high school, and he is not good at baseball, though he is on the varsity team.*)

For **listening support** for students at varying proficiency levels, see the **Text X-Ray** on page 362C.

ENGLISH LEARNER SUPPORT

Think Out Loud If students struggle with the story, ask a series of related questions and encourage students to give one-word answers that come to mind, and then jot the answers on the board so students can write them down. Ask: *Who is the narrator?* (Mitchell) *How old is he?* (teenage). Provide answers to the questions in instances when students don't know them. When done, have students read their lists back to you and congratulate them for keeping up with the storyline. **MODERATE**

CRITICAL VOCABULARY

clique: Since a clique is a small group of people, it's a comic note that the school could hardly have any.

ASK STUDENTS what connotation they think the word *clique* has, as opposed to group or team. (*The word* clique *has a negative connotation, suggesting a group of people who don't let others into their group.*)

Ball Hawk **367**

TEACH

✏️ SET A PURPOSE

Remind students that **characterization** is anything about a character in a story, from physical appearance to thoughts, speech, actions, and dreams. (**Answer:** *Mitchell seems to be a character with a chip on his shoulder about baseball—to be a little resentful of people's expectations.*)

✏️ ANALYZE POINT OF VIEW

Remind students of the differences between **third-person limited** (knows just one character's perspective and experience) and **third-person omniscient** perspective (knows all). (**Answer:** *Seeing this description from Mitchell's point of view makes the reader feel sorry for him. It helps the reader feel the pain that his father's death has caused.*)

📖 For **reading support** for students at varying proficiency levels, see the **Text X-Ray** on page 362D.

CRITICAL VOCABULARY

consecutive: Mitchell is being very detailed about his failures, noting how many times he struck out in a row.

ASK STUDENTS what other things in life generally appear consecutively. (*A new pack of playing cards are consecutive, as are days in the week.*)

mascot: He seems deeply aware of the derisive way Native Americans are often portrayed in wider American culture.

ASK STUDENTS when they've seen a mascot and what makes a good one. (*Mascots are at most sporting events and a good one is memorable, costumed, and usually based on an animal.*)

368 Unit 5

✏️ **NOTICE & NOTE**

SET A PURPOSE
Annotate: Remember the purpose you have set: noting how the author uses characterization. In paragraph 6, mark Mitchell's thoughts about playing baseball.

Infer: How does Mitchell's attitude toward baseball help to characterize him?

consecutive
(kən-sĕk′yə-tĭv) *adj.* When things are *consecutive*, they follow one after another without interruption.

mascot
(măs′kŏt′) *n.* A *mascot* is a person, animal, or object used as the symbol of an organization, such as a sports team.

ANALYZE POINT OF VIEW
Annotate: In paragraph 10, mark Mitchell's description of the aftermath of his father's death.

Critique: How does seeing this description through Mitchell's eyes affect the reader?

368 Unit 5

---

4   Uncle Tommy, though, saved me from turning my back on being a skin. I'd been hanging around Uncle Tommy ever since he moved up here to work in the Indian Village and my mom introduced him to me in her German accent.

5   "Mitchell, it vould be gut for you to meet anudder real Indianishe mann und he vas ein freund of you vater."

6   It wasn't just that Uncle Tommy was, indeed, a real Indian, albeit of a different tribe than my father. Or that this broad-shouldered old Indian guy with long gray braids and a friendly face really did seem to like me and enjoy taking on that role of being an uncle. Or that he knew more about being Indian, really being Indian, than anyone else I'd ever met. He also had a sense of humor and we both needed it when it came to me and baseball. For some reason, everyone thought I should be playing it. True, I'd always been good at other sports like football and wrestling, but baseball had me buffaloed. My mother had gotten it into her head that being an Indian I should of course not just play baseball but excel at it. Even striking out in nineteen consecutive at-bats had failed to disabuse her of that certainty.

7   Why baseball? Well, as little as my mom knew about American sports, she had heard of the Cleveland Indians and the Atlanta Braves. So she figured it was a game that honored Indians and thus I should be part of it. Yeah, I know. But try to explain to an eager German immigrant mother about stereotyping and American Indians being used as **mascots**.

8   Plus my dad had been a really great baseball player. He'd been playing armed forces ball when Mom met him in Germany.

9   He was the best baseball player in the history of our family. He was even better than his grandfather, who'd played baseball at the Carlisle Indian School and in the summer Carolina semi-pro leagues with Jim Thorpe.[2] On the ball field, my Dad was unstoppable. He could hit almost any pitch. If he'd had the right breaks, and hadn't gotten his right knee ruined when he was in the service, he could have gone pro.

10 We played pitch and catch together almost every day during the seven years we shared before his truck was hit head-on by a drunk driver, leaving his half-Indian son to be raised in the sticks by the wife he had brought back with him at the end of his tour of duty with the marines, which had concluded in der Vaterland.[3]

---
[2] **Jim Thorpe:** Native American athlete (1887–1953), most famous as a track-and-field star and All-American football player but also excelling in a variety of other sports.
[3] **der Vaterland:** German for "the Fatherland," or land of one's ancestors. (Mitchell's mother is German.)

NOTICE & NOTE

11   Anyhow, going back to that day when I was ready to pack it all in, it was a game we were sure to win. But even though we were leading the Hurleytown Hornets by a score of 6–0 and it was the bottom of the seventh inning, I still had to take at least one more turn at bat. When there's only twelve guys on your whole team and you're the center fielder, you can't avoid it.

12   I wiped my hands on my knees, knocked imaginary dirt off my cleats. Nineteen, I thought.

13   The Hurleytown pitcher smiled when he saw me come up to the plate. All the pitchers in the Northern league did that. Then he mouthed the words. Easy out. I hate it when they do that.

14   I looked over toward the stands. My mom was smiling and nodding at me, even though she had both fists clenched around her soda can so hard that it looked like an hourglass. Uncle Tommy, who was next to her, just kept his face blank. I was grateful for that.

15   The pitcher wound up, kicked high just to show off, and let it go. Fastball, high and outside just where I like it. I took a cut that would have knocked down a wall if I'd been holding a sledgehammer. Unfortunately all I had was a bat. WHIFFF!

16   Strike one.

17   I don't have to tell you what happened with the next two pitches. Just the usual. Twenty in a row.

18   Mercifully, we finished the game without my coming around in the batting order again and us winning 7–1. I took my time in the locker room, soaped my long black hair and rinsed it out twice. Half of me hoped everybody would be gone by the time I came out. But the other half of me desperately wanted to not be alone, wanted somebody to be there waiting for me.

SET A PURPOSE
Annotate: In paragraph 18, mark words and phrases that reveal what Mitchell looks like and how he feels after the game. (Remember: these are methods of characterization.)

Infer: Why do you think Mitchell is confused after the game? What does it suggest about his character?

Ball Hawk   369

TEACH

WORDS OF THE WISER

Remind students that the **Words of the Wiser** signpost is often identifiable through context or **setting**. When two characters, one older and one younger, retire to a quiet place to talk seriously, this often becomes a moment for wisdom to be shared by the elder with the younger character. Have students think and talk about why Uncle Tommy might have taken this moment to share his words with his nephew Mitchell. (**Answer:** *Uncle Tommy is trying to tell Mitchell that baseball is part of his heritage, part of who he is. Mitchell needs to be reminded of this because he seems to want to give baseball up because he thinks that he is useless on the field.*)

CRITICAL VOCABULARY

federal: Mitchell seems to imply that government officials sometimes intrude on his uncle and other members of his Native American community.

ASK STUDENTS what other things they can think of are *federal*, as opposed to state or local. (*The mail system as well as most holidays are federal because they are nationwide, and most laws are federal because they are passed and implemented by the U.S. government.*)

370   Unit 5

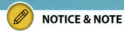
NOTICE & NOTE

19 That's what I was thinking as I shuffled out of the gym, my duffel bag in one hand and my towel in the other. Then I saw Uncle Tommy still sitting there, all alone in the bleachers. He raised a hand, gesturing for me to join him.

20 It might have been my mom who encouraged Uncle Tommy to stay around and wait for me. But maybe not. After all, Uncle Tommy had been faithfully watching in the stands each time I whiffed out. He came to all my games, not just football in the fall, where I'd found my groove in my sophomore year at both tight and D-end. Tackling other ballplayers, blocking and snagging the occasional pass were right up my alley. Unlike trying to tag that white little pill with either glove or bat.

WORDS OF THE WISER

Notice & Note: In paragraph 21, underline Uncle Tommy's comment to Mitchell. Then, circle the later paragraph that explains the meaning of that comment.

Analyze: What is Uncle Tommy trying to tell Mitchell? Why does Mitchell need to be reminded of this?

21 "Indians invented baseball," Uncle Tommy said again. We were sitting at the very top of the stands where we had a great view of the high peaks that were beginning to turn red in the setting April sun. I knew he had to get back to his place and check on the hawks before dark, but he wasn't making a move to stand up, so I stayed put. My uniform was in my bag, but I had pulled my glove out and I was punching my left fist into it.

22 I looked up at him, ready to smile if I saw him grinning. But his face was serious.

23 "You know what I mean," he said.

24 Well, I did. I'd heard the whole rap before. There were no team sports in Europe before those early explorers stumbled into the new world and found Indians playing all kinds of team games—from lacrosse to basketball. Rubber balls were invented by Indians.

25 But I didn't say anything. I just pounded my glove a little harder.

26 Uncle Tommy looked up and nodded his head. I followed his gaze. There was a distant speck getting closer. A very big bird, the circle of its soaring flight carrying it closer to us. It wasn't Hawk or any of the other birds that Uncle Tommy was nursing back to health. It was bigger. An eagle. Pretty soon it was right overhead. I wondered how Uncle Tommy could do that. Call a great bird like that to us.

27 Folks around here knew that whenever anyone came across a big bird that had been hurt, maybe tangled with a power line or sideswiped by a truck, a hawk or an owl or even an eagle like the one above us, they could bring it to Uncle Tommy. He didn't have one of those **federal** licenses to care for birds of prey, but whenever game wardens came out to check on him, they never found anything. Uncle Tommy never caged or tied down any of his birds. He let them fly free. If they were too hurt to fly he kept them somewhere safe that the federal people couldn't find.

federal
(fĕd′ər-əl) *adj.* Something that is *federal* relates to the U.S. government in Washington, D.C., and not to state and local governments.

370   Unit 5

WHEN STUDENTS STRUGGLE . . .

Gallery Walk Help students follow along by having them respond to a few simple questions about the storyline in an interactive gallery walk.

Think of some basic questions about "Ball Hawk," such as: *Who is the narrator? Where is the story taking place? What sport is being played?* Paste these questions on posters around the classroom and have students work in pairs to respond to them. Establish a time for pairs to move on to the next posted question. Then, when students have answered them all and have returned to their seats, recap the story with the class.

NOTICE & NOTE

28   Sometimes Uncle Tommy made it all seem so easy.
29   "Mitchell," he said, "things that are supposed to come easy aren't always that easy to do."
30   Uncle Tommy, the mind-reading Zen master.
31   "Meaning what?" I said, like I was supposed to do.
32   "Do you like playing baseball?" Uncle Tommy asked. Of course he was not answering my question.
33   "Baseball is great," I said. "It's just me. I stink."
34   "Hmm," Uncle Tommy said. Not a question, not a comment, but a lot more than both.
35   "Okay, so I'm good at running bases. Better than most, I guess. And when I do finally get the ball I can throw it hard and straight. But half the time I go out to shag a fly ball, I miss it. You ever notice how when I yell 'I've got it,' all the other fielders start praying?"
36   "Hmm," Uncle Tommy said again. He really wasn't going to let go of this, was he?
37   "Well, what about my batting?" I asked. "The only way I could ever get a hit was if the ball was as big as a watermelon and you set it up on a tee."
38   "And painted a bull's-eye on it?" Uncle Tommy said.
39   I couldn't help it. I had to laugh. For a while. Then I stopped, feeling empty inside.
40   "I quit!" I yelled, standing up and throwing my glove out onto the field. "I'm done with it."
41   Uncle Tommy didn't bat an eye at my temper tantrum. He just kept looking out at the mountains. So I stood there, not sure whether I should climb out of the stands and stomp off or go down on the field and pick up my glove.
42   "Why'd you say that?" Uncle Tommy finally asked in a soft voice.
43   "I hate this game!"
44   Uncle Tommy shook his head. "Why did you keep playing it so long?"
45   "Because the other guys won't let me quit. No . . . because my mom wants so bad for me to play baseball."
46   "And why is that?"
47   "Because she's got some idea that Indians should play baseball."
48   "Why?"
49   "Because there are teams with Indian names. Right?"
50   I looked over at Uncle Tommy and he shook his head.
51   "Mitchell," he said, "I knew your dad when he played ball at Haskell Indian School. My playing days were way behind me then, but I was there teaching in the crafts program. He was

TOUGH QUESTIONS

Notice & Note: In paragraphs 33–40, mark the complaints that Mitchell has about the way he plays baseball.

Analyze: What internal conflict or struggle do these lines reveal?

LANGUAGE CONVENTIONS

Annotate: To recognize the correct spelling of a commonly misspelled word, pay attention to its use in texts. Underscore the words in paragraph 49 that are often misspelled.

Compare: Choose one word and write down the other ways to spell the word. Think of a sentence where each word is used correctly.

Ball Hawk   371

TEACH

AHA MOMENT

Remind students that an **Aha Moment** comes at a critical juncture in the text when a character realizes he or she has to make a tough or important decision. At this moment, a character will pivot toward a new way of doing things, a new solution to a problem, or a new philosophy or understanding of life. In this case, Mitchell realizes that he's been trying too hard to connect with his father while playing baseball because he knows how much his father loved the game. (**Possible answer:** *He may try to get Uncle Tommy to help him play better.*)

SET A PURPOSE

Remind students that the **narrator** of any story may not be aware of himself or herself as much as the reader is and that it's up to the reader to infer motivations, attitudes, and beliefs through the actions, not only the words, of a **character**. (**Answer:** *The response suggests that Mitchell is very motivated to become a better baseball player.*)

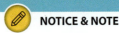 **NOTICE & NOTE**

AHA MOMENT

Notice & Note: Mark the two things that Mitchell suddenly realizes in paragraphs 52 and 53.

Predict: What do you think Mitchell will do, now that he knows why he hasn't been playing well?

SET A PURPOSE

Annotate: In paragraph 58, mark Mitchell's response to Uncle Tommy's telling him that they would start training the next day.

Infer: What does this response suggest about Mitchell?

was good enough to have pro scouts looking at him until he decided to go with the military instead. But even then he was a star on those armed forces teams."

52 I started crying then. Uncle Tommy was right. My mom wanted me to play baseball because she knew how much Dad loved the game. She'd met him when she came to one of his games on the base in Germany. She fell in love with the way he ran like a deer after hitting the ball over the fence. Then she fell in love with him.

53 But he'd never be here in the bleachers to watch me play the game he loved best of all. I wanted so badly to connect with him that—even though I knew it was impossible—my mind was twisted against itself whenever I went out onto the field.

54 Uncle Tommy's hand was on my shoulder. He stayed silent until I'd cried myself out. Then he climbed down out of the stands with me when I went to pick up my glove—which had landed far out in left field.

55 "Time to check on the hawks," he said.

56 Uncle Tommy never drove. Instead he'd let me take him places in the old beater truck I'd bought with the money I'd earned working summers with him at the Indian Village, teaching the tourists about real Native people. Neither one of us said anything until we were almost at his place.

57 "Mitchell, maybe your mind is getting clear now, but you still need to train your eye," he said as we pulled in the drive. "We'll start tomorrow morning."

58 <u>I came back at dawn.</u> Of course he was already up and waiting for me with his own glove, a beautiful old Louisville Slugger,[4] and a whole box of baseballs. All stuff that he'd stored in that little attic of his, which somehow seemed to have more storage space than a cargo ship. He'd never let me go up there, but he was always producing unexpected things from it. Like that time he brought down two saddles and blankets and all the gear for riding and roping calves. But that's another story.

59 "Batting practice," he said, pointing at the home plate he had set up against the side of his house.

60 Uncle Tommy had been a pitcher when he was in Indian school and it turned out he could still bring it—fastball, slider, even a tricky little curve.

61 "Focus," he'd say. "Don't see anything except that ball getting bigger. Connect." Then he would whiz another one past me. But by Sunday afternoon I started making contact.

62 "Are you slowing the pitches down?" I said.

---

[4] **Louisville Slugger:** official bat of Major League Baseball, originally designed by "Bud" Hillerich of Louisville, Kentucky.

372 Unit 5

IMPROVE READING FLUENCY

Targeted Passage Pair students and tell them that they will focus on paragraph 58 for a reading fluency exercise. After modeling reading the passage aloud, ask students to begin reading the paragraph to each other. Encourage them to record their readings with a camera, cell phone, or Dictaphone and listen to it repeatedly to focus on word pronunciations and passages (such as "Louisville" or "riding and roping calves") with which they may struggle. For more advanced students, ask them to discuss the concepts and ideas in the paragraph with their partners.

 Go to the **Reading Studio** for additional support in developing fluency.

63 "Nope." Uncle Tommy smiled. "You are." He got ready to throw again. "Relax with power," he said. "Hard and easy."

64 He had another trick up his sleeve. "The way we always used to learn," he said, "was by watching nature. I got another teacher for you here."

65 He wrapped a deerskin around his arm and we walked out back.

66 "Hawk," he called, holding up his arm. Uncle Tommy never gave names to wild animals more than that. A deer was just "Deer," a bear was just "Bear." But when he called out the word "Hawk," the one hawk he was calling to was always the one that would come. This time it was the big red-tail. It dove down out of the tree, braked with its wings, and reached out its big **talons** to grasp his arm.

67 "How can this hawk catch a bird in flight at ninety miles an hour?" Uncle Tommy said.

68 "Because he sees it?" I asked.

69 Uncle Tommy shook his head. He wanted me to think.

70 "Because he sees where it's going to be," I said.

71 "Go ahead," Uncle Tommy said. He lifted his arm and the hawk took flight. It whistled as it rose and then began circling overhead. I cut a piece of meat from the flank of the road-killed doe we'd picked up from the main road that morning. It was a piece about the size of a baseball. I cocked my left arm and heaved it.

72 Before it could hit the ground, that red-tail caught it out of midair with its claws.

73 Our next game was Wednesday afternoon. Instead of the usual heavy feeling of hopeless despair, I was feeling sick to my stomach. I felt like I might even throw up. And that wasn't a bad thing. Whenever I threw up in the locker room before I went out on the mat to wrestle, I usually ended up doing good. In another couple of minutes we'd be heading out on the field. My gut roiled.

NOTICE & NOTE

ANALYZE POINT OF VIEW

Annotate: Mark the words and phrases in paragraph 66 that suggest that Mitchell thinks Uncle Tommy has a special connection with animals.

Analyze: How does reading about Uncle Tommy from Mitchell's perspective shape the way readers feel about the character of Uncle Tommy?

talon
(tăl´ən) *n.* A *talon* is the claw of a bird of prey.

SET A PURPOSE

Annotate: In paragraph 73, mark words and phrases that describe how Mitchell usually feels before a game and how he is feeling before this game.

Infer: How does this change help to characterize Mitchell?

Ball Hawk   373

TEACH

ANALYZE POINT OF VIEW

Remind students of the concept of **first-person** perspective and how this narrative form shapes the reader's perception by filtering images, characters, ideas, and events through the mind of a **narrator**. (*Answer:* Mitchell is very fond of Uncle Tommy and presents him as wise, caring, and almost superhuman. Because this is the only view we have of Uncle Tommy, it makes us like and respect him just as Mitchell does.)

> **EL ENGLISH LEARNER SUPPORT**
>
> **Point of View** Assist students in understanding point of view by having them search the text of "Ball Hawk" for pronouns. On the board, list first-person pronouns (*I, me, my, we, our*) and third-person pronouns (*he, she, her, his, they, their*). Have them circle these pronouns as they read the text. Intermediate students may make a list of their findings and read it aloud. Students should use their notes and lists to identify the perspective in which the story is written.
>
> **MODERATE**

SET A PURPOSE

Explain that just as in real life, characters in stories constantly go through changes of all kinds. In paragraph 73, the author is encouraging the reader to infer that Mitchell's changes aren't just emotional, but are happening throughout his body. (*Answer:* The change suggests that Mitchell is becoming more confident as a baseball player and that he is not as depressed about his skills.)

CRITICAL VOCABULARY

talon: Biologists use the specialized term *talons* to identify the hooked feet with which large birds of prey hunt.

ASK STUDENTS to think about what body parts of other animals correlate to the *talons* of large birds. (*Humans have hands/feet, lions have claws, bears have paws, and horses have hooves.*)

Ball Hawk   373

TEACH

AHA MOMENT

Remind students that **Aha Moments** come with their own language, which usually includes phrases like "Suddenly, I knew" or "All at once everything was clear." Ask students to pay close attention to the text here and make note of the specific language that tells us this is probably an **Aha Moment** for Mitchell. (**Answer:** *He won't be so depressed and resentful about baseball. He may even embrace it and enjoy it as a connection to his father.*)

NOTICE & NOTE

74 "Excuse me, guys," I said, heading for the john.

75 "Hey," Robby Mills, our shortstop said, "Sabattis is about to lose his lunch."

76 "Cool," Zach Branch said. He was on the wrestling team with me.

77 It wasn't that big a game that day for most of us. It was the Carrier Falls Cougars we were playing and we'd beaten them already a few weeks ago by a score of 4–1, despite my striking out three times. But it was big enough for me. It started in the top of the third inning when I called for a fly ball and not only caught it, but threw it back in quick and hard enough to catch the Cougars runner who'd been on base between second and third. My first double play! Robbie almost cracked my ribs when he came running out from shortstop to hug me.

78 Bottom of the third, I was the second batter up. I looked up just before the pitch and thought I saw a bird circling above the field. Then the pitcher reared back and let it fly. It was a curveball. I saw that clearly as it came toward me. I swear I could even see that there was a smudge of green from the turf on the ball's lacing as it rotated toward me. My swing was strong, but relaxed at the same time. Hard and easy. And I connected.

AHA MOMENT

Notice & Note: In paragraph 79, mark Mitchell's accomplishment.

Predict: What do you think this will mean for Mitchell?

79 The ball hit the sweet spot on the bat. It was a sound half crack and half chunk, a sound I had heard before, just plain music. And the ball was rising, heading up and out, and I knew it was going far past any of the fielders, way out beyond the fence. People were yelling at me to run, but I was just standing there, watching it go, flying toward the sun.

80 And that was when the yelling stopped. It stopped as that hawk dove. It caught the ball in its claws, banked, flapped its wings, and floated off toward the distant mountains, taking what should have been my first home run with it.

81 "You got it, Dad," I whispered. Don't ask me why I said that or if it makes any sense. I mean, I knew it was just Uncle Tommy's red-tail.

82 I turned to the umpire, whose mouth was open as he watched the big bird disappear.

83 "Hey," I said in a soft voice, "I think I know what you should call it." Then I told him.

84 A big grin came to his face and he pointed off in the direction the hawk had gone.

85 He yelled it out and everybody in the park went wild.

86 The pitcher was so rattled by what had happened that he threw me an easy one on his next pitch that I stroked over the third baseman's head for a double.

374 Unit 5

TO CHALLENGE STUDENTS . . .

Write It Your Way Have students reread paragraph 79 and imagine how such a moment would feel if they had been Mitchell. Talk to students about feelings of accomplishment, triumph, and joy, and ask them to think of a time when they did something important or achieved something special. Now ask students to rewrite paragraph 79, substituting themselves for Mitchell and substituting his moment of achievement for an important moment from their own lives. Circulate and ensure students consider character, setting, the narrator, and point of view.

87   I ended up that day with two more doubles and a sacrifice bunt to my credit. We won 5–2. And I played out the rest of that season with a batting average of .285 and a reputation as a better than average fielder. I even had a grand slam home run the last game of the season. But the best moment I ever had in baseball came that day against the Cougars. It came to me because of what Uncle Tommy taught me about letting go of anger and putting my heart in the game. It allowed me to have my best hit ever, even if it ended up being a foul ball.

NOTICE & NOTE

ANALYZE POINT OF VIEW

Annotate: In paragraph 87, mark sentences that reveal that the narrator is reflecting on that day and what he has learned.

Analyze: Why do you think that the narrator tells this story from the perspective of looking back on events, rather than as they actually are happening? What benefit does this perspective have?

CHECK YOUR UNDERSTANDING

Answer these questions before moving on to the **Analyze the Text** section on the following page.

1 According to Mitchell, what is Uncle Tommy's best characteristic?

   A The fact that Uncle Tommy knew Mitchell's father

   B The fact that Uncle Tommy is a *real Indian*

   C His sense of humor about dealing with life

   D His spiritual connection with the natural world

2 The author has Mitchell tell about Uncle Tommy's care for injured birds of prey in order to —

   F emphasize Uncle Tommy's compassionate nature

   G suggest that Uncle Tommy has a hidden past

   H compare Uncle Tommy to a fierce predator

   J praise Uncle Tommy's knowledge of Indian folklore

3 According to Mitchell, why was the hit that the hawk intercepted his best hit ever?

   A The fact that a hawk had taken his hit earned him the respect of his teammates.

   B It was the first hit he made because he truly cared and was no longer angry.

   C He knew that the hit was powerful enough to produce a home run.

   D It was a great hit, which he followed with other good hits in the same game.

Ball Hawk   375

TEACH

ANALYZE POINT OF VIEW

Inform students that some of the benefits of a first-person singular, past-tense point of view are the ability for the narrator to be reflective, thoughtful, and to build his character slowly and carefully. For contrast, suggest students think or write about what a third-person plural, present-tense point of view (we, our) would sound like. (**Answer:** *Telling the story from the perspective of looking back on events allows the narrator to weave wisdom and life lessons into the story.*)

CHECK YOUR UNDERSTANDING

Have students answer the questions independently.

Answers:

1. C
2. F
3. B

If they answer any questions incorrectly, have them reread the test to confirm their understanding. Then they may proceed to ANALYZE THE TEXT on p. 376.

ENGLISH LEARNER SUPPORT

Oral Assessment   Use the following questions to assess students' comprehension and speaking skills:

1. Is Uncle Tommy a kind character? *(yes.)* Provide a sentence frame to help students describe Uncle Tommy: Uncle Tommy is ____. *(kind)* He helps Mitchell play ____. *(baseball)*

2. What is Uncle Tommy's relationship to birds? Is this an important detail? Tell why or why not. *(Uncle Tommy helps birds that are hurt. It is am important detail because it shows he cares about others and nature.)*

3. At what time of day do Uncle Tommy and Mitchell begin their practice? *(They begin at dawn, the very beginning of the day.)*

SUBSTANTIAL/MODERATE

Ball Hawk   **375**

APPLY

ANALYZE THE TEXT
Possible answers:

1. **DOK 4:** Mitchell uses a first-person point of view to say that he lives "in the sticks." He recognizes that he is on the varsity baseball team only because there are very few students. Uncle Tommy's connection with nature helps shape him, and Mitchell's work in the village.

2. **DOK 2:** Because Mitchell is a Native American, as was Mitchell's father, Tommy wants Mitchell to remember that baseball is part of his heritage.

3. **DOK 2:** "Ball hawk" literally refers to the hawk that catches Mitchell's ball at the end of the story. It is symbolic of the way that Mitchell improves by taking Uncle Tommy's words to heart.

4. **DOK 4:** The scene in which Uncle Tommy calls Hawk and discusses how it can catch a bird in flight foreshadows the climax of the story, in which the hawk catches Mitchell's home run hit.

5. **DOK 4:** Uncle Tommy offers Mitchell advice and is patient with him. He helps Mitchell see his anger and the reason that he isn't playing baseball well. He is like a substitute for Mitchell's late father.

RESEARCH
Tell students that they should confirm the information they gather by double checking it with other credible sources.

Extend Some good resources for this are the histories of Native Americans in baseball found at the Major League Baseball website (www.mlb.com) and www.baseball-almanac.com. Ask students to think about what hurdles these players, like Mitchell, must have had to overcome to play the game they loved.

376 Unit 5

 RESPOND

ANALYZE THE TEXT
Support your responses with evidence from the text. 📓 NOTEBOOK

1. **Analyze** Review paragraphs 3 and 10. What point of view is used in describing the setting in which Mitchell lives? How does this setting affect Mitchell as a character?

2. **Infer** Refer to your "Set a Purpose" notes about Mitchell's characterization. Why do you think that Uncle Tommy twice reminds Mitchell that "Indians invented baseball"? Why are these words an important part of Mitchell's characterization?

3. **Interpret** In the language of baseball, a "ball hawk" is a player who is skilled in catching fly balls. Why is "Ball Hawk" an appropriate title for this story?

4. **Analyze** When a writer provides hints that suggest future events in a story, it's called **foreshadowing.** Identify and explain an example of foreshadowing in "Ball Hawk."

5. **Notice & Note** What does Uncle Tommy do to help Mitchell overcome his anger and work on his baseball skills?

RESEARCH TIP
When you scan search results, look for websites that are more likely to include information that is accurate and current. This includes sites that end in *.gov, .org,* and *.edu.* For sites that end in *.com,* use your judgment. Ask yourself who published the information and what the purpose might be. Evaluate whether the information seems credible, well researched, and unbiased.

RESEARCH
Like Mitchell's father, many well-known Major League Baseball players were (and are) Native Americans. Research these baseball players. Record details abut their origins, teams, and achievements.

BASEBALL PLAYER	ACHIEVEMENTS
Louis Sockalexis	*Born on the Penobscot Indian reservation in Maine in 1871 he was the first well-known Native American in the big leagues. He played three years for the Cleveland Spiders.*
Charles Albert Bender	*Born in Minnesota, he played for the Philadelphia Athletics from 1903 to 1917. He was the first Native American inducted into the National Baseball Hall of Fame.*
Zachariah Davis Wheat	*From Hamilton, Missouri, his mother was a Cherokee. Wheat played for the Brooklyn Dodgers. He was the 2nd Native American inducted into the Baseball Hall of Fame, in 1959.*

Extend In the first paragraph of Bruchac's story, Uncle Tommy notes that "Indians invented baseball." In fact, there were other ways that Indians became familiar with the game. Find out how a lot of Native Americans were introduced to baseball in the 1800s and 1900s.

376 Unit 5

 LEARNING MINDSET

Questioning Students should always feel comfortable asking questions. Curiosity is always a good thing, no matter how silly the inquiry might feel. The only way to grow, learn new things, and feel comfortable taking on a problem is to ask the right things and pursue new ideas according to the answers. Remind students that the pursuits of science, technology, education, and so much more are all predicated on important but surprisingly simple questions: How does the world work? How can we make it work better? How can people learn to work well together? Questioning is essential for learning, growing, and understanding your surroundings. Never hesitate if you feel curious—and never hesitate to ask!

CREATE AND ADAPT

Write an Epilogue Write a three- to four-paragraph epilogue or concluding section in which you describe Mitchell's views of baseball a year after the story ends.

- ❏ Brainstorm how you think Mitchell will feel about baseball and about himself in a year.
- ❏ Begin your epilogue by noting where Mitchell is in a year and what he's doing. You may want to continue to write the story from the first-person point of view to help you explore Mitchell's concerns.
- ❏ End the epilogue by explaining how Mitchell feels about baseball and whether he plans to continue playing.

Create a Baseball Card Using details from the story and your own imagination, create a baseball card for Mitchell.

- ❏ As a group, review the text and note details about Mitchell's appearance, background, and batting average. Find baseball cards online to use as a reference for the card's design and layout.
- ❏ Create your card. Draw a picture of Mitchell on the front. Put biographical information and batting average on the back.
- ❏ Share and compare your card with the cards that a few classmates created. Discuss the differences in how you portrayed Mitchell and what specific details from the story shaped your portrayal.

RESPOND TO THE ESSENTIAL QUESTION

 How do sports bring together friends, families, and communities?

Gather Information Review your annotations and notes on "Ball Hawk." Then, add relevant details to your Response Log. As you determine which information to include, think about:

- how Mitchell changed
- why Uncle Tommy was important
- how seeing events through Mitchell's eyes affected the story

At the end of the unit, use your notes to help you write a short story.

RESPOND

Go to **Writing Narratives** in the **Writing Studio** to help with the epilogue.

Go to **Participating in Collaborative Discussions** in the **Speaking and Listening Studio** for help.

ACADEMIC VOCABULARY

As you write and discuss what you learned from the short story, be sure to use the Academic Vocabulary words. Check off each of the words that you use.

- ❏ attitude
- ❏ consume
- ❏ goal
- ❏ purchase
- ❏ style

APPLY

CREATE AND ADAPT

Write an Epilogue Inform students that *epilogue* literally means "extra text" in Greek. Encourage them to stick to the list on page 377 in writing their epilogues, but to use their creativity in continuing and expanding Mitchell's story in their own words.

For **writing support** for students at varying proficiency levels, see the **Text X-Ray** on page 362D.

Create a Baseball Card Remind students that they may use preexisting knowledge about baseball cards if they have it, but that additional research is probably necessary to get the details—like batting averages and stats—correct. Working in groups is also acceptable; group members can share information and responsibilities for the project.

RESPOND TO THE ESSENTIAL QUESTION

Allow time for students to add details from "Ball Hawk" to their Unit 5 Response Logs.

APPLY

CRITICAL VOCABULARY

Answers:

1. *a. The president is the head of the federal (national) government.*

2. *a. An eagle needs talons because it is a bird of prey; a sparrow is not.*

3. *b. Sports teams have animal mascots, which symbolize competitiveness and athleticism.*

4. *b. Thursday, Friday, and Saturday follow each other without interruption.*

5. *a. People in a clique gather together as friends; athletes, especially those on different teams, may not know each other at all.*

VOCABULARY STRATEGY:
Word Origins

Answers:

1. **clique:** *from the (old) French **cliquer**: to make a sound or noticeable noise; originated in 18th century France.*

2. **mascot:** *from the 19th century French **mascotte**, and Provençal **mascoto** meaning "witchcraft" or "charm" and possibly the Latin **masca** meaning "ghost."*

378   Unit 5

 RESPOND

WORD BANK
clique
consecutive
mascot
federal
talon

CRITICAL VOCABULARY

Practice and Apply Mark the letter of the answer to each question.

1. Which of the following is an example of a **federal** employee?
   a. the president of the U.S.   b. the governor of your state

2. Which of the following would have a **talon**?
   a. an eagle   b. a sparrow

3. Which of the following would more likely be a team **mascot**?
   a. a ship   b. a panther

4. Which of the following is three **consecutive** days?
   a. Monday, Wednesday, Friday   b. Thursday, Friday, Saturday

5. Which of the following would more likely be found in a **clique**?
   a. a popular group of friends   b. the best athletes in a league

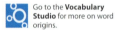 Go to the **Vocabulary Studio** for more on word origins.

VOCABULARY STRATEGY: Word Origins

Etymologies show the origin of a word across time. Being aware of the origin and historical development of an unfamiliar word can help you understand how the current word form evolved. Study this example of the etymology of the Critical Vocabulary word *talon*.

> Middle English *taloun* < Old French *talon*, heel < Latin *talus*, ankle

The etymology for *talon* shows that the word is from Middle English but has its root in a Latin word meaning "ankle."

Practice and Apply Use a dictionary to find the etymology of each Critical Vocabulary word in the chart below. Record what you learn.

CRITICAL VOCABULARY WORD	ETYMOLOGY
clique	
mascot	

378   Unit 5

 ENGLISH LEARNER SUPPORT

Vocabulary Strategy Put learners in pairs to practice sketching or acting out the new vocabulary words. After clearly defining all new words, give the student pairs two separate lists of vocabulary terms taken from the new vocabulary on this page. Then ask students to either sketch or mime the words in a way that will get their partners to guess the right word. Model for them first, using the word *talon*. Partners take turns until they run through the entire list.
MODERATE

RESPOND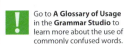

LANGUAGE CONVENTIONS:
Commonly Confused Words

Words that sound alike but have different meanings and different spellings can cause problems for writers. Look at this example from "Ball Hawk."

> "Baseball is great," I said. "It's just me. I stink."

In this example, *it's* (meaning "it is") is often confused with *its* (the possessive form of *it*). Some other commonly confused words include *accept/except*, *past/passed*, *affect/effect*, *there/their/they're*, and *to/two/too*.

It is important to review your writing to make sure that you are using commonly confused words correctly. People reading your work may not understand your message if you use words incorrectly. Rereading your writing to correct any errors will help you communicate more effectively. If you are unsure about which spelling to use in a sentence, consult a dictionary and determine which word has the meaning that will fit in your sentence.

Practice and Apply Mark the word that correctly completes each sentence. Then write the meaning of the word on the line.

1. Janine didn't want the game to (**affect/effect**) her friendship with Laila.
   _____

2. The basketball players wanted (**their/there/they're**) own jerseys.
   _____

3. Mitchell swung the bat (**to/two/too**) soon.
   _____

4. Everyone in the bleachers (**accept/except**) Jake's parents cheered the referee's call.
   _____

5. Uncle Tommy didn't want the (**past/passed**) to upset Mitchell.
   _____

> Go to **A Glossary of Usage** in the **Grammar Studio** to learn more about the use of commonly confused words.

APPLY

LANGUAGE CONVENTIONS:
Commonly Confused Words

Review the information about commonly confused words with students. Explain that even accomplished writers occasionally misspell or misuse words that sound alike but have different meanings. This usually happens when writers are in a hurry or not giving full attention to reviewing their work. Most words that sound alike but are spelled differently do not have similar meanings—such as *to* and *two*. There are some words which can be more difficult to use correctly; *affect* and *effect* are often confused with each other. In its verb form, *effect* means "to make something happen," as in: *The manual explains how to effect repairs*, i.e., make, or accomplish repairs. This can easily be confused with the verb form of *affect* which means *to influence*. When trying to decide which verb to use, writers can ask themselves if they mean that they want to talk about influencing change in something that already exists, or making something to happen. If the sentence above read *the manual explains how to affect repairs* it would imply that the manual explains how to cause changes in, or influence repairs that are already being made.

Practice and Apply Words that sound the same but have different meanings are often confused with one another; playing close attention to context can be helpful in determining which word should be used.

Use Commonly Confused Words
Answers:

1. **affect:** *to influence*
2. **their:** *possessive for of and they*
3. **too:** *excessively*
4. **except:** *excluding; other than*
5. **past:** *a period of time before the present time.*

🆔 ENGLISH LEARNER SUPPORT

Language Conventions Help students learn to distinguish between commonly confused words. Display *to*, *two*, and *too*. Model their meanings. For example, say *I am walking to the door*. Point at *to* while walking. Point to the word *two* and say *I have two pencils* while holding two pencils. Model *too* as in *too much*, and in *addition to*. Guide students to choose the correct words: I am going to/two/too the store. I would like two/too/to tickets. You made two/to/too many cookies. I want to go to/too/two! **SUBSTANTIAL**

PLAN

GET IN THE ZONE: THE PSYCHOLOGY OF VIDEO GAME DESIGN

Informational Text by Aaron Millar

GENRE ELEMENTS
INFORMATIONAL TEXT

Remind students that the aim of an **informational text** is to present readers with facts and information about a specific topic in order to inform, entertain, or persuade. Informational texts often include supporting testimony from experts on the topic and may use features such as headings, sidebars, and graphics to organize and communicate information. Examples of informational texts are magazine articles, historical writing, and biographies.

LEARNING OBJECTIVES

- Distinguish between the subjective and objective point of view.
- Make predictions about a text.
- Write an objective summary of an informational text.
- Discuss a video game analytically.
- Use semicolons to connect independent clauses.
- Use context to determine the meaning of unfamiliar words.
- **Language** Discuss a video game.

TEXT COMPLEXITY

Quantitative Measures	Get in the Zone: The Psychology of Video Game Design	Lexile: 800L
Qualitative Measures	**Ideas Presented** Literal, explicit, and direct; purpose or stance clear	
	Structure Used Conventional, supported through subheads	
	Language Used Some unfamiliar vocabulary, but support is offered	
	Knowledge Required Begins to rely more on outside knowledge	

380A Unit 5

PLAN

Online

RESOURCES

- Unit 5 Response Log
- Selection Audio
- Reading Studio: Notice & Note
- Writing Studio: Using Textual Evidence
- Speaking and Listening Studio: Participating in a Collaborative Discussion
- Vocabulary Studio: Context Clues
- Grammar Studio: Module 14: Lesson 6: Semicolons
- "Get in the Zone" Selection Test

SUMMARIES

English

Author Aaron Millar explains why some video games absorb us completely while others frustrate us to the point of losing focus and interest. What makes the difference? Millar attributes it to the psychology of gaming design. The best-designed games are ones that manipulate players into feeling a sense of mastery and self-satisfaction as they proceed from level to level. Games that strike the perfect balance between challenging and just possible keep players hooked—and even increase their dopamine levels.

Spanish

El autor Aaron Millar explica por qué ciertos videojuegos nos absorben completamente mientras que otros nos frustran al punto de perder la concentración y el interés. ¿A qué viene la diferencia? Millar se lo atribuye a la psicología del diseño de juegos. Los juegos mejor diseñados son los que manipulan a los jugadores para que sientan un sentido de dominio y de satisfacción personal a medida que pasan de nivel en nivel. Los juegos que llegan al equilibrio perfecto entre dificultad y posibilidad mantienen a los jugadores enganchados e incluso aumentan sus niveles de dopamina.

SMALL-GROUP OPTIONS

Have students work in small groups to read and discuss the selection.

Activate Academic Vocabulary

- Provide students with a list of Academic Vocabulary words (*attitude, consume, goal, purchase, style*).
- Ask students to discuss video games while integrating each of the Academic Vocabulary words into their discussion.
- Ask one student to be the record keeper to see who in the group uses which word and how many times.
- Set the clock for 10 minutes and see who can get the most use out of the words.

Pinwheel Discussion

- After students have read the excerpt from "Get in the Zone: The Psychology of Video Game Design," ask them to create pinwheel formations of six per group.
- For the first rotation, ask students to discuss the "Challenge" section of the text.
- For the second rotation, ask students to discuss the "Focus" section of the text.
- For the third rotation, ask students to discuss the "Reward" section of the text.

Get in the Zone: The Psychology of Video Game Design

PLAN

Text X-Ray: English Learner Support
for "Get in the Zone: The Psychology of Video Game Design"

Use the Text X-Ray and the supports and scaffolds in the Teacher's Edition to help guide students at different proficiency levels through the selection.

INTRODUCE THE SELECTION
DISCUSS FRUSTRATED AND CHALLENGED

In this lesson, students will read and discuss why some video games frustrate players while others challenge them. Provide the following explanations:

- **frustrated:** feeling annoyed and defeated because you can't change or achieve something
- **challenged:** feeling that a task is difficult but doable

Explain to students that when people feel frustrated they want to give up, and they lose the concentration they need to succeed. When people feel challenged, they want to keep going because they think they can overcome any difficulties and succeed.

Have students share times or experiences when they felt frustrated and times or experiences when they felt challenged.

I felt frustrated when I _____. I felt challenged when I _____.

CULTURAL REFERENCES

The following words and phrases may be unfamiliar to students:

- *Stone ramparts* (paragraph 1): fortification consisting of an embankment; usually found surrounding castles
- *lap time* (paragraph 4): a racing term, but can be applied to how long it takes to do something
- *state of mind* (paragraph 5): a person's mood
- *delicate balancing act* (paragraph 7): trying to do two things at a time
- *feedback* (paragraph 7): receiving evaluation on the progress of one's work
- *blows a fuse* (paragraph 9): idiom from overloading an electrical circuit
- *open-ended* (bullets at conclusion): having no end

LISTENING

Listen for the Main Idea

Draw students' attention to the "Challenge" subheading on p. 385. Explain that a subheading of a section can help them figure out the main idea of the section.

Have students listen as you read aloud the "Challenge" section of the article. Use the following supports with students at varying proficiency levels:

- Tell students that you will ask questions about what you just read aloud. Model that they should give a thumbs up for yes and a thumbs down for no. Ask: *Should videos games be very, very hard to play?* (no) *Should video games be very easy to play?* (no) **SUBSTANTIAL**
- Have students talk about not being frustrated by a video game that is too hard or not being bored by a video game that is too easy. **MODERATE**
- Have students explain what the author means by "a delicate balancing act." What is being balanced and why? **LIGHT**

PLAN

SPEAKING

Discuss a Video Game

Direct students to the Discuss a Video Game assignment on p. 389. Use the following prompts to facilitate their discussions.

Use the following supports with students at varying proficiency levels:

- Provide sentence frames. *My favorite game video is _____ . I like _____ . I don't like _____ .* **SUBSTANTIAL**
- .Have student pairs find a video game they both have played. Provide sentence frames. (*Name of game*) has _____ music. (*Name of game*) was not _____ to learn. (*Name of game*) reminds me of _____.
- Challenge them to come up with questions to ask each other about the video game that incorporate the concepts presented in the selection. **MODERATE**
- Have student pairs find a video game they both have played. Challenge them to discuss it in terms of the concepts presented in the selection. **LIGHT**

READING

Understand the Main Idea

Direct student attention to the "Reward" section of the article on p. 386. Ask students to keep the subheading in mind as they read the section.

Work with students to reread the "Reward" section. Use the following supports with students at varying proficiency levels:

- Have students echo read the section. Ask whether they need clarification of any words or phrases, and provide them accordingly. Then ask students to underline the words in the text that explain why rewards feel good. **SUBSTANTIAL**
- Pair students to identify the reasons why, according to the section, the players of video games respond to rewards. **MODERATE**
- Pair students to explain what micro-rewards are, in their own words. **LIGHT**

WRITING

Write a Summary

Direct students to the Writing an Objective Summary assignment on p. 389. Review the qualities of a good summary.

Use the following supports with students at varying proficiency levels:

- Help students reread paragraph 3. Use gestures, cognates, and images to check for understanding. Then, have students label images with words from their home languages, cognates, and the corresponding words in English. Tell them that they are making a word-image bank they will use for the assignment. Help them pronounce and use words that go with the images, e.g., the word *frustrated* that goes with an image of a frustrated player. Continue for other key words: *zone, entertaining, complicated, difficult,* and *easy.* **SUBSTANTIAL**
- Have students write the titles of the subheadings on a sheet of paper. Then ask them to write a two- to three-sentence summary of the main points of each section. **MODERATE**
- Have students write the titles of the subheadings on a sheet of paper. Then ask them to write a brief summary of each section. **LIGHT**

TEACH

? Connect to the ESSENTIAL QUESTION

This informational text explores the connection between games and people by examining the psychological influence that video games have on players.

ANALYZE & APPLY

GET IN THE ZONE: THE PSYCHOLOGY OF VIDEO GAME DESIGN

Informational Text by **Aaron Millar**

? ESSENTIAL QUESTION:

How do sports bring together friends, families, and communities?

GET READY

QUICK START

Describe an experience that you or a character in a film or TV show has had while playing a video game. What was the player's focus? Did anything unexpected happen?

PREDICT

Making predictions as you read nonfiction texts means making an educated guess about what the author will discuss next. As you read on, you may confirm or change that prediction. Identifying clues in elements such as the following can help you make predictions.

- **Text Features:** Subheadings, boldfaced words, and graphics often reveal ideas that you can use to inform your predictions.
- **Structures:** The organization of the text (for example, cause/effect or sequence) helps you predict what the author will explain next.

Use the chart below as you analyze the selection.

PREDICTION	TEXT EVIDENCE THAT CONFIRMS IT

GENRE ELEMENTS: INFORMATIONAL TEXT
- provides factual information and/or explanations
- presents evidence to support key ideas
- often contains text features, such as subheadings
- includes magazine and newspaper articles, legal documents, essays, and speeches

ANALYZE SUBJECTIVE AND OBJECTIVE POINT OF VIEW

Point of view refers to the perspective from which an article is written. A first-person point of view uses pronouns such as *I*, *me*, and *we*. A third-person point of view uses pronouns such as *he*, *she*, *it*, and *they*. Authors of nonfiction write in a subjective or objective point of view.

- When using a **subjective point of view,** an author includes personal thoughts, opinions, and emotions.
- When using an **objective point of view,** an author presents fact-based information in an unbiased way.

The author uses language to develop his or her **voice,** or unique style, and **tone,** or attitude toward a subject. Voice and tone can influence point of view. As you read the selection, consider how the author's use of language shapes voice and tone and develops point of view, and think about the author's purpose in choosing a specific point of view.

TEACH

QUICK START

Have students read the Quick Start question and think about it independently for a few minutes. Guide them by asking what makes them lose interest in a video game. Have students respond to the question in a brief whole-class discussion.

PREDICT

Explain to students that making predictions while reading is something good readers do regularly, whether they realize they are doing it or not. To demonstrate how students may already be making predictions, indicate their textbook's features and structure. Ask students how, after reading through several units, they can now predict what kind of help they will receive with each selection.

ANALYZE SUBJECTIVE AND OBJECTIVE POINT OF VIEW

Explain to students that a writer's **bias** is not necessarily a bad thing. Bias is simply an inclination toward a particular judgment on a topic or issue. Most people have a bias against war and poverty, for example. But an author's bias could also unfairly prejudice readers against a topic. Advise students to ask themselves these questions as they determine the author's voice:

- What is the author's attitude toward the topic?
- What kinds of facts is the author presenting?
- Do the author's words have positive or negative connotations?

TEACH

CRITICAL VOCABULARY

Encourage students to read all the sentences before deciding which word best completes each one. Remind them to look for context clues that match the meaning of each word.

Answers:

1. *disorient*
2. *absorb*
3. *irrelevant*
4. *immerse*
5. *wholly*

■ **English Learner Support**

Use Cognates Tell students that several of the Critical Vocabulary words have Spanish cognates (*absorb/absorber, irrelevant/irrelevante, disorient/desorientar*). Help them pronounce the words properly. **ALL LEVELS**

LANGUAGE CONVENTIONS

Explain that semicolons, like all punctuation, are used to make written language clearer to the reader. Tell students that they can think of the period in a semicolon separating two independent clauses and the comma in a semicolon indicating that the sentence hasn't come to a full stop yet.

 ANNOTATION MODEL

Remind students to circle the signal words that suggest what the text will be discussing next. Have them underline sentences that indicate the author's voice. Point out that they may use their own annotation system, like color-coding, if they prefer. Inform students to note in the margins any questions about ideas that are unclear or topics they want to learn more about.

382   Unit 5

GET READY

CRITICAL VOCABULARY

absorb   wholly   immerse   irrelevant   disorient

To see how many Critical Vocabulary words you already know, use them to complete these sentences.

1. Waking up in the middle of the night can _____ someone.
2. While traveling in Spain, Becca tried to _____ local customs.
3. The committee ignored Raul's objections to the new regulations, calling them _____ to the discussion.
4. Jonathan would _____ himself in his notes to study for tests.
5. She dedicated her time _____ to learning to play guitar.

LANGUAGE CONVENTIONS

Comma Splices and Run-On Sentences A comma splice is a punctuation error. It happens in compound sentences when a comma is used when there is no coordinating conjunction. One way to correct this error is to use a semicolon (;) to separate the independent clauses.

I played the video game for two hours, I finally won.

I played the video game for two hours; I finally won.

A run-on sentence occurs when two or more sentences are written as if they were one sentence. Authors avoid run-ons by separating the sentences or with punctuation and coordinating conjunctions.

ANNOTATION MODEL   **NOTICE & NOTE**

As you read, look for places where you might make predictions. You can also mark details that suggest the author's point of view. In the model, you can see one reader's notes about one part of the text.

> 2   (Sound familiar?)
>
> 3   Frustration is something every gamer knows all too well. But why do some video games completely absorb us in their world while others leave us howling at the screen? The answer has less to do with your ability to press buttons than it does with what's happening in your brain. Good games are designed to get you "in the zone" —a heightened state of concentration, and enjoyment, that psychologists call flow.

The author asks a question. I predict that he'll explain why gaming experiences vary.

Facts are given with no emotion or opinion.

382   Unit 5

BACKGROUND

There's no question that video games are a popular pastime. From the appearance of the first video-game consoles and arcade video games in the 1970s to today's generation of online 3D and virtual reality games, they have captured the attention of players of all ages. Players have their favorite games—but what makes some games more popular than others? In this selection, author Aaron Millar gives his answer to that question.

GET IN THE ZONE: THE PSYCHOLOGY OF VIDEO GAME DESIGN
Informational Text by Aaron Millar

SETTING A PURPOSE

As you read, pay attention to clues in the text that help you predict what the author will discuss in each section. Think, too, about whether the author's point of view is largely subjective, largely objective, or a mix of both—and how you can tell.

1   The dragon rises above me, breathing flames into the night air. Stone ramparts crumble in the township; houses burn. Screams echo all around me. I have only one chance. His jaws open. I draw my sword. But before I can react he's snatching me into his talons, throwing me in his mouth, and the hero … dies. In exactly the same place. Again. It's completely unfair. I throw my control pad on the floor, scream at the screen, and walk out of my bedroom in disgust.

2   Sound familiar?

3   Frustration is something every gamer knows all too well. But why do some video games completely **absorb** us in their world while others leave us howling at the screen? The answer has less to do with your ability to press buttons

NOTICE & NOTE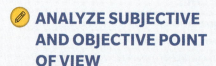

Notice & Note

Use the side margins to notice and note signposts in the text.

ANALYZE SUBJECTIVE AND OBJECTIVE POINT OF VIEW
Annotate: Mark details in paragraph 1 in which the author is talking about himself.

Critique: Why do you think the author chose this point of view? How does this convey the author's voice?

absorb
(əb-zôrb′) v. Things that *absorb* you occupy your time or attention.

Get in the Zone: The Psychology of Video Game Design 383

ENGLISH LEARNER SUPPORT

Understand First-Person Point of View Read paragraph 1 to students, stopping after each sentence to see if they need any clarification of words or phrases. Ask yes-or-no questions to help them identify the first-person point of view. *Does the writer use I and me? Is he talking about his own experience? (Yes, yes)* Continue identifying the point of view in subsequent paragraphs. **SUBSTANTIAL/MODERATE**

TEACH

BACKGROUND

After students read the Background note, tell them that Millar never actually mentions any specific video games in the text, so students should ask themselves as they read if any of the author's information applies to the video games they play.

SETTING A PURPOSE

Direct students to use the Setting a Purpose prompt to focus their reading.

ANALYZE SUBJECTIVE AND OBJECTIVE POINT OF VIEW

Direct students to look for first-person pronouns like *I, me, we,* and *us*. Also tell them to look for verbs and adjectives that convey emotions. These are clues to the subjective point of view. (**Answer:** *The author uses a first-person, subjective point of view. He probably does so to make an immediate connection with his readers by revealing his love of video games.*)

ENGLISH LEARNER SUPPORT

Identify Informal English Read aloud and display the text title on page 383. Explain that "get in the zone" is an example of informal English that is used to get the reader's attention.

- Form small groups of beginning and intermediate learners. Then have students use words from images you have labeled to construct story titles that catch readers' attention with informal English. For example, label an image of the Hoover Dam with the words *water, dam,* and *river,* and share the expression "Hold everything!" Circulate among students to offer help as necessary.
  SUBSTANTIAL/MODERATE

- Ask students to write titles and the opening sentences of a story using informal English to catch the reader's attention. **LIGHT**

CRITICAL VOCABULARY

absorb: When we really get involved in a game, it takes all our attention.

ASK STUDENTS how this definition of *absorb* is like a sponge absorbs water. (*Possible answer: When a sponge absorbs water, it takes it all in and doesn't leave anything.*)

Get in the Zone: The Psychology of Video Game Design **383**

TEACH

QUOTED WORDS

Remind students that this signpost is used to indicate opinions or conclusions of someone who is an expert on the subject. *(Answer: Madigan explains what a "flow state" is. He is qualified because he is a psychologist who has authored a website on the subject.)*

ENGLISH LEARNER SUPPORT

Understand Quotations Have students locate the complete quotation in paragraph 4. Explain to them why the quotation is broken up. Have volunteers read the text within the quotation marks. Then explain and model "air quotes" with your fingers.

ASK STUDENTS Write the following sentence (without the quotes) on the board and have students read it while making "air quotes" at the appropriate times. ("It is a beautiful day," said the bus driver, "so I am going to enjoy the drive.") **LIGHT**

NOTICE & NOTE

QUOTED WORDS

Notice & Note: Mark the explanation that Jamie Madigan gives in paragraph 4.

Evaluate: What topic is Madigan explaining? Why is he qualified to speak about this topic?

wholly
(hō´lē) *adv.* If a speech deals *wholly* with the history of the solar system, that is the only topic the speaker discusses.

than it does with what's happening in your brain. Good games are designed to get you "in the zone"—a heightened state of concentration, and enjoyment, that psychologists call flow.

4   In a state of flow even the most difficult tasks feel effortless and easy to complete. Just beat your best lap time by 10 seconds? That's flow. Killed the monster you were stuck on for two weeks? Welcome to the zone. "In a flow state," explains psychologist Jamie Madigan, author of psychologyofvideogames.com, "you don't have to think. Your performance is automatic. The rest of the world falls away and you are **wholly** focused on the screen." Top athletes and rock stars describe this state of mind when they're performing at their best. But gamers have an edge: unlike the real world, video games are designed to get us into this state as quickly as possible—and keep us there. It's why we play: flow is fun. But some games are better than others. And here's why.

CRITICAL VOCABULARY

wholly: The writer uses *wholly* to explain how completely the gamer is focused.

ASK STUDENTS how *wholly focused* and *absorbed* are similar in meaning. *(They both mean that someone is giving their complete attention to something.)*

Challenge

5   If you kill the dragon the first time, it's boring; don't kill him the hundredth time and it's just plain annoying. Flow happens only when there's a perfect balance between the challenge of the game and the skill level of the player. "It should be difficult," Madigan says, "but just possible."

6   The reason has to do with the amount of information our minds can hold at any one time. Imagine your brain is like a backpack. If it's filled to the top with just the skills required for the game, there's no room left for any distractions. You're completely **immersed** in that imaginary world. But put in too much and your backpack will break—you'll get stressed and fed up with playing; too little, and you'll start thinking about that party next week.

7   It's a delicate balancing act: in order to keep us in the zone, games have to increase their level of difficulty at precisely the same rate at which players improve their level of skill. And

NOTICE & NOTE

PREDICT
Annotate: Mark the subheading that introduces paragraphs 5–7. Predict what you think will be discussed under that subheading.

Analyze: Review your prediction after you read the section. Did the text reflect your predictions? Explain.

immerse
(ĭ-mûrs´) v. If you *immerse* yourself in an activity, that activity is the only thing that you are focused on.

Get in the Zone: The Psychology of Video Game Design 385

APPLYING ACADEMIC VOCABULARY

☑ attitude   ☐ consume   ☑ goal   ☑ purchase   ☐ style

Write and Discuss Have students turn to a partner to discuss the following questions. Guide students to include the academic vocabulary words *attitude*, *goal*, and *purchase* in their responses. Ask volunteers to share their responses with the class.

- What is the author's overall **attitude** toward video games?
- What is the author's **goal** in writing this article?
- Does this article make you want to **purchase** a new video game?

TEACH

 LANGUAGE CONVENTIONS

Explain to students that there must always be a relationship between two independent clauses that are in the same sentence—they can't be unrelated ideas. (**Answer:** *The semicolon joins the two independent clauses: "If you kill the dragon the first time, it's boring" and "don't kill him the hundredth time and it's just plain annoying." The clauses are related because they both refer to different levels of interest in the same video game.*)

■ **English Learner Support**

Language Conventions Have students choral-read the first sentence in paragraph 5. Explain how the semicolon joins the two independent clauses. Have students find the sentence with the semicolon in paragraph 6.

Ask students to explain why the author uses a semicolon in that sentence. (*To join two complete ideas/independent clauses.*) **SUBSTANTIAL/MODERATE**

For **listening support** for students at varying proficiency levels, see the **Text X-Ray** on page 380C.

 PREDICT

Remind students that predicting content will prepare them to understand the text more easily. (**Answer:** *Students should recognize that this section will present information about how video games challenge people's abilities and why this is an important psychological element.*)

CRITICAL VOCABULARY

immerse: The author suggests that when your brain is completely involved in the video game, you are immersed in it.

ASK STUDENTS how *immersed* relates to *wholly focused* and *absorbed*. (*This is the third such term the author uses to describe being wrapped up in a video game.*)

Get in the Zone: The Psychology of Video Game Design **385**

TEACH

PREDICT

Remind students that making predictions means thinking about the information you have been given before, combining it with the information you are reading at the moment, and guessing the information the author will give you next. (**Predict:** *In this section, the author will probably discuss the various kinds of rewards players get in video games and how they feel about them.*)

EL **ENGLISH LEARNER SUPPORT**

Confirm Understanding Write the word *dopamine* on the board, pronounce it, and have students repeat it after you. Point out the Spanish cognate *dopamina*. Help students understand how success can cause chemicals to be released in the brain. These chemicals can cause people to feel good. Ask students to underline the words in the text that explain why the dopamine is released. **SUBSTANTIAL/MODERATE**

 For **reading support** for students at varying proficiency levels, see the **Text X-Ray** on page 380D.

CRITICAL VOCABULARY

irrelevant: Too much information is a problem and so is information that doesn't relate to what you're focusing on.

ASK STUDENTS what happens when there is irrelevant information on the screen. (*We lose focus and become uncertain.*)

disorient: The wrong kind of information confuses the mind.

ASK STUDENTS how we feel when we lose focus. (*We feel lost and unsure.*)

386 Unit 5

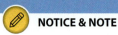 **NOTICE & NOTE**

everyone's different. "The secret," according to Madigan, "is designing games that have really clear feedback so that you know when you're doing something well or poorly, and why."

Focus

8 Imagine fighting a horde of zombies while being distracted by something out the window. Not easy, right? Flow requires focus. The games we love force us to concentrate at just the right level—but in order to get us in the zone, they must *direct* our concentration in the right way too.

9 That's because focus, our ability to pay attention, is like a flashlight beam—it can only shine on one or two things at a time. Too much information, or **irrelevant** info, on screen and our focus blows a fuse. We become **disoriented,** unmotivated, and unsure of what to do. The zombies win.

10 Ever been lost in a dungeon, not sure if you're supposed to find a key, move a block, or start again? That's bad flow. The best game designers keep us in the zone by steering our attention, like movie directors, from one challenge to the next—we're simply along for the ride.

Reward

11 Fighting the dragon should be fun, but we need a reason to keep trying too. Goals are built into games to keep us coming back for more. But goals without <u>rewards</u> are like pancakes without maple syrup: hard to swallow and a lot less sweet.

12 That's because rewards release a chemical called dopamine in our brain, which feels good. When you get an A+ on your test, that warm feeling inside is the reward center of your brain having a party. And that same chemical is released by virtual rewards too. Just leveled up, or beat your best score? Hello, dopamine.

13 The key, according to Madigan, is designing games with "micro-rewards that are linked to longer term goals." Saving the king is a worthy mission, but should I storm the castle or sneak in undetected? The best games break long-term goals into clear, manageable chunks and reward us for achieving each one: search the store room for a grappling hook; steal the key from the guards; scale the tallest tower. Bingo. The king's free and has just given me my own province to rule.

14 Rewards are like fuel for flow. We need to keep filling up if we're going to slay the dragon, build our empire, and make it to the end of the game.

irrelevant
(ĭ-rĕl′ə-vənt) *adj.* Something that is *irrelevant* is unrelated to the matter under consideration.

disorient
(dĭs-ôr′ē-ĕnt′) *v.* To *disorient* is to make someone or something lose a sense of direction.

PREDICT
Annotate: In paragraph 11, mark where the author says that goals need to become "sweet."

Predict: What do you predict will be the author's focus in this final section?

ANALYZE SUBJECTIVE AND OBJECTIVE POINT OF VIEW
Annotate: Mark one opinion that appears in this section.

Analyze: Does the fact that an opinion is included mean that this whole section has a subjective point of view? Why or why not?

386 Unit 5

WHEN STUDENTS STRUGGLE . . .

Use Graphic Organizers Provide students with a main-idea-and-details graphic organizer. Ask them to work individually to complete an organizer for each subheading in the article, including one for the introduction. Then have small groups compare their organizers, decide on the best main idea statements and most important details, and create a revised version that reflects their decisions.

 For additional support, go to the **Reading Studio** and assign the following **Level Up tutorial: Main Idea and Supporting Details**

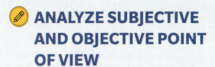

PSYCHOLOGICAL EDGE: TIPS FOR GAMERS
- Games are most fun when the level of difficulty is just above your level of skill. It should be hard, but not impossible. If you're screaming at the screen, it's probably a mismatch. Try manually adjusting the level of challenge instead.
- Increase your gaming flow by removing distractions before you play: turn off the lights, stop texting, and focus all your attention on the screen.
- If the game feels too open-ended, or you're not sure what to do next, try breaking down big goals into more immediate and manageable chunks.

CHECK YOUR UNDERSTANDING

Answer these questions before moving on to the **Analyze the Text** section on the following page.

1. In paragraph 3, the author introduces the idea of "flow" in order to —

   A describe a strategy used by successful players of video games

   B explain why some video games are better than others

   C show how creators of video games work together

   D encourage readers to try different kinds of video games

2. According to the section called CHALLENGE, why do players of video games often give up?

   F The game requires too much button pressing in complicated patterns.

   G The game has been designed to be impossible to win.

   H The game contains too much information that is not really important.

   J The game requires concentration but does not offer much enjoyment.

3. What is the purpose of the bulleted points in the final section?

   A They give readers advice about how to play video games better and enjoy them more.

   B They summarize the kinds of rewards that players of video games like best.

   C They present the main points regarding "flow."

   D They list and rate several popular video games.

TEACH

ANALYZE SUBJECTIVE AND OBJECTIVE POINT OF VIEW

Inform students that the use of a word such as *fun* is a subjective term because it depends on individual experience. For instance, what if someone does not enjoy video games at all? They would consider no game as the "most fun." (**Answer:** *Students may suggest that the overall presentation in that section is objective and that even though an opinion is stated, it is a generally accepted opinion rather than the author's personal view.*)

CHECK YOUR UNDERSTANDING

Have students answer the questions independently.

Answers:

1. B
2. H
3. A

If they answer any questions incorrectly, have them reread the test to confirm their understanding. Then they may proceed to ANALYZE THE TEXT on p. 388.

ENGLISH LEARNER SUPPORT

Oral Assessment Use the following questions to assess students' comprehension and speaking skills.

1. Do people get bored if a game is too easy? Why? *(Yes. If a game is too easy, players they lose interest.)*

2. Do people get upset or give up if a game is too hard? Why? *(Yes. Players become frustrated and give up if a game is too difficult.)*

3. How can bulleted sentences help the reader? *(bullets help readers to understand and synthesize the most important points to consider in a text.)* **SUBSTANTIAL/MODERATE**

APPLY

ANALYZE THE TEXT
Possible answers:

1. **DOK 2:** *Flow occurs when a person is completely focused on a video game and the player's actions come automatically.*

2. **DOK 4:** *The author uses a subjective point of view in paragraph 1 and then shifts to an objective point of view in paragraph 3. The first paragraph sets a tone of fun in dealing with a technical subject.*

3. **DOK 2:** *Micro-rewards keep the player focused on the long-term goal by providing satisfaction along the way.*

4. **DOK 4:** *The author provides (1) evidence based on personal experiences and (2) scientific evidence provided by psychologists. Both are effective because one connects readers to the article and the other proves the points in a more objective way.*

5. **DOK 4:** *Because of Madigan's background, it is logical to assume that he has read or been involved in psychological studies of gamers.*

RESEARCH

Explain to students that a good place to get information about careers in video game development would be websites for schools that provide training in these areas.

Extend Student responses will vary. Among the careers they might discover in their research are software developer, game designer, game producer, animator, artist, technical director, and creative director. Software developers and designers will need a college degree, and most artists and animators go to art school.

RESPOND

ANALYZE THE TEXT
Support your responses with evidence from the text. NOTEBOOK

1. **Summarize** Reread paragraphs 3 and 4. Then summarize in a few sentences what the author means by "flow" in video games.

2. **Analyze** Where in the text does the point of view change, and how does it change? How does the structure of the article help express the author's attitude toward the subject?

3. **Cause/Effect** According to the article, how do micro-rewards affect the player's experience of the game? How are they related to the achievement of long-term goals?

4. **Analyze** What are two different types of evidence the writer offers to support his discussion of the concept of flow? Which type of evidence do you think is more effective? Explain.

5. **Notice & Note** Reread Madigan's quotation in paragraph 7. Based on what you know about him from paragraph 4, how do you think he came to understand feedback in video games?

RESEARCH

RESEARCH TIP
General questions, like the ones in this chart, are a good way to start doing your research. However, be ready to get more specific. As you start to see results, you may want to rephrase your questions, or create new and more precise questions, to search for the best, most interesting information.

In a small group, research a career in video game development. Think about which aspects of video game development you want to know more about. For example, are you interested in coming up with gaming concepts, programming them, or creating visuals? Find out about the skills needed for this career.

QUESTION	ANSWER
Which career in video games interests me the most?	
What kind of training and education do I need for this career?	
What are some of the challenges and rewards of this career?	

Extend Find out about a video gaming convention that takes place each year. Which companies exhibit during these conferences? What are some of the career-related activities that take place?

388 Unit 5

TO CHALLENGE STUDENTS...

Consult Multiple Sources This informational text presents video games in a favorable light, but it is only one opinion of a topic. Assign students to research other articles that cite different scientific studies about video games. They may also want to branch out to the economics involved in video gaming and the psychology behind "micro-rewards" and whether these are really positive or negative in the long run. Have students produce a 3–5 page essay comparing and contrasting "Get in the Zone: The Psychology of Video Game Design" with one or more articles with a different view of the topic.

CREATE AND ADAPT

Write an Objective Summary Write a summary of "Get in the Zone: The Psychology of Video Game Design."

- Review the text, your answers to the guided reading questions, and any other notes you made while reading.
- Remember that the text is organized into sections. Write a summary for each section; then put section summaries together.
- Make sure that the summary includes only the most important information. You don't want to include every detail.
- Use your own words, but stick to the facts. To make the summary objective, leave out your personal feelings and opinions.

Discuss a Video Game Adapt what you learned in "Get in the Zone: The Psychology of Video Game Design" to a discussion about another game. In a small group, give a rating to a video game you have played (or would like to play) in terms of the concept of flow.

- Choose a specific game. In the discussion, include precise details about the game.
- Describe your experience (real or imagined) in playing the game. In particular, evaluate its flow—that is, how well it makes you concentrate on and enjoy the action.
- Offer praise about the game or suggestions for improving it.

RESPOND TO THE ESSENTIAL QUESTION

? How do sports bring together friends, families, and communities?

Gather Information Review your notes on "Get in the Zone: The Psychology of Video Game Design." Then, add details to your Response Log. As you determine which information to include, think about:

- your experience with video games
- what makes playing video games enjoyable

At the end of the unit, use your notes to help you write a short story.

RESPOND

Go to **Using Textual Evidence** in the **Writing Studio** for more on summarizing.

Go to **Participating in Collaborative Discussions** in the **Speaking and Listening Studio** to learn more.

ACADEMIC VOCABULARY

As you write about and discuss what you learned from the informational text, be sure to use the Academic Vocabulary words. Check off each of the words that you use.

- ❏ attitude
- ❏ consume
- ❏ goal
- ❏ purchase
- ❏ style

Get in the Zone: The Psychology of Video Game Design 389

APPLY

CREATE AND ADAPT

Write an Objective Summary Explain to students that rereading a text is a good way to remind themselves of key points and to notice points they missed in the first reading. Remind them that:

- quoting specific facts and phrases may be helpful, but using block quotes or paraphrasing every sentence will not result in a good summary.
- using their own words but not expressing their feelings is a good way to write objectively.

For **writing support** for students at varying proficiency levels, see the **Text X-Ray** on page 380C.

Discuss a Video Game If students have no experience playing video games, they may modify the discussion by choosing a sport, playground game, or board game. Remind students to encourage participation from all group members.

RESPOND TO THE ESSENTIAL QUESTION

Allow time for students to add details from "Get in the Zone: The Psychology of Video Game Design" to their Unit 5 Response Logs. Encourage students to think about the video games that challenged them and frustrated them.

ENGLISH LEARNER SUPPORT

Discuss a presentation Help students describe their own experience of playing video games. Encourage them to draw and/or find images of players whose expressions show how they feel about the video games they are playing. Tell them they may use some of the images they created earlier for their word-image bank. Guide students in writing text that will go with the images. Use sentence frames to get them started, for example: *I like playing (name of the video game) it is (easy/difficult/challenging); I enjoy the (images/characters).* Circulate around the room helping students. **SUBSTANTIAL/MODERATE**

Get in the Zone: The Psychology of Video Game Design 389

APPLY

CRITICAL VOCABULARY

1. b
2. a
3. a
4. c
5. b

VOCABULARY STRATEGY:
Use Context

Possible answer: *Saving the king is a worthy mission, but should I storm the castle or sneak in without anyone realizing that I'm there?*

 **RESPOND**

WORD BANK
absorb
wholly
immerse
irrelevant
disorient

CRITICAL VOCABULARY

Practice and Apply Mark the letter of the word whose meaning is similar to each Critical Vocabulary word. Verify your answers using an online dictionary or thesaurus.

1. **absorb:** a. bleed | **b. consume** | c. sing
2. **wholly:** **a. totally** | b. partially | c. fortunately
3. **immense:** **a. enormous** | b. intelligent | c. miniature
4. **irrelevant:** a. dreamlike | b. appropriate | **c. unnecessary**
5. **disorient:** a. clarify | **b. confuse** | c. doubt

Go to the **Vocabulary Studio** for more on context clues.

VOCABULARY STRATEGY: Context Clues

When you come across an unfamiliar word in a text, use the following strategy to determine the word's meaning.

Step 1 ▶	Step 2 ▶	Step 3 ▶	Step 4
Determine the likely meaning using **context**, the surrounding words and sentences.	Substitute the likely meaning for the word in the sentence to see if it makes sense.	Look up the word in a print or digital dictionary to verify the likely meaning.	Determine which definition after the entry word best fits with the context.

Look at this example from "Get in the Zone: The Psychology of Video Game Design":

> We become *disoriented*, unmotivated, and unsure what to do.

The nearby phrase *unsure what to do* provides a clue: The meaning of *disoriented* has something to do with a feeling of confusion. Try using *confused* instead of *disoriented* in the sentence. Both meanings make sense. A dictionary verifies the meaning by giving this definition for *disoriented*: "mentally confused or losing a sense of direction."

Practice and Apply Find the sentence containing the word *undetected* in paragraph 13 of the selection. Then, use the four steps above to determine the word's meaning. Write it below.

 ENGLISH LEARNER SUPPORT

Vocabulary Strategy If students are unable to determine the meaning of words in the article by using context clues, provide them with additional practice that makes the task more easily understood. Write on the board: I am very *agitated/excited* because I found out that my dog is sick. He was *elated/depressed* because he just won $1,000 in the lottery. The *impressive/insignificant* building was more than 30 stories high. The *inquisitive/incurious* man kept asking me questions. Ask students to justify their choice of words by citing cognates (*agitato, insignificante*) or other reasons. **MODERATE**

LANGUAGE CONVENTIONS:
Comma Splices and Run-On Sentences

The **semicolon** (;) is a punctuation mark that has a variety of uses. For example, when two independent clauses express complete and related ideas, a semicolon can be used to connect them, rather than a comma plus a coordinating conjunction. In this example from "Get in the Zone: The Psychology of Video Game Design," the semicolon takes the place of a comma and the coordinating conjunction *and*.

> Stone ramparts crumble in the township; houses burn.

Because semicolons have this use, they can be used to correct **comma splices** (which occur when only a comma is used to connect independent clauses) and **run-on sentences** (which occur when there is no punctuation or conjunction to connect independent clauses). Note these examples.

> COMMA SPLICE: This new video game is terrific, in fact, I could play it every day.
> REVISION: This new video game is great; in fact, I could play it every day.
>
> RUN-ON SENTENCE: I'm going to tell Jalayne about this game she will probably want to play it with me.
> REVISION: I'm going to tell Jalayne about this game; she will probably want to play it with me.

Practice and Apply Use semicolons to correct the error in each of the following sentences. Then identify whether the original sentence had a comma splice or was a run-on sentence.

1. Jalayne is an experienced player I'm just a beginner.
2. There are some terrific video games on sale this weekend the store is clearing the shelves to make room for a new shipment.
3. Jalayne has been to a video game conference in San Antonio, Texas, next week she will attend one in Richmond, Virginia.
4. I quickly ditched my plans for shopping on Saturday I went to Jalayne's house and played video games with her and her brother instead.
5. Jalayne hopes to be a video game designer for action/adventure games someday, on the other hand, she may become a martial arts instructor with her own studio.

RESPOND

Go to **Run-On Sentences** and **Semicolons** in the **Grammar Studio** to learn more.

APPLY

LANGUAGE CONVENTIONS:
Semicolons

Remind students that first they must determine whether a sentence has two independent clauses. If it does, the next step is to see whether those clauses are joined by the proper punctuation. No punctuation between the two clauses means that the sentence is a **run-on**. A comma all by itself means the sentence is a **comma splice**.

Practice and Apply

1. *semicolon after* player; *run-on*
2. *semicolon after* weekend; *comma splice*
3. *semicolon after* Texas; *comma splice*
4. *semicolon after* Saturday; *run-on*
5. *semicolon after* someday; *comma splice*

ENGLISH LEARNER SUPPORT

Language Conventions Use the following supports with students at varying levels:

- Provide students with the following sentence and ask them if a semicolon or a comma should replace the dash. *The bowl has a hole in it—there were no cherries left in the bowl.* **SUBSTANTIAL**
- Where should a semicolon be placed in the following sentence: *We were happy to eat the fresh food (;) we were bored with the fried food.* **MODERATE**
- Ask students to correctly punctuate the following sentences: *If you have the time (,) video games can be a lot of fun. I've lost all track of time (;) I've never played such a wonderful video.* **LIGHT**

PLAN

IT'S NOT JUST A GAME
Informational Text by Lori Calabrese

GENRE ELEMENTS
INFORMATIONAL TEXT
Remind students that the purpose of **informational text** is to present facts and information. It has a main topic and provides facts and details that support the topic. Informational text answers *who*, *what*, *where*, and *why* and/or *how* questions. It often includes subheadings and other text features that help organize information. In this lesson, students will use subheadings to help them explore the reasons sports are a serious matter and not merely done for amusement.

LEARNING OBJECTIVES
- Identify organizational patterns and use text features to navigate informational text.
- Conduct research about a sport of their choice.
- Write a poem about their favorite sport.
- Present an infographic that describes the positive and negative aspects of sports.
- Identify subject-verb agreement in complex sentences.
- **Language** Discuss with a partner how to use subheads to learn how a text is organized.

TEXT COMPLEXITY

Quantitative Measures	It's Not Just a Game	Lexile: 990L
Qualitative Measures	**Ideas Presented** Simple, single meaning; literal, explicit, and direct; purpose or stance clear	
	Structures Used Primarily explicit; varies from chronological order; largely conventional	
	Language Used Explicit, literal, contemporary language; vocabulary simple	
	Knowledge Required Requires no special knowledge; situations and subjects familiar	

PLAN

RESOURCES

- Unit 5 Response Log
- 🔊 Selection Audio
- 📗 Close Read Screencasts: Modeled Discussions
- 📖 Reading Studio: Notice & Note
- 💬 Writing Studio: Writing as a Process
- 💬 Speaking and Listening Studio: Using Media in a Presentation
- 🔤 Vocabulary Studio: Reference Resource
- ❗ Grammar Studio: Module 8: Lesson 1: Agreement of Subject and Verb
- ✓ "It's Not Just a Game" Selection Test

SUMMARIES

English

Sports began in prehistoric times, possibly to aid survival. Ancient peoples engaged in some sports that are still familiar today. Children instinctively play games. Sports are intended to be enjoyable. Some people play organized sports; others prefer to watch them. Research has shown that playing sports benefits people's minds and bodies. Engaging in sports helps people to integrate all of their talents and abilities. Many forms of play teach the skill of negotiation and foster mutual respect between players.

Spanish

Los deportes comenzaron en épocas prehistóricas, posiblemente para ayudar a la supervivencia. En la antigüedad, la gente participaba en deportes que aún nos son familiares. Los niños juegan instintivamente desde temprana edad. Los deportes están destinados a ser disfrutables. Hay quienes practican deportes organizados; otros prefieren verlos. Hacer deporte beneficia nuestras mentes y cuerpos. Practicar deportes nos permite integrar todos nuestros talentos y capacidades. Nos enseña la destreza de negociación y fomenta el respeto mutuo.

SMALL-GROUP OPTIONS

Have students work in small groups to read and discuss the selection.

Give One and Get One

- Ask: *How do sports utilize all of our talents and abilities?*
- Students write several responses.
- They exchange lists with a partner and add one of the partner's ideas to their own list, noting the partner/source.
- They repeat the process with new partners.
- Call on a student to give an idea and its source. The source gives an idea from someone else. Continue through the class.
- Make a master list as the basis for a writing assignment.

Numbered Heads

- Number students from 1-4 in teams of four.
- Ask: *Which is the most important benefit of playing a sport?*
- Allow teams time to come up with a response.
- Ask students with a number (from 1-4) to raise their hands.
- Choose from students with the chosen number to answer on behalf of their team.
- Continue until all groups have responded. Encourage groups to compare their responses.

It's Not Just a Game! 392B

PLAN

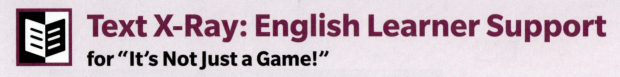

Text X-Ray: English Learner Support
for "It's Not Just a Game!"

Use the Text X-Ray and the supports and scaffolds in the Teacher's Edition to help guide students at different proficiency levels through the selection.

INTRODUCE THE SELECTION
DISCUSS THE VALUE OF GAMES

In this lesson, students will need to be able to understand and discuss the importance of games. Read paragraph 3 with students. Point out the phrase *serious play*. Provide the following explanation:

- Play that involves rules and special skills is considered serious.
- Not all play is serious; sometimes it is spontaneous and just for fun.

Explain to students that all play is important because it teaches people how to get along with one another, how to use their skills and talents, and how to enjoy being part of a group. Have volunteers share their experience of sports. Use the following sentence frames to structure responses. Supply labeled images of sports and games to help students complete the sentences.

My favorite game when I was small was _____ . (tag, kickball, hide and seek, jump rope) I used to play the game with my _____ . (brothers, sisters, friends) Now that I am older, my favorite sport is _____ . (softball, basketball, other)

CULTURAL REFERENCES

The following words and phrases may be unfamiliar to students:

- *came into play* (paragraph 2): had an effect
- *support network* (paragraph 7): a group of people who offer help when you are in trouble emotionally
- *birthright* (paragraph 9) something to which one is entitled when one is born
- *walking encyclopedias* (paragraph 13) people who have great knowledge of a particular subject

LISTENING

Understand Words and Meaning

Gather images of activities that appear in paragraph 5. Help students label them with the correct words. Tell students that the general idea of the paragraph is that exercise is good for people. Ask them to listen for the main ideas in the article, and to be prepared to retell what they have heard.

Have students listen as you read aloud paragraph 5. Use the following supports with students at varying proficiency levels:

- Display student-labeled images of people playing sports as well as several content-related infographics—including one of the human brain. Ask: *What are sports good for?* (body, mind/brain). Work with students to listen for the vowel digraph *ai* in brain. Help them to listen for other *ai* words such as *rain* from a supplied word bank. **SUBSTANTIAL**
- Say: *This is exercise*. Use gestures and images to demonstrate what exercise is. Ask students to listen to a sentence you read aloud. Have them finish it: *Play not only exercises our brain, it also exercises our _____. (body)*. Ask students to retell any words, phrases, and ideas they remember from the paragraph. **MODERATE**
- Ask pairs to take turns retelling the main points and ideas in paragraph 5. **LIGHT**

392C Unit 5

PLAN

SPEAKING

Use Subheads to Set a Purpose

Discuss the importance of subheads in informational articles. Tell students that subheads are helpful for organizing the different parts of an article; they help readers remember where information is located— particularly for later study.

Use the following supports with students at varying proficiency levels:

- Read, explain, and display the subhead "Forgetting the Fun," and the sentence *"Playing sports is usually fun, but sometimes we can get frustrated."* (*frustrado*) Have students pronounce the short vowel *u* in *fun*, say the word *fun*, and repeat for other short *u* words such as *cup*. **SUBSTANTIAL**
- Display the subhead "Different Sports for Different Folks." Have students echo read it with you. Supply the cloze sentence *The sports I like best are_____*. Help students choose words to complete the sentence, Ask: *What sports do you like?* Invite volunteers to respond. **MODERATE**
- Pair students. Have them read aloud and discuss paragraph 2. Ask them what kinds of information they might want to know more about as they prepare to read or reread the article. Have volunteers share their results with the class. **LIGHT**

READING

Use Supports for Understanding

Help students comprehend longer sentences and unfamiliar topics by using visual supports and analytical skills.

Help students read paragraph 14. Use the following supports with students at varying proficiency levels:

- Display and read the sentence "We feel self-confident and experience joy when our favorite team wins." Use gestures, images of a winning team and its fans, and cognates such as *confianza* and *favorito* to explain the meaning. Model choosing "happy" from a word bank to describe the fans. Write "happy" on the board and have them say it. Practice the short vowel *a* with other words such as *hat, bat*, and *tap*. Allow students to use their home language to seek clarification. **SUBSTANTIAL/MODERATE**
- Pair students to silently read paragraph 14, and then retell the content of the paragraph to each other. Encourage them to seek clarification. Ask for volunteers to share with the class. **LIGHT**

WRITING

Write a Poem

Explain to students that many poems are about feelings and thoughts. Poets use ordinary words that are heard in conversation and as well as unusual or made-up words. A poem can be rhymed or unrhymed. Point out graphic elements in various poems.

Use the following supports with students at varying proficiency levels:

- Tell students to think of the words they know in English that describe their favorite sport. Model using words and drawings together to create a poem about the sport, such as a ball, a bat, or a goal. **SUBSTANTIAL**
- Pair students to brainstorm about all the action words and sounds that relate to their favorite sports, such as *throw/snap* or *catch/plop*. Then let them work together to write a poem. Provide word banks to help them find words for their poems **MODERATE**
- Suggest that students think of all the sights, sounds, and feelings they experience while playing their favorite sport. Tell them to use this memory as the basis of a descriptive poem. **LIGHT**

TEACH

? Connect to the ESSENTIAL QUESTION

"It's Not Just a Game" explains the many benefits of sports. The article points out that playing a sport teaches us many lessons, such as respect for others, the ability to negotiate, and practice in following directions. Sports fill many emotional and physical needs. They are good for the brain as well as the body.

ANALYZE & APPLY

IT'S NOT JUST A GAME!

Informational Text by **Lori Calabrese**

? ESSENTIAL QUESTION:

How do sports bring together friends, families, and communities?

 LEARNING MINDSET

Grit A student's attitude toward learning is a key element in acquiring new skills and knowledge. Remind students that just as athletes develop stronger muscles by exercising, they will build stronger brains by exercising them. When they choose the more difficult route – for example, reading a newspaper instead of checking the Internet – their brains will grow stronger and they will become smarter.

QUICK START

Do you like to play sports? Watch sports? Discuss with a partner how important you think sports are to people's lives today, and why.

SET A PURPOSE

Before reading an informational text, you'll want to **set a purpose**—that is, make a plan for what you want to get out of your reading. One tool for setting a purpose is a K-W-L Chart. You can use a chart like this one to list what you already know about the topic (in this case, sports) and what you want to know as you read. Then, as you read and afterward, you can record what you learned from the text.

What I **K**now	
What I **W**ant to Know	
What I **L**earned	

This technique can help you monitor your comprehension and decide when you need to reread, ask questions, use what you already know, or make notes to help you understand the text.

ANALYZE ORGANIZATIONAL PATTERNS

Effective informational writing almost always follows an **organizational pattern,** or structure. For example, an author may present information in chronological order (the time order in which events happened) or in order of importance (usually with the most important information at the end).

Sometimes, however, an author chooses a **descriptive pattern.** The author presents a variety of kinds of information about the topic—historical background, characteristics, examples, comments from experts, comparisons, and so on. To give structure to the presentation, the author may use subheadings, such as these examples from "It's Not Just a Game!"

> **Different Sports for Different Folks**
> **Making Sports Work for Us**

As you read "It's Not Just a Game!" look for the ways in which the author presents various kinds of information. Consider how each kind of information helps you understand the topic.

GET READY

GENRE ELEMENTS: INFORMATIONAL TEXT
- provides facts and explanations
- includes details that support a main idea about the topic
- answers *who*, *what*, *where*, *when*, *why*, and/or *how* questions
- may include text features such as subheadings to help organize information

TEACH

QUICK START

Have students read the Quick Start question, and invite them to share their sports interests with a partner. Tell them not to be shy about mentioning nontraditional sports that they may know, e.g., cricket, jai alai, or hurling.

SET A PURPOSE

Tell students that setting a purpose for reading helps them focus on information in the text. Tell them to jot down in the chart what they already know about the benefits of sports and what they might want to know about the effects of sports on their minds and bodies. Explain that they will complete the "What I Learned" section of the chart after reading the article.

ANALYZE ORGANIZATIONAL PATTERNS

Students may be familiar with the usual patterns of organization, such as sequence, cause-and-effect, and order of importance. Point out the writers are not obliged to use a particular pattern. They choose the pattern that suits the information they want to present.

The descriptive pattern used in "It's Not Just a Game" allows the author to include a wide variety of information that would not fit into other organizational patterns. Suggest that students think of the descriptive pattern as a wheel in which the center is the topic and each of the spokes is a different kind of information. Tell them to look for the "spokes" in the subheadings as they read.

TEACH

CRITICAL VOCABULARY

Encourage students to read all the sentences before deciding which word best completes each one. Remind them to look for context clues that match the meaning of each word.

Answers:

1. *isolate*
2. *accomplishment*
3. *mutual*
4. *negotiate*
5. *utilization*

■ English Learner Support

Use Cognates Point out the vocabulary words that have Spanish cognates: *mutual/mutuo, negotiate/negociar*. The base word of *utilization (utilize)* also has a Spanish cognate: *utilizar*. Guide students as they pronounce each word in English. Repeat until they have pronounced the word correctly. **SUBSTANTIAL**

LANGUAGE CONVENTIONS

Tell students to analyze a sentence by first identifying the clauses. They should then find the subject of each clause and determine whether it is singular or plural. Next, they should look for the verb and verify that it agrees with the subject in number. Clauses may have multiple verbs, but they must all agree with the subject.

ANNOTATION MODEL

Remind students of the descriptive pattern they learned about in Analyze Organizational Patterns. Point out that they may follow this suggestion or use their own system for marking up text.

394   Unit 5

 GET READY

CRITICAL VOCABULARY

accomplishment   negotiate   mutual   isolate   utilization

To see how many Critical Vocabulary words you already know, write the word asked for in each question.

1. Which word goes with *separate*? _____
2. Which word goes with *achievement*? _____
3. Which word goes with *shared*? _____
4. Which word goes with *discuss* and *bargain*? _____
5. Which word goes with *use* and *implementation*? _____

LANGUAGE CONVENTIONS

Complex Sentences and Subject-Verb Agreement In this text, you will see several **complex sentences**—sentences made from one independent clause and at least one subordinate clause. A complex sentence, therefore, contains at least two examples of a subject and verb working together. In every case, the subject and verb need to **agree** in number. Note these examples:

Whether <u>you</u> <u>run</u> a race, <u>bounce</u> a basketball, or <u>hurl</u> a baseball home, <u>you</u> <u>do</u> it because it's [<u>it is</u>] fun.

That <u>might explain</u> why <u>sports</u> <u>are</u> likely to be as old as humanity.

As you read and write about "It's Not Just a Game!" remember the importance of subject-verb agreement in complex sentences.

ANNOTATION MODEL   NOTICE & NOTE

As you read, mark details you connect to and details you want to learn more about. You can also mark information that the author uses to describe her topic and note how it helps you understand. In the model, you can see one reader's notes about a section of "It's Not Just a Game!"

> 1 Whether you <u>run a race</u>, <u>bounce a basketball</u>, or <u>hurl a baseball home</u>, you do it because it's fun. Some scientists claim play is a natural instinct—just like sleep. That might explain why [sports are likely to be as old as humanity.]

These are sports I know. I like running and playing hoops.

"as old as humanity" = I hope the author follows up with more historical info about sports.

394   Unit 5

BACKGROUND

Lori Calabrese *worked as a TV producer for ten years before deciding to become a writer after the birth of her children. Her first book was the well-received picture book* The Bug That Plagued the Entire Third Grade. *She also has written many nonfiction articles for young people, including "It's Not Just a Game!" Calabrese says that she is "forever probing people and places in search of information." "I love research," she admits—"in fact, I can't get enough."*

IT'S NOT JUST A GAME!
Informational Text by Lori Calabrese

SETTING A PURPOSE

As you read, think about what you like and dislike about sports. How does the information the author presents give you more insights into the wide world of sports—and into your own experiences with them?

1   Whether you run a race, bounce a basketball, or hurl a baseball home, you do it because it's fun. Some scientists claim play is a natural instinct—just like sleep. That might explain why sports are likely to be as old as humanity.

2   Some claim sports began as a form of survival. Prehistoric man ran, jumped, and climbed for his life. Hunters separated themselves by skill, and competition flourished. Wall paintings dating from 1850 B.C., that depict wrestling, dancing, and acrobatics, were discovered in an Egyptian tomb at Bani Hasan.[1] The Ancient Greeks

---

[1] **Bani Hasan** (bän′ē hä-sŏn′): ancient Egyptian burial site, located along the Nile River.

NOTICE & NOTE

Notice & Note

Use the side margins to notice and note signposts in the text.

ANALYZE ORGANIZATIONAL PATTERNS

Annotate: In paragraph 2, mark references to three groups of people from the past.

Analyze: Review the entire paragraph. How does the author use time order to organize information?

It's Not Just a Game!   395

TEACH

BACKGROUND

After students read the Background note, explain that nonfiction writers spend much of their time doing research so they will make accurate statements and find new information to share with their readers.

SETTING A PURPOSE

Direct students to use the Setting a Purpose prompt to focus their reading.

ANALYZE ORGANIZATIONAL PATTERNS

Remind students that the descriptive pattern of organization is flexible. The writer can use any type of order within a paragraph because he or she is not following a more formal pattern of organization.

(The author organizes information chronologically: She starts with prehistoric people; then refers to ancient Egypt, followed by ancient Greece; then goes to the early nineteenth century; and finally discusses the sports today.)

ENGLISH LEARNER SUPPORT

Getting Organized Review the characteristics of descriptive organization with students. Ask them to draw a small circle on a sheet of paper and write the word *Sports* in the center of the page. Point out the subheadings in the article. Tell them to draw a line from the center of the circle each time they see a subheading. They will write the subheading on the line. Tell students that this will help them understand the organization of the article. It will also help them complete the chart on the student page. Circulate among students to be sure they understand the task. **SUBSTANTIAL**

It's Not Just a Game!   395

TEACH

ENGLISH LEARNER SUPPORT

Understand Word Play Have students locate the sentence in parentheses in paragraph 2. Discuss the meaning of the word *pun* (*using a word in a way that suggests more than one meaning*). Then point out the idiom *came into play*. Explain that it means "to have had an effect."

ASK STUDENTS to read the sentence before "Pardon the pun." Point out the word *sports*. Ask students why the word *play* is a pun. (*People* play *sports, but the author is humorously apologizing for using the word* play *in the idiom in the same sentence as the word* sports.)
LIGHT

SET A PURPOSE

Suggest that students look for the qualities that describe a serious activity. (*Students probably will mention times when they have had to follow rules and to exhibit skill and strategy—if not in a traditional organized sport, then in informal play and even in board games.*)

QUOTED WORDS

Explain that quotations have value in proportion to the authority being quoted. Students should always consider the source of information that is quoted. (*There are many organizations that evaluate the impact of various activities on the health of children. Finding experts who do not have a vested interest in sports or a personal bias about the value of sports is important. Many experts have examined the "well-being of children and youth" in relation to organized sports.*)

CRITICAL VOCABULARY

accomplishment: Succeeding in an effort to do something well is an accomplishment that makes us proud.

ASK STUDENTS what kinds of accomplishments are more important than winning when playing sports. (*getting along with teammates and sharing responsibility*)

negotiate: When we negotiate on the playing field, we learn to compromise so everyone feels they have been treated fairly.

ASK STUDENTS what is the value of being able and willing to negotiate. (*Negotiation allows us to settle differences without creating conflict.*)

396 Unit 5

 **NOTICE & NOTE**

SET A PURPOSE
Annotate: In paragraph 3, mark the evidence that supports the idea that organized sports are serious play.

Connect: Did you already know this information? Explain.

accomplishment
(ə-kŏm´plĭsh-mənt) *n.* An *accomplishment* is a task that you succeed in doing.

QUOTED WORDS
Notice & Note: Mark the source of the quotation in paragraph 5.

Evaluate: Why would this source be a valuable one to quote?

negotiate
(nĭ-gō´shē-āt´) *v.* When you *negotiate*, you work with others to reach an agreement.

---

revolutionized sports by holding the world's first Olympic games at Olympia in 776 B.C. But it wasn't until the early nineteenth century, that sports as we know them came into play. (Pardon the pun!) Modern sports such as cricket,[2] golf, and horse racing began in England and spread to the United States, Western Europe, and the rest of the world. These sports were the models for the games we play today, including baseball and football.

3 All organized sports, from swimming to ice hockey, are considered serious play. There are rules to obey, skills and positions to learn, and strategies to carry out. But Peter Smith, a psychology professor at Goldsmiths, University of London, and author of *Understanding Children's Worlds: Children and Play* (Wiley, 2009), says, "Sport-like play is usually enjoyable, and done for its own sake."

Different Sports for Different Folks

4 Sports come in many shapes and sizes. Both team and individual sports have advantages and disadvantages, but most people find that from an early age, they are drawn toward one or the other. In a team sport like soccer, you're part of a group, striving to be a winning team. That means putting the team ahead of your own **accomplishments.** You must learn to get along with your teammates and share responsibility. In an individual sport like tennis, you're usually only concerned about your own performance. That can make these sports more challenging.

The Ultimate Value of Sports

5 Whether it's football or golf, there's little doubt about the value of sports. According to the American Academy of Pediatrics (AAP), "play is essential to the cognitive, physical, social, and emotional well-being of children and youth." Play not only exercises our bodies, it also exercises our minds. Sports teach us about ourselves and our world. We learn how to **negotiate** plans, settle disagreements, and how to monitor our attitude. The skills we learn playing can be applied to school and work. Since organized sports are a hands-on, minds-on learning process, they stimulate our imagination, curiosity, and creativity. The growing science of play is armed with research claims that play, and thus sports, is important to healthy brain development. We use language during play to solve problems, we use thinking when we follow directions to a game, and we

---
[2] **cricket** (krĭk´ĭt): English team sport, played with a bat, ball, and wickets.

use math skills to recognize averages and odds of each sports play.

6   Sports also raise our energy level and act as antidepressants. Activity increases the brain's level of chemicals called *endorphins*, which boost mood. When we start moving and having fun, we feel good about ourselves.

Forgetting the Fun

7   In a perfect world, everyone would have fun playing sports. But that's not always the case. Sports can get aggressive and cause scrapes, bruises, and broken bones. They can also hurt us psychologically. David Elkind, professor emeritus of Child Development at Tufts University and author of *The Power of Play*, says that when young children play self-initiated games such as tag or hide and seek, "misunderstandings and hurt feelings are part of the learning process, and happen in a context of **mutual** respect. Those that arise in organized team sports, don't have the same supportive network, the sense of competition outweighs the sense of cooperation, and can be hurtful to the child's sense of self and self-esteem." Playing sports is usually fun, but sometimes we can get frustrated. It might be because of the pressure to win, parents who yell and scream from the stands, or coaches who treat us unfairly. Sports are supposed to bring people together, but they can also drive people apart. When sports are separated into skill level, gender, or ethnicity, some players feel **isolated**, begin to forget the fun in sports, and even want to quit. Sports may not always be a

NOTICE & NOTE

LANGUAGE CONVENTIONS
Annotate: The last sentence of paragraph 6 is a complex sentence, made of an independent clause and a subordinate clause. In each clause, mark the subject and its verb.

Identify: How do you know that each verb agrees with its subject?

ANALYZE ORGANIZATIONAL PATTERNS
Annotate: Mark the subheading that introduces paragraph 7.

Analyze: Review the first few sentences of paragraph 7. How does the subheading help readers understand the author's change in focus?

mutual
(myōo´choo-əl) *adj.* Something is *mutual* when everyone treats each other the same way or shares the same feeling.

isolate
(ī´sə-lāt´) *v.* When you *isolate* something, you separate it so that it is apart or alone.

TEACH

LANGUAGE CONVENTIONS

Review subject-verb agreement in complex sentences. Remind students to identify the independent and dependent clauses and look for the subject and verb in each part of the sentence. (*In each clause the subject is* we, *which is plural, so the verbs,* start *and* feel, *have the form that agrees with a plural subject.*)

ANALYZE ORGANIZATIONAL PATTERNS

Remind students that the author is using a descriptive pattern of organization. This pattern allows the writer to address topics in whatever order he or she wishes. (*Up to this point, the author has focused on the positive—"fun"—aspect of sports. Now, she will explore some possible negative aspects. The subheading signals this shift in focus.*)

For **listening and speaking support** for students at varying proficiency levels, see the **Text X-Ray** on pages 392C–D.

ENGLISH LEARNER SUPPORT

Confirm Understanding Write the word *endorphins* on the board and draw lines to separate the word into syllables. Draw attention to the digraph *ph*, and remind them that it is pronounced *f*. Pronounce the word several times. Have students say it with you. Then ask them to pronounce it on their own. (Note that some Asian students from the Philippines pronounce *f* as *p* and may have difficulty with the word.) Tell students that endorphins act to temporarily decrease pain and (often) make people feel happier.   **SUBSTANTIAL**

CRITICAL VOCABULARY

mutual: Children who choose to play together have mutual respect and deal with misunderstandings.

ASK STUDENTS some reasons children who play informally have mutual respect. (*They know each other; they can choose to play or not play.*)

isolate: Being isolated from other players because of age or skill makes some players want to quit a game.

ASK STUDENTS why feeling isolated makes players want to quit. (*People feel as though they do not have an equal chance of being part of the team or sport.*)

TEACH

SET A PURPOSE

Discuss the task to be sure that students understand that they are to mark only the facts they have not previously known. *(Annotations will vary. Students may mark the Elkind quotation, for example, or the reference to play as "a right of every child." Answers to the skill question will vary depending on the fact chosen. For example, the Elkind quotation is valuable because it shows how play can address many aspects of a person's life; the reference to play as a "birthright" shows that many forms of it are valued for a variety of reasons.)*

ENGLISH LEARNER SUPPORT

Identify Quotations Draw quotation marks on the board. Remind students that these are used to show someone's exact words. Have students look for quotation marks on the student page. Ask them to point out where they occur (at the end of paragraph 8). Ask students to identify who said the words. If they have difficulty identifying the name *Elkind*, explain that the name of the person being quoted is usually near the quotation. **MODERATE**

ANALYZE ORGANIZATIONAL PATTERNS

Point out to students that a descriptive organizational pattern allows the writer to present information in any order. *(Answers will vary, but students probably will focus on the entertainment value and/or social aspect of being a sports fan.)*

CRITICAL VOCABULARY

utilization: Full utilization of all our abilities in play makes us feel whole and completely engaged in what we are doing.

ASK STUDENTS why utilization of all your abilities is a good thing. *(Using all our abilities allows each of them to be developed to their full potential.)*

398   Unit 5

NOTICE & NOTE

SET A PURPOSE
Annotate: Mark new information that you learned from reading paragraphs 8 and 9.
Critique: Why do you think this information is valuable for everyone to know?

utilization
(yōōt´l-ĭ-zā´shən) *n.* Utilization is when you put something to use in an effective way.

ANALYZE ORGANIZATIONAL PATTERNS
Annotate: In paragraphs 11–13, mark three positive effects of sports when people watch others play them.
Connect: Which effect means the most to you? Why?

---

positive experience, but even when they're not, they give us a dose of how to face life's challenges.

Making Sports Work for Us

8   Playing sports doesn't mean you have to play on a varsity team. And very few people have what it takes to be a professional athlete. But your school basketball coach or gymnastics teacher has found a way to make play their work. And in doing so, they've found the work best suited to who they are. According to Elkind, "Whenever we combine play with work, as in our hobbies, cooking, gardening, sewing, and carpentry, it is the full **utilization** and integration of all our interests, talents, and abilities. It's an activity that makes us feel whole."

9   Play is so important to our development that the United Nations High Commission for Human Rights has included it as a right of every child.[3] In other words, it's your birthright to play! And there's no better place to play and learn about the world than on a sports field. So regardless of *your* sport— from swimming to soccer—play to have fun and you'll automatically win!

Keep Your Eye on the Ball

10   Are your eyes glued to the TV when a basketball superstar takes the court or a baseball superstar steps to the plate? While fans fill arenas, even more click their TVs on at home to watch athletes slam a puck into a net or hit a ball with a fat stick. Play is not only something to do, it's something to watch others do.

11   Sports are a form of entertainment. The joy you and your teammates get by working together is the same joy your family, friends, and other spectators get when they watch. Fans experience the thrill of victory and the agony of defeat,[4] just like the players on the field. Think of all the applauding, shouting, and yelling that happen at sporting events. It's a way for many of us to live vicariously through the players' actions.

12   Sports are also social events, opportunities for strangers to cheer together and debate outcomes. A Saturday morning game is a great way to spend time with family.

13   Sports involve learning, too. Fans research players, teams, and the sports themselves. How many fans do you know who are walking encyclopedias of sports trivia?

---

[3] **United Nations High Commission for Human Rights:** In 1989, the United Nations passed the *Convention on the Rights of the Child*, a treaty that protects the human rights of every child.
[4] **the thrill of victory and the agony of defeat:** This common sports phrase was originally part of the introduction to *Wide World of Sports*, a popular TV program that ran from 1961 to 1998.

398   Unit 5

WHEN STUDENTS STRUGGLE...

Using Graphic Organizers Have students read paragraphs 11–15. Ask them to draw a circle and put the words "Benefits of Sports" inside it. Tell them to draw smaller circles around the center circle. In each smaller circle, they should write one of the benefits of sports mentioned in the paragraphs. Have students share their graphic organizers with each other and add any points that they have missed.

 For additional support, go to the **Reading Studio** and assign the following Level Up tutorial: Reading for Details.

NOTICE & NOTE

14 Why do so many of us watch sports and have a favorite team? Studies show that it fills both emotional and psychological needs. We feel self-confident and experience joy when our favorite team wins. Sports fulfill our human need to belong, and many fans, whether their team wins or loses, enjoy the suspense that allows them to release their emotions. Where we live, our family background, peer pressure, and our own sense of self *(identity)* all determine which baseball cap we wear and why we root for *our* team.

15 So the next time you put your Red Sox cap on and tune in to the game, remember it's not just about the amazing pitchers and batters, but about the way you feel when you watch *your team* play.

CHECK YOUR UNDERSTANDING

Answer these questions before moving on to the **Analyze the Text** section on the following page.

1. The author includes information about the Greeks in order to —
   A explain how we know which sports ancient peoples played
   B prove that "sports" was once a means for survival
   C encourage readers to play the games the Greeks once played
   D show that an ancient people had a high regard for sports

2. According to paragraph 7, why can a negative experience in sports still have a positive effect?
   F It encourages people to work together to solve problems.
   F It can make people more compassionate toward their enemies.
   G It can help people learn to deal with other difficult experiences.
   J It teaches people to think carefully about their priorities.

3. What does the section <u>Keep Your Eye on the Ball</u> contribute to this text?
   A It explains why entertainment is the greatest benefit of sports.
   B It explains that sports benefit spectators as well as players.
   C It quotes experts about the various benefits of sports.
   D It outlines the physical benefits that result from playing sports.

It's Not Just a Game! 399

TEACH

 CHECK YOUR UNDERSTANDING

Have students answer the questions independently.

Answers:

1. D
2. G
3. B

If they answer any questions incorrectly, have them reread the text to confirm their understanding. Then they may proceed to ANALYZE THE TEXT on page 400.

For **reading support** for students at varying proficiency levels, see the **Text X-Ray** on page 392D.

 ENGLISH LEARNER SUPPORT

Oral Assessment Use the following questions to assess students' comprehension and speaking skills:

1. Where were the first Olympic Games held? *(Olympia, Greece)*
2. In a team sport like soccer (football), what is an *accomplishment* for the whole team? *(teamwork, playing as well as possible by relying on each other's talents)*
3. If you have *respect* for someone, are you *isolated* from that person? *(no.)*

4. What does the section "Keep your eye on the Ball" add to this text? *(It quotes experts about the various benefits of sports.)*
   SUBSTANTIAL/MODERATE

It's Not Just a Game! 399

APPLY

ANALYZE THE TEXT

Possible answers:

1. **DOK 2:** *Even though there is a "fun" element to sports, there are significant health benefits from participation.*

2. **DOK 2:** *In team sports, the team shares responsibility. In individual sports, one person bears all of the responsibility, making that situation more challenging.*

3. **DOK 2:** *Sports can help people learn to negotiate, to control their attitude, and to become more curious and imaginative. Sports can also help develop language and math skills. Playing sports releases endorphins that can decrease pain and create an overall "good" feeling.*

4. **DOK 3:** *By "win," the author means "be successful." She supplies quotations from experts and provides verifiable facts to explain the various benefits of sports*

5. **DOK 4:** *The quotation states that sports can be for fun, or for "serious play." In the final two sections of the text, the author provides readers with a perspective on the importance of sports around the world.*

RESEARCH

Point out to students that there are many sources online and in print that they can access for information about any sport. Tell them to consult a variety of sources to cross-check the accuracy of their information.

Connect Tell students that as they fill out the graphic organizer they should keep a record of their sources.

RESPOND

ANALYZE THE TEXT

Support your responses with evidence from the text. 📓 NOTEBOOK

1. **Interpret** How does the title "It's Not Just a Game!" reflect the main idea of this text?

2. **Cause/Effect** According to the author, why can individual sports be more challenging than team sports?

3. **Summarize** How does the author support the idea that sports can build our brains, not just our bodies?

4. **Evaluate** In paragraph 9, the author tells readers, "[P]lay to have fun and you'll automatically win!" Do you agree with this statement? Why?

5. **Notice & Note** Reread the quotation in paragraph 3. How does it contribute to a greater understanding of sports?

RESEARCH

RESEARCH TIP
Don't believe everything you read online. It's always a good idea to get information from sites you know are reliable— and from more than one site. It's especially smart to check multiple reliable sites if you have any doubts about whether a piece of information is correct.

In "It's Not Just a Game!" the author includes a little information about sports history in general. Now it's time to get specific. Choose a sport that you enjoy or are curious about. Do some research to learn about its history and complete the graphic organizer below.

_____ (NAME OF SPORT)
When and Where It Began
Invented by James Naismith late in autumn 1891, at the YMCA Training School in Springfield, MA, where Naismith was an instructor; meant to give students something to do when cold weather made outdoor activities difficult.
How It Spread and Became Popular
Spread to other YMCAs and then to basketball leagues and college teams; some professional teams after World War I; first national championship in March 1938; much more growth in the prosperous times that followed World War II (NBA founded in 1949); even more popularity with the spread of TV.
Differences in How It Is Played Today
Played with a special ball, not the original soccer ball; a larger court today; five players on the court instead of nine; the ball can now be dribbled, not just thrown from player to player; the basket is now open at the bottom; games today last for four quarters instead of two halves.

Connect Compare your findings with those of a classmate who chose a different sport. What can you learn from each other?

LEARNING MINDSET

Questioning Explain to students that asking questions is a way to learn about new ideas and experiences. Remind them that asking questions is closely related to "grit." You need courage to ask questions; never fear being embarrassed. And remember to ask your question again, in a different way, if you don't understand the answer. Don't give up!

CREATE AND ADAPT

Write a Poem Write a poem about your favorite sport.

- ❏ Include characteristics of the sport that make it your favorite. (You may get some ideas by thinking about some of the positive aspects of sports discussed in "It's Not Just a Game!")
- ❏ Focus on the main idea or feeling you want to convey. Then brainstorm for vivid details that will make your ideas clear to readers.
- ❏ Decide whether to use rhyme and rhythm in your poem or to have your poem flow in an unstructured way.

Present an Infographic Meet with a partner and use the information from your research to create an infographic poster that shows both the positive and the negative aspects of the sport or sports that you learned about. Then present the graphic to the class.

- ❏ Use information from "It's Not Just a Game!" to discuss ways in which the sport(s) you chose benefits players and fans and the ways in which it is challenging. Make lists of these benefits and challenges.
- ❏ Choose images and decide on text to include—and how to present that text visually (for example, through captions or callout boxes).
- ❏ Sketch out possible designs. Revise to keep text brief and to ensure that the images and text work together. When you have a sketch that you both like, create a final version to present.

RESPOND TO THE ESSENTIAL QUESTION

 How do sports bring together friends, families, and communities?

Gather Information Review your annotations and notes on "It's Not Just a Game!" Then, add relevant details to your Response Log. As you determine which information to include, think about:

- what people can learn by playing sports
- how sports can be used to benefit all students and their schools

At the end of the unit, you can refer to your notes when you write a short story.

RESPOND

Go to **Writing as a Process** in the **Writing Studio** for help in writing a poem.

Go to **Using Media in a Presentation** in the **Speaking and Listening Studio** to learn more.

ACADEMIC VOCABULARY

As you write and discuss what you learned from the informational text, be sure to use the Academic Vocabulary words. Check off each of the words that you use.

- ❏ attitude
- ❏ consume
- ❏ goal
- ❏ purchase
- ❏ style

APPLY

CREATE AND ADAPT

Write a Poem Remind students to use figurative language and vivid words in their poems. Tell them to avoid vague words and that originality is an important ingredient in a good poem.

For **writing support** for students at varying proficiency levels, see the **Text X-Ray** on page 392D.

Present an Infographic Remind students that their infographic should present information clearly and simply. Tell them to take their time and use rulers and circular objects to aid them. Point out that clear organization will help them present their work in a smooth and logical way.

RESPOND TO THE ESSENTIAL QUESTION

Allow time for students to add details from "It's Not Just a Game" to their Unit 5 Response Logs.

APPLY

CRITICAL VOCABULARY

Answers:

1. *The senator's greatest* **accomplishment** *was when she had the new automobile safety law passed.*
2. *Because the two sides agreed to* **negotiate**, *they reached a settlement that made everyone happy.*
3. *Fans of the same sports team have a* **mutual** *interest in its players.*
4. *Doctors decided to* **isolate** *the patient because they didn't want to risk having other patients catch his illness.*
5. *Plans for* **utilization** *of the empty building included a children's museum, a fitness studio, and a homeless shelter.*

VOCABULARY STRATEGY:
Reference Aids

Possible synonyms appear in **boldface**:

(Sports are also **friendly** *events, opportunities for strangers to celebrate together and* **argue** *outcomes. A Saturday morning game is a* **wonderful** *way to spend time with family.)*

 RESPOND

WORD BANK
accomplishment
negotiate
mutual
isolate
utilization

 Go to the **Vocabulary Studio** for more on reference resources.

CRITICAL VOCABULARY

Practice and Apply Complete each sentence to show that you understand the meaning of the vocabulary word.

1. The senator's greatest **accomplishment** was when she . . .
2. Because the two sides agreed to **negotiate**, . . .
3. Fans of the same sports team have a **mutual** . . .
4. Doctors decided to **isolate** the patient because . . .
5. Plans for **utilization** of the empty building included . . .

VOCABULARY STRATEGY:
Reference Resources

A **thesaurus** is a reference aid that lists synonyms, or words with similar meanings. Writers can use a print or digital thesaurus to help them find the exact word they need. A thesaurus entry usually looks something like this:

isolate *v.* confine, cut off, disconnect, keep apart, remove, quarantine, seclude, segregate, separate, set apart

The fact that a thesaurus shows you several synonyms doesn't mean that all of the synonyms would work equally well in a sentence. Choose the synonym that best captures the meaning you want to convey and reflects your style as a writer.

Practice and Apply Choose four words in paragraph 12 of "It's Not Just a Game!" Use a print or digital thesaurus to find synonyms for those words. Then, rewrite the paragraph, using what you think are appropriate synonyms for the words you chose.

 ENGLISH LEARNER SUPPORT

Using Articles Some Asian students may forget to use definite and indefinite articles in spoken and written language. Work with these students to use the new vocabulary in writing their own sentences. Have them speak the sentences aloud. If they have left out articles, have them repeat the sentences correctly. Then suggest that they add the articles to their written work as a reminder. Supply them with quick reference charts that show the proper use of articles. **SUBSTANTIAL/MODERATE**

RESPOND

LANGUAGE CONVENTIONS:
Complex Sentences and Subject-Verb Agreement

A subject and its verb work together to create meaning in a sentence. In a **complex sentence,** that work happens at least twice: once in an independent clause and once in each subordinate clause. No matter how many times that work happens in a sentence, it is important for the subject and its verb to **agree** in number. A singular subject takes a singular verb form; a plural subject takes a plural verb form. Note these examples from "It's Not Just a Game!":

> Since organized <u>sports</u> <u>are</u> a hands-on, minds-on learning process, <u>they</u> <u>stimulate</u> our imagination, curiosity, and creativity.

> <u>Play</u> <u>is</u> not only something to do, <u>it's</u> something to watch others do. (Note that one verb is part of a contraction.)

> <u>We</u> <u>feel</u> self-confident and <u>experience</u> joy when our favorite <u>team</u> <u>wins</u>. (*Team* is considered a singular noun. Note that the subject in the independent clause, *we*, works with two verbs.)

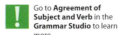
Go to **Agreement of Subject and Verb** in the **Grammar Studio** to learn more.

Practice and Apply These complex sentences are based on "It's Not Just a Game!" Whenever you see a choice of verbs in parentheses, mark the correct verb and then mark the subject with which it agrees.

1. I (wonder/wonders) if wrestlers (was/were) as popular in ancient Egypt as they (is/are) today.
2. Rules (keeps/keep) games functioning in an orderly way, especially when a player (makes/make) a mistake.
3. Because people (has/have) different interests, (there's/there are) a sport for just about everyone.
4. After the game (ends/end), the players of both teams (shakes/shake) hands as they (heads/head) to the locker rooms.
5. When my friends (follows/follow) directions, our game nights (runs/run) smoothly and (is/are) a lot of fun.

It's Not Just a Game! 403

APPLY

LANGUAGE CONVENTIONS:
Complex Sentences and Subject-Verb Agreement

Review the information about subject-verb agreement in complex sentences. Remind students to separate the clauses in a sentence when they are checking for subject-verb agreement.

Point out that sometimes there is a word in one clause that is referred to in another. Have students note the first example sentence on this page. The word *they* in the independent clause refers to the word *sports* in the dependent clause.

Practice and Apply

Answers:

1. <u>I</u> (<u>wonder</u>/wonders) if <u>wrestlers</u> (was/<u>were</u>) as popular in ancient Egypt as <u>they</u> (is/<u>are</u>) today.
2. <u>Rules</u> (keeps/<u>keep</u>) games functioning in an orderly way, especially when a <u>player</u> (<u>makes</u>/make) a mistake.
3. Because <u>people</u> (has/<u>have</u>) different interests, (<u>there's</u>/there are) a <u>sport</u> for just about everyone.
4. After the <u>game</u> (<u>ends</u>/end), the <u>players</u> of both teams (shakes/<u>shake</u>) hands as <u>they</u> (heads/<u>head</u>) to the locker rooms.
5. When my <u>friends</u> (follows/<u>follow</u>) directions, our game <u>nights</u> (runs/<u>run</u>) smoothly and (is/<u>are</u>) a lot of fun.

PLAN

THE CROSSOVER
Novel in Verse by Kwame Alexander

GENRE ELEMENTS
NOVEL IN VERSE

Inform students that the aim of a **novel in verse**, like all creative writing, is to entertain and interest the reader. All of the elements present in prose novels are present in verse novels too, and students will once again be asked to be mindful of things like setting, character, plot, and conflict. The primary differences between the two kinds of novels are form and style. Novels in verse look and sound like poetry; prose novels do not.

LEARNING OBJECTIVES

- Analyze a novel in verse.
- Analyze metaphor and personification.
- Conduct research on rules of a team sport.
- Write a letter asking for information.
- Create a podcast.
- **Language** Use the key words *verse novel* in a discussion.

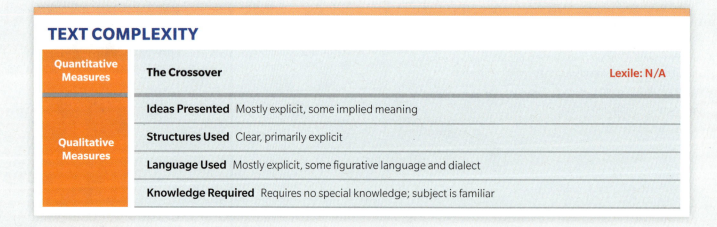

TEXT COMPLEXITY

Quantitative Measures	The Crossover	Lexile: N/A
Qualitative Measures	**Ideas Presented** Mostly explicit, some implied meaning	
	Structures Used Clear, primarily explicit	
	Language Used Mostly explicit, some figurative language and dialect	
	Knowledge Required Requires no special knowledge; subject is familiar	

404A Unit 5

PLAN

Online Ed

RESOURCES

- Unit 5 Response Log
- 🔊 Selection Audio
- Interpreting Graphic Elements
- 📖 Reading Studio: Notice & Note
- Writing Studio: Writing as a Process
- 💬 Speaking and Listening Studio: Participating in a Collaborative Discussion; Using Media in a Presentation
- ✓ "The Crossover" Selection Test

SUMMARIES

English

This excerpt from the verse novel *The Crossover* is an example of narrative poetry. It features a thirteen-year-old speaker who excels at basketball. He talks lovingly but competitively of his twin brother, JB, who also excels at basketball. Although they are twins and play on the same school basketball team, the speaker makes it quite clear that he and his brother are very different kinds of people.

Spanish

Este pasaje de la novela en verso El paso es un ejemplo de poesía narrativa. Presenta a un narrador de trece años que se destaca en el baloncesto. Él habla cariñosa y competitivamente de su hermano gemelo, JB, quien también se destaca en el baloncesto. A pesar de ser gemelos idénticos y jugar en el mismo equipo escolar de baloncesto, el narrador deja bastante claro que él y su hermano son personas muy distintas.

SMALL-GROUP OPTIONS

Have students work in small groups to read and discuss the selection.

Pinwheel Discussion

- After students have read the excerpt from *The Crossover*, ask them to create pinwheel formations of six per group.
- For the first rotation, ask students to discuss what the speaker is saying in the first section.
- For the second rotation, ask students to discuss what the speaker is saying in the second section.
- For the third rotation, ask students to discuss what the speaker is saying in the third section.

Jigsaw with Experts

- Divide the excerpt into its three component sections.
- Have students count off, or assign each student a numbered section.
- After they read their section, have students form groups with other students who read the same section. Each expert group should discuss its section.
- Then, have students form new groups with a representative for each section. These groups should discuss the excerpt as a whole.

The Crossover **404B**

PLAN

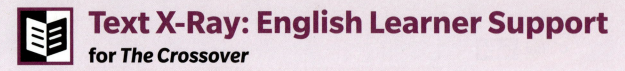

Text X-Ray: English Learner Support
for *The Crossover*

Use the Text X-Ray and the supports and scaffolds in the Teacher's Edition to help guide students at different proficiency levels through the selection.

INTRODUCE THE SELECTION
DISCUSS SPORTS AND FAMILY

In this lesson, students will need to be able to discuss the dynamics within a family as they are affected by sports. These words and the concepts they represent will be helpful to students in their discussions:

- **Competition**. In competition, people try to win by being or doing better than the people they **compete** against. Brothers and sisters are often **competitive** with each other, and that is brought out when they play sports together.
- **Cooperation**. In both sports and families, cooperation is more important than competition. Cooperation means "working together." Teams have to **cooperate** to win, and families have to cooperate to thrive.

Have volunteers share the things they feel competitive about and the ways they cooperate, either with their teammates or with their families.

CULTURAL REFERENCES

The following words and phrases may be unfamiliar to students:

- *Sunday school* (poem 1, line 7): a class held on Sundays that teaches children about their religion
- *warm-ups* (poem 2, title): preparation and practice before a game
- *A.K.A.* (poem 2, line 23): also known as; another name or nickname for a person
- *Phil Jackson* (poem 2, line 28): a famous basketball player and championship-winning coach
- *play-by-play* (poem 3, line 20): an analysis of the moves in a game

LISTENING

Listen for Details

Remind students that the things speakers say in a personal narrative are important details that help readers understand the speakers' feelings, ideas, and attitudes about themselves and others.

Have students listen as you read aloud "At the End of Warm-Ups, My Brother Tries to Dunk." Use the following supports with students at varying proficiency levels:

- Tell students that you will ask questions about what they just heard. Ask questions that require a yes-or-no or one-word answer. For example, ask: *Is the speaker trying to tease his brother?* (yes) *Who is giving advice?* (the coach) **SUBSTANTIAL**
- Have students describe in their own words what happens near the end of the warm-ups. **MODERATE**
- Ask students to work in pairs and discuss the speaker's feelings about his brother, using evidence from the narrative. **LIGHT**

PLAN

SPEAKING

Deliver a Podcast

Draw students' attention to the Create a Podcast assignment on p. 413. Use this practice to help them prepare for the recording. Circulate around the room to make sure students are speaking correctly.

Use the following supports with students at varying proficiency levels:

- Ask students what comment or note they would like to contribute to the podcast. Allow short answers, e.g., *Basketball is fun, exciting, competitive, cooperative*. Write their responses on the board in the form of complete sentences. Have students pronounce the responses properly. **SUBSTANTIAL**
- Have students work in pairs, asking each other questions about designated parts of the text and then answering the questions asked of them. **MODERATE**
- Have students record their podcast and then evaluate their performance in it and its overall clarity and organization. **LIGHT**

READING

Read Narrative Poetry

Inform students that reading narrative poetry requires the same analytical skills as reading any kind of literary text. The reader is looking for details about the characters and their behavior.

Work with students to read one of the three sections in the excerpt. Use the following supports with students at varying proficiency levels:

- Have students echo read "The Sportscaster." Ask them to raise their hands if they need clarification of a word or phrase and provide it. Ask a yes-or-no question to see if they understand the word or phrase. **SUBSTANTIAL**
- Ask students to reread "JB and I." Then ask them to identify three ways that the speaker and his twin are different. **MODERATE**
- Ask students to reread "At the End of Warm-Ups, My Brother Tries to Dunk." Then ask them to describe what the speaker is feeling during the warm-up. **LIGHT**

WRITING

Write a Letter

Work with students to read the writing assignment on p. 413. Point out to speakers of Spanish and Arabic that in questions the verb comes before the subject, and there's often another verb after the subject. (*Do you live here?*) In statements the subject comes first.

Use the following supports with students at varying proficiency levels:

- Help students to understand the form for questions they would like to ask the author of *The Crossover* by writing sentence frames: *Are you ____ (excited/unexcited) by basketball? Do you think different basketball teams are ____ (cooperative/competitive) with each other?* **SUBSTANTIAL**
- Provide sentence frames, such as the following, that students can use to craft their letters: *I would like you to know that I am ____. The question I would most like to ask you is ____.* **MODERATE**
- Remind students to use transitions to link their details to their opinions. Have pairs find three places in their essays where they can use a transition. **LIGHT**

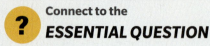

TEACH

? Connect to the ESSENTIAL QUESTION

In *The Crossover* excerpt, playing basketball brings out the love and connection a young teenage boy shares with his brother and father, proving that sports do indeed bring families together.

COMPARE THEME

Point out to students that poems come in many different forms and styles. Some rhyme and some don't. Some follow strict patterns while others have a free form. Some are two lines long, and some go on for volumes. Nonetheless, they all share many of the devices and techniques detailed in the unit.

COLLABORATE & COMPARE

NOVEL IN VERSE
from
THE CROSSOVER
by **Kwame Alexander**
pages 407–411

COMPARE THEME

From sonnets to haiku, from ballads to epic poems, from odes to elegies, poets are always seeking creative freedom in poetic forms, old and new. Think about how the form of each poem—along with its use of rhythm, sound devices, and figurative language—creates layers of meaning.

 ESSENTIAL QUESTION:

How do sports bring together friends, families, and communities?

POEM
DOUBLE DOUBLES
by **J. Patrick Lewis**
pages 417–419

404 Unit 5

from The Crossover

QUICK START

Have you ever heard a rap with a story that caught your imagination? What happened? What about the rap made it special?

ANALYZE NOVEL IN VERSE

A **narrative poem** tells a story. Some narrative poems are brief, like old ballads that were originally sung. Others are book-length, including ancient works such as the *Odyssey* and *Beowulf*.

Throughout history, new forms of narrative poetry have emerged. For example, the **verse novel** is a novel-length narrative told in poetry instead of prose. As you read "JB and I," "At the End of Warm-Ups, My Brother Tries to Dunk," and "The Sportscaster" by Kwame Alexander, note examples of these characteristics of verse novels:

Organized into **scenes**, each with a setting and a plot

Presents a **speaker** and other characters, often interacting and even conflicting; usually shows the speaker's emotions

May include **graphical elements** (unusual line breaks and line length; unusual punctuation and type styles/sizes)

Expresses a **theme** in each scene, working together for a "life lesson" that relates to the verse novel as a whole

GET READY

GENRE ELEMENTS: VERSE NOVEL

- has many of the characteristics of a story, including setting, characters, and plot (which may include conflict)
- is structured in groups of lines instead of in paragraphs
- usually uses vivid word choices and figurative language to make the topic easy to visualize
- expresses a theme, or a lesson about life

The Crossover 405

TEACH

QUICK START

Have students read the Quick Start question, and invite them to share their thoughts with a partner or in small groups. Explain that rap and poetry have many similarities: they both use rhyme, rhythm, images, and figurative language to tell a story.

ANALYZE NOVEL IN VERSE

Help students understand the terms and concepts related to analyzing novels in verse. Tell them that even though a novel is in verse, they should analyze it as they would any other story, by examining the main characters, the events in the plot, and the conflict.

Suggest that students ask themselves these questions as they analyze novels in verse:

- What qualities and attitudes does the main character have?
- What does the main character feel about the other characters?
- How does the author's choice of words express these feelings?

The Crossover **405**

TEACH

ANALYZE METAPHOR AND PERSONIFICATION

Explain to students that figurative language isn't exclusive to poetry. Authors of all genres use metaphors and personification to make their writing more interesting. Tell students that figurative language is especially present in poetry because it is a way to express feelings and ideas in few words with more impact.

To help students analyze figurative language, have them ask the following questions:

- What are the two things being compared?
- How are the two things alike?
- Does the comparison help to create an effective visual image?
- Does the comparison help to express a feeling or idea?

■ English Learner Support

Language Conventions Inform students that metaphor and personification have Spanish cognates (*metáfora* and *personificación*). Provide students with easy-to-understand examples of each: *The night was as black as ink. The moon smiled at me.* **SUBSTANTIAL/MODERATE**

ANNOTATION MODEL

Remind students that they are looking for examples of metaphor and personification, but that they are welcome to annotate other interesting choices like unusual capitalization and punctuation. Point out that students may choose to circle metaphors, box examples of personification, and underline other interesting details. Or they may create their own annotation methods, like color-coding. Encourage students to comment on what the use of the figurative language adds to the text.

406 Unit 5

 GET READY

ANALYZE METAPHOR AND PERSONIFICATION

Poets often use **figurative language** to express their ideas in imaginative ways. Figurative language is not literally true, but it can be used to emphasize ideas, create mental images, or stir readers' emotions. Two common types of figurative language used in poetry are metaphor and personification.

In a **metaphor**, the poet compares two basically unlike things that have one or more qualities in common. A metaphor makes a direct comparison and does not use the words *like* or *as*.

> **The basketball court was a swarm of activity.**

This metaphor compares the players to a swarm of insects. It helps create a feeling of intense, fast-moving action.

In **personification**, the poet gives human qualities to an animal, object, or idea.

> **The ball thought about things for a moment and then dropped through the net.**

This personification creates the mental image of a basketball that does not fall through the net right away. It adds suspense to the scene.

As you read these three poems by Kwame Alexander, look for examples of figurative language. Think about what the poet wants to say and the kind of mental image or feeling he wants to create.

ANNOTATION MODEL NOTICE & NOTE

As you read, think about the elements of verse novels. You can also mark examples of figurative language and other interesting details. In the model, you can see one reader's notes about a scene from *The Crossover*.

>   . . . I snicker
> but it's not funny to him,
> 5 especially when I take off from center court,
> my hair like wings,
> each lock lifting me higher and HIGHER
> like a 747 ZOOM ZOOM!

This may be an important moment in the plot.

The figurative language helps me "see" the scene.

The different sizes of types remind me of the sound of a plane taking off.

406 Unit 5

NOTICE & NOTE

BACKGROUND

Kwame Alexander *(b. 1968) is an American poet, novelist, and educator. He has written more than two dozen books and has won numerous literary awards. These include the prestigious John Newbery Award, the Coretta Scott King Author Honor Book Award, and the Lee Bennett Hopkins Poetry Award, all in recognition of The Crossover. Alexander frequently travels to schools—both in the United States and around the world—where he reads and discusses poetry and leads writing workshops.*

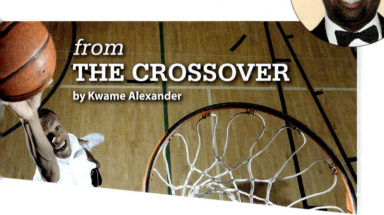

from THE CROSSOVER
by Kwame Alexander

PREPARE TO COMPARE

As you read these three poems, think about the story that they tell and the way that Alexander tells it. Note the ways in which he brings the sport of basketball to life and relates it to personal relationships.

JB and I

are almost thirteen. Twins. Two basketball goals at
opposite ends of the court. Identical.
It's easy to tell us apart though. I'm

an inch taller, with dreads to my neck. He gets
5 his head shaved once a month. I want to go to Duke,
he flaunts Carolina Blue. If we didn't love each other,

we'd HATE each other. He's a shooting guard.
I play forward. JB's the second
most phenomenal baller on our team.

Notice & Note

Use the side margins to notice and note signposts in the text.

ANALYZE NOVEL IN VERSE
Annotate: In lines 1–9, underline examples of unusual line breaks. Circle an unusual type style.
Analyze: Why do you think the poet used these graphical elements?

The Crossover **407**

ENGLISH LEARNER SUPPORT

Confirm Understanding Have students choral read the first three stanzas of "JB and I." Stop after each sentence or two to ask students whether they need any words or phrases clarified. Check for comprehension by asking yes-and-no questions (*Are the boys related? Are they cousins?*) or questions with one-word answers (*Who is taller? Who plays guard?*)
SUBSTANTIAL

TEACH

BACKGROUND

Inform students that the three sections in the unit are selections from a full-length novel in verse in which the author tells a complete story with all the usual elements of a novel—main characters, secondary characters, a plot, conflict, and resolution. Encourage students to read the entire book if they are interested in finding out more about the narrator, JB, and their father.

PREPARE TO COMPARE

Direct students to use the Prepare to Compare prompt to focus their reading.

TEXT IN FOCUS

Interpreting Graphic Elements Have students view the **Text in Focus** video on this page of their ebook to learn how to use graphic elements to aid their understanding of a story. Then have students use **Text in Focus Practice** to apply what they have learned.

ANALYZE NOVEL IN VERSE

The author uses unusual line breaks to emphasize points about the two brothers and to keep readers in a bit of suspense until they find out the information in the next line. The capitalization of the word *hate* emphasizes the great difference the speaker sees between himself and his brother.

(Answer: *The author uses unusual line-breaks in the first three stanzas to highlight the differences (and competition) between the two brothers. The graphical elements are often at odds with the punctuation and capitalization that create sentence structure. For example, "I'm" is the last word at the end of the first stanza instead of the first word at beginning of the second stanza. The graphical elements direct the reader's attention to the contrasts and comparisons the author is creating.*)

The Crossover **407**

TEACH

CONTRASTS AND CONTRADICTIONS

Remind students that this signpost is used to indicate sharp contrasts, in this case the way JB used to behave and the way he behaves now. Have students identify the clue words ("Ever since") that signal this contrast. Then have them answer the question to determine the purpose of the contrast. (**Answer:** *Students may suggest that a big change in someone close to them might make them feel uncomfortable or worried that the friendship may change as well.*)

 ANALYZE NOVEL IN VERSE

Remind students that a novel in verse still has many of the features of prose fiction, such as conflict. (**Answer:** *The speaker's taunt points to a conflict he has about his brother's basketball skills and might even suggest other conflicts, such as JB's newfound interest in girls.*)

ANALYZE METAPHOR AND PERSONIFICATION

Remind students, if necessary, of the definition of each term and of the enhanced meaning and beauty figurative speech brings to a poem. (**Answer:** *These figures of speech create vivid mental images that make the reader understand the action—the successful dunk—and the feelings—near dizziness about the crowd and the game—that the speaker is describing.*)

 For **listening support** for students at varying proficiency levels, see the **Text X-Ray** on page 404C.

 **NOTICE & NOTE**

CONTRASTS AND CONTRADICTIONS

Notice & Note: Mark the way in which the speaker says that JB has changed.

Connect: Imagine a big change in someone close to you. How do you think that change would make you feel?

ANALYZE NOVEL IN VERSE
Annotate: In lines 1–8, mark the words that the speaker is either saying to or thinking about JB.

Infer: A narrative's plot usually focuses on a conflict. What conflict do you see in these lines?

ANALYZE METAPHOR AND PERSONIFICATION
Annotate: In lines 9–18, mark an example of a metaphor and an example of personification.

Critique: How does this figurative language contribute to the reader's understanding and enjoyment of the poem?

10 He has the better jumper, but I'm the better
     slasher. And much faster. We both
     pass well. Especially to each other.

     To get ready for the season, I went
     to three summer camps. JB only went to
15 one. Said he didn't want to miss Bible school.

     What does he think, I'm stupid? Ever since
     Kim Bazemore kissed him in Sunday school,
     he's been acting all religious,

     thinking less and less about
20 basketball, and more and more about
     GIRLS.

At the End of Warm-Ups, My Brother Tries to Dunk

Not even close, JB.
What's the matter?
The hoop too high for you? I snicker
but it's not funny to him,
5 especially when I take off from center court,
my hair like wings,
each lock lifting me higher and HIGHER

like a 747 ZOOM ZOOM!
I throw down so hard,
10 the fiberglass trembles.   *personification*
BOO YAH, Dad screams
from the top row.
I'm the only kid
on the team
15 who can do that.

The gym is a loud, crowded circus.
My stomach is a roller coaster.
My head, a carousel.   *metaphors*
The air, heavy with the smell
20 of sweat, popcorn,
and the sweet perfume
of mothers watching sons.

408 Unit 5

IMPROVE READING FLUENCY

Targeted Passage Have students work with partners to read the section "At the End of Warm-Ups, My Brother Tries to Dunk." First, use lines 1 through 5 to model how to read verse. Have students follow along in their books as you read the text with appropriate phrasing, feeling, and emphasis. Then, have partners take turns reading aloud the entire section. Encourage students to provide feedback and support for achieving a dramatic effect. Inform students that when they are reading verse aloud for an audience, they should be expressive and convey feeling.

 Go to the **Reading Studio** for additional support in developing fluency.

408 Unit 5

Our mom, a.k.a. Dr. Bell, a.k.a. The Assistant Principal,
is talking to some of the teachers
25 on the other side of the gym.
I'm feeling better already.
Coach calls us in,
does his Phil Jackson impersonation.
Love ignites the spirit, brings teams together, he says.
30 JB and I glance at each other,
ready to bust out laughing,
but Vondie, our best friend,
beats us to it.
The whistle goes off.
35 Players gather at center circle,
dap[1] each other,
pound each other.
Referee tosses the jump ball.
Game on.

---

[1] **dap** (dăp): to give a congratulatory greeting by tapping a closed fist on top ot and on the bottom of the other person's fist.

NOTICE & NOTE

> **WORDS OF THE WISER**
>
> **Notice & Note:** Mark the advice that the coach offers to the players.
>
> **Interpret:** What lesson does the coach want the players to learn?

The Crossover 409

APPLYING ACADEMIC VOCABULARY

☐ attitude   ☑ consume   ☐ goal   ☑ style   ☐ purchase

Write and Discuss Have students turn to a partner and discuss the following questions before they write their responses. Guide students to include the Academic Vocabulary words *consume* and *style*.

- Why is the speaker in the poem **consumed** by his twin brother's actions?
- In what ways are their basketball **styles** different?

TEACH

▶ WORDS OF THE WISER

Remind students that this signpost is used to indicate advice or insight that a wiser character who is usually older offers about life to the main character. Then have students answer the question. (**Answer:** *Brotherly love for your teammates makes everyone play better.*)

 ENGLISH LEARNER SUPPORT

Identify Formal and Informal English Read aloud and display the Background information on page 407. Explain that it is an example of formal English. Every word means the same thing as its dictionary definition. Then read aloud lines 30–34 of "JB and I." Point out the playful tone. The expression "ready to bust out laughing" is an example of informal English; it's closer to the way people talk to each other when they are comfortable and want to convey a specific feeling.

- Use gestures, cognates, and intonation to aid student comprehension. Read aloud and display sentences written in both formal and informal English and ask students to identify them. For example: *I laughed so hard, I thought my mouth would break.* (informal). **SUBSTANTIAL**

- Supply students with sentences in formal and informal English. Ask them to distinguish between the two. For example: *I would really like to work for that company.* (formal). *I'd give my right arm for that job.* (informal). **MODERATE**

- Ask students to compose their own sentences and/or paragraphs in both formal and informal English. Challenge them to convey the same meaning in formal and informal language. **LIGHT**

The Crossover   **409**

TEACH

ANALYZE NOVEL IN VERSE

Explain to students that poets use line breaks to guide readers and, sometimes, to make them pay attention. When reading a poem, students may be surprised and feel that a line is not finished. For example, "JB likes to taunt and." For just an instant, before the reader goes on to the next line, he or she wonders what else JB likes to do. (**Answer:** *Students may say that the author uses lines with only a few words and many breaks in order to emphasize phrases or to create a particular mood, a change from what went before.*)

EL
ENGLISH LEARNER SUPPORT

Language Conventions Direct students' attention to lines 11 through 13. Read the words, giving each emphasis.

- Have students echo your reading. Give students this sentence frame to complete to describe the effect of the three words. "The poet makes the narrator seem _____." *(careful,fast, smart)*
  SUBSTANTIAL/MODERATE

- Have pairs of students read the lines to each other and discuss the effect of the lines in showing JB's character.
  LIGHT

 For **reading support** for students at varying proficiency levels, see the **Text X-Ray** on page 404D.

NOTICE & NOTE

ANALYZE NOVEL IN VERSE
Annotate: Mark examples of unusual punctuation, capitalization, and line length in "The Sportscaster."

Analyze: Why do you think the poet chose these unique graphical elements?

The Sportscaster

JB likes to taunt and
trash talk
during games
like Dad
5 used to do
when he played.

When I walk onto
the court
I prefer silence
10 so I can
Watch
React
Surprise.

I talk too,
15 but mostly
to myself,
like sometimes
when I do
my own
20 play-by-play
in my head.

410 Unit 5

WHEN STUDENTS STRUGGLE . . .

Read Poetry If students are having difficulty understanding the text because of the many unusual line breaks and the fragmented language, advise them to disregard the line breaks and read the poems as though they were regular prose, joining words and phrases that logically belong together and stopping when there is an end period. For additional support, ask students what each sentence is saying, using their own words.

 For additional support, go to the **Reading Studio** and assign the following **Level Up tutorial: Paraphrasing.**

NOTICE & NOTE

CHECK YOUR UNDERSTANDING

Answer these questions before moving on to the **Analyze the Text** section on the following page.

1. According to the speaker in "JB and I," why is JB more interested in being religious than in playing basketball?

   A JB had a spiritual experience at camp.

   B JB is not as good a slasher as the speaker is.

   C JB is interested in a girl at church.

   D JB is trying to please his parents.

2. Near the end of "At the End of Warm-Ups, My Brother Tries to Dunk," the brothers probably are tempted to laugh because —

   F they already have been trying hard to make the coach's advice work

   G their teammate Vondie is making fun of the coach as he talks

   H the coach does a terrible job of imitating a famous NBA coach

   J the coach's advice is the opposite of their feelings toward each other

3. Which statement best describes the brothers' father as we see him in the second and third scenes?

   A He misses the days when he was a basketball player.

   B He has a bond with his sons because of basketball.

   C He is not as impressed with his two sons as his wife is.

   D He attends his sons' games only because he must.

The Crossover 411

TEACH

CHECK YOUR UNDERSTANDING

Have students answer the questions independently.

Answers:

1. C
2. J
3. B

If they answer any questions incorrectly, have them reread the text to confirm their understanding. Then they may proceed to ANALYZE THE TEXT on p. 412.

ENGLISH LEARNER SUPPORT

Oral Assessment Use the following questions to asses students' comprehension and speaking skills:

1. Is JB interested in a girl? *(yes, at church)*

2. At the end of "At the End of Warm-Ups, My Brother Tries to Dunk," who gives them advice, which the boys laugh at? *(the coach)*

3. Which sport did the boy's father used to play? *(basketball)*

SUBSTANTIAL/MODERATE

The Crossover **411**

APPLY

ANALYZE THE TEXT

Possible answers:

1. **DOK 2:** *The speaker is an inch taller than JB and has dreadlocks; JB shaves his head. The speaker wants to go to Duke; JB flaunts "Carolina Blue," a different college. The speaker plays forward; JB is a shooting guard. JB is a better jumper; the speaker is a better slasher. The speaker went to three basketball camps; JB went to only one.*

2. **DOK 2:** *The brothers love each other but are very competitive. They probably know that they have different basketball skills but are both good players.*

3. **DOK 4:** *JB tries to dunk the ball but fails. The speaker taunts him, but JB isn't laughing. The speaker shows off by flying down court like a jet, jumping, and dunking the basketball as Dad cheers him on from the stands.*

4. **DOK 4:** *The three scenes suggest that the brothers acknowledge a competitive spirit but also have a lot in common. The theme may be that family relationships don't always go smoothly but that there usually is a basis for getting along with each other.*

5. **DOK 4:** *The speaker is the more likely "sportscaster" because he does a "play-by-play" analysis, which is the kind of talk that a sportscasters do.*

RESEARCH

Review the Research Tip with students. Remind them to use reputable, reliable sources of information, such as sites published by established news and sports organizations.

Connect Answers will vary, depending on which sport students choose to examine. Remind students to document their sources.

412 Unit 5

 RESPOND

ANALYZE THE TEXT

Support your responses with evidence from the text. 📓 **NOTEBOOK**

1. **Compare** In lines 1–2 of "JB and I," the speaker compares JB and himself to "goals at / opposite ends of the court." According to lines 3–15, how are the speaker and JB different?

2. **Infer** How does the use of capital letters in "JB and I" and "At the End of Warm-Ups, My Brother Tries to Dunk" affect your understanding of the speakers' personality?

3. **Connect** Review lines 16–18 of "At the End of Warm-Ups, My Brother Tries to Dunk." What mental images do these metaphors create and how do they help express what the speaker is feeling?

4. **Synthesize** Think about these three verse novel scenes. What theme do the scenes, taken together, suggest?

5. **Notice & Note** How does the speaker contrast himself with his brother in "The Sportscaster"? To which brother do you think the term *sportscaster* applies better, and why?

RESEARCH TIP
The rules of a sport can change over time. As you research the rules of the sport you have chosen, check the date for each source and make sure that your information is current.

RESEARCH

Research the rules of another team sport that you play or that interests you. Use the graphic organizer to analyze some of its key elements.

QUESTION	ANSWER
How many players are on each team?	
What is the role of each type of player?	
How are points scored?	
What are some key rules of the game? What happens if a rule is not followed?	

Connect With a small group, discuss the rules for the game. Which rules do you think make for a better game? Which rules do you think should be changed, and why?

412 Unit 5

TO CHALLENGE STUDENTS . . .

Historical Research Have students conduct more intensive research to learn how an organized sport has changed through history. Inform students that a sport like baseball has been around for more than a century. Encourage students to address not only the change in rules but also organizational changes and why those changes were made. This kind of activity lends itself well to a timeline; challenge students to create one. Have students write an essay about their findings or present them to the class in an oral report.

CREATE AND DISCUSS

Write a Letter Write a letter to the poet requesting information about what inspired him to write *The Crossover*.

❏ Write a friendly letter that includes a heading with an address and a date, a greeting, the body of the letter, and a closing (such as Sincerely,) and a signature.
❏ Introduce yourself and say something about what you liked about the scenes from *The Crossover* that you read.
❏ Ask him questions about why he wrote these poems. (Possible questions: Did you play any sports in your youth? Which character in *The Crossover* do you identify with the most?)
❏ Ask him why he chose the form of a verse novel and what was the most difficult part of creating it.
❏ Throughout, use a friendly but respectful tone.

Create a Podcast Work in a small group to create a podcast in which participants discuss their responses to the excerpt from *The Crossover*.

❏ Review your answers and notes that you made while reading. Highlight notes that you would want to share in a discussion.
❏ As a group, plan your questions. Be sure to ask how the text makes you curious about the rest of this verse novel. Plan a role for each member of your group, including a moderator.
❏ Practice your discussion before you record it. Work with your teacher to record the podcast and possibly post it.

RESPOND TO THE ESSENTIAL QUESTION

 How do sports bring together friends, families, and communities?

Gather Information Review your annotations and notes on these scenes from *The Crossover*. Then, add relevant details to your Response Log. As you determine which information to include, think about:

- how sports affect people's lives
- what makes someone a good player at a sport
- how competition shapes players' attitudes

At the end of the unit, refer to your notes as you write a short story.

RESPOND

Go to **Writing as a Process** in the **Writing Studio** for help.

Go to **Participating in Collaborative Discussions and Using Media in a Presentation** in the **Speaking and Listening Studio** for guidance.

ACADEMIC VOCABULARY
As you write and discuss what you learned from the verse novel, be sure to use the Academic Vocabulary words. Check off each of the words that you use.

❏ attitude
❏ consume
❏ goal
❏ purchase
❏ style

The Crossover 413

APPLY

CREATE AND DISCUSS

Write a Letter Point out that the first three bullet points of the list on page 417 can serve as an outline for the students' letters. Each item can be one paragraph. Advise students to select their details from the novel before they begin to write their letters.

 For **writing support** for students at varying proficiency levels, see the **Text X-Ray** on page 404D.

Create a Podcast Remind students that a podcast is a conversation that requires careful planning and timing. Suggest that each question they discuss should have a time limit so everyone can participate equally and all questions can be answered effectively.

RESPOND TO THE ESSENTIAL QUESTION

Allow time for students to add details from *The Crossover* to their Unit 5 Response Logs. Remind them that the Essential Question is about the effect of sports on families.

 ENGLISH LEARNER SUPPORT

Discuss with a Small Group To assist them with the creation of their podcasts, ask students to discuss which specific notes they wish to share with the group so they can prevent repetition of the same notes. Then ask students to select a moderator and finalize the order of questions. Allow students to rehearse their podcast. Encourage them to find ways to make the transitions move faster before you start recording. **SUBSTANTIAL**

The Crossover 413

PLAN

DOUBLE DOUBLES
Poem by J. Patrick Lewis

GENRE ELEMENTS
POEM
Remind students that the aim of a **poem** is to entertain and interest readers with its use of figurative and descriptive language, unusual graphical elements, rhythm (or lack of rhythm) and special way of expressing feelings, emotions, and ideas. A **two-voice poem**, like the one presented in this unit, has the added quality of presenting two different characters at one time, so it is up to readers to examine and "hear" both characters as individuals and as a pair.

LEARNING OBJECTIVES
- Analyze two voices in a poem.
- Make inferences based on information in the text.
- Compare poetic literary works.
- Conduct research about the Williams sisters.
- Write a two-voice poem.
- **Language** Discuss the role of the speakers in a poem.

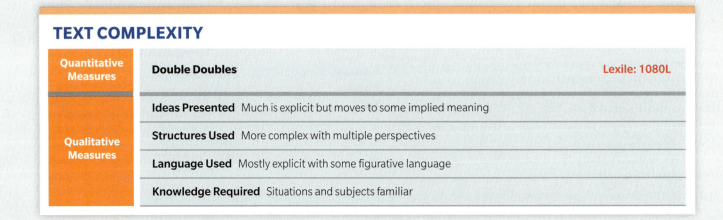

TEXT COMPLEXITY

Quantitative Measures	Double Doubles	Lexile: 1080L
Qualitative Measures	**Ideas Presented** Much is explicit but moves to some implied meaning	
	Structures Used More complex with multiple perspectives	
	Language Used Mostly explicit with some figurative language	
	Knowledge Required Situations and subjects familiar	

414A Unit 5

PLAN

Online Ed

RESOURCES

- Unit 5 Response Log
- 🔊 Selection Audio
- 📖 Reading Studio: Notice & Note
- ✏️ Writing Studio: Writing as a Process
- 💬 Speaking and Listening Studio: Participating in a Collaborative Discussion
- ✓ "Double Doubles" Selection Test

SUMMARIES

English
"Double Doubles" finds Venus and Serena Williams side by side on the tennis court—and the page—playing in a doubles tennis match. The poem expresses their love and admiration for each other and for the game, as well as the unique bond that they share as sisters and teammates. The poem features lines that the two women say simultaneously as well as individually.

Spanish
"Dobles dobles" encuentra a Venus y Serena Williams lado a lado en la cancha (y en la página) jugando tenis en un partido de dobles. El poema expresa el amor y admiración de la una por la otra y por el juego, así como el lazo único que comparten como hermanas y compañeras de equipo. El poema presenta líneas que ambas mujeres dicen simultáneamente, así como individualmente.

SMALL-GROUP OPTIONS

Have students work in small groups to read and discuss the selection.

Pinwheel Discussion
- After students have read "Double Doubles," ask them to create pinwheel formations of six per group.
- For the first rotation, ask students to discuss what the speakers say together.
- For the second rotation, ask students to discuss what the speakers say individually.
- For the third rotation, ask students to discuss the different information the two sisters provide about each other.

Think-Pair-Share
- After students have read "Double Doubles," pose this question: *What makes the Williams sisters such excellent teammates?*
- Have students think about the question individually and jot down ideas.
- Then, have pairs discuss their ideas about the question.
- Finally, ask pairs to share their responses with the class.

Double Doubles **414B**

PLAN

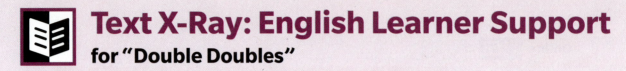

Text X-Ray: English Learner Support
for "Double Doubles"

Use the Text X-Ray and the supports and scaffolds in the Teacher's Edition to help guide students at different proficiency levels through the selection.

INTRODUCE THE SELECTION
DISCUSS PARTNERSHIP

In this lesson, students will need to be able to discuss the relationship between partners so they can understand why the Williams sisters work so well together. Give students these words and explanations to help them.

Goals: Partners in sports and in other areas of life share goals, results they want to achieve. They work together in many ways to reach those goals.

Communication: One of the most important things in a partnership is the ability to communicate, to share information well. People communicate with words, of course, but good partners also communicate without words because they know each other well.

Have students fill in sentence frames like those below. Ask volunteers to read their sentences aloud:

One thing I'd like you two know about me is _____. My friend and I make a good team because we _____.

CULTURAL REFERENCES

The following words and phrases may be unfamiliar to students:

- *lob* (line 7): a ball hit in a high arc over an opponent
- *volleys* (line 8): strikes of the ball before it hits the ground
- *love* (line 14): having a score of zero in tennis
- *tie-break* (line 25): a move that ends an even score
- *match point* (line 26): a point needed to win a match
- *Venus* is the name of the of one of the Williams sisters; it is also the name of the planet between Earth and Mercury.

LISTENING

Listen for Clues

Remind students that authors provide clues in literary works which readers can use to better understand the characters. Have students listen to the selection audio. Clarify unfamiliar terms and cultural references. Read the poem again aloud; pause to offer clarification as necessary.

Have students listen as you play the selection audio of "Double Doubles." Then, read it more slowly aloud, combining both Venus and Selena's parts. Use the following supports with students at varying proficiency levels:

- Tell students that you will ask questions about what they just heard. Ask questions that require a yes-or-no or one-word answer or provide sentence frames: For example, ask: *What game are the sisters playing? The game the sisters are playing is _____. How do you know this? I know they are playing tennis because the poem says _____.* **SUBSTANTIAL**
- Ask students to identify specific words that the author uses that suggest that the sisters love each other and love tennis. **MODERATE**
- Ask students to work in pairs to discuss the feelings that the sisters express in the poem. **LIGHT**

414C Unit 5

PLAN

SPEAKING

Critique a Poem

Draw students' attention to the Critique a Poem assignment on p. 421. Use this practice to help them prepare for the critique. Circulate around the room to make sure students are speaking correctly.

Use the following supports with students at varying proficiency levels:

- Ask students what they liked about the poem and what they didn't. Allow one- or two-word answers. Use sentence frames: *I liked when Venus said that_____. I didn't like the poem because _____.* Write their responses on the board in the form of complete sentences. Have students pronounce the responses correctly. **SUBSTANTIAL**
- Have students work in pairs to determine which criticisms they would like to include in their critiques. Encourage student pairs to defend their choices. **MODERATE**
- Have students deliver their critiques to a group in a trial run. Have the group evaluate their presentations and recommend areas for improvement. **LIGHT**

READING

Understand and Analyze a Poem

Inform students that reading two-voice poems requires the same analytical skills as reading any kind of literary text—the reader is looking for details about the characters.

Work with students to reread the poem. Use the following supports with students at varying proficiency levels:

- Have students follow the text on the page as you read it aloud. Spot-check to see whether they need clarification of a word or phrase and provide it. Then ask a yes-or-no question to see if they understand the word or phrase. Review cultural references that may continue to confuse students. **SUBSTANTIAL**
- Ask student pairs to reread "Double Doubles." Then ask them to identify three feelings Venus and Serena express in the poem. **MODERATE**
- Ask student pairs to reread "Double Doubles." Then ask them to note the lines Venus and Serena say together and discuss what they show about the sisters. **LIGHT**

WRITING

Write a Two-Voice Poem

Work with students to read the writing assignment on p. 421.

Use the following supports with students at varying proficiency levels:

- Help students choose the characters and subjects for their poems. Ask them for one- or two-word comments that the characters might say about their subjects. Write a short paragraph on the board using those comments. Then have students copy the paragraph in their notebooks. **SUBSTANTIAL**
- Provide sentence frames that students can use to plan their poems: *The perspective the two characters share about the subject is _____. The two characters feel differently about _____.* **MODERATE**
- Ask students to explain how they will lay out their poems graphically. Review their poems for execution of these elements. **LIGHT**

Double Doubles **414D**

TEACH

 Connect to the
ESSENTIAL QUESTION

Like *The Crossover*, "Double Doubles" celebrates the love two siblings have for a sport and how that sport brings them even closer together as sisters.

COMPARE THEME

Point out to students that *The Crossover* is a full-length novel of which they have read only three scenes; "Double Doubles" is a poem that is a complete work unto itself. Explain that apart from this difference, they both use similar poetic elements, including unusual line breaks and figurative language.

COLLABORATE & COMPARE

POEM
DOUBLE DOUBLES
by **J. Patrick Lewis**
pages 417–419

COMPARE THEME

Now that you've read three scenes from the verse novel *The Crossover*, read "Double Doubles," in which siblings who play another sport share their thoughts about their sport—and about each other. As you read, think about the similarities and differences in how each poet presents his speakers. After you are finished, you will collaborate with a small group on a final project that involves an analysis of both poets' work.

 ESSENTIAL QUESTION:

How do sports bring together friends, families, and communities?

NOVEL IN VERSE
from
THE CROSSOVER
by **Kwame Alexander**
pages 407–411

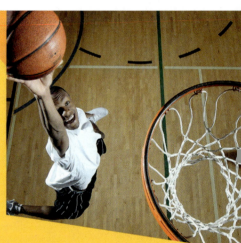

Double Doubles

QUICK START

Have you ever heard a duet, a song in which two artists sing—sometimes singing to each other and sometimes singing together? What makes the "conversation" in a duet different from a performance in which only one person sings?

ANALYZE A TWO-VOICE POEM

Most poems have a single voice. It is the voice of the speaker, who tells about personal experiences, feelings, and thoughts. A popular new form of poetry, however, is known as the **two-voice poem.** In this kind of poem, two distinct voices are heard. They may be conversing with each other, or they both may be trying to talk to you at the same time. Reading this kind of poem, or hearing it read aloud, allows you to see two points of view about a topic or theme at the same time. It also encourages you to explore similarities and differences between the poem's speakers.

Note these characteristics of two-voice poems:

- They are meant to be read aloud by two people, each assuming the voice of one of the speakers.
- Graphical elements are very important. Two-voice poems are usually set up in two columns, with each column representing just one speaker's voice. If both speakers are meant to speak the same words at the same time, either the shared words appear in both columns or the poet creates a middle column for those words. (Sometimes, the poet may choose to write in alternating stanzas, with every other stanza spoken by the same speaker.)
- They should be read sequentially, from left to right, line by line and from top to bottom.

Watch for and make notes about these characteristics as you read "Double Doubles."

GET READY

GENRE ELEMENTS: TWO-VOICE POETRY

- is more about thoughts and feelings than about a story
- expresses ideas about a topic or theme from the perspective of two different speakers
- is structured in a way that makes it clear which lines are spoken by one voice and which are spoken by both voices
- like other kinds of poems, expresses a theme, or a lesson about life

TEACH

QUICK START

Have students read the Quick Start question, and invite them to discuss their thoughts with a partner. Explain that in a duet, the two singers usually share a feeling or an experience with each other during the course of a song. The same is true for the characters in a two-voice poem.

ANALYZE A TWO-VOICE POEM

Explain to students that poems that are meant to be read by more than one person are not new, although they were once more popular than they are now. In the plays of ancient Greece and Shakespeare's England, there were groups of actors called the **chorus** who spoke lines of verse together. Combining voices increases the possibilities for beautiful and interesting sounds.

The two-voice poem, in particular, also allows the poet to explore a relationship between two people in a way that is almost like a play but keeps the emotional intensity of a short poem.

To help students focus on the similarities and differences of the two characters, suggest that they keep these questions in mind as they read:

- What words and phrases do they say together?
- What words and phrases do they say separately?
- What does this technique say about the characters?

TEACH

MAKE INFERENCES

Help students understand inferences by explaining that authors of literary works may be very explicit and direct about information they tell the reader or they may be indirect about it, so it's up to the reader to figure things out. Tell them that the author of "Double Doubles" could have had the character say "My name is Venus." That would be explicit and direct. Instead, the author chose an indirect way of saying this, allowing the name to find its own way into the reader's mind and, at the same time, leading to the imagery of the next lines.

■ English Learner Support

Making Inferences Provide students with more practice making inferences by creating scenarios with clues. Allow them to respond in their own language if necessary. Help them translate their words into English, asking them to repeat the words.

ASK STUDENTS what they know about a character if he is sweating, wipes his head with a handkerchief, and takes off his jacket. Use gestures to show what a person who is hot would do. *(The man is hot or nervous.)*
SUBSTANTIAL/MODERATE

ANNOTATION MODEL

Remind students that **inferences** are hints that reveal information about what characters think or feel. Tell students that the kinds of inferences they are looking for in this poem are hints indicating what the sisters feel about themselves, about each other, and about playing tennis. Point out that students may use circles and boxes to indicate inferences drawn from what the sisters say individually and underline inferences drawn from what they say simultaneously. Or they may create their own annotation methods, like color-coding.

 GET READY

MAKE INFERENCES

Poets rarely state directly every idea they want to express. However, since poets choose their words carefully, you often can find clues in the text that help build understanding. If you combine these clues with what you already know, you will be well on your way to identifying a poem's speaker or speakers and the ideas expressed in the poem.

An **inference** is a logical guess based on text evidence—the "clues" in the text—plus your own knowledge and experience. For an inference to be reasonable, it must be supported by **textual evidence** along with **previous knowledge and personal experience.** Using a diagram like the one below can help you make reasonable inferences.

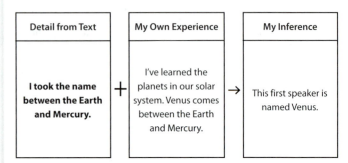

ANNOTATION MODEL NOTICE & NOTE

As you read, think about the elements of two-voice poems. You can also mark inferences that you make as you read. In the model, you can see one reader's notes about part of "Double Doubles."

The Williams sisters	The Williams sisters	*Each column represents one of the two sisters' voices.*
20 (Read each other better)	than <u>a</u> to <u>z</u>	
and everything between. Momentum	Momentum takes us to	*I can infer from this detail that the sisters have a close bond.*
the final tie-break. <u>Match point is only one</u>	<u>Match point is only one</u> quick ace away. . . .	*I wonder why they both speak this line but not the next one?*

416 Unit 5

BACKGROUND

J. Patrick Lewis (b. 1942) is an American poet who served as the Poetry Foundation's Children's Poet Laureate from 2011 to 2013. He has published numerous books of poetry; indeed, he says, "[W]hat truly transports me is poetry, and so I spend most of my working hours thinking of themes to develop into manuscripts." In addition to his prolific writing and editing career, Lewis regularly visits classrooms to spread appreciation for poetry.

DOUBLE DOUBLES
by J. Patrick Lewis

PREPARE TO COMPARE

As you read, keep track of who is speaking, and when. Add your knowledge to clues in the text to make inferences about the speakers and their perspective on their sport and their relationship.

I took the name
between the Earth
and Mercury.
We took our game   We took our game
5 to beaded stars above.   to beaded stars above.
My sister's   My sister's
   lobs and
volleys
so astonish me,   so astonish me,
10 the score
   our score
   is usually
plenty—   plenty—
   love.

NOTICE & NOTE

Notice & Note

Use the side margins to notice and note signposts in the text.

MAKE INFERENCES

Annotate: In lines 1–14, mark words that you think are sports terms.

Infer: Which sport are these speakers discussing? Who are these speakers? (Skim the rest of the poem to check.)

ANALYZE A TWO-VOICE POEM

Annotate: Mark examples of lines that are spoken by both voices.

Analyze: Why you think the poet chose these lines to be spoken by both voices?

Double Doubles 417

ENGLISH LEARNER SUPPORT

Confirm Understanding Have students choral read the poem. Start with Venus's voice first and then read Serena's voice. Stop after each sentence to ask students whether they need any words or phrases clarified. Explain the various tennis terms that appear in the text. Check for comprehension by asking yes-or-no questions (*Are the sisters playing against each other? Is the game almost over?*) or questions with one-word answers (*What are the sisters doing? When will the game end?*). **SUBSTANTIAL**

TEACH

AGAIN AND AGAIN

Remind students that this signpost refers to events, images, ideas, or particular words or phrases that repeat in a text. Authors use this kind of repetition to emphasize a point. In this poem, where repetition often means the combination of two voices, that emphasis is even more effective. (**Answer:** *The sisters will probably win this doubles match.*)

 ENGLISH LEARNER SUPPORT

Repeated Language Help students locate repeated words and phrases in the poem. Have them say the words. Check for proper pronunciation of vowels and consonants— especially the short *i* in *sisters*, the two consecutive voiceless consonants in *sisters, stars, astonish,* and the final trigraph in *match*. **SUBSTANTIAL**

 **NOTICE & NOTE**

AGAIN AND AGAIN

Notice & Note: In lines 19–32, mark two examples of teamwork.

Cause/Effect: What is the likely result of the teamwork, given this repeated idea?

15 where she'll be going.
We move together

The Williams sisters
20 read each other better,
and everything between.
Momentum

25 the final tie-break.
Match point is only one

30 I know why
double doubles
players play.

I play as if I know

We move together
like a fine machine.
The Williams sisters

than *a* to *z*.

Momentum
takes us to

Match point is only one
quick ace away.
As soon as I see sister
Venus rising,

double doubles
players play.

418 Unit 5

WHEN STUDENTS STRUGGLE...

Adjust for Graphic Elements If students are having difficulty understanding or following the text because of the graphic layout of the two voices, have them read each sister's portion of the poem separately. If the unusual line breaks and fragmented language pose challenges, advise students to read the poem as though it were regular prose, joining words and phrases that logically belong together and stopping when there is an end period.

NOTICE & NOTE

CHECK YOUR UNDERSTANDING

Answer these questions before moving on to the **Analyze the Text** section on the following page.

1 The back-and-forth between the two speakers is meant to represent —

   A a family argument

   B the age difference between the sisters

   C the way a tennis match is played

   D a cheering crowd

2 Which set of lines indicates that the Williams sisters consider each other an extraordinary tennis player?

   F *We took our game / to beaded stars above.* (lines 4–5)

   G *My sister's / lobs and / volleys / so astonish me* (lines 6–9)

   H *The Williams sisters / read each other better / than <u>a</u> to <u>z</u>.* (lines 19–21)

   J *Match point is only one / quick ace away.* (lines 26–27)

3 According to this poem, what advantage do the Williams sisters have over other players?

   A The moves of both sisters are always identical.

   B They both have been playing tennis for a long time.

   C Love for the game of tennis makes both of them great.

   D They each know everything about the way the other plays.

TEACH

CHECK YOUR UNDERSTANDING

Have students answer the questions independently.

Answers:

1. *C*

2. *G*

3. *D*

If they answer any questions incorrectly, have them reread the text to confirm their understanding. Then they may proceed to ANALYZE THE TEXT on p. 420.

Double Doubles 419

 ENGLISH LEARNER SUPPORT

Oral Assessment Use the following questions to asses students' comprehension and speaking skills:

1. Who are the two speakers in the poem? *(Venus and Serena Williams)*

2. Does each sister think the other is a great player? Which lines show it? *(My sister's / lobs and / volleys / so astonish me, lines 6–9.)*

3. Do the Williams sister have a special form of communication? Does this help them when they play tennis? *(Yes, they each know everything about the way the other plays.)*
   MODERATE/LIGHT

APPLY

ANALYZE THE TEXT
Possible answers:

1. **DOK 2:** The sisters respect and love each other. In lines 3–4, both took their game "to beaded stars above," meaning they played well. In line 9, each says that the other's tennis abilities "so astonish me." In lines 11–14, they both say "plenty" when they refer to "love," a pun on the tennis term.

2. **DOK 2:** Venus says, "the score," but Serena corrects her by saying "our score." The correction emphasizes that the two sisters are a unified team.

3. **DOK 2:** That they say things simultaneously and complete each other's thoughts reflect their sisterly bond and sense of teamwork.

4. **DOK 4:** In lines 29–30, "Venus rising" is another "sky" reference; it means that Venus is playing well. These references emphasize the sisters' importance in the world of tennis and the "out of this world" thrill that comes from winning a game.

5. **DOK 4:** In lines 15–18, the sisters anticipate each other's moves and play like "a fine machine." The theme these examples suggest is that people (specifically, siblings) can succeed by knowing each other well and working together.

RESEARCH
Review the Research Tip with students. Remind them to use reputable, reliable sources of information, like sites published by established news and sports organizations.

Extend Students may infer that the Williams sisters have played so well that their game has gone as far "up" as it can go; that "beaded stars above" refers to a heavenly tapestry; that "beaded stars" made by people represent the brightness of stars; both sisters are known for beaded hairstyles, and both are tennis stars; they have both challenged the tennis stars who came before them.

420 Unit 5

 RESPOND

ANALYZE THE TEXT
Support your responses with evidence from the text. 📓 **NOTEBOOK**

1. **Make Inferences** How do you think the sisters feel about each other? Which details support your inference?

2. **Interpret** In lines 10–11, how does the sister (Serena) correct what Venus says? Why do you think she makes this correction?

3. **Identify Patterns** Except for the first sentence, every sentence in the poem is "shared," with each speaker taking part. Why do you think the poet chose to include both speakers in almost every sentence?

4. **Synthesize** Lines 1–5 include references to the sky. What other lines make a similar reference? What do these references add to your understanding of the poem?

5. **Notice & Note** Earlier in this lesson, you identified two examples of teamwork in lines 19–32 of "Double Doubles." What is another example, earlier in the poem? What do the examples suggest about a theme for this poem?

RESEARCH TIP
As you research the careers of living people, consider watching interviews, news clips, commentary, and other video sources that you find at reliable websites.

RESEARCH
Research the tennis careers of Serena and Venus Williams. Use the organizer below to gather information and make comparisons.

QUESTION	VENUS	SERENA
When was each sister born?	1980	1981
Who introduced each sister to tennis?	Father	Father
As of 2017, what was each sister's highest ranking in singles? In doubles?	1 ; 1	1 ; 1
As of 2017, how many Grand Slam singles titles had each sister won?	7	23
As of 2016, how many Olympic gold medals had each sister won?	4	4

Extend With a partner, discuss the reference to "beaded stars" (line 5). How does it seem to apply to the sisters' careers? How does it add to the mental image created in lines 4–5 of the poem?

420 Unit 5

CREATE AND PRESENT

Write a Two-Voice Poem Write a two-voice poem that expresses two viewpoints about a subject.

- ❏ Choose two speakers (two real or imaginary people, or even two objects) who might have a perspective on the same topic.
- ❏ Draft the poem. Allow each speaker to voice his or her own thoughts and feelings and to respond to the other speaker. Remember that some lines should be voiced by both speakers.
- ❏ Review your draft with a classmate. Revise to make each speaker's views clearer or to point more clearly to a theme.
- ❏ You may wish to work with a partner to present your final version of the poem orally to the class.

Critique a Poem With a partner, plan and present an oral critique of "Double Doubles." Use the ideas below to guide your discussion.

- ❏ Review your notes about "Double Doubles," and then read the poem aloud with your partner.
- ❏ Consider how successfully the poet created two speakers and structured the poem to show each speaker's thoughts and feelings. Is the poem easy to read or challenging? In addition, discuss the poem's theme. Include text evidence for your views.
- ❏ Together, organize your comments. Practice and work to communicate your ideas, speaking clearly and at a good volume. Use gestures to help your audience understand. Be prepared to respond to questions after you present your critique.

RESPOND TO THE ESSENTIAL QUESTION

How do sports bring together friends, families, and communities?

Gather Information Review your notes on "Double Doubles." Then, add relevant details to your Response Log. As you determine which information to include, think about:

- the admiration that athletes may have for each other
- the nature and advantages of teamwork
- the feeling of being close to winning a game

At the end of the unit, use your notes to help you write a short story.

RESPOND

Go to **Writing as a Process** in the **Writing Studio** to learn more.

Go to **Participating in a Collaborative Discussion** in the **Speaking and Listening Studio** for more help.

ACADEMIC VOCABULARY

As you write about and discuss what you learned from the two-voice poem, be sure to use the Academic Vocabulary words. Check off each of the words that you use.

- ❏ attitude
- ❏ consume
- ❏ goal
- ❏ purchase
- ❏ style

Double Doubles 421

APPLY

CREATE AND PRESENT

Write a Two-Voice Poem Point out to students that the list on p. 421 should be used to plan their poems. Help students choose a subject with two different viewpoints by suggesting they consider two eyewitness accounts of a famous historical event, an athletic game, or even a family function. Explain that these accounts could be drastically different or similar but with a slightly different perspective.

For **writing support** for students at varying proficiency levels, see the **Text X-Ray** on page 414D.

Critique a Poem Remind students that they are expressing their opinions in a critique and to address the questions detailed on p. 421. Encourage partners to participate equally in the preparation and presentation of their critiques.

RESPOND TO THE ESSENTIAL QUESTION

Allow time for students to add details from "Double Doubles" to their Unit 5 Response Logs. Encourage students to write about their own experiences with successful teamwork.

ENGLISH LEARNER SUPPORT

Discuss with Partners Restate the oral critique activity as a question: What features of the poem did you like or dislike and why? Allow students to work with partners to review their notes and the text for details that answer the question. Provide these sentence frames to help students formulate their ideas for the critiques: *The lines which successfully show two speakers communicated are _____. The lines which successfully show each speaker's thoughts and feelings are _____. The lines that were easy/difficult to read are _____.* **MODERATE**

Double Doubles 421

APPLY

COMPARE THEME

Before groups work on completing their Venn diagrams, emphasize that they are looking for details that suggest a theme or a message, about family and sports, not poetic or graphical elements that the two works have in common.

ANALYZE THE TEXTS

Possible answers:

1. **DOK 3:** *The Crossover is a verse novel with one speaker telling his view of a situation. "Double Doubles" is a poem in which two characters speak. The organizational structure of each is appropriate to its content: The Crossover is composed of separate scenes, like a novel; "Double Doubles" is a self-contained poem.*

2. **DOK 2:** *In both selections, the siblings are competitive but love and appreciate each other. In* The Crossover, *the brother says, "If we didn't love each other, / we'd HATE each other." In "Double Doubles," the sisters say, "the/our score / is usually / plenty / love."*

3. **DOK 4:** *In* The Crossover, *the poet uses similes, metaphors, and personification. They help him support his theme with movement, excitement, and conflict. In "Double Doubles" the poet uses similes and metaphors to support a theme of strength that comes from love and sharing.*

4. **DOK 4:** *Answers will vary.* **Possible answer**: *Family members can compete in sports but still respect and love each other.*

 RESPOND

from **THE CROSSOVER**
Novel in Verse
by Kwame Alexander

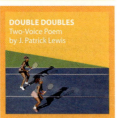

DOUBLE DOUBLES
Two-Voice Poem
by J. Patrick Lewis

Collaborate & Compare

COMPARE THEME

The scenes from both *The Crossover* and "Double Doubles" are about siblings who play sports. Because the poems are about the same topic, they share many similarities—but there are differences, too.

A poem's **theme** is a message about life that the poet wishes to convey to the reader. Poets rarely state themes directly. The reader must infer the theme based on details from the text. Work with a group and complete the diagram below to help you analyze and record similarities and differences in the two poets' work. Think about how these details affect your understanding of the poems' themes. One detail has been included.

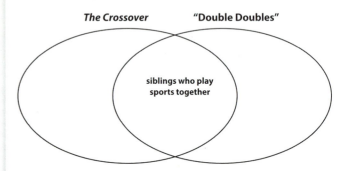

ANALYZE THE TEXTS

Discuss these questions in your group.

1. **Critique** With your group, discuss the organizational structure of each selection. How are the selections' structures different? Is the organization of each selection appropriate to its content? Explain.

2. **Compare** With your group, review details from both selections that express how playing a sport affects the siblings' relationship. Cite text evidence in your discussion.

3. **Analyze** What types of figurative language appear in each poem? How do they help you understand each poem's theme?

4. **Synthesize** What have you learned from these selections about how sports can affect siblings who play together?

422 Unit 5

ENGLISH LEARNER SUPPORT

Ask Questions Use the following questions to help students compare the selections:

1. What does each work say about being siblings?
2. What does each work say about being an athlete?
3. How is the brothers' relationship different from the sisters' relationship?

Remind students that they are looking for details in the texts that support their ideas.
MODERATE/LIGHT

422   Unit 5

RESPOND

COLLABORATE AND PRESENT

Now, your group can continue exploring the ideas in these texts by identifying and comparing their themes. Follow these steps:

Go to **Giving a Presentation** in the **Speaking and Listening Studio** for help.

1. **Identify Important Details** With your group, review your completed Venn Diagram. Identify the most important details from each poem that you listed. Discuss points of agreement and disagreement about these details and try to come to a consensus. Remember to cite evidence from the texts.

2. **Determine Themes** Work together to infer the theme of each poem based on details. Then, decide on a statement that concisely expresses each theme. Use the graphic organizers below to help organize your thoughts as you work together.

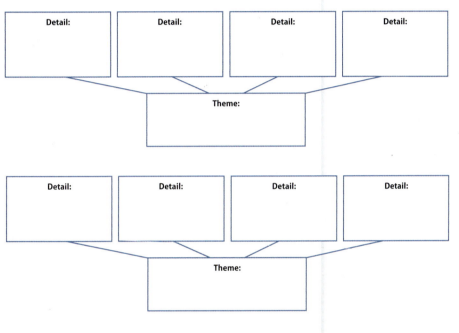

3. **Compare Themes** As a group, decide whether the themes of the selections are similar or different. Use details from your analysis of the poems to support your theme statements.

4. **Make a Class Presentation** In your group, practice making a presentation of your ideas to other students in the class. Be sure to clearly state your position about whether the poems have similar or different themes. Use your graphic organizers or other visuals to make your presentation clear and concise.

Collaborate & Compare 423

WHEN STUDENTS STRUGGLE . . .

Identify Themes Students might find it difficult to identify and articulate themes in two works that do not have a clear moral to the story. To help them, ask students to try a different approach by seeing things from the perspectives of the characters themselves. Ask students what Venus or Serena might have to say about being sisters and teammates, or what the speaker of *The Crossover* might have to say about playing on the same team as his brother. By imagining themselves in the lives of the characters, students might find the theme that is escaping them.

APPLY

COLLABORATE AND PRESENT

Explain that a collaboration means that group members are working together as a team. Remind students to allow each member of the group to participate and contribute his or her perspective on the topic.

1. **Identify Important Details** As students identify their details, circulate among the groups, and check that each student is getting the opportunity to participate. Encourage members of the group to evaluate how well their list of details can be used to determine a theme.

2. **Determine Themes** Circulate among the groups, making sure students are completing the graphic organizer properly. Suggest that students come up with multiple themes. Remind them that a theme is not a topic like "sports." A theme makes a statement *about* some aspect of life.

3. **Compare Themes** Explain to students that they may decide that the themes are similar, different, or a little of each. Recommend that the groups seek consensus about their choice of themes.

4. **Make a Class Presentation** Before students deliver their presentations, have them decide on the format. For example, one student might play the role of the moderator, who introduces the other group members. Pairs could then present themes and supporting details.

Depending on the size of the group, students who might not have a chance to present a theme or details can answer questions for the group during the final segment.

INDEPENDENT READING

READER'S CHOICE

Select and Preview Have students review their Unit 5 Response Log and consider what they've already learned about sports as a unifying force. As they select their Independent Reading selections, encourage them to ask themselves what more they want to know.

NOTICE & NOTE

Explain that some selections may contain multiple signposts; others may contain only one. And the same type of signpost can occur many times in the same text.

LEARNING MINDSET

Persistence Fans love watching athletes reach deep and try hard to succeed — but you don't have to be on a field or a court to persist and bring home a win. Classroom victories may not be dramatic, but it is a point in anyone's favor to acquire a skill or insight they may not have had yesterday. Encourage students to ask for help when they need it, and their peers to share help graciously. Those who persist can prevail.

INDEPENDENT READING

 ESSENTIAL QUESTION:

How do sports bring together friends, families, and communities?

Reader's Choice

Setting a Purpose Select one or more of these options from your eBook to continue your exploration of the Essential Question.

- Read the descriptions to see which text grabs your interest.
- Think about which genres you enjoy reading.

Notice & Note

In this unit, you practiced noticing and noting three signposts: **Words of the Wiser, Tough Questions,** and **Aha Moment.** As you read independently, these signposts and others will aid your understanding. Below are the anchor questions to ask when you read literature and nonfiction.

Reading Literature: Stories, Poems, and Plays		
Signpost	Anchor Question	Lesson
Contrasts and Contradictions	Why did the character act that way?	p. 99
Aha Moment	How might this change things?	p. 3
Tough Questions	What does this make me wonder about?	p. 362
Words of the Wiser	What's the lesson for the character?	p. 363
Again and Again	Why might the author keep bringing this up?	p. 3
Memory Moment	Why is this memory important?	p. 2

Reading Nonfiction: Essays, Articles, and Arguments		
Signpost	Anchor Question(s)	Lesson
Big Questions	What surprised me?	p. 265
	What did the author think I already knew?	p. 183
	What challenged, changed, or confirmed what I already knew?	p. 437
Contrasts and Contradictions	What is the difference, and why does it matter?	p. 183
Extreme or Absolute Language	Why did the author use this language?	p. 182
Numbers and Stats	Why did the author use these numbers or amounts?	p. 264
Quoted Words	Why was this person quoted or cited, and what did this add?	p. 437
Word Gaps	Do I know this word from someplace else? Does it seem like technical talk for this topic? Do clues in the sentence help me understand the word?	p. 265

424 Unit 5

ENGLISH LEARNER SUPPORT

Describe in Writing Support students at varying proficiency levels:

- Guide students to find sight words in a sample text and copy them into their notebooks. Then model reading those words aloud, defining them when possible with mime or gesture. (For example: *I, you, he, she, this, that, come, go, yes, no, on, off.*) **SUBSTANTIAL**

- Furnish the following sentence stem: *Well-chosen verbs and modifiers bring ____ to a short story.* (power, nuance, sensory elements, musicality, definition) Ask students to identify strong verbs and modifiers in a sample text. **MODERATE**

- Challenge students in groups to write a group story about benign aliens who arrive on Earth just in time to celebrate the last day of school. Advise the group to elect one student who will make notes and write the story. Encourage all students to suggest characters, a conflict, a plot, and a resolution. Invite a group member to read the story to the class. **LIGHT**

424 Unit 5

INDEPENDENT READING

You can preview these texts in Unit 5 of your eBook.

Then, check off the text or texts that you select to read on your own.

☐
SHORT STORY
Batting After Sophie
Sue Macy

Find out how a young softball player learns to respect her coach's decisions and become a true team player.

☐
SHORT STORY
Amigo Brothers
Piri Thomas

Learn how Felix and Antonio respond to an opportunity to box that threatens to undermine their friendship.

☐
BLOG
Bridging the Generational Divide Between a Football Father and Soccer Son
John McCormick

Can people who are passionate about different sports ever understand each other's point of view?

☐
SCIENCE WRITING
Arc of Triumph
Nick D'Alto

How can understanding the science of the parabola, or curve, improve your performance in sports?

Collaborate and Share   Work with a partner to discuss what you learned from at least one of your independent readings.

- Give a brief synopsis or summary of the text.
- Describe any signposts that you noticed in the text and explain what they revealed to you.
- Describe what you most enjoyed or found most challenging about the text. Give specific examples.
- Decide if you would recommend the text to others. Why or why not?

 Go to the **Reading Studio** for more resources on **Notice & Note**.

Independent Reading 425

INDEPENDENT READING

MATCHING STUDENTS TO TEXTS

Use the following information to guide students in choosing their texts.

Batting After Sophie   **Lexile: 760L**
  Genre: short story
  Overall Rating: Accessible

Bridging the Generational Divide Between a Football Father and Soccer Son   **Lexile: 1040L**
  Genre: blog
  Overall Rating: Challenging

Arc of Triumph   **Lexile: 830L**
  Genre: science writing
  Overall Rating: Accessible

Amigo Brothers   **Lexile: 910L**
  Genre: short story
  Overall Rating: Accessible

Collaborate and Share   To assess how well students read the selections, walk around the room and listen to their conversations. Encourage students to be focused and specific in their comments.

 for Assessment

- Independent Reading Selection Tests

 Encourage students to visit the **Reading Studio** to download a handy bookmark of **NOTICE & NOTE** signposts.

WHEN STUDENTS STRUGGLE . . .

Keep a Reading Log   As students read their selected texts, have them keep a reading log for each selection to note signposts and their thoughts about them. Use their logs to assess how well they are noticing and reflecting on elements of the texts.

Reading Log for (title)		
Location	**Signpost I Noticed**	**My Notes about It**

Independent Reading 425

PLAN

UNIT 5 Tasks

- **WRITE A SHORT STORY**

MENTOR TEXT
BALL HAWK
Short Story by
JOSEPH BRUCHAC

LEARNING OBJECTIVES

Writing Task
- Write a short story about sports or game-playing.
- Use strategies to plan and organize material.
- Develop a focused, structured draft.
- Use the mentor text as a model for writing strong introductions and descriptive language.
- Revise drafts, incorporating feedback from peers.
- Edit drafts for correct punctuation of dialogue.
- Use a rubric to evaluate writing.
- Publish writing to share it with an audience.
- **Language** Brainstorm ideas for a story, develop its essential elements, and then take a meaningful role in writing the story with classmates.

Speaking Task
- Adapt a short story for presentation.
- Present a short story to a class.
- Use appropriate verbal and nonverbal techniques.
- **Language** Share information using the sentence stem *A good short story is* _____.

Assign the Writing Task in *Ed.*

RESOURCES
- Unit 5 Response Log
- Writing Studio: Writing Narratives
- Grammar Studio : Module 15: Lesson 1: Quotation Marks

426A Unit 5

PLAN

Language X-Ray: English Language Support

Use the instruction below and the supports and scaffolds in the Teacher's Edition to help you guide students of different proficiency levels.

INTRODUCE THE WRITING TASK

Explain that **short stories** are an ancient form of entertainment: before books were printed (and before most people could read) people told one another stories based on events or things they "made up." Bedtime stories and beloved folk tales from every culture on Earth are all a part of the short story tradition.

In groups, invite students to make up a story based on a sentence stem or a topic of their choosing. (For example, *I knew I was in trouble when ____. Or: I was sure I was right, but then I found out ____.*) As one or two students take notes, invite group members to suggest or act out characters, setting, or a problem or conflict, a sequence of events, or a conclusion. To generate ideas, invite students to tell one another familiar stories and encourage them to invent and add details. Challenge one or more students to take the group's notes and use them to create a short story. Invite a group member to present the story to the class.

WRITING

Use Descriptive Language

Tell students that descriptive language choices can change what readers think about things, people, and ideas in a short story. Have students note the differences in meaning in these word sets: *small* and *puny, careful* and *careless, bold* and *wild*.

Use the following supports with students at varying proficiency levels:

- Model spelling and reading adjectives with close correspondents in Spanish: *curious/curioso; delicious/delicioso; numerous/numeroso*. Invite students to suggest other examples. (*fabulous/fabuloso; glorious/glorioso; mysterious/misterioso*) **SUBSTANTIAL**
- Present sentence frames for practice using descriptive language. For example: *She was ___, ___, and ___. He was ___, ___, and ___.* **MODERATE**
- Have students work in groups to identify descriptive language in a sample text and come up with synonyms or antonyms for the words. **LIGHT**

SPEAKING

Tell Stories

Encourage students to tell and share stories of their choosing. Guide them to understand the short story elements present in the stories they have chosen and help them use this understanding to shape and refine their writing ideas.

Use the following supports with students at varying proficiency levels:

- Ask students questions about stories, such as *What is your favorite story? Who is the main character? How does the story end?* Offer supports with Spanish cognates where possible. **SUBSTANTIAL**
- Invite volunteers to read a brief section from a piece of fiction aloud. Ask students to identify and describe the main character. **MODERATE**
- Invite volunteers to read a brief section from a piece of fiction aloud. Ask others to identify colorful descriptive language and offer synonyms. **LIGHT**

WRITING

WRITE A SHORT STORY

Introduce students to the Writing Task by reviewing the introductory paragraph with them. Encourage students to refer to the notes they recorded in the Unit 5 Response Log for inspiration and ideas about characters, conflict, and plot. Stress the importance of addressing the theme of sports as something that can unite friends, family, and community.

 For **writing support** for students at varying proficiency levels, see the **Language X-Ray** on p. 426B.

USE THE MENTOR TEXT

Author's Craft Note that "Ball Hawk" is told in first-person narration from the point of view of the main character, Mitchell. The narrator tells the story the way you might tell a story to a friend. He begins with a quote about Uncle Tommy and then launches into the story. Suggest that students look at the order in which the narrator unveils the plot and the narrator's use of dialogue and language for ideas for their own writing.

Vivid Descriptive Language Have students note the author's use of language in paragraphs 71 and 72. What details make the flight of the hawk come alive? ("*caught it out of midair with its claws*") Point out other examples of vivid descriptive language and have students note how they bring the story to life.

WRITING PROMPT

Review the prompt with students. Encourage them to ask questions about any part of the assignment that is unclear. Remind students that they can consider a broad range of possibilities as they frame their stories: the sport, the setting, the characters, and the conflict. Invite them to brainstorm with each other alternatives before they settle on the defining elements of their short stories.

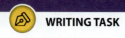 **WRITING TASK**

Write a Short Story

 Go to the **Writing Studio** for help writing your short story.

This unit focuses on the ways in which sports and games affect society and individuals. For this writing task, you will write a short story that portrays some aspect of sports or game-playing. For an example of a well-written short story you can use as a mentor text, review the story "Ball Hawk."

As you write your short story, you can use the notes from your Response Log, which you filled out after reading the texts in this unit.

Writing Prompt

Read the information in the box below.

This is the topic or context for your short story.

> Many people enjoy playing individual and team sports and games, ranging from soccer to chess to video games. Competition can teach us many things about ourselves.

Think carefully about the following question.

This is the Essential Question for this unit. How would you answer this question based on the texts in this unit?

> How do sports bring together friends, families, and communities?

Now mark the words that identify exactly what you are being asked to produce.

Write a short story about a character who is involved in a team or individual sport, or in a game played by one or more people. You may present either a positive view or a critical view of the sport or game.

Be sure to—

Review these points as you write and again when you finish. Make any needed changes.

- ❏ establish, develop, and resolve a conflict
- ❏ introduce and develop characters, events, and setting with dialogue, pacing, and descriptive details
- ❏ include a series of related events that lead to a climax
- ❏ use transitions among paragraphs to show sequence
- ❏ end with a conclusion that reveals a theme

 LEARNING MINDSET

Try Again It is not easy to write good fiction. Encourage students to revisit their drafts and try another approach if the first one is not effective. Or, they might consider trying an entirely new approach. Persistence pays dividends in every endeavor. Suggest that students might enjoy taking on a challenge and then well-earned pride in rising to meet it.

WRITING TASK

1 Plan

Authors of narratives make many choices as they plan their work. Think about these questions as you begin planning your story.

- **CHARACTERS:** What does the main character look like? How does he or she speak and act? Who are the other characters in the story?
- **POINT OF VIEW:** Who tells the story? If a character narrates the story, using pronouns *I* or *we*, the author is using a first-person point of view. If the narrator is not a story character, the author is using a third-person point of view. A third-person narrator may be limited (describing events as characters see them) or omniscient (revealing characters' thoughts and feelings).
- **SETTING:** The setting of your story is the time and place in which it occurs. Where does the story take place?
- **CONFLICT:** Conflict is the struggle between people or ideas that the main character must overcome. What does he or she want? What obstacles must he or she overcome to achieve that goal?

Short Story Planning Table	
Characters	
Point of View	
Setting	
Conflict	

Background Reading Review the notes you have taken in your Response Log after reading the texts in this unit. These texts provide background reading that may give you some ideas that you can use when planning your short story.

Go to **Writing Narratives: Point of View and Characters** for help in planning your short story.

Notice & Note
From Reading to Writing

As you plan your story, apply what you've learned about signposts to your own writing. Remember that writers use common features, called signposts, to help convey their message to readers.

Think about how you can incorporate evidence of an **Aha Moment** into your story.

Go to the **Reading Studio** for more resources on **Notice & Note**.

Use the notes from your Response Log as you plan your short story.

Write a Short Story 427

WRITING

1 PLAN

Allow time for students to discuss the topic with partners or in small groups and then to complete the planning chart independently.

English Learner Support

Understand Academic Language Make sure students understand words and phrases used in the chart, such as *characters, setting,* and *conflict*. Work with them to fill in the blank sections, providing text that they can copy into their charts as needed. **MODERATE**

NOTICE AND NOTE

AHA MOMENT Ask students to use signposts in their story. One of the most important signposts is the Aha moment. Remind students that these moments show visible shifts in the thinking or understanding of a character about something important. When a detective realizes that a piece of evidence that was previously thought to be unimportant will probably solve a mystery, he or she is having an Aha moment. Ask students to brainstorm ideas for how one of their characters comes to understand something important.

Background Reading As they plan their essays, remind students to refer to the notes they took in the Response Log. Their notes will provide clues as to how they responded to various selections and what most interests them about sports and games. Suggest that they also review the selections to find additional ideas about what they might want to include in their writing.

TO CHALLENGE STUDENTS...

Expand Themes Sports can be a lens through which a writer zeroes in on big ideas. Challenge students to plan a story by choosing an angle or issue they'd like to address before they settle on writing about a baseball or some other sport. They might want to address issues of gender or ethnicity, culture and subcultures, misplaced hopes or thwarted ambitions, family, trustworthiness, or love. Ask them to imagine a conflict through which they might deliver their broader message. Then invite them to explore and develop that conflict through characters engaged in sports.

Write a Short Story 427

WRITING

Organize Your Ideas Review with students the structure for short story plots.

Point out that some writers might begin their drafts "in the middle," with the climax or most important event around which the story is built happening in the first pages. Stress to students that the important thing is to find a way to draw their readers in right away.

2 DEVELOP A DRAFT

Remind students to follow their charts as they draft their stories, but point out that they can still make changes to their writing plan during this stage. As they write, they may decide to consider modifying their opening, refining their character development, or adding details to their plot.

■ English Learner Support

Create a Collaborative Short Story Simplify the writing task and provide direct support by having students work in pairs to draw and write captions for the main events of their stories. **SUBSTANTIAL/MODERATE**

 WRITING TASK

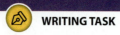 Go to **Writing Narratives: Narrative Structure** for help organizing your short story.

Organize Your Ideas After gathering ideas for your story's characters, point of view, setting, and conflict, you need to determine the plot. The term *plot* refers to the series of events in a story. The major events in the plot of most stories are defined in the story map below. You can use a similar diagram to record ideas for the plot of your own story.

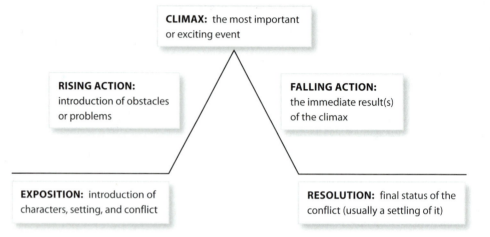

- **CLIMAX:** the most important or exciting event
- **RISING ACTION:** introduction of obstacles or problems
- **FALLING ACTION:** the immediate result(s) of the climax
- **EXPOSITION:** introduction of characters, setting, and conflict
- **RESOLUTION:** final status of the conflict (usually a settling of it)

2 Develop a Draft

 You may prefer to draft your short story online.

Once you have completed your planning activities, you will be ready to draft your short story. Refer to your plot diagram and any notes you took as you studied the texts in the unit. These will provide a kind of map for you to follow as you write. Using a word processor or online writing application makes it easier to make changes or move sentences around later when you are ready to revise your first draft.

428 Unit 5

WHEN STUDENTS STRUGGLE...

Develop a Draft Writers sometimes find plot development challenging; when they get stuck they may wonder "what ought to happen next?" If students struggle with the plots of their short stories, suggest a chronological structure. Ask: *How could you develop your work around an eventful evening, a long weekend, or a soccer season?* Likewise, a condensed plot could track an event with a built-in narrative arc: an away game with a crosstown rival or a Homecoming Day parade. Remind them that a strong plot can be relatively simple. Whatever happens next can be important to your characters, and a good fit for your short story.

WRITING

WRITING TASK

Use the Mentor Text

▶ **Author's Craft**
Your introduction is your first chance to draw readers into your story. Introduce the conflict early to create suspense. Note how the author captures the readers' attention, introduces a conflict, and creates suspense in the opening sentences of "Ball Hawk."

"Indians invented baseball."
   That's what Uncle Tommy Fox said on the day I was ready to throw in my glove and quit the Long Pond High School team for good. It was one of his typically cryptic remarks and, as usual, it started me thinking.
   Quite frankly, if Uncle Tommy hadn't come into my life when he did, I probably would have ended up dyeing my hair purple and going goth.

The author opens the story with an intriguing quotation that makes readers want to know more. Then he introduces the conflict of the story: The narrator wants to quit the team, but Uncle Tommy doesn't want him to.

Apply What You've Learned To capture your readers' attention, you might open your story with dialogue. Providing clues about characters and the obstacles they have to overcome is another good way to begin.

▶ **Genre Characteristics**
To develop characters and make them believable, authors may describe how characters look, act, talk, and think. Notice how the author of "Ball Hawk" creates a vivid picture of Uncle Tommy.

Or that this broad-shouldered old Indian guy with long gray braids and a friendly face really did seem to like me and enjoy taking on that role of being an uncle. Or that he knew more about being Indian, really being Indian, than anyone else I'd ever met. He also had a sense of humor and we both needed it when it came to me and baseball.

The author (speaking through the main character, the narrator) shows what the character looks like, tells us what he knows, and tells us that he has a sense of humor.

Apply What You've Learned To help your readers understand and visualize your characters, include vivid, precise words and phrases as well as sensory details in your description.

Write a Short Story   **429**

WHY THIS MENTOR TEXT?

"Ball Hawk" serves as a solid example of short-story form. Use the instruction below to help students model the mentor text for writing strong introductions and vivid, precise detail in their short stories.

USE THE MENTOR TEXT

Author's Craft Ask a volunteer to read aloud the introduction to "Ball Hawk." Note that the author introduces the main character, establishes point of view, presents a conflict, and perhaps gives a hint to his plot, all in the second sentence. Ask: *How do you think this conflict might play out?* (Mitchell may wrestle with his desire to quit baseball. We will see what he chooses to do.)

Invite students to propose aloud conflicts they can summarize concisely to kick off an entertaining short story. Ask: *What kind of a conflict or problem could drive your story? How could you rephrase that, so a character was thinking or saying it?*

Genre Characteristics Ask students to identify the adjectives that paint a textual portrait of Uncle Tommy. (*broad-shouldered, old; long, gray, friendly*) Then suggest that they practice the art of descriptive prose with basic observation and note-taking. They might start with lively moments like a family gathering or the school cafeteria in the minutes before the bell. Say: *Try studying what you see and hear, like a reporter or secret agent. Take notes on it. Fine-tune them as you continue to watch and listen, to try to make word pictures.*

 ENGLISH LEARNER SUPPORT

Use the Mentor Text Use the following supports with students at varying proficiency levels:

- In their consumable texts, ask students to circle sight words in the selection. Display the words you want students to find and model pronunciation of each word. Choose words that can be defined with gesture or pantomime. (For example: *I, you, up, down, on, off, he, she, sit, stand, walk, write.*) **SUBSTANTIAL**

- Ask students to circle or underline descriptive language in their consumable text. In groups, invite them to draw pictures based on people or things vividly described in the story. **MODERATE**

- In groups, challenge students to come up with an alternative conflict that could drive a story about the same characters, in the same setting as "Ball Hawk." Ask them to craft a basic plot based on five-part structure. **LIGHT**

Write a Short Story   **429**

WRITING

3 REVISE

Have students answer each question in the chart to determine how they can improve their drafts. Invite volunteers to model their revision techniques.

With a Partner Have students ask peer reviewers to evaluate the form and content of their short stories. Guide reviewers to make notes that answer the following questions:

- Does my introduction grab your attention?
- Have I established a clear conflict? How might I improve this element?
- How did I handle exposition, or setting the background, for my story?
- Are my characters believable?
- How well-structured is my plot? What parts of it may need to be strengthened?
- What could I do to improve the descriptive detail in my story?

Students should use the reviewer's feedback to strengthen structure, characterization, and language in their short stories.

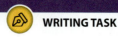 **WRITING TASK**

 Go to **Writing Narratives: The Language of Narratives** for help revising your short story.

3 Revise

On Your Own Once you have written your draft, go back and look for ways to improve your short story. As you reread and revise, think about whether you have achieved your purpose. The Revision Guide will help you focus on specific elements to make your writing stronger.

Revision Guide

Ask Yourself	Tips	Revision Techniques
1. Does my introduction grab readers' attention?	**Highlight** the introduction.	**Introduce** a character. **Add** dialogue and descriptions of setting.
2. Are my characters easy to imagine and believable?	**Underline** examples of characters' authentic words and actions.	**Add** words and actions that seem authentic.
3. How well does the setting affect characters and help shape the plot?	**Highlight** details of setting. **Underline** details that affect characters and help shape the plot.	**Add** sensory details to descriptions of setting.
4. Is the conflict in the story clear? Do events build to a climax?	**Circle** details about the conflict. **Highlight** the climax.	**Mark** the beginning of each event. **Add** a strong climax.
5. Does the pacing keep the action moving, building interest and suspense?	**Underline** events that build interest and suspense.	**Delete** any unnecessary events.
6. Does my conclusion reflect a theme, or message about life?	**Highlight** the conclusion. **Underline** phrases or sentences that reflect the theme.	**Insert** phrases or sentences that give strong hints about and/or state the theme.

ACADEMIC VOCABULARY
As you conduct your **peer review,** be sure to use these words.

☐ attitude
☐ consume
☐ goal
☐ purchase
☐ style

With a Partner Once you and your partner have worked through the Revision Guide on your own, exchange papers and evaluate each other's stories in a **peer review**. Provide revision suggestions for at least three of the items in the guide. Explain why you think your partner's draft should be revised and what your suggestions are.

When receiving feedback from your partner, listen attentively and ask questions to make sure you understand the revision suggestions.

 ENGLISH LEARNER SUPPORT

Use Modifiers Explain that writers use modifiers to add color and definition to their work. Have students identify the adjectives in this passage:

> Gracie was a *tall, athletic* girl, with a *proud* way of walking and an *easy, open* smile that soon put strangers at ease.

Encourage students to revise their short stories to include colorful modifiers.
LIGHT

4 Edit

Once you have addressed the organization, development, and flow of ideas, improve the finer points of your draft. Edit for the proper use of standard English conventions and correct any misspellings or grammatical errors.

Language Conventions

Correct Punctuation of Dialogue Dialogue is what characters say to each other in a story. Errors in the punctuation of dialogue can confuse readers about who is speaking or about when characters stop speaking and action resumes. Here are some rules for punctuating dialogue.

Use quotation marks to enclose a direct quotation—a character's exact words.

- "Time to check on the hawks," he said.

Direct quotations usually begin with an uppercase letter. However, when the speaker interrupts a quoted sentence, the second part of the quotation begins with a lowercase letter.

- "Mitchell," he said, "things that are supposed to come easy aren't always that easy to do."

A period or a comma is always placed inside the closing quotation marks. The same is true of a question mark or an exclamation point unless the entire sentence is a question or an exclamation.

- "I quit!" I yelled, standing up and throwing my glove out onto the field. "I'm done with it."

Begin a new paragraph each time the speaker changes.

- "Why'd you say that?" Uncle Tommy finally asked in a soft voice. "I hate this game!"

5 Publish

Finalize your short story and choose a way to share it with your audience. Consider these options:

- Read your short story aloud to the class.
- Post your short story on a classroom or school website.
- Submit your short story to a literary magazine.

WRITING TASK

Go to **Quotation Marks** in the **Grammar Studio** to learn more.

Write a Short Story **431**

WHEN STUDENTS STRUGGLE . . .

Correct Punctuation of Dialogue If students are struggling with the fine points of attribution, have them review sports news stories. Distribute among students a sports story of local interest, and ask them to circle or underline quotations marks, commas, and periods, as well as split paragraphs denoting speech. Encourage students to read similar stories independently, noting dialogue punctuation style.

WRITING

4 EDIT

Suggest that students read their stories aloud to assess how clearly and smoothly they have presented their ideas. Guide them to edit for descriptive language to add color and definition to their texts. Remind them of the basics of story craft: a central conflict or problem; solid characterization; a credible plot built around a climactic event.

LANGUAGE CONVENTIONS

Correct Punctuation of Dialogue Review the information about punctuation with students. Then discuss the sample sentences in the chart, noting that *attribution* is a term referring to who said what: as in *she said* this and *he said* that.

Display the following examples of incorrectly punctuated dialogue and ask students to correct them.

- "I'm not sure I can run fast enough, he said. (*Quote should be closed after the word* enough.)
- "That's it", she said. "I've had it." (*Closing quote after* first it *is incorrect.*)

■ **English Learner Support**

Correct Punctuation of Dialogue Display punctuation marks, including opened and closed quotes, a comma, and a period. Model reading a sample passage, with changes in intonation and pauses at each mark. Refer to each displayed mark as you read it.

5 PUBLISH

Students can read their short stories to the class and/or post their work to a classroom or school website. Encourage others to read each other's texts and write constructive comments about them. The authors can then respond to their comments.

Write a Short Story **431**

WRITING

USE THE SCORING GUIDE

Allow students time to read the scoring guide and to ask questions about any words, phrases, or ideas that are unclear. Then have partners exchange final drafts of their short stories. Ask them to score their partner's essay using the scoring guide. To support their analysis, encourage partners to make notes on their partner's work as a teacher might, with brief comments as to strengths or shortcomings in content and form. Ask them to use a colored pen or marker for their notes.

WRITING TASK

Use the scoring guide to evaluate your short story.

Writing Task Scoring Guide: Short Story

	Organization/Progression	Development of Ideas	Use of Language and Conventions
4	• The event sequence is smooth and clearly structured, creating suspense and building to a strong, satisfying conclusion. • The pacing is effective. • Transition words are successfully used to signal shifts in setting. • The conclusion clearly reflects a theme, or message, about life.	• A conflict is skillfully introduced, developed, and resolved. • A clear setting is effectively used to shape the plot. • Characters are well developed, compelling, and believable. • Dialogue and descriptions are used successfully.	• A consistent point of view is maintained. • Vivid, precise words and phrases, as well as sensory language, are used to describe the setting and the characters. • Spelling, capitalization, and punctuation are correct. • Grammar and usage are correct.
3	• The event sequence is generally well structured and creates some suspense, but it includes some extraneous events. • Pacing is somewhat uneven and confusing. • Transition words are used sporadically. • The conclusion hints at a possible theme or message but does not present it clearly.	• A conflict is introduced, developed, and resolved. • The setting somewhat shapes and affects the characters and the conflict. • Characters are interesting and have some believable traits. • Dialogue and descriptions are not consistently effective.	• The point of view is mostly consistent. • Some descriptive words and phrases are used, but there could be more sensory details. • Spelling, capitalization, and punctuation are correct. • Some grammatical and usage errors are repeated in the story.
2	• Some of the story's events are structured unclearly and distract from the plot. • Pacing is choppy or distracting. • Transition words are used ineffectively, if at all. • The conclusion does not reflect a theme, or message, about life.	• The conflict is introduced but not developed or resolved. • The setting is not clearly established and does not impact the story. • Characters are not adequately developed. • The story lacks sufficient dialogue and descriptions.	• The point of view is inconsistent. • The story lacks precise words and phrases and has little sensory language. • Spelling, capitalization, and punctuation are often incorrect but do not make reading difficult. • There are some grammar and usage errors, but the ideas are often still clear.
1	• The story does not have a clear sequence of events or plot. • There is no evidence of pacing. • Transition words are not used. • The conclusion is inappropriate to the story or is missing.	• The story has no identifiable conflict. • The setting is vague. • Characters are underdeveloped or not believable. • Dialogue and descriptions are missing.	• A clear point of view has not been established. • The story lacks precise language and sensory details. • Many spelling, capitalization, and punctuation errors are present. • Many grammatical and usage errors obscure the meaning of the writer's ideas.

Reflect on the Unit

By completing your short story, you have created a writing product that pulls together and expresses your thoughts about the reading you have done in this unit. Now is a good time to reflect on what you have learned.

Reflect on the Essential Question

- How do sports bring together friends, families, and communities? How has your answer to this question changed since you first considered it when you started this unit?

- What are some examples from the texts you've read that show the kinds of lessons people can learn from sports and how sports can create conflict and/or bring people together?

Reflect on Your Reading

- Which selections were the most interesting or surprising to you?

- From which selection did you learn the most about the value of sports?

Reflect on the Writing Task

- As you were writing your story, where did you get your ideas? Did new ideas send you in a new direction with your plot?

- What difficulties did you encounter while working on your short story? How might you avoid them next time?

- What improvements did you make to your short story as you were revising?

 REFLECT

UNIT 5 SELECTIONS
- "Ball Hawk"
- "Get in the Zone: The Psychology of Video Game Design"
- "It's Not Just a Game!"
- from *The Crossover*
- "Double Doubles"

REFLECT ON THE UNIT

Have students reflect on the questions independently, and write some notes in response to each one. Then have students meet with partners or in small groups to discuss their reflections. Circulate during these discussions to identify the questions that are generating the liveliest conversations. Wrap up with a whole-class discussion focused on these questions.

 LEARNING MINDSET

Self-Reflection Explain that self-reflection is important part of assessing our personal strengths and acknowledging our areas of struggle. Remind students that each of us will encounter difficulties with various projects we undertake. Encourage students to keep pushing ahead even when the goal seems difficult to attain. Stress that they should take pride in their sincere efforts both in and out of the classroom.

UNIT 6

Instructional Overview and Resources

		Instructional Focus	Resources
	Unit Instruction **Change Agents**	Unit 6 Essential Question Unit 6 Academic Vocabulary	**Stream to Start:** Change Agents **Unit 6 Response Log**

ANALYZE & APPLY

"Craig Kielburger Reflects on Working Toward World Peace" Essay by Craig Kielburger **Lexile 1080L** **NOTICE & NOTE** READING MODEL **Signposts** • Extreme or Absolute Language • Quoted Words • Big Questions	**Reading** • Question • Analyze Author's Point of View **Writing:** Write a Research Report **Speaking and Listening:** Discuss with a Small Group **Vocabulary:** Word Origin **Language Conventions:** Commas	🔊 **Audio** **Text in Focus:** Understanding Data **Close Read Screencast:** Modeled Discussion **Reading Studio:** Notice & Note **Writing Studio:** Conducting Research **Speaking and Listening Studio:** Participating in Collaborative Discussions **Vocabulary Studio:** Word Origins **Grammar Studio:** Punctuation

from It Takes a Child Documentary by Judy Jackson	**Media** • Analyze a Documentary **Writing:** Write a Personal Essay **Speaking and Listening:** Produce a Podcast	**Reading Studio:** Notice & Note **Writing Studio:** Writing as a Process **Speaking and Listening Studio:** Using Media in a Presentation

"Sometimes a Dream Needs a Push" Short Story by Walter Dean Myers **Lexile 770L**	**Reading** • Analyze Realistic Fiction • Analyze Character Qualities **Writing:** Write an Informational Article **Speaking and Listening:** Create a Video Critique **Vocabulary:** Context Clues **Language Conventions:** Consistent Verb Tense	🔊 **Audio** **Reading Studio:** Notice & Note **Writing Studio:** Informative Texts **Speaking and Listening Studio:** Using Media in a Presentation **Vocabulary Studio:** Context Clues **Grammar Studio:** Module 9: Using Verbs Correctly

"A Poem for My Librarian, Mrs. Long" Poem by Nikki Giovanni	**Reading** • Analyze Free Verse Poetry • Analyze Theme **Writing:** Write a Free Verse Poem **Speaking and Listening:** Write a Letter	🔊 **Audio** **Reading Studio:** Notice & Note **Writing Studio:** Writing as a Process

SUGGESTED PACING: 30 DAYS

Unit Introduction	Craig Kielburger Reflects on Working Toward World Peace	from It Takes a Child	Sometimes a Dream Needs a Push	A Poem for My Librarian, Mrs. Long
1	2 3 4 5 6	7 8 9	10 11 12 13 14	15 16 17 18

PLAN

English Learner Support		Differentiated Instruction	Assessment
• Learn Vocabulary			
• Text X-Ray • Question • Use Cognates • Learn New Vocabulary • Idioms • Language Conventions • Oral Assessment • Learn New Language Structures	• Vocabulary: Suffix –ion • Combine Clauses Correctly	**When Students Struggle** • Language Conventions	**Selection Test**
• Text X-Ray • Look it Up • Aspects of a Documentary Film • Write it Up • The Big Ideas		**When Students Struggle** • Possible Sentences	**Selection Test**
• Text X-Ray • Monitor Comprehension • Figurative Language • Understand Contrasts and Contradictions • Confirm Understanding • Language Conventions		**When Students Struggle** • Make a Chart **To Challenge Students** • Conduct Research	**Selection Test**
• Text X-Ray • Analyze Language • Use Cognates • Learning Strategies • Internalize Language • Oral Assessment • Write a Letter		**When Students Struggle** • Analyze Poetry Elements **To Challenge Students** • Conduct Research	**Selection Test**

Frances Perkins and the Triangle Factory Fire / The Triangle Factory Fire
19 › 20 › 21 › 22 › 23 › 24 › 25

Independent Reading
26 › 27

End of Unit
28 › 29 › 30

Change Agents **434B**

PLAN

UNIT 6 Continued | **Instructional Focus** | **Online Ed Resources**

COLLABORATE & COMPARE

"Frances Perkins and the Triangle Factory Fire"
History Writing by David Brooks
Lexile 930L

Reading
- Analyze History Writing
- Determine Key Ideas

Writing: Write an Ode
Speaking and Listening: Discuss Primary Sources
Vocabulary: Latin Roots
Language Conventions: Pronoun-Antecedent Agreement

🔊 **Audio**
Reading Studio: Notice & Note
Writing Studio: Writing as a Process
Speaking and Listening Studio: Participating in Collaborative Discussion
Vocabulary Studio: Latin Roots
Grammar Studio: Module 8: Lesson 8: Pronoun Agreement

Mentor Text
"The Story of the Triangle Factory Fire"
History Writing by Zachary Kent
Lexile 1110L

Reading
- Paraphrase
- Analyze Text Structure

Writing: Write Historical Fiction
Speaking and Listening: Create a Graphic Novel Page
Vocabulary: Connotations and Denotations
Language Conventions: Subject-Verb Agreement and Prepositional Phrases

🔊 **Audio**
Reading Studio: Notice & Note
Writing Studio: Writing Narratives
Speaking and Listening Studio: Giving a Presentation
Vocabulary Studio: Connotations and Denotations
Grammar Studio: Module 8: Lesson 2: Prepositional Phrase Interrupters

---

Collaborate and Compare

Reading
- Compare Authors' Purposes and Messages
- Analyze the Texts

Speaking and Listening: Research and Share

Speaking and Listening Studio: Giving a Presentation

INDEPENDENT READING

 The independent Reading selections are only available in the eBook.
Go to the Reading Studio for more information on Notice & Note.

"Difference Maker: John Bergman and Popcorn Park"
Article by David Karas
Lexile 1130L

from *Walking with the Wind*
Autobiography by John Lewis
Lexile 940L

END OF UNIT

Writing Task: Write a Research Report

Speaking and Listening Task: Participate in a Panel Discussion

Reflect on the Unit

Writing: Write a Research Report
Language Conventions: Paraphrasing and Plagiarizing
Speaking and Listening: Participate in a Panel Discussion

Unit 6 Response Log
Mentor Text: Notice & Note
Writing Studio: Conducting Research
Writing Studio: Using Textual Evidence
Speaking and Listening Studio: Participating in a Collaborative Discussion
Grammar Studio: Module 14: Punctuation

PLAN

English Learner Support	Differentiated Instruction	Online Ed Assessment
• Text X-Ray • Critical Vocabulary • Imagine and Learn • Comprehension Check • Oral Assessment • Chronological Summaries • Name that Pronoun	**When Students Struggle** • Tone **To Challenge Students** • Modern Parallels	**Selection Tests**
• Text X-Ray • Cognates • Oral Assessment • Describe a Character • Vocabulary Strategy • Language Conventions	**When Students Struggle** • Learning Strategy	**Selection Tests**
• Ask Questions	**When Students Struggle** • Learning Strategy	
"Doris is Coming" Short Story by ZZ Packer **Lexile 880L**	"Seeing is Believing" Informational Text by Mary Morton Cowan **Lexile 1100L**	**Selection Tests**
• Language X-Ray • Understand Academic Language • Write a Collaborative Research Report • Use the Mentor Text • Use Negatives and Contractions • Paraphrasing and Plagiarizing • Adapt the Research Report	**When Students Struggle** • Develop a Draft • Paraphrasing and Plagiarizing • Take Notes **To Challenge Students** • Conduct Research	**Unit Test**

Change Agents

TEACH

Connect to the ESSENTIAL QUESTION

Ask a volunteer to read aloud the Essential Question. Discuss how the images on p. 434 relate to the question. Ask: *How can we make the world a better place? What can we learn from individuals committed to social change?* Encourage students to think of real-life situations where good souls help those in need.

■ English Learner Support

Learn Vocabulary Make sure students understand the Essential Question. If necessary, explain the following terms:

- *Inspire* means "cause you to feel and/or think you should do something or make something"
- *Make a difference* means "to change something"

Help students reframe the question: *Why is social change important?* **SUBSTANTIAL/MODERATE**

DISCUSS THE QUOTATION

Ann Lesley Cotton (born 1950) of the United Kingdom, is the founder of Camfed, a nongovernmental organization (NGO) that has benefited more than 3 million African children. Through Camfed, girls and young women in rural Africa receive education and further support in becoming entrepreneurs and community leaders. What kinds of things do you think these African women might go on to do?

UNIT 6

CHANGE AGENTS

ESSENTIAL QUESTION:

What inspires you to make a difference?

> " Be greedy for social change, and your life will be endlessly enriched. "
>
> — Ann Cotton

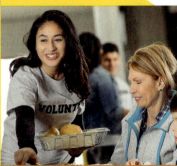

434 Unit 6

⚙ LEARNING MINDSET

Growth Mindset Remind students that a growth mindset means believing one can grow intellectually and emotionally by taking on challenges and pushing oneself. Encourage students to look at every selection as an opportunity to set higher goals and stretch past their comfort zone. Provide 2–3 growth mindset expressions, such as "Mistakes are an opportunity to improve" and "Effort and dedication help us learn and grow," to help students understand that as they take on more challenges, they will discover areas of strength they didn't know they had.

UNIT 6

ACADEMIC VOCABULARY

Academic Vocabulary words are words you use when you discuss and write about texts. In this unit you will practice and learn five words.

✓ contrast ❑ despite ❑ error ❑ inadequate ❑ interact

Study the Word Network to learn more about the word **contrast**.

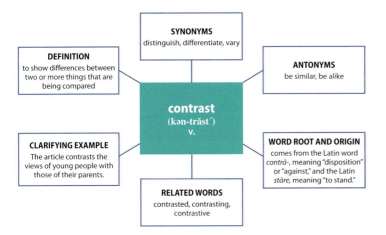

Write and Discuss Discuss the completed Word Network with a partner, making sure to talk through all of the boxes until you both understand the word, its synonyms, antonyms, and related forms. Then, fill out Word Networks for the remaining four words. Use a dictionary or online resource to help you complete the activity.

 *Go online to access the **Word Networks**.*

RESPOND TO THE ESSENTIAL QUESTION

In this unit, you will explore how and why people work to change societies and the communities in which they live. As you read, you will revisit the **Essential Question** and gather your ideas about it in the **Response Log** that appears on page R6. At the end of the unit, you will have the opportunity to write a **research report.** Filling out the Response Log will help you prepare for this writing task.

 *You can also go online to access the **Response Log**.*

Change Agents 435

TEACH

ACADEMIC VOCABULARY

As students complete Word Networks for the remaining four vocabulary words, encourage them to include all the categories shown in the completed network if possible, but point out that some words do not have clear synonyms or antonyms. Some words may also function as different parts of speech—for example, *contrast* may be a verb or a noun.

contrast ((kən-trăst´) *intr. v.* to show differences compared to other things (Spanish cognate: *contraste*)

despite (dĭ-spīt´) *prep.* instead of; in spite of.

error (ĕr´ər) *n.* something that unintentionally deviates from what is right; a mistake (Spanish cognate: *error*)

inadequate (ĭn-ăd´ Ĭ-kwĭt) *adj.* not enough to fulfill a need

interact (ĭn´tər-ăkt´) *intr. v.* to act on one another (Spanish cognate: *interactuar*)

RESPOND TO THE ESSENTIAL QUESTION

Direct students to the Unit 6 Response Log. Explain that students will use it to record ideas and details from the selections that help answer the Essential Question. When they work on the writing task at the end of the unit, their Response Logs will help them think about what they have read and make connections between texts.

Change Agents 435

PLAN

READING MODEL
CRAIG KIELBURGER REFLECTS ON WORKING TOWARD PEACE
Personal Essay by Craig Kielburger

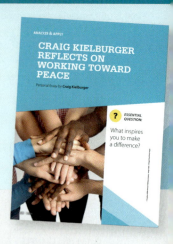

GENRE ELEMENTS
PERSONAL ESSAY
An **essay** is a short work of nonfiction that deals with a single subject. Some essays are formal—that is, tightly structured and written in an impersonal style. Others are informal, with a looser structure and a more personal style. A **personal essay** is usually an informal essay in which the writer expresses his or her thoughts and feelings about a subject, focusing on the meaning of events and issues in his or her own life.

LEARNING OBJECTIVES
- Generate questions about a text before, during, and after reading.
- Analyze the author's point of view.
- Write an informative essay about WE Charity.
- Understand word origins.
- Use commas to set off introductory or nonessential elements and to separate clauses.
- **Language** Rephrase sentences that have an extra "balancing" word in the main clause.

TEXT COMPLEXITY

Quantitative Measures	Craig Kielburger Reflects on Working Toward Peace	Lexile: 1080L
Qualitative Measures	**Ideas Presented** Single purpose; explicitly stated	
	Structure Used Clearly stated; sequential organization of main ideas and details	
	Language Used Clear, direct language; some sophisticated vocabulary	
	Knowledge Required Everyday knowledge required	

PLAN

RESOURCES

- Unit 6 Response Log
- 🔊 Selection Audio
- Text in FOCUS Understanding Data
- Close Read Screencasts: Modeled Discussions
- Reading Studio: Notice & Note
- Level Up Tutorial: Reading for Details
- Writing Studio: Conducting Research
- Speaking and Listening Studio: Participating in a Collaborative Discussion
- Vocabulary Studio: Word Origins
- Grammar Studio: Module 14: Punctuation
- "Craig Kielburger Reflects On Working Toward Peace" Selection Test

SUMMARIES

English
When Craig Kielburger was twelve years old, he read about another twelve-year-old boy. The story of that boy, a Pakistani rug weaver and slave laborer who was murdered, inspired Craig to found the organization Free the Children. He has traveled around the world meeting and talking to children everywhere and now believes that each person has a gift that can help make the world a better place.

Spanish
Cuando Craig Keilburger tenía doce años, leyó acerca de otro niño de doce años. La historia de un niño paquistaní tejedor de alfombras y esclavo que fue asesinado inspiró a Craig a fundar la organización Free the Children. Así ha recorrido el mundo, conociendo y hablando con niños de todas partes, y ahora cree que cada persona posee un don que puede cambiar al mundo para mejor.

SMALL-GROUP OPTIONS

Have students work in small groups to read and discuss the selection.

Send a Problem
- Pose a question about the ideas described in "Craig Kielburger Reflects on Working Toward Peace." Call on a student to respond.
- If student does not have a response, then he or she must call another student by name to answer the same question.
- Wait up to 11 seconds.
- The student asking the question, repeats the question as he or she calls on another for assistance.
- Monitor responses and redirect or ask another question at any time.

Numbered Heads Together
- Form groups of four students and then number off 1 – 2 – 3 – 4 within the group.
- Ask students: "Why do you think the story of the rug weaver affected Craig so strongly?"
- Have students discuss their responses in their groups.
- Call a number from 1 to 4. That "numbered" student will then respond for the group.
- If you like, groups may adopt names, such as "Wildcats," to identify their groups. You will then call on Wildcat number 4.

Craig Kielburger Reflects on Working Toward Peace **436B**

PLAN

Text X-Ray: English Learner Support
for "Craig Kielburger Reflects on Working Toward Peace"

Use the Text X-Ray and the supports and scaffolds in the Teacher's Edition to help guide students at different proficiency levels through the selection.

INTRODUCE THE SELECTION
DISCUSS CHANGE AGENTS

In this lesson, students will discuss what inspires people to make a difference in the world. To provide students with the vocabulary they may need to discuss this question, introduce them to these phrases:

- *social change*: Social change refers to a change in social structures and behaviors that occurs over a period of time. The Civil Rights Movement brought about social change in the United States.
- *change agent*: A change agent is a person who works to bring about social change. Cesar Chavez and other leaders of the farm workers movement have been change agents in the United States.

Explain to students that social change usually does not happen without a strong effort. Change agents work hard and long to bring about more justice and freedom in society. Model using research sites where students can find images and linguistically accommodated material about agents of change.

CULTURAL REFERENCES

- The following words and phrases may be unfamiliar to students:
- *sold into bondage* (paragraph 2): Technically, slavery is illegal everywhere in the world, but there are still many places where people are actually slaves.
- *garbage dump* (paragraph 4): a place where people dump trash and garbage
- *absolute poverty* (paragraph 7): is the condition of not having the income needed to support basic human needs.

LISTENING

Understand Point of View

Draw students' attention to the way Craig Kielburger combines subjective and objective points of view when talking about working toward achieving peace in the world.

Have students listen as you read aloud paragraph 8. Use the following supports with students at varying proficiency levels:

- Help students understand the difference between "I know" *(in Spanish, "Lo sé)* to state a fact and "I believe" *(in Spanish, Creo)* to state an opinion. Say, *"I know I have ten fingers. I believe it is a pretty day."* **SUBSTANTIAL**
- Have students identify subjective and objective statements by raising their left hands for objective and their right hands for subjective. Say: *People spend millions of dollars on cosmetics. That is a bad thing. Peace must begin with children. (left, right, right)* **MODERATE**
- Review the meanings of *subjective* and *objective*. Pair students to read the paragraph to each other and identify two subjective and two objective statements. **LIGHT**

PLAN

SPEAKING

Discuss Young People as Change Agents

Draw students' attention to the discussion topic on p. 447. Give them some preparation for participating in the discussion.

Use the following supports with students at varying proficiency levels:

- Clarify the meaning of the word *kind*. Model using thumbs up to mean yes and down to mean no. Say: *Joe helped his friend. Is that kind? Kim called someone a name. Is that kind?* **SUBSTANTIAL**
- Give students sentence frames to express thoughts about the topic. *Craig was a _____ boy. He felt _____ for the boy in Pakistan. He needed _____ to do what he did.* (kind, sorry, courage) **MODERATE**
- Pair students to talk about Craig Kielburger. Have each pair come up with two sentences about Craig Kielburger to contribute to the discussion. **LIGHT**

READING

Understand the Author's Point of View

Draw students' attention to the description of point of view on p. 439. Then help students to understand how a writer's tone, or attitude, can be expressed in word choices.

Reread paragraph 11. Help students see how the author's point of view is expressed in tone and word choice. Use the following supports with students at varying proficiency levels:

- Say the word *no*, using several different tones of voice—angry, hesitant, questioning, surprised. Ask students to describe in words or to show on their own faces the attitude or emotion expressed each time. **SUBSTANTIAL**
- Give student partners a pair of synonyms with different connotations—*young, childish*. Ask students to tell you which one is a good quality and which one is a bad quality. (young, *good*; childish, *bad*) **MODERATE**
- Pair students and ask them to focus on the phrase "most precious" in paragraph 11. Ask: *What other words could the author have used to describe the shirt?* (best, most valuable, nicest) **LIGHT**

WRITING

Write a Thesis Statement

Draw students' attention to the Research Report instructions on p. 447. Help students write a clear thesis statement for their reports.

Focus on the word *statement*. Explain that a statement is something you say or write. It gives information in a clear, formal way. Use the following supports with students at varying proficiency levels:

- Model making statements, such as "Kind people are helpful, "Many people live in poverty, "We need to help children," **SUBSTANTIAL**
- Explain that a thesis statement gives the main idea of a report. Display these two sentences. Ask students to tell you which one is the better thesis statement: "Young people can help each other," "Kids can do better," **MODERATE**
- Pair students to discuss the topic of the Research Report and work together to write a thesis statement on that topic. **LIGHT**

TEACH

EXPLAIN THE SIGNPOSTS

Explain that **Notice & Note Signposts** are significant moments in the text that help readers understand and analyze works of fiction or nonfiction. Use the instruction on these pages to introduce students to the signposts **Extreme or Absolute Language, Quoted Words,** and **Big Questions**. Then use the selection that follows to have students apply the signposts to a text.

For a full list of the fiction and nonfiction signposts, see p. 502.

EXTREME OR ABSOLUTE LANGUAGE

As signposts go, **Extreme or Absolute Language** stands taller: It is written to stick up and stand out of context with exaggerated, possibly overblown, claims. You'll find it where various nouns take strong modifiers, such as *never, none, smallest, biggest, perfectly, absolutely,* or *entirely*.

Review the example passage. Ask: *What is the one word that most plainly signifies extreme or absolute language?* (*all*) Point out that savvy writers will use these kinds of terms sparingly. The more Extreme or Absolute Language turns up in a text, the less impactful it tends to be.

Tell students that when they spot Extreme or Absolute Language, they should pause, mark it in their consumable texts, and ask the anchor question to determine the **author's purpose**: *Why did the author use this language?*

436 Unit 6

Notice & Note
READING MODEL

CRAIG KIELBURGER REFLECTS ON WORKING TOWARD PEACE

You are about to read the personal essay "Craig Kielburger Reflects on Working Toward Peace." In it, you will notice and note signposts that will give you clues about the author's purpose and message. Here are three key signposts to look for as you read this personal essay and other works of nonfiction.

For more information on these and other signposts to Notice & Note, visit the **Reading Studio.**

When you read language like the following, pause and consider whether it might be an **Extreme or Absolute Language** signpost:

terms that indicate certainty or completeness—*all, none, everyone, no one, always, never, totally*

statements that express an uncompromising position—*we must all agree; no one should . . .*

language that is provocative—*spinach should be outlawed*—or that is exaggerated—*nothing in the universe . . .*

Extreme or Absolute Language Suppose that a friend invites you on an amusement park ride. She says it is *the best ride ever* and that you are going to *love it*. The friend may think you'll like the ride, but it may also be that she doesn't want to go alone.

Similarly, when authors use **Extreme or Absolute Language,** they usually have a purpose for doing so. Paying attention to Extreme or Absolute Language signposts can provide clues to the author's purpose and biases, point to the main idea the author wants to convey, and help you draw conclusions about the author's key points.

The paragraph below shows a student's annotation within Kielburger's essay and a response to an Extreme or Absolute Language signpost:

> 1 When I was very young I dreamed of being Superman, soaring high above the clouds and swooping down to snatch up <u>all of the bad people seeking to destroy our planet</u>. I would spend hours flying across the park, stopping momentarily to kick a soccer ball in my path or to pat my dog, Muffin, who ran faithfully at my heels.

Anchor Question
When you notice this signpost, ask: Why did the author use this language?

What language is provocative or exaggerated?	"all of the bad people seeking to destroy our planet"
Why might the author have used this language?	The author may want to emphasize his commitment to a cause, even at an early age.

436 Unit 6

Quoted Words If you read that a well-known children's doctor advises, "Exercising every day is essential to good health," what would you think? Does using a quotation make the advice more convincing?

Authors use **Quoted Words** to provide support for a point. Quoted Words might be the thoughts of an expert on the subject, someone who is important to the author, or someone who witnessed an event. When you read quoted words, ask yourself why the author included them and what they help you understand. Here a student marked an example of Quoted Words in Kielburger's essay:

> 14 When I returned home my mother asked me, "Are you certain you aren't gifted?" I realized that I had given the wrong answer. I was gifted, and the more I reflected, the more I concluded that I had never met a person who was not special or talented in some way.

Anchor Question When you notice this signpost, ask: Why was this person quoted or cited, and what did this add?

What quoted words does the author include?	"Are you certain you aren't gifted?"
Why might the author have included this quotation?	The author shows how important his mother's question was to him and how it changed his thinking.

Big Questions In nonfiction texts, you will find facts that support your understanding of an issue. Sometimes you will also read details that make you rethink how you look at that issue. As you read, ask yourself: What is challenging, changing, or confirming what I already know? Here a student marked up a detail in Kielburger's essay related to a Big Question that prompted rethinking.

> 5 I have met children like eight-year-old Muniannal, in India, with a pretty ribbon in her hair, but no shoes or gloves, who squats on the floor every day separating used syringes gathered from hospitals and the streets for their plastics. When she pricks herself, she dips her hand into a bucket of dirty water. She dreams of being a teacher.

When you see details like these, pause and consider the **Big Questions** signpost:
- Identify details that confirm what you already know.
- Note details that prompt you to reexamine what you think, feel, or believe.

What detail challenged what you thought?	"She dreams of being a teacher."
Why might the author have included this challenging detail?	The author may be asking us to think about how every child has dreams and how those dreams can come true.

Notice & Note 437

TEACH

▶ **QUOTED WORDS**

Point out that **Quoted Words** are easy to spot: just look for the quotation marks. Then ask: *Why do nonfiction writers use them?*

Quoted Words add personal perspectives, bringing human voices into storytelling. **Citations** from experts lend authority to an author's claim. And when multiple speakers are quoted in succession, an **argument** gains strength in numbers.

Tell students that when they spot Quoted Words, they should pause, mark them in their consumable texts, and ask the anchor question to determine why a particular **quotation** is included: *Why is this person cited? What does the quotation add?*

▶ **BIG QUESTIONS**

A **Big Question** is like a red flag hanging from a signpost. **Big Questions** arise when we encounter information:
- that may seem hard to believe
- that challenges us to look at the world differently
- that gives us a new outlook on things we already know

Read the example passage. Tell students that the Big Question is a tool they can use to **evaluate** details in a text. Ask: *How does the big question "stick out" in this context?* (*The paragraph describes circumstances more likely to crush dreams than nurture them.*)

Tell students that when they spot Big Questions, they should pause, mark them in their consumable texts, and ask the anchor question: *What surprised me?*

APPLY THE SIGNPOSTS

Have students use the selection that follows as a model text to apply the signposts. As students encounter signposts, prompt them to stop, reread, and ask themselves the anchor questions that will help them understand author's purpose.

Tell students to continue to look for these and other signposts as they read the other selections in the unit.

WHEN STUDENTS STRUGGLE . . .

Use Strategies Use the Poster strategy to help students flag **Big Questions**. Tape copies of a sample passage in large type to flip-chart paper, one sheet to a group. In groups of four or five, ask students to read along with you, writing their responses to the text (including **Big Questions**) on the chart. Say: *This exercise has a no-talking ground rule. Let's have a "conversation" about the text on paper.* Circulate around the room, reviewing notes and making suggestions to stimulate student engagement. When a time limit has expired, invite students to discuss their responses to the sample.

TEACH

? Connect to the ESSENTIAL QUESTION

"Craig Kielburger Reflects on Working Toward Peace" explains what inspired a twelve-year-old boy to found an organization that is making a difference for children around the world.

ANALYZE & APPLY

CRAIG KIELBURGER REFLECTS ON WORKING TOWARD PEACE

Personal Essay by **Craig Kielburger**

? ESSENTIAL QUESTION:

What inspires you to make a difference?

438 Unit 6

QUICK START

Have you ever seen something on TV that made you want to take action? Or perhaps you read a story that highlighted an injustice. With a group, discuss how you felt and your ideas for what you could do.

QUESTION

Effective readers **question** what they are reading and look for answers in the text. Asking questions helps you deepen your understanding and gain information. Readers' questions often focus on the following:

- What is the **controlling idea** or thesis of the text? What is the writer's position on the topic or subject of the text?
- What **supporting evidence,** such as examples and other text details, does the author provide to support the controlling idea? Why is the author including certain details?
- Does what the author is saying make sense to me? Why or why not?

Taking notes and writing down questions as you read is an effective strategy for deepening your understanding of the text. Use a T-chart like the one below to take notes and list questions about the essay.

CRAIG KIELBURGER REFLECTS ON WORKING TOWARD PEACE	
NOTES	QUESTIONS
Author read about a boy his age forced to work long hours. . . .	Why did this happen? Can it be stopped from happening again?

ANALYZE AUTHOR'S POINT OF VIEW

The author of a personal essay often writes from a first-person **point of view,** using first-person pronouns, such as *I, me,* and *we.* The author might write from an objective or a subjective point of view, or both. When writing from an **objective point of view,** the writer presents information in an unbiased way. When writing from a **subjective point of view,** the writer includes personal ideas, values, feelings, and beliefs.

As you read the personal essay, think about the author's point of view by noting these features in the text:

- statements of the author's opinions
- details and examples from the author's experiences
- words and descriptions that have emotional impact
- the writer's **tone,** or attitude toward a subject
- the use of language that allows you to hear the writer's **voice,** or unique personality

GET READY

GENRE ELEMENTS: PERSONAL ESSAY

- short work of nonfiction that deals with a single subject
- written from a first-person point of view
- includes author's opinions, feelings, and/or insights based on personal experience
- often written in casual language to feel like a conversation with readers

Craig Kielburger Reflects on Working Toward Peace 439

TEACH

QUICK START

Bring the question of change home to students by talking with them about issues that involve them and others their age, including bullying, poverty, and materialism.

QUESTION

To bring home the interactive nature of reading, suggest that students read the selection as though they were interviewing Craig Kielburger. As they go along, they should think of questions they would like to ask and read closely to see whether their questions are answered. Explain that good readers ask questions as they read, sometimes without even realizing it.

ANALYZE AUTHOR'S POINT OF VIEW

Explain that an author's point of view is the unique combination of ideas, values, feelings, and beliefs that influences the way he or she views and evaluates at a topic. Authors express their points of view in many ways. Suggest that students ask themselves these questions to help them determine the author's point of view:

- What words and descriptions that convey emotions does the author use?
- What specific facts and examples does the author present?
- What message does the author want to convey to the reader?

TEACH

CRITICAL VOCABULARY

Encourage students to read all the sentences before deciding which word best completes each one. Remind them to look for context clues for help in determining the meaning of each word.

Answers:

1. *exploitation*
2. *inquire*
3. *syringe*
4. *capacity*
5. *possession*

■ English Learner Support

Use Cognates Tell students that all of the Critical Vocabulary words have Spanish cognates: *exploitation/explotación, inquire/inquirir, syringe/jeringa, capacity/capacidad, possession/posesión.*
ALL LEVELS

LANGUAGE CONVENTIONS

Explain to students that commas, like all punctuation, help to make writing clearer and more understandable. The rules guiding the use of commas help readers interpret an author's words with more confidence.

ANNOTATION MODEL

Note that **Extreme or Absolute Language** leaves no doubt about a situation. The **Quoted Words** are used as a confirmation by an expert or witness to support a claim. Have students look at the Annotation Model, which suggests underlining important details and circling words that signal important parts of the text. Point out that they may follow this suggestion or use their own system for marking up the selection in their write-in text. They may want to color-code their annotations by using highlighters. Their notes in the margin may include questions about ideas that are unclear or topics they want to learn more about.

440   Unit 6

 **GET READY**

CRITICAL VOCABULARY

syringe   possession   inquire   capacity   exploitation

To see how many Critical Vocabulary words you already know, use them to complete the sentences.

1. Congress passed a law to prevent the _____ of migrant workers.
2. José decided to _____ about the new bike that he saw for sale on the corner.
3. The nurse drew the liquid medicine into the _____.
4. She saw many promising engineers in her _____ as a science teacher.
5. Dalia packed every _____ into the back of her car and drove across the country.

LANGUAGE CONVENTIONS

Commas In this lesson, you will learn about the effective use of commas. In general, commas are used to separate words, phrases, clauses, and ideas in a sentence. As you read "Craig Kielburger Reflects on Working Toward Peace," note how the author's use of commas clarifies his ideas.

ANNOTATION MODEL   **NOTICE & NOTE**

As you read, notice and note signposts, including **Extreme or Absolute Language** and **Quoted Words**. Ask yourself this **Big Question:** What changed, challenged, or confirmed what I already knew? Here is an example of how one reader responded to a paragraph in "Craig Kielburger Reflects on Working Toward Peace."

> 7 Poverty is the biggest killer of children. More than 1.3 billion people—one-quarter of the world's population—live in absolute poverty, struggling to survive on less than one dollar a day. Seventy percent of them are women and children. I dream of a day when people learn how to share, so that children do not have to die.

I didn't know that! Why is this so?

These are dramatic words. I think the author may be trying to convince me of something.

440   Unit 6

BACKGROUND

In 1995—when **Craig Kielburger** (b. 1982) was only twelve years old—he and several classmates founded Free the Children, an organization to help young people. Now called WE Charity, the organization raises social awareness in schools and works in developing countries to provide education and healthcare programs. *This essay comes from* Architects of Peace: Visions of Hope in Words and Images, *published when Kielburger was a teenager.*

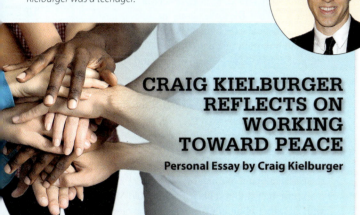

CRAIG KIELBURGER REFLECTS ON WORKING TOWARD PEACE

Personal Essay by Craig Kielburger

SETTING A PURPOSE

In this essay, Kielburger calls for a fairer, more just world. As you read, pay attention to how he describes his experiences as a young activist.

1 When I was very young I dreamed of being Superman, soaring high above the clouds and swooping down to snatch up all of the bad people seeking to destroy our planet. I would spend hours flying across the park, stopping momentarily to kick a soccer ball in my path or to pat my dog, Muffin, who ran faithfully at my heels.

2 One day, when I was twelve years old and getting ready for school, I reached for the newspaper comics. On the front page was a picture of another twelve-year-old boy from Pakistan, with a bright red vest and his fist held high. According to the article, he had been sold into bondage[1] as

---
[1] **bondage:** the state of being held as a slave.

NOTICE & NOTE

Notice & Note

Use the side margins to notice and note signposts in the text.

ANALYZE AUTHOR'S POINT OF VIEW

Annotate: Mark sentences in paragraph 2 that have an emotional impact.

Analyze: How do these sentences affect the reader? How would you describe the author's point of view, or perspective, in this paragraph?

Craig Kielburger Reflects on Working Toward Peace   441

TEACH

BACKGROUND

In this essay, Craig Kielburger talks about child labor around the world. Explain to students that in the United States most child labor was outlawed in 1939, although exceptions were made for agricultural labor. But children are still forced to work in most of the world, usually for little money, and sometimes as slaves.

SETTING A PURPOSE

Direct students to use the Setting a Purpose prompt to focus their reading.

 ANALYZE AUTHOR'S POINT OF VIEW

Explain to students that the author's **tone**, the attitude expressed by his or her language, is an important clue to the author's point of view. (**Answer**: *The author, in a very serious tone, describes a personal experience that affected him deeply. His description probably is meant to make the reader feel anger at such an injustice.*)

 ENGLISH LEARNER SUPPORT

Learn New Vocabulary Read the first paragraph of the selection to students. Use vocal and facial expressions and gestures to reinforce the meanings of the descriptive phrases, such as "soaring high above the clouds" and "swooping down," "flying across the park." Then ask for a volunteer to provide the gestures while you read the words and phrases again.
SUBSTANTIAL/MODERATE

Craig Kielburger Reflects on Working Toward Peace   **441**

TEACH

ENGLISH LEARNER SUPPORT

Understand Idioms Explain to students that the phrase in paragraph 4, "over the past four years," means "starting four years ago and happening several times during those four years."

ASK STUDENTS to explain what Craig Kielburger has been doing during this four-year period. *(He has been traveling and meeting children around the world.)*

MODERATE/LIGHT

For **listening support** for students at varying proficiency levels, see the **Text X-Ray** on page 436C.

QUESTION

Explain to students that skipping over information they don't quite understand can lead to problems further along as they read. Remind them that it is important to ask questions that will help them understand what they are reading. (**Answer**: *Would it cost an extra $7 billion more than all of these numbers put together? Or would it just cost $7 billion? What point is the author making here? Is the author saying that poverty can be ended just by educating children?*)

TEXT IN FOCUS

Understanding Data Have students view the **Text in Focus** video on this page of their eBook to learn how to interpret data in nonfiction writing. Then have students use **Text in Focus Practice** to apply what they have learned.

CRITICAL VOCABULARY

syringe: The girl in India is taking apart syringes that have been used to give people injections.

ASK STUDENTS what danger might the syringes present to the girl. *(They might have germs on them that would give the girl a disease.)*

442 Unit 6

NOTICE & NOTE

a weaver and forced to work twelve hours a day tying tiny knots to make carpets. He had lost his freedom to laugh and to play. He had lost his freedom to go to school. Then, when he was twelve years old, the same age as me, he was murdered.

3   I had never heard of child labor and wasn't certain where Pakistan was—but that day changed my life forever. I gathered a group of friends to form an organization called Free the Children.

4   Over the past four years, in my travels for Free the Children, I have had the opportunity to meet many children around the world—children like Jeffrey, who spends his days in a Manila garbage dump, alongside rats and maggots, where he sifts through decaying food and trash, trying to salvage a few valuable items to help his family survive. He dreams of leaving the garbage dump one day.

5   I have met children like eight-year-old Muniannal, in India, with a pretty ribbon in her hair, but no shoes or gloves, who squats on the floor every day separating used **syringes** gathered from hospitals and the streets for their plastics. When she pricks herself, she dips her hand into a bucket of dirty water. She dreams of being a teacher.

6   I have met children in the sugarcane fields of Brazil who wield huge machetes close to their small limbs. The cane they cut sweetens the cereal on our kitchen tables each morning. They dream of easing the hunger pains in their stomachs.

7   Poverty is the biggest killer of children. More than 1.3 billion people—one-quarter of the world's population—live in absolute poverty, struggling to survive on less than one dollar a day. Seventy percent of them are women and children. I dream of a day when people learn how to share, so that children do not have to die.

8   Every year, the world spends $800 billion on the military, $400 billion on cigarettes, $160 billion on beer, and $40 billion playing golf. <u>It would only cost an extra $7 billion a year to put every child in school by the year 2010</u>, giving them hope for a better life. This is less money than Americans spend on cosmetics in one year; it is less than Europeans spend on ice cream. People say, "We can't end world poverty; it just can't be done." The 1997 United Nations Development Report carries

syringe
(sə-rĭnj´) *n.* A *syringe* is a medical instrument used to inject fluids into the body.

QUESTION
Annotate: Underline words, phrases, or sentences that are unclear or confusing to you in paragraph 8.

Connect: What questions could you ask to help clarify any confusion?

442   Unit 6

CLOSE READ SCREENCAST

Modeled Discussion Have students click the *Close Read* icon in their eBook to access a screencast in which readers discuss and annotate paragraph 2, a key passage that discusses an important moment of discovery in the author's life.

As a class, view and discuss the video. Then have students pair up to do an independent close read of the author's conclusion in paragraph 18. Students can record their answers on the Close Read Practice PDF.

Close Read Practice PDF

a clear message that poverty can be ended, if we make it our goal. The document states that the world has the materials and natural resources, the know-how, and the people to make a poverty-free world a reality in less than one generation.

9   Gandhi[2] once said that if there is to be peace in the world it must begin with children. I have learned my best lessons from other children—children like the girls I encountered in India who carried their friend from place to place because she had no legs—and children like José.

10 I met José in the streets of San Salvador, Brazil, where he lived with a group of street children between the ages of eight and fourteen. José and his friends showed me the old abandoned bus shelter where they slept under cardboard boxes. They had to be careful, he said, because the police might beat or shoot them if they found their secret hideout. I spent the day playing soccer on the streets with José and his friends—soccer with an old plastic bottle they had found in the garbage. They were too poor to own a real soccer ball.

11 We had great fun, until one of the children fell on the bottle and broke it into several pieces, thus ending the game. It was getting late and time for me to leave. José knew I was returning to Canada and wanted to give me a gift to remember him by. But he had nothing—no home, no food, no toys, no **possessions**. So he took the shirt off his back and handed it to me. José didn't stop to think that he had no other shirt to wear or that he would be cold that night. He gave me the most precious thing he owned: the jersey of his favorite soccer team. Of course, I told José that I could never accept his shirt, but he insisted. So I removed the plain white T-shirt I was wearing and gave it to him. Although José's shirt was dirty and had a few small holes, it was a colorful soccer shirt and certainly much nicer than mine. José grinned from ear to ear when I put it on.

12 I will never forget José, because he taught me more about sharing that day than anyone I have ever known. He may have been a poor street child, but I saw more goodness in him than all of the world leaders I have ever met. If more people had the heart of a street child, like José, and were willing to share, there would be no more poverty and a lot less suffering in this world. Sometimes young people find life today too depressing. It all seems so hopeless. They would rather escape, go dancing or listen to their favorite music, play video games or hang out with their friends. They dream of true love, a home of their own, or

---

[2] **Gandhi:** Mohandas Karamchand Gandhi (1869–1948, more commonly called Mahatma Gandhi), a leader of India whose belief in justice inspired many people around the world.

NOTICE & NOTE

QUOTED WORDS

Notice & Note: Whose idea does the author reference (as an indirect quotation) in paragraph 9?

Analyze: Why do you think the author used this quotation?

BIG QUESTIONS

Notice & Note: What changed, challenged, or confirmed what you already knew in paragraphs 10 and 11?

Analyze: Why might the author have included this information?

possession
(pə-zĕsh´ən) *n.* A *possession* is something you own.

EXTREME OR ABSOLUTE LANGUAGE

Notice & Note: Mark statements in paragraph 12 that seem to exaggerate or overstate a point.

Evaluate: How does this use of extreme language affect how you feel about the author's message?

TEACH

QUOTED WORDS

Remind students that an author may quote the words of someone who is considered an expert or a respected person to support a point. (**Answer:** *The author indirectly quotes Mohandas Gandhi, a very respected leader. The quotation supports the author's view that helping children is an important part of making the world a better place.*)

BIG QUESTIONS

Explain to students that authors often surprise or deliberately try to shock the reader when they want to bring up a big question. They do this to make the reader stop and think. (**Answer:** *The fact that the police might beat or shoot homeless children [paragraph 10] challenged what I thought I knew. The author probably wanted to include shocking details to help support his point that we need to address the problem of children living in poverty.*)

EXTREME OR ABSOLUTE LANGUAGE

Explain to students that it's important to pay attention when a writer of nonfiction uses extreme language. It may be a sign that the writer is exaggerating his or her argument, or it may be use of **hyperbole**. Hyperbole is a form of figurative language that is not meant to be taken literally but is used to emphasize a point. (**Answers will vary:** *Some students may be moved by the exaggeration; others may feel that it makes his argument seem too simplistic.*)

CRITICAL VOCABULARY

possession: The author tells how a poor boy in Brazil gave him a T-shirt, the boy's favorite possession.

ASK STUDENTS to tell what it shows when someone like José, who has very little, is willing to give a new friend one of his few possessions. (*It shows that he thinks sharing is more important than owning things.*)

TEACH

✏️ LANGUAGE CONVENTIONS

Explain to students that commas are used to set apart introductory words and phrases, as well as words and phrases that are not essential to the sentence. They may also be used to separate clauses within a sentence. (**Answer**: *First two commas separate a nonessential element; third comma separates clauses; fourth comma separates an introductory element; fifth comma separate clauses.*)

■ English Learner Support

Language Conventions Explain to students that periods and commas are both used to separate things. Periods are used to separate one sentence from another sentence. Commas are used to separate one part of a sentence from another part. Read aloud the following sentences, pausing for the punctuation. During the pauses, have students raise their right hands for commas and their left hands for periods: Last night at dinner (,) my uncle told me that everyone has a gift to share(.) "That's very true(,)" my aunt replied(.)
MODERATE

CRITICAL VOCABULARY

inquire: It's the job of television interviewers to ask questions. This interviewer inquired whether Craig was gifted.

ASK STUDENTS what the interviewer likely wanted to know when he asked whether Craig was gifted. (*He probably wanted to know whether Craig was unusually smart.*)

capacity: The author uses the word *capacity* when he talks about how people create things when they are acting as carpenters, artists, or builders.

ASK STUDENTS to explain what a person would create in his or her capacity as a musician. (*music*)

444   Unit 6

 **NOTICE & NOTE**

having a good time at the next party. At sixteen, I also like to dance, have fun, and dream for the future. But I have discovered that it takes more than material things to find real happiness and meaning in life.

13   One day I was the guest on a popular television talk show in Canada. I shared the interview with another young person involved in cancer research. Several times during the program this young man, who was twenty years old, told the host that he was "gifted," as indicated by a test he had taken in third grade. Turning my way, the host **inquired** whether I, too, was gifted. Never having been tested for the gifted program, I answered that I was not.

14   When I returned home my mother asked me, "Are you certain you aren't gifted?" I realized that I had given the wrong answer. I was gifted, and the more I reflected, the more I concluded that I had never met a person who was not special or talented in some way.

15   Some people are gifted with their hands and can produce marvelous creations in their **capacity** as carpenters, artists, or builders. Others have a kind heart, are compassionate, understanding, or are special peacemakers; others, again, are humorous and bring joy into our lives. We have all met individuals who are gifted in science or sports, have great organizational skills or a healing touch. And, of course, some people are very talented at making money. Indeed, even the most physically or mentally challenged person teaches all of us about the value and worth of human life.

16   I think that God(,)in fact(,)played a trick on us. He gave each and every person special talents or gifts(,)but he made no one gifted in all areas.

17   Collectively(,)we have all it takes to create a just and peaceful world(,)but we must work together and share our talents. We all need one another to find happiness within ourselves and within the world.

inquire
(ĭn-kwīr´) *v.* If you *inquire* about something, you ask about it.

capacity
(kə-păs´ĭ-tē) *n.* A person's *capacity* is his or her role or position.

LANGUAGE CONVENTIONS
Annotate: Mark the commas in paragraphs 16 and 17.
Identify: Why is each comma necessary?

444   Unit 6

WHEN STUDENTS STRUGGLE . . .

Understand Genre Elements   To guide comprehension about elements of personal essays, have students work independently or with a partner to complete a genre elements chart.

Point of View	Author's Personal Details	Author's Thoughts and Feelings
First-person:"I" statements	Craig was a guest on a television show as a teenager.	Craig believes everyone is "special or talented in some way."

 For additional support, go to the **Reading Studio** and assign the following Level Up tutorial: **Informational Text.**

18   I realize, now, that each of us has the power to be Superman and to help rid the world of its worst evils—poverty, loneliness, and **exploitation.** I dream of the day when Jeffrey leaves the garbage dump, when Muniannal no longer has to separate used syringes and can go to school, and when all children, regardless of place of birth or economic circumstance, are free to be children. I dream of the day when we all have José's courage to share.

NOTICE & NOTE

exploitation
(ĕk´sploi-tā´shən) *n.* Exploitation is the unfair treatment or use of something or someone for selfish reasons.

CHECK YOUR UNDERSTANDING

Answer these questions before moving on to the **Analyze the Text** section on the following page.

1. The author refers to <u>dreams</u> at the end of paragraphs 4, 5, 6, and 7 in order to —

   A indicate that every child has hope for a better future

   B explain what happens to children who live in poverty

   C point out how different the children are from each other

   D prove that poverty affects children all around the world

2. The author's main purpose in telling the story of José is to —

   F describe how some homeless children live

   G encourage sharing by showing that everyone has something to offer

   H show that children who live in poverty still find time for play

   J explain that although childhood poverty seems hopeless, it is not

3. Which statement best expresses the author's controlling idea in this personal essay?

   A Child bondage is a problem faced by children around the world.

   B Education is the key to ending childhood poverty.

   C Everyone has the capacity to help end poverty, but it requires cooperation.

   D Every person is gifted, but each person is gifted in his or her own way.

Craig Kielburger Reflects on Working Toward Peace   445

TEACH

CHECK YOUR UNDERSTANDING

Have students answer the questions independently.

Answers:

1. A
2. G
3. C

If they answer any questions incorrectly, have them reread the text to confirm their understanding. Then they may proceed to ANALYZE THE TEXT on p. 446.

CRITICAL VOCABULARY

exploitation: The author uses the word *exploitation* to describe one of the world's "worst evils."

ASK STUDENTS to identify examples the author provides to show how children are exploited. (*Jeffrey has to sift through a garbage dump; Muniannal has to separate dangerous used syringes.*)

 ENGLISH LEARNER SUPPORT

Oral Assessment Use the following questions to assess students' comprehension and speaking skills:

1. What is the author expressing when he talks about dreams at the ends of paragraphs 4, 5, 6, and 7? (*Every child has hope for a better future.*)

2. What is the author's main purpose in telling the story of José? (*Showing the importance of sharing what we have.*)

3. What is Craig Kielburger's main idea in this personal essay? (*Everyone has the capacity to help end poverty, but we need to cooperate with each other.*) **SUBSTANTIAL/MODERATE**

APPLY

ANALYZE THE TEXT

Possible answers:

1. **DOK 2:** *The sudden awareness of injustice against a boy like himself opened Kielburger's eyes to what was happening in the world.*

2. **DOK 4:** *The facts and figures support his claim that poverty can be ended. He probably hopes that readers will consider spending money on poor people instead of on luxury items. The information is effective.*

3. **DOK 3:** *He says that he and all people are gifted with talents they can share. His purpose is to emphasize that everyone has the potential to do great things.*

4. **DOK 4:** *The essay's introduction and conclusion both refer to Superman. In the introduction, Superman is a fantasy hero. In the conclusion, he says that everyone has the power to be a real "Superman" and end real evils in the world.*

5. **DOK 4:** *The effect of the absolute language in many cases is to include the reader and convince the reader of a particular point. But the dramatic language occasionally may make readers feel that they are being manipulated.*

RESEARCH

Remind students that it's good to have more than one source of information when doing research. Remind them that there are sites that review charities and other nongovernmental organizations (NGOs).

Connect Students may note that for every dollar donated to WE Charity, 91 cents goes to the charity's actual programs. This is a very good percentage for a charity. Tell students that it is also important to find out how charitable organizations treat their own workers.

 RESPOND

ANALYZE THE TEXT

Support your responses with evidence from the text. 📓 NOTEBOOK

1. **Cause/Effect** How does the story about the murdered boy reflect Kielburger's subjective point of view on life and the world?

2. **Critique** Reread paragraphs 6 and 7. Why do you think Kielburger provides this kind of supporting evidence? What effect might he hope this information has on the reader? How effective is this information in supporting his controlling idea?

3. **Draw Conclusions** What is Kielburger's purpose in saying that he is gifted in paragraph 14?

4. **Analyze** How does Kielburger connect the introduction and conclusion of his essay?

5. **Notice & Note** Throughout the essay, Kielburger uses extreme or absolute language—for example, "We have all met individuals who are gifted . . ." and ". . . so that children do not have to die." Explain the effect that such language has on the reader and whether you think it helps the author achieve his purpose.

RESEARCH

RESEARCH TIP
Most charities have a domain name that ends in *.org* or *.net*. A charity's homepage usually features a menu across the top that helps users navigate the site and directs them to the information they seek, including how they can support the organization's mission.

Today, WE Charity includes many of the goals of Free the Children. Research the following programs of WE Charity. With a partner, generate questions about WE Charity and then research the answers. Record what you learn in this chart.

PROGRAM	WHAT IT IS/WHAT IT DOES
WE Villages	*WE Villages is a model for ending poverty. It addresses the five primary causes of poverty, focusing on solutions for each one: Education, clean water and sanitation, healthcare, food security, and alternative income*
WE Schools	*This is a year-long educational program that nurtures compassion in students, helps them identify local and global issues, and provides tools to help them create social change.*
WE Day	*This series of stadium-sized events celebrates youth who have taken action through the WE Schools program. WE Day is filled with inspirational stories and speakers and performers, all encouraging young people making a difference in their community and globally.*

Connect Meet with a small group to share and discuss your findings. Which program or programs interest you the most? Why?

CREATE AND DISCUSS

Write a Research Report Write a short (1–2 pages) research report about WE Charity.

- ❏ Review your findings from the Research on the previous page.
- ❏ Organize your findings and ideas by creating an outline. Then write a working thesis statement.
- ❏ Write your report, using your outline as a guide. Include details and other evidence from your research to support your ideas.

Discuss with a Small Group A slogan of the WE movement is "Making doing good, doable." Discuss whether Craig Kielburger was a rare example of a young humanitarian or whether all young people have the capacity to act on their social awareness.

- ❏ As a group, review the essay and discuss the qualities that you think allowed Craig Kielburger to do what he did.
- ❏ Then talk about whether these qualities are rare or if all young people share them. How much help do you think he received from his parents and teachers? How important is this support?
- ❏ Finally, discuss how a person who wants to make a difference might get started.

RESPOND

Go to **Conducting Research** in the **Writing Studio** to learn more.

Go to **Participating in Collaborative Discussions** in the **Speaking and Listening Studio** for help.

RESPOND TO THE ESSENTIAL QUESTION

 What inspires you to make a difference?

Gather Information Review your annotations and notes on "Craig Kielburger Reflects on Working Toward Peace." Then, add relevant details to your Response Log. As you determine which information to include, think about:

- what caused Kielburger to start his charity
- what kinds of problems children around the world face
- what solutions Kielburger has identified

At the end of the unit, use your notes to help you write a research report.

ACADEMIC VOCABULARY

As you write about and discuss what you learned from the personal essay, be sure to use the Academic Vocabulary words. Check off each of the words that you use.

- ❏ contrast
- ❏ despite
- ❏ error
- ❏ inadequate
- ❏ interact

APPLY

CREATE AND DISCUSS

Write a Research Report Point out to students that doing research begins with deciding what you need to find out. One of the best ways to do that is to formulate a set of questions that you hope to answer about WE Charity.

 For **writing support** for students at varying proficiency levels, see the **Text X-Ray** on page 436D.

Discuss with a Small Group Remind students that a successful discussion depends on the participation of everyone in the group. If students think they will have trouble expressing their opinions, have them write a sentence ahead of time that communicates a thought or feeling. Then they can read that sentence when their turn to speak comes in the discussion.

RESPOND TO THE ESSENTIAL QUESTION

Allow time for students to add details from "Craig Kielburger Reflects on Working Toward Peace" to their Unit 6 Response Logs.

APPLY

CRITICAL VOCABULARY

Answers:

1. inquire: When you inquire, or ask, you expect to get an answer.
2. syringe: A needle is part of a syringe, which is a medical instrument that injects or draws out fluids.
3. exploitation: Underpaid workers are used unfairly, which is an example of exploitation.
4. possession: Something that you own, or possess, is a possession.
5. capacity: If you have the capacity to do something, you have the skill to do it.

VOCABULARY STRATEGY: WORD ORIGIN

Answers:

1. Latin: sÿringa meaning "injection" The meaning is related because a syringe is used to make an injection.
1. Latin: possidere meaning "to have or control" The meaning is related because a possession is something you have or own.
1. Latin: inquīrere, same meaning.
1. Old French, exploitation, "use for profit." The meaning is related because exploitation means using a person for profit.

 ENGLISH LEARNER SUPPORT

Spell Suffixes That Sound Alike Tell students that a base word ending in -t, -te, or -ate, such as *decorate*, will often take the *-tion* suffix to form a noun. Words ending in -s often take an *-sion* ending to form a noun. Guide students to use the correct spellings with the following words: *discuss, suggest, possess, depress, inspect, educate, create*. Point out that there are exceptions—such as *submit/submission*.
MODERATE/LIGHT

---

448 Unit 6

 RESPOND

WORD BANK
syringe
possession
inquire
capacity
exploitation

CRITICAL VOCABULARY

Practice and Apply Identify the Critical Vocabulary word that is most closely related to the boldfaced word in each question. Be prepared to explain your choices.

1. Which word goes with **answer**? _____
2. Which word goes with **needle**? _____
3. Which word goes with **underpaid**? _____
4. Which word goes with **ownership**? _____
5. Which word goes with **skill**? _____

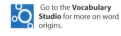 Go to the **Vocabulary Studio** for more on word origins.

VOCABULARY STRATEGY: Word Origin

Word origin, or etymology, tells you which language a word came from and gives you the historical development of the word. For example, if you look in a dictionary, you will see that the word *capacity* comes most recently from Middle English. However, it can be traced back through Old French and finally to the Latin word *capācitās,* from *capāx,* which means "spacious." *Capacity* has several meanings, one of which is "the maximum amount that something can hold."

Practice and Apply Follow these steps to explore the origin of each of this lesson's other Critical Vocabulary words.

- Look up each word in a print or online dictionary. You may want to look at a simpler form of the word as noted in the chart below.
- Find each word's origin or etymology. For help, look at the front or back of a dictionary. There will be a section that explains how the etymology is noted and what the abbreviations used mean.
- Write each word's origin and original meaning in the chart. Is the word's meaning related to the original meaning? How?

VOCABULARY WORD	ORIGIN/MEANING
syringe	
possession (possess)	
inquire	
exploitation (exploit)	

448 Unit 6

 ENGLISH LEARNER SUPPORT

Understand the Suffix -ion Explain to students that English words often have parts that change their meaning or the way they can be used in a sentence. Display the word *possession*. Underline the base word, *possess*. Say: *This word is a verb. Possess. It means "to own something."* Underline the suffix *–ion*. Then explain that *-ion* is a word part that changes a verb to a noun. It is like the Spanish suffixes *-ción/* and *sion*. Circle the whole word *possession*. Say: *the word possession is a noun that means "something that is owned."* Repeat the process with one or two more words, such as *prediction* and *action*. **MODERATE/LIGHT**

RESPOND

LANGUAGE CONVENTIONS: Commas

Commas have a variety of purposes. Used correctly, they help writers communicate effectively. They show readers which words and phrases go together and indicate which part of a sentence is most important. They can also create pauses, which give readers a moment to think about what they are reading. In "Craig Kielburger Reflects on Working Toward Peace," commas are used for several reasons, including these:

- To set off introductory words or phrases:

    Indeed, even the most physically or mentally challenged person teaches all of us about the value and worth of human life.

- To set off nonessential words, phrases, and clauses:

    If more people had the heart of a street child, like José, and were willing to share, there would be no more poverty and a lot less suffering in this world.

- To separate dependent clauses from independent clauses:

    Although José's shirt was dirty and had a few small holes, it was a colorful soccer shirt and certainly much nicer than mine.

- To separate two independent clauses joined by one of the coordinating conjunctions: *and, but, or, for, nor, so,* or *yet*:

    He may have been a poor street child, but I saw more goodness in him than all of the world leaders I have ever met.

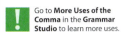 Go to **More Uses of the Comma** in the **Grammar Studio** to learn more uses.

Practice and Apply Write your own sentences with commas using the examples from "Craig Kielburger Reflects on Working Toward Peace" as models. Your sentences can be about Craig Kielburger's work or about a topic related to helping others. When you have finished, share your sentences with a partner and compare your use of commas.

 ENGLISH LEARNER SUPPORT

Combine Clauses Correctly In some languages, including Cantonese, Korean, and Vietnamese, speakers sometimes use a "balancing" word in the main clause after an introductory adverbial clause. For example, *Because the book is long,* **so** *it may take me a while to read it.* Or *After the program starts,* **then** *I don't like to talk.* **MODERATE/LIGHT**

Work with students to help them avoid adding that additional connecting word in English.

APPLY

LANGUAGE CONVENTIONS: COMMAS

Review the information about commas, and then provide further information and examples of each comma usage.

To set off introductory words or phrases. Explain that an introductory word or phrase may give information about when, where, how, or why.

- Yesterday, I ate lunch with Josie.
- In the backyard, the flowers are blooming.
- With a shovel, digging was easy.
- Just to be sure, I checked the lock twice.

To set off nonessential words, phrases, and clauses. Explain that some modifying elements are essential to the meaning of a sentence. "I chose the shirt with long sleeves." The phrase "with long sleeves" identifies the shirt and is essential to the meaning. Some modifying elements are not essential. "My sister, a teacher, makes good coffee." The phrase "a teacher" is not essential.

- The cat, licking its paw, ignored me.
- The cat with the black spots is my favorite.

To separate dependent clauses from independent clauses. When a dependent clause comes before an independent clause, it is separated by a comma.

- When I looked again, the bird was gone.
- I will call you when I get home.

To separate two independent clauses joined by a coordinating conjunction. If two independent clauses are not joined by a conjunction, they are separated by a semicolon.

- He was late, but it didn't really matter.
- I walked home; it was a nice day.

Have students read the following example sentences and delete the word that does not belong:

- Because I was late, *(so)* I had to run the last block to school.
- When I finished my homework, *(then)* I helped fix dinner.

Practice and Apply Have partners discuss whether commas are used correctly in their sentences. *(Students' sentences will vary.)*

PLAN

MEDIA
from IT TAKES A CHILD
Documentary by Judy Jackson

GENRE ELEMENTS
DOCUMENTARY

Inform students that most **documentary** films capture aspects of reality and present them in the form of a nonfiction story or a journalistic report; still others are more artistic in nature. All involve making creative choices that stem from the point of view of the filmmaker. Many documentaries feature interviews, scripted voice-over narration, sound effects, visual effects, and music. Others rely more on sound recorded synchronously with the image and little else in the way of effects: these films tend to follow the action of the film's subjects rather than depending on interviews. The earliest documentaries had subtitles and no recorded sound.

LEARNING OBJECTIVES

- Analyze documentary film.
- Conduct research on child and youth activists.
- Write a personal essay about social activism.
- Create a podcast film review of "It Takes a Child."
- Analyze sound effects and film footage.
- **Language** Discuss with a partner elements of an interview.

TEXT COMPLEXITY

Qualitative Measures	It Takes a Child	Lexile: N/A
Qualitative Measures	**Ideas Presented** Simple, single meaning, basic and explicit	
	Structure Used Easily identified structure	
	Language Used Explicit, literal, and contemporary language	
	Knowledge Required Requires no special knowledge	

PLAN

Online

RESOURCES

- Unit 6 Response Log
- 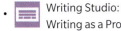 Reading Studio: Notice & Note
- Writing Studio: Writing as a Process
- Speaking and Listening Studio: Using Media in a Presentation
- "It Takes a Child" Selection Test

SUMMARIES

English

In 1995, child-rights activist Craig Kielburger went to India chaperoned by a family friend. He went specifically to research the dangerous world of child labor there. Filmmaker Judy Jackson documented what he discovered while there. The resulting film, "It Takes a Child," shows just how far a gritty, devoted young person can go when he really wants to get involved and become an agent of global change.

Spanish

En 1995, al joven e inexperimentado activista infantil Craig Kielburger le permitieron que fuera a la India solo, a la edad de doce años, para investigar el peligroso mundo del trabajo infantil. La cineasta Judy Jackson lo siguió cámara en mano, grabando cada momento de la investigación del intrépido niño. El resultado fue la película It Takes a Child, que muestra qué tan lejos puede llegar una persona joven, enérgica y ferviente cuando verdaderamente quiere involucrarse y convertirse en un agente del cambio global.

SMALL-GROUP OPTIONS

Have students work in small groups to read and discuss the selection.

Sticky Note Review

- Break students into groups or pairs.
- Provide each group with pads of sticky notes.
- Ask the groups to re-watch the film and to jot down one of each of the following: one positive comment, one critical comment, and one question about the text.
- Students then exchange the sticky notes, marking the notes they agree with or have questions or answers to add.
- Students discuss and exchange ideas.

Think-Pair-Share

- After students have read and digested "It Takes a Child," ask the class a question, such as: *How inspired do you have to be to become a change agent?*
- Have students think about the question individually, and take notes on their thoughts.
- Put students into pairs so they can discuss their answers.
- Finally, ask students to share their answers with the class.

PLAN

Text X-Ray: English Learner Support
for "It Takes a Child"

Use the Text X-Ray and the supports and scaffolds in the Teacher's Edition to help guide students at different proficiency levels through the selection.

INTRODUCE THE SELECTION
DISCUSS DOCUMENTARY FILM

In this lesson, students will need to be able to discuss how filmmaking elements and techniques are used to document activism and social justice issues. Help students understand the terms: *interview, footage, sound,* and *voice-over narration.* Have them consider and discuss what a documentary film can convey that text cannot by using:

- Visual media: this includes unedited footage, and the edited film.
- Audio: Sound recorded synchronously with the image, sound effects, voice-over narration, and music

Tell students they are going to watch a documentary in which the interviewer travels to South Asia to learn more about poverty, child labor, slavery, and the complex web of people and institutions that either profit from these practices or allow them to continue. Provide students with illustrated literature, and ask them to complete the following: *I would like to learn more about_____.*

CULTURAL REFERENCES

The following words and phrases may be unfamiliar to students:

- *child labor*: the largely illegal but still occurring practice of forcing small children to work
- *South Asia*: the global region that includes Nepal, India, Pakistan, Bangladesh, and Sri Lanka
- *Camcorder*: small, handheld video cameras
- *AIDS*: acquired immune deficiency syndrome, AIDS, is a life threatening disease spread through the blood and through sexual contact
- *first-hand*: an adjective meaning *direct* or *in person*; when something is *firsthand knowledge* it is not read in a book but learned in a real-life situation

LISTENING

Understand the Power of Voice

Ask students to pay close attention to the information contained in the narration and the interviews. Have them note the tone of voice used by the interviewer and the filmmaker. Explain that Judy Jackson was the filmmaker and one of the two narrators.

Have students watch the film and pay close attention to narration. Use the following supports with students at varying proficiency levels:

- Ask questions about the narration, and have students respond with thumbs up or down or brief answers. Ask: *Did Craig Kielburger go to India? (yes) Did he study child labor? (yes) Who was doing most of the talking? (Craig Kielburger)* **SUBSTANTIAL**
- Have students take notes during the film, and then ask them questions. *Why did Craig Kielburger go to India? (to study child labor) Who is the filmmaker? (Judy Jackson) Who was doing the voice-over narration? (Craig Kielburger and Judy Jackson)* **MODERATE**
- Ask pairs to seek clarification about anything they might not have understood, then ask: *How would you describe the tone of Craig Kielburger's voice-over? How did he sound while delivering speeches in the film? Was it effective? Why or why not?* **LIGHT**

PLAN

SPEAKING

Understand Interviews

Help students understand that many documentaries depend on interviews to provide structure and depth for exploring their subjects.

Use the following supports with students at varying proficiency levels:

- Play a section of the film in which Craig Kielburger is interviewing someone, and say: *This is an interview. This is the interviewer. This is the interviewee.* Have students repeat after you. **SUBSTANTIAL**
- Point to the illustrated literature from the selection introduction, and use gestures to indicate that students should pick an issue that interests them. Provide the sentence frame, model using it, and have students verbally complete it by using a word from the literature: *I would like to interview people about_____.* **MODERATE**
- Pair students and have them interview each other about their views of the film "It Takes a Child." Circulate to be sure that students are asking clear, respectful questions and giving clear answers. **LIGHT**

READING

Research Nonfiction Subjects

Have students research Craig Kielburger, poverty, and child labor.

Use the following supports with students at varying proficiency levels:

- Provide illustrated background reading related to the subject of the video. Help students to identify, decode, and define key words in the captions or in the text. Have them label images and their own drawings with the key words, then paste them into word web/concept graphic organizers. **SUBSTANTIAL**
- Have students create cause and effect graphic organizers using key words from illustrated pamphlets and literature. Encourage them to seek clarification when necessary. **MODERATE**
- Pair students and ask them retell what they discovered in their research about child labor and/or another activist whose work has been the subject of a documentary. **LIGHT**

WRITING

Write a Personal Essay

Draw students' attention to the writing assignment on p. 453. Suggest that they think about people and events that have inspired them.

Use the following supports with students at varying proficiency levels:

- Ask students to review their labeled images and parts of the video; have them use word banks to find words that will help them describe what they felt as they viewed "It Takes a Child." Write the words on the board, and have students copy them into their notebooks. Help students use the words to describe any other social issue they have encountered **SUBSTANTIAL**
- Provide sentence frames, such as the following, that students can use to create outlines for their essays: *I felt that the interviews were _____. I thought that the footage and sound were effective because_____.* Help students use the frames to describe any other social issue they know about. **MODERATE**
- Have students work individually to jot down ideas. Then, have them work in pairs to create timelines of the action that will help them to write outlines for their essays. Finally, have them work on their outlines. **LIGHT**

TEACH

Connect to the
ESSENTIAL QUESTION

"It Takes a Child" documents the international activist work of Craig Kielburger. The documentary portrays how and why Kielburger was inspired to travel to South Asia at the age of twelve. The camera follows him as he meets children who work virtually as slaves. In order to show the different ways he has worked to make a difference in the world, the film features footage from other periods of Kielburger's life.

QUICK START

Have students form small groups to discuss social issues that they find crucial or that affect them directly. Call on students to talk about an issue they feel is important for the class, their school, or the community in general.

ANALYZE A DOCUMENTARY

Review the terms and concepts from the introduction. Then, remind students of the ways documentaries are related to articles and stories. Films and stories share elements such as perspective, tone, narrative, mood, and dialogue.

Inform students that understanding the separate elements will help them better understand and enjoy documentary films. Have them take notes on the following questions as they watch:

- Who is interviewed in the film and why?
- How does the film use different kinds of footage and for what effect?
- In what ways is the voice-over helpful to the viewer?
- How are sound effects used? (For example, how do the street sounds in India compare with what the viewer has heard before?)

■ English Learner Support

Look It Up Have student pairs watch the film while making notes on words, terms, and ideas they don't know (e.g., *AIDS, unemployed, development*). With their joint list, partners will then look up the words and discuss them to get a better understanding of their meaning. Circulate to make sure students define and use the words correctly.
MODERATE/LIGHT

ANALYZE & APPLY

MEDIA

from
IT TAKES A CHILD

Documentary by **Judy Jackson**

? ESSENTIAL QUESTION:

What inspires you to make a difference?

QUICK START

What problem or issue do you feel strongly about? What would you be willing to do to solve that problem? Discuss your ideas with a partner.

ANALYZE A DOCUMENTARY

GENRE ELEMENTS: DOCUMENTARY
- includes interviews filmed specifically for the documentary
- contains filmed material—or footage—that gives information about the topic
- features voice-over narration—the voice of an unseen speaker—to give facts or explain
- includes sound effects used for a variety of purposes

A **documentary** is a nonfiction film about important people, events, issues, or places. Documentaries include **interviews, film footage, voice-over narration,** and **sound effects** to convey information, mood, and tone, or the author's attitude toward the subject. As you watch the film clip, think about how these features work together.

FEATURE	STRATEGIES FOR VIEWING
Interviews feature experts on the subject or someone close to the person or event.	Consider the person being interviewed. Does he or she have special knowledge or present another side of the story?
Footage can include film clips, reports, photos, and interviews about a subject.	Consider why the footage was chosen. Does it reveal the filmmaker's attitude toward the topic? Does it show emotions?
Voice-over narration is scripted to present key facts and explain their importance.	Listen to the voice-over narration. Does it change from speaker to speaker? Does the language contribute to mood or tone?
Sound effects include music and sounds that show mood and signal shifts in the topic.	Follow music cues. Do they signal a change in setting or mood? Listen for sound effects. Do they clarify events?

450 Unit 6

 ENGLISH LEARNER SUPPORT

Understand Features of Documentary Film Help students understand the meaning of the following: *interview, footage,* and *voice-over narration*. Use the following sentence frames to determine whether students understand the different features.

1) Video of a journalist asking questions is an example of an _____.

2) Moving images with sound is an example of _____.

3) The voice of an unseen speaker that explains something in film is _____.
MODERATE

GET READY

BACKGROUND

When child activist Craig Kielburger was twelve years old, he became interested in the plight of child laborers. Inspired by the story of twelve-year-old Iqbal, a child labor activist who had been murdered in South Asia, Kielburger realized that a child could make a difference in the world. Kielburger then traveled to South Asia to see child labor first hand. With the help of a film crew, he documented his journey so that the world could see what he had witnessed.

SETTING A PURPOSE

As you view the documentary, think about why Kielburger decided to make this journey and what he wanted to find out. Notice the ways that filmmaking and news reporting come together to help you understand Kielburger's reasons for traveling to South Asia. Write down any questions you have during viewing. 📓 **NOTEBOOK** .

For more online resources, log in to your dashboard and click on **"from It Takes a Child"** from the selection menu.

As needed, pause the documentary to make notes about what impresses you or about ideas you might want to talk about later. Replay or rewind so that you can clarify anything you do not understand.

WHEN STUDENTS STRUGGLE . . .

Organize Prior Knowledge Help students prepare for viewing the documentary. Ask them to seek clarification of the following words and terms: *children's rights, activism, child labor, South Asia, research, documentary film, Toronto*. Ask students to match their drawings or found images to these words and places. Have students create a KWL chart that will help them keep track of important vocabulary and facts that they learn during the course of watching the film. Tell them that the goal is to obtain descriptive references for unfamiliar words that will come up in the course of activities related to the film.

TEACH

BACKGROUND

Have students read the Background note. Tell them that in the 20th century, many progressive reforms were written into law throughout the world; children were protected from abusive practices for the first time in the industrial era. Point out that in many countries where poverty is prevalent, many of these laws are unenforced and children still work as slaves or bonded labor. According the film, in 1995 there were 55 million child workers in India. Encourage students to research how things have changed since then.

SETTING A PURPOSE

Direct students to use the Setting a Purpose prompt to focus their viewing.

APPLY

ANALYZE MEDIA

Possible answers:

1. **DOK 2:** *The controlling idea is that some children are forced to work and that this practice is unjust. In the scenes that depict this, the author interviews laborers and shows visuals of the lives of child laborers.*

2. **DOK 4:** *The filmmaker's purpose is to inform and persuade the viewer that child labor is unjust. The footage of the girl with the syringes is startling and sad.*

3. **DOK 2: Interviews:** *The interview with a man concerning the girl with the syringes shows how indifferent some people are to child labor.*

   Footage: *Footage of Kielburger observing the work shows how passionately he views his subject.*

   Voice-over: *A woman's voice-over gives details about the trip. Kielburger's voice, as a fifteen-year-old, describes his goals and his reactions.*

   Sound effects: *We hear music from India, which stops at certain points for emphasis.*

4. **DOK 4:** *The opening footage, with scenes and music from India, gives viewers a sense of the culture.*

5. **DOK 4:** *The unnamed narrator provides a factual account of why Kielburger visited India and background information on child labor. The boy's narration provides a personal response to India.*

RESEARCH

Remind students to confirm their research by checking several sources, such as print and digital newspapers, journals, and encyclopedias.

Connect Put students in pairs and ask them to choose an activist to study. Encourage them to study "It Takes a Child" as well as other documentary films to find strong approaches for portraying their own film ideas.

 RESPOND

ANALYZE MEDIA

Support your responses with evidence from the documentary.

📓 **NOTEBOOK**

1. **Infer and Summarize** What is the controlling idea, or thesis, of the documentary? Describe the scenes that take place in the film and how those scenes support the key idea.

2. **Analyze** Identify the filmmaker's purpose(s) in making the documentary. What key parts of the film convey the purpose(s)?

3. **Infer** Think about the features the filmmaker uses. Explain how the filmmaker uses interviews, film footage, voice-over, and sound effects to clarify the issues presented in the documentary.

4. **Analyze** How does the opening introduce the setting? What combination of features works together in the opening to create a sense of the place Kielburger is visiting and to help you understand the setting?

5. **Compare and Contrast** The voice-over narration includes two narrators: an unnamed speaker and Craig Kielburger. The unnamed narrator is objective, while Craig Kielburger's narration is subjective. Compare and contrast the language and types of information given by the two narrators. How does each contribute to the mood and tone of the documentary?

RESEARCH

RESEARCH TIP
Because information on the Internet is not regulated for accuracy, ensure accuracy either by using only reputable sources (those ending in *.edu*, *.gov*, and *.org*) or by verifying by using multiple sources.

Many other young activists are currently working to solve problems they care about. With a partner, do some research to find two examples of other young activists and the problems they are working to solve. Record your information in the chart.

ACTIVIST	PROBLEM
Malala Yousafzai	*lack of education for girls in Pakistan and other countries*

Connect How would you present your information in a documentary about one of the young activists you researched? With your partner, sketch out the sound and visual elements you would include to convey this information.

RESPOND

CREATE AND PRESENT

Write a Personal Essay Write a personal essay about an encounter with a social activist or an experience with social action that was inspirational.

- ❏ Jot down ideas about the experience and why it was meaningful.
- ❏ Use your ideas to create an outline. Your outline should show the events in a logical order.
- ❏ Write your essay, using the first-person point of view. Use colorful and specific words to describe exactly what you saw, heard, and felt.
- ❏ In your conclusion, summarize why the event or person was inspirational.

Produce a Podcast With a partner, create an audio recording for a podcast review of the documentary clip from *It Takes a Child*.

- ❏ Make notes about visual and sound elements in the documentary that particularly impressed you, both positively and negatively.
- ❏ Explain how the choice of screen scenes affects the impact of the words spoken in the interviews. Include an assessment of whether viewers should see the entire documentary.
- ❏ Create the recording of your review with a partner, speaking in a conversational tone and enunciating clearly. Share your podcast with a larger group.

 Go to **Writing as a Process** in the **Writing Studio** for more help.

 Go to **Using Media in a Presentation** in the **Speaking and Listening Studio** to learn more.

RESPOND TO THE ESSENTIAL QUESTION

 What inspires you to make a difference?

Gather Information Review your annotations and notes on the film clip from *It Takes a Child*. Then, add relevant details to your Response Log. As you determine which information to include, think about:

- what motivated Craig Kielburger's journey
- how you think people might react to the documentary

At the end of the unit, use your notes to help you write a research report.

ACADEMIC VOCABULARY
As you write about and discuss what you learned from the documentary, be sure to use the Academic Vocabulary words. Check off each of the words that you use.

- ❏ contrast
- ❏ despite
- ❏ error
- ❏ inadequate
- ❏ interact

It Takes a Child 453

APPLY

CREATE AND PRESENT

Write a Personal Essay Assist students who haven't been directly involved in social justice activism by encouraging them to brainstorm about the acts of others whom they admire. Tell them to think about inspirational experiences they may have had with classmates, friends, or family. Remind students that the point is to write an essay about a person or moment that was inspired them.

For **writing support** for students at varying proficiency levels, see the Text X-Ray on page 450D.

Produce a Podcast Remind students that they should critique all the features of documentary media—interviews, footage, voice-over, and sound effects—in their podcast review. Encourage students to use the list on p. 453 as a blueprint and to script their podcast as thoroughly as possible before recording.

RESPOND TO THE ESSENTIAL QUESTION

Allow time for students to add details from "It Takes a Child" to their Unit 6 Response Logs.

 ENGLISH LEARNER SUPPORT

Oral Assessment Use the following questions to assess students' comprehension and speaking skills:

- Who is Craig Kielburger in the film "It Takes a Child"? *(Craig Kielburger is a child activist who went to India.)* **SUBSTANTIAL**
- What is the basic story of Craig Kielburger in the film "It Takes a Child"? *(Craig Kielburger is a Canadian children's-rights activist who went to India to study child labor practices in 1995.)* **MODERATE**
- What inspired Craig Kielburger to do what he did in the film "It Takes a Child" and why do you believe his work is important? *(Answers will vary. Craig Kielburger's trip to India was inspired by the harsh child labor practices going on there and Craig's desire to change them. It's important because child labor laws can work and have worked in many countries.)* **LIGHT**

It Takes a Child 453

PLAN

SOMETIMES A DREAM NEEDS A PUSH

Short Story by Walter Dean Myers

GENRE ELEMENTS
REALISTIC FICTION

Remind students that the purpose of **realistic fiction** is to tell the reader a story about real-life obstacles as well as real-life lessons. In a **short story**, the characters, their traits, and the conflicts will be introduced very quickly. The author of realistic fiction will fill the prose with details that come from everyday life, but write them in such a way as to make them seem anything but mundane. By the end, the character(s) will have overcome an obstacle and learned a valuable life lesson that readers will be able to relate to experiences in their own lives.

LEARNING OBJECTIVES

- Analyze features of realistic fiction.
- Research wheelchair basketball.
- Write an informative article about wheelchair basketball.
- Create a video critique of the story
- Use consistent verb tenses.
- Use context clues to determine word meaning.
- **Language** Identify character qualities in a short story.

TEXT COMPLEXITY

Quantitative Measures	Sometimes a Dream Needs a Push	Lexile: 770L
Qualitative Measures	**Ideas Presented** Much is explicit but moves to some implied meaning	
	Structure Used Clear, chronological, conventional	
	Language Used Some dialect, some figurative language	
	Knowledge Required Begins to rely more on outside knowledge	

454A Unit 6

PLAN

RESOURCES

- Unit 6 Response Log
- 🔊 Selection Audio
- 📖 Reading Studio: Notice & Note
- Level Up Tutorial: Short Stories and Novels.
- Writing Studio: Introduction: Informative Texts
- Speaking and Listening Studio: Using Media in a Presentation
- Vocabulary Studio: Context Clues
- Grammar Studio: Module 9: Using Verbs Correctly
- "Sometimes a Dream Needs a Push" Selection Test

SUMMARIES

English
Chris, the son of a former pro basketball player, is involved in a car crash and loses the use of his legs. Chris's father has grown distant from him. When an elder at the family's church invites Chris to join the church's new wheelchair basketball team, Chris's father displays little interest. However, when Chris's father does start coming to basketball practice, he lends his expertise to the boys' team. By the end, Chris has rediscovered his bond with his father.

Spanish
Chris, el hijo de un antiguo jugador profesional de baloncesto, tiene un accidente de tránsito y pierde la movilidad en las piernas. Su padre se ha alejado de él. Cuando una persona mayor de la iglesia invita a Chris a unirse al nuevo equipo de baloncesto sobre sillas de ruedas de la iglesia, su padre muestra poco interés. Sin embargo, cuando el padre de Chris comienza a ir a las prácticas de baloncesto, presta su pericia al equipo. Al final, Chris ha redescubierto su vínculo con su padre.

SMALL-GROUP OPTIONS

Have students work in small groups to read and discuss the selection.

Pinwheel Discussion
- Divide students into groups of eight. Have four students sit in a square, facing out. Then, have each of the other four students sit facing the students in the inner square.
- Instruct students in the inner square to remain stationary throughout the discussion.
- Have students in the outer square move to face the student to their right after discussing each question.
- Control the discussion by providing a question for each rotation. For example, "Why does Chris's dad grumble?" "What do you think happens after the story ends?"

Double-Entry Journal
- Have students divide a piece of notebook paper down the middle, and add the following headings to each column: "Quotes from the Text" and "My Notes."
- Instruct students to record significant or perplexing passages in the left column.
- In the right column, have students write their own interpretations, summaries, questions, and restatements opposite the quoted material, leaving space for more notes if necessary.

Sometimes a Dream Needs a Push **454B**

PLAN

Text X-Ray: English Learner Support
for "Sometimes a Dream Needs a Push"

Use the Text-X-Ray and the supports and scaffolds in the Teacher's Edition to help guide students at different proficiency levels through the selection.

INTRODUCE THE SELECTION

DISCUSS GOALS AND DREAMS

Tell students that the word *dream* has multiple meanings. It can be the thoughts and images you have while sleeping, but in this story it means a special goal that someone wants to achieve.

Guide students to come up with specific goals. Tell them that this could be a job they want to do, a skill they want to learn, or a place they'd like to visit or live. Provide sentence frames:

My dream is to _____. When I grow up, I want to be a _____.

Explain that sometimes things happen that make it hard to achieve dreams. In the story, Chris can no longer walk, but he still finds a way to play basketball. Guide students to describe how they will achieve their dreams:

I will _____ to achieve my dream.

CULTURAL REFERENCES

The following words and phrases may be unfamiliar to students:

- *she was all for it* (paragraph 7): eagerly agreeable
- *under his breath* (paragraph 7, 24): saying something so low no one can hear it
- *pj's* (paragraph 11): short for pajamas
- *My heart sank* (paragraph 22): feeling sad when hearing bad news
- *baseline* (paragraph 35): boundary line
- *bumper cars* (paragraph 61): carnival game in which people drive small cars and bump into each other
- *layup* (paragraph 61): in basketball, a shot made near the basket that bounces off the backboard and (hopefully) into the basket

LISTENING

Understand Character Qualities

Work with students to read the Analyze Character Qualities section on p. 455. Draw students' attention to details in the story that identify character qualities.

Have students listen as you read aloud paragraphs 3–7. Use the following supports with students at varying proficiency levels:

- Tell students you will ask some questions about what they just heard. Model that they should give a thumbs up if the answer is yes, and a thumbs down for no. For example, ask: *Does Chris's mom want him to play basketball?* (yes) **SUBSTANTIAL**
- Have students identify the character qualities (shy, guilty, helpful) described in the excerpt. Ask: *How did the paragraph help you better understand the characters?* **MODERATE**
- After listening to the excerpt, ask students to work in pairs to list details from the excerpt that support their impressions of the characters. **LIGHT**

454C   Unit 6

PLAN

SPEAKING

Critique the Story

Help students prepare for the Video Critique assignment outlined on p. 465. Explain that to critique something means to review it in detail. Have students note any important or interesting details in the story that they can discuss in their critiques.

Use the following supports with students at varying proficiency levels:

- Have students prepare their critiques with a partner using the following sentence frames: *I liked/disliked this story because _____. I liked/disliked [character name] because he/she _____. I did/didn't like it in the story when _____. The story would have been better/not as good if _____.* **SUBSTANTIAL**

- Help students underline ten or more words that seem "most important" to the story. Guide pairs to critique the story, using as many of the underlined words as possible in their discussion. **MODERATE**

- Provide student pairs with the following sentence frames when they first discuss their critiques: *What do you mean by _____? That's a good point because _____. I agree with your point, but _____.* **LIGHT**

READING

Read Realistic Fiction

Tell students that authors of realistic fiction set their stories in real places, during a recent time period, and the events and characters of the story are meant to seem like real people. There will also be many vivid details and descriptions that add more flavor to everyday life.

Work with students to reread paragraphs 18–22. Use the following supports with students at varying proficiency levels:

- Echo read the excerpt. Read aloud one sentence at a time, then have students repeat the sentence back to you. Point out aspects of realism, such as when Chris thinks, "which is a little irritating when you've got a ton of homework." Ask yes or no questions: *Does Chris act like a real teenager?* (yes) **SUBSTANTIAL**

- Ask students to identify the tension in the excerpt. (*Chris is nervous that his coach called his dad.*) Have them explain whether they felt suspense in this excerpt. **MODERATE**

- Pair students to analyze the excerpt. Ask: *What makes the excerpt realistic and how does the author build suspense using realism?* (*Chris and his mom talk like normal people; Suspense is built when it is revealed Mr. Evans called for his father, but we have to wait until dinner to find out why.*) **LIGHT**

WRITING

Write an Informational Article

Work with students to read and understand the writing assignment on p. 465.

Use the following supports with students at varying proficiency levels:

- Work with students to identify words and phrases in the text that they can use in their final product. Have students copy these to their notebooks. Help them use these terms from the story to seek out information in their research. If needed, students can present their articles in graphic form. **SUBSTANTIAL**

- Provide sentence frames students can use to craft their articles: *What I didn't know about wheelchair basketball before was _____. One difference between wheelchair basketball and traditional basketball is _____. The nearest wheelchair basketball league is _____.* **MODERATE**

- Encourage students to compare the information they found in the research to what they read in the short story. How realistic was it depicted in the story? **LIGHT**

TEACH

? Connect to the ESSENTIAL QUESTION

This selection tells the story of a family who suffered a tragic accident in which the son is left unable to walk. The son has trouble connecting with his father, a former pro-basketball player who dreamed his son would someday play too. But then the son joins a wheelchair basketball team. Students will see that after a tragic setback, dreams don't have to die, after all.

ANALYZE & APPLY

SOMETIMES A DREAM NEEDS A PUSH

Short Story by **Walter Dean Myers**

? ESSENTIAL QUESTION:

What inspires you to make a difference?

LEARNING MINDSET

Plan/Predict Remind students that planning is essential to completing work efficiently and exceptionally. Encourage them to make a plan for completing an assignment, including mapping out the steps. For this section, they can flip ahead to see that they will be writing an informational article and creating a video critique. As they are reading the selection, they can begin noting important details. Explain that careful planning makes the final product much more impressive.

GET READY

QUICK START

How might guilt, or feelings of regret, affect your relationship with someone? List some ideas and then discuss them with a small group.

ANALYZE REALISTIC FICTION

Realistic fiction is fiction that is set in the real, modern world. The characters, setting, problems, and resolution are all believable.

- The characters behave like real people when faced with modern life's problems and conflicts.
- The dialogue reflects the age and culture of the characters.
- The setting is a real or realistic place (for example, a modern city). The story takes place in the present or recent past.
- The conflicts that the characters face can be internal or external. These conflicts often reflect social issues or problems that real people are likely to face.

As you read "Sometimes a Dream Needs a Push," look for these realistic elements to help you analyze the story.

GENRE ELEMENTS: REALISTIC FICTION
- includes the basic elements of fiction: setting, characters, plot, conflict, and theme
- centers on one particular moment or event in life
- if in the form of a short story, can be read in one sitting

ANALYZE CHARACTER QUALITIES

Character **qualities** may be physical traits (such as athletic ability) or personality traits (such as shyness). Just as in real life, a fictional character's qualities can influence events and relationships. Characters' qualities can affect how they interact and how they resolve both internal and external conflicts in a story. As you read "Sometimes a Dream Needs a Push," make inferences about the qualities of Chris and his father based on their words, thoughts, and actions. Here is one example. You can use a similar chart to record your own ideas.

CHARACTER	WORDS, THOUGHTS, ACTIONS	INFERENCE
Chris	I hadn't told any of the kids about my father coming to practice. I wasn't even sure he was going to show up.	Chris doesn't want to get his hopes up. He has been disappointed before.
Chris's father	"Sometimes I think he blames himself," Mom said. "Whenever he sees you in the wheelchair he wants to put it out of his mind."	Chris's dad feels guilty. He is more quiet and distant because of his guilt.

TEACH

QUICK START

Guilt and regret are very complex emotions, and it may be too personal for some students to openly discuss their own examples. You can keep this discussion general and impersonal by citing examples from past selections and popular culture that students can discuss with more comfort.

ANALYZE REALISTIC FICTION

Have students make a list of genre elements that are not commonly associated with realistic fiction, such as:

- The setting being in the distant past or future, or another world altogether
- The characters displaying larger-than-life qualities, being fantastical creatures, or having superpowers
- The dialogue is unnatural, does not sound the way people really talk.
- The conflicts are extreme, like end-of-the-world scenarios.

ANALYZE CHARACTER QUALITIES

Explain to students that Chris and his father are the main characters, therefore they will receive the most **characterization**. However, some of the supporting characters (Chris's mother, Mr. Evans) will receive enough characterization that readers can understand how they help move the story along. Chris's mother is characterized as busy with work, but she is also encouraging her husband and son to come together. Mr. Evans, the basketball coach, is also in a wheelchair, and is knowledgeable of what Chris's life in a wheelchair will be like.

TEACH

CRITICAL VOCABULARY

Encourage students to read all the sentences before deciding which word best completes each one. Remind them to look for context clues that match the meaning of each word.

Answers:

1. *congestion*
2. *concession*
3. *turnover*
4. *collision*
5. *fundamentals*

■ English Learner Support

Use Cognates Tell students that several of the Critical Vocabulary words have Spanish cognates: *congestion/congestión, collision/colisión, fundamentals/fundamentos.*

LANGUAGE CONVENTIONS

Have students convert the following sentence from paragraph 10 in the text into present tense: *Mom looked at me and her mouth tightened just a little.*

(**Possible Answer:** *Mom looks at me and her mouth tightens just a little.*)

Ask whether present tense or past tense sounds more natural for a narrator telling a story. Next, explain that while this story is told in the past tense, it will at times shift into present tense. For example, when characters are speaking, their dialogue remains in the present tense. Ask students why they think that is. (*While action is written in past tense, dialogue is representative of how people actually speak, which is in the present tense.*)

ANNOTATION MODEL

Students may use their own system for marking up the selection in their write-in text. They may want to color-code their annotations by using highlighters. Their notes in the margin may include questions about wheelchair basketball or any other ideas or topics they want to learn more about.

456 Unit 6

 GET READY

CRITICAL VOCABULARY

concession   collision   congestion   turnover   fundamental

To see how many Critical Vocabulary words you already know, use them to complete the sentences.

1. There was so much _____ in the hallway that students were late getting to their classes.

2. The _____ stand at the theater sells great popcorn.

3. The play resulted in a _____ when the point guard lost possession of the ball.

4. Texting while driving resulted in a deadly _____.

5. She learned the _____ skills of creating a smartphone app.

LANGUAGE CONVENTIONS

Consistent Verb Tense In this lesson, you will learn about using verb tenses, which indicate the times of events, correctly. Consistent verb tenses help show the sequence of events.

Afterward, the team <u>voted</u>, and the Hartsdale Posse all <u>agreed</u> that we <u>wanted</u> to play in the league.

Here, the time frame for the three actions (*voted*, *agreed*, and *wanted*) are the same: the past. Therefore, all three verbs use the past tense. As you read "Sometimes a Dream Needs a Push," pay attention to the author's use of consistent verb tenses.

ANNOTATION MODEL   **NOTICE & NOTE**

As you read, look for realistic text details. You can also mark up details that suggest each character's qualities. In the model, you can see one reader's notes about part of "Sometimes a Dream Needs a Push."

> 1   You might have heard of my dad, Jim Blair. He's six five and played a year of good basketball in the pros before tearing his knee up in his second year. The knee took forever to heal and was never quite the same again. Still, he played pro ball in Europe for five years before giving it up and becoming an executive with a high-tech company.

Chris probably admires his dad. His dad was a good athlete and may be rather competitive.

The setting is in the present-day United States.

456   Unit 6

BACKGROUND

Walter Dean Myers (1937–2014) was born in West Virginia but grew up in the Harlem community of New York City. He developed a love of reading and writing in school and went on to write at least five pages a day over his lengthy career. He published more than 100 books for young people, often focusing on the experiences of young African Americans. Myers received great recognition, including two Newbery Honor Book Awards and several Coretta Scott King Awards.

SOMETIMES A DREAM NEEDS A PUSH

Short Story by Walter Dean Myers

SETTING A PURPOSE

As you read, pay attention to how the father and son interact with each other. How do these characters' thoughts, feelings, and actions reveal their individual qualities—and help you understand their relationship?

Notice & Note

Use the side margins to notice and note signposts in the text.

1 You might have heard of my dad, Jim Blair. He's six five and played a year of good basketball in the pros before tearing his knee up in his second year. The knee took forever to heal and was never quite the same again. Still, he played pro ball in Europe for five years before giving it up and becoming an executive with a high-tech company.

2 <u>Dad loved basketball and hoped that one day I would play the game. He taught me a lot, and I was pretty good until the accident.</u> It was raining and we were on the highway, approaching the turnoff toward our house in Hartsdale, when a truck skidded across the road and hit our rear bumper. Our little car spun off the road, squealing as Dad tried to bring it under control. But he couldn't avoid the light pole. I remember seeing the broken windows, hearing Mom yelling, amazingly bright lights flashing crazily in front of me. Then everything

ANALYZE CHARACTER QUALITIES

Annotate: Mark words and phrases in paragraphs 2 and 3 that tell you about Chris and his father.

Analyze: How would you describe each character? How do you think Chris's becoming physically disabled has changed their relationship?

Sometimes a Dream Needs a Push **457**

TEACH

BACKGROUND

Have students read the information about the author. As they read the short story, have them notice details that may be linked to Myers's background. Also ask them to pay attention to Myers's use of language and think about how his style made him a successful author of books for young people.

SETTING A PURPOSE

Direct students to use the Setting a Purpose prompt to focus their reading.

ANALYZE CHARACTER QUALITIES

Explain to students that in a **short story,** character qualities and **conflict** will likely be introduced in the first few paragraphs. (**Answer:** *Chris is accepting and seems level-headed. His father seems quiet, sullen, and maybe a little angry. His father taught him a lot about basketball, but since the accident his father talks less and seems to have taken it hard. Their relationship may be strained and they find less in common with each other.*)

ENGLISH LEARNER SUPPORT

Monitor Comprehension Have students listen as you read aloud paragraphs 1–3. Tell students that you will ask questions about what you just read. Model that they should give a thumbs up if the answer is yes, and a thumbs down for no. For example, ask the following questions:

- Does Chris's dad still play basketball? *(no)*
- Was Chris in a car crash? *(yes)*
- Can Chris use his legs? *(no)*
- Does Chris's dad talk very much? *(no)*

Sometimes a Dream Needs a Push **457**

TEACH

ANALYZE REALISTIC FICTION

Instruct students that *modern* usually means within the last 20 years, but can mean as long ago as a century. *Contemporary* would mean very recent, within the past few years. Some of the details, such as Chris's father reading a newspaper, not a tablet or smartphone, may not seem contemporary to readers. (**Answer:** *Chris uses words that a real young person would use, and he describes modern wheelchairs. These realistic details make the story seem as though it could happen, allowing the reader to engage with the story and relate to the characters and their problems.*)

ENGLISH LEARNER SUPPORT

Understand Idioms Explain that idioms are phrases or sayings that have a different meaning than their literal meaning.

ASK STUDENTS to identify the idiom "chewing up his words" in paragraph 7. Ask: *Is Chris's dad actually chewing on his words?* (no) Explain that when someone chews their words, that means they do not speak clearly. Have pairs of varying proficiency work together to locate the context clue that helps define the idiom. (*mumbled something under his breath*)

ANALYZE CHARACTER QUALITIES

Ask students whether they expected Chris's father to be excited at the game. Remind them that characters are unlikely to change very much during the **rising action**, the action in the story leading up to the **climax**. (**Answer:** *His father is reminded of his guilt when he sees kids in wheelchairs playing basketball. It tells us that Chris is a little confused and wants his dad to be involved in the same way he would have been if they were playing conventional basketball.*)

CRITICAL VOCABULARY

concession: When Chris and his parents go to watch a wheelchair basketball game, his mother sits with him while his father goes and stands next to the concession stand.

ASK STUDENTS why it would be odd to be at the concession stand for an entire game. (*A concession stand is located away from the stands and the best view of the game.*)

458 Unit 6

NOTICE & NOTE

was suddenly dark. The next thing I remember is waking up in the hospital. There were surgeries and weeks in the hospital, but the important thing was that I wasn't going to be walking again.

3   I didn't like the idea, but Mom and I learned to live with it. Dad took it hard, real hard. He was never much of a talker, Mom said, but he talked even less since I was hurt.

4   "Sometimes I think he blames himself," Mom said. "Whenever he sees you in the wheelchair he wants to put it out of his mind."

5   I hadn't thought about that when Mr. Evans, an elder in our church, asked me if I wanted to join a wheelchair basketball team he was starting.

6   "We won't have the experience of the other teams in the league," he said. "But it'll be fun."

7   When I told Mom, she was all for it, but Dad just looked at me and mumbled something under his breath. He does that sometimes. Mom said that he's chewing up his words to see how they taste before he lets them out.

8   Our van is equipped with safety harnesses for my chair, and we used it on the drive to see a game between Madison and Rosedale. It was awesome to see guys my age zipping around in their chairs playing ball. I liked the chairs, too. They were specially built with rear stabilizing wheels and side wheels that slanted in. Very cool. I couldn't wait to start practicing. At the game, Mom sat next to me, but Dad went and sat next to the **concession** stand. I saw him reading a newspaper and only looking up at the game once in a while.

9   "Jim, have you actually seen wheelchair games before?" Mom asked on the way home.

10   Dad made a little motion with his head and said something that sounded like "Grumpa-grumpa" and then mentioned that he had to get up early in the morning. Mom looked at me, and her mouth tightened just a little.

11   That was okay with me because I didn't want him to talk about the game if he didn't like it. After washing and getting into my pj's I wheeled into my room, transferred to the bed, and tried to make sense of the day. I didn't know what to make of Dad's reaction, but I knew I wanted to play.

12   The next day at school, tall Sarah told me there was a message for me on the bulletin board. Sarah is cool but the nosiest person in school.

13   "What did it say?" I asked.

14   "How would I know?" she answered. "I don't read people's messages."

ANALYZE REALISTIC FICTION
Annotate: In paragraph 8, circle words and phrases that Chris uses that reflect his age. Underline text details that describe a modern setting for the story.

Critique: How do these details make the story seem realistic? Why are details such as these important to how the reader perceives the story?

concession
(kən-sĕsh´ən) *n.* Sporting and entertainment events often feature *concession* stands where food and drinks are sold.

ANALYZE CHARACTER QUALITIES
Annotate: In paragraph 11, mark Chris's thoughts about his dad's reaction to the game.

Infer: Why do you think Chris's dad reacts this way? What does Chris's desire to play wheelchair basketball tell you about Chris's character?

458 Unit 6

TO CHALLENGE STUDENTS...

Analyze Character Have students examine some of the author's subtle ways of revealing character qualities. For example, on p. 459 Chris's mom tells him that his coach called, even though the call was for his dad. Then she brings it up at family dinner. Ask students what this conveys about the character of Chris's mother. (*She is artfully guiding the other characters.*) From there, you can have students work alone or in pairs to find other examples throughout the story in which the author uses subtle methods to reveal characters' qualities.

NOTICE & NOTE

15 "Probably nothing important," I said, spinning my chair to head down the hall.

16 "Just something about you guys going to play Madison in a practice game and they haven't lost all season," Sarah said. "From Nicky G."

17 "Oh."

18 The school has a special bus for wheelchairs and the driver always takes the long way to my house, which is a little irritating when you've got a ton of homework that needs to get done, and I had a ton and a half. When I got home, Mom had the entire living room filled with purple lace and flower things she was putting together for a wedding and was lettering nameplates for them. I threw her a quick "Hey" and headed for my room.

19 "Chris, your coach called," Mom said.

20 "Mr. Evans?"

21 "Yes, he said your father had left a message for him," Mom answered. She had a big piece of the purple stuff around her neck as she leaned against the doorjamb. "Anything up?"

22 "I don't know," I said with a shrug. <u>My heart sank.</u> I went into my room and started on my homework, trying not to think of why Dad would call Mr. Evans.

23 With all the wedding stuff in the living room and Mom looking so busy, I was hoping that we'd have pizza again. No such luck. Somewhere in the afternoon she had found time to bake a chicken. Dad didn't get home until nearly seven-thirty, so we ate late.

24 While we ate Mom was talking about how some woman was trying to convince all of her bridesmaids to put a pink streak in their hair for her wedding. She asked us what we thought of that. Dad grunted under his breath and went back to his chicken. He didn't see the face that Mom made at him.

25 "By the way"—Mom gave me a quick look—"Mr. Evans called. He said he had missed your call earlier."

26 "I spoke to him late this afternoon," Dad said.

27 "Are the computers down at the school?" Mom asked.

28 <u>"No, I was just telling him that I didn't think that the Madison team was all that good,"</u> Dad said. <u>"I heard the kids saying they were great. They're okay, but they're not great. I'm going to talk to him again at practice tomorrow."</u>

29 "Oh," Mom said. I could see the surprise in her face and felt it in my stomach.

30 The next day zoomed by. It was like the bells to change classes were ringing every two minutes. I hadn't told any of the kids about my father coming to practice. I wasn't even sure

ANALYZE CHARACTER QUALITIES

Annotate: Mark text details in paragraph 22 that show how Chris feels when his mother tells him about the phone call.

Interpret: Why might Chris feel this way? What does this scene suggest about Chris's feelings toward his father?

CONTRASTS AND CONTRADICTIONS

Notice & Note: Mark Chris's dad's comments in paragraph 28.

Compare: How do these comments differ from his attitude up to this point in the story? What does this new information suggest about Chris's dad?

Sometimes a Dream Needs a Push 459

APPLYING ACADEMIC VOCABULARY

 contrast   ☐ despite   ☐ error   inadequate   ☐ interact

Write and Discuss Have students turn to a partner to discuss the following questions. Guide students to include the Academic Vocabulary words *contrast* and *inadequate* in their responses. Ask volunteers to share their responses with the class.

- How does Chris's mom's behavior **contrast** with his dad's?
- How does Chris's behavior express that he feels **inadequate** to his father?

TEACH

✏️ ANALYZE CHARACTER QUALITIES

Remind students that this story is told in first person, which means we are only being told what Chris thinks and how he feels. The information we learn about other characters comes only through his filter. (**Answer:** *Chris knows that his dad is uncomfortable with the wheelchair basketball and he may be worried that his father doesn't want him to play. This suggests that he really wants to play basketball but that he is also concerned about what his father thinks.*)

▶ CONTRASTS AND CONTRADICTIONS

Instruct students that as they compile their impressions of character qualities, they will from time to time come up against behavior that contradicts previous behavior or well-established patterns by a character in the story. This is one technique authors use to develop characters. (**Answer:** *Chris's dad has shown no interest in wheelchair basketball, but the comments suggest that he has been paying attention and is suddenly interested in the team's chances. This suggests that maybe he is changing his mind about wheelchair basketball and even beginning to accept that Chris is in a wheelchair.*)

■ English Learner Support

Understand Contrasts and Contradictions Point out the dialogue in paragraph 28. Ask: *What does Chris's dad think about the Madison team?* Provide sentence frames to guide their responses: *Chris's dad thinks the Madison team is _____.* (not very good) Ask: *Does Chris's dad care about wheelchair basketball now?* (yes) *Is this the same as or different from how he felt earlier in the story?* (different)

 For **reading support** for students at varying proficiency levels, see the **Text X-Ray** on page 454D.

Sometimes a Dream Needs a Push 459

TEACH

ANALYZE CHARACTER QUALITIES

Explain to students that **dramatic action** happens when a character does something that reveals their inner feelings. **(Answer:** *Chris's admiration for his father and his desire to make him proud makes him behave nervously and play poorly.*)

CONTRASTS AND CONTRADICTIONS

Remind students that a contrast is a sharp difference between what we would expect and what we observe happening. **(Answer:** *Chris's dad is confident and skillful when he is shooting the ball from a standing position, but when he is in the wheelchair, he is not confident in himself. I think he will realize that the game takes a lot of skill.*)

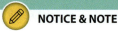 **NOTICE & NOTE**

ANALYZE CHARACTER QUALITIES

Annotate: In paragraph 31, mark text details that show what Chris thinks, feels, and does when his father shows up to practice.

Infer: How does Chris's reaction reflect his internal conflict about his father's presence?

CONTRASTS AND CONTRADICTIONS

Notice & Note: Review paragraphs 37–39. How do Chris's dad's skill and confidence change when he sits in the wheelchair?

Predict: What do you think he will come to realize about wheelchair basketball?

---

he was going to show up. He had made promises before and then gotten called away to work. This time he had said he was coming to practice, which was at two-thirty, in the middle of his day.

31   He was there. He sat in the stands and watched us go through our drills and a minigame. <u>I was so nervous, I couldn't do anything right. I couldn't catch the ball at all, and the one shot I took was an air ball from just behind the foul line.</u> We finished our regular practice, and Mr. Evans motioned for my father to come down to the court.

32   "Your dad's a giant!" Kwame whispered as Dad came onto the court.

33   "That's how big Chris is going to be," Nicky G said.

34   I couldn't imagine ever being as tall as my father.

35   "I was watching the teams play the other day." Dad had both hands jammed into his pockets. "And I saw that neither of them were running baseline plays and almost all the shots were aimed for the rims. Shots off the backboards are going to go in a lot more than rim shots if you're shooting from the floor."

36   Dad picked up a basketball and threw it casually against the backboard. It rolled around the rim and fell through. He did it again. And again. He didn't miss once.

37   "I happen to know that you played pro ball," Mr. Evans said, "and you're good. But I think shooting from a wheelchair is a bit harder."

38   "You have another chair?" Dad asked.

39   Mr. Evans pointed to his regular chair sitting by the watercooler. Dad took four long steps over to it, sat down, and

460   Unit 6

WHEN STUDENTS STRUGGLE . . .

Make a Chart Have students fill out a graphic organizer like the one shown for each major character in the story. They can do these multiple times for each character.

Character	Setting	Conflict	Dialogue	Actions	Outcome
Mom	Home	Wants Chris to play basketball	"Chris, your coach called."	Tells Chris his coach called for his dad.	Finds out Chris's dad is going to help

 For additional support, go to the **Reading Studio** and assign the following **Level Up** tutorial: **Short Stories and Novels.**

wheeled himself back onto the floor. He put his hands up and looked at me. I realized I was holding a ball and tossed it to him. He tried to turn his chair back toward the basket, and it spun all the way around. For a moment he looked absolutely lost, as if he didn't know what had happened to him. He seemed a little embarrassed as he glanced toward me.

40 "That happens sometimes," I said. "No problem."

41 He nodded, exhaled slowly, then turned and shot a long, lazy arc that hit the backboard and fell through.

42 "The backboard takes the energy out of the ball," he said. "So if it does hit the rim, it won't be so quick to bounce off. Madison made about twenty percent of its shots the other day. That doesn't win basketball games, no matter how good they look making them."

43 There are six baskets in our gym, and we spread out and practiced shooting against the backboards. At first I wasn't good at it. I was hitting the underside of the rim.

44 "That's because you're still thinking about the rim," Dad said when he came over to me. "Start thinking about a spot on the backboard. When you find your spot, really own it, you'll be knocking down your shots on a regular basis."

45 Nicky G got it first, and then Kwame, and then Bobby. I was too nervous to even hit the backboard half the time, but Dad didn't get mad or anything. He didn't even mumble. He just said it would come to me after a while.

46 Baseline plays were even harder. Dad wanted us to get guys wheeling for position under and slightly behind the basket.

47 "There are four feet of space behind the backboard," Dad said. "If you can use those four feet, you have an advantage."

48 We tried wheeling plays along the baseline but just kept getting in each other's way.

49 "That's the point," Dad said. "When you learn to move without running into each other you're going to have a big advantage over a team that's trying to keep up with you."

50 Okay, so most of the guys are pretty good wheeling their chairs up and down the court. But our baseline plays looked more like a **collision** derby. Dad shook his head and Mr. Evans laughed.

51 We practiced all week. Dad came again and said we were improving.

52 "I thought you were terrible at first," he said, smiling. I didn't believe he actually smiled. "Now you're just pretty bad. But I think you can play with that Madison team."

53 Madison had agreed to come to our school to play, and when they arrived they were wearing jackets with their school colors and CLIPPERS across the back.

NOTICE & NOTE

ANALYZE REALISTIC FICTION
Annotate: Circle words and phrases that Chris's dad uses in paragraphs 44 and 47 that provide realistic details about playing wheelchair basketball.

Evaluate: What do details such as these add to the story?

LANGUAGE CONVENTIONS
Annotate: Mark the verbs in paragraph 50.

Analyze: Why is there a change in verb tense between the first sentence of the paragraph and the last two sentences?

collision
(kə-lĭzh´ən) n. When the two things crash into each other, the result is a collision.

Sometimes a Dream Needs a Push 461

TEACH

ANALYZE REALISTIC FICTION

Explain to students that when reading **realistic fiction**, the details of **realism** may not hit them at first. This is because they may be reading something that is so familiar to them, they may miss the specific little details the author included to make the story feel realistic. (**Answer:** Specific, realistic details such as these make the story more believable and they help readers better visualize the scene because readers can use their own prior knowledge of traditional basketball, wheelchair basketball, or both.)

LANGUAGE CONVENTIONS

Instruct students to read the paragraph out loud if they are having trouble understanding the change in verb tense. Explain that Chris is telling the story in past tense, but to write the first sentence in past tense would take away from the flow and immediacy of the story. (**Answer:** The present tense is used in the first sentence because it shows a continuous state [they are good at wheeling . . .] and is in the present as Chris tells the story. The past tense is used later in the paragraph because it shows actions that were completed in the past.)

IMPROVE READING FLUENCY

Targeted Passage Read aloud paragraphs 46–52, emphasizing Chris's dad's matter-of-fact tone in paragraphs 47 and 49, then his humorous tone in paragraph 52. Note how the attribute "he said, smiling," marks how the dialogue should be read. Read paragraph 50 with Chris's casual and humorous tone.

Break students into pairs to practice these shifts in tone by reading paragraphs 46–52 to each other, one taking the voice of the narrator, the other the voice of Chris's father. Then have them switch roles and repeat.

 Go to the **Reading Studio** for additional support in developing fluency.

CRITICAL VOCABULARY

collision: Chris describes his team as looking like a collision derby whenever they are bunched up together at the baseline.

ASK STUDENTS why the team does not want to look like a collision derby when they are playing basketball. *(If they keep colliding with one another, they are not going to be very effective at moving the ball.)*

Sometimes a Dream Needs a Push **461**

TEACH

ANALYZE REALISTIC FICTION

Tell students that the rising action, the events that occur once the conflict is set in motion, are more subtle in realistic fiction than in other forms of stories they may have read. (**Answer:** *It isn't unusual for a son to look for approval and support from his father. A father's guilt over being involved in his son's accident is understandable because parents want to protect their children. The story's conflict is realistic because a father withdrawing from a son when he seeks support and approval is a believable experience.*)

ENGLISH LEARNER SUPPORT

Understand Vocabulary Use the following supports with students at varying proficiency levels to help them understand the word *fundamental*. (paragraph 63)

- Write *fundamental* on the board, and draw lines to separate the syllables. Pronounce the word several times, with students repeating after you. Explain that *fundamentals* are basic things one learns about something. In basketball the fundamentals are dribbling and shooting.

- Have students pronounce *fundamental*, and help them understand that in basketball it means the basics of the game. Prompt them to state what Chris's dad taught the team, followed by the phrase, "____ is a *fundamental* of basketball."

CRITICAL VOCABULARY

turnover: The team lost possession (turnover) a lot because their passes were not accurate.

ASK STUDENTS why Chris would say "wild passes" are the reason for turnovers. (*Because his team was not passing well, it made it easier for the other team to steal the ball.*)

congestion: The team's plays along the baseline are compared to the congestion of bumper cars.

ASK STUDENTS why congestion is not a good thing in this situation. (*Chris has already described his team's trouble with baseline plays. This means they are still crowding at the baseline.*)

462   Unit 6

 **NOTICE & NOTE**

54   We started the game and Madison got the tip-off. The guy I was holding blocked me off so their guard, once he got past Nicky G, had a clear path to the basket. The first score against us came with only ten seconds off the clock.

55   I looked up in the stands to see where Mom was. I found her and saw Dad sitting next to her. I waved and she waved back, and Dad just sat there with his arms folded.

56   Madison stopped us cold on the next play, and when Bobby and Lou bumped their chairs at the top of the key, there was a man open. A quick pass inside and Madison was up by four.

turnover
(tûrn´ō´vər) *n.* In basketball, a *turnover* is a loss of possession of the ball.

57   We settled down a little, but nothing worked that well. We made a lot of wild passes for **turnovers,** and once, when I was actually leading a fast break, I got called for traveling when the ball got ahead of me, and I touched the wheels twice before dribbling. The guys from Madison were having a good time, and we were feeling miserable. At halftime, we rolled into the locker room feeling dejected. When Dad showed up, I felt bad. He was used to winning, not losing.

58   "Our kids looked a little overmatched in the first half," Mr. Evans said.

59   "I think they played okay," Dad said, "just a little nervous. But look at the score. It's twenty-two to fourteen. With all their shooting, Madison is just eight points ahead. We can catch up."

60   <u>I looked at Dad to see if he was kidding</u>. He wasn't. He wasn't kidding, and <u>he had said "we." I liked that.</u>

ANALYZE REALISTIC FICTION
Annotate: In paragraph 60, mark Chris's reaction to his dad's assessment of the team.

Evaluate: What makes Chris's reaction to his father realistic? How realistic is the conflict in their relationship? Why?

congestion
(kən-jĕs´chən) *n. Congestion* is overcrowding, such as when too many vehicles cause a traffic jam.

61   We came out in the second half all fired up. We ran a few plays along the baseline, but it still seemed more like bumper cars than basketball with all the **congestion.** Madison took twenty-three shots in the second half and made eight of them plus three foul shots for a total score of forty-one points. We took seventeen shots and made eleven of them, all layups off the backboard, and two foul shots for a total of thirty-eight points. We had lost the game, but everyone felt great about how we had played. We lined up our chairs, gave Madison high fives before they left, and waited until we got to the locker room to give ourselves high fives.

62   Afterward, the team voted, and the Hartsdale Posse all agreed that we wanted to play in the league. Dad had shown us that we could play, and even though we had lost we knew we would be ready for the next season.

fundamental
(fŭn´də-mĕn´tl) *n.* A *fundamental* is a basic but essential part of an object or a system.

63   Dad only comes to practice once in a while, but he comes to the games when they're on the weekend. At practice he shows us **fundamentals,** stuff like how to line your wrist up for a shot, and how the ball should touch your hand when you're ready to shoot. That made me feel good even if he would never

462   Unit 6

---

fundamental: When Chris's dad comes to practice, he helps out by showing the team the fundamentals of basketball.

ASK STUDENTS why Chris's dad would be good at teaching the fundamentals. (*Chris's dad was a pro basketball player; he would know the fundamentals very well.*)

talk about the games when he wasn't in the gym. I didn't want to push it too much because I liked him coming to practice. I didn't want to push him, but Mom didn't mind at all.

64 "Jim, if you were in a wheelchair," she asked, "do you think you could play as well as Chris?"

65 Dad was on his laptop and looked over the screen at Mom, then looked over at me. Then he looked back down at the screen and grumbled something. <u>I figured he was saying that there was no way he could play as well as me in a chair</u>, but I didn't ask him to repeat it.

NOTICE & NOTE

ANALYZE CHARACTER QUALITIES
Annotate: In paragraph 65, underline Chris's interpretation of his father's grumbles.

Analyze: What does this interpretation suggest about Chris's confidence? What does it suggest about his relationship with his father?

CHECK YOUR UNDERSTANDING

Answer these questions before moving on to the **Analyze the Text** section on the following page.

1 Which statement best explains why this story is an example of realistic fiction?

   A The characters are people whom the author knows.

   B The author includes details about an actual sport.

   C The conflict in the story is one that happens to everyone.

   D The author included only details that really happened.

2 Read this sentence from paragraph 7.

> Mom said that he's chewing up his words to see how they taste before he lets them out.

The sensory language in this sentence highlights the father's —

   F confusion

   G hesitation

   H sense of humor

   J wish for secrecy

3 Using the first-person point of view allows the author to —

   A explain why the father takes an interest in wheelchair basketball

   B describe each character's feelings about the accident

   C reveal the narrator's relationship with his father

   D inform readers about the rules of wheelchair basketball

Sometimes a Dream Needs a Push 463

TEACH

ANALYZE CHARACTER QUALITIES

Tell students that while some character qualities may achieve an arc, or change over the course of the story, there are still some consistent character qualities that will remain the same as they were in the beginning. In this case, Chris's father still grumbles! (**Answer:** *It shows that he's more confident than he used to be, and it suggests that he thinks that his father now appreciates his skill on the basketball court. It also suggests that his relationship with his father has improved.*)

CHECK YOUR UNDERSTANDING

Have students answer the questions independently.

Answers:

1. B
2. G
3. C

If they answer any questions incorrectly, have them reread the text to confirm their understanding. Then they may proceed to ANALYZE THE TEXT on p. 464.

🗨 ENGLISH LEARNER SUPPORT

Oral Assessment Use the following questions to assess students' comprehension and speaking skills:

1. Name one detail that shows the story is realistic fiction. Use the sentence frames: *The characters in the story play _____.* (basketball) *I know this story is realistic fiction because _____ is a real sport.* (basketball)

2. Why do you think Chris's dad chews, or mumbles, his words? Use the sentence frame: *I think Chris's dad chews his words because he does not know what to _____.* (say)

3. The author tells the story using the word *I*. Who is telling the story? (Chris) What do you learn about Chris when the author uses the word *I*? (how Chris feels)

SUBSTANTIAL/MODERATE

Sometimes a Dream Needs a Push   **463**

APPLY

ANALYZE THE TEXT
Possible answers:

1. **DOK 2:** *Chris says at the beginning of the story that he liked playing basketball. He also says it was awesome to see guys his age zipping around in the chairs. So he probably joined to have fun.*

2. **DOK 4:** *Chris and his dad still don't talk a lot by the end of the story, but Chris's father seems to have worked through his guilt, and Chris seems to be satisfied with his father's involvement with the team. Chris also thinks that his dad is proud of his ability at wheelchair basketball, and this seems to make their relationship less strained.*

3. **DOK 3:** *Chris's mom is supportive of Chris, but she sees the strain between Chris and his dad. Chris admires his dad and wants to please him. His dad's interaction with him is limited because of his job, which is realistic. It is also limited because of the guilt he feels, which seems like an emotion that any parent in that situation might feel.*

4. **DOK 4:** *At the beginning of the story, the narrator explains how his father wanted him to play basketball and how he wanted to play. The dream is one they both share. The push may refer to the wheelchair, as using a wheelchair requires pushing, but in the larger sense, the title refers to Chris and his dad both needing a little encouragement to achieve their dream.*

5. **DOK 4:** *Chris's dad doesn't appear to be interested in wheelchair basketball at first. When he starts going to games and Chris's team's practices, though, he begins to see what a challenge it is to play in a wheelchair. He also realizes how his experience as a pro player can help Chris's team, which makes him decide to become more involved.*

RESEARCH
Suggest to students that they check local resources to see whether there are any wheelchair basketball leagues in their area.

Extend The game emerged around 1946, when soldiers who had played basketball but had been injured in World War II began playing wheelchair basketball.

RESPOND

ANALYZE THE TEXT
Support your responses with evidence from the text. 📓 NOTEBOOK

1. **Make Inferences** Consider what you know about Chris's character. What do you think motivates him to join the wheelchair basketball team? Why?

2. **Analyze** In what ways has the relationship between Chris and his dad changed by the end of the story?

3. **Evaluate** Think about the relationship between Chris and his mom and between Chris and his dad. What elements of the story make each relationship seem realistic?

4. **Synthesize** Think about the story's title. Whose dream is the author referring to? What do you think the dream is? Explain the significance of the title.

5. **Notice & Note** How does Chris's dad's opinion of and interest in wheelchair basketball change from the beginning of the story to the end? Why?

RESEARCH TIP
The best sources for information about the rules of a sport are often organizations dedicated to or related to that sport. These web addresses usually end in *.org*. Also, as you scroll through your search results, scan the brief description under each result to find the sites that are most likely to have the information you seek.

RESEARCH
In the short story, Chris joins a wheelchair basketball team. Research wheelchair basketball. Record what you learn in the chart.

QUESTION	ANSWER
What are the key rules of wheelchair basketball?	*The rules are the same as regular basketball with the following exceptions: 1) players must dribble once for every two pushes; 2) no double dribble violation; 3) only the rear wheels of the chair must be behind free-throw and three-point line during a shot; 4) a three-second lane violation won't be called if a player tries to exit but is trapped in the lane*
How do the wheelchairs used for the game differ from everyday wheelchairs?	*Athletic wheelchairs are lighter and have no brakes. The wheels are angled more so that the chair can make sharper turns.*

Extend When and why did people first begin playing wheelchair basketball? Find out about the origins of wheelchair basketball.

LEARNING MINDSET

Problem Solving If students get stuck when trying to respond to the Analyze the Text questions, help them by asking them to apply problem-solving strategies as they work through the questions. Encourage students to look at a question from a different angle or to try a different learning strategy. Remind them that there are many different ways to solve problems (being patient; changing strategies; asking for help, etc.) and that everyone solves problems in their own unique way.

RESPOND

CREATE AND PRESENT

Write an Informational Article Using the research you found on wheelchair basketball, write a one- to two-page informational article about this sport.

- ❏ Review your research. Decide what information you want to include and how you want to organize it.
- ❏ Include the controlling idea or thesis you want to convey in the first paragraph. In each paragraph that follows, include a key idea that connects to the controlling idea or thesis and is supported by evidence from your research.
- ❏ In your final paragraph, summarize your findings and restate the main idea in an engaging way.

Go to **Introduction: Informative Texts** in the **Writing Studio** for more.

Create a Video Critique In pairs, tape brief critiques, or reviews, of the story. Switch roles as the on-camera reviewer and the recorder.

- ❏ Discuss the story with your partner. Go beyond a discussion of likes and dislikes. For example, what part of the story did you most connect with?
- ❏ Write the outline of a short critique. Include a brief summary and your responses to the story's characters, setting, and plot.
- ❏ Before taping your critiques, practice delivering them. Speak clearly; use appropriate gestures and facial expressions. Consider ways to add interest to your videos, such as using a basketball court as a location and a basketball as a prop.

Go to **Using Media in a Presentation** in the **Speaking and Listening Studio** for help.

RESPOND TO THE ESSENTIAL QUESTION

 What inspires you to make a difference?

Gather Information Review your annotations and notes on "Sometimes a Dream Needs a Push." Then, add relevant details to your Response Log. As you determine which information to include, think about:

- the reasons that people become involved in sports
- how athletes train for competition
- the value of teamwork

At the end of the unit, refer to your notes to help you write a research report.

ACADEMIC VOCABULARY

As you write and discuss what you learned from the short story, be sure to use the Academic Vocabulary words. Check off each of the words that you use.

- ❏ contrast
- ❏ despite
- ❏ error
- ❏ inadequate
- ❏ interact

Sometimes a Dream Needs a Push   465

APPLY

CREATE AND PRESENT

Write an Informational Article Suggest students organize their articles by dividing each paragraph into subjects, such as the rules of the game, followed by the specifications of the wheelchairs. Encourage students to use **transitions** or **headings** to clearly distinguish each section.

 For **writing support** for students at varying proficiency levels, see the **Text X-Ray** on p. 454D.

Create a Video Critique Have students consider ways to enhance their videos with photos, graphics, audio, and other features. Remind them that careful planning and rehearsal will make for a better outcome. After viewing the videos, students can offer constructive criticism of each pair's videos, or offer to help in polishing them. They may even wish to post their finished videos on a school or class website. If your time or resources are limited, have students simply present detailed plans for their video critiques.

RESPOND TO THE ESSENTIAL QUESTION

Allow time for students to add details from "Sometimes a Dream Needs a Push" to their Unit 6 Response Logs.

APPLY

CRITICAL VOCABULARY

Answers:

1. b
2. b
3. a
4. a
5. b

VOCABULARY STRATEGY:
Context Clues

Answers:

GUESSED DEFINITION	DICTIONARY DEFINITION
Furnished	supplied with tools
Curve	shaped like an arch or curve
Sad	depressed

 RESPOND

WORD BANK
concession
collision
congestion
turnover
fundamental

CRITICAL VOCABULARY

Practice and Apply Mark the letter of the answer to each question. Be prepared to explain your response.

1. Where would you be more likely to find a **concession** stand?
   a. a forest
   b. a football stadium

2. Which of the following might be involved in a **collision**?
   a. two buildings
   b. two bicycles

3. Which of the following is more likely to cause highway **congestion**?
   a. a stalled car
   b. mild temperatures

4. Which of the following would more likely lead to a **turnover** during a sports game?
   a. misplaying the ball
   b. taking a timeout

5. Which of the following is a **fundamental** of learning to ride a bike?
   a. exercise
   b. braking

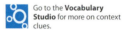 Go to the **Vocabulary Studio** for more on context clues.

VOCABULARY STRATEGY: Context Clues

When you encounter an unfamiliar word, **context clues**—hints that appear in surrounding words, sentences, or paragraphs—can help you determine the meaning. Consider this example from the story:

> We ran a few plays along the baseline, but it still seemed more like bumper cars than basketball with all the congestion.

Look for clues to the meaning of *congestion* in the surrounding text. Running the plays seemed "more like bumper cars than basketball." This phrase helps you contrast wheelchairs moving on a basketball court with the way that bumper cars move in a limited area. You can infer, then, that *congestion* means "crowded."

Practice and Apply Use context clues to define these words from "Sometimes a Dream Needs a Push."

WORD	CONTEXT CLUES	MY GUESSED DEFINITION	DICTIONARY DEFINITION
equipped	(paragraph 8)	furnished	supplied with tools
arc	(paragraph 41)	curve	shaped like an arch or a curve
dejected	(paragraph 57)	sad	depressed

 ENGLISH LEARNER SUPPORT

Identify Sound Transfer Issues Speakers of Vietnamese may struggle producing voiceless consonants, such as the *f* in *fundamental* and the voiceless *s* and *sh* sounds in *concession*. Demonstrate how to make these sounds and have students echo them. As fluency improves, encourage students to read the vocabulary words aloud as you monitor for correct pronunciation. **ALL LEVELS**

LANGUAGE CONVENTIONS:
Consistent Verb Tense

A verb's **tense** shows a particular time that an action occurs.

Present: Chris plays basketball.

Present perfect: Chris has played basketball.

Past: Chris played basketball.

Past perfect: Chris had played basketball.

Future: Chris will play basketball.

Future perfect: Chris will have played basketball.

Shifting tenses within sentences or paragraphs can be confusing unless it is done correctly. Follow these two rules to help you control verb tense shifts in your writing:

- Shift verb tense within a sentence only when there is a shift in the time frame.
- Shift verb tense within a paragraph only when it is necessary to refer to events that occurred in the past or to events that will occur in the future.

The chart shows examples from "Sometimes a Dream Needs a Push."

SENTENCE TYPE	EXAMPLE
Consistent Verb Tense (past tense)	Mom looked at me, and her mouth tightened just a little.
Correct Shift in Verb Tense (from past tense to past perfect tense)	I looked at Dad to see if he was kidding. He wasn't. He wasn't kidding, and he had said "we." I liked that.

Practice and Apply Write your own sentences using consistent verb tenses or correctly shifting verb tenses. Your sentences can be about the story's events or characters. When you have finished, share your sentences with a partner and compare them.

 RESPOND

 Go to **Using Verbs Correctly** in the **Grammar Studio** for more.

APPLY

LANGUAGE CONVENTIONS:
Consistent Verb Tense

Explain to students that when verb tenses shift incorrectly, a text can become confusing for the reader. Shifts in verb tense are very common in works of fiction, particularly when an author uses dialogue.

Illustrate the confusion that can arise when authors shift verb tenses incorrectly by rewriting the second example from the chart on the board:

> I <u>look</u> at Dad to see if he <u>is</u> kidding. He <u>wasn't</u>. He <u>wasn't</u> kidding and he <u>had said</u> "we." I <u>liked</u> that.

Have students note that the verb tense in the first sentence is in the present tense while the rest of the sentences are in past and past perfect tense.

If students struggle, choose example sentences from the story and have them substitute different verb tenses. Have them read both the correct and incorrect sentences aloud and discuss the difference with a partner.

Practice and Apply Have partners discuss whether they are using consistent verb tenses and whether they are correctly shifting between verb tenses. *(Students' sentences will vary.)*

 ENGLISH LEARNER SUPPORT

Language Conventions Use the following supports with students at varying proficiency levels:

- Have student pairs practice saying the sample sentences on p. 467. Then, have them use their own names in place of "Chris" and another game instead of basketball. **SUBSTANTIAL**

- Have student pairs practice saying the sample sentences on p. 467. Then, have them substitute different verbs and verb phrases for the different tenses. **MODERATE**

- Have students read paragraph 62 and identify which tense each sentence is in. *(past, past perfect)* **LIGHT**

PLAN

POETRY

A POEM FOR MY LIBRARIAN, MRS. LONG
Poem by Nikki Giovanni

GENRE ELEMENTS
POETRY
Remind students that the purpose of **poetry** is to tell a story and/or convey a message using creative language. A **free verse poem** is a poem that does not follow a specific structure. A free verse poem can be anything a poet wants it to be, and does not follow a strict set of rules. It may include irregular rhythm and lines, little or no rhyme, unconventional capitalization and punctuation, sound devices and figurative language.

LEARNING OBJECTIVES
- Identify a theme, or central message in a poem.
- Identify unconventional capitalization and punctuation.
- Recognize free verse poetry.
- Research a poet and her poetry.
- Write a free verse poem.
- **Language** Discuss with a partner how free verse poems are structured.

TEXT COMPLEXITY

Quantitative Measures	A Poem for My Librarian, Mrs. Long
Qualitative Measures	**Ideas Presented** Multiple levels, use of imagery, figurative language and demand for inference.
	Structure Used Unconventionally structured stanzas, includes one speaker.
	Language Used Meanings are implied, more figurative and metaphorical language.
	Knowledge Required More complex themes, necessitates more cultural and historical references.

PLAN

RESOURCES

- Unit 6 Response Log
- Selection Audio
- Reading Studio: Notice & Note
- Level Up Tutorial: Elements of Poetry
- Writing Studio: Writing as a Process
- "A Poem for My Librarian, Mrs. Long" Selection Test

SUMMARIES

English

"A Poem for My Librarian, Mrs. Long" uses a free verse structure to tell the story of a little girl who loved to read. As she got older, she realized the librarian at her local library made sure she could read as many books as she wanted, even though it was sometimes a hard thing for her to do. The poem is the poet's thank-you to her librarian for making a difference in her life.

Spanish

En "Un poema para mi bibliotecaria, la Sra. Long" se utiliza una estructura de verso libre para contar la historia de una niñita a quien le encantaba leer. Al hacerse mayor, se dio cuenta de que la bibliotecaria de su biblioteca local se aseguraba de que ella leyera tantos libros como quisiera, aun cuando fuesen difíciles. El poema es el agradecimiento de la poeta a su bibliotecaria por marcar la diferencia en su vida.

SMALL-GROUP OPTIONS

Have students work in small groups to read and discuss the selection.

Numbered Heads Together

- Divide students into equally numbered groups. Assign each student a number. They will later respond to a question when their number is called.
- Ask students: *Who makes a difference to the speaker of the poem? How does she make a difference?* Have students share their responses with their group, and give each other feedback on their ideas.
- Call on each number. Each student should respond to the question when his or her number is called.

Think-Pair Share

- After students have read and analyzed the poem pose this question: *Why are books special to the speaker?*
- Have students think about the question individually and take notes.
- Then, have pairs discuss their ideas about the question.
- Finally, ask pairs to share their responses with the class.

PLAN

Text X-Ray: English Learner Support
for "A Poem for My Librarian, Mrs. Long"

Use the Text X-Ray and the supports and scaffolds in the Teacher's Edition to help guide students at different proficiency levels through the selection.

INTRODUCE THE SELECTION
DISCUSS MAKING A DIFFERENCE

In this lesson, students will need to be able to understand why poetry is a good medium for expressing feelings and discuss how people can make a difference in someone's life. When someone makes a difference in someone's life, they influence who they are as a person, and make them feel special. Poetry is a good way to tell a story and express how a person who makes a difference can make someone feel.

Have students discuss how to make a difference, using sentence frames to guide them.

- A doctor can make a difference. A doctor can _____.
- A teacher can make a difference. A teacher can _____.
- A parent can make a difference. A parent can _____.
- A brother or sister can make a difference. A brother or sister can _____

CULTURAL REFERENCES

The following words and phrases may be unfamiliar to students:

- *easy listening or smooth jazz* (line 10): a kind of music, particularly popular in the 1940s in America
- *portable* (line 11): a hand held radio
- *Nat King Cole, Matt Dennis, June Christy, Ella Fitzgerald, Sarah Vaughan*. (lines 12-14): Famous singers and musicians from the 1940s
- *Leaves of Grass* (line 28): A long poem by Walt Whitman
- *hat in hand* (line 30): an expression meaning to show humbleness

LISTENING

Understand the Theme

Draw students' attention to the title of the poem and the **Essential Question**. Point out that the poem is a tribute, or a piece of writing that honors another person. Tell them that the title and the essential question will help them understand the themes in the poem.

Have students listen as you read aloud lines 27–30. Use the following supports with students at varying proficiency levels:

- Tell students you will ask some questions about what they just heard. Model that they should give a thumbs up if the answer is yes, and a thumbs down for no. For example, ask: *Do you think the speaker believes Mrs. Long is special?* (yes) **SUBSTANTIAL**
- Help students identify the theme of the excerpt. Ask: *What sort of person goes through a lot of trouble to help a child?* (a good, helpful person) *Why do you think the speaker wrote a poem about Mrs. Long?* (the poem was written to honor Mrs. Long) **MODERATE**
- After listening to the excerpt read aloud, ask students to work in pairs to list details that support the idea of the poem being a tribute to Mrs. Long. **LIGHT**

468C   Unit 6

SPEAKING

Discuss Unconventional Poetry Structures

Draw students' attention to the differing line lengths and stanzas in the poem. Ask them to think about why the poet would write this way as they discuss the poem's structure.

Use the following supports with students at varying proficiency levels:

- Have students point to lines 12-16. Tell them they can use one-word responses to answer the questions. Ask: *Is line 12 shorter or longer than 11?* (shorter) *What is on line 13?* (a name) **SUBSTANTIAL**
- Point out that on lines 13-15, there is a list of jazz musicians. *Why might Ella Fitzgerald have a short line all to herself?* (She is special to the speaker.) *Why might the next line also have just one musician, but be a long line?* (Sarah Vaughn has a different sound than the others.) **MODERATE**
- Pair students up to discuss the following questions. *What kind of poem has lines and stanzas that are different lengths?* (free verse) *Why does the poet write this way?* (to sound like talking and tell a story) **LIGHT**

READING

Understand Free Verse

Remind students that free verse poetry doesn't look like standard English. Some words that should be capitalized are not, and punctuation can be missing. Guide students to identify the unconventional techniques used in the poem.

Use the following supports with students at varying proficiency levels:

- Tell students to look for names in the stanza. Ask: *Are names usually capitalized?* (yes) *Are they capitalized here?* (no) **SUBSTANTIAL**
- Have students identify the unconventional capitalization in the stanza. (*The names should be capitalized, but they are not.*) **MODERATE**
- Have students circle three examples of incorrect punctuation and three of incorrect capitalization. **LIGHT**

WRITING

Write a Letter

Draw students' attention to the letter writing activity on p. 475.

Use the following supports with students at varying proficiency levels:

- Provide students with sentence frames and a word bank to begin writing their letters: *Dear, _____. I liked your ___. I liked that ___ helped you.* Word bank: *Nikki Giovanni, poem, Mrs. Long* **SUBSTANTIAL**
- Have students brainstorm a list of things they would like to say to Nikki Giovanni about her poem. Then have them compare their list with a partner before writing their sentences. Provide vocabulary assistance as necessary. **MODERATE**
- Have student pairs discuss the poem and what they would like to say to Nikki Giovanni. Then, have students write short paragraphs independently. Monitor students' writing production, and check that they have structured their letters correctly. **LIGHT**

TEACH

? Connect to the ESSENTIAL QUESTION

In "A Poem for My Librarian, Mrs. Long" the speaker uses carefully chosen language to illustrate how one person's actions made a difference to her as a child. The librarian, Mrs. Long, faces adversity to make sure the speaker has access to books. So many things may have inspired her to help the young girl with a thirst for the knowledge and a desire to escape into a book. Perhaps she saw herself in the girl or believed knowledge should be available to everyone. Think about what might have inspired Mrs. Long as you read.

ANALYZE & APPLY

A POEM FOR MY LIBRARIAN, MRS. LONG

(You never know what troubled little girl needs a book)

Poem by **Nikki Giovanni**

? ESSENTIAL QUESTION:

What inspires you to make a difference?

GET READY

QUICK START

The poem you are about to read is about a person who influenced the poet's life. Make some notes about a person who has helped to shape your character, personality, likes, or dislikes.

Description of the Person	How This Person Affected Me

ANALYZE FREE VERSE POETRY

"A Poem for My Librarian, Mrs. Long" is an example of **free verse poetry,** a form with no set patterns of rhythm and rhyme. Instead, the language flows like everyday speech. Although free verse differs from conventional poetry in form, it may include some of the same literary techniques, such as imagery and figurative language. Here are some of the techniques poets use in free verse poetry and an example of each from Nikki Giovanni's poem.

TECHNIQUE	EXAMPLE
Use of punctuation and capitalization in unique ways	And up the hill on vine street / (The main black corridor) sat our carnegie library
Varied length of stanzas and lines to suit stylistic effects	Late at night with my portable (that I was so proud of) / Tucked under my pillow
Use of sensory language to create vivid mental images	Which I visited and inhaled that wonderful odor / Of new books
Use of sound devices, such as repetition and alliteration to create a mood and convey meaning	Hat in hand to ask to borrow so that I might borrow

As you read the poem, note other examples of these techniques and think about the meaning they convey in the poem.

GENRE ELEMENTS: FREE VERSE POETRY

- uses irregular rhythm and line length; may group lines into stanzas
- may use little or no rhyme; often resembles natural speech
- may use unconventional punctuation or capitalization
- may use sound devices and figurative language

TEACH

QUICK START

Tell students that the people who influence them can be relatives, friends, or members of a community. To get students thinking about the kinds of people who have influenced them ask, *What is one thing you have learned from another person? What did that person teach you?* Have volunteers share their responses with the class, then have students fill in their charts independently.

ANALYZE FREE VERSE POETRY

Point out to students that what makes free verse poetry interesting and fun to read is its lack of strictly enforced structure. Poets who write free verse poems often include traditional poetry elements, but they get to do so in a personal and less restrictive way.

Remind students to look for literary techniques as they read. When they come across unconventional punctuation, figurative language, or other techniques, suggest that students use these questions to help them analyze the poem.

- What literary technique do I see in this line?
- Why did the poet include this literary technique here?
- What does this literary technique add to the poem's meaning?
- What does this literary technique add to the poem's structure?

TEACH

ANALYZE THEME

Tell students that one way to determine the theme or themes in a poem is to determine the main idea. Students should look for the main idea and lesson as they read, and use text evidence to support their ideas. Provide the following questions to help students understand the main idea and lesson in the poem:

- What can you infer about how the speaker feels about Mrs. Long based on her words and actions?
- What is the poem mostly about?
- What did you learn from the poem?

Tell students that poems may have several main ideas that come together to present the theme. Remind students that they can also use the essential question as a guide to help them determine the theme of the poem.

■ English Learner Support

Use Cognates Point to the word *tone* on p. 470 and provide the Spanish cognate *tono*. Tell students that tone, or the mood, refers to the tone or mood in the poem itself. Write a list of possible *tones* on the board (angry, happy, grateful,) and have students use gestures and simple language to define them, providing support as necessary. **SUBSTANTIAL**

ANNOTATION MODEL

Tell students to look for elements of free verse poetry as they read. Students should annotate by underlining and circling sensory details, unusual punctuation or line lengths, descriptive details, figurative language, and other elements of poetry that add to the mood or tone of the poem. Point out that they may follow this suggestion or use their own system for marking up the selection in their write-in text. They may want to color-code their annotations by using highlighters. Their notes in the margin may include questions about ideas that are unclear or language they do not understand.

GET READY

ANALYZE THEME

A **theme** is a message about life or human nature that an author shares with the reader. Readers can infer one or more themes by thinking about an author's **tone**, or attitude toward the subject, and by considering what is said and how ideas come together.

In "A Poem for My Librarian, Mrs. Long," the poet is also the speaker, reflecting on her childhood experiences. After describing everyday activities, she turns her attention to her love of books. The poem is dedicated to Mrs. Long, a librarian who likely endured adversity so that the young girl could read the books she wanted.

To determine a theme in a poem, look for ideas that the poet develops over the course of the poem and how they build on one another. This chart shows text evidence for one theme in the poem.

Text evidence:	Text evidence:	Text evidence:
And up the hill on vine street / (The main black corridor) . . .	Hat in hand to ask to borrow so that I might borrow . . .	Probably they said something humiliating since southern / Whites like to humiliate southern blacks

Theme: Helping someone may mean standing up to prejudice.

As you read the poem, consider what seems most important about the poet's relationship with Mrs. Long. What theme might that suggest?

ANNOTATION MODEL   NOTICE & NOTE

As you read, notice the author's descriptions and use of sensory language, and the mood and mental images that they create. You can also mark up unusual line lengths, capitalization, and punctuation. This model shows one reader's notes for the first stanza of "A Poem for My Librarian, Mrs. Long."

> At a time when there was no (tv) before 3:00 P.M.
> And on Sunday none until 5:00
> <u>We sat on front porches watching</u>
> <u>The (jfg) sign go on and off greeting</u>
> 5 <u>The neighbors, discussing the political</u>
> <u>Situation congratulating the preacher</u>
> <u>On his sermon</u>

lowercase tv and jfg suggest they are not important

line break emphasizes "watching"

image of a close family and neighborhood; warm mood

BACKGROUND

Nikki Giovanni (b. 1943) has been one of the best known American poets since publishing her first book of poetry in 1968. Giovanni grew up in the racially segregated South. When Giovanni attended college, she became a part of a movement of African American writers who were finding new ways to express pride in their distinct culture. In addition to her poetry collections, Giovanni is also an award-winning children's author.

A POEM FOR MY LIBRARIAN, MRS. LONG
(You never know what troubled little girl needs a book)

Poem by Nikki Giovanni

SETTING A PURPOSE

In the poem, Nikki Giovanni looks back at her childhood and the people who most influenced her. As you read, think about how Giovanni's childhood experiences shaped her dreams and her writing.

At a time when there was no tv before 3:00 P.M.
And on Sunday none until 5:00
We sat on front porches watching
The jfg[1] sign go on and off greeting
5   The neighbors, discussing the political
Situation congratulating the preacher
On his sermon

---
[1] **jfg:** a brand of coffee that was popular in Knoxville, Tennessee; an old electrically lit sign for the coffee is a famous landmark in Knoxville, Tennessee.

Notice & Note

Use the side margins to notice and note signposts in the text.

MEMORY MOMENT

Notice & Note: According to lines 1–7, what were the main activities for the poet as a child?

Critique: There's no mention of a librarian yet. Why might that be so?

TEACH

BACKGROUND

When Nikki Giovanni was growing up in the early 1950s, life for African Americans was very different than it is today. In the Southern states, there were many laws that required the separation of blacks and whites. During the time of the Civil Rights Movement, Giovanni became inspired to begin writing poetry. In this poem, the speaker considers the obstacles faced by her Jim Crow–era librarian in obtaining a diverse selection of books to open the wider world to young people.

SETTING A PURPOSE

Direct students to use the Setting a Purpose prompt to focus their reading.

MEMORY MOMENT

Explain to students that this signpost can be used to help students identify how the speaker's character is developed and how it ties into the theme. Ask students: *Why does the poet give details about the speaker's childhood? What do these details tell us about the speaker?* (**Answer:** *watching TV, watching the "jfg sign," and talking to neighbors about various things. Perhaps the poet has not brought up the librarian yet is because she is trying to establish the setting and tell a little bit about the speaker first.*)

For **listening support** for students at varying proficiency levels, see the **Text X-Ray** on page 468C.

ENGLISH LEARNER SUPPORT

Understand Prepositions Read aloud lines 1 and 2 as students follow along. Write the phrase "no tv before 3:00 p.m." on the board. Underline the word *before*. Pair students of differing proficiencies and have them work together to use the preposition correctly in sentences: *We eat dinner ___ dessert. We do our homework ___ we watch TV.*
SUBSTANTIAL/MODERATE

TEACH

ENGLISH LEARNER SUPPORT

Internalize Language Provide students with note cards divided into quadrants. In the top-right quadrant, have students copy an unfamiliar word from the poem. Model how to fill out the remaining quadrants with a definition/illustration, synonyms or related words, and foreign language equivalent. Allow advanced students to choose words from the poem, while providing vocabulary words from the poem for beginning learners. Students should keep their cards and review them throughout the lesson.

ASK STUDENTS to find the word *sing* in line 14 and write it on their note card. Model completing the card for *sing*. Then have students work independently or with a partner to complete another card for the word *bookstore* or another word they do not understand.

ALL LEVELS

ANALYZE FREE VERSE POETRY

Remind students that poets utilize literary techniques with a purpose in mind. As they identify the unconventional capitalization and line lengths, students should ask themselves why the poet would use those techniques. Ask: *What might the effect be in these lines if the poet had used conventional capitalization and standardized line lengths?* (**Answer:** *Not capitalizing gay street tends to de-emphasize it. However, the effect of the shorter lines is to emphasize the words in each. In line 19, the poet is emphasizing books, a dominant idea in the poem. In line 21, the phrase a last resort is emphasized as the last words in the last line of a stanza.*)

ANALYZE THEME

Remind students that analyzing what the speaker says and does gives clues to the theme in a poem. Point out line 29 and ask: *What does the speaker know now that she did not know before? Why is this detail important?* (**Answer:** *The poet admires Mrs. Long because she went to great lengths to help her. She suggests that educators and librarians like Mrs. Long have the power to influence children and change their lives, just as Mrs. Long influenced the poet as a child.*)

472 Unit 6

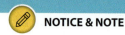 **NOTICE & NOTE**

There was always radio which brought us
Songs from wlac in nashville and what we would now call
10 Easy listening or smooth jazz but when I listened
Late at night with my portable (that I was so proud of)
Tucked under my pillow
I heard nat king cole and matt dennis, june christy and
      ella fitzgerald
And sometimes sarah vaughan sing black coffee
15 Which I now drink
It was just called music

There was a bookstore uptown on gay street
Which I visited and inhaled that wonderful odor
Of new books
20 Even today I read hardcover as a preference paperback only
As a last resort

And up the hill on vine street
(The main black corridor) sat our carnegie library[2]
Mrs. Long always glad to see you
25 The stereoscope[3] always ready to show you faraway
Places to dream about

Mrs. Long asking what are you looking for today
When I wanted *Leaves of Grass* or alfred north whitehead
She would go to the big library uptown and I now know
30 Hat in hand to ask to borrow so that I might borrow
Probably they said something humiliating since southern
Whites like to humiliate southern blacks

But she nonetheless brought the books
Back and I held them to my chest
35 Close to my heart
And happily skipped back to grandmother's house
Where I would sit on the front porch
In a gray glider and dream of a world
Far away

---

[2] **carnegie library:** a library built with money donated by the businessman Andrew Carnegie.
[3] **stereoscope:** an optical instrument with two eyepieces used to create a three-dimensional effect when looking at two photographs of the same scene.

ANALYZE FREE VERSE POETRY

Annotate: In lines 17–21, circle words that normally would be capitalized. Underline short lines in the stanza.

Analyze: What effect does the unconventional capitalization have? How do the shorter lines convey meaning?

ANALYZE THEME

Annotate: Mark what Mrs. Long said and did in lines 24–39.

Interpret: How does the poet feel about Mrs. Long? What message is the poet sending about the power of people like Mrs. Long?

472 Unit 6

WHEN STUDENTS STRUGGLE...

Analyze Poetry Elements Have partners work together to identify and analyze the unconventional punctuation and capitalization in lines 12–16.

Have partners read the lines aloud, pausing briefly at the end of each line. Have partners work together to rewrite the lines with conventional punctuation and capitalization. Then ask: *What do these lines tell you about the speaker?*

 For additional support, go to the **Reading Studio** and assign the following **Level Up Tutorial: Elements of Poetry.**

40 I love the world where I was
   I was safe and warm and grandmother gave me neck kisses
   When I was on my way to bed

   But there was a world
   Somewhere
45 Out there
   And Mrs. Long opened that wardrobe
   But no lions or witches⁴ scared me
   I went through
   Knowing there would be
50 Spring

---

⁴ **wardrobe . . . lions or witches:** refers to *The Lion, the Witch and the Wardrobe*, a fantasy novel by C.S. Lewis; in the story, four children visit a land called Narnia via the wardrobe, or closet, in a spare room.

NOTICE & NOTE

ANALYZE FREE VERSE POETRY

Annotate: In the final stanza of the poem, mark words that rhyme.

Analyze: What idea does this use of rhyme help to emphasize? How does it contribute to a theme?

CHECK YOUR UNDERSTANDING

Answer these questions before moving on to the **Analyze the Text** section on the following page.

1. The poem's speaker discovers another world through —
   A drinking coffee
   B reading books
   C talking to neighbors
   D watching television

2. What does the stanza break between lines 42 and 43 help the poet convey most clearly?
   F the contrast between the poet's two worlds
   G the distance the poet sometimes traveled
   H the respect she has for Mrs. Long and other librarians
   J the childhood dreams the poet had for her future

3. Why is the first stanza important to the poem?
   A It provides clues about the poem's main theme.
   B It conveys the personality of the poet.
   C It introduces the poet's childhood world.
   D It states a problem the poet had as a child.

A Poem for My Librarian, Mrs. Long   473

TEACH

ANALYZE FREE VERSE POETRY

Point out that rhyme creates a musical quality to poetry. The poet waits to use rhyme until the last stanza when she is also referencing a famous children's book that deals with the theme of childlike wonder: *The Lion, the Witch and the Wardrobe*. Ask: *Considering how rhymes help people connect to songs, movies, and literature, why might the poet use rhyme in this stanza?* (**Answer:** *The rhyme emphasizes the idea of books offering the poet another world. It contributes to a theme of the importance of books to children.*)

CHECK YOUR UNDERSTANDING

Have students answer the questions independently.

Answers:
1. B
2. F
3. C

If they answer any questions incorrectly, have them reread the text to confirm their understanding. Then they may proceed to ANALYZE THE TEXT on p. 474.

ENGLISH LEARNER SUPPORT

Oral Assessment Use the following questions to assess students' comprehension and speaking skills:

1. How does the speaker of the poem discover a new world? *(through books)* How does she feel about books? *(happy)*

2. Note the break between lines 42 and 43. What does this break show? *(the two different worlds that the speaker inhabits)*

3. Why is the first stanza important? *(It shows the speaker's childhood, a time long ago.)* **SUBSTANTIAL/MODERATE**

APPLY

ANALYZE THE TEXT

Possible answers:

1. **DOK 2:** One of the poem's themes is the power of books to transport people to different places. The subtitle refers to a troubled girl's need for a book, which emphasizes the idea of a book's ability to take a person out of their world.

2. **DOK 3:** The tone of the poem could best be described as grateful, because the poem is dedicated to Mrs. Long and because the poet describes how the librarian helped her get the books she wanted.

3. **DOK 2:** Because the poem deals with the importance of books in childhood, it ends with an allusion to a popular children's novel. The poet might have included this allusion because it is a novel about children who find a magical world behind a wardrobe, just like the magical world made available by Mrs. Long. In addition, the poem ends with the idea of spring, and the novel ends with the end of a long-lasting winter.

4. **DOK 4:** The punctuation and capitalization are used in unconventional ways, or not at all, to draw attention to certain words and phrases and to emphasize ideas.

5. **DOK 4:** The poet was imaginative because she liked to dream of faraway places. Her words create images about the place she lived and the people around her. She was intelligent because she read challenging books, like Walt Whitman's Leaves of Grass and the philosopher Alfred North Whitehead. She was loving because of her affectionate relationship with her grandmother. She was hopeful because she knew that somewhere out in the world she would find "spring."

RESEARCH

Remind students that biographical information can help a reader understand a poet better. Point out that it is important to use reputable sources so that they can effectively interpret a poet's life and body of work. **(Answer: Row 1**: Nikki Giovanni's grandmother was outspoken and a storyteller, and both traits influenced the poet. **Row 2:** Nikki Giovanni explores themes of race, family, politics, anger and grief, among others in her poetry. **Row 3:** "My First Memory (of Librarians)" and "A Library (for Kelli Martin).")

Connect Students may note that Nikki Giovanni's other poems are also written as free verse poems and include details from her childhood. They also have themes dealing with the wonder of learning and books.

474   Unit 6

RESPOND

ANALYZE THE TEXT

Support your responses with evidence from the text.   NOTEBOOK

1. **Infer** The subtitle of the poem is "(You never know what troubled little girl needs a book)." What might that subtitle suggest about a theme of the poem?

2. **Evaluate** Words like *amused, thoughtful, grateful, hopeful,* and *angry* can be used to describe the tone of a poem. In your opinion, which of these words best fits the poem? Explain.

3. **Interpret** An **allusion** is a reference to a well-known person, place, event, or work of literature. The final stanza of this poem makes an allusion to C. S. Lewis's novel *The Lion, the Witch and the Wardrobe,* in which the heroes end a witch's curse of endless winter. Why might the poet have ended the poem with this allusion?

4. **Analyze** How does the poet's use of punctuation and capitalization contribute to the poem's meaning?

5. **Notice & Note** Reread the last stanza of the poem. What words would you use to describe the poet as a child? Think about the mental images that the descriptions of her childhood memories created as you read the poem. Why do your words fit?

RESEARCH

RESEARCH TIP
Use specific search terms when searching online. For example, you might search "library poems by Nikki Giovanni" to find more poems about libraries. As you scan search results, look for reputable websites, usually those that end in *.org* and *.edu*.

Find out more about Nikki Giovanni and then answer these questions.

QUESTION	ANSWER
Ms. Giovanni refers to her grandmother in the poem. What influence did her grandmother have on her?	*Her grandmother was outspoken and was a storyteller, both of which influenced the poet.*
What other kinds of themes does Nikki Giovanni explore in her poetry?	*She explores themes of race, family, politics, anger, and grief, among others*
What other poems about libraries has she written?	*"My First Memory (of Librarians)" and "A Library (for Kelli Martin)"*

Connect In a small group, discuss how the other poems about libraries that Nikki Giovanni wrote are similar to "A Poem for My Librarian, Mrs. Long."

474   Unit 6

TO CHALLENGE STUDENTS . . .

Conduct Research Challenge students to find other poems on libraries, librarians, or books written by different poets. Have students examine the poetry techniques and elements of the poem, and identify its themes. Have students compare and contrast Nikki Giovanni's "A Poem for My Librarian, Mrs. Long" with the poem they select. They should compare the way each poet uses poetry elements and what effect these have on the theme and tone in each poem.

CREATE AND WRITE

Write a Free Verse Poem Pay tribute to a person whom you admire by writing a free verse poem about that person.

- ❏ Include specific examples of qualities or actions that make this person exceptional.
- ❏ Choose sensory words and phrases to describe the person or your feelings about the person.
- ❏ Consider how you will use punctuation, capitalization, and line breaks to emphasize specific ideas and create meaning.

Write a Letter Write a letter to Nikki Giovanni. In it, share your opinion of "A Poem for My Librarian, Mrs. Long" and any other of her poems you have read. Adapt any notes you took while reading her work. Use these guidelines to help you plan and draft your letter.

- ❏ Open with the date and an appropriate greeting (for example, "Dear Ms. Giovanni").
- ❏ State your opinion clearly and politely, using descriptive words and phrases. Support your opinion with specific examples from the poems. Use transitions to move from one point to the next.
- ❏ Provide a concluding thought that sums up your opinion. Remember to end the letter with an appropriate closing (for example, "Sincerely") and your signature.

RESPOND TO THE ESSENTIAL QUESTION

 What inspires you to make a difference?

Gather Information Review your annotations and notes on "A Poem for My Librarian, Mrs. Long." Then, add relevant details to your Response Log. As you determine which information to include, think about:

- the jobs people do that can inspire others
- the importance of books
- how people make a difference to other people

At the end of the unit, refer to your notes as you write a research report.

RESPOND

Go to **Writing as a Process** in the **Writing Studio** for more help.

ACADEMIC VOCABULARY
As you write and discuss what you learned from the poem, be sure to use the Academic Vocabulary words. Check off each of the words that you use.

- ❏ contrast
- ❏ despite
- ❏ error
- ❏ inadequate
- ❏ interact

APPLY

CREATE AND WRITE

Write a Free Verse Poem Remind students that there are no rules about how to apply poetry techniques when writing a free verse poem. Once they decide on a theme, they can use traditional poetry elements—such as rhythm— in any way they like: or not use them at all. Encourage students to use their favorite poetry elements, as well as common free verse poetry elements such as unconventional line lengths, capitalization, and punctuation. When students are finished, have them work with a partner to make sure they are using the poetry elements they have chosen correctly.

 For **writing support** for students at varying proficiency levels, see the **Text X-Ray** on page 468D.

Write a Letter Remind students to support their opinions of Nikki Giovanni's work by using text evidence from her poems. They may also reference the biographical information they have discovered during their research. Encourage them to imagine how Nikki Giovanni would feel if she read their words, and remind them to be polite.

RESPOND TO THE ESSENTIAL QUESTION

Allow time for students to add details from "A Poem for My Librarian, Mrs. Long" to their Unit 6 Response Logs.

PLAN

FRANCES PERKINS AND THE TRIANGLE FACTORY FIRE
History Writing by David Brooks

GENRE ELEMENTS
HISTORY WRITING

Tell students that **history writing** is a form of **informational text** that focuses on real people and events from the past. Authors attempt to tell a true story that is based on research; they use primary sources—such as eyewitness accounts, official records, and photographs—and secondary sources, such as newspaper accounts and the writings of historians. Organized using both narrative and key ideas, it presents the interactions between people and events. Although historical writing is primarily objective, it often reveals the author's view of the topic.

LEARNING OBJECTIVES

- Analyze history writing.
- Determine key ideas.
- Conduct research about Frances Perkins.
- Write an ode.
- Discuss primary sources.
- Identify Latin roots of English words.
- Practice subject-verb agreement.
- **Language** Identify word choice that express the author's tone.

TEXT COMPLEXITY

Quantitative Measures	Frances Perkins and the Triangle Factory Fire	Lexile: 930L
Qualitative Measures	**Ideas Presented** Mostly explicit but moves to some implied meaning	
	Structure Used Primarily explicit; primarily single perspective	
	Language Used Mostly explicit, but sentence structure more complex	
	Knowledge Required More complex problems; experiences may be unfamiliar to some	

PLAN

Online

RESOURCES

- Unit 6 Response Log
- 🔊 Selection Audio
- 📖 Reading Studio: Notice & Note
- LEVELUP Level Up Tutorial: Tone
- Writing Studio: Writing as a Process
- Speaking and Listening Studio: Participating in a Collaborative Discussion
- Vocabulary Studio: Latin Roots
- Grammar Studio: Module 8: Lesson 8: Pronoun Agreement
- ✓ "Frances Perkins and the Triangle Factory Fire" Selection Test

SUMMARIES

English

David Brooks tells the story of the catastrophic Triangle Factory Fire from the perspective of Frances Perkins. Perkins was an educator and activist who later became the Secretary of the Department of Labor; she was the first woman to hold a cabinet position in the United States. Brooks describes the horrors of the fire and the women who had to choose between death by fire and a nine-story fall. He also tells of the working conditions that led to the fire and the deaths of 123 women and 23 men. This human-created disaster led many people to change their attitudes about the labor reform movements.

Spanish

David Brooks cuenta la historia del catastrófico incendio en la fábrica *Triangle Shirtwaist* desde la perspectiva de Frances Perkins, una activista de Nueva York, quien se convirtió en funcionaria de gobierno y quien fue luego nombrada la primera mujer del gabinete presidencial. Brooks describe los horrores del incendio y las mujeres que tuvieron que elegir entre la muerte en el fuego o una caída de nueve pisos. También describe cómo las condiciones laborales llevaron directamente al incendio y a las muertes.

 ## SMALL-GROUP OPTIONS

Have students work in small groups to read and discuss the selection.

Three Before Me

- Have students bring in a piece of writing to class, for instance a draft of their ode (see p. 487 for details of this assignment).
- Each student asks three other students to edit the writing before turning it in. Students can be asked to edit only for pronoun-antecedent agreement or for all general grammatical errors.
- Each student is responsible for evaluating editorial comments from the three student editors before turning in the assignment.

Reciprocal Teaching

- Present lecture on a relevant topic.
- Offer a list of generic question stems, and have each student write three to five questions on the topic (students do not need to know answers to their questions).
- Put students into groups of three, with each group settling on two questions.
- Groups answer those questions to collective satisfaction, and then locate textual evidence to support their answers.

Frances Perkins and the Triangle Factory Fire **476B**

PLAN

 Text X-Ray: English Learner Support
for "Frances Perkins and the Triangle Factory Fire"

Use the Text X-Ray and the supports and scaffolds in the Teacher's Edition to help guide students at different proficiency levels through the selection.

INTRODUCE THE SELECTION

DISCUSS WORKERS' RIGHTS

In this lesson, students will need to be able to discuss the treatment of workers and the movement to improve their safety and health. Give students the following definitions as they apply to the text to help them:

- *exploit:* to treat someone unfairly in order to make more money from their work
- *working conditions:* the environment of a worker's job, including: levels of heat and cold, cleanliness, number of hours of work, breathable air, treatment by supervisors and employers, and pay
- *reform:* making changes in something in order to improve it

Give students the following sentence frames to help them discuss the labor movement:

- *Dangerous and exploitative working conditions can cause _____ .*
- *Labor activists work to _____ working conditions.*

CULTURAL REFERENCES

The following words and phrases may be unfamiliar to students:

- *society matron* (paragraph 1): a well-known, wealthy, married woman; the opposite of a friendless, poor woman
- *trace its lineage* (paragraph 2): had ancestors (e.g., grandparents, great-grandparents)
- *picketers* (paragraph 18): striking workers: by refusing to work—which is expensive for a company—workers try to negotiate for better conditions
- *...we have found you wanting!* (paragraph 19): not good enough, a biblical reference (Daniel 5:27)
- *pinion* (paragraph 21): tie or bind oneself to something

LISTENING

Understand Key Vocabulary and Ideas

Read aloud the first two paragraphs of the selection after helping students label period images that will help them internalize new vocabulary. Find key words they will need to understand the overall point of the text, e.g., *workers, society matron, protests, strikes,* and *factory.*

Have students listen as you read aloud paragraphs 2–3, pause for clarification and read it again. Use the following supports with students at varying proficiency levels:

- Point to the relevant labeled photographs. Ask yes-no questions, and have students give thumbs up or thumbs down responses. For example: *Was Frances Perkins a worker? (no.) Was she helping to end child labor? (Yes) Was the burning building a factory? (yes)* **SUBSTANTIAL**
- Have students use labeled images and a word bank to listen to two readings of paragraphs 2–3 before engaging in a basic retelling of the text with partners. **MODERATE**
- Have student pairs read paragraphs 1–3 to each other twice. Have each student retell what he or she heard while the listener tallies the remembered details. **LIGHT**

476C Unit 6

PLAN

SPEAKING

Discuss Dialogue and Intonation

Read paragraph 15 aloud. Point out the quotation marks and remind students that they enclose dialogue; in this case, one person is speaking. Have students discuss the probable expression and intonation of the speaker.

Use the following supports with students at varying proficiency levels:

- Say the word *No*, using several different tones of voice to indicate what is being expressed—calm, angry, hesitant, surprised. Ask students to name in words or to show on their own faces the attitude or emotion expressed each time. Have volunteers decide which tone of voice should be used to read the dialogue in paragraph 15 starting with "I was only looking for my own life…" Have students choral read the dialogue with you. Read it twice: use two different tones of voice. Define the word *distinguish* as it used here, and have students sound it out with you: first by each syllable and then all at once. **SUBSTANTIAL/MODERATE**

- Pair students and have them take turns reading paragraphs 15–16 aloud to each other; circulate to check for proper intonation and expression. **LIGHT**

READING

Spot the Pronouns

Call attention to the pronouns in paragraphs 2 and 3. Review the material about pronouns and their antecedents. Remind students that pronouns must agree with their antecedents in number, gender, and person.

Work with students to read paragraphs 2–3. Use the following supports with students at varying proficiency levels:

- List personal pronouns on the board. Choral read paragraphs 2–3 with students. Have them pause and raise their hands when they spot a pronoun. **SUBSTANTIAL**

- List four nouns on the board—for example, *the butler, Perkins, the Revolution, the ladies*—and ask students to pick the correct pronoun and mark it in their texts as they read. (Answers: *he, she, it, they*). **MODERATE**

- Have students silently read paragraphs 2–3. Then have them underline in their texts: 1) all the pronouns and 2) all nouns that could be replaced by pronoun. **LIGHT**

WRITING

Write an Ode

Work with students to read the writing assignment on p. 487.

Use the following supports with students at varying proficiency levels:

- Ask students simple questions about a topic for an ode. Ask: *Name a person you respect. What does he or she do? What one word would describe that person?* Have students begin a word bank for an ode. Supply students with stems from simple modern odes as models for the form. **SUBSTANTIAL**

- Give students a choice of first lines for their odes: *I honor _____.* OR *_____ was a hero.* Suggest that the rest of the poem be about the reasons they honor and respect the subject of their ode. **MODERATE**

- Ask partners to discuss the person they have chosen to write about. Have them make a list of qualities and/or achievements they will mention in their odes. Have students work separately on the opening lines of their odes, and then read them to their partners. **LIGHT**

Frances Perkins and the Triangle Factory Fire **476D**

TEACH

 Connect to the ESSENTIAL QUESTION

"Frances Perkins and the Triangle Factory Fire" tells the story of a person who was inspired to make a difference in the world. What inspired Frances Perkins was a catastrophe that had a direct affect on her community and her way of evaluating her own responsibilities. She chose to see that moment as a call to action, and her life was never the same again.

COMPARE AUTHORS' PURPOSES AND MESSAGES

Encourage students to take notes on both articles in preparation for the final project in the Collaborate & Compare section. Ask the class to think deeply about David Brooks's message in writing about Frances Perkins and the Triangle Factory fire, and to consider it in contrast with Zachary Kent's rendition of the same events, which they will read next.

COLLABORATE & COMPARE

HISTORY WRITING

FRANCES PERKINS AND THE TRIANGLE FACTORY FIRE

by **David Brooks**
pages 479–485

COMPARE AUTHORS' PURPOSES AND MESSAGES
When authors write about history, their purpose is often to explain what happened. As you read these texts—two texts about the same topic—note what is similar and what is different about their explanations. Think about what main idea, or message, each one expresses. After you read both selections, you will collaborate with a small group on a final project.

 ESSENTIAL QUESTION:

What inspires you to make a difference?

HISTORY WRITING

from

THE STORY OF THE TRIANGLE FACTORY FIRE

by **Zachary Kent**
pages 493–495

476 Unit 6

 LEARNING MINDSET

Persistence Remind students that in life sometimes the going can get tough—and when it does positive self-talk can help. Model positive self-talk for the class: *I know I can do this!* or *I never fail because I try again!* Have students chorally repeat after you. Tell students that when a person has energy and effort there really isn't anything that can hold him or her back. Persistence doesn't mean striving for perfection, it simply means dusting yourself off and redoubling your efforts when you fail. Pursuing an unselfish goal or something you know you want for good reasons often requires a balance of passion and determination.

Frances Perkins and the Triangle Factory Fire

QUICK START

If you and a friend both described the same event, would your accounts be the same? In a small group, discuss why they might differ.

ANALYZE HISTORY WRITING

History writing is a type of literary nonfiction that combines the features of a narrative text (a true story with a setting, characters, and a plot) and an informational text (paragraphs covering key ideas and factual details). Authors write from a unique perspective, or view of topics, which the following clues can help you identify.

CLUE	WHAT CLUE TELLS YOU
Tone	**Tone** is the author's attitude toward the topic. Consider how the author's language expresses emotions that affect your understanding of the topic.
Point of View	A **subjective** point of view means that the author includes personal opinions. An **objective** point of view means that the author focuses only on the facts.
Emphasis	Note which facts the author emphasizes. Why do you think the author highlights those facts?
Portrayals	Does the author include any **primary sources,** such as quotations from people who witnessed or took part in an event? If so, what do the primary sources tell you?

As you read "Frances Perkins and the Triangle Factory Fire," look for clues like the ones in the chart.

GENRE ELEMENTS: INFORMATIONAL TEXT

- focuses on real people and events from the past
- often tells a true story, with factual details acquired through research
- presents the interactions between people and events
- may hint at the author's own view of the topic

DETERMINE KEY IDEAS

Selections that are history writing will have a **controlling idea,** or thesis. The controlling idea is also called a **key idea,** or the most important idea about the topic. It may be stated explicitly in a sentence, or it may be implied. Each paragraph or section also will have a key idea that provides support for the controlling key idea.

Key ideas are supported by **details,** facts, and other information that clarifies the key ideas. As you read history writing, think about key ideas and information that answers questions such as *Where and when did the event take place? Who was involved? What were the event's causes and effects? How does this information help me understand the topic?*

TEACH

QUICK START

After students read the Quick Start question, take a volunteer out of the classroom and give him or her directions to run in to the room, pick something up, run back out. Return to the room and ask students to describe what they saw in detail— including what the volunteer was wearing, what he or she picked up, what he or she said or did not say, and what expression the person had. Discuss any differences in accounts.

ANALYZE HISTORY WRITING

Explain to students that what we call history is often a series of educated guesses about what happened in the past. Historians investigate and use as many clues as they can find to try to determine exactly what happened. These clues include:

- **primary sources**, including eye witness accounts, oral histories, photographs, official records
- **secondary sources**, including newspaper articles from the time, stories handed down to children and grandchildren, accounts written by other historians

Historians usually maintain an objective point of view. However, when writing for a general audience, they frequently allow their own feelings and opinions to show in **tone** and in what they choose to **emphasize.**

DETERMINE KEY IDEAS

Remind students that every paragraph has its own **key idea** that is supported by **details** and facts. Encourage students to seek these controlling ideas out in each paragraph as practice for their group project.

TEACH

CRITICAL VOCABULARY

Encourage students to read all the sentences before deciding which word best completes each one. Remind them to look for context clues that match the meaning of each word.

Answers:

1. *fatal*
2. *distinguish*
3. *lobby*
4. *indifferent*

■ **English Learner Support**

Access New Vocabulary Pair students of varying English proficiency, and ask them to examine the Spanish cognates for three of the new Critical Vocabulary words (fatal: *fatal*, distinguish: *distinguir*, and indifferent: *indiferente*).
ALL LEVEL

LANGUAGE CONVENTIONS

Explain to students that pronouns are used to avoid repetition, such as "Tom put Tom's book in Tom's backpack." However, pronouns can be confusing if the antecedents are not clear.

(The pronoun for elevator would be it, because an elevator has no gender and it is not plural.)

 ## ANNOTATION MODEL

Tell students they may follow the suggestion on p. 478 or use their own system for marking up the selection. They may want to color-code their annotations with highlighters. Their notes in the margin may include questions about ideas that are unclear or topics they want to learn more about.

 GET READY

CRITICAL VOCABULARY

lobby   fatal   distinguish   indifferent

To preview the Critical Vocabulary words, complete each sentence with a word from the list.

1. Without treatment, that disease could become _____ .
2. In the snowstorm, the truck driver could not _____ the road from the ditch beside it.
3. The workers decided to _____ their boss for a raise.
4. No one in the neighborhood was _____ about the need for a new school.

LANGUAGE CONVENTIONS

Pronoun-Antecedent Agreement In this lesson, you will learn about making sure that pronouns agree with their antecedents (the nouns or other pronouns to which they refer) in number, gender, and person. In this example, notice that the singular pronoun *it* agrees with *elevator*, its singular antecedent:

> The people rode to the first floor in an **elevator. It** got stuck on the second floor, and the people had to wait.

As you read, see how pronoun-antecedent agreement helps you understand key ideas and details.

ANNOTATION MODEL   NOTICE & NOTE

As you read, note how the author presents the historical topic. You can also mark up key ideas and the information that supports them. In the model, you can see one reader's notes about part of "Frances Perkins and the Triangle Factory Fire."

> 1 . . . But back <u>in 1911, there were (nice) brownstones on the northern side of the park and factories on its eastern and southern sides</u>, drawing young and mostly Jewish and Italian immigrant workers. One of the (nice) homes was owned by Mrs. Gordon Norrie, a society matron descended from two of the men who signed the Declaration of Independence.

The contrast between the brownstones and the factories may be a key idea.

The author uses "nice" twice, but not to describe the factories.

478   Unit 6

BACKGROUND

David Brooks *(b. 1961) was born in Canada and grew up in New York City. He started his career as a police reporter in Chicago. Today, Brooks is perhaps best known as a newspaper columnist and television analyst. His commentary and writings often focus on culture and social issues. In his book* The Road to Character, *in which this piece of history writing appears, Brooks explores what inspired individuals such as Frances Perkins to become leaders and help change society for the better.*

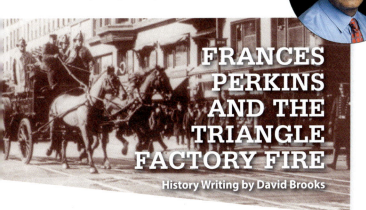

FRANCES PERKINS AND THE TRIANGLE FACTORY FIRE

History Writing by David Brooks

PREPARE TO COMPARE

As you read, consider how the author presents facts and other evidence to explain a tragic but significant historical event and its effects. This information will help you compare Brooks's account of the fire with an account of the same event by Zachary Kent, which follows it.

NOTICE & NOTE

Notice & Note

Use the side margins to notice and note signposts in the text.

ANALYZE HISTORY WRITING

Annotate: Mark the facts presented about Frances Perkins in paragraph 2.

Infer: Why do you think the author includes these facts about Perkins? What do they tell you about her?

1   Today, the area around Washington Square Park in lower Manhattan is surrounded by New York University, expensive apartments, and upscale stores. But back in 1911, there were nice brownstones on the northern side of the park and factories on its eastern and southern sides, drawing young and mostly Jewish and Italian immigrant workers. One of the nice homes was owned by Mrs. Gordon Norrie, a society matron descended from two of the men who signed the Declaration of Independence.

2   On March 25, Mrs. Norrie was just sitting down to tea with a group of friends when they heard a commotion outside. One of her guests, Frances Perkins, then thirty-one, was from an old but middle-class Maine family, which could also trace its lineage back to the time of the

Frances Perkins and the Triangle Factory Fire   **479**

TEACH

BACKGROUND

After students read the Background note, remind them that the Triangle Shirtwaist Factory fire of 1911 is considered by many social historians to be a turning point in modern American history. The catastrophic fire set in motion a series of events that eventually led to improved conditions for workers, a ban of child labor, and expanded and robust union activity across the country.

PREPARE TO COMPARE

Direct students to use the Prepare to Compare prompt to focus their reading.

ANALYZE HISTORY WRITING

Remind students that to be **objective** is to attempt to remain outside of the events by reporting only facts, events, and research. (**Answer:** *The author may want to show the contrast between Perkins's life and the lives of the factory workers, as well as what Perkins was like before the fire. The facts suggest that Perkins lived a comfortable life but also tried to influence politicians on social issues.*)

> For **listening support** for students at varying proficiency levels, see the **Text X-Ray** on page 476C.

ENGLISH LEARNER SUPPORT

Imagine and Learn Help students imagine the thoughts and feelings of the people who had protested against the conditions at the Triangle Shirtwaist Factory *before* the fire. Have them complete sentence frames with words covered in the introduction to the selection: *exploiting, working conditions, reform, picketers*. Sound out the words with students, and define them using images, gestures, and cognates. Then, have students use them as if writing to a friend, for example: I did not know *(working conditions)* at the factory were so dangerous. It is now clear that the owners' had been *(exploiting)* the workers for a long time. We have to *(reform)* by changing laws. No wonder there were so many *(picketers!)*   **MODERATE**

Frances Perkins and the Triangle Factory Fire   **479**

TEACH

BIG QUESTIONS

This **Big Questions** signpost is an example of both a salient **detail** and a specific **emphasis** made by the author. By researching the event, Brooks learned what the onlookers experienced and chose to include this specific detail in order to emphasize the catastrophe. (**Answer:** *The truth was a surprise to the people watching, but I suspected the truth. The repeated they thought was a clue, as was the information that workers were crowded around the windows of the burning building.*)

 DETERMINE KEY IDEAS

Remind the class that **details** and how they are chosen are an integral part of the author's chosen tone and emphasis. (**Answer:** *This probably is a key idea. The thought that 47 people were so desperate that jumping to their deaths was preferable to burning alive is so dramatic that it may shape the rest of what the author presents.*)

 NOTICE & NOTE

lobby
(lŏb´ē) v. To *lobby* is to attempt to influence politicians to support the cause that you represent.

BIG QUESTIONS

Notice & Note: In paragraph 4, circle what people thought they were seeing. Then underline what they actually were seeing.

Connect: Did the truth surprise you, or did it confirm what you already knew? Explain.

DETERMINE KEY IDEAS
Annotate: In paragraph 7, mark details that help explain why some workers decided to jump.

Predict: Do you think that this is a key idea in the text? Why or why not?

Revolution. She had attended Mount Holyoke College and was working at the Consumers' League of New York,[1] **lobbying** to end child labor.

3   A butler rushed in and announced that there was a fire near the square. The ladies ran out. Perkins lifted up her skirts and sprinted toward it. They had stumbled upon the Triangle Shirtwaist Factory, one of the most famous fires in American history. Perkins could see the eighth, ninth, and tenth floors of the building ablaze and dozens of workers crowding around the open windows. She joined the throng of horrified onlookers on the sidewalk below.

4   Some saw what they thought were bundles of fabric falling from the windows. They thought the factory owners were saving their best material. As the bundles continued to fall, the onlookers realized they were not bundles at all. They were people, hurling themselves to their death. "People had just begun to jump as we got there," Perkins would later remember. "They had been holding on until that time, standing in the windowsills, being crowded by others behind them, the fire pressing closer and closer, the smoke closer and closer.

5   "They began to jump. The window was too crowded and they would jump and they hit the sidewalk," she recalled. "Every one of them was killed, everybody who jumped was killed. It was a horrifying spectacle."

6   "The firemen held out nets, but the weight of the bodies from that great height either yanked the nets from the firemen's hands or the bodies ripped right through. One woman grandly emptied her purse over the onlookers below and then hurled herself off.

7   Perkins and the others screamed up to them, "Don't jump! Help is coming." It wasn't. The flames were roasting them from behind. Forty-seven people ended up jumping. One young woman gave a speech before diving, gesticulating passionately, but no one could hear her. One young man tenderly helped a young woman onto the windowsill. Then he held her out, away from the building, like a ballet dancer, and let her drop. He did the same for a second and a third. Finally, a fourth girl stood on the windowsill; she embraced him and they shared a long kiss. Then he held her out and dropped her, too. Then he himself was in the air. As he fell, people noticed, as his pants ballooned out, that he wore smart tan shoes. One reporter wrote, "I saw his face before they covered it. You could see in it that he was a real man. He had done his best."

---
[1] **Consumers' League of New York:** organization founded in 1891 and dedicated to improve working conditions and other social issues.

480   Unit 6

CRITICAL VOCABULARY

lobby: At her job, Perkins worked to try to get politicians to make laws against child labor.

ASK STUDENTS what Perkins might have done to lobby for the end of child labor. (*She might have talked to politicians and tried to convince them that children shouldn't have to work.*)

480   Unit 6

8   The fire had started at about 4:40 that afternoon, when somebody on the eighth floor threw a cigarette or a match into one of the great scrapheaps of cotton left over from the tailoring process. The pile quickly burst into flames.

9   Somebody alerted the factory manager, Samuel Bernstein, who grabbed some nearby buckets of water and dumped them on the fire. They did little good. The cotton scraps were explosively flammable, more so than paper, and there was roughly a ton of the stuff piled on the eighth floor alone.

10 Bernstein dumped more buckets of water on the growing fire, but by this point they had no effect whatsoever, and the flames were spreading to the tissue paper patterns hanging above the wooden work desks. He ordered workers to drag a fire hose from a nearby stairwell. They opened the valve, but there was no pressure. As a historian of the fire, David Von Drehle, has argued, Bernstein made a **fatal** decision in those first three minutes. He could have spent the time fighting the fire or evacuating the nearly five hundred workers. Instead, he battled the exploding fire, to no effect. If he had spent the time evacuating, it is possible that nobody would have died that day.

11 When Bernstein finally did take his eyes off the wall of fire, he was astonished by what he saw. Many of the women on the eighth floor were taking the time to go to the dressing room to retrieve their coats and belongings. Some were looking for their time cards so they could punch out.

12 Eventually, the two factory owners up on the tenth floor were alerted to the fire, which had already consumed the eighth floor and was spreading quickly to their own. One of them, Isaac Harris, gathered a group of workers and figured it was probably suicidal to try to climb down through the fire. "Girls, let us go up on the roof! Get on the roof!" he bellowed. The other owner, Max Blanck, was paralyzed by fear. He stood frozen with a look of terror on his face, holding his youngest daughter in one arm and his elder daughter's hand with the other. A clerk, who was evacuating with the firm's order book, decided to throw it down and save his boss's life instead.

13 Most of the workers on the eighth floor were able to get out, but the workers on the ninth floor had little warning until the fire was already upon them. They ran like terrified schools of fish from one potential exit to another. There were two elevators, but they were slow and overloaded. There was no sprinkler system. There was a fire escape, but it was rickety and blocked. On normal days the workers were searched as they headed home, to prevent theft. The factory had been designed

NOTICE & NOTE

LANGUAGE CONVENTIONS
Annotate: Circle the pronouns *them* and *they* in paragraph 9. Then underline the phrase that is the antecedent for both pronouns.

Analyze: How does this example of pronoun-antecedent agreement help you understand the author's explanation of the attempt to control the fire?

fatal
(fāt´l) *adj.* A *fatal* decision is a choice that results in death.

ANALYZE HISTORY WRITING
Annotate: In paragraph 11, mark text details of what was happening on the eighth floor.

Infer: What do you think the author's point of view is about this scene, and why?

DETERMINE KEY IDEAS
Annotate: In paragraph 13, mark words and phrases that describe the conditions of the factory.

Analyze: How did the factory conditions force workers to make "life-and-death decisions"?

Frances Perkins and the Triangle Factory Fire   481

IMPROVE READING FLUENCY

Targeted Passage   Put students in pairs and ask them to turn to paragraphs 8–10 for a targeted reading. Have students read the paragraphs back and forth slowly, offering comments and corrections to each other as they go. Once they've read it twice, ask students to identify the main idea of the three paragraphs and to summarize the events that occurred. Have them read again and then ask them to identify the key idea in each individual paragraph. Finally, have students look up any words they don't know in the passage.

   Go to the **Reading Studio** for additional support in developing fluency.

TEACH

🖉 LANGUAGE CONVENTIONS

Remind students that an **antecedent** (in Latin meaning "to go before") is the original noun that is later replaced by a corresponding pronoun. (**Answer:** *By making sure that* they *and* them *agree with the antecedent* buckets of water, *the writer makes a clear image of how the first attempts to fight the fire were ineffectual and helped worsen the fire.*)

🖉 ANALYZE HISTORY WRITING

Tell the class, readers can often identify an author's personal point of view on a subject by paying close attention to which details he includes. (**Answer:** *The fact that the author points out that many women were stopping to take care of other tasks instead of evacuating as quickly as possible suggests that he may feel as astonished as Bernstein did.*)

🖉 DETERMINE KEY IDEAS

Remind students that a **key idea** is the same thing as a thesis or controlling idea. It acts as a core for the text and guides the story forward. (**Answer:** *The factory had limited means of escape. Worse, most escape routes were unsafe because they were in poor condition or were blocked. During a fire with limited ways to escape, many workers would not be able to get out and all the workers had no time to think or plan and had to make quick, risky decisions.*)

CRITICAL VOCABULARY

fatal: The company owner made a decision that caused a great many people to die.

ASK STUDENTS what decision Bernstein could have made that would not have been fatal. (*He could have focused on evacuating workers instead of trying to save his property.*)

Frances Perkins and the Triangle Factory Fire   **481**

TEACH

✏️ ANALYZE HISTORY WRITING

Remind students that an author's **portrayal** relies on deep research into primary resources, like newspapers and journals. To get this information about Weiner, Brooks must have studied reports of the incident from 1911. (**Answer:** *Weiner's dramatic action, made vivid through the detail suggests that the author sees her as courageous. His tone seems to be one of admiration.*)

CRITICAL VOCABULARY

distinguish: In the confusion, the workers couldn't tell one thing from another.

ASK STUDENTS to what, besides confusion, might have made it difficult to distinguish things in the factory. (*There was probably a lot of smoke that made it difficult to distinguish specific things.*)

482   Unit 6

 **NOTICE & NOTE**

to force them through a single choke point[2] in order to get out. Some of the doors were locked. As the fire surrounded them, the workers were left to make desperate life-and-death decisions with limited information in a rising atmosphere of fire, smoke, and terror.

14   Three friends, Ida Nelson, Katie Weiner, and Fanny Lansner, were in the changing room when the screams of "Fire!" reached them. Nelson decided to sprint for one of the stairwells. Weiner went to the elevators and saw an elevator car descending the shaft. She hurled herself into space, diving onto the roof. Lansner took neither course and didn't make it out.

15   Mary Bucelli later described her own part in the vicious scramble to get out first: "I can't tell you because I gave so many pushes and kicks. I gave and received. I was throwing them down wherever I met them," she said of her co-workers. "I was only looking for my own life. . . . At a moment like that, there is big confusion and you must understand that you cannot see anything. . . . You see a multitude of things, but you can't **distinguish** anything. With the confusion and the fight that you take, you can't distinguish anything."

16   Joseph Brenman was one of the relatively few men in the factory. A crowd of women were pushing between him and the elevators. But they were small, and many of them were faint. He

ANALYZE HISTORY WRITING
Annotate: In paragraph 14, mark the sentences that describe Katie Weiner's actions.
Interpret: How would you describe the author's tone at this point? Explain.

distinguish
(dĭ-stĭng´gwĭsh) *v.* To *distinguish* one thing from another means perceiving them as being different or distinct.

---
[2] **choke point** a narrow passage; a point of congestion or blockage.

The *New York World,* a major newspaper of the early 20th century, conveyed the dramatic details of what became known as a major industrial disaster.

482   Unit 6

WHEN STUDENTS STRUGGLE . . .

Understand Tone To help students understand tone, read aloud the third and fourth sentences of paragraph 14. Point out the words Brooks uses to describe Katie Weiner's jump onto the roof of the elevator—"hurled herself into space, diving onto the roof." Then rephrase the sentence: *She jumped onto the roof of the elevator.* Ask students whether the words Brooks uses communicate his attitude towards Katie Weiner's actions.

📖   For additional support, go to the **Reading Studio** and assign the following **Level Up tutorial: Tone.**

shoved them aside and barreled his way onto the elevator and to safety.

17   The fire department arrived quickly but its ladders could not reach the eighth floor. The water from its hoses could barely reach that high, just enough to give the building exterior a light dousing.

Shame

18   The horror of the Triangle Shirtwaist Fire traumatized the city. People were not only furious at the factory owners, but felt some deep responsibility themselves. In 1909 a young Russian immigrant named Rose Schneiderman had led the women who worked at Triangle and other factories on a strike to address the very issues that led to the fire disaster. The picketers were harassed by company guards. The city looked on **indifferently**, as it did upon the lives of the poor generally. After the fire there was a collective outpouring of rage, fed by collective guilt at the way people had self-centeredly gone about their lives, callously **indifferent** to the conditions and suffering of the people close around them. "I can't begin to tell you how disturbed the people were everywhere," Frances Perkins remembered. "It was as though we had all done something wrong. It shouldn't have been. We were sorry. Mea culpa! Mea culpa!"[3]

---
[3] **Mea culpa!** (mā´ə kŭl´pə): a cry meaning "I am at fault!"

NOTICE & NOTE

DETERMINE KEY IDEAS
Annotate: In paragraph 18, mark the descriptive word that appears twice (once as an adverb, once as an adjective) and refers to the general attitude of people toward factory workers before the fire.

Critique: Why is the idea that these words represent a key idea in the text?

indifferent
(ĭn-dĭf´ər-ənt) adj. Someone who is *indifferent* has no feelings one way or another about something.

Frances Perkins and the Triangle Factory Fire   483

TO CHALLENGE STUDENTS . . .

Research to Connect Past and Present Times Ask students to research child labor laws.

- In what year was child labor outlawed in the United States?
- What exceptions were made to those laws?
- What exceptions still exist?
- Are there any children working in the United States today?

TEACH

DETERMINE KEY IDEAS

Tell students that authors sometimes use repetition to reinforce the importance of a concept or idea. After students have located the words *indifferently* and *indifferent* in the text, ask them to think about how these words represent society's attitude towards the struggles workers faced. (**Answer:** *The words indifferently and indifferent support the key idea that society failed to protect workers because they did not care about the struggles of their neighbors, which ultimately lead to tragedy.*)

ENGLISH LEARNER SUPPORT

Comprehension Check Help students understand the phrase *mea culpa*. Display the phrase and pronounce it. Explain that it is a Latin phrase that means "I am guilty" and that, in Spanish, the phrase is *mi culpa*. Ask students to come up with some synonyms or similar phrases to *mea culpa* (e.g., *my bad, my mistake, my fault, my responsibility, I'm responsible, I'm guilty*).

ALL LEVELS

CRITICAL VOCABULARY

indifferent: The people of the city never worried about working conditions for others.

ASK STUDENTS why being indifferent before made people feel guilty after the fire. (*People felt that they should not have been indifferent to other people's danger.*)

Frances Perkins and the Triangle Factory Fire   **483**

TEACH

 ANALYZE HISTORY WRITING

Remind students that **primary sources** are resources like journals, diaries, photographs, and eye-witness accounts in newspapers, which come directly from the era and the people involved. (**Answer:** *The author included this primary source because it shows the passion of someone who had tried, unsuccessfully, to bring about change before the fire. Her rejection of* fellowship *shows her determination to make change.*)

 DETERMINE KEY IDEAS

Remind students that important details that can be used to support key ideas come from strong research into primary and secondary sources, which the author clearly did before writing this text. (**Answer:** *Brooks describes how achieving reform became more important to Perkins than the "structure of her life." In addition, she became more active in politics instead of continuing as a "genteel progressive" and she even worked with corrupt people to help achieve reform.*)

 **NOTICE & NOTE**

ANALYZE HISTORY WRITING
Annotate: In paragraphs 19–20, mark what Rose Schneiderman says about the idea of "fellowship."

Infer: Why do you think the author included this primary source? What additional information does it provide?

DETERMINE KEY IDEAS
Annotate: In paragraph 21, mark the first sentence that tells you about the change in Frances Perkins after the fire.

Cite Evidence: How does the author support this key idea?

19   A large memorial march was held, and then a large meeting, with all the leading citizens of the city. Perkins was on stage as a representative of the Consumers' League when Rose Schneiderman electrified the crowd: "I would be a traitor to those poor burned bodies if I were to come here to talk good fellowship. We have tried you, good people of the public—and we have found you wanting! . . .

20   "We have tried you, citizens! We are trying you now and you have a couple of dollars for the sorrowing mothers and brothers and sisters by way of a charity gift. But every time the workers come out in the only way they know to protest against conditions which are unbearable, the strong hand of the law is allowed to press down heavily upon us. . . . I can't talk fellowship to you who are gathered here. Too much blood has been spilled!"

21   The fire and its aftershocks left a deep mark on Frances Perkins. Up until that point she had lobbied for worker rights and on behalf of the poor, but she had been on a conventional trajectory, toward a conventional marriage, perhaps, and a life of genteel good works. After the fire, what had been a career turned into a vocation.[4] Moral indignation set her on a different course. Her own desires and her own ego became less central and the cause itself became more central to the structure of her life. The niceties of her class fell away. She became impatient with the way genteel progressives went about serving the poor. She became impatient with their prissiness, their desire

---
[4] **vocation** (vō-kā′shən): a strong commitment to a certain course of action.

In 1933, Frances Perkins became the first female U.S. Cabinet member as Secretary of Labor.

484   Unit 6

APPLYING ACADEMIC VOCABULARY

☐ contrast   ☑ despite   ☑ error   ☐ inadequate   ☑ interact

Write and Discuss Have students turn to a partner to discuss the following questions. Guide students to include the Academic Vocabulary words *despite*, *error*, and *interact* in their responses. Ask volunteers to share their responses with the class.

- How did Perkins carry on advocating for labor rights **despite** how her colleagues and her "fellowship" felt about it?

- What were the major **errors** that led to the Triangle Factory fire being more catastrophic than it should have been?
- By what method did labor activists of the time **interact** with the public in order to spread word of their working conditions and their demands?

484   Unit 6

to stay pure and above the fray. Perkins hardened. She threw herself into the rough and tumble of politics. She was willing to take morally hazardous action[5] if it would prevent another catastrophe like the one that befell the women at the Triangle factory. She was willing to compromise and work with corrupt officials if it would produce results. She pinioned herself to this cause for the rest of her life.

---

[5] **morally hazardous action:** an action that may result in increased risk to oneself or others and that some may consider to be inappropriate.

NOTICE & NOTE

CHECK YOUR UNDERSTANDING

Answer these questions before moving on to the **Analyze the Text** section on the following page.

1. What key idea could a reader most likely determine from the details in paragraph 10?

   A No one could have prevented the fire.

   B Cotton dust and scraps are flammable.

   C Poor decisions made the fire much worse.

   D A growing fire cannot be stopped.

2. In paragraph 15, the author includes a direct quotation from Mary Bucelli in order to —

   F explain the factory workers' actions during the fire

   G persuade readers that the fire could have been prevented

   H explain why the fire spread so quickly

   J describe what happened after the fire

3. Which sentence best explains why Frances Perkins devoted the rest of her life to bringing reform to the lives of workers?

   A She always had been interested in helping the poor.

   B She was deeply affected by the tragic fire at the factory.

   C She was unhappy about the indifference that city leaders showed toward the poor.

   D She wanted workers' children to have a better life than their parents had had.

TEACH

CHECK YOUR UNDERSTANDING

Have students answer the questions independently.

Answers:

1. C
2. F
3. B

If they answer any questions incorrectly, have them reread the text to confirm their understanding. Then they may proceed to ANALYZE THE TEXT on p. 486.

 ENGLISH LEARNER SUPPORT

Oral Assessment Use the following questions to assess students' comprehension and speaking skills:

1. Look at the details in paragraph 10. What is the key idea of this paragraph? *(Poor decisions made the fire much worse.)*

2. Read what Mary Bucelli says in paragraph 15. What is the purpose of this quote? *(It helps explain the factory workers' actions during the fire.)*

3. Which sentence explains why Frances Perkins helped workers? *(Paragraph 18 shows that she was deeply affected by the tragic fire at the factory.)*

SUBSTANTIAL/MODERATE

APPLY

ANALYZE THE TEXT
Possible answers:

1. **DOK 3:** *The Triangle factory was unsafe and its workers were not trusted. Evidence includes: the absence of a sprinkler system, the fire escape was in poor shape, the doors were locked and workers were forced to leave through a "choke point" in order to prevent suspected theft.*

2. **DOK 4:** *The author's choice of details—the careless toss of a cigarette, the flammable scraps of cotton on the floor, the attempt to stop the fire with buckets of water—suggests anger that such conditions existed. That feeling is intensified by the inclusion of a historian's point that loss of life could have been prevented.*

3. **DOK 2:** *Details such as nets that failed and weak fire hoses imply that equipment was not up to the challenges of fighting fires in the booming cities.*

4. **DOK 3:** *Each person's story is moving, and the fact that they are not named makes them symbolic of all victims. The information emphasizes the human and tragic aspects.*

5. **DOK 4:** *Perkins led a comfortable life before the fire, but she'd been lobbying for social reforms. Because the fire so deeply affected her, it's not surprising that she decided to fully advocate for reforms in working conditions.*

RESEARCH

Remind students to double check their sources, using newspapers and encyclopedias, both online and off, to confirm information about Perkins's life.

Extend Help students elect a facilitator for the group discussion. Ensure that all students participate equally, that they listen to each other's comments and questions, and that they make a list of at least three additional questions about Perkins's life.

 RESPOND

ANALYZE THE TEXT
Support your responses with evidence from the text. 📓 **NOTEBOOK**

1. **Cite Evidence** What does the information in paragraph 13 indicate about working conditions in the factory? Cite details from the text that support your answer.

2. **Analyze** Reread paragraphs 8–10. What are the author's tone and point of view as he describes the start of the fire and the first attempts to extinguish it? How can you tell?

3. **Infer** What can you infer from text details about the quality of firefighting equipment at this time in history?

4. **Critique** In paragraph 7, the author describes several people who jumped to their death. What does this information add to your understanding of the most important key idea about the event?

5. **Notice & Note** Review the details about Frances Perkins's life before and after the fire. How did the fire change Perkins's life? Did this change surprise you? Why or why not?

RESEARCH TIP
The best research sources are accurate, credible, and balanced. What should you do, though, if two quality sources provide different information about the same topic, such as different birthdates for a historical figure? It's always helpful to compare multiple sources with one another—and then try to find a few additional quality sources to use for comparison as well. If most of the sources agree, and they're all reliable, then you can feel more confident about the information you present.

RESEARCH

Find out more about Frances Perkins. Research the two questions below and one more that you generate on your own. Note what you learn in the chart.

RESEARCH QUESTIONS	DETAILS ABOUT PERKINS'S LIFE
What was Perkins's childhood like?	*Perkins was raised in a middle-class family in which education was stressed. She became interested in history and social causes at an early age.*
Why was Perkins called "the woman behind the New Deal"?	*Perkins was the first woman ever to serve in a U.S. president's cabinet, serving under Franklin D. Roosevelt. As such, she was one of the leaders of the New Deal, a series of laws and reforms passed during the Great Depression to help improve people's lives.*

Extend With a small group, share your questions and discuss what you learned about Perkins's life. After your discussion, do you have more questions about Perkins's life? With your group, list these and discuss how you could research them.

 LEARNING MINDSET

Problem Solving Tell students that many problems have a number of good solutions, which is why it's a great thing that different people view problems in different ways. Every student will view problems differently and every problem needs a range of viewpoints to be solved well. Having a strategy is important: if your strategy doesn't work on one problem, it may be what works when the next problem comes around. Thinking critically and solving problems is a big part of learning and growing, so don't be afraid of trying new solutions, methods, and strategies.

CREATE AND DISCUSS

Write an Ode Use what has inspired you from reading this piece of history writing to create an ode. (An ode is a short, serious poem in which a speaker expresses personal thoughts and feelings, often as a tribute to a person or event.) Perhaps your ode could honor the factory workers who died or Frances Perkins and her work as a reformer.

- ❏ Choose the specific topic for your ode and the message you will convey.
- ❏ Draft your ode, using any poetic structure you like. Choose details and language that will help readers share your feelings about the topic.
- ❏ Review your draft. Make revisions that will show the speaker's feelings and the overall message of the ode more clearly.

Discuss the Primary Sources With a partner, review what each quotation in the text adds to your understanding of the event.

- ❏ Use clues within the primary source itself to help you discuss its main idea, or message. For example, what is the speaker's point of view of the event? What is the speaker's tone, and why does the tone matter?
- ❏ To build on your partner's ideas, ask clarifying questions. For example, what do you think Rose Schneiderman means to convey by her use of the word *traitor* (paragraph 19)?

RESPOND TO THE ESSENTIAL QUESTION

 What inspires you to make a difference?

Gather Information Review your annotations and notes on "Frances Perkins and the Triangle Factory Fire." Then, add relevant details to your Response Log. As you determine which information to include, think about:

- people's responses to tragic events
- ways to support people affected by a tragic event
- steps that may help prevent a similar event from happening again

At the end of the unit, you can use your notes to help you write a research report.

RESPOND

Go to **Writing as a Process** in the **Writing Studio** for help.

Go to **Participating in Collaborative Discussions** in the **Speaking and Listening Studio** to learn more.

ACADEMIC VOCABULARY

As you write and discuss what you learned from the piece of history writing, be sure to use the Academic Vocabulary words. Check off each of the words that you use.

- ❏ contrast
- ❏ despite
- ❏ error
- ❏ inadequate
- ❏ interact

Frances Perkins and the Triangle Factory Fire 487

APPLY

CREATE AND DISCUSS

Write an Ode Inform students that the range of possible poetic forms for odes is quite wide and that they should look up some forms online to decide which works best for their ode. Encourage students to choose the form that best suits their chosen topic.

 For **writing support** for students at varying proficiency levels, see the **Text X-Ray** on p. 476D.

Discuss Primary Sources Encourage students to take turns, listen carefully, and cooperate with one another on this task. Ask students to get a strong sense of the primary source by reading and rereading it before offering an idea of what its message is.

RESPOND TO THE ESSENTIAL QUESTION

Allow time for students to add details from "Frances Perkins and the Triangle Factory Fire" to their Unit 6 Response Logs.

ENGLISH LEARNER SUPPORT

Summarize Events Tell students to clarify the events in the piece by creating time line graphic organizers of the events using the headings *First, Next, Then,* and *Later.* Have them gather details from the text, words from the images they labeled earlier, cognates, and home language descriptions to place under each head: all according to when the events occurred. **SUBSTANTIAL**

Have students use cause and effect graphic organizers to summarize the events in David Brooks's piece on the Triangle Shirtwaist Factory Fire. **MODERATE**

APPLY

CRITICAL VOCABULARY

Answers:

1. *indifferent:* When people feel indifferent about something, they think it is not worth caring about; in other words, it is unimportant.

2. *fatal:* A fatal fire or other tragic event is disastrous, resulting in death and destruction.

3. *distinguish:* Being able to distinguish one thing from another means being able to see what is distinct, or unique, among them so you can tell them apart.

4. *lobby:* When people call or email politicians, they are lobbying, or trying to influence politicians to support the cause they represent.

VOCABULARY STRATEGY:
Latin Roots

Answers:

1. *indistinguishable* means that people cannot tell one thing from another, usually because those things are very similar.

2. *extinguish* refers to an act that puts an end to something. In the example, critics try to put an end to some people's dream.

3. *undistinguished* means something that cannot be separated from the other things into a different category. It is ordinary or unnoticed.

4. *extinguisher* refers to a device that puts out fires, often by smothering the fire and separating the elements that a fire needs to have all together to burn.

488   Unit 6

 RESPOND

WORD BANK
lobby
fatal
distinguish
indifferent

CRITICAL VOCABULARY

Practice and Apply Identify the Critical Vocabulary word that is most closely related to the boldfaced word in each question. Be prepared to explain your choices.

1. Which vocabulary word goes with **unimportant**?
   _____

2. Which vocabulary word goes with **disastrous**? _____

3. Which vocabulary word goes with **distinct**? _____

4. Which vocabulary word goes with **influence**? _____

VOCABULARY STRATEGY: Latin Roots

A **root** is a word part that came into English from an older language. Roots from Latin appear in many English words. Note this comment by Mary Bucelli in "Frances Perkins and the Triangle Factory Fire":

> You see a multitude of things, but you can't distinguish anything. (paragraph 15)

The word *distinguish* contains a root, *sting*, from the Latin word *distinguere*, which means "to separate." You can see the root meaning in the word *distinguish*; it literally means separating what you perceive, or being able to tell things apart. Recognizing the root *sting* can help you figure out the meanings of other words that include this root.

 Go to the **Vocabulary Studio** for more on Latin roots.

Practice and Apply In each sentence, identify the word with the Latin root *sting* or its variation *ting*. Write what each word means. Use a print or digital dictionary to check your ideas.

1. There are many kinds of maple trees, but most people think that one maple tree is indistinguishable from another.
   _____

2. Despite the criticism they got, they would not let anyone extinguish their dream.
   _____

3. Although many of her players were undistinguished, the coach led them to win games by inspiring them to work hard as a team.
   _____

4. A fire extinguisher works by removing one or more of the three elements of every fire: oxygen, heat, and fuel.
   _____

488   Unit 6

LANGUAGE CONVENTIONS:
Pronoun-Antecedent Agreement

To keep your writing clear, make sure that the pronouns that you use agree with their antecedents in number (singular or plural), gender (male, female, or neuter), and person (first, second, or third).

	SINGULAR PRONOUNS	PLURAL PRONOUNS
First person	I / me / my, mine	we / us / our, ours
Second person	you / you / your, yours	you / you / your, yours
Third person	he, she, it / him, her, it / his, her, hers, its	they / them / their, theirs

Look at these examples from "Frances Perkins and the Triangle Factory Fire" and examine the pronouns and their antecedents.

- Notice how the pronouns *his* and *he* agree with their antecedent, *Bernstein,* in number (singular), gender (male), and person (third):

    When Bernstein finally did take his eyes off the wall of fire, he was astonished by what he saw. (paragraph 11)

- Notice how the pronoun *its* agrees with its antecedent, *fire department,* in number (singular), gender (neutral), and person (third):

    The fire department arrived quickly but its ladders could not reach the eighth floor. (paragraph 17)

- Notice how the pronoun *she* agrees with its antecedent, *Perkins,* in number (singular), gender (female), and person (third):

    Perkins hardened. She threw herself into the rough and tumble of politics. She was willing. . . . (paragraph 21)

Practice and Apply Write 4 or 5 sentences that summarize this piece of history writing. Try to use different pronouns. As you do, check to make sure that the pronouns agree with their antecedents. Use the examples and chart above as guides.

RESPOND

! Go to **Pronoun-Antecedent Agreement** in the **Grammar Studio** to learn more.

APPLY

LANGUAGE CONVENTIONS:
Pronoun-Antecedent Agreement

Review the rules of pronoun-antecedent agreement with students. Clarify the concept of "person" by explaining that it is the distinction between the speaker (first person), the person spoken to (second person), and other people (third person). Have students look at the following sentences and determine whether the pronoun agrees with the antecedent.

- *The man next door was pretty unhappy before she met Sylvia.* (She *is incorrect, because its antecedent is* man *and should be* he.)
- *I took the cat to the vet's office, but they said there was nothing wrong with him.* (They *refers correctly to the doctors at the vet's office; because the antecedent* cat *can be male,* him *is also correct.*)
- *"Hassan, would you pick up a book for me."* (You *is correct for the antecedent* Hassan, *and* me *is correct for the speaker.*)

Practice and Apply Have partners review each other's sentences to check for correct prounoun-antecedent agreement. (**Possible Answer:** *The Triangle Factory Fire was a* tragedy, *but* it *could have been prevented. Unsafe working conditions were a main cause of the Triangle Factory Fire.* Frances Perkins *was a witness to the* fire, *and* she *was deeply affected by* it. *After the fire,* Perkins *devoted* her *life to improving working conditions and the lives of the poor.*)

 ENGLISH LEARNER SUPPORT

Reinforce Pronoun Agreement Remind students that pronoun subjects must agree in number with the subjects they replace.

- Read aloud and display sentence frames for students to complete orally. Have them use the correct pronouns to replace subjects. Here are two examples to help students practice using the correct pronouns: Cora (He/She/It/They) is in eighth grade. (**She** is in eighth grade.) The girls (He/She/It/They) are going to the beach. (**They** are going to the beach.) **SUBSTANTIAL**

- Have students read sentence frames such as the one above to themselves. Have them use the correct pronouns. **MODERATE**

- Have students write paragraphs about a recent trip or family experience in which they correctly demonstrate pronoun usage. Remind them to use both singular and plural subject pronouns in their paragraphs. **LIGHT**

 ENGLISH LEARNER SUPPORT

Practice Consonant Clusters Have students practice the *sh* and *th* sounds in the following sentences while echo reading with you. Before beginning, display and pronounce a few *sh* and *th* words. Have students practice with you: *she, should show, shirtwaist, that, they, thought*.

Rose Schneiderman protested against the Triangle Shirtwaist Factory three years before the fire. She went on strike with twenty thousand other shirtwaist workers. **MODERATE**

PLAN

MENTOR TEXT

from THE STORY OF THE TRIANGLE FACTORY FIRE

History Writing by Zachary Kent

> This excerpt serves as a **mentor text**, a model for students to follow when they come to the Unit 6 Writing Task: Writing a Research Report.

GENRE ELEMENTS
HISTORY WRITING

Remind students that the purpose of **history writing**, a form of **informational text**, is to present accurate information about the past. Explain to students that the organization of history writing is almost always strictly chronological, but also uses other structures, such as problem and solution and key idea and details. Although the history writer uses an objective point of view, the language of the text can be emotional.

LEARNING OBJECTIVES

- Paraphrase text.
- Analyze chronological text structure.
- Examine subject-verb agreement with prepositional phrases.
- Conduct research about the Triangle Factory fire.
- Write a short historical fiction narrative.
- Understand connotations and denotations.
- Create a graphic novel page.
- Compare author's message and purpose.
- **Language** Speak and write using chronological transition words.

TEXT COMPLEXITY

Quantitative Measures	The Story of the Triangle Factory Fire	Lexile: 1110L
Qualitative Measures	**Ideas Presented** Offers basic information; mostly explicit; clear purpose	
	Structure Used Primarily explicit; chronological	
	Language Used Mostly explicit; some Tier II words	
	Knowledge Required Experiences may be less familiar	

490A Unit 6

PLAN

Online

RESOURCES

- Unit 6 Response Log
- 🔊 Selection Audio
- 📖 Reading Studio: Notice & Note
- Level Up Tutorial: Chronological Order
- Writing Studio: Writing Narratives
- Speaking and Listening Studio: Giving a Presentation
- Vocabulary Studio: Connotations and Denotations
- Grammar Studio: Module 8: Lesson 2: Prepositional Phrase Interrupters
- *The Story of the Triangle Factory Fire* Selection Test

SUMMARIES

English

This excerpt from *The Story of the Triangle Factory Fire* deals with the aftermath of the tragedy: the fault-finding in the days after the fire, the ensuing trial against the factory owners, and in the years that followed, the movement to end unsafe working conditions through legislation. The excerpt includes many compelling quotations from people who were present at the fire and the trial. The author's point is that this tragedy led to awareness and change.

Spanish

Este pasaje de *La historia del incendio de la fábrica Triangle* trata de las repercusiones de la tragedia: el descubrimiento de las fallas en los días que siguieron al incendio, el consiguiente juicio contra los dueños de la fábrica y, en los años siguientes, el movimiento para acabar con las peligrosas condiciones de trabajo a través de la ley. El pasaje incluye muchas citas persuasivas de quienes estuvieron presentes en el incendio y el juicio. El punto del autor es que esta tragedia llevó a la conciencia y al cambio.

SMALL-GROUP OPTIONS

Have students work in small groups to read and discuss the selection.

Pinwheel Discussion

- After students have read the excerpt from *The Story of the Triangle Factory Fire*, ask them to create pinwheel formations of six per group.
- For the first rotation, ask students to discuss what happened days after the fire.
- For the second rotation, ask students what happened at the trial.
- For the third rotation, ask students to discuss what happened in the years after the trial.

Think-Pair-Share

- After students have read the excerpt from *The Story of the Triangle Factory Fire*, pose this question: *Could a fire like that start in a factory today?*
- Have students think about the question individually and jot down ideas.
- Then, have pairs discuss their ideas about the question.
- Finally, ask pairs to share their responses with the class.

The Story of the Triangle Factory Fire **490B**

PLAN

Text X-Ray: English Learner Support
for "The Story of the Triangle Factory Fire"

Use the Text X-Ray and the supports and scaffolds in the Teacher's Edition to help guide students at different proficiency levels through the selection.

INTRODUCE THE SELECTION
DISCUSS RESPONSIBILITY AND CHANGE

In this lesson, students will be asked to discuss the events that followed the Triangle Factory Fire of 1911. Several agencies worked together to determine who was to blame for the tragedy. As students discuss the investigations and the trial, these words will be useful:

- **responsible**: The person or people who are *responsible* for something happening, have to *make sure* that something happens or takes place.
- **prevent**: When you *prevent* something, that something will *not happen*.

Have students complete sentence frames that use these words.

Barry is _____ for getting breakfast to the students.

Nobody is _____ for the mess.

She can _____ the dog from playing on the grass.

CULTURAL REFERENCES

The following words and phrases may be unfamiliar to students:

- *fix the fault* (paragraph 1): decide who is responsible
- *invite disaster* (paragraph 1): be very dangerous
- *manslaughter* (paragraph 2): the crime of killing someone without planning to do so
- *weighing the evidence* (paragraph 2): considering all the information
- *firetraps* (paragraph 3): places where people would be trapped during a fire

LISTENING

Listen for Opinions

Tell students that quotations are a good places to look for opinions. Explain that historical writing frequently presents different opinions about the same historical event.

Have students listen as you read aloud paragraph 2. Use the following supports with students at varying proficiency levels:

- Tell students that you will ask questions about what you just read aloud. Model that they should give a thumbs up for yes and a thumbs down for no. Ask: *Did everyone agree with the jury's decision?* (no) *Did New York take action?* (yes) **SUBSTANTIAL**
- Have students identify the different opinions expressed in the paragraph about the owners' legal responsibility for the fire. **MODERATE**
- Have students explain their feelings about the verdict. Then ask: *After hearing how citizens reacted during the trial, do you think they'll be happy with the jury's verdict?* **LIGHT**

490C Unit 6

PLAN

SPEAKING

Discuss Quotations

Have students discuss how primary source material can directly connect the reader to a time and place in the past. Explain that both quotes and photographs are primary sources.

Reread paragraphs 5 and 6. Use the following supports with students at varying proficiency levels:

- Read aloud to students, and have them repeat: *A primary source is something that someone actually said in the past, a quotation. A primary source is a picture someone took in the past, a photograph.* **SUBSTANTIAL**
- Read aloud to students the Perkins quotation in paragraph 6. Explain that to "die in vain" means to "die for no reason," or *morir en vano* in Spanish. Then ask students to discuss if the phrase "die in vain" is stronger than "die for no reason." **MODERATE**
- Read aloud the Perkins quotation in paragraph 5. Ask pairs of students to discuss the images, "frozen horror," and "hands on our throats," that Perkins creates in the quotation. **LIGHT**

READING

Understand Problems and Solutions

Draw students' attention to the problem described in paragraph 1, dangerous conditions for workers, and the solution described in paragraphs 3 and 4, labor laws that create safe conditions for workers.

Reread paragraphs 1 and 3–4 and explain that recognizing problems and solutions is an important part of understanding the text. Use the following supports with students at varying proficiency levels:

- Write the words *problem* and *solution* on the board. Then write: *Rafael is very hungry. Rafael is going to eat lunch.* Ask: *What is the problem?* (Rafael is hungry.) *What is the solution?* (to eat lunch) **SUBSTANTIAL**
- Write the words *fire* and *disaster* on the board. Then ask student pairs to name two problems connected with these words in paragraph 1. **MODERATE**
- Pair students and ask them to explain which problems named in paragraph 1 were addressed by which solutions in paragraphs 3–4. **LIGHT**

WRITING

Write a Fictional Historical Narrative

Work with students to read the writing assignment on p. 497.

Use the following supports with students at varying proficiency levels:

- As a group, decide on a character to write about. Help students write a one- or two-word description of the character and a short phrase about what they did. (*Fire Chief Crocker tries to protect people from fires.*) **SUBSTANTIAL**
- Provide sentence frames such as the following that students can use to craft their narratives: *The main character is _____. He/She is connected to the Triangle Factory fire because _____. My character escapes because _____.* **MODERATE**
- Remind students to use chronological signal words to link their details and events. Have pairs look for additional places in their essays where they can use chronological signal words. **LIGHT**

TEACH

 Connect to the ESSENTIAL QUESTION

The Triangle Factory fire inspired people like Frances Perkins to make a difference in the lives of others by ending life-threatening working conditions in American factories.

COMPARE AUTHORS' PURPOSES AND MESSAGES

Point out to students that their comparison of the two texts will include several different aspects: what the authors are writing about and how they present their information. Tell students that although both texts are about the same historical event, they focus on different aspects of the fire, its causes, and the aftermath.

MENTOR TEXT

At the end of the unit, students will be asked to write a research report. This excerpt from *The Story of the Triangle Factory Fire* as well as "Frances Perkins and the Triangle Factory Fire" provide models of how authors present historical information they have gathered through research.

COLLABORATE & COMPARE

HISTORY WRITING
from
THE STORY OF THE TRIANGLE FACTORY FIRE
by **Zachary Kent**
pages 493–495

COMPARE AUTHORS' PURPOSES AND MESSAGES

Now that you've read "Frances Perkins and the Triangle Factory Fire," read an excerpt from *The Story of the Triangle Factory Fire*. As you read, think about the similarities and differences in how each author presents information about the same event. After you are finished, you will collaborate with a small group on a final project that involves an analysis of both texts.

 ESSENTIAL QUESTION:

What inspires you to make a difference?

HISTORY WRITING
FRANCES PERKINS AND THE TRIANGLE FACTORY FIRE
by **David Brooks**
pages 479–485

490 Unit 6

from The Story of the Triangle Factory Fire

QUICK START

What can a person do after learning of a tragic event such as a fire, flood, or tornado? Brainstorm ideas with a partner or small group.

PARAPHRASE

When you **paraphrase,** you restate information that you read or hear using your own words. Here is one way you might paraphrase a sentence from *The Story of the Triangle Factory Fire*.

ORIGINAL TEXT	PARAPHRASE
They examined workers' filthy living conditions and witnessed the dangers of crippling machinery and long work hours in dusty, dirty firetraps. (paragraph 3)	They inspected where the workers lived and worked. They found unhealthy homes and dangerous working conditions.

Paraphrasing key ideas and important details can help you understand and remember what you read. As you read the selection, write short paraphrases next to important information.

ANALYZE TEXT STRUCTURE

Effective history writing has a **text structure**—a particular way of organizing ideas and information to support multiple topics and categories and subcategories in a text.

- **Chronological order,** or time order, is the arrangement of events in the sequence in which they occur—what happens first, second, and so on. When reading history writing, pay attention to dates, times, and signal words such as *next, then, before, after, later,* and *finally.*

Days after the fire, city officials searched the rubble for clues. → Then the owners were charged with manslaughter. → After a three-week trial, a jury found the owners not guilty.

- **Problem-solution** refers to a structure in which a problem is stated and then solutions are proposed and analyzed. Words that may signal a problem include *challenge* and *issue*. Words that may signal a solution include *propose, answer,* and *conclude.*

As you read the selection, look for words and phrases that signal how the information is arranged to help you understand the text.

GENRE ELEMENTS: INFORMATIONAL TEXT

- a blend of narrative and informational writing that deals with people and events from the past
- presents the interactions between people and events to maintain interest
- uses an organizational pattern to present key ideas and supporting details
- may use language that suggests the author's perspective

TEACH

CRITICAL VOCABULARY

Remind students to look for context clues that suggest the meaning of each word.

Answers:

1. ugly; disgusting
2. passageway; hallway
3. pass; vote in
4. protestor; activist

■ **English Learner Support**

Use Cognates Explain to students that two of the Critical Vocabulary words have Spanish cognates: *corridor/corredor, reformer/reformador.* **ALL LEVELS**

LANGUAGE CONVENTIONS

Remind students that agreement between subjects and verbs in English is usually simple.

- Most verbs show the difference between singular and plural only in the third person of the present tense.
- In the present tense, the third-person singular form ends in –s.
- A verb agrees only with its subject. When words come between a subject and a verb, ignore them when considering proper agreement.

ANNOTATION MODEL

Remind students to look for signal words that indicate text structure and to choose important ideas or points to paraphrase. Point out that students may choose to circle structural elements and underline text they wish to paraphrase or create their own annotation methods, like color-coding.

 GET READY

CRITICAL VOCABULARY

hideous   corridor   enact   reformer

To preview the Critical Vocabulary words, replace each boldfaced word with a different word or words that have the same meaning.

1. The building once was beautiful, but now it was falling apart and looked (**hideous**) _____.
2. The (**corridor**) _____ was crowded with busy people.
3. After a tragic event, people often demand that politicians (**enact**) _____ laws to prevent a similar event from happening.
4. One (**reformer**) _____ can make a positive difference in the lives of many people.

LANGUAGE CONVENTIONS

Subject–Verb Agreement and Prepositional Phrases In sentences, verbs must agree (or match) their subjects in number. If subjects and verbs don't agree, readers may be confused. Look at this sentence:

The workers in the factory are weaving.

Are weaving (the verb) agrees with *workers* (the subject). Notice the prepositional phrase *in the factory* does not change the subject-verb agreement. As you read the excerpt from *The Story of the Triangle Factory Fire,* notice subject–verb agreement.

ANNOTATION MODEL **NOTICE & NOTE**

As you read, note the text structure. You can also mark up passages and paraphrase them. In the model, you can see one reader's notes about this text from *The Story of the Triangle Factory Fire.*

> 3 . . . In October 1911 the city established a Bureau of Fire Prevention to inspect safety standards in other buildings. Five months earlier the New York State legislature created a special Factory Investigating Commission. Through the next four years Commission investigators crawled and pried through the rooms and cellars of factories and tenement houses all across the state.

These phrases tell me that the special commission was created before the Bureau of Fire Prevention was established.

My paraphrase: "Investigators spent four years inspecting factories and run-down apartment buildings."

492   Unit 6

BACKGROUND

Zachary Kent *(b. 1951) is the author of more than fifty books for young readers. He writes primarily about history. A historical event such as the Triangle Factory Fire can be so dramatic and so haunting that it compels generations that follow to dissect its details and trace its impact. In Kent's account, he recounts what happens and examines the fire's long-term effects.*

from THE STORY OF THE TRIANGLE FACTORY FIRE

History Writing by Zachary Kent

PREPARE TO COMPARE

As you read, pay attention to the way in which the author presents information about this deadly fire, especially how he structures or organizes facts and other details. Consider what you learn about the aftermath of the fire and why the author includes this information.

Notice & Note

Use the side margins to notice and note signposts in the text.

1   In the days following the fire, city officials sifted through the charred rubble at the Asch Building and tried to fix the fault for the tragedy. Fire Chief Croker angrily stated, "There wasn't a fire escape anywhere fronting on the street by which these unfortunate girls could escape." Doors that opened inward instead of outward, overcrowding in work areas, and blocked exits also were to blame. Fire Marshal William Beers stunned New Yorkers by soon declaring, "I can show you 150 loft buildings far worse than this one." Lillian D. Wald of the Joint Board of Sanitary Control also reported on the general situation. "The conditions as they now exist are **hideous**. . . . Our investigators have shown that there are hundreds of buildings which invite disaster just as much as did the Asch structure."

PARAPHRASE

Annotate: Mark text details in paragraph 1 that reveal the building's condition when the fire occurred.

Interpret: In your own words, describe the condition of the building when the fire took place.

hideous
(hĭd′ē-əs) *adj.* When something is *hideous*, it is repulsive or revolting.

TEACH

QUOTED WORDS

Remind students that this signpost is used to indicate the opinions or conclusions of someone who is an expert on the subject or an eyewitness. (**Answer:** *The quotations provide perspectives from three different parties: angry citizens, a member of the jury, and a newspaper. The author presents all three to give a full account of the public's reaction.*)

 For **listening support** for students at varying proficiency levels, see the **Text X-Ray** on page 490C.

 PARAPHRASE

Remind students that paraphrasing will help them understand, remember, and summarize a text. (**Answer:** *Quotation choices will vary, as will reasons for choices. Possible paraphrases: We rushed over when we heard about the fires. What we saw horrified us. OR We will always remember the deaths of the workers and they will inspire us to make changes*)

ANALYZE TEXT STRUCTURE

Remind students that authors use words that signal time so readers can follow the sequence of events. (**Answer:** *The phrase "by 1914" indicates that legislators took swift action after the fire; the word soon indicates that other states followed New York's example quickly after.*)

CRITICAL VOCABULARY

corridor: The women were not in the courtroom itself; they were right outside the door in the corridors.

ASK STUDENTS why the women were in the corridors. (*There probably wasn't enough room for them in the courtroom; the judge might have been afraid that they would disrupt the trial.*)

enact: By enacting new laws, state governments made bad working conditions illegal.

ASK STUDENTS how new state laws get enacted. (*They have to be presented to the state legislature and the members vote on them.*)

494   Unit 6

NOTICE & NOTE

corridor
(kôr´ĭ-dər) *n.* A *corridor* is a narrow hallway or passageway.

QUOTED WORDS
Notice & Note: In paragraph 2, mark the three speakers whom the author quotes.

Infer: Why do you think the author includes three very different quotations in this paragraph?

ANALYZE TEXT STRUCTURE
Annotate: In paragraph 4, mark words and phrases that signal chronology, or time order.

Analyze: Remember that the fire happened in 1911. What does this later chronology of events tell the reader about the effects of the fire?

enact
(ĕn-ăkt´) *v.* If you *enact* something, you make it into a law.

PARAPHRASE
Annotate: Reread paragraphs 5–6. Mark the quotation by Frances Perkins that you connect with more.

Interpret: In your own words, paraphrase that quotation. Why did you choose it?

494   Unit 6

---

2   Accused of ignoring their employees' safety, Triangle owners Blanck and Harris were charged with manslaughter. During the three week trial angry citizens packed the courtroom. Outside, in the **corridors,** women screamed, "Murderers! Murderers! Make them suffer for killing our children!" Lawyers argued that Blanck and Harris kept all of the Triangle doors locked during the workday, therefore causing many of the deaths. Weighing the evidence, however, the jury returned a verdict of not guilty. "I cannot see that anyone was responsible for the disaster," explained juror H. Houston Hierst. "It seems to me to have been an act of the Almighty."[1] The New York *Call* viewed the matter differently. "Capital can commit no crime," it angrily declared, "when it is in pursuit of profits."

3   Furious New Yorkers refused to let the issue rest. In October 1911 the city established a Bureau of Fire Prevention to inspect safety standards in other buildings. Five months earlier the New York State legislature created a special Factory Investigating Commission. Through the next four years Commission investigators crawled and pried through the rooms and cellars of factories and tenement houses[2] all across the state. They examined workers' filthy living conditions and witnessed the dangers of crippling machinery and long work hours in dusty, dirty firetraps.

4   As a result of the Commission's shocking findings, New York State quickly passed thirty-three new labor laws by 1914. These laws formed the foundation of New York State's Industrial Code, the finest in the nation. Soon other states followed New York's example and **enacted** protective labor laws.

5   One Factory Commission investigator had witnessed the fateful Triangle fire. Frances Perkins said, "We heard the fire engines and rushed . . . to see what was going on. . . . We got there just as they started to jump. I shall never forget the frozen horror which came over us as we stood with our hands on our throats watching that horrible sight, knowing that there was no help."

---

[1] **an act of the Almighty:** a term that refers to events or actions that are beyond the control of human beings (and, therefore, that happen through the will of God).
[2] **tenement houses:** very run-down city apartments where the poor and immigrants often live.

6   In 1933 President Franklin Roosevelt named Frances Perkins secretary of labor. She and other social **reformers** dedicated their lives to insuring worker safety throughout the country. "They did not die in vain and we will never forget them," vowed Perkins. From the ashes of the tragic Triangle factory fire came help for millions of United States laborers today.

NOTICE & NOTE

reformer
(rĭ-fôrm´) *n.* A *reformer* seeks to improve or correct practices or behaviors that cause harm.

ANALYZE TEXT STRUCTURE

Annotate: In paragraph 6, mark words and phrases that help you determine the chronology, or time order, of this paragraph.

Critique: Do you agree that the workers would not be forgotten, even today? Why or why not?

CHECK YOUR UNDERSTANDING

Answer these questions before moving on to the **Analyze the Text** section on the following page.

1. According to the author, what statement by Fire Marshal William Beers stunned New Yorkers?

   A The Triangle Factory building was going to be rebuilt.
   B Other factory buildings were in even worse condition.
   C The Triangle Factory owners were being charged with crimes.
   D There was no more money left to fight other fires.

2. In paragraph 2, how does the juror's viewpoint compare to that of angry citizens?

   F Only the citizens felt that the fire could have been prevented.
   G Jurors believed that the fire was the fault of the workers.
   H Only the jurors believed that the fire was not the owners' fault.
   J Jurors and citizens agreed that the fire was no one's fault.

3. Which conclusion is best supported by the information in this piece of history writing?

   A The fire resulted in New York City's becoming the safest city in the United States.
   B After the fire, American industry saw a decline in the number of women in the workplace.
   C Even after the fire, the problem of unsafe working conditions was never addressed.
   D The fire resulted in new laws being passed to improve the safety of workers.

TEACH

ANALYZE TEXT STRUCTURE

Remind students that chronological order is the most common way of structuring history writing, and it is usually combined with other structures. (**Answer:** *Yes—Students of history are still reading about this tragic event. No—Working conditions are still bad in many places, and we don't change them.*)

CHECK YOUR UNDERSTANDING

Have students answer the questions independently.

Answers:

1. B
2. H
3. D

If they answer any questions incorrectly, have them reread the text to confirm their understanding. Then they may proceed to ANALYZE THE TEXT on p. 496.

ENGLISH LEARNER SUPPORT

Oral Assessment Use the following questions to asses students' comprehension and speaking skills:

1. What did Fire Marshal William Beers say that surprised New Yorkers? *(Other factories were in even worse condition.)*
2. How is what the people on the jury thought different from what the people of New York thought? *(Only the jurors believed the owners were not guilty.)*
3. What does the selection say happened because of the fire? *(New laws were passed to improve the safety of workers.)* **SUBSTANTIAL/MODERATE**

CRITICAL VOCABULARY

reformer: Social reformers are people who work hard to pass laws that will make life better for all.

ASK STUDENTS what causes they would support if they became reformers. *(Answers will vary but might include environmental or social justice issues.)*

APPLY

ANALYZE THE TEXT

Possible answers:

1. **DOK 3:** *In paragraph 1, the author details the unsafe conditions in the factory and provides two quotations stating that other factories at the time were just as unsafe or worse and that similar tragedies could occur.*

2. **DOK 2:** *In the first four years after the fire, which took place in March 1911, officials investigated other factories and tenements, which led to the passage of new labor laws in 1914 and subsequent worker safety measures in New York and in other states.*

3. **DOK 3:** *The author uses chronological organization, starting with the fire and ending in the present. Chronological order helps readers understand that the tragic fire led to significant positive results, including new labor laws and improvements in worker safety.*

4. **DOK 4:** *The primary source quotations provide readers with multiple perspectives on the trial and present firsthand evidence that supports the idea that new laws were enacted as a result of the fire.*

5. **DOK 4:** *The author uses Perkins's words to bring the text to a powerful close and to support his claim that the fire led to many positive changes.*

RESEARCH

Have students read the Research Tip. Remind them to use reliable websites from reputable governmental and academic institutions.

Connect Answers will vary but should address factory working conditions before the Triangle fire and the legislation, improved conditions, and reformers that followed.

RESPOND

ANALYZE THE TEXT

Support your responses with evidence from the text. 📓 NOTEBOOK

1. **Cite Evidence** What was true of factories in New York City before the Triangle Factory Fire? Cite details from the text that support your answer.

2. **Summarize** In two or three sentences, summarize the changes that occurred in the aftermath of the tragedy. Be sure to mention the time period over which the changes happened.

3. **Critique** What is the author's main method of organization in this piece of history writing? Why is it useful for the author's purpose?

4. **Evaluate** Review the primary source quotations in the text. How well do they help readers better understand the fire's aftermath?

5. **Notice & Note** Review the statement by Frances Perkins in the final paragraph. Why did the author include Perkins's comment? What does it add to this account of the Triangle Factory Fire?

RESEARCH

RESEARCH TIP
For many historical topics, consider looking for both primary and secondary sources. Primary sources provide personal, subjective views of the event because they are created by someone who took part or witnessed it. Primary sources include diaries, autobiographies, and photographs. Secondary sources provide an overview of the event and factual details.

Think of something or someone you want to learn more about in connection with the Triangle Factory Fire. For example, do you want to learn more about the working conditions before the fire? More about the laws that were enacted after the fire? More about the historical figures named in the article? Choose a topic that interests you and is related to the fire. Research the topic and record what you learn in the chart. Also use the chart to keep track of the sources you used.

TRIANGLE FACTORY FIRE What or Who: _____	
Explanation/description	**Primary sources**
Answers will vary but should include important facts and other information that gives readers a basic understanding of the topic	*https://trianglefire.ilr.cornell.edu https://www.osha.gov/oas/trianglefactoryfire.html*
Significance	**Secondary sources**
Answers will vary but should be directly related to the fact and other information provided above	*: https://www.smithsonianmag.com/history/uncovering-the-history-of-the-triangle-shirtwaist-fire-124701842/ http://www.pbs.org/wgbh/americanexperience/films/triangle/*

Connect In the final paragraph, Frances Perkins is quoted as saying, "They did not die in vain. . . ." With a small group, discuss how what you learned relates to Perkins's statement.

WHEN STUDENTS STRUGGLE . . .

Use Graphic Organizers If students are having difficulty discerning the chronology of events and the author's purpose in writing this text, distribute a three-column, three-row graphic organizer. The column headings should read: What Happened, Why It Happened, and Quotations. The row names should read: Days After, Months After, and Years After. Work with students to complete the graphic organizer.

 For additional support, go to the **Reading Studio** and assign the following Level Up Tutorial: Chronologial Order.

CREATE AND ADAPT

Write Historical Fiction Create a fictional narrative based on information from the selection and your own research. Remember: historical fiction includes real places, people, and events, but writers use their imagination to create scenes, dialogue, and characters.

- ❏ Choose a situation related to the fire. Establish a point of view: a first-person narrator or third-person narrator. Review information from the selection and your research to gather details.
- ❏ List key events in chronological order. Use vivid language to describe feelings and actions. Include a conclusion that follows from the sequence of events.
- ❏ Read your narrative aloud to yourself or to a classmate and make any revisions that you think will make the story more powerful.

Create a Graphic Novel Page Adapt the courtroom scene described in paragraph 2 of *The Story of the Triangle Factory Fire* into a page for a graphic novel.

- ❏ Visualize the scene. Then, identify the key images so that your readers also can visualize it.
- ❏ In a graphic novel, space for words is limited, so decide which dialogue and descriptive words and phrases are most essential for the scene.
- ❏ Share your first draft with a classmate and ask for feedback. Revise the images or words for the greatest impact; then share your final version in a brief presentation.

RESPOND TO THE ESSENTIAL QUESTION

? What inspires you to make a difference?

Gather Information Review your notes on the excerpt from *The Story of the Triangle Factory Fire*. Then, add relevant details to your Response Log. As you determine which information to include, think about:

- the sequence of key events that took place after the fire
- why these events took place when they did

At the end of the unit, use your notes to help you write a research report.

RESPOND

Go to **Writing Narratives: Point of View and Characters** in the **Writing Studio** for more help.

Go to **Using Media in a Presentation** in the Speaking and Listening Studio to learn more.

ACADEMIC VOCABULARY
As you write and discuss what you learned from the piece of history writing, be sure to use the Academic Vocabulary words. Check off each of the words that you use.

- ❏ contrast
- ❏ despite
- ❏ error
- ❏ inadequate
- ❏ interact

APPLY

CREATE AND ADAPT

Write Historical Fiction Help students create a main character for their narrative. Have them answer the following questions about the worker they are going to write about.

Explain that students don't have to include all this information in their narrative, but knowing it will help them make their character more real.

 For **writing support** for students at varying proficiency levels, see the **Text X-Ray** on page 490D.

Create a Graphic Novel Page Review the list of guidelines with students. Remind them that they must come up with ideas for images as well as text. Allow students to work independently to jot down ideas before working with a partner.

RESPOND TO THE ESSENTIAL QUESTION

Allow time for students to add details from *The Story of the Triangle Factory Fire* excerpt to their Unit 6 Response Logs. Encourage them to use chronological order to organize their details.

APPLY

CRITICAL VOCABULARY

Possible answers:

1. It can be very upsetting to see something so ugly that it is called hideous.
2. People won't be able to get to the elevator if the hallway, or corridor, has obstacles.
3. People can persuade local politicians to enact, or pass, laws by protesting.
4. A reformer is a person who is dedicated to bringing about improvements in society.

VOCABULARY STRATEGY: Connotations and Denotations

Answers:

1. *determined: It has a stronger positive connotation than serious and better suits the word refused.*
2. *disgusting: It has a stronger negative connotation tan messy and better suits the word filthy.*
3. *alarming: It has a stronger negative connotation than surprising and better suits the word shocking.*
4. *devoted: It has a stronger positive connotation than helpful and better suits the word dedicated.*

498   Unit 6

 **RESPOND**

WORD BANK
hideous
corridor
enact
reformer

Go to the **Vocabulary Studio** for more on connotations and denotations.

CRITICAL VOCABULARY

Practice and Apply Answer each question by using the Critical Vocabulary word in a complete sentence.

1. Why might people react with shock if they saw something that was **hideous**?
2. Why is it important to keep a **corridor** clear of obstacles?
3. What can people do to persuade local politicians to **enact** a law?
4. How would you describe a **reformer** who helps bring about a positive change in society?

VOCABULARY STRATEGY: Connotations and Denotations

A word's **denotation** is its literal, dictionary meaning. A word's **connotation** comes from the ideas and feelings associated with the word. The author of *The Story of the Triangle Factory Fire* chose some words because of their connotation. He also chose quotations whose speakers likely did the same, as in this comment by Lillian D. Wald:

> **The conditions as they now exist are hideous. . . .**

The choice of *hideous* suggests that the conditions were terrible and revolting. The word suggests an image that would upset most readers.

Some words have positive connotations; other words have negative connotations. To determine a word's connotation, examine the context of the phrase, sentence, or paragraph in which the word appears.

Practice and Apply For each item, mark the word you think better expresses the meaning of the sentence. Use a print or online dictionary to help you. Then explain your choice to a partner.

1. "Furious New Yorkers refused to let the issue rest."
   The people were (**serious, determined**).
2. "They examined workers' filthy living conditions. . . ."
   The workers' living conditions were (**disgusting, messy**).
3. "As a result of the Commission's shocking findings, New York State quickly passed thirty-three new labor laws. . . ."
   The findings were (**surprising, alarming**).
4. "She and other social reformers dedicated their lives to insuring worker safety. . . ."
   These reformers were (**helpful, devoted**).

498   Unit 6

 ENGLISH LEARNER SUPPORT

Use Prior Knowledge Provide students with additional practice with positive and negative connotations. Write the following word pairs on the board: *funny/silly, childish/childlike, inexpensive/cheap, slim/skinny, curious/nosy etc.* Ask students to identify which word in the pair has the more positive or negative connotation. Allow them to look up words in the dictionary if necessary.   **MODERATE/LIGHT**

LANGUAGE CONVENTIONS:
Subject–Verb Agreement and Prepositional Phrases

As you know, the subject and verb in a clause must agree in number. **Agreement** means that if the subject is singular, the verb is also singular, and if the subject is plural, the verb is also plural. Most verbs show the difference between singular and plural only in the third person of the present tense. In the present tense, the third-person singular forms ends in *-s*.

Singular	Plural
I work	we work
you work	you work
she, he, it works	they work

However, the verb *be* causes subject-verb agreeement issues because this verb doesn't follow the usual patterns. It is important to pay particular attention to agreement with this verb.

FORMS OF *BE*			
Present Tense		Past Tense	
Singular	Plural	Singular	Plural
I am	we are	I was	we were
you are	you are	you were	you were
she, he, it is	they are	she, he, it was	they were

In addition, you need to pay attention to words between a subject and a verb. A verb only agrees with its subject. Therefore, when a prepositional phrase or other words come between a subject and a verb, ignore them and focus on identifying the subject and making sure the verb agrees with it. Notice the prepositional phrase "of the tragic Triangle factory fire" does not change the agreement of *ashes* and *came* in this example from *The Story of the Triangle Factory Fire*:

> From the <u>ashes</u> of the tragic Triangle factory fire <u>came</u> help for millions of United States laborers today.

Practice and Apply Choose the verb that agrees with the subject.

1. Today, the victims of the Triangle factory fire (**is** / **are**) remembered.
2. The safety of workers (**wasn't** / **weren't**) as important as today.
3. Citizens in the courtroom (**was** / **were**) furious with the verdict.
4. Investigators in the tenement buildings (**was** / **were**) searching for dangerous conditions.
5. The details of the 1911 fire (**anger** / **angers**) public safety officials.

The Story of the Triangle Factory Fire 499

RESPOND

Go to **Intervening Prepositional Phrases** in the **Grammar Studio** for more help.

APPLY

LANGUAGE CONVENTIONS:
Subject-Verb Agreement and Prepositional Phrases

Explain to students that if subject and verb don't agree, a text will become confusing for the reader. Demonstrate the awkward and incorrect form a sentence can take when the verb *be* causes subject-verb disagreement:

People protested against conditions they think is unsafe.

Tell students that it takes practice to use the verb *be* correctly.

Model using the correct verb in the following sentences:

I am/are going to the market with my mother.

They is/are very good friends of mine.

Tell students that because the verb *be* doesn't follow rules that may be more familiar to them, they should refer to the forms of *be* in the chart on p. 499 until they become accustomed to using it correctly.

Practice and Apply Have partners check whether they have chosen the correct verb form for each sentence.

Answers:
1. *are*
2. *wasn't*
3. *were*
4. *were*
5. *anger*

🄴🄻 ENGLISH LEARNER SUPPORT

Language Conventions Provide students with more subject/verb agreement practice. Choose a verb, write it on the board, and have students use the correct present tense form of the verb to complete your prompts. For example: think: I _____. You _____. The boy _____. The boys _____. The girl _____. Then add prepositional phrases to the prompts: *The boys in the room _____.* Make sure students pronounce the final 's' sound for each third-person singular response. **SUBSTANTIAL/MODERATE**

APPLY

COMPARE AUTHORS' PURPOSES AND MESSAGES

Before students work with their partners to complete the chart, review the meaning of *tone* (mood/attitude) and *point of view* (objective/subjective). Explain that examining these elements, along with the details each author emphasizes, will help students identify the authors' purpose and message. Tell students that although both pieces of historical writing cover the same event, they focus on somewhat different aspects. Advise students to keep these differences in mind as they proceed.

ANALYZE THE TEXTS

Possible answers:

1. **DOK 2:** *The Story of the Triangle Factory Fire*; it covers the short-term and long-term effects in more detail than the other account does.

2. **DOK 2:** Frances Perkins actually witnessed the fire. The tragedy affected her deeply and motivated her to improve working conditions for factory workers, which she did as a Factory Commission investigator and as President Franklin Roosevelt's Secretary of Labor.

3. **DOK 2:** Both used primary sources, including eyewitness accounts.

4. **DOK 4:** Both authors emphasize the importance of safe working conditions and of people working to improve worker safety. Today, we have fire and other emergency drills, and our buildings have smoke alarms and fire and safety inspections. These measures are the results of laws and regulations designed to prevent tragedies like the Triangle Factory Fire.

 RESPOND

Collaborate & Compare

COMPARE AUTHORS' PURPOSES AND MESSAGES

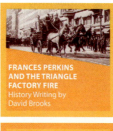

FRANCES PERKINS AND THE TRIANGLE FACTORY FIRE
History Writing by David Brooks

from **THE STORY OF THE TRIANGLE FACTORY FIRE**
History Writing by Zachary Kent

Why compare the **purpose** (reason for writing) and **message** (most important idea) of two authors who wrote about the same historical event? Comparing the texts can give you a greater understanding of the event and new insights into the lives of the people involved.

With a partner, complete the chart and then determine each author's purpose and message. Finally, discuss how the texts are similar and how they differ. Cite text evidence in your discussion.

	DAVID BROOKS'S ACCOUNT	ZACHARY KENT'S ACCOUNT
Author's tone Author's point of view Emphasized details		
What is the author's purpose and message?		

ANALYZE THE TEXTS

Discuss these questions in your group.

1. **Cause/Effect** Which of the two texts would you use to research the effects of the Triangle Fire? Why?

2. **Compare** Look back at both texts to find mention of Frances Perkins. Why is she an important person to know about?

3. **Infer** What kinds of sources did both authors use in researching this topic?

4. **Connect** What idea presented by both authors is most relevant to us today? Why?

 ENGLISH LEARNER SUPPORT

Ask Questions Use the following questions to help students focus their comparisons as they work on their charts:

1. What text is better to use for researching the effects of the Triangle Fire? Why?

2. Why is Frances Perkins an important person in both texts?

3. What kinds of sources did both authors use to research the Triangle fire?

4. Where does the information in each piece fit into the fire's overall chronology?

Remind students that their goal is to find similarities and differences between the two texts. **MODERATE/LIGHT**

RESPOND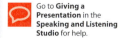

RESEARCH AND SHARE

Now, your group can continue exploring the ideas presented in these texts. As a team, collaborate on research about another significant fire in history and its effects. Then present your findings in an oral presentation. Follow these steps:

1. **Focus Your Research** As a group, decide on a historic fire to research. Begin by searching general terms such as "great fires in history" or specific historic fires such as the Great Fire of London (1666), the Great Fire of Chicago (1871), or the Iroquois Theater Fire (1903). Use your search results to help you choose the fire you all want to explore.

2. **Gather Information** Once you've agreed on the focus of your research, plan how you will each gather information using credible online and print resources. You can use a **web** to guide your research and to record information about the fire. Then use it as a framework for an oral presentation of your findings.

Go to **Giving a Presentation** in the **Speaking and Listening Studio** for help.

RESEARCH TIP
When incorporating information from the sources you find, be sure to guard against plagiarism—that is, using someone else's words and not giving the person credit for them. If you quote or paraphrase a source, keep information about the source and give credit in your work.

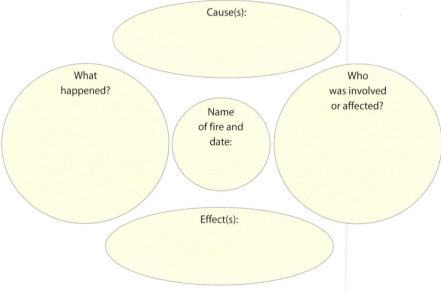

3. **Present What You Learn** Everyone in your group is now an expert on this historic fire and its effects. Discuss which aspects of the fire you each will present and how you will present the information. Consider including a timeline and other images to enhance your presentation. Also prepare for follow-up questions from your audience.

APPLY

RESEARCH AND SHARE
Remind students that they are conducting research for an oral presentation. Have them decide on the role each group member will play both in the research and the presentation so that everyone participates equally.

1. **Focus Your Research** Encourage students to do preliminary research on all three of the fires mentioned to determine which one they would like to choose for their presentation. Allow students to write about a different fire, provided that there is enough researchable information about it. Help groups achieve consensus on their choice.

2. **Gather Information** Point out the Research Tip. Remind students to record where they got their information. Encourage them to look for eyewitness accounts and other primary sources whenever possible. Advise them to include quotations and record them accurately and to be mindful of chronology. Point out that they should use the web to record their information. Encourage students to look for images as well.

3. **Present What You Learn** To prepare for the presentation, help students shape their research so it has a purpose, a message, and an overall structure. Remind them to include important elements like causes and effects. Then have them decide on the format. Allow groups to rehearse their presentations.

WHEN STUDENTS STRUGGLE . . .

Use Timelines If students find it difficult to organize their research, encourage them to use a timeline for a more visual approach. If students have difficulty focusing their presentations and structuring them accordingly, work with them to develop an overall strategy. Ask them to think about the kind of a presentation they would like to give and provide them with options: Will it focus on cause and effect? Will it be a chronological account? Will it be more of a narrative that is based on eyewitness accounts? Will it be some combination of these elements? Then assist students in creating an outline for their presentations.

INDEPENDENT READING

READER'S CHOICE

Setting a Purpose Have students review their Unit 6 Response Log and think about what inspires people to make a difference. As they choose their Independent Reading selections, encourage them to consider what more they want to know.

NOTICE NOTE

Explain that some selections may contain multiple signposts; others may contain only one. And the same type of signpost can occur many times in the same text.

LEARNING MINDSET

Grit Good things start to happen when inspiration yields perspiration: when sturdy people push hard in a positive direction. Remind students to summon again (and again) the grit they found in themselves in taking on and surmounting an obstacle. If there's some part of a lesson they struggle with, encourage students to dig in and keep trying —and to ask for help when they could use some.

 INDEPENDENT READING

ESSENTIAL QUESTION:

What inspires you to make a difference?

Reader's Choice

Setting a Purpose Select one or more of these options from your eBook to continue your exploration of the Essential Question.
- Read the descriptions to see which text grabs your interest.
- Think about which genres you enjoy reading.

Notice Note

In this unit, you practiced asking **Big Questions** and noticing and noting two signposts: **Extreme or Absolute Language** and **Quoted Words**. As you read independently, these signposts and others will aid your understanding. Below are the anchor questions to ask when you read literature and nonfiction.

Reading Literature: Stories, Poems, and Plays		
Signpost	**Anchor Question**	**Lesson**
Contrasts and Contradictions	Why did the character act that way?	p. 99
Aha Moment	How might this change things?	p. 3
Tough Questions	What does this make me wonder about?	p. 362
Words of the Wiser	What's the lesson for the character?	p. 363
Again and Again	Why might the author keep bringing this up?	p. 3
Memory Moment	Why is this memory important?	p. 2

Reading Nonfiction: Essays, Articles, and Arguments		
Signpost/Strategy	**Anchor Question(s)**	**Lesson**
Big Questions	What surprised me? What did the author think I already knew? What challenged, changed, or confirmed what I already knew?	p. 265 p. 183 p. 437
Contrasts and Contradictions	What is the difference, and why does it matter?	p. 183
Extreme or Absolute Language	Why did the author use this language?	p. 182
Numbers and Stats	Why did the author use these numbers or amounts?	p. 264
Quoted Words	Why was this person quoted or cited, and what did this add?	p. 437
Word Gaps	Do I know this word from someplace else? Does it seem like technical talk for this topic? Do clues in the sentence help me understand the word?	p. 265

 ENGLISH LEARNER SUPPORT

Develop Fluency Select a passage from a text that matches students' reading abilities. Read the passage aloud while students follow along silently.

- Have students echo read two to three sentences from the passage after you. Check their comprehension by asking yes/no questions about the passage. Encourage students to respond verbally instead of with gestures. **SUBSTANTIAL**
- Have students work with a partner to read the passage aloud. Encourage them to ask and answer questions if they come across confusing or unfamiliar text in the passage. **MODERATE**
- Have students take turns reading the passage aloud to a partner, correcting each other's pronunciation and rate as they read. Provide students with written comprehension questions about the passage. Instruct students to respond to the questions using complete sentences. **LIGHT**

INDEPENDENT READING

You can preview these texts in Unit 6 of your eBook.
Then, check off the text or texts that you select to read on your own.

ARTICLE
Difference Maker: John Bergmann and Popcorn Park
David Karas

Learn how people are making a difference to the condition of wildlife and domesticated animals that are distressed.

AUTOBIOGRAPHY
from **Walking with the Wind**
John Lewis

Explore how the words of a young preacher inspired a lifetime of political activism.

SHORT STORY
Doris Is Coming
ZZ Packer

What happens when a young girl in the early 1960s refuses to be intimidated by the racist rules of her hometown?

INFORMATIONAL TEXT
Seeing Is Believing
Mary Morton Cowan

Find out how the work of a single photographer helped change the lives of America's poorest children.

Collaborate and Share Get with a partner to discuss what you learned from at least one of your independent readings.

- Give a brief synopsis or summary of the text.
- Describe any signposts that you noticed in the text and explain what they revealed to you.
- Describe what you most enjoyed or found most challenging about the text. Give specific examples.
- Decide if you would recommend the text to others. Why or why not?

Go to the **Reading Studio** for more resources on **Notice & Note**.

PLAN

UNIT 6 Tasks

- **WRITE A RESEARCH REPORT**
- **PARTICIPATE IN A PANEL DISCUSSION**

MENTOR TEXT
THE STORY OF THE TRIANGLE FACTORY FIRE
History Writing by
ZACHARY KENT

LEARNING OBJECTIVES

Writing Task
- Write a research report about an inspirational person from Unit 6.
- Use strategies to plan and organize material.
- Develop a focused, structured draft.
- Use the mentor text as a model for descriptive language, literary devices, and strong supporting detail.
- Revise drafts, incorporating feedback from peers.
- Edit drafts to avoid plagiarism.
- Use a rubric to evaluate writing.
- Publish writing to share it with an audience.
- **Language** Write a research report using strong descriptive language.

Speaking Task
- Participate in a panel discussion.
- Practice presentation skills in less structured settings.
- Use appropriate verbal and nonverbal techniques.
- Listen actively to a presentation.
- **Language** Share information using the sentence stem *I am inspired by _____.*

Assign the writing Task in **Ed.**

RESOURCES

- Unit 6 Response Log
- Reading Studio: Notice & Note
- Writing Studio: Conducting Research
- Writing Studio: Using Textual Evidence
- Speaking and Listening Studio: Participating in a Collaborative Discussion
- Grammar Studio: Module 14: Punctuation

PLAN

Language X-Ray: English Language Support

Use the instruction below and the supports and scaffolds in the Teacher's Edition to help you guide students of different proficiency levels.

INTRODUCE THE WRITING TASK

Explain that writing a **research report** means working like a student *and* a teacher. The writer must choose a subject, sift through sources, synthesize and organize information: the kinds of tasks students take on every day. When it's time to create the report, the student becomes the instructor: refining material and putting it in a well-structured, engaging form, thus sharing newfound knowledge and insight as a teacher would.

Remind students that the subject of their report will be one of the inspiring individuals profiled in the unit. Prompt students to discuss people they know who inspire them by their unselfishness, hard work, and generosity of spirit. Ask: *What are some of the qualities that these kinds of people, famous or otherwise, have in common?*

WRITING

Paraphrase Sentences

Tell students that paraphrase is a verb that means "to express the same meaning in a different way." Ask them to paraphrase the following example: I take a bus to school every day.

Use the following supports with students at varying proficiency levels:

- Tell students that paraphrasing is a valuable tool when writing a report. Display a sentence from the text: "*The conditions as they now exist are hideous. . .*" Model paraphrasing: *The working conditions are very bad*. Repeat with students guiding you with words from their word banks. **SUBSTANTIAL**
- Ask students to paraphrase the following: *Soccer originated more than 2,000 years ago*. **MODERATE**
- Review vocabulary for the Writing Task. Model restating words such as *research*. The discoveries made during their *investigation* angered many people. **LIGHT**

SPEAKING

Discuss Inspirational People

Provide students with the sentence stem *I am inspired by ____*. Circulate around the room to make sure students are using the sentence stem correctly.

Use the following supports with students at varying proficiency levels:

- Work with students to complete the sentence stem with a person's name. Ask them to practice reciting the completed sentence to a partner. **SUBSTANTIAL**
- Have students build on the sentence stem *I am inspired by ____ because (he/she) ____ .* Ask: *What has that person done that inspires you?* **MODERATE**
- In groups, ask students to discuss the qualities that inspire them. Challenge volunteers to pick up on the subject(s) addressed by the student who spoke before them. **LIGHT**

Unit 6 Tasks **504B**

WRITING

WRITE A RESEARCH REPORT

Introduce students to the Writing Task by reading the introductory paragraph with them. Remind students to refer to the notes they recorded in the Unit 6 Response Log as they plan and draft their research reports. The Response Log should contain ideas about role models for social change. Drawing on these different perspectives should help students engage with the assignment.

 For **writing support** for students at varying proficiency levels, see the **Language X-Ray** on page 504B.

USE THE MENTOR TEXT

"The Story of the Triangle Fire" is a model of a fact-based report on social change. Point out to students that the mentor text follows both chronological *and* problem-solution structure. Also note the author's flair for graphic, rhythmic language. Remind students that their report should closely track the life and work of one person; their reports must go into more detail about the person as an agent of change than what is found in the mentor text.

WRITING PROMPT

Review the prompt with students. Encourage them to ask questions about any part of the assignment that is unclear. Refer students to the elements of form under **Research and Write**. Encourage them to review the mentor text and note the author's approach to structure, continuity, and detail.

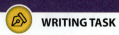 **WRITING TASK**

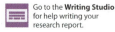 Go to the **Writing Studio** for help writing your research report.

Write a Research Report

This unit focuses on people working for social change—the many challenges they encounter, as well as their accomplishments. For this writing task, you will research and write a report about a person you read about in the unit whom you admire and would like to know more about. For an example of a well-written report you can use as a mentor text, review the excerpt from *The Story of the Triangle Factory Fire*.

As you write your research report, you can use the notes from your Response Log, which you filled out after reading the texts in this unit.

Writing Prompt

Read the information in the box below.

This is the topic or context for your research report.

> Some people are willing to do whatever is necessary to make the world a better place—no matter how difficult the task.

This is the Essential Question for this unit. How would you answer this question, based on the text in this unit?

Think carefully about the following question.

> What inspires you to make a difference?

Now mark the words that identify exactly what you are being asked to produce.

Research and write about one of the figures you read about in this unit. In your report, write about the challenges that person faced and the accomplishments he or she ultimately achieved.

Be sure to—

Review these points as you write and again when you finish. Make any needed changes.

- ❏ provide a strong controlling idea or thesis statement and an introduction that catches the reader's attention and states the topic
- ❏ develop the topic using specific facts, definitions, and examples to support the thesis statement
- ❏ clearly organize ideas and concepts to make connections
- ❏ use appropriate transitions to connect ideas and to create coherence within and across paragraphs
- ❏ identify, gather, and document various sources of information
- ❏ provide a conclusion that summarizes main points and refers to the controlling idea or thesis statement

504 Unit 6

 LEARNING MINDSET

Asking for Help Explain that asking for help can get students "unstuck" so they can move forward. Remind them not to judge themselves when they stumble. Tell them that comparing themselves to others can lead to negative self-talk. Seeking help is a way to honestly be oneself rather than silently wishing to be different. Everyone can make progress if they reach out and keep trying to learn more.

1 Plan

First you need to look at all the people in the unit and decide which person you would like to research and write about. Are you interested in someone who is doing things now or someone in the past?

Develop Research Questions Once you have decided who you will write about, you can narrow your topic by generating questions. For example, you might ask "What unique background and experiences motivated this person?" or "Who was most affected by his or her actions?" After you have done some preliminary research, you may need to refine your research questions to narrow your focus or find a more interesting angle to write about. Use the table below, or one like it, to assist you in planning your draft.

Research Report Planning Table	
Initial Research Question	What caused Frances Perkins to become interested in worker safety?
Refined Research Question	How did Frances Perkins and other reformers help make workplaces safer?

Preview Sources After you have questions that seem correctly focused, search for a variety of sources to find available information. Skim the sources you find to decide if they are are **relevant**—covering the target aspect of your topic; **accurate**—including information that can be verified by more than one source; and **objective**—presenting multiple, and unbiased, viewpoints on the topic. As you continue to conduct research for your report, you can use these initial previewed sources to decide if other sources are credible, or reliable and trustworthy.

Background Reading Review the notes you have taken in your Response Log after reading the texts in this unit. This background reading will help you choose someone to write about and the aspects of his or her life and work you will focus on.

WRITING TASK

Go to **Conducting Research: Starting Your Research** for help planning your research report.

Notice & Note
From Reading to Writing

As you plan your research report, apply what you've learned about signposts to your own writing. Remember that writers use common features, called signposts, to help convey their message to readers.

Think about how you can incorporate **Quoted Words** into your report.

Go to the **Reading Studio** for more resources on Notice & Note.

Use the notes from your Response Log as you plan your report.

Write a Research Report 505

WRITING

1 PLAN

Allow time for students to discuss the topic with partners or in small groups and then to complete the planning chart independently.

■ English Learner Support

Understand Academic Language Make sure students understand words and phrases used in the chart, such as *initial research, refined research,* and *background experiences*. Work with them to fill in the blank sections, providing text that they can copy into their charts as needed.
SUBSTANTIAL/MODERATE

▶ NOTICE AND NOTE

From Reading to Writing

Remind students that they can use quoted words to include the opinions or conclusions of someone who is an expert on the topic. Students can also use Quoted Words to provide support for a point they are trying to make. Remind students to formate direct quotations correctly and to give credit to the source.

Background Reading As they plan their reports, remind students to refer to the notes they took in the Response Log. These notes and their affinities for one of the people profiled in the unit should help them select their subject.

TO CHALLENGE STUDENTS . . .

Conduct Research Encourage students to dig into multimedia to stimulate ideas and provide the basis for further research on their subject. An archive that may include drawings, photos, documentaries, and dramatizations puts faces on stories, and adds depth and texture to their engagement and understanding. The Internet is a good place to start, and further resources should be available at the library.

Write a Research Report 505

WRITING

Research Your Report Remind students that they must cite a range of sources, including print. Encourage them to be curious as information from one source leads them to another: for example, from an encyclopedia entry to a personal journal or a video clip (remind them to check the credibility of their sources).

Organize Your Information Remind students to structure the notes from their research according to the form in the chart:

I. Introduction

II. Person's Background

III. Challenges Faced

IV. Accomplishments

V. Conclusion

Encourage them to keep a writer's eye and ear out for telling elements and well-turned phrases. Well-chosen primary sources can furnish supporting detail that might add color, strength, and a ring of authenticity to their reports.

2 DEVELOP A DRAFT

Remind students to follow their notes, chart, and outlines as they begin their drafts. As they write, they may choose to add, subtract, or modify detail, and make adjustments to the structure of their reports as new findings warrant.

■ English Learner Support

Write a Collaborative Paragraph Simplify the writing task and provide direct support by having students work in groups to write collaborative paragraphs that address the Essential Question. Have students think about the unit and discuss what inspires them to make a difference. Help them to create an outline with strong ideas from their discussion. Then, help them synthesize their ideas by developing a controlling idea in the form of an opening sentence. Build on that with sentence frames and words from their word bank.
SUBSTANTIAL/MODERATE

 **WRITING TASK**

Go to **Conducting Research: Types of Sources** in the **Writing Studio** for help.

Research Your Report The next step in planning your report is to use your list of previewed sources and expand your research to decide on at least three relevant and reliable sources, both online and in print. These might include **primary sources** such as letters or diary entries, as well as **secondary sources** such as encyclopedias.

Organize Your Information You can use the chart below to take notes from your sources. These notes might include direct quotations, summaries, or paraphrases to support your ideas. Be sure to keep accurate records about your sources so that you can create **academic citations** that include the author, title, and publication information for each print and digital source. Ask your teacher about the format that you should use for your citations.

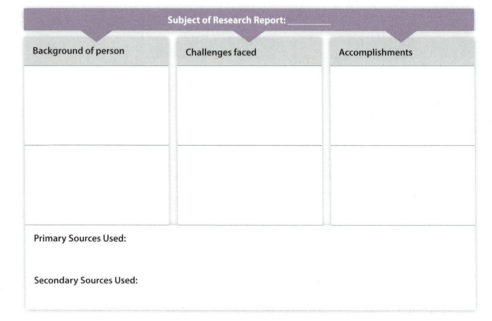

 You may prefer to draft your research report online.

2 Develop a Draft

After research and planning, draft your report. Refer to your planning table, the chart, as well as any notes you took as you studied the texts in the unit. Using a word processor or online writing application can make it easier to create and revise your first draft. As you work, keep in mind that you should identify the sources of your information. Recording your sources as you write will make your work accurate and help you avoid **plagiarizing,** or using someone else's words or ideas.

WHEN STUDENTS STRUGGLE . . .

Develop a Draft If students are struggling to get started, remind them that their research need not be linear: they may want to learn first about the accomplishments of their subject, before they explore personal backgrounds and challenges faced. For concise overviews, encyclopedias may be the best place to start. Encourage students to use a dictionary and thesaurus when they encounter terms and references that are new to them. These basic reference tools should remain handy when students are paraphrasing source material.

WRITING TASK

Use the Mentor Text

Author's Craft
Fiction authors and poets are not the only writers to use descriptive language and literary devices. To capture your readers' attention and help them visualize what you describe, use precise words. You might also consider using devices like alliteration and parallel structure to create interest and emphasize certain key ideas.

> Through the next four years Commission investigators crawled and pried through the rooms and cellars of factories and tenement houses all across the state. They examined workers' filthy living conditions and witnessed the dangers of crippling machinery and long work hours in dusty, dirty firetraps.

The writer uses strong verbs and adjectives and employs alliteration (dusty, dirty) and parallel structure (crawled and pried through the rooms and cellars of factories and tenement houses).

Apply What You've Learned To maintain your reader's attention, use strong verbs, specific adjectives, and concrete nouns.

Genre Characteristics
Supporting details are words, phrases, sentences, and quotations that tell more about a key idea. Notice how the author of *The Story of the Triangle Factory Fire* uses a quotation by the fire chief to support a key idea about why so many people died in the fire.

> In the days following the fire, city officials sifted through the charred rubble at the Asch Building and tried to fix the fault for the tragedy. Fire Chief Croker angrily stated, "There wasn't a fire escape anywhere fronting on the street by which these unfortunate girls could escape."

The author provides evidence, including quotations, to explain why the girls died.

Apply What You've Learned The details you include in your report should be clearly related to ideas about the person you are researching. Quotations might come from the subject of your report, his or her family members, coworkers, and government officials.

Write a Research Report   507

WRITING

WHY THIS MENTOR TEXT?
The excerpt from *The Story of the Triangle Factory Fire* is a concise, well-crafted example of a research report. Use the instruction below to help students model the mentor text for descriptive language, literary devices, and strong supporting detail.

USE THE MENTOR TEXT
Author's Craft Invite a volunteer to read aloud the example paragraph. Ask: *Can you identify some of the sensory terms, or references to the way things looked, felt, or smelled?* (crawled, pried, filthy, crippling, long, dusty, dirty) Then ask: *What effect does that language have in the parallel verb structure of the first sentence?* (Answers will vary. The parallel structure reinforces and sharpens the image of investigators on their knees in nasty places. The text paints a picture most readers can envision and imagine further details to complete.)

Genre Characteristics Read the example paragraph aloud. Ask: *Why is a direct quote here stronger than a paraphrase would have been?* (A direct quote from a trusted source serves as strong evidence, in a court of law or public opinion.) Then ask: *What are good sources for uncovering such quotes?* (Newspapers and magazines are often primary sources for first-hand quotes and responses to noteworthy events.)

 ENGLISH LEARNER SUPPORT

Use the Mentor Text Use the following supports with students at varying proficiency levels:

- Use images of the factory interior after the fire along with gestures to help illustrate the words *charred rubble*. Show images of tenements and difficult working conditions for the words *filthy, dusty, and dirty*. Be sure not to confuse images of people with descriptions of places. Have students chorally pronounce the words with you in sentences, i.e., *This is charred rubble.* **SUBSTANTIAL**

- Guide students to use descriptive language. Supply these sentence frames: *This room is_____.* (dusty, dirty). *This machine is _____.* (dangerous) Have them copy the sentences into their notebooks. **MODERATE**

- Help students identify parallel structure and alliteration. Have them create their own sentences using the words *jumped, leaped, pulled open, stained, smeared,* and *smudged.* **LIGHT**

Write a Research Report   **507**

WRITING

3 REVISE

Have students answer each question in the chart to determine how they can improve their drafts. Invite volunteers to model their revision techniques.

With a Partner Have students ask peer reviewers to evaluate the form and content of their reports. Guide reviewers to make notes that answer the following questions:

- Is the thesis statement strong and explicit?
- Do the topic sentences properly frame the details that follow? Are there sound logical links between topic sentences and supporting details?
- Does the text flow? Are there well-chosen transitions between ideas?
- Where information has been paraphrased, is the text clear, and clearly original?
- Is the conclusion clear and concise?
- Does the descriptive language need improvement?

Students should use the reviewer's feedback to strengthen form and content in their reports.

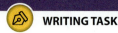 **WRITING TASK**

3 Revise

Go to **Conducting Research: Refocusing Your Inquiry** for help with revising your report.

On Your Own Once you have written your draft, go back and look for ways to improve your research report. As you reread and revise, think about whether you have achieved your purpose. The Revision Guide will help you focus on specific elements to make your writing stronger.

Revision Guide		
Ask Yourself	**Tips**	**Revision Techniques**
1. Is my topic clear?	**Mark** the thesis statement.	**Add** a thesis statement.
2. Does each paragraph have a topic sentence related to the controlling idea, or thesis statement?	**Highlight** the topic sentence of each paragraph.	**Delete** unrelated ideas or **rearrange** information into separate paragraphs. **Add** a topic sentence.
3. Are there supporting facts and examples for each key idea?	**Underline** facts, examples, and quotations that support your key idea.	**Add** more facts, examples, and quotations from your notes.
4. Are ideas organized logically? Do transitions connect ideas? Is there coherence within and across paragraphs?	**Highlight** transitional words and phrases within and between paragraphs.	**Rearrange** sentences and paragraphs to organize ideas logically. **Add** transitions to connect ideas and create coherence.
5. Is information gathered from a variety of sources, all cited correctly?	**Underline** references to sources.	**Add** more sources for variety. **Cite** all sources correctly.
6. Does the conclusion summarize the key ideas?	**Underline** the summary.	**Review** the topic sentence in each paragraph. **Add** a summary statement.

ACADEMIC VOCABULARY
As you conduct your **peer review**, be sure to use these words.

- ❏ contrast
- ❏ despite
- ❏ error
- ❏ inadequate
- ❏ interact

With a Partner After working through the Revision Guide on your own, exchange papers with a partner and evaluate each other's drafts in a **peer review**. Take turns reading or listening to each other's reports and offer suggestions based on the Revision Guide to make the reports more effective. When receiving feedback from your partner, listen attentively and ask questions to make sure you fully understand the revision suggestions.

508 Unit 6

 ENGLISH LEARNER SUPPORT

Use Negatives and Contractions Explain to students that there is often more than one negative form for a given verb phrase. Display the following quote from the mentor text and ask students to express the negative in different terms.

"I shall never forget the horror that came over us as we stood with our hands on our throats . . ." *(will never forget, won't ever forget)*

Encourage students to review their use of negatives and contractions in their research reports.
LIGHT

508 Unit 6

4. Edit

Once you have revised your research report, you can improve the finer points of your draft. Edit for the proper use of standard English conventions, such as correct punctuation, and be sure to correct any misspellings or grammatical errors.

Paraphrasing to Avoid Plagiarism

Finding sources is an important part of developing a research report. But equally important is paraphrasing those sources correctly to avoid plagiarism and citing all of your sources.

- When you **paraphrase,** you restate information in your own words.
- **Plagiarism** is the unauthorized use of someone else's work. When you plagiarize, you present someone else's work as if it was your own.

Learning to paraphrase correctly can help you avoid plagiarism. The chart below contains an excerpt from *The Story of the Triangle Factory Fire* and two paraphrases. The first paraphrase uses too many of the author's original words. The second paraphrase is done correctly.

Original text	Furious New Yorkers refused to let the issue rest. In October 1911 the city established a Bureau of Fire Prevention to inspect safety standards in other buildings.
Incorrect paraphrase	Angry New Yorkers would not let the issue rest. The city set up a Bureau of Fire Prevention in October 1911 to inspect other buildings' safety standards.
Correct paraphrase	New Yorkers pressed for change, resulting in the establishment of the Bureau of Fire Prevention in 1911. The bureau's job was to ensure that other buildings met safety standards.

5. Publish

Finalize your research report by examining your work for interest, accuracy, and correct citations. Choose a way to share your report with your audience. Consider these options:

- Post your report on a school website.
- Produce a multimodal presentation of your essay.

WRITING TASK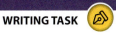

 Go to the **Grammar Studio: Punctuation** to learn more.

 Go to **Using Textual Evidence: Attribution** in the **Writing Studio** for more help with research.

WHEN STUDENTS STRUGGLE . . .

Avoid Plagiarism The distinctions between paraphrasing and plagiarizing are sometimes subtle. If students are struggling to "say it in their own words," suggest they recast their notes to include key information and minimize original language. For example, "Bureau of Fire Prevention created in October 1911" encapsulates an important point from the sample text above, without "borrowing" modifiers, verbs or sentence structure. Referring back to such notes, a writer must use his or her own tools and terms to contextualize the information.

WRITING

4. EDIT

Suggest that students read their drafts aloud to assess how clearly and smoothly they have presented their ideas. Review the fundamental elements of their assignment: a clear, concise thesis statement; a series of topic sentences buttressed with supporting evidence; a smooth, logical unity between sentences, paragraphs and ideas; and a summary in conclusion. Encourage students to look closely at their descriptive language with an eye and ear toward color and rhythm.

LANGUAGE CONVENTIONS

Paraphrasing to Avoid Plagiarizing Review the information about paraphrasing and plagiarizing with students. Then discuss the samples in the chart, asking students to mark the words and phrases that suggest plagiarism in the **incorrect paraphrase**. (Constructions are too much alike. Changing Furious to Angry and established to set up doesn't go far enough in adapting original text.) Encourage students to try to channel their own way of explaining things or ideas through their text, to develop and maintain a voice and style of their own in their reports.

■ English Learner Support

Use Your Own Words Explain the chart on p. 509 and then model paraphrasing the sentence "Furious New Yorkers refused to let the issue rest." Use a Think-Aloud. Say: *New Yorkers are people, so I can change those words to People in New York. I can ask myself what they wanted. I know from the reading that they wanted changes; I can use the vocabulary word reform: People in New York wanted reforms.*
MODERATE/LIGHT

5. PUBLISH

Students can present their work on a school website. Encourage others to read the research reports and write constructive comments about them. The authors can then respond to the comments.

WRITING

USE THE SCORING GUIDE

Allow students time to read the scoring guide and ask questions about any words, phrases, or ideas that are unclear. Then have partners exchange final drafts of their research reports. Ask them to score their partner's report using the scoring guide. Each student should write a paragraph explaining the reasons for the score he or she awarded in each category, referring to specific strengths and shortcomings in their partner's work.

 **WRITING TASK**

Use the scoring guide to evaluate your research report.

Writing Task Scoring Guide: Research Report

	Organization/Progression	Development of Ideas	Use of Language and Conventions
4	• The organization is effective and logical throughout the report. • Transitions clearly show the relationship among ideas from one paragraph to another. • There is coherence within and across paragraphs.	• The thesis statement is clear and the introduction is engaging, reflecting depth of thought. • The thesis statement is well developed with relevant facts, concrete details, interesting quotations, and specific examples from reliable sources. • The conclusion effectively summarizes the information presented.	• The writing maintains a formal style throughout. • Language is strong and precise. • There is sentence variety. • Spelling, capitalization, and punctuation are correct. • Grammar and usage are correct. • Research sources are cited and paraphrased correctly.
3	• The organization is confusing in a few places. • A few more transitions are needed to connect related ideas. • There is coherence within and across paragraphs.	• The thesis statement is clear, reflecting some depth of thought, but the introduction could do more to grab readers' attention. • The thesis statement needs more support from relevant facts, details, quotations, and examples from reliable sources. • The conclusion summarizes the information presented.	• The style is inconsistent in a few places. • Language is too general is some places. • There is some sentence variety. • A few spelling, capitalization, and punctuation errors are present. • Some errors in grammar and usage are repeated. • Sources are not cited or punctuated consistently.
2	• The organization is logical in some places but often doesn't follow a pattern. • More transitions are needed throughout to connect ideas. • There is little coherence within and across paragraphs.	• The thesis statement is unclear and does not reflect depth of thought. The introduction could be more engaging. • The development of ideas is minimal. The facts, details, quotations, and examples are not relevant or are ineffectively presented. • The conclusion is only partially effective.	• The style is informal in many places. • Overly general language is used. • Most sentences are structured in the same way. • Spelling, capitalization, and punctuation are often incorrect but do not make reading difficult. • Grammar and usage are often still clear. • Only one or two research sources are cited, using incorrect format and punctuation.
1	• A logical organization is not used; information is presented randomly. • Transitions are not used, making the report difficult to understand. • There is no coherence within and across paragraphs.	• The thesis statement is unclear, or the introduction is missing or confusing. • Facts, details, quotations, and examples come from unreliable sources or are missing. • The conclusion is missing.	• The style is inappropriate for the report. • Language is too general to convey the information. • There is no sentence variety. • Many spelling, capitalization, and punctuation errors are present. • Many grammatical and usage errors appear. • Research sources are not cited.

Participate in a Panel Discussion

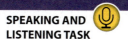

SPEAKING AND LISTENING TASK

In this unit, you read about people who were inspired to solve problems. In this activity, you will draw from the selections you read to participate in a panel discussion about commitment to a cause. Recognize that a successful participant in a panel discussion—

- makes a clear, logical generalization about the topic
- uses quotations and specific examples to illustrate ideas
- responds politely to the moderator and other group members
- evaluates other group members' contributions
- summarizes the discussion by synthesizing ideas

Go to **Participating in Collaborative Discussions** in the **Speaking and Listening Studio** for help developing your panel discussion.

1 Prepare for a Panel Discussion

Work with your classmates to prepare for the discussion.

- Form a group. Choose three selections from this unit, including the excerpt from *The Story of the Triangle Factory Fire*, for the discussion.
- Select one student to be the moderator. The rest of your classmates will be your audience during the panel discussion.
- Create a schedule that shows the order in which panel members will speak and for how long. Develop rules for the appropriate times for the moderator or the audience to ask panel members questions.
- **Gather Evidence** Work individually to analyze what your chosen selections suggest about commitment to a cause. Note specific details, examples, and quotations that support your views. Then consider your experiences. Ask yourself questions as you take notes.

QUESTION	EVIDENCE
What degree of positive change might one person or group hope to accomplish?	
Are good intentions enough? How knowledgeable does a person need to be in order to take on an issue?	
What are the benefits or drawbacks of committing to a cause?	

Participate in a Panel Discussion 511

SPEAKING AND LISTENING

PARTICIPATE IN A PANEL DISCUSSION

Introduce students to the Speaking and Listening Task by noting some of the parallels to their research report: a clear, logical generalization about the topic that is analogous to a thesis statement, and quotations and specific examples that provide supporting detail. Note that a panel discussion is a collaborative presentation of ideas that will call on students to listen attentively; take careful notes; ask insightful questions; and participate supportively in a verbal exchange of ideas and information.

1 PREPARE FOR A PANEL DISCUSSION

Have students review the guidelines and chart on p. 511. Then work with the class to list some general principles for presenting information orally. (**Examples:** *Use short sentences. Repeat important ideas. Integrate your part in the presentation into the group effort.*) Point out that the questions in the chart can be reshaped into general statements specific to your chosen selections. Those statements should then be substantiated with supporting evidence.

 For **speaking support** for students at varying proficiency levels, see the **Language X-Ray** on page 504B.

 ENGLISH LEARNER SUPPORT

Adapt the Research Report Have students gather evidence for their reports using the chart on p. 511. Use the following supports with students at varying proficiency levels:

- Have students identify questions about needed reforms (e.g., How can people make buildings safer for workers?) Help them find text evidence to answer their questions. **SUBSTANTIAL**

- Ask students to use evidence from a selection to answer the questions they put to themselves. Have students work in pairs to gather evidence from other selections. **MODERATE**

- Tell students that responsible investigators share information. Have students share evidence from unit selections to include in reports they've adapted for presentation. **LIGHT**

Participate in a Panel Discussion **511**

SPEAKING AND LISTENING

② PRACTICE THE PANEL DISCUSSION

Review the information and tips with the class, ensuring that all the terms and ideas are clear. Stress the importance of rehearsing in an informal setting, to help work through some of the anxieties that invariably attend public speaking. Encourage students to be supportive of one another, offering constructive criticism without judgment in a sincere effort to advance a collective endeavor.

③ PRESENT THE DISCUSSION

Set aside time for all students to give their presentations. When everyone has finished, ask students to share their thoughts on how their classmates' feedback improved their performance.

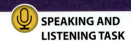

SPEAKING AND LISTENING TASK

As you work collaboratively, be sure to follow discussion rules:
- ❑ listen closely to each other
- ❑ don't interrupt
- ❑ stay on topic
- ❑ ask only helpful, relevant questions
- ❑ provide only clear, thoughtful, and direct answers

② Practice the Panel Discussion

Work individually to outline your ideas and develop a clear controlling idea. Then prepare to "think on your feet" as you present your ideas to your group. The moderator and group members will ask questions about your ideas to prepare you for the real discussion. The moderator should time each panel member's contribution and suggest length adjustments. The moderator should also write notes for opening remarks and concluding remarks. Based on the practice session, make changes to your written response to the texts.

Provide and Consider Advice for Improvement

As a listener, pay close attention. Take notes about ways that presenters can improve their presentations and more effectively use verbal and nonverbal techniques. Paraphrase and summarize each presenter's key ideas to confirm your understanding, and ask questions to clarify any confusing ideas.

As a presenter, listen closely to questions and consider ways to revise your work to make sure your points are clear and logically sequenced.

- Effective **verbal techniques** include clearly enunciating words and speaking at an appropriate rate and volume.
- Effective **nonverbal techniques** include making eye contact, varying facial expressions, and using meaningful gestures.

③ Present the Discussion

Now it's time to present your panel discussion before the rest of the class. Have your outline at hand for reference. Here are some guidelines for the discussion:

- Have the moderator use his or her notes for opening remarks to introduce the topic, panelists, and format for the discussion. The moderator will ask the first question and facilitate discussion.
- Speak directly to the panel and audience. Refer to your notes for your main points, but don't just read from your notes.
- Listen closely so that you can respond appropriately.
- After the panel discussion, have the moderator invite panelists and the audience to ask questions.
- Conclude by having the moderator summarize the discussion and thank the panelists for their participation.

WHEN STUDENTS STRUGGLE . . .

Take Notes If students have difficulty taking notes during their classmates' presentations, divide the task between several students. One student may focus on the list of effective verbal techniques, checking off techniques that are used well and jotting down brief notes about ones that need improvement. Another student may do the same for the list of effective nonverbal techniques. A third may listen for key ideas and write those down. This student may choose to listen with eyes closed to tune out distractions.

Reflect on the Unit

By completing your research report and engaging in a panel discussion, you have expressed your thoughts about the reading you have done in this unit as well as the information you discovered in your research. Now is a good time to reflect on what you have learned.

Reflect on the Essential Question

- What inspires you to make a difference? How has your answer to this question changed since you first considered it?
- What are some examples you've read of people who are inspired to make a difference—both from the unit and from other sources?

Reflect on Your Reading

- Which selections were the most interesting or surprising to you?
- From which selection did you learn the most about how people become inspired to make the world a better place?

Reflect on the Writing Task

- What difficulties did you encounter while working on your research report? How might you avoid them next time?
- What parts of the report were the easiest and hardest to write? Why?
- What improvements did you make to your report during revision?

Reflect on the Speaking and Listening Task

- Were you able to defend your ideas? Did the discussion cause you to rethink your point of view? If so, why?
- What was your favorite part of participating in the panel discussion?
- In what ways was the panel discussion successful? What might you do differently the next time?

REFLECT

UNIT 6 SELECTIONS
- "Craig Kielburger Reflects on Working Toward Peace"
- from *It Takes a Child*
- "Sometimes a Dream Needs a Push"
- "A Poem for My Librarian, Mrs. Long"
- "Frances Perkins and the Triangle Factory Fire"
- from *The Story of the Triangle Factory Fire*

Reflect on the Unit 513

SPEAKING AND LISTENING

REFLECT ON THE UNIT

Have students reflect on the questions independently and write some notes in response to each one. Then have students meet with partners or in small groups to discuss their reflections. Circulate during these discussions to identify the questions that are generating the liveliest conversations. Wrap up with a whole-class discussion focused on these questions.

LEARNING MINDSET

Self-Reflection Remind students that patience and persistence are fundamental attributes of those who inspire us by example. Ask them to model those qualities in the work they do, in and out of the classroom. As students reflect on the unit, encourage them to ask themselves these questions: *Did I ask questions if I needed help? Did I review my work for possible errors? Did I do my part in a group effort? Was I careful in my feedback to be constructive? Did I give other students chances to ask questions?*

Reflect on the Unit 513

Student Resources

Response Logs	R1
Using a Glossary	R7
Pronunciation Key	R7
Glossary of Academic Vocabulary	R8
Glossary of Critical Vocabulary	R9
Index of Skills	R13
Index of Titles and Authors	R21
Acknowledgments	R22

 HMH *Into Literature* Studios
For more instruction and practice,
visit the HMH *Into Literature* Studios.

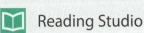 Reading Studio

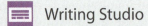 Writing Studio

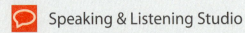 Speaking & Listening Studio

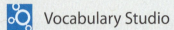 Grammar Studio

Vocabulary Studio

UNIT 1 RESPONSE LOG

Use this Response Log to record your ideas about how each of the texts in Unit 1 relates to or comments on the **Essential Question.**

? Essential Question:
What helps people rise up to face difficulties?

Text	
Rogue Wave	
The Flight of Icarus	
Icarus's Flight	
Women in Aviation	
Thank You, M'am	
A Police Stop Changed This Teenager's Life	

UNIT 2 RESPONSE LOG

Use this Response Log to record your ideas about how each of the texts in Unit 2 relates to or comments on the **Essential Question.**

? Essential Question:
What can blur the lines between what's real and what's not?

Heartbeat	
The Camera Does Lie	
Two Legs or One?	
The Song of Wandering Aengus	
Eldorado	
The Governess *from* The Good Doctor	
from The Governess	

R2 Response Log

UNIT 3 RESPONSE LOG

Use this Response Log to record your ideas about how each of the texts in Unit 3 relates to or comments on the **Essential Question.**

? Essential Question:
What does it mean to be in harmony with nature?

Never Retreat *from* Eyes Wide Open	
from Mississippi Solo	
The Drought	
Allied with Green	
Ode to enchanted light	
Sleeping in the Forest	
from Trash Talk	
You're Part of the Solution	

UNIT 4 RESPONSE LOG

Use this Response Log to record your ideas about how each of the texts in Unit 4 relates to or comments on the **Essential Question.**

? Essential Question:
Why is the idea of space exploration both inspiring and unnerving?

Martian Metropolis	
Dark They Were, and Golden-Eyed	
Challenges for Space Exploration	
What If We Were Alone?	
Seven Minutes of Terror	
Space Exploration Should Be More Science Than Fiction	
Humans Should Stay Home and Let Robots Take to the Stars	

UNIT 5 RESPONSE LOG

Use this Response Log to record your ideas about how each of the texts in Unit 5 relates to or comments on the **Essential Question.**

? Essential Question:
How do sports bring together friends, families, and communities?

Ball Hawk	
Get in the Zone: The Psychology of Video Game Design	
It's Not Just a Game!	
from The Crossover	
Double Doubles	

UNIT 6 RESPONSE LOG

Use this Response Log to record your ideas about how each of the texts in Unit 6 relates to or comments on the **Essential Question.**

 Essential Question:
What inspires you to make a difference?

Craig Kielburger Reflects on Working Toward Peace	
from It Takes a Child	
Sometimes a Dream Needs a Push	
A Poem for My Librarian, Mrs. Long	
Frances Perkins and the Triangle Factory Fire	
from The Story of the Triangle Factory Fire	

Using a Glossary

A glossary is an alphabetical list of vocabulary words. Use a glossary just as you would a dictionary—to determine the meanings, parts of speech, pronunciation, and syllabification of words. (Some technical, foreign, and more obscure words in this book are defined for you in the footnotes that accompany many of the selections.)

Many words in the English language have more than one meaning. This glossary gives the meanings that apply to the words as they are used in the selections in this book.

The following abbreviations are used to identify parts of speech of words:

adj. adjective   *adv.* adverb   *n.* noun   *v.* verb

Each word's pronunciation is given in parentheses. A guide to the pronunciation symbols appears in the Pronunciation Key below. The stress marks in the Pronunciation Key are used to indicate the force given to each syllable in a word. They can also help you determine where words are divided into syllables.

For more information about the words in this glossary or for information about words not listed here, consult a dictionary.

Pronunciation Key

Symbol	Examples	Symbol	Examples	Symbol	Examples
ă	pat	m	mum	ûr	urge, term, firm, word, heard
ā	pay	n	no, sudden* (sud´n)		
ä	father	ng	thing	v	valve
âr	care	ŏ	pot	w	with
b	bib	ō	toe	y	yes
ch	church	ô	caught, paw	z	zebra, xylem
d	deed, milled	oi	noise	zh	vision, pleasure, garage
ĕ	pet	ŏŏ	took		
ē	bee	ōō	boot	ə	about, item, edible, gallop, circus
f	fife, phase, rough	ŏŏr	lure		
g	gag	ôr	core	ər	butter
h	hat	ou	out		
hw	which	p	pop	**Sounds in Foreign Words**	
ĭ	pit	r	roar	KH	German ich, ach; Scottish loch
ī	pie, by	s	sauce	N	French, bon (bôn)
îr	pier	sh	ship, dish	œ	French feu, œuf; German schön
j	judge	t	tight, stopped		
k	kick, cat, pique	th	thin	ü	French tu; German über
l	lid, needle* (nēd´l)	th	this		
		ŭ	cut		

*In English the consonants *l* and *n* often constitute complete syllables by themselves.

Stress Marks
The relevant emphasis with which the syllables of a word or phrase are spoken, called stress, is indicated in three different ways. The strongest, or primary, stress is marked with a bold mark (´). An intermediate, or secondary, level of stress is marked with a similar but lighter mark (´). The weakest stress is unmarked. Words of one syllable show no stress mark.

GLOSSARY OF ACADEMIC VOCABULARY

abnormal (ăb-nôr′məl) *adj.* not typical, usual, or regular; not normal

affect (ə-fĕkt′) *v.* to have an influence on or effect a change in something

aspect (ăs′pĕkt) *n.* a characteristic or feature of something

attitude (ăt′ĭ-tōōd′) *n.* a manner of thinking that reflects a person's feelings; a particular state of mind

complex (kŏm′plĕks′) *adj.* consisting of many interwoven parts that make something difficult to understand

consume (kən-sōōm′) *v.* to buy things for your own use or ownership

contrast (kən-trăst′) *v.* to show differences between two or more things that are being compared

cultural (kŭl′chər-əl) *adj.* of or relating to culture or cultivation

despite (dĭ-spīt′) *prep.* in spite of; even though

element (ĕl′ə-mənt) *n.* a part or aspect of something

ensure (ĕn-shoor′) *v.* to make sure or certain

error (ĕr′ər) *n.* a mistake

evaluate (ĭ-văl′yoo-āt′) *tr.v.* to examine something carefully to judge its value or worth

feature (fē′chər) *n.* a prominent or distinctive part, quality, or characteristic

focus (fō′kəs) *v.* to direct toward a specific point or purpose

goal (gōl) *n.* the object toward which your work and planning is directed; a purpose

inadequate (ĭn-ăd′ĭ-kwĭt) *adj.* not enough or sufficient to fulfill a need or meet a requirement

interact (ĭn′tər-ăkt′) *v.* to act upon each other

participate (pär-tĭs′ə-pāt′) *v.* to be active and involved in something or to share in something

perceive (pər-sēv′) *v.* to become aware of something directly through any of the senses

potential (pə-tĕn′shəl) *adj.* capable of doing or being something; having possibility

purchase (pûr′chĭs) *v.* to buy

rely (rĭ-lī′) *v.* to depend on something or someone for support, help, or supply

resource (rē′sôrs′) *n.* something that can be used for support or help

specify (spĕs′ə-fī′) *v.* to state exactly or in detail what you want or need

stress (strĕs) *v.* to put emphasis on something

style (stīl) *n.* the combination of techniques that a writer uses to make his or her work effective and unique

task (tăsk) *n.* an assignment or work done as part of one's duties

text (tĕkst) *n.* a literary work that is regarded as an object of critical analysis

valid (văl′ĭd) *adj.* convincing or having a sound reason for something

GLOSSARY OF CRITICAL VOCABULARY

absolute (ăbʹsə-lo͞otʹ) *adj.* Something that is without qualifications or exceptions is *absolute.*

absorb (əb-zôrbʹ) *v.* Things that *absorb* you occupy your time or attention.

accelerate (ăk-sĕlʹə-rātʹ) *v.* When something *accelerates*, its speed increases.

accomplishment (ə-kŏmʹplĭsh-mənt) *n.* An *accomplishment* is a task that you succeed in doing.

adaptability (ə-dăpʹtə-bĭlʹĭ-tē) *n.* People who have *adaptability* can change to survive and fit in with new circumstances.

addiction (ə-dĭkʹshən) *n.* An *addiction* is a habit upon which a person becomes physically or emotionally dependent.

administration (ăd-mĭnʹĭ-strāʹshən) *n.* A president's *administration* is his or her term of office.

advancement (ăd-vănsʹmənt) *n.* Something that is an *advancement* is an improvement or step forward.

anxiety (ăng-zīʹĭ-tē) *n. Anxiety* is an uneasy, worried feeling.

aquifer (ăkʹwə-fər) *n.* An *aquifer* is an underground layer of rock that contains water.

arboretum (ärʹbə-rēʹtəm) *n.* An *arboretum* is a place where many trees are grown for educational or viewing purposes.

atmosphere (ătʹmə-sfîrʹ) *n.* An *atmosphere* is the gaseous mass or envelope that surrounds a planet.

avalanche (ăvʹə-lănchʹ) *n.* An *avalanche* is a large mass of snow, ice, dirt, or rocks falling quickly down the side of a mountain.

barren (bărʹən) *adj.* Something that is empty and lacking interest or charm is *barren.*

beneficial (bĕnʹə-fĭshʹəl) *adj.* When something is *beneficial*, it is good or favorable.

bogus (bōʹgəs) *adj.* Something that is *bogus* is fake or not genuine.

burden (bûrʹdn) *v.* If you *burden* someone, you create a situation that is difficult or stressful for him or her.

capacity (kə-păsʹĭ-tē) *n.* A person's *capacity* is his or her role or position.

clique (klĭk) *n.* If you are part of a *clique*, you belong to a small group of friends that doesn't allow outsiders.

collision (kə-lĭzhʹən) *n.* When the two things crash into each other, the result is a *collision.*

colonize (kŏlʹə-nīzʹ) *v.* When you *colonize* a place, you send a group of people to a new place to establish a colony or settlement.

combustion (kəm-bŭsʹchən) *n. Combustion* is the process of burning, which produces heat and light.

commute (kə-myo͞otʹ) *n.* A *commute* is a person's travel to and from work or school.

concession (kən-sĕshʹən) *n.* Sporting and entertainment events often feature *concession* stands where food and drinks are sold.

congestion (kən-jĕsʹchən) *n. Congestion* is overcrowding, such as when too many vehicles cause a traffic jam.

consecutive (kən-sĕkʹyə-tĭv) *adj.* When things are *consecutive*, they follow one after another without interruption.

continuity (kŏnʹtə-no͞oʹĭ-tē) *n.* In the movies, *continuity* refers to making sure that things that were filmed at different times or out of sequence look as if they were filmed at the same time or in the intended sequence.

convivial (kən-vĭvʹē-əl) *adj.* A person who is *convivial* enjoys the company of others in a sociable manner.

corridor (kôrʹĭ-dər) *n.* A *corridor* is a narrow hallway or passageway.

crucial (kro͞oʹshəl) *adj.* Something that is *crucial* is extremely important or significant.

deck (dĕk) *n.* The *deck* is the platform on a ship or boat where people stand.

Glossary of Critical Vocabulary   R9

GLOSSARY OF CRITICAL VOCABULARY

delirious (dĭ-lîr´ē-əs) *adj.* Someone who is *delirious* is temporarily confused, often because of fever or shock.

dignified (dĭg´nə-fīd´) *adj.* Someone or something that is *dignified* has or shows honor and respect.

discrepancy (dĭ-skrĕp´ən-sē) *n.* When there is a *discrepancy* between two things, there is a difference or disagreement.

disorient (dĭs-ôr´ē-ĕnt´) *v.* To *disorient* is to make someone or something lose a sense of direction.

distinguish (dĭ-stĭng´gwĭsh) *v.* To *distinguish* one thing from another means perceiving them as being different or distinct.

donate (dō´nāt´) *v.* To *donate* is to give, or contribute, something to a person, cause, or fund.

dubious (dōō´bē-əs) *adj.* If something is *dubious*, it is questionable or not to be relied upon.

elaborate (ĭ-lăb´ər-ĭt) *adj.* Something that is *elaborate* has been carefully planned and constructed with great attention to detail.

embarrass (ĕm-băr´əs) *v.* To *embarrass* is to cause to feel uncomfortable or self-conscious.

enact (ĕn-ăkt´) *v.* If you *enact* something, you make it into a law.

encounter (ĕn-koun´tər) *n.* An *encounter* is a short meeting that is unplanned or unexpected.

entail (ĕn-tāl´) *v.* To *entail* means to have or require.

erupt (ĭ-rŭpt´) *v.* When something *erupts*, it develops suddenly.

ethereal (ĭ-thîr´ē-əl) *adj.* If something is *ethereal*, it is light and airy.

exhibition (ĕk´sə-bĭsh´ən) *n.* An *exhibition* is an organized presentation or show.

exploitation (ĕk´sploi-tā´shən) *n.* *Exploitation* is the unfair treatment or use of something or someone for selfish reasons.

fatal (fāt´l) *adj.* A *fatal* decision is a choice that results in death.

federal (fĕd´ər-əl) *adj.* Something that is *federal* relates to the U.S. government in Washington, D.C., and not to state and local governments.

forlorn (fər-lôrn´) *adj.* Something that is *forlorn* appears lonely or sad.

frantic (frăn´tĭk) *adj.* If you do something in a *frantic* way, you do it quickly and nervously.

fundamental (fŭn´də-mĕn´tl) *n.* A *fundamental* is a basic but essential part of an object or a system.

futile (fyōōt´l) *adj.* When something is *futile*, it has no useful or meaningful result.

geothermal (jē´ō-thûr´məl) *adj.* *Geothermal* relates to the internal heat of the earth.

habitat (hăb´ĭ-tăt´) *n.* In this instance, a *habitat* is a structure that provides a controlled environment for living in very hostile or even deadly locations.

heirloom (âr´lōōm´) *n.* An *heirloom* is a valued possession that was passed down in a family.

hideous (hĭd´ē-əs) *adj.* When something is *hideous*, it is repulsive or revolting.

hoax (hōks) *n.* A *hoax* is something that is meant to trick or fool someone.

idle (īd´l) *v.* When you *idle*, you pass time without doing anything purposeful.

immerse (ĭ-mûrs´) *v.* If you *immerse* yourself in an activity, that activity is the only thing that you are focused on.

indifferent (ĭn-dĭf´ər-ənt) *adj.* Someone who is *indifferent* has no feelings one way or another about something.

Inferior (ĭn-fîr´ē-ər) *adj.* If something is *inferior*, it is lower in value and quality.

infinitely (ĭn´fə-nĭt-lē) *adv.* *Infinitely* means to a great extent, or with no limits.

inquire (ĭn-kwīr´) *v.* If you *inquire* about something, you ask about it.

insulate (ĭn´sə-lāt´) *v.* When you *insulate* something, you prevent the passage of heat through it.

GLOSSARY OF CRITICAL VOCABULARY

interaction (ĭn′tər-ăk′shən) *n.* An *interaction* occurs when people speak or otherwise are in contact with one another.

inundate (ĭn′ŭn-dāt′) *v.* To *inundate* is to overpower with a huge amount of something.

irrelevant (ĭ-rĕl′ə-vənt) *adj.* Something that is *irrelevant* is unrelated to the matter under consideration.

isolate (ī′sə-lāt′) *v.* When you *isolate* something, you separate it so that it is apart or alone.

latch (lăch) *v.* To *latch* means to hold onto or get hold of.

lobby (lŏb′ē) *v.* To *lobby* is to attempt to influence politicians to support the cause that you represent.

madame (mə-dăm′) *n. Madame* is a form of polite address for a woman.

mascot (măs′kŏt′) *n.* A *mascot* is a person, animal, or object used as the symbol of an organization, such as a sports team.

median (mē′dē-ən) *n.* A *median* is a dividing area between opposing lanes of traffic on a highway or road.

metabolism (mĭ-tăb′ə-lĭz′əm) *n.* A living thing's *metabolism* is the chemical processes that give it energy and produce growth.

mistrust (mĭs-trŭst′) *v.* To *mistrust* is to be without confidence or trust.

moderate (mŏd′ər-ĭt) *adj.* When something is kept *moderate*, it is kept within a certain limit.

moot (mo͞ot) *adj.* Something that is *moot* is unimportant or irrelevant.

muse (myo͞oz) *v.* When you *muse*, you say something thoughtfully.

mutual (myo͞o′cho͞o-əl) *adj.* Something is *mutual* when everyone treats each other the same way or shares the same feeling.

navigation (năv′ĭ-gā′shən) *n.* The *navigation* of a ship or boat is the act of guiding it along a planned course.

negotiate (nĭ-gō′shē-āt′) *v.* When you *negotiate*, you work with others to reach an agreement.

obituary (ō-bĭch′o͞o-ĕr′ē) *n.* An *obituary* is a public notice of a person's death.

obsess (əb-sĕs′) *v.* If you *obsess* over something, your mind is filled with thinking about a single topic, idea, or feeling.

pendulum (pĕn′jə-ləm) *n.* A *pendulum* is a weight that is hung so that it can swing freely. Sometimes it is used in timing the workings of certain clocks.

plague (plāg) *v.* To *plague* something is to cause hardship or suffering for it.

porthole (pôrt′hōl′) *n.* A *porthole* is a circular window on a boat or ship.

possession (pə-zĕsh′ən) *n.* A *possession* is something you own.

precaution (prĭ-kô′shən) *n.* A *precaution* is an action taken to avoid possible danger.

procession (prə-sĕsh′ən) *n.* In a *procession*, people or things move along in an orderly and serious way.

prominent (prŏm′ə-nənt) *adj.* If something is *prominent*, it stands out.

prowess (prou′ĭs) *n. Prowess* is the strength and courage someone has.

radiation (rā′dē-ā′shən) *n. Radiation* is energy transmitted in the form of waves or particles.

recede (rĭ-sēd′) *v.* To *recede* means to become fainter or more distant.

reformer (rĭ-fôrm′ər) *n.* A *reformer* seeks to improve or correct practices or behaviors that cause harm.

reliable (rĭ-lī′ə-bəl) *adj.* A person or object that can be trusted, or depended on, is *reliable*.

remorseful (rĭ-môrs′fəl) *adj.* If you are *remorseful*, you feel very sorry about something that you have done.

repulse (rĭ-pŭls′) *v.* Something that *repulses* you makes you want to reject it because you find it disgusting.

restrictive (rĭ-strĭk′tĭv) *adj.* When something is *restrictive*, it is limiting in some way.

ruse (ro͞oz) *n.* A *ruse* is a plan meant to deceive someone.

GLOSSARY OF CRITICAL VOCABULARY

scarcity (skâr′sĭ-tē) *n.* When you experience a *scarcity* of something, you have a shortage or lack of that thing.

scurry (skûr′ē) *v.* To *scurry* means to hurry along with light footsteps.

sketchy (skĕch′ē) *adj.* If someone or something seems *sketchy*, you doubt its authenticity or trustworthiness.

splinter (splĭn′tĕr) *v.* To *splinter* means to break up into sharp, thin pieces.

submerge (səb-mûrj′) *v.* To *submerge* is to descend beneath the surface of the water.

subtly (sŭt′lē) *adv.* To do something *subtly* means to do it in a manner hard to notice or perceive—that is, not obviously.

suede (swād) *n.* *Suede* is leather that is treated to be fuzzy and soft.

swell (swĕl) *n.* A *swell* is a long, unbroken wave.

syringe (sə-rĭnj′) *n.* A *syringe* is a medical instrument used to inject fluids into the body.

talon (tăl′ən) *n.* A *talon* is the claw of a bird of prey.

token (tō′kən) *n.* A *token* serves as an expression or a sign of something else.

turnover (tûrn′ō′vər) *n.* In basketball, a *turnover* is a loss of possession of the ball.

upright (ŭp′rīt′) *adv.* Someone or something that sits or stands *upright* is in a strictly vertical position.

utilization (yōōt′l-ĭ-zā′shən) *n.* *Utilization* is when you put something to use in an effective way.

wholly (hō′lē) *adv.* If a speech deals *wholly* with the history of the solar system, that is the only topic the speaker discusses.

Index of Skills

Key

Teacher's Edition subject entries and page references are printed in **boldface** type. Subject entries and page references that apply to both the Student Edition and the Teacher's Edition appear in lightface type.

A

abbreviations, 277
absolute language. *See* Extreme or Absolute Language (Notice & Note)
academic citations, 506
Academic Vocabulary, 1, 21, 33, 43, 55, 67, 79, 97, 109, 121, 131, 143, 159, 167, 176, 181, 193, 205, 215, 225, 235, 239, 249, 258, 263, 275, 301, 311, 321, 325, 335, 343, 354, 361, 377, 389, 401, 413, 421, 430, 435, 447, 453, 465, 475, 487, 497, 508
acknowledgments, 267
active listening, 145, 241
adjectives, 26, 29, 35
adverbs, 72, 75, 81
Again and Again (Notice & Note), 3, 9, 11, 15, 84, 99, 105, 170, 222, 231, 252, 293, 348, 418, 424, 502
Aha Moment (Notice & Note), 3, 15, 16, 84, 98, 106, 129, 170, 252, 255, 290, 348, 363, 372, 374, 424, 427, 502
alliteration, 37, 136, 144, 234, 469
allusions, 474
analysis. *See also* Analyze the Text
    arguments, 185, 188, 190, 327, 329, 332, 338–339
    author's purpose, 305, 308
    characters, 59, 61–63, 65, 101, 103, 107
    conflict, 59, 61, 63, 101, 104, 106
    digital texts, 244
    documentaries, 450
    drama, 147, 149–151, 153, 155–156
    figurative language, 197, 200
    folk tales, 125, 128
    form in poetry, 37, 40
    free verse poetry, 469, 472–473
    graphical elements, 315, 318
    history writing, 477, 479, 481–482, 484
    humor, 125, 127, 147, 150–151, 153–154
    key ideas, 481
    lyric poetry, 230, 237
    media, 163–164, 166, 243, 248, 250, 324, 452
    memoirs, 199, 202
    metaphor and personification, 406, 408
    mood, 136–137, 140, 279–295
    myths, 25, 27–28
    odes, 229, 232
    organizational patterns, 267, 393, 395, 397–398
    plot, 5, 8, 10, 17–18
    point of view, 185, 188–189, 365–368, 373–376, 381–383, 386, 439–441
    predictions, 385
    punctuation and tone, 38, 39
    realistic fiction, 455, 458, 461–462
    repetition, 305, 308
    rhetorical devices, 327, 330, 332, 340, 342
    rhyme and rhyme scheme, 135, 137, 140, 210, 212
    science fiction, 279, 282, 285, 288, 296, 298
    setting, 59, 61, 63
    sonnets, 209, 212
    sound devices, 136–137
    text structure, 71–77, 267, 270, 273, 491, 494–495
    themes, 217, 220, 222, 316, 318, 470, 472
    two-voice poetry, 415, 417
    verse novels, 405, 407–408, 410
Analyze the Text, 20, 32, 42, 54, 66, 78, 82, 108, 120, 130, 142, 144, 158, 192, 204, 214, 224, 234, 238, 240, 274, 300, 310, 320, 334, 342, 346, 376, 388, 400, 412, 420, 422, 446, 464, 474, 486, 496, 500
Anchor Questions (Notice & Note), 2–3, 84, 98–99, 170, 182–183, 252, 264, 265, 348, 362–363, 424, 436–437, 502
animation, 244, 322
annotate
    arguments, 188, 190, 329, 332, 338–339
    author's purpose, 47, 50, 52, 115, 117, 308
    characters, 61–63, 65, 103, 107
    complex sentences, 220, 331
    conflict, 104, 106
    drama, 149–151, 153, 155–156
    figurative language, 200
    free verse poetry, 472–473
    graphical elements, 318
    history writing, 479, 481–482, 484
    humor, 127, 150–151, 153–154
    inferences, 7, 14, 17, 417
    key ideas, 480–481, 484
    lyric poetry, 237
    memoirs, 199, 202
    metaphor and personification, 408
    as monitoring strategy, 217
    mood, 137, 140, 281–295
    myths, 27–28
    odes, 232
    organizational patterns, 270, 395, 397–398
    paraphrasing, 493–494
    plot, 8, 10, 17–18
    poetic form, 40
    point of view, 188–189, 367–368, 373, 375, 383, 386, 441
    predictions, 385–386
    punctuation and tone, 39
    questions generated about text, 442
    realistic fiction, 458, 461–462
    repetition, 308
    rhetorical devices, 330, 332, 340
    rhyme and rhyme scheme, 137, 140, 212
    science fiction, 282, 285, 288, 296, 298
    setting and conflict, 61, 63
    set a purpose, 368–369, 372–373, 396, 398
    sonnets, 212
    text structure, 73–77, 270, 273, 494–495
    themes, 30, 220, 222, 318, 472
    traits of characters, 457–460, 463
    two-voice poetry, 417
    verse novels, 407–408, 410
Annotation Model, 6, 26, 38, 46, 60, 72, 102, 114, 126, 136, 148, 186, 198, 210, 218, 230, 268, 280, 306, 316, 328, 366, 382, 394, 406, 416, 440, 456, 470, 478, 492
antecedents, 123, 355, 478, 481, 489
Applying Academic Vocabulary, 9, 28, 49, 105, 117, 152, 189, 201, 291, 331, 385, 409, 459, 484
argumentative essay, 350–356
    conclusion, 350
    develop, 352–353
    edit, 355
    introduction, 350, 353
    plan, 263, 351–352
    publish, 355
    revise, 354
    scoring guide, 356
    writing prompt, 350
arguments. *See also* argumentative essays
    analysis of, 185, 188, 190, 327, 329, 332, 338–339
    claims in, 185, 305, 327
    comparison of, 192, 310, 326, 346
    counterarguments, 185, 327
    critique of, 342
    drawing conclusions from, 334
    evaluation of, 310, 332, 342
    evidence for, 192, 327, 334
    Genre Elements, 185, 305, 327, 353
    inferences from, 190, 334
    reasons for, 327
    setting a purpose in, 187, 307
    summaries of, 192, 310, 342
    support for, 185, 327
    tracing reasoning of, 327
articles
    author's purpose in, 113, 115, 117
    informational, 465
    news, 45, 79
association appeals, 243
assonance, 136, 144
audience
    for arguments, 351
    eye contact with, 94
    for infographics, 109
    for informational essays, 86
    for narratives, 255
    in panel discussions, 511
    persuasive media and, 243
    for presentations, 173
author's message, 476, 490, 500
author's point of view, 439, 477
author's purpose
    analysis of, 305, 308
    in articles, 113, 115, 117
    comparison of, 476, 490, 500
    connections and, 52
    critiques of, 50, 117
    drawing conclusions regarding, 47, 446
    inferences regarding, 120
    in informational texts, 45, 47, 50, 52

B

background reading, 87, 173, 255, 351, 427, 505
bandwagon appeals, 243
bias, 243
Big Questions (Notice & Note), 84, 170, 183, 190, 252, 265, 271, 348, 424, 437, 443, 480, 502
biography, 45
brainstorming, 83, 87, 169, 251, 321, 377

C

capitalization
    as graphical element, 315
    in poetry, 209, 469
    proper nouns, 60, 268, 272, 277
    uses of, 62, 69
cause-and-effect relationships, 78, 267, 324, 388, 400, 446
characterization, 59, 168, 365
characters
    analysis of, 59, 61–63, 65, 101, 103, 107
    cast of, 147, 163
    comparison of, 32, 42, 82, 300
    connections and, 224
    costumes of, 166
    critique of, 224
    discussion of, 67
    inferences regarding, 103, 464
    interpretations and, 61, 108, 300
    motivations of, 101
    personality of, 59, 101, 455
    predictions regarding, 66, 300
    in realistic fiction, 455
    setting as influence on, 5
    in short story, 427
    traits of, 59, 101, 167, 455, 457–460, 463
chronological order, 71, 254, 256, 393, 491
citations, academic, 506
Cite Evidence
    for arguments, 192, 334
    for drawing conclusions, 54, 113, 117–118
    for fake videos, 120
    in history writing, 486, 496
    from informational texts, 45, 48, 50, 274
    for key ideas, 484
    for memoir, 204
    from myth, 32
    from short story, 108
    of structure informing readers of events, 78

claims, in arguments, 185, 305, 327
classification patterns, 267
clauses, 23, 111, 337. *See also* dependent clauses; independent clauses
climax, 5, 428
Close Read Screencast, 10, 155, 200, 232, 397, 442
coherence of ideas, 350, 504
Collaborate & Compare, 82–83, 144–145, 168–169, 240–241, 250–251, 346–347, 422–423, 500–501
commas
    in compound sentences, 23
    conjunctive adverbs and, 81
    coordinate adjectives and, 35
    effective use of, 26, 440, 444
    interpretation of, 29, 128
    for introductory phrases, 306, 307, 313, 449
    in pace of stories, 126
    for pauses, 133
    uses of, 449
comma splices, 227, 345, 382, 391
commonly confused words, 259, 366, 379
compare and contrast
    characters and characterization, 108, 168
    narrators, 452
comparisons. *See also* Collaborate & Compare; compare and contrast
    arguments, 192, 310, 326, 346
    author's purpose and message, 476, 490, 500
    characters, 32, 42, 82, 300
    conflict, 20
    genres, 58, 70
    graphical elements, 318
    in informational texts, 54
    media, 242, 250
    memoir, 202
    moods, 134, 144
    poetry, 228, 240–241, 320, 404
    sources, 486
    text structure, 274
    themes, 422–423
    versions, 146, 162, 168
complete predicates, 23
complete subjects, 23
complex sentences
    annotations, 220, 331
    comma splices, 227, 345, 382, 391
    complete, 345
    dependent clauses in, 6, 195, 218, 227, 328, 337
    independent clauses in, 6, 23, 161, 195, 218, 227, 337
    subject-verb agreement in, 227, 345, 394, 397, 403

    subordinating conjunctions in, 148, 161, 186, 195, 328
composition, 164
compound sentences, 6, 23
comprehension monitoring, 217, 219–220, 393
conclusions. *See also* drawing conclusions
    argumentative essay, 350
    friendly letter, 131
    informational essay, 86
    personal narrative, 159, 254
    research report, 504
    short story, 426
conflict
    analysis of, 59, 61, 63, 101, 104, 106
    comparison of, 20
    in drama, 147
    external, 59, 101
    foreshadowing, 20
    internal, 59, 101
    in realistic fiction, 455
    resolution of, 5, 101, 428
    setting as influence on, 5, 101
    in short story, 427
conjunctions. *See also* subordinating conjunctions
    coordinating, 23, 81, 449
    correlative, 114, 123, 186, 195
conjunctive adverbs, 72, 75, 81
connect
    in arguments, 188
    author's purpose and, 52
    characters and, 224
    in comparison of texts, 82
    in folk tales, 128
    foreshadowing and, 20
    to graphical elements, 214
    in informational texts, 78
    in media, 250
    metaphors and, 412
    as monitoring strategy, 217
    in organizational patterns, 398
    questions generated about text and, 442
    in setting a purpose for texts, 396
    research, 20, 54, 67, 78, 108, 120, 128, 158, 188, 214, 224, 238, 274, 324, 396, 408, 412, 452, 474, 480, 500
    themes and, 220
connotations, 56, 243, 336, 498
consistent verb tenses
    analysis of, 461
    exceptions to, 57, 207, 303, 467
    importance of, 46, 198, 280, 456
    in sentences and paragraphs, 91
consonance, 136, 144
constructive feedback, 55, 131

context clues, 80, 110, 194, 226, 390, 456
contradictions. *See* Contrasts and Contradictions (Notice & Note)
contrast clues, 80
Contrasts and Contradictions (Notice & Note), 74, 76, 84, 99, 105, 116, 170, 183, 187, 202, 252, 284, 348, 408, 424, 459–460, 502. *See also* compare and contrast
controlling ideas
    of documentaries, 452
    in explanatory paragraphs, 33
    in film adaptations, 21
    in history writing, 477
    identifying, 439
    in informational essays, 55, 86, 89
    in informative reports, 275
    in literary analysis, 205
    in multimodal presentations, 172, 175
    in play versions, 169
    of news articles, 79
    in research reports, 504
coordinate adjectives, 26, 29, 35
coordinating conjunctions, 23, 81, 449
correlative conjunctions, 114, 123, 186, 195
correspondence. *See* letters
counterarguments, 185, 327
couplets, 209
credibility of sources, 192, 347
Critical Vocabulary, 6, 22, 26, 34, 46, 56, 60, 68, 72, 80, 102, 110, 114, 122, 126, 132, 148, 160, 186, 194, 198, 206, 218, 226, 268, 276, 280, 302, 306, 312, 328, 336, 344, 366, 378, 382, 390, 394, 402, 440, 448, 456, 466, 478, 488, 492, 498
critique
    arguments, 342
    author's purpose, 50, 117
    characters, 224
    history writing, 486, 496
    memoirs, 199
    metaphor and personification, 408
    oral, 43, 169
    play, 169
    poetry, 43, 142, 238, 421
    point of view, 188, 368, 383
    posters, 248–250
    production images, 163, 164, 166, 169
    realistic fiction, 458
    rhymes, 214
    setting a purpose for texts, 398
    supporting evidence, 446
    text structure, 495
    themes, 30

verb tense, 52
videos, 93–94, 324, 465

D

denotations, 56, 336, 498
dependent clauses
    in complex sentences, 6, 195, 218, 227, 328, 337
    subordinating conjunctions in, 23, 328, 337
descriptive patterns, 393
details
    evaluation of, 45, 48, 50
    supporting, 89, 477
dialogue
    in drama, 147, 163
    humor in, 125
    punctuation of, 431
    in realistic fiction, 455
    writing, 167
diction, 135, 144, 230
dictionary, 122, 206, 344
direct address, nouns/pronouns of, 133, 327
direct quotations, 431
disadvantages and advantages pattern, 267
discuss
    advertisements, 55
    characters, 67
    explanations, 33
    informational texts, 55
    opinions, 79, 225
    panel discussions, 511–512
    plot, 21
    presentations, 145
    primary sources, 487
    research reports, 447
    rules for, 512
    storyboard, 121
    sustainability, 193
    timelines, 275
    video games, 389
    Word Networks, 1, 97, 181, 263, 361, 435
documentary, 450–452
draft
    argumentative essay, 352–353
    edit, 91, 259, 355
    informational essay, 88–89
    multimodal presentation, 174–175
    peer review of, 90, 176, 258, 354, 430, 508
    personal narrative, 256–257
    research report, 506–507
    revise, 90, 176, 258, 354
    short story, 428–429
    two-voice poetry, 421

drama, 147, 149–151, 153, 155–156
dramatic readings, 143
draw conclusions
    from argument, 334
    from author's purpose, 47, 446
    for characters, 63, 107
    for conflict, 104
    in drama, 151, 158
    evidence for, 54, 113, 117–118
    in folk tales, 130
    from mood, 291
    in myth, 27
    in plot analysis, 17
    in poetry, 214
    in short story, 66
    from themes, 318, 320
    from videos, 248, 250, 324

E

edit
    argumentative essay, 355
    informational essay, 91
    multimodal presentation, 176
    personal narrative, 259
    research report, 509
    short story, 431
emotional appeals, 243
encyclopedias, 324
endnotes, 267
end rhyme, 135, 225
enunciation, 94, 177, 205, 358, 512
English Learner Support, 1, 2, 6, 9, 10, 11, 12, 13, 14, 15, 17, 19, 21, 22, 23, 24, 25, 29, 30, 31, 32, 33, 34, 35, 36, 37, 38, 39, 40, 41, 43, 45, 46, 48, 49, 50, 51, 52, 53, 55, 56, 57, 59, 62, 63, 64, 67, 68, 69, 71, 73, 75, 76, 77, 79, 80, 81, 82, 84, 87, 88, 89, 90, 91, 93, 96, 97, 101, 102, 103, 104, 107, 109, 110, 111, 113, 114, 115, 116, 117, 118, 119, 121, 122, 123, 125, 127, 128, 129, 132, 133, 137, 138, 139, 141, 143, 144, 145, 147, 148, 149, 150, 151, 152, 154, 156, 157, 159, 160, 161, 163, 164, 165, 167, 168, 169, 170, 173, 174, 175, 176, 177, 180, 186, 189, 191, 194, 195, 198, 199, 200, 201, 202, 203, 206, 207, 210, 211, 212, 213, 215, 219, 221, 223, 226, 227, 229, 230, 231, 232, 233, 235, 236, 237, 239, 240, 244, 245, 247, 248, 250, 255, 256, 257, 258, 259, 262, 268, 269, 271, 272, 273, 275, 276, 277, 280, 281, 283, 284, 285, 286, 289,
290, 292, 299, 302, 303, 306, 307, 309, 312, 316, 317, 318, 322, 324, 325, 328, 329, 331, 333, 338, 341, 344, 345, 346, 348, 351, 352, 353, 354, 355, 357, 360, 366, 367, 369, 371, 373, 375, 378, 379, 382, 383, 384, 385, 386, 387, 389, 390, 391, 394, 395, 396, 397, 398, 399, 402, 406, 407, 409, 410, 411, 413, 416, 417, 418, 419, 421, 422, 424, 427, 428, 429, 430, 431, 434, 440, 441, 442, 444, 445, 448, 449, 450, 453, 456, 457, 458, 459, 462, 463, 466, 467, 470, 471, 472, 473, 478, 479, 483, 485, 487, 489, 492, 495, 498, 499, 500, 502, 506, 507, 508, 509, 511

essays. See also argumentative essays; informational essays
    opinion, 121
    personal, 439, 441, 453
etymology, 160, 312, 378, 448
evaluate
    argument, 310, 332, 342
    details, 45, 48, 50
    drama, 158
    figurative language, 204
    folk tales, 130
    informational text, 54, 400
    media, 166
    poetic, 234, 238
    primary sources, 496
    realistic fiction, 461–462, 464
    rhetorical devices, 340
    tone, 474
    videos, 324
    visual elements, 248
evidence. See also Cite Evidence
    for arguments, 192, 327, 334
    for controlling ideas, 439
    critique of, 446
    for drawing conclusions, 54, 113, 117–118
    for inferences, 5, 416, 420
    for panel discussion, 511
    supporting details as, 89
    for theme, 470
exaggeration, 125
exposition, 5, 428
expository essays. See informational essays; writing activities
external conflict, 59, 101
Extreme or Absolute Language (Notice & Note), 84, 170, 182, 188, 190, 252, 332, 348, 424, 436, 443, 502
eye contact, 94, 169, 177, 358, 512

F

facial expressions, 94, 143, 163, 164, 169, 177, 358, 512
falling action, 5, 428
feedback
    constructive, 55, 131
    listening to, 90, 176, 258, 354, 430, 508
    positive, 321
fiction. See also short story
    historical, 497
    realistic, 5, 455, 458, 461–462, 464
    science fiction, 279–282, 285, 288, 296, 298
figurative language
    analysis of, 197, 200
    annotations, 200
    evaluation of, 204
    metaphors, 197, 240, 406, 408, 412
    mood and, 125
    personification, 197, 240, 406, 408
    in poetry, 37, 229, 240
films. See videos
first-person point of view, 365, 439
folk tales, 125, 127–128
footage, 244, 322, 450
footnotes, 267, 274
For Struggling Students, **358**
foreshadowing, 5, 20, 376
form of poetry, 37, 40, 43, 209
free verse poetry, 225, 230, 315, 469, 472–473, 475

G

gathering information
    argument, 275, 301, 311, 321, 325, 335, 343
    informational essay, 21, 33, 43, 55, 67, 79
    multimodal presentation, 109, 121, 131, 143, 159, 167
    personal narrative, 193, 205, 215, 225, 235, 239, 249
    research, 224, 251, 347, 501
    research report, 447, 453, 465, 475, 487, 497
    short story, 377, 389, 401, 413, 421
generalizations, 243, 327
generating questions, 166, 388, 439, 442, 505
Genre Elements
    argument, 185, 305, 327, 353
    comparison of, 58, 70
    documentary, 450
    drama, 147
    folk tale, 125

informational text, 45, 71, 113, 267, 381, 393, 477, 491
media, 163, 243, 322
memoir, 197
myth, 25, 27–28
personal essay, 439
personal narrative, 257
poetry, 37, 135, 209, 229, 315
realistic fiction, 455
research of, 300
science fiction, 279
short story, 5, 59, 101, 217, 365, 429
two-voice poetry, 415
verse novel, 405
gestures, 94, 143, 167, 169, 177, 358, 512
glittering generalizations, 243
glossaries, 132, 344
Glossary of Academic Vocabulary, R8
Glossary of Critical Vocabulary, R9–R12
graphical elements
    analysis of, 315, 318
    in poetry, 209, 214, 315, 415
    in verse novels, 405
    in videos, 322
graphic novels, 497
graphic organizers, 279, 301
Greek roots, 276
group work. *See* discussions

H

haikus, 37
historical fiction, 497
historical sources, 142, 166
history writing, 477, 479, 481–482, 484, 486, 496
how-to instructions, 45
human-interest stories, 79
humor
    in drama, 147, 150–151, 153–154
    in folk tales, 125, 127
    in production images, 164
    opinions on, 131

I

ideas. *See also* controlling ideas
    clarification of, 94, 225
    coherence of, 350, 504
    key ideas, 477, 480–481, 484
    organization of, 88, 174, 256, 352, 428, 506
    transitions between, 33, 55, 121, 159, 161
illusions, 121, 172–175
illustrations, 109

imagery, 37, 125, 135, 229
Improve Reading Fluency, 40, 50, 138, 153, 222, 232, 288, 372, 408, 461, 481
indefinite pronouns, 355
independent clauses
    in complex sentences, 6, 23, 161, 195, 218, 227, 337
    in compound sentences, 6
    conjunctive adverbs in connection of, 72, 81
Independent Reading, 84–85, 170–171, 252–253, 348–349, 424–425, 502–503
inference
    annotations for, 7, 14, 17
    argument, 190, 334
    author's purpose, 120
    characters, 103, 464
    comparison of texts, 82
    defined, 416
    documentary, 452
    drama, 150, 158
    evidence to support, 5, 416, 420
    from footnotes, 274
    history writing, 479, 481, 484, 486
    humor, 151, 153
    interpretation of, 7, 14, 17
    mood, 286, 293
    myth, 28
    plot, 18
    poetry, 40, 214, 320, 416–417
    punctuation and tone, 39
    from repetition, 310
    rhetorical devices, 340
    setting and conflict, 63
    short story, 66
    speaker, 142, 412
    text structure, 73–74, 77
    theme, 25, 224, 474
    traits of characters, 458, 460
    verse novel, 408
infographic, 109, 401
informational article, 465
informational essay, 86–94
    conclusion, 86
    develop, 88–89
    edit, 91
    introduction, 55, 86, 89
    plan, 1, 87–88
    present, 93–94
    publish, 91
    revise, 90
    scoring guide, 92
    writing prompt, 86
informational text
    author's purpose, 45, 47, 50, 52

cite evidence and evaluate details, 45, 48, 50, 274
comparison, 54
connections, 78
discussion, 55
evaluation, 54, 400
Genre Elements, 45, 71, 113, 267, 381, 393, 477, 491
interpretation, 54
prediction, 381, 385–386
structure, 71–77, 267, 270, 273, 491, 494–495
information gathering. *See* gathering information
information requests, 67, 193, 413
informative report, 275
Instructional Overview and Resources, 1A–1D, 96A–96D, 180A–180D, 262A–262D, 364A–364D, 436A–436D
internal conflict, 59, 101
interpret
    allusions, 474
    argument, 329, 338
    author's purpose, 308
    character, 61, 108, 300, 459
    conflict, 106, 130
    history writing, 482
    inference, 7, 14, 17
    informational text, 54, 120
    lyric poetry, 237
    memoir, 204
    mood, 137, 140, 281, 284, 287, 289
    ode, 232
    paraphrasing, 493–494
    poetry, 42, 142, 234, 238, 320, 420
    production images, 166
    rhetorical devices, 342
    rhyme and rhyme scheme, 137, 140, 212
    science fiction, 282
    short story, 66
    theme, 222, 472
    titles, 376, 400
    video, 324
    visual elements, 248
interview, 450
introductory phrases, 306, 307, 313, 449
irony, 125, 147
Italian sonnet, 209, 210

K

key ideas, 477, 480–481, 484

L

Language Conventions. *See also* capitalization; clauses; commas; complex sentences; subject-verb agreement; subordinating conjunctions; tense of verbs
    comma splices, 227, 345, 382, 391
    commonly confused words, 259, 366, 379
    conjunctive adverbs, 72, 75, 81
    coordinate adjectives, 26, 29, 35
    correlative conjunctions, 114, 123, 186, 195
    introductory phrases, 306, 307, 313, 449
    prepositional phrases, 102, 105, 111, 133, 492, 499
    pronoun-antecedent agreement, 123, 355, 478, 481, 489
    proper nouns, 60, 268, 272, 277
    punctuation of dialogue, 431
    relative pronouns, 328, 331, 337, 339
    run-on sentences, 227, 345, 382, 391
    sentence structure, 6, 13, 23
Language X-Ray: English Learning Support, 86B, 172B, 350B, 426B, 504B
Latin roots, 22, 34, 302, 488
Learning Mindset, 2, 4, 5, 20, 45, 58, 66, 84, 86, 95, 96, 100, 134, 135, 136, 142, 146, 158, 166, 170, 172, 179, 180, 184, 192, 196, 204, 252, 254, 261, 262, 266, 274, 278, 300, 348, 350, 359, 360, 364, 376, 392, 400, 424, 426, 433, 434, 454, 464, 476, 486, 502, 504, 513
letter
    expression of opinion, 249, 301, 475
    formal, 335
    friendly, 131, 193, 301, 413
    request, 67, 193, 413
lighting, 164
limerick, 37
lines in poetry, 37, 209, 315, 469
listening
    active, 145, 241
    alliterative sounds, 37
    feedback, 90, 176, 258, 354, 430, 508
    group discussions, 55, 79
    poetry, 235, 239, 311, 321
    presentations, 94, 145, 177, 241, 358
    retelling, 131
    sonnet, 215
loaded language, 243, 327, 335
logical appeals, 243
logical fallacies. *See* loaded language; sweeping generalizations

loyalty appeals, 243
lyric poetry, 229, 230, 237, 239

M

main ideas and details, 79, 176, 178
media. *See also* videos
    analysis, 163–164, 166, 243, 248, 250, 324, 452
    comparison, 242, 250
    digital text, 244
    documentary, 450–452
    Genre Elements, 163, 243, 322
    persuasive, 243, 250
    podcast, 205, 357–358, 413, 453
    poster, 244, 248–251
media campaign, 201
melody, 230, 239
memoirs, 197, 199, 202, 204
Memory Moment (Notice & Note), 2, 13, 16, 64, 84, 170, 236, 252, 348, 424, 471, 502
mental images, 125, 406, 412, 469
Mentor Text, 44A, 86, 89, 112A, 172, 175, 196A, 254, 257, 304A, 350, 353, 362A, 364, 426, 439, 490A, 504, 507
message of author, 476, 490, 500
metaphors, 197, 240, 406, 408, 412
meter, 37, 209, 229
monitoring comprehension, 217, 219–220, 393
mood
    analysis of, 136–137, 140, 279–295
    lighting and, 164
    of plays, 147
    of poetry, 38, 134–137, 140, 144, 229, 469
motivations of characters, 101
multimodal presentation, 172–178
    deliver, 177
    develop, 174–175
    introduction, 175
    plan, 97, 173–174
    practice, 177
    revise, 176
    scoring guide, 178
    storyboard, 121
    write prompt, 172
music, 244, 322
myths, 25, 27–28

N

narration, 244, 322, 450, 452
narrative structure, 254–260, 365, 426–432
narrators, 59, 365
natural gestures, 143, 169, 177
negative connotations, 336, 498
nonverbal techniques, 94, 177, 358, 512
Notice & Note
    Again and Again, 3, 9, 11, 15, 84, 99, 105, 170, 222, 231, 252, 293, 348, 418, 424, 502
    Aha Moment, 3, 15, 16, 84, 98, 106, 129, 170, 252, 290, 348, 363, 372, 374, 424, 502
    Anchor Questions, 2–3, 84, 98–99, 170, 182–183, 252, 264–265, 348, 362–363, 424, 436–437, 502
    Annotation Model, 6, 26, 38, 46, 60, 72, 102, 114, 126, 136, 148, 186, 198, 210, 218, 230, 268, 280, 306, 316, 328, 366, 382, 394, 406, 416, 440, 456, 470, 478, 492
    Big Questions, 84, 170, 183, 190, 252, 265, 271, 348, 424, 437, 443, 480, 502
    Contrasts and Contradictions, 74, 76, 84, 99, 105, 116, 170, 183, 187, 202, 252, 284, 348, 408, 424, 459–460, 502
    Extreme or Absolute Language, 84, 170, 182, 188, 190, 252, 332, 348, 424, 436, 443, 502
    Memory Moment, 2, 13, 16, 64, 84, 170, 236, 252, 348, 424, 471, 502
    Numbers and Stats, 84, 170, 252, 264, 270, 340, 348, 424, 502
    Quoted Words, 48, 84, 170, 252, 348, 384, 396, 424, 437, 443, 494, 502
    Tough Questions, 84, 170, 252, 348, 362, 371, 424, 502
    Word Gaps, 84, 170, 252, 265, 269, 271, 348, 424, 502
    Words of the Wiser, 28, 84, 156, 170, 252, 317, 348, 363, 370, 409, 424, 502
nouns
    of direct address, 133
    proper, 60, 268, 272, 277
novels, 405, 407–408, 410, 497
Numbers and Stats (Notice & Note), 84, 170, 252, 264, 270, 340, 348, 424, 502

O

objective point of view, 185, 188–189, 381, 383, 386, 439, 477
objective sources, 505
objective summaries, 79, 389
odes, 229, 232, 235, 487
omniscient point of view, 365

opinion essays, 121
opinions
    in arguments, 185
    discussion of, 79, 225
    on humor, 131
    in letters, 249, 301, 475
oral critiques, 43, 169
oral traditions, 125, 130
organizational patterns, 267, 270, 393, 395, 397–398
organization of ideas, 88, 174, 256, 352, 428, 506
organizations, 277, 464

P

panel discussion, 511–512
parallel structure, 123
paraphrasing, 491, 493–494, 509
parts of speech, 122, 123, 206, 344. *See also specific parts of speech*
past perfect tense, 57, 207
past tense, 52, 57, 201, 207, 290, 303
patterns
    descriptive, 393
    identifying, 420
    organizational, 267, 270, 393, 395, 397–398
    repetition, 136, 144, 305, 308, 310–311
    structural, 71
peer review, 90, 176, 258, 354, 430, 508
personal essays, 439, 441, 453
personal experiences
    for inferences, 416
    in memoirs, 197
    in personal narratives, 254, 257
    use in essay planning, 87
personality of characters, 59, 101, 455
personal narrative, 254–260
    conclusion, 159, 254
    develop, 256–257
    edit, 259
    genre characteristics, 257
    introduction, 254, 257
    plan, 181, 255–256
    publish, 259
    revise, 258
    scoring guide, 260
    write, 159, 254–260, 325
personification, 197, 240, 406, 408
persuasive media, 243, 250
phrases
    introductory, 306, 307, 313, 449
    prepositional, 102, 105, 111, 133, 492, 499

plagiarism, 501, 506, 509
plan
    argumentative essay, 263, 351–352
    film critique, 93
    informational essay, 1, 87–88
    multimodal presentation, 97, 173–174
    personal narrative, 181, 255–256
    podcast, 357
    poster, 251
    research report, 435, 505–506
    short story, 361, 427–428
    video, 251
plays and playwrights, 147, 161, 163, 168
plot
    analysis of, 5, 8, 10, 17–18
    annotations, 8, 10, 17–18
    conflict in, 59
    discussion of, 21
    in drama, 147
    draw conclusions, 17
    inferences, 18
    stages of, 5, 428
plural pronouns, 111, 123
podcasts, 205, 357–358, 413, 453
poetic elements and devices. *See also poetry; rhyme and rhyme scheme*
    alliteration, 37, 136, 144, 234, 469
    capitalization, 209, 469
    end rhyme, 135, 225
    figurative language, 37, 229, 240
    lines, 37, 209, 315, 469
    meter, 37, 209, 229
    mood, 38, 134–137, 140, 144, 229, 469
    punctuation, 38, 39, 43, 209, 469
    refrain, 230
    repetition, 136, 144, 469
    rhythm, 37, 43, 136, 143–144, 209, 239
    stanzas, 37, 142, 316, 469
    themes, 316–321, 422–423, 470
poetry. *See also poetic elements and devices*
    comparisons, 228, 240–241, 320, 404
    critiques of, 43, 142, 238, 421
    draw conclusions, 214
    evaluation of, 234, 238
    form of, 37, 40, 43, 209
    free verse, 225, 230, 315, 469, 472–473, 475
    Genre Elements, 37, 135, 209, 229, 315
    inferences, 40, 214, 320, 416–417
    interpretations of, 42, 142, 234, 238, 320, 420

Index of Skills **R17**

listen, 235, 239, 311, 321
lyric, 229, 230, 237, 239
narrative, 405
odes, 229, 232, 235, 487
present, 143, 145
punctuation in, 38, 39, 43, 209
set a purpose, 39, 317, 471
sonnets, 37, 209–212, 215
sound devices in, 37, 135–137, 144, 240
speaker in, 142
tone of, 38, 39, 43, 135, 229, 470, 474
two-voice, 415, 417, 421
voice in, 42, 135, 229, 415
write, 43, 143, 225, 239, 311, 321, 401, 421
point of view
    analysis of, 185, 188–189, 365–368, 373–376, 381–383, 386, 439–441
    author's, 439, 477
    first-person, 365, 439
    objective, 185, 188–189, 381, 383, 386, 439, 477
    omniscient, 365
    in short story, 427
    subjective, 185, 188–189, 381, 383, 386, 439, 477
    third-person, 365
positive connotations, 243, 336, 498
posters, 244, 248–251, 401
predicates, complete, 23
predictions
    author's purpose and, 115
    characters, 66, 300
    humor and, 127
    in informational texts, 381, 385–386
    key ideas, 480
    in plot analysis, 8, 10
    in science fiction, 298
prepositional phrases, 102, 105, 111, 133, 492, 499
presentations. *See also* multimodal presentations
    deliver, 94, 177
    discussion of, 145
    infographic, 401
    informational essay, 93–94
    listen to, 94, 145, 177, 241, 358
    media campaign, 201
    plan, 93
    play version, 169
    podcast, 205, 357–358
    poetry, 143, 145
    poster critique, 249
    practice, 94, 177, 358
    timing in, 177
present tense, 52, 57, 207, 303

primary sources, 477, 487, 496, 505–506
print elements, 244
problem-solution structure, 491
production images, 163, 164, 165, 169
pronouns
    antecedent agreement with, 123, 355, 478, 481, 489
    of direct address, 327
    indefinite, 355
    relative, 328, 331, 337, 339
    singular vs. plural, 111, 123
pronunciation, 122, 132, 206, 344
pronunciation key, R7
proper nouns, 60, 268, 272, 277
publish
    argumentative essay, 355
    informational essay, 91
    personal narrative, 259
    research report, 509
    short story, 431
punctuation. *See also specific types of punctuation*
    of dialogue, 431
    as graphical element, 315
    in poetry, 38, 39, 43, 209, 469
purpose. *See* author's purpose; setting a purpose

Q

qualities of characters. *See* traits of characters
questions
    about text, 439, 442
    as monitoring strategy, 217
    focused, 20, 108
    for research, 388, 505
quotation marks, 431
Quoted Words (Notice & Note), 48, 84, 170, 252, 348, 384, 396, 424, 437, 443, 494, 502

R

rate of speaking, 94, 177, 205, 358, 512
reference resources
    dictionaries, 122, 206, 344
    encyclopedias, 324
    endnotes, 267
    footnotes, 267, 274
    glossaries, 132, 344
    thesaurus, 206, 402
register, 79

relative pronouns, 328, 331, 337, 339
reports, 275. *See also* research reports
research. *See also* search terms; sources
    of author or publisher works, 42
    on careers of living people, 420
    on charities, 446
    of contextual factors, 234
    encyclopedias for, 324
    focused questions in, 20, 108
    generalized, 238
    generate questions, 166, 388, 505
    of genres, 300
    job descriptions, 347
    leads for, 342
    on organizations, 464
    of problems and solutions, 248
    recent, 334
    stay on topic, 120
    trickster tales, 130
research report
    conclusion, 504
    develop, 506–507
    edit, 509
    introduction for, 504
    plan, 435, 505–506
    publish, 509
    revise, 508
    scoring guide, 510
    write, 435, 447, 504–510
resolution of conflict, 5, 101, 428
Resource Logs, R1–R6
revise
    argumentative text, 354
    informational text, 90
    multimodal presentation, 176
    personal narrative, 258
    research report, 508
    short story, 430
rhetorical devices, 136, 144, 305, 308, 310–311, 327, 330, 332, 340, 342, 469
rhetorical questions, 185, 243, 327
rhyme and rhyme scheme
    annotations, 137, 140, 212
    critique, 214
    end rhyme, 135, 225
    interpretation, 137, 140, 212
    mood and, 135, 144
    in odes, 229
    in sonnets, 210, 214
rhythm, 37, 43, 136, 143–144, 209, 239
rising action, 5, 428
roots, 22, 34, 276, 302, 488
rubrics. *See also* scoring guides
    argument, 356
    informational essay, 92
    multimodal presentation, 178
    personal narrative, 260

research report, 510
short story, 432
run-on sentences, 227, 345, 382, 391

S

science fiction, 279–282, 285, 288, 296, 298
science writing, 267
scoring guides
    argumentative text, 356
    informational text, 92
    multimodal presentation, 178
    personal narrative, 260
    research report, 510
    short story, 432
search terms
    general nature, 66
    online research, 32, 66, 214
    specificity, 54, 66, 158, 204, 474
    subtopics, 320
secondary sources, 496, 506
self-sustained reading. *See* Independent Reading
semicolons, 23, 81, 391
sensory language, 469
sentences. *See also* complex sentences
    comma splices, 227, 345, 382, 391
    compound, 6, 23
    consistent verb tenses, 91
    fragmented, 195, 227, 345
    run-on, 227, 345, 382, 391
    simple, 6, 23
    structure, 6, 13, 23
    variety, 86
setting
    analysis of, 59, 61, 63
    conflict and, 5, 101
    in drama, 147
    mood and, 144
    in realistic fiction, 455
    in short story, 427
set a purpose, 365, 368–369, 372–373, 376, 393, 395–396, 398
setting a purpose, 7, 27, 39, 47, 103, 115, 127, 187, 199, 211 219, 269, 281, 307, 317, 323, 367, 383, 441, 451, 457, 471
Shakespearean sonnets, 209, 210
short story
    characters, 59
    conclusion, 426
    develop, 428–429
    edit, 431
    Genre Elements, 5, 59, 101, 217, 365, 429
    introduction, 429
    plan, 361, 427–428

R18   Student Resources

publish, 431
revise, 430
scoring guide, 432
set a purpose, 7, 103, 219, 367, 457
theme, 217, 220, 222, 224
write, 343, 361, 426–432
similes, 197, 240
simple sentences, 6, 23
singular pronouns, 111, 123
small group discussions. *See* discussions
sonnets, 37, 209–212, 215
sound devices, 37, 135–137, 144, 240, 469
sound effects, 163, 450
sound elements, 244, 322, 325
sources. *See also* research
   academic citations, 506
   accuracy of, 505
   comparison of, 486
   credibility of, 192, 347
   current nature of, 412
   historical, 142, 166
   newspapers, 83
   objective, 505
   online research, 42, 78, 83, 192, 310
   patience with, 130
   primary, 477, 487, 496, 505–506
   relevant, 505
   reliability of, 83, 166, 192, 274, 310, 347, 400
   reputable, 452, 474
   secondary, 496, 506
speaker
   inferences, 142, 412
   mood and, 144
   in poetry, 142
   rate of, 94, 177, 205, 358, 512
   in verse novels, 405
   volume of, 94, 177, 205, 358, 512
Speaking and Listening Task
   film critique, 93–94
   panel discussion, 511–512
   podcast, 357–358
spelling, 259, 344, 366, 371, 379
stagecraft, 163, 164, 169
stage directions, 147, 159, 163, 167, 168
stanzas, 37, 142, 316, 469
statistics. *See* Numbers and Stats (Notice & Note)
structure
   of argumentative text, 185, 188, 190, 243, 305, 327, 329, 332, 338, 339, 346, 350–356
   of complex sentences, 6, 23, 161, 218, 227

of informational texts, 71–77, 267, 270, 273, 491, 494–495
parallel, 123
of narratives, 254–260, 365, 426–432
of poetry, 37, 38, 215, 228, 229, 230, 315, 405, 415, 422
of sentences, 6, 13, 23
of texts, 381, 393, 491
style of poetry, 229
subheadings, 393
subjective point of view, 185, 188–189, 381, 383, 386, 439, 477
subjects, complete, 23
subject-verb agreement
   in complex sentences, 227, 345, 394, 397, 403
   correlative conjunctions and, 123
   prepositional phrases and, 102, 105, 111, 492, 499
subordinate clauses. *See* dependent clauses
subordinating conjunctions
   annotations, 150, 190
   in complex sentences, 148, 186, 195, 328
   in dependent clauses, 23, 161, 328, 337
suffixes, 68
summarize
   arguments, 192, 310, 342
   history writing, 496
   main ideas, 400
   objective, 79, 389
   paragraphs, 32, 388
   stanzas, 142
support for arguments, 185, 327
supporting details, 89, 477
supporting evidence. *See* evidence
suspense, 5, 21
sweeping generalizations, 327
syllabication, 344
synonyms, 206, 402
synthesizing
   character costumes, 166
   in comparison of texts, 82
   informational texts, 120
   myths, 32
   poetry, 420
   research information, 251
   themes, 412
   titles, 464

T

tense of verbs, 52, 57, 201, 207, 290, 303. *See also* consistent verb tenses
Text Complexity, 2A, 24A, 36A, 44A, 58A, 70A, 100A, 112A, 124A, 134A, 146A, 162A, 182A, 196A, 208A, 216A, 228A, 242A, 278A, 304A, 314A, 322A, 326A, 362A, 380A, 392A, 404A, 414A, 436A, 450A, 454A, 468A, 476A, 490A
text features, 244, 267, 381
Text in Focus, 7, 27, 115, 199, 231
textual evidence. *See* evidence
Text X-Ray: English Language Support, 2C–2D, 24C–24D, 36C–36D, 44C–44D, 58C–58D, 70C–70D, 100C–100D, 112C–112D, 124C–125D, 146C–146D, 162C–162D, 182C–182d, 196C–196D, 208C–208D, 216C–216D, 228C–228D, 242C–242D, 278C–278D, 304C–304D, 314C–314D, 322C–322D, 326C–326D, 362C–362D, 380C–380D, 392C–392D, 404C–404D, 414C–414D, 436C–436D, 450C–450D, 454C–454D, 468C–468D, 476C–476D, 490C–490D
themes, 25, 30, 217, 220, 222, 224, 316–321, 405, 412, 422–423, 470, 472, 474
thesaurus, 206, 402
thesis statements. *See* controlling ideas
third-person point of view, 365
To Challenge Students..., 18, 29, 48, 63, 87, 130, 156, 169, 173, 214, 224, 241, 246, 255, 271, 287, 295, 340, 351, 374, 388, 412, 427, 458, 474, 483, 505
tone, 21, 38, 39, 43, 79, 125, 131, 135, 147, 229, 305, 381, 439, 470, 474, 477 Tough Questions (Notice & Note), 84, 170, 252, 348, 362, 371, 424, 502
tracing reasoning of arguments, 327
traits of characters, 59, 101, 167, 455, 457–460, 463
transitions, 33, 55, 121, 159, 161

V

verbal techniques, 94, 177, 358, 512
verbs. *See* subject-verb agreement; tense of verbs
verse novels, 405, 407–408, 410
version comparisons, 146, 162, 168
video
   adaptation of, 21
   critique of, 93–94, 324, 465
   draw conclusions, 248, 250, 324
   informational, 322–324
   interpretation, 324
   plan, 251
   sound elements, 244, 322
   visual elements, 244, 322
visual elements, 244, 248, 322, 325
Vocabulary Strategy. *See also* Academic Vocabulary; Critical Vocabulary
   connotations, 56, 243, 336, 498
   context clues, 80, 110, 194, 226, 390, 456
   denotations, 56, 336, 498
   etymology, 160, 312, 378, 448
   glossaries, 132, 344
   reference resources, 122, 206, 344, 402
   roots, 22, 34, 276, 302, 488
   suffixes, 68
   word origins, 160, 206, 312, 378, 448
voice
   author's point of view and, 439
   author's purpose and, 305
   modulation of, 94, 177, 358
   of narrator, 59
   pitch of, 94, 177, 358
   of playwright, 147
   in poetry, 42, 135, 229, 415
   point of view and, 381
   tone of, 21, 79
voice-over narration, 450, 452
volume of speaking, 94, 177, 205, 358, 512

W

When Students Struggle, 3, 11, 13, 30, 42, 54, 60, 75, 83, 85, 88, 91, 94, 99, 106, 108, 118, 140, 154, 164, 171, 174, 177, 183, 190, 202, 210, 212, 221, 234, 236, 251, 252, 253, 256, 259, 265, 268, 283, 284, 294, 301, 310, 320, 323, 332, 339, 347, 349, 352, 355, 363, 370, 386, 398, 410,

418, **423**, **425**, **428**, **431**, **437**, **444**, **451**, **460**, **472**, **482**, **496**, **501**, **503**, **506**, **509**, **512**

word choice
  in informational essays, 86
  mental images and, 125
  in poetry, 37, 135, 229
  point-of-view and, 185
  rhetoric and, 305

Word Gaps (Notice & Note), 84, 170, 252, 265, 269, 271, 348, 424, 502

Word Networks, 1, 97, 181, 263, 361, 435

words. *See also* word choice
  commonly confused, 259, 366, 379
  connotations, 56, 243, 336, 498
  context clues for, 80, 110, 194, 226, 390, 456
  denotations, 56, 336, 498
  historical development of, 160, 344
  meaning of, 22, 34, 194, 226, 344, 466
  origin of, 160, 206, 312, 378, 448
  pronunciation of, 122, 132, 206, 344
  rhyming, 135
  roots, 22, 34, 276, 302, 488

suffixes, 68
syllabication of, 344

Words of the Wiser (Notice & Note), 28, 84, 156, 170, 252, 317, 348, 363, 370, 409, 424, 502

writing activities
  argumentative text, 350–356
  dialogue, 167
  epilogue, 377
  explanation of expressions, 33
  free verse poetry, 475
  historical fiction, 497
  informational text, 86–92, 465
  informative report, 275
  job description, 347
  letters, 67, 193, 249, 301, 335, 413, 475
  literary analysis, 205
  multimodal presentation, 172–178
  objective summaries, 79, 389
  odes, 235, 487
  opinion essay, 121
  personal essay, 453
  personal narratives, 159, 254–260, 325

  poetry, 43, 143, 225, 239, 311, 321, 401, 421
  research reports, 435, 447, 504–510
  short stories, 343, 361, 426–432
  sonnet, 215
  text for infographic, 109
writing process. *See* draft; edit; revise
writing prompts
  argument, 350
  informational essay, 86
  multimodal presentation, 172
  personal narrative, 254
  research report, 504
  short story, 426

INDEX OF TITLES AND AUTHORS

A
Alarcón, Claudia, 329
Alexander, Kwame, 407
Allied with Green, 219

B
Ball Hawk, 367
Benson, Sally, 27
Bradbury, Ray, 281
Brooks, David, 479
Bruchac, Joseph, 367

C
Caffall, Eiren, 338
Calabrese, Lori, 395
Camera Does Lie, The, 115
Challenges for Space Exploration, 307
Craig Kielburger Reflects on Working Toward Peace, 441
Crossover, The, 407

D
Dark They Were, and Golden-Eyed, 281
Dobyns, Stephen, 39
Double Doubles, 417
Drought, The, 212

E
Eldorado, 140

F
Fleischman, Paul, 187
Flight of Icarus, The, 27
Frances Perkins and the Triangle Factory Fire, 479

G
Get in the Zone: The Psychology of Video Game Design, 383
Giovanni, Nikki, 471
Governess, The (drama), 149
Governess, The (production images), 165

H
Harris, Eddy, 199
Heartbeat, 103
Helfrich, Amy, 211
Hughes, Langston, 61
Humans Should Stay Home and Let Robots Take to the Stars, 338

I
Icarus's Flight, 39
It Takes a Child (documentary), 451
It's Not Just a Game!, 395

J
Jackson, Judy, 451

K
Kent, Zachary, 493
Kielburger, Craig, 441

L
Leckie, Ann, 307
Lewis, J. Patrick, 417

M
Martian Metropolis, 269
McKissack, Fredrick, 47
McKissack, Patricia, 47
Millar, Aaron, 383
Mississippi Solo, 199
Moss, Meg, 115
Myers, Walter Dean, 457

N
National Aeronautics and Space Administration, 323
National Oceanic and Atmospheric Administration, 245
Neruda, Pablo, 231
Never Retreat, 187
Nye, Naomi Shihab, 219

O
Ode to enchanted light, 231
Oliver, Mary, 236

P
Poe, Edgar Allan, 140
Poem for My Librarian, Mrs. Long, A, 471
Police Stop Changed This Teenager's Life, A, 73

R
Rogue Wave, 7

S
Seven Minutes of Terror (video), 323
Sherman, Josepha, 127
Simon, Neil, 149
Sleeping in the Forest, 236
Sometimes a Dream Needs a Push, 457
Song of Wandering Aengus, The, 137
Space Exploration Should Be More Science Than Fiction, 329
Stafford, William, 317
Story of the Triangle Factory Fire, The, 493

T
Taylor, Theodore, 7
Thacher, Meg, 269
Thank You, M'am, 61
Trash Talk (video), 245
Two Legs or One?, 127

W
Wang, Amy B, 73
What If We Were Alone?, 317
Women in Aviation, 47

Y
Yeats, W. B., 137
Yoo, David, 103
You're Part of the Solution (poster), 247

ACKNOWLEDGMENTS

"Allied with Green" from *There is No Long Distance Now: Very Short Stories* by Naomi Shihab Nye. Text copyright © 2011 by Naomi Shihab Nye. Reprinted by permission of HarperCollins Publishers.

Excerpts from *The American Heritage Dictionary of The English Language, Fifth Edition.* Text copyright © 2016 by Houghton Mifflin Harcourt Publishing Company. Reprinted by permission of Houghton Mifflin Harcourt Publishing Company.

"Ball Hawk" by Joseph Bruchac from *Baseball Crazy* by Nancy Mercado. Text copyright © 2008 by Joseph Bruchac. Reprinted by permission of Barbara Kouts, Literary Agent.

"The Camera Does Lie" by Meg Moss from *Muse,* July/August 2013. Text copyright © 2013 by Carus Publishing Company. Reproduced by permission of Carus Publishing Company. All Cricket Media material is copyrighted by Carus Publishing Company d/b/a Cricket Media, and/or various authors and illustrators. Any commercial use or distribution of material without permission is strictly prohibited. Please visit http://cricketmedia.com/licensing for licensing and http://www.cricketmedia.com for subscriptions.

"Chapter 2: The Summoned Self" from *The Road to Character* by David Brooks. Text copyright © 2015 by David Brooks. Reprinted by permission of Random House, an imprint and division of Penguin Random House LLC and Penguin Books Ltd. All rights reserved. Any third party use of this material, outside of this publication, is prohibited. Interested parties must apply directly to Penguin Random House LLC for permission.

"Craig Kielburger Reflects on Working Toward Peace" (retitled from "Reflections on Working Toward Peace") from *Architects of Peace* by Michael Collopy. Text copyright © 2000 by Michael Collopy. Used by permission of Michael Collopy.

Excerpt from *The Crossover* by Kwame Alexander. Text copyright © 2014 by Kwame Alexander. Reprinted by permission of Houghton Mifflin Harcourt.

"Dark They Were, and Golden-Eyed" by Ray Bradbury. Text copyright © 1949 by Standard Magazines, renewed © 1976 by Ray Bradbury. Reprinted by permission of Don Congdon Associates, Inc. Photocopying, printing and other reproduction rights are strictly prohibited.

"Double Doubles" from *Vherses: A Celebration of Outstanding Women* by J. Patrick Lewis. Text copyright © 2005 by J. Patrick Lewis. Reprinted by permission of the Creative Company.

"The Drought" by Amy Helfrich. Text copyright © by Amy Helfrich. Reprinted by permission of Amy Helfrich.

"Get in the Zone: The Psychology of Video Game Design" by Aaron Millar from *Muse,* May/June 2015. Text copyright © 2015 by Carus Publishing Company. Reprinted by permission of Carus Publishing Company. All Cricket Media material is copyrighted by Carus Publishing Company d/b/a Cricket Media, and/or various authors and illustrators. Any commercial use or distribution of material without permission is strictly prohibited. Please visit http://cricketmedia.com/licensing for licensing and http://www.cricketmedia.com for subscriptions.

"The Governess" from *The Good Doctor* by Neil Simon. Text copyright © 1974 by Neil Simon. Reprinted by permission of Gary N. DaSilva. Caution: Professionals and amateurs are hereby warned that *The Good Doctor* is fully protected under the Berne Convention and the Universal Copyright Convention and is subject to royalty. All rights, including without limitation professional, amateur, motion picture, television, radio, recitation, lecturing, public reading and foreign translation rights, computer media rights and the right of reproduction, and electronic storage or retrieval, in whole or in part and in any form, are strictly reserved and none of these rights can be exercised or used without written permission from the copyright owner. Inquiries for stock and amateur performances should be addressed to Samuel French, Inc., 45 West 25th Street, New York, NY 10010. All other inquiries should be addressed to Gary N. DaSilva, 111 N. Sepulveda Blvd., Suite 250, Manhattan Beach, CA 90266-6850.

"Heartbeat" by David Yoo. Text copyright © 2005 by David Yoo. Reprinted by permission of Writers House, LLC, on behalf of David Yoo.

"Icarus's Flight" by Stephen Dobyns. Originally appeared in *Ploughshares* Winter 1996/1997. Text copyright © 1996 by Stephen Dobyns. Reprinted by permission of Harold Ober Associates Incorporated.

"It's Not Just a Game" by Lori Calabrese from *Odyssey,* July 2009. Text copyright © 2009 by Carus Publishing Company. Reprinted by permission of Carus Publishing Company. All Cricket Media material is copyrighted by Carus Publishing Company d/b/a Cricket Media, and/or various authors and illustrators. Any commercial use or distribution of material without permission is strictly prohibited. Please visit http://cricketmedia.com/licensing for licensing and http://www.cricketmedia.com for subscriptions.

"Martian Metropolis" by Meg Thatcher from *Muse,* July/August 2016. Text copyright © 2016 by Carus Publishing Company. Reprinted by permission of Carus Publishing Company. All Cricket Media material is copyrighted by Carus Publishing Company d/b/a Cricket Media, and/or various authors and illustrators. Any commercial use or distribution of material without permission is strictly prohibited. Please visit http://cricketmedia.com/licensing for licensing and http://www.cricketmedia.com for subscriptions.

Excerpt from *Mississippi Solo* by Eddy Harris. Text copyright © 1988 by Eddy L. Harris. Reprinted by permission of Lyons Press.

"Never Retreat" from *Eyes Wide Open* by Paul Fleischman. Text copyright © 2014 by the Brown-Fleischman Family Trust. Reprinted by permission of Candlewick Press.

"Ode to Enchanted Light" from *Odes to Opposites* compiled by Ferris Cook. Originally published in Spanish as "Oda a la luz encantada" by Pablo Neruda, translated by Ken Krabbenhoft. Translation copyright © 1995 by Ken Krabbenhoft. Text copyright © 1995 by Pablo Neruda and Fundación Pablo Neruda. Text compilation copyright © 1995 by Ferris Cook. Reprinted by permission of Bullfinch/Hachette Book Group USA and Agencia Literaria Carmen Balcells S.A. All rights reserved.

ACKNOWLEDGMENTS

"Poem for My Librarian, Mrs. Long" from *Acolytes* by Nikki Giovanni. Text copyright © 2007 by Nikki Giovanni. Reprinted by permission of HarperCollins Publishers.

Quote by Ann Cotton from "Leading Questions" by Alison Benjamin from The Guardian, March 28, 2007. Text copyright © 2007 by Guardian News & Media Limited. Reprinted courtesy of Guardian News & Media Limited.

Quote by Amelia Earhart. Text copyright © by Amelia Earhart. Reprinted by permission of CMG Worldwide.

Quote by Phiona Mutesi from "Game of her life" by Tim Crothers, originally published in ESPN The Magazine, January 10, 2011. Text copyright © 2011 by ESPN, Inc. Reprinted by permission of ESPN. All rights reserved.

Excerpt from *Red-Tail Angels: The Story of the Tuskegee Airmen of World War II* by Patricia and Fredrick McKissack. Text copyright © 1995 by Patricia and Frederick McKissack. Reprinted by permission of Bloomsbury Publishing Inc.

"Rogue Wave" from *Rogue Wave and Other Red-Blooded Sea Stories* by Theodore Taylor. Text copyright © 1996 by Theodore Taylor. Reprinted by permission of the Theodore Taylor Estate and the Watkins/Loomis Agency.

"Sleeping in the Forest" from *Twelve Moons* by Mary Oliver. Text copyright © 1972, 1973, 1974, 1976, 1977, 1978, 1979 by Mary Oliver. Reprinted by permission of Charlotte Sheedy Literary Agency on behalf of the author and Little, Brown and Company. All rights reserved.

"Sometimes a Dream Needs a Push" from *Flying Lessons* by Walter Dean Myers. Text copyright © 2017 by Walter Dean Meyers. Reprinted by permission of DeFiore and Company. *Flying Lessons* published by Crown Books for Young Readers/Random House Children's Books in partnership with We Need Diverse Books. The story first appeared in *Boys' Life* © 2007.

"The Song of Wandering Aengus" from *The Wind in the Reeds* by William Butler Yeats. Text copyright © 1989 by Anne Yeats. Reprinted by permission of United Agents, LLP, a subsidiary of A.P. Watt, on behalf of Caitríona Yeats.

Excerpt from *Stories of the Gods and Heroes* by Sally Benson. Text copyright 1940 and renewed © 1968 by Sally Benson. Reprinted by permission of Dial Books for Young Readers, an imprint of Penguin Young Readers Group, a division of Penguin Random House LLC. All rights reserved. Any third-party use of this material, outside of this publication, is prohibited. Interested parties must apply directly to Penguin Random House LLC for permission.

Excerpt from *The Story of the Triangle Factory Fire* by Zachary Kent. Text copyright © 1989 by Children's Press, Inc. Reprinted by permission of Children's Press, an imprint of Scholastic Library Publishing, Inc. All rights reserved.

"Thank you, M'am" from *Short Stories* by Langston Hughes. Text copyright © 1996 by Ramona Bass and Arnold Rampersad. Reprinted by permission of Hill and Wang, a division of Farrar, Straus & Giroux, Inc. and Harold Ober Associates, Inc.

"This Teenager Was Walking for Hours to and from Work - Until a Police Stop Changed His Life" by Amy B. Wang from *The Washington Post* September 30, 2016. Text copyright © 2016 The Washington Post. Reprinted by PARS International on behalf of the Washington Post. All rights reserved. Protected by the Copyright Laws of the United States. The printing, copying, redistribution, or retransmission of this Content without express written permission is prohibited. www.washingtonpost.com

"The 12 Greatest Challenges for Space Exploration" by Annie Leckie from *Wired* February 16, 2016. Text copyright © 2016 by Condé Nast. Reprinted by permission of Condé Nast.

"Two Legs of One?" from *Forty Folk Stories from Around the World* retold by Josepha Sherman. Text copyright © 1996 by Josepha Sherman. Reprinted by permission of Marian Reiner on behalf of the publisher August House, Inc.

"What If We Were Alone?" from *The Way It Is: New and Selected Poems* by William Stafford. Text copyright © 1987, 1998 by William Stafford and the Estate of William Stafford. Reprinted by permission of The Permissions Company, Inc. on behalf of Graywolf Press, Minneapolis, Minnesota, www.graywolfpress.org and Kim Stafford.